International Environmental Law and Policy

International Environmental Law and Policy

Edith Brown Weiss
Georgetown University School of Law

Stephen C. McCaffrey
McGeorge School of Law

Daniel Barstow Magraw
Washington, D.C.

Paul C. Szasz
Germantown, N.Y.

Robert E. Lutz
Southwestern University School of Law

ASPEN LAW & BUSINESS
A Division of Aspen Publishers, Inc.
Gaithersburg New York

Permissions
Aspen Law & Business
1185 Avenue of the Americas
New York, NY 10036

Printed in the United States of America

Library of Congress Cataloging-in-Publication Data

International environmental law and policy / Edith Brown Weiss . . . [et al.].
p. cm.
Includes index.
ISBN 0-7355-0146-7
1. Environmental law, International—Cases. I. Weiss, Edith Brown, 1942-
K3585.3.I568 1998
341.7′62—dc21 98-41335
CIP

About Aspen Law & Business, Legal Education Division

In 1996, Aspen Law & Business welcomed the Legal Education Division of Little, Brown and Company into its growing business—already established as a leading provider of practical information to legal practitioners.

Acquiring much more than a prestigious collection of educational publications by the country's foremost authors, Aspen Law & Business inherited the long-standing Little, Brown tradition of excellence—born over 150 years ago. As one of America's oldest and most venerable publishing houses, Little, Brown and Company commenced in a world of change and challenge, innovation and growth. Sharing that same spirit, Aspen Law & Business has dedicated itself to continuing and strengthening the integrity begun so many years ago.

ASPEN LAW & BUSINESS
A Division of Aspen Publishers, Inc.
A Wolters Kluwer Company

To Chuck, Tamara, and Jed

—EBW

To Susan, Kevin, Brooke, Darren, and Amanda

—SCM

To Sean, Caitlin, Kendra, Kim, and Cindy [Lucinda],
and Dan and Jean Magraw

—DBM

To Frances and our daughters, Catherine Dibble and Ree Brennin

—PCS

To my children, Ryan and Erin, that they may live in
a sustainably developed world, and to my deceased
parents, Robert and Claire Lutz, for the many
environmental lessons they taught me.

—REL

Summary of Contents

Contents

PART THREE

■

PART FOUR

■

TRADE AND FINANCE 1033

Chapter XX Environment and Trade 1035

Preface

Since 1970 international environmental issues have increasingly seized local, national, and international attention. In 1992 at the United Nations Conference on Environment and Development in Rio de Janeiro, Brazil, states confirmed that environmental protection and economic development are integrally linked and called for "sustainable development" worldwide. Governments, international organizations, and nongovernmental organizations have stepped up their efforts to address the rapidly increasing threats to the quality of air, water, soil, and the oceans; to the existence of countless species; and to human, plant, and animal health. Major multinational enterprises, from Exxon and Unilever to Dow Chemical, as well as local industries, deal with environmental issues on a daily basis. The World Bank and other multilateral development banks have set up offices to examine the environmental implications of Bank-funded projects. Still, the threats continue.

International law plays a key role in addressing environmental problems. As of 1998 there are over a thousand international legal instruments (bilateral and multilateral agreements and important nonbinding instruments) concerned with environmental protection. Every country has at least one piece of environmental legislation; most have far more. In addition, there are other relevant sources of law: customary international law, general principles of law, decisions and actions of international organizations, and nonbinding legal instruments negotiated by governments or developed transnationally in the private sector. Environmental protection is also treated in other areas of international law, such as trade and human rights.

Thus, there is now a substantial and significant body of international environmental law and practice. As countries and societies become more interdependent and globalized, law schools and universities increasingly need to address international legal issues. This book is intended to provide a basis for studying one field of international law: international environmental law.

The Field of International Environmental Law

The field of international environmental law has several components: public international law as reflected in international agreements and other sources of international law, domestic environmental and natural resource protection law, and transnational private law. It is foremost, however, a field of international law.

While the field of international environmental law is "new" or "emerging" as a field of international law, it is also ancient. The field is new in the sense that most international agreements concerned with protecting the environment (and most domestic environmental laws) have been developed since 1970. At the turn of the twentieth century, there were few multilateral or bilateral international environmental agreements. Those agreements that existed concerned primarily boundary waters, navigation, fishing rights along shared waterways, and the protection of commercially valuable species. Global environmental problems, such as marine protection, ozone depletion, and climate change, were not addressed until the latter half of this century. At the same time, international environmental law has ancient roots in international law and in the diplomatic exchanges and international agreements developed for centuries to handle local resource problems. Moreover, some of the most important legal precedents in the field, such as the Trail Smelter arbitration, date from the first half of the twentieth century.

The field of international environmental law should be understood as encompassing both international law and national environmental laws that relate to international environmental problems. Routinely, national legislation and regulations implement international agreements. Some national statutes contain provisions addressing transfrontier pollution problems or other international environmental issues for which international agreements do not yet exist. Sometimes national legislation provides the impetus for international lawmaking. Moreover, occasionally subfederal governmental units take actions directed at international environmental problems based on their local laws.

Nongovernmental organizations and the private sector are increasingly developing transnational codes of behavior and practice that are technically nongovernmental, nonbinding international legal instruments. They are, however, relevant to understanding the development and implementation of international environmental law.

Approach to the Materials

Our approach to the course book has been informed by our accumulated experience in the field. This experience suggests the tools that are needed to function effectively in this complex and rapidly growing area. Various of us have served, or are serving, as teachers, scholars, officials of national government agencies and international organizations, members of national and international expert bodies, international arbitrators, and counsel to governments in international environmental disputes. We are also informed by our scholarly and professional experience in other areas of international law and in domestic environmental and natural resources law. We have all gained from our experiences in teaching international environmental law for more than a dozen years using versions of the materials included here.

International Environmental Law and Policy provides an overview of the field. It combines analytical materials with in-depth treatment of real life issues. The course book reflects a recognition that the international system today consists of many different relevant actors: states, subnational governmental units, international organizations, nongovernmental organizations, corporate entities, *ad hoc* transnational groupings, and individuals. The materials emphasize the links between international and domestic law in developing and implementing international law, the merging of public and private international law in certain cases, and the relevance of social and natural sciences to understanding the development and implementation of international environmental law. Several chapters explicitly address the links between environmental issues and other areas of international law: trade, human rights, and national security.

This book is designed to provide students with basic materials on the wide range of knowledge and perspectives needed to be an effective, "three-dimensional" international environmental lawyer. Mastering this field requires not only expertise in specific international environmental regimes but also knowledge of public international law, institutions, and processes more generally, and an understanding of domestic legal approaches to environmental protection. An effective international environmental lawyer must also be able to appreciate the complexity and interrelationships of our natural environment, the role of scientific uncertainty and risk assessment in protecting health and the environment, and even the nature of the scientific process. Similarly, he or she must be sensitive to the ethical and cultural dimensions of environmental protection, familiar with the basic economic concepts frequently encountered in this area, and aware of how poverty, differences in levels of economic development among various countries, and political considerations relate to environmental degradation and attempts to remedy it. For these reasons, the principles related to sustainable development and stewardship of the planet figure prominently in our approach to the course.

International environmental law functions within the context of the more general field of public international law. Since many students taking this course will not have studied international law, we believe some introduction should be provided. The challenge is to determine how much time should be devoted to this task: A lengthy treatment would leave little room for the examination of international environmental problems; yet too little attention would leave the student ill-equipped to function in the field of international environmental law. We have decided on what we hope is a *via media:* succinct, textual coverage of the international legal system, including coverage of public international law and institutions, written especially for this book (Chapter 5). The material is designed both to allow the teacher who does not which to consume class time on the subject to assign the chapter as outside or background reading and to facilitate class discussion of the materials.

Organization of the Materials

The material in the book is organized in four parts. Part I sets forth an analytical framework that can be applied to any international environmental legal problem. It provides an introduction to the environmental and social/political systems in the context of sustainable development (Chapter 1). Chapter 2 addresses the underlying philosophical issues of our relations with present and future generations and with nature. Chapter 3 examines the relevance of economic analysis to international environmental legal issues and explores the economic implications of international legal rules. Chapter 4 explores the principles and measures for addressing risk and scientific uncertainty. Chapter 5 provides a basic introduction to international law and organization and draws attention to issues of compliance with international law. The materials include both basic analytical pieces and specific case studies and examples. The authors intend to provide students with material that can be drawn upon throughout the other parts of the casebook. Students and teachers will recognize that this—or any single—course book cannot cover these issues in depth, but the materials should enable the reader to become acquainted with fundamental concepts and approaches.

The remainder of the book addresses specific international environmental problems and related issues. Part II examines the many-faceted and difficult subject of pollution, as it is broadly defined. General and specific norms concerning this problem are treated in Chapters 6-9. Chapter 6 is devoted to explicating the four major cases that have been most influential in the field, beginning with the *Trail Smelter* arbitration. Our experience as teachers, scholars, and practicing lawyers is that, for whatever reasons, discussion of these cases often occurs without a full appreciation of their factual contexts and actual legal holdings; it is our hope that this chapter will enable students to avoid that pitfall. Thereafter we examine general norms of prevention (including both substantive and procedural norms and international human rights law) (Chapter 7), the norms applicable to environmental disasters such as Bhopal and Chernobyl (Chapter 8), and traditional and innovative measures to promote accountability and compliance (Chapter 9). Part II also considers the legal and policy issues of specific pollution related problems: regional transboundary air and water pollution (Chapter 10), stratospheric ozone depletion (Chapter 11), global climate change (Chapter 12), marine environmental degradation (Chapter 13), hazardous substances (Chapter 14), and environmental harms related to military activities (Chapter 15).

Part III explores issues relating to the management of Earth's natural resources. It examines norms of allocation and use of fresh water (Chapter 16), and it considers legal issues related to the international protection of national sites such as world heritage sites and wetlands (Chapter 17), the conservation of biological diversity (Chapter 18), and the protection of endangered species (Chapter 19).

The book concludes with material devoted to issues of trade and finance (Part IV). The two chapters in this part address, respectively, the interface between promoting trade liberalization and protecting health and the environment (Chapter 20), and the financing of environmental protection (Chapter 21). The materials in Chapter 20 on environment and trade cover efforts in the private sector to development transnational codes of behavior as well as public and private initiatives on ecolabeling.

In addition to the foregoing, we have included three appendices to provide readers with in depth background material for the course. Appendix I provides material on conducting research in the field of international environmental law. Appendix II contains information on international organizations that supplements the material on that subject contained in Chapter 5. And Appendix III describes the general steps that are followed in formulating multilateral agreements, to give the student a fuller appreciation of the treaty-making process.

Finally, we would like to welcome you to what is not only one of the most challenging and important areas of the law, but also one of the most fascinating. Developments in international environmental law have already had important effects on the development of international law generally. We look forward to learning with you in the years to come.

Edith Brown Weiss (Washington, DC)
Stephen C. McCaffrey (Sacramento, CA)
Daniel Barstow Magraw (Washington, DC)
Paul C. Szasz (Germantown, NY)
Robert E. Lutz (Los Angeles, CA)

August 1998

ACKNOWLEDGEMENTS

Many people have been involved in the preparation of these materials. Since this book has been in gestation for nearly a decade, however, it is virtually impossible for us to thank properly all of those who have contributed in one way or another. We do wish to extend special thanks to the following, hoping as we do so that anyone who has inadvertently been omitted will understand and forgive us.

Edith Brown Weiss would like to thank Christina Carroll, Brett Frischmann, Richard Holbrook, Lainie Kropp, Andrea Lachenmayr, Krista Nadakavaukaren, Carrie Rhoads, Stephanie Tai, and Michael Willis, present and former students at Georgetown University Law Center, who provided invaluable research and editing assistance over the years. She would also like to give special thanks to Ellen Schaffer, the International Law Librarian at the Georgetown University Law Center, for her outstanding and tireless efforts in finding materials and bringing items to our attention, to the administrative staff of the Georgetown University Law Center for their fine assistance in preparing various versions of the manuscript, and to Dean Judith Areen for her support.

Stephen McCaffrey would like to extend his appreciation to the following present and former students at the University of the Pacific (UOP) McGeorge School of Law for their assistance with research and preparation of the manuscript: Rebecca McCarty Petty, J.D. (1993); Timothy M. Harris, J.D. (1996); Jeffrey B. Carra, J.D. (1996); Anita Millers, J.D. (1998); Tara

Lynch, J.D. (1998); and Eunice Bonaparte (class of 2001). He would like to extend warm thanks to Dale Riston for her cheerful and highly competent assistance with the preparation of the manuscript and to the Reference Librarians of the Gordon D. Schaber Law Library, particularly Susan Van Syckel, for assistance readily provided on numerous occasions. Thanks are also due to the UOP McGeorge School of Law for its unstinting support of the project over the years.

Daniel Magraw would like to express his gratitude to the librarians at the University of Colorado (CU) School of Law, particularly to Barbara Bintliff and Jane Thompson; their expertise, good humor, enthusiasm, and creativity were of immense assistance and were greatly appreciated. The unstinting assistance of the Faculty Secretaries at CU, in particular Anne Guthrie, Marge Bruner, Marcia Murphy, and Kay Wilkie, was also essential to the book, and he would like to express his deep gratitude to them. He would also like to thank then-Dean of the law school Gene Nichol for his support and encouragement. Special thanks are in order to Dan's excellent research assistants over the years, including especially Debra Donahue, Gwen Fleener, Mary Lee, Valeria Neale, Rebecca Rains, Julia Roig, Dana Rose, Mary Scherschel, Paul Schmidt, and Serena Wilson. Research Librarian Susan Van Syckel, of the UOP McGeorge School of Law, deserves special mention for her excellent work in updating and improving Appendix I, Researching International Environmental Law.

Paul Szasz would like to express his deep appreciation to Lee A. Kimball for her insightful comments concerning environmental institutions.

Robert Lutz would like to acknowledge the very able assistance of the following former students at Southwestern University School of Law in the preparation of materials for this book: Lynne McGhee; Dina DeLaurentis; James Murphy; Debra Belanger; Stacy Abrams; Irene Borromeo; Lara Yeretsian; and Douglas Schwab. The Support Center staff—especially Jeannie Nicholson, Sandra Montgomery, and Martha Fink—were most helpful in preparing the manuscript and readying drafts for distribution. David McFadden, Southwestern's Senior Research Librarian, was always resourceful in aiding him and his students in their research. He is also grateful to Southwestern and its Dean, Leigh H. Taylor, for their support and encouragement throughout.

All the authors have deeply appreciated the many helpful comments on the materials that they have received over the years from those who have used or read various drafts of this book, including the many students who have used versions of these materials in courses we have taught on international environmental law: we thank them for their reactions, insights, and contributions. We would also like to express our sincere appreciation to the Georgetown University Law Center for making facilities available to us for an intensive drafting and editing session among the co-authors. It truly has been a collaborative effort.

We alsogratefully acknowledge the permission granted by the authors, publishers, and organizations to reprint portions of the following copyrighted materials.

Chapter 1

Brown Weiss, Edith, The Changing Structure of International Law, Georgetown University Law Center, May 23, 1996, reprinted in Georgetown Law—Res Ipsa Loquitur 52 (Spring 1997). Reprinted with permission of the author.

Caldwell, Lynton, International Environmental Policy (first edition). © 1984 Duke University Press. Reprinted with permission.

Easterbrook, Gregg, A Moment on the Earth, 1995. Used by permission of Viking Penguin, a division of Penguin Putnam Inc.

Gleick, James, Chaos: Making a New Science. Reprinted by permission of James Gleick. Chaos: Making a New Science. © 1987.

Lawrence, Gary, Will Habitat II Matter to the Members of the OECD? Unpublished paper. OECD-Germany Conference on Sustainable Urban Development, Berlin, March 1996. The views are those of the author and do not necessarily represent the OECD. Reprinted with permission of the author.

Matthews, Jessica Tuchman, Redefining Security, 68 For. Aff. 162 (1989). Reprinted by permission of Foreign Affairs, 1989. © 1989 by the Council on Foreign Relations, Inc.

Turnbull, Colin, The Mountain People, 1972. Reprinted with permission of Simon & Schuster from The Mountain People by Colin M. Turnbull. © 1972 by Colin Turnbull.

United Nations Environment Programme, Poverty and the Environment. © United Nations Environment Programme 1995. Reprinted with permission.

World Commission on Environment and Development, Our Common Future, 1987. Reprinted with permission of Oxford University Press.

Yellen, John, Bushmen, 42 Science 41 (1985). © 1985 American Association for the Advancement of Science. Reprinted with permission from John Yellen.

Chapter 2

D'Amato, Anthony and Sudhir K. Chopra, Whales: Their Emerging Right to Life, 85 American Journal of International Law 21 (1991). Reproduced with permission, © The American Society of International Law.

Brown Weiss, Edith, In Fairness to Future Generations: International Law, Common Patrimony and Intergenerational Equity, 1989. Reprinted with the permission of Transnational and United Nations University Press.

Norton, Bryan, Environmental Ethics and the Rights of Future Generations, 4 Environmental Ethics 322 (1982). Reprinted with the permission of Bryan Norton and Environmental Ethics, Department of Philosophy and Religion, University of Georgia, Athens, GA 30602.

John Passmore, Man's Responsibility to Nature: Ecological Problems and Western Tradition (1974). Reproduced with the permission of Duckworth General Publishers.

Sagoff, Mark, On Preserving the Natural Environment, 84 Yale Law Journal 205 (1974). Reprinted by permission of the Yale Law Journal Company and Fred B. Rotharn & Company from The Yale Law Journal, Vol. 84, pp. 205-267 and Mark Sagoff.

Stone, Christopher D., Should Trees Have Standing?—Toward Legal Rights for Natural Objects, 45 S. Cal. L. Rev. (1972). Reprinted with the permission of the Southern California Law Review.

Chapter 3

Applegate, John S., Worst Things First: Risk, Information, and Regulatory Structure in Toxic Substances Control, 9 Yale Journal of Regulation 277 (1992). Reprinted with the permission of the Yale Journal of Regulation.

Brown Weiss, Edith, The Planetary Trust: Conservation and Intergenerational Equity, 11 Ecology Law Quarterly 495 (1984). Reprinted with the permission of author.

Costanza, Robert, Ralph D'Arge, Rudolf de Groot, Stephen Farber, Monica Grasso, Bruce Hannon, Karin Limburg, Shahid Naseem, Robert O'Neill, Jose Paruelo, Robert G. Raskin, Paul Sutton, and Marjan van den Belt, The Value of the World's Ecosystem Services and Natural Capital, Nature, May 15, 1997. Reprinted by permission from Nature, vol. 387, p. 253, © 1997 Macmillan Magazines Ltd.

Cross, Frank B., Natural Resource Damage Valuation, 42 Vanderbilt L. Rev. 269 (1989). Reprinted with the permission of the Vanderbilt Law Review.

D'Arge, Ralph C. and Allen V. Kneese, State Liability for International Environmental Degradation: An Economic Perspective, 20 Natural Resources Journal 427 (1980). Reprinted with the permission of the Natural Resources Journal, University of New Mexico School of Law.

Dorfman, Robert, An Economist's View of Natural Resource and Environmental Problems, in The Global Possible (Robert Repetto, ed. 1985). © 1985 Yale University Press. Reprinted with the permission of Robert Dorfman and Yale University Press.

Fox, Sean T., Responding to Climate Change: The Case for Unilateral Trade Measures to Protect the Global Atmosphere, 84 Georgetown Law Journal 2499 (1996). Reprinted with the permission of the publisher, Georgetown University and Georgetown Law Journal © 1996.

Hardin, Garrett, Tragedy of the Commons, 162 Science 1243 (1968). Excerpted with permission, © 1968 American Association for the Advancement of Science.

Herfindahl, Orris C. National Resource Information for Economic Development (1969). Reprinted with the permission of John Hopkins University Press.

Page, Talbot, Economics of a Throwaway Society in Economics of Environmental and Natural Resources Policy (J. Butlin, ed. 198 1). Reproduced with permission the permission of Talbot Page.

Polinksy, A. Mitchell, An Introduction to Law and Economics (1983). Excerpted with permission from Little, Brown and Company.

Repetto, Robert and William McGrath, Michael Wells, Christine Beer, & Fabrizio Rossini, Wasting Assets: Natural Resources in the National Income Accounts (1989). Reprinted with the permission of the World Resources Institute.

Sagoff, Mark, Economic Theory and Environmental Law, 79 Michigan Law Review 1393 (1981). Reprinted with the permission of Mark Sagoff and the Michigan Law Review.

Steer, Andrew and Jocelyn Mason, The Role of Multilateral Finance and the Environment: A View from the World Bank, 3 Indiana Journal of Global Legal Studies 35 (1995). Reprinted with the permission of the Indiana Journal of Global Legal Studies.

Williams, Deborah Lee, Benefit-Cost Analysis in Natural Resources Decisionmaking: An Economic and Legal Overview, 4 Natural Resources Lawyer 761 (1979). Reprinted by permission of the American Bar Association Natural Resources Law Section. Copyright © 1979 American Bar Association.

Chapter 4

Kindall, M.P.A., UNCED and the Evolution of Principles of International Environmental Law, 25 John Marshall Law Review 19 (1991). Reprinted with the permission of the John Marshall Law Review.

Richard Wilson and E.A.C. Crouch, 236 Science 267 (April 17, 1987). Reprinted with permission from Science. Copyright 1987 American Association for the Advancement of Science.

Chapter 5

Magraw, Daniel, Legal Treatment of Developing Countries. Originally published in the Colorado Journal of International Environmental Law & Policy, © 1990. All rights reserved.

Chapter 7

Alston, Phillip, Making Space for New Human Rights: The Case of the Right to Development, 1 Harvard Human Rights Yearbook 3, 4 (1988). Reprinted by permission.

Alston, Phillip, Conjuring Up New Human Rights: A Proposal for Quality Control. Reproduced with permission from American Journal of International Law 607, 607-17 (1984), © The American Society of International Law.

Bodansky, Daniel, Panel on New Developments in International Environmental Law, 85 A.S.I.L. PROC. 413 (1991) Transcript from a Presentation at the American Society of International Law, Proceedings of the 85th Annual Meeting 413, 414-417 (1991). Reproduced with permission from 85 A.S.I.L. PROC. 413, 414-17 (1991), © The American Society of International Law.

Gibson, Noralee, The Right to a Clean Environment, 54 Saskatchewan Law Review 5, pp.12, 16-17 (1990). Reprinted by permission.

Handl, Günther, Human Rights and Protection of the Environment: A mildly "Revisionist" View, in Human Rights, Sustainable Development and the Environment 117, pp.120-122 (A. Cancado Trindade ed., 1992). Reprinted by permission.

Kimmerling, Judith, Disregarding Environmental Law: Petroleum Development in Protected Natural Areas and Indigenous Homelands in the Ecuadorian Amazon. University of California, Hastings College of the Law (1991). Reprinted from Hastings International and Comparative Law Review, Vol. 14, No. 4, pp.849-855 by permission.

Leighton Schwartz, Michelle, International Legal Protection for Victims of Environmental Abuse, 18 Yale Journal of International Law 355, pp.359-361, 364-366, 368, 370, 370, 375-378 (1993). Reprinted by permission.

Magraw, Daniel B., Legal Treatment of Developing Countries: Differential, Contextual & Absolute Norms, 1 Colo. J. Int'l L. & Pol'y 69, 69-76 (1990) (Originally published in the Colorado Journal of International Environmental Law & Policy, Copyright 1990. All rights reserved). Reprinted with permission of University Press of Colorado.

McCaffrey, Stephen, A Human Right to Water: Domestic and International Implications, 5 Georgetown International Environmental Law Review 1, pp.5-12 (1992). Reprinted with the permission of the publisher, Georgetown University and the Georgetown International Environmental Law Review, © 1992.

Shelton, Dinah, Human Rights, Environmental Rights, and the Right to Environment, 28 Stanford Journal of International Law 103, pp.105-07, 112-13, 116, 122-24, 133 (1991). Reprinted with the permission of the Stanford Journal of International Law. Copyright © 1991 by the Board of Trustees of the Leland Stanford Junior University.

Sohn, Louis B., The New International Law: Protection of the Rights of Individuals Rather Than State, 32 American University Law Review 1, pp. 17-21 (1982). Reprinted by permission.

Sohn, Louis B., The Stockholm Declaration on the Human Environment, 14 Harvard International Law Journal 423, 496-502 (1973). Reprinted with permission of Harvard International Law Journal.

Symonides, Janusz, The Human Right to a Clean, Balanced and Protected Environment, 20 International Journal of Legal Information 24, pp. 28-29 (1992). Reprinted by permission.

Chapter 8

Adede, Andronico O., Overview of Legal & Technical Aspects of Nuclear Accident Pollution, International Law & Pollution (D. Magraw, ed.) (1991), 129-132, 136-138. Reprinted with permission of the University of Pennsylvania Press.

Brown Weiss, Edith, Environmental Disasters in International Law, Anuaria Juridico Interamerican, 1986, 141-____. Reprinted with permission of the Organization of American States.

Gündling, Lothan, The Status in International Law of the Principle of Precautionary Action, 5 Int'l J. Estuarine & Coastal L. 23, 23-24, 25-30 (1990). Reprinted with the permission of Kluwer Law International.

Handl, Günther, Internationalization of Hazard Management in Recipient Countries: Accident Preparedness & Response, Transferring Hazardous Technologies & Substances: The International Challenge (G. Handl & R. Lutz, eds.) (1989) 106-107, 111-117. Reprinted with the permission of Kluwer Law International.

Magraw, Daniel B., The Bhopal Disaster: Structuring a Solution, 57 University of Colorado Law Review 835, 815, 838, 840-847 (1986). Reprinted with permission of University of Colorado Law Review, Inc.

Nanda, Ved P. and Bruce C. Bailey, Nature and Scope of the Problem, Transferring Hazardous Technologies & Substances: The International Challenge (G. Handl & R. Lutz, eds.) (1989) 3-11, 16-19. Reprinted with the permission of Kluwer Law International.

Chapter 9

Birnie, Patricia and Alan Boyle, International Law and the Environment (pp. 136-137, 160-163, 208-210) (1992). Reprinted with permission of Oxford University Press.

Brown Weiss, Edith, Strengthening National Compliance with International Environmental Agreements, Environmental Policy and Law, vol. 27, No. 4 (1997), p. 297. This article first appeared in Environmental Policy and Law, vol. 27, No. 4 (1997), at p. 297. Reprinted with permission of IOS Press.

Brunnee, Jutta, Acid Rain & Ozone Layer Depletion: International Law & Regulation (1988) 103-111. Reprinted with permission of Transnational Publishers, Inc.

Charney, Jonathan, Third State Remedies for Environmental Damage to the World's Common Spaces, International Responsibility for Environmental Harm (Francesco Francioni & Tullio Scovazzi, eds.) (1991) pp. 149-150, 175-177. Reprinted with permission of Kluwer Academic Publishers.

McCaffrey, Stephen C., Crimes Against the Environment, 1 International Criminal Law 541, 541-561 (M. Cherif Bassoiuni, ed.) (1986). Reprinted with permission of Transnational Publishers, Inc.

McCaffrey, Stephen C., Water, Politics, and International Law, from Water in Crisis: A Guide to the World's Fresh Water Resources (Peter H. Gleick, ed.) pp. 92, 93-96. Copyright © 1993 by Oxford University Press, Inc. Used by permission of the Oxford University Press, Inc.

Pisillio-Mazzeschi, Ricardo, Forms of International Responsibility for Environmental Harm (Francesco Francioni & Tullio Scovazzi, eds.) (1991) pp. 15, 16-17, 29, 34-35. Reprinted with permission of Kluwer Academic Publishers.

Rosencranz, Armin, The Uniform Transboundary Pollution Reciprocal Access Act, 15 Environmental Policy & Law 105 (1985), p. 105. Reprinted with permission of IOS Press.

Sachariew, Kamen Promoting Compliance with International Legal Standards: Reflections on Monitoring and Reporting Mechanisms (1991), Yearbook of International Environmental Law 31 (1992). Reprinted with permission of Kluwer Academic Publishers.

Sand, Peter, Lessons Learned in Global Environmental Governance (pp. 30-34) (1990). Reprinted with permission of World Resources Institute.

Chapter 10

Bilder, Richard, Controlling Great Lakes Pollution: A Study in U.S.–Canadian Environmental Cooperation, 70 Michigan L. Rev. 469, 473-475, 480-484 (1972). Reprinted with permission of Michigan Law Review Association and Richard Bilder.

Dominice, Christian, Institute of International law, Resolution on the Pollution of Rivers and Lakes and International Law (Athens Resolution), Annuaire de l'Institut de droit International (Yearbook of International Law), Vol. 59-I, Athens Session, Sept. 1979 p. 197 (1980). Reprinted with permission of Christian Dominice at the Institut de droit International.

Dominice, Christian, Resolution on the Use of International Non-Maritime Waters, Annuaire de l'Institut de droit International, Vol. 49-II (Year Book Institute of International Law) Salzburg Session, Sept. 1961. Reprinted with permission of Christian Dominice at the Institut de droit International.

Francis, George, Binational Cooperation for Great Lakes Water Quality: A Framework for the Groundwater Connection, 65 Chicago Kent Law Review 39 (1989), pp. 361-368. Reprinted with permission of Chicago-Kent College of Law, Illinois Institute of Technology. This article first appeared in 65 Chicago-Kent Law Review 359 (1989) [Copyright © 1989] and is reprinted by special permission of Chicago-Kent College of Law, Illinois Institute of Technology.

Gaines, Sanford, Taking Responsibility for Transboundary Environmental Effects, Hastings International & Comparative Law Review Vol. 14 No. 4, pp. 801, 802-807, (1991), copyright 1991 by University of California, Hastings College of the Law. Reprinted with permission from Hastings Comparative Law Review Vol. 14, No. 4, pp. 801, 802-807.

The Great Lakes Water Quality Agreement: An Evolving Instrument for Ecosystem Management 2 (1985), National Research Council for the United States and Royal Society of Canada, pp. 2,3, 4, 7-9, 77-78, 80, 83-84, 85-86, 91-92, 93. Reprinted with permission of both the National Research Council for the United States and Royal Society of Canada.

Helsinki Rules on the Uses of Waters of International Rivers (adopted by the International Law Association at its 52d conference held in Helsinki, 1966), International Law Association, Report of the 52d Conference, Helsinki, 14-20 August, 1966, 484 (1967). Reprinted with permission of the International Law Association.

Lammers, Johan G., The European Approach to acid Rain, International Law and Pollution 265 (D. Magraw, ed.) 267-282 (1991). Reprinted with permission of the University of Pennsylvania Press.

Chapter 11

Benedick, Richard E., Ozone Diplomacy, 1991. Reprinted by permission of the publisher, Harvard University Press, Copyright © 1991 by the World Wildlife Fund and the Conservation Foundation and the Institute for the Study of Diplomacy, Georgetown University.

Brown Weiss, Edith and Harold K. Jacobson, Engaging Countries: Strengthening Compliance with International Environmental Accords (1998), Table 5-6: Montreal Protocol Ozone Depleting Substances. Reprinted with permission of MIT Press.

Enders, Alice and Amelia Porcres. Successful Conventions and Conventional Success: Saving the Ozone Layer in The Greening of World Trade Issues (K. Anderson and R. Blackhurst, eds. 1991). Reprinted with the permission of Harvester Wheatsheaf.

Jachtenfuchs, Markus, The European Community and the Protection of the Ozone Layer, Journal of Common Market Studies 261 (Mar. 1990). Reprinted with permission. Copyright © 1990 Blackwell Publishers Ltd.

Nangle, Orval E., Stratospheric Ozone: United States Regulation of Chlorofluorocarbons, 16 Boston College Environmental Affairs Law Review 531 (1989). Reprinted with the permission of the Boston College Environmental Affairs Law Review.

Williams, Sylvia Maureen, A Historical Background on the Chlorofluorocarbon Ozone Depletion Theory and Its Legal Implications in Transboundary Air Pollution (Flinterman, Kwiatkowska, and Lammers, eds. 1986). Reprinted with the kind permission of Kluwer Law International.

Chapter 12

Breidenich, Clare, Daniel Magraw, Anne Rowley, and James Rubin, Current Development: The Kyoto Protocol to the United Nations Framework Convention on Climate Change, 92 American Journal of International Law 317 (1998). © The American Society of International Law. Reprinted with permission.

Brown Weiss, Edith and M.P.A. Kindall. Emissions Trading and Climate Change (mimeo 1992). Reprinted with the permission of the authors.

Committee on Science, Engineering and Public Policy, National Academy of Sciences, National Academy of Engineering, Institute of Medicine, Policy Implications of Greenhouse Warming. Reprinted with permission. Copyright © 1991 by the National Academy of Sciences. Courtesy of the National Academy Press, Washington, D.C.

Chapter 13

Haas, Peter, Saving the Mediterranean: The Politics of International Environmental Cooperation,1990. Reprinted with the permission of the publisher. Copyright © 1990, Columbia University Press.

Sielen, Alan B., Sea Changes? Ocean Dumping and International Regulation, 1 Georgetown International Environmental Law Review 2 (1988). Reprinted with the permission of the publisher, Georgetown University and Georgetown International Environmental Law Review, © 1988.

Chapter 14

Christrup, Judy, Clamping Down on the International Waste Trade, 13 Greenpeace 8 (Nov./Dec. 1988). Reprinted with the permission of Greenpeace Magazine.

Colbom, Theo, Dianne Dumanoski, and John Peterson Myers, To the

Ends of the Earth from Our Stolen Future 91-104 (1996). Copyright © 1996 by Theo Colborn, Dianne Dumanoski, and Dr. John Peterson Myers, Used by permission of Dutton, a division of Penguin Putnam, Inc.

Kummer, Katharina, International Management of Hazardous Wastes (1995). Reprinted by permission of Oxford University Press.

Lallas, Peter and Steve Wolfson, International Cooperation to Address Risks from Pesticides and Hazardous Chemicals (mimeo 1997). Reprinted with the permission of the authors.

Chapter 15

Apple, R.W., Jr., The New York Times, January 28, 1991, section A, page 1, column 3. © The New York Times Company. Reprinted with permission of The New York Times.

Lorch, Donatella, The New York Times, March 6, 199 1, section A, page 1, column 4. © The New York Times Company. Reprinted with permission of The New York Times.

McFadden, Robert D., The New York Times, January 26, 1991, section 1, page 1, column 3. © The New York Times Company. Reprinted with permission of The New York Times.

Simons, Marlise, The New York Times, March 16, 1991, Section 1, page 1, column 4. © The New York Times Company. Reprinted with permission of The New York Times.

Weisskopf, Michael, The Washington Post, April 4, 1991, section A, page 25. © Washington Post. Reprinted with permission of The Washington Post.

Chapter 16

Bourne Charles, The International Law Commission's Draft Articles on the Law of International Watercourses, 3 Colo. J. Int'l L. & Pol'y 65, 89-91 (1992). Reprinted with the permission of University of Colorado School of Law. This article was originally published in the Colorado Journal of International environmental Law & Policy, Copyright 1992. All rights reserved.

McCaffrey, Stephen C., Austrian Journal of Public and International Law, The Evolution of the Law of International Watercourses, 45 Austrian J. Pub. Int'l. Law 87 (1993), pp. 88-89.

McCafffrey, Stephen C., Background & Overview of the International Law Commission's Study of the Non-Navigational Uses of International Watercourses, 3 Colo. J. Int'l L. & Pol'y 17, 22-23, 25-29 (1992). Reprinted with permission of University of Colorado School of Law. This article was originally published in the Colorado Journal of International environmental Law & Policy, Copyright 1992. All rights reserved.

Chapter 17

Magraw, Daniel, International Law and Park Protection: A Global Responsibility in Our Common Lands (David J. Simon, ed. 1988). © National Parks and Conservation Association. Reprinted with the permission of Island Press, Washington, D.C. and Covelo, CA. For more information, contact Island Press directly at 1-800-828-1302, info@islandpress.org (E-mail), or www.islandpress.org (website).

Chapter 18

Bodansky, Daniel M., International Law and the Protection of Biological Diversity, 28 Vand. J. Transnatl. L. 623, 627 (1995). Copyright © 1995, Vanderbilt Journal of Transnational Law. Reprinted with permission.

Bordwin, Harold J., The Legal and Political Implications of the International Undertaking on Plant Genetic Resources, 12 Ecology L.Q. 1053, 10533-1054, 1059-1069 (1985). Copyright © 1985 by the Ecology Law Quarterly. Reprinted with permission.

Brown Weiss, Edith, In Fairness to Future Generations: International Law, Common Patrimony and Intergenerational Equity 193, 204-205, 219-223, 1989. Reprinted with the permission of Transnational and United Nations University Press.

De Klemm, Cyril, Conservation of Species: The Need for a New Approach, 9 Envtl. Poly. & L. 122 (1982). Reprinted with the permission of Environmental Policy and Law.

Sedjo, Robert A., Property Rights for Plants, 97 Resources 1-4 (Fall 1989). Reprinted with the permission of Resources for the Future.

Wilson, E. O., The Current State of Biological Diversity in Biodiversity (E. O. Wilson, ed. 1988). Copyright © 1988 by the National Academy of Sciences. Reprinted with permission. Courtesy of National Academy Press, Washington, D.C.

Chapter 19

Brown Weiss, Edith and Harold K. Jacobson, Engaging Countries: Strengthening Compliance with International Environmental Accord (1998), Figure 5.7, Annual Reports Required of CITES Parties. Reprinted with permission of MIT Press.

Glennon, Michael J., Has International Law Failed the Elephant?, 84

American Journal of International Law 1 (1990). © The American Society of International Law. Reprinted with permission.

Heppes, John B. and Eric J. McFadden, The Convention on International Trade in Endangered Species of Wild Flora and Fauna: Improving the Prospects for Preserving Our Biological Heritage, 5 Boston University International Law Journal 229 (1987). Reprinted with the permission of the Boston University International Law Journal.

Kosloff, Laura H. and Mark C. Trexler, The Convention on International Trade in Endangered Species: No Carrot, But Where's the Stick?, 17 Envtl. L. Rep. 10, 222 (1987). Reprinted with the permission of the Environmental Law Institute.

Simmons, Randy and Urs Kreuter, Save and Elephant—Buy Ivory, The Washington Post, October 1, 1989, at D3. Reprinted with permission of the authors.

Sutton, Michael, Don't Let Them Buy Ivory, The Washington Post, October 9, 1989, at A21. © Washington Post. Reprinted with permission of The Washington Post.

Chapter 20

Brown Weiss, Edith and Charles Weiss, Jr., Transnational Norms of Environmental Behavior and the Spread of the Industrial Ecology Ethic (1997). Reprinted with permission of authors.

Frosch, Robert A., Adapting Technology for a Sustainable World, 37 Environment 16 (1995). Reprinted with the permission of Heldref Publications.

Lallas, Peter, and Andreas Ziegler, International Economics, Trade and the Environment, in International Occupational and Environmental Medicine (Jessica Herzstein et al., eds., Mosby, 1988). Reprinted with the permission of the authors.

Magraw, Daniel, NAFTA and the Environment-. Substance and Process, Section of International Law and Practice, American Bar Association (1995). Reprinted by permission from the American Bar Association © 1995.

Nash, Jennifer and John Ehrenfeld, Code Green, 8 Environment 16 (1996). Reprinted with the permission of Heldref Publications.

Chapter 21

Conservation International, The Debt for Nature Exchange: A Tool for International Conservation, pp. 11, 17-19, 23-30, 37-40 (September 1989). Reprinted by permission.

Fuller, Kathryn S., & Williamson, Douglas F., Debt-for-Nature Swaps, A

New Means of Funding Conservation in Developing Nations. Reprinted with permission from International Environment Reporter, Vol. 11, No. 5, pp.301, 302-303 (May 11, 1988). Copyright 1988 by The Bureau of National Affairs, Inc. (800-372-1033) <http://www.bna.com>

Goldberg, Donald M., The Montreal Protocol Multilateral Fund: A Model for the Framework Convention on Climate Change. Reprinted with permission from International Environment Reporter, Vol. 16, No. 6, pp.233-235 (March 24, 1993). Copyright 1993 by The Bureau of National Affairs, Inc. (800-372-1033) <http://www.bna.com>

Klitgard, Robert, Tropical Gangsters, Excerpts from pp.8-12, 207 (1991). Copyright © 1990 by BasicBooks, Inc. Reprinted by permission of BasicBooks, a subsidiary of Perseus Books Group, LLC.

Rich, Bruce, The Multilateral Development Banks, Environment Policy, and the United States, 12 Ecology Law Quarterly 681. © 1985 by California Law Review, Inc. Reprinted from California Law Review, Vol. 12, No. 4, pp.682-688 by permission.

PART ONE

THE NATURE OF INTERNATIONAL ENVIRONMENTAL ISSUES—BASIC CONCEPTS AND CONTEXT

> Nature is the only superpower.
>
> *Timothy E. Wirth*

> This we know: the earth does not belong to man, man belongs to the earth. All things are connected like the blood that unites us all. Man did not weave the web of life, he is merely a strand in it. Whatever he does to the web, he does to himself.
>
> *Attributed to Chief Seattle, patriarch of the Duwamish and Squamish Indians of Puget Sound, ca. 1855*[1]

The image of the web of life on Earth is a powerful one. It is also a useful and important point of entry into the field of international environmental law, for at least three reasons. First, it conveys the critical message of the interconnectedness of all forms of life on Earth. Because of this interdependence, actions in one part of the web can effect other parts. An appreciation of these phenomena is essential to an understanding of

1. Whether Chief Seattle actually uttered these or similar words is controversial. *See generally* Paul S. Wilson, What Chief Seattle Said, 22 Envtl. L. 1451 (1992); Rudolf Kaiser, A Fifth Gospel, Almost, Chief Seattle's Speech(es): American Origins and European Reception, in Indians and Europe: An Interdisciplinary Collection of Essays 505, at 519-520 (1987). Despite the difficulty of locating an authentic text, the tenor of the sentiments quoted above is not inconsistent with the only extant report of Chief Seattle's remarks on the signing of the Point Elliott Treaty, contained in an appendix to Professor Wilson's article, above, at 1463.

environmental problems themselves and equips us to evaluate policy and legal responses to those problems.

Second, the image of the web of life emphasizes that humans are part of that set of interrelationships. Regardless of whether one takes an anthropocentric view of environmental issues, it is clear that human welfare is affected by the health of nonhuman aspects of the web, and vice versa.

Third, the image reminds us that we are dealing with the conditions that make life possible and define its quality. International environmental law involves human, plant, and animal health and the well-being of entire ecosystems, as well as allocation of natural resources and the more aesthetic, but still important, issues such as preservation of, and access to, natural and cultural sites. The health aspect of international environmental law often is not understood or appreciated, a fact that may lead to more resistance to "environmental" initiatives than would otherwise arise.

Interdependence is a feature of the various elements of the environment of local communities and individual countries no less than it is a characteristic of the global biosphere. But as we will see, it can be dangerous to conceive of environmental problems in terms of political units, whether on the local, national, or regional (e.g., North American or European) level. For illustrations of the fundamental principle that natural systems and associated environmental problems do not respect political boundaries we need only consider such situations as the following, which unfortunately are not at all uncommon: acid rain in one country resulting from sulphur dioxide emissions in another; pollution problems in border-crossing rivers; pesticides applied in one county that cause illness in another; logging in an upstream jurisdiction causing flooding in one downstream; and aircraft noise from an airport in an adjoining city.

International cooperation is normally essential to dealing with such issues. A central task for international environmental policymakers and lawyers is to determine what form(s) such cooperation should take—e.g., what forms of social organization, including institutional and normative aspects, will be effective—and how to bring into existence, as well as to monitor and revise the forms decided on.

That task is complicated because it is not only the elements of ecosystems and the biosphere as a whole that are interrelated with one another. Other interrelationships need also to be kept in mind. Threats to human health and the environment are linked, making it futile to address one without dealing with the other. What is more, protecting health and the environment cannot be approached in isolation from other human activities, such as industrial activity and business investment, or from social conditions, such as degree of poverty/affluence and educational level. In addition, political relationships and conditions, such as the relationship between the nation-states concerned and whether those countries have strong central governments or are beset with civil war, are significant. Finally, it is useful to bear in mind that environmental protection and conservation typically depend on changes in behavior not only of nation-states but also of other agglomerations of individuals such as business organizations and even of individuals themselves. The behavior, attitudes, and psychology of individuals in a particular culture are thus also part of the equation.

All of this makes international environmental law one of the most interesting and challenging areas of legal practice. Quite apart from the diverse scientific, economic, philosophical, and other nonlegal issues involved, the field requires an unusual breadth of substantive legal knowledge. For example, a good international environmental lawyer needs to be knowledgeable about both domestic environmental law and public international law, as well as about the particular aspects of international environmental law with which she or he works. This reality presents challenges to students and teachers of international environmental law, most of whom cannot be assumed to have had the opportunity to study all of the relevant legal and nonlegal areas.

This coursebook thus begins by providing basic material on the nonlegal and legal issues that constitute the context for international environmental law and institutions. Examples of nonlegal topics include global population growth, intergenerational equity, risk assessment, and the tension between industrialized and developing countries; these are covered in Part One, Chapters 1-4. The legal background topics covered in this book are public international law and international institutions; these are treated in Part One, Chapter 5.

Because these issues provide necessary background rather than being the primary focus of the course, this coursebook approaches them differently than it does the actual components of international environmental law. The materials provided regarding the nonlegal background issues are intended to introduce basic concepts, relationships, and questions; in no sense will they provide a complete coverage of these complex topics. Similarly, public international law and institutions (Chapter 5) are the subject of a three-unit (or more) course in most law schools—a luxury not available here. Instead, we cover that topic primarily via textual material written specifically for this book, interspersed with selective excerpts from cases and legal literature and with Notes and Questions, rather than by focusing primarily on excerpts from cases or articles as in more traditional coverage. The latter approach is used for the actual components of international environmental law in Parts Two, Three, and Four, although even in these portions we occasionally resort to text specifically written for this coursebook in order to deal with the fact that there are not many international environmental law cases and to fill in gaps in the relevant literature.

I

Interdependence

The materials in this chapter are intended to convey a sense of the richness of the interconnections described in the Introduction, above, and of the complexity of the issues pertaining to them.

A. THE NATURE OF INTERNATIONAL ENVIRONMENTAL ISSUES

■ THE EARTH: A FRAGILE, INTERDEPENDENT WHOLE

World Commission on Environment and Development [The "Brundtland Commission"], Our Common Future 1 (1987)

In the middle of the 20th century, we saw our planet from space for the first time. Historians may eventually find that this vision had a greater impact on thought than did the Copernican revolution of the 16th century, which upset the human self-image by revealing that the Earth is not the center of the universe. From space, we see a small and fragile ball dominated not by human activity and edifice but by a pattern of clouds, oceans, greenery, and soils. Humanity's inability to fit its doings into that pattern is changing planetary systems, fundamentally. Many such changes are accompanied by life-threatening hazards. This new reality, from which there is no escape, must be recognized—and managed.

Fortunately, this new reality coincides with more positive developments new to this century. We can move information and goods faster around the globe than ever before; we can produce more food and more goods with less investment of resources; our technology and science gives us at least the potential to look deeper into and better understand natural systems. From space, we can see and study the Earth as an organism whose health depends on the health of all its parts. . . .

■ REMARKS OF JOHN S. PERRY

United States Academy of Sciences, April 15, 1988

It is an interesting exercise to design *de novo* an optimum habitat for creatures like us. We would start, of course, with a suitably sized planet a reasonable distance from a warm enough star. We would make the planet big enough so that its gravity could hold captive useful amounts of water and a bit of air. It would be wise to have the planet rotate like a chicken on a spit so that the star's heat would be nicely spread out.

But the rest of the recipe for a habitable planet is not so easy. A look at our neighbors shows the pitfalls. The moon is a complete failure. Too small to hold an atmosphere, and rotating too slowly, it goes through a monthly cycle from furnace heat to unthinkable cold. Something clearly went wrong with Venus, too—the surface temperature is hot enough to melt lead! Mars is somewhat more successful—the air is a bit thin, but even its summers are hardly warmer than Siberian Januaries.

Clearly, designing an Earth isn't as easy as it seems. What's the trick? To maintain a planet at a reasonable temperature, one needs some sort of ingenious one-way valve that will let in the sun's energy, but somehow keep just the right amount of heat down at the surface. Here, physics comes to our rescue. An incandescent body such as our sun emits most of its energy in the short wavelengths of visible light. A warm body such as the earth, however, radiates most of its energy in much longer infrared wavelengths. Solid bodies radiate and absorb energy at all wavelengths, just as a black surface absorbs light of whatever color. Gases, however, absorb and radiate energy in only a finite number of discrete wavelengths; radiation of other frequencies passes through unimpeded. We can thus arrange to trap the earth's heat by providing our atmosphere with gases that do not absorb much of the sun's energy, but which do soak up the earth's rising heat. These gases will then warm, and re-radiate heat back from the atmosphere to Earth. This clever trick is the famous "greenhouse effect."

The most convenient gases for us to use for this planetary down comforter are water vapor and carbon dioxide. Both are plentiful, and both are in any event essential working materials in the business of life. The mechanics of the greenhouse effect has been well understood since the 1860s, and quite realistic numerical calculations of its magnitude were made by Arrhenius around the turn of the century. Thanks to the greenhouse effect, the surface of the Earth is on the average about 34 degrees Celsius warmer than it would be without an atmosphere.

With the heating system now in hand, a planet-constructor must turn to public health. What to do about this flood of potentially damaging ultraviolet radiation coming from our star? Here again, the atmosphere comes to the rescue. With a reasonable amount of oxygen in the atmosphere, solar radiation itself will create a good supply of ozone molecules, and these will soak up the worst of the ultraviolet high in the atmosphere.

So now we know how to build a habitable planet—and somehow we did it, for here we are! But how did we do it? The details are by no means clear, but it seems evident that somehow life itself shaped a planetary environment to its liking. Certainly the very early Earth had an atmosphere and a climate quite unlike today's. A thin film of green stuff gained a foothold, and slowly extracted excess carbon from the air to be buried safely in sediments of the earth's crust. At the same time, the green stuff liberated oxygen, the raw material for shielding ozone and the fuel for air-breathing creatures like us.

In this way, the basic ingredients of a habitable planet were put together by living things in the first billion and a bit years of the Earth's history. Since then, despite the slow evolution of our star and the slow wandering of continents, the Earth as a whole has always had a climate that will support the life that shaped it. But this stability does not imply constancy. Climate, in particular, has always been at once the most regular and the most variable element of our natural environment: the most regular, for the inexorable march of the seasons has been unbroken; the most variable, for we have passed through eras of balmy warmth, great ice ages, and climatic fluctuations on all time scales.

The current geological epoch, for example, is a period of ice ages. For the quarter billion years of the Quaternary epoch, ice has always lurked somewhere on the globe. We know from careful analysis of sediments and glacial ice that ice sheets have dominated the globe for most of this period, interrupted at intervals of about 120,000 years by brief warm interglacial periods such as the Holocene period in which we live. These changes seem to be paced by small oscillations in the Earth's orbit that produce small fluctuations in our supply of heat from the sun.

Since the retreat of the last great glaciation, which was complete about 8,000 years ago, we have enjoyed a generally favorable climate. There have been, however, a few notable fluctuations such as the "Little Ice Age" most clearly felt in Europe in the 17th and 18th centuries. On a lesser scale, the workings of the ocean and atmosphere on a spinning globe not surprisingly give rise to some turbulence that we feel as weather, floods, droughts, and the like. However, other things being equal, what we know about the Earth's history would lead us to expect a rather placid future until the onset of the next glacial period in a few thousand years.

Why, then, are we worried about climate today? What new enemy has appeared to threaten the Earth's sunny stability? To quote that great sage, Pogo, "we have met the enemy, and it is us." Human society, ever growing in numbers and capabilities, is making radical changes in the planetary environment. The most significant changes are evident in the atmosphere, and result from our use of fossil fuels and the land, and our introduction of new materials into the air. By burning fossil fuels—coal and oil—we release back into the atmosphere atoms of carbon that were laboriously extracted and entombed millions of years ago. One might say that we are rewinding the tape of the Earth's history at high speed. . . . We are changing our planet in a massive way, in what has been termed a "great geophysical experiment."

■ INTERNATIONAL ENVIRONMENTAL POLICY—EMERGENCE AND DIMENSIONS

Lynton Caldwell
9 (1984)

Humanity lives in two realities. The abiding reality is that of the *earth*—the planet—independent of man and his works; the other reality—the transient reality—is that of the *world*, which is a creation of the human mind. The earth and its biosphere form a grand synthesis of complex interactive systems within systems, organic and inorganic, animate and inanimate. The world is the way humanity understands and has organized its occupancy of the earth: an expression of imagination and purpose materialized through exploration, invention, labor, and violence. Oceans, islands, species and ecosystems are integral parts of the earth, but the world is not integrated—its cultures and their values do not comprise a unity. All living men may be of one species, but their values are diverse. Physically, men belong to the earth, yet intellectually they may transcend it—a dangerous liberty when dissociated from regard for the necessities of life on earth.

The environmental crisis of the modern world derives from this physical and intellectual duality. Unlike the environmental disasters encountered by prehistoric and primitive man, the modern crisis is largely man-made—a consequence of the failure of human insight and ingenuity to predict and prevent the ill effects of human imagination and purpose. . . .

■ REDEFINING SECURITY

Jessica Tuchman Mathews
68 For. Aff. 162 (1989)

. . . Individuals and governments alike are beginning to feel the cost of substituting for (or doing without) the goods and services once freely provided by healthy ecosystems. Nature's bill is presented in many different forms: the cost of commercial fertilizer needed to replenish once naturally fertile soils; the expense of dredging rivers that flood their banks because of soil erosion hundreds of miles upstream; the loss in crop failures due to the indiscriminate use of pesticides that inadvertently kill insect pollinators; or the price of worsening pollution, once filtered from the air by vegetation. Whatever the immediate cause for concern, the value and absolute necessity for human life of functioning ecosystems is finally becoming apparent. . . .

An important paradox to bear in mind when examining natural resource trends is that so-called nonrenewable resources—such as coal, oil and minerals—are in fact inexhaustible, while so-called renewable resources can be finite. As a nonrenewable resource becomes scarce and more expensive, demand falls, and substitutes and alternative technologies appear. For that reason we will never pump the last barrel of oil or anything close to it. On the other hand, a fishery fished beyond a certain point will not recover, a species driven to extinction will not reappear, and eroded topsoil cannot be replaced (except over geological time). There are, thus, threshold effects for renewable resources that belie the name given them, with unfortunate consequences for policy.

The most serious form of renewable resource decline is the deforestation taking place throughout the tropics. An area the size of Austria is deforested each year. Tropical forests are fragile ecosystems, extremely vulnerable to human disruption. Once disturbed, the entire ecosystem can unravel. The loss of the trees causes the interruption of nutrient cycling above and below the soil, the soil loses fertility, plant and animal species lose their habitats and become extinct, and acute fuelwood shortages appear (especially in the dry tropical forests). The soil erodes without the ground cover provided by trees and plants, and downstream rivers suffer siltation, causing floods and droughts, and damaging expensive irrigation and hydroelectric systems. Traced through its effects on agriculture, energy supply and water resources, tropical deforestation impoverishes about a billion people. This pattern is endemic throughout Central America, much of Asia, sub-Saharan Africa and South America.

The planet's evolutionary heritage—its genetic diversity—is heavily concentrated in these same forests. It is therefore disappearing today on a scale not seen since the age of the dinosaurs, and at an unprecedented pace. Biologists estimate that species are being lost in the tropical forests 1,000-10,000 times faster than the natural rate of extinction. As many as 20 percent of all the species now living may be gone by the year 2,000. The loss will be felt aesthetically, scientifically and, above all, economically. These genetic resources are an important source of food, materials for energy and construction, chemicals for pharmaceuticals and industry, vehicles for health and safety testing, natural pest controls and dozens of other uses.

The only reason that species loss is not a front-page issue is that the majority of species have not yet been discovered, much less studied, so that none but a few conservation biologists can even guess at the number and kinds of species that are vanishing. The bitter irony is that genetic diversity is disappearing on a grand scale at the very moment when biotechnology makes it possible to exploit fully this resource for the first time.

Soil degradation is another major concern. Both a cause and a consequence of poverty, desertification, as it is generally called, is causing declining agricultural productivity on nearly two billion hectares, 15 percent of the earth's land area. The causes are overcultivation, overgrazing, erosion, and salinization and waterlogging due to poorly managed irrigation. In countries as diverse as Haiti, Guatemala, Turkey and India, soil erosion has sharply curtailed agricultural production and potential, sometimes destroying it completely. Though the data are uncertain, it is estimated that the amount of land permanently removed from cultivation due to salinization and waterlogging is equal to the amount of land newly irrigated at great expense each year.

Finally, patterns of land tenure, though not strictly an environmental condition, have an immense environmental impact. In 1975, seven percent of landowners in Latin America possessed 93 percent of all the arable land in this vast region. In Guatemala, a typical case, two percent of the population in 1980 owned 80 percent of the land, while 83 percent of farmers lived on plots too small to support a household. At the same time, even in Costa Rica, with its national concern for social equity, three percent of landowners held 54 percent of the land. These large holdings generally include the most desirable land. The great mass of the rural population is pushed onto the most damage-prone land, usually dry or highly erodible slopes and into the forests. Land reform is among the most difficult of all political undertakings but without it many countries will be unable to create a healthy agricultural sector to fuel economic growth. . . .

A different kind of environmental concern has arisen from mankind's new ability to alter the environment on a planetary scale. The earth's physiology is shaped by the characteristics of four elements (carbon, nitrogen, phosphorous and sulfur); by its living inhabitants (the biosphere); and by the interactions of the atmosphere and the oceans, which produce our climate.

Mankind is altering both the carbon and nitrogen cycles, having increased the natural carbon dioxide concentration in the atmosphere by 25 percent. This has occurred largely in the last three decades through fossil-fuel use and deforestation. The production of commercial fertilizer has doubled the amount of nitrogen nature makes available to living things. The use of a single, minor class of chemicals, chlorofluorocarbons, has punched a continent-sized "hole" in the ozone layer at the top of the stratosphere over Antarctica, and caused a smaller, but growing loss of ozone all around the planet. Species loss is destroying the work of three billion years of evolution. Together these changes could drastically alter the conditions in which life on earth has evolved. . . .

Despite important uncertainties about aspects of greenhouse warming, a virtually unanimous scientific consensus exists on its central features. If present emission trends continue, and unless some as yet undocumented phenomenon (possible increased cloudiness) causes an offsetting cooling, the planet will, on average, get hotter because of the accumulation of these gases. Exactly how large the warming will be, and how fast it will occur, are uncertain. . . .

Hotter temperatures will be only one result of the continuing greenhouse warming. At some point, perhaps quite soon, precipitation patterns are likely to shift, possibly causing dustbowl-like conditions in the U.S. grain belt. Ocean currents are expected to do the same, dramatically altering the climates of many regions. A diversion of the Gulf Stream, for example, would transform Western Europe's climate, making it far colder than it is today. Sea level will rise due to the expansion of water when it is warmed and to the melting of land-based ice. . . . [A] large rise in the sea level would inundate vast coastal regions, erode shorelines, destroy coastal marshes and swamps (areas of very high biological productivity), pollute water supplies through the intrusion of salt water, and put at high risk the vastly disproportionate share of the world's economic wealth that is packed along coastlines. The great river deltas, from the Mississippi to the Ganges, would be flooded. Estimates are that a half-meter rise in Egypt would displace 16 percent of the population, while a two meter rise in Bangladesh would claim 28 percent of the land where 30 million people live today and where more than 59 million are projected to live by 2030.

Positive consequences would be likely as well. Some plants would grow more quickly, fertilized by the additional carbon dioxide. (Many of them, however, will be weeds.) Rainfall might rise in what are now arid but potentially fertile regions, such as parts of sub-Saharan Africa. Conditions for agriculture would also improve in those northern areas that have both adequate soils and water supplies. Nonetheless, as the 1988 drought in the United States vividly demonstrated, human societies, industrial no less than rural, depend on the normal, predictable functioning of the climate system. Climate undergoing rapid change will not only be less predictable because it is different, but may be inherently more variable. Many climatologists believe that as accumulating greenhouse gases force the climate out of equilibrium, climate extremes—such as hurricanes, droughts, cold snaps and typhoons—will become more frequent and perhaps more intense. . . .

Greenhouse change is closely linked to stratospheric ozone depletion, which is also caused by chlorofluorocarbons. The increased ultraviolet radiation resulting from losses in that protective layer will cause an increase in skin cancers and eye damage. It will have many still uncertain impacts on plant and animal life, and may suppress the immune systems of many species.

Serious enough in itself, ozone depletion illustrates a worrisome feature of man's newfound ability to cause global change: it is almost impossible to predict accurately the long-term impact of new chemicals or processes on the environment. Chlorofluorocarbons were thoroughly tested when first introduced, and found to be benign. Their effect on the remote stratosphere was never considered.

Not only is it difficult to anticipate all the possible consequences in a highly interdependent, complex system, the system itself is poorly understood. When British scientists announced the appearance of a continent-sized "hole" in the ozone layer over Antarctica in 1985, the discovery sent shock waves through the scientific community. Although stratospheric ozone depletion had been the subject of intense study and debate for more than a decade, no one had predicted the Antarctic hole and no theory could account for it.

The lesson is this: current knowledge of planetary mechanisms is so scanty that the possibility of surprise, perhaps quite nasty surprise, must be rated rather high. The greatest risk may well come from a completely unanticipated direction. We lack both crucial knowledge and early warning systems.

. . . The planet is not destined to a slow and painful decline into environmental chaos. There are technical, scientific and economical solutions that are feasible to many current trends, and enough is known about promising new approaches to be confident that the right kinds of research will produce huge payoffs. Embedded in current practices are vast costs in lost opportunities and waste, which, if corrected, would bring massive benefits. Some such steps will require only a reallocation of money, while others will require sizable capital investments. None of the needed steps, however, requires globally unaffordable sums of money. What they do demand is a sizable shift in priorities. . . .

But if the technological opportunities are boundless, the social, political and institutional barriers are huge. Subsidies, pricing policies and economic discount rates encourage resource depletion in the name of economic growth, while delivering only the illusion of sustainable growth. Population control remains a controversial subject in much of the world. The traditional prerogatives of nation states are poorly matched with the needs for regional cooperation and global decisionmaking. And ignorance of the biological underpinning of human society blocks a clear view of where the long-term threats to global security lie. . . .

■ A MOMENT ON THE EARTH

Gregg Easterbrook
49-51 (1995)

The Magnitude of Natural Time

The cosmos is thought to be eight to 20 billion years old; Earth and its companion sun 4.5 billion years old; simple microbial life 3.8 million years old; complex microorganisms perhaps 2.8 billion years old; animal life perhaps 600 million years old; mammalian life about 200 million years old. Given time in such vastness, researchers are prone to describing as "recent" events that occurred within the last few hundred million years. Recently, the land mass called North America was located at the South Pole. Recently, life was already very old.

By contrast, the world of intellect is in childhood. The lineage of genus *Homo* stretches perhaps 30,000 centuries into the past; toolmaking humankind may be 8,000 centuries old; *Homo sapiens*, the creatures that look like us, appeared around 350 centuries ago; civilization, defined by agriculture, is thought to have begun perhaps 80 centuries ago; technology may be said to have begun around 50 centuries ago, with Egyptian pyramids and sailing vessels; the human attempt to take over Earth's ecosphere began about two centuries ago, with the industrial era.

Tricks can be played with such expanses of time. Express the age of the Earth as a single year, as Carl Sagan likes to, and the first mammal draws breath on Thanksgiving Day. Our shaggy ancestor *Homo erectus* first beholds light on New Year's Eve. Anyone alive today is born as some blow-dried ninny cries out "two . . . one . . ." to the image of the gaudy ball descending toward inebriated Boeotians in Times Square. . . .

Natural processes that are central to environmental events often engage boundless spans of time. . . .

Some commentators have described the vastness of geologic time as a sort of natural wonder drug. Something dreadful like an ice age renders much of the globe hostile to life; or an asteroid or comet strikes Earth, triggering a "nuclear winter" and acid rain from hell. In the time-as-miracle drug view a catastrophic natural event transpires, immense numbers of years tick by, and then one morning everything is fine again, the birds sweetly singing and fair pastures of lilies turning their lineaments toward the sun. This view overlooks an elementary consideration: Between the catastrophe and the idyllic restoration, *life continues.* Nature has shown itself able to keep creatures alive through protracted periods when ecological conditions are horrible. . . .

That nature can endure painful trials does not mean acts of human malfeasance against the ecology are insignificant. Any damage that occurs to the environment during each person's moment on the Earth frames that person's experience of the planet and diminishes his or her one chance at life, regardless of whatever corrections occur in the long run. And since your lifetime is all that matters to you, even a relatively small human environmental affront can be ample to inspire outrage. But your lifetime is not all that matters to the Earth. It is one of multiple trillions of considera tions in an ongoing endeavor of astounding duration and complexity—an endeavor that, far from being on its last legs, may be just getting under way. . . .

■ CHAOS: MAKING A NEW SCIENCE

James Gleick
3-4, 7-8, 23, 59-64 (1987)

Where chaos begins, classical science stops. For as long as the world has had physicists inquiring into the laws of nature, it has suffered a special ignorance about disorder in the atmosphere, in the turbulent sea, in the fluctuations of wildlife populations, in the oscillations of the heart and the brain. The irregular side of nature, the discontinuous and erratic side—these have been puzzles to science, or worse, monstrosities.

But in the 1970s a few scientists in the United States and Europe began to find a way through disorder. They were mathematicians, physicists, biologists, chemists, all seeking connections between different kinds of irregularity. Physiologists found a surprising order in the chaos that develops in the human heart, the prime cause of sudden, unexplained death. Ecologists explored the rise and fall of gypsy moth populations. Economists dug out old stock price data and tried a new kind of analysis. The insights that emerged led directly into the natural world—the shapes of clouds, the paths of lightning, the microscopic intertwining of blood vessels, the galactic clustering of stars.

. . . The simplest systems are now seen to create extraordinarily difficult problems of predictability. Yet order arises spontaneously in those systems—chaos and order together. Only a new kind of science could begin to cross the great gulf between knowledge of what one thing does—one water molecule, one cell of heart tissue, one neuron—and what millions of them do.

Watch two bits of foam flowing side by side at the bottom of a waterfall. What can you guess about how close they were at the top? Nothing. . . . The modern study of chaos began with the creeping realization in the 1960s that quite simple mathematical equations could model systems every bit as violent as a waterfall. Tiny differences in input could quickly become overwhelming differences in output. . . . In weather, for example, this translates into what is only half-jokingly known as the Butterfly Effect—the notion that a butterfly stirring the air today in Peking can transform storm systems next month in New York.

When the explorers of chaos began to think back on the genealogy of their new science, they found many intellectual trails from the past. But one stood out clearly. For the young physicists and mathematicians leading the revolution, a starting point was the Butterfly Effect. . . .

The Butterfly Effect acquired a technical name: sensitive dependence on initial conditions. And sensitive dependence on initial conditions was not an altogether new notion. It had a place in folklore:

> "*For want of a nail, the shoe was lost;*
> *For want of a shoe, the horse was lost;*
> *For want of a horse, the rider was lost;*

For want of a rider, the battle was lost;
For want of a battle, the kingdom was lost!"

In science as in life, it is well known that a chain of events can have a point of crisis that could magnify small changes. But chaos meant that such points were everywhere. They were pervasive. In systems like the weather, sensitive dependence on initial conditions was an inescapable consequence of the way small scales intertwined with large. . . .

Ravenous fish and tasty plankton. Rain forests dripping with nameless reptiles, birds gliding under canopies of leaves, insects buzzing like electrons in an accelerator. Frost belts where voles and lemmings flourish and diminish with tidy four-year periodicity in the face of nature's bloody combat. The world makes a messy laboratory for ecologists, a cauldron of five million interacting species. Or is it fifty million? Ecologists do not actually know.

Mathematically inclined biologists of the twentieth century built a discipline, ecology, that stripped away the noise and color of real life and treated populations as dynamical systems. Ecologists used the elementary tools of mathematical physics to describe life's ebbs and flows. Single species multiplying in a place where food is limited, several species competing for existence, epidemics spreading through host populations—all could be isolated, if not in laboratories then certainly in the minds of biological theorists.

In the emergence of chaos as a new science in the 1970s, ecologists were destined to play a special role. They used mathematical models, but they always knew that the models were thin approximations of the seething real world. . . .

. . . To describe a population changing each year, a biologist uses a formalism that a high school student can follow easily. Suppose next year's population of gypsy moths will depend entirely on this year's population. You could imagine a table listing all the specific possibilities—31,000 gypsy moths this year means 35,000 next year, and so forth. Or you could capture the relationship between all the numbers for this year and all the numbers for next year as a rule—a function. The population (x) next year is a function (F) of the population this year: $x_{next} = F(x)$. Any particular function can be drawn on a graph, instantly giving a sense of its overall shape.

In a simple model like this one, following a population through time is a matter of taking a starting figure and applying the same function again and again. To get the population for a third year, you just apply the function to the result for the second year, and so on. The whole history of the population becomes available through this process of functional iteration—a feedback loop, each year's output serving as the next year's input. Feedback can get out of hand, as it does when sound from a loudspeaker feeds back through a microphone and is rapidly amplified to an unbearable shriek. Or feedback can produce stability, as a thermostat does in regulating the temperature of a house: any temperature above a fixed point leads to cooling, and any temperature below it leads to heating.

Many different types of functions are possible. A naive approach to population biology might suggest a function that increases the population by a certain percentage each year. That would be a linear function—$x_{next} = rx$—and it would be the classic Malthusian scheme for population growth, unlimited by food supply or moral restraint. The parameter r represents the rate of population growth. Say it is 1.1; then if this year's population is 10, next year's is 11. If the input is 20,000, the output is 22,000. The population rises higher and higher, like money left forever in a compound-interest savings account.

Ecologists realized generations ago that they would have to do better. An ecologist imagining real fish in a real pond had to find a function that matched the crude realities of life—for example, the reality of hunger, or competition. When the fish proliferate, they start to run out of food. A small fish population will grow rapidly. An overly large fish population will dwindle. . . .

. . . Anyway, if the population kept bouncing back and forth, ecologists assumed that it was oscillating around some underlying equilibrium. The equilibrium was the important thing. It did not occur to the ecologists that there might be no equilibrium.

■ OUR COMMON FUTURE

World Commission on Environment and Development
[The "Brundtland Commission"]
4-6 (1987)

The planet is passing through a period of dramatic growth and fundamental change. Our human world of 5 billion must make room in a finite environment for another human world. The population could stabilize at between 8 billion and 14 billion sometime next century, according to UN projections. More than 90 per cent of the increase will occur in the poorest countries, and 90 per cent of that growth in already bursting cities.

Economic activity has multiplied to create a $13 trillion world economy [$18 trillion in 1997—EDS.], and this could grow five- or tenfold in the coming half-century. Industrial production has grown more than fiftyfold over the past century, four-fifths of this growth since 1950. Such figures reflect and presage profound impacts upon the biosphere, as the world invests in houses, transport, farms, and industries. Much of the economic growth pulls raw material from forests, soils, seas, and waterways.

A mainspring of economic growth is new technology, and while this technology offers the potential for slowing the dangerously rapid consumption of finite resources, it also entails high risks, including new forms of pollution and the introduction to the planet of new variations of life forms that could change evolutionary pathways. Meanwhile, the industries most heavily reliant on environmental resources and most heavily polluting are growing most rapidly in the developing world, where there is both more urgency for growth and less capacity to minimize damaging side effects.

These related changes have locked the global economy and global ecology together in new ways. We have in the past been concerned about the impacts of economic growth upon the environment. We are now forced to concern ourselves with the impacts of ecological stress—degradation of soils, water regimes, atmosphere, and forests—upon our economic prospects. We are now forced to accustom ourselves to a sharp increase in economic interdependence among nations. We are now forced to accustom ourselves to an accelerating ecological interdependence among nations. Ecology and economy are becoming ever more interwoven—locally, regionally, nationally, and globally—into a seamless net of causes and effects. . . .

International economic relationships pose a particular problem for environmental management in many developing countries. Agriculture, forestry, energy production, and mining generate at least half the gross national product of many developing countries and account for even larger shares of livelihoods and employment. Exports of natural resources remain a large factor in their economies, especially for the least developed. Most of these countries face enormous economic pressures, both international and domestic, to overexploit their environmental resource base. . . .

Notes and Questions

1. *Interrelationships and interdependence.* What interrelationships in nature are identified in the foregoing excerpts? What relationships between nature and human activity? What relationships between specific international environmental issues, or between possible solutions to those problems?

Do you agree that the world is increasingly interdependent—culturally, economically, politically, ecologically? In terms of ecological interdependence, is it accurate to say that aspects of the biosphere (i.e., the layer of land, water, and atmosphere that supports life) are increasingly interdependent or that humans have become increasingly aware of that interdependence or that anthropogenic (i.e., human generated) activity is increasingly affecting the details of that interdependence? What does interdependence imply for coexistence or cooperation among nation-states?

2. *Feedback and self-correction.* What sorts of feedback, reinforcement, and self-correcting mechanisms and effects are evident in the foregoing excerpts?

3. *Feedback, self-correction, and logic.* Does the presence of feedback loops and reinforcement or self-correction effects make linear logic unsuit-

able and require the adoption of a new ecologic that takes account of these phenomena?

4. *Uncertainty.* Chaos Theory, as described in the excerpt by James Gleick, obviously has implications for our ability to predict the behavior and fate of species and ecosystems. It is also evident from the excerpts by Matthews and others that considerable uncertainty exists regarding the details of many specific international environmental issues. This is perhaps most obvious with respect to climate change, but scientific uncertainty also exists in many other areas, such as what health and environment risks are posed by the proposed import of a new, untested chemical. In addition, the final excerpt above (from *Our Common Future*) reminds us that we are dealing with a dynamic situation that is changing rapidly in many respects (e.g., population and economic activity), which creates even more uncertainties. Scientific and other uncertainty and how the international legal system can take account of it are discussed in Chapter 4.

5. *Specific international environmental issues.* Parts Two, Three, and Four, below, address specific international problems mentioned in the foregoing excerpts. When you read those materials, we suggest you bear in mind the issues raised in the present chapter.

B. HUMAN POPULATION

> In many parts of the world, the population is growing at rates that cannot be sustained by available environmental resources, at rates that are outstripping any reasonable expectations of improvements in housing, health care, food security, or energy supplies.
>
> *World Commission on Environment and Development (The "Brundtland Commission"), Our Common Future 9 (1987)*

> If we lift our gaze from the frightening daily headlines . . . we shall see that economic life in the United States and the rest of the world has been getting better rather than worse during recent centuries and decades. There is, moreover, no persuasive reason to believe that these trends will not continue indefinitely. . . . [A]dditional children have positive long-run effects on the standard of living.
>
> *Julian Simon (1990)*

Human population growth is often raised either as a problem in itself or as a factor significantly affecting international environmental issues. As the two quotations above indicate, however, opinions differ greatly (and passionately) regarding the effect of increases in human population. What is not in question is that the world is experiencing massive human population growth and that the vast majority of that growth will occur in developing countries for the foreseeable future. The materials below provide a historical description of human population growth and then present two excerpts expressing different views on the subject.

The world's population has increased dramatically since 10,000 years ago, when human society shifted from hunter-gatherer to agricultural. In 8000 B.C., the world's population is estimated to have been approximately 8 million. By mid-1997 A.D., world population was about 5.8 billion.

The population growth rate, determined by the relative levels of birth and death rates, increased exponentially. It took about 600 years to double the population from its level of 265,000,000 in 1000 A.D. (to 545,000,000 in 1600); and world population was only 900,000,000 around the start of the Industrial Revolution at the end of the eighteenth century. In contrast, it took only 40 years to double 1950's population of 2,500,000,000.

Mortality is declining in most countries of the world. Life expectancy at birth reached 64.4 years in 1990-1995 at the global level, an increase of 6.5 years since 1970-1975. Life expectancy at birth in the more-developed regions was 74.4 years, more than 12 years higher than in the less-developed regions where it was 62.3 years, which was in turn 11 years higher than the average life expectancy, 51.2 years, for the least-developed countries. Women are expected to live about four years longer than men. For the world as a whole, life expectancy for men is 62.4 years, while that for women is 66.5 years. In 1996, life expectancy for men in some countries, e.g., Russia, decreased.[1]

The population growth rate appears now to have slowed. World population is still expected to increase, although estimates vary regarding how much. For example, respectable estimates of world population in the year 2025 range from 7,280,000,000 to 9,190,000,000. United Nations projections are that world population will reach 10 billion in the year 2050 and level off at approximately 11.6 billion. A higher projection is that global population will reach 21 billion by 2150; a lower projection estimates a peak of 7.5 billion in 2050.[2] Table 1-1 illustrates these trends.

The disparate population-growth projections reflect differing estimates regarding initial population size and age-sex structure and varying assump-

1. The information in the text is derived from several sources, mostly United Nations or World Bank publications such as United Nations Economic and Social Council, Review of Population Trends, Policies and Programmes: Monitoring of World Populations Trends and Policies, E/CN.9/1995/2 and The World Bank Atlas 1994 and 1995. Some of that material is taken verbatim for purposes of this text only.

2. For a discussion of population projections, *see* Ygdrassil, Gold, Anderson & Hizsnyik, A Critical Review of Population Projections for the Study of Long-term, Large-scale Interactions between Development and Environment, in Scenario of Socioeconomic Development for Studies of Global Environmental Change: A Critical Review (IIASA: F.L. Toth, E. Hizsnyik & W.C. Clark, eds. 1989).

Table 1-1
World Population (in millions)

8000 B.C.	8
200 B.C.	190
1000 A.D.	265
1300 A.D.	360
1400 A.D.	350 (after the Plague)
1600 A.D.	545
1800 A.D.	900
1900 A.D.	1,600
1950 A.D.	2,500
1975 A.D.	3,900
1990 A.D.	5,400
2025 A.D.	7,280-9,190

Sources: McNamara, Time Bomb or Myth: The Population Problem, 62 For. Aff. 1107 (1985) (for 8000 B.C.); C. McEvedy & R. Jones, Atlas of World Population History (1978) (for 200 B.C.-1975 A.D.); United Nations, World Population Prospects, Estimates and Projections as assessed in 1982, U.N. Pop. Studies No. 855, ST/ESA/SER.A/86 (low estimate for 2025); Keyfitz, The Growing Human Population, Sci. Am., Sept. 1989, at 120 (high estimate for 2025).

tions about fertility, migration, and, to a lesser extent, mortality. Factors such as fertility, in turn, are subject to a variety of influences.

Historically, there has been an inverse correlation between a society's level of economic wealth and its birthrate: the more wealthy a society, the lower its birthrate. Similarly, industrialization and urbanization have tended to lead to lower birthrates. This general pattern continues today: developed industrialized countries generally have significantly lower birthrates (some were less than replacement level in 1997) than do developing countries, although there are notable differences among countries and the correlation is not perfect. This relationship is evident in Table 1-2.

This phenomenon is called demographic transition. It has been universally observed and documented, but many different theories purport to explain it. The largest single factor in decreasing birthrates appears to be increased social status and education for women. The latter effect, at least, tends to occur as per capita income increases. Nevertheless, affecting population growth rates is a very sensitive process. Consider the following quotation:

> Achieving [a balance between the needs and wishes of a population and the environmental means to sustain them] is the most difficult of environment-related public policies. The beliefs and values of people concerning human numbers are rooted in the distant past when human circumstances differed radically. Population as an issue includes family formation, birth or

Table 1-2

Population growth rate 1980-90	*Number of countries*	*GNP (US$000.000) 1990*	*Population (000,000) 1990*	*Per capita income (US$) 1990*
More than 3.0%	52	743,000	684	1,170
2.2%—3.0%	43	961,000	832	1,150
1.5%—2.1%	27	1,575,000	2,478	640
1.0%—1.4%	16	5,881,000	341	17,240
Less than 1.0%	47	11,679,000	960	12,170
No data	—	—	—	—

Source: The World Bank Atlas 1995.

> conception control, and the meaning of life itself. The issue is meshed in a cultural context, bound up with considerations of social status (personal, familial, ethnic, and communal), property and legal rights, religion and concepts of morality and social justice. A denominator common to these issues is political power. In human society numbers "count"—no less in egalitarian democracies than in expansionist despotisms, no less in market economies than in Marxist socialism.
>
> More than any other aspect of public policy, population in its fullest sense is clouded by emotional and intuitive miasmas. Its issues are more often characterized by rationalization than by reality-tested rationality. Although solutions to the problems require technological assistance the "population problem" per se has no technical solution. It is fundamentally a problem of social philosophy, and the nature of its *political* reality, as distinguished from its *ecological* or *environmental* reality, is a construct of the human mind.[3]

Estimates about mortality differ, for example, because of uncertainties about death rates from diseases such as Aquired Immunity Deficiency Syndrome (AIDS). AIDS has already struck very hard in Africa, and some researchers predict an exponential growth in HIV-infection rates in Asia over the next decade; projections vary widely because they depend on unknowable factors such as advances in medical science, access of low-income people to such advances, and changes in human behavior. Another negative effect on population growth may be chemicals that disrupt the human body's endocrine (hormone) system. As is discussed in Chapter 13 below, serious concerns exist that these chemicals interfere significantly with humankind's ability to reproduce (as well as causing other serious health and environmental problems).

As of 1992, 77 percent of the world's approximately 5.3 billion people

3. Lynton Caldwell, International Environmental Policy: Emergence and Dimensions 170-171 (2d ed. 1990).

lived in developing countries. Approximately 800,000,000-1,000,000,000 of them exist in what Robert McNamara called "absolute poverty," a condition so fraught with malnutrition, lack of resources, exposure to the elements, and illiteracy as to be beneath any reasonable level of human decency. Although globally the percentage of poor is decreasing, the number of poor people continues to expand. The population situation in most developing countries appears unlikely to change soon, in spite of some success in population control. Even taking into account migration between countries, approximately 95 percent of the world's population growth over the next three decades is expected to occur in developing countries. For example, projections are that the population of Africa—where the population growth rate is expected to be highest—will increase by more than 200 percent between 1994 and 2050. The projected 2.1 billion people will be three times Africa's 1994 population and almost 10 times its 1950 population.

In the aggregate (and even taking into account the AIDS pandemic), developing countries face a population increase over the next 30 years that exceeds the total population of those countries in 1950. Even if average developing country birthrates were somehow reduced to a replacement level, population size would continue to increase dramatically over the next 25 years, as today's children (a large proportion of developing countries' populations) come of childbearing age.

Developing countries thus face the task of integrating massive numbers of people into their societies. This is occurring amidst an ongoing effort to improve, as rapidly as possible, the low living standards prevalent in developing countries. The current infrastructure of developing countries will need to expand rapidly with respect to the creation of jobs, schools, and other general facilities for these people. Historically, such development has inflicted severe stress on the environment as nations delayed coping with environmental concerns until after they had attained a level of prosperity. Moreover, the massive increase in absolute numbers of people in developing countries will place additional pressures on the environment. That will occur even though much of the population, at least in the foreseeable future, will probably continue to move to cities, creating—among other things—Third World megaglopolises characterized by overcrowding and pollution.

As of mid-1994, 2.5 billion persons, i.e., 45 percent of world population, were urban dwellers. Of these, 1.7 billion resided in the less-developed regions. The world's urban population is growing at a rate of 2.5 percent per annum, three times that of rural populations (0.8 percent per annum). As a result, urban areas are absorbing 61 million persons each year compared with 25 million for rural areas. United Nations projections are that sometime over the next ten years the earth will no longer be predominantly rural: over half the world's population will live in cities. This is the largest population movement in history.

Patterns of urbanization differ markedly between the more-developed and the less-developed regions, as well as among the less-developed regions. In 1994, 75 percent of the population of the more-developed regions were urban residents. However, the less-developed regions are undergoing a rapid process of urbanization in contrast to the more-developed regions where the urbanization process has slowed. Latin America is more highly urbanized than Africa or Asia. For a table listing the world's 15 largest urban agglomerations in 1994 and as projected in 2015, see World Urbanization Prospects: The 1994 Revision (United Nations).

In both rural and urban areas, population growth places stress on water supplies. Water is already a scarce resource in many parts of the world. Some 80 countries, with 40 percent of the world population, suffer from serious water shortages. The bulk of world water use is claimed by irrigated agriculture, which accounts for about 70 percent of total withdrawals. Rates of water use are expected to continue to increase well into the next century, led by still increasing rates of irrigation in many parts of the world. Projections made by hydrologists indicate that meeting demands by 2000 could require virtually all the usable freshwater supplies in northern Africa and western Asia.

Developed nations, and even relatively well-off developing nations, may be besieged by increased migration as more people search for a better life or attempt to escape environmental catastrophes—anthropogenic or nonanthropogenic. Thus all countries, regardless of their stage of development, are affected by population growth.

A major question for decisionmakers thus is what to do about population growth. What are the probable effects of substantial population growth on economic development? On resource availability? On environmental quality? On political stability? On international relations?

These questions are not new, of course, just as many other environmental issues are not new. Plato wrote that agricultural practices had degraded Attica's land into the "bones of a wasted body . . . the richer and softer parts of the soil having fallen away, and the mere skeleton being left."[4] In the eighteenth century, Thomas Robert Malthus lamented the disasters he saw as inevitable as human population increased relative to natural resources.[5] Malthus believed that high population growth can only lead to lower living standards and a return of high mortality rates as humans deplete the earth's natural resources. For over a decade, beginning in 1820, Malthus's theories prevailed over strong criticism from economist David Ricardo, scholar William Godwin, and others who believed that more people would stimulate economies and new technology would develop to fulfill any unmet needs. Malthus, however, had indeed underestimated technology, particularly in agriculture, and the theories of Ricardo and Godwin

4. Plato's *Critias, quoted in* R. Dubos, A God Within 3-4 (1973).
5. *See, e.g.,* T.R. Malthus, Essay on the Principle of Population 9 (1960).

quickly regained public support. For a long time, it seemed that Malthus had lost the argument.

The battle has now been joined again, this time with an expressly ecological thrust, debating not only the possible limits imposed by natural resources (e.g., air, water, soil, and living space) but also the dangers posed by unmanaged (and perhaps unmanageable) pollution. The broader question of the carrying capacity of the earth has reemerged. The following excerpts illustrate the debate between the two population theory camps, which have been called the "Malthusians," "Conservationists," and "Doomsters" on the pessimistic side and the "Cornucopians," "Possibilists," and "Boomsters" on the optimistic side.[6]

■ THE GROWING HUMAN POPULATION

Nathan Keyfitz
Sci. Amer. 118 (Sept. 1989)

. . . Only in the past few decades have humans brought about changes comparable in magnitude to those wrought by nature during long epochs of geological time. Forests that grew over centuries and soils that took millions of years to develop are now being used up in a single human lifetime.

Can one be glad that the rate of increase [of population] is slowing when it is not rates that wreak ecological destruction but absolute numbers of people? . . .

Today rapid population growth is occurring simultaneously with improvements in production methods. . . . Labor-saving technology makes it more difficult to turn unequipped workers into gold. . . .

Are the unemployed evidence of overpopulation? Or are they not, rather, evidence of a badly run economy, in which the wages of those who do have jobs are kept artificially high? . . .

Population increases, then, abetted by various aspects of technology and political structure, threaten social and political stability in the less developed countries. In addition, environmental issues are now emerging in the less developed as well as in the developed regions. One such issue is the flooding caused by deforestation; overlogging is directly related to the demand from ever-expanding populations for building material, firewood, additional farmland and foreign capital. . . .

High birth rates in the countryside have forced many subsistence farmers onto marginal lands. . . .

. . . A case might therefore be made for the ecological innocuousness of cities—were it not for one feature of modern urban dwellers: their

6. *See* Clark, Sustainable Development of the Biosphere: Themes for a Research Program,

unprecedented mobility. . . . [M]uch of the damage to the ecosphere is related to movement and travel [by cars, buses, and planes].

. . . There must be some natural limit, some ultimate constraint [on population growth]. [P]rogress in agriculture does not exorcise other limits set by, for example, the availability of suitable living space, constraints on production and the limited capacity of the environment to absorb insults to it. . . .

■ POPULATION MATTERS: PEOPLE, RESOURCES, ENVIRONMENT, AND IMMIGRATION

Julian Simon
22-25, 40-54 (1990)

[E]conomic life in the United States and the rest of the world has been getting better rather than worse during recent centuries and decades. There is, moreover, no persuasive reason to believe that these trends will not continue indefinitely.

Life expectancy [has risen]. . . . Health has improved, too. . . . The main air pollutants—particulates and sulfur dioxide—have declined since 1960 and 1970, respectively. . . . [F]urther increases in income [in developing countries] almost surely will bring about pollution abatement, just as increases in income in the United States have provided the wherewithal for better garbage collection and cleaner air and water. . . .

Food is an especially important resource, and the evidence indicates that its supply is increasing despite rising population. The long-run prices of food relative to wages, and even relative to consumer goods are down. Famine deaths have decreased in the past century even in absolute terms, let alone relative to the much larger population. . . .

But does not a larger population necessarily mean "more pressure" on the land . . . ? [T]he more general trend points in the opposite direction. In all the higher-income industrialized countries in Europe, North America, and in Japan, a smaller absolute number of farmers are producing much more food and feeding much larger populations than in the past.

. . . Population growth and productivity increase are not independent forces running a race. Rather, additional persons cause technological advances by inventing, adapting, and diffusing new productive knowledge. . . .

In short, economic theory that includes key elements left out of previous models, together with the empirical data, suggests that additional children have positive long-run effects upon the standard of living.

---

in Sustained Development of the Biosphere 9 (IIASA: W.C. Clark & R.E. Munn eds. 1986); J. Tierney, Betting the Planet, N.Y. Times Mag. (Dec. 2, 1990).

Notes and Questions

1. *Examining population theories.* What are some of the underlying assumptions involved in the different population theories? Are they valid? Why or why not? Is Keyfitz correct in asserting that it is the absolute number of people that creates ecological damage, not the rate of growth? What would Simon say about that?

2. *Population and the Rio Declaration.* The only reference to population in the Rio Declaration—the statement of principles on environment and development adopted at the 1992 UN Conference on Environment and Development (UNCED)—is in Principle 8: "To achieve sustainable development and a higher quality of life for all people, States should reduce and eliminate unsustainable patterns of production and consumption and promote appropriate demographic policies." What guidance does this provide? *See also* Chapter 5 (Demographic Dynamics and Sustainability) of Agenda 21, also adopted at UNCED.

3. *Population and development.* The relationship between population and development was addressed at the United Nations-sponsored International Conference on Population and Development (ICPD), held in Cairo in 1994. Chapter 3 of the ICPD Plan of Action addressed the relationship between environment and population. Some relevant provisions follow:

> 3.3. Sustainable development implies, *inter alia,* long-term sustainability in production and consumption relating to all economic activities, including industry, energy, agriculture, forestry, fisheries, transport, tourism and infrastructure, in order to optimize ecologically sound resource use and minimize waste. Macroeconomic and sectoral policies have, however, rarely given due attention to population considerations.
>
> 3.24. Meeting the basic human needs of growing populations is dependent on a healthy environment. These human dimensions need to be given attention in developing comprehensive policies for sustainable development in the context of population growth.
>
> 3.25. Demographic factors, combined with poverty and lack of access to resources in some areas, and excessive consumption and wasteful production patterns in others, cause or exacerbate problems of environmental degradation and resource depletion and thus inhibit sustainable development.
>
> 3.26. Pressure on the environment may result from rapid population growth, distribution and migration, especially in ecologically vulnerable ecosystems. Urbanization and policies that do not recognize the need for rural development also create environmental problems.
>
> 3.27. Implementation of effective population policies in the context of sustainable development, including reproductive health and family-planning programmes, require new forms of participation by various actors at all levels in the policy-making process.

3.28. Consistent with Agenda 21, the objectives are:

(a) To ensure that population, environmental and poverty eradication factors are integrated in sustainable development policies, plans and programmes;

(b) To reduce both unsustainable consumption and production patterns as well as negative impacts of demographic factors on the environment in order to meet the needs of current generations without compromising the ability of future generations to meet their own needs.

4. *Population growth and economic growth.* Economic structures in most countries are based on growth. Can economies remain or become stable or strong if the national population is declining? What are some of the effects of fewer people in a society? If you were a government leader, under what circumstances would you be concerned about a stable population size? A declining population? Who will pay for retirement and other social programs for the elderly if population declines such that there are fewer people working than there are retired persons?

5. *Mandating population control?* Robert McNamara grouped the consequences of population growth into two broad categories: "First are the effects that bear on the pace of national economic development and on political stability and human rights in the developing countries. . . . [S]econd are the effects on the international system: principally, the perpetuation of the gap between rich and poor countries and all that implies for international economic and political relationships." Robert S. McNamara, Time Bomb or Myth: The Population Problem, 62 For. Aff. 1107 (1985). One thing he feared was a time when countries would feel forced to mandate population control and the effect that would have, *inter alia*, on human rights. If you were drafting international legislation on population control what would it look like? Consider the following possible norms:

A: Each state shall institute a population-control program to ensure that, by the year 2020, no couple shall have more than two children. To prevent illegal childbearing, every person shall, after replacing herself or himself, be sterilized. Rules shall be adopted for allocating children to parents for purposes of determining whether a particular person has reproduced herself or himself.

B: Each state shall institute a family planning program. Every state shall ensure that a full variety of contraceptive devices are available to all residents. Parents will be urged to have small families. Every child, as he or she comes of childbearing age, shall receive education concerning procreation. No one will be allowed to reproduce until they are of a specified age.

C: A state's overall birthrate shall not exceed replacement level.

6. *Population and climate change.* How might the evidence of gaseous buildup in the atmosphere leading to climate change affect one's approach to population growth? Should the virtual certainty that some countries (such as the United States and China) will experience population growth, while others (such as Italy and Germany) will have stable or reduced populations, affect the formulation of norms to control climate change—e.g., should limits be based on per capita emissions of greenhouse gasses or on per country emissions of the same gasses? *See* chapter 12, below.

7. *Cornucopians vs. Malthusians.* Julian Simon, determined to prove his "Cornucopian" theory, offered to bet anyone $1,000 that commodity prices would decrease over a ten-year period. Paul Erlich, a leader of modern Malthusian theory, accepted the offer. Erlich chose five metals (chrome, copper, nickel, tin, and tungsten) that he believed would increase in price over ten years, due to increased pressure from growing populations. The bet was in the form of a futures contract. Simon "bought" quantities of each metal for $200 each and in 1990 would sell these to Erlich at 1980 prices. Thus if the combined 1990 price of these metals was higher than $1,000, Simon would pay Erlich the difference; if the quantities were worth less than $1,000, Erlich would pay the difference.

In 1990, Erlich wrote Simon a check for $576.07 to pay off the bet. Does this add credibility to Simon's population theory? Would he assert that it shows that natural resources are not really "scarce" and that we are not running out of them? Does it detract from the Malthusian theory of more mouths, less food? What about other implications of population growth?

8. *Illustration: population growth in a bottle.* For an illustration of the phenomenon of steady growth in a finite environment, consider the case used by Al Bartlett of the University of Colorado of a strain of bacteria that doubles its numbers inside a bottle every minute:[7] Suppose that one bacterium is placed in a bottle at 11 A.M., and it is observed that the bottle is full at noon. When was the bottle half-full? At what time would an average bacterium first realize—assuming it had the capacity to realize anything—that it and its fellow bacteria were running out of room? At 11:55 A.M., when the bottle is only 3 percent filled and 97 percent empty, how many would perceive that there was a problem? Suppose further that at 11:58, when the bottle is still 75 percent empty, a search for new bottles is undertaken and that three new empty bottles are discovered at 11:59. For how long will the discovery allow the bacteria to continue growing? Would Simon say that this thought game contains any lessons for human population growth?

9. *Optimism and population growth.* One commentator has said that one's view of whether population growth is a serious environmental problem depends ultimately on whether one is fundamentally optimistic or pessimistic and that his own view seems to depend on whom he has spoken

7. University of Colorado, Summit Magazine (1991).

to about the issue most recently. Do you agree with the first proposition? What information is needed to proceed beyond the quandary he describes?

C. SOCIAL AND CULTURAL CONTEXT

The relationship between the environment and the cultural and social aspects of society is to some extent intuitively obvious: one would expect that a society will reflect the ecological conditions in which that society exists—e.g., that diet, hunting practices, and living arrangements will bear a relationship to the abundance and migration patterns of game and to the agricultural potential of a particular locale. The relationship is also complicated, however, not only because it involves human psychology and because different effects may offset each other but also because humans have developed means of coping with limitations that otherwise would be placed on us by our environments (e.g., heating and air conditioning systems, pesticides, agricultural irrigation, and synthetic materials). In addition, decisions made in distant geographic locations now often affect living conditions at a particular place (e.g., a decision to test nuclear weapons in a specific locale or to build a dam on an international river), and individuals' and groups' aspirations and expectations are now influenced by global communications. The following two excerpts explore some aspects of the relationship between environment and the cultural and social aspects of society.

■ BUSHMEN

John Yellen
42 Science 41 (1985)

. . . I had expected the Kalahari Desert to be bare open sand. I had imagined myself looking out over vast stretches that swept across to the horizon. But to my surprise, I found that the dunes were covered with trees and that during the rains the grasses grew high over my head. The bare sand, where I could see it, was littered with leaves, and over these the living trees and brush threw a dappled pattern of sunlight and shade. To look in the far distance and maintain a sense of direction, to narrow my focus and pick a way between the acacia bushes and their thorns, and then to look down, just in front of my feet to search out menacing shapes, was too much for me. Already, in that first month, the Bushmen had shown me a puff adder coiled motionless by the base of an acacia tree, but not until Cumsa the Hunter came up close to it, ready to strike it with a spear, could I finally see what all those hands were pointing at. . . .

We dug day after day in the old camps—and found what Dau said we should. Bones, decomposing, but still identifiable: bones of wildebeest and steenbok among the charcoal and mongongo nut shells.

We dug our squares, sifting through the sand for bones. And when I dumped the bones, the odd ostrich eggshell bead, and other bits and pieces out onto the bridge table to sort, so much of what my eyes and ears told me was confirmed in this most tangible form. If excavation in one square revealed the bones of a wildebeest or kudu or other large antelope, then the others would contain them as well. In an environment as unpredictable as the Kalahari, where the game was hard to find and the probability of failure high, survival depended on sharing, on spreading the risk. And the bones, distributed almost evenly around the individual family hearths confirmed that. What also impressed me was how little else other than the bones there was. Most archeological sites contain a broad range of debris. But in those years the Bushmen owned so little. Two spears or wooden digging sticks or strings of ostrich eggshell beads were of no more use than one. Better to share, to give away meat or extra belongings and through such gifts create a web of debts, of obligations that some day would be repaid. In 1948, even in 1965, to accumulate material goods made no sense. . . .

So we left the 1940s, collapsed the bridge table and the folding chairs and went to that site that played such a crucial role for anthropologists: DBC 12, the 1963 camp where those old myths about hunters and gatherers came up against the hard rock truth. . . .

What [Richard Lee] found in that desert camp, that dry, hard land, set the anthropological world back on its collective ear. What his scale and his wristwatch and his systematic scribbles showed was that we were fooled, that we had it all wrong. To be a hunter and gatherer wasn't that bad after all. They didn't work that hard, even in this land of thorns: For an adult, it came to less time than a nine-to-five office worker puts in on the job. They lived a long time, too, didn't wear out and die young but old-looking, as we had always thought. Even in this camp, the camp with the good hunting dogs, it was plants, not meat, which provided the staff of life. Women walked through the nut groves and collected nuts with their toes, dug in the molapos and sang to each other through the bush. Unlike the game, which spooked so easily and followed the unpredictable rains, the nuts, roots, and berries were dependable, there in plenty, there for the picking. Another distinguished anthropologist, Marshall Sahlins, termed those DBC 12 people "the original affluent society"—something quite different from the traditional conception of hunting and gathering as a mean, hard existence half a step ahead of starvation and doom.

Over the years that name was held—but life in the Kalahari has changed. That kind of camp, with all the bones and mongongo nuts and dogs, is no more.

By the mid-1970s, things were different at Dobe. Diane Gelburd, another of the anthropologists out there then, only needed to look around her to see how the Bushman lifestyle had changed from the way Richard recorded it, from how Sahlins described it. But what had changed the people at DBC 12 who believed that property should be commonly held and shared? What had altered their system of values? That same winter Diane decided to find out. . . .

First knowledge, then belief, and finally material culture. She did the less sensitive questions first. "Do you have a field? What do you grow? What kind of animals do you have? How many of what?" Then came the hard part: She needed to see what people actually owned. I tagged along with her one day and remember the whispers inside one dark mud hut. Trunks were unlocked and hurriedly unpacked away from the entrance to shield them from sight. A blanket spread out on a trunk revealed the secret wealth that belied their statements: "Me? I have nothing." In the semidarkness she made her inventory. Then the trunks were hastily repacked and relocked with relief.

She went through the data, looked at those lists of belongings, itemized them in computer printouts. Here's a man who still hunts. The printout shows it. He has a bow and quiver and arrows on which the poison is kept fresh. He has a spear and snares for birds. He has a small steenbok skin bag, a traditional carryall that rests neatly under his arm.

He also has 19 goats and two donkeys, bought from the Herero or Tswana, who now get Dobe Bushmen to help plant their fields and herd their cows. They pay in livestock, hand-me-down clothing, blankets, and sometimes cash. He has three large metal trunks crammed full: One is packed to the top with shoes, shirts, and pants, most well-worn. He has two large linen mosquito nets, 10 tin cups, and a metal file. He has ropes of beads: strand upon strand—over 200 in all, pounds of small colored glass beads made in Czechoslovakia that I had bought in Johannesburg years earlier. He has four large iron pots and a five-gallon plastic jerry can. He has a plow, a gift from the anthropologists. He has a bridle and bit, light blankets, a large tin basin. He has six pieces of silverware, a mirror and hairbrush, two billycans. His wife and his children together couldn't carry all that. The trunks are too heavy and too large for one person to carry so you would have to have two people for each. What about the plow, those heavy iron pots? Quite a job to carry those through bush, through the thick thorns.

But here is the surprising part. Talk to that man. Read the printout. See what he knows, what he believes. It isn't surprising that he speaks the Herero language and Setswana fluently or that he has worked for the Herero, the anthropologists. Nothing startling there. A budding Dobe capitalist. But then comes the shock: He espouses the traditional values.

"Bushmen share things, John. We share things and depend on each other, help each other out. . . ."

But the same person, his back to the door, opens his trunks, unlocks them one by one, lays out the blankets, the beads, then quickly closes each before he opens the next.

Multiply that. Make a whole village of people like that, and you can see the cumulative effect: You can actually measure it. As time goes on, as people come to own more possessions; the huts move farther and farther apart.

In the old days a camp was cozy, intimate and close. You could sit there by one fire and look into the other grass huts, see what the other people were doing, what they were making or eating. You heard the conversations, the arguments and banter. . . .

You read Diane's interviews and look at those lists of how much people own. You see those shielded mud huts with doors spaced, so far apart. You also listen to the people you like and trust. People who always have been honest with you. You hear their explanations and realize the evasions are not for you but for themselves. You see things they can't. But nothing can be done. It would be ludicrous to tell these brothers: "Don't you see, my friends, the lack of concordance between your values and the changing reality of your world?"

Now, years after the DBC study, I sit with data spread out before me and it is so clear. Richard's camp in 1963: just grass huts, a hearth in front of each. Huts and hearths in a circle, nothing more. 1968: more of the same. The following year though the first *kraal* appears, just a small thorn enclosure, some acadia bushes cut and dragged haphazardly together for their first few goats. It's set apart way out behind the circle of huts. On one goes, from plot to plot, following the pattern from year to year. The huts change from grass to mud. They become larger, more solidly built. Goats, a few at first, then more of them. So you build a fence around your house to keep them away from the grass roofs. The *kraals* grow larger, move in closer to be incorporated finally into the circle of huts itself. The huts become spaced farther and farther apart, seemingly repelled over time, one from the next. People, families move farther apart.

The bones tell the same story. 1947: All the bones from wild animals, game caught in snares or shot with poisoned arrows—game taken from the bush. By 1964 a few goat bones, a cow bone or two, but not many. Less than 20 percent of the total. Look then at the early 1970s and watch the line on the graph climb slowly upwards—by 1976 over 80 percent from domesticated stock.

But what explains the shattering of this society? Why is this hunting and gathering way of life, so resilient in the face of uncertainty, falling apart? It hasn't been a direct force—a war, the ravages of disease. It is the internal conflicts, the tensions, the inconsistencies, the impossibility of reconciling such different views of the world.

At Dobe it is happening to them all together. All of the huts have moved farther apart in lockstep, which makes it harder for them to see how incompatible the old system is with the new. . . .

THE MOUNTAIN PEOPLE

Colin M. Turnbull
20-32, 129-139 (1972)[8]

It seemed that just before World War II the [Ik] had all been encouraged to settle in northern Uganda, in the mountainous northeast corner bordering on Kenya to the east and Sudan to the north. Until then they had roamed in nomadic bands, as hunters and gatherers, throughout a vast region in all three countries. It was only with the advent of nationhood, following the war, that the boundaries became a major significance, but the process of settlement had begun well before.

From what I was able to learn later, their way of life then had been very different from what it was now. The area in which they are now confined, between the Kenya-Uganda escarpment and Mount Morungole, on the eastern edge of what is now Kidepo National Park, used to be a temporary resting place in the annual nomadic cycle. Kidepo Valley, below Morungole, formed their major hunting territory. It was some thirty-five miles across, almost completely hemmed in by Morungole to the south and east, the Didinga Mountains to the north, and the Niangea Mountains to the west. The only opening was in the southwest corner. The valley is full of game throughout the year, but when the heavy rains come the valley floor tends to get sodden and the large game, especially elephant, used to move out either through the southwestern corridor or up into the Didinga Mountains. At this point the hunters began moving, following the game, especially through the Didinga Mountains and into the Sudan, hunting the game and gathering wild vegetables and roots and berries as they went, seldom staying in one place more than a few days. Then with the end of the rains the hunters came down into northern Kenya, west of Lake Rudolf, and made their way back toward the escarpment, collecting honey as they went, especially in the Zingout Mountains. They then climbed up the two-thousand-foot escarpment back into Uganda, over to Morungole and back down into Kidepo.

Kidepo was undoubtedly where they spent the best part of the year, but, like most hunters and gatherers, these depended as much on vegetable resources as they did on game, and vegetable supplies can be exhausted even more quickly and permanently than game if a band stays in one place too long. Mobility is essential to the hunting and gathering way of life, and

8. [Several commentators have questioned Turnbull's analysis, but none have disproven it—Eds.].

nomadism is by no means the random, aimless meandering it is sometimes thought to be. At the same time, hunting and gathering, even in a marginal environment, are neither as hard nor as precarious as they may seem. . . .

. . . Kidepo was taken over as a National Park and the Ik were excluded, in this way, from their major hunting ground . . . .

With hunters a child is brought up to regard any adult living in the same camp as a parent, any age-mate as a brother or sister. These are the real and effective relationships, constantly shifting and changing as the composition of the band changes and the camps are abandoned and rebuilt. The Ik no less than any others had this essentially social attitude toward kinship, and it readily lent itself to the rapid and disastrous changes that took place following the restriction of their movement and hunting activities. The family simply ceased to exist.

In such a fluid society of hunters the environment invariably provides the central theme that holds them together, that gives them a sense of common identity; it is the hub around which their life revolves. It provides all the necessities such as food, shelter and clothing, and often some kind of spiritual existence of its own is attributed to it. Just as the Mbuti Pygmies in their lush tropical rain forest regard the forest as a benevolent deity, so do the Ik, in their rocky mountain stronghold, think of the mountains as being peculiarly and specially theirs. People and mountains belong to each other and are inseparable. It is not just that the Ik would not know how to live, to hunt or farm, in the flat, arid plateau below them, because they are as intelligent as any and a great deal sharper, quicker to learn and more adaptable than many. But with regard to the mountains it is different, and their adaptability seems to reach its limits. The Ik, without their mountains, would no longer be the Ik and similarly, they say, the mountains without the Ik would no longer be the same mountains, if indeed they continued to exist at all. . . . The mountains themselves seem to be, like the Ik, in a state of perpetual motion. And so the two live together, a part of each other. . . .

The smaller the society, the less emphasis there is on the formal system, and the more there is on inter-personal and inter-group relations, to which the system is subordinated. Security is seen in terms of these relationships, and so is survival. The result, which appears so deceptively simple, is that hunters frequently display those characteristics that we find so admirable in man: kindness, generosity, consideration, affection, honesty, hospitality, compassion, charity and others. This sounds like a formidable list of virtues, and so it would be if they *were* virtues, but for the hunter they are not. For the hunter in his tiny, close-knit society, these are necessities for survival, without them society would collapse. It is a far cry from our society, in which anyone possessing even half these qualities would find it hard indeed to survive, yet we are given to thinking that somehow these are virtues inherent in man.

It was not foremost in my mind, I suppose, but . . . I took it for granted that the Ik [in their new location] would possess these same qualities. It was a shock to find myself wrong on almost all counts. [T]hey were not hunters, they were farmers, their mountain villages were far from livable, the food was uneatable because there was not any, and the people were unfriendly, uncharitable, inhospitable and generally mean as any people can be. For those positive qualities we value so highly are no longer functional for the Ik; even more than in our own society they spell ruin and disaster. . . .

I suppose one cannot blame [a dead boy's parents] too much [for trying to hide the fact of the boy's death in order to avoid having to hosting a funeral feast]. They had little enough to eat for themselves, and to try to provide for parasitical relatives because their son had died would only add injury to injury. What they did does not in any way indicate that they were incapable of love. What it does indicate, as did the whole lack of family life seen so far, was that there simply was not room, in the life of these people, for such luxuries as family and sentiment and love. So close to the verge of starvation, such luxuries could mean death, and is it not a singularly foolish luxury to die for someone already dead, or weak, or old? This seemed to strike hard at the assumption that there are such things as basic human values, at the very notion of virtue, or goodness even. I was not yet ready to accept that the hunger was as serious as all that, and if it was, I wished to ignore that it was deliberately, consciously confined by the young and relatively healthy to the aged, left to be abandoned . . . , and now, it seemed, extended to the children. Yet biologically it made good sense. The children were as useless as the aged, or nearly so; as long as you keep the breeding group alive you can always get more children. So let the old go first, then the children. Anything else is racial suicide, and the Ik, I almost regret to say, are anything but suicidal.

Hunger was indeed more severe than I knew, and the children were the next to go. It was all quite impersonal. . . .

It is [in the relationship between parents and their children] that we can see most clearly the reason for the collapse of those family values we like to cherish and hold to be basic. Under the circumstances that surround the Ik, the larger a family grows, the less security it can offer. The ideal family, economically speaking and within restricted temporal limitations, is a man and his wife and no children. Children are useless appendages, like old parents. Anyone who cannot take care of himself is a burden and a hazard to the survival of others. I found it difficult to see why they bother having children, the likelihood of their being able and willing to contribute to the family as a whole being as small as it is. There is always the chance of a good year in the fields during which the family proper—that is to say, parents with children—finds mutual advantage in cooperation, which is the only reason conceivable to the Ik. The family, otherwise, is for the insane, for it spells death, not life. . . . The other quality of life that we hold to be necessary for survival, love, the Ik also dismiss as idiotic and highly dangerous. . . .

So we should not be surprised when the mother throws her child out at three years old. She has breast-fed it, with some ill humor, and cared for it in some manner for three whole years, and now it is ready to make its own way. . . .

At the age of three a series of *rites de passage* begins. In this environment a child has no chance of survival on his own until he is about thirteen years old, so children divide themselves into two age levels and form age bands. The junior band consists of children between the ages of three and seven, the senior age band caters for the eight- to twelve-year-olds. . . . Initiation into a band is as rough as the *rite de passage* by which you are moved out of it. . . .

The final *rite de passage* is into manhood and womanhood, at the age of twelve or thirteen, depending on how long the candidate for adult status has been able to fight off the attacks of his competitors. By now he has learned the wisdom of acting on his own, for his own good, while acknowledging that on occasion it is profitable to associate temporarily with others. That such associations must be temporary he has had plenty of opportunity to observe as he has grown from junior member to senior member of each band, from the bullied and beaten to the bully and beater. . . .

Notes and Questions

1. *Relationship between environment and social conditions.* What do the foregoing excerpts suggest about the relationship between environment and social conditions and practices? What evidence is there in the articles about the Ik and the Bushmen that cultural integrity is affected by changes in the physical environment in which the culture exists? What effect did culture have on the environment of those groups? (Note that the Ik were displaced from their traditional hunting grounds and way of life by the creation of a national park.) In what ways has the physical environment in the United States or in your region or locality affected the culture in which you grew up or now live?

2. *Culture's effect on attitudes.* In what ways does your culture affect your attitudes or behavior toward protecting health and the environment?

3. *Religious backgrounds.* Do you think persons with Buddhist, Islamic, Christian, Judaic, Hindu, and atheistic backgrounds are likely to have the same reactions or approaches to environmental protection or sustainable development (the subject of section F, below)?

4. *Future tensions over cultural differenes?* Several authors have argued that cultural differences will increasingly cause international tension. *See, e.g.,* Samuel P. Huntington, The Clash of Civilizations?: The Debate (1996).

D. ECONOMIC CONTEXT: POVERTY AND ECONOMIC DISPARITIES

Vast numbers of people in the world—perhaps four out of ten, or 40 percent—live in poverty, with perhaps one billion people living in a state of "absolute poverty" beneath any reasonable standard of human decency. The need to improve the living conditions of these people puts what are often perceived as irresistible pressures on policymakers, e.g., in terms of choosing short-term gains in employment or in exploiting natural resources over more sustainable policies.

At the same time, massive economic disparities exist among countries and regions. These disparities are typically linked to other social and environmental differences, such as literacy, access to safe drinking water, access to healthcare facilities, and access to open spaces. These disparities affect the policies adopted by developing countries. The disparities also strongly influence the political setting in which discussions of international environmental issues occur, e.g., because developing countries have banded together into the "Group of 77" (also referred to as the "Group of 77 and China" and the "G 77"), even though there are now many more than 77 members. There are also significant disparities in income and wealth distribution within countries—both developed and developing.

The following excerpt indicates the extent of the disparities in per capita income between countries, explores some questions about the relationship between poverty and the environment, and addresses related issues. Other aspects of the relationship between international environmental issues and economic analysis and activity are covered in Chapter 3 (The Economic Perspective), Chapter 19 (Environment and Trade), and Chapter 20 (Financing Environmental Protection).

■ POVERTY AND THE ENVIRONMENT

7-11, 24-25 (United Nations Environment Programme (UNEP) 1995)

This report arises from a deep concern with the issues of poverty and environmental degradation and their interrelationships. The concern stems from the observations that (1) poverty and environmental degradation have the same or related root causes, (2) poverty reduction is a prerequisite for sustainable development, and (3) that past attempts to address these issues have mostly suffered from a lack of integration. However, it is fair to say that this is changing, due to a process of adaptation of world views to the realities of the poverty degradation trap that faces so many people—if not the human species as such. This chapter briefly deals with the phenomena of poverty and environmental degradation and outlines the main dimensions of a more integrated approach towards them.

Table 1-3

GNP per capita, 1993	*Number of economies*	*GNP (US$000.000) 1993*	*Population (000,000) 1993*	*GNP per capita (US$) 1993*
Low	59	1,165,000	3,094	380
Lower-middle	69	1,635,000	1,099	1,490
Upper-middle	42	2,153,000	498	4,320
High	39	19,304,000	834	23,150
World	209	24,257,000	5,525	4,390

The Growth of Poverty, Disparity and Environmental Degradation

POVERTY, ENVIRONMENT AND DEVELOPMENT

The protection of the environment and of natural resources is an essential part of development: without adequate environmental capital, development is undermined and this in turn may reduce the resources available for investing in maintaining and enhancing the environmental resource base (World Bank 1992). The poor are both victims and agents of environmental damage, and hence alleviating poverty is not only a moral imperative but also a prerequisite for environmental sustainability and sustainable development (World Bank 1992).

In 1978, Robert McNamara, former president of the World Bank, described absolute poverty as "a condition of life so limited by malnutrition, illiteracy, disease, squalid surroundings, high infant mortality, and low life expectancy as to be beneath any reasonable definition of human decency." Poverty, however, is not merely a condition but is the result of a process of impoverishment that may be characterized as a downward spiral that flows from one generation to the next, drawing in increasing numbers of people.

From a developmental perspective, the primary task is to eliminate poverty, as is recognized in the Declaration of Rio and Agenda 21. Even though substantial progress has taken place in terms of the average levels of consumption and life expectancy, yet more than one-fifth of humanity lives in acute poverty and the percentage of the population in developing countries below the poverty line is around 30%. Up to 40% of the world population may be defined as poor, if poverty is measured according to whether they have a standard of living that includes adequate food, safe and sufficient supplies of water, secure shelter and access to education and health care (WHO 1992).

The relationship between poverty and environment first emerged as a divisive issue at the United Nations Stockholm Conference on the Human Environment in 1972, where former Indian Prime Minister Indira Gandhi attributed pollution primarily to poverty and underdevelopment. At that conference, developing countries expressed concern that environmental goals could detract from their development goals. *The World Conservation Strategy*, released in 1980 by IUCN—The World Conservation Union, UNEP and WWF—World Wide Fund for Nature, recognized that conservation could not be achieved without alleviating poverty and coined the term "sustainable development." These concerns also provided the impetus for the work of the World Commission on Environment and Development, also known as the Brundtland Commission, which recognized the need for the integration of environment and development concerns, and for international equity. The Commission's report, *Our Common Future* (WCED 1987), and its recommendations, provided the basis for the agenda at the 1992 Earth Summit on Environment and Development (UNCED), which was largely a dialogue between the North and South on strategies for moving towards a sustainable future. The UNCED conference recognized both the relationship between poverty and environmental degradation in underdeveloped countries, as well as the problem of unsustainable production and consumption patterns in the developed countries. A concerted effort to alleviate poverty was established as a priority for the 21st century. In the long run all human beings should be capable of mobilizing and developing an adequate and sustainable supply of the means of living (UNCED, Agenda 21).

THE DEVELOPMENT OF POVERTY

. . . During the 1980s, in spite of an overall increase in economic growth, the numbers of people living in absolute poverty increased from approximately three-quarters of a billion to the current 1.4 billion or one-fourth of humanity (UNDP 1992). Absolute numbers of poor people have increased with growing populations, even though there has been a fall in the percentage of the population below the poverty line. In Africa, however, the poor have also increased in proportion to the rest of the population. Largely as a result of high population growth rates in the developing world, the number of people living in poverty is expected to continue to increase unless there are profound changes in the structure of the world economy.

Exceptions are found in some East Asian countries, where there has been a decline in both the absolute numbers of poor and in the percentage of the population that is poor. Although circumstances in individual countries differ, much of the progress in human development in East Asia is based on the redistribution of assets through land reform; investment in health, education, and skill development; and government support for building economic capacity. . . . East Asian countries also had lower rates of unemployment than OECD countries (UNDP 1993).

The relationship of poverty to environmental degradation is a direct one in developing countries, as their economies rely relatively heavily on extraction of primary commodities. Developed countries also saw an increase in poverty in the 1980s. In the United States for example, the average level of poverty rose from 24,792 [million] or 11.8% in the 1970s, to 32,893 [million] or 13.8% from 1980-91. In 1992, one in five or 14.6 million children (21.9%) were in poverty, up from 11,543 (18.3%) in 1980. Estimates of homelessness range from 228,000 to 600,000 a night, of which 100,000 are children. In addition, 5.5 million children a year experience hunger. Conditions of poverty in developed countries are different from those in undeveloped countries because there is greater access to infrastructure and government assistance programmes. However, even in the United States, poor children are much more likely than non-poor children to die from infections and parasitic disease, from accidents and violence, and from all causes combined. Others suffer needless health and learning problems, abnormally stunted growth, and physical wasting that lead to low test scores and behaviour problems. In both developed and undeveloped countries, poor and low-income people are disproportionately affected by environmental degradation and are more likely to be exposed to toxic pollutants in their homes and workplaces.

Disparity

Between 1960 and 1990, there was also an increase in economic disparity. In 1960, the richest 20% of world population had incomes 30 times greater than the poorest 20%. By 1990, the richest 20% of the population had 60 times more than the poorest 20%, measured *between* countries. If maldistribution *within* countries is included, the income of the richest 20% is 150 times *greater* than that of the poorest 20%. The poorest 20% receive 0.2% of global commercial bank lending, 1.3% of global investment, 1% of global trade and 1.4% of income. These figures have decreased since 1960. It is expected that this disparity will continue to widen.

Although general indicators of development, such as GNP per capita, life-expectancy at birth, infant mortality and calories per capita, have steadily improved as a result of technological innovations, poverty is growing and the environment is being stressed on larger scales than ever before (Gallopin *et al.* 1989).

Poverty and Environment

Poor people may become trapped into short time-horizons with respect to resources over which they have little or no control because they lack assurances of future access to resources and because they lack other economic opportunities. To the extent that they are excluded from participation in the market economy, they also rely directly on non-marketed natural resources for their immediate survival.

Population growth and landlessness (or near landlessness) create pressure for poor people to exploit increasingly marginal rural and urban environments for survival in the short term, in a manner that leads to resource degradation, which creates more poverty and jeopardizes survival in the long term. These marginal land areas are either remote and ecologically fragile rural areas, or are, increasingly, at the edges of growing urban areas. Ecologically fragile rural areas in developing countries are primarily arid and semi-arid lands, hillsides and tropical forests.

Deforestation in tropical countries, allegedly for the purpose of increasing food production, has instead often decreased it. For example, Haiti has 2% of its forests intact but agricultural production has dropped 15% in the last decade. The correlation between poverty and environmental degradation is particularly acute in Africa, where a map of absolute poverty coincides with areas of deforestation (Leonard 1993). The poorest countries are also located in places where water is either scarce for part of the year or drought occurs in intermittent years, or where high evaporation makes it unavailable for human use (Falkenmark and Lindh 1993). These circumstances also occur in developed countries that have, so far, managed to overcome regional water scarcities through the use of technology, because of their greater access to technical knowledge, energy resources, other inputs and money. Twenty years of land clearing in the Amazon rain forest did not improve the human condition, but led instead to the exponential growth of malaria cases, a high prevalence of trauma, increased child mortality and malnutrition and, in some areas, the endemism of schistosomiasis. . . .

. . . Poor countries in general also rely heavily on exports of natural capital, in the form of primary commodities, which does not contribute to development because the proceeds are primarily used to pay national debts rather than to invest in the development of other forms of capital. . . .

Types, Locations and a Broad Socio-economic Profile of the Poor

. . . The majority of the poor (80%) live in rural areas and the numbers of rural poor have increased by 40% over the last two decades despite 40 years of international development assistance. The number of poor in urban areas, currently over 130 million, is increasing even faster—squatter settlements are estimated to be increasing their population at approximately 7% a year compared to 3.5% for urban areas as a whole and 2.1% annually for developing countries in general. By the turn of the century, it is expected that most of the poor population will be urban. These squatter settlements normally lack urban infrastructure and access to basic water and sanitation services. Poverty disproportionately affects particular social groups including women, households headed by women, children and indigenous populations. In the last 20 years, the number of rural women in poverty rose by 50% from 370 million to 565 million compared to 30% for men. More than 250,000 children die of malnutrition and related

Table 1-4
Widening Economic Gaps between Regions (% of global figures)

	Global population		*Global GNP*	
	1960	*1989*	*1960*	*1989*
Sub-Saharan Africa	7.1	9.5	1.9	1.2
South Asia	19.8	22.7	3.1	2.8
East and Southeast Asia (excl. China)	8.8	9.9	1.7	2.9
China	21.8	21.6	3	2
Arab States	3.9	5	1.5	2.5
Latin America and the Caribbean	7.1	8.4	4.7	4.4
Developing countries	68.5	77.1	15.9	15.8
Least developed	6.8	8.4	1	0.5
Industrial countries	31.5	22.9	84.1	84.2

disease each week. Children in sub-Saharan Africa, of which over 40% are malnourished, have the highest infant mortality rate in the world (180 per 1000), which continues to increase.

Indigenous peoples are another group at more than average risk. In Bolivia, where the overall poverty rate is over 50%, almost three-quarters of the monolingual indigenous population are poor and two-thirds of the bilingual population are poor. In Guatemala, where over 60% of the population is indigenous, only 150 out of 25,000 students in higher education are from the indigenous groups. Even in developed countries, the conditions of indigenous populations sometimes resembles those in developing countries. For example, in Canada, infant mortality among indigenous people is twice the national average; in New Zealand, they are 7 times more likely to be unemployed; and in Australia, they have a 20-year lower life expectancy and are 14 times more likely to be imprisoned.

The majority of those in absolute poverty are clustered in South Asia and sub-Saharan Africa. Post-1988 data indicate that 939 million of those below nationally defined absolute poverty lines reside in rural areas, including 633 million in Asia, 204 million in sub-Saharan Africa, 76 million in Latin American and the Caribbean, and the remainder reside in the Near East and in North Africa. It is also estimated that 80% of the poor people in Latin America live in marginal land areas; the figures for Asia and Africa are 60% and 50%. Table 1-4 shows a comparison between the share of global population and the share of global GNP in industrial and less-developed countries and the differences between 1960 and 1989.

Notes and Questions

1. *Economic disparities and environmental cooperation.* How do economic disparities between countries and regions complicate environmental cooperation efforts? Are poorer countries likely to face the same threats to health and environment as richer countries face? Are they likely to prioritize dealing with environmental threats in the same way? Is public participation regarding environmental issues likely to be the same in the two sets of countries? Will these differences affect the likelihood that poor and rich countries will be able to reach agreement on an international regime to address a particular environmental problem? Consider the following quotation from Our Common Future 17 (1987): "Two conditions must be satisfied before international economic exchanges can become beneficial for all involved. The sustainability of ecosystems on which the global economy depends must be guaranteed. And the economic partners must be satisfied that the basis of exchange is equitable. For many developing countries, neither condition is met."

2. *Participation of poor countries in environmental protection efforts.* Is a poorer country likely to be able to commit the same resources to an international environmental cooperation effort as a richer one? Is the poorer country likely to have the capacity to comply with international legal obligations to the same extent as a richer country? Will these differences affect the effectiveness of international environmental regimes? Will they affect the substantive content of those regimes? During negotiations of the Basel Convention on International Transport of Hazardous Waste, many developing countries sought an outright ban on international trade in hazardous waste, rather than the prior informed consent regime eventually adopted (see Chapter 13, section A, below), arguing that they do not have the capacity to administer a prior informed consent approach. The situation confronting developing countries with respect to hazardous chemicals is discussed in the excerpt from Lallas & Wolfson in Chapter 13, section B, below.

3. *Poverty and the environment.* Does environmental degradation cause poverty? Does poverty lead to threats to health and the environment?

4. *Health and environmental tradeoffs.* What tradeoffs would a policymaker in a developing country face with respect to investments in human health and the environment?

5. *Patterns of production and consumption.* Agenda 21 and subsequent international instruments such as the declaration adopted at the Special Session of the United Nations General Assembly in June 1997 (held to conduct a five-year review of UNCED) stated that unsustainable patterns of production and consumption, especially among developed countries, are the primary cause of the degradation of the global environment. Similar patterns are evident in developing countries, particularly among the middle

and upper income segments of their populations (which in absolute numbers are approaching the size of similarly situated populations in developed countries). A commonly asked question is what the world would be like if every person in China and India (which together account for about 40 percent of the world's population) had the same access to automobiles as do people in Japan, the United States, and Europe. The prospect of negotiating or overseeing a decline in the standard of living is anathema to political leaders. Does the path to sustainable patterns of consumption and production necessarily lead in that direction?

6. *Private capital flow.* One of the most important economic phenomena of the 1990s is the fact that the international flow of private investment capital now vastly exceeds that of public assistance—both multilateral and bilateral. One of the great challenges is thus how to ensure that those investments are socially and environmentally responsible. It also emphasizes the need for international finance institutions and bilateral assistance agencies to consider the impact of private investment.

E. POLITICAL CONTEXT

The political context in which international environmental protection efforts occur can be viewed at several levels—e.g., local, national, regional, global—and in terms of various players—e.g., various levels of government, individuals, nongovernmental organizations, business entities, international finance institutions, and other regional and global international organizations. The following excerpts provide some insights into the interaction of those levels and players.

■ INTERNATIONAL ENVIRONMENTAL POLICY

Lynton Keith Caldwell
14-15 (1984)

Environmental policy tends to be focused, at least initially, on specific and concrete emergencies or events. Environmental issues are numerous and disparate; but public attention is drawn to immediate, comprehensible concerns more readily publicized than are the larger, more complex developments of which they are manifestations. It is easier to attract public attention to the effects of acid rain, the plight of fur seals, or pollution from pesticides than to the more fundamental problems of biogeochemical cycles or species-habitat relationships. . . .

Critical issues as categorized by science do not always correspond to the perceptions and priorities prevailing in governments and international agencies.

THE POLITICAL ECONOMY OF CHANGE

Ilchman & Uphoff
3-7, 39-47 (1971)

In the face of frequent mutual exclusiveness of demands and the persistent scarcity of resources, the statesman has various options. He may choose to meet some demands wholly or in part. Some demands he will ignore or explicitly reject. Sometimes when a demand from the sectors cannot be met, the statesman may seek to substitute resources that he thinks will be temporarily acceptable; in some situations he may give the sectors currency as claims on resources in the future. He may employ coercion to remove the effects of certain demands, or he may institute education to remove the causes. Each option requires the spending of resources now and in the future. For each, calculations must be made to determine its potential for increasing the total stock of political capital at the disposal of the regime. Such calculations are the foundations of choice. Given the necessity of choices, the statesman must figure out on whom, how much, in what combination, when, where, why, and for what return the regime's scarce political resources should be spent. . . .

REDEFINING SECURITY

Jessica Tuchman Mathews
68 For. Aff. 162 (1989)

The 1990s will demand a redefinition of what constitutes national security. In the 1970s the concept was expanded to include international economics as it became clear that the U.S. economy was no longer the independent force it had once been, but was powerfully affected by economic policies in dozens of other countries. Global developments now suggest the need for another analogous, broadening definition of national security to include resource, environmental and demographic issues.

The assumptions and institutions that have governed international relations in the postwar era are a poor fit with these new realities. Environmental strains that transcend national borders are already beginning to break down the sacred boundaries of national sovereignty, previously rendered porous by the information and communication revolutions and the instantaneous global movement of financial capital. The once sharp dividing line between foreign and domestic policy is blurred, forcing governments to grapple in international forums with issues that were contentious enough in the domestic arena. . . .

Environmental decline occasionally leads directly to conflict, especially when scarce water resources must be shared. Generally, however, its impact on nations' security is felt in the downward pull on economic performance and, therefore, on political stability. The underlying cause of turmoil is often ignored; instead governments address the poverty and instability that are its results.

In the Philippines, for example, the government regularly granted logging concessions of less than ten years. Since it takes 30-35 years for a second-growth forest to mature, loggers had no incentive to replant. Compounding the error, flat royalties encouraged the loggers to remove only the most valuable species. A horrendous 40 percent of the harvestable lumber never left the forests but, having been damaged in the logging, rotted or was burned in place. The unsurprising result of these and related policies is that out of 17 million hectares of closed forests that flourished early in the century only 1.2 million remain today. Moreover, the Philippine government received a fraction of the revenues it could have collected if it had followed sound resource management policies that would have also preserved the forest capital. This is biological deficit financing writ large. . . .

Conditions in sub-Saharan Africa, to take another case, have reached catastrophic dimensions. . . . [N]early three-quarters of the population makes its living off of the land, which also supplies, as fuelwood, 80 percent of the energy consumed. The land's capacity to produce is ebbing away under the pressure of rapidly growing numbers of people who do not have the wherewithal to put back into the land what they take from it. A vicious circle of human and resource impoverishment sets in. As the vegetative cover—trees, shrubs and grass—shrinks from deforestation and overgrazing, soil loses its capacity to retain moisture and nourish crops. The decline accelerates as farmers burn dung and crop residues in place of fuelwood, rather than using them to sustain the soil. Agricultural yields then fall further, and the land becomes steadily more vulnerable to the naturally variable rainfall that is the hallmark of arid and semiarid regions, turning dry spells into droughts and periods of food shortage into famines. Ethiopia is only the most familiar case. The sequence is repeated throughout the region with similarly tragic results.

If such resource and population trends are not addressed, as they are not in so much of the world today, the resulting economic decline leads to frustration, resentment, domestic unrest or even civil war. Human suffering and turmoil make countries ripe for authoritarian government or external subversion. Environmental refugees spread the disruption across national borders. Haiti, a classic example, was once so forested and fertile that it was known as the "Pearl of the Antilles." Now deforested, soil erosion in Haiti is so rapid that some farmers believe stones grow in their fields, while bulldozers are needed to clear the streets of Port-au-Prince of topsoil that flows down from the mountains in the rainy season. While many of the boat people who fled to the United States left because of the brutality of the Duvalier regimes, there is no question that—and this is not widely recognized—many Haitians were forced into the boats by the impossible task of farming bare rock. Until Haiti is reforested, it will never be politically stable.

Haitians are by no means the world's only environmental refugees. In Indonesia, Central America and sub-Saharan Africa, millions have been forced to leave their homes in part because the loss of tree cover, the disappearance of soil, and other environmental ills have made it impossible to grow food. Sudan, despite its civil war, has taken in more than a million refugees from Ethiopia, Uganda and Chad. Immigrants from the spreading Sahel make up one-fifth of the total population in the Ivory Coast. Wherever refugees settle, they flood the labor market, add to the local demand for food and put new burdens on the land, thus spreading the environmental stress that originally forced them from their homes. Resource mismanagement is not the only cause of these mass movements, of course. Religious and ethnic conflicts, political repression and other forces are at work. But the environmental causes are an essential factor. . . .

On the political front, the need for a new diplomacy and for new institutions and regulatory regimes to cope with the world's growing environmental interdependence is . . . compelling. Put bluntly, our accepted definition of the limits of national sovereignty as coinciding with national borders is obsolete. The government of Bangladesh, no matter how hard it tries, cannot prevent tragic floods, such as it suffered [in 1988]. Preventing them requires active cooperation from Nepal and India. The government of Canada cannot protect its water resources from acid rain without collaboration with the United States. Eighteen diverse nations share the heavily polluted Mediterranean Sea. Even the Caribbean Islands, as physically isolated as they are, find themselves affected by others' resource management policies as locusts, inadvertently bred through generations of exposure to [be impervious to] pesticides and now strong enough to fly all the way from Africa, infest their shores.

The majority of environmental problems demand regional solutions [and] encroach upon what we now think of as prerogatives of national governments. This is because the phenomena themselves are defined by the limits of watershed, ecosystem, or atmospheric transport, not by national borders. Indeed, the costs and benefits of alternative policies cannot often be accurately judged without considering the region rather than the nation. . . .

THE CHANGING STRUCTURE OF INTERNATIONAL LAW

Edith Brown Weiss
***Georgetown University Law Center, May 23, 1996,* reprinted in**
Georgetown Law—Res Ipsa Loquitur 52 (Spring 1997)

The Peace of Westphalia that ended the Thirty Years War three hundred and fifty years ago established a new international order based on sovereign, independent, territorially defined States, each striving to maintain political independence and territorial integrity. . . .

The international system is rapidly changing and with it the structure of international law. Two changes have profound implications for the structure of international law: the simultaneous push toward integration and fragmentation; and the rise of thousands of organizations and millions of individuals as relevant actors.

As we approach the third millennium, our world is becoming both more integrated and more fragmented. Evidence of global integration abounds: regional trading units, global communication networks such as the worldwide web, international regimes covering issues ranging from banking and trade, to human rights, environmental protection, and arms control. The information revolution, the spread of financial markets, the penetration of industries across borders, the rapid technological advances, the global environmental problems and other economic interdependencies compel greater integration. Future problems will require global cooperation to address them effectively.

At the same time nationalism, ethnicity, and the need for personal affiliations and satisfaction push toward fragmentation and decentralization. Less than 10% of the more than 185 states are homogeneous ethnically. Only about 50% of the states have one ethnic group that accounts for three-quarters of the population. Scholars write of the rise of "tribalism" and the revealed need for community bonds. States are relinquishing elements of sovereignty to transnational networks of nonstate actors; the sense of community (with intense loyalty and identification) that served to bind together the citizens of the state is not being extended to the networks. . . .

The emerging system has many new international actors other than states. The 1995/96 edition of the Yearbook of International Organizations records 5,668 intergovernmental organizations and 36,054 nongovernmental organizations, for a total of 41,722 international organizations. There are other relevant actors in addition: multinational corporations, ethnic minorities, subunits of national governments, local nongovernmental organizations, illicit actors such as transnational drug cartels or terrorist networks, and *ad hoc* transnational associations of individuals. These new transnational elites are interested in particular outcomes, and may have extensive resources at their disposal. They are bound together in complex ways that change frequently. Most are part of the integrative pulse that is sweeping the globe.

New information technologies empower groups other than states to participate in developing and implementing international law. They empower publics to participate in the process of governance. Since 1994, communiques of rebels in Chiapas, Mexico, have been transmitted across the world through internet bulletin boards to seek support for the rebels' cause. Political factions and separatists in other areas of the world also circulate their messages through internet. Pressure groups now form almost instantaneously on the internet to oppose actions in a given country, as almost every college student knows. Letter writing campaigns have gone electronic. . . .

[Political scientists have suggested] that two-level games, internationally and domestically, are being played in all international negotiations and in the implementing and compliance theater that ensues after agreements go into effect. Robert Putnam offered in 1988 a theory of two-level games in which a state is engaged in separate games at the international and the national level, each influencing the other. "At the national level, domestic groups pursue their interests by pressuring the government to adopt favorable policies, and politicians seek power by constructing coalitions among those groups. At the international level, national governments seek to maximize their own ability to satisfy domestic pressures, while minimizing the adverse consequences of foreign developments. Neither of the two games can be ignored by central decision-makers, so long as their countries remain interdependent, yet sovereign."[9] Those who have been involved in international negotiations, whether over trade, environment, military security, or energy, have experienced this first hand. . . .

Traditionally states have been accountable to each other as sovereign independent states for assuring compliance with international law. This is still true. But the communications revolution has made governance more transparent and hence public involvement greater. The negotiations in June 1995 between the Prime Minister of Russia and the Chechen rebel leader for a truce in the Chechen republic and the release of hostages from a hospital in Budyonnovsk took place over television for the public to observe. Meetings of the parties to the Convention controlling trade in endangered species and to the World Heritage Convention are promptly available on the internet. Televised images of civilians suffering in internal conflicts have generated pressure on governments by nongovernmental organizations and domestic public opinion to take collective action in response.

However, accountability for the many nonstate actors has yet to emerge. Many are constructive in their influence; others not. Their sheer number poses congestion problems.

In a very important sense, participation by nonstate actors in the international legal system greatly enhances accountability, because it can give a voice to citizens who would otherwise be unrepresented, ensure that actions taken meet local needs, counter effects of high-level governmental corruption, and therefore produce outcomes that maximize human welfare efficiently. Information technology can assist because it makes information readily accessible to groups and individuals across the world and empowers them. It makes governments and international organizations more transparent. . . .

Two problems arise: how to structure constructively NGO [nongovernmental organization] and private sector participation in international gov-

9. Robert D. Putnam, Diplomacy and Domestic Politics: The Logic of Two-Level Games, 42 Intl. Org. 427, 434 (1988).

ernmental and international organization deliberations and how to ensure that the transnational norms developed largely outside of governments are responsive to public needs and concerns.

Particularly in international environmental law, nonstate actors are now prominent participants, either formally or informally, in international negotiations, conferences of parties, and other meetings. Some are membership-based and accountable to their members, while others are loosely accountable to their funders, who may be dispersed. While the UN ECOSOC still determines accreditation to intergovernmental meetings, the sheer number of NGOs suggests that the system needs to be reconsidered to ensure effective representation. Moreover, it is time to consider additional processes that legitimate NGO participation in the international legal system.

On the other hand, nongovernmental organizations also need to be held accountable for their actions. Spurious information, unrelenting pressures for special interest pleading outside the intergovernmental forum, unlimited demands for transparency, and similar concerns mean that pressures are building for at least an informal code of conduct. Leading nongovernmental organizations, who have contributed so much to developing and implementing international law in fields such as human rights and environment, may find it in their best self-interest to take the lead in initiating this.

A second major issue of accountability stems from the emerging transnational standards and management practices being developed, largely in the private sector. In the West, at least, industries and corporations are accountable through the market system. Thus, nonstate actors should eventually find that consumer preferences both drive and limit what they can do. But accountability through the market place is tenuous and works imperfectly. . . .

■ END OF THE THIRD WORLD

Robert J. Samuelson
Newsweek, July 23, 1990, at 45

The Third World is gone. It has been vanishing for a long while, but now it has completely disappeared. Oh, the countries once assigned to the Third World are still there, but the concept of the Third World is no longer connected to any reality.

We will still deal (quite obviously) with the Brazils, Indonesias, Nigerias, and Indias. But the idea that these many nations represent anything like a single bloc with similar characteristics and interests is shattered forever. It is yet another casualty of the end of the cold war. The term Third World originally reflected a globe divided into the First World (the industrialized democracies), the Second World (the communist bloc) and everyone else. . . .

[D]eveloping countries, as a group, have lost much of their political leverage. [During the cold war] countries could subtly (or not so subtly) tout their importance in the cold-war contest as a way of winning more foreign assistance. No longer.

[P]oorer countries will increasingly be thrown back on their own resources: they're not likely to get much help unless they demonstrate the ability to organize legitimate governments and to stimulate internal economic development.

The discipline will be imposed not only by stingy taxpayers in richer countries but also by the multinational companies that control large private investment. Companies will locate plants where they think they can count on productive workers and political stability.

What has also fragmented the Third World are huge differences in economic growth. . . . With rapid population growth, poverty has deepened in sub-Saharan Africa, and disruptions in food production threaten famine. In Latin America, middle-class living standards have declined, and the poor have gotten poorer. Meanwhile, much of East Asia has boomed. . . .

■ OUR COMMON FUTURE

World Commission on Environment and Development
17 (1987)

Multilateral financial institutions have a crucial role to play. The World Bank is presently reorienting its programmes towards greater environmental concerns. This should be accompanied by a fundamental commitment to sustainable development by the Bank. It is also essential that the regional Development Banks and the International Monetary Fund incorporate similar objectives in their policies and programmes. A new priority and focus is also needed in bilateral aid agencies.

Notes and Questions

1. *Coming anarchy?* For an alarming view of how the serious tensions facing the world will be resolved, *see* Robert D. Kaplan, The Coming Anarchy, The Atlantic Monthly 44 (Feb. 1994). For example, Kaplan states:

> West Africa is becoming *the* symbol of worldwide demographic, environmental, and societal stress, in which criminal anarchy emerges as the real "strategic" danger. Disease, overpopulation, unprovoked crime, scarcity of resources, refugee migrations, the increasing erosion of nation-states and international borders, and the empowerment of private armies, security firms, and international drug cartels are now most tellingly demonstrated through a West African prism [but they] will soon confront our civilization.

Id. at 46.

2. *Prospects for cooperation.* What do the excerpts above suggest about the prospects and mechanisms for dealing with international environmental problems? Even during the height of the Cold War, the United States and the USSR often cooperated on environmental issues. *See* Magraw & Vinogradov, Environmental Law, in Beyond Confrontation: International Law for the Post-Cold War Era (L.F. Damrosch, G.M. Danilenko & R. Mullerson, eds. 1995).

3. *Developing countries and climate change.* What might the situation described by Samuelson portend for resolving issues such as climate change? Do small island developing states have the same interests as Bolivia or China? Climate change is discussed in Chapter 12, below.

4. *Roles of various players.* What obstacles exist to the potential roles of individuals, non-governmental organizations, and various levels of government envisioned in the following excerpt from Gary Lawrence, Will Habitat II Matter to the Members of the Organization for Economic Cooperation and Development? 14-15 (1996):

> [S]ome of the forces now at work which will affect public expectations on the legitimate role of national governments [are:]
>
> - Globalization of information, business and finance suggests that Ned Beatty's chilling line in the movie "Network"—"there are no nations . . . there are only corporations"—is true. If it were true, would the public think this better or worse?
> - Numerous examples of alternative ways of living, many of them make-believe, blanket the globe through movies, television and advertising, changing ideas of what constitutes a "normal" or "good" life. What will it mean to be German, Norwegian, Japanese or Australian if one's wants and desires are shaped by the same sources?
> - Changes from homogeneous to multi-cultural populations who bring expectations that differ from traditional expectations, thereby increasing complexity and diversity of interests within communities, making it much more difficult to develop national solutions which will work.
>
> Coupled with these trends toward homogenization of norms, values and expectations is an increased desire for individual identity. People will be looking for ways to demonstrate that they are part of a community, whether it is a community of place or community of interest. The most important factor will be that the community is small enough so that the individual can get some sense that his or her life matters and that his or her fate is somewhat within the individual's control. . . .

How do these views compare with those in the excerpt from Edith Brown Weiss, above?

5. *Accountability.* The excerpt from Edith Brown Weiss describes two-level game theory and notes that civil society has come to play a much

more influential role in the international system than previously was the case. Does two-level game theory apply to business associations? To environmental non-governmental organizations (NGOs)? For a discussion of two-level game theory, *see* Robert D. Putnam, Diplomacy and Domestic Politics: The Logic of Two-Level Games, 42 International Organizations 427 (1988). Are the problems of accountability as great as Brown Weiss indicates? If so, how can they be dealt with?

F. SUSTAINABLE DEVELOPMENT

Policymakers have not found it easy to deal with the relationship between environmental protection and other aspects of human behavior. As the foregoing materials indicate, the protection of health and the environment is inextricably related to economic activity and social conditions. But what precisely are those relationships, and how is a policymaker to approach dealing with them?

The concept of "sustainable development" gained prominence as a way of explaining that relationship with the publication of *Our Common Future* (1987), the report of the World Commission on Environment and Development (also known as the Brundtland Commission). Sustainable development was adopted by the world community as the overarching paradigm for improving the quality of life of all people in 1992, at the United Nations Conference on Environment and Development (UNCED).

One view is that sustainable development may best be viewed as a process rather than as a static end-point—a process that is not necessarily the same for all countries but that is founded on informed public input from all and the use of integrating tools such as environmental and social impact analysis, cost-benefit analysis, cost-internalization techniques, indicators, and natural resource accounting. But there is no universally agreed-upon definition of sustainable development. Contrast the following excerpts.

■ DECLARATION OF SANTA CRUZ DE LA SIERRA AND PLAN OF ACTION FOR THE SUSTAINABLE DEVELOPMENT OF THE AMERICAS

December 1996, para. 5

We recognize that the needs and responsibilities facing the countries of the Hemisphere today are diverse. Sustainable development does not assume that all the countries are at the same level of development, have the same capabilities, or can necessarily use the same model to attain it.

In view of the different contributions to global environmental degradation, states have common but differentiated responsibilities in the global quest for sustainable development. We should make efforts to ensure that the benefits of sustainable development reach all countries in the Hemisphere, in particular those that are less developed, and all segments of our populations.

■ STATE OF THE WORLD 1996

A Worldwatch Institute Report on Progress Toward a Sustainable Society 11-12 (1996)

[W]e know what an environmentally sustainable economy would look like. We know how to build an economic system that will meet our needs without jeopardizing prospects for future generations. And with some trends already headed in the right direction, we have the cornerstones on which to build such an economy.

In a sustainable economy, human births and deaths are in balance, soil erosion does not exceed the natural rate of new soil formation, tree cutting does not exceed tree planting, the fish caught do not exceed the sustainable yield of fisheries, the cattle on a range do not exceed its carrying capacity, and water pumping does not exceed aquifer recharge. It is an economy where carbon emissions and carbon fixation are also again in balance. The number of plant and animal species lost does not exceed the rate at which new species evolve.

The Brundtland Commission's definition, set forth in the following excerpt from Our Common Future 8-9, 43 (1987), is probably the most subscribed to:

Humanity has the ability to make development sustainable—to ensure that it meets the needs of the present without compromising the ability of future generations to meet their own needs. The concept of sustainable development does imply limits—not absolute limits but limitations imposed by the present state of technology and social organization on environmental resources and by the ability of the biosphere to absorb the effects of human activities. But technology and social organization can be both managed and improved to make way for a new era of economic growth. The commission believes that widespread poverty is no longer inevitable. Poverty is not only an evil in itself, but sustainable development requires meeting the basic needs of all and extending to all the opportunity to fulfil their aspirations for a better life. A world in which poverty is endemic will always be prone to ecological and other catastrophes.

Meeting essential needs requires not only a new era of economic growth for nations in which the majority are poor, but an assurance that those poor get their fair share of the resources required to sustain that growth. Such equity would be aided by political systems that secure effective citizen participation in decision making and by greater democracy in international decision making.

Sustainable global development requires that those who are more affluent adopt lifestyles within the planet's ecological means—in their use of energy, for example. Further, rapidly growing populations can increase the pressure on resources and slow any rise in living standards, thus sustainable development can only be pursued if population size and growth are in harmony with the changing productive potential of the ecosystem.

Yet in the end, sustainable development is not a fixed state of harmony, but rather a process of change in which the exploitation of resources, the direction of investments, the orientation of technological development, and institutional change are made consistent with future as well as present needs. We do not pretend that the process is easy or straightforward. Painful choices have to be made. Thus, in the final analysis, sustainable development must rest on political will. . . .

Sustainable development is development that meets the needs of the present without compromising the ability of future generations to meet their own needs. It contains within it two key concepts:

- the concept of "needs," in particular the essential needs of the world's poor, to which overriding priority should be given; and
- the idea of limitations imposed by the state of technology and social organization on the environment's ability to meet present and future needs.

A less complicated view, at least in part consistent with that of the Brundtland Commission, is that sustainable development has two primary characteristics: decisionmakers must think not only about the present but also about the future; and environmental, economic, and social issues cannot be considered in isolation but must be integrated. Such statements, however, provide no detail regarding how to make what are, or can appear to be, difficult tradeoffs, leading some to argue that the term is meaningless or even oxymoronic.

In addition, diplomats from some developing countries have expressed fundamental distrust of the idea of sustainable development. As reflected in the excerpt from Lawrence, below, these persons argue that: the primary need of developing countries is sustained economic growth in the short term to alleviate absolute poverty and environmental damage can be repaired later (if necessary or desirable); the industrialized countries did just that, so the developing countries have the right to, as well; industrialized countries even now do not practice sustainable development (citing, for example, the cutting of old growth forests in the Pacific Northwest of the United States); and sustainable development is really a ruse by which industrialized countries will condition international trade on environmental and social performance in a way detrimental to developing countries and their (often desperately poor) residents. There has even been an effort to place "sustained economic growth" as an equally important goal with sustainable development. That effort has been resisted by industrialized countries. These countries argue, *inter alia,* that long-term economic prosperity requires a healthy environment, and vice versa, so that a one-dimensional focus on economic growth—or on environmental protection, for that matter—is doomed to be self-defeating.

After particularly intense negotiations, sustainable development was reaffirmed as the overarching paradigm at the World Summit on Social Development in 1995, in paragraph 6 of the Copenhagen Declaration:

> We are deeply convinced that economic development, social development and environmental protection are interdependent and mutually reinforcing components of sustainable development, which is the framework for our efforts to achieve a higher quality of life for all people. . . .

This language, or close paraphrases of it, was repeated in subsequent United Nations conferences on women (Cairo, 1995) and human settlements (Istanbul, 1996) and at the Special Session of the U.N. General Assembly to follow up on UNCED (1997). Notably, Copenhagen paragraph 6 also indicates the importance of sustained economic growth ("in the context of sustainable development") and attention to the needs of the poor. The paragraph continues:

> Equitable social development that recognizes empowering the poor to utilize environmental resources sustainably is a necessary foundation for sustainable development. We also recognize that broad-based and sustained economic growth in the context of sustainable development is necessary to sustain social development and social justice.

The tension—at least in diplomatic circles—between sustainable development and sustained economic growth seems likely to continue, as indicated in the following excerpt, written for the Organization for Economic Cooperation and Development (OECD) in preparation for the Second United Nations Conference on Human Settlements (Habitat II), which was held in Istanbul in June 1996.

■ WILL HABITAT II MATTER TO THE MEMBERS OF THE ORGANISATION FOR ECONOMIC CO-OPERATION AND DEVELOPMENT?

J. Gary Lawrence
7-9 (1996)

Should the guiding principle of Habitat II be *sustainable development* or *sustained economic growth?* . . .

In the debates at the Preparatory Conferences, the G-77 have insisted upon the formulation *sustained economic growth.* The U.S. has insisted upon *sustainable development,* as have most of the member nations of the OECD. The conflicts appear to go very deep.

For the G-77, *sustainable development* has become loaded with imagery of maintained dominance by traditional colonial powers and denial of opportunity to achieve a standard of living equivalent to that of the developed world. To paraphrase a number of G-77 delegate's descriptions: "You have used up all of your own resources, and many of ours, to create economic security for your citizens. Now, after you find out that you have pursued a path which brings into question your ability to maintain your quality of life, you tell us that we can not pursue the same path as you. One can only assume that you are trying to get us to save what is left so that you can use it to develop the products you are telling us we should buy. The sustainability you seem committed to is your quality of life at the expense of ours."

The G-77 has insisted upon *sustained economic growth* as the paradigm. *Sustained economic growth* is seen by its detractors as economic expansion as a legitimate and justifiable end in itself. Sustainability definitions, in which economic security, environmental stewardship and social goals are the three basic elements, set forth balance as the measure of success. *Sustained economic growth* is seen to assume that social and environmental goals, by necessity, must be subjugated to economic security for the State. . . . Many members of the developed world have been insistent upon *sustainable development* as the only acceptable formulation. While agreeing with the arguments the G-77 has put forward about the developed world's un-sustainable past, the emphasis here is upon the future. . . .

Many statistics related to air and water quality, human health, species diversity, and distribution of wealth are brought forward to bolster the argument that maintaining our existing growth models will lead to the inevitable doom of human society and many of the other species with whom we share the planet. Some of the science is suspected by those arguing for *sustained economic growth* as "convenient" in supporting the argument for changing the growth ground rules, but most, it is generally agreed, correctly reflect the trends if not the specifics. It is easy to wonder why, if we can agree upon the consequences of our choices, we have such a difficult time agreeing on a paradigm for growth which seeks to avoid these consequences. . . .

Notes and Questions

1. *Sustainable development and the Third World.* Are the developing countries' concerns about sustainable development valid? Do they reflect an adequate understanding of the interrelationship among economic, social, and environmental issues? Would a focus on sustained economic

growth be a return to the pure growth/trickle down strategies of the past? What might Robert Samuelson, quoted above, say about this debate?

2. *Sustainable development and the First World.* Does the industrialized countries' position adequately reflect the realities of developing countries, particularly of the approximately one billion people who live in absolute poverty, that is, in a condition of malnutrition, exposure to the elements, illiteracy, and lack of resources that is below any reasonable standard of human decency?

3. *Is the concept nevertheless useful?* Does the concept of sustainable development actually provide detailed guidance? Is the vision of sustainable development presented in *State of the World 1996* satisfying? Is the concept nevertheless useful? If sustainable development is not the appropriate paradigm, what should the overarching model be? Can there be one? If there is not one, can a successful international dialogue occur?

4. *Homemade sustainable development.* Local Agenda 21s have been referred to as "homemade sustainable development." How should local, national, and global sustainable development concerns and efforts be coordinated?

5. *Sustainable development in case law.* In the recent decision of the International Court of Justice in the *Gabcikovo-Nagymaros* case (Hungary/Slovakia), Sept. 25, 1997, 1997 I.C.J.—, extracted in Chapter 15, Vice President Weeramantry devoted an entire section of his separate opinion to "The Concept of Sustainable Development." He stated that while the Court "referred to it as a concept . . . I consider it to be more than a mere concept, but as a principle with normative value. . . ." He also wrote that "the principle of sustainable development . . . , in my view, . . . is an integral part of modern international law. It is clearly of the utmost importance, both in this case and more generally."

6. *Sustainable development in the United States.* For a practical assessment of what sustainable development might entail in the United States, *see* Report of the President's Council on Sustainable Development (1995).

7. *Implementation of sustainable development.* It is sometimes said that sustainable development is essentially an approach that requires consideration of various components (economic, social, environmental) and of the interests not only of the present generation but also of future generations and that also requires both transparency and meaningful public participation. What tools are useful in carrying out such an approach? Some that might be considered include environmental impact assessments, social impact assessments, cost-benefit analyses, and public hearings. Can you think of others?

II

The Philosophical Framework

There are two philosophical dimensions that underpin the content of international environmental law: our relationship to future generations and our relationship to nature. What is the desirable relationship in both of these cases? What does the present international legal regime assume about these relationships? What institutional and procedural measures are available to effectuate different relationships in either or both?

A. THE INTERGENERATIONAL DIMENSION

1. Intergenerational Environmental Issues

The following article sets out the author's view that any generation must address three problems of fairness among generations: depletion of resources resulting in the loss of options or diversity in resources, degradation in the quality of the environment and its resources, and discriminatory access to resources among generations and within the present generation.

■ IN FAIRNESS TO FUTURE GENERATIONS: INTERNATIONAL LAW, COMMON PATRIMONY AND INTERGENERATIONAL EQUITY

Edith Brown Weiss
ch. 1 (Transnational & UNU 1989)

As we develop and use the natural and cultural resources of our planet, we will face problems in allocating the wealth from these resources between members of the present generation and those of future generations. Since future generations are not represented in the processes for making decisions today, potential trade-offs between the preferences of present and future generations are usually ignored. Thus, the present generation may benefit from these resources at the expense of future generations.

Development and use of our natural and cultural resources raise three kinds of equity problems between generations: depletion of resources for future generations, degradation in quality of resources for future generations, and discriminatory access to use and benefit from the resources received from past generations.

A. Depletion of Resources

At least three kinds of actions by the present generation may deplete resources and thereby conflict with the interest of future generations: (1) consumption of higher quality resources, leading to higher real prices of resources for future generations; (2) consumption of resources not yet identified as valuable by the present generation or prior to discovery of their best use; and (3) exhaustion of resources, resulting in the narrowing of the range of available natural resources. The effects of these actions, particularly of the last two, may be effectively irreversible.

The most common problem of equity will arise from differentials in the price of a resource to different generations. Although many natural resources may not become scarce in the sense that they will be physically used up, the consumption of the higher grade resources by the present generation may result in only lower quality resources being available, which may lead to real increases in the cost of the resources to later generations. This may apply in particular to future generations in those countries that rely on particular resources, such as oil or coal, for their economic development.

Some economists would object to the possibility of a rise in real prices of natural resources on the grounds that there is infinite substitution of resources and unlimited capacity of improvement in extraction technology. If a rise in real prices occurs, they would contend that it may be due to higher labor costs or costs of other factors in the production process. But this is optimistic. Countries may not be able to find alternative energy supplies at the same real price as they have paid for oil or coal, or they may not find equally cheap alternatives for the products derived from particular species of plants and animals.

If we assume that the net price of a given natural resource will be higher for future generations than for the present one, there is an equitable issue as to which communities in future generations must bear the burden of these higher costs. The increase in the real price may fall on those in the future generation least able to pay for them. Future generations in countries dependent upon those resources will arguably be worse off than their predecessors. While it is possible that these generations may inherit a sufficiently higher income level and investment in capital and technology to offset increases in the price of natural resources relative to other items, this is not assured.

The second problem of equity among generations arises because natural resources are often exploited in ignorance of their potential economic importance, which may deplete potentially valuable resources. History offers many examples. Companies flared the natural gas which was a by-product of extracting oil, because the cost of delivery exceeded the price that it could command at that time. More recently, companies have exploited natural gas reserves containing helium, which is a potentially valuable resource and one for which we have no known substitute. This points to a major intergenerational problem in exploiting natural resources: recognizing that a given substance may be a valuable resource to future generations and properly assessing its potential value. Unless we proceed cautiously, we will discard natural resources which future generations would have wanted to pay us handsomely to retain.

The third problem arises from the exhaustion of resources, which leads to a narrowing of the diversity of the resource base that we pass to future generations and, in some cases, eliminates resources that people depend upon. To the extent that we consume all or nearly all known quantities of an existing natural resource, we reduce the natural resource options available to future generations. This reduces the economic soundness of the natural resource base for future generations, because we lost important options for developing new beneficial products. For example, through the rapid extinction of species, we can lose important options for developing new food crops and new medicines. We may or may not be able to develop substitutes for these products, and the price of doing so may be considerably higher than if the natural resources were available to use. Moreover, loss of varieties in particular crops may make it more difficult and costly to develop strains that are resistant to particular pests or less susceptible to climatic variations. These losses are irreversible.

If we exhaust known supplies of nonrenewable or essentially nonrenewable resources, such as natural gas deposits containing helium, we also narrow the diversity of the natural resource base. For example, helium, the lightest of known gases, appears indispensable for certain energy-related uses that may be important several decades from now, such as long-distance cryogenic transmission of electrical power. By then, helium-bearing natural gas deposits may be exhausted. Since the present demand for helium is lower than productive capacity, a great amount of helium is being lost to the atmosphere as natural gas is burned for fuel. Recapturing helium from the air, even if it becomes technically feasible, will be extremely expensive.

Reducing the diversity of known reserves of nonrenewable resources raises several problems for future generations. It forecloses applications for the resources that the present generation has not yet appreciated, but which could be very valuable for future generations. Substitutes may be found, but the price of developing them may be substantially higher. It also reduces the range of nonrenewable resources available to tackle any given problem, which may lead to inferior solutions or to more costly ones, particularly for those communities that were once rich in the nonrenewable resource.

[A similar analysis applies to cultural resources, particularly the knowledge that we have acquired about how natural and social systems work.]

B. Degradation in Environmental Quality

In this century we have seen increasing degradation of the quality of the global natural environment, particularly air, water, and soils, caused by pollution and, in some cases, exhaustion of resources. From an ecological perspective, waste products are an integral part of our system. We can either produce fewer, recycle them, or dispose of them in land, air, fresh waters, or marine areas, and now conceivably in outer space or under the seabed. We cannot ignore them.

As we dispose of our wastes, we affect the uses that future generations can make of the natural environment and the costs that they must bear in doing so. While some of our actions will enhance the utility of the natural environment to future generations, others will cause significant damage to it. The problem is that the present generation may reap short-term benefits from cheap disposal of wastes and pass along the substantial costs of this disposal to future generations.

Similarly, our actions may degrade the quality of the environment by destroying the environmental services that forests, soils, and watersheds now provide. Forests, for example, prevent soil erosion, facilitate water recharge, harbor wildlife, maintain the productivity of soils, and buffer climate—all essential environmental services.

Problems of intergenerational equity relating to degradation of quality arise from the following uses: (1) disposal of wastes that trigger damaging, costly and essentially irreversible changes in the quality of the environment; (2) actions that reduce the variety of uses to which any given resource can be put; (3) uses that so degrade the quality of the environment that they lead to depletion of specific resources in it; and (4) actions that degrade the environmental services which natural resources otherwise provide. In many instances the focus of concern is the risk that our actions will have these effects in the future; in other instances the problems are already apparent.

The first problem arises when the present generation uses the natural environment as a free or cheap resource in which to dump its physical wastes. In doing so, the present generation may impose serious health effects and welfare costs on future generations and pass on to them the severe costs of cleaning up the degraded quality of the environment, if they can do so at all. Problems of air and water pollution, and increasingly of groundwater pollution, illustrate this. For example, sulphates and nitrous oxides cause acid precipitation, which results in the biological impoverishment of lakes, the degradation of soils, and damage to plant life, which may persist for generations. Persistent toxic chemicals in lakes, which may either flow directly into the lake or be transported from disposal sites elsewhere, represent serious long-term dangers for future generations. The time necessary to remove them through natural processes can be exceedingly long. While the impact from the deterioration in lake quality may sometimes be reversed through the removal of the toxic contaminants from the bottoms of lakes, rivers or landfill sites, the costs of doing so are staggering.

At the global level, it is predicted that the increasing concentrations of greenhouse gases, such as carbon dioxide and methane, will lead in the first half of the next century to a rise in global mean temperature "which is greater than any in man's history." This will profoundly affect global climate patterns, with effects on ecosystems, agriculture, water resources and ocean levels. Activities contributing to these changes may occur several generations before their full effects are felt. Similarly, emissions of chlorofluorocarbons lead to the depletion of the global ozone layer, which can seriously damage human health and plant activity. . . . The disposal of nuclear wastes in permanent geologic sites on land or in other areas can also lead to irreversible changes in the quality of the immediate environment since the hazards of nuclear radiation continue for thousands of years.

The second problem of intergenerational equity related to degradation of environmental quality arises because some actions of the present generation so degrade environmental quality that future generations will have less flexibility in using their natural resources. Areas may become so heavily polluted that certain uses are precluded. For example, lakes may become so polluted that uses, such as for contact recreation (swimming, etc.) and municipal water supplies, are precluded. Examples are legion throughout the world. Tropical forests may be so mismanaged as to preclude some uses by future generations, such as for sustainable forestry or agriculture or for certain river fisheries dependent upon the forest fauna and flora. Or temperate forests suffering from acid deposition and other pollutants become unsuited for recreational and other uses.

The third problem arises when actions that pollute the natural environment directly lead to depletion of plant and animal life. For example, pollution of lakes may contaminate fisheries in the lakes and destroy certain plant and animal life in the region. Damage to fisheries from toxic pollution has been particularly acute in the Great Lakes between the United States and Canada. Similarly, air pollution is believed to be responsible for the "Waldsterben" of large areas in Europe, where even deciduous trees such as oak and beech are now affected.

The loss of natural environmental services caused by mismanaging natural resources raises another intergenerational problem of degraded environmental quality. For example, tropical forests may be so mismanaged that the fragile soils are unable to sustain productive growth, including sustainable agriculture. Clearcutting of forested slopes can cause soil erosion and degradation of the watershed, with resulting siltation of rivers, lakes and dams downstream, loss of wildlife, and changes in climate. The environmental services provided by the former forests can be essential to the ecological well-being of the region. As the Report of the World Commission on Environment and Development makes clear, the loss of natural environmental services is inconsistent with developing the planet on a sustainable basis, which, it emphasizes, is essential for the well-being of both present and future generations. [Again, a similar analysis applies to cultural resources.]

C. Discriminatory Access and Use of Resources

As beneficiaries of a planetary trust, each generation has an equitable right to use and benefit from the planetary resources. The two previous sections identified actions which the present generation might take to benefit itself at the expense of future generations. This section identifies factors that prevent the present generation from fully using and benefiting from the legacy.

There are three problems of equity regarding access to and use of the legacy: (1) the needs of future generations, which foreclose the present generation from consuming all of the fruits of the natural and cultural resources of its ancestors; (2) the severe impoverishment of some communities, which prevents them from being able to share equitably in the planetary legacy; and (3) actions by members of the present generation that prevent other members from enjoying the fruits of the legacy.

The first problem of access use arises if the present generation is viewed as having no right to exploit and use the natural and cultural resources of the planet, because they must be conserved for future generations. This is the preservationist argument. Taken to its extreme, it deprives the present generation of its legitimate claim to use and benefit from the earth's natural resources and the cultural resources of our species. This position can also easily become an apology for failing to assist those currently in economic need. Extreme poverty of certain parts of the global community remains one of our most pressing problems. Preserving all resources for future generations would seriously aggravate the problems of access that those in need already have, and would be untenable. Moreover, it would exacerbate the inequities in poverty and wealth that would be passed on unchanged to future generations.

The second problem of equitable access is an intragenerational problem, which is related to the first. It is theoretically based on the relationship which all members of the present generation have as beneficiaries of the natural and cultural resources of the planet. Although all members have an equitable right of access to and use of these resources, many are effectively unable to realize this right because of the great economic disparities in the world community. Those who now receive the benefits from exploiting the planetary resources have more to pass on to future generations, but this may result only in more to pass on to their own descendants, which perpetuates the inequality.

Members of the present generation may also prevent other members of their generation from enjoying natural and cultural resources when their activities cause environmental or other damage to them. In this perspective, one person's disposal of wastes, as in public lakes or streams, directly confronts another person's right as beneficiary to use resources for his or her own benefit. Parties externalize the costs of their own activities by imposing them upon other parties, who must then bear the burden without the benefit. The problems are particularly acute when parties dispose of their pollutants and waste in global commons, such as the oceans, where the benefits of externalizing the cost are reaped by a few and the costs ultimately borne by many. Such examples raise problems of equitable access and use among members of the present generation, and in such instances as toxic contamination, also among generations.

The three problems of intergenerational equity—depletion of resources for future generations, degradation in quality of resources, and [discriminatory] access to the benefits from and use of the resources—are interrelated. To the extent that the natural resource base is significantly depleted, its quality is also degraded. Similarly, degradations in quality can lead to effective depletion of resources and to less variety in the uses for the resources. Problems of access encompass concerns about the depletion and the quality of the resources for which access is sought, since degradations in either may mean less effective access, particularly to the benefits. While it is important to recognize these interconnections, the problems need to be addressed separately if we are to develop effective principles of equity among generations.

Notes and Questions

1. Can you think of specific environmental situations that raise intergenerational concerns? Do the categories suggested in the article above cover them?

2. What intergenerational issues do you see in the protection of cultural resources?

2. *Theoretical Perspectives*

Conceptually there are several approaches to intergenerational issues. The first is a preservationist approach, in which the present generation saves all resources for future generations. People can use resources so long as they do not deplete them in any way. This approach has deep roots in the natural flow theory in English water law and in efforts to preserve such unique places as the Grand Canyon. If carried to the extreme, it would promote the status quo over any change. While the approach is consistent with a subsistence economy, it is not consistent with an industrial economy.

At the opposite end of the spectrum is the opulent approach, in which the present generation consumes all that it wants today and generates as much wealth as it can, in the belief that maximizing consumption today is the best way to maximize wealth for future generations. This approach ignores long-term degradations, such as irreversible losses of species diversity and non-renewable resources.

Still another approach is to view the earth as an investment, with each generation living off the interest on the capital.

Consider the following excerpt in the context of these three perspectives.

■ INTERGENERATIONAL EQUITY: TOWARD AN INTERNATIONAL LEGAL FRAMEWORK

Edith Brown Weiss
Global Accord 332-353 (Nazli Choucri, ed. 1993)

Sustainable development rests on a commitment to equity with future generations. Sustainability . . . is possible if we look at the earth and its resources not only as an investment opportunity but as a trust, passed to us by our ancestors, to be enjoyed and passed on to our descendants for their use. Such a "planetary trust" conveys to us both rights and responsibilities. Most important, it implies that future generations, too, have rights, although these rights have meaning only if we, the living, respect them and if this respect transcends the differences among states, religions, and cultures. The notion that each generation holds the earth as a steward or in trust for its descendants strikes a deep chord with men and women of all cultures, religions, and nationalities. . . .

There are two relationships that must shape any theory of intergenerational equity: our relationship to other generations of our own species and our relationship to the natural system of which we are a part. . . . The theory of intergenerational equity stipulates that all generations have an equal place in relation to the natural system. There is no basis for preferring the present generation over future generations in their use of the planet. This assumption finds deep roots in international law. The preamble to the Universal Declaration of Human Rights begins, "Whereas recognition of the inherent dignity and of the equal and inalienable rights of all members of the human family is thc foundation of freedom, justice and peace in the world." The reference to all members of the human family has a temporal dimension that brings all generations within its scope. The reference to equal and inalienable rights affirms the basic equality of such generations in the human family.

. . . The anchor of a legal framework is thus the notion of equality as the norm connecting sequential generations in their use and care of the environment. The corollary is the concept of partnership between humans and nature and between sequences of humans born. . . . In this partnership no generation knows beforehand when it will be the living generation, how many members it will have, or even how many generations there will ultimately be. It is useful, then, to take the perspective of a generation that is placed somewhere along the spectrum of time, but does not know in advance where it will be located. (See John Rawls, Theory of Justice (1971).) Such a generation would want to inherit the earth in a condition at least as good as the condition it has been in for any previous generation and to have as much access to it as previous generations have had. This requires each generation to pass the planet on in no worse condition than in which it received it and to provide equitable access to its resources and benefits. Each generation is thus both a trustee for the planet with obligations to care for it and a beneficiary with rights to use it.

One of the questions that always arises in any discussion of intergenerational equity is how we can afford to address equity to future generations when there are widespread inequities today.

The author of the reading above comments as follows:

> While intergenerational equity may be viewed as in conflict with achieving intragenerational equity, the two are consistent and in fact must go together. Members of the present generation have an intragenerational right of equitable access to use and benefit from the planet's resources, which derives from the underlying equality which all generations have with each other in relation to their use of the natural system. Moreover, even the most selfish members of the present generation who care only about their own descendants must, as they extend their time horizon further, increasingly care about the general environment that their descendants will inherit. Since no one country or group of countries alone has the power to ensure a healthy environment, all must cooperate to ensure a robust planet in the future. This means meeting

> the basic needs of the poor so that they will have both the desire and ability to fulfill their intergenerational obligations to conserve the planet.

Id. at 336.

The article below questions how much a generation must do for future generations. Note the difference which arises from whether happiness or justice is the standard for our actions.

■ MAN'S RESPONSIBILITY FOR NATURE: ECOLOGICAL PROBLEMS AND WESTERN TRADITION

John Passmore
75-77, 86-87 (1974)

So the conservationist programme confronts us with a fundamental moral issue: ought we to pay any attention to the needs of posterity? To answer this question affirmatively is to make two assumptions: first, that posterity will suffer unless we do so; secondly that if it will suffer, it is our duty so to act as to prevent or mitigate its sufferings. Both assumptions can be, and have been, denied. To accept them does not, of course, do anything to solve the problem of conservation, but to reject them is to deny that there is any such problem, to deny that our society would be a better one—morally better—if it were to halt the rate at which it is at present exhausting its resources. . . .

To begin with the assumption that posterity will suffer unless we alter our ways, it is still often suggested that, on the contrary, posterity can safely be left to look after itself, provided only that science and technology continue to flourish. This optimistic interpretation of the situation comes especially from economists and from nuclear physicists. So Norman McRae, writing in the *Economist,* happily informs us that with the aid of the new sensors, carried by satellites, which are now available to geologists, vastly increased reserves of fossil fuels and minerals will soon be available for man's use. (They would certainly have to be vast: if our rate of consumption increases at the rate at which it has been increasing over the last decade even resources five times as great as those already known would be exhausted within the life-time of most children now less than ten years old.) "My own guess," he writes of fossil fuel in particular, "is that we will have an embarrassingly large fuel surplus"—this by the year 2012, when so many calculations predict the exhaustion of petroleum. "And nuclear fusion . . . should [by that time]," he continues, "give to mankind a virtually unlimited source of industrial power, with the oceans serving as a boundless reservoir of fuel—even for a world population far larger and many times richer than today's." If there is a problem, in his view, it lies only in the disposal of wastes—a pollution rather than a conservation problem. The nuclear physicist Alvin Weinburg is no less confident that "the problem of source depletion is a phony." With the exception of phosphorus, he tells us, "the most essential resources are virtually inexhaustible." . . . If these scientists, these economists, are right, there simply is no "problem of conservation."

Very many scientists, of course, take the opposite view, especially if they are biologists. Expert committees set up by such scientific bodies as the American National Academy of Sciences have, in fact, been prepared to commit themselves to definite estimates of the dates at which this resource or that will be exhausted. This is always, however, on certain assumptions. It makes a considerable difference whether one supposes or denies that rates of consumption will continue to increase exponentially as they have done since 1960; it makes a very great—in many cases an overwhelming—difference whether one supposes or denies that substitutes will be discovered for our major resources. The Academy's extrapolations are best read as a *reductio ad absurdum* of the supposition that our present patterns of resource consumption can continue even over the next century.

The possibility that substitutes will be discovered introduces a note of uncertainty into the whole discussion, an uncertainty which cannot be simply set aside as irrelevant to our moral and political decisions about conservation, which it inevitably and properly influences. At the moment, for example, the prospect of developing a fuel-cell to serve as a substitute for petrol is anything but bright; confident predictions that by 1972 nuclear fusion would be available as an energy source have proved to be unrealistic. But who can say what the situation will be in twenty years time? The now common-place comparison of earth to a space-ship is thus far misleading: the space-ship astronaut does not have the facilities to invent new techniques, nor can he fundamentally modify his habits of consumption. Any adequate extrapolation would also have to extrapolate technological advances. But by the nature of the case—although technologists have a bad habit of trying to persuade us otherwise—we cannot be at all certain when and whether those advances will take place, or what form they will assume. . . .

The uncertainties, however, remain. We can be confident that some day our society will run out of resources, but we do not know when it will do so or what resources it will continue to demand. The Premier of Queensland recently swept aside the protests of conservationists by arguing that Queensland's oil and coal resources should be fully utilised now, since posterity may have no need for them. This is not a wholly irrational attitude. One can readily see the force of an argument which would run thus: we are entitled, given the uncertainty of the future, wholly to ignore the interests of posterity, a posterity whose very existence is hypothetical—granted the possibility of a nuclear disaster—and whose needs, except for such fundamentals as air and water, we cannot possibly anticipate. . . .

Man considered as a pure consumer or a pure producer, economic man, has, indeed, only a very limited concern for posterity. As the economist Joan Robinson has freely admitted: "This problem [of sacrifices for posterity] cannot be resolved by any kind of calculation based on 'discounting the future,' for the individuals concerned in the loss and gain are different. . . . The benefit from their sacrifices will come later and they may not survive to see it. The choice must be taken somehow or other, but the principles of Welfare Economics do not help to settle it."

A somewhat different line of argument—which takes justice rather than happiness as its starting point—has been put forward by John Rawls. He does not so much as mention the saving of natural resources. (How rare it is for moral philosophers to pay any attention to the world around them!) But he has a good deal to say about the general concept of saving for posterity; that we ought to save for posterity, he in general argues, is a consequence of the fact that we ought to act justly, to posterity as to our contemporaries. The utilitarian principle of impartiality, taken literally, demands too much from us; we cannot reasonably be expected to share our resources between ourselves and the whole of posterity. What we can reasonably be expected to do is to hand on to our immediate posterity a rather better situation than we have ourselves inherited. Anything less than this would be unfair to them, anything more would be unfair to the present generation. Rawls is Kantian in so far as he presumes that the final aim of our efforts is an ideal society we shall not live to see realised. But he so far compromises with much of Kant's critics as Herder and Herzen as to argue that we can best work towards that society by improving the conditions of life *now* and passing on the results to our immediate descendants, for them to do likewise. Exactly to what degree we should save for posterity, it is not possible, he admits, accurately to determine. But about the general character of what we ought to do he has no doubts. "Each generation," he writes, "must not only preserve the gains of culture and civilisation, and maintain intact those just institutions that have been established, but it must also put aside in each period of time a suitable amount of real capital accumulation." The "capital accumulation" may take various forms—investment in learning and education as well as in machinery, factories, agriculture.

Note that, as Rawls sees the situation, we have a threefold task: first to "preserve the gains of our civilisation"; secondly to "maintain intact" our "just institutions"; thirdly to hand over to posterity an accumulation of capital greater than we received from our ancestors. Many nowadays would, of course, challenge the assumptions inherent in this conception of our task. What we have been accustomed to call "gains," they would argue, are not really such; none of our institutions are just; we should be doing no kindness to posterity by handing over to them a greater capital accumulation. But for my part, I am prepared to accept the view, at least, that if our situation were a normal one, Rawls has accurately described what posterity would expect, and all it could properly expect, from us. So far, so good. But it is not very far.

Each generation, Rawls is suggesting, should decide what it ought to save for posterity by answering in particular terms a general question: what is reasonable for a society to expect, at the stage of development it has reached, from its predecessor? If it then acts upon the answer at which it arrives, each generation will be better off than its predecessor but no generation will be called upon to make an exceptional sacrifice. This is as far as we can go, I should agree, if our relationship with succeeding generations is to be governed by the principle of justice. The consequence is that each generation is concerned, when it is considering what sacrifices it should make, only with the next succeeding generation, not with some remote posterity. And this, as contrasted with classical utilitarianism, presents it with an easier set of calculations to make, difficult although they still are.

But although this means that, up to a point, each generation is in a unique position, unique in respect to exactly what it inherits and exactly what it has a duty to hand on, it does not allow for the position of a generation which is unique in a quite different sense: it cannot calculate what it should do for posterity by reflecting on what its predecessors did for it. The sacrifice required of such a generation may be heroic, and Rawl's theory is based on the concept of justice, fairness, equal shares; it leaves no room for the heroic sacrifice. Yet if the conservationists are right it is precisely such a heroic sacrifice we are now called upon to make, a sacrifice far beyond anything our ancestors had to make. And this transforms the situation.

Not everyone agrees that future generations have rights that obligate individuals in the present generation to act in a prescribed manner. The following is an example of the reasoning behind the idea that future generations do not have rights.

■ ENVIRONMENTAL ETHICS AND THE RIGHTS OF FUTURE GENERATIONS

Bryan Norton
4 Envtl. Ethics 19, 322-324 (1982)

We can now return to the main question, Is there a concept of the rights of future generations according to which individuals currently have rights that impose obligations on present individuals? Can one base an ethic of environmental preservation on this? Criticisms of such rights are based on two separable grounds—their futurity and their referential ambiguity. The futurity objection, offered by Richard De George, is as follows: "Future generations by definition do not exist now. They cannot now, therefore, be the present bearer or subject of anything, including rights." But this futurity objection is unconvincing. One can respond that future people have hypothetical rights in the present. These are the rights they will have when they in fact exist. If we believe that an individual has a certain hypothetical right and if we also have strong evidence that the individual will exist, how can the hypothetical right in question be ignored? Since a person's date of birth is morally irrelevant, canons of impartiality demand that future individuals be accorded rights equal to those of present individuals, provided of course that they are brought into existence. De George's argument is inconclusive because it concentrates on irrelevant temporal differences.

My line of attack concentrates rather on the concept of future personhood which, I believe, is necessarily incoherent in the context of environmental preservation. This incoherence can be introduced by "Parfit's Paradox." Parfit describes two social policies, which he calls High Consumption and Low Consumption.

> If we choose High rather than Low Consumption, the standard of living will be higher over the next century. This effect implies another. The people who will live more than a century from now would be different on the two policies. Given the effects of two such policies on the details of our lives, different marriages would increasingly be made. More simply, even in the same marriages, the children would increasingly be conceived at different times. As we have seen, this would in fact be enough to make them different children. . . .
>
> Return next to the moral questions. If we choose High Consumption, the quality of life will be lower more than a century from now. But the particular people who will then live would never have existed if instead we have chosen Low Consumption. Is our choice of High Consumption worse for these people? Only if it is against their interest to have been born. Even if this makes sense, we can suppose that it would not go as far as this. We can conclude that, if we choose High Consumption, our choice will be worse for no one.

This argument may appear to have an air of sleight of hand about it. Indeed, its being dubbed a "paradox" suggests that it is a minor conceptual anomaly, rather than a cogent, substantive point. Nevertheless, the argument deserves serious consideration.

Three consequences follow from Parfit's argument:

(1) No one is harmed by a policy of High Consumption.
(2) No future person's rights are infringed by a policy of High Consumption.
(3) Rights of future generations are an inadequate basis for an environmental ethic.

Consequence (1) is Parfit's conclusion. Consequence (2) follows from (1) together with the principle that rights must be possessed by some actual individual. If rights must be possessed by some individual and if no harm has occurred to any individual, then no rights have been infringed upon by a policy of depletion. If (2) is true, (3) seems to follow. High consumption is precisely what an ethic of environmental protection is intended to forbid. If an environmental ethic cannot rule out such a policy by invoking infringements of rights, it is surely inadequate.

It might be responded that Parfit's result become effective only after two or three generations. But a policy of depletion would undoubtedly affect the immediately subsequent generation, and be ruled out because it would infringe upon their rights. This response does not help. Suppose one generation, while pursuing a policy of depletion, causes levels of radioactivity which sterilize all living beings. All would agree that, if this consequence resulted from informed actions, the generation in question would have done wrong. Yet by a simple extension of the above reasoning, no future individual would have been harmed. While one might object on the grounds that the sterilizing infringes upon the rights of present people to reproduce, this objection would be giving up the original goal of developing an environmental ethic based upon the rights of future generations. [Norton favors general obligations based in multi-generational community.]

For more discussion on Parfit's Paradox, *see* Anthony D'Amato, Do We Owe a Duty to Future Generations to Preserve the Global Environment?, in AGORA: What Obligation Does Our Generation Owe to the Next? An Approach to Global Environmental Responsibility, 84 A.J.I.L. 190-198 (1990) (asserting that under the reasoning of Parfit's Paradox, we have no moral obligation to future generations). *See also* Paul. A. Barresi, *Beyond Fairness to Future Generations: An Intragenerational Alternative to Intergenerational Equity in the International Environmental Arean,* 11 Tul. Envtl. L.J. 59 (1997) (arguing that individual rights held by the present generation suffice); Edith Brown Weiss, *A Response to Barresi's "Beyond Fairness to Future Generations,"* 11 Tul. Envtl. L.J. 89 (1997).

Notes and Questions

1. Why should we care about future generations? As the saying goes, what have future generations ever done for us?

Sociologists would agree that we innately act in ways calculated to promote the survival and reproduction of our genes. Others would say that caring about future generations represents a primordial social value, necessary for maintaining human communities. Only when a community is fighting a losing battle for survival does it no longer care for its children. *See* Colin Turnbull, The Mountain People (1972) (excerpted in Chapter

1C above) for a description of the desperate plight of the Ik tribe in Kenya-Uganda.

Still others contend that there is a basic psychological need in all of us to transcend the self, which is expressed through the creation of books, artistic works, institutions, music, and other things that may last beyond our lifetime. Kenneth Boulding has written, "the most satisfactory individual identity is that which identifies not only with a community in space but also with a community extending over time from the past into the future. . . . There is a great deal of historical evidence to suggest that a society which loses its positive image of the future loses also its capacity to deal with present problems and soon falls apart." Kenneth Boulding, The Economics of the Coming Spaceship Earth, in The Environmental Handbook 99-100 (G. de Bell, ed. 1970). *See also,* Edith Brown Weiss, In Fairness to Future Generations: International Law, Common Patrimony and Intergenerational Equity, ch. 2, 1989.

2. What assumption should we make about intergenerational equity?

- Should we *preserve* the planet intact? If so, doesn't this thwart economic growth and ignore poverty?
- Alternatively, should we consume as much as we can today to generate more wealth to pass to future generations in the form of capital investments, technology, knowledge, and infrastructure? Are significant environmental costs then ignored?
- Should we promote equality among generations in their access to and use of the environment? Are we trustees/custodians of the environment?
- How would John Rawls's *Theory of Justice* apply to our care and use of the natural system?

3. How could the interests of future generations be represented in our legal system?

4. Do future generations have rights in relation to the natural system?

5. What is the difference between having a right and relying only on an obligation? How are rights and obligations related? How are the two terms—"rights" and "obligations"—relevant to the way one generation handles the earth's resources?

Consider the following:

> Planetary rights and obligations coexist in each generation. In the *inter*generational dimension, the generations to which the obligations are owed are future generations. Thus, the rights of future generations are linked to the obligations of the present generation. In the *intra*generational context, planetary obligations and rights exist between members of the present generation. . . . Thus, intergenerational obligations to conserve the planet flow from the present generation, who have the right to use and enjoy the planetary legacy.
>
> . . . Can intergenerational obligations exist without rights? While rights are always connected to obligations, the reverse is not always true.

Edith Brown Weiss, Our Rights and Obligations to Future Generations for the Environment, in AGORA: What Obligation Does Our Generation Owe to the Next? An Approach to Global Environmental Responsibility, 84 Am. J. Intl. L. 198, 202-203 (1990) (asserting that future generations have a right to live in an environment at least as healthy as the present generation's).

6. What would be our corresponding obligations toward future generations if we accepted the proposition that they had rights?

ADDITIONAL READINGS

For more reading on our intergenerational relationships, *see* Ernest Partridge, ed., Responsibilities to Future Generations (Prometheus Books, 1981); Future Generations Journal (International Environment Institute Foundation for International Studies); Lothar Guendling, Our Responsibility to Future Generations, Am. J. Intl. L. 207 (1990); Catherine Redgewell, Intergenerational Equity and Global Warming, in Robin Churchill and David Freestone, eds., International Law and Global Climate Change 41-56 (1991).

3. Implementation of Intergenerational Equity

The idea of considering future generations has been much discussed in environmental policy circles. The following Guidelines were developed by the Advisory Group for the United Nations University Project on International Law, Common Patrimony and Intergovernmental Equity. The statement was made in Goa, India, on February 15, 1988.

■ GUIDELINES ON INTERGENERATIONAL EQUITY

The Advisory Committee established to the United Nations University Project on "International Law, Common Patrimony and Intergenerational Equity" adopts, on the basis of the major study undertaken, the following statement.

The increasing concerns over the depletion of natural resources and the degradation of environmental quality and the recognition of the need to conserve the natural and cultural heritage have evoked responses at all levels: national, regional and international; governmental and non-governmental. These concerns have been expressed in new political initiatives, in incipient economic adjustments and in significant developments in the legal field.

One innovative response to these concerns is represented by the present project which attempts to introduce for the first time in a systematic and comprehensive manner, a long-term temporal dimension into international law as a complement to the traditional spatial dimension.

The temporal dimension is articulated through the formulation of the theory of intergenerational equity: all members of each generation of human beings, as a species, inherit a natural and cultural patrimony from past generations, both as beneficiaries and as custodians under the duty to pass on this heritage to future generations. As a central point of this theory the right of each generation to benefit from and develop this natural and cultural heritage is inseparably coupled with the obligation to use this heritage in such a manner that it can be passed on to future generations in no worse condition than it was received from past generations. This requires conservation and, as appropriate, enhancement of the quality and diversity of this heritage. The conservation of cultural diversity is as important as the conservation of environmental diversity to ensure options for future generations.

Specifically, the principle of intergenerational equity requires conserving the diversity and the quality of biological resources, of renewable resources such as forests, water and soils which form an integrated system, as well as of our knowledge of natural and cultural systems. The principle requires that we avoid actions with harmful and irreversible consequences for our natural and cultural heritage and that we dispose of nuclear and other wastes without unduly shifting the costs to coming generations.

Planetary rights and planetary obligations follow from the principles of equity governing the relationship between generations. These pertain to valued interests of past, present and future generations, covering natural and cultural resources. They will become enforceable as they find expression in customary and conventional international law. In case of violations, claims should be raised on behalf of present and future generations. There is a complementarity between recognized human rights and the proposed intergenerational rights.

To implement intergenerational rights and obligations, the following strategies are proposed: (a) representation by States not only of present but also of future generations; (b) designation of ombudsman or commissioners for protecting the interests of future generations; (c) monitoring systems for cultural and natural resources; (d) conservation assessments giving particular attention to long-term consequences; (e) measures to ensure use of renewable resources and ecological systems on a sustainable basis; (f) commitment to scientific and technical research to advance the purposes set out above and (g) programmes of education and learning at all social levels and age groups especially the young generations. It is particularly important to give attention to the proper functioning and maintenance of facilities and services. It is crucial not only to establish services and facilities for conserving natural and cultural resources but also to take appropriate measures for maintaining them.

National institutions and decision-makers and international organizations concerned with the conservation and development of natural resources and cultural systems should be encouraged to integrate as a matter of course the intergenerational perspective in their activities and in the elaboration of international principles and agreements respecting our common heritage.

Notes and Questions

1. What status do the Guidelines have in international law?
2. What problems do you foresee in implementing the Guidelines? What changes would you recommend to them?

In the maritime boundary delimitation case of Denmark v. Norway before the International Court of Justice, 1993 I.C.J. 38, Judge Weeramantry issued a concurring opinion in which he discusses the role of equity. He notes that a broader perspective on equity comes from traditional legal systems such as the African, the Pacific, and the Amerindian, "which contained a deeply ingrained respect for the earth, the atmosphere, the lakes and the seas, which the evolving law of the sea can consider with profit. . . . Respect for these elemental constituents of the inheritance of succeeding generations, dictated rules and attitudes based upon a concept of an equitable sharing which was both horizontal in regard to the present generation and vertical for the benefit of generations yet to come." Judge Weeramantry then cites In Fairness to Future Generations (excerpted above) for the proposition that principles of intergenerational equity "can build upon the increasing use by the International Court of Justice of equitable principles to achieve a result that the Court views as fair and just."

In the 1995 Nuclear Test Case (New Zealand v. France), 1995 I.C.J. 288, New Zealand argued that France's proposed underground nuclear tests constituted a violation of international law and/or that it was "unlawful for France to conduct such nuclear tests before it has undertaken an Environmental Impact Assessment according to accepted international standards." Formally the case arose as a request to examine the proposed nuclear tests in accordance with the ICJ's 1974 Judgment in the Nuclear Test Cases involving atmospheric nuclear tests by France. In that case, the Court decided that the issue was moot because of declarations by France that it would not carry out further atmospheric nuclear tests but noted in paragraph 63 of the Judgment that "if the basis of this Judgment were to be affected, the Applicant could request an examination of the situation in accordance with the provisions of the Statute."

The 1995 Judgment of the Court declined to accept the request since underground rather than atmospheric tests were now involved. Order of

September 22, 1995. Two of the dissenting opinions discussed the importance of intergenerational equity to the dispute. Judge Weeramantry wrote as follows:

> **The Concept of Intergenerational Rights**
>
> The case before the Court raises, as no case ever before the Court has done, the principle of intergenerational equity—an important and rapidly developing principle of contemporary environmental law.
>
> . . . Having regard to the information before us that the half life of a radioactive by-product of nuclear tests can extend to over 20,000 years, this is an important aspect that an international tribunal cannot fail to notice. In a matter of which it is duly seised, this Court must regard itself as a trustee of those rights in the sense that a domestic court is a trustee of the interests of an infant unable to speak for itself. If this Court is charged with administering international law, and if this principle is building itself into the corpus of international law, or has already done so, this principle is one which must inevitably be a concern of this Court. The consideration involved is too serious to be dismissed as lacking in importance merely because there is no precedent on which it rests.
>
> New Zealand's complaint that its rights are affected does not relate only to the rights of people presently in existence. The rights of the people of New Zealand include the rights of unborn posterity. Those are rights which a nation is entitled, and indeed obliged, to protect. In considering whether New Zealand has made out a prima facie case of damage to its interests sufficient to bring the processes of this Court into operation in terms of paragraph 63, this is therefore an important aspect not to be ignored.
>
> In the words of an important recent work on this question:
>
>> The starting proposition is that each generation is both a custodian and a user of our common natural and cultural patrimony. As custodians of this planet, we have certain moral obligations to future generations which we can transform into legally enforceable norms.[1]

On July 8, 1996, the International Court of Justice handed down its Advisory Opinion on The Legality of the Threat or Use of Nuclear Weapons. 35 I.L.M. 809 (1996). The opinion responded to the request from the United Nations General Assembly in December 1994. The court found that there was no specific authorization nor any comprehensive and universal prohibition in customary or conventional international law on the threat or use of nuclear weapons as such. In the most controversial finding, a divided court in a seven to seven vote, found that . . . "the threat or use of nuclear weapons would generally be contrary to the rules of international law applicable in armed conflict, and in particular the principles and rules of humanitarian law. However, in view of the current state of international law, and of the elements of fact at its disposal, the court cannot conclude

1. *See* E. Brown Weiss, In Fairness to Future Generations: International Law, Common Patrimony, and Intergenerational Equity 21 (1989).

definitively whether the threat or use of nuclear weapons would be lawful or unlawful in an extreme circumstance of self-defence, in which the very survival of a state would be at stake." In its opinion, the court explicitly referred to the interests of future generations: "it is imperative for the court to take account of the unique characteristics of nuclear weapons, and in particular . . . their ability to cause damage to generations to come." (para. 36).

In his dissenting opinion, Judge Weeramantry discussed the damage to future generations and wrote:

> This Court, as the principal judicial organ of the United Nations, empowered to state and apply international law with an authority matched by no other tribunal must, in its jurisprudence, pay due recognition to the rights of future generations. If there is any tribunal that can recognize and protect their interests under the law, it is this court.
>
> It is to be noted in this context that the rights of future generations have passed the stage when they were merely an embryonic right struggling for recognition. They have woven themselves into international law through major treaties, through juristic opinion and through general principles of law recognized by civilized nations. [at 17.]

Notes and Questions

1. On June 26, 1992, the International Court of Justice decided that it had jurisdiction to hear the dispute between Nauru and Australia, Case Concerning Certain Phosphate Lands in Nauru, 1992 I.C.J. 240 (jurisdictional issues). Nauru argued that it suffered large-scale environmental damage as a result of Australia's violation of its rights under the United Nations Trusteeship and under general principles of international law. Article 5 of the Trusteeship Agreement referred to the well-being of both "present and future interests" of Nauru's inhabitants. The case was subsequently settled before the court decided the merits of the case. Do you think a principle of intergenerational equity could have been applicable in this case? What difference would it make?

2. Hungary and the Slovak Republic agreed to have the International Court of Justice decide a dispute over the flow of the Danube river. Among other items, Hungary alleged that the Slovak Republic had diverted the waters of the Danube river and deprived Hungary of groundwater and made Hungarian land near the Danube arid. Are there any intergenerational issues that you see in this dispute? What difference would the application of a principle of intergenerational equity make? What problems do you foresee? The court handed down its decision in September 1997, which reaffirmed its statement in the 1996 Nuclear Weapons Advisory Opinion

that states have a general obligation "to ensure that activities within their jurisdiction and control respect the environment of other states or of areas beyond national control." Judge Weeramantry, in a separate opinion, affirmed the principle of intergenerational rights and further identified a principle of trusteeship of earth's resources.

3. The United Nations Commission on Sustainable Development's Expert Group Meeting on Identification of Principles of International Law for Sustainable Development identified intergenerational equity as one of the principles. The report discussed equity as including both intergenerational equity (relating to the rights of future generations and our obligations to them) and intragenerational equity (relating to members of generations existing today). Report of the Expert Group Meeting on Identification of Principles of International Law for Sustainable Development, September 1995, United Nations Commission for Sustainable Development, Background Paper #3, April-May 1996 Session, New York, at 11-14. The United Nations Environment Programme's Expert Group Workshop also identified equity within and among generations as one of the principles of international law aiming at sustainable development. Final Report of the Expert Group Workshop on International Environmental Law Aiming at Sustainable Development, Oct. 4, 1996, UNEP/IEL/WS/3/2 at 13-14.

On August 9, 1993, the Supreme Court of the Republic of the Philippines granted standing to a group of children as representative of themselves and of future generations to bring a case against the Environment and Natural Resources Department to seek cancellation of existing timber license agreements and to ban the approval of new ones.

The Supreme Court said

> [w]e find no difficulty in ruling that they can, for themselves, for others of their generation and for the succeeding generations, file a class suit. Their personality to sue in behalf of the succeeding generations can only be based on the concept of intergenerational responsibility insofar as the right to a balanced and healthful ecology is concerned. Such a right, as hereinafter expounded, considers the "rhythm and harmony of nature." Nature means the created world in its entirety. Such rhythm and harmony indispensably include, inter alia, the judicious disposition, utilization, management, renewal and conservation of the country's forest, mineral, land, waters, fisheries, wildlife, off-shore areas and other natural resources to the end that their exploration, development and utilization be equitably accessible to the present as well as future generations. Needless to say, every generation has a responsibility to the next to preserve that rhythm and harmony for the full enjoyment of a balanced and healthful ecology. Put a little differently, the minors' assertion of their right to a sound environment constitutes, at the

> same time, the performance of their obligation to ensure the protection of that right for generations to come.

The Supreme Court found the right to balanced and healthful ecology in the Constitution of the Philippines. Minors Oposa v. Secretary of the Department of the Environment and Natural Resources, 33 I.L.M. 173 (1994). For analysis of the case, *see* Ted Allen, The Philippine Children's Case Recognizing Legal Standing for Future Generations, 6 Geo. Intl. Envtl. L. Rev. 713 (1994).

Notes and Questions

1. Do you agree with the Supreme Court of the Philippines that children can represent the interests of those generations yet unborn?
2. What consequences do you foresee in granting standing to representatives of future generations?
3. Critics of deforestation and other such actions have often argued that the economic instruments that we have to consider future costs and benefits inherently discriminate in favor of exploiting resources in the present. Dr. Mostafa K. Tolba, Executive Director of UNEP in 1990, addressed this issue. He wrote, "Action [to protect the environment] will entail at times sweeping economic reforms, whereby irrational discounting practices witnessed by economic decisions geared for short-term, high income yields at the expense of lower or even negative income for future generations, become a thing of the past. Such economic impatience reflects market price structures that embody immediate, not future, economic conditions." In Salvino Busuttil et al., eds., Our Responsibilities Towards Future Generations, "Foreward," at 11 (Foundation for International Studies, Malta, 1990).

Additional Readings

For insightful economic analyses of ways to consider the future, *see* Richard B. Norgaard, Sustainability and the Economics of Assuring Assets for Future Generations (1992); Jerome Rothenberg, Economic Perspectives on Time Comparisons: An Evaluation of Time Discounting and Economic Perspectives on Time Comparisons: Alternative Approaches to Time Comparisons, in Global Accord: Environmental Challenges and International Responses 307-332, 355-398 (Nazli Choucri, ed. 1993). *See generally* Laurence J. Kotlikoff, Generational Accounting: Knowing Who Pays and When, for What We Spend (1992) (comparing the fiscal treatment of different generations in general accounting).

B. RELATIONSHIP OF HUMANS TO THE NATURAL SYSTEM

1. *Flora*

■ SHOULD TREES HAVE STANDING?—TOWARD LEGAL RIGHTS FOR NATURAL OBJECTS

Christopher D. Stone
45 S. Cal. L. Rev. 450 (1972)

INTRODUCTION: THE UNTHINKABLE

In *Descent of Man,* Darwin observes that the history of man's moral development has been a continual extension in the objects of his "social instincts and sympathies." Originally each man had regard only for himself and those of a very narrow circle about him; later, he came to regard more and more "not only the welfare, but the happiness of all his fellowmen"; then "his sympathies became more tender and widely diffused, extending to men of all races, to the imbecile, maimed, and other useless members of society, and finally to the lower animals. . . ."

History of the law suggests a parallel development. Perhaps there never was a pure Hobbesian state of nature, in which no "rights" existed except in the vacant sense of each man's "right to self-defense." But it is not unlikely that so far as the earliest "families" (including extended kinship groups and clans) were concerned, everyone outside the family was suspect, alien, rightless. And even within the family, persons we presently regard as the natural holders of at least some rights had none. Take, for example, children. . . .

The legal rights of children have long since been recognized in principle, and are still expanding in practice. Witness, just within recent time, *In re Gault,* guaranteeing basic constitutional protections to juvenile defendants, and the Voting Rights Act of 1970. We have been making persons of children although they were not, in law, always so. And we have done the same, albeit imperfectly some would say, with prisoners, aliens, women (especially of the married variety), the insane, Blacks, foetuses, and Indians.

Nor is it only matter in human form that has come to be recognized as the possessor of rights. The world of the lawyer is peopled with inanimate right-holders: trusts, corporations, joint ventures, municipalities, Subchapter R partnerships, and nation-states, to mention just a few. Ships, still referred to by courts in the feminine gender, have long had an independent jural life, often with striking consequences. We have become so accustomed to the idea of a corporation having "its" own rights, and being a "person" and "citizen" for so many statutory and constitutional purposes, that we forget how jarring the notion was to early jurists.

It is this note of the *unthinkable* that I want to dwell upon for a moment.

Throughout legal history, each successive extension of rights of some new entity has been, theretofore, a bit unthinkable. We are inclined to suppose the rightlessness of rightless "things" to be a decree of Nature, not a legal convention acting in support of some status quo. . . .

The fact is, that each time there is a movement to confer rights onto some new "entity," the proposal is bound to sound odd or frightening or laughable. This is partly because until the rightless thing receives its rights, we cannot see it as anything but a *thing* for the use of "us"—those who are holding rights at the time. . . . There is something of a seamless web involved: there will be resistance to giving the thing "rights" until it can be seen and valued for itself; yet it is hard to see it and value it for itself until we can bring ourselves to give it "rights"—which is almost inevitably going to sound inconceivable to a large group of people.

The reason for this little discourse on the unthinkable [is that] I am quite seriously proposing that we give legal rights to forests, oceans, rivers and other so-called "natural objects" in the environment—indeed, to the natural environment as a whole.

TOWARD HAVING STANDING IN ITS OWN RIGHT

It is not inevitable, nor is it wise, that natural objects should have no rights to seek redress in their own behalf. It is no answer to say that streams and forests cannot have standing because streams and forests cannot speak. Corporations cannot speak either; nor can states, estates, infants, incompetents, municipalities or universities. Lawyers speak for them, as they customarily do for the ordinary citizen with legal problems. One ought, I think, to handle the legal problems of natural objects as one does the problems of legal incompetents—human beings who have become vegetable. If a human being shows signs of becoming senile and has affairs that he is de jure incompetent to manage, those concerned with his well being make such a showing to the court, and someone is designated by the court with the authority to manage the incompetent's affairs. The guardian (or "conservator" or "committee"—the terminology varies) then represents the incompetent in his legal affairs. Courts make similar appointments when a corporation has become "incompetent"—they appoint a trustee in bankruptcy or reorganization to oversee its affairs and speak for it in court when that becomes necessary.

On a parity of reasoning, we should have a system in which, when a friend of a natural object perceives it to be endangered, he can apply to a court for the creation of a guardianship. Perhaps we already have the machinery to do so. California law, for example, defines an incompetent as "any person, whether insane or not, who by reason of old age, disease, weakness of mind, or other cause, is unable, unassisted, properly to manage and take care of himself or his property, and by reason thereof is likely to be deceived or imposed upon by artful or designing persons." Of course, to urge a court that an endangered river is "a person" under this provision will call for lawyers as bold and imaginative as those who convinced the Supreme Court that a railroad corporation was a "person" under the fourteenth amendment, a constitutional provision theretofore generally thought of as designed to secure the rights of freedom.

■ SIERRA CLUB v. MORTON, SECRETARY OF THE INTERIOR

405 U.S. 727 (1971)
Prior History: Certiorari to the United States Court of Appeals for the Ninth Circuit

SYLLABUS

No. 70-34 Argued November 17, 1971—Decided April 19, 1972. Petitioner, a membership corporation with "a special interest in the conservation and sound maintenance of the national parks, game refuges, and forests of the country," brought this suit for a declaratory judgment and an injunction restraining federal officials from approving an extensive skiing development in the Mineral King Valley in the Sequoia National Forest. Petitioner relies on §10 of the Administrative Procedure Act, which accords judicial review to a "person suffering legal wrong because of agency action, or [who is] adversely affected or aggrieved by agency action within the meaning of a relevant statute." On the theory that this was a "public" action involving questions as to the use of natural resources, petitioner did not allege that the challenged development would affect the club or its members in their activities or that they used Mineral King, but maintained that the project would adversely change the area's aesthetics and ecology. The District Court granted a preliminary injunction. The Court of Appeals reversed, holding that the club lacked standing, and had not shown irreparable injury. Held: a person has standing to seek judicial review under the Administrative Procedure Act only if he can show that he himself has suffered or will suffer injury, whether economic or otherwise. In this case, where petitioner asserted no individualized harm to itself or its members, it lacked standing to maintain the action. Pp. 4-14, 433 F.2d 24 affirmed.

STEWART, J., delivered the opinion of the Court in which BURGER, C.J., and WHITE and MARSHALL, J.J., joined.

MR. JUSTICE DOUGLAS, dissenting.

I share the views of my Brother, BLACKMUN and would reverse the judgment below.

The critical question of "standing" would be simplified and also put neatly in focus if we fashioned a federal rule that allowed environmental issues to be litigated before federal agencies or federal courts in the name of the inanimate object about to be despoiled, defaced, or invaded by roads and bulldozers and where injury is the subject of public outrage. Contemporary public concern for protecting nature's ecological equilibrium should lead to the conferral of standing upon environmental objects to sue for their own preservation. See Stone, Should Trees Have Standing? Toward Legal Rights for Natural Objects, 45 S. Cal. L. Rev. 450 (1972). This suit would therefore be more properly labeled as *Mineral King v. Morton.*

Inanimate objects are sometimes parties in litigation. A ship has a legal personality, a fiction found useful for maritime purposes. The corporation soul—a creature of ecclesiastical law—is an acceptable adversary and large fortunes ride on its cases. The ordinary corporation is a "person" for purposes of the adjudicatory processes, whether it represents proprietary, spiritual, aesthetic, or charitable cases.

So it should be as respects valleys, alpine meadows, rivers, lakes, estuaries, beaches, ridges, groves of trees, swampland, or even air that feels the destructive pressures of modern technology and modern life. The river, for example, is the living symbol of all the life it sustains or nourishes—fish, aquatic insects, water ouzels, otter, deer, elk, bear, and all other animals, including man, who are dependent on it or who enjoy it for its sight, its sound, or its life. The river as plaintiff speaks for the ecological unit of life that is part of it. Those people who have a meaningful relation to that body of water—whether it be a fisherman, a canoeist, a zoologist, or a logger—must be able to speak for the values which the river represents and which are threatened with destruction.

I do not know Mineral King. I have never seen it nor traveled it, though I have seen articles describing its proposed "development," notably Hano, *Protectionists v. Recreationists*—the Battle of Mineral King, N.Y. Times Mag., Aug. 17, 1969; and Browning Mickey Mouse in the Mountains, Harper's, March 1972, p. 65. The Sierra Club in its complaint alleges that "[o]ne of the principal purposes of the Sierra Club is to protect and conserve the national resources of the Sierra Nevada Mountains." The District Court held that this uncontested allegation made the Sierra Club "sufficiently aggrieved" to have "standing" to sue on behalf of Mineral King.

Mineral King is doubtless like other wonders of the Sierra Nevada such as Tuolumne Meadows and the John Muir Trail. Those who hike it, fish it, hunt it, camp in it, or frequent it, or visit it merely to sit in solitude and wonderment are legitimate spokesmen for it, whether they may be a few or many. Those who have that intimate relation with the inanimate object about to be injured, polluted, or otherwise despoiled are its legitimate spokesmen.

The Solicitor General, whose views on this subject are in the Appendix to this opinion, takes a wholly different approach. He considers the problem in terms of "government by the Judiciary." With all respect, the problem is to make certain that the inanimate objects, which are the very core of

America's beauty, have spokesmen before they are destroyed. It is, of course, true that most of them are under the control of a federal or state agency. The standard given those agencies are usually expressed in terms of the "public interest." Yet "public interest" has so many differing shades of meaning as to be quite meaningless on the environmental front. Congress accordingly has adopted ecological standards in the National Environmental Policy Act of 1969, Pub. 91-90, 83 Stat. 852, 42 U.S.C. §4321. L.N. *et seq.*, and guidelines for agency action have been provided by the Council on Environmental Quality of which Russell E. Train is Chairman. See 36 Fed. Reg. 7724.

Yet the pressures on agencies for favorable action one way or the other are enormous. The suggestion that Congress can stop action which is undesirable is true in theory; yet even Congress is too remote to give meaningful direction and its machinery is too ponderous to use very often. The federal agencies of which I speak are not venal or corrupt. But they are notoriously under the control of powerful interests who manipulate them through advisory committees, of friendly working relations, or who have that natural affinity with the agency which in time develops between the regulator and the regulated. . . .

The voice of the inanimate object, therefore, should not be stilled. That does not mean that the judiciary takes over the managerial functions from the federal agency. It merely means that before these priceless bits of Americana (such as a valley, an alpine meadow, a river, or a lake) are forever lost or are so transformed as to be reduced to the eventual rubble of our urban environment, the voice of the existing beneficiaries of these environmental wonders should be heard.

Perhaps they will not win. Perhaps the bulldozers of "progress" will plow under all the aesthetic wonders of this beautiful land. That is not the present question. The sole question is, who has standing to be heard?

Those who hike the Appalachian Trail into Sunfish Pond, New Jersey, and camp or sleep there, or run Allagash in Maine, or climb the Guadalupes in West Texas or who canoe and portage the Quetico Superior in Minnesota, certainly should have standing to defend those natural wonders before courts or agencies, though they live 3,000 miles away. Those who merely are caught up in environmental news or propaganda and flock to defend these waters or areas may be treated differently. That is why these environmental issues should be tendered by the inanimate object itself. Then there will be assurances that all of the forms of life which it represents will stand before the court—the pileated woodpecker as well as the coyote and bear, the lemmings as well as the trout in the streams. Those inarticulate members of the ecological group cannot speak. But those people who have so frequented the places as to know its values and wonders will be able to speak for the entire ecological community.

Ecology reflects the land ethic; and Aldo Leopold wrote in A Sand County Almanac 204 (1949), "The land ethic simply enlarges the boundaries of the community to include soils, waters, plants, and animals, or collectively, the land."

That, as I see it, is the issue of "standing" in the present case and controversy.

See also Laurence H. Tribe, Ways Not to Think About Plastic Trees: New Foundations for Environmental Law, 83 Yale L.J. 1315 (1974); Christopher D. Stone, Should Trees Have Standing Revisited: How Far Will Law and Morals Reach? A Pluralist Perspective, 59 S. Cal. L. Rev. 1 (1985) (setting out the author's views on what he calls Moral Pluralism, elaborating on the 1972 article); D. Paul Emond, Co-operation in Nature: A New Foundation for Environmental Law, 22 Osgoode Hall L.J. 323 (1984).

For criticisms of the idea that nonhumans should have rights, *see* Martin H. Krieger, What's Wrong with Plastic Trees? 179 Science 446 (1973); P.S. Elder, Legal Rights for Nature—The Wrong Answer to the Right(s) Question, 22 Osgoode Hall L.J. 285 (1984) (arguing that "deep ecologist" views do not help the environment's legal status); Mark Sagoff, Animal Liberation and Environmental Ethics: Bad Marriage, Quick Divorce, 22 Osgoode Hall L.J. 297, 306-307 (1984) ("A humanitarian ethic—an appreciation not of nature, but of the welfare of animals—will not help us to understand or to justify an environmental ethic. It will not provide necessary or valid foundations for environmental law."); John Livingston, Rightness or Rights, 22 Osgoode Hall L.J. 309, 321 (1984) ("To extend the concepts of rights into nature—Caesar's ultimate exercise of power—would be to export and legitimate a pathological obsession with hierarchical relationship.").

The idea of rights for natural objects is highly controversial. The following article criticizes the ideas previously expounded.

■ ON PRESERVING THE NATURAL ENVIRONMENT

Mark Sagoff
84 Yale L.J. 205, 221-222 (1974)

What is wrong with this suggestion? [That natural objects have rights.] We have already seen that it is a little vague as it stands. But suppose it were put into effect. Even then we would have no rationale for preserving the natural environment. When only human interests are considered, as Stone admits, there is no "utilitarian" argument against development. [Humans have] learned to enjoy plastic forests and artificial parks. Man has chosen to live in manufactured habitats ever since he came down from the trees; there is no reason to think his trend away from nature will change today. But what about the interests of animals and other natural things? There is every reason to suppose that these interests differ very little from those of man. This conclusion follows from the example with which Stone himself defends the thesis that "natural objects can communicate their wants (needs) to us, and in ways that are not terribly ambiguous." Stone explains: "The lawn tells me that it wants water by a certain dryness of the blades and soil—immediately obvious to the touch—the appearance of bald spots, yellowing, and a lack of springiness after being walked on." Notice that nature is unlikely to take care of Stone's lawn. He has to water it with a hose, and this is a step toward an artificial, not a natural environment. Now consider how trees choke one another and gasp for air, water, and light. How much happier they would be planted in neat rows, as the timber companies would have them, and saved from their struggle for life! Consider animals. Many animals already inhabit our houses; no one can maintain that pets, rodents, and vermin would do as well in the wild. And wild animals often show their preference for the sanctuary of a domestic environment. The fawn would take its dinner in a kennel rather than its chances in a wilderness, and thus be sure of eating, rather than being eaten. Geese find the shore of the Schuylkill, where they are fed by the park police, so attractive that they forget their long flight south. The salmon might prefer the aquarium or the fish tank, where it can lay its eggs quietly, without making the arduous journey upstream. There is no reason to think that the interests of animals must differ from ours. Nature is a war of each against all, as Hobbes said, and man and beast alike prefer the safety and comfort of an artificial environment.

The interests of nonliving things are a little harder but perhaps not impossible to imagine. Let us suppose, for the sake of argument, that resorts, factories, and electric plants are not among the objects which have to be represented in court. That leaves us with rivers, mountains, lakes and other natural things. Environmentalists always assume that the interests of these objects are *opposed* to development. How do they know this? Why wouldn't Mineral King want to host a ski resort, after doing nothing for a billion years? In another few millennia it will be back to original condition just the same. The Sequoia National Forests tells the developer that it wants a ski lift by a certain declivity of its hills and snowiness during the winter—immediately obvious to the sight—and that it needs a four lane highway by the appearance of certain valley passages and obvious scenic turnouts on the mountainsides. The seashore, meanwhile, indicates its willingness to entertain poor people from Oakland by becoming covered with great quantities of sand. Finally, it is reasonable to think that Old Man River might like to do something for a change, like make electricity, and not just keep on rolling along. It is an incredible optimism which assumes the guardians appointed to represent nature would take an environmentalist position. These guardians would be chosen by the government, in other words by the lobbies, and thus nature could enter suits on the side of development. Man is a part of nature, as Tribe and Stone never weary of telling us; therefore his interests and those of his environment ultimately are the same. A Ho Jo's in the Rockies, then, would benefit nature since it benefits man. If such improvements do not benefit nature, however, it can only be because human interests and those of nature conflict. If so, can we rule out a priori the possibility that since man is the most dangerous animal, a rigorous cost-benefit analysis equitable to all nature would send him back to the caves? This is a real possibility—if objects of nature are always the victims, and never beneficiaries of development.

Notes and Questions

1. What is our relationship to the natural system? Does the human species have a right to exploit it without limit for its own benefit? Is there an equality between the human species and other species? What does it mean to say, as human ecologists do, that the human species is part of the natural system? What legal constraints does this imply?

2. Should we give standing to trees, rivers, and plants? How do we know the interests of these objects? Would a redwood tree prefer to remain alive in the Redwood National Park or be made into a table and put in the Oval Office in the White House? What is the value of giving standing to trees? Couldn't you accomplish the same goal by liberalizing current judicial standing requirements?

3. What legal approaches can be used to ensure that natural objects are not always the "victims of development"? What approaches could be used to reconcile development with conservation of the environment? How does the Planetary Trust model of our relationship to the environment address development?

2. *Fauna*

As already noted, there is a subtle difference between having rights and being owed an obligation. In the context of the environment, some scholars argue that a sense of moral obligation to protect the animals is not sufficient.

The following passage argues that whales must have a legal status to adequately protect their lives.

■ WHALES: THEIR EMERGING RIGHT TO LIFE

Anthony D'Amato & Sudhir K. Chopra
85 A.J.I.L. 21, 50-53 (1991)

The middle four stages of the legal progression that we traced in part II—from (2) regulation, to (3) conservation, to (4) protection, to (5) preservation—might be thought to serve whales well enough for all practical and legal purposes. What need is there to move to the sixth, entitlement, stage? Specifically, what particular value is added by ascribing rights to whales, as distinct from recognizing a duty of nations and individuals toward whales?

We contend, first, that it is intelligible to regard whales as rights holders and, second, that viewing the rights in this way makes a difference. On both these points, we employ the pioneering analysis of Christopher Stone.

History has seen a widening of the circle of rights holders. When infanticide was freely practiced, infants had no rights; now of course their right to life is protected in nearly all countries by the law against murder. Convicted felons used to be stripped of all rights; now they have certain basic protections (e.g., equal medical care). The laws of most countries have seen a gradual progression in ascribing rights to aliens, married women, the mentally enfeebled and racial minorities. Rights have also been extended to inanimate, intangible entities: trusts, corporations, joint ventures, partnerships and municipalities. In recent years corporations have been prosecuted and convicted of crimes. International law classically regards nation-states as having rights and responsibilities. In this broad context, there is nothing strange about recognizing the rights of whales—creatures that are more animate than corporations, more communicative than infants and mentally enfeebled persons, more communal than the society of nations, and perhaps more intelligent than the smartest human beings.

Professor Stone has suggested the important differences that would accrue if we ascribed rights to natural objects in the environment. The first is what we might call the aspect of generality: that having rights is a generalized legal competence, whereas being the beneficiary of the obligations of others breaks down into a series of specialized, specific rules. For example, suppose a person signs a contract with a corporation, then attempts to avoid his obligations under the contract by pointing to the corporation's charter and showing that the terms of the contract were, strictly construed, *ultra vires.* Under a strict interpretation of the idea of incorporation, the corporation only exists by virtue of the specific competencies listed in its corporate charter. But such an approach would hardly ever be adopted by any court. Instead, the corporation is said to have certain generalized "rights," including the right to enter into contracts. These rights bestow a competence on the corporation that, in Professor Stone's words, is flexible and open-ended.

Second, the idea of having "rights" includes a notion of moral rights that can inform existing law or even push it in a certain direction. Take, for example, a battered wife suing her husband in the nineteenth century. Courts routinely dismissed such cases on the ground that they had no jurisdiction over what happened in the home, and in any event a wife had an adequate remedy under the laws of divorce. But at some point, courts changed their approach and began recognizing tort claims by wives against their husbands. Suppose that just prior to the turning point an attorney advised a wife that she had no legal right to sue her husband in tort. The advice, though grounded in precedent, would have been misleading since, by hypothesis, in the very next case the court "found" such a right. What happened is that the court accepted the powerful moral claim of right and recognized it as somehow subsisting in the common law all along, even though legal precedent was to the contrary. We say that the court "articulated" the preexisting right, much as we argue that an international court could articulate an entitlement of whales arising from the customary law practice of their preservation.

Third, the burden of proof in litigation and negotiation can turn on which party is a rights claimant. Courts may be predisposed to giving a far more "liberal" construction of applicable rules to a party that claims to be asserting rights than to one that claims to be a third-party beneficiary of asserted rights. Even the rules regarding burden of proof, Professor Stone suspects, would be more liberally interpreted in favor of a rights claimant.

Fourth, the development of a jurisprudence regarding whales is more likely if whales are perceived by courts as rights holders, just as a jurisprudence of corporate law has developed as a result of viewing corporations as legal entities entitled to sue and be sued and even to be prosecuted for corporate crime.

Finally, standing is facilitated for rights holders. Standing may be a lesser problem in American law than in the law of many other countries because of the separation-of-powers tradition of contesting many forms of governmental action in the courts. Yet even in U.S. courts when the protection of whales arises, the need to assert harm to one's own interests, as opposed to the interests of whales, may exert a subtle negative influence upon the petitioners. In *Japan Whaling Association v. American Cetacean Society,* although the Supreme Court found (in a footnote) that the American Cetacean Society, Greenpeace, Friends of the Earth and other environmental organizations had "alleged a sufficient 'injury in fact' in that the whale watching and studying of their members will be adversely affected by continued whale harvesting," the Court ultimately held against those organizations on the merits. Watching and studying whales seems a slender reed on which to mount a lawsuit to protect whales. The real party in interest is the whale. Perhaps the very tenuousness of the "standing" the Supreme Court allowed the environmental groups contributed to the lack of empathy toward whales in the Court's ultimate decision on the merits.

For these reasons, and similar ones that could be adduced, the extension of legal rights to whales would have significant legal consequence. To move from "preservation" to "entitlement" is not just a way of talking. Rather, it acknowledges the creation of a new subject of international law.

A "right" may be legal or moral or both. The attempt to draw a sharp distinction between legal and moral rights often founders on two grounds.

First, as H.L.A. Hart has demonstrated, moral considerations influence the content of law over time. Second, there may be a deeper connection between law and morality than positivists such as Professor Hart are willing to admit. Although this connection may not be a "necessary" one in the substantive sense of Cicero or in the procedural sense of Lon Fuller, it exists in the claim of legitimacy that the law makes—a claim that surpasses that which can be enforced and spills over into the realm of that which is morally persuasive. For these general reasons, we have not attempted in this article to draw lines between the moral and the legal in our discussion of the emerging rights of whales. Although we have indicated when we are primarily talking about moral rights and when we are primarily talking about legal rights, the considerable degree of overlap between the two, we submit, reflects the way a norm develops over time.

Notes and Questions

1. What rights do animals have? Who represents them? Should a representative of whales be allowed to enforce the provision of the International Whaling Convention? If we do not give standing to animals, won't the protection of their interests be subordinate to economic and political considerations which may have little to do with a need to protect the whales?

2. One author has argued that it makes a difference whether nonhumans are treated "as though they have rights" or treated so as not to violate the rights they actually possess. Richard A. Watson, Self-Consciousness and the Rights of Nonhuman Animals and Nature, in The Animal Rights/ Environmental Ethics Debate: The Environmental Perspective, 1-35, 12 (Eugene C. Hargrove, ed. 1992).

3. Could there be a conflict between intergenerational rights and animal rights? Don't we regularly conduct animal research to sustain the present quality of human life and the robustness of the natural environment? An Australian Senate Report stated, "Experiments are . . . conducted on wildlife to obtain more effective and humane methods of controlling them with less detrimental effects on non-target species. Within this area of research specific projects may present difficult decisions . . . such as research using traps to check on the contents of dingos' stomachs and LD50 tests to examine the effect of 1080 baiting on non-target species." Report by the Senate Select Committee on Animal Welfare, Animal Experimentation 130 (1989).

How could the rights of future generations of people and those of individual animals be reconciled?

4. Consider the following as a comparative view of animal rights:

Germany's Federal Law for the Protection of Animals (Tierschutzgesetz, TierSchG)

[The] aim of this federal statute is the protection of individual animals in their own right (sect. 1, sentence 1). No animal shall be subjected to pain, suffering or damage without reasonable justification (sect. 1, sentence 2). The law sets out detailed provisions for the accommodation of animals by humans, justified circumstances and ways of killing animals (whoever kills a "Wirbeltier," [a vertebrate animal] without proper reason, faces up to two years in prison, sect. 17) and the possibilities for animal experiments (limited for the enhancement of medicine, the detection of environmental dangers and for testing substances and products within a research project of fundamental nature and the pain, suffering or damage to the animals has to be proportional to the purpose of the experiment; experiments for the development of tobacco products, washing detergent and cosmetics are prohibited, sect. 7, people carrying out the experiments have to obtain permits, sect. 8. Furthermore, the raising of animals is restricted, e.g., warm-blooded animals may not be given to persons under 16 years of age (sects. 11 and 11(c)).*

*The Editors thank Torsten Bartsch of Germany, L.L.M., Georgetown, for the above note.

III

The Economic Perspective

Although we are addressing legal issues, economic perspectives provide useful insights into managing common areas and shared resources, addressing spillover effects of pollution onto neighboring areas, considering effects of activities on the well-being of future generations, and valuing damage to the environment. Moreover, costs limit the actions of all entities, whether they be public sector industries, private companies, nongovernmental groups, or individuals. We cannot avoid prioritizing in international environmental law.

This chapter* sets out several economic perspectives relevant to international environmental law. It also addresses some of the arguments about the extent to which environmental issues can be usefully looked at in this way.

A. PROTECTION OF COMMON AREAS

In the study of international environmental law, we are dealing with a shared resource: Earth. Throughout history, humans have taken from Earth

*The Editors thank Andrea Lachenmayer, J.D. candidate, Georgetown University Law Center, for assisting with the sections on valuing natural resources and on cost effectiveness.

to maximize our standard of living. Today, we realize that Earth's resources may not be capable of continuing to sustain the rate of use to which we have become accustomed.

One of the problems facing humans is balancing individual needs and desires with the needs of Earth as a system. Garrett Hardin writes of the problem caused by humans whose individual actions taken alone may be rational in using a commons but whose activities collectively lead to the demise of the commons.

■ THE TRAGEDY OF THE COMMONS*

Garrett Hardin
162 Science 1243, 1244-1245 (1968)

The tragedy of the commons developed in this way. Picture a pasture open to all. It is to be expected that each herdsman will try to keep as many cattle as possible on the commons. Such an arrangement may work reasonably satisfactorily for centuries because tribal wars, poaching, and disease keep the numbers of both man and beast well below the carrying capacity of the land. Finally, however, comes the day of reckoning, that is, the day when the long-desired goal of social stability becomes a reality. At this point, the inherent logic of the commons remorselessly generates tragedy.

As a rational being, each herdsman seeks to maximize his gain. Explicitly or implicitly, more or less consciously, he asks, "What is the utility to me of adding one more animal to my herd?" This utility has one negative and one positive component.

1. The positive component is a function of the increment of one animal. Since the herdsman receives all the proceeds from the sale of the additional animal, the positive utility is nearly +1.
2. The negative component is a function of the additional overgrazing created by one more animal. Since, however, the effects of overgrazing are shared by all the herdsmen, the negative utility for any particular decision-making herdsman is only a fraction of −1.

Adding together the component partial utilities, the rational herdsman concludes that the only sensible course for him to pursue is to add another animal to his herd. And another; and another . . . But this is the conclusion reached by each and every rational herdsman sharing a commons. Therein is the tragedy. Each man is locked into a system that compels him to increase his herd without limit—in a world that is limited. Ruin is the destination toward which all men rush, each pursuing his own best interest in a society that believes in the freedom of the commons. Freedom in a commons brings ruin to all.

Pollution

In a reverse way, the tragedy of the commons reappears in problems of pollution. Here it is not a question of taking something out of the commons, but of putting something in—sewage, or chemical, radioactive, and what wastes into water; noxious and dangerous fumes into the air; and distracting and unpleasant advertising signs into the line of sight. The calculations of utility are much the same as before. The rational man finds that his share of the cost of the wastes he discharges into the commons is less than the cost of purifying his wastes before releasing them. Since this is true for everyone, we are locked into a system of "fouling our own nest," so long as we behave only as independent, rational, free-enterprises.

The tragedy of the commons as a food basket is averted by private property, or something formally like it. But the air and waters surrounding us cannot readily be fenced, and so the tragedy of the commons as a cesspool must be prevented by different means, by coercive laws or taxing devices that make it cheaper for the polluter to treat his pollutants than to discharge them untreated. We have not progressed as far with the solution of this problem as we have with the first. Indeed, our particular concept of private property, which deters us from exhausting the positive resources of the earth, favors pollution. The owner of a factory on the bank of a stream—whose property extends to the middle of the stream—often has difficulty seeing why it is not his natural right to muddy the waters flowing past his door. The law, always behind the times, requires elaborate stitching and fitting to adapt it to this newly perceived aspect of the commons.

How to Legislate Temperance?

Analysis of the pollution problem as a function of population density uncovers a not generally recognized principle of morality, namely: the morality of an act is a function of the state of the system at the time it is performed. A hundred and fifty years ago a plainsman could kill an American bison, cut out only the tongue for his dinner, and discard the rest of the animal. He was not in any important sense being wasteful. Today, with only a few thousand bison left, we would be appalled at such behavior.

Notes and Questions

1. The classic prisoner's dilemma case illuminates the tragedy of the commons. In the prisoner's dilemma, there are two prisoners who, during

a private interrogation, must decide whether to confess to a moderate crime or to accuse the other prisoner of a serious crime. The accuser goes free unless the other prisoner has also accused him or her of a serious crime, in which case both receive a much heavier sentence than if they had confessed to a moderate crime in common. If you were a prisoner who would never see the other person again after this event, what would you choose?

Would it make a difference if you played this game and knew that the two of you would encounter the same situation together at least 20 times? Would it make a difference if you could communicate with the other prisoner before making your choice? If there were 20 other prisoners instead of two?

Does it change your opinion to know that real prisoners in this situation rarely confess or implicate their partner? See Brian Forst and Judith Lucianovic, The Prisoner's Dilemma: Theory and Reality, 5 J. Crim. Justice 55-64 (1977).

In the tragedy of the commons, the goal is to move from a situation in which countries are increasingly worse off to one in which they use the commons on a sustainable basis and make modest gains. What are the different kinds of approaches that a community can take to manage a commons on a sustainable basis? What does each require? What are the limitations of each? What are the transaction costs?

In general, *see* M. Olson, The Logic of Collective Action (1965); Cox, No Tragedy of the Commons, 7 Envirn. Affrs. 49 (1985); Carol Rose, The Comedy of the Commons, 53 U. Chi. L. Rev. 711 (1986). For other approaches to environmental problems, *see* Barry Commoner, The Closing Circle (1971) (arguing that advanced technology is to blame for most environmental problems); White, The Historical Roots of Our Ecologic Crisis, 155 Science 1203 (1967) (arguing that the Judeo-Christian ethic of dominating nature is to blame).

2. Consider how the international system now addresses the management of the globally shared commons of Earth. The starting position is an international system of sovereign states with national sovereignty over the resources located within their borders. This principle is basic to international law and is reflected in the famous Principle 21 of the 1972 Stockholm Declaration on the Human Environment, from the first international intergovernmental conference on environmental issues. Is there an analogy here to the private property regime that is basic in the United States?

3. Much has been written on the economics of sustainable development. Most of the authors of these works agree on the basic goal: development by methods that retain the capacity of Earth to support life in the future. Consider the following passage as an example of the philosophy.

> For much of this century, economic debate has focused on whether capitalism or socialism is the best way to organize a modern industrial econ-

omy. That argument now seems to be over. . . . Yet . . . a new, more fundamental question has arisen: How can we design a vibrant economy that does not destroy the natural resources and environmental systems on which it depends?

The vast scale and rapid growth of the 20,000-billion-dollar global economy are hailed as great achievements of our time. But as the pace of environmental deterioration quickens, the consequences of failing to bridge the gap between the workings of economic systems and natural ones are becoming all too clear.

Redirecting the global economy towards environmental sustainability requires fundamental reforms at both the international and national levels.

Lester R. Brown, Sandra Postel, & Christopher Flavin, From Growth to Sustainable Development, Environmentally Sustainable Economic Development 93 (1991).

For the fundamental work on sustainable development, *see* World Commission on Environment and Development, Our Common Future 8 (1987) ("The concept of sustainable development does imply limits—not absolute limits but limitations imposed by the present state of technology and social organization on environmental resources and by the ability of the biosphere to absorb the effects of human activities. But technology and social organization can be both managed and improved to make way for a new era of economic growth."). *See also* chapter 1F.

Additional Reading

For further reading, *see* Joel Darmstadter, ed., Global Development and the Environment (1992); Stephen Schmidheiny, Changing Course: A Global Business Perspective on Development and the Environment (1992) (advocating a change in business practices to a more environmentally aware stance).

B. BEARING THE COSTS FOR EXTERNALITIES

1. *The Polluter Pays Principle*

The costs of building or using environmentally sound instruments or of installing cleaning devices on existing production plants can be very high. So can the cost of cleaning up the environment after it has been polluted.

The question of who is going to pay for the environmentally sound practices is key. The OECD has advocated an approach based on what economists refer to as internalizing costs, called the "polluter pays principle."

The OECD polluter pays principle is not, as may seem at first, a liability principle. Rather, it states that those who pollute should bear the costs of installing and maintaining pollution controls. That is, these costs should be internalized and can then be passed on to the consumer. OECD Council Recommendation on the Implementation of the Polluter-Pays Principle, November 14, 1974, reprinted in 14 I.L.M. 234 (1975).

One of the reasons governments have been reluctant to embrace the polluter pays principle is the political problem of hurting industry supporters. The principle requires the elimination of subsidies to producers. At any given price, a subsidy makes production more profitable for the producer since costs are lowered. This, therefore, distorts the results of a cost-benefit analysis and may cause less environmentally desirable options to be chosen.

What does this imply for assistance to developing countries to achieve environmental standards set by the industrialized countries? What about European Union assistance in the form of economic subsidies to certain member countries to allow them to comply with community requirements? Should economic subsidies be treated as legal subsidies?

2. *Liability*

While traditionally states have relied upon a tortlike negligence standard in their relations with each other, some authors call for a more rigid stance.

Strict liability is another possibility for a state liability scheme. This would require the state to assume the costs of cleaning up damage to another state caused by an environmental accident even if the first state's government had imposed and enforced all of its treaty obligations.

Think about whether strict liability would enhance or hold back a state's willingness to become a party to a treaty. Would it help or hurt the use of risk-reducing devices?

In the following excerpt, the author describes various economic tools for controlling pollution that lawmakers can use.

■ SEVENTH APPLICATION—POLLUTION CONTROL

A. Mitchell Polinsky
Introduction to Law and Economics 89-93 (1983)

. . . [W]e will investigate the efficiency of different legal rules for controlling pollution when the polluters are firms in a competitive industry in long-run equilibrium. The discussion will be based on an example in which firms emitting air pollution harm households downwind of the pollu-

Table 10
Pollution Control Example

Behavior of Firm	*Firm's Production COst Per Unit (1)*	*Victim's Pollution Damage Per Unit (2)*	*Full Cost Per Unit (3)*	*Firm's Cost Per Unit under Negligence (4)*	*Firm's Cost Per Unit under Strict Liability (5)*
Don't filter	$100	$40	$140	$140	$140
Filter	$115	$10	$125	$115	$125

tion. For simplicity, it is assumed that the victims of the pollution are not also consumers of the product manufactured by the firms. In the example, the harm to the victims depends on whether the polluters filter their smoke before discharging it into the atmosphere. The filtering process reduces the level of pollution but does not eliminate it entirely. It also increases the polluters' cost of production. The victims of the pollution are assumed to be reconsidered below. The data for this example are described in Table 10 for a representative firm (ignore for now the last three columns). Note that, once the filtering decision has been made, there is no uncertainty with respect to the harm; thus, the issue of risk allocation does not arise in this example.

Given the data in Table 10, it is clear that the efficient solution involves filtering the pollution before discharging it. Although filtering increases production costs by $15 for each unit of the firm's output, it reduces pollution damages by $30 for each unit produced. Another way to express this is to note that the full cost of the product—the firm's production cost plus the victims' pollution damage—is $140 if filtering does not occur but only $125 if it does occur. This is shown in the third column of Table 10.

Only Polluters Determine Harm

We will now examine whether the liability rules of negligence and strict liability lead to the efficient control of pollution. Under negligence, suppose firms are liable only if they do not filter. Then, as shown in the fourth column in Table 10, a firm's cost, including its liability payments, would be $140 if it does not filter and $115 if it does. Clearly, each firm will choose to filter. Thus, in long-run equilibrium, the price will be $115 per unit. If the price were higher, entry would occur due to the profit opportunities, and if the price were lower, firms would leave the industry since they would be losing money. But if the equilibrium price is $115, excessive consumption of the good will occur. Given that firms filter, the full cost is $125, including the $10 residual pollution damage borne by victims (see Table 10). Thus, at a price of $115, there will be persons who value the good at less than its full cost—for example, at $120—but who will buy it nonetheless.

This example illustrates a general point about the effects of negligence rules in competitive markets: Even though the rule of negligence can, with an appropriate standard of care, induce firms to take an efficient amount of care, it generally leads to an inefficient level of output because the market price does not completely reflect the full cost of the product. Specifically, the price does not reflect the residual damages that occur even when each firm is taking an efficient amount of care. Consequently, too much of the good will be consumed.

Now consider the rule of strict liability, under which firms will be made liable for the victims' pollution damages whether they filter or not. Then, as shown in the last column of Table 10, each firm's cost, including liability payments, would be $140 if it does not filter and $125 if it does. Each firm will therefore choose to filter. Thus, in long-run equilibrium, the price of the good will be $125, and, since the full cost is also $125, the amount of the good bought by consumers will be efficient. This example illustrates a general observation about strict liability in competitive markets: Strict liability can induce firms to take an efficient amount of care and can induce consumers to purchase an efficient amount of the good. The latter effect occurs because the market price reflects the full cost of the product, including the damages that remain even when each firm is taking an efficient amount of care.

Victims Also Affect Harm

In many pollution situations, the victims of the pollution also can affect their damages from pollution. For example, they might be able to paint their homes with more expensive pollution-resistant paint or move to a less polluted neighborhood. The conclusions in this chapter regarding the rules of negligence and strict liability would have to be modified somewhat if both the polluters' behavior and the victims' behavior can affect the level of damages.

Suppose for concreteness that the efficient solution now requires not only that the polluters filter but also that the victims paint their homes with special paint. This paint reduces the victims' damages, but it does not eliminate the damages. The efficient solution still requires that only those consumers who value the good more than its full cost purchase it. Note, however, that the appropriate full cost now equals the polluters' cost of production plus the residual damages that occur both when the polluter is filtering and when the victims are using the special paint.

Under the rule of negligence, a polluter will choose to filter in order to avoid the liability costs that he would otherwise incur. Given this decision, the victims will bear their own losses and will therefore have an appropriate incentive to use the pollution-resistant paint. Thus, as in the automobile accident example, the negligence rule can induce both the injurer and the victim to take appropriate care. However, the negligence rule will still fail to induce efficient decisions by consumers since the price of the good will not reflect the damages that occur even when the polluters and the victims are taking appropriate care.

Under strict liability, polluters will also choose to filter, as before. However, pollution victims will not have any incentive to use pollution-resistant paint since they will be fully compensated for their damages. Thus, for reasons described in Chapter 6 in the context of the automobile accident example, it is necessary to add a defense of contributory negligence in order to induce the pollution victims to take appropriate care. With this defense, the rule of strict liability will be efficient with respect to both parties' care. Since the victims will choose not to be contributorily negligent, the polluters will be liable for the victims' residual damages. Thus, the price of the product will reflect these damages and an efficient amount will be purchased.

STATE LIABILITY FOR INTERNATIONAL ENVIRONMENTAL DEGRADATION: AN ECONOMIC PERSPECTIVE

Ralph C. d'Arge & Allen V. Kneese
20 Nat. Res. J. 427 (1980)

INTRODUCTION

State responsibility and liability are not clearly defined with respect to environmental degradation. But a limited number of cases and declarations by international tribunals do point in a definable direction. In the famous Trail Smelter Case, the tribunal declared: "A State owes at all times a duty to protect other states against injurious acts by individuals from within its jurisdiction." The Organization for Economic Cooperation and Development (OECD) adopted the "polluter pays" principle (PP) in 1972, which states that the waste discharger must pay for any ameliorating measures which are caused to be undertaken. This principle does not apply to any residual damages which may remain. However, the German government has recently issued an interpretation which requires payment of an effluent charge which presumably, in some manner, is meant to reflect remaining damages within German territory. The Stockholm Declarations could also be interpreted as placing responsibility upon those undertaking the actions which result in environmental degradation, although the emphasis is upon "common action" among states. The tendency then is to interpret state responsibility as requiring that states within whose boundaries harmful actions occur must pay or cause to be paid the cost of ameliorating those actions and, possibly, must pay for the remaining damages as well.

In this paper, we shall define and analyze four major principles of assigning state responsibility and discuss the economic meaning of those principles. The first principle is that each state is responsible for all waste discharge control costs internally and externally but is not responsible for compensation of remaining damages following installation of the agreed-upon controls. This is a variant of the OECD principle cited above in that we apply it, as an area of major concern, to transfrontier pollution problems; application of the principle to such problems was explicitly excluded by OECD member nations. The second major principle is the full costing principle (FC), which requires the state responsible for waste discharge to pay compensation for remaining damages as well as control costs. The third principle is the "victim pays" principle (VP), which requires the affected state to compensate the affecting state (or internal parties creating harmful residuals) for all costs of control and to absorb all residual damages after controls are implemented. The fourth principle, in its simplest form, requires the establishment of an internal or international autonomous agency to regulate the joint use of common property resources by individual or multiple states. In the international case, the various states would give powers to the agency to regulate waste discharges into the commonly shared environment. For lack of a better description, we term this principle of responsibility the common property resources institution principle (CPRI).

Direct Technological Externalities

THE BILATERAL CASE

The current implied legal doctrine that each country must pay for transnational pollution by ceasing activities that cause it may for various reasons (including the difficulty of estimating damages, especially internationally) be adopted as the best practical type of polluter pays principle, but it can be shown to be inefficient in many instances. Let us suppose that agriculture in Arizona is very much more productive than downstream in Mexico and that the only way to reduce salt content downstream is to take land out of cultivation upstream. Then the current legal doctrine offers the following choice: let the Mexicans continue to suffer uncompensated losses or take more productive land out upstream and replace it with less productive land downstream. Other considerations aside, a PP principle with compensatory flexibility would be more efficient, since agricultural production across both countries could be maintained at a higher level and the parties involved could share the gain through compensation arrangements to the betterment of both.

Under certain simplified conditions, it can be shown that the VP and PP principles applied to transnational pollution problems both produce Pareto efficiency in the short run and the long run if consumers and factors of production are immobile internationally. The only difference between the two is in the international distribution of income. This result might lead one to favor the VP principle for the simple reason that it can be implemented without international enforcement machinery which in the past has proved so intractable. The damaged party has an incentive both to get information and to bargain with the sovereignty within which the offending activity is taking place. The principle also has the advantage that the willingness of the affected sovereignty to pay for reduction provides a quantitative estimate of the damage loss, which might otherwise be very hard to calculate. But aside from the fact that most people would probably consider the arrangement quite inequitable, it has another basic flaw. If the VP principle is applicable, the externality-generating country may threaten (by giving high estimates of future loads) to discharge materials as an incidental aspect of the production of other goods simply to obtain compensation for not doing so. One may hypothesize that polluting material could be produced at low cost. Thus, if the VP principle were to be applied, an aspect of state responsibility would have to be structured to remove the incentives underlying "pollution for profit."

Of course, under the PP or FC principles, the injured country could also exaggerate its losses, but it is not in the superior position which would permit it to exact retribution if its demands are not met. Thus, there seem to be significant preliminary grounds for preferring the FC or PP principles for both efficiency and equity reasons.

Before turning to the multilateral case, we should point out that the theoretical symmetry among the PP, FC, and VP principles indicated above is dependent upon the assumption (usually made in the classical international trade literature) that resources are immobile internationally. If this is not the case, capital or labor movements will cause the outcomes of the principles to differ.

THE MULTILATERAL CASE

With multi-country environmental problems, assessment of the efficiency of the previously stated principles in allocating global resources is much less clear than in the bilateral case just analyzed. As an example, consider one upstream country with waste discharges affecting two downstream countries. With the FC principle, there is the problem of arriving at an agreement between the downstream countries about which is damaged the most and which should consequently be compensated the most. The PP principle contains similar problems in that there must be joint agreement on acceptable levels of upstream control. Finally, the VP principle is fraught with so-called "free-rider" problems in that, if one country provides a substantial amount of the necessary controls, the second downstream country receives reduced damages at no cost. If, in general, there are more receptor countries than emitters, then it will be more difficult, in terms of coordination, for a solution to emerge under the VP principle than under the FC principle. This result follows because the agreement on compensation requires a greater number of sovereignties arranging to make a payment, which inherently seems more difficult to negotiate than those same sovereignties agreeing to receive a payment.

SUMMARY

The various principles of state responsibility have substantially different impacts on the global efficiency of resources unless there are no transfers of resources among nations. With no transfers or movements, the various principles lend to affect only the distribution of wealth among nations. In terms of allocative efficiency, the "best" principle would be one of converting all CPRs to internationally operated and regulated resources. But such a conversion may imply substantial changes in wealth and therefore may be unacceptable. The principle with the most desirable efficiency properties would appear to be a modified FC principle where the emitter country's government taxed internal firms according to receptor country damages but did not provide compensation to the receptor country.

Notes and Questions

1. Is the polluter pays principle described by Kneese and d'Arge a liability standard? How would Polinsky characterize it? Do you agree with Kneese and d'Arge's characterization? Compare it with the OECD principle described above at 99–100.

2. Kneese and d'Arge identify a victim pays principle. In Table 10 of the Polinsky excerpt, how much does the firm pay if it filters and doesn't filter under the victim pays principle? Under these two scenarios, what are the costs to the victim under a victim pays principle? Does it ever make economic sense for the victim to pay the polluter to install a filter to control the emission of pollutants? What would the full costs to the victim be in this case? The Federal Republic of Germany helped the former state of Czechoslovakia to install air pollution control technology on a factory near the border. Could this make economic sense? Should a developed country that is a victim of pollution from a neighboring developed country pay for the installation of control technology by the polluter? If not, why not?

3. In thinking about liability, consider two recent cases. In the first action, the EPA sued Louisiana-Pacific, one of the largest timber corporations in the United States, for pollution caused by its production of wood-fiber construction panels. *See* 682 F. Supp. 1141 (D.C. Colo. 1988).

On May 24, 1993, Pacific-Louisiana agreed to settle the case. The settlement of $11.1 million, including $2 million punitive damages and $9 million for benefits the company received through violating the Clean Air Act, was the largest air pollution fine ever imposed in the United States (LEXIS/NEXIS Hot Topics—Natural Resources, EPA, DOJ Announce 11.1 Million

Settlement with Louisiana-Pacific). In addition, Louisiana-Pacific agreed to install $70 million worth of pollution control equipment within two years.

In response to the settlement announcement, Attorney General Janet Reno and EPA Administrator Carol M. Browner declared that the amount of the fine sent a "loud and clear message" to the violators and other corporations. *See* Keith Schneider, $11.1 Million Pollution Fine Too Soft?, The New York Times, June 2, 1993, at D22.

The second case was brought by the Canadian government against Tioxide Canada, Inc. Again, a historically high fine was issued—$1 million plus $3 million to restore the damaged areas along the St. Lawrence River. *See* Glenn Bohn, Record Pollution Fine Sends Big Message to Companies, The Vancouver Sun, June 5, 1993, at B4.

A Canadian pollution investigator commented that although company officials may now start considering the costs of penalties before deciding to engage in environmentally damaging practices, he believes that some just internalize the potential fines as a business cost.

What are the effects of imposing large fines to deter polluters? When do such fines deter unwanted behavior? When are they just added into the costs of doing business and reflected in the price of the product? When do they encourage innovation in developing and adopting pollution control technology? What affects this decision?

4. Some authors have argued that neither negligence nor strict liability is the suitable standard for environmental damages. Instead, criminal liability should be imposed. What do you think about this? Are the reasons for making certain actions a crime consistent with criminalizing environmental degradation? Note that there is no international crime of polluting the environment in an unsafe manner. While the international community has developed the concept of crimes against humanity, there is no agreement yet to the proposition that these include serious, widespread, and irreversible environmental degradation. Should this be included?

ADDITIONAL READINGS

For more reading on environmental crimes, *see:*

Mark A. Cohen, Environmental Crime and Punishment: Legal/Economic Theory and Empirical Evidence on Enforcement of Federal Environmental Statutes, 82 J. Crim. L. & Criminology 1054 (1992) (supporting the imposition of criminal sanctions for violators of environmental laws).

Gary S. Lincenberg, Sentencing Environmental Crimes, 29 Am. Crim. L. Rev. 1235 (1992) (discussing the growth of criminal penalties for environmental crimes and the use of the environmental sentencing Guidelines).

Vincent J. Marella, The Department of Justice Prosecutive Guidelines in Environmental Cases involving Voluntary Disclosure—A Leap Forward or a Leap of Faith?, 29 Am. Crim. L. Rev. 1179 (1992) (discussing and comparing guidelines for voluntary environmental disclosures).

C. VALUING NATURAL RESOURCES

Economists rely on quantified values to determine the benefits society assumes from a specific good. While in many cases the value chosen is the price at which the product is sold, when one is judging the value of a nonsalable good, additional problems arise.

The natural environment is an extreme example of a nonsalable good, and its valuation is correspondingly difficult. Not only do people tend to value the environment more highly than they are willing to pay for, making private pricing techniques inaccurate, but the environment as a whole may be much more valuable than the sum of every individual organism and resource.

Various methods have been formulated for determining the "correct" measure for assessing the value of natural resources. As you read the materials, think of the problems associated with each one, and try to come up with other possibilities.

For a critique of the use of monetary valuation of resources as set out by members of the Green Party in the Federal Republic of Germany, *see* The Group of Green Economists, Ecological Economies, especially pp. 47-48 (1992).

1. Investments: The Problem of Valuing Natural Resources

■ WASTING ASSETS: NATURAL RESOURCES IN THE NATIONAL INCOME ACCOUNTS

Robert Repetto, William McGrath, Michael Wells, Christine Beer, & Fabrizio Rossini
2-3, 20 (1989)

The neo-classical economists virtually dropped natural resources from their model and concentrated on labor and invested capital. . . . As a result, there is a dangerous asymmetry today in the way we measure, and hence the way we think about, the value of natural resources. Man-made assets—buildings and equipment, for example—are valued as productive capital, and are written off against the value of production as they depreciate. This practice recognizes that a consumption level maintained by drawing down the stock of capital exceeds the sustainable level of income. Natural resources are not so valued, and their loss entails no debit charge against current income that would account for the decrease in potential future production. A country could exhaust its mineral resources, cut down its forests, erode its soils, pollute its aquifers, and hunt its wildlife and fisheries to extinction, but measured income would not be affected as these assets disappeared. (at p. 2.)

. . . [T]his difference in the treatment of natural resources and other tangible assets provides false signals to policymakers. It reinforces the false dichotomy between the economy and the "environment" that leads policymakers to ignore or destroy the latter in the name of economic development. It confuses the depletion of valuable assets with the generation of income. Thus it promotes and seems to validate the idea that rapid rates of economic growth can be achieved and sustained by exploiting the resource base. The result can be illusory gains in income and permanent losses in wealth. (at p. 3.)

. . . By failing to measure an appropriate depletion allowance, conventional national accounting procedures allocate a disproportionate share of current income flows to present generations at the expense of future generations. [For example] Kiribati, the small atoll republic of the Solomon Islands depended throughout the 20th century on its phosphate mines for income and government revenues. While the mines ran, gross domestic product was high and rising, but the mining proceeds were treated as current income rather than as capital consumption. When the deposits were mined out in the 1970s, income and government revenues declined drastically because far too little had been set aside for investment that would replace the lost revenues. (at p. 20.)

2. *Approaches to Measuring Damage to Natural Resources*

■ NATURAL RESOURCE DAMAGE VALUATION

Frank B. Cross
42 Vanderbilt L. Rev. 269-341 (1989)

Values Attributable to Natural Resources

The first difficulty in valuation is determining the meaning of value itself and then determining which value characteristics of natural resources should be compensable. A useful approach recognizes at least three analytically distinct types of natural resource value that could be compensable: use value, existence value, and intrinsic value. Use value recognizes that natural resources only have value to humans when the resources are used for practical human ends, such as for fishing or hunting. Use value seeks to measure the monetary importance of the loss of these human uses. Existence value acknowledges that the presence of natural resources, even unused, may have value to humans. For example, some people may want to preserve the availability of resources for future generations. Intrinsic value recognizes that natural resources may have value independent of humans, based on their status as natural creatures or objects.

Use value is more precise and less speculative than other types of resource value because it isolates the extent to which people put their money where their mouth[s are]. Use value measures actual behavior, rather than attitudes and therefore is a more certain means of ascertaining damages. Complete reliance on use value has some shortcomings however. Greater public use of recreation sites actually may diminish the recognized public value of those facilities. Most significantly, use value ignores the reality that natural resources may have value beyond their use by humans. Surely a fish is worth something even if a fisherman never catches it.

Emphasis on market value for natural resources strikes many people as exalting economics above other socially held values. In the context of natural resources, unthinking reliance on economic principles would recommend selling the Grand Canyon to the highest bidder for commercial development, if that sale would yield the most profit. Not long ago, Milton Friedman proposed closing the national parks in which the commercial value of lumber or minerals exceeded the value of recreational use. The democratic process has rejected this result unequivocally.

Natural resources may possess intertemporal value. If society values these resources today, future generations almost certainly will value the preservation of these resources. This generation may regret the extinction of the passenger pigeon because of the actions of past generations and should consider the consequences that our acts may have for people living in the future.

However, there is no good behavioral test for existence value. Because the concept is demonstrated attitudinally, and not behaviorally, an economist may question how strongly the value is truly held. For skeptics, the absence of a behavioral test of existence value renders the concept impossible to measure accurately. Existence has other troublesome aspects. Under the existence value and use value paradigms, nature's only value is its value to human beings. The human-based or anthropocentric valuation can prescribe undue environmental destruction. The occasional practice of "planting" plastic artificial trees in place of real trees provides an example. Humanity might someday be persuaded to prefer plastic trees to growing trees. Should this occur, existence value would recognize no harm in replacing all of nature with man-made objects. Intuitively, this result seems wrong. Nature surely must have some value even when humans fail to recognize it.

Some ecologists contend that man must recognize his fiduciary obligation to other species of life. According to modern "deep ecologists," all living things have inherent value and have moral significance independent of their use by human beings, or even of human existence. Perhaps only recognition of intrinsic value can protect mankind from a future of forests comprised of plastic trees. For these ecologists, relying on economics is "technocratic" and the root of environmental degradation; monetary natural resource damages contribute to the problem rather than the solution. These people refuse to place a monetary value on nature. [However,] their refusal leaves the law only two options: economically valuing natural resources at zero or infinity. The former alternative inevitably creates an incentive to destroy the resources; the latter is transparently unworkable. Valuing natural resources at infinity also reflects a lack of understanding of nature. As Darwin proved, destruction of some elements of nature is itself natural. When a snake eats a mouse, it is fulfilling nature, not destroying it. Humans themselves are part of nature and should not be hesitant to destroy some other parts of nature when necessary. The desire to protect nature may be best understood as an effort to prevent unnecessary damage.

Methods for Monetizing Damage to Natural Resources

The four leading procedures for valuing natural resource damage are: (a) restoration and replacement costs, (b) market valuation, (c) behavioral use valuation, and (d) contingent valuation.

When natural resources are damaged, one obvious policy option is to restore or replace them. When restoration is effective, the remedy at least partially can cure the injuries to use value (by providing repaired resources for recreational use), existence value (by restoring to existence of any destroyed resources), and intrinsic value (by reproducing intrinsically valuable natural resources). If a state were to select this option, then the correct measure of natural resource damages would be the cost of their restoration or replacement.

However, ecologists dispute the practicality of restoration. Because wildlife systematics and ecology is a complex science, government may be unable to reproduce preexisting environmental conditions. The greatest objection to restoration is probably the enormous cost that the process sometimes entails.

A readily available and appealing approach to valuing natural resources uses existing free market value as the measure of damages. For at least some natural resources, a court can determine value by consulting a price list. For example, commercial hatcheries provide an established price for certain species of fish. Even if no market exists for a resource, a court can measure damages by the reduction in land value from the loss of the resource. Market valuation is easy to measure and promotes economic efficiency.

For some naturalists, particularly those who find some intrinsic value in nature, complete reliance on market valuation is illegitimate or even immoral. A remarkable example illustrates this point well. Certain rare butterflies lived only in isolated corners of Africa. Reportedly, unscrupulous collectors would collect a few specimens and then burn the surrounding grassland to destroy as many others of the species as possible, thereby enhancing the uncommonness of their own collection and increasing their value. This natural response to market incentives obviously is contrary to the goals of applicable environmental legislation and illustrative of the shortcomings of market valuation. Senator Max Baucus of Montana, a critic of market valuation, has observed that it "is inconceivable that any reasonable person would suggest measuring the [value of the] Grand Canyon or Yellowstone Park on the basis of a land appraisal."

Economists seeking to overcome the shortcomings of market valuation of public goods have developed new methods for valuing natural resources based on human behavior, including travel cost studies and hedonic valuation. Travel cost valuation is based on the intuitive assumption that the value of a site to visitors is reflected in the expense they incur to visit the site. Hedonic valuation measures the extent to which the value of a nonmarketed commodity, such as a pristine environment, is captured directly in the price of marketed commodities, such as land. The best example of hedonic price valuation measures the value of air quality changes by linking high levels of pollution to lowered housing prices or wage rates.

Contingent valuation simplifies the process of valuing natural resources by asking people directly what monetary value they place on identified resources. Contingent valuation is controversial. Empirical studies suggest that people's expressed attitudes do not accurately predict their actual behavior.

Notes and Questions

1. To what extent are debates over different conceptions of value (use value, existence value, and intrinsic value) really debates over differing values and to what extent are they driven by measurement problems?

Modern social sciences, such as economics, are founded on a methodology of logical positivism. Positivists developed a concept known as "the empiricist criteria of meaningfulness," which argued that only those things that can be operationalized truly exist. Thus, economic science focuses on values as revealed in the market in part because these values *can* be measured and downplays other types of values because they cannot be measured. To what extent does this create a methodological bias? Does such an approach fall prey to the fallacy illustrated by the familiar joke of looking for a contact lens, not where you lost it, but where the light is good?

2. To what extent can the different ways of measuring value (replacement costs, market price, behavioral use, and contingent valuation) be combined? Which types of environmental problems should use which type of measurement?

Additional Reading

See Robert F. Copple, The New Economic Efficiency In Natural Resource Damage Assessments, 66 U. Colo. L. Rev. 675 (1995); Murray B. Rutherford, Jack L. Knetsch, and Thomas C. Brown, Assessing Environmental Losses: Judgements Of Importance and Damage Schedules, 22 Harv. Envtl. L. Rev. 51 (1998).

3. *The Value of Ecological Services and the Total Value of Earth*

The following article, appearing in *Nature* and authored by a group of economists and ecologists, is an attempt to value the services provided by the ecosystems of Earth. The authors suggest that the value of these services, which are outside the market, may be higher than the global gross national product.

■ THE VALUE OF THE WORLD'S ECOSYSTEM SERVICES AND NATURAL CAPITAL

Robert Costanza, Ralph d'Arge, Rudolf de Groot, Stephen Farber, Monica Grasso, Bruce Hannon, Karin Limburg, Shahid Naseem, Robert O'Neill, Jose Paruelo, Robert G. Raskin, Paul Sutton, & Marjan van den Belt
Nature, May 15, 1997, at 253*

The services of ecological systems and the natural capital stocks that produce them are critical to the functioning of the Earth's life-support system. They contribute to human welfare, both directly and indirectly, and therefore represent part of the total economic value of the planet. We have estimated the current economic value of 17 ecosystem services for 16 biomes, based on published studies and a few original calculations. For the entire biosphere, the value (most of which is outside the market) is estimated to be in the range of US$16-54 trillion ($10^{12}$) per year, with an average of US$33 trillion per year. Because of the nature of the uncertainties, this must be considered a minimum estimate. Global gross national product total is around US$18 trillion per year.

Because ecosystem services are not fully "captured" in commercial markets or adequately quantified in terms comparable with economic services and manufactured capital, they are often given too little weight in policy decisions. This neglect may ultimately compromise the sustainability of humans in the biosphere. The economies of the Earth would grind to a halt without the services of ecological life-support systems, so in one sense their total value to the economy is infinite. However, it can be instructive to estimate the "incremental" or "marginal" value of ecosystem services (the estimated rate of change of value compared with changes in ecosystem

*Reprinted by permission from *Nature,* vol. 387, p. 253, ©1997 Macmillan Magazines Ltd.

services from their current levels). . . . [W]e have estimated values for ecosystem services per unit area by biome, and then multiplied by the total area of each biome and summed over all services and biomes. . . .

Ecosystem Functions and Ecosystem Services

Ecosystem functions refer variously to the habitat, biological or system properties or processes of ecosystems. Ecosystem goods (such as food) and services (such as waste assimilation) represent the benefits human populations derive, directly or indirectly, from ecosystem functions. For simplicity, we will refer to ecosystem goods and services together as ecosystem services. . . . For the purposes of this analysis we grouped ecosystem services into 17 major categories. These groups are listed in Table 1. . . .

Natural Capital and Ecosystem Services

In general, capital is considered to be a stock of materials or information that exists at a point in time. Each form of capital stock generates, either autonomously or in conjunction with services from other capital stocks, a flow of services that may be used to transform materials, or the spatial configuration of materials, to enhance the welfare of humans. The human use of this flow of services may or may not leave the original capital stock intact. Capital stock takes different identifiable forms, most notably in physical forms including natural capital, such as trees, minerals, ecosystems, the atmosphere and so on; manufactured capital, such as machines and buildings; and the human capital of physical bodies. In addition, capital stocks can take intangible forms, especially as information such as that stored in computers and in individual human brains, as well as that stored in species and ecosystems.

Ecosystem services consist of flows of materials, energy, and information from natural capital stocks which combine with manufactured and human capital services to produce human welfare. Although it is possible to imagine generating human welfare without natural capital and ecosystem services in artificial "space colonies," this possibility is too remote and unlikely to be of much current interest.

Thus we can consider the general class of natural capital as essential to human welfare. Zero natural capital implies zero human welfare because it is not feasible to substitute, in total, purely "non-natural" capital for natural capital. Manufactured and human capital require natural capital for their construction. Therefore, it is not very meaningful to ask the total value of natural capital to human welfare, nor to ask the value of massive, particular forms of natural capital. It is trivial to ask what is the value of the atmosphere to humankind, or what is the value of rocks and soil infrastructure as support systems. Their value is infinite in total.

However, it is meaningful to ask how changes in the quantity or quality of various types of natural capital and ecosystem services may have an impact on human welfare. Such changes include both small changes at large scales and large changes at small scales.

Valuation of Ecosystem Services

. . . The exercise of valuing the services of natural capital "at the margin" consists of determining the differences that relatively small changes in these services make to human welfare. Changes in quality or quantity of ecosystem services have value insofar as they either change the benefits associated with human activities or change the costs of those activities. These changes in benefits and costs either have an impact on human welfare through established markets or through non-market activities. For example, coral reefs provide habitats for fish. One aspect of their value is to increase and concentrate fish stocks. One effect of changes in coral reef quality or quantity would be discernible in commercial fisheries markets, or in recreational fisheries. But other aspects of the value of coral reefs, such as recreational diving and biodiversity conservation, do not show up completely in markets. Forests provide timber materials through well established markets, but the associated habitat values of forests are also felt through unmarketed recreational activities. The chains of effects from ecosystem services to human welfare can range from extremely simple to exceedingly complex. Forests provide timber, but also hold soils and moisture, and create microclimates, all of which contribute to human welfare in complex, and generally non-marketed ways.

Valuation Methods

. . . Many of the valuation techniques used in the studies covered in our synthesis are based, either directly or indirectly, on attempts to estimate the "willingness-to-pay" of individuals for ecosystem services. For example, if ecological services provided a $50 increment to the timber productivity of a forest, then the beneficiaries of this service should be willing to pay up to $50 for it. In addition to timber production, if the forest offered non-marketed, aesthetic, existence, and conservation values of $70, those receiving this non-market benefit should be willing to pay up to $70 for it. The total value of ecological services would be $120, but the contribution to the money economy of ecological services would be $50, the amount that actually passes through markets. In this study we have tried to estimate the total value of ecological services, regardless of whether they are currently marketed.

. . . In this study we estimated the value per unit area of each ecosystem service for each ecosystem type. To estimate this "unit value" we used (in order of preference) either: (1) the sum of consumer and producer surplus; or (2) the net rent (or producer surplus); or (3) price times quantity as a

Table 1
Ecosystem Services and Functions Used in This Study

Number	*Ecosystem service**	*Ecosystem functions*	*Examples*
1	Gas regulation	Regulation of atmospheric chemical composition.	CO_2/O_2 balance, O_3 for UVR protection, and SO_2 levels.
2	Climate regulation	Regulation of global temperature, precipitation, and other biologically mediated climatic processes at global or local levels.	Greenhouse gas regulation, DMS production affecting cloud formation.
3	Disturbance regulation	Capacitance, damping, and integrity of ecosystem response to environmental fluctuations.	Storm protection, flood control, drought recovery and other aspects of habitat response to environmental variability mainly controlled by vegetation structure.
4	Water regulation	Regulation of hydrological flows.	Provisioning of water for agricultural (such as irrigation) or industrial (such as milling) processes or transportation.
5	Water supply	Storage and retention of water.	Provisioning of water by watersheds, reservoirs, and aquifers.
6	Erosion control and sediment retention	Retention of soil within an ecosystem.	Prevention of loss of soil by wind, runoff, or other removal processes, storage of silt in lakes and wetlands.
7	Soil formation	Soil formation processes.	Weathering of rock and the accumulation of organic material.
8	Nutrient cycling	Storage, internal cycling, processing and acquisition of nutrients.	Nitrogen fixation, N, P, and other elemental or nutrient cycles.

9	Waste treatment	Recovery of mobile nutrients and removal or breakdown of excess or xenic nutrients and compounds.	Waste treatment, pollution control, detoxification.
10	Pollination	Movement of floral gametes.	Provisioning of pollinators for the reproduction of plant populations.
11	Biological control	Trophic-dynamic regulations of populations.	Keystone predator control of prey species, reduction of herbivory by top predators.
12	Refugia	Habitat for resident and transient populations.	Nurseries, habitat for migratory species, regional habitats for locally harvested species, or overwintering grounds.
13	Food production	That portion of gross primary production extractable as food.	Production of fish, game, crops, nuts, fruits by hunting, gathering, subsistence farming or fishing.
14	Raw materials	That portion of gross primary production extractable as raw materials.	The production of lumber, fuel, or fodder.
15	Genetic resources	Sources of unique biological materials and products.	Medicine, products for materials science, genes for resistance to plant pathogens and crop pests, ornamental species (pets and horticultural varieties of plants).
16	Recreation	Providing opportunities for recreational activities.	Eco-tourism, sportfishing, and other outdoor recreational activities.
17	Cultural	Providing opportunities for non-commercial uses.	Aesthetic, artistic, educational, spiritual, and/or scientific values of ecosystems.

*We include ecosystem "goods" along with ecosystem services.

proxy for the economic value of the service. . . . We then multiplied the unit values times the surface area of each ecosystem to arrive at global totals.

Ecosystem Values, Markets and GNP

As we have noted, the value of many types of natural capital and ecosystem services may not be easily traceable through well functioning markets, or may not show up in markets at all. For example, the aesthetic enhancement of a forest may alter recreational expenditures at that site, but this change in expenditure bears no necessary relation to the value of the enhancement. Recreationists may value the improvement at $100, but transfer only $20 in spending from other recreational areas to the improved site. Enhanced wetlands quality may improve waste treatment, saving on potential treatment costs. For example, tertiary treatment by wetlands may save $100 in alternative treatment. Existing treatment may cost only $30. The treatment cost savings does not show up in any market. There is very little relation between the value of services and observable current spending behaviour in many cases.

There is also no necessary relationship between the valuation of natural capital service flows, even on the margin, and aggregate spending, or GNP, in the economy. This is true even if all capital service flows had an impact on well functioning markets. A large part of the contributions to human welfare by ecosystem services are of a purely public goods nature. They accrue directly to humans without passing through the money economy at all. In many cases people are not even aware of them. Examples include clean air and water, soil formation, climate regulation, waste treatment, aesthetic values and good health, as mentioned above. . . .

Total Global Value of Ecosystem Services

. . . We estimated that at the current margin, ecosystems provide at least US$33 trillion dollars worth of services annually. The majority of the value of services we could identify is currently outside the market system, in services such as gas regulation (US$1.3 trillion yr-1), disturbance regulation (US$1.8 trillion yr-1), waste treatment (US$2.3 trillion yr-1) and nutrient cycling (US$17 trillion yr-1). About 63% of the estimated value is contributed by marine systems (US$20.9 trillion yr-1). Most of this comes from coastal systems (US$10.6 trillion yr-1). About 38% of the estimated value comes from terrestrial systems, mainly from forests (US$4.7 trillion yr-1) and wetlands (US$4.9 trillion yr-1). . . .

Discussion

What this study makes abundantly clear is that ecosystem services provide an important portion of the total contribution to human welfare on this planet. We must begin to give the natural capital stock that produces these services adequate weight in the decision-making process, otherwise current and continued future human welfare may drastically suffer. We estimate in this study that the annual value of these services is US$16-54 trillion, with an estimated average of US$33 trillion. The real value is almost certainly much larger, even at the current margin. US$33 trillion is 1.8 times the current global GNP. One way to look at this comparison is that if one were to try to replace the services of ecosystems at the current margin, one would need to increase global GNP by at least US$33 trillion, partly to cover services already captured in existing GNP and partly to cover services that are not currently captured in GNP. This impossible task would lead to no increase in welfare because we would only be replacing existing services, and it ignores the fact that many ecosystem services are literally irreplaceable.

If ecosystem services were actually paid for, in terms of their value contribution to the global economy, the global price system would be very different from what it is today. The price of commodities using ecosystem services directly or indirectly would be much greater. The structure of factor payments, including wages, interest rates and profits would change dramatically. World GNP would be very different in both magnitude and composition if it adequately incorporated the value of ecosystem services. One practical use of the estimates we have developed is to help modify systems of national accounting to better reflect the value of ecosystem services and natural capital. Initial attempts to do this paint a very different picture of our current level of economic welfare than conventional GNP, some indicating a leveling of welfare since about 1970 while GNP has continued to increase. A second important use of these estimates is for project appraisal, where ecosystem services lost must be weighed against the benefits of a specific project. Because ecosystem services are largely outside the market and uncertain, they are too often ignored or undervalued, leading to the error of constructing projects whose social costs far outweigh their benefits.

Notes and Questions

1. The excerpt above omits the authors' detailed discussion of valuation methods and the sources of their values, as well as a detailed account of the values assigned to each ecosystem service. However, the description of this study illuminates what a daunting task it is to value the services which are often thought of as free or as having an indeterminate value. How would the global economy change if we all had to pay for ecosystem services?

2. Do you think the work described by the authors above adequately values Earth? It may seem the difficulty stems from the fact that we would simply be comparing apples and oranges. Considering the uncertainty and complexity of the task, is it worth it to denominate such nonmarket services in market terms? Stuart L. Pimm, commenting on the study above, notes:

> Market prices are the easier objects of study, recorded abundantly in units (currencies) with known, if varying, calibrations. Values are more slippery, being likely to vary widely from person to person and from generation to generation. Prices, moreover, reflect incremental (or "marginal") costs. Diamonds trade for a higher price than does fresh water. Yet the value of all fresh water is infinite: we could not survive without it. For ecologists, prices are woefully incomplete measures of nature's value that poorly prefigure the consequences of humanity's exponential growth. For economists, the challenge is how to assess an ecosystem's non-market values and predict their future trends.

Stuart L. Pimm, The Value of Everything, *Nature,* May 15, 1997, at 231.

4. *United States Law: CERCLA and the Natural Resources Trustee*

The Federal Comprehensive Environmental Response, Compensation and Liability Act (CERCLA, 42 U.S.C. 9601 et seq.) is a program designed to give the federal government the authority to clean up hazardous waste sites and get reimbursed from the owners or those responsible for the pollution (*see generally* Noel W. Nellis & Carl I. Seneker II, The Effect of Federal and State Hazardous Waste Laws on Real Estates Transactions in the United States—Annotated Outline (International Bar Association, 1986)). The Act also created the "Superfund," which is actually two funds—one to provide money to clean up the damage, and the other to repay property damage resulting from the release of hazardous substances (Nellis, at 4-5).

Section 107 of CERCLA (U.S.C. 9407) provides a joint and several, strict liability scheme for injuries resulting from "injury to, destruction of, or loss of natural resources . . ." owned by the federal or state government or by Native Americans. *See* Town of Boonton v. Drew Chemical Corp., 621 F. Supp. 663 (D.N.J. 1985) (even a local government may recover damages under CERCLA). That means that any or all of the parties contributing to the pollution may be held liable for all of the removal or remedial costs; "any other necessary costs of response" (9407(b)); compensation, including the costs of assessing losses; and the costs of human health effects or studies (9407(4)).

The issue of damages naturally presented the question of how to determine the value of the resources themselves. When amending CERCLA in 1986, therefore, Congress included a provision for government officials to perform the evaluation. CERCLA 107(f)(2)(A) provides that the president "shall designate . . . Federal officials who shall act on behalf of the public as trustees for natural resources under this chapter. . . ." Governors of the states have similar authority, subject to the president's approval. 42 U.S.C.A. 9407(f)(2)(B) (West 1991 & Supp. 1993).

These trustees, who may be federal agencies, are to serve traditional fiduciary duties for the resources themselves. The duties include initiating lawsuits for harm to the resource and then assessing, requesting, and collecting damage awards when a suit is successful. Significantly, the trustee also has the authority to enter into negotiations with the relevant parties and come to a settlement of the claim. 42 U.S.C.A. 9622(j)(1). Thus, cleanup of the environment is given priority over litigation. *See* F. Henry Habicht II, The Expanding Role of Natural Resource Damage Claims under Superfund, 7 Va. J. Nat. Resources L. 1, 14 (1987). The trustee then delivers the fee to the government.

The trustees are provided with regulations from the Department of the Interior to be followed at their option. 43 C.F.R. 11 (1986). However, when the Natural Resources Damage Assessment guidelines are adhered to, the trustee's assessment of damages becomes rebuttably presumed. *See* Roger Marzulla, Superfund 1991: How Insurance Firms Can Help Clean Up the Nation's Hazardous Waste, 4 Toxics L. Rep. (BNA) 685 (Nov. 8, 1989); Douglas M. Garrou, The Potentially Responsible Trustee: Probable Target for CERCLA Liability, 77 Va. L. Rev. 113 (1991) ("With only slight exaggeration, one government lawyer has described a [CERCLA] trial as requiring only that the Justice Department lawyer stand up and recite: 'May it please the Court, I represent the government and therefore I win'").

The natural resource damage assessment provisions originally used a measure of the decrease in the level of services that the resource provides after damage as the basis for calculating the loss of value. 43 C.F.R. 11.72. The trustee was to quantify the amount of service the resource provided to humans and that to the environment before and after the damage occurred. The two would be compared, and any difference regarded as the amount of damage. Once the loss of service value was determined, the trustee had to calculate the cost of replacement or restoration. The lesser of replacement/restoration cost or loss of value was to be used as the damage claimed. 43 C.F.R. 11.80(c).

This provision has been challenged by ten states and three environmental organizations, who argued that since the value of lost use will in most cases be lower than the cost of restoration, the provisions will result in awards that do not cover restoration costs. In State of Ohio v. United States Dept. of the Interior, 880 F.2d 432 (D.C. Cir. 1989), rehearing denied, 897 F.2d 1151 (D.C. Cir. 1989), the court agreed that the "lesser of" rule contradicted the congressional mandate. According to the court, CERCLA made it clear that replacement cost and use value are not to be accorded equal presumptive legitimacy in the assessment process. *Id.* at 444. In 1994, the Department of the Interior revised the process to allow natural resource damage actions to be used to restore or acquire equivalent natural resources; 59 Fed. Reg. 14262 (1994). The NRDA process under 43 C.F.R.

pt. 11 applies to the Clean Water Act as well as CERCLA and has been amended by the DOI. *See e.g.,* 62 Fed. Reg. 60457-01 (1997). In addition, the National Oceanic and Atmostpheric Administration (NOAA) has promulgated regulations for the assessment of natural resource damages under the Oil Pollution Act of 1990. *See* 15 C.F.R. pt. 990.

Additional Readings

For more reading on valuation under United States law, *see generally* Frank B. Cross, Natural Resource Damage Valuation, 42 Vanderbilt L. Rev. 269 (1989); Kevin M. Ward & John W. Duffield, Natural Resource Damages: Law and Economics (1992); Charles B. Anderson, Damage To Natural Resources And The Costs Of Restoration, 72 Tul. L. Rev. 417 (Dec. 1997) (analyzing the natural resource damage assessment process in the U.S. under the Clean Water Act, CERCLA, and the Oil Pollution Act of 1990).

D. COST-BENEFIT ANALYSIS

Cost-benefit analysis is the prevailing method of evaluating the economic wisdom of projects or regulations in the United States today. The analysis is based on a comparison of the calculation of the costs of a given project and the calculated benefits that would derive from the project over time. In theory, if the costs are greater than the benefits, that alternative should be rejected; if the benefits are greater, the project should be acted upon unless an alternative exists with a higher net benefit.

Cost-benefit analysis, however, is far more problematic in practice than it is in theory. Not only do the actual costs have to be measured and quantified, but a complete analysis necessitates the calculation of opportunity costs, or the costs incurred by putting resources in one place rather than another.

Next, benefits must be calculated for the present and future. Not only must the benefits be estimated and monetarized, but the future income must be discounted to take into account the interest that would accrue if the money were left in the bank.

Finally, an accurate cost-benefit analysis would account for externalities, or those costs or benefits that arise outside of the immediate actors paying for the project.

The use of cost-benefit analysis for environmental decisionmaking must confront the inherent problems of the analytical method as well as the additional uncertainties of how to value the resources themselves. Because the most prevalent way of determining the value of a good is price, the cost- or benefit-valuation of a nonpriced resource becomes an additional step in the analysis.

For an easily understandable economic introduction to cost-benefit analysis, *see* E.J. Mishan, Cost-Benefit Analysis (1976). For a more quantitative discussion, *see* O.J. Kuik, F.H. Oosterhuis, H.M.A. Jansen, K. Holm, & H.-J. Ewers, Assessment of Benefits of Environmental Measures (1992) (written as a policy proposal advocating the usage of environmental assessments in the European Community; especially helpful is Appendix 3.1, setting out questions for assessing environmental benefits, at 34-35).

Before you read the next articles, consider also the following passages from Cost-Benefit Analysis (citation above):

> But why bother with cost-benefit analysis at all? What is wrong with deciding whether or not to undertake any specific investment, or to choose among a number of specific investment opportunities, guided simply by proper accounting practices and, therefore, guided ultimately by reference to profitability? The answer is provided by the familiar thesis that what counts as a benefit or a loss to one part of the economy—to one or more persons or groups—does not necessarily count as a benefit or loss to the economy as a whole. And in cost-benefit analysis we are concerned with the economy as a whole, with the welfare of a defined society and not any smaller part of it. [p. *x* (Foreword).]
>
> The economist engaged in the cost-benefit appraisal of a project is not, in essence, then, asking a different sort of question from that being asked by the accountant of a private firm. Rather, the same sort of question is being asked about a wider group of people—who comprise society—and is being asked more searchingly. . . . [T]he economist asks whether society as a whole will become better off by undertaking this project rather than not undertaking it, or by undertaking instead any of a number of alternative projects. [p. *xii.*]

1. The Techniques of Cost-Benefit Analysis

The following article provides a brief overview of cost-benefit analysis, particularly in the context of environmental law.

■ BENEFIT-COST ANALYSIS IN NATURAL RESOURCES DECISIONMAKING: AN ECONOMIC AND LEGAL OVERVIEW

Deborah Lee Williams
4 Nat. Resources L. 761, 766-767 (1979)

[The author distinguishes three types of benefit-cost analysis:]

1. Informal benefit-cost analysis: an analysis which compares in a systematic manner the benefits and costs of alternative projects,

but which does not quantify or monetize all the benefits and costs. This analysis often uses a large amount of qualitative description.

2. Quantitative benefit-cost analysis: an analysis which compares quantified, but not necessarily monetized, benefits and costs of alternative projects. Quantification involves measuring all benefits and costs in terms of measurable units such as square miles, gallons and decibels.
3. Monetized (or formal) benefit-cost analysis: an analysis which defines all benefits and costs in terms of their dollar value.

Virtually all economic writings have focused on monetized benefit-cost analysis. . . .

To do this [benefit-cost analysis] relies upon the theory of consumer sovereignty. Any benefit, under this theory, can be measured by how much a consumer would be willing to pay for the good, service, or opportunity. A cost is the minimum amount a consumer would be willing to accept to forego the good, service, or opportunity. The preferences of all persons affected by the project in question are included in the calculations on a one dollar one vote basis.

Since benefits and costs accrue over time and since a dollar today is worth more than a dollar a year from today, to facilitate a direct comparison between all benefits and costs, analysts discount them to their present value. . . . Assuming the annual interest rate were 5 percent, $1.05 a year from today would be equal to a dollar today.

In benefit-cost analysis it is useful to distinguish between primary costs and secondary costs and between primary benefits and secondary benefits. "Primary costs" refers to the goods and services needed to develop and operate a project. "Primary benefits" refers to the immediate value of the goods and services produced, such as the value of irrigation water from a dam to farmers, or treated municipal waste water to industry. "Secondary costs" and "secondary benefits" refer to all other costs and benefits associated with the project that can be measured in the marketplace, such as increased employment in an associated industry in the region because of materials made available in the targeted project. There are also intangible costs and benefits, namely those costs and benefits that cannot be adequately captured in the marketplace, such as the value of a biologically diverse forest or coral reef. *See* Deborah Lee Williams, Benefit-Cost Analysis in Natural Resources Decisionmaking: An Economic and Legal Overview, 4 Nat. Resources L. 761, 766-767 (1979).

The next article supports the use of cost-benefit analysis by setting out the problems in its present use.

■ AN ECONOMIST'S VIEW OF NATURAL RESOURCE AND ENVIRONMENTAL PROBLEMS

Robert Dorfman
The Global Possible 80-86 (R. Repetto, ed. 1985)

Although benefit-cost analysis is a banner to some people and a red flag to others, it is unavoidable. To choose among courses of action, one must compare the advantages and drawbacks of the permissible alternatives. Since this must be done, it is best done consciously and systematically.

Nevertheless, the use of benefit-cost analyses is a subject of controversy, and the results are regarded with skepticism.

There are numerous reasons for this costly and unsatisfactory state of affairs. A half-dozen of the leading problems that can be corrected will be discussed below.

Absence of Standards. It is not too much to say that every benefit-cost analysis is ad hoc, an exercise in the analyst's judgment and ingenuity. Every analyst goes about this work in a distinctive way and, in general, carries out each task differently. This state of affairs has numerous disastrous consequences. The analogy that comes to mind is auditing, in many ways a similar enterprise. How much confidence would financial reports deserve if every auditor had wide latitude to define the various classes of assets and liabilities and to devise valuation assumptions? That is essentially the situation with benefit-cost analysis.

There is need for some influential agency or group of agencies concerned with environmental problems to set forth specifications for benefit-cost evaluations and to require that studies submitted to, or generated by, the agency conform to them. That is not easy in the present state of the art. To be useful, the specifications would have to be explicit and detailed. Undoubtedly, several formats would have to be permitted, to allow for differences in the scale of the appropriate analytic effort, in the availability of data, and in the nature of the problem. Preparing such a document will require difficult negotiations and some experimentation. The effort would certainly not be worthwhile if the need were not so urgent. But considering the amount of effort now devoted to preparing benefit-cost analyses of doubtful usefulness and questionable validity, it would be a sure winner.

The promulgation of acceptable standards is only the first step, though a major one. The standards would have to be brought up to date from time to time as experience and knowledge accumulated. Most important, any benefit-cost analysis invokes numerous assumptions—about population growth, trends in price levels and interest rates, and other matters. For comparability of studies, therefore, standard sets of assumptions would need to be prescribed. They need not pretend to precision and in fact should not. The important thing is that they impose uniformity and be reasonably plausible.

Neglect of Distributional Effects. At least nine out of ten benefit-cost studies adopt the time-honored procedure of adding up benefits and costs "to whomsoever they may accrue." This alone is enough to disqualify them as guides for making practical decisions. Decisions about environmental policies are—and ought to be—political decisions. Their effectiveness depends ultimately on public acceptance. Under any form of government, the officials who make the decisions must be alert to the reactions of the constituencies to which they owe their positions and influence. Analyses that omit the effects of policies on relevant population groups—farmers in the affected region, workers in the affected industries, richer and poorer nations, the poor wherever they may be—thereby leave out the very information that is or should be most significant to the people who make the decisions. A major concern of political decision-makers is to get that information. If it is left out of benefit-cost analyses, they will get it from other sources, ignoring the analyses in the process.

Practical politicians and administrators often point out that it is indiscreet to be explicit about who benefits and who pays for environmental measures, that it can lead to nothing but dissension. It can be countered that it is impossible to hide the fact of distributional consequences and that it is far better to admit them openly than to leave a vacuum to be filled by tendentious claims.

Unpersuasive Treatment of Nonmonetary Effects. Environmental problems are undoubtedly the most difficult field of application of benefit-cost analysis. This is because the major benefits and many of the costs have no natural monetary values: examples are protection of public health, preservation of natural areas and wildlife, improvement in air quality, reduction in urban noise levels. There have been endless efforts to put dollar values on these things and equally endless debates about those efforts. The very propriety of trying to place dollar values on such ultimate goods has been challenged. The problem is built in and it is also inescapable. It has been pointed out many times that every decision involving an environmental problem entails an implicit or explicit judgment about how much we ought to be spending on the goals that it is designed to achieve.

Since there is no generally accepted way of assigning monetary value to many of the benefits that motivate environmental programs, benefit-cost analyses will not be persuasive if their conclusions depend on monetary values selected by the analyst. Instead, estimates of the physical results (for example, number of untimely deaths averted, number of hectares preserved, increase in the level of dissolved oxygen) should stand at the heart of the analyses, so that the reader can judge whether the results are worth the cost according to his or her own scale or values.

The reader will often be helped if the physical results are translated, after they are presented, into monetary equivalents by applying a plausible range of values to those results. Occasionally this translation will show the cost to be so small or so great as to force a decision but the analyst has no right to presume this.

Neglect of Uncertainty. The future is always uncertain, but never more so than when attempting to foresee the benefits and costs of environmental interventions. We know painfully little about the effects of human actions on environmental or ecological conditions, or about the way in which people respond to programs intended to alter their behavior with respect to the environment. Thus, the effects of environmental programs cannot be predicted with any accuracy, and it is pretense to behave otherwise. Yet that is the almost invariable practice. It is standard for benefit-cost analyses to present point estimates of decreases in death rates, increases in net social benefits, and the like, with no indication of how uncertain those estimates are.

No reader, of course, takes those estimates literally, but neither does he have a basis for judging how skeptical he should be about them. It is the responsibility of the analyst to provide such a basis, by indicating the ranges within which there is good reason to believe the true values lie.

This aspect of benefit-cost analyses has an important link with the implementation problems to be discussed below. The choice of implementation strategy often depends on where the uncertainties lie. For example, one of the critical choices may be whether to rely on economic incentives or to impose direct regulations. Poor information about the private costs of abating emissions will produce less confidence in estimates of the effects of economic incentives than in those of the effects of regulations. On the other hand, if the major uncertainties relate to the beneficial effects of abatement, then the economic and administrative advantages of economic incentives will loom large. Information about the reliability of the various estimates in a benefit-cost analysis is therefore critically important to the design of an implementation plan.

Inadequate Attention to Alternatives. There are always a number of potential responses to an unsatisfactory environmental condition—in fact often more than one can conceive of, much less analyze. The possible alternatives differ in the amount of protection they afford and in their cost, side effects, and methods of implementation. Sound planning requires, first, identifying a variety of plausible responses to a problem, though a complete listing is out of the question. Second, it requires that the identified alternatives be assigned a price tag and compared incrementally—that is, that each alternative be compared with the one whose costs are just below its own so that readers can see what improvements are bought with the additional expense.

Superficial Treatment of Costs. So much effort is generally expended in estimating the benefits of environmental protection measures that cost is relatively neglected. But this neglect can be costly. For example, when the use of a dangerous pesticide is banned or restricted, farmers are likely to resort to some other pesticide that may also be dangerous. Then dangers imposed by the second pesticide are one of the costs of restricting the first, and they should be taken into account. Again, when tall stacks were recommended as a means of dispersing the sulfur dioxide generated in congested areas, the effects of long-distance transport were not taken into account. We are now worrying about them, a bit late. Many other examples could be cited of adverse but foreseeable side effects that might well have influenced environmental decisions. It is a mistake to assume that the visible expenses of implementation are the only costs of environmental policies.

Allowance for Degree of Effectiveness. Finally, benefit-cost studies invariably take it for granted that the policies studied will be executed with 100-percent faithfulness by all concerned. Alas, life isn't like that. Emissions, for example, are never abated by quite as much as a plan calls for; endangered species continue to be trapped and gathered despite determined efforts to protect them; and so on. Benefit estimates should not presume 100-percent efficiency in execution; the actuality may be far lower.

Thus far the discussion has concentrated on some technical aspects of planning, which is where the most pervasive and serious shortcomings lie at present. There are naturally substantive issues as well, at least one of which should be mentioned.

No planner leaves costs—in the narrow dollars-and-cents sense—entirely out of account in environmental planning, although sometimes the United States pretends to do so. However, one implication of these costs is rarely taken into account, perhaps because it is so unpleasant. It is that some countries and communities can afford more protection than others. Many countries adopt American or German environmental standards to avoid the onerous task of establishing their own. The World Health Organization has recommended some uniform environmental standards as guides to individual nations. All such blanket proposals are misguided. In environmental matters, as in education, nutrition, health care, and so on, sound planning requires that aspiration levels be adapted to available resources. In any country, the stricter the environmental standards the greater the resources that will be required to attain them, and the less the resources that will be available for other urgent needs such as health care and developmental investments.

The poorer countries of the world confront tragic choices. They cannot afford drinking water standards as high as those to which the industrial countries are accustomed. They cannot afford to close their pristine areas to polluting industries that would introduce technical know-how and productive capital and thereby earn urgently needed foreign exchange. They cannot afford to bar mining companies from unexploited regions. Nor can they afford to impose on those companies antipollution requirements that are as strict and expensive as those in richer industrialized countries. They should always realize that environmental protection measures are financed out of the stomachs of their own people, since the multinationals cannot be made to pay for them. It follows that every country, and particularly the poorer ones, has to choose its own environmental standards, adapted to its needs and resources.

These remarks apply to global pollutants, particularly carbon dioxides, as well as to local and regional pollutants. The richer countries are beginning to cut back on globally polluting emissions. The poorer countries can say, justly, "You fellows have increased the carbon dioxide concentration in the atmosphere by at least 12 percent. Now it's our turn." Is there any really satisfactory response to that? The world can neither stand by complacently while India, China, and the others pour carbon dioxide into the atmosphere, nor can it expect them to desist. A partial response would be for a consortium of the richer countries to subsidize the more expensive fuels and processes that would permit poorer countries to expand their production of energy with small emissions of carbon dioxide than they could otherwise afford.

For further reading, *see* J.T. Winpenny, Values for the Environment: A Guide to Economic Appraisal (1991) (setting out techniques of valuing environmental resources, including cost-benefit and cost-effectiveness analysis, among others).

Notes

Cost-benefit analysis can be used as a guide in determining appropriate standards for existing regulations and for choosing among alternative legislative schemes.

For more on this topic in the context of developing countries, *see* World Resources Institute Report, Improving Environmental Cooperation: The Roles of Multinational Corporations and Developing Countries 22-28 (1984).

2. *Discounting*

Discounting is a tool economists use for considering the long-term effects on the environment and for considering the economic wisdom of conserving natural resources. This tool is an essential part of cost-benefit analysis.

The term "discounting" refers to the adjustment of amounts of money upward or downward to account for interest rates over time. Of utmost importance to any discounting calculation for a cost-benefit analysis, then, is the rate of interest.

There are two methods for determining the appropriate rate of interest.

One is the private discount rate. The other is the social discount rate. The private rate is based on how much interest an individual would demand in order to defer having use of a specified sum and instead take it later. The social discount rate is that interest rate at which society values the use of the money. Generally, the social discount rate is calculated to be lower. Which of the two rates should be used as the environmental discount rate is a policy question.

As you read the following materials, consider whether the instrument of a discount rate is sufficient to protect the environment in a cost-benefit regime.

The passage below discusses the need for using a discount rate in determining the value of our resources if future generations are to be equitably treated.

■ THE PLANETARY TRUST: CONSERVATION AND INTERGENERATIONAL EQUITY

Edith Brown Weiss
11 Ecol. L.Q. 495, 516-519 (1984)

C. The Economically Efficient Use

The economic efficiency approach to the development and use of resources has dominated Western thought for the last few centuries and is widely reflected in the common law. It counsels that we maximize, for present consumers, the present value of consumption over time. According to this theory, we best fulfill our obligation to future generations by maximizing consumption, the fruits of which can then be passed on to future generations in the form of knowledge, technology, capital instruments and institutions. This economic heritage is therefore of greater value to future generations than the reservation of specific natural resources for their use.

Economists use the discount method to decide whether or not a natural resource should be exploited at a given time. The discount rate is defined as the opportunity cost of capital—the rate of return that could be earned by investing money in alternative investments of the same risk. A potential investor takes the current money value of the natural resource and applies the formula for compound interest, using the discount rate as the interest rate, to calculate the value that the investment would achieve by some future date if it were invested in an alternative opportunity. The investor compares this value to the value the natural resource is anticipated to have achieved by the same future date if it is reserved for development. To determine this anticipated value, the investor estimates the return from the future sales of the resource, less the costs of extraction, to yield a net price.

At the point of equilibrium, when the net price is expected to increase at the same rate as the value of the alternative investment (that is, at the compound interest rate), the investor is, in theory, indifferent to holding or extracting the resource. If the net price rise exceeds that yielded by the compounded rate of interest, the investor will hold the resource for later development; if the net price rises more slowly than that rate, he will choose to extract it and thus exhaust it sooner.

From the point of view of public policy, the private discount rate can be used to determine the wisdom of exploiting or holding natural resources only if we assume that each individual unit, acting separately, inherently works in the best interests of the whole, extended over time. Hotelling, Pigou, Solow, and others challenge this assumption, pointing out that the long-term interests of society may not be identical to the interests of individuals.

If the private discount rate derived from the market is too high natural resources will be exploited too soon. There are several reasons to suspect that private discount rates are too high. Individuals may discount for some risks, such as wealth transfers, that society as a whole does not share. Equally important, private time preferences may favor the present generation at the expense of future generations, because future generations cannot bid in the market place.

To allow quantitative analysis of the gap between societal preferences and the individual's interest, economists have developed the conceptual tool of social discount rate. The social discount rate is usually lower than the private discount rate. Thus, even if the anticipated increase in value of resources held in the ground is not so high as to encourage private investors to forego immediate development, public decisionmakers may determine, by applying a lower social discount rate, that preservation is warranted. In effect, the choice of a social discount rate is a policy decision about the intertemporal distribution of income.

The major problem with using social discount rates to make investment or policy decisions is that the decisions rendered are still likely to favor the present generation over future ones. Traditionally, the discount rate has been applied over a period of ten years or, sometimes, twenty years. Some agricultural investments, such as forestry, however, require thirty to fifty years or more to reach maturity for commercial harvest. Hardwoods, like white oak, may require 200 years to reach maturity. Moreover, in analyzing certain investments, like nuclear power plants, economists often ignore substantial long-term costs by discounting them, in effect, to zero; but they may not be zero. Thus, while the discount rate may be a suitable tool for analyzing the relative merits of short-term investments, it is not particularly useful for taking account of posterity.

Solow has responded to this problem by proposing a standard under which per capita consumption would be held constant over time, so that no generation would be favored over others. Under this proposal, the discount rate would vary with time to yield the largest sustainable per capita consumption. Like other social discount rates, however, Solow's runs into the practical difficulty that it would require unattainable accuracy in technological forecasting.

For a short discussion of intergenerational and environmental considerations in deciding on the proper discount rate, *see* Raymond F. Mikesell, The Rate of Discount for Evaluating Public Projects 18-27 (1977).

The importance of choosing the correct discount rate is demonstrated in the following excerpt.

■ NATIONAL RESOURCE INFORMATION FOR ECONOMIC DEVELOPMENT

Orris C. Herfindahl

Appendix to Chapter 1, at 16-18: The Theory of Discounting

To understand the nature of the process of discounting, we must first realize that at all times a society has the option of investing another $1,000—but only at a later point in time. In a market economy, this return will tend to be the same for all lines of investment.

The return will be the same in a special sense, however. The longer the period between the investment and the return, the greater must be the return. And it must be greater in a very special way if the following two situations are to be equivalent:

	Now	*One year from now*	*Two years from now*
Situation A:	Invest $1		Receive $1 plus return for 2 years = S_2
Situation B:	Invest $1	Receive $1 plus return for 1 year	Receive S_1 plus return on S_1 = S_1 for one year at the rate of (S_1 = 1) per dollar invested = $S_1 + (S_1 - 1)S_1$

The initial market investment is the same in both situations. Hence competition in the market should insure that the sum of money available two years from now should be the same in both situations. . . .

Because of the very existence of the opportunity to invest now and to secure a return on this investment later, a dollar spent or received now should not be regarded as having the same value *as* a dollar spent or received at some other time. . . .

This process by which dollars spent or received at different times are made comparable by converting them to "present value" as of *a given date* is called discounting. . . .

In calculating the profitability of an investment, all expenditures and receipts must be converted to a present value as of some given date. The timing of the receipts and expenditures is of a very great importance, as the following example illustrates. Suppose that an investment opportunity involves the following products and outlays, all at the end of the year designated:

	1966	*1967*	*1968*	*1969*	*Total*
Product	$ 0	$90	$160	$54	$304
Outlay	100	70	60	42	272

Without discounting, the value of product exceeds the outlays. To compare product and outlay correctly, however, we must discount them to the same date. Any date will do, but let us pick the end of 1968. Then if the rate of discount is 20 per cent per year, the 1966 outlay of 100 has a 1968 value of $100(1.20)(1.20) = 100(1.20)^2 = 144$, because the 100 could have produced a capital good which would have yielded say, 144 after two years.

The 1969 outlay has a 1968 value of $\frac{42}{1.20} = 35$.

The complete values discounted to 1968 are as follows:

	1966	*1967*	*1968*	*1969*	*Total*
Product	$ 0	$108	$160	$45	$313
Outlay	144	84	60	35	323

Thus when proper account is taken of interest, the investment does not pay.

In the next excerpt, the author discusses the problems of policymaking for equitable inter- and intragenerational distribution of income.

■ ECONOMICS OF A THROWAWAY SOCIETY: THE ONE-WAY ECONOMY

T. Page
Economics of Environmental and Natural Resources Policy
Chapter 5 (J. Butlin, ed. 1981)

> Upon our own generation lies the responsibility for passing onto the next generation the prospects of continued well-being.
>
> *Paly Commission Report*

Criteria

By one school of thought it is possible for the market to provide its own criteria to determine the right ("socially optimal") balances of material flows. This view holds that if the market is working properly, there should be no active policies toward recycling or the provision of resources for the future. Whatever amount of recycling or provision the market provides for the future is the "right amount." Recycling is not a good in itself, nor is the preservation of resources. When costs from depletion and waste generation fall upon the future, they should be discounted by a market rate of interest just the way other costs, and benefits as well, from market activities are discounted by market rates of interest.

If one feels that somehow the market is recycling too little and not providing sufficiently for the future, he is directed by this view to look for market failures which might explain why the flows are not "socially optimal." The three most often cited are the failure of the tax system to be neutral, the failure of the freight rate structure to count adequately the cost of shipment, and the failure of the price system to include the costs of disposal in product price. All three of these failures are considered to favor virgin material extraction over scrap recycling and thus to explain why there is "too" little recycling and "too" much depletion. Once these failures are corrected we will automatically achieve the right balance of material flows, which will incidentally imply more recycling and lower rates of depletion than are presently occurring.

While the costs of waste generation are included, conspicuously absent from this list of market failures is the inability of the market to count the costs of depletion which fall upon future generations. It is absent because in this school of thought it is believed that the market does provide adequately for the future. The mechanism is explained by a concept called resource reservation. The owner of a stock of some particular natural resource will decide upon his most profitable rate of extraction by balancing what he can get now for the material and what he may be able to get in the future. As his stock is depletable, he knows that if sold at one time he won't have the stock to sell at another time. Anticipating future scarcity, he reserves some of his stock in order to take advantage of the better market and higher prices associated with future scarcity. Thus material is reserved for future use.

One may wonder if this motivation, which amounts to speculation on future price increases, is not overwhelmed by more immediate considerations. The planning period of the resource holder must be very long, and uncertainties over new technologies and the tenure of resource ownership may lead the present owner to discount heavily (by more than market rate of interest) the worth to him of possible future price increases. And, in fact, economists who have studied the behavior of firms in the extractive industries have found little or no evidence of resource reservation.

The above is a very simplified version of the economic theory of natural resources. The policy prescription is to remove market failures. In this school of thought the criterion is to let the perfected market decide. We call this the efficiency criterion. The resulting market allocation will depend heavily on the distribution of market power (the distribution of wealth) and discounting, which incorporates the present generation's time preference and partial sense of altruism towards the future.

By a second school of thought, the above is morally indefensible. As decisions concerning the generation of long-lived wastes and depletion of resources affect the means of survival for the future, these decisions should not be made solely by the market in response to the present's appetite and selfishness. Such decisions should be made on ethical grounds.

The ethical problem has been transformed without being solved. In the past the costs from depletion were perceived as certain, with certain dates of exhaustion. Now we have begun to perceive the costs as probabilistic. How well can we guarantee that the new technology will come on line in time and that new reserves will be found in time?

In leaving the decision process to the market, even a perfected market, there is no guarantee that the economy will not gradually drift off course, become ever more polluted and depleted until it becomes unlivable. And so, according to the second school of thought, the decisions concerning basic resource flow are too important to be left completely to the market, even a perfect one. Some fundamental decisions to guarantee permanent livability should be made explicitly without discounting, but on the grounds of fairness between generations.

These two schools of thought are not so irreconcilable as might be imagined. The theory of resource economics and the theory of resource reservation, so briefly mentioned above (and in the previous readings) is microeconomic theory. This theory asks what is best for a single small mine in the midst of a large industry and whether or not what is best for the individual mine is also best for society as a whole. The analysis proceeds along the assumption that certain conditions hold. The most important for our purposes is that the distribution of wealth is ethically satisfactory and that possible changes contemplated are small enough not to effect the distribution of wealth in a socially undesirable way. This along with other conditions such as full employment and no inflation are macroeconomic conditions and they form an environment in which microeconomic firms and markets operate.

The second school of thought is concerned directly with the macro environment. The ethical problem raised by this school can be illustrated in an economic context by comparing the market allocation of resources over time with the market allocation of resources at a given moment of time. It is true that the market provides a well-defined and explicit distribution of goods and services at a given moment of time. But is this distribution ethically desirable? This question immediately invites another question: "Is the distribution of market power socially desirable?" If this distribution of wealth, and hence market power, is found in some way ethically undesirable then the market allocation stemming from this distribution of wealth is also ethically unsatisfactory. It is well known in economic theory that the ethical question of the distribution of economic well-being is logically prior to the market allocation of goods and services.

One can see the difference between concepts of altruism and fairness by comparing the resource allocation problem intergenerationally with another resource allocation problem which is occurring across groups of people at the present moment of time. Many people think that the ocean's resources are owned jointly by all people in the present generation. One rule of fairness would be to establish compacts among the fishing nations to ensure that each one got an equitable catch and the stock as a whole was not overfished. Another way of allocating the fisheries resources would be to give control and full rights for the entire resource stock to Japan for the first year, to the US the second year, to Russia the third year, and so on. Management of the stock would depend on the "present generation's" inability to exhaust the resource in a single year and upon its altruism toward the "next generation." Relying on the altruism of previous nations would doubtless make successor nations feel uneasy. Yet this is roughly the situation with natural resources intertemporally.

In the case of income distribution intratemporally, the poor and the rich are present at the same time and there are political mechanisms to move towards what is considered a fair distribution. The poor and the rich can both be represented legislatively (the fairness of the representation is another matter) and a progressive income tax established. But the future is not around to press any claims against the present, and potentially the present does have all the market power.

3. *Cost-Effectiveness*

Cost-effectiveness analysis is a method of comparing the attractiveness of alternative investment opportunities. It assumes that the decisionmaker has limited resources to accomplish a goal—say, the cleanup of toxic contaminants. The most cost-effective investment alternative for this goal would give the greatest bang for the buck, by eliminating the most or worst toxic contaminants.

Like cost-benefit analysis, the results of a cost-effectiveness inquiry depend on the political context: whether the benefits that will count toward cost-effectiveness are local or global and whether regulatory incentives, including taxes or subsidies, make certain alternatives more or less expensive than others.

As the next article notes, the reason decisionmakers rely on cost-effectiveness comparisons is that their funds, for enactment of a regulatory scheme or for investment in some environmental technology, are always limited.

WORST THINGS FIRST: RISK, INFORMATION, AND REGULATORY STRUCTURE IN TOXIC SUBSTANCES CONTROL

John S. Applegate
9 Yale J. on Reg. 277, 286-288, 295-296 (Summer 1992)

A. Sources of Scarcity

. . . Information is not the only scarce commodity in toxic substances regulation. The government has finite resources with which to investigate problems, develop regulations, and enforce its decisions. A major regulatory initiative that will have a significant economic impact on the regulated industry is likely to be, for that reason alone, highly controversial. Controversy costs money: the information and analysis costs associated with developing a major regulation are high in any event, but intensive industry involvement requires extensive analysis during the rulemaking process to respond to arguments and to prepare for the inevitable court challenge. As a result, agencies are unable to regulate "more than two or three controversial chemicals in any year."

B. Priority Setting

. . . The present regulatory scheme for toxic substances requires far greater informational and other regulatory resources than are available or can be obtained. Therefore, apart from developing better and cheaper ways to generate information, accepting highly imprecise regulatory standards, or adopting largely untried market-based controls, effective control of toxic substances requires that EPA use its scarce resources as efficiently as possible. The agency's first task, upon which the overall efficacy and efficiency of the rest of the process depends, is the allocation of resources among potential regulatory efforts. Agencies must set priorities among the risks within their purview.

C. Cost-Effectiveness

As a general proposition, faced with limited resources and the need to make choices, we should accomplish our environmental goals (however defined) in a cost-effective way. That is, [b]ased on the assumption that the objective is to achieve the greatest possible health benefits for the amount of resources expended, cost-effective resource allocation would give the highest priority to actions that achieve the greatest health benefit per dollar drawn from the resource pool. Given a fixed resource pool, a cost-effective scheme sets priorities so as to achieve as much in total environmental protection as possible, usually but not necessarily in terms of reducing risk. It is also firmly in the technocratic tradition that these priorities must be based on "sound scientific data and analysis . . . 'to develop realistic, achievable, cost effective, environmentally sound goals.' "

Getting the most "bang for the buck" is particularly important when comparing risks of potential concern. An agency ought to prefer to exercise control where it would be fairly easy to do so, because it could reduce risks with fewer resources from both agency and industry. Because the premise of cost-effectiveness is uncontroversial, and because cost-effectiveness does not require the wide-ranging inquiry contemplated by cost-benefit analysis, Congress and agencies have been more willing to adopt it. A more ambitious version of this idea is the so-called risk portfolio approach. The inverse of an investment portfolio, its overall goal is "the progressive reduction of the risk in the existing portfolio" of environmental hazards. The portfolio, like other comparisons, assumes an objective, tolerably reliable, and presumably quantitative risk assessment on which to base its technocratic analysis. . . .

Notes and Questions

1. The last part of the article above suggests that cost-effectiveness analysis is politically palatable because it can be considered value-neutral. Choosing among policy options on a cost-effectiveness basis requires, in theory, little political debate—the obvious choice is always the one which results in a bigger pile of some quantifiable benefit for the same investment.

Yet consider that private actors usually have a very defensible cost-effectiveness basis for making choices that are nonetheless socially undesirable. If you, a commuter, want to drive as many miles as possible on a tank of gas this winter, your cost-effective fuel choice would not be reformulated gasoline (RFG), which decreases your car's miles per gallon and costs more than conventional gasoline. Yet, in requiring RFG in certain polluted metropolitan areas, the government may have concluded that the RFG requirement was the most cost-effective policy for reducing ozone emissions in those areas.

2. In some areas, the first dollars spent toward the achievement of a goal may be more or less effective than the next dollars spent toward the achievement of that goal—that is, the marginal costs of additional benefits may increase as the policy goal is approached. For example, when the policy goal is the total phaseout of certain chemicals used in industry, it may be cheaper, or more cost-effective, to eliminate or replace the first 90 percent of the targeted chemicals. The phaseout of the remaining 10 percent of the targeted chemicals may be far more expensive because, for

example, the increased demand for alternatives resulting from the first 90 percent phaseout leads to greater scarcity and higher prices of those alternatives available for phasing out the last 10 percent.

3. As the author below suggests in his Note, the difference in cost-effectiveness of the first stage of the phaseout and subsequent stages of a phaseout may have important consequences when the goal is global—such as the reduction of greenhouse gases.

■ RESPONDING TO CLIMATE CHANGE: THE CASE FOR UNILATERAL TRADE MEASURES TO PROTECT THE GLOBAL ATMOSPHERE

Sean T. Fox
84 Geo. L.J. 2499 (1996)

B. Applying Theory to the Climate Change Context

Early efforts to develop a comprehensive multilateral response to climate change have highlighted the difficulties associated with negotiating a cooperative agreement among all countries of the world. . . .

[R]adically different cost-benefit calculations regarding reductions of GHGs [greenhouse gases] will hinder any negotiations in the climate change context. On the cost side, some states will be able to reduce GHGs more efficiently than others because of the current composition of their energy sources, the availability of substitutes for fossil fuels, their tax policies, and their current levels of energy efficiency. The United States, for example, has a relatively high output of GHGs per unit of energy consumed. As a result, the United States would likely be able to reduce its GHG emissions more cost effectively than Japan or the EU because the United States can undertake relatively cheap actions that the EU and Japan have already exhausted. More dramatically, consider the cost-benefit analysis of OPEC countries that rely on the consumption of fossil fuels as their primary source of income. These states would suffer devastating economic losses if the demand for oil fell significantly as a result of policies aimed at reducing GHG emissions. Not surprisingly, some of the most vigorous opposition to the Climate Change Treaty came from oil-producing states.

On the benefit side of the equation, some states, such as the island countries and other low-lying countries, stand to benefit disproportionately from GHG emissions reductions made by other states. In fact, the actual existence of some islands may be threatened by changes in the sea level prompted by climate change.

Finally . . . [u]nanswered questions about the timing, magnitude, and nature of climate change create greater room for disagreement among negotiators. This uncertainty increases the difficulty of developing consensus at both the national and international level, and as a result complicates efforts to reach a negotiated international agreement to reduce GHG emissions.

Government agencies may induce private action toward a policy goal by changing the inputs to cost-effectiveness calculations of the private actors who must choose, for example, among technologies or fuels for energy production on the basis of cost-effectiveness. The following authors describe how multilateral financial institutions (MFIs) can induce private action to help achieve international environmental goals, even when the cost-effectiveness calculation would lead private actors to reject the environmentally preferred alternative in the absence of the MFI's involvement.

■ THE ROLE OF MULTILATERAL FINANCE AND THE ENVIRONMENT: A VIEW FROM THE WORLD BANK

Symposium: International Environmental Law and Agencies: The Next Generation
Andrew Steer
Jocelyn Mason
3 Ind. J. of Global Legal Studies 35, 44 (1995)

C. Multiplying Resources for the Environment

The job of [MFIs] is to use the small amount of "paid-in" capital, taxpayers' money, from their member countries to leverage large sums of private funding. Since the World Bank was founded in 1944, it has been playing this multiplication role, turning paid-in capital totaling roughly $10 billion into total loans of $250 billion and total investments in development of over $500 billion.

. . . [In addition] MFIs can help multiply environmental efforts at the international level by administering a wide range of international funds, most notably the Global Environment Facility (GEF). The GEF is jointly implemented by the World Bank, the United Nations Development Programme (UNDP), the United Nations Environment Programme, and the Multilateral Fund for the Implementation of the Montreal Protocol. MFIs can integrate these funds with other forms of funding, such as bilateral funds, into the broader development process.

The World Bank's role in the GEF illustrates this well. The $2 billion committed to the GEF over three years is clearly inadequate on its own to have any real effect on the facility's areas of concern: the urgent global problems of climate change, biodiversity loss, pollution of international waters, and depletion of the ozone layer. Success of the GEF requires that these funds be leveraged to have an impact much greater than the core funds by being used to catalyze change within a much larger program of action. At the project level, a modest amount of GEF funding can be used to tip the scale and make a project with global environmental benefits financially attractive. For example, power generated by coal may be more cost-effective when judged by national interests. However, it might be more beneficial from a global perspective to avoid the global warming effects of carbon emissions from coal-generated power and invest in generating power from geothermal energy. In this case, a GEF grant can be used to fund the incremental cost difference between coal and geothermal energy production, thereby aligning national and global interests behind the less polluting alternative.

Similarly, at the program level, GEF funding can be used to change the balance of costs and benefits for a whole group of investors. For example, the World Bank and its private sector associate, the International Finance Corporation, are currently developing venture capital funds for renewable energy and biodiversity protection. A principal barrier to attracting private investors to these areas is the uncertainty due to unfamiliarity and lack of reliable information. Modest support from the GEF, as well as the added confidence brought from association with the International Finance Corporation, is expected to help take these investments across the threshold of profitability and obviate the need for any additional concessional funding.

E. CRITIQUE OF ECONOMIC ANALYSIS

As you read the articles above, you may have had doubts about the suitability of a purely economic analysis to protect the environment. If so, you were not alone. Several authors have complained that the valuation of the environment and assessments of costs and benefits are simply too complex and uncertain to be credible. Do you agree with the following articles? Do they adequately address the problems with economic analysis and offer alternatives?

■ ECONOMIC THEORY AND ENVIRONMENTAL LAW

Mark Sagoff

79 Mich. L. Rev. 1393, 1410-1419 (1981)

Economic methods cannot supply the information necessary to justify public policy. Economics can measure the intensity with which we hold our beliefs; it cannot evaluate those beliefs on their merits. Yet such evaluation is essential to political decision making. This is my greatest single criticism of cost-benefit analysis. The many problems involved in applying the concept of shadow pricing are secondary, because the concept itself rests on a mistake.

To recognize this mistake, we must first understand what it is that economists attempt to measure. If they measure consumer interests, market data are appropriate and relevant. The pricing mechanism can suggest when resources used to satisfy certain wants might be more efficiently employed to satisfy others. When economists approach issues that concern us as citizens, however, they do not, as they should, abandon the pricing mechanism. They believe that they can account for citizen-preferences as well as consumer-preferences by determining their dollar value. They do this, for example, by asking citizens what they would pay for a certain level of environmental protection. But this attempt to measure the convictions or values of citizens by pricing them as market externalities confuses what the individual wants as an individual and what he or she, as a citizen, believes is best for the community.

This confusion involves what logicians call a category-mistake. One makes category-mistake by treating facts or concepts as if they belong to one logical type or category, when they actually belong to another. Several examples are illustrative. It is logically correct to predicate whiteness of snow or even of coal. (It may not be true, but it is intelligible.) To say that the square root of four is white, however, makes no sense because it is impossible meaningfully to predicate color of a number. When two concepts are in different categories, one cannot measure the first by methods that are appropriate only to the second. . . .

Private and public preferences also belong to different logical categories. Public "preferences" do not involve desires or wants, but opinions or beliefs. They state what a person believes is best or right for the community or group as a whole. These opinions or beliefs may be true or false, and we may meaningfully ask the individual for the reasons that he or she holds them. But an economist who asks how much citizens would pay for opinions that they advocate through political association commits a category-mistake. The economist asks of objective beliefs a question that is appropriate only to subjective wants.

When an environmentalist argues that we ought to preserve wilderness areas because of their cultural importance and symbolic meaning, he or she states a conviction and not a desire. When an economist asserts that we ought to attain efficient levels of pollution, he or she, too states a belief. But beliefs are to be supported by arguments, not by money. One cannot establish the validity of these beliefs by pricing them, nor can that mechanism measure their importance to society as a whole. One can judge how strongly people hold their beliefs by asking how much they would pay to see them implemented, but that is not how we make policy decisions. Those who think that Creationism should be taught in the public schools, for example, are able to raise a lot of money. But the amount of money that partisans raise does not demonstrate the merit of their position. A person who wants his or her child taught a particular doctrine is free to pay for that; willingness to pay may correctly measure the strength of that desire. When a person advocates a policy as being right or appropriate for society as a whole, however, the intensity of the desire is no longer relevant. Rather, advocates must present arguments that convince the public or its representatives to adopt a policy. Political decision makers judge ideas on their merits, and make decisions based on what is good for us all. These policymakers may consider economic factors, but they should not use the economic method to evaluate competing beliefs.

The distinction between public and private interests is indispensable to the study of political philosophy. "To abolish the distinction," as one commentator has written, "is to make a shambles of political science by treating things that are different as if they were alike." Markets are the appropriate arena for the competition of private interests. This competition may best be understood and regulated in terms of individual willingness to pay. When one advocates not a special or private interest of all, however, the framework of debate completely changes. Public discussion must then be carried on in public terms. . . . What matters is whether the argument that he or she offers is sound. . . . This is not to say that economic data are irrelevant in public decision making. It is to argue that the satisfaction of revealed preferences is only one goal among others that policymakers must take into account.

The blurring of the distinction between public and private interest—and, therefore, between the competition of preferences and the contradiction of ideas—produces results that we should do well to avoid. First, the policymaker, employing the willingness-to-pay criterion, attempts to remain neutral among contending positions. As a result, the analyst must grant equal credibility to every position, no matter how bizarre or preposterous. . . .

Second, the willingness-to-pay approach to public policy removes the basis of legitimacy from the political process. I do not mean merely that it crushes the "cherished illusion" that policy comes from the minds of elected officials in Congress rather than from the computer of economists in the back room. I refer, rather, to the fact that cost-benefit approaches deal only with values of preferences already extant in society. A political process—a process of debate and compromise—is supposed to be creative. The ability of the political process to change values and to rise above self-interest is crucial to its legitimacy. Political leaders are supposed to educate and elevate public opinion; they are not supposed merely to gratify preexisting desires.

A third likely consequence in public policy may be the most disastrous. Economic analysis limits conflict to those parties who have something at stake for which they are willing to pay. This approach would prevent the socialization of conflict that is crucial to the functioning of a democracy. Consider an example. Suppose a corporation proposes and an environmentalist group opposes the building of a shopping center in a rural area just outside of town. An economist might make a recommendation based upon prices assigned to the various wants or preferences of relevant interest groups. This would effectively limit conflict to the immediate parties. The genius of democracy, however, is to let the conflict spread to a larger audience. The institutions of democratic government—legislatures, agencies, parties, courts, and the press—depend and thrive on the potential for conflicts of this kind to widen beyond their original bounds. This happens when one side—usually the side that otherwise would be defeated—finds a public issue (e.g., a "snail darter") and moves the conflict into the press, the legislature, and the courts. The shopping center may then never be built because it takes so long to work through the resulting political process.

This might seem grossly inefficient to economists, and perhaps it is, but it is what democratic government is all about. An alternative—technocracy—quarantines or localizes conflict so that it may be resolved by the application of some mechanical rule or decision procedure. Cost-benefit approaches to public policy, if taken to their extreme, would do this, and thus they would make useless the institutions of democratic government. Cost-benefit analysis localizes conflict among affected individuals and prevents it from breaking open into the public realm. This suggests that the reason that industry favors economic approaches to public policy is not necessarily the obvious one, namely, that cost-benefit is sensitive to the costs of regulation. The deeper reason may be that cost-benefit analysis defines a framework for conflict that keeps the public qua public and the citizen qua citizen out.

Once we recognize the logical difference between wants and beliefs, it becomes clear that cost-benefit analysis can measure only the former. To conduct such an analysis, the economist asks how much we would pay for certain policies. How much would you pay to save Lange's metalmark? How much would you pay to preserve the quality of the air in the Southwest? Our responses indicate only the degree to which we care about the issues. If the analyst prices these views by willingness-to-pay criteria, or makes any similar economic trade-off, he tests neither the validity of the views nor the reasons for them, but only the intensity with which they are held.

Economic efficiency is usually defined in terms of the maximum satisfaction of the wants or preferences of individuals in the order that those individuals rank them. A market in which competition is perfect, in theory, achieves this kind of efficiency. . . .

If we were to pursue efficiency as our goal in environmental policy, I believe that we would quickly turn all of our natural beauty into commercial blight. This is what happens when self-fueling and irreversible consumer markets have their way. To forestall this result by "pricing" beliefs, values, and ideals as if they were consumer benefits, I have argued, is to commit a category-mistake. Cost-benefit analysis, at that point, disintegrates into storytelling; it becomes a bad exercise in ad hoc justification.

The environmental legislation of the last twenty years has consistently indicated our preference for national policies that respond to concerns other than economic efficiency. This legislation rejects markets as the indicator of the national will. There is nothing in this legislation or in the public debate on environmental protection that remotely suggests that most people regard pollution as a problem only because pollution is inefficient. Rather, we regard it as a problem because it is efficient. The "gospel of efficiency" is now as anachronistic as is the Lochner decision that is its most typical expression. . . .

THE ROLE OF ECONOMICS

E.F. Schumacher
Small Is Beautiful 40-51 (1973)

Economics plays a central role in shaping the activities of the modern world, inasmuch as it supplies the criteria of what is "economic" and what is "uneconomic," and there is no other set of criteria that exercises a greater influence over the actions of individuals and groups as well as over those of governments. . . .

But what does it *mean* when we say something is uneconomic? . . . [S]omething is uneconomic when it fails to earn an adequate profit in terms of money. Society, or a group of individuals within society, may decide to hang on to an activity or asset *for non-economic reasons*—social, aesthetic, moral, or political—but this does in no way alter its *uneconomic* character. . . .

Economics . . . deals with goods in accordance with their market value. . . . The buyer . . . is not concerned with the origin of the goods or the conditions under which they have been produced. . . . If a buyer refused a good bargain because he suspected that the cheapness of the goods in question stemmed from exploitation or other despicable practices he would be open to the criticism of behaving "uneconomically." . . .

Economics operates legitimately and usefully within a "given" framework which lies altogether outside the economic calculus. . . . [I]f [the economist] remains unaware of the fact that there are boundaries to the applicability of the economic calculus, he is likely to fall into a similar kind of error as that of certain medieval theologians who tried to settle questions of physics by means of biblical quotations. . . .

IV

Risk Assessment and Scientific Uncertainty

International environmental law requires, more than most areas of law, scientific understanding of the environmental system. Some of the complexities and interrelationships are evident from the materials in Chapter 1. While our knowledge of the global environmental system and its associated local systems has been rapidly growing, it is still far from complete. Our understanding is constantly changing as we acquire new knowledge about the environment. We often realize that what we thought we knew was actually not true or that newly discovered knowledge changes our ideas about our old knowledge, leading us to a different understanding of the environment as a system. Moreover, contrary to popular myth, it is rare that we can be nearly one hundred percent sure of anything. From the scientific perspective there is always an element of uncertainty, as is particularly apparent from the excerpt regarding chaos theory in Chapter 1.

When studying international environmental law, it is necessary to realize that perceptions of environmental threats, as well as "hard" facts, play a large role in determining what issues will be accepted as suitable subjects for an international agreement or other international legal instrument. Different people will perceive the same data differently. The perceptions depend not only on the reliability of the data but on differing assessments of how serious the risk is, how effective and costly the measures to address it may be, and priorities in addressing risk.

This chapter explores the implications of scientific uncertainty for international environmental law. It introduces the concepts of risk assessment and risk management and tries to relate these to emerging international principles and existing international agreements. Since at least some scientific uncertainty always exists, and our scientific understanding of environmental issues is constantly changing, we should consider possible approaches in drafting international legal instruments that would provide flexibility to parties to adapt to advances in our scientific understanding.

A. RISK ANALYSIS AND INTERNATIONAL ENVIRONMENTAL LAW

A distinction has frequently been made between identifying and assessing a risk and doing something about the risk, that is, managing the risk. Since William Ruckelshaus first set out the two processes as distinct when he was administrator of the United States Environmental Protection Agency, there has been considerable discussion of whether this distinction is an artificial one. However, the distinction may be useful for understanding the development of international environmental law. One can view risk assessment as the international processes for determining whether a risk exists that merits action by the international community and risk management as those actions the international community takes to minimize or to respond to the risk.

1. The Process of Risk Assessment

■ RISK ASSESSMENT AND COMPARISONS: AN INTRODUCTION

Richard Wilson & E.A.C. Crouch
236 Science 267-270 (Apr. 17, 1987)

Most of us act semi-automatically to minimize our risks. We also expect society to minimize the risks suffered by its members, subject to overriding moral, economic, or other constraints. In some cases these constraints will dominate, in others there will be trade-offs between the values assigned to risks and the constraints. Risk assessments, except in the simplest of circumstances, are not designed for making judgments, but to illuminate them. To effectively illuminate, and then to minimize, risks requires knowing what they are and how big they are. This knowledge usually is gained through experience, and the essence of risk assessment is the application of this knowledge of past mistakes (and deliberate actions) in an attempt to prevent new mistakes in new situations.

Risk Estimation Based on Historical Data

The way in which risks are perceived is strongly correlated with the way in which they are calculated. Risks based on historical data are particularly easy to understand and are often perceived reliably. It is therefore easy to illustrate a risk calculated from historical data to understand some characteristics of risk estimation. There are plenty of data on automobile accidents. . . . One thing that these data can tell us is the frequency of such accidents in the past and their trend through time. To make predictions, however, we must use a model. The simplest model is that there will be as many accidents next year as last, to within a statistical error of the square root of the number. A slightly more complicated, but perhaps more accurate, model might be to fit a mathematical function to numbers from previous years and to argue that next year's accidents will follow the trend given by this function. A possibly better and possibly more accurate model still might use all available information that might influence accident trends. For example, an oil embargo with a concomitant rise in oil price and reduction in automobile travel would be likely to reduce the risk of accident. In any event, it becomes clear that it is impossible to calculate any risk without a model of some sort, even the simple one that tomorrow will be like today.

Risks of New Technologies

We can only use the historical approach to estimating risks when the hazard (for example, technology, chemical, or simply some action) has been present for some time and the risk is large enough to be directly measured (although when it is not large enough to be measured, an upper limit may be calculated, if one assumes some sort of model). If there is no historical database for the hazard (of a new power plant or industrial facility, for instance), one approach is to consider it in separate parts, calculating the risks from each part and adding them together to estimate a risk for the whole. For example, all possible chains of events from an initiator to a final accident are followed in an "event tree," with the probabilities of each event in the tree being estimated from historical data in different situations.

Risks by Analogy: Carcinogenic Risks

Some carcinogenic risks may be estimated from historical data. But this is complicated by the time delay between the insult and the final cancer, one reason why causality is hard to prove if the risk is small. This is the difficult field of epidemiology.

Although some of the largest cancer risks have been identified through the use of epidemiology, preventive public health suggests that we endeavor to estimate risks even where no historical data exist and the risk is small. This is often done by analogy with the cancer risks to animals, usually rodents, which are deliberately exposed to large enough quantities of pollutant so that an effect is observed. To use these data to estimate the risk of low doses in people involves (to oversimplify matters) two difficult steps, the comparison of carcinogenic potency in animal and man and the extrapolation from a high dose to a low dose. Because both steps require a certain amount of theory, they are controversial. Indeed, there are those who regard the uncertainty as so great that they prefer not to provide numerical estimates of risk, although they may order materials in carcinogenic potency. The difference between this and providing a numerical estimate is important, but is one of presentation rather than substance.

Risk Value Versus Certainty of Information

After risks of a number of situations have been assessed, we often want to order them in order to decide which should command our attention. It is not always the order of increasing risk that is used for such purposes. There have been proposals to order potential carcinogens on other factors, such as the certainty of information.

We can compare this with the possible cancer incidence that was predicted by the Food and Drug Administration (FDA) in 1977 from use of saccharin. This was based on experiments with rats, leading to an additional uncertainty. More people ate saccharin than were exposed to vinyl chloride, and nearly 500 cancers per year were estimated for the United States alone. For vinyl chloride we therefore have the situation that the individual risk is now low, yet there is considerable certainty that there is a risk. For saccharin the risk is higher, but there is more uncertainty about the value of the risk. Some persons, in some situations, may demand that more attention be given to the risk from vinyl chloride than to the risk from saccharin; for other persons or situations the reverse may be the case.

Comparison of Risks

The purpose of risk assessment is to be useful in making decisions about the hazards causing risks, and so it is important to gain some perspective about the meaning of the magnitude of the risk. Comparisons can be useful. We are not born with an instinctive feeling for what a risk of one in a million per lifetime means, although we do learn that some risks are small and others large. It is particularly helpful to compare risks that are calculated in a similar way. For example, the risk of traveling by automobile can be compared to that of traveling by horse with the use of historical data.

Contrasting Risks

Objections have been raised to risk comparison on the ground that they are misleading. This would be true if all risks of the same numerical magnitude were treated in the same way. But they are not. In some cases it is useful to contrast risks to indicate different ways in which they are treated in society.

The small risk of a large accident in a nuclear power plant can also be contrasted with the more numerous small accidents or events that occur every day in the mining, transport, and burning of coal. One feature that is brought out clearly here is that we do not always compare the risk averaged over time, but worry more about risks that are sharply peaked in time.

Expression of Risks

It is important to realize that risks appear to be very different when expressed in different ways. One example of this can be seen if we consider the cancer risk to those persons exposed to radionuclides after the Chernobyl disaster. According to the Soviets, the 24,000 persons between 3 and 15 kilometers from the plant, but excluding the town of Pripyat, received and are expected to receive 1.05 million man-rems total integrated dose, or about 44 rems average. Even if we assume a linear dose-response relation, with 8000 man-rems per cancer, the risk may be expressed in different ways. Dividing 1.05 million man-rems by 8000 gives 131 cancers expected in the lifetime of that population. This is larger than, and for some people more alarming than, the 31 people within the power plant itself who died within 60 days of acute radiation sickness combined with burns. Dividing the 131 again by the approximately 5000 cancer deaths expected from other causes, the accident caused "only" a 2.6% increase in cancer. This seems small compared to the 30% of cancers attributable to cigarette smoking. The difference is even more striking if we consider the 75 million people in Byelorussia and the Ukraine who received and will receive 29 million man-rems over their lifetimes. On the line as dose-response relation this leads to 3500 "extra cancers" surely a large number for one accident. But dividing by the 15 million cancers expected in this population leads to an "insignificant" increase of 0.004%. Of course, none of the methods of expressing the risk can be considered "right" in an absolute sense. Indeed, it is our belief that a full understanding of the risk involves expressing it in as many different ways as possible.

Cost of Reducing a Risk

Another interesting and instructive way of comparing risks is by comparing the amount people have paid in the past to reduce them. It might be thought that people would try to adjust their activities until the amount spent is roughly the same. Cohen has shown that the amounts spent vary by a factor of more than a million. He shows that it would be possible even for an American to save lives in Indonesia by aiding in immunization at $100 per life saved. Society is willing to spend more on environmental protection to prevent cancer (over $1 million per life) than on cures (about $50,000 per life with the high value of $200,000 for kidney dialysis raising some objections). This ratio is in rough accord with the maxim "an ounce of protection is better than a pound of cure." People are willing to spend still more on radiation protection at nuclear power plants and on waste disposal. Economists and others often argue that efficiency depends on adjusting society until the amounts spent to save lives in different situations are equalized. It seems to us that society does not work that way. People are aware of the order of magnitude of these differences, and approve of them. Nonetheless, we believe that providing this information to a decision-maker is essential for an informed decision.

2. *Risk Assessment and Risk Management*

Risk assessment is used to determine the magnitude and likelihood of the risk and to clarify the assumptions and uncertainties involved.

While assessments may help in determining what actions would not be overly restrictive or themselves harmful to either the environment or the economy, risk management is the tool used to choose the means used to reduce risks. The "management decision may involve economic, social, and political considerations and is subject to the constraints of particular statutes, which differ in the way they allow risk to be considered." Risk management helps to minimize the economic impact of risk reduction policies.

Risk assessment and risk management schemes as policymaking tools are not without critics. John Atcheson, for instance, writes, "Risk reduction . . . does not allow adequate consideration of resource conservation and patterns of development. Further it is reactive, difficult to communicate to the public, may be resource-limiting, and involves a high level of uncertainty." John Acheson, The Department of Risk Reduction or Risky Business, 21 Envtl. L. 1375 (1991).

Milton Russell and Martin Gruber recognize that assessment methods may either over- or underestimate risks. Russell and Gruber, *Risk Assessment in Environmental Policy-making,* 236 Science 4799 (1987). Nevertheless, they say these types of problems are not necessarily inherent to the process of risk assessment itself. They can be alleviated by better information and communication.

More important than the shortcomings, say the authors, are the benefits risk assessment and risk management have on the community:

> Risk-based approaches confront people with the fact that they are inevitably, as a consequence of their membership in an industrial society, exposed to risks. Public officials are understandably uncomfortable with bearing such news and most people are not comfortable with receiving it. Recent studies suggest, however, that communicating risk has become important to policymakers at the national level.
>
> Confronting risk in this way also raises disturbing questions about what kind of society we want to have and about the distribution of risk among different areas and social sectors. Such questions are as vexing ethically and as politically sensitive as the more familiar ones about the distribution of income and opportunities among our people. Much of the heat generated by the risk assessment policies described here derives from the association, perhaps barely sensed by most, between such policies and the profound issues that arise from our conflicting desires for prosperity, justice equity, and environmental quality. *Id.*

Notes and Questions

1. *Risk and negligence law.* Traditionally, issues of risk have been dealt with through tort law. However, given the nature of environmental risks, such individualized adjudication is impractical:

> Negligence law is simply inadequate to deal with these emergent problems and opportunities. Environmental pollutants are often impossible to trace to their source. Their health effects are uncertain, and their harms may not show up for years or even generations. Such uncertainty makes a finding of negligence liability unlikely, inappropriate and therefore ineffective in protecting society. Moreover, a case-by-case approach cannot match the scale of impact from pollution.

David L. Bazelon, Science and Uncertainty: A Jurist's View, 5 Harv. Envtl. L. Rev. 209, 211 (1981).

2. *Risk and technology.* Debates often take a static view of risk; that is, they fail to include future reductions in risk made possible by initially risky technology. Similarly, they often fail to include reductions in risks in some areas that are made possible by increases in risks in other areas. For a discussion of these issues, *see* Peter Huber, *Safety and the Second Best: The Hazards of Public Risk Management in the Courts,* 85 Colum. L. Rev. 277 (1985).

3. *Who takes the risk?* Who should decide to accept certain risks and prevent others? Why should a majority, which may be risk-accepting, be able to impose those risks on a minority that is risk-averse? Conversely, why should a majority that is risk-averse be able to deny the minority the benefits of potentially risky activities? Richard Abel, for example, has argued that "Each person ought to be able to control the risk to which he or she is exposed . . . no one ought to be subjected to a risk whose nature or level

is determined by another." Richard Abel, A Socialist Approach to Risk, 41 Mary. L. Rev. 695, 702 (1982).

However, is there any way around the fact that some people (be they scientists, bureaucrats, or a majority of voters) are going to decide to impose risks that others are unwilling to accept? Does this help to explain the growing phenomenon of NIMBY (Not In My Back Yard)? On these issues, *see* Daniel J. Fiorino, *Environmental Risk and Democratic Process: A Critical Review,* 14 Colum. J. Envtl. L. 501 (1989). How would this analysis apply to the transboundary shipment of hazardous and nuclear wastes for disposal and storage?

4. *Familiar risks.* The scientific approach to risk management emphasizes quantitative mortality rates. Social psychology research has found other principles that people use. Thus David Farber has argued that

> People find two other factors important to assessing risk. One is the unfamiliarity of the risk. Familiar risks are given less weight than those involving mysterious technology or esoteric scientific knowledge. The other major factor is voluntariness. The most dramatic example is cigarette smoking, which poses the most serious health risk of any known toxic substance. Cigarettes kill approximately 350,000 people per year. Nevertheless, because smoking at least appears voluntary, most people think government intervention is much less warranted than for hazardous waste sites or drinking water contamination. The result is that we spend vast sums of money dealing with relatively minute health hazards, but very little on controlling cigarettes. Yet cutting smoking in half would save more lives than every environmental statute ever passed.

Daniel A. Farber, Risk Regulation in Perspective: Reserve Mining Revisited, 21 Envtl. L. 1321, 1338-1339 (1991).

For other findings, *see* Roger G. Noll & James E. Krier, Some Implications of Cognitive Psychology for Risk Regulation, 19 J. Legal Stud. 747 (1990).

Additional Readings

For background on the history of legal attempts to deal with environmental risk, *see* Larry D. Silver, The Common Law of Environmental Risk and Some Recent Applications, 10 Harv. Envtl. L. Rev. 61 (1986). For additional reading on all aspects of risk assessment and risk management, *see* Risk: Issues in Health and Safety (1990). For a comprehensive overview of risk assessment in the U.S. Environmental Protection Agency, *see* Volume 21:4 of Environmental Law (1991).

For the problems of legislating acceptable risks, *see* Alon Rosenthal, et al., Legislating Acceptable Cancer Risk from Exposure to Toxic Chemicals, 19 Ecol. L.Q. 269 (1992) (using cancer risks as the basis for a case study, the authors set out the steps of quantitative risk analysis and argue that brightline legislation is ineffective in limiting administrative risk management discretion, since the discretion in risk assessment is so great). For a study of the relationship between environmental surprise and risk assessment, *see* Robert Kates and William Clark, Expecting the Unexpected? (Environmental Surprises) 38 Environment 6 (1996) (using Legionnaire's Disease, Bhopal, and ozone depletion as case studies).

For an overview of comparative risk assessment (CRA), *see* J. Clarence Davies, ed., Comparing Environmental Risks: Tools for Setting Government Priorities. Washington, DC: Resources for the Future, 1996 (defining the concept of comparative risk assessment and providing guidance on its application to national environmental policymaking). *See also* R. M. Perhac, Comparative Risk Assessment: Where Does the Public Fit In? 23 Science Technology and Human Values 221-241 (1998) (examining the political, normative, and epistemic rationales for public involvement in CRA). For an example of a comparative risk assessment conducted in a developing country, see Roger K. Raufer, Particulate and Lead Air Pollution Control in Cairo: Benefits Valuation and Cost-effective Control Strategies, 21 Natural Resources Forum 209-219 (Aug. 1997).

3. Risk Assessments and Environmental Impact Assessments

One instrument for assessing risk is the environmental impact statement (EIS) or environmental impact assessment (EIA), which requires an evaluation of the likely environmental effects of proposed actions and, in the United States, the discussion of alternative courses of actions and their effect on the environment.

The United States National Environmental Policy Act of 1969 set forth the now famous requirement of an environmental impact statement (EIS) for all major federal actions that significantly affect the environment. 42 U.S.C. 4332 (1988). Under this statute, federal projects must "identify and develop methods and procedures, . . . which will insure that presently unquantified environmental amenities and values may be given appropriate consideration in decisionmaking along with economic and technical considerations" (2B). The goal is to ensure that environmental effects are considered throughout the decisionmaking process and that the concerned public be able to participate in this process.

For analysis of the difficulties in assessing cumulative environmental impacts, *see* V. Alaric Sample, Assessing the Cumulative Environmental Impacts: The Case of National Forest Planning, 21 Envtl. L. 839 (1991); for articles that focus on the role of public participation in managing risks, *see* 1 Risk: Issues in Health and Safety (1990).

The European Community has issued a Directive on Environmental Assessment (87/337/EC), which requires environmental impact assessments in member countries. According to EC law, countries are to implement the Directive by adopting measures at the national level requiring environmental impact assessments. Shortly after the EC Directive was passed, the EC surveyed countries to determine whether they had in fact adopted the appropriate legislation or regulations. Many but not all countries had. For a critique of environmental impact assessments, *see* W.R. Sheate, Public Participation: The Key to Effective Environmental Assessment, 21 Environmental Policy and Law 156 (July 1991) (arguing that to maintain citizens' confidence in the governance of the environment, there should be more public input in the making of an environmental impact assessment report).

At the international level, the United Nations Environment Programme's (UNEP) Governing Council requested in 1982 that "guidelines, standards and model legislation" be developed for environmental impact assessments. This led to UNEP approval in 1987 of 13 principles of environmental impact assessment, which included notification to any other State that was significantly affected of relevant information contained in the environmental impact assessment. UNEP Report No. 9, 1987. For analysis of the UNEP principles, *see* Peter Thacher, Changing Requirements for International Information, Environmental Change and International Law 90-94 (Edith Brown Weiss ed., 1993).

Most recently, under the auspices of the United Nations Economic Commission for Europe, countries have negotiated an international agreement requiring environmental impact assessments for actions significantly affecting the environment and setting forth in considerable detail the proposed coverage of the assessments. Convention on Environmental Impact Assessment in a Transboundary Context, Feb. 25, 1991, 30 I.L.M. 800 (1990) (not yet in force as of July 1998).

Should there be an international requirement for the international community to prepare an environmental impact assessment for each international agreement negotiated that affects the environment? What problems would you foresee? What are the advantages? Would it be preferable to handle this at the national level? In the United States, the Executive Branch is to prepare an environmental assessment of international agreements that affect the environment and transmit it to the Senate along with the agreement. Usually these have been prepared after the agreement is negotiated. The Executive Branch prepared two environmental reviews regarding the North American Free Trade Agreement—one at the beginning of negotiations and one after all negotiations were finished. *See* Daniel Magraw, NAFTA and the Environment (1995) (containing excerpts from both reports).

4. Scientific Uncertainty and the Precautionary Principle

Decisions on international environmental issues must always be made in the face of some scientific uncertainty and the likelihood that our scientific understanding of the issues will change. In some cases this may mean new scientific information confirming the assessment of risk. In others, it may mean that the risks are less serious than believed or differ in kind or impact. While scientists can define risks, the decision about how to respond is, in the end, a political one. Politics plays as important a role in environmental risk management as science does in deciding what to do about a risk. *See* William Y. Brown, Environmental Leadership: The Search for Priorities and Power, 21 Envtl. L. 1413 (1991) (arguing that sociological and psychological factors complicate risk assessment but cannot be ignored).

Many scholars and diplomats argue that there is a precautionary principle emerging in international law to provide a norm to determine whether actions are justified to address a given risk. The principle appears in a number of international declarations but has never been codified. There is still no agreement on its precise content. Moreover, there is some uncertainty whether precaution is a principle or an approach. The Rio Declaration on Environment and Development refers to a "precautionary approach," rather than a principle, but does so under the caption of a principle—Principle 15. The United States has traditionally argued against recognizing precaution as a binding principle of customary international law. Does it matter whether it is regarded as a principle or an approach?

How would you define a precautionary principle? Consider the following materials.

a. The Precautionary Principle

■ UNCED AND THE EVOLUTION OF PRINCIPLES OF INTERNATIONAL ENVIRONMENTAL LAW

M.P.A. Kindall
25 John Marshall L. Rev. 19, 23-25 (1991)

"The precautionary principle" is another suggested addition to the Earth Charter. This principle addresses the problem of decision making in the face of scientific uncertainty over the effects of proposed activities on health and the environment. When should activities be permitted which could cause environmental harm, and when should they be forbidden? Most formulations of the precautionary principle attempt to analyze this question with reference to the magnitude of the harm that might occur and the probability that it will occur. Some formulations also examine the value of the proposed activity and the possibilities for getting the benefits of the activity while decreasing the risks.

The precautionary principle has been discussed and debated in many international fora over the past few years, and several formulations have been advanced. The portion of the Ministerial Declaration of the G7 1990 Houston Summit concerning climate change stated that "in the face of threats of irreversible environmental damage, lack of full scientific certainty is no excuse to postpone actions which are justified in their own right." This is a fairly limited principle; it only concerns "irreversible" harm, and the required preventative actions are painless. It only admonishes states not to use the absence of "full scientific certainty"—which never exists—as an excuse for not taking actions that already make sense for other reasons. In this formulation, the lack of significant scientific certainty about potentially catastrophic and irreversible damage could justify a refusal to take mitigating actions that had little cost, no cost, or even provided a net economic benefit.

The 1990 Bergen Declaration suffered from the same drawbacks, but was slightly stronger. It stated: "Where there are threats of serious or irreversible damage, lack of full scientific certainty should not be used as a reason for postponing measures to prevent environmental degradation." While this applies to serious harm as well as irreversible damage, and the range of requisite mitigating actions is not limited to those that make sense for other reasons, it still hinges on "full scientific certainty."

A more detailed definition of a precautionary principle was developed at the Second International Conference on the Protection of the North Sea.

> [The ministers] accept the principle of safeguarding the marine ecosystem of the North Sea by reducing pollution emissions of substances that are persistent, toxic and liable to bioaccumulate at source by the use of the best available technology and other appropriate measures. This applies especially when there is reason to assume that certain damage or harmful effects on the living resources of the sea are likely to be caused by such substances, even where there is no scientific evidence to prove a causal link between emissions and effects ("the principle of precautionary action").

This formulation focuses on a slightly different situation from that of the Houston Summit statement. In this situation, a "precautionary" approach is warranted when pollution loadings will reach levels that are "likely" to cause "damage or harmful effects," a rather lower threshold than "irreversible damage." Moreover, the real uncertainty lies not in the damage but in the causal link to emissions.

The discussions in international fora over the past few years, as the above examples indicate, have not succeeded in producing any uniform, commonly-accepted formulation of a precautionary principle. UNCED, thus, has an opportunity to build on what has been done before without being bound by it.

Not surprisingly, the proposals for a "precautionary principle" that have been advanced in the UNCED preparatory process echo some of the debates that have been generated in other fora on the topic. The EC, for example, submitted a formulation that was similar to the compromise worked out in the Bergen declaration quoted above. Virtually all of the suggested formulations stressed an element that was not highlighted in many prior discussions of the principle: the need for comprehensive assessments of environmental impacts. Several submissions also listed the need to notify potentially affected parties of proposed development activities. On the more substantive issues, however, there was little consensus in the submissions.

. . . At the risk of adding yet another voice to an already cacophonous debate, I suggest that any precautionary approach include the following elements:

(1) The environmental impacts of human actions on the environment are frequently unknown; scientific debate and uncertainty are the rule rather than the exception.
(2) Steps should be taken to analyze the environmental impacts of proposed actions and notify potentially affected parties. The comprehensiveness of such an analysis should depend upon the magnitude of the proposed action.
(3) Efforts should be taken to prevent or minimize pollution and reduce risks of environmental harm through clean technologies and good management practices.
(4) To the extent that the risks of environmental harm from proposed activities cannot be eliminated or reduced:
    (a) the activities should not be permitted where there is a significant risk of serious or irreversible damage to the environment; in such cases, our obligation to protect our patrimony for present and future generations requires such an outcome;
    (b) where there is no significant risk of serious or irreversible harm to health or the environment, the benefits from such activities should be weighed against the potential environmental damage, considering both the likelihood and magnitude of the damage;
    (c) where activities are permitted, appropriate steps should be taken to mitigate anticipated environmental harm.

Addressing these points would make for a fairly detailed "principle." Arguably, what is described is an approach rather than a principle per se. No simple formulation of a precautionary principle, however, would be likely to address adequately the tension between the need for development and the uncertainties of its consequences.

b. The Bergen Declaration

In May 1990, the conference on Sustainable Development, Science and Policy, organized primarily by the Norwegian Research Council for Science and the Humanities, observed that

> Where the environmental changes are *global* in scale, *irreversible,* and *transgenerational,* anticipatory assessments aimed at *narrowing uncertainties* and estimating types and magnitudes of effects are particularly needed. In such cases, early intervention by policy-makers may be crucial to prevent costly harms.

Norwegian Research Council for Science and the Humanities, Sustainable Development, Science and Policy: The Conference Report 33 (1990).

c. The 1992 Rio Declaration on Environment and Development

> **Principle 15**
>
> In order to protect the environment, the precautionary approach shall be widely applied by States according to their capabilities. Where there are threats of serious or irreversible damage, lack of full scientific certainty shall not be used as a reason for postponing cost-effective measures to prevent environmental degradation.

d. The 1996 Protocol to the London Convention of 1972

In November 1996, parties to the 1992 London Convention on the Prevention of Marine Pollution by Dumping of Wastes and Other Matter adopted a protocol to the convention, which will replace the 1972 Convention when it goes into effect. The 1996 Protocol provides in Article 3, General Obligations, that in implementing the protocol,

> Contracting Parties shall apply a precautionary approach to environmental protection from dumping of wastes or other matter whereby appropriate preventative measures are taken when there is reason to believe that wastes or other matter introduced into the marine environment are likely to cause harm even when there is no conclusive evidence to provide a causal relation between inputs and their effects.

1996 Protocol to the 1972 Convention on the Prevention of Marine Pollution by Dumping of Wastes and Other Matter, 36 I.L.M. 1 (1997).

Notes and Questions

1. *The precautionary principle and United States environmental law.* Can you argue that United States environmental law is a prime example of the implementation of a precautionary principle, or approach?

2. *Ozone depletion, climate change and the precautionary principle.* How

would you apply a precautionary principle to the problems of climate change and ozone depletion?

Consider two current problems in the management of global environmental risks: the depletion of the ozone layer from human made chemicals and global climate change. As you read the materials in the chapters coming up, ask yourself whether it is possible to develop a principle in international law to guide decisionmakers in addressing these problems. Keep in mind that the option of "no action" is just as much a decision as the option of "action." Decisions both for action and inaction as to risk share the potential to profoundly affect the global environment.

3. *The precautionary principle.* The precautionary approach/principle is developed in further detail in Chapter 7. For further analysis of the precautionary principle, *see* Daniel Bodansky, Scientific Uncertainty and the Precautionary Principle, 33 Environment 4 (1991) (providing a critical analysis) and James Cameron & Jacob D. Werksman, The Precautionary Principle: A Policy for Action in the Face of Uncertainty (paper presented at the Centre for International Environmental Law, Kings College, London, Jan. 1991). *See also* Interpreting the Precautionary Principle (Timothy O'Riordan & James Cameron, eds. 1994) (providing a history of the precautionary principle and analyses of its scientific, management, and international implications, and arguing that the precautionary principle will not explode onto the stage of environmental policymaking internationally but rather will seep through political consciousness gradually if the tide of the times so permits).

B. CLIMATE CHANGE AS A CASE STUDY FOR RISK ASSESSMENT

Both the problems of depletion of the ozone layer by human made chemicals and of climate change caused by human activities raise important problems in long-term risk assessment and management. In both cases countries have had to consider what actions to take in the face of scientific uncertainty about potentially serious risks of irreversible harm to present and future generations.

The materials here focus on climate change, but as you read the chapter on ozone depletion, you should reconsider the materials in this chapter.

1. *Conference at Villach, Austria*

One of the earliest examples of assessment of the risks posed by climate change came out of a conference in Villach, Austria, on the role of carbon dioxide and other greenhouse gases. The 1985 conference was sponsored jointly by the International Council of Scientific Unions, the World Meteorological Organization, and the United Nations Development Programme. Excerpts from the Conference Statement follow.

■ CONFERENCE STATEMENT: INTERNATIONAL ASSESSMENT OF THE ROLE OF CARBON DIOXIDE AND OF OTHER GREENHOUSE GASES IN CLIMATE VARIATIONS AND ASSOCIATED IMPACTS

Sponsored by UNEP/WMO/ISCU
Villach, Austria, Oct. 9-15, 1985

A joint UNEP/WMO/ISCU Conference was convened in Villach (Austria) from 9 to 15 October 1985, with scientists from twenty-nine developed and developing countries to assess the role of increased carbon dioxide and other radiatively active constituents of the atmosphere (collectively known as greenhouse gases and aerosols) on climate changes and associated impacts. The other greenhouse gases reinforce and accelerate the impact due to CO_2 alone. As a result of the increasing concentrations of greenhouse gases, it is now believed that in the first half of the next century a rise of global mean temperature could occur which is greater than any in man's history.

- The amounts of some trace gases in the troposphere, notably carbon dioxide (CO_2), nitrous oxide (N_2O), methane (CH_4), ozone (O_3) and chloro-fluorocarbons (CFC) are increasing.
- The role of greenhouse gases other than CO_2 in changing the climate is already about as important as that of CO_2. If present trends continue, the combined concentrations of atmospheric CO_2, and other greenhouse gases would be radiatively equivalent to a doubling of CO_2 from pre-industrial levels possibly as early as the 2030's.
- The most advanced experiments with general circulation models of the climatic system show increases of the global mean equilibrium surface temperature for a doubling of the atmospheric CO_2 concentration, or equivalent, of between 1.5 and 4.5 degrees C. Because of the complexity of the climatic system and the imperfections of the models, particularly with respect to ocean-atmosphere interactions and clouds, values outside this range cannot be excluded.
- While other factors such as aerosol concentrations, changes in solar energy input, and changes in vegetation may also influence climate,

the greenhouse gases are likely to be the most important cause of climate change over the next century.

- Regional scale changes in climate have not yet been modeled with confidence.
- It is estimated on the basis of observed changes since the beginning of this century, that global warming of 1.5 degrees C to 4.5 degrees C would lead to a sea-level rise of 20-140 centimeters. A sea level rise in the upper portion of this range would have major direct effects on coastal areas and estuaries.
- Based on analyses of observational data, the estimated increase in global mean temperature during the last one hundred years of between 0.3 and 0.7 degree C is consistent with the projected temperature increase attributable to the observed increase in CO_2 and other greenhouse gas, although it cannot be ascribed in a scientifically rigorous manner to these factors alone.
- Based on evidence of effects of past climatic changes, there is little doubt that a future change in climate of the order of magnitude obtained from climate models for a doubling of the atmospheric CO_2 concentration could have profound effects on global ecosystems, agriculture, water resources and sea ice.

2. *Intergovernmental Panel on Climate Change*

In response to the growing concern about climate change, countries formed an intergovernmental body to address the risk of climate change, which was called the Intergovernmental Panel on Climate Change, or IPCC. The IPCC drew upon the programs of the World Meteorological Organization and the United Nations Environment Programme and more than 350 scientists worldwide.

In November 1988, the first meeting of the International Panel on Climate Change took place in Geneva to address the global concerns caused by greenhouse gases. The official objectives set out the goals of "assess[ing] the scientific information . . . that is needed to enable the environmental and socio-economic consequences of climate change to be evaluated . . . [and] formulat[ing] realistic response strategies for the management of the climate change issue." Introduction, Formulation of Response Strategies, Report Prepared for IPCC by Working Group III, June 1990, at 1.

The panel was composed of three working groups: Working Group I on a scientific assessment of climate change; Working Group II on assessment of the social, economic, and environmental impacts of climate change; and Working Group III on proposed response strategies.

The Intergovernmental Panel on Climate Change reached its conclusions after several years of often heated deliberations. On the basis of the report, countries agreed to open negotiations for a convention to address climate change.

The IPCC approved new reports from each of the three working groups again in 1995. The report, prepared by Working Group I on the science of climate change, noted that the anthropogenic influences climate, in particular by including the effects of sulphate aerosols into the calculations. The IPCC noted that as of 1995, "the balance of evidence suggests that there is a discernible human influence under global climate" and observed that the available evidence suggested that the twentieth century "global mean temperature is at least as warm as any other century since at least 1400 A.D." The 1995 report concluded that under different scenarios the estimate of global mean surface air temperature relative to 1990 ranged from 1 degree to 3.5 degrees centigrade by the year 2100. Temperature changes would continue to increase after 2100, even if greenhouse gas concentrations were stabilized by the year 2100. IPCC, Climate Change 1995, 5-6 (WMO, UNEP, 1996). The report of Working Group I was compiled by 78 lead authors from 20 countries, with input from over 900 contributing authors and reviewers from over 40 countries. The Working Group approved in detail the summary of the lengthy report at a November 1995 meeting in Madrid, Spain.

Notes and Questions

1. *The risk assessment triangle.* Why should a group composed of governmental representatives decide scientific issues? Doesn't this politicize the risk assessment?

Is it possible in such a group to ensure that the assumptions and data are scientifically credible? How can you adequately consider and reflect the range of risks reflected in the scientific literature?

On the other hand, will governments be willing to rely on scientific assessments that they have not had a chance to participate in collectively? Are there advantages to the IPCC process for the negotiation and implementation of international agreements?

The traditional view of the relationship of science to policy and to legal instruments is that there is a bilateral relationship between government and scientists. Governments consult scientists, and scientists inform governments. But some argue that the correct metaphor is triangular, with scientists informing the public as well as government, and the public conveying science to governments (through parliaments and Congress) as well as having input into scientific deliberations. What difference does this triangular model make for the drafting and implementation of international environmental agreements and other legal instruments? To what extent does it depend on a political system in which people are used to having a voice?

2. *The climate change convention.* In May 1992, countries concluded a

climate change convention. While the convention establishes a framework for countries to develop policies to limit greenhouse gases, it does not explicitly set targets for reducing any greenhouse gas by a specific date. It provides for a body to review available scientific information on global warming and the impacts of climate changes and to inform the parties so that they may take appropriate actions. It also provides for the development of national inventories of greenhouse gases and strategies to control greenhouse gas emissions. In December 1997, parties negotiated the Kyoto Protocol, which limits emissions of six greenhouse gases for industrialized countries. For more details, see Chapter 12, Global Climate Change.

C. SCIENTIFIC CHANGE AND INTERNATIONAL AGREEMENTS

Our scientific understanding of environmental issues is always changing. Lawyers face the problem of drafting international agreements that will be sufficiently flexible to enable the parties to respond to changes in scientific knowledge. Consider the devices countries have developed to address this issue. Can you think of others?

One technique is the use of a framework agreement to which protocols and annexes may subsequently be negotiated as scientific understanding advances or political consensus is reached. These include the Montreal Protocol on Substances That Deplete the Ozone Layer to the Vienna Convention on Protecting the Ozone Layer; the protocols on sulphur emissions, nitrogen oxides, volatile organic compounds, heavy metals, and persistent pollutants to the Convention on Long Range Transboundary Air Pollution; the annexes to the Great Lakes Water Quality Agreement; the annex to the Convention on the Conservation of Antarctic Seals; and the protocols to many of the regional seas conventions.

International agreements also use appendices or lists attached to the agreement to indicate specifically which substances or activities may be subject to the agreement. In some instances the appendices set forth scientific criteria for placing items on the list. These agreements include the Great Lakes Water Quality Agreement between Canada and the United States, which lists hazardous and potentially hazardous pollutants in appendices; the London Ocean Dumping Convention; the Rhine Convention Against Pollution by Chlorides; the Convention on the Conservation of Migratory Species of Wild Animals; and the Convention on International Trade in Endangered Species of Wild Fauna and Flora.

One of the most promising approaches is the use of scientific advisory boards that are established as part of the conventions. These boards are usually authorized to advise on issues relevant to implementing the conventions. For example, the Migratory Species Scientific Council, attached to the Convention on the Conservation of Migratory Species of Wild Animals, is to provide scientific advice to the parties, recommend and evaluate relevant research, recommend migratory species for inclusion in the agreement, and suggest conservation measures. Similarly, the Great Lakes Water Quality Agreement establishes a Science Advisory Board to assist the Water Quality Board and members of the International Joint Commission and ultimately the parties in implementing the Agreement. The Environmental Protocol to the Antarctic Treaty, the Convention on the Conservation of Antarctic Marine Living Resources, and the Convention for the Conservation of Antarctic Seals also establish scientific advisory bodies. *See* Edith Brown Weiss, Climate Change, Intergenerational Equity and International Law: An Introductory Note, 15 Climatic Change 327, 333 (1989).

The early international environmental agreements did not have, however, any special processes for adjusting to changes in the scientific understanding of the problem.

> Even if there were schedules attached to the agreements, they could be amended only by the traditional process of establishing a negotiating forum, agreeing upon the changes, adopting them, and then obtaining the number of ratifications required by the treaty for them to enter into force. This traditional procedure has proved to be too cumbersome to address rapid scientific advances. Later agreements have eased the process by providing for periodic meeting of the parties, for the formulation of technical changes by experts or international secretariats subject to confirmation by the parties, and entry into force by agreement of the parties without ratification.

Edith Brown Weiss, International Environmental Law: Contemporary Issues and the Emergence of a New World Order, 91 Georgetown L.J. 688-689 (1993).

The Montreal Protocol offers an excellent example of countries consciously trying to negotiate an agreement that would enable them to respond flexibly to new scientific evidence. It calls for regular meetings of the parties, more flexible procedures for adjusting the phase out of chemicals on the controlled list than the amendment procedures required to list new ones, and regular technical assessments to be provided to the parties.

The protocol provides in Article 6 that

> [b]eginning in 1990, and at least every four years thereafter, the parties shall assess the control measures provided for in Article 2 on the basis of available scientific, environmental, technical and economic information. At least one year before each assessment, the parties shall convene appropriate panels of experts qualified in the fields mentioned and determine the composition and terms of reference of any such panels. Within one year of being convened, the panels will report their conclusions, through the secretariat, to the parties.

Article 9 provides that

> (a) Based on the assessment pursuant to Article 6, the parties may decide whether:
>
> (i) adjustments to the ozone-depleting potentials specified in Annex A and/or Annex B should be made and, if so, what the adjustments should be; and
>
> (ii) further adjustments and reductions of production or consumption of the controlled substances should be undertaken and, if so, what the scope, amount and timing of any such adjustment and reductions should be.
>
> (b) Proposals for such adjustments shall be communicated to the Parties by the secretariat at least six months before the meeting of the Parties at which they are proposed for adoption.
>
> (c) In taking such decisions, the parties shall make every effort to reach agreement by consensus. If all efforts at consensus have been exhausted, and no agreement reached, such decisions shall, as a last resort, be adopted by a two-thirds majority vote of the parties present and voting representing a majority of the parties operating under Article 5(1) present and voting and a majority of the parties not so operating present and voting.
>
> (d) The decisions, which shall be binding on all parties, shall forthwith be communicated to the parties by the Depositary. Unless otherwise provided in the decisions, they shall enter into force on the expiry of six months from the date of the circulation of the communication by the Depositary.

Montreal Protocol on Substance that Deplete the Ozone Layer, Done at Montreal on 16 September 1987, *reprinted in* 26 I.L.M. 1150 (1987).

D. RISKS AND DEVELOPING COUNTRIES

Developing countries, faced with the need to provide shelter, food, and potable water to their populations, may assess risks differently from wealthier countries. Some risks, such as ozone depletion or climate change, may seem less pressing than more immediate risks of disease and starvation. This in turn affects the willingness of countries to enter into international environmental accords and their ability to implement them.

The economic structure of the economy may also significantly affect the prioritization of risks. In many developing countries the reliance on one product, industry, or small group of investors will affect the government's willingness to give priority to stopping environmental damage caused by it.

A number of factors may exacerbate risks in countries. High population densities may result in either a higher probability of harm or a greater severity of harm from environmental accidents. In Bhopal, India, for example, the gas that escaped from the Union Carbide plant killed more citizens than if it had been located in a less populous area. For a short treatment of various views of the risks posed by population growth, *see* Ronald G. Ridkeer, Population Issues, in Global Development and the Environment 7-14 (Joel Darmstadter, ed. 1992).

Similarly, financial problems along with lower levels of training among the workforce may make probabilities of harm greater for threats which are easily controlled by technologies widely available in a wealthier economy. The risks from an industrial accident, for instance, could be much greater in a country that relied upon technical experts to arrive from distant countries to minimize immediate damage than in one where the experts lived within a short distance and could be on hand in case of problems.

What effects should these factors have in the formulation and implementation of international legal principles that address risk? *See also* Roger Kasperson, et al., The Social Amplification of Risk: A Conceptual Framework, 8 Risk Analysis 177 (1988) (discussing impact of culture on risk perception).

V

A Short Course on the International Legal System

The possibilities and limitations of international environmental law and institutions as a means of helping resolve environmental problems can be understood only in the context of the international legal system considered as a whole. The fundamental charateristics of that system apply, of course, to the part of it that is environmental; and norms often apply across all of international law, so that their application to environmental issues must be consistent with their application to nonenvironmental issues. Discerning the precise meaning of international environmental norms—even those in treaties—may require recourse to other aspects of public or even private international law. In addition, the functioning of international environmental institutions is determined at least in part by the general international law principles relating to international organizations. It is thus clear that a competent international environmental lawyer must possess a knowledge of the fundamentals of public international law and insitutions.

This chapter is designed to provide an introduction to these fundamentals for those who have not yet studied them, utilizing examples relating to environmental issues. Because of the richness and bulk of these topics, which are covered in a course of three or more units in a typical United States law school, we have taken an approach somewhat different from that used in most other chapters of the coursebook. The primary material in this chapter consists of text written specifically for this book, interspersed with selected excerpts of cases and other readings, plus Notes and Questions.

The international legal system governs the interaction of nation-states, of which nearly 200 exist at the end of the twentieth century. Though precursors of such a system can be found as far back as the reach of recorded history, for example, in respect to the states in classic Greece and the Hindu states of ancient India, the current system originated in eighteenth century Europe.

After a relatively long static period, the international legal system has recently, especially since the end of World War II, seen rapid evolution. In particular, the system has been broadened to (1) include states all over the world, including many that only recently achieved independence; (2) regulate the rights and obligations of actors other than states, such as international organizations, transnational corporations, and even individuals; and (3) cover new fields of activities such as those in space, new concerns such as those for the protection of the environment, and even old ones that previously had been considered to be exclusively domestic, such as human rights. Finally, while through the end of the nineteenth century relations between and among states were for the most part direct, in recent years these increasingly take place within, or are mediated by, international intergovernmental organizations (IGOs).

The international legal system can to some extent be analogized to the domestic legal system of a state, though in doing so one must be conscious of important differences. In particular, the international legal system, for most purposes, does not have a lawmaking authority to promulgate international norms of the type common to domestic legal systems, there is no overarching adjudicative body with compulsory and binding jurisdiction to settle disputes regarding alleged violations of international law, and there is no centralized enforcement authority to enforce international law. On the other hand, there are international laws or norms, as well as an international normmaking or legislative process, which are examined in section A below; there are processes for avoiding and, if necessary, resolving international disputes, examined in section B; and there are, albeit only rudimentary and generally very weak, devices to further compliance with international norms, examined in section C. These quasi-legislative, judicial and quasi-judicial, and quasi-executive functions are increasingly being carried out by IGOs—and these are described below in section D. Although these examinations and description are in part general in nature, they focus as much as possible on norms, processes, and institutions relevant to the protection of the environment.

Finally, it should be noted that it is somewhat of a misnomer to speak of *an* international legal system. Instead, it is necessary to recognize that there are a number of different systems, which have at best a partially hierarchical relationship. Thus there is a universal system, for the most part within or related to the United Nations (UN). This chapter largely concentrates on this system. However, there are also regional systems (such as those of Africa and the Americas, and several overlapping ones in Europe), subregional ones (such as those of Central America, the Caribbean, the Nordic states, Sub-Saharan Africa, the ASEAN states, etc.), and bilateral ones. There are also systems and corresponding IGOs that are primarily economic or functional (e.g., the International Whaling Commission) or political rather than geographically based.

A. INTERNATIONAL LAW

1. *General Considerations*

International law is the set of norms that governs the interaction between nation-states. As is described at greater length below, international law is largely if not exclusively made by states and reflects their will and consent. However, the obligations and rights set out in that law govern not only those states but also the establishment and functioning of international governmental and non-governmental organizations and, to a lesser extent and usually only mediately through the states of their nationality, corporations and individuals.

As pointed out above in connection with the international legal system, international law may be worldwide (also referred to as "general" or "universal"), regional, subregional, restricted multilateral, or bilateral. Because the international system is hierarchical only to a most limited extent, it cannot be assumed that norms of a broader scope necessarily supersede or govern those of a lesser scope. It is for each state to see to it that new norms it consents to will not be inconsistent with a previous one by which it is bound and which it cannot change.

As is true of domestic or "municipal" law (as the internal law of states is called in international law), there are many different types of international law—but these generally do not correspond to the various forms of domestic law. The most important of these types are listed in Article 38(1) of the Statute of the International Court of Justice (ICJ or World Court). However, that listing was established over 75 years ago (for the predecessor of the ICJ), and it is generally recognized that it is no longer complete. Full agreement as to the components of such a list does not currently exist. The following types of law are described and characterized below: (1) customary law; (2) international agreements, herein referred to as "treaties" but which also have many other names such as conventions (hence the term "conventional law"); (3) general principles of law; (4) international administrative law; and (5) "soft law."

There are various means of establishing or determining the existence of international law, some of which are also listed in Article 38(1) of the Statute ICJ. These means include the decisions of intergovernmental organizations (IGO) organs; judicial decisions; and the teachings of recognized publicists.

The diverse types of international law that have just been mentioned can be characterized in several overlapping ways:

(1) Some types of international law can be found in black-letter form, i.e., as written texts (in particular, treaties and many forms of soft law, such as decisions of IGO organs and certain rules, guidelines, etc. generated by them), while others have no precise, definitive statements (such as customary law and general principles). This distinction resembles that in domestic law between, on the one hand, statutes and regulations and, on the other, judge-made common law.

(2) Some legal obligations, particularly those originating in certain types of treaties, are merely reciprocal—i.e., they exist between pairs of states (e.g., the parties to bilateral agreements or to certain types of multilateral agreements that basically establish networks of bilateral relationships, such as those concerning trade or diplomacy). Other legal obligations are characterized as *erga omnes,* i.e., they run from states bound by these obligations to all other states or rather to the world (or the regional) community as a whole. Although certain environmental norms, such as those relating to a particular river that flows along or through a boundary between two states, fall into the first category, those environmental obligations that relate to a global commons (such as the high seas or Antarctica) are *erga omnes. See* Chapter 6, sec. D.2.c., below.

(3) Although the creation of international law depends on the will and sometimes on the continuing consent of states, it is increasingly recognized that certain norms—usually of customary law but also some deriving from important treaties like the UN Charter or even from general principles—may have or gradually acquire such a compelling and universal respect that states cannot be permitted to change or supersede them by treaty or otherwise. These are called preemptory norms or *jus cogens*[1]. It should be noted that while by no means all *erga omnes* norms are also *jus cogens,* normally all *jus cogens* norms are likely to function *erga omnes.* In the absence of any definitive list of preemptory international norms, it is difficult to say whether any environment-related norms may at present be considered as falling into this category, but it seems likely that as this field matures and gains in generally recognized importance, certain of these norms will soon be characterized as *jus cogens.*

1. *See* Articles 53, 64, and 71 of the 1969 Vienna Convention on the Law of Treaties, May 23, 1969, 1155 U.N.T.S. 331, 8 I.L.M. 679 (1969).

(4) Some types of international law, in particular customary law, treaties, and general principles of law, are binding on those states subject to them, and are therefore referred to as "hard law." Other statements—including political commitments—are at most hortatory or partially compelling. These are sometimes therefore characterized as "soft law." As is explained below, the characterization of even certain nonbinding statements as "law" arguably can be justified by the fact that states actually do largely conform to them.

2. *Customary Law*

Customary international law consists of the set of norms derived from the actual practice of states undertaken by these states in the belief that such practices are required by international law. To identify such norms it is therefore necessary to study how states (i.e., their official organs, which include executive, legislative, and judicial ones) actually behave. Although it is not necessary to document the practice of *all* states, a customary norm is one that can be shown to be generally followed (worldwide in respect to universal customary law, or regionally or subregionally in respect to geographically restricted customary law) by the states concerned. It can be seen that this is no easy task and not one that is likely to result in unambiguous formulations. Consequently, to the extent that a senior court (in particular the World Court) or some other tribunal determines the existence (or not) of some alleged customary norm, such determinations may constitute persuasive evidence for the existence of the norm. Similar effect may be attributed to a determination by a group of recognized legal scholars (such as the members of the International Law Commission (ILC), who are elected by the UN General Assembly) of the existence of a norm or sometimes to a statement of a senior IGO organ (such as the UN General Assembly).

It should be noted that in order to establish the normative nature of a practice it is necessary to determine that it is based on a belief by the state organs concerned that such is required by international law—i.e., that it is not merely a normal courtesy, a clearly advantageous act, or a means of seeking favor, creating good will, or escaping a threat. This requirement is called *opinio juris* [*sive necessitatis*]. *Opinio juris* often is not easy to establish strictly because the motivations for particular state actions are by no means always clear, though an action against a state's interest can be assumed to be motivated by a perception of legal obligation.

Though customary international law is therefore normally created by unconscious and inchoate processes that persuade states generally that they should behave in a particular way, there are devices—whether used deliberately or not—to induce states to consider that acting in a particular way is legally required. These include resolutions of senior IGO organs encouraging such behavior, particularly if these suggest that there is a legal requirement. The adoption of multilateral treaties may also have such an effect even before they have entered into force, either in anticipation or because states may consider that such treaties largely codify preexisting international law. Finally, the creation of soft law, which, though technically nonbinding, may still induce states to act in the indicated mode in the belief that such action is at least legally desirable.

As indicated above, in order for customary law to come into being, it is necessary that the norm in question be generally observed by states; but it is unnecessary, and in many instances impractical, to establish compliance by all the states concerned (whether of all countries in the world or those of a particular region or subregion). Once it comes into being, a customary law norm is binding on all states concerned. However, a state may, by persistently and from the beginning objecting to the norm (and not observing it), exempt itself from being bound by it. Of course, if there are too many such "persistent objectors," then the norm does not become binding as part of customary law.

An important customary norm, relevant but not peculiar to environmental law, is that every state may use its territory and carry out activities thereon as it wishes, but only to the extent that no harm is caused thereby to other states.[2]

Historically the oldest source of general international law (as distinguished from the particular international law created by two parties to a bilateral international treaty), customary law is rapidly being superseded in importance by the massive quantities of blackletter law being created by the lawmaking multilateral treaties discussed immediately below.

Notes and Questions

1. How does one determine whether (and when) a practice has become customary international law? The *North Sea Continental Shelf Cases*, 1969 I.C.J. Reports 3, involved the Federal Republic of Germany's claim against Denmark and the Netherlands for a boundary delimitation of the continental shelf. The ICJ was faced with the issue of what principles and rules of international law it should apply in delimiting the boundaries between these opposite and adjacent states. Denmark and the Netherlands argued that the "equidistance-special circumstances" principles in Article 6(2) of the 1958 Geneva Convention on the Continental Shelf applied. The concave nature of the coastline shared by the three countries—with Germany in

2. *See* Principle 21 of the Stockholm Declaration of the 1972 UN Conference on the Human Environment, 11 I.L.M. 1416 (1972), and Principle 2 of the Rio Declaration of the 1992 UN Conference on Environment and Development, 31 I.L.M. 874 (1992).

the middle—meant that the application of this principle would render to Germany a much smaller portion of the continental shelf than it would receive by the application of other delimitation rules. Accordingly, Germany opposed the application of this rule, partly on the ground that it was not then a party to the Geneva Convention. It also opposed the Danish and Dutch contentions that the equidistance rule was customary international law at the time of the Convention, was "crystallized" as a rule of customary international law by the process of creating the Convention, or had come to be regarded as a rule of customary international law since the Convention. The following excerpt focuses on the latter question:

> 70. The Court must now proceed to the next stage in the argument put forward on behalf of Denmark and the Netherlands. This is to the effect that even if there was at the date of the Geneva Convention no rule of customary international law in favour of the equidistance principle, and no such rule was crystallized in Article 6 of the Convention, nevertheless such a rule has come into being since the Convention, partly because of its own impact, partly on the basis of subsequent State practice,—and that this rule, being now a rule of customary international law binding on all States, including therefore the Federal Republic, should be declared applicable to the delimitation of the boundaries between the Parties' respective continental shelf areas in the North Sea.
>
> 71. In so far as this contention is based on the view that Article 6 of the Convention has had the influence, and has produced the effect described, it clearly involves treating that Article as a norm-creating provision which has constituted the foundation of, or has generated a rule which, while only conventional or contractual in its origin, has since passed into the general *corpus* of international law, and is now accepted as such by the *opinio juris*, so as to have become binding even for countries which have never, and do not, become parties to the Convention. There is no doubt that this process is a perfectly possible one and does from time to time occur: it constitutes indeed one of the recognized methods by which new rules of customary international law may be formed. At the same time this result is not lightly to be regarded as having been attained. . . .
>
> 72. The Court must now consider whether State practice in the matter of continental shelf delimitation has, subsequent to the Geneva Convention, been of such a kind as to satisfy this requirement. Leaving aside cases which, for various reasons, the Court does not consider to be reliable guides as precedents, such as delimitations effected between the present Parties themselves, or not relating to international boundaries, some 15 cases have been cited in the course of the present proceedings, occurring mostly since the signature of the 1958 Geneva Convention, in which continental shelf boundaries have been delimited according to the equidistance principle—in the majority of the cases by agreement, in a few others unilaterally—or else the delimitation was foreshadowed but has not yet been carried out. Amongst these 15 are the four North Sea delimitations, United Kingdom/Norway-Denmark-Netherlands, and Norway/Denmark already mentioned in paragraph 4 of this Judgment. But even if these various cases constituted more

> than a very small proportion of those potentially calling for delimitation in the world as a whole, the Court would not think it necessary to enumerate or evaluate them separately, since there are, *a priori*, several grounds which deprive them of weight as precedents in the present context.
>
> 76. To begin with, over half the States concerned, whether acting unilaterally or conjointly, were or shortly became parties to the Geneva Convention, and were therefore presumably, so far as they were concerned, acting actually or potentially in the application of the Convention. From their action no inference could legitimately be drawn as to the existence of a rule of customary international law in favour of the equidistance principle. As regards those States, on the other hand, which were not, and have not become parties to the Convention, the basis of their action can only be problematical and must remain entirely speculative. Clearly, they were not applying the Convention. But from that no inference could justifiably be drawn that they believed themselves to be applying a mandatory rule of customary international law. There is not a shred of evidence that they did and . . . there is no lack of other reasons for using the equidistance method, so that acting, or agreeing to act in a certain way, does not of itself demonstrate anything of a juridical nature. . . .
>
> 81. The Court accordingly concludes that if the Geneva Convention was not in its origins or inception declaratory of a mandatory rule of customary international law enjoining the use of the equidistance principle for the delimitation of continental shelf areas between adjacent States, neither has its subsequent effect been constitutive of such a rule; and that State practice up-to-date has equally been insufficient for the purpose.

Id. at paras. 70-81, 8 I.L.M. 340, at 373-77 (1969).

From a temporal perspective, what are the possible relationships between the creation of a rule of customary international law and the finalization of a treaty that expresses the same content as is contained in the customary norm? What types of state practice did the ICJ examine, and how much did it insist on before a norm could be created?

Judge Manfred Lachs, in dissent, wrote:

> For in the world today an essential factor in the formation of a new rule of general international law is to be taken into account: namely that States with different political, economic and legal systems, States of all continents, participate in the process. No more can a general rule of international law be established by the fiat of one or of a few, or—as it was once claimed—by the consensus of European States only.
>
> [The States Parties to the Convention on the Continental Shelf] include States of all continents, among them States of various political systems, with both new and old States representing the main legal systems of the world.
>
> It may therefore be said that, from the viewpoints both of number and or representativity, the participation in the Convention constitutes a solid basis for the formation of a general rule of law. It is upon that basis that further more extensive practice has developed.

[After concluding that the principles and rules in the Convention had been accepted by sufficient states to "be viewed as evidence of a practice widespread enough to satisfy the criteria for a general rule of law," Judge Lachs continued.] Can the practice summarized be considered as having been accepted as law, having regard to the subjective element [*opinio juris*] required? The process leading to this effect is necessarily complex. There are certain areas of State activity and international law which by their very character may only with great difficulty engender general law, but there are others, both old and new, which may do so with greater ease. Where continental shelf law is concerned, some States have at first probably accepted the rules in question, as States usually do, because they found them convenient and useful, the best possible solution for the problems involved. Others may also have been convinced that the instrument elaborated within the framework of the United Nations was intended to become and would in due course become general law. . . . Many States have followed suit under the conviction that it was law.

Thus at the successive stages in the development of the rule the motives which have prompted States to accept it have varied from case to case. It could not be otherwise. At all events, to postulate that all States, even those which initiate a given practice, believe themselves to be acting under a legal obligation is to resort to a fiction—and in fact to deny the possibility of developing such rules. For the path may indeed start from voluntary, unilateral acts relying on the confident expectation that they will find acquiescence or be emulated; alternatively, the starting-point may consist of a treaty to which more and more States accede and which is followed by unilateral acceptance. It is only at a later stage that, by the combined effect of individual or joint action, response and interaction in the field concerned, i.e., of that reciprocity so essential in international legal relations, there develops the chain-reaction productive of international consensus.

. . . In sum, the practice of States should be recognized as prima facie evidence that it is accepted as law. Such evidence may, of course, be controverted—even on the test of practice itself, if it shows "much uncertainty and contradiction." . . .

What did Judge Lachs mean by "representative" state practice? What types of factors are relevant to that determination?

2. In *The Paquete Habana*, 175 U.S. 677 (1900), the United States Supreme Court was posed the question of whether fishing vessels could be seized as prizes of war under international law. In determining what was the customary international rule to be applied, the Court undertook the following examination, demonstrating the methodology courts employ:

By an ancient usage among civilized nations, beginning centuries ago, and gradually ripening into a rule of international law, coast fishing vessels, pursuing their vocation of catching and bringing in fresh fish, have been recognized as exempt, with their cargoes and crews, from capture as prize of war.

This doctrine, however, has been earnestly contested at the bar; and no complete collection of the instances illustrating it is to be found, so far as we are aware, in a single published work, although many are referred to and discussed by the writers on international law. . . .

The earliest acts of any government on the subject, mentioned in the books, either emanated from, or were approved by, a King of England. In 1403 and 1406, Henry IV issued orders to his admirals and other officers [and] he took into his safe conduct . . . the fisherman of France . . . in regard to their fishery, while sailing . . . and lawfully fishing "without molestation", [and he ordered that fisherman should not be interfered with.] The treaty made October 2, 1521, between the Emperor Charles V and Francis I of France, through their ambassadors, recited that a great and fierce war had arisen between them . . . [and] agreed that the subjects of each sovereign, fishing in the sea, could . . . without incurring any attack . . . or hindrance . . . safely and freely take herrings and every other kind of fish, the existing war by land and sea notwithstanding. The herring fishery was [also] permitted, in time of war, by French and Dutch edicts in 1536.

The doctrine which exempts coast fishermen with their vessels and cargoes from capture as prize of war has been familiar to the United States from the time of the War of Independence. On June 5, 1779, Louis XVI, our ally in that war, addressed a letter to his admiral, [giving] orders to the commanders of all his ships not to disturb English fishermen, nor to arrest their vessels laden with fresh fish, even if not caught by those vessels; provided they had no offensive arms, and were not proved to have made any signals creating a suspicion of intelligence with the enemy. . . .

Among the standing orders made by Sir James Marriott, Judge of the English High Court of Admiralty, was one of April 11, 1780, by which it was "ordered that all causes of prize of fishing boats or vessels taken from the enemy may be consolidated . . . , if under 50 tons burthen, and not more than 6 in number." Marriott's Formulary, 4. But by the statements of his successor, and of both French and English writers, it appears that England, as well as France, during the American Revolutionary War, abstained from interfering with the coast fisheries. The Young Jacob and Johanna, 1 C. Rob. 20; 2 Ortlan, 53; Hall, §148.

In the treaty of 1785 between the United States and Prussia, article 23 provided that, if war should arise between the contracting parties, "all women and children, scholars of every faculty, cultivators of the earth, artisans, manufacturers and fishermen, unarmed and inhabiting unfortified towns, villages or places, and in general all others whose occupations are for the common subsistence and benefit of mankind, shall be allowed to continue their respective employments, and shall not be molested in their persons." . . .

In the war with Mexico in 1846, the United States recognized the exemption of coast fishing boats from capture. In proof of this, counsel have referred to records of the Navy Department, which this court is clearly authorized to consult upon such a question.

International law is part of our law, and must be ascertained and administered by the courts of justice of appropriate jurisdiction, as often as questions of right depending upon it are duly presented for their determination. For

> this purpose, where there is no treaty, and no controlling executive or legislative act or judicial decision, resort must be had to the customs and usages of civilized nations; and, as evidence of these, to the works of jurists and commentators, who by years of labor, research and experience, have made themselves peculiarly well acquainted with the subjects of which they treat. Such works are resorted to by judicial tribunals, not for the speculations of their authors concerning what the law ought to be, but for trustworthy evidence of what the law really is.
>
> Wheaton places, among the principal sources of international law, "Text-writers of authority, showing what is the approved usage of nations, or the general opinion respecting their mutual conduct, with the definitions and modifications introduced by general consent." As to these he forcibly observes: "Without wishing to exaggerate the importance of these writers, or to substitute, in any case, their authority for the principles of reason, it may be affirmed that they are generally impartial in their judgment. They are witnesses of the sentiments and usages of civilized nations, and the weight of their testimony increases every time that their authority is invoked by statesmen, and every year that passes without the rules laid down in their works being impugned by the avowal of contrary principles." Wheaton's International Law, (8th ed.) §15. . . .
>
> This review of the precedents and authorities on the subject appears to us abundantly to demonstrate that at the present day, by the general consent of the civilized nations of the world, and independently of any express treaty or other public act, it is an established rule of international law. . . .
>
> This rule of international law is one which prize courts administering the law of nations are bound to take judicial notice of and to give effect to, in the absence of any treaty or other public act of their own government in relation to the matter. . . .

What kinds of state conduct did the Court look to for incidents of state practice? What did the Court consider to be evidence of the existence of norms? How did the Court deal with inconsistent state practice? What did the Court mean by the phrase, "in the absence of any . . . public act of their own government"? Why should that matter?

3. Professor Louis Sohn has written that unratified treaties may also be a source of customary international law. He states:

> The [International] Court [of Justice] is thus willing to pay attention not only to a text that has codified a pre-existing customary law but also to one that has crystallized an "emergent rule of international law." It is sufficient for that purpose to have the rule in question adopted by an international conference by consensus or . . . without a dissenting vote. Later formalities, such as signing and ratification merely add icing to the cake. What is relevant is the fact that one can observe here the primordial creative force at work. It is generally recognized that international law has only one source—the common will of States. A new rule is created by its general acceptance by all the States concerned. The States themselves are the masters of the method

> by which they agree to express their common will. If they agree that a particular rule represents a satisfactory product of "mutual accommodation, reasonableness and co-operation, they can agree in addition that they accept this rule as of that moment as binding upon them. Sometimes this second agreement is explicit, sometimes it is implicit, and its existence has to be deduced from the circumstances of the case." If most States, including almost all States having a special interest in the application of the rule, act in accordance with it, there is a clear presumption that the rule agreed upon at the conference, though the agreement has not yet been ratified, has become an accepted rule of customary international law.[3]

4. In Nicaragua v. United States (officially referred to as *Military and Paramilitary Activities in and against Nicaragua*), Merits, 1986 I.C.J. Rep. 14 (Judgment of June 27, 1986), the International Court of Justice determined, somewhat controversially, that certain multilateral treaties agreed to by the parties (e.g., the United Nations Charter) in part reflected customary international legal principles that bound the parties. Thus, even though multilateral treaties were excluded (by the United States reservation contained in its Article 36(2) acceptance of the compulsory jurisdiction of the ICJ) from consideration by the ICJ in deciding the case, the Court held it could apply such derived customary international law to the facts of the case in arriving at a judgment. The Court stated:

> [E]ven if two norms belonging to two sources of international law appear identical in content, and even if the States in question are bound by these rules both on the level of treaty-law and on that of customary international law, these norms retain a separate existence.

Id. at 95.

5. It has been said that "reciprocity is the foundation of international law." Do you agree?

3. *Treaties*

a. General

Treaties are the other great, and increasingly predominant, form of binding international law. Unlike customary law, treaties are black-letter law—whose wording, but not necessarily meaning, is clearly established. Many different terms are used to describe agreements between states or IGOs that are governed by international law, for example, treaty, convention, agreement, covenant, protocol, constitution, statute, articles of

3. Louis B. Sohn, Unratified Treaties as a Source of Customary International Law, in Realism in Law-Making: Essay on International Law in Honor of Willem Riphagen (1986).

agreement, executive agreement, memorandum of understanding, and so on. Generally speaking, that terminology does not have independent legal significance.

Originally treaties were usually bilateral instruments. There are many significant bilateral treaties that relate wholly or partially to environmental matters; for example, the many concluded between Canada and the United States relating to the boundary waters, including the Great Lakes and the St. Lawrence Seaway. Starting in the nineteenth century, and with increasing rapidity after World War II, a number of states, and often a significant fraction of all states (or of all states in a particular region), concluded multilateral treaties. Many of these treaties establish general environmental norms (such as those relating to the protection of the ozone layer or the prevention of marine pollution) or create international institutions with exclusively or at least significant environmental functions.

Because of the growing number of states (their number more than tripled from about 60 at the end of World War II to nearly 200 as of 1998) and the ever greater number, intensity, and complexity of their interactions on an increasing number of subjects, the number of treaties is constantly rising. As of 1998, there are well over 30,000, of which some 1,500 are multilaterals with a significant number of parties. The United States is a party to some 7,500 international agreements in force.

The law relating to treaties, their formulation, entry into force, effect, interpretation, revision, and termination is largely the subject of well-established customary norms. Many of these have been codified, and some have been revised, in a series of UN-sponsored treaties. The first and most important of these is the 1969 Vienna Convention on the Law of Treaties (VCLT).[4] That Convention covers all agreements between states set out in written form and governed by international law—no matter how designated. The most important rule regarding treaties is set out in Article 26 of the VCLT, which codifies preexisting customary law in requiring that the obligations under treaties must be carried out: *pacta sunt servanda.*

b. Treaty-Making

Unlike the domestic legislative process, which when completed results in an instrument (e.g., a statute) that is automatically binding on all subjects of the state, the international process has two quite different phases: an international one, by which a treaty is formulated and adopted; and a domestic one, by which each interested and qualified state decides whether or not to become a party to the treaty (and sometimes on what terms). Often the international phase precedes the domestic phase, but sometimes the two proceed concurrently. Normally a treaty does not enter into force

4. 1155 U.N.I.T.S. 331; 8 I.L.M. 679 (1969).

until the requisite number of states (specified in the treaty in question) have expressed their consent to be bound by it[5] and then only for those states that have done so.

(i) The International Process[6]

The formulation of bilateral treaties is basically a process of negotiation between the pair of states concerned. The nature and length of this process depends largely on the complexity and urgency of the subject and the substantive differences between the parties in relation thereto.

The formulation of multilateral agreements is more complicated, tending to increase in difficulty with the number of potential parties. Nowadays, this process normally takes place within or under the auspices of an IGO—ideally the one whose membership and mandate best corresponds to the scope and subject of the proposed instrument. The process also tends to follow some general patterns and, in some IGOs, special procedural rules. The general steps in this process are described in Appendix III.[7]

All steps in the formulation process include, and in many instances principally consist of, negotiations. Negotiations may start even before the first proposal concerning a treaty is publicly revealed and to some extent affects all the political decisions taken, including whether to initiate the process formally, the choice of fora, aspects of timing, and the decisions relating to the conclusion of the instrument. Negotiations may, in effect, even take place in expert organs (whose members are normally chosen by states even if they do not formally represent them) and in technical fora such as drafting committees. Moreover, the negotiations are not necessarily confined to the issue at hand, as state representatives may well engage in bargaining involving some of the thousands of other issues concurrently being considered in connection with the hundreds of items on the agendas of numerous international organs. In all this, the international legislative process fully mimics the corresponding domestic one. Moreover, negotiations may continue even after an instrument has been formally adopted, i.e., during the domestic phase and even after entry into force when changes to the treaty may be considered.

The methods of taking decisions in international bodies are diverse

5. There are several processes whereby a state may definitively signal its consent to be bound by a treaty, which may be done by: a definitive signature, not requiring any subsequent expression of consent to be bound; a signature *ad referendum,* confirmed by ratification, adoption, or approval; accession without prior signature; and in some cases, notification of succession to a previous party to a treaty. The domestic requirements for taking such steps are discussed below.

6. Appendix III, General Steps in Formulating Multilateral Agreements, contains more detail on this process.

7. The stages of the multilateral treaty-making process are described at some length by Paul C. Szasz in a chapter on The UN System as a Source of Law, in 1 United Nations Legal Order 35 (O. Schachter & C.C. Joyner, eds. 1994).

and somewhat complex. In a few international financial institutions (IFIs, such as the World Bank), votes are allocated to members roughly in accordance to their investments in or contributions to the organization. In most other IGO organs, each member (large or small, rich or poor, powerful or weak, democratic or authoritarian) is allocated one vote; substantive decisions normally require a two-thirds majority and procedural ones, a simple one. However, because that formula permits a large number of states with insignificant population and little economic or military strength to adopt decisions that are opposed by a number of powerful or otherwise significant states whose participation in a proposed treaty is essential for its proper functioning, the tendency has been to avoid formal votes at most stages of the treaty-making process. In particular, an attempt is made at all stages to achieve consensus, which normally requires achieving a sufficient measure of agreement so that no member vigorously opposes a decision. This search for consensus is likely to take longer than the resolution of issues by votes. And to some extent, it holds the process hostage to those who would impede it either to achieve a particular negotiating goal, out of fundamental opposition, merely capriciously, or sometimes in connection with some unrelated matter; through all this the process may be delayed—sometimes for years or even decades, and the resulting text is apt to be watered down to a low common denominator. On the other hand, a successful negotiation is likely to signal the willingness of most participants to become parties to the adopted treaty (which may be a requirement for it to enter into force at all) and to implement it thereafter.

Usually at a late stage in the international phase of the treaty-making process the "Final Clauses" of the proposed treaty are formulated. These may include provisions regarding the making of reservations and other options to be available to prospective parties (*see* below); which states or IGOs, such as the European Union, are eligible to become parties; any preconditions for participation (e.g., the prior adoption of relevant legislation); the formal steps to be taken by prospective parties (normally signature during a specified period—usually one year—at a specified place—usually the headquarters of the IGO), to be confirmed by ratification, approval or adoption, or accession without prior signature for states that missed the signature deadline; and conditions for entry into force (minimum number of parties and usually a time delay of some months after a sufficient number have acted).

Though many of these conditions and provisions tend to be standard, at least for a particular type of treaty (e.g., environmental or human rights), those relating to entry into force may require some substantive decisions. Some multilateral treaties (e.g., human rights) are valuable even with a minimal number of participants. Others, such as those regulating a global commons, make sense only if substantially all important users of that commons participate; otherwise the parties to the treaty restrain themselves to improve the commons, leaving more resources (e.g., fish or waste disposal sites) to be exploited by nonparties that benefit as "free riders." Also, if a significant IGO is to be established by the treaty, then it is necessary that the parties include states able and willing to bear most of the costs thereof.

(ii) The Domestic Process

Each state has its own domestic requirements and procedures for becoming a party to a treaty. In some cases this decision is taken merely by the executive. In others, one or more branches of the legislature must agree. In certain federal states, the consent of the constituent states must be obtained in respect to obligations to be carried out by the latter. Substantively, a state must examine to what extent the proposed treaty is compatible with its own legal system—e.g., are there constitutional obstacles, are there laws or regulations that must be adopted or amended—and what steps need be taken to correct any deficiencies. It must also examine to what extent the proposed treaty is compatible with its other international legal obligations, perhaps flowing from earlier treaties or from customary law, and how any possible obstacles can be overcome.

All this may require the translation of the proposed treaty and perhaps any commentary thereto into the official language(s) of the country and the preparation of reports to the executive and legislature, explaining the treaty, analyzing its advantages, costs, and other disadvantages, proposing necessary legislative or regulatory texts, and so on. These requirements are likely to strain the capacities of even well-staffed bureaucracies. They may overwhelm those of smaller or less developed states, resulting in delays or often complete inaction based not on any opposition to an instrument but merely on an inability to cope rapidly with the requirements for bringing it into force domestically.

Some IGOs are equipped or are equipping themselves to assist members in processing treaties adopted under the auspices of the particular IGO. Such assistance in many instances need merely be technical to meet the requirements listed in the previous paragraph. In other instances, technical or even material assistance may be required to enable a state to comply substantively, e.g., to carry out monitoring of particular environment-relevant factors.

(iii) Options Available to Treaty Parties

In order to facilitate the participation of states in treaties—and thus their entry into force and the broadest possible coverage—a number of indulgences or options may be offered to them.

First, and especially in respect to certain environmental treaties, their substantive obligations may be adjusted to the capacities of specified groups of states, for example, by delaying the date by which they must comply with certain requirements.[8] This is discussed further in Chapter 8, below.

States may also, in becoming parties to a treaty—though not normally later—indicate "reservations" designed to alter their obligations with respect to certain provisions of a treaty. For example, both the United States and the USSR made a reservation that they would not be bound by the mandatory dispute settlement article in the 1986 Convention on Early Notification of a Nuclear Accident.[9] The Final Clauses of a treaty should specify whether or not any reservations are "admissible" (i.e., permissible or recognizable), and, if so, which ones. If there is no such specification, the 1969 Vienna Convention on the Law of Treaties states that reservations not incompatible with the basic purpose of the treaty are admissible. The Vienna Convention also indicates how these are to be made and to what extent these change the respective treaty obligations of the reserving state and of other parties, which may or may not object to the reservation. States may use reservations in order to enable them to become parties to treaties of which they basically approve but some features of which are incompatible with provisions of their constitution or would face great resistance from domestic groups. For the same purpose, treaties may also offer parties the opportunity to exercise certain options built into the instrument (e.g., a choice of dispute settlement procedures) or of ancillary instruments (such as specialized protocols).

Finally, some treaties may offer relatively easy withdrawal provisions, so that a state may feel reassured that its acceptance of certain obligations is not irrevocable if these prove to be too onerous or if relevant conditions should change.

All the above-described devices are intended to facilitate the conclusion and entry into force of treaties by granting a certain measure of flexibility as to when, how, and to what extent states are to be bound by obligations under these instruments. The disadvantage is that they can result in a very uneven patchwork of international legal obligations. With respect to a particular treaty, some states may be parties and others not (either not having become so, or having withdrawn); some states may have made reservations, to which others may or may not have objected; and various combinations of options may have been exercised with respect to provisions of the treaty or of ancillary instruments. In this respect, the international legislative process differs significantly from the domestic one, in which all subjects automatically have the same obligations.

8. *E.g.,* Article 5 to the Montreal Protocol on Substances that Deplete the Ozone Layer, 1987, 26 I.L.M. 1550 (1987).

9. *See* Article 11 of the International Atomic Energy Agency (IAEA) Convention on Early Notification of a Nuclear Accident, 1986, 25 I.L.M. 1370 (1986).

(iv) Living Treaties

Historically, the relatively few multilateral treaties, once adopted, remained unchanged indefinitely. Often there was no urgency about changing them, and even if there was some reason to do so it was not an enterprise that could conveniently be undertaken. These treaties were adopted at *ad hoc* meetings of states rather than under the auspices of an IGO with a continuing interest in the subject, and they normally did not themselves establish any organs charged with their implementation and review. Eventually, once they became entirely obsolete, they might be superseded by a new instrument on the same subject.

In the modern fast-moving and changing world, with many treaties—particularly those in the environmental field—dealing with scientific and technical developments that either create new problems or promise novel solutions, this former rigid pattern is no longer appropriate. Nor is it necessary, because with respect to almost every significant multilateral treaty there exists a competent and concerned IGO that either participated in formulating the treaty or was established by it. However, if every change or addition requires a process comparable to that needed to formulate the treaty and to have it enter into force, then it would still be difficult to keep treaty law sufficiently up-to-date to respond to rapid developments in the real world, such as changes in scientific knowledge. Consequently, a number of devices have been developed to shortcut either the international or the domestic phase of the treaty-making process, or both, so as to facilitate changing an existing instrument. To be effective, the legal basis for these devices must normally be written into the particular treaty or alternatively into a constitutional instrument of the IGO responsible for the amending process.

These devices often differentiate among (1) substantive amendments to the basic treaty, which normally require, at least in the domestic phase, the same steps and procedures as required for the treaty itself; (2) amendments to technical provisions, especially those set out in annexes, for which often both the international and the domestic phases of the legislative process are simplified; and (3) the adoption of additional technical protocols that also may have one or both phases streamlined.

With respect to the international phase, instead of establishing an ad hoc procedure as is usually required for a new treaty instrument, the consideration of amendments and of new protocols is often automatically assigned to standing expert and/or representative organs, assisted by a knowledgeable secretariat, which can formulate new texts expeditiously. Adoption can take place at a regularly or specially scheduled session of a general representative organ (e.g., a conference of the parties).

With respect to the domestic phase, various devices for facilitating entry into force can be used:

(1) Some amendments, particularly to the constitutional instruments of IGOs, require normal procedures with respect to signature, ratification, and so on and require such steps to be taken by a certain fraction (usually two-thirds) of the membership for entry into force; but such entry then applies automatically to all members, including those that have not acted.

(2) Some adopted amendments provide that they automatically enter into force for all states except those that by a given date indicate their intention to opt out—a decision that the states can then reverse at any time. It is usually also provided that if a certain fraction of the parties opts out, then the amendment fails.

(3) Some adopted amendments provide that they enter into force for states by a simple notification to the secretariat, which may enable many of the states to circumvent the domestic requirements regarding the ratification of treaties.

Notes and Questions

1. Reservations to multilateral treaties pose some particularly complex problems that the International Court of Justice addressed in a 1951 advisory opinion named *Reservations to the Convention on the Prevention and the Punishment of the Crime of Genocide.*[10] The UN General Assembly requested the opinion with respect to whether states making reservations to the convention became parties thereto, when some of the states which had negotiated the convention objected to the reservations. The Court recalled the principle that a state could not be bound without its consent, and that no reservation could be made without a state-party's agreement.[11] Thereafter, the Court concluded:

> [A] State which has made and maintained a reservation which has been objected to by one or more of the parties to the Convention but not by others, can be regarded as being a party to the Convention if the reservation is compatible with the object and purpose of the Convention, otherwise, that State cannot be regarded as being a party to the Convention. . . . [I]f a party to the Convention objects to a reservation which it considers to be incompatible with the object and purpose of the Convention, it can in fact consider that the reserving State is not a party to the Convention; if, on the other hand, a party accepts the reservation as being compatible with the object and purpose of the Convention, it can in fact consider that the reserving State is a party to the Convention.[12]

10. 1951 I.C.J. Reports 15.
11. *Id.* at 21, 24.
12. *Id.* at 29-30.

The United States Senate gave its advice and consent to the Genocide Convention in 1986; however, it was accompanied by two reservations, five understandings, and one declaration.[13]

2. The 1982 UN Convention on the Law of the Sea prohibited reservations. *See* Article 309. The United States refused to sign the convention because of its opposition to the part of the convention that—Part XI—dealt with international seabed mining development. Twelve years after its completion, a separate agreement, 1994 Agreement Relating to the Implementation of Part XI of the United Nations Convention on the Law of the Sea of 10 December 1982 (Part XI Agreement),[14] was negotiated to allow states (primarily the United States) to join the 1982 Law of the Sea Convention without having to accept Part XI of the Convention.

3. Do you think international environmental conventions should permit reservations? Does your answer depend on which states you want to be a party? The subject matter? How many states will be parties?

4. *General Principles of Law*

A relatively minor source of international law listed in Article 38(1)(c) of the ICJ Statute is "the general principles of law recognized by civilized nations." In this context, "civilized nations" means states that have an organized legal system.

It should be noted that the reference here is not to "general principles of international law," which are the rules of customary international law. Rather, what is referred to here are those common elements of all, or virtually all, domestic legal systems, which thus can be presumed also to pertain to the international domain. Though scholars have from time to time identified certain such principles, the World Court itself has relatively rarely relied on them and then only in respect to procedural principles (e.g., no one can be a judge in one's own case) rather than in respect to substantive matters.

The international legislative process never directly attempts to create new general principles. However, to the extent that certain state behavior is encouraged through hortatory declarations (which may constitute soft law) or other means and such behavior is then absorbed into national legal systems, it is possible that with time some new general principle may be recognized and thus also enter the international legal canon.

13. *See* Leich, Contemporary Practice of the United States Relating to International Law, 80 Am. J. Intl. L. 612 (1986); *see also* Liesbeth Lijnzaad, Reservations to U.N.-Human Rights Treaties: Ratify and Ruin? (1995); 1969 Vienna Convention on the Law of Treaties, 1155 U.N.T.S. 336, *reprinted in* 63 Am. J. Intl. L. 875 (1969); and American Law Institute, Restatement (Third) of the Foreign Relations Law of the United States §313, Reporter's Note 1 (1987).

14. 33 I.L.M. 1309 (1994).

Note and Question

For an early attempt to identify the consistency of national law concepts and principles in addressing environmental concerns—some of which today might qualify as "general principles of law"—*see* Robert E. Lutz, The Laws of Environmental Management: A Comparative Study, 24 Am. J. Comp. L. 447 (1976). Do you think the "polluter pays principle" can be considered a "general principle of law"? In the article cited, Professor Lutz wrote that "[the polluter pays principle] has received wide acceptance among countries and international organizations" and cites the European Communities, Organisation for Economic and Co-operation and Development, Council of Europe, Australia, Canada, the United Kingdom, Federal Republic of Germany and Japan, as having adopted the principle.

5. International Administrative Law

International administrative law (not mentioned in the ICJ Statute) is the law that governs IGOs. Its principal manifestations are the constitutional law of IGOs, the procedural rules governing the business of international organs, the privileges and immunities of IGOs and their staffs, the rules governing the granting of assistance by IGOs to states, the rules governing the various types of activities carried out by IGOs within states (e.g., meetings; peacekeeping operations; humanitarian assistance; inspections and other types of monitoring), and the personnel and financial regime of IGOs. Some of that law is created mostly by treaties, some by decisions of competent IGO organs, and some by the practices of these organizations, which largely are carried out by their secretariats. There are also a number of international courts (e.g., the World Court and the European Court of Justice) and administrative tribunals (the personnel courts of almost every IGO or group of IGOs, such as those of the UN and the International Labour Organisation) that interpret and to some extent even create this type of law.

Because of the narrow subject matter of this area of international law, little of it is directly relevant to environmental matters. Only to the extent that the activities of IGOs active in relation to the environment are governed by international administrative law may that law have some relevance to the subject of this volume.

6. Other Norms and Instruments

a. Soft Law

Hard international law (i.e., those types mentioned above) is, by definition, legally binding, at least on some international entities (states and

IGOs), although not necessarily on all. By contrast, what some commentators refer to as "soft international law" is not binding, though perhaps superficially it may appear to be so. Nevertheless, the international entities concerned habitually comply with it, and it is this feature that arguably makes it appropriate to refer to it as "law."

Soft law manifests itself in various ways. One is in hortatory rather than obligatory language set out in otherwise binding instruments, such as when in a treaty in force certain actions to be taken are preceded by "should" rather than by "shall."[15] (This needs to be differentiated from obligations that are by their very nature vague, such as to consult or negotiate before taking certain actions, because the performance of such obligations must always be judged by the standard of good faith.) Perhaps more frequent are obligations expressed as such but set out in an instrument that is not binding, such as a resolution of a senior international organ (such as the World Charter for Nature promulgated by the UN General Assembly) or of a high-level conference (such as the Stockholm and Rio Declarations adopted at the 1972 Stockholm Conference on the Human Environment and the 1992 UN Conference on Environment and Development, respectively).

According to one view, such nonbinding precepts (rather than obligations) can be considered as soft law only if international entities, particularly states, habitually comply with them—or at least pretend to do so, thus in effect acknowledging their authority. Such behavior, even in the absence of a strict legal obligation, may be due to various factors, such as the existence of a control mechanism that notes and may report on noncompliance; it may also be due to a mere expectation of compliance expressed by other states and by the general public (including their own citizens) with respect to precepts that a government has helped to negotiate and include in an instrument adopted with the concurrence of its representatives in an international organ. Others use the term "soft law" to refer to any hortatory (or sometimes precatory) international statement.

Soft law is often generated as a compromise between those who desire a certain matter to be regulated definitively and those who, while not denying the merits of the substantive issue, do not wish (at least for a time) to be bound by a rigid and obligatory rule—perhaps because they cannot obtain the necessary domestic legislative approval. At other times a particular set of norms may not be considered ready to become a binding measure, though what is essentially voluntary compliance can be sought. Finally, certain matters may be considered to be too technical, trivial, or perhaps ephemeral for inclusion in a treaty instrument.

In any event, there is an ever-growing amount of soft law, most particularly in respect to the environment, expressed in the form of standards,

15. *See, e.g.*, Article 3 of the Framework Convention on Climate Change (1992), *reprinted in* 31 I.L.M. 849 (1992).

guidelines, and rules formulated by expert organs and often promulgated by the executive head of a technical IGO or organ, such as UNEP. While in principle the development of such norms mimics that of the process of formulating multilateral treaties, the process is apt to be a great deal quicker, more technical, and less political. Similarly, when such norms are to be amended or supplemented, this often can be done much more rapidly and simply than even a simplified treaty-amending procedure.

Inherently even less binding than soft law instruments that at least in form suggest an expectation of compliance, are those that are merely presented as model legislation, regulations, or treaties—for example, those merely designed to assist states that wish to benefit from the technical expertise of an IGO without feeling under a legal obligation to do so. If formulated so as to be truly useful, such instruments may achieve a high level of acceptance, especially in technical fields in which many countries do not have the expertise to consider formulating standards of their own, while at the same time feeling the need to include appropriate provisions in their domestic legislation.

Notes and Questions

1. Is it accurate, or even helpful, to use the term "soft law"? How can something not legally binding be considered "law"? Does this usage provide fuel to those who doubt that even international obligations that are clearly legally binding are truly "law" as that term is used domestically (e.g., because there is not, generally speaking, any centralized judicial or enforcement mechanism in the international system)? On the other hand, how else can one take account of the normative effect of some non-legally binding statements?

2. Quite apart from the questions of terminology raised in note 1, it is important to recognize the fact that non-legally binding statements and commitments often are complied with by states.

> [R]ecognition of a moral obligation does not in itself create legal obligations and rights. Rather it is a stage in the evolution of the public conscience. When this evolution has achieved a certain degree of maturity—the definition of which is impossible *in abstracto*—legal obligations and rights are formulated. This is the first condition for the legal protection by society.
>
> In international law, we must regard planetary obligations and planetary rights as in the formative stage. Concern for future generations exists, although there is limited awareness of the issues. The first step is for society to formulate planetary obligations and planetary rights, as by a solemn declaration of principles. Such declarations have been frequent since 1945 for other principles, and have assumed the crucial role of formulating social values. These declarations constitute only "soft law" instruments, which are not mandatory and may not be applied. But we can speak of pre-legal rules or emerging principles which can either prepare "hard law" rules (conclusion

of treaties) or contribute to the creation of rules of customary international law.[16]

3. Equally important is that non-legally binding statements sometimes are transformed into legally binding obligations, either by becoming customary international law or through incorporation in a treaty. Consider the following excerpt from Daniel Magraw, International Pollution, Economic Development and Human Rights, in International Law and Pollution 30, 49-50 (Daniel Barstow Magraw, ed. 1991):

> One of the most striking developments in substantive international law since World War II has been the rapid transformation of aspirational goals to binding customary obligations in the international human rights area (i.e., as some describe it, from "soft" law to "hard" law). It is now widely acknowledged, for example, that many human rights norms are part of customary international law and that some of those have even risen to the status of *jus cogens,* that is, peremptory norms that cannot be abrogated by agreement. It has been strongly argued that the entire 1948 Universal Declaration of Human Rights, which unquestionably was aspirational when originally adopted, has become part of customary international law.
>
> Many reasons account for this transformation. Several human-rights or analogous norms, for example, prohibition of slavery and State responsibility for injuries to aliens (although the latter, in particular, retains a separate policy basis and jurisprudence), existed before World War II. The fundamental concept of human rights is widely accepted, at least in word (such as in national constitutions), if not in deed. Human rights have a powerful moral appeal. Moreover, perhaps because of the previously mentioned factors, States are extremely reluctant to speak out against human rights (even if failing to do so is blatantly hypocritical, such as was the case when the General Assembly unanimously approved the Convention Against Torture). Nevertheless, the transformation of human rights aspirations to customary norms, in particular, is remarkable for several reasons: the time frame was relatively short, a substantial amount of contrary State practice occurred during the period, most of the consistent State practice was comprised of refraining from acting, and much of that refraining was already required by international agreements.

As you proceed through the materials in this book, consider whether international environmental law shares these characteristics and whether other circumstances favor or disfavor this process?

4. An example of an attempt to harden soft law into treaty law is the effort to transform the Guidelines for the Exchange of Information on Chemicals in International Trade (adopted by the United Nations Environment Programme Governing Council in 1987 and known as the UNEP PIC—prior informed consent—Guidelines) into a binding international agreement on prior informed consent. (This instrument was finalized as this book went to press in early 1998).

16. Edith Brown Weiss, In Fairness to Future Generations 103 (1989).

5. One commentator (Günther Handl) has referred to soft law as "the Trojan Horse of international environmental law" because soft law often contains environmentally preferable language that would not have been agreed to as legally binding when it was adopted, yet it will, over time, become hard law, or at least sufficiently obligatory that environmental activists can argue it is legally binding.

6. Are soft law obligations subject to sanctions for noncompliance?[17]

b. Decisions of International Organizations

Except in respect of certain parts of international administrative law, the decisions of IGO organs, no matter how senior, are not binding on states. The only exceptions are those in which states have empowered a particular organ to take decisions binding on them. This is rare, but when it is done it is normally accomplished through a treaty such as the constitutional instrument of an IGO. The prime example is Chapter VII of the UN Charter, which authorizes the UN Security Council to determine the existence of a threat to the peace, a breach of the peace, or an act of aggression and thereupon require all UN members (i.e., not only the offending state) to take specified economic, diplomatic, or even military actions to maintain or restore international peace and security.

The only instance in which the Security Council used this authority on an explicitly environmental matter was in providing that Iraq is responsible and must pay compensation for the environmental harm that it caused during the Gulf War.[18] More directly relevant to environmental protection are those instances in which states have empowered certain specified organs to make minor technical adjustments to a treaty or to issue binding regulations of a narrowly circumscribed nature. Even then, states usually reserve the right to opt out of such amendments or standards or to be bound only if they specifically opt in (see above).

Most frequently, the decisions of IGO organs constitute, at most, recommendations to members of the organization. Such recommendations can relate to a treaty, such as to comply with its substantive or procedural obligations (e.g., to submit required reports). Recommendations to take certain substantive actions can also encourage behavior leading to the creation of customary law or the acceptance of soft law.

17. *See generally* Gochalla-Wesierski, A Framework for Understanding "Soft Law," 30 McGill Law J. 37 (1984). For a discussion about the use of codes of conduct in regulating multinational enterprises, particularly with respect to their applicability to transfers of hazardous technologies and substances. *See* Robert E. Lutz & George D. Aron, Codes of Conduct and Other International Instruments, in Transferring Technologies and Substances: The International Legal Challenge, 129, 151-157 (G. Handl and R. Lutz, eds. 1989).

18. *See* para. 16 of UN Security Council Resolution 687, April 3, 1991; 30 I.L.M. 847, at 852 (1991). *See also* Chapter 15 below.

Note and Questions

Consider the following excerpt from the Texaco/Libya Arbitration Award of Jan. 19, 1977, 17 I.L.M. 1 (1978):

> The general question of the legal validity of the Resolutions of the United Nations has been widely discussed by the writers. This Tribunal will recall first that, under Article 10 of the U.N. Charter, the General Assembly only issues "recommendations," which have long appeared to be texts having no binding force and carrying no obligations for the Member States.
>
> Refusal to recognize any legal validity of United Nations Resolutions must, however, be qualified according to the various texts enacted by the United Nations. These are very different and have varying legal value, but it is impossible to deny that the United Nations' activities have had a significant influence on the content of contemporary international law. In appraising the legal validity of the above-mentioned Resolutions, this Tribunal will take account of the criteria usually taken into consideration, *i.e.,* the examination of voting conditions and the analysis of the provisions concerned.

Suppose a UN General Assembly resolution declares that States are obligated to prohibit the import and sale of elephant ivory tusks from any African state. Even though all European states and African states and most North and South American states vote for this resolution, virtually all Asian and some Third World countries from other regions vote against it, making the vote two-thirds for and one-third against. What is the international legal value of the resolution? Would it have mattered if the vote had been unanimous in favor of the resolution?[19]

c. Other Legal Statements

Although Article 38(1)(d) of the ICJ Statute specifically refers to "judicial decisions and the teachings of the most highly qualified publicists of the various nations," it characterizes these not as a type or source of law but merely as "subsidiary means for the determination of rules of law" (i.e., evidence of the existence of law). With respect to judicial decisions, this is in part because the international system lacks any hierarchy of courts (in which a senior one can effectively bind a junior one) and in part by deliberate decision that the doctrine of *stare decisis*[20] does not apply.

These subsidiary means are, however, valuable in identifying, authenticating, and clearly expressing (e.g., in converting unwritten law into *lex scripta*) rules of customary international law or general principles of law,

19. *See* Schachter, Resolutions of the General Assembly as Evidence of Law, 178 *Rec. des Cours* 114-121 (1982-V); and S. Rosenne, Practice and Methods of International Law, 111-17 (1984).

20. *See* Article 59 of the ICJ Statute.

or in interpreting controverted texts in a treaty. They are not, however, independent sources of law, and thus there can be no legislative process in respect to them.

Notes and Questions

1. The case of Filartiga v. Pena-Irala, 630 F.2d 876 (2d Cir. 1980), 19 I.L.M. 966 (1980), indicates how a court might utilize "subsidiary means" to determine the applicable international legal rule. In that case, the court, applying the Alien Tort Statute, 28 U.S.C. §1350, decided that torture committed by a state official against a person held in detention violated the law of nations. Consider this excerpt:

> [A]lthough there is no universal agreement as to the precise extent of the "human rights and fundamental freedoms" guaranteed to all by the Charter, there is at present no dissent from the view that the guaranties include, at a bare minimum, the right to be free from torture. This prohibition has become part of customary international law, as evidenced and defined by the Universal Declaration of Human Rights. The General Assembly has declared that the Charter precepts embodied in this Universal Declaration "constitute basic principles of international law." G.A. Res. 2625 (XXV) (Oct. 24, 1970).
>
> Particularly relevant is the Declaration on the Protection of All Persons from Being Subjected to Torture, General Assembly Resolution 3452 . . . This Declaration, like the Declaration of Human Rights before it, was adopted without dissent by the General Assembly.
>
> These U.N. declarations are significant because they specify with great precision the obligations of member nations under the Charter. Since their adoption, "(m)embers can no longer contend that they do not know what human rights they promised in the Charter to promote." Moreover, a U.N. Declaration is, according to one authoritive definition, "a formal and solemn instrument, suitable for rare occasions when principles of great and lasting importance are being enunciated." Accordingly, it has been observed that the Universal Declaration of Human Rights "no longer fits into the dichotomy of 'binding treaty' against 'non-binding pronouncement,' but is rather an authoritative statement of the international community." Thus, a Declaration creates an expectation of adherence, and "insofar as the expectation is gradually justified by State practice, a declaration may by custom become recognized as laying down rules binding upon the States." Indeed, several commentators have concluded that the Universal Declaration has become, in toto, a part of binding, customary international law.
>
> Turning to the act of torture, we have little difficulty discerning its universal renunciation in the modern usage and practice of nations. The international consensus surrounding torture has found expression in numerous international treaties and accords. E.g., American Convention on Human Rights Art. 5; International Covenant on Civil and Political Rights, U.N.

General Assembly Res. 2200 (XXI)A (identical language); European Convention for the Protection of Human Rights and Fundamental Freedoms, Art. 3. The substance of these international agreements is reflected in modern municipal, i.e., national law as well. Although torture was once a routine concomitant of criminal interrogations in many nations, during the modern and hopefully more enlightened era it has been universally renounced. According to one survey, torture is prohibited, expressly or implicitly, by the constitutions of over fifty-five nations, including both the United States and Paraguay. Our State Department reports a general recognition of this principle.

On what grounds did the court reach its conclusion? How did it treat declarations of the General Assembly?

7. *Relationship Between International and Domestic Law*

Broadly speaking, there are two alternative approaches to the relationship between international and domestic (or municipal) law:

1. the "monistic" approach, which considers that both systems of law constitute part of a single whole, in which international law is therefore necessarily hierarchically superior to domestic law. This is similar to a federal system in which federal law is, within its designated limits, superior to the law of the constituent entities of the federation. In such a system, even provisions of the national constitution must yield to international law binding on that state; and
2. the "dualist" approach, in which international and domestic law are considered to be basically separate. Usually the municipal rules ultimately determine the hierarchical relationship between the two. The United States follows this dualist approach, as is described below.

International law itself relies on the monistic approach. Thus, for example, Article 37 of the 1969 Vienna Convention on the Law of Treaties provides that a state may not advance any provision of its domestic law (including its constitution) as an excuse for a failure to comply with a treaty obligation. However, states following the dualist system are in effect able to do so, because ultimately states can rarely be compelled to act in a particular way (*see* section C, below). Fortunately, direct clashes between international and domestic law are relatively rare.

The United States clearly takes a dualist approach. The Supremacy Clause of the United States Constitution (Article VI, section 2), provides:

> This Constitution, and the Laws of the United States which shall be made in Pursuance thereof; and all Treaties made, or which shall be made, under

> the Authority of the United States, shall be the supreme Law of the Land; and the Judges in every State shall be bound thereby, any Thing in the Constitution or Laws of any State to the Contrary notwithstanding.

Congress is given the power to—but not required to—"define and punish . . . [o]ffenses against the Law of Nations" in Article I, section 8 of the Constitution. The terminology here bears some examination. We would now refer to the "Law of Nations" as international law.

The term "treaty" requires more explanation when discussing United States law. Domestically, it is customary to distinguish between a "treaty," which requires approval of two-thirds of the Senate present (according to Art II, section 2 of the Constitution), and executive agreements, which may be entered into by the president without such approval. Article VI, quoted above, makes clear that "treaties" have equivalent status with federal statutes. But what about executive agreements? For most purposes, executive agreements are treated like treaties, but the situation is not entirely clear. In exploring the uncertainties, it is helpful to distinguish among three types of executive agreements: (1) "treaty executive agreements" entered into pursuant to a treaty; (2) "congressional executive agreements" that have been approved by a majority of each House of Congress (e.g., the North American Agreement on Environmental Cooperation); and "sole executive agreements" that are entered into by the President on his/her sole authority (e.g., the United States-Mexico La Paz Agreement for Cooperation on Environmental Programs and Transboundary Problems). Taking into account the United States Constitution, decisions of the Supreme Court and other tribunals, and the Restatement (Third) of the Foreign Relations Law of the United States (1987), the current situation appears to be as follows.

1. The Constitution is superior to treaties. Thus the United States may not enter into a treaty violative of any part of the Constitution, and if it did so, the treaty may not be complied with to the extent it so violates, even if thereby the United States fails to comply with international law.
2. Treaties are at the same hierarchical level as federal laws; if they conflict, the later in time prevails—though, under a rule of interpretation applied by the courts, a later statute will only be allowed to cause a violation of an earlier treaty if it is (utterly) clear that Congress intended that the treaty be violated.
3. Treaties are always superior to federal regulations and to all rules of state laws, including even their constitutions.
4. Customary law has for the purpose of the above rules practically the same status as treaties.
5. The situation regarding (2) and (3) above is more complicated regarding executive agreements, depending on whether they were

entered into pursuant to a Senate-approved treaty, with the approval of both Houses of Congress, or on the sole authority of the President. Generally speaking, the first two are treated like treaties. The authority of the third (sole executive agreements) is not fully settled and probably depends, at least in large part, on the subject of the agreement and its relation to any specific allocations of power in the Constitution (e.g., to recognize ambassadors or regulate commerce with foreign nations).

Another aspect of the relationship between international and municipal law relates to the customary international law rules regarding when it is permissible for a state to exercise jurisdiction, that is, to regulate behavior via legislation (called "jurisdiction to prescribe"), to adjudicate, or to enforce a law. For present purposes, it suffices to note that international law recognizes jurisdiction to prescribe based on the principle of territoriality (e.g., conduct within a state's territory or intended to have an effect within its territory); the principle of nationality (e.g., activities, relations or status of a state's nationals); the protective principle (e.g., offenses committed against the security of the state, such as counterfeiting); and the principle of universality (e.g., a universally condemned crime, such as piracy). A fifth principle—passive personality—is also gaining recognition. It would allow protection of a state's nationals from, for example, terrorism. *See generally* Restatement (Third) of the Foreign Relations Law of the United States §§402-416 (1987).

Notes and Questions

1. Recall the language of the Supreme Court in *The Paquette Habana* (pp. 177-79) regarding the relationship of international law to United States law: "International law is part of our law. . . ."

2. Treaties and executive agreements may be either self-executing or non-self-executing. Self-executing instruments become immediately part of the domestic (municipal) law of the United States upon their international entry into force for the United States and may be used by courts for the rule of decision in cases before them. Non-self-executing agreements, on the other hand, require implementing legislation in order to execute them domestically. In some cases determining whether a treaty or an international agreement is self-executing or not can be a challenge. Does the following language from People of Saipan v. United States Department of Interior, 502 F.2d 90 (9th Cir. 1974), suggest workable criteria for distinguishing between self- and non-self-executing international agreements?

> The extent to which an international agreement establishes affirmative and judicially enforceable obligations without implementing legislation must

be determined in each case by reference to many contextual factors: the purposes of the treaty and the objectives of its creators, the existence of domestic procedures and institutions appropriate for direct implementation, the availability and feasibility of alternative enforcement methods, and the immediate and long-range social consequences of self- or non-self-execution. . . .

The preponderance of features in this . . . Agreement suggests the intention to establish direct, affirmative, and judicially enforceable rights. The issue involves the local economy and environment, not security; the concern with natural resources and the concern with political development are explicit in the agreement and are generally international concerns as well; the enforcement of these rights requires little legal or administrative innovation in the domestic fora; and the alternative forum . . . would present to the plaintiffs obstacles so great as to make their rights virtually unenforceable. . . .

B. AVOIDANCE AND SETTLEMENT OF DISPUTES

It is evident that in respect to the environment, a number of types of disputes can arise between states. Disputes also arise with respect to other international entities, such as IGOs and NGOs. These may include accusations of causing specific harms through transboundary pollution and the measure of the resulting damages; accusations of damage to a global commons, such as the atmosphere or the high seas, or of the improper exploitation of a shared resource; questions involving the interpretation of environmental treaties or the degree of compliance by particular states with these treaties; and questions whether certain environmental principles not set out in treaties constitute customary law or merely nonbinding soft law. Some such disputes involve only the parties directly concerned. Others potentially involve all states in a particular region or pursuing a particular activity (e.g., fishing), or the world community as a whole.

International law requires that disputes between states be settled peacefully.[21] This means more than just avoiding the use of force, which is prohibited by UN Charter Article 2(4), as well as by customary international law. It also requires that every state must make good faith efforts toward resolving any international disputes to which it is a party.

No state, however, is under any obligation to consent to any particular method of settling disputes peacefully, unless on the basis of some applicable agreement. It is therefore said that states have a free choice of means

21. UN Charter, Articles 2(3) and 33(1). *See* the Manila Declaration on the Peaceful Settlement of International Disputes, formulated by the UN General Assembly's Special Committee on the Charter of the United Nations and on Strengthening the Role of the Organization and approved by the Assembly by A/RES/37/10, of Nov. 15, 1982, to which the Declaration is annexed.

in this respect. The effect, however, is that the obligation to settle disputes peacefully establishes an imperfect obligation, because it is usually difficult to prove a clear violation, as long as each state asserts that it is eager to settle the impasse but merely considers inappropriate the particular method of dispute settlement proposed by the other side.

With respect to the environment, these principles are set out in a number of instruments including:

(1) [UNEP] Principles of Conduct in the Field of the Environment for the Guidance of States in the Conservation and Harmonious Utilization of Natural Resources Shared by Two or More States, Principle 11;[22]
(2) WCED Experts Group on Environmental Law: General Principles Concerning Natural Resources and Environmental Interferences, Article 22;[23]
(3) Antarctic Treaty, Article XI;[24]
(4) Vienna Convention for the Protection of the Ozone Layer, Article 11.[25]

Article 33(1) of the UN Charter contains an essentially complete catalogue of the methods available for the peaceful settlement of international disputes. Each of these is described and discussed at some length in the *Handbook on the Peaceful Settlement of Disputes between States* that was prepared by the Secretary-General at the request of the General Assembly.[26] These several methods are analyzed, with particular reference to environmental disputes, under the sub-headings below. In comparing and evaluating various methods for the peaceful settlement of disputes, it is useful to examine particularly the following features:

(1) Is the method useful in avoiding or deflecting incipient disputes?
(2) Does the method involve only the parties to the dispute, or does a neutral "third party" participate in some capacity?
(3) How structured is the method: is it entirely ad hoc or partly or wholly institutional?
(4) How easily can the method be frustrated by the intransigence of

22. E. Brown Weiss, D.B. Magraw, & P.C. Szasz, International Environmental Law: Basic Instruments and References (hereinafter "IEL") 183 (1991).

23. *Id.* at 194.

24. *Id.* at 518.

25. *Id.* at 282.

26. Report of the Special Committee on the Charter of the United Nations and on Strengthening the Role of the Organization, 46 GAOR Supp. No. 33 (A/46/33), Annex (1991), *reproduced in* UN doc. OLA/COD/2394 (UN, New York 1992), UN Publication Sales No. E.92.V.7, ISBN 92-1-133428-4. *See also* Dag Hammarskjöld Library, Peaceful Settlement of Disputes between States: A Selective Bibliography (UN 1991), UN doc. ST/LIB/SER.B/39; UN Publication Sales No. E.91.I.49, ISBN 92-1-100464-0.

any of the parties? (In general, methods that involve third parties and particularly those that involve established institutions are more difficult to frustrate.)

(5) Is any resolution of the dispute binding on some or all of the parties?

(6) Is the resolution of the dispute enforceable in respect of any or all of the parties?

1. *Consultation and Exchange of Views*

Consultations and exchanges of views are, as these terms indicate, informal methods normally pursued by two or more states or other entities, usually without the assistance or participation of any third party and usually without any defined structure. In some instances there are arrangements, usually provided for in a treaty, for regular consultations to take place, perhaps within a body set up for that purpose.

In effect, these methods are designed less for settling any dispute than for preventing disputes from arising, by reaching understandings before any actions are taken that could constitute the basis for a dispute.

There is no general obligation in international law to consult or to exchange views, but such obligations may arise from particular bilateral or multilateral treaties or be proposed in nonbinding declarations and other instruments. It should be noted that even where there is a duty to consult or to "take into account," there is no duty to agree or to conform one's behavior or attitude to that urged by another party. There is, however, an obligation to listen in good faith; for example, not to delay consultations until after a decision has in effect already been taken.

For environmentally relevant examples, *see:* (1) [UNEP] Principles of Conduct in the Field of the Environment for the Guidance of States in the Conservation and Harmonious Utilization of Natural Resources Shared by Two or More States, Principles 6(1) and 7;[27] (2) WCED Experts Group on Environmental Law: General Principles Concerning Natural Resources and Environmental Interferences, Article 17;[28] and (3) Convention on the Protection of the Environment, among Denmark, Finland, Norway, and Sweden, Article 11.[29]

2. *Negotiations*

Negotiations in the international sphere means essentially the same as it does domestically: an attempt by the parties to communicate their posi-

27. IEL, *supra* note 22, at 183.
28. *Id.* at 192.
29. *Id.* at 238.

tions and to identify and narrow their differences until complete agreement can be reached. Negotiation differs from mere consultations and exchanges of views, because in these there is no implication of the need for a party to be prepared to change its position (which characterizes true negotiations). For this reason, an obligation to consult or to exchange views should not be construed as an obligation to negotiate.

Negotiation is not only one, indeed the basic, method for resolving disputes; it normally is a prerequisite for the other methods of settling disputes, sometimes as a formal requirement for embarking on methods such as arbitration or resort to a court, but more often just as the natural means of establishing (1) whether a dispute exists; (2) what it is about; and (3) by what means it might be resolved. Negotiation, of course, is not only a means of dispute resolution, but also the basic method for reaching agreement on any question, such as establishing a new regime between the parties. Sometimes such an agreement can obviate the necessity of formally resolving an earlier dispute, which can then be set aside.

Negotiation normally permeates all other methods of settling disputes. That is, even while other methods (e.g., mediation, arbitration, or judicial proceedings) are being pursued, negotiations are likely to continue between the parties, which, if they show prospects of success, may lead to the suspension or termination of any formal proceedings. In turn, the likely outcome of these proceedings will influence the progress of the negotiations. In effect, there is a symbiotic relation between negotiations and other methods of disputes resolution.

A refusal to negotiate, except during the pendency of another agreed proceeding, is likely to be prima facie evidence of a violation of the general international duty of good faith and of the obligation to attempt to resolve disputes peacefully. However, there is no general duty to negotiate in certain situations, in particular in respect of matters essentially within a state's domestic jurisdiction. Frequently in the environmental field, however, there may be a disagreement about whether a particular matter (e.g., the damming of an international river or the release of pollutants into the stratosphere) can be considered as essentially domestic.

Negotiations can be entirely unstructured, consisting of only casual contacts or exchanges of communications. Indeed, parties may maintain different views as to the nature of such contacts, one asserting that negotiations are taking place while the other may (perhaps for domestic consumption) deny that and admit to only informal consultations. On the other hand, many negotiations are essentially formal, with teams of negotiators facing each other at scheduled sessions. Even then, however, much progress may be made in the course of informal contacts. Between states, negotiations normally take place on a diplomatic level, for example, between a foreign ministry on one side and a country's diplomatic mission on the other; more frequently, such contacts take place between diplomats accredited to a particular IGO, in particular one whose mandate is relevant to the issue at hand. On technical questions (such as many relating to the environment) the diplomats may be advised by scientists or other experts, or the negotiations may in part take place directly between experts. Because of the basically unstructured nature of negotiations, their venue often changes. Indeed, it is a well-established technique to shift negotiations that appear to be stuck to either a higher (e.g., Foreign Minister) or a lower (e.g., group of experts) level in the hope of thus making progress on at least some issues.

As a method of resolving disputes, negotiations can easily be frustrated either by the intransigence of one or more parties, or, even with their good will, by the natural difficulty of the problem. Consequently, there is never any assurance about resolving a dispute by negotiations or about how long negotiations will require. Thus a party that insists on resolution of a dispute merely by negotiations and rejects all other methods is likely not to be acting in good faith.

Whether a resolution reached by negotiation is binding on the parties and whether it is enforceable depends on the method of resolution. If that takes the form of an international agreement—which may be a formal treaty or merely implicit in an official statement on behalf of each party that it will abide by the agreed resolution—then it becomes binding under the *pacta sunt servanda* rule applicable to all international agreements (see p. 181). Enforceability depends on other agreements between the parties, including their mutual participation in IGOs that have enforcement powers or as mutually agreed with regard to the matter at hand.

For some environmentally relevant examples, *see:* (1) International Convention Relating to Intervention on the High Seas in Cases of Oil Pollution Casualties, Article VIII;[30] (2) [ECE] Convention on Long-Range Transboundary Air Pollution (LRTAP), Article 13;[31] and (3) USA-Canada Agreement on Air Quality, Article XIII.[32] *See also* chapter 6, sec. C, Notes and Questions 3, 4, & 5, below.

3. Enquiry or Fact-Finding

Enquiry or fact-finding is a method of resolving or assisting in resolving disputes and perhaps in avoiding them altogether by establishing or agreeing on certain facts relevant to such disputes or potential disputes.

The facts in question (e.g., the degree of pollution of a river or the number of fish in a lake) may be investigated unilaterally (e.g., by one of the parties), by some joint organ (such as a commission of scientists) of the parties or possibly also of some neutral states, or by an agreed IGO or even NGO. Some environmental treaties establish permanent or standby bodies for this purpose. Any technique of fact-finding may be used, includ-

30. 970 U.N.T.S. 911; 26 U.S.T. 765.
31. IEL *supra* note 22, at 255.
32. *Id.* at 268.

ing the expertise and experience of the persons conducting the enquiry, contributions of other experts, research in the literature, experiments and measurements in the field, the testimony of witnesses, and so on.

After the body charged with the enquiry has established the facts, the parties have to decide whether to accept them, unless they have agreed in advance to accept the report of that body. To consider whether to do so, the diplomatic representatives of the parties may consider the expertise of the fact-finders, their methodology, or other matters. How much scope there is for this depends on the matter at hand. For example, to establish the flow or salinity of a river at a given time and place may not require complex studies, but there may be considerable disagreement about the time and place to be specified.

The UN General Assembly has recently approved a Declaration on Fact-Finding by the United Nations in the Field of the Maintenance of International Peace and Security.[33] Though probably few environmental disputes would fall directly within the purview of this declaration, it is not to be excluded that as these issues are taken more seriously by states some such disputes may escalate from threats of economic retaliation to those that actually endanger the peace.

As is true of other methods for the avoidance and resolution of international disputes, enquiry in most instances is likely to be more effective the more structured it is, and the more neutral third parties (e.g., a state or an organization) are involved. To the extent that fact-finding must take place within areas under the jurisdiction of any of the parties (e.g., to determine emissions from a particular facility), that state can, of course, completely or partially frustrate their work by refusing to cooperate with the fact-finders.

As fact-finding can rarely resolve a dispute by itself, the issue of the binding or enforceable nature of the outcome of the process rarely arises. Of course the parties may agree, in advance or afterward, that facts established in a particular way are binding on them in further negotiations or that they may or must be taken into account by any arbitral or judicial tribunal to which the dispute is referred.

Some environmentally relevant examples are:

(1) [UNEP] Principles of Conduct in the Field of the Environment for the Guidance of States in the Conservation and Harmonious Utilization of Natural Resources Shared by Two or More States, Principles 8 and 10;[34] and
(2) Convention on the Prohibition of Military and Other Hostile Use of Environmental Modification Techniques (ENMOD), Article V.1-2, Annex.[35]

33. A/RES/46/59 of Dec. 9, 1991, Annex.
34. IEL, *supra* note 22, at 182-183.
35. *Id.* at 636, 637-638, *reprinted* below, in Chapter 15.

4. Good Offices and Mediation

Good offices and mediation are both methods by which a third (i.e., neutral) party—which may be a state or group of states, an IGO or an IGO official—assists parties to a dispute to negotiate a resolution. Though the two methods cannot be strictly distinguished, it is sometimes said that

(1) the exercise of good offices merely involves the encouragement of parties to negotiate and perhaps the facilitation of such negotiations by passing messages back and forth, when the parties are otherwise reluctant to engage in them at all or to pursue them seriously (perhaps because they have no diplomatic relations or do not even recognize each other); while
(2) mediators, by contrast, may also involve themselves in the substance of the dispute by introducing proposals of their own. This may be useful both because an impartial outsider may be in a position to sponsor proposals that did not occur to the parties involved or that a party may be reluctant to advance itself, or because these parties may seek to save face by accepting a neutrally sponsored proposal rather than one presented by an opponent.

A third party that is on reasonably good terms with all the parties to the dispute and not particularly close to just some of them may offer to exercise good offices or to mediate their dispute. Such an offer may be made publicly, though generally this is done only after first exploring privately whether such an offer would be welcome, unless an untested public offer is designed to force the hand of one or more parties to the dispute. Sometimes the intervention of a third party may be requested jointly by the parties to the dispute and sometimes unilaterally by one of them. In the latter case, there is a danger that other parties will become suspicious and reject the initiative.

Once all parties concerned agree to a particular good offices exercise or to mediation, or at least through silence indicate that they are willing to tolerate it, the third party can begin to function. Its efforts may be exercised largely in its own capital (e.g., through contacts with the respective diplomatic representatives there) or at the seat of an IGO at which all parties are represented; or special meetings may be called. The third party may succeed in getting all the parties to meet together or may instead meet in turn with the representatives of each party separately (so-called shuttle diplomacy or proximity talks, depending on how close the delegations of the parties are located), passing messages back and forth or seeking to establish whether particular proposals originating with one party, or with a mediator, are acceptable to the others.

The outcome of a successful good offices exercise or mediation is a negotiated agreement among the disputing parties. Sometimes such a resolution may be facilitated by having it merely announced by the mediator, while the parties at issue indicate their agreement either explicitly or by not objecting.

Because good offices and mediation merely facilitate negotiations, their ultimate effectiveness is essentially the same as for direct negotiations. However, because of the involvement of the third party, especially if it is able to exercise some leverage over all parties or at least the most obdurate one(s), such negotiations are somewhat less likely to be frustrated. Moreover, they are less likely to extend indefinitely, as unassisted negotiations may, because there the pace is usually set by the most reluctant party, while the pace of assisted negotiations is likely to be set or at least influenced by the third party.

Similarly, the binding nature and also the enforceability of a resolution reached by assisted negotiations may be enhanced if the third party in effect becomes, formally or informally, a guarantor of the agreement reached.

Environmentally relevant examples include: (1) Vienna Convention on the Protection of the Ozone Layer, Article 11(1, 2);[36] and (2) ILA: Helsinki Rules on the Uses of the Waters of International Rivers, Chapter 6 (Art. XXXII).[37]

5. *Conciliation*

Conciliation involves the establishment or choice by the parties to a dispute of an impartial body to resolve their dispute. In this sense, it is similar to arbitration (*see* section B.6, below). The most significant difference between conciliation and arbitration is that: (1) a conciliation commission issues a nonbinding report, but (2) an arbitral tribunal issues a binding award.

Any party to a conciliation proceeding may unilaterally declare, at any time, that it accepts or will accept the outcome as binding. However, if all the parties to such a proceeding agree in advance to accept a conciliation report as binding, they are in effect arbitrating, though they may not wish to admit this. Similarly, if the parties to a so-called arbitral proceeding agree in advance that the award is not to be binding on them, they are in effect merely conciliating. In some disputes settlement regimes, an unsuccessful effort at conciliation (e.g., an inability of the conciliators to prepare proposals acceptable to all the parties) is a prerequisite for subsequent arbitral or judicial proceedings.

Because of its binding character, arbitration is generally taken more seriously than conciliation by the parties. They (particularly the party whose case is weaker) are more likely to agree to conciliation than to arbitration,

36. *Id.* at 282.
37. *Id.* at 401.

and having agreed to either procedure they often are less likely to try to frustrate conciliatory rather than an arbitral proceeding. Consequently the terms of an arbitration are likely to be more detailed and precise than those for a conciliation.

In other respects, the two procedures are in principle so similar that only arbitration will be discussed in detail (*see* immediately below, in which some features that distinguish conciliation are mentioned).

Some environmentally relevant examples of conciliation provisions are (1) African Convention on the Conservation of Nature and Natural Resources, Article XVIII;[38] (2) Vienna Convention for the Protection of the Ozone Layer, Article 11(3-5);[39] (3) ILA: Helsinki Rules on the Uses of the Waters of International Rivers, Article XXXIII and Annex;[40] (4) United Nations Convention on the Law of the Sea, Article 284 and Annex V.

6. *Arbitration*

As already mentioned in connection with conciliation, arbitration involves the establishment or choice, by the parties, of an impartial body charged with resolving their dispute in a quasi-judicial proceeding. An arbitral tribunal issues a binding award. It may thus be considered as an ad hoc court established by the parties to the dispute.

a. Agreement to Arbitrate

An agreement to engage in arbitration can be concluded before a dispute arises and is then normally included as a "compromissory clause" in an agreement. The agreement can either be generally concerned with the peaceful settlement of future disputes between the parties or regulate a substantive matter as to which the parties expect that disputes may arise. Many bilateral and multilateral arbitration agreements (*see* examples at end of this section) contain such clauses. Alternatively, such an agreement can be concluded with respect to a particular dispute that has already arisen, in which case it is normally called a "*compromis.*" The relative advantages and disadvantages of these two approaches are discussed in section 7.a.vi, below with reference to international courts, but these considerations are also relevant here.

An agreement to arbitrate must specify how the arbitral tribunal is to be established (*see* section 6.b, below) and what its jurisdiction and proce-

38. *Id.* at 209-210.
39. *Id.* at 282.
40. *Id.* at 401, 402-403.

dures will be. Several observations provide perspective on various aspects of such agreements.

(1) It is important in respect of arbitration (which is designed to lead to a definitive settlement of the dispute) that the procedures for the establishment and operation of the tribunal be such that they cannot be frustrated by the obduracy of any party or parties. That is, if at least one party persists it should be able to cause the proceeding to move to a conclusion.
(2) In a compromissory clause (*see* above), the jurisdiction of the tribunal is described in terms of the types of disputes that may be submitted, and possibly some preliminary requirements for submission, such as prior negotiations. A *compromis,* on the other hand, must contain a sufficient description of the dispute being submitted and of the issues to be decided. In either case it is useful to provide that the tribunal has the power to decide any question concerning its own jurisdiction, unless there is some standing outside body to which such questions can be referred.
(3) An arbitral tribunal can be charged with establishing facts in dispute, to determine the law, and/or to act *ex aequo et bono* (i.e., on the basis of what is equitable and good). If the arbitral tribunal is to act according to legal rules, these may be specified explicitly or by reference to a governing legal system (e.g., a particular treaty regime), or they may be left to the tribunal to determine. In many cases the specification of the applicable legal regime may in effect resolve the contentious issue; and for just that reason the parties may find it difficult to agree on it.
(4) The procedures to be followed by the tribunal can be specified in great detail; but they generally need not be because the parties can leave it to that body itself to adopt most of these—except for those that are basic to its operations. Thus it is necessary to specify the voting rules if there is more than one arbitrator (normally a simple or qualified majority is preferable because a unanimity requirement enables any member—including one appointed by a party—to prevent any decision), the quorum (again only a majority should be required, in order to prevent possible sabotage), and the extent of the power of the tribunal to establish rules. In any event, whatever rules the parties specify in their agreement and whatever rules a tribunal may adopt, the parties jointly retain complete control over the proceeding and its procedures and thus can take any decisions thereon that all can agree to. Thus, for example, time limits may be set aside to enable the parties to engage in negotiations, for whatever period they wish.
(5) The agreement may limit or constrain the tribunal in respect of

its output. For example, it is customary to require that an award be reasoned and relate to every aspect of the dispute.

(6) Though implied by the use of the term "arbitration," it is useful for the agreement to specify the effect of the arbitral award, normally that it will be considered final and binding and will be complied with by all the parties. (In case of a conciliation, the agreement might specify that the parties will give serious or good faith consideration to or endeavor to follow the conciliation report or that it may be considered as a basis of any future litigation.)

b. Establishment of an Arbitral Tribunal

An arbitral tribunal (like a conciliation commission) normally consists of an uneven number of members. If the tribunal consists of more than one person, an equal number of persons are appointed by each of the parties, subject to whatever constraints are provided for in the agreement—for example, that only so many may be their own nationals, that they should have particular expertise, or that they must be chosen from a list maintained by some institution. The rest of the arbitrators (one of whom will preside) are appointed by them jointly or are selected by the party-appointed members, which amounts to almost the same thing. If there are more than two parties and they cannot be divided into two sides, usually the only satisfactory disposition is that all the members must be appointed jointly.

To prevent any party from sabotaging the proceeding by simply not appointing its own members, it should either be provided that after a certain delay any party may petition a neutral "default" appointing authority to appoint such members or, more rarely, that the proceeding can go forward without such members. Similarly, if the parties or the tribunal member(s) they have appointed are unable to agree on the neutral members, then any party should be able to request the appointing authority to make the appointment(s). The appointing authority must be specified in the arbitral agreement. It can be either a named individual or a designated official (most frequently, in interstate proceedings, the President of the ICJ or the UN Secretary-General, or the executive head of a regional organization), or an institution (such as the International Chamber of Commerce (ICC)). It is best to make certain before the agreement is finalized that the designated appointing authority is prepared to accept the specified task, either because it is within its terms of reference or customary functions, or by specifically asking. Normally such an authority will carry out its designated functions in consultation with the parties. It should be understood that by acting the authority does not decide whether the body to be established will have jurisdiction over the dispute (often the noncooperating party will claim that the agreed arbitral procedure is for some reason inapplicable), since that is to be decided by the tribunal itself (*see* above).

Suitable provisions should be also made for replacing members of the tribunal whenever that proves necessary. Again, it should be kept in mind that no party should have the possibility of frustrating the proceeding through any means of noncooperation by itself or through persons it has appointed to the tribunal.

c. The Proceeding

Basically it is for the parties to decide, either in their original agreement or at any time thereafter, how their tribunal is to carry out its task. To the extent they fail to do so, that body should be empowered, either explicitly or implicitly through normal custom, to make the necessary determinations. There also exist several ready-made sets of arbitral rules (such as those of the UN Commission on International Trade Law (UNCITRAL), which, for example, were designated for use in the Iran-United States Claims Tribunal established in 1981); and it usually suffices to incorporate by reference one of these "off-the-shelf" texts into an arbitral agreement.

Such proceedings are normally quasi-judicial. This means, inter alia, (1) that the tribunal as a whole must be impartial, though not necessarily each of its members (i.e., the party-appointed ones); and (2) that each party must have a fair and equal opportunity to present its case, both as to the substantive issues and with respect to any preliminary or procedural questions that may arise.

In general, arbitral proceedings tend to follow a rather standard pattern:

(1) almost always one or more rounds of written pleadings are provided for, submitted either alternately by the parties or simultaneously;
(2) there generally also are oral proceedings, either just to hear the arguments of the parties or also for the presentation and questioning of witnesses;
(3) other appropriate means of fact-finding may also be employed, such as visits to relevant sites, the appointment of masters, or the consultation of experts;
(4) the proceedings are normally not open to the public and are conducted confidentially—a point usually considered desirable by the states parties but not necessarily by any concerned NGOs; and
(5) in due course an arbitral award is issued, generally in writing and supplied with reasons and indicating any dissenting views; the award is usually supplied only to the parties, and published only if they all agree.

Generally no challenges or appeals are possible in respect to an arbitral award. However, sometimes the arbitral agreement may provide, or the institution within which the proceeding takes place may foresee, certain limited challenges, such as charging corruption by a member of the tribunal or that the award does not fulfill certain substantive or formal requirements (e.g., that every point at issue must be decided and that reasons must be given). Such challenges are then submitted to another body and, if sustained, may lead to a reopening of the original proceeding or to an entirely new one.

d. Institutionalization

International arbitration may be arranged entirely ad hoc by the parties or may take place within the framework of an institution specified by the parties. It should be noted that even in respect of an entirely ad hoc proceeding, the general practice of relying on a default appointing authority to assist, if necessary, in the constitution of the tribunal may introduce an element of institutionalization if that authority is an official of a particular international organization (such as the UN Secretary-General or the ICJ President). If the proceeding is fully entrusted to an institution, it may be sufficient merely to specify so in the compromissory clause or the *compromis,* leaving all other decisions to the rules of that body.

e. Evaluation of Arbitration as a Dispute Settlement Method

Arbitration necessarily involves reliance on a type of third party, i.e., the tribunal, or in any event the independent members of these bodies. In addition, any default appointing authority is of course a neutral "third party," as is any institution under whose aegis the proceeding takes place.

As already pointed out, arbitration can be almost entirely ad hoc but certain standing institutions exist, and more are likely to be created to which parties to a dispute can agree to entrust all or many aspects of the proceeding. As of mid-1998, there were no such institutions with specifically environmental terms of reference.

A well-designed arbitration clause can generally not be frustrated by a party (or a combination less than all parties). The most important requirement is that if even one party insists on the proceeding, the tribunal must be able to be established under all circumstances, usually with the assistance of a default appointing authority. It is therefore important to select an appointing authority that will be able and willing to function in all contingencies, and that once appointed, the tribunal be empowered to take all necessary procedural and substantive decisions. To the extent that the proceeding is entrusted to a standing institution, it is more difficult to frustrate.

Almost by definition, arbitral awards are generally binding on all parties and are final, in the sense that they cannot normally be appealed. Whether it is "enforceable" depends on the framework within which the proceeding is conducted or within which the parties are acting. Normally international obligations, whether arising through a treaty, through customary law, through a unilateral commitment, or through an arbitral or judicial decree, are not enforceable in the sense that their domestic equivalents are (*see* section c below). However, parties acting within certain institutions may incur penalties if they violate its rules (such as compliance with arbitral awards) and, if such a violation threatens international peace and security, the UN Security Council may intervene.

Finally, it should be noted that the entire costs of the proceedings, both those incurred directly by the parties and those required for the tribunal, must be borne by the parties. Unless otherwise agreed, or unless the tribunal is authorized and does direct a different allocation, these latter expenditures, which may be considerable, are borne equally by the parties.

f. Environmentally Relevant Examples

(1) Paris Convention for the Prevention of Marine Pollution from Land-Based Sources, Article 21 and Annex B.[41]

(2) ILA: Helsinki Rules on the Uses of the Waters of International Rivers, Articles XXXIV-XXXVI.[42]

(3) Bonn Convention for the Protection of the Rhine River Against Pollution, Article 15 and Annex B.[43]

(4) Trail Smelter Arbitration, extracts from:
   (a) Ottawa Convention for the Establishment of a Tribunal to Decide Questions of Indemnity Arising from the Operation of the Smelter at Trail, British Columbia (162 L.N.T.S. 73, 49 Stat. 3245);
   (b) Award of the Tribunal (3 UN R.I.A.A. 1911 (1941)); and
   (c) Supplementary Agreement to Decide Questions of Indemnity and Future Regime (151 U.N.T.S. 171, 3 U.S.T. 539).

(5) Convention on International Liability for Damage Caused by Space Objects, Articles XII, XIV-XX.[44] N.B.: These provisions call for the establishment of a claims commission, which is a type of arbitral tribunal usually charged with deciding a whole series of disputes between the parties arising out of the same incident or legal situation.

41. *Id.* at 366, 368-369.
42. *Id.* at 401-402.
43. *Id.* at 447-448.
44. Done on March 29, 1972, 961 U.N.T.S. 187, 24 U.S.T. 2389, T.I.A.S. 7762.

7. *International Courts*

An international court is in many ways like a domestic one: it is a standing institution with incumbent judges charged with settling disputes properly submitted to it, for example, those that are within the competence of the institution and are brought within its jurisdiction. However, it does differ from its domestic counterparts in several important ways, which recall the arbitral origins of international judicial organs: (1) the jurisdiction of an international court normally requires the consent of all states parties to the dispute; (2) all parties are normally "represented" on the court; and (3) the court is likely to be more responsive to the desires of the parties as to certain aspects of the procedures to be followed, especially the timing of successive steps.

a. Locating a Competent Court

Only a very few international courts exist that have competence for disputes between states relating to the environment. The only such institution on the worldwide level is the International Court of Justice (ICJ)—the so-called World Court—which is the principal judicial organ of the United Nations. All UN members and most of the significant nonmember states are parties to the Statute of the ICJ and thus can litigate with other such parties about any question of international law. Because only states may be parties, disputes involving international organizations or other nonstate entities cannot be submitted to the ICJ directly. However, an alternative procedure, involving the Court's competence to give "advisory opinions," may be used to resolve such disputes (*see* below).

The Court has only recently (September 1997) decided a dispute with an important clearly environmental component[45] and another was settled and therefore withdrawn.[46] In addition, the Court has given at least one advisory opinion (*see* below) in which environmental considerations figured importantly.[47] To respond to the question whether its classically trained and generally scientifically unversed judges would be factually competent in respect of this essentially modern subject, the Court in July 1993 established a seven-member standing Chamber for Environmental Matters. The

45. Gabcikovo-Nagymaros Project (Hungary/Slovakia), 1997—I.L.M.—(199_), in which the issue is whether Hungary was justified in cancelling a project to which it had agreed to by treaty, on the asserted ground that it is likely to cause great environmental harm.

46. Certain Phosphate Lands in Nauru (Nauru v. Australia), which revolved about the issue of the exhaustion of a natural resource.

47. Legality of the Threat or Use of Nuclear Weapons, Advisory Opinion of July 8, 1996, 1996 I.C.J.; 35 I.L.M. 869 and 1343 (1996). The environmentally relevant parts of the Opinion are reproduced in Chapter 15 on Military Activities.

Court could also resort to the use of expert assessors, which is foreseen in its Statute.[48]

The International Tribunal for the Law of the Sea, which is provided for in the 1982 United Nations Convention on the Law of the Sea, is competent, inter alia, in respect of the convention's extensive environmental provisions. The tribunal was actually set up in 1996 and decided its first case (partially environmental) in 1997.

Aside from the ICJ and the Law of the Sea Tribunal, the only actually functioning international court with extensive competence including environmental matters is the Court of Justice of the European Union (EU). That court has jurisdiction not only in respect of the 12 member states of the EU but also in respect of all the organs of the union as well as private individuals and entities. It has handed down a number of significant decisions relating to the environmental regime of the EU (and its predecessor, the European Communities). However, because of its geographically restricted competence and general atypical nature (the EU is characterized as a supranational entity rather than as an international one) it will not be considered further here.

No exclusively environmental court exists, either on the worldwide or regional level. Though from time to time proposals have been made for the establishment of such courts to deal with the increasing number of environmental regimes and the potential disputes concerning them, there are no current projects actually under consideration at the political level.

In light of the above, the further discussion of international environmental litigation below will be restricted to the ICJ. The most relevant provisions of the UN Charter and of the ICJ Statute (which is an Annex to the Charter) are Charter Article 94 and Statute Articles 4(1) (first clause), 26, 31(1-3), 34(1-2), 36(1-3), 38, 41, 43(1-2, 5), 46, 50-51, 53, 55-57, 59-60, 61(1), 62.

b. Consent to Litigation

As pointed out above, for any international court, including the ICJ, to have jurisdiction in respect of a dispute, all the parties thereto must consent to submit it to the Court. As in respect of conciliation and arbitration, that consent can be given in two different ways: (1) an abstract submission, before any dispute has arisen, of all future disputes or of those in some defined categories (e.g., all environmental disputes or all disputes with reference to a particular environmental regime), or (2) the concrete submission of a particular existing dispute.

An abstract submission to an international court can be made either by a general bilateral or multilateral agreement relating to dispute settle-

48. Article 30(2) of the ICJ Statute; *see also* Articles 9 and 21(2) of the Rules of Court.

ment or also by a particular treaty with respect to any disputes that might arise in respect thereto (i.e., in a "compromissory clause"). In respect of the ICJ, an abstract submission can also be made, under Article 36(2) of its Statute, by a declaration accepting the Court's jurisdiction in respect of all or of defined classes of disputes, but only on the basis of strict reciprocity in respect of other states making similar declarations. This, in effect, is the functional equivalent of a multilateral disputes settlement agreement.

The submission of an actual dispute is done by means of an ad hoc agreement between all the disputing parties, for example, by a *compromis.*

Although legally these two methods are equivalent, in practice there are important differences. While abstract consent to the submission of undefined future disputes may often be easier to secure than consent after a dispute has arisen (when relations among the parties may be embittered and one party may realize that it is likely to lose on a strictly legal basis), experience has shown that an ad hoc submission testifies to a real desire to have the dispute resolved and a willingness to abide by the court's judgment. In contrast, an advance consent that may have been given decades earlier by a politically different regime is in practice often disavowed by the current government, which may then refuse to cooperate with the proceeding and disregard its legally binding outcome.

c. Composition of the World Court

Because the ICJ already exists and its 15 judges have been elected, there is no need or opportunity to compose the Court (unlike an arbitral tribunal), with two exceptions. In a throw-back to its essentially arbitral origins, if any state party to a dispute before the ICJ does not have a judge of its nationality on the Court, it may appoint an ad hoc judge to sit for that case. (N.B.: in a national court, one might instead expect that if any judges on a standing panel *are* affiliated with one of the parties, they will recuse themselves.) Also, the parties jointly may request that the case not be heard by all the judges but by only a small chamber. If that occurs, the parties may be consulted in composing the panel.

d. Procedures of the World Court

As a standing body, the ICJ has established procedures (e.g., as to the written and oral proceedings) set out in its Statute and the Rules of Court. Therefore the parties do not have to agree on any such points, though if they do the Court will do its best to accommodate them, in particular in respect of the timing of the various steps. This flexibility may enable the parties privately to negotiate in the shadow of the public litigation, and perhaps to resolve the dispute in a face-saving manner so as to obviate the need for a judgement, much as often happens in domestic courts. Thus the often lengthy proceedings in the World Court sometimes merely reflect the wishes of the parties rather than any inherent sluggishness of the Court.

The Court's proceedings are public (unlike conciliation and arbitral ones). Aside from the parties, no one can participate in the proceeding, i.e., neither other states (except in the event of rarely allowed formal interventions by a state necessarily affected by the outcome of the litigation), nor inter- or non-governmental organizations, nor private entities. There is no possibility of submitting amicus briefs to the World Court in contentious cases. Except to the extent that any of the states parties may invite some private entity (e.g., an environmental NGO) to join its legal team, there is thus no opportunity for participation by the public.

If any party defaults before the ICJ (e.g., it fails to appear, either altogether or from a given point of the proceeding), this does not result in a discontinuance of the proceeding. However, unlike in a domestic litigation where a defaulting party normally automatically loses, the ICJ under Article 53(2) of its Statute must in deciding the case "satisfy itself, not only that it has jurisdiction . . . , but also that the claim is well founded in fact and law."

Unlike many domestic courts, the ICJ cannot give binding injunctive relief to a party during the pendency of a proceeding. It can, however, under Article 41 of its Statute, "indicate, if it considers that circumstances so require, any provisional measures to be taken to preserve the respective rights of either party." Though not considered as binding, such suggested measures are automatically reported to the Security Council, which presumably can consider whether compliance therewith should be urged on or even required of the parties (if considered necessary to maintain peace and security).

Under Article 59 of the Court's Statute, its decisions have binding force only between the parties and in respect of the particular case—there is no *stare decisis* (though there is *res judicata*). However, like any court, the ICJ naturally strives for consistency in its jurisprudence, and therefore it frequently cites its earlier judgments and advisory opinions. Moreover, other international courts, arbitral tribunals, international organs, states, and legal scholars routinely cite pronouncements by the World Court as authoritative statements of international law (*see also* section A.6.c, above).

e. Evaluation of ICJ Litigation as a Disputes Settlement Method

Litigation, in any court, by definition involves a "third party" and is necessarily highly structured, though, as indicated, the ICJ is usually responsive to procedural wishes of any party and particularly if all are in agreement. Technically, ICJ proceedings cannot be frustrated by an intransigent party, because the Court, if it finds that it has jurisdiction (which requires a finding that every party has in some way and at some time "consented"), will proceed to a judgment, even if a party defaults. It is, however, true that noncooperation by a party may make the Court's task of establishing the facts and the law more difficult and, though the resulting judgment is binding and enforceable, actually there is likely to be noncompliance.

Under the UN Charter and the ICJ Statute, its judgments are legally binding on the parties to the litigation. This requires no special advance agreement of the parties—indeed, if they should agree ahead of the litigation that they will not consider the judgment as binding the Court would probably decline to hear the case.

If a party to an ICJ litigation refuses to comply with the resulting judgment, the other party may refer the matter to the Security Council "which may, if it deems necessary, make recommendations or decide upon measures to give effect to the judgment."[49] The Council, of course, can orchestrate measures of enforcement by the world community in the form of economic or diplomatic sanctions or even military force if it considers that such measures are required to preserve peace and security,[50] which may sometimes, though probably rarely, be endangered by noncompliance with a judgment in an environmental dispute.

Finally, it should be noted that (in contrast to ad hoc conciliation or arbitration), the institutional costs of maintaining the ICJ, including any costs associated with a particular case before it, are borne by the regular budget of the United Nations.

f. The Advisory Competence of the World Court

In addition to its function in resolving interstate disputes, the ICJ also may give advisory opinions at the request of a restricted number of specified organs of IGOs within the UN system. That competence can be used in two significant ways. First, to advise the requesting organ as to legal questions—which in case of the UN General Assembly and Security Council can be "any legal question" but in the case of other organs would have to be one "arising within the scope of [its] activities." Thus the Court answered the query of the General Assembly as to the Legality of the Threat or Use of Nuclear Weapons, in which it took into account environmental considerations.[51] In the same way, the opinion of the Court could be secured as to the interpretation of environmental treaties, unless this was already

49. UN Charter, Article 94(2).

50. UN Charter, Chapter VII, in particular Articles 41 and 42.

51. *See* footnote 47 above. At the same time it declined to respond to a similar query from the World Health Assembly of the World Health Organization, on the ground that it did not arise within the scope of WHO's activities.

an issue between states parties to the treaty that they could submit to the Court under its contentious competence.

The second way to use the advisory competence of the ICJ is to resolve disputes involving a party or between parties that do not all have a right to participate in a contentious proceeding. What is required is that the dispute, with the consent of the parties thereto, be formulated as a question (or series of questions) that is then addressed to the Court by an IGO organ competent to do so. The consent so required can in effect be given in the same ways as indicated in B.7.b, above. However, as such submissions are not under the contentious competence of the Court, the responses of the Court are not automatically binding on the parties, unless they have agreed to make them so. Such disputes could, for example, relate to the respective competencies of two or more IGOs in respect of an environmental matter.

Environmentally relevant examples include:

(1) Basel Convention on the Transboundary Movements of Hazardous Wastes and their Disposal, Article 20;[52]
(2) Convention on Early Notification of a Nuclear Accident, Article 11(2 (first sentence), 3-4).[53]

8. *Resort to Regional Agencies or Other International Organizations*

A dispute may be taken up on submission by one or more parties or sometimes even *sua sponte* by an international organization, whether created by a regional treaty or one that relates to a particular subject matter (e.g., the exploitation of a particular resource or species), when all the parties to the dispute are parties to the treaty establishing the organization: the competent IGO organs can then either assist the parties in negotiating a solution or can propose and perhaps even impose a solution on them.

Some treaties that establish IGOs require the members (i.e., the parties to the treaty) to submit certain disputes to specified organs of the organization. Other treaties simply give an opportunity to the parties to do so by mutual consent. If the submission is compulsory, then the consent thereto has, in effect, been given by becoming party to the treaty that so provides.

Several types of IGO organs could consider interstate disputes. These include the standing organs of the IGO, or it may be one created ad hoc by a competent standing organ to deal with the particular submission. It may even be an essentially political one, such as a representative organ of the IGO. Alternatively, there may be a standing expert and/or quasi-judicial

52. IEL, *supra* note 22, at 616.
53. *Id.* at 586.

organ, or one may be created ad hoc. The body to consider the dispute may have competence to perform one or more of many of the third party functions discussed above: it may provide good offices, mediation, impartial fact-finding, conciliation, arbitration, or, in principle, even judicial settlement.

What procedures are applied to resolve disputes in this manner obviously depends on the nature and functions of the organ considering the dispute. In general the considerations recited above will apply to the corresponding methods relied on by an IGO. Of course, as such methods are by definition institutional, it will be less necessary to secure the agreement of the parties to every aspect of the creation and functioning of a fact-finding, conciliation, or arbitral organ.

The methods of resolving disputes through IGOs are quite varied, but the actual experience with such methods is relatively sparse. The following general observations are possible. First, because these methods involve a standing body, for example, the IGO, acting as a "third party," they may be generally more difficult to frustrate than ones that are purely created by the parties to the dispute. Second, whether the outcome is binding depends on the treaty pursuant to which the IGO is performing the dispute settlement function. And third, given that an IGO is involved, it may be able to enforce or at least to press for compliance by various measures taken within the IGO or that it can encourage or require the other members to take in respect of a recalcitrant state.

Following are some environmentally relevant examples: (1) Montreal Protocol on Substances That Deplete the Ozone Layer, interim procedures and institutional mechanisms adopted by the parties at their second (London) Meeting;[54] (2) Convention on the Prohibition of Military or any Other Hostile Use of Environmental Modification Techniques (ENMOD), Article V and Annex;[55] and (3) the World Trade Organization's Understanding on Rules and Procedures Governing the Settlement of Disputes.[56]

C. COMPLIANCE WITH INTERNATIONAL LAW

As discussed in the two previous sections of this chapter, there are many forms of international law. There is also a functioning international legislative process, and numerous procedures for the avoidance and the settlement of disputes, though the latter are often rendered ineffective by the general requirement that all parties concerned must consent to any form of international litigation. This section briefly examines the questions

54. *Id.* at 312-313.
55. *Id.* at 636-638.
56. 33 I.L.M. 1226 (1994).

of the extent to which international law is actually complied with and, to the extent that it is not, what tools the international community has to deal with the situation.

Compliance with international obligations, in particular those arising from treaties, is important from several points of view. First and foremost, compliance is necessary in order to accomplish the objectives of a particular treaty (e.g., with respect to the Montreal Protocol on Substances That Deplete the Ozone Layer, to reduce the quantity of CFCs emitted into the atmosphere). Moreover, even in respect of countries whose violation of a treaty (e.g., emissions in violation of the Montreal Protocol) would in any event be insignificant, compliance is important to reinforce the principle of the sanctity of treaty obligations. In addition, compliance is significant in order to prevent noncomplying countries from, in effect, getting a "free ride" from the restraint shown by others. This has two aspects. First, the violating country benefits from the restraint shown by others in that, for example, the ozone layer is less diminished than it would be without that restraint. Second, the violating country also benefits in not having to assume, or having its industry assume, the costs of compliance, which savings can either be considered as a form of unjustified income or as enabling the country to compete unfairly on the world market, in that it can produce certain goods more cheaply than a complying state can. Because such unfair competition may not be tolerable to competitors who are subject to the restraint, they may consider violating the regime or withdrawing from it—which, in turn, can lead to the unravelling of the entire system of a universally beneficial restraint.

For most purposes, there may be little practical distinction between a state that has not subjected itself to a particular regime and one that, having done so, violates it. Nevertheless, the former would not be breaking international law and the latter would be. It is therefore one of the problems of ensuring the functioning of various treaty regimes (e.g., environmental and disarmament) to decide whether and how parties to such a regime can and should differentiate between nonparties to the regime and parties that do not comply with it.

1. *Voluntary Compliance*

It has been observed that generally speaking most states comply with most of their international legal obligations most of the time.[57] In the 1990s, a number of studies have been undertaken to document the actual extent of compliance with international instruments, in particular with respect to environmental obligations, and to determine what factors, such

57. *See* Louis Henkin, How Nations Behave 47 (2d ed. 1979).

as the binding or nonbinding nature of the obligation or the availability of sanctions, affect the degree of compliance.[58]

Why states should generally comply with their international legal obligations is not difficult to understand. In the first place, as pointed out in section A above, international legal obligations are almost without exception voluntarily assumed by or consented to by states, and presumably they would not do so unless they actually intended to comply. Furthermore, the reasons that motivated the acceptance of the obligation, whether it is the desire to behave appropriately or to ensure that other states do so, normally continue to be valid and to affect a state's decision as to how to act. To the extent that the state in effect yielded to pressures in accepting the obligation—whether these are ones exerted by the international community as a whole, the other states in the region, by one or more states with significant economic, political, or military power, or because of internal political forces—all these are likely to be as insistent about compliance as they were about acceptance of the obligation.

Many of the considerations mentioned above in respect of binding obligations (i.e., those flowing from treaties or from customary law) also apply in respect of the provisions of nonbinding soft law instruments, such as solemn declarations of the UN General Assembly or of high-level worldwide conferences (e.g., concerning the environment, the 1972 Stockholm and the 1992 Rio Conferences). Thus states whose representatives, or possibly even heads of state or government, agreed to a declaration calling for certain behavior, may feel constrained by internal and external considerations to conform to such declarations, even though they are not strictly binding.

2. *Sanctions*

When states do not comply with their international obligations, the question arises: what can the international community do about it?

It has often been remarked that the international community—in contrast to national governments—lacks an executive or that the apparent executives (i.e., the executive heads of IGOs, such as the Secretary-General of the United Nations) lack executive power. From this some observers draw the conclusion that international law is not really "law" because it cannot be enforced. This conclusion disregards the facts that for various reasons actual compliance with international regimes is very high (as is discussed above); that it can be enhanced even more by some of the devices discussed below (under subsection 3); and that, in certain situations the

58. *See, e.g.,* Abram Chayes & Antonia Handler Chayes, The New Sovereignty: Compliance with International Regulatory Agreements (1995); The Implementation and Effectiveness of International Environmental Commitments: Theory and Practice (David G. Victor, Kal Raustida & Eugene B. Skolnikoff eds., 1998).

international community can indeed act to counter violations. These "sanctions" are discussed in this section.

a. Unilateral Sanctions

Modern international law absolutely forbids the threat or use of military force (except in self-defense against an armed attack)[59] and increasingly it prohibits or at least discourages the use of unilateral (as distinguished from properly organized collective) economic power to accomplish a country's own purposes. However, in general such power can be used in retaliation for a direct bilateral affront[60] and in some instances has been used—occasionally very effectively—to discourage an affront against a collective interest.

Thus the United States has used its economic power (e.g., by either barring certain fishing-related imports from the American market or by closing its fishing zones to certain states) in order to discourage states from conducting whaling operations in violation of rules established by the International Whaling Commission (*see* Chapter 19), in spite of the fact that these rules are not necessarily binding on the target states and that there is no provision in the relevant treaties for the imposition of either unilateral or collective sanctions.

The danger in such unilateral measures is that, even if not abused, they tend to lead to the enforcement of only such international measures of which one or more powerful states particularly approve, while leaving unsanctioned violations of regimes in which they have a lesser interest. There also are questions about how such measures relate to treaties, for example, the World Trade Organization agreements (*see* Chapter 20).

b. Collective Sanctions

Some international regimes provide for the imposition of collective sanctions on violators. To the extent that these sanctions are imposed only on violating parties, and not on nonparties, legal problems are diminished, because all parties to the regime can be considered to have consented to the imposition of the specified sanctions under the specified conditions.

The actual sanctions that can be imposed under such a regime are normally only economic ones and usually directly related to the violation—such as the prohibition of trade with the violator in goods that are in some

59. *See* UN Charter, Articles 2(4) and 51.

60. Thus, the new World Trade Organization (WTO) is charged with conducting elaborate quasi-judicial proceedings to determine what retaliatory action a WTO party may take against another party that allegedly has injured the former through particular trade measures that it considers to be in violation of a WTO-sponsored regime.

way affected by the violation. Whether a regime, such as an environmental one, could allow stricter or different sanctions is a matter largely untested in international law. It can be argued that the UN Security Council has a monopoly on the imposition of undifferentiated economic and diplomatic sanctions, on which it itself can rely under Article 41 of the UN Charter.

The real difficulties with the imposition of any collective sanctions are, however, procedural and political. To impose sanctions, it is generally necessary to take the following steps:[61]

(1) To establish facts suggesting that a violation has occurred. This can often be done by the secretariat of the IGO responsible for administering the regime in question, though the original impetus may come from an accusation by another state party, or perhaps by an NGO.
(2) To have a political body (usually an organ of the IGO) evaluate the facts to determine whether these actually prove a violation. In this connection it should be noted that generally (except perhaps in respect of a pariah state) governmental representatives are most reluctant to find a clear violation in the actions of another government.
(3) To determine what sanctions, within the purview of the regime and the authority of the IGO, should be imposed.
(4) To determine which states parties are to be authorized or perhaps required to take the sanctions measures decided on.
(5) To determine how the costs of the sanctions regime are to be distributed, lest certain parties be unfairly penalized—particularly if they are ones that can themselves be punished by the target state.

Because of these obstacles, few if any effective collective sanctions regimes have yet been developed.

c. Publicity

One potentially effective sanctioning measure is less subject to the complications discussed in the section above: to publicize the violations, leaving it to the "discipline of shame" to result in corrective action. Experience does show that states, or rather their governments, are most reluctant to be pilloried as treaty violators by a competent IGO, and an effective threat that may result in compliance (or at least the promise thereof) is that of a critical mention in an international report, particularly if it is

61. *See* Paul C. Szasz, Sanctions and International Nuclear Controls, 11 Conn. L. Rev. 545-581 (1979).

high-profile. A different way of viewing this is that publicity—e.g., through a system of monitoring, reporting, and verifying—can provide an effective incentive to implement and thereby comply with international obligations in the first instance, thus avoiding a dispute altogether.

3. Inducing Compliance and Implementation

Studies of why states may, in spite of the considerations mentioned in section C.1, fail to comply with their international obligations, show that this is only infrequently due to willful defiance and is more often due to ignorance or to technical or economic disability. This suggests that the corrective measures, rather than sanctions, should instead consist of education and of the rendering of appropriate assistance. Although this can be undertaken by another state (in a sort of "big-sibling" capacity), this is more often and more appropriately assigned to the secretariat or a special organ of the competent IGO.

Compliance with international regimes, particularly environmental ones, is apt to require a degree of scientific and technical expertise that not all countries can command. So, in some instances education is all that may be required (i.e., a clear explanation of the steps a state needs to take in order to comply). More often, however, the assistance may have to go beyond mere explanations, to actual technical aid in carrying out certain required functions, such as monitoring the emission of pollutants. Assistance may also be required in drafting necessary legal instruments, such as a set of technical regulations to be enacted by a competent ministry, or even laws to be adopted by the national legislature to create domestic regulatory bodies.

Aside from technical difficulties, some states may for economic reasons be unable or unwilling to comply with the requirements of a particular environmental regime. If this is evident during the negotiation of a treaty, special provisions may be included to relieve certain states or usually categories of states (e.g., the "least developed") from full or immediate compliance. In some cases, instead of building into the treaty a rigid set of exceptions, an organ of the competent IGO may be charged with determining what are genuine cases of need and what indulgences might be offered. In order to achieve a high measure of compliance, it may therefore be necessary or advisable to depart from an ideally rigid regime and to impose instead more differentiated obligations that will enable all parties of good will to comply with the appropriately relaxed obligations.

In addition, some treaties establish non-compliance mechanisms to assist or otherwise deal with states who may be experiencing difficulty in complying. The Montreal Protocol is perhaps the clearest example of this, as is discussed in chapter 11, sec. C.3, below. *See also* the discussion of non-confrontational approaches to compliance in chapter 9, sec. E, below.

Note and Questions

Chapter 7, section C contains an excerpt from Daniel Magraw, Legal Treatment of Developing Countries: Differential, Contextual, and Absolute Norms, 1 Colo. J. Intl. Envtl. L. & Poly. 69-70, 98-99 (1990). In the article, Professor Magraw writes:

> International norms, including international environmental norms, take three general forms. One form is to provide what I call "differential" treatment to developing countries. The second form is what I call "contextual" treatment; i.e., the norm, without specifically mentioning developing countries, requires or allows consideration of characteristics that typically vary according to the economic developmental situation in a country. The third general form of norm is what I call "absolute" norms, i.e., norms that provide a common standard for all countries and that do not require or allow contextual treatment. These three types of norms have different advantages and disadvantages, and thus are appropriately used in different situations.
>
> . . .
>
> Although absolute norms predominate, the contemporary international legal system is replete with differential and contextual norms. Instances of each type occur in the evolving and interconnected areas of economic development, human rights, and environmental protection/resource management law. Indeed, there arguably is an existing, general customary obligation, stemming primarily from State practice in those three areas, to take the effect on sustainable development in developing countries into account—in order to foster, or at least avoid unduly interfering with, such development and in order to ensure that norms are not impossible to comply with—when fashioning international environmental norms. Similarly, it is arguable that developed countries have a customary law duty to assist developing countries meet international environmental norms relating to progressive realization of international human rights.
>
> The most important customary international environmental principles already contain a contextual element, although this is not always expressed. Customary environmental law does not contain any examples of differential treatment, with the possible exceptions of the principles discussed in the immediately preceding paragraph.

Under what circumstances are various forms of norms most useful in promoting compliance? What are the advantages and disadvantages of using different types of norms? Is it possible to apply a contextual or differential norm in a principled manner? Do any difficulties in that regard affect the likelihood of compliance with norms by developing countries? By developed countries?

In analyzing the international environmental norms identified in subsequent chapters, evaluate into which of the above categories they may fall. Further evaluate whether, in the case of developing counties, differential or contextual treatment is warranted.

D. THE INTERNATIONAL INSTITUTIONAL FRAMEWORK

This section briefly introduces international organizations and provides an overview of some of the more important of those organizations active in the environmental field.

1. *Background: The Nature of International Organizations*

As many of the users of the present volume may not have taken a general course in international law or in international organizations, the present section starts with a brisk review of the taxonomy of international organizations. Those interested in more general background on international organizations and additional detail concerning environmental organizations will find a discussion of these issues in Appendix II.

There are two main types of international organizations (IOs): Intergovernmental Organizations (IGOs) and International Non-Governmental Organizations (INGOs). Perhaps not surprisingly, there may be ambiguities about the precise classification of a particular organization.[62] The widely respected *Handbook of International Organizations* lists some 300 "conventional" IGOs and over 4,000 "conventional" INGOs. It should be noted that there also are national NGOs (NNGOs), but these are only minimally mentioned herein.

The principal subjects of this section are IGOs, which have a primary role in the formulation, promulgation, and monitoring of compliance with international environmental legal norms, and may often directly contribute to their implementation. In all these respects INGOs and some NNGOs may play an important, sometimes arguably crucial, but still secondary role.

2. *United Nations Organs with Environmental Functions*[63]

Within the UN there is one organs that is primarily focused on environmental protection and a number of others for which this is one of many concerns. There have also been a number of environmental conferences, and UN organs have also sponsored numerous environmental treaties whose implementation in turn depends on treaty organs associated with such organs. These bodies are discussed below.

62. A prime example is the World Conservation Union—formerly known as the International Union for Conservation of Nature and Natural Resources (IUCN)—described briefly below.

63. Portions of this section are adapted from P.C. Szasz, Restructuring the International Organizational Framework (part A, The current structure), in Environmental Change and International Law, Chapter 11 (Edith Brown Weiss ed. 1992).

a. Primarily Environmental Institutions—United Nations Environment Programme (UNEP)

UNEP is a standing quasi-autonomous subsidiary organ of the UN General Assembly, established as a result, but not strictly speaking on the recommendation, of the 1972 UN [Stockholm] Conference on the Human Environment (discussed below).[64] Actually, the Assembly did not, strictly speaking, establish UNEP as such, but rather it created[65] a number of organs that, together, constituted the complex subsidiary organ referred to as UNEP. These organs were the 58-member Governing Council of the United Nations Environment Programme (a restricted representative organ); the Environment Secretariat (explicitly characterized as "small"), headed by the Executive Director of the United Nations Environment Programme; the Environment Fund; and the Environment Co-ordination Board (with an undefined membership, but clearly meant to consist of representatives of all environmentally active UN System organs and organizations, under the chairmanship of the UNEP Executive Director[66]). The primary function of these organs (except for the Fund) was to be the promotion of international cooperation and the coordination of environmental programs within the UN System.

Considering the handicaps of its somewhat oblique establishment (due to a reluctance to create any new international institutions at that time), of its location (for political reasons) in the rather remote Nairobi, far from the institutions it was supposed to coordinate, and of its always rather scanty funding,[67] UNEP actually became a remarkably effective centerpiece of the world organization's efforts to protect the environment. It has over the past two decades operated a strikingly varied and important set of programs, which include the stimulation of research, the collection and co-ordination of data, publications, education, the sponsorship of negotiations leading to the adoption of international treaties, and the establishment of numerous specialized environmental organs, as well as the issuing of guidelines and

64. Indeed, the Action Plan for the Human Environment adopted by the Conference (A/CONF.48/14/Rev. 1, Chapter II) did not call for the establishment of any UN organ, but principally for enhancing a number of organs and activities of various existing organs and organizations of the UN System, largely to be co-ordinated by the UN Secretary-General.

65. By A/RES/2997 (XXVII) of Dec. 15, 1972, on Institutional and Financial Arrangements for International Environmental Cooperation, which was reaffirmed by A/RES/31/112 of 16 December 1976, with the same title.

66. The Board was replaced in 1977 by the interagency board of Designated Officials on Environmental Matters (DOEM), a UNEP-created quasi-subsidiary of the UN System's Administrative Committee on Co-ordination (ACC).

67. In 1990, for example, UNEP received only about $4.8 million from the UN regular budget (which is financed by assessed contributions), an amount that in real terms represented no increase since 1980. $52.3 million came from voluntary contributions to the Environment Fund, $18.7 million from technical cooperation trust funds (which, in effect, require UNEP to carry out specified assistance programs) and $5.2 million from counterpart contributions (work performed nominally for other organizations). This compares with the United States EPA's 1990 budget of approximately $6 billion.

other types of "soft law." Some of the most important activities, projects, and accomplishments are the following:[68]

(i) *Ozone Layer.* UNEP sponsored the negotiations leading first to the 1985 Vienna Convention for the Protection of the Ozone Layer and to its 1987 Montreal Protocol, and provides the secretariat for the treaty organs (e.g., the Meetings of the Parties) established by either instrument; in the latter capacity it assisted in the Helsinki, London, and Copenhagen meetings at which important amendments to the protocol were negotiated and adopted.

(ii) *Climate.* UNEP and WMO cosponsor the Intergovernmental Panel on Climate Change (IPCC) in which the scientific, technical, and political foundations were laid for the negotiation of the 1992 Framework Convention on Climate Change, which is to create a regime to protect the global climate from greenhouse warming, as well as the 1997 Kyoto Protocol thereto.

(iii) *Hazardous Wastes.* In 1987 the UNEP Governing Council adopted the Cairo Guidelines and Principles for the Environmentally Sound Management of Hazardous Wastes, and UNEP sponsored the negotiations that led to the adoption of the 1989 Basel Convention on the Control of Transboundary Movements of Hazardous Wastes and Their Disposal.

(iv) *Marine Environment.* In 1974 UNEP initiated its Regional Seas Program,[69] which now covers some 11 distinct international seas, for each of which an action plan has been adopted by the states concerned (some 120 in all the Programs), some eight of which are being implemented by a respective framework convention supplemented by one or more protocols[70] (approximately 18 in all as of 1996).

(v) *Fresh Water.* Under its Program for the Environmentally Sound Management of Inland Water (EMINWA), UNEP sponsored the 1987 Zambezi Action Plan, and is assisting in the negotiation and preparation of such plans for Lake Chad and for the Aral Sea.

(vi) *Land Degradation.* With the assistance of FAO and UNESCO,

68. Systematic information about UNEP activities can be obtained since 1982 from the Annual Reports of the Executive Director, and from the recently introduced and episodically published UNEP Profiles (which set out cumulative information). The *Reports* of the UNEP Governing Council to the General Assembly (always published as Supplement No. 25 to the Official Records of the General Assembly), merely report on the Council's biannual (and sometimes special) sessions, and are not particularly informative. UNEP also issues a very considerable number of miscellaneous publications reporting on or describing particular programs, projects, subsidiary or associated organs, or reproducing the texts of various legal instruments or expert committee reports; unfortunately, these papers are rarely numbered and are thus hard to cite and even harder to find; no complete publications catalogue exists. Information about selected technical assistance and other projects can be found in the annual *Evaluation Reports* (e.g., that for 1989 reports on 15 projects).

69. Described in a series of publications entitled *UNEP Regional Seas Reports and Studies.*

70. For example, the 1976 Barcelona Convention for the Protection of the Mediterranean Sea against Pollution, supported by two simultaneously adopted Protocols for the Prevention of Pollution of the Mediterranean Sea by Dumping from Ships and Aircraft and concerning Co-operation in Combatting Pollution of the Mediterranean Sea by Oil and Other Harmful Substances in Cases of Emergency, the 1980 Athens Protocol for the Protection of the Mediterranean Sea against Pollution from Land-Based Sources, and the 1982 Geneva Protocol concerning Mediterranean Specially Protected Areas.

UNEP prepared and in 1982 the Governing Council adopted a World Soils Policy.

(vii) *Forests.* UNEP has cooperated with a number of other UN agencies in developing FAO's 1985 Tropical Forest Action Plan, and assisted in formulating the environmental provisions of the 1985 International Tropical Timber Agreement.

(viii) *Biological Diversity.* In 1987 UNEP initiated the preparation of a framework convention on the protection and preservation of biological diversity. It also acts as the secretariat of both the 1973 Washington Convention on International Trade in Endangered Species of Wild Fauna and Flora (CITES) and of the 1979 Bonn Convention on the Conservation of Migratory Species of Wild Animals (CMS).

(ix) *Monitoring and Information Systems.* Under its "Earthwatch" program, UNEP has established the Global Environment Monitoring System (GEMS), in which four specialized agencies, as well as IUCN and over 140 states participate. It also established INFOTERRA, a decentralized international mechanism for the exchange of environmental information, maintains the International Register of Potentially Toxic Chemicals (IRPTC), and with ILO and WHO operates the International Programme on Chemical Safety (IPCS).

In addition, UNEP has taken a number of important initiatives for setting or resetting the UN System's environmental agenda, such as the formulation of The United Nations System-Wide Medium-Term Environment Programmes for 1984-1989[71] and 1990-1995,[72] The formulation of the Programme for the Development and Periodic Review of Environmental Law (1982) (Montevideo Programme) and the Programme for Development and Periodic Review of Environmental Law for the 1990s(1993) (Montevideo Programme II), and the establishment of both the Intergovernmental Inter-sessional Preparatory Committee on the Environmental Perspective to the Year 2000 and Beyond and of the World Commission on Environment and Development (Brundtland Commission), the reports of which were endorsed by the General Assembly.[73] It also provides secretariat services for such interagency organs as the Designated Officials for Environmental Matters (DOEM)[74] and the Committee of International Development Institutions on the Environment (CIDIE).[75]

71. UNEP/GC/DEC/10/13 of May 31, 1982.

72. UNEP/GC/DEC/SS.I/3 of March 18, 1988. The plan is reproduced in document UNEP/GCSS.I/7/Add. 1, and inter alia, sets out, in over 400 paragraphs, the "Problems addressed," the "General objective," the detailed "Specific objectives," the "System-wide strategy" and the "Implementation of the strategy" on some 32 programmatic items grouped under 16 headings.

73. A/RES/42/186 and 187 of Dec. 11, 1987.

74. Over a dozen UN organs and some eight agencies participate in this body. *See* note 66, above.

75. This is a joint body of 16 multilateral development/finance institutions, including several outside the UN system.

b. Institutions to Integrate Environmental Policies with Other Policies

(i) Commission on Sustainable Development (CSD)

Just as UNEP originated in the 1972 Stockholm Conference, CSD is an offspring of the 1992 UN [Rio] Conference on Environment and Development, discussed below. It was established by the UN Economic and Social Council (ECOSOC) as one of its Functional Commissions (under Article 68 of the UN Charter) at the direction of the General Assembly,[76] which in turn was following recommendations incorporated by the Rio Conference into its "Agenda 21." CSD's task is to define and promote the reconciliation of the ostensibly antagonistic topics combined in the official name of UNCED—protection of the *environment,* more recognized as a concern by the developed countries, and *development,* often associated with economic growth, the striving of the developing countries—as well as of *social* issues. It is a simple 53-member representative organ, without the operational functions of the two quasi-autonomous UN organs, UNEP and the United Nations Development Program (UNDP), whose contrasting cultures it is to bridge.

Each year CSD examines certain general issues affecting the whole range of environmental topics covered by Agenda 21 (e.g., resource availability, technology transfer, science, education, and trade), and also reviews a cluster of related topics from among those included in Agenda 21. It makes recommendations on these to all parts of the UN System and especially to ECOSOC and the General Assembly.

(ii) High-level Advisory Board on Sustainable Development

Like CSD, the High-level Advisory Board on Sustainable Development was established by ECOSOC on the direction of the General Assembly, acting on recommendations contained in Agenda 21. Unlike CSD, the Advisory Board is an expert organ, whose "eminent" members are to have "recognized expertise on the broad spectrum of issues to be dealt with by [CSD], drawn from relevant scientific disciplines, industry, finance, and other major non-governmental constituencies, as well as various disciplines related to environment and development," be representative of all regions of the world and with due account for gender balance.[77] It advises the Secretary-General, CSD, ECOSOC, and the General Assembly.

c. UN-Related Treaty Bodies

In relation to many of the new or more acute environmental concerns, such as long-range transboundary air pollution, threats to the ozone layer,

76. A/RES/47/191 of Dec. 22, 1992.
77. *Id.*, para 29.

or the need to protect some particularly threatened or fragile environment or species, special treaties have been concluded under the auspices of some of the above-mentioned organs. Aside from establishing and defining relevant obligations for the states parties, some of these treaties have created full-fledged though small international organizations, with their own political organs and secretariats, or sometimes merely political or expert treaty organs without their own secretariats. These mini-organizations and treaty organs in effect function within the UN and thus constitute crucial parts of its machinery for dealing with environmental matters. For the most part the secretariat functions for servicing these organs have been assigned, sometimes on a permanent and sometimes on merely an interim or experimental basis, to some existing subsidiary UN organ, such as UNEP or a UN Regional Commission. A list of some environmental treaty regimes, together with their respective secretariats, follows:

(1) 1973 Washington Convention on International Trade in Endangered Species of Wild Fauna and Flora (CITES), administered by UNEP in Geneva;
(2) 1979 Convention on Long-Range Transboundary Air Pollution with its several protocols, administered by the Economic Commission for Europe (ECE) in Geneva;
(3) 1979 Bonn Convention on the Conservation of Migratory Species of Wild Animals (CMS), administered by UNEP in Bonn;
(4) 1985 Vienna Convention for the Protection of the Ozone Layer and the 1987 Montreal Protocol on Substances that deplete the Ozone Layer, administered by UNEP in Nairobi, except that the Multilateral Fund established by the 1990 London Amendments to the Montreal Protocol is administered by a separate secretariat in Montreal;
(5) 1989 Basel Convention on the Control of Transboundary Movements of Hazardous Wastes and Their Disposal, administered by UNEP in Geneva;
(6) 1992 UN Framework Convention on Climate Change, administered independently in Bonn;
(7) 1992 Biodiversity Convention, administered independently in Montreal.

d. Environmental Conferences

Another type of IGO activity are conferences convened for the purpose of adopting environmental treaties and other related instruments or merely to give an international platform for the exploration of a particular theme. Although these conferences can be characterized as ad hoc high-level representative organs of the convening IGOs, it should be recognized that an international conference does not consist of merely the relatively short meeting denominated as such, but that almost always there are several other stages and manifestations.

(i) General Environmental Conferences

There have been two general environmental conferences, both convened by the United Nations:

(1) *1972 Stockholm Conference.* The 1972 United Nations Conference on the Human Environment served both to awaken the international community to the importance of protecting the environment and was followed by a number of institutional arrangements for that purpose (in particular, UNEP). Its formal work was embodied in a declaration (known as the Stockholm Declaration) including 26 Principles, as well as in a more detailed Action Plan for the Human Environment.

(2) *1992 Rio Conference.* The 1992 United Nations Conference on Environment and Development (also called UNCED and the Earth Summit), convened two decades after the Stockholm Conference as a follow-up thereto, addressed the more obviously divergent views of developed and developing countries towards environmental issues and sought to bridge these by the concept of "sustainable development." To implement this concept it recommended the establishment of standing organs, such as the Commission on Sustainable Development and the High Level Advisory Board on Sustainable Development. It issued the Rio Declaration on Environment and Development with 27 Principles; Agenda 21, consisting of 40 somewhat lengthy Chapters; and a Non-legally Binding Authoritative Statement of Principles for a Global Consensus on the Management, Conservation and Sustainable Development of all Types of Forests. The Conference also provided the forum for the opening for signature of the Convention on Biological Diversity and the Framework Convention on Climate Change, which had been negotiated and formulated separately from but in parallel with the preparations for the Conference.

(ii) Specific Environment-Related Conferences

Ever since the Stockholm Conference, the United Nations has convened a number of much more narrowly focused, environment-related conferences. Some of these again have been essentially thematic, to focus attention on a particular problem; others have been charged with formulating treaties to formalize cooperative solutions to such problems. Following are some of the more important such meetings:

(1) The 1974 World Population Conference, Bucharest, adopted the World Population Plan of Action. It was followed by the 1984 International Conference on Population, which adopted the Mexico City Declaration on Population and Development, and the 1994 International Conference on

Population and Development, Cairo, which adopted a 20-year Programme of Action (including a chapter on population and environment).

(2) The 1976 Conference on Human Settlements (Habitat), Vancouver, which adopted the Vancouver Declaration on Human Settlements leading to the establishment of the UN Centre for Human Settlements (Habitat) in Nairobi. Habitat II was convened in Istanbul in 1996.

(3) The 1977 Conference on Desertification, Nairobi, produced the Plan of Action to Combat Desertification. After years of work on the subject within UNEP, the General Assembly in 1992 established the International Negotiating Committee for the Elaboration of an International Convention to Combat Desertification in Those Countries Experiencing Serious Drought and/or Desertification, particularly in Africa, which in 1994 adopted the eponymous Convention.

(4) The 1977 United Nations Water Conference, Mar del Plata (Argentina), approved the Mar del Plata Action Plan and several specific agreements.

(5) The 1981 United Nations Conference on New and Renewable Sources of Energy, Nairobi, adopted the Nairobi Programme of Action for the Development and Utilization of New and Renewable Sources of Energy.

(6) The 1994 Global Conference on the Sustainable Development of Small Island Developing States, Bridgetown (Barbados), adopted the Declaration of Barbados and the Programme of Action for the Sustainable Development of Small Island Developing States.

(7) The 1995 Conference on Straddling Fish Stocks and Highly Migratory Fish Stocks, New York, adopted the eponymous Convention.

3. *International Non-Governmental Organizations*[78]

There are two areas of international intercourse where NGOs have made (and are making) a particularly significant impact: the protection of human rights and of the environment. In both fields these organizations, both INGOs and NNGOs, carry out important functions vis-à-vis both IGOs and national governments. In both fields, but particularly in the latter, these functions include:

(1) Monitoring of the condition of the environment, the impact on those conditions of particular anthropogenic events, and the impact on the latter of particular protective measures imposed by international or national regimes. The results of these studies are communicated to IGOs and national governments, as well as, through the media, to the public.

(2) Lobbying IGOs and governments, directly or through the genera-

78. For a general discussion on NGOs, *see* Appendix II, Part II.

tion of public pressure, for the establishment of regimes designed to protect the environment, whether in the form of treaties, statutes, regulations, guidelines, or other forms of international and national laws.

(3) Assisting IGO and governmental organs in formulating appropriate legal texts.

(4) In a few instances, actually participating in the administration of certain aspects of environmental regimes.

There are a great number of environmental NNGOs and also a certain number of INGOs. Most of the latter and some of the former have consultative status with ECOSOC. Listed below are the more important INGOs active in this field in Category II status with ECOSOC (organizations with special competence but concerned with only a few of the Council's activities):

(1) Environment Liaison Centre;

(2) Greenpeace International—well known for its forceful public advocacy;

(3) International Centre for Industry and the Environment;

(4) International Council of Environmental Law;

(5) International Petroleum Industry Environmental Conservation Association;

(6) World Conservation Union—formerly known as the International Union for Conservation of Nature and Natural Resources—(IUCN); this is arguably the most important of these INGOs and was originally established as the International Union for the Protection of Nature. Quite unlike most NGOs, it was created by a treaty, and its members include over 50 states, over 100 government agencies and some 350 NNGOs and INGOs. It works in close collaboration with a number of IOs and organs, in particular FAO and UNEP, and with INGOs such as the WWF. On commission by UNEP, IUCN developed the World Conservation Strategy in 1980. It has also prepared the initial drafts of or helped in formulating a number of environmental treaties.

4. *Summary and Conclusions*

The international institutional structure relevant to the protection of the environment in some ways resembles national regimes, but in many important ways differs from these. In both there are norm-creating legislative organs; in both there are executive ones charged with implementing these regimes, but the national ones are clearly better equipped to do so effectively; and both have disputes settlement mechanisms, though the national ones are clearly far more developed and effective, in particular because these, unlike most international ones (with the notable exception of the European Union (EU)), have compulsory jurisdiction.

International regimes are more complex and decentralized than national ones. The reason of course is that there does not exist any world government, or even a regional one, with the possible exception of the EU for most of Western Europe. But a more fundamental reason probably is that the international community is far more diverse that any national one, which becomes obvious when one compares the actors (principally states) on the international scene, according to size, power, wealth, or state of development. Consequently it is difficult to achieve agreement on any but the narrowest aspects of international governance (such as the establishment of a regime meant to protect against a very specific threat), which therefore is assigned somewhat haphazardly to numerous largely independently established intergovernmental organizations, with essentially no hierarchical relationships; at most there are certain weak coordinating mechanisms within the groups into which many, but by no means all, international organizations are clustered. Because there is no central authority that could undertake to rearrange international organizations and organs into a more logical pattern, and because there is (and has been for some time) an aversion to the creation of any more significant new institutions, improvements can only be incremental. At present most of these consist of ad hoc additions, either to the functions of existing organizations or in a minor way to the international machinery by the creation of treaty organs or mini-IGOs.

This having been said, it should be noted that as far as environmental affairs are concerned, the world community has been able to formulate instruments and to create institutions essentially as fast as agreements can be reached on these—which of course is not always easy given the diversity in both the nature and the interests of the nearly 200 states now involved in the process. Naturally, these agreements often reflect a low common denominator—but this is a phenomenon often observed in legislation produced in democratically governed states.

What the international system to a considerable extent lacks is simplicity and elegance, and the transparency that would go with these characteristics. Outsiders may find it difficult to disentangle the multiplicity of institutions that may be dealing with a particular issue and to try to establish responsibility for failures. Nevertheless, once such understanding has been achieved—and this has been done by those operating many of the NGOs in this field and accounts for their ability to influence the process—it will be seen that international institutions respond to essentially the same stimuli as national ones, and that the ability to secure and to present relevant facts persuasively, to be able to identify the competent centers of power and to analyze their special interests and concerns, and above all to negotiate with those whose interests are different, are the elements essential to success in achieving improvements in both international and national environmental regimes.

Notes and Questions

1. *A single IGO for the environment?* Would it be sensible to try to create a single international IGO, to embrace all or at least most of the existing environmental IGOs and IGO organs? What might be the arguments for and against? For an analysis favoring such an organization, *see* Daniel C. Esty, Greening the GATT: Trade Environment and the Future (1994).

2. *More specifically tasked IGOs?* If you conclude that the comprehensive IGO suggested in Question 1 is too ambitious, would it be sensible to create one or more environmental IGOs that would deal with at least the following:

(1) All atmosphere related matters, such as ozone-layer protection; greenhouse gases; air pollution?
(2) All ocean and regional sea-related matters?
(3) All UN System environmental activities?

3. *Voting.* Would it be better if voting in environmental IGOs were based, instead of the now normal one-member-one-vote basis, on population and/or on financial contributions to the IGO?

4. *Funding of environmental IGOs.* Should contributions to environmental IGOs be on an assessed contribution, voluntary contribution, or some other basis?

5. *The role of non-governmental organizations:*

(1) Should environmental INGOs and NNGOs be given a greater role in shaping the work of IGOs? What might such increased roles be?
(2) Do you consider INGOs and NNGOs better representatives of the interests of normal citizens than the governmental representatives who determine the policies of IGOs? Why? *See generally* Edith Brown Weiss, The Changing Structure of International Law, excepted in chapter 1, sec. E, above.

PART TWO

POLLUTION CONTROL: GENERAL AND SPECIFIC NORMS

Controlling pollution is one of the great challenges confronting the international legal system. It is a complex and difficult task because many different activities cause pollution. Moreover, those activities often are part of our everyday lives and are associated with fundamental aspects of our economy. Automobiles, for example, emit exhaust into the air, causing smog.

A. WHAT IS "POLLUTION"?

An initial question is, what do we mean by "pollution"? The Organisation for Economic Co-operation and Development (OECD) has defined pollution as follows:

> the introduction by humankind, directly or indirectly, of substances or energy into the environment resulting in deleterious effects of such a nature as to endanger human health, harm living resources and eco-systems, impair amenities or interfere with other legitimate uses of the environment.[1]

1. OECD Res. C(77) 28 (Final), Annex, Introduction, 17 May 1977, in OECD, OECD and the Environment 151 (1986).

What does this definition encompass? Does it include the emission of sulphur dioxide from power plants that causes acid rain? Radioactive material from the Chernobyl reactor? Nitrogen oxides emitted from automobile tailpipes? Spills of chemicals into rivers? Litter dropped by hikers? Cigarette smoke?

Does the OECD definition include carbon dioxide emitted from automobiles? Recall the Perry excerpt in Chapter 1: carbon dioxide is already present in significant quantities in the atmosphere.[2] Some have argued that adding carbon dioxide to the atmosphere is not pollution because of that fact. Does that fact matter? Assuming the emission of carbon dioxide can constitute pollution, does the OECD definition include carbon dioxide exhaled by competitors in the Olympics? Oxygen (or carbon dioxide) emitted by plants or trees?[3] Does the answer depend on whether the plants or trees were planted by humans? What about the release into a river of water heated by use in a nuclear reactor, or the presence of heat from a human body swimming in the ocean? Or the disposal of diapers in a landfill?

Does the OECD definition include the introduction of foreign species into an ecosystem? Does the answer turn on whether the introduction was intentional (such as the introduction of plant species in Hawaii[4] and African bees in South America[5]) or accidental (such as presumably was the case with the Zebra mussel in the Great Lakes[6])? What about the creation and introduction of faster-growing varieties of rice through selective breeding—is the Green Revolution a form of pollution? Or new life forms through genetic engineering? Does it matter if the new life forms are confined to a laboratory, rather than released into nature at large?

Regardless of whether the OECD definition encompasses the effects just mentioned, should society consider them to be, or treat them as, pollution? Does it matter whether effects are characterized as pollution if the difficulties associated with them are addressed? Does the characterization affect the likelihood that the difficulties will be addressed?

2. *See generally* Chapter 12, below.

3. Plants emit oxygen during photosynthesis and carbon dioxide during respiration.

4. It is estimated that approximately 200 species of plants in Hawaii have become extinct, in part due to the introduction of foreign plants and animals into the islands.

5. High honey-yielding, aggressive bees from Africa were bred with nonaggressive, low-yielding bees in South America in the hopes of obtaining a nonaggressive, high-yielding strain of bees. Unfortunately, the result was a highly aggressive, low-yielding bee that has emigrated north. The bees are expected to cross the Mexico-United States border soon.

6. The Zebra mussel is thought to have been deposited in the Great Lakes from the ballast of ships travelling up the St. Lawrence River from Europe. The small inedible shellfish reproduces rapidly and adheres to the hulls of boats, clogs intake pipes of power plants, and ingests food in competition with native fish.

B. THE INTERNATIONAL COMMUNITY'S INTEREST IN POLLUTION

Another threshold question is, under what circumstances is pollution legitimately of interest to the international community? The clearest instance most probably involves a situation where the activities of a state (the state of origin) in its territory create pollution that causes damage to the territory of another state (the affected state). The international community has a strong interest in resolving disputes and preventing conflict between states, including conflict generated by transboundary harm; and international law traditionally has focused (almost exclusively) on the rights and duties of states.

Suppose, however, that the activity creating the pollution is within the state of origin's territory but is private. Or that the harm is to private interests in the affected State. The OECD's definition of "transfrontier pollution" (also sometimes referred to as "transboundary pollution") includes the situations just mentioned:

> any intentional or unintentional pollution whose physical origin is subject to, and situated wholly or in part within the area under, the national jurisdiction of one State and which has effects in the area under the national jurisdiction of another State.[7]

Suppose that an activity, which causes pollution damage in a state, occurs on a global commons such as the high seas but is nevertheless within another state's control (i.e., that state has the legal authority to regulate the activity): is that "transfrontier pollution" as defined by the OECD? In any event, is it of concern to the international community?

Suppose that the pollution harms only a global commons, for example, an area that belongs to all states and over which no state has exclusive authority. Does the international community have a legitimate interest in such "commons pollution"?

Suppose that the direct harm is wholly within the state of origin's territory (sometimes this type of pollution is referred to as "intrastate pollution"). Does the international community have a legitimate interest in intrastate pollution if some identifiable right or duty (e.g., an international human right to health or a duty established by an international agreement such as the World Heritage Convention[8]) is abridged? Suppose the intrastate pollution endangers the survival of a species?

Do the transfrontier, commons, and intrastate effects just described fall within the OECD definition of "pollution"?

7. OECD Res. C(77) 28 (Final), Annex, Introduction, 17 May 1977, in OECD, OECD and the Environment 151 (1986).

8. Convention for the Protection of the World Cultural and Natural Heritage, 23 November 1972, 27 U.S.T. 37, T.I.A.S. No. 8226, *reprinted in* 11 I.L.M. 1358 (1972).

C. ECONOMIC ANALYSIS OF POLLUTION

In Chapter 3, four aspects of economic environmental analysis were introduced: protection of common areas, externalities, benefit-cost analysis, and discounting. It is useful to review those materials at this point, in order to consider how they apply to analyzing international pollution.

Regarding protection of common areas, how does Garrett Hardin's analysis apply to pollution?

Regarding the other three issues, is it important to require polluters to internalize the externalities of the pollution they cause? If so, how can that best be done? How should the costs and benefits of externalities be measured, especially when they affect something for which there is no readily ascertainable market? What other things subject to pollution damage are in that category? Should there always be an offset against costs for external benefits? Should Canada compensate the United States for benefits to its agriculture due to increased nitrogen brought by transboundary acid rain?

Assuming the relevant benefits and costs and their values can be agreed upon, how should the temporal factor—the fact that benefits and costs accrue over time—be taken into account: what discount rate should be used? Is it appropriate to use a standard discount rate, regardless of the type of activity causing the pollution, the type of damage, and the location of the activity and damage?

D. OVERVIEW OF INTERNATIONAL POLLUTION: ISSUES RAISED AND NORMS USED IN RESPONSE

A question important to efforts to settle disputes or make rules about future behavior—and to understanding those efforts—is, what types of legal and policy issues are actually raised by international pollution (whether transfrontier pollution, commons pollution, or intrastate pollution)? Phrased differently, what specifically are the affected state or private person and the international community concerned about?

Consider the cases of acid rain and the Chernobyl disaster. What specific concerns do they raise? How do they differ?

One author distinguishes between pollution resulting from a single event (such as an accidental or intentional discharge of a pollutant) and pollution resulting from a chronic condition (such as long-term, low-level emission of toxic fumes):

> Generally speaking, with respect to single-event pollution, the community is concerned with (1) the probability that an event will occur and corresponding

> safety standards for the State in which the activity is occurring (the State of origin); (2) immediate response mechanisms, such as notification of States that potentially may be harmed (affected States) and assistance mechanisms to facilitate terminating the pollution, providing medical treatment, evacuating nearby populations, or other mitigation measures in all States concerned; (3) determination of accountability for injuries suffered, that is, ascertaining whether the State of origin met the appropriate standard of care; and (4) compensation of those who are actually injured. In contrast, in the case of chronic transboundary pollution, the community is concerned with (1) proving that the chronic problem has caused a recognizable injury in the affected state(s); (2) either eliminating or minimizing the chronic pollution without necessarily ending the activity causing the pollution, whose economic viability often depends on the chronic release; and (3) possibly compensating those injured by the chronic pollution, particularly if it is not eliminated completely.[9]

Is this distinction helpful? Into which categories do acid rain and the Chernobyl disaster fall? Does the quotation identify all the important issues?

Another way of classifying those issues is whether they have to do with preventing pollution, mitigating the effects of pollution (including rehabilitating or restoring the situation to what it was before the pollution occurred), or compensating for pollution damage. Chapters 7 and 9 consider the norms relating to those issues.Those norms are either customary international law or general principles of law recognized by civilized nations (those sources of law are discussed in Chapter 5). Discussion of pollution-control regimes that have been developed by international agreement in order to protect against particular pollution threats or in order to protect particular resources from pollution follows. The materials on each conventional regime include principles and rules relating to each of prevention, mitigation, and compensation, as well as rules regarding the major cross-cutting issues, such as how to deal with scientific uncertainty, how to treat developing countries, and how to deal with future generations, to the extent such rules exist. Relevant "soft law," a precept or guideline that is not legally binding,[10] is also included in those materials.

Norms (and soft law) regarding pollution control vary greatly and can be quite complex. For example, it is generally recognized that states have an obligation to cooperate to prevent pollution.[11] This obligation, which has substantive and procedural aspects, can be articulated with more or less specificity, and it relates to several stages of pollution prevention, as well as shading into mitigating the effects of pollution. These stages include: conducting international environmental impact assessments of proposed activities; notifying other states of potential risks before undertaking projects; consulting with such states, regarding plans; monitoring (e.g., regard-

9. Magraw, International Law and Pollution 6, in International Law and Pollution (D. Magraw, ed. 1991).

10. Soft law is discussed in Chapter 5 sec. A.6.a.

11. *See* Chapter 7, below.

ing the condition of dams on international rivers); regularly exchanging environmentally pertinent data and information; warning potentially affected states that polluting accidents have occurred; and assisting states in which such accidents have occurred.

Generally speaking (and as seen in greater detail below), the pollution-control principles and rules are of three types: contextual, differential, and absolute. A "contextual" norm is a norm that on its face provides identical treatment to all states affected by the norm but requires in its application consideration of characteristics that might vary from country to country. Applying a contextual norm thus usually involves balancing multiple interests and characteristics. The principle that shared natural resources should be utilized in a "reasonable and equitable manner"[12] is an example of a contextual norm, as is the requirement that states "cooperate" in preventing pollution.[13]

A "differential" norm is a norm that on its face provides different, presumably more advantageous, standards for one group of states than for another group. The groups of states can be distinguished on any ground (other than simply that one group is composed of states that are the actors and the other group consists of states that are affected by the actions). The differential norms of greatest interest with respect to the environment are those that treat developing countries differently than developed countries. Examples include the rules contained in the 1987 Montreal Protocol on Substances That Deplete the Ozone Layer, as adjusted in 1990, that allow developing states (defined in terms of annual consumption of controlled substances) ten years longer to eliminate chlorofluorocarbons than it allows developed countries,[14] and a provision of the Law of the Sea Convention requires that "developing States" (a term that is not defined in the Convention) be given preference in the provision of scientific and technical assistance for the protection of the marine environment.[15]

An "absolute" norm is a norm that provides identical treatment to all countries and does not require or permit consideration of factors that vary between countries. The 1987 Nuclear Accident Notification Convention's requirement of "forthwith" notification of pending transboundary harm is an example of an absolute norm,[16] as is the obligations agreed upon by Mexico and the United States that Mexico is to receive 1.5 million acre-feet of Colorado River water per year and that the salinity concentration of that water shall not exceed 115 parts per million over the concentrations

12. *See* Chapter 16, below.

13. Montreal Protocol on Substances That Deplete the Ozone Layer, Sept. 16, 1987, art. 5, *reprinted in* 26 I.L.M. 1550 (1987), as adjusted on June 27, 1990.

14. Footnote 13, above.

15. United Nations Convention on the Law of the Sea, Dec. 10, 1982, art. 202, U.N. Doc. A/CONF. 62 (1988), *reprinted in* 21 I.L.M. 1261 (1982).

16. IAEA Convention on Early Notification of a Nuclear Accident, 26 Sept. 1986, art. 2, *reprinted in* 25 I.L.M. 1370 (1986).

of the water delivered to the Imperial Dam in California.[17] Applying absolute norms typically involves an inquiry into the facts of the specific case (e.g., when did a nuclear accident occur and when did notification occur, in order to determine whether notification was "forthwith"); and reasonable people may differ about which facts are relevant to such inquiries. No bright line exists between absolute and contextual norms, therefore, although it is usually clear which type of norm is involved.

Absolute norms have the capacity for being highly precise, as do differential norms that do not contain contextual elements. The ten-year period referred to above regarding the differential treatment of developing countries is such an example: it is more precise than a term such as "reasonable period of time." Precision is sometimes desirable regarding pollution control because the behavior or effect can be described specifically. Absolute norms also provide greater certainty and less room for States to argue that behavior is permissible or impermissible. Contextual norms (and even, to a lesser extent, differential norms), on the other hand, allow greater flexibility and are more sensitive to variations in circumstances, which can be desirable with respect to some environmental issues (e.g., as a prospective norm regarding the allocation of shared natural resources in light of future uses and needs that cannot be foreseen). Even the lack of certainty may be beneficial in the sense that it may allow states to agree on some standard, in situations where agreement otherwise would be impossible.

Contextual norms also allow individual developing countries to be treated differently than other countries, because the factors taken account of in the contextual analysis may be affected by the fact that the country in question is a developing country.[18]

17. Treaty Relating to the Utilization of Waters of the Colorado and Tijuana Rivers and of the Rio Grande, Feb. 3, 1944, art. 10, Mexico-United States, 59 Stat. 1219, T.S. No. 994, 3 U.N.T.S. 313; Agreement on Colorado River Salinity Confirming Minute No. 242, Aug. 30, 1973, Mexico-United States, 24 U.S.T. 1968, T.I.A.S. No. 7408.

18. For a discussion of the advantages and disadvantages of using these types of norms, *see* Magraw, Legal Treatment of Developing Countries: Differential, Contextual, and Absolute Norms, 1 Colo. J. Intl. Envtl. L. & Poly. 69 (1990).

VI

The Basic Cases

Despite variations in their authoritative value, cases are an important source of law in most legal systems. As you have already seen in Chapter 5, the international legal system is no exception. There are four major cases that most commentators regard as the principle sources of the "common law" of international environmental problems. Perhaps because of their comparative rarity, these cases seem to invite attempts to inflate their authoritative value and to apply them to problems far removed from their fact situations. One of our tasks in this chapter will therefore be to examine these cases carefully with a view to determining their proper use as sources of authority and policy. We begin with the classic in the field, the one case in which a final decision was rendered in a dispute concerning transfrontier pollution.

A. TRANSFRONTIER POLLUTION: THE *TRAIL SMELTER* ARBITRATION

In the 1920s and 1930s, the Consolidated Mining and Smelting Company of Canada, Ltd. (known as COMINCO since the 1960s) operated a large zinc and lead smelter at Trail, British Columbia, Canada (the smelter is still operating as of this writing). The smelter is located on the Columbia

River just north of the international boundary, about seven miles as the crow flies, or about 11 miles along the course of the river. The smelting process produced sulphur dioxide, which was discharged into the air through tall stacks. Certain atmospheric conditions prevailing from time to time carried these fumes down the Columbia River valley into the United States, to Washington State, where they caused damage to private farms and timber lands.

Lawyers at the time were generally of the view that British Columbia courts would decline to assert jurisdiction in any action to recover for the property damage in Washington because of the rule announced by the House of Lords in British South Africa Company v. Companhia de Moçambique, [1893] A.C. 602. That case held that suits for damage to foreign land are local actions and must be brought in the state where the land is located. Yet the Washington property owners would fare no better in that state since at the time it had no long-arm statute that would have permitted a Washington court to assert jurisdiction over the Canadian smelter. In 1928 the United States and Canadian governments referred the problem to the International Joint Commission (IJC), established by the two countries under the 1909 Boundary Waters Treaty, for an investigation and report. In 1931 the IJC submitted its report in which it found that the smelter had caused damage in the amount of $350,000 and made certain recommendations. The unacceptability of these recommendations to the United States led to negotiations that resulted in a convention signed on April 15, 1935, in which the parties agreed to submit the matter to an arbitral tribunal.[1] The convention contains two other provisions of present interest. In Article I, Canada agreed to pay the United States $350,000 to cover all damage that had occurred prior to January 1, 1932. And in Article IV, the parties instructed the Tribunal as to the standards to be applied in arriving at its decision: "The Tribunal shall apply the law and practice followed in dealing with cognate questions in the United States of America as well as International Law and Practice, and shall give consideration to the desire of the High Contracting Parties to reach a solution just to all parties concerned." The Tribunal's second and final decision is excerpted here.

■ *TRAIL SMELTER* ARBITRATION

(United States v. Canada)
Ad Hoc International Arbitral Tribunal, 1941
3 U.N. Rep. Intl. Arb. Awards 1911, 1938 (1941)[2]

The controversy is between two Governments involving damage occurring, or having occurred, in the territory of one of them (the United

1. Convention for the Final Settlement of the Difficulties Arising through Complaints of Damage Done in the State of Washington by Fumes Discharged from the Smelter of the Consolidated Mining and Smelting Company, Trail, British Columbia, April 15, 1935, 49 Stat. 3245 (1935), T.S. No. 893, 162 L.N.T.S. 74 (effective Aug. 3, 1935).

2. Reprinted in 35 Am. J. Intl. L. 684 (1941).

States of America) and alleged to be due to an agency situated in the territory of the other (the Dominion of Canada). . . .

As between the two countries involved, each has an equal interest that if a nuisance is proved, the indemnity to damaged parties for proven damage shall be just and adequate and each has also an equal interest that unproven or unwarranted claims shall not be allowed. For, while the United States' interests may now be claimed to be injured by the operations of a Canadian corporation, it is equally possible that at some time in the future Canadian interests might be claimed to be injured by an American corporation. . . .

Considerations like the above are reflected in the provisions of the Convention in Article IV, that "the desire of the high contracting parties" is "to reach a solution just to all parties concerned." And the phraseology of the questions submitted to the Tribunal clearly evinces a desire and an intention that, to some extent, in making its answers to the questions, the Tribunal should endeavor to adjust the conflicting interests by some "just solution" which would allow the continuance of the operation of the Trail Smelter but under such restrictions and limitations as would, as far as foreseeable, prevent damage in the United States, and as would enable indemnity to be obtained, if in spite of such restrictions and limitations, damage should occur in the future in the United States.

In arriving at its decision, the Tribunal has had always to bear in mind the further fact that in the preamble to the Convention, it is stated that it is concluded with the recognition of "the desirability and necessity of effecting a permanent settlement."

The duty imposed upon the Tribunal by the Convention was to "finally decide" the following questions:

(1) Whether damage caused by the Trail Smelter in the State of Washington has occurred since the first day of January, 1932, and, if so, what indemnity should be paid therefor?
(2) In the event of the answer to the first part of the preceding question being in the affirmative, whether the Trail Smelter should be required to refrain from causing damage in the State of Washington in the future and, if so, to what extent?
(3) In the light of the answer to the preceding question, what measures or régime, if any, should be adopted or maintained by the Trail Smelter?
(4) What indemnity or compensation, if any, should be paid on account of any decision or decisions rendered by the Tribunal pursuant to the next two preceding questions?

On April 16, 1938, the Tribunal reported its "final decision" on Question No. 1, as well as its temporary decisions on Questions No. 2 and No. 3, and provided for a temporary régime thereunder. The decision reported on April 16, 1938, will be referred to hereinafter as the "previous decision."

Concerning Question No. 1, in the statement presented by the Agent for the Government of the United States, claims for damages of $1,849,156.16 with interest of $250,855.01—total $2,100,011.17—were presented, divided into seven categories, in respect of (*a*) cleared land and improvements; (*b*) of uncleared land and improvements; (*c*) live stock; (*d*) property in the town of Northport; (*e*) wrong done the United States in violation of sovereignty, measured by cost of investigation from January 1, 1932, to June 30, 1936; (*f*) interest on $350,000 accepted in satisfaction of damage to January 1, 1932, but not paid on that date; (*g*) business enterprises. The area claimed to be damaged contained "more than 140,000 acres," including the town of Northport.

The Tribunal disallowed the claims of the United States with reference to items *(c), (d), (e), (f)* and *(g)* but allowed them, in part, with respect to the remaining items *(a)* and *(b)*.

In conclusion (end of Part Two of the previous decision), the Tribunal answered Question No. 1 as follows:

> Damage caused by the Trail Smelter in the State of Washington has occurred since the first day of January, 1932, and up to October 1, 1937, and the indemnity to be paid therefor is seventy-eight thousand dollars ($78,000), and is to be complete and final indemnity and compensation for all damage which occurred between such dates. Interest at the rate of six per centum per year will be allowed on the above sum of seventy-eight thousand dollars ($78,000) from the date of the filing of this report and decision until date of payment. This decision is not subject to alteration or modification by the Tribunal hereafter. The fact of existence of damage, if any, occurring after October 1, 1937, and the indemnity to be paid therefor, if any, the Tribunal will determine in its final decision.

Answering Questions No. 2 and No. 3, the Tribunal decided that, until a final decision should be made, the Trail Smelter should be subject to a temporary régime (described more in detail in Part Four of the present decision) and a trial period was established to a date not later than October 1, 1940, in order to enable the Tribunal to establish a permanent régime based on a "more adequate and intensive study," . . .

I

By way of introduction to the Tribunal's decision, a brief statement, in general terms, of the topographic and climatic conditions and economic history of the locality involved in the controversy may be useful.

The Columbia River has its source in the Dominion of Canada. At a place in British Columbia named Trail, it flows past a smelter located in a gorge, where zinc and lead are smelted in large quantities. From Trail, its course is easterly and then it swings in a long curve to the international boundary line, at which point it is running in a southwesterly direction; and its course south of the boundary continues in that general direction.

The distance from Trail to the boundary line is about seven miles as the crow files or about eleven miles, following the course of the river (and possibly a slightly shorter distance by following the contour of the valley). At Trail and continuing down to the boundary and for a considerable distance below the boundary, mountains rise on either side of the river in slopes of various angles to heights ranging from 3,000 to 4,500 feet above sea-level, or between 1,500 to 3,000 feet above the river. The width of the valley proper is between one and two miles. On both sides of the river are a series of bench lands at various heights. . . .

The most important industry in the area formerly was the lumber industry. It had its beginning with the building of the Spokane and Northern Railway. Several saw mills were constructed and operated, largely for the purpose of furnishing ties to the railway. In fact, the growing trees—yellow pine, Douglas fir, larch, and cedar—were the most valuable asset to be transformed into ready cash. In the early days, the area was rather heavily wooded, but the timber has largely disappeared and the lumber business is now of small size. On about 57,000 acres on which timber cruises were made in 1927-1928 and in 1936 in the general area, it may be doubtful whether there is today more than 40,000 thousands of board feet of merchantable timber.

As to agricultural conditions, it may be said that farming is carried on in the valley and upon the benches and mountain slopes and in the tributary valleys. . . .

In general, the crops grown on the farms are alfalfa, timothy, clover, grain cut green for hay, barley, oats, wheat, and a small amount of potatoes. Wild hay is cut each year to some extent. The crops, in general, are grown for feed rather than for sale, though there is a certain amount of wheat and oats sold. . . .

Milch cattle are raised to a certain extent and they are grazed on the wild grasses on the hills and mountains in the summer months, but the dairying business depends on existence of sufficient land under cultivation as an adjunct to the dairy to provide adequate forage for the winter months. . . .

II

In 1896, a smelter was started under American auspices near the locality known as Trail, B.C. In 1906, the Consolidated Mining and Smelting Company of Canada, Limited, obtained a charter of incorporation from the Canadian authorities, and that company acquired the smelter plant at Trail as it then existed. Since that time, the Canadian company, without interruption, has operated the Smelter, and from time to time has greatly added to the plant until it has become one of the best and largest equipped smelting plants on the American continent. In 1925 and 1927, two stacks of the plant were erected to 409 feet in height and the Smelter greatly increased its daily smelting of zinc and lead ores. This increased production resulted in more sulphur dioxide fumes and higher concentrations being emitted into the air. In 1916, about 5,000 tons of sulphur per month were emitted; in 1924, about 4,700 tons; in 1926, about 9,000 tons—an amount which rose near to 10,000 tons per month in 1930. In other words, about 300-350 tons of sulphur were being emitted daily in 1930. (It is to be noted that one ton of sulphur is substantially the equivalent of two tons of sulphur dioxide or SO_2.)

From 1925, at least, to 1937, damage occurred in the State of Washington, resulting from the sulphur dioxide emitted from the Trail Smelter as stated in the previous decision. . . .

Since the Tribunal has, in its previous decision, answered Question No. 1 with respect to the period from the first day of January, 1932, to the first day of October, 1937, it now answers Question No. 1 with respect to the period from the first day of October 1937, to the first day of October, 1940, as follows:

(1) No damage caused by the Trail Smelter in the State of Washington has occurred since the first day of October, 1937 and prior to the first day of October, 1940, and hence no indemnity shall be paid therefor.

PART THREE

The second question under Article III of the Convention is as follows:

> In the event of the answer to the first part of the preceding question being in the affirmative, whether the Trail Smelter should be required to refrain from causing damage in the State of Washington in the future and, if so, to what extent?

Damage has occurred since January 1, 1932, as fully set forth in the previous decision. To that extent, the first part of the preceding question has thus been answered in the affirmative.

[T]he report of the International Joint Commission . . . contained a definition of the word "damage" excluding "occasional damage that may be caused by SO_2 fumes being carried across the international boundary in air pockets or by reason of unusual atmospheric conditions," as far, at least, as the duty of the Smelter to reduce the presence of that gas in the air was concerned.

The correspondence between the two Governments during the interval between that report and the conclusion of the Convention shows that the problem thus raised was what parties had primarily in mind in drafting Question No. 2. Whilst Canada wished for the adoption of the report, the United States stated that it could not acquiesce in the proposal to limit consideration of damage to damage as defined in the report. . . . The view was expressed that "so long as fumigations occur in the State of Washington with such frequency, duration and intensity as to cause injury," the conditions afforded "grounds of complaint on the part of the United

States, regardless of the remedial works . . . and regardless of the effect of those works." . . .

The first problem which arises is whether the question should be answered on the basis of the law followed in the United States or on the basis of international law. The Tribunal, however, finds that this problem need not be solved here as the law followed in the United States in dealing with the quasi-sovereign rights of the States of the Union, in the matter of air pollution, whilst more definite, is in conformity with the general rules of international law.

Particularly in reaching its conclusions as regards this question as well as the next, the Tribunal has given consideration to the desire of the high contracting parties "to reach a solution just to all parties concerned."

As Professor Eagleton puts in (*Responsibility of States in International Law*, 1928, p. 80): "A State owes at all times a duty to protect other States against injurious acts by individuals from within its jurisdiction." A great number of such general pronouncements by leading authorities concerning the duty of a State to respect other States and their territory have been presented to the Tribunal. These and many others have been carefully examined. International decisions, in various matters, from the Alabama case onward, and also earlier ones, are based on the same general principal, and, indeed, this principle, as such, has not been questioned by Canada. But the real difficulty often arises rather when it comes to determine what, *pro subjecta materie*, is deemed to constitute an injurious act.

A case concerning, as the present one does, territorial relations, decided by the Federal Court of Switzerland between the Cantons of Soleure and Argovia, may serve to illustrate the relativity of the rule. Soleure brought a suit against her sister State to enjoin use of a shooting establishment which endangered her territory. The court, in granting the injunction, said: "This right (sovereignty) excludes . . . not only the usurpation and exercise of sovereign rights (of another State) . . . but also an actual encroachment which might prejudice the natural use of the territory and the free movement of its inhabitants." As a result of the decision, Argovia made plans for the improvement of the existing installations. These, however, were considered as insufficient protection by Soleure. The Canton of Argovia then moved the Federal Court to decree that the shooting be again permitted after completion of the projected improvements. This motion was granted. "The demand of the Government of Soleure," said the court, "that all endangerment be absolutely abolished apparently goes too far." The court found that all risk whatever had not been eliminated, as the region was flat and absolutely safe shooting ranges were only found in mountain valleys; that there was a federal duty for the communes to provide facilities for military target practice and that "no more precautions may be demanded for shooting ranges near the boundaries of two Cantons than are required for shooting ranges in the interior of a Canton." . . .

No case of air pollution dealt with by an international tribunal has been brought to the attention of the Tribunal nor does the Tribunal know of any such case. The nearest analogy is that of water pollution. But, here also, no decision of an international tribunal has been cited or has been found.

There are, however, as regards both air pollution and water pollution, certain decisions of the Supreme Court of the United States which may legitimately be taken as a guide in this field of international law, for it is reasonable to follow by analogy, in international cases, precedents established by that court in dealing with controversies between States of the Union or with other controversies concerning the quasi-sovereign rights of such States, where no contrary rule prevails in international law and no reason for rejecting such precedents can be adduced from the limitations of sovereignty inherent in the Constitution of the United States.

In the suit of the *State of Missouri v. the State of Illinois,* (200 U.S. 496, 521) concerning the pollution, within the boundaries of Illinois, of the Illinois River, an affluent of the Mississippi flowing into the latter where it forms the boundary between that State and Missouri, an injunction was refused. "Before this court ought to intervene," said the court, "the case should be of serious magnitude, clearly and fully proved, and the principle to be applied should be one which the court is prepared deliberately to maintain against all considerations on the other side. (See *Kansas v. Colorado,* 185 U.S. 125.)" The court found that the practice complained of was general along the shores of the Mississippi River at that time, that it was followed by Missouri itself and that thus a standard was set up by the defendant which the claimant was entitled to invoke.

As the claims for public health became more exacting and methods for removing impurities from the water were perfected, complaints ceased. It is significant that Missouri sided with Illinois when the other riparians of the Great Lakes' system sought to enjoin it to desist from diverting the waters of that system into that of the Illinois and Mississippi for the very purpose of disposing of the Chicago sewage.

In the more recent suit of the State of New York against the State of New Jersey (256 U.S. 296, 309), concerning the pollution of New York Bay, the injunction was also refused for lack of proof, some experts believing that the plans which were in dispute would result in the presence of "offensive odors and unsightly deposits," other equally reliable experts testifying that they were confidently of the opinion that the waters would be sufficiently purified. The court, referring to *Missouri v. Illinois,* said: ". . . the burden upon the State of New York of sustaining the allegations of its bill is much greater than that imposed upon a complainant in an ordinary suit between private parties. Before this court can be moved to exercise its extraordinary power under the Constitution to control the conduct of one State at the suit of another, the threatened invasion of rights must be of serious magnitude and it must be established by clear and convincing evidence."

What the Supreme Court says there of its power under the Constitution equally applies to the extraordinary power granted this Tribunal under the Convention. What is true between States of the Union is, at least equally true concerning the relations between the United States and the Dominion of Canada.

In another recent case concerning water pollution ([New Jersey v. New York,] 283 U.S. 473 [1931]), the complainant was successful. The City of New York was enjoined, at the request of the State of New Jersey, to desist, within a reasonable time limit, from the practice of disposing of sewage by dumping it into the sea, a practice which was injurious to the coastal waters of New Jersey in the vicinity of her bathing resorts.

In the matter of air pollution itself, the leading decisions are those of the Supreme Court in the *State of Georgia v. Tennessee Copper Company and Ducktown Sulphur, Copper and Iron Company, Limited.* Although dealing with a suit against private companies, the decisions were on questions cognate to those here at issue. Georgia stated that it had in vain sought relief from the State of Tennessee, on whose territory the smelters were located, and the court defined the nature of the suit by saying: "This is a suit by a State for an injury to it in its capacity of quasi-sovereign. In that capacity, the State has an interest independent of and behind the titles of its citizens, in all the earth and air within its domain."

On the question whether an injunction should be granted or not, the court said (206 U.S. 230):

> It (the State) has the last word as to whether its mountains shall be stripped of their forests and its inhabitants shall breathe pure air. . . . It is not lightly to be presumed to give up quasi-sovereign rights for pay and . . . if that be its choice, it may insist that an infraction of them shall be stopped. This court has not quite the same freedom to balance the harm that will be done by an injunction against that of which the plaintiff complains, that it would have in deciding between two subjects of a single political power. Without excluding the considerations that equity always takes into account . . . it is a fair and reasonable demand on the part of a sovereign that the air over its territory should not be polluted on a great scale by sulphurous acid gas, that the forests on its mountains, be they better or worse, and whatever domestic destruction they may have suffered, should not be further destroyed or threatened by the act of persons beyond its control, that the crops and orchards on its hills should not be endangered from the same source. . . . Whether Georgia, by insisting upon this claim, is doing more harm than good to her own citizens, is for her to determine. The possible disaster to those outside the State must be accepted as a consequence of her standing upon her extreme rights.

Later on, however, when the court actually framed an injunction, in the case of the Ducktown Company (237 U.S. 474, 477) (an agreement on the basis of an annual compensation was reached with the most important of the two smelters, the Tennessee Copper Company), they did not go beyond a decree "adequate to diminish materially the present probability of damage to its (Georgia's) citizens."

Great progress in the control of fumes has been made by science in the last few years and this progress should be taken into account.

The Tribunal, therefore, finds that the above decisions, taken as a whole, constitute an adequate basis for its conclusions, namely, that, under the principles of international law, as well as of the law of the United States, no State has the right to use or permit the use of its territory in such a manner as to cause injury by fumes in or to the territory of another or the properties or persons therein, when the case is of serious consequence and the injury is established by clear and convincing evidence.

The decisions of the Supreme Court of the United States which are the basis of these conclusions are decisions in equity and a solution inspired by them, together with the regime hereinafter prescribed, will, in the opinion of the Tribunal, be "just to all parties concerned," as long, at least, as the present conditions in the Columbia River Valley continue to prevail.

Considering the circumstances of the case, the Tribunal holds that the Dominion of Canada is responsible in international law for the conduct of the Trail Smelter. Apart from the undertakings in the Convention, it is, therefore, the duty of the Government of the Dominion of Canada to see to it that this conduct should be in conformity with the obligation of the Dominion under international law as herein determined.

The Tribunal, therefore, answers Question No. 2 as follows: (2) So long as the present conditions in the Columbia River Valley prevail, the Trail Smelter shall be required to refrain from causing any damage through fumes in the State of Washington; the damage herein referred to and its extent being such as would be recoverable under the decisions of the courts of the United States in suits between private individuals. The indemnity for such damage should be fixed in such manner as the Governments, acting under Article XI of the Convention, should agree upon.

PART FOUR

The third question under Article III of the Convention is as follows: "In the light of the answer to the preceding question, what measures or regime, if any, should be adopted and maintained by the Trail Smelter?"

Answering this question in the light of the preceding one, since the Tribunal has, in its previous decision, found that damage caused by the Trail Smelter has occurred in the State of Washington since January 1, 1932, and since the Tribunal is of opinion that damage may occur in the future unless the operations of the Smelter shall be subject to some control, in order to avoid damage occurring, the Tribunal now decides that a regime or measure of control shall be applied to the operations of the Smelter and shall remain in full force unless and until modified in accordance with the provisions hereinafter set forth in Section 3, Paragraph VI of the present part of this decision. . . .

Section 3

In order to prevent the occurrence of sulphur dioxide in the atmosphere in amounts, both as to concentration, duration and frequency, capable of causing damage in the State of Washington, the operation of the Smelter and the maximum emission of sulphur dioxide from its stacks shall be regulated as provided in the following regime. [The Tribunal set forth a detailed set of requirements under the following headings: I. Instruments; II. Documents; III. Stacks; IV. Maximum Permissible Sulphur Emission (containing two tables, concerning the growing season and the non-growing season, and setting forth maximum hourly permissible emissions at various times and under various weather conditions); V. Definition of Terms and Conditions; and VI. Amendment or Suspension of Regime (providing for the establishment of a scientific commission to deal with requests for amendment or suspension of the regime).]

PART FIVE

The fourth question under Article III of the Convention is as follows:

> What indemnity or compensation, if any, should be paid on account of any decision or decisions rendered by the Tribunal pursuant to the next two preceding Questions?

The Tribunal is of opinion that the prescribed regime will probably remove the causes of the present controversy and, as said before, will probably result in preventing any damage of a material nature occurring in the State of Washington in the future.

But since the desirable and expected result of the regime or measure of control hereby required to be adopted and maintained by the Smelter may not occur, and since in its answer to Question No. 2, the Tribunal has required the Smelter to refrain from causing damage in the State of Washington in the future, as set forth therein, the Tribunal answers Question No. 4 and decides that on account of decisions rendered by the Tribunal in its answers to Question No. 2 and Question No. 3 there shall be paid as follows: (a) if any damage as defined under Question No. 2 shall have occurred since October 1, 1940, or shall occur in the future, whether through failure on the part of the Smelter to comply with the regulations herein prescribed or not withstanding the maintenance of the regime, an indemnity shall be paid for such damage but only when and if the two Governments shall make arrangements for the disposition of claims for indemnity under the provisions of Article XI of the Convention; (b) if as a consequence of the decision of the Tribunal in its answers to Question No. 2 and Question No. 3, the United States shall find it necessary to maintain in the future an agent or agents in the area in order to ascertain whether damage shall have occurred in spite of the regime prescribed herein, the reasonable cost of such investigations not in excess of $7,500 in any one year shall be paid to the United States as a compensation, but only if and when the two Governments determine under Article XI of the Convention that damage has occurred in the year in question, due to the operation of the Smelter, and "disposition of claims for indemnity for damage" has been made by the two Governments; but in no case shall the aforesaid compensation be payable in excess of the indemnity for damage; and further it is understood that such payment is hereby directed by the Tribunal only as a compensation to be paid on account of the answers of the Tribunal to Question No. 2 and Question No. 3 (as provided for in Question No. 4) and not as any part of indemnity for the damage to be ascertained and to be determined upon by the two Governments under Article XI of the Convention.

PART SIX

Since further investigations in the future may be possible under the provisions of Part Four and of Part Five of this decision, the Tribunal finds it necessary to include in its report, the following provision:

Investigators appointed by or on behalf of either Government, whether jointly or severally, and the members of the Commission provided for in Paragraph VI of Section 3 of Part Four of this decision, shall be permitted at all reasonable times to inspect the operations of the Smelter and to enter upon and inspect any of the properties in the State of Washington which may be claimed to be affected by fumes. This provision shall also apply to any localities where instruments are operated under the present regime or under any amended regime. Wherever under the present regime or under any amended regime, instruments have to be maintained and operated by the Smelter on the territory of the United States, the Government of the United States shall undertake to secure for the Government of the Dominion of Canada the facilities reasonably required to that effect.

The Tribunal expresses the strong hope that any investigations which the Governments may undertake in the future, in connection with the matters dealt with in this decision, shall be conducted jointly.

(Signed) *Jan Hostie*
(Signed) *Charles Warren*
(Signed) *R.A.E. Greenshields*

Notes and Questions

1. *The wellspring.* The *Trail Smelter* arbitration has been described as a "milestone" in the development of state responsibility for "environmental injury" (Jan Schneider, World Public Order of the Environment: Towards an International Ecological Law and Organization 50 (1979)) and "as

having laid out the foundations of international environmental law, at least regarding transfrontier pollution" (Alexandre Kiss & Dinah Shelton, International Environmental Law 107 (1991)). Indeed, it is the only decision of an international court or tribunal that deals specifically, and on the merits, with transfrontier pollution. A number of writers have treated as an expression of a norm of customary international law the following now-famous declaration of the tribunal: "[U]nder the principles of international law, . . . no State has the right to use or permit the use of its territory in such a manner as to cause injury by fumes in or to the territory of another or the properties or persons therein, when the case is of serious consequence and the injury is established by clear and convincing evidence." *See, e.g.*, Experts Group on Environmental Law of the World Commission on Environment and Development, Environmental Protection and Sustainable Development 76 (1987); J. Brunnée, Acid Rain and Ozone Layer Depletion: International Law and Regulation 88-89 (1988); P.-M. Dupuy, Overview of the Existing Customary Legal Regime Regarding International Pollution, in International Law and Pollution 61, 63 (D. Magraw, ed. 1991); L. Goldie, A General View of International Environmental Law—A Survey of Capabilities, Trends and Limits, in Hague Academy of International Law, Colloquium 1973, The Protection of the Environment and International Law 25, 66-69 (1973); and A. Kiss, Problèmes Juridiques de la Pollution de l'Air, in *id.* 145, at 156-157, 169-174.

2. *An "environmental" case?* But did the arbitration involve "environmental injury" as such? Do you think the tribunal would have decided the case the same way if it had involved no damage to private property? More basically, do you think the dispute would have arisen and gone to arbitration absent damage to private property?

3. *What does it stand for?* Turning to the value of the decision as legal precedent, can *Trail Smelter* be said to have established a new principle—or indeed *any* principle—of law? Samuel Bleicher has argued that because of Canada's "voluntary acceptance of responsibility . . . the Tribunal overstated the scope of state responsibility in saying that Canada was obligated 'apart from the undertakings in the Convention.'" Samuel Bleicher, An Overview of International Environmental Regulation, 2 Ecology L.Q. 1, at 22 (1972). Do you agree?

4. *What does it stand for (II)?* Still considering the authoritative value of the decision, do you agree with the following assessment?

> The *Trail Smelter* arbitration provides clear authority for saying that international tribunals may both require the payment of compensation for past pollution damage and prescribe regimes which either prohibit the activity causing the harm, or permit it to continue on a reduced scale so as not to cause pollution injury at all, or at least not above certain levels of permissible and presumably non-deleterious environmental impairment. Thus international law, here and now, provides a basis for prohibiting outright, or regulat-

ing with an even-handed justice, the pollution damage of one state, or its citizens, by another, or its citizens.

L. Goldie, The Nuclear Tests Cases: Restraints on Environmental Harm, 5 J. Mar. L. & Com. 491, 502-503 (1974).

5. *Attribution of private conduct to the state.* The *Trail Smelter* arbitration involved a private activity in Canada that caused harm to private property in the United States, yet the arbitration was between the two states and Canada was held responsible. This is not surprising since Canada voluntarily agreed, through the convention, to pay for damage caused prior to January 1932, and to accept the tribunal's findings concerning subsequent damage, compensation therefor, and the regime to be imposed on the smelter. But what would the situation have been if Canada had not voluntarily accepted responsibility for the smelter's actions? Would Canada be responsible under international law for transboundary injury caused by a purely private activity within its borders? To put the question another way, would the smelter's conduct be "attributable" to Canada? In his analysis of the *Trail Smelter* decision, Bleicher has written that the award goes "well beyond . . . the general principles of the law of state responsibility to aliens, which would reach only to state-controlled activities. . . ." Bleicher, above, at 28-29. Indeed, the draft articles on State Responsibility adopted by the United Nations International Law Commission indicate (with exceptions not pertinent here) that a state is responsible only for the acts of its organs, entities exercising government authority, or those acting on its behalf. [1980] Y.B. I.L.C., vol. 2, pt. 2, at 31 (articles 5-15) (1981). The smelter would not qualify under any of these categories. But does this principle apply in the case of transfrontier pollution? Or do states have an affirmative duty to prevent activities under their jurisdiction, be they public or private, from causing transfrontier pollution damage? Most contemporary writers believe that the latter approach is applicable in cases of transfrontier pollution. Thus it is the content of the obligation itself that is determinative. *See, e.g.,* P.-M. Dupuy, Overview of the Existing Customary Legal Regime Regarding International Pollution, in International Law and Pollution 61, 63 (D. Magraw, ed. 1991). *Cf.* G. Handl, Balancing of Interests and International Liability for the Pollution of International Watercourses: Customary Principles of Law Revisited, 1975 Can. Y.B. Intl. L. 156, 164 (1976). *See also United States Diplomatic and Consular Staff in Iran* (United States v. Iran), 1979 I.C.J. Rep. 7, in which the World Court held Iran responsible for not "taking appropriate steps to ensure the protection" of the United States embassy and staff against attacks by private persons even though the actions of these persons were not, at the time they occurred, attributable to Iran. The obligations in question were those owed by Iran to the United States under the 1961 Vienna Convention on Diplomatic Relations and other treaties. Therefore, the fact that it had not been established that the militants were in fact acting on Iran's behalf and thus that their conduct was not

attributable to Iran was not fatal to the case of the United States. We will further examine the question dealt with in this note in connection with the *Corfu Channel* case, below.

6. *Implementation of the tribunal's orders.* The fact that the damage in Washington was caused by a private entity and not the Canadian government per se also gave rise to potential problems concerning the implementation of the convention and the tribunal's decision: How could the Canadian government be sure that the smelter would carry out the tribunal's orders? In the words of John Read, who served as Agent (chief counsel) for Canada during the case, "[i]t would not have been easy—and perhaps impossible—to prepare a formal contract with the [Consolidated Mining and Smelting] Company [obligating it to carry out the obligations under the Convention and award], taking into account all contingencies that might arise in the course of the arbitration." J. Read, The Trail Smelter Dispute, 1963 Can. Y.B. Intl. L. 213, 228 (1963). Instead, another approach was taken. According to Read, "the Company and the government were yoked together as a team," with representatives of the company participating in the drafting of the convention and the general counsel of the company serving as counsel for Canada in the arbitration. Read states that there was never any question as to the company's implementation of the tribunal's orders. However, he indicates that if the company had refused to comply at any stage, the Canadian Parliament would have had the authority to enact legislation for the implementation of the treaty. *Id.* at 229.

7. *The precise relief sought by the United States.* Did the United States insist on a complete cessation of harmful emissions? Reread the second question put to the arbitration tribunal. That question, in conjunction with the next two, indicates that the United States in effect gave the tribunal the authority to legalize future damage if that was necessary to the establishment of an effective regime of control. According to John Read, "the regime of control prescribed by the Tribunal has brought about a position in which effective operation of the smelter is possible and in which there has been cessation of damage; but such a result did not seem to be certain at the time of negotiation." Read, above, at 224. Indeed, one might wonder why the United States effectively left open the possibility that the tribunal would create an easement for the sulphur dioxide fumes. (In fact, as we have seen, the tribunal's award recognized the possibility that damage might occur even if the smelter complied with the regime, and provided for the payment of compensation for any such damage.) Again, John Read: "The acceptance of the principle of absolute cessation of damage might have shut down the Trail Smelter; but it would also have brought Detroit, Buffalo and Niagara Falls to an untimely end." *Id.* at 224-225. Does the failure of the United States to insist on prevention of all transfrontier pollution damage from the smelter weaken the precedential value of the *Trail Smelter* award? How does it affect, if at all, the tribunal's ringing declaration that "no State has the right to use or permit the use of its

territory in such a manner as to cause injury by fumes in or to the territory of another"? Since customary international law is a reflection of state practice (*see* Chapter 5, sec. A.2, above), does the failure of the United States to insist on absolute cessation of damage mean (1) that it did not believe international law required such or (2) that if international law did embody such a requirement, the contrary practice of the United States could contribute to a change in the law?

8. *Parsing the "holding."* The declaration of the tribunal, quoted in part at the end of the preceding note, would oblige states to prevent transfrontier pollution injury only "when the case is of serious consequence and the injury is established by clear and convincing evidence." The tribunal drew these requirements from the United States cases it reviewed.

a. How "serious" must the damage be for the prohibition to apply? Does the requirement of seriousness apply only where injunctive relief (i.e., cessation or partial abatement) is sought, or must it also be satisfied before the state of origin has a duty to pay compensation? Several paragraphs after it enunciated the "seriousness" requirement, the tribunal held that "the Trail Smelter shall be required to refrain from causing *any* damage through fumes in the State of Washington; the damage herein referred to and its extent being such as would be recoverable under the decisions of the courts of the United States in suits between private individuals." (Emphasis added.) Is this statement consistent with the "seriousness" standard? In light of the maxim, *de minimis non curat lex,* is any qualifying term necessary? According to Handl, "[t]here is a general consensus . . . that not any and every transboundary impact is to be avoided. The international legal threshold of impermissible natural resource use will be deemed transgressed only when 'serious,' 'significant,' or similarly qualified transboundary effects occur." Handl, National Uses of Transboundary Air Resources: The International Entitlement Issue Reconsidered, 26 Nat. Res. J. 405, 412 (1986). For a survey of international agreements, judicial decisions and state practice other than agreements relating to the question of the definition of harm in the context of the obligations of prior notification and consultation, *see generally* U.N. Secretariat, Survey of State Practice Relevant to International Liability for Injurious Consequences Arising Out of Acts Not Prohibited by International Law, 1985 Y.B. Intl. L. Commn., vol. 2, part 1, 1, 26-40 (1989).

b. What about the "clear and convincing evidence" standard? Presumably it is not enough merely to establish injury by such evidence; causation must also be shown. While this did not pose a problem in *Trail Smelter* because of the topography and meteorological conditions involved, it could well be an obstacle in other cases: "Proof of actual causation is often particularly difficult in pollution cases because the injury may be of a cumulative or gradual nature; because a number of concurrent sources may have contributed to the injury; or because it may be difficult to trace the pollution to its source." Note by the Canadian Delegation, Transfrontier Pollution (TFP): Liability and Compensation, in OECD, Legal Aspects of Transfrontier Pollution 283, 290 (1977). Should scientific certainty be required as to the cause and effect relationship (as argued by the United States administration during the 1980s with regard to acid deposition in Canada)? Conversely, even if causation is established, should there be a requirement on the international level that the polluting activity be the reasonably proximate cause of the harm? Or should it be sufficient if the harm would not have occurred but for the activity, no matter how attenuated the causal chain (in terms of either distance or such factors as foreseeability)? For a discussion of causation problems in private air pollution litigation, *see* J. Fischer, The Availability of Private Remedies for Acid Rain Damage, 9 Ecology L.Q. 429, 449-464 (1981).

9. *Actual versus threatened injury.* Must injury already have occurred for the *Trail Smelter* test to be met, or would it suffice if injury were only threatened? *See* Bleicher, *above,* at 25.

10. *Technical assistance for the tribunal.* The two governments anticipated that the members of the arbitral tribunal would need assistance with the highly technical issues of fact involved in the case. They accordingly provided in Article II of the convention that each country could designate a scientist to assist the tribunal. Two scientists were so designated, and the tribunal itself later appointed an additional scientist to assist them. The tribunal made extensive use of the scientists, who prepared a report entitled Meteorological Investigations Near Trail, B.C., 1938-1940. The tribunal described the report as "an elaborate document of 374 pages accompanied by numerous scientific charts, graphs and photographs." 3 U.N. Rep. Intl. Arb. Awards, at 1967. The tribunal characterized its investigations as "probably the most thorough study ever made of any area subject to atmospheric pollution by industrial smoke." *Id.* at 1973.

11. *The role of the International Joint Commission.* The United States and Canada initially referred the problem of transboundary pollution from the smelter at Trail to the International Joint Commission (IJC), a body established under the 1909 Boundary Waters Treaty[3] between the two countries. The reference was made under Article IX of the treaty. While Article VIII envisions that the IJC will "pass upon" certain cases involving boundary waters, Article IX provides in part that "any other questions or matters of difference arising between [the parties] involving the rights, obligations or interests of either in relation to the other, or to the inhabitants of the other, along the common frontier between the United States and the Dominion of Canada shall be referred from time to time to the Interna-

3. Treaty Relating to the Boundary Waters and Questions Arising Along the Boundary between the United States and Canada, Jan. 11, 1909, entered into force May 5, 1910, 36 Stat. 2448, T.S. 548, 12 Bevans 319.

tional Joint Commission for examination and report" at the request of either of the parties. As indicated in the prefatory note to the case, the United States declined to accept the IJC's recommendations, resulting ultimately in the agreement to submit the dispute to arbitration. For a discussion of the IJC's activities through 1958, *see* L.M. Bloomfield & G.F. Fitzgerald, Boundary Water Problems of Canada and the United States: The International Joint Commission 1912-1958 (1958). The authors discuss the IJC's work as an investigative body under Article IX in Chapter 4, at 38.

12. *Jurisdictional obstacles to private remedies.* The jurisdictional problems that prevented private lawsuits against the smelter have been addressed, if not entirely resolved. In August 1982, the National Conference of Commissioners on Uniform State Laws of the United States and the Uniform Law Conference of Canada jointly adopted the Uniform Transboundary Pollution Reciprocal Access Act. The Act provides that actions concerning actual or threatened pollution injury suffered in a reciprocating jurisdiction on the other side of the border (i.e., a state or province that has enacted the Uniform Act or provides comparable rights of access) may be brought in the jurisdiction from which the pollution originates or may originate (§2). This would effectively abolish—for these kinds of lawsuits in enacting jurisdictions—the "local action rule" laid down by the House of Lords in the 1893 *Moçambique* case. The Act also provides that a plaintiff in such an action has the same rights to relief as if the injury had occurred or was threatened within the state of origin (§3), and that the applicable law is that of the latter state (§4). The Uniform Act has been enacted in the Provinces of Manitoba, Ontario, and Prince Edward Island, and the states of Colorado, Michigan, New Jersey, Oregon, and Wisconsin. Uniform Laws Ann., Matrimonial, Family and Health Laws, 1992 Supp. (Pocket Part). Unfortunately, these jurisdictions do not yet include Washington and British Columbia. For a discussion of the case law prior to the Act, *see* Stephen McCaffrey, Transboundary Pollution Injuries: Jurisdictional Considerations in Private Litigation between Canada and the United States, 3 Cal. West. Intl. L.J. 191 (1973).

13. *Postscript.* Some recent press reports have boasted that the metallurgical operation in Trail, British Columbia, is "a technically advanced, environmentally friendly" operation. Patrick Whiteway, A Century of Smelting at Trail, Canadian Mining J., Oct. 1, 1996, at S10, *available in* 116 WL 9853081. However, 1994 press accounts did not treat COMINCO as favorably. Various reports attributed health problems experienced by residents of Washington to the COMINCO smelter at Trail. For example, in the city of Northport, in Stevens County, Northeastern, Washington, located ten miles downwind of Trail, residents suffered health problems, particularly gastrointestinal illnesses and respiratory problems, that they believed were linked to exposure to pollution from the Trail lead and zinc smelter. Julie Titone, More Lake Roosevelt Fish to Be Tested, The Spokesman

Rev., Feb. 18, 1994, at B2, *available in* 1994 WL 4512126. A year-long study by the Washington Health and Ecology Departments revealed some of the highest levels of cadmium and arsenic ever recorded, as well as high levels of airborne lead. *Id.* The same report revealed that hospital rates in Northport for bowel diseases, e.g., ulcerative colitis and Crohn's disease, were higher than the state average. Mark Jewell/Associated Press, Air Pollution Clouds Border Relationship, Canadian Smelter May Cause Illness, The News Tribune, Tacoma, May 10, 1994, at B3, *available in* 1994 WL 4629985.

COMINCO was pressured by British Columbia's provincial government, as well as by downstream residents and agencies in Washington, to reduce the pollutants that had been poured into the river for decades. Julie Titone, Pollutants in Lake Roosevelt Still Too High: Environmental Scientist Cites Ceasing Dumping of Slag as Integral in Making a Difference, The Spokesman Rev., Nov. 15, 1994, at B3, *available in* 1994 WL 4513182. On July 1, 1995, COMINCO stopped dumping slag (a cinderlike by-product of smelting that contains mercury, lead, zinc, and other metals and can cause nerve damage, *id.*) into the Columbia River, thereby ending the 65-year practice that it had previously considered harmless. Firm Ends 65 Years of Dumping in Columbia (The Associated Press), Portland Oregonian, Sept. 12, 1995, at B04, *available in* 1995 WL 9190670.

14. *Problem.* You are counsel to the affected individuals. What course of action would you advise them to follow? A private lawsuit? An appeal to the Washington State government? To the United States government? What are the strengths and weaknesses of each of these approaches?

B. THE HARMLESS USE OF TERRITORY: THE *CORFU CHANNEL* CASE

On October 22, 1946, two British warships were seriously damaged when they struck mines while passing through the Corfu Strait in Albanian territorial waters. The explosions also resulted in the deaths of 44 British seamen and personal injuries to many more. The two governments submitted the case to the International Court of Justice by a Special Agreement they had concluded in response to a resolution of the UN Security Council. In the agreement the parties asked the court to decide upon two questions, the first of which was the following: "Is Albania responsible under international law for the explosions which occurred on the 22nd October 1946 in Albanian waters and for the damage and loss of human life which resulted from them and is there any duty to pay compensation?" In the second question the court was asked whether the UK had violated the sovereignty of Albania. As to the latter question, the court found that the British vessels were exercising their right of innocent passage in transiting the Straits of

Corfu and thus had not violated Albanian sovereignty. As to the former, the court was confronted with a problem of proof as to which state had laid the mines and whether Albania had knowledge of their presence in its waters. The UK made a pro forma contention, unsupported by evidence, that Albania had laid the mines, but Albania had no navy and the court dispensed with this claim. In the alternative, the UK alleged that the mines had been laid by Yugoslavia with the "connivance" of Albania. The court also found insufficient evidence to support this contention. Thus, "the authors of the minelaying remain[ed] unknown." 1949 I.C.J. Rep. at 17. The court's findings continue, below.

■ *CORFU CHANNEL* CASE (MERITS)[4]

(United Kingdom v. Albania)
International Court of Justice, 1949
1949 I.C.J. Rep. 4

Finally, the United Kingdom Government put forward the argument that, whoever the authors of the minelaying were, it could not have been done without the Albanian Government's knowledge.

It is clear that knowledge of the minelaying cannot be imputed to the Albanian Government by reason merely of the fact that a minefield discovered in Albanian territorial waters caused the explosions of which the British warships were the victims. It is true, as international practice shows, that a State on whose territory or in whose waters an act contrary to international law has occurred, may be called upon to give an explanation. It is also true that that State cannot evade such a request by limiting itself to a reply that it is ignorant of the circumstances of the act and of its authors. The State may, up to a certain point, be bound to supply particulars of the use made by it of the means of information and inquiry at its disposal. But it cannot be concluded from the mere fact of the control exercised by a State over its territory and waters that that State necessarily knew, or ought to have known, of any unlawful act perpetrated therein, nor yet that it necessarily knew, or should have known, the authors. This fact, by itself and apart from other circumstances, neither involves prima facie responsibility nor shifts the burden of proof.

On the other hand, the fact of this exclusive territorial control exercised by a State within its frontiers has a bearing upon the methods of proof available to establish the knowledge of that State as to such events. By reason of this exclusive control, the other State, the victim of a breach of international law, is often unable to furnish direct proof of facts giving rise

4. The Court's prior decision on the question of jurisdiction is reported in 1947-1948 I.C.J. Rep. 15. The Court's decision on the question of damages may be found in 1949 I.C.J. Rep. 244.

to responsibility. Such a State should be allowed a more liberal recourse to inferences of fact and circumstantial evidence. This indirect evidence is admitted in all systems of law, and its use is recognized by international decisions. It must be regarded as of special weight when it is based on a series of facts linked together and leading logically to a single conclusion.

The Court must examine therefore whether it has been established by means of indirect evidence that Albania has knowledge of minelaying in her territorial waters independently of any connivance on her part in this operation. The proof may be drawn from inferences of fact, provided that they leave no room for reasonable doubt. The elements of fact on which these inferences can be based may differ from those which are relevant to the question of connivance.

In the present case, two series of facts, which corroborate one another, have to be considered: the first relates to Albania's attitude before and after the disaster of October 22nd, 1946; the other concerns the feasibility of observing minelaying from the Albanian coast.

1. It is clearly established that the Albanian Government constantly kept a close watch over the waters of the North Corfu Channel, at any rate after May 1946. . . .

As the Parties agree that the minefield had been recently laid, it must be concluded that the operation was carried out during the period of close watch by the Albanian authorities in this sector. This conclusion renders the Albanian Government's assertion of ignorance a priori somewhat improbable. . . .

Another indication of the Albanian Government's knowledge consists in the fact that that Government did not notify the presence of mines in its waters, at the moment when it must have known this, at the latest after the sweep on November 13th, and further, whereas the Greek Government immediately appointed a Commission to inquire into the events of October 22nd, the Albanian Government took no decision of such a nature, nor did it proceed to the judicial investigation incumbent, in such a case, on the territorial sovereign.

This attitude does not seem reconcilable with the alleged ignorance of the Albanian authorities that the minefield had been laid in Albanian territorial waters. It could be explained if the Albanian Government, while knowing of the minelaying, desired the circumstances of the operation to remain secret.

2. As regards the possibility of observing minelaying from the Albanian coast, the Court regards the following facts, relating to the technical conditions of a secret minelaying and to the Albanian surveillance, as particularly important.

The Bay of Saranda and the channel used by shipping through the Strait are, from their geographical configuration, easily watched; the entrance of the bay is dominated by heights offering excellent observation points, both over the bay and over the Strait; whilst the channel throughout is close to the Albanian coast. The laying of a minefield in these waters could hardly fail to have been observed by the Albanian coastal defences.

On this subject, it must first be said that the minelaying operation itself must have required a certain time. . . . The report of the [court-appointed] Experts reckons the time that the minelayers would have been in the waters, between Cape Kiephali and St. George's Monastery, at between two and two and a half hours. This is sufficient time to attract the attention of the observation posts. . . .

The Court cannot fail to give great weight to the opinion of the Experts who examined the locality in a manner giving every guarantee of correct and impartial information. Apart from the existence of a look-out post at Cape Denta, which has not been proved, the Court, basing itself on the declarations of the Albanian Government that look-out posts were stationed at Cape Kiephali and St. George's Monastery, refers to the following conclusions in the Experts' Report: (1) that in the case of minelaying from the North towards the South, the minelayers would have been seen from Cape Kiephali; (2) in the case of minelaying from the South, the minelayers would have been seen from Cape Kiephali and St. George's Monastery.

From all the facts and observations mentioned above, the Court draws the conclusion that the laying of the minefield which caused the explosions on October 22nd, 1946, could not have been accomplished without the knowledge of the Albanian Government.

The obligations resulting for Albania from this knowledge are not disputed between the Parties. Counsel for the Albanian Government expressly recognized that [translation] 'if Albania had been informed of the operation before the incidents of October 22nd, and in time to warn the British vessels and shipping in general of the existence of mines in the Corfu Channel, her responsibility would be involved. . . .'

The obligations incumbent upon the Albanian authorities consisted in notifying, for the benefit of shipping in general, the existence of a minefield in Albanian territorial waters and in warning the approaching British warships of the imminent danger to which the minefield exposed them. Such obligations are based, not on the Hague Convention of 1907, No. VIII, which is applicable in time of war, but on certain general and well-recognized principles, namely: elementary considerations of humanity, even more exacting in peace than in war; the principle of the freedom of maritime communication; and every State's obligation not to allow knowingly its territory to be used for acts contrary to the rights of other States.

In fact, Albania neither notified the existence of the minefield, nor warned the British warships of the danger they were approaching. [The court found that even if the mines had been laid at the last possible moment Albania would have had time to warn the British vessels.]

In fact, nothing was attempted by the Albanian authorities to prevent the disaster. These grave omissions involve the international responsibility of Albania.

The Court therefore reaches the conclusion that Albania is responsible under international law for the explosions which occurred on October 22nd, 1946, in Albanian waters, and for the damage and loss of human life which resulted from them, and that there is a duty upon Albania to pay compensation to the United Kingdom. . . .

Notes and Questions

1. *The relevance of the decision.* The *Corfu Channel* case is often cited in support of the proposition that a state is under an obligation to prevent activities within its borders from causing transfrontier pollution harm. *See, e.g.,* Dupuy, above, at 63-64; A. Kiss and D. Shelton, International Environmental Law 107 (1991); L. Goldie, Liability for Damage and the Progressive Development of International Law, 14 Intl. & Comp. L.Q. 1189, 1229-1231 (1965); Bleicher, above, at 28; and A. Lester, River Pollution in International Law, 57 Am. J. Intl. L. 828, 839-840 (1963). This has sometimes been referred to as the principle of the "harmless use of territory." *See, e.g.,* P.-M. Dupuy, International Liability of States for Damage Caused by Transfrontier Pollution, in OECD, Legal Aspects of Transfrontier Pollution 345, 349 (1977). Use of the case as authority for this proposition is usually based on the passage in which the court refers to "every State's obligation not to allow knowingly its territory to be used for acts contrary to the rights of other States." Can this be characterized as *the* or even *a* holding of the case? If not, what in your view is the authoritative value of the case for the stated proposition? Is your answer affected by the court's characterization of the doctrine expressed in the passage as a "general and well-recognized principle?" Is the value of the case as authority for the stated proposition affected by Albania's admission that it would be responsible if it knew that the mines had been laid in time to warn the British vessels?

2. *The "rights" of other states.* Still focusing on the passage quoted in the previous note, does it beg the question to make the obligation in question hinge on the "*rights* of other States?" That is, does this decision say anything about whether a state has a "right" to be free from harm whose source is beyond its borders and, *a fortiori,* foreign-source pollution?

3. *The decision's applicability to environmental cases.* Is the authoritative value of the decision diminished at all by the fact that the case did not involve pollution or environmental problems, per se? Bleicher has written that "the injury was not a by-product of an economically useful activity, but the intended result of the symbolic and actual collision of two military machines." Bleicher, above, at 17. He therefore concludes that "the decision may be a rather weak reed to lean upon" as the basis of state responsibility in transfrontier pollution cases involving private parties at both ends of the causal chain. *Id.* Similarly, Schneider views the *Corfu Channel* and *Lake Lanoux* cases below as being "somewhat far-fetched [as precedents establish-

ing state responsibility for environmental injury] and reveal the lengths to which environmental lawyers have had to go in order to find sources in the field of international environmental law." Jan Schneider, World Public Order of the Environment: Towards an International Ecological Law and Organization 50 (1979). Do you agree? Professor Ian Brownlie declares that "it would not occur to anyone to say that the *Corfu Channel* case was irrelevant to a pollution problem because it did not concern pollution as such." Brownlie, State Responsibility and International Pollution: A Practical Perspective, in International Law and Pollution 122 (D. Magraw, ed. 1991) (footnote omitted). Can you articulate how, precisely, the case is relevant to pollution problems? Does its relevance depend upon whether the pollution in question is chronic or the result of an incident? Upon whether actual harm or the risk of harm is involved?

4. *Problem.* For those concerned with transfrontier pollution problems, some of the most interesting aspects of the court's opinion have to do with the circumstances under which a state will be held responsible for activities on its territory, including standards of proof. Suppose Chemcorp, a multinational chemical company, operates a fertilizer plant in Angeria, a developing country, under an agreement with that state. The plant is situated in a rural area on the Brown River, a stream flowing from Angeria into neighboring Botseria. If Botseria is harmed by chemical waste dumped into the Brown River by the Chemcorp plant, does the *Corfu Channel* case suggest that Angeria could be held liable if it could be established that the harm emanated from Angerian territory, whether or not Angeria knew of the dumping? Does the fact that the harmful pollution originated within Angeria shift the burden of proof? Would your answers be any different if the transfrontier pollution harm were the result of an oil spill by an unknown ship in Angeria's territorial waters, a spill that crossed into Botseria's waters and fouled its coastline? Would it matter whether Angeria had knowledge of the spill and of the danger of harm to Botseria?

5. *The* Island of Palmas *case.* Another decision that factually has nothing to do with pollution or environmental problems, but that has been cited in support of the principle of the "harmless use of territory," is the award of the sole Arbitrator, Max Huber, in the *Island of Palmas* case (United States v. Netherlands), 2 U.N. Rep. Intl. Arb. Awards 829 (1928). The case involved a dispute between the United States and the Netherlands as to whether the island, situated between Mindanao in the Philippines (then United States territory) and Nanusa in Indonesia (then the Dutch East Indies), was in the territory of the United States or the Netherlands. The award contains the following passage:

> Territorial sovereignty . . . involves the exclusive right to display the activities of a State. This right has as corollary a duty: the obligation to protect within the territory the rights of other states, in particular their right to integrity and inviolability in peace and in war, together with the rights which

> each state may claim for its nationals in foreign territory. Without manifesting its territorial sovereignty in a manner corresponding to circumstances, the State cannot fulfil this duty. Territorial sovereignty cannot limit itself to its negative side, i.e. to excluding the activities of other States; for it serves to divide between nations the space upon which human activities are employed, in order to assure them at all points the minimum of protection of which international law is the guardian.

2 U.N. Rep. Intl. Arb. Awards at 839. The facts of this case are perhaps even further removed from international environmental problems than those of the *Corfu Channel* case, and Huber's declarations more abstract than those of the Court. Nevertheless, the general principles enunciated by Huber can be taken as support for the idea that the principle of the harmless use of territory "is a natural corollary of a sovereign State's exclusive jurisdiction over its territory." Dupuy, above, at 64. The International Court of Justice went further in its Advisory Opinion in the *Namibia* case, holding that actual control over territory is a sufficient basis for state responsibility: "Physical control of a territory, and not sovereignty or legitimacy of title, is the basis of State liability for acts affecting other States." Legal Consequences for States of the Continued Presence of South Africa in Namibia (South West Africa) Notwithstanding Security Council Resolution 276 (1970), Order No. 3 of 26 January 1971, 1971 I.C.J. Rep. 42, para. 118.

6. *The duty to warn.* The *Corfu Channel* case is of obvious relevance with regard to the procedural duty to warn or notify of known dangers. This duty, which may come into play in connection with a variety of environmental problems from natural disasters and chemical spills to the operation of activities involving risk, is explored in Chapter 8, below. In a more recent case, the court reaffirmed the duty to warn of the danger posed by a minefield, quoting and relying upon the passage of the *Corfu Channel* decision concerning the obligations of Albania to notify and warn. *See* Case Concerning Military and Paramilitary Activities in and Against Nicaragua (Nicaragua v. United States) (Merits), Judgment of June 27, 1986, 1986 I.C.J. Rep. 4. While the vote on this aspect of the case was not unanimous (14 to 1), no judge disputed the existence of the duty to warn of a known danger (Judge Oda dissented on jurisdictional grounds).

7. *Subsequent developments in the case.* In a subsequent decision in the *Corfu Channel* case, the Court assessed damages against Albania of approximately £850,000 (1949 I.C.J. Rep. 244). Notwithstanding the obligation of Albania under Article 94 of the United Nations Charter to comply with decisions of the Court,[5] the judgment went unsatisfied for over 40 years.

5. Article 94, paragraph 1 of the UN Charter provides as follows:

> 1. Each Member of the United Nations undertakes to comply with the decision of the International Court of Justice in any case to which it is a party.

This was partly due to a controversy over the ownership of gold removed from Rome in 1943. *See generally* Monetary Gold Removed from Rome in 1943 (Italy v. France, United Kingdom, United States) (Prelimary Question), June 15, 1954, I.C.J. Reports, 1954, at 19. The case was finally resolved when the two states reached a settlement agreement on May 8, 1992. Under the terms of the agreement, Albania is to pay the UK £1.1 million in settlement of all outstanding claims. The UK, in turn, agreed to release to Albania 1547 kg of gold it had been holding since World War II, pending Albania's payment of the amount awarded the UK by the Court. The gold was Albania's share of the precious metal amassed by the Nazis during their occupation of Europe and ultimately confiscated from them by the Allies. Financial Times, May 9, 1992, p. 2.

C. SHARED NATURAL RESOURCES: THE *LAKE LANOUX* ARBITRATION

The case involved a French plan to divert from Lake Lanoux water, which in its natural course flowed into Spain. The Spanish government claimed that the plan violated an 1866 Treaty and Additional Act between the two states and that the French project could not be executed without the prior agreement of the parties. The following paragraphs describe the background of the dispute in some detail[6] because the discussions between France and Spain leading to the arbitration are believed to hold important lessons concerning state practice in the field of shared natural resources.

"Lake Lanoux is situated on the south slope of the Pyrenees and on the territory of the French Republic. . . . It is fed by streams all of which rise on French territory and traverse only that territory. Its waters flow out through a single stream, the Font-Vive, which is one of the sources of the Carol River. [The latter] river, after having flowed about twenty-five kilometres measured from Lake Lanoux on French territory, crosses the Spanish boundary at Puigcerdá. . . ."[7] In 1950, Electricité de France applied to the French government for a concession to construct and operate a hydroelectric facility using water diverted from Lake Lanoux. The plan called for the construction of a dam that would increase the capacity of Lake Lanoux from 17 to 70 million cubic meters and the diversion of the lake's waters through a tunnel down a steep incline to a power station, from which it would flow toward the Ariège River. Thus, under normal conditions, no water would flow out of the lake through the Font-Vive to the Carol. The Carol and the Ariège are in different drainage basins. Waters

6. For the full description, *see* 12 U.N. Rep. Intl. Arb. Awards at 291-295. *See also* 24 Intl. L. Rep. at 105-111; and 53 Am. J. Intl. L. at 157-159.

7. 1974 ILC Y.B. at 196; 12 U.N. Rep. Intl. Arb. Awards, at 287-288.

of the former empty into the Mediterranean while those of the latter ultimately drain into the Atlantic. According to the French Memorial (brief) in the case, the project would produce sufficient electricity to meet the needs of a city of 326,000 throughout the year. The French Memorial also stated that approximately 18,000 farmers in Spain depend upon the waters of the Carol; a quarter of those waters came from Lake Lanoux.

The proposal of Electricité de France called for restoring all of the diverted waters to the Carol River in France by means of a tunnel from the Ariège to the Carol. However, the French government initially took the position that it was required to return only as much water as was necessary to satisfy the actual needs of the Spanish users. France notified Spain in 1953 that it would proceed to develop Lake Lanoux on this basis. In response, Spain requested that no work be undertaken on the project until after a meeting of the Mixed Commission of Engineers the two countries had established in 1949[8] to study the question of the utilization of the waters of Lake Lanoux. France agreed to a meeting of the Mixed Commission and offered assurances that no construction was planned or imminent, but noted that the relevant treaty[9] did not require suspension of works likely to affect the system of waters at the request of the other party.

Before any meeting was held, however, France changed its position. It decided to accept the original proposal of Electricité de France to fully restore to the Carol the waters diverted from Lake Lanoux. It accordingly provided the Spanish authorities with the technical information concerning that proposal. Spain objected on the ground that the project would cause serious prejudice to Spanish interests and again requested a meeting of the Mixed Commission. France replied that since the plan in its current form would not result in any change as far as Spanish users were concerned the relevant agreement was not applicable.[10] This meant that the agreement's requirement of prior notification did not apply. France also denied that it was under any obligation to postpone commencement of work on the project pending a meeting of the Mixed Commission. It did not object to such a meeting being held, however.

The Mixed Commission of Engineers met in August 1955, but the meeting was without result. A subsequent exchange of views between the two governments led to the formation of a Special Mixed Commission charged with preparing a proposal for the utilization of the water of Lake Lanoux for submission to the two governments. France stressed, however, that it would consider itself free to proceed, within the bounds of its rights, if the Special Commission had not concluded its work within three months.

8. The Mixed Commission of Engineers was established in February 1949, at a meeting of the International Commission for the Pyrenees. The latter commission had been formed by an exchange of notes of May and July 1875 between France and Spain.

9. France referred in this connection to the Additional Act of May 26, 1866, between Spain and France.

10. France referred here, in particular, to Article 11 of the Additional Act.

The Special Commission met in December 1955. At that meeting France offered a series of guarantees that would ensure the delivery to Spain of a quantity of water equivalent to the amount that would have flowed from Lake Lanoux but for the project. These guarantees included a double set of valves that would allow water to be released from Lake Lanoux itself in the event of technical difficulties with the restoration tunnel; a proposal to establish a mixed Franco-Spanish Commission to oversee the works and the restoration of water; the granting of access to the proposed works by a member of a Spanish Consulate who would enjoy appropriate privileges and immunities; and an assurance that irrespective of the amount of water flowing into Lake Lanoux, at least 20 million cubic meters of water per year would be restored to the Carol River, such restoration to be regulated so as to correspond to Spanish needs regardless of the quantities flowing into Lake Lanoux. Spain remained fundamentally opposed to the French plan, however, and the meeting came to naught.

A second meeting of the Special Commission was held in March 1956. France indicated at the meeting that it could offer additional guarantees to protect Spanish interests. Spain, for its part, submitted a counterproposal that involved no diversion of the waters of Lake Lanoux but would have produced 10 percent less electricity than the French plan. This initiative proved unacceptable to France. Once again, the meeting ended without result, whereupon the Special Commission terminated its work. Later in March 1956, France informed Spain that in accordance with its earlier statement it would now consider itself free to proceed with its plans, within the limits of its rights. Work on the project, which up to that point had consisted only of the construction of a road and a *téléphérique,* was accordingly resumed in April. By the time the arbitral tribunal (described below) rendered its award the project had been largely completed, although no water had yet been diverted.

France and Spain referred the matter to arbitration pursuant to a 1929 Arbitration Treaty between the two countries.[11] By a *compromis* signed in November 1956, the parties established an arbitral tribunal[12] to which they submitted the following question:

> Is the French Government justified in its contention that, in carrying out, without a prior agreement between the two Governments, works for the use of the waters of Lake Lanoux on the terms laid down in the plan and in the French proposals mentioned in the preamble to this *compromis,* it would

11. In the treaty the two countries agreed to resolve by arbitration all disputes that could not be settled through diplomatic channels.

12. In accordance with Article 2 of the *compromis,* the tribunal consisted of four members and a President. The members were Plinio Bolla and Paul Reuter, appointed by the French government; and Fernand de Visscher and Antonio de Luna, appointed by the Spanish government. The President, Sture Petrén, was appointed by the King of Sweden. *Id.* at 195.

not commit a violation of the provisions of the Treaty of Bayonne of 26 May 1866 and of the Additional Act of the same date?[13]

The tribunal rendered its award on November 16, 1957. The award is excerpted, below.

■ LAKE LANOUX ARBITRATION

(France v. Spain)
Ad Hoc International Arbitral Tribunal, 1957
12 U.N. Rep. Intl. Arb. Awards 281[14]

1. The public works contemplated in the French plan are situated entirely in France; the greater part, if not all, of their effects will be felt on French territory; they relate to water which is subject to French territorial sovereignty according to article 8 of the Additional Act. . . .

2. . . . The Spanish Government bases its arguments first on the text of the Treaty and of the Additional Act of 1866. . . . But, in addition, the Spanish Government relies both on the general and traditional features of the Pyrénées boundary system and on certain rules of customary international law to interpret the Treaty and the Additional Act of 1866.

Moreover, the French Memorial . . . examines the question submitted to the Tribunal in the light of the "law of nations." The French Counter-Memorial does the same, with the following reservation: "although the question submitted to the Tribunal is clearly confined to the interpretation, in the case under consideration, of the Treaty of Bayonne . . . and of the Additional Act. . . ." In his oral pleadings, the agent of the French Government said: "the *compromis* does not charge the Tribunal with determining whether there are on the subject general principles of the law of nations applicable in the present case" . . . , and: "A treaty is interpreted in the context of positive international law at such time as it may be applied." . . .

Since the question submitted by the *compromis* relates solely to the Treaty and the Additional Act of 1866, the Tribunal will apply, with regard to each particular point, the following rules:

Clear provisions of treaty law do not call for any interpretation; . . . when there is matter for interpretation, this should be done according to international law; international law does not establish any absolute and

13. *Id.* at 195.

14. This report carries the award in the original French. The full French text is reprinted in 62 Revue générale de droit international public 79 (1958). For English translations of the award, or major portions thereof, *see* 24 Intl. L. Rep. 101 (1961); 53 Am. J. Intl. L. 156 (1959); and 1974 Y.B. Intl. L. Commn., vol. 2, part 2, p. 194 (1976) (hereafter 1974 ILC Y.B.). The present excerpts consist in part of the Editors' translation of the French text of the award and in part of the translation contained in the 1974 ILC Y.B.

rigid system of interpretation; it is, therefore, permissible to take into consideration the spirit which governed the Pyrénées treaties as well as the rules of customary international law. . . .

3. This dispute may be reduced to two fundamental questions:

(*a*) Would the works for the use of the waters of Lake Lanoux . . . constitute in themselves a violation of the rights granted to Spain by the substantive provisions of the Treaty of Bayonne of 26 May 1866 and the Additional Act of the same date?

(*b*) If the answer to the preceding question is in the negative, would the execution of these works constitute a violation of the provisions of the Treaty . . . and . . . the Additional Act . . . , on the ground that these provisions made execution subject in any event to a prior agreement between the two Governments or because other rules of article 11 of the Additional Act concerning the negotiations between the two Governments had not been observed?

I. As to the First Question (Stated under 3, *A*)

[The Tribunal discussed articles 9-11 and 18 of the Additional Act. Article 9 provides as follows:

> For watercourses flowing from one country to the other, or which form a boundary, each government recognizes, subject to verification when appropriate, the legality of irrigations, works and domestic uses currently existing in the other state, by virtue of concession, title or by prescription, except that only such water will be used as is necessary to satisfy actual needs, that abuses must be eliminated and that this recognition will in no way infringe the respective rights of the governments to authorize works of public utility, on condition that just compensation be paid.

Article 10 provides that any water remaining after actual needs have been satisfied is to be apportioned between the parties. Article 11 requires that when new works are proposed that might affect users of a watercourse in the other country, prior notice be given to the appropriate administrative authority in that country so that the users in question may lodge a timely claim with the competent authorities in the country in which the works have been proposed. Article 18 provides that an international commission of engineers is to determine the present use of water in each country in order to allocate the necessary quantity of water and to eliminate abuses, as required by Article 9 and other articles.]

6. Indeed, thanks to the restitution effected by the mechanism described above, no guaranteed user will be injured in his enjoyment of the waters (this has not been the subject of any claim founded on Article 9); at the lowest water level, the volume of the surplus waters of the Carol at the boundary would at no time suffer a diminution; it may even, by virtue

of the minimum guarantee by France, enjoy an increase in volume assured by the waters of the Ariège that flow naturally to the Atlantic.

This conclusion might have been attacked in several ways.

It could have been argued that the works would result in the pollution of the waters of the Carol, or that the returned waters would have a chemical composition or a temperature or some other characteristic that could injure Spanish interests. Spain could then have claimed that its rights had been impaired in violation of the Additional Act. Neither the dossier nor the arguments in this case bear any trace of such an allegation.

It could also have been claimed that, by their technical character, the works contemplated by the French plan could not in fact ensure the restitution of a volume corresponding to the natural contribution of Lake Lanoux to the Carol, because of defectiveness either of the measuring instruments or of the restoration mechanisms. The question was touched upon in the Spanish Counter-Memorial . . . , which underlined the "extraordinary complexity" of the control procedures, their "very onerous" character and the "risks of damage or of negligence, in the handling of the gates and of the barrier in the tunnel." But it has never been alleged that the planned works have any other character or entail any other risks than works of the same kind that are today widespread all over the world. It has not been clearly asserted that the planned works would entail a risk that is abnormal in neighborly relations or in the utilization of waters. As we have seen above, the technical guarantees for the restitution of the waters are as satisfactory as possible. If, despite the precautions that have been taken, the restitution of the waters were to suffer from an accident, such would only be an occasional occurrence and, according to the two parties, would not constitute a violation of Article 9.

7. But the Spanish government takes a different position. In the arbitration *compromis,* it had already claimed that the French plan "alters the natural conditions of the hydrographic basin of Lake Lanoux, by diverting its waters to the Ariège and thereby making the return of the waters to the Carol physically dependent on the will of man, which will lead to the *de facto* predominance of one Party instead of the equality of the two Parties contemplated by the Treaty of Bayonne of 26 May 1866 and by the Additional act of the same date."[15]

. . . In the statement of its case, [the Spanish government] referred to article 12 of the Additional Act:

> [The lower lands are subject to receiving from the higher lands of the neighboring country the waters that naturally flow therefrom including what they carry, without the hand of man having contributed thereto. There may be constructed neither a dam nor an obstacle of any kind capable of harming

15. Arbitration *compromis,* at 195-196 (the passage is from the third preambular paragraph of the arbitration *compromis*) [—EDS.].

the upper riparians, who are likewise prohibited from doing anything that might increase the burden of the servitude of the lower lands.[16]]

According to the Spanish Government, this provision confirms the notion that neither of the Parties may, without the consent of the other, alter the natural order of the water's flow. The Spanish Counter Memorial . . . acknowledges, however, that: "From the moment that the will of man intervenes to carry out any hydraulic development whatever, an extra-physical element acts on the current and alters what Nature established." Consequently, the Spanish Government does not attribute an absolute meaning to respect for natural order; according to the Counter Memorial . . . : "A State has the right to use unilaterally the part of a river which traverses it to the extent that this use is likely to cause on the territory of another State a limited harm only, a minimal inconvenience, which comes within the bounds of what is implied by good neighbourliness."

In reality, it seems that the Spanish thesis is twofold and covers, on the one hand, the prohibition, without the consent of the other Party, of compensation between two basins, in spite of the equivalence of withdrawal and return and, on the other hand, the prohibition, without the consent of the other Party, of all actions that may create along with a *de facto* inequality, the physical possibility of a violation of law.

The two points should be examined in order.

8. The prohibition of compensation between two basins, without the consent of the other Party, despite the equivalence of withdrawal and return, would result in a general bar to the taking of water from a waterway belonging to river basin A for the benefit of river basin B, even if this withdrawal was offset by a strictly equivalent return from a waterway of river basin B for the benefit of river basin A. The Tribunal, from the viewpoint of physical geography, cannot disregard the reality of each river basin, which constitutes, as the Spanish case . . . contends, "a whole." But this fact does not justify the absolute consequences which the Spanish thesis seeks to draw from it. The unity of a basin is supported at the legal level only to the extent that it conforms to the realities of life. Water, which is by nature a fungible thing, may be restored without alteration of its qualities from the viewpoint of human needs. A withdrawal with return, as contemplated in the French plan, does not alter a state of affairs established in response to the demands of life in society.

The state of modern technology leads more and more frequently to the acknowledgement that water used in the generation of electric power need not be returned to its natural course. The water is taken from a constantly higher point and it is carried still lower, and in the course of this process it is sometimes diverted to another river basin, in the same State or in another [state] within the same federation or even in a third

16. [Our translation—Eds.].

State. In federations, court decisions have recognized the validity of this latter practice [the tribunal cited Wyoming v. Colorado, 259 U.S. 419; cases cited by the authors D.J.E. Berber and G. Sauser-Hall; and case law of the Swiss Federal Tribunal].

The Tribunal considers, therefore, that withdrawal with return, as provided in the French plan and proposals, is not in conflict with the Treaty and Additional Act of 1866.

9. In another connexion, the Spanish Government challenged the legality of works carried out on the territory of one of the signatories of the Treaty and of the Additional Act, if they were calculated to enable it, even in violation of its international commitments, to bring pressure to bear on the other signatory. This rule was said to follow from the fact that the treaties in question established the principle of equality among States. Specifically, Spain feels that France does not have the right to procure for itself, by public works, the physical possibility of stopping the flow of the Lanoux water or the return of an equivalent quantity of water. It is not for the Tribunal to judge the reasons or experiences which might lead the Spanish Government to give expression to a certain anxiety. But it is not alleged that the purpose of the works in questions, aside from the satisfaction of French interests, is to create a means of at least potential injury to Spanish interests; that would be all the more unlikely as France could only partially exhaust the resources represented by the discharge of the Carol, as she would also affect all the French land irrigated by the Carol, and as she would expose herself along the whole boundary to formidable reprisals.

On the other hand, the French Government's proposals, which are an integral part of its plan, include "the assurance that it will not in any case, interfere with the regime thus established." . . . The Tribunal must, therefore, answer the question submitted by the *compromis* on the basis of this assurance. It could not be alleged that despite this commitment Spain would not have a sufficient guarantee, for it is a well-established general principle of law that bad faith is not presumed. Furthermore, it has not been contended that either of the two States at any time intentionally infringed a rule relating to the regime of the waters to the detriment of the other. Moreover, although based on a just spirit of reciprocity, the Treaties of Bayonne established only equality in law and not equality in fact. If it were otherwise, they would have had to forbid on both sides of the boundary any installations and works of a military order which could give to one of the States a *de facto* predominance which it might use to violate its international commitments. But it is necessary to go farther still; man's growing mastery of the forces and secrets of nature has placed in his hands instruments which he may use to violate his obligations or for the common good; the danger of misuse has not resulted, up to the present, in making the possession of these means dependent on the authorization of the States which may be threatened. Even if viewed solely from the standpoint of the relations of neighbours, the political danger alleged by the Spanish Government would be not more exceptional than the technical risk mentioned above. In any case, there is not, in the Treaty and Additional Act of 26 May 1866 or in the generally accepted principles of international law, a rule which forbids a State, acting to protect its legitimate interests, from placing itself in a situation which enables it in fact, in violation of its international obligations, to do even serious injury to a neighbouring State.

It remains still to be determined whether the French plan conflicts with the substantive rules laid down by article 11. This question will be examined further on, in connexion with the general terms of this article . . . .

Subject to this last reservation, the Tribunal replies in the negative to the first question, set forth in paragraph 3 *a.*

II. As to the Second Question (Stated under 3, B)

10. In the *compromis,* the Spanish Government had already declared that in its opinion the execution of the French plan required "the prior agreement of the two Governments, and that in the absence of such agreement the country that proposed the project is not free to undertake the works."

In the proceedings, both written and oral, the Government developed this approach, completing it in particular by a statement of the principles which should govern the negotiations leading to this prior agreement. Two obligations were said to rest upon the State which wished to undertake the proposed works: the most important was to reach a prior agreement with the other State concerned; the other which was only secondary, was to observe the other rules laid down by article 11 of the Additional Act.

The arguments submitted by the Spanish Government are put forth, moreover, at two levels; the Spanish Government bases its position, on the one hand, on the Treaty and Additional Act of 1866, and on the other hand on the system of joint community pasturage rights (*faceries* and *compascuités*) which exits at the Pyrénées frontier and on the generally accepted rules of international law. The last two sources would make it possible first, to interpret the Treaty and Additional Act of 1866, and then, in a broader perspective, to demonstrate the existence of an unwritten general rule of international law. There are said to be precedents establishing that rule in the traditions of the system of joint community pasturage rights, in the provisions of the Pyrenees treaties, and in the international practice of States concerning the industrial use of international waterways.

11. Before considering the Spanish arguments, the Tribunal believes it would be useful to make some very general observations on the nature of the obligations alleged to be incumbent on the French Government. To admit that in a given matter competence may no longer be exercised except on the condition of or by means of an agreement between two States is to place an essential restriction on the sovereignty of a State, and it

may be allowed only if there is conclusive proof. Undoubtedly international practice discloses some specific cases in which this assumption is proved; thus, sometimes two States exercise jurisdiction jointly over certain territories (indivisum, co-imperium or condominium); similarly, in certain international institutions, the representatives of States exercise jointly a certain competence on behalf of States or on behalf of organizations. But these cases are exceptional and international case law does not readily recognize their existence, especially when they infringe upon the territorial sovereignty of a State, which would be true in the present case.

In fact, to evaluate in its essence the need for a prior agreement, it is necessary to adopt the hypothesis that the States concerned cannot arrive at an agreement. In that case, it would have to be admitted that a State which ordinarily is competent has lost the right to act alone as a consequence of the unconditional and discretionary opposition of another State. This is to admit a "right of consent," a "right of veto," which at the discretion of one State paralyses another State's exercise of its territorial competence.

For this reason, international practice prefers to resort to less extreme solutions, limiting itself to requiring States to seek the terms of an agreement by prior negotiations without making the exercise of their competence conditional on the conclusion of this agreement. Thus reference is made, although often incorrectly, to "an obligation to negotiate an agreement." In reality, the commitments thus assumed by States take very diverse forms, and their scope varies according to the way in which they are defined and according to the procedures for their execution; but the reality of the obligations thus assumed cannot be questioned, and they may be enforced, for example, in the case of an unjustified breaking off of conversations, unusual delays, disregard of established procedures, systematic refusal to give consideration to proposals or adverse interests, and more generally in the case of infringement of the rules of good faith. (The Tacna-Arica Case, in United Nations, *Reports of International Arbitral Awards*, Vol. II, pp. 921 *et seq.*; Case concerning Railway Traffic between Lithuania and Poland, in P.C.I.J., *Series A/B* 42, pp. 108 *et seq.*)

In the light of these general observations and with reference to the present case, we shall consider successively whether a prior agreement is necessary and whether the other rules established by article 11 of the Additional Act have been observed.

A) NECESSITY OF A PRIOR AGREEMENT

12. We shall consider first, therefore, whether the proposition that the execution of the French plan is conditional on the prior consent of the Spanish Government is justified by reference to the system of joint community pasturage rights or to the generally accepted principles of international law; the data collected is supposed to help, if necessary, to interpret the Treaty and Additional Act of 1866 or, better still, according to the more general form given to the Spanish thesis, to establish the existence of a

general principle of law or custom which was recognized, *inter alia*, by the Treaty and the Additional Act of 1866. . . .

[After examining the question, the Tribunal concluded that] it is impossible to extend the system of joint community pasturage rights beyond the bounds assigned to it by the Treaties, or to derive from it an idea of a generalized "community" which would have any legal content whatever. As for the appeal to the idea of a "frontier zone," an obligation cannot be added to those laid down by positive law merely by the use of the vocabulary of legal doctrine.

13. The Spanish Government also attempted to establish the existing positive international law. . . . Some of the principles for which proof is offered, assuming them to be established, are without relevance to the matter now under consideration. Thus, while admittedly there is a rule prohibiting the upper riparian State from altering the waters of a river in circumstances calculated to do serious injury to the lower riparian State, such a principle has no application to the present case, since it was agreed by the Tribunal, with respect to the first question considered above, that the French plan did not alter the waters of the Carol. In fact, States today are well aware of the importance of the conflicting interests involved in the industrial use of international rivers and of the necessity of reconciling some of these interests with others through mutual concessions. The only way to achieve these compromises of interests is the conclusion of agreements on a more and more comprehensive basis. International practice reflects the conviction that States should seek to conclude such agreements; there would thus be an obligation for States to agree in good faith to all negotiations and contacts which should, through a wide confrontation of interests and reciprocal goodwill, place them in the best circumstances to conclude agreements. This point will be considered later on in establishing the obligations of France and Spain concerning contacts and negotiations prior to the execution of a plan such as the one for Lake Lanoux.

But international practice does not permit us, so far, to go beyond this conclusion; the rule that States may use the hydraulic power of international watercourses only if a *prior* agreement between the States concerned has been concluded cannot be established as a custom or, still less, as a general principle of law. In this connexion the history of the drafting of the multilateral Geneva Convention of 9 December 1923 relating to the Development of Hydraulic Power affecting more than one State[17] is very significant. The initial draft was based on the idea of compulsory prior agreements for developing the hydraulic power of international waterways. But this proposal was rejected, and the Convention, in its final form, provided (art. 1) that it "in no way affects the right belonging to each State, within the limits

17. [36 L.N.T.S. 75—Eds.].

of international law, to carry out on its own territory any operations for the development of hydraulic power which it may consider desirable;" it is merely provided that the signatory States concerned have an obligation to agree to a joint investigation of a scheme of development; the carrying out of this program is not compulsory except for States which have formally undertaken to do so.

No more than the traditions of the Pyrenees does generally accepted international law provide a basis for interpreting the Treaty and Additional Act of 1866 in a sense favourable to the necessity of a prior agreement or, still less, for concluding that there is a general principle of law or custom to this effect.

14. A rule requiring an agreement prior to the hydraulic development of an international waterway can exist between Spain and France only as a result of a treaty. . . . [The Tribunal, after examining the agreements in force between the parties, held that they contained no such rule.]

[With respect to the other obligations under article 11 of the Additional Act, the Tribunal said:]

21. Article 11 of the Additional Act imposes a twofold obligation on States in which works or new concessions susceptible of changing the regime or the volume of a watercourse traversing the two States are proposed. One is to give prior notice to the competent authorities of the neighbouring country; the other is to develop a system of complaints and of safeguards for all the interests involved on one side and the other.

[France claimed that since it had found that the planned works would cause no harm to Spanish interests, it had no obligation to notify the Spanish authorities.] A State that may suffer the repercussions of works undertaken by a neighboring State is the sole judge of its interests, and if the latter has not taken the initiative, the right of the other [i.e., the potentially affected State] to demand notification of planned works or concessions cannot be denied.

It has not been disputed that France has satisfied the obligation of notice as far as the development of Lake Lanoux is concerned.

22. The content of the second obligation is more difficult to determine. The "complaints" mentioned in article 11 relate to the various rights protected by the Additional Act, but the main question is to establish how "all the interests involved on one side and the other" should be safeguarded.

First, it is necessary to determine which "interests" should be safeguarded. A strict interpretation of article 11 would support the conclusion that only interests corresponding to a right of the riparian population were involved. Various considerations already pointed out by the Tribunal lead however to a broader interpretation. Consideration must be given to all interests, whatever their nature, which may be affected by the works undertaken, even if they do not amount to a right. Only this solution is in accord with the terms of article 16, the spirit of the Pyrénées Treaties, and the trends apparent in current international practice as regards hydro-electric development.

The second question is to determine the procedure whereby these interests can be safeguarded. Although this procedure necessarily involves negotiations, it cannot be reduced to purely formal requirements, such as taking note of complaints, protests or expressions of displeasure submitted by the lower riparian State. The Tribunal considers that the upper riparian State, under the rules of good faith, has an obligation to take into consideration the various interests concerned, to seek to give them every satisfaction compatible with the pursuit of its own interests and to show that it has, in this matter, a real desire to reconcile the interests of the other riparian with its own.

It is difficult to determine if such an obligation has been met. Nevertheless, without substituting himself for the Parties, the judge is able to undertake this determination on the basis of the evidence furnished by the negotiations.

23. In the present case, the Spanish Government charges that the French Government did not draw up the development plan for the waters of Lake Lanoux on a basis of absolute equality. This charge is twofold: it relates to both procedure and substance. With regard to procedure, it is suggested that the French Government imposed its plan unilaterally without associating the Spanish Government in a joint search for an acceptable solution. As to substance, it is contended that the French plan does not maintain an equitable balance between French interests and Spanish interests. The French plan, it is argued, perfectly serves French interests, especially those directed toward electric power production designed to meet peak demand, but does not take sufficient account of Spanish interests in respect of irrigation. According to the Spanish Government, the French Government refused to consider plans which, in the Spanish Government's opinion, would have involved a slight sacrifice for French interests and great advantages for the Spanish agricultural economy. Spain bases its argument specifically on the following facts: during the meeting of the Special Joint Commission at Madrid (12-17 December 1955), the French delegation made a comparison of three development plans for Lake Lanoux and pointed out the considerable advantages which, in its opinion, the first plan (corresponding to the final plan) had in comparison with the other two. The Spanish delegation, having no particular objection to these latter plans, declared that it was prepared to accept either of the two. The French delegation deemed itself unable to renounce the execution of plan No. 1, which was more favourable to French interests and based, in its opinion, on a right. . . .

From the standpoint of principle, the Spanish thesis cannot be accepted by the Tribunal, for it is inclined to put rights and mere interests on the same level. Article 11 of the Additional Act makes a distinction between them, which both Parties have reproduced in the fundamental statement of their theses at the beginning of the *compromis*:

> Considering that, in the opinion of the French Government, the carrying out of its plan . . . would not prejudice any of the rights or interests referred to in the Treaty of Bayonne of 26 May 1866 and in the Additional Act of the same date;
>
> Considering that, in the opinion of the Spanish Government, the carrying out of this plan would prejudice Spanish interests and rights.

France may exercise its rights; it may not disregard Spanish interests.

Spain may demand respect for its rights and consideration of its interests.

As to procedure, the upper riparian State has, procedurally, a right of initiative; it is not obliged to involve the lower riparian State in the preparation of its plans. If during the negotiations the lower riparian State submits plans to it, the upper riparian State should examine them, but it has the right to prefer the solution embodied in its plan, if it takes into consideration in a reasonable manner the interests of the lower riparian State.

24. In the case of Lake Lanoux, France adhered throughout to the solution which involved a diversion of the water of the Carol to the Ariège, with complete return. In making this choice, France is merely exercising a right; the Lake Lanoux development works are being carried out on French territory, the burden and the responsibility of the undertaking rests on France, and France is the sole judge of the public works to be carried out on its territory, subject to article 9 and 10 of the Additional Act, which the French plan does not infringe.

For its part, Spain may not invoke a right to have the development of Lake Lanoux based on the needs of Spanish agriculture. In fact, if France renounced all the works planned on its territory, Spain could not require other works which conformed to its wishes to be carried out. It, therefore, may assert its interests simply to obtain terms providing reasonable safeguards for them within the limits of the plan adopted by France.

It remains to be decided whether this requirement has been met. . . .

In determining whether France, both in its negotiations and in its proposals, took Spanish interests sufficiently into consideration, note must be taken of the intimate connection between the obligation to take adverse interests into account in the course of negotiations and the obligation to give a reasonable place to such interests in the solution adopted. A State which has conducted negotiations with understanding and good faith in accordance with article 11 of the Additional Act is not released from the obligation to give a reasonable place to adverse interests in the solution adopted because the conversations have been interrupted, even by the intransigence of its partner. Conversely, in appraising the way in which a plan takes account of the interests concerned, the manner in which the negotiations have been conducted, the interests presented and the price which each of the Parties was prepared to pay to safeguard them, are the main factors in establishing the merit of the plan in relation to the obligations of article 11 of the Additional Act.

In view of all the above-mentioned circumstances of the case, the Tribunal is of the opinion that the French plan satisfies the obligations of article 11 of the Additional Act.

FOR THESE REASONS

The Tribunal decides to reply in the affirmative to the question set forth in article 1 of the *compromis.* In carrying out, without a prior agreement between the two Governments, works for the use of the waters of Lake Lanoux on the terms laid down in the Plan for the Utilization of the Waters of Lake Lanoux, due notice of which was given to the Governor of Gerona Province on 21 January 1954 and of which the representatives of Spain on the Pyrénées Commission were informed during the Commission's session from 3 to 14 November 1955, and in accordance with the proposals submitted by the French delegation to the Special Joint Commission on 13 December 1955, the French Government would not commit a violation of the provisions of the Treaty of Bayonne of 26 May 1866 and of the Additional Act of that date.

Notes and Questions

1. *The award's significance.* As with *Trail Smelter* and *Corfu Channel,* broad significance has been attributed to the *Lake Lanoux* award. *See, e.g.,* S. Bleicher, An Overview of International Environmental Regulation, 2 Ecology L.Q. 1, 25-29 (1972). "[F]rom the point of view of establishing some substantive principles for environmental protection, the case is of great interest as a virtual catalogue of potential grounds for relief." *Id.* at 27 (footnote omitted). Strictly speaking, can the decision be taken as anything other than an interpretation and application of the relevant agreements between France and Spain? If not, of course, it would be of considerably less assistance in disputes involving other countries. It would also contribute little to the formation of principles of general international law.

2. *The role of general international law.* Both France and Spain evidently believed that general international law had an important role to play in the resolution of the case, despite the fact that the question they posed to the tribunal was confined to whether the Treaty of Bayonne and the Additional Act required the prior consent of Spain for the French project. The two countries, in their memorials, extensively analyzed customary international law as it applied to the dispute. *See* J. Laylin & R. Bianchi, The Role of Adjudication in International River Disputes: The Lake Lanoux Case, 53 Am J. Intl. L. 30, n.34, at 42-43 (1959). And, in its award, the tribunal

had broad recourse to customary international law in interpreting and filling gaps in the relevant agreements. Note in this connection that Spain appears to have argued, inter alia, that the relevant agreements simply recognized a general principle of law or custom concerning the necessity of a prior agreement. See paragraph 12 of the award. What would be the effect of the tribunal's acceptance of this argument?

3. *The obligation to negotiate.* Perhaps the most notable area in which the tribunal elaborated on principles of general international law as they applied to the dispute was that of the obligation to negotiate. In holding that France was not required to obtain Spain's consent prior to implementing its plans, the tribunal explained that "international practice prefers to resort to less extreme solutions," namely, requiring the states concerned to attempt to reach an agreement through negotiations. But is the obligation to negotiate a meaningful one? Can states satisfy it simply by being polite and appearing reasonable? Does it encourage states to inflate their initial positions in order to be able to modify their "demands" without really conceding anything of importance to them? What functions or interests of the international community does it serve, if any? Finally, do you believe France satisfied the obligation to negotiate as that obligation was defined by the tribunal? Is your answer affected by the fact that France resumed work on the project some seven months before the arbitration tribunal was established and had largely completed it by the time the tribunal handed down its award? In the *Electricity at Sofia* case, the Permanent Court of International Justice (the predecessor of the International Court of Justice) referred to

> the principle universally accepted by international tribunals . . . to the effect that the parties to a case must abstain from any measure capable of exercising a prejudicial effect in regard to the execution of the decision to be given and, in general, not allow any step of any kind to be taken which might aggravate or extend the dispute.

P.C.I.J. Ser. A/B, No. 79, at 199 (1939). Did France's continued work on the project violate this principle?

4. *The obligation to negotiate: other decisions.* The obligation to negotiate has also been addressed by the International Court of Justice in cases involving fisheries and the delimitation of maritime boundaries. *See* the *Fisheries Jurisdiction* cases (United Kingdom v. Iceland; Germany v. Iceland), 1974 I.C.J. Rep. 3, 175; the *North Sea Continental Shelf* cases (Germany/Denmark; Germany/The Netherlands), 1969 I.C.J. Rep. 3; the case concerning the *Continental Shelf* (Tunisia/Libya), 1982 I.C.J. Rep. 18, at 59-60, paras. 70-71; and the case concerning *Delimitation of the Maritime Boundary in the Gulf of Maine Area* (Canada/United States), 1984 I.C.J. Rep. 246, at 339-340, para. 230. In the *North Sea Continental Shelf* cases, for example, the

Court explained the meaning of the obligation to negotiate in the following way:

> [T]he parties are under an obligation to enter into negotiations with a view to arriving at an agreement, and not merely to go through a formal process of negotiation as a sort of prior condition for the automatic application of a certain method of delimitation in the absence of agreement; they are under an obligation so to conduct themselves that the negotiations are meaningful, which will not be the case when either of them insists upon its own position without contemplating any modification of it; . . .
>
> . . . So far as [this] rule is concerned, the Court would recall . . . that the obligation to negotiate . . . merely constitutes a special application of a principle which underlies all international relations, and which is moreover recognized in Article 33 of the Charter of the United Nations as one of the methods for the peaceful settlement of international disputes. . . .
>
> . . . Defining the content of the obligation to negotiate, the Permanent Court [of International Justice], in its Advisory Opinion in the case of *Railway Traffic between Lithuania and Poland,* said that the obligation was "not only to enter into negotiations but also to pursue them as far as possible with a view to concluding agreements," even if an obligation to negotiate did not imply an obligation to reach agreement (*P.C.I.J., Series A/B, No. 42,* 1931, at p. 116). . . .

1969 I.C.J. Rep. at 47-48. How does this definition of the obligation to negotiate compare with the statements of the *Lake Lanoux* tribunal concerning that obligation?

5. *The obligation to negotiate: UN Watercourses Convention.* The 1997 United Nations Convention on International Watercourses contains a set of provisions on notification, consultation, and negotiation concerning new uses of those watercourses. Those provisions are set forth in section B of Chapter 7.

6. *Interbasin transfers.* One of Spain's objections to the French plan was that it involved a transfer of water from one river basin to another. In fact, while Lake Lanoux naturally drained into a system that flowed through Spain and emptied into the Mediterranean, the French project channeled the lake's waters into a wholly French basin (the Garonne) that empties into the Atlantic. The tribunal's response to Spain's complaint was that water "is by nature a fungible thing [and] may be restored without alteration of its qualities from the viewpoint of human needs." (Paragraph 8.) While an inter-basin transfer may have been harmless in the context of the *Lake Lanoux* dispute, it is not always so. This is especially true in light of current knowledge of the harm that can be done through the introduction of alien species into an ecosystem. *See generally* D. Bederman, International Control of Marine "Pollution" by Exotic Species, 18 Ecology L.Q. 677 (1991). An illustration is the vast American irrigation project known as the Garrison

Diversion Unit (GDU). The GDU involves the transfer of water from the Missouri River basin (which ultimately drains into the Gulf of Mexico) to the Red River and Hudson Bay drainage basins. One of Canada's concerns with regard to the project was that along with the water would come not only agricultural pollution runoff but also biota (living plant and animal organisms, including diseases) that would be harmful to aquatic life in the Hudson Bay and Red River watersheds in Canada. The problem was referred by the United States and Canada to the International Joint Commission (discussed in note 11 following the *Trail Smelter* case), which found that if the project did result in an interbasin transfer of biota into Canada, it would violate the 1909 Boundary Waters Treaty between the two countries. *See generally* J. Carroll, Environmental Diplomacy 174-182 (1983). The project was ultimately discontinued, although some still advocate it.

7. *Problem.* Assume that state A is planning to construct a state-of-the-art nuclear power plant in the region of its border with state B, and that B claims the plant would impermissibly place B in danger of being seriously harmed. A's foreign minister has asked you to draft a diplomatic note covering the legal aspects of the case. Would you cite and rely upon the *Lake Lanoux* award? *See, e.g.*, paragraph 9. What about the *Trail Smelter* award? Would your answer be any different if the plant were of the Chernobyl type? What rights to prior notification, consultation and negotiation, if any, would B have vis-à-vis A under *Lake Lanoux* in either situation?

8. *The threat posed by upstream dams.* One of Spain's concerns about the project was that it would place France in a position to "bring pressure to bear on the other [party]." (Paragraph 9.) The tribunal answered in part that "the danger of misuse [of works] has not resulted, up to the present, in making the possession of these means dependent on the authorization of the States which may be threatened." (*Id.*) In December 1959, the Malpasset Dam in southern France ruptured, killing 423 people in that country. If this incident had occurred before the *Lake Lanoux* arbitration do you think the tribunal would have responded in the same way to Spain's concern?

In 1986 North Korea began construction on a dam on the Han River that would hold some 20 billion gallons of water. The Han crosses the border and flows through the South Korean capital of Seoul. South Korea feared that the massive facility was intended to produce a "water bomb." According to this scenario, North Korea would blow up the dam, which would send a 20 billion-ton wall of water down the Han River Valley through Seoul, 80 miles downriver, causing untold damage and fatalities. South Korea responded to the perceived threat by constructing a new $250 million "Peace Dam," whose purpose was to catch the deadly wave of flood waters. *See, e.g.*, Dam, Double Dam, Time, Dec. 15, 1986, p. 47; and Seoul's "Water Bomb" Defense Left High and Dry, Washington Post, August 1, 1988, p. A17, col. 1. While South Korea's fears appear to have been groundless, would the tribunal's response to the concern of Spain described above have been the same if this Korean case had arisen prior to the Lake Lanoux dispute? Should different principles apply in situations like the Korean one?

D. ATMOSPHERIC NUCLEAR TESTING

1. *ICJ Opinion*

■ *NUCLEAR TESTS* CASES

(Australia v. France)[18]
Interim Protection, Order of 22 June 1973
International Court of Justice, 1973
1973 I.C.J. Rep. 99

The International Court of Justice,

Having regard to the Application by Australia filed in the Registry of the Court on 9 May 1973, instituting proceedings against France in respect of a dispute concerning the holding of atmospheric tests of nuclear weapons by the French Government in the Pacific Ocean, and asking the Court to adjudge and declare that the carrying out of further atmospheric nuclear weapon tests in the South Pacific Ocean is not consistent with applicable rules of international law, and to order that the French Republic shall not carry out any further such tests,

Makes the following Order:

1. Having regard to the request . . . whereby the Government of Australia . . . asks the Court to indicate, pending the final decision in the case brought before it by the Application of the same date, the following interim measures of protection:

> The provisional measures should be that the French Government should desist from any further atmospheric nuclear tests pending the judgment of the court in this case; . . .

6. Whereas by a letter dated 16 May 1973 from the Ambassador of France to the Netherlands, handed by him to the Registrar the same day, the French Government stated that it considered that the Court was manifestly not competent in the case and that it could not accept the Court's jurisdiction, and that accordingly the French Government did not intend to appoint an agent, and requested the Court to remove the case from its list; . . .

18. A parallel case was brought by New Zealand. 1973 I.C.J. Rep. 135 [—Eds.].

11. Noting that the French Government was not represented at the hearings; and whereas the non-appearance of one of the States concerned cannot by itself constitute an obstacle to the indication of provisional measures; . . .

13. Whereas on a request for provisional measures the Court need not, before indicating them, finally satisfy itself that it has jurisdiction on the merits of the case, and yet ought not to indicate such measures unless the provisions invoked by the Applicant appear, *prima facie*, to afford a basis on which the jurisdiction of the Court might be founded; . . .

15. Whereas, according to the letter of 16 May 1973 handed to the Registrar by the French Ambassador to the Netherlands, the French Government considers, *inter alia*, that . . . paragraph 3 of [its declaration of 20 May 1966 under Article 36, paragraph 2, of the Statute of the Court] excepts from the French Government's acceptance of compulsory jurisdiction disputes concerning activities connected with national defence; and that the present dispute concerning French nuclear tests in the Pacific incontestably falls within the exception contained in that paragraph;

16. Whereas in its oral observations the government of Australia maintains, *inter alia*, that . . . if the reservation in paragraph 3 of the French declaration of 20 May 1966 relating to "disputes concerning activities connected with national defence" is to be regarded as one having an objective content, it is questionable whether nuclear weapon development falls within the concept of national defence; that if this reservation is to be regarded as a self-judging reservation, it is invalid, and in consequence France is bound by the terms of that declaration unqualified by the reservation in question;

17. Whereas the material submitted to the Court leads it to the conclusion, at the present stage of the proceedings, that the provisions invoked by the Applicant appear, *prima facie*, to afford a basis on which the jurisdiction of the Court might be founded; and whereas the Court will accordingly proceed to examine the Applicant's request for the indication of interim measures of protection; . . .

22. Whereas the claims formulated by the Government of Australia in its Application are as follows:

(i) The right of Australia and its people, in common with other States and their peoples, to be free from atmospheric nuclear weapon tests by any country is and will be violated;

(ii) The deposit of radio-active fall-out on the territory of Australia and its dispersion in Australia's airspace without Australia's consent:
  (a) violates Australian sovereignty over its territory;
  (b) impairs Australia's independent right to determine what acts shall take place within its territory and in particular whether Australia and its people shall be exposed to radiation from artificial sources;

(iii) The interference with ships and aircraft on the high seas and in the superadjacent airspace, and the pollution of the high seas by radio-active fall-out, constitute infringements of the freedom of the high seas; . . .

24. Whereas by the terms of Article 41 of the Statute the Court may indicate interim measures of protection only when it considers that circumstances so require in order to preserve the rights of either party;

[The following summary of the principal facts of the case is taken from the Court's order of December 20, 1974, 1974 I.C.J. Rep. 253, 258.—Eds.

"17. Prior to the filing of the Application instituting proceedings in this case, the French Government had carried out atmospheric tests of nuclear devices at its Centre d'experimentations du Pacifique, in the territory of French Polynesia, in the years 1966, 1967, 1968, 1970, 1971 and 1972. [France had conducted nuclear tests in Algeria both in the atmosphere and underground from 1959-1963, but moved the test site to French Polynesia after the UN General Assembly adopted resolutions calling for the termination of nuclear weapons tests in Africa.[19]] The main firing site used has been Mururoa atoll some 6,000 kilometres to the east of the Australian mainland. The French Government has created 'Prohibited Zones' for aircraft and 'Dangerous Zones' for aircraft and shipping, in order to exclude aircraft and shipping from the area of the tests centre; these 'zones' have been put into effect during the period of testing in each year in which tests have been carried out.

"18. As the United Nations Scientific Committee on the Effects of Atomic Radiation has recorded in its successive reports to the General Assembly, the testing of nuclear devices in the atmosphere has entailed the release into the atmosphere, and the consequent dissipation in varying degrees throughout the world, of measurable quantities of radio-active matter. It is asserted by Australia that the French atmospheric tests have caused some fall-out of this kind to be deposited on Australian territory; France has maintained in particular that the radio-active matter produced by its tests has been so infinitesimal that it may be regarded as negligible, and that such fall-out on Australian territory does not constitute a danger to the health of the Australian population."]

25. Whereas the government of Australia alleges, *inter alia,* that . . . during recent months there has been a growing body of reports, not denied by the French government, to the effect that the French Government is planning to carry out a further series of atmospheric nuclear tests in the Pacific in 1973; that this series of tests may extend to 1975 and even beyond that date; that in diplomatic correspondence and in discussions earlier in

19. U.N.G.A. Resolutions 1379 (XIV), 14 UN GAOR Supp. 16, p. 3 (1969); and 1652 (XVI), 16 UN GAOR Supp. 17, p. 4 (1969).

the present year the French Government would not agree to cease nuclear testing in the atmosphere in the Pacific and would not supply Australia with any information as to the dates of its proposed tests or the expected size and yield of its explosions; and that in a statement made in the French Parliament on 2 May 1973 the French Government indicated that, regardless of the protests made by Australia and other countries, it did not envisage any cancellation or modification of the programme of nuclear testing as originally planned;

26. Whereas these allegations give substance to the Australian Government's contention that there is an immediate possibility of a further atmospheric nuclear test being carried out by France in the Pacific;

27. Whereas the Government of Australia also alleges that the atmospheric nuclear explosions carried out by France in the Pacific have caused wide-spread radio-active fall-out on Australian territory and elsewhere in the southern hemisphere, have given rise to measurable concentrations of radio-nuclides in foodstuffs and in man, and have resulted in additional radiation doses to persons living in that hemisphere and in Australia in particular; that any radio-active material deposited on Australian territory will be potentially dangerous to Australia and its people and any injury caused thereby would be irreparable; that the conduct of French nuclear tests in the atmosphere creates anxiety and concern among the Australian people; that any effects of the French nuclear tests upon the resources of the sea or the conditions of the environment can never be undone and would be irremediable by any payment of damages; and any infringement by France of the rights of Australia and her people to freedom of movement over the high seas and superjacent airspace cannot be undone;

28. Whereas the French Government, in a diplomatic Note dated 7 February 1973 and addressed to the government of Australia, the text of which was annexed to the Application in the present case, called attention to Reports of the Australian National Radiation Advisory Committee from 1967 to 1972, which all concluded that the fall-out from the French tests did not constitute a danger to the health of the Australian population; whereas in the said Note the French Government further expressed its conviction that in the absence of ascertained damage attributable to its nuclear experiments, they did not violate any rule of international law, and that, if the infraction of the law was alleged to consist in a violation of a legal norm concerning the threshold of atomic pollution which should not be crossed, it was hard to see what was the precise rule on which Australia relied;

29. Whereas for the purpose of the present proceedings it suffices to observe that the information submitted to the Court, including Reports of the United Nations Scientific Committee on the Effects of Atomic Radiation between 1958 and 1972, does not exclude the possibility that damage to Australia might be shown to be caused by the deposit on Australian territory of radio-active fall-out resulting from such tests and to be irreparable;

30. Whereas in the light of the foregoing considerations the Court is satisfied that it should indicate interim measures of protection in order to preserve the right claimed by Australia in the present litigation in respect of the deposit of radio-active fall-out on her territory; . . .

33. Whereas the decision given in the present proceedings in no way prejudges the question of the jurisdiction of the Court to deal with the merits of the case, or any questions relating to the admissibility of the Application, or relating to the merits themselves, and leaves unaffected the rights of the French Government to submit arguments in respect of those questions; . . .

Accordingly,
The COURT
Indicates, by 8 votes to 6, pending its final decision in the proceedings instituted on 9 May 1973 by Australia against France, the following provisional measures:

The Governments of Australia and France should each of them ensure that no action of any kind is taken which might aggravate or extend the dispute submitted to the Court or prejudice the rights of the other Party in respect of the carrying out of whatever decision the Court may render in the case; and, in particular, the French Government should avoid nuclear tests causing the deposit of radio-active fall-out on Australian territory; . . .

(Signed) F. AMMOUN, Vice-President.
(Signed) S. AQUARONE, Registrar

[The declarations of four judges and dissenting opinions of an additional four judges are omitted.]

Notes and Questions

1. *France's subsequent testing.* In spite of the court's order of interim measures of protection of June 22, 1973, France resumed atmospheric tests the following month. Specifically, two further series of tests were conducted at the Pacific test site, in July and August 1973, and June-September 1974. 1974 I.C.J. Rep. 253, 258, para. 19. In letters to the Court concerning the new tests, Australia stated that "fall-out had been recorded on Australian territory which . . . was clearly attributable to these tests, and that 'in the opinion of the Government of Australia the conduct of the French Government constitutes a clear and deliberate breach of the Order of the Court of 22 June 1973.'" *Id.* at 259.

The court held hearings on the questions of jurisdiction and admissibility in July 1974. Again, France did not participate, nor did it file pleadings. In its Order of December 20, 1974, the Court found that it would not be appropriate to remove the case from its docket, as France had requested in its letter of May 16, 1973. In that decision the court also considered the effect of a series of statements by the French Government concerning its nuclear testing program. The first statement was contained in a communique issued by the Office of the President of France on June 8, 1974. The communique stated in part:

> The Office of the President of the Republic takes this opportunity of stating that in view of the stage reached in carrying out the French nuclear defence programme France will be in a position to pass on to the stage of underground explosions as soon as the series of tests planned for this summer is completed.

Id. at 265, para. 34. Subsequent statements of a similar nature were made in a note of June 10, 1974 from the French embassy in Wellington to the New Zealand Ministry of Foreign Affairs; a press conference by the President on July 25, 1974; a television interview by the French Minister of Defense on August 16, 1974; an address by the French Foreign Minister to the U.N. General Assembly on September 25, 1974; and a press conference by the Minister of Defense on October 11, 1974.

The court, in an opinion that provoked much comment, held that France's unilateral declarations that it would halt its atmospheric testing program in the Pacific produced "a situation in which the objective of the Applicant [Australia] has in effect been accomplished. . . ." 1974 I.C.J. Rep. 270, para. 52. The court found that "France has undertaken the obligation to hold no further nuclear tests in the atmosphere in the South Pacific," *id.*, that "no question of damages arises in the present case" since Australia had raised none, *id.*, para. 53, and that "the original and ultimate objective of Applicant has been to seek protection 'against any further atmospheric test' . . . ," *id.* The Court therefore concluded that, "the dispute having disappeared, the claim advanced by Australia no longer has any object. It follows that any further finding would have no *raison d'être.*" *Id.*, para. 56. In the operative paragraph of its order, the Court found, by a vote of nine to six, "that the claim of Australia no longer has any object and that the Court is therefore not called upon to give a decision thereon." *Id.*, para. 62. New Zealand's claim was disposed of in the same manner. *Id.* at 457.

2. *The effect of France's declarations.* Was Australia's objective in fact accomplished by the French declarations? Would there have been any value in a finding by the court that the tests conducted prior to the initial application violated obligations owed by France to Australia? What about a finding as to the permissibility of the tests conducted by France after the Court's indication of protective measures?

The relief requested by Australia and New Zealand, respectively, was as follows:

> [T]he Government of Australia Asks the Court to Adjudge and Declare that . . . the carrying out of further atmospheric nuclear weapon tests in the South Pacific Ocean is not consistent with applicable rules of international law.
>
> And to Order
>
> that the French Republic shall not carry out any further such tests.

I I.C.J., Pleadings, Nuclear Tests (Australia v. France) 14-15 (1978) (hereafter I Pleadings).

> New Zealand Asks the Court to Adjudge and Declare:
>
> That the conduct by the French Government of nuclear tests in the South Pacific region that give rise to radioactive fallout constitutes a violation of New Zealand's rights under international law, and that these rights will be violated by any further such tests.

II I.C.J., Pleadings, Nuclear Tests (New Zealand v. France) 9 (1978) (hereafter II Pleadings). Jan Schneider has observed that: "A basic contention of the dissenters [in the 1974 decision] was that the objective of the applicants was too narrowly circumscribed by the Court, in that a declaratory judgment on the illegality of the tests was also sought and would have had value in and of itself." J. Schneider, World Public Order of the Environment 42 (1979).

3. *Australia's claimed relief.* Does the fact that Australia did not claim damages or "satisfaction" (a form of reparation, dealt with in Chapters 5 and 9) foreclose it from making such a claim later, either through diplomatic channels or in a separate proceeding? If a subsequent damages claim would not be foreclosed, would a declaration by the court concerning the legality of the French tests have been of value with regard to such claims?

4. *Further reading.* For comment on the court's decisions in the *Nuclear Tests* cases, *see, e.g.*, Thomas M. Franck, Word Made Law, 69 Am. J. Intl. L. 612 (1975); L.F.E. Goldie, The Nuclear Tests Cases: Restraints on Environmental Harm, 5 J. Mar. L. & Com. 491 (1974); Peter J. Goldsworthy, Interim Measures in the ICJ, 68 Am. J. Intl. L. 258 (1974); Pierre Lellouche, The Nuclear Tests Cases, 16 Harv. Intl. L.J. 614 (1975); R. St. J. Macdonald & Barbara Hough, "The Nuclear Tests Case Revisited," 20 Germ. Y.B. Intl. L. 337 (1977); and Alfred P. Rubin, Findings on Legal Effects of Unilateral French Declaration Concerning Nuclear Tests, 71 Am. J. Intl. L. 1 (1977).

5. *The value of the court's decision.* Does the court's Order of June 22, 1973 indicating interim measures of protection have any general normative value? Alexandre Kiss and Dinah Shelton have written that because the merits were never reached in *Nuclear Tests*, "[i]t is . . . difficult to consider

this case as constituting a legal precedent which would demonstrate the existence of a specific rule of international law forbidding transfrontier pollution." A. Kiss & D. Shelton, International Environmental Law 126 (1991). Do you agree?

6. *Pleadings and separate opinions.* In terms of their contribution to international environmental law, the *Nuclear Tests* cases may, in fact, be more significant for the wealth of material contained in the applicants' pleadings and in dissenting opinions than for the court's opinions themselves. Do you see how the positions taken by the parties and dissenting judges might qualify as "sources" of international law under Article 38 of the Statute of the International Court of Justice? The following section will review some of the points addressed in these pleadings and opinions.

2. *Applicants' Pleadings and Dissenting Opinions*

a. Norms Concerning Transfrontier Pollution

In its application, New Zealand claimed with regard to the French nuclear testing that, inter alia:

> *(c)* it violates the right of New Zealand that no radioactive material enter the territory of New Zealand, . . . including [its] air space and territorial waters, as a result of nuclear testing. . . . [and]
>
> *(d)* it violates the right of New Zealand that no radioactive material, having entered the territory of New Zealand, . . . including [its] air space and territorial waters, as a result of nuclear testing, cause harm, including apprehension, anxiety and concern, to the people and Government of New Zealand. . . .

II Pleadings 8.[20] The claims of Australia concerning French responsibility for causing deposition of radioactive fallout in Australian territory are set forth in paragraph 22 of the Court's 1973 Order, reprinted above, under (ii).

In its oral argument on the Request for the Indication of Interim Measures of Protection, Australia (per Mr. Ellicott, counsel for Australia) developed the thesis that "atmospheric nuclear testing is illegal in international law." I Pleadings 184. It cited the Stockholm Declaration on the Human Environment, specifically Principles 6 (which "deals with the discharge of toxic substances into the environment"), 7 (which "refers to the pollution of the seas") and 21. It continued:

20. These claims and the others asserted by New Zealand are compared and contrasted with each other in New Zealand's memorial on jurisdiction and admissibility, II I.C.J., Pleadings, Nuclear Tests (N.Z. v. Fr.) 203-205 (1978).

> While [the first] two principles provide evidence of community concern to eliminate pollution of the environment by substances which are released by atmospheric nuclear tests, it is the third, Principle 21, which is even more directly pertinent—for this goes to the very centre of the problem in the present case.
>
> > States have, in accordance with the Charter of the United Nations and the principles of international law, the *sovereign right* to exploit their own resources pursuant to their own environmental policies and the *responsibility* to ensure that activities within their jurisdiction or control do not cause damage to the environment of other States or of areas beyond the limits of national jurisdiction. (Emphasis added.)

I Pleadings 185. Australia went on to "suggest the significance of pronouncements of this character as evidencing the evolution of a rule of customary international law which prohibits State conduct tending towards pollution and the creation of hazards to human health and the environment and in particular a rule prohibiting the conduct of atmospheric nuclear tests." *Id.* Australia's argument continued:

> The specific function of the Stockholm resolution and declarations is that they reflect what the community regards as an acceptable standard of conduct in these matters—and correlatively what the community regards as an unacceptable standard. In view of the fact that the protection of human health and the environment is a matter of which the international community has only relatively recently become conscious, it stands to reason that the traditional standards of State freedom to pursue activities which may affect them must undergo some restriction. This being so, the Court may well feel that the criteria which normally govern the determination of the contents of customary international law are satisfied when the *opinio juris* of the vast majority of States is evidenced in this form.

Id. (What is Mr. Ellicott driving at in the last sentence just quoted?) Australia then turned to "other arguments . . . [which] are in a sense more specific and would in themselves be sufficiently comprehensive and strong to bear the whole weight of the contention that the conduct by France of atmospheric tests violates Australia's rights in international law." *Id.* at 186. The one most relevant for present purposes is that the fallout from French tests violated Australian sovereignty. Australia invoked the finding of the Court in the *Corfu Channel* case (1949 I.C.J. Rep. at 35) that while a minesweeping operation by the British Navy in Albanian territorial waters caused no damage, it nonetheless violated Albanian sovereignty. It then asked whether there was any "difference between the intrusion of naval vessels into the territory of another State which causes no damage, on the one hand, and, on the other, the deposit on the territory of another State of radio-active fall-out which, for this purpose alone, I shall assume not to be dangerous. The answer is, of course, that there is no difference; and as the former was a violation of territorial sovereignty so is the latter." *Id.* at 186-187. Australia's argument continued:

> In the present case . . . it might be suggested that the tests carried out on Mururoa Atoll represent no more than a legitimate use by France of territory under her sovereignty and that, accordingly, the situation must be governed by the law governing the mutual conduct of neighbours, if that is a correct description of the territorial relationship between Mururoa Atoll and Australia. . . .
>
> [After reserving its position on the question whether "Mururoa may be treated like any other part of French territory," Australia continued:] One is . . . bound to ask whether there is any rule of international law which permits a State by virtue of the use of its territory to infringe the sovereignty of another State. To answer this question absolutely in the negative might be to go too far. At the same time, Australia will contend that in the circumstances of this case, France's conduct infringes the rights of Australia. Though it is inappropriate to develop this contention fully at this moment [i.e., at the jurisdictional phase of the case], two elements may be mentioned as relevant to it:
>
> First, one may say that France simply has no right to conduct atmospheric nuclear tests. [Here Australia quoted Judge Jiménez de Aréchaga's statement that "[i]f a nuclear test produces fall-out beyond the territorial limits of the State conducting it the State should be absolutely liable under the normal rules of State responsibility."[21]]
>
> The second factor relevant to the infringement of Australia's rights lies in the nature of the act and of the damage to which it gives rise. The Court has already heard some scientific detail about the tests. It is manifest that they constitute an unusual, abnormal, non-natural and ultra-hazardous activity. Any analogy drawn between them and other uses of a State's territory which may trouble a neighbour are unhelpful because the degree of difference is so great as to amount to a difference of kind. Nuclear tests are not comparable to the use of waters by an upper riparian or to the emission of noxious fumes by factories. They are an activity *sui generis* by reason of their motivation, their sheer physical size and their potential consequences. The trespass to which they give rise is not transient or short-lived; it is long-enduring. . . . It is worth noting again Principle 21 of the Stockholm Declaration which makes no concession to the sovereign right of States to use their territory to cause damage to the environment. The obligation of States is expressed absolutely and without qualification: [Australia quoted the second, or "responsibility" clause of Principle 21.]
>
> There is another aspect of Australian sovereignty which is infringed by French nuclear testing in the atmosphere . . . . That is Australia's independent right to determine what acts shall take place within its territory and in particular whether Australia and its people shall be exposed to the effects of

21. Jiménez de Aréchaga, International Responsibility, in Manual of Public International Law 533, 540 (M. Sorensen, ed. 1968). This conclusion was reached on the ground that "a state is not entitled to conduct nuclear tests in its territory or on the high seas which cause damage in or to foreign states." *Id.*

> ionizing radiation from artificial sources. . . . [Australia] pointed to the universally accepted principle that there should be no additional exposure of people or territory to radiation without a compensating benefit. The right to decide this must rest with each sovereign country. It alone can decide whether the benefit to its population will outweigh the risk of harm.

Id. at 187-188. Is this line of argument apposite to the normal case of transfrontier pollution? Or is it relevant only to transfrontier pollution caused by nuclear testing and, possibly, other "ultrahazardous" activities?

In its Request for the Indication of Interim Measures of Protection, II Pleadings 49, New Zealand addressed the "Consequences for the Environment" of the French tests (*id.* at 54). After declaring that "[i]n varying degrees, the local, regional and global environment and its resources will be contaminated" by the tests (*id.*), the New Zealand argument continues:

> 29. The contamination of the South Pacific is of special significance; for this region is as yet relatively free from the pollution seriously affecting many other parts of the world. The preservation of the South Pacific environment is of obvious importance to the countries and territories which are located in the region. For many of these countries and territories the sea and its resources are a vital element in their subsistence and economy. Their smallness, their limited resources and their isolation in a vast ocean constitute a significant barrier both to their relations with the rest of the world and to their development. They can legitimately expect to have these disadvantages offset by an environment free from pollution.
>
> 30. The international community as a whole also has a large interest in the preservation of the South Pacific environment: it is one of the few remaining large areas which can serve as a base for the regeneration of gravely depleted marine resources upon which all countries will increasingly depend as a source of food.

Id. at 54-55. Should different standards apply when the environment of the polluted or threatened country or area is more pristine than the world at large? What about where the country is especially small or remote?

Like Australia's argument, New Zealand's Request invoked the 1972 Stockholm Conference on the Human Environment, which it characterized as having "represented the first comprehensive attempt to grapple with the problems of pollution and to articulate the norms which regulate the use of the environment." *Id.* at 55. After reviewing statements adopted at the Conference concerning nuclear weapons and the testing thereof, the Request continued:

> 35. The Stockholm Conference also proclaimed a number of norms which are more general in scope but which have a direct bearing on the testing of nuclear weapons that gives rise to radio-active fall-out. Paragraph 6 of the Declaration endorsed the view that:

> A point has been reached in history when we must shape our actions throughout the world with a more prudent care for their environmental consequences. Through ignorance or indifference we can do massive and irreversible harm to the earthly environment on which our life and well-being depend.

Id. at 56. The Request went on to quote Principles 6, 7, and 21 of the Stockholm Declaration. Do you agree that these elements of the Stockholm Declaration are "norms"? Technically, could the Stockholm Conference "proclaim[]" norms? If your answers to these questions are in the negative, do the texts referred to have any authoritative value? Does the fact that they are invoked by a state in a case before the World Court affect your answer?

This brief survey of positions taken in *Nuclear Tests* concerning transfrontier pollution norms would not be complete without mention of the opinion of Judge de Castro. In his dissent to the 1974 judgment in Australia v. France, Judge de Castro stated as follows:

> The right relied on by the Applicant with regard to the deposit of radioactive fall-out on its territory was considered in the Order of 22 June 1973 (para. 30). We must now consider whether reliance on this right makes the request admissible. The applicant's complaint against France of violation of its sovereignty by introducing harmful matter into its territory without its permission is based on a legal interest which has been well known since the time of Roman law. The prohibition of *immissio* (of water, smoke, fragments of stone) into a neighboring property was a feature of Roman law. . . . The principle *sic utere tuo ut alienum non laedas* is a feature of law both ancient and modern. It is well known that the owner of a property is liable for intolerable smoke or smells, "because he oversteps [the physical limits of his property], because there is *immissio* over the neighbouring properties, because he causes injury."

Nuclear Tests (Australia v. France), 1974 I.C.J. Rep. 253 (Judgment of Dec. 20, 1974), Dissenting Op. Judge de Castro, *id.*, 372, at 388-389, quoting from H. & L. Mazeaud & A. Tunc, 1 Traité théorique et pratique de la responsabilité civile, paras. 597, 679, *et seq.* (5th ed. 1957) (bracketed language in original).

Judge de Castro continued:

> In international law, the duty of each State not to use its territory for acts contrary to the rights of other States might be mentioned [citing the *Corfu Channel* case]. The arbitral awards [in the *Trail Smelter* case] mention the lack of precedents as to pollution of the air, but also the analogy with pollution of water, and the Swiss litigation between the cantons of Solothurn and Aargau. The conflict between the United States and Canada with regard to the Trail Smelter was decided on the basis of the following rule:
>
> > No State has the right to use or permit the use of its territory in such a manner as to cause injury by fumes in or to the territory of another . . . when

> the case is of serious consequence and the injury is established by clear and convincing evidence. . . .

> If it is admitted as a general rule that there is a right to demand prohibition of the emission by neighbouring properties of noxious fumes, the consequence must be drawn, by an obvious analogy, that the Applicant is entitled to ask the Court to uphold its claim that France should put an end to the deposit of radio-active fall-out on its territory.

Id. at 388-389 (footnotes omitted). In footnote 21, following the quotation from the *Trail Smelter* award, Judge de Castro stated in part as follows:

> The award has been regarded as "basic for the whole problem of interference. Its bases are now part of customary international law," A. Randelzhofer, B. Simma, "Das Kernkraftwerk an der Grenze—Ein 'ultra-hazardous activity' im Schnittpunkt von internationalem Nachbarrecht und Umweltschutz," Festschrift für Friedrich Berber, Munich, 1973, p. 405. This award marks the abandonment of the theory of Harmon (absolute sovereignty of each State in its territory with regard to all others[22]); Krakan, Die Harmon Doktrin: Eine These der Vereinigten Staaten zum internationalen Flussrecht, Hamburg, 1966, p. 9.

Id. Is the authoritative value of these statements diminished by the fact that, technically, they concerned the "admissibility" of Australia's application, and not the merits of the case?

b. Threshold of Legally Recognizable Damage

An issue that was much discussed in the *Nuclear Tests* cases was whether the French tests had caused legally recognizable damage to Australia and New Zealand. In a note of January 3, 1973 from the Australian Ambassador in Paris to the French Foreign Minister, Australia expressed the view that the conducting of nuclear tests "would be unlawful—particularly in so far as it involves modification of the physical conditions of and over Australian territory; [and] pollution of the atmosphere and of the resources of the seas. . . ." I Pleadings 27. France responded in a note of February 7, 1973 from the French Ambassador in Canberra to the Australian Prime Minister and Foreign Minister. The latter note stated in part that France was convinced that its nuclear tests violated no rule of international law. Specifically with regard to the violations alleged by Australia concerning the pollution and physical modifications of Australian territory, the sea, and the superadjacent airspace, France noted that Australia had not claimed it had suffered actual, physical harm as a result of the tests. In the absence of such harm, France continued, Australia would have to show that France had violated

22. [This doctrine is considered in Chapter 16—Eds.]

an international legal norm concerning the threshold of atomic pollution that may not be crossed. But France said it failed to understand what precise rule was being invoked by Australia in this connection and that, in any event, Australia had not established that atmospheric nuclear testing is automatically unlawful. I Pleadings 28, at 30.

The issue of the threshold of legally recognizable damage was addressed by Australia and New Zealand in response to a question asked during oral argument by Judge Sir Humphrey Waldock. The question related to the following passage from Australia's memorial on the question of admissibility: " 'France's activities in the South Pacific area are inconsistent with its obligation under general international law to respect the sovereignty of Australia over and in respect of its territory and thus to abstain from producing alterations of any kind in the Australian environment (atmosphere, soil, waters) by the deposit on its territory and the dispersion in its air space of radio-active fall-out.' " I Pleadings 524 (as quoted in Judge Sir Humphrey Waldock's question, from paragraph 432 of Australia's memorial, I Pleadings at 331; *see also id.*, para. 454, at 336). Judge Sir Humphrey said:

> I should be glad if Australia's representatives would state whether they consider that every transmission by natural causes of chemical or other matter from one State into another State's territory, air space or territorial sea automatically constitutes in itself a legal cause of action in international law without the need to establish anything more. . . . In other words, do they draw a line and if so where between a deposit or dispersion of matter within another State which is unlawful and one which has to be tolerated as merely an incident of the industrialization or technological development of modern society. Do they consider that . . . harm or the potentiality of harm . . . is a *sine qua non* for establishing the breach of an international obligation in such cases?

I Pleadings 524. In reply Mr. Byers, Counsel for Australia, stated:

> . . . [T]he Government of Australia . . . does *not* consider that every transmission by natural causes of chemical or other matter from one State into another State's territory, air space or territorial sea automatically constitutes in itself a legal cause of action in international law without the need to establish anything more.
>
> The Government of Australia considers that where, as a result of a normal and natural use by one State of its territory, a deposit occurs in the territory of another, the latter has no cause of complaint unless it suffers more than merely nominal harm or damage. The use by a State of its territory for the conduct of atmospheric nuclear tests is not a [n]ormal or natural use of its territory. The Australian Government also contends that the radio-active deposit from the French tests gives rise to more than merely nominal harm or damage to Australia. . . .

> . . . [T]he Australian Government states that it *does* draw a line between lawful and unlawful deposit or dispersion of matter within another State.
>
> . . . The Australian Government assumes that in referring to an incident of the industrialization or technological development of modern society the question is contemplating a normal and natural use of territory. Hence deposit or dispersion of chemical or other matter arising from such use may be lawful. The use of territory to conduct atmospheric nuclear explosions is . . . not a normal or natural use of territory.
>
> [Australia] says that a deposit of radio-active fall-out resulting from France's conduct of atmospheric testing is, without more, a breach of its territorial [and decisional[23]] sovereignty. In neither case is it necessary to show more. Further and additionally it says that radio-active fall-out is harmful and causes damage.
>
> [As to whether harm must be shown, Australia] states that it does *not* regard the harm or the potentiality of harm as the *sine qua non* for the establishment of the breach of obligation. This is because . . . the intrusion constitutes a breach of sovereignty. Where that intrusion upon sovereignty is accompanied by harm—as it is in the case of atmospheric nuclear testing—the affected State has an even greater right to complain.
>
> [T]he basic principle is that intrusion of any sort into foreign territory is an infringement of sovereignty. Needless to say, the Government of Australia does not deny that the practice of States has modified the application of this principle in respect of the interdependence of territories. . . . It concedes that there may be no illegality in respect of certain types of chemical fumes in the absence of special types of harm. What it does emphasize is that the legality thus sanctioned by the practice of States is the outcome of the toleration extended to certain activities which produce these emissions, which activities are generally regarded as natural uses of territory in modern industrial society and are tolerated because, while perhaps producing some inconvenience, they have a community benefit.
>
> Any such practice of States is not a denial of the basic principle. Unless an exception recognized by customary international law can be established, that principle continues to govern the relations of States. There have been, for example, many references in connection with international telecommunications to the absence of any right in a State to transmit radio beams to foreign territory.

I Pleadings 525-526. New Zealand's answer to the same question was as follows:

> We do not consider that every transmission of the kind described from one territory to another constitutes in itself a legal cause of action. A line does have to be drawn between different types of intrusion into areas over which another State has sovereignty; and, as new activities arise and different

23. Mr. Byers used the expression "decisional sovereignty" to refer to a state's right "to decide for itself, or in agreement with other States, whether or not it accepts and, if so, the circumstances and extent of any acceptance by it of artificial radiation risk." *Id.* at 525.

> dangers are perceived, that line may have to be extended. It will not, however, . . . be necessary for the Court . . . to fix the exact line between lawful and unlawful transmissions, as the present case falls clearly within the latter category. One of the principal factors to be taken into account in the present case is that the intrusion complained of and the activity which gives rise to it, are condemned by the international community. This condemnation of nuclear testing in the atmosphere is based on the dangers to mankind presented by the proliferation of nuclear weapons, by its harmful consequences for the health of present and future generations of mankind, and by the contamination of man's environment by radioactive substances. . . .
>
> [As to the necessity of establishing harm,] we do not consider that harm or the potentiality of harm is an element that the law requires to be proved in order to establish the breach of an international obligation under this head.

Letter from the Agent of New Zealand to the Registrar of 15 July 1974, II Pleadings 429, at 430.

Judge Barwick, the Australian Judge ad hoc in the case, took the following position in his dissent to the 1974 judgment:

> Is there a possible limitation or qualification of the right to territorial and environmental integrity which springs from the nature of the activity which generates the substance which is deposited or intruded into the State's territory and environment? There are doubtless uses of territory by a State which are of such a nature that the consequences for another State and its territory and environment of such a use must be accepted by that other State. It may very well be that a line is to be drawn between depositions and intrusions which are lawful and must be borne and those which are unlawful; on the other hand it may be that because of the unique nature of nuclides and the internationally unnecessary and unprofitable activity which gives rise to their dissemination, no more need to be decided than the question whether the intrusion of such nuclides so derived is unlawful.

Nuclear Tests (Aus. v. Fr.), 1974 I.C.J. Rep. at 433.

Are these responses consistent with the *Trail Smelter* holding? Where "natural and normal" uses of neighboring territory result in only minor transboundary harm, is it preferable to treat the causing of such harm as lawful, or to treat it as a technical wrong that does not, however, entitle the "invaded" state to compensation or injunctive relief? If the latter, should an apology or other form of satisfaction be required? Would the express or implied consent of the "invaded" state be sufficient? Compare the approach of the common law of trespass to land: a "harmless" invasion such as setting foot on another's property qualifies as a trespass but entitles the landowner to only nominal damages. On the question of whether physical harm is necessary to a cause of action under international law for transfrontier pollution, *see* Günther Handl, Territorial Sovereignty and the Problem of Transnational Pollution, 69 Am J. Intl. L. 50 (1975). Handl examines Australia's argument and, after surveying state practice, concludes that in the case of lawful state activities "international law requires proof of material damage as a precondition of the polluting state's responsibility to the affected state. . . . Indeed, the mere fact of [a] transfrontier crossing [of pollutants into a state's territory] does not in itself amount to a violation of sovereignty which could engage the polluting state's liability." *Id.* at 75. *See also* Jerome B. Elkind, Footnote to the Nuclear Tests Cases: Abuse of Right—A Blind Alley for Environmentalists, 9 Vand. J. Transnatl. L. 57 (1976).

What kinds of activities other than atmospheric nuclear testing, if any, might arguably be "unlawful" such that any transfrontier intrusion they occasion would engage the responsibility of the state of origin without proof of material damage?

c. Representation of Common Interests

In its Application instituting proceedings against France, New Zealand asserted not only its own rights but also those of the international community. Specifically, New Zealand contended with regard to the French atmospheric nuclear testing, inter alia, that:

> *(a)* it violates the right of all members of the international community, including New Zealand, that no nuclear tests that give rise to radioactive fallout be conducted;
>
> *(b)* it violates the rights of all members of the international community, including New Zealand, to the preservation from unjustified artificial radioactive contamination of the terrestrial, maritime and aerial environment and, in particular, of the environment of the region in which the tests are conducted and in which New Zealand [and associated territories] are situated . . . .

II Pleadings 3, at 8. It has been seen that Australia, for its part, referred in its Application to a violation of "[t]he right of Australia and its people, in common with other States and their peoples, to be free from atmospheric nuclear weapon tests by any country. . . ." I Pleadings at 3, at 14.

Does New Zealand or Australia have "standing," or *locus standi,* to assert the rights of the international community or other states? Need a state have suffered a direct injury to bring a claim against the state allegedly responsible for inflicting the injury? If New Zealand may not assert the rights and interests of the international community, who may?

In its Memorial on Jurisdiction and Admissibility, New Zealand argued as follows with regard to the rights asserted in the above excerpt:

> 191. . . . The rights listed under *(a)* and *(b)* are shared in the sense that their violation in relation to any one nation will necessarily involve a violation

of the same rights vested in other members of the international community. The degree of attention which individual countries are prepared to give to the protection of these rights and the degree of anxiety displayed in the event of their violation may, and obviously does, vary. Yet the rights are the same for all. They reflect a community interest in the protection of the security, life and health of all peoples and in the preservation of the global environment. The rights are held in common and the corresponding obligation imposed on France . . . is owed in equal measure to New Zealand and to every other member of the international community. It is an obligation *erga omnes*. . . .

195. . . . International law has never been concerned exclusively with the protection of the material interests, narrowly defined, of individual States. It has long been acknowledged that States may have a legitimate—and legal—interest in matters which cannot readily be related to their financial, economic or other tangible interests. And, in an increasingly interdependent world, there has been an accelerating shift in the emphasis of substantive rules of international law away from the protection of rights of individual States towards the protection of the general welfare, of community interests shared by all.

196. The development of substantive rules of law for the protection of the general welfare has been accompanied by a recognition of the interests of individual States in the judicial enforcement of those rules. Had this parallel development not occurred, there would have been an increasingly large body of international law rules lacking any means of judicial protection. In this respect, the protection of international community interests differs markedly from the protection of the public interest in many municipal law systems. . . .

II Pleadings 204-205 (footnotes omitted). After quoting from works of De Visscher[24] and Abi-Saab[25] and citing other writers,[26] New Zealand's Memorial continued:

198. . . . [T]he separate and dissenting opinions of Judge Jessup in the *South West Africa* cases[27] . . . reveal that there is an imposing body of precedent which establishes a legal interest in the general welfare in fields as diverse as slavery, minorities, dependent peoples, labour, genocide, racial discrimination and human rights in general. Following his survey of these precedents . . . Judge Jessup stated his general conclusion in the following terms:

> I agree that there is no generally established *actio popularis* in international law. But international law has accepted and established situations in which States are given a right of action without any showing of individual prejudice or individual substantive interest as distinguished from the general interest.[28]

24. C. De Visscher, Aspects récents du droit procédural de la Cour international de Justice 70-71 (1966).
25. G. Abi-Saab, Les exceptions préliminaires dans la procédure de la Cour internationale 142-143 (1967).
26. C. Jenks, The Prospects of International Adjudication 524 (1964).
27. South West Africa, Preliminary Objections, I.C.J. Reports 1962, pp. 425-433 and South West Africa, Second Phase, I.C.J. Reports 1966, pp. 373-388.
28. I.C.J. Reports 1966, pp. 387 and 388.

199. Guidance as to what these situations are is to be found in the most recent pronouncement by the Court on the subject of legal interest in its judgment in the case concerning the *Barcelona Traction, Light and Power Company, Limited.*[29] . . . [T]he Court characterized the different kinds of international law obligation which may be incumbent on States as follows:

> . . . an essential distinction should be drawn between the obligations of a State towards the international community as a whole, and those arising vis-à-vis another State in the field of diplomatic protection. By their very nature the former are the concern of all States. In view of the importance of the rights involved, all States can be held to have a legal interest in their protection; they are obligations *erga omnes.*
>
> Such obligations derive, for example, in contemporary international law, from the outlawing of acts of aggression, and of genocide, as also from the principles and rules concerning the basic rights of the human person, including protection from slavery and racial discrimination. Some of the corresponding rights of protection have entered into the body of general international law (*Reservations to the Convention on the Prevention and Punishment of the Crime of Genocide, Advisory Opinion, I.C.J. Reports 1951,* p. 23); others are conferred by international instruments of a universal or quasi-universal character.

II Pleadings 206-207 (some footnotes omitted). New Zealand emphasized that in the passage just quoted from *Barcelona Traction,* "it is acknowledged, with specific reference to genocide that customary law as well as treaty law may give rise to obligations *erga omnes* and to the corresponding rights of protection." *Id.* at 207-208 (footnote omitted). New Zealand also maintained in its oral argument that the French tests affected "the common heritage of mankind," "inevitably conflict with international environmental law," and violate an obligation "of a universal character, an obligation *erga omnes.*" *See* II Pleadings 264-266. *See also* the argument of Australia in its Memorial on Jurisdiction and Admissibility, I Pleadings 330, 332-335.

The Court never passed on these arguments. Several judges addressed them in their separate and dissenting opinions, however. While Judges Gros[30] and de Castro[31] denied the capacity of the Applicants to assert community interests, Judge Petren thought the lack of a mechanism for asserting violations of obligations *erga omnes,* which admittedly exist, was a "self-contradiction."[32] Judges Onyeama, Dillard, Jiménez de Arechaga, and Waldock, in their joint dissenting opinion, stated as follows:

> Although we recognize that the existence of a so-called *actio popularis* in international law is a matter of controversy, the observations of this Court in the *Barcelona Traction, Light and Power Company, Limited* case suffice to show that the question is one that may be considered as capable of rational legal argument and a proper subject of litigation before this Court.[33]

29. I.C.J. Reports 1970, p. 3.
30. 1974 I.C.J. Rep. 253, 276, at 290 (Sep. Op.).
31. *Id.* at 390 (Dissenting Op.).
32. *Id.* 298, at 303 (Dissenting Op.).
33. *Id.* 312, at 370 (Joint Dissenting Op.).

The four judges need go no further than they did since the questions before the Court at that stage of the proceedings were whether the Court had jurisdiction and whether the claims of Applicants were admissible. Nevertheless, the quoted passage indicates that they at least had open minds on the question of the Applicant's capacity to assert community interests. Jan Schneider has remarked: "[I]f the World Court had specifically considered the claim of the applicants to be representing inclusive common interests in addition to their own exclusive interests, might it not have decided to issue a declaratory judgment instead of merely finding that the sole objective of Australia and New Zealand—that is, termination of the specific series of tests—had been fulfilled?" J. Schneider, above, at 130. What do you think?

What would be the advantages and disadvantages of permitting Australia and New Zealand to assert the interests of the international community in the *Nuclear Tests* cases? Of permitting a country outside the affected area—say, Poland or Brazil—to assert those interests? Is there a better way to handle the problem of "obligations" that no one has standing to enforce? *See generally* F. Kirgis, Standing to Challenge Human Endeavors that Could Change the Climate, 84. Am. J. Intl. L. 525 (1990).

3. *France's Subsequent Testing*

a. Nuclear Testing and Pacific Island States

Lori Osmundsen has written:

> Most Pacific Island states have expressed deep-seated fear and resentment of nuclear activities in the South Pacific. Since the founding of the South Pacific Forum in 1971, atmospheric testing of nuclear weapons in French Polynesia has generated considerable concern among Pacific Island heads of state. The fact that nuclear fallout poses potential dangers to marine ecosystems as well as human life has been long understood; in fact, Western Samoa and the Cook Islands lodged formal protests against British and American tests in the region as early as 1956. Although Australia and New Zealand were the lone petitioners against France in the *Nuclear Tests* cases . . . , the South Pacific Forum members firmly supported the effort launched in The Hague to prohibit atmospheric testing.
>
> When France began to conduct underground tests [in the South Pacific] in 1975, formal protests temporarily ceased. However, science soon verified the risks of detonating nuclear devices beneath coral ledges, and regional concerns were reignited. Researchers speculated that the blasts would lead to cracks in the underwater bases of the atolls, eventually resulting in two devastating effects: collapse of the atolls themselves and leakage of radioactive material into the surrounding sea. However, in order to determine whether the blasts were causing cracks and leakage in the coral base, researchers needed to perform independent on-site inspections, which the French refused to allow until 1983.

> Three separate research teams conducted investigations at Moruroa between 1983 and 1987, the last of which was led by Jacques Cousteau. Cousteau's report warned that deep cracks existed in the atoll. While he found no dangerous levels of radioactivity, Cousteau was unwilling to dismiss the risk of potential contamination in the future. These findings led in large part to the French decision in March 1989 to shift testing to the Fangataufa atoll to prevent the already-existing cracks in Moruroa from expanding.

Lori Osmundsen, Paradise Preserved? The Contribution of the SPREP Convention to the Environmental Welfare of the South Pacific, 19 Ecology L.Q. 727, 760-761 (1992) (footnotes omitted). The "SPREP Convention" is the Convention for the Protection of the Natural Resources and Environment of the South Pacific Region, Nov. 25, 1986, *reprinted in* 26 I.L.M. 38 (1987). *See also* the two protocols to the SPREP Convention, Protocol Concerning Co-operation in Combating Pollution Emergencies in the South Pacific Region, *reprinted in* 26 I.L.M. 59 (1987), and Protocol for the Prevention of Pollution of the South Pacific Region by Dumping, *reprinted in* 26 I.L.M. 65 (1987). These agreements entered into force August 18, 1990.

b. France's 1995 Tests

On August 21, 1995, New Zealand filed a "Request for an Examination of the Situation" under paragraph 63 of the ICJ's 1974 judgment in the *Nuclear Tests* case (New Zealand v. France). Paragraph 63 of that judgment stated: "Once the Court has found that a State has entered into a commitment concerning its future conduct it is not the Court's function to contemplate that it will not comply with it. However, the Court observes that if the basis of this Judgment were to be affected, the Applicant could request an examination of the situation in accordance with the provisions of the Statute." France had announced in June 1995 that it "would conduct a final series of eight nuclear weapons tests in the South Pacific starting in September 1995." These tests would be carried out underground at Mururoa and Fangataufa Atolls. New Zealand contended that this entitled it to invoke paragraph 63, reopening the case.

On September 22, 1995, the court dismissed New Zealand's request by a vote of 12 to 3 (Judges Weeramantry and Koroma and Judge ad hoc Sir Geoffrey Palmer, dissenting). Its rationale was essentially that the subject matter of the 1974 judgment concerned exclusively *atmospheric* nuclear tests and not underground or other forms of testing. The court found that the "basis" of the 1974 judgment was France's undertaking not to conduct any further *atmospheric* nuclear tests; this, in the court's view, prevented it from taking into consideration questions relating to *underground* nuclear tests. The court noted, however, that its Order was without prejudice to the obligations of States in general to protect the natural environment. Judge Shahabuddeen in his separate opinion, and Judges Weeramantry and Koroma in their dissenting opinions, all stressed that the case was important because it involved issues of environmental protection.

How would you have ruled in this case? Was the court hypertechnical? Or simply prudent?

4. *The Court's Advisory Opinion on the Legality of the Threat or Use of Nuclear Weapons*

On July 8, 1996, the ICJ issued its Advisory Opinion on the question contained in UN General Assembly Resolution 49/75 K of December 15, 1994:[34] "Is the threat or use of nuclear weapons in any circumstance permitted under international law?" 35 I.L.M. 809 (1996). The issue proved so controversial, even within the court, that it had to be decided by the president's "casting vote"—i.e., a second vote the president may cast in case of a tie. (There are normally 15 members of the court; the tie was made possible by the death of one of the judges.) The court found that "the threat or use of nuclear weapons would generally be contrary to the rules of international law applicable in armed conflict, and in particular the principles and rules of humanitarian law. . . ." Dissenting were Vice-President Schwebel and Judges Oda, Shahabuddeen, Weeramantry, Koroma, and Higgins—albeit for different reasons. Judge Weeramantry, in dissent, found that the threat or use of nuclear weapons is illegal in any circumstances whatsoever. (Judge Koroma agreed with this conclusion.) He noted that nuclear weapons endanger the human environment in a manner that threatens the entirety of life on the planet. 35 I.L.M. at 888. In this connection, he referred to the prohibition under international humanitarian law of causing damage to the environment. 35 I.L.M. at 905.

Do you believe Judge Weeramantry would have reached a similar conclusion concerning France's atmospheric nuclear tests in the 1970s?

The World Health Organization (WHO), by resolution WHA46.40 of May 14, 1993 adopted by the World Health Assembly, submitted the following question to the court for an advisory opinion: "In view of the health and environmental effects, would the use of nuclear weapons by a State in war or other armed conflict be a breach of its obligations under international law including the WHO Constitution?" The Court concluded, by an 11 to 3 vote, that it was not able to give the requested opinion. It found that while (1) the agency requesting the opinion had been duly authorized

34. Article 96 of the United Nations Charter provides that the General Assembly and Security Council may request the ICJ "to give an advisory opinion on any legal question." In addition, other UN organs and specialized agencies that are authorized by the General Assembly may request such opinions "on legal questions arising within the scope of their activities."

under the UN Charter to request opinions from the court, and (2) the opinion requested was on a legal issue, as required, the question was not one arising within the scope of activities of the WHO. The court reasoned that while under its Constitution the WHO is authorized to deal with the effects on health of the use of nuclear weapons, or of any other hazardous activity, and to take preventive measures to protect the health of populations in the event that such weapons are used or activities engaged in, the question put to the court relates not to the effects of nuclear weapons but to the legality of their use, in light of their effects on health and the environment. According to the court, the competence of the WHO to deal with those effects is not dependent on the legality of the acts that caused them. ICJ, Communiqué No. 96/22, July 8, 1996; 35 I.L.M. 809 (1996).

Notes and Questions

1. *The legal value of the decisions.* While the foregoing cases relate, in particular, to transfrontier pollution and shared resource problems, they are in fact the major decisions in the broader field of international environmental law. They are often cited by commentators as evidence of rules of customary international law in that field. Can you distill one or more general legal propositions from these cases? If your answer is yes, try to state the proposition(s) with precision.

2. *The legal value of the decisions II.* Samuel Bleicher has written:

> Taken together, the *Corfu Channel* case and the *Trail Smelter* and *Lake Lanoux* arbitrations establish a consistent if somewhat surprising set of principles governing state responsibility for transnational environmental damage. The overriding proposition is that a state may not use or permit the use of its territory in such a manner as to cause substantial damage in another state. There is no requirement of a balancing of interests or any prerequisites involving the use the plaintiff state is presently making of either the resource itself or the injured property. The restriction extends beyond state-initiated activity to private activity, which will be imputed to the defendant state if it knew of its injurious character; such knowledge can be imputed on the basis of a liberal policy of inferences from circumstantial evidence. At the same time, a state is not automatically responsible for activities which only create a risk of injury or the capability to cause injury. . . .
>
> . . . However appealing such an absolute rule may be to conservationists and ecologists, one might expect a tribunal to retreat from it when faced with the prospect of actually terminating an activity that produces significant benefits in the defendant state.

S. Bleicher, An Overview of International Environmental Regulation, 2 Ecology L.Q. 1, 28-29 (1972). Do you agree with this assessment? Can the holdings of the respective tribunals be generalized in the way Bleicher does?

3. *The legal value of the decisions III.* Jan Schneider offers the following appraisal:

> The international decisions [referring to the *Trail Smelter, Corfu Channel* and *Lac Lanoux* cases] can in general be said to indicate acceptance of a standard of strict liability for damage caused or deprivations resulting from manipulation of environmental variables.

J. Schneider, World Public Order of the Environment 48 (1979). *See also* L. Goldie, A General Review of International Environmental Law: A Survey of Capabilities, Trends and Limits, in Hague Academy of International Law, Colloquium 1973: The Protection of the Environment and International Law 25, at 70 (C. Kiss, ed. 1975); *id.*, International Principles of Responsibility for Pollution, 9 Colum. J. Transnatl. L. 283, 306 (1970); and C. Jenks, Liability for Ultra-Hazardous Activities in International Law, 117 Recueil des Cours 99, 122 (1966 I). For a contrary view *see, e.g.*, G. Handl, Balancing of Interests and International Liability for the Pollution of International Watercourses: Customary Principles of Law Revisited, 1975 Canadian Y.B. Intl. L. 156, 164, 166-170 (1976):

> The truth is, of course, that state responsibility is rarely based on the principle of risk-creation, and almost never on the fault of state officials attributable to the state. In the overwhelming majority of cases liability arises simply from what might be called an "objective violation" of an international obligation. . . . In other words, an unqualified identification of liability in the absence of fault, in the sense of *dolus* or *culpa*, with responsibility for risk, is inappropriate in international law.

Id. at 164 (footnotes omitted). After analyzing the *Corfu Channel, Trail Smelter,* and *Lake Lanoux* cases, Handl concludes: "In the light of the foregoing considerations it is obvious that the international judicial precedents do not indicate a trend towards responsibility for risk [an expression Handl prefers to 'strict liability,' *see id.* at 165] as a general category of international liability." *Id.* at 170.

Who is right? Is the standard a strict one? If not, what is the applicable standard of responsibility and liability? Is it, or should it be, different for different kinds of harmful or risk-producing activities?

VII

General Norms of Prevention

The old adage, "an ounce of prevention is worth a pound of cure," is perhaps more apt in the field of the environment than in any other. In fact, as applied to the environment it probably does not go far enough: not only is environmental damage often very difficult and expensive to repair, because of the fragility and uniqueness of the elements of nature, it may not be reparable at all. In short, once the genie of environmental harm is out of the bottle, it is at best costly[1] and at worst impossible[2] to put it back in.

The idea of prevention of environmental harm is thus a very attractive one. Prevention has been called "the Golden Rule for the environment,"[3] and with good reason. For example, dolphins killed "incidentally" in purse-

1. For example, the complaint in the *Amoco Cadiz* case sought $2.2 billion in damages for oil pollution harm to the French coastline and seabed due to the spill from the *Amoco Cadiz. See* In Re Amoco Cadiz, 20 ERC [Environment Reporter—Cases] 2041 (N.D. Ill. 1984). The total damages from the Chernobyl incident were probably even greater.

2. This is the case, most obviously, with loss of biological diversity. "The current rate of species and ecosystem loss far exceeds that at which evolution is creating new diversity, and the rate of loss continues to rise." Holly Doremus, Patching the Ark: Improving Legal Protection of Biological Diversity, 18 Ecology L.Q. 265, 267 (1991) (footnotes omitted).

3. A. Kiss & D. Shelton, International Environmental Law 6 (1991). *See also* J. Schneider, World Public Order of the Environment 144-150 (1979). "Within the overall realm of state environmental responsibility, the first objective of international sanctioning or implementing processes is that of the long-term prevention of environmental losses." *Id.* at 144.

seine tuna nets cannot be brought back to life;[4] ancient forests cannot be regrown overnight; the marine environment may take years to recover from a massive oil spill and may never recover fully; extinct species cannot be resurrected; forests and lakes may take decades to recover from acid deposition damage; stabilization of atmospheric concentrations of substances that deplete the stratospheric ozone layer will be costly and time consuming; and, assuming it can be accomplished, halting anthropogenic climate change will be enormously expensive and will require, among other things, the development of new technologies and, in many countries, fundamental behavioral changes.

A preventive approach to environmental protection seeks to anticipate and avoid problems such as those just mentioned, or at least keep them from becoming worse. But the law does not prevent conduct lightly. On the municipal level, one seeking an injunction—that is, a judicial order forbidding the defendant to engage in or to continue certain conduct or commanding the defendant to perform certain acts—must normally satisfy a number of preconditions designed to protect the defendant from unjustified interferences with its freedom of action. The injunction has been called "an instrument of some danger in a free society, as well as an instrument of considerable power."[5] On the international level, state sovereignty itself stands as a formidable obstacle to any effort to constrain the conduct of nations, whether through treaty provisions or court orders.[6] States are understandably hesitant to surrender their freedom of action in any field, but they are particularly reluctant to do so with regard to their economic development activities (which may result, e.g., in air and water pollution), in general and the exploitation of their natural resources (e.g., logging), in particular.

A question that should be kept in mind in studying the materials in this chapter is, therefore, to what extent have states accepted obligations of prevention of international environmental harm? Specifically, where obligations of prevention are found in customary international law, in treaty provisions or in "soft law" instruments such as resolutions, declarations

4. *See generally* GATT, *United States—Restrictions on Imports of Tuna, Report of the Panel,* GATT Doc. DS21/R, 3 Sept. 1991, paras. 2.1-2.2. *See* Chapter 20.

5. D. Dobbs, Law of Remedies 105 (1973). For these reasons, "[t]he form of relief, the standards under which it is granted or denied, and the procedures for obtaining such relief, are . . . of considerable importance in providing protections against abuse." *Id.*

6. For example, Article 41 of the Statute of the International Court of Justice authorizes the court to "*indicate,* if it considers that circumstances so require, any provisional measures which ought to be taken to preserve the respective rights of either party." Statute of the International Court of Justice, Art. 41, para. 1 (emphasis added). Under this provision, the court may "take steps roughly equivalent to the interim injunction which domestic courts are frequently empowered to issue pending the final determination." S. Rosenne, The World Court, What It Is and How It Works 75 (3d rev. ed. 1973). The "freezing" of the positions of the states involved is so potentially sensitive that paragraph 2 of Article 41 requires the court to provide notice of the measures not only to the parties of the measures but also to the United Nations Security Council. In addition, note that the statute permits the court only to "indicate" provisional measures, not to "order" them.

and expert drafts, are these obligations "strict"—in the sense that they are breached if the state of origin fails to prevent the harm in question, regardless of whether, or the extent to which, it attempted to do so? Or may a state comply with these obligations by exercising its best efforts to prevent environmental harm, even if those efforts are not successful? A related question is whether obligations of prevention apply in the same way to all countries, regardless of their level of development. This issue is considered in Chapter 9 on Accountability and Compliance, below, but should be borne in mind in connection with this chapter as well.

The most fundamental "customary" norms of international environmental law have already been foreshadowed in the cases contained in Chapter 6. In this chapter, we divide international environmental norms into two categories: substantive norms and procedural norms. While this dichotomy may be artificial in some ways, it is one that is generally familiar to lawyers and is helpful for purposes of analysis. The norms examined in this chapter deal with international pollution and not with the important problem of allocation of shared natural resources (such as international rivers and lakes), which is treated in Chapter 16.

The materials in this chapter illustrate how the fundamental principles announced in the basic cases (Chapter 6) have been enshrined, elaborated upon, or supplemented in subsequent instruments. You should carefully consider the authoritative value of each of the instruments as you study it: Is it binding or merely exhortative? Even if it is not technically binding does it have normative force? For example, does such a nonbinding instrument reflect a principle of customary international law that *is* binding on states? If the instrument is binding, how strict are its provisions? Is there an inverse relationship between the "bindingness" of the instrument and the "strictness"/specificity and stringency of the obligations it contains? Is there any value to nonbinding instruments whose provisions go beyond existing law?[7] Answers to these questions are important both for assessing the value of the instrument in question and for developing strategies and making policy for the field as a whole.

A. SUBSTANTIVE NORMS

In this section we will examine the fundamental substantive norms of international environmental law. By "substantive norms" we mean norms that establish rights and obligations concerning the environment, as opposed to "procedural norms" that prescribe the method or process for implementing substantive norms or for their enforcement, or that deal

7. *See generally* P.-M. Dupuy, Soft Law and the International Law of the Environment, 12 Mich. J. Intl. L. 420 (1991).

principally with procedures states must follow. Both substantive and procedural norms embody international legal obligations whose breach entails the international responsibility of the offending state. The latter subject is dealt with in Chapter 9 on Accountability and Compliance. This section provides an overview of the most fundamental of the substantive norms of international environmental law. We begin with the obligation that is perhaps the cornerstone of the law in the field.

1. *The Obligation Not to Cause Transboundary Environmental Harm*

■ STOCKHOLM DECLARATION ON THE HUMAN ENVIRONMENT, PRINCIPLE 21

Adopted 16 June 1972 at the United Nations Conference on the Human Environment, Stockholm. Report of the U.N. Conference on the Human Environment, U.N. Doc. A/CONF.48/14/Rev.1 at 3 (1973), U.N. Doc. A/CONF.48/14 at 2 and Corr.1 (1972),* reprinted in *11 I.L.M. 1416 (1972).

PRINCIPLE 21

States have, in accordance with the Charter of the United Nations and the principles of international law, the sovereign right to exploit their own resources pursuant to their own environmental policies, and the responsibility to ensure that activities within their jurisdiction or control do not cause damage to the environment of other States or of areas beyond the limits of national jurisdiction.

Notes and Questions

1. *The Stockholm Conference and Declaration:*

The United Nations Conference on the Human Environment, held 5-16 June 1972 in Stockholm, marked the emergence of international environmental law as a separate branch of international law. Much preparatory work preceded the Stockholm Conference, in which 113 States participated (the Soviet Union and other Eastern European States [except Romania] boycotted the Conference because of the exclusion of the German Democratic Republic), together with 13 specialized agencies, several intergovernmental organizations, and numerous non-governmental organizations. . . .

The Declaration on the Human Environment, which was adopted by acclamation, contains a preamble . . . and 26 principles covering many international environmental issues, including human rights, natural resource management, pollution prevention, the relation between environment and development, institutional arrangements, education, the obligation to prevent pollution (the famous principle 21), whether standards should be the

> same for developed and developing countries, and nuclear weapons. The Declaration does not cover some important topics, however. For example, a draft principle requiring notification of the risk of adverse transboundary effects was deleted from the Declaration.
>
> The Stockholm Declaration was subsequently endorsed by the General Assembly on 15 December 1972 (UNGA Res. 2994), by 112 to none, with ten abstentions. Although the language of the Declaration often is normative ("shall") rather than precatory ("should"), the Declaration was intended not to be legally binding. However, at least one portion of the Declaration—principle 21—is now generally viewed as customary international law (though there is disagreement about its precise meaning). More generally, the Stockholm Declaration has had great and widespread influence.

E. Brown Weiss, D. Magraw & P. Szasz, International Environmental Law: Basic Instruments and References 171-172 (1992). *See also* Jutta Brunnée, Acid Rain and Ozone Layer Depletion: International Law and Regulation 84 (1988): "Principle 21 . . . was endorsed in the preamble of the 1979 ECE convention on Long-Range Transboundary Air Pollution [which was] signed and ratified by the USSR, the GDR, Czechoslovakia, Poland, and Hungary, and signed by several other east block countries. . . . The leading notion with respect to transfrontier pollution is that expressed in Principle 21. . . . Principle 21 draws upon important precedents and has since been incorporated in environmental policies and agreements on all levels."

2. *Principle 21 and* Trail Smelter. Principle 21 has become a true classic in the field. One of the "important precedents" for Principle 21 was the *Trail Smelter* arbitration, considered in the previous chapter. Are there significant differences between Principle 21 and the *Trail Smelter* tribunal's statement of the rule concerning transfrontier pollution? If so, what are they?

3. *From Stockholm to Rio in 20 years.* Twenty years after the Stockholm Conference, the United Nations held a second meeting on the environment. The United Nations Conference on Environment and Development, or UNCED (popularly known as the Earth Summit), met in Rio de Janeiro from June 3-14, 1992. The 178 states participating in UNCED adopted a statement of principles, as had been done at the Stockholm Conference. The UNCED principles are entitled the Rio Declaration on Environment and Development. U.N. Doc. A/CONF.151/5/Rev.1, 14 June 1992, adopted 14 June 1992, *reprinted in* 31 I.L.M. 874 (1992). The counterpart of Principle 21 in the Rio Declaration is Principle 2, which provides as follows:

> *The United Nations Conference on Environment and Development,*
> *Proclaims that:*
>
> **Principle 2**
>
> States have, in accordance with the Charter of the United Nations and the principles of international law, the sovereign right to exploit their own

> resources pursuant to their own environmental and developmental policies, and the responsibility to ensure that activities within their jurisdiction or control do not cause damage to the environment of other States or of areas beyond the limits of national jurisdiction.

A comparison of the Rio Declaration's Principle 2 with the Stockholm Declaration's Principle 21 reveals only one difference in language: the words "and developmental" have been added in Principle 2. What is the legal significance, if any, of the addition of those words? Do they weaken the Stockholm Declaration's version of the principle from an environmental protection point of view? Do they imply that in exploiting its resources, a state may give equal consideration to environmental and developmental considerations? Is the concept of "sustainable development" implicit in the phrase "environmental and developmental policies"?

4. *The progeny of Principle 21.* Principle 21 is incorporated verbatim in Article 3 of the Convention on Biological Diversity of June 5, 1992, 31 I.L.M. 818 (1992); and in Principle 1(a) of the Statement of Principles for a Global Consensus on the Management, Conservation and Sustainable Development of All Types of Forests (the "Forest Principles"), 31 I.L.M. 881 (1992). The Desertification Convention recites Principle 2 of the Rio Declaration verbatim in its fifteenth preambular paragraph (Convention to Combat Desertification in Those Countries Experiencing Serious Drought and/or Desertification, Particularly in Africa, Paris, June 17, 1994, U.N. Doc. A/AC.241/15/Rev.3, 33 I.L.M. 1332 (1994)), and the Framework Convention on Climate Change does so in its eighth preambular paragraph (New York, May 9, 1992, 31 I.L.M. 849 (1992)).

What is the legal significance of the repetition of Principles 21 and 2? Does it indicate that they are accepted as norms of customary international law? Or does it mean that states believe these principles are not binding unless they are incorporated into an agreement? In *Legality of the Threat or Use of Nuclear Weapons, Advisory Opinion,* 1996 I.C.J.—, 241-242, para. 29, the International Court of Justice stated: "The existence of the general obligation of States to ensure that activities within their jurisdiction and control respect the environment of other States or of areas beyond national control is now part of the corpus of international law relating to the environment." This statement was reaffirmed in the court's decision in *Gabcikovo-Nagymaros Project (Hungary/Slovakia),* 1997 I.C.J. —, Sept. 25, 1997, para. 53.

5. *The difficult birth of Principle 21.* The luster Principle 21 has taken on over the years tends to obscure the controversy that attended its birth. Professor Louis Sohn, in his commentary on the principle, describes its drafting history and discusses a number of versions proposed by different delegations, including the following:

> Each State has a sovereign right to its environment and to dispose of its natural resources and a right to take all necessary and appropriate measures to protect its environmental integrity.

> In support of this proposal, it was argued that as a first step in the development of international environmental law it is necessary to make clear the principle that "sovereignty includes the right to environmental integrity and the right to maintain that integrity in a wholesome and unimpaired condition." Another delegation supported this proposal, subject to the condition that any such right can be exercised only in accordance with the Charter of the United Nations and the general principles of international law. Several other delegations opposed these proposals, however. They observed that, unlike the concept of sovereignty, the concept of the human environment did not have any clearly established limits; consequently, the proposed new principle could be interpreted as 'implying that each State was left free to define the extent of its environment' to the prejudice of the established principles of international law.

Louis Sohn, The Stockholm Declaration on the Human Environment, 14 Harv. Intl. L.J. 423, 488-489 (1973) (footnotes omitted).

At the Stockholm Conference, the United States made the following statement concerning its interpretation of Principle 21:

> [N]othing contained in this principle, or elsewhere in the Declaration, diminishes in any way the obligation of States to prevent environmental damage or gives rise to any right on the part of States to take actions in derogation of the rights of other States or of the community of nations. The statement on the responsibility of States for damage caused to the environment of other States or of areas beyond the limits of national jurisdiction is not in any way a limitation on the above obligation, but an affirmation of existing rules concerning liability in the event of default on the obligation.

U.N. Doc. A/CONF.48/14, at 118 (1972). Professor Sohn describes the reaction to this and other proposals as follows:

> The consensus reached in the Working Group of the Preparatory Committee on this principle was so fragile that the Working Group of the Conference not only refused to clarify the text, as suggested by the United States, but also rejected a number of amendments of the kind that it had no trouble in accepting in connection with other principles. Thus it rejected a Brazilian proposal to delete the restrictive reference to the Charter of the United Nations and the principles of international law, as well as another Brazilian proposal to restore an earlier text allowing each state to follow, without any restriction, not only its environmental policies but also its "standards and criteria." The Working Group also refused to make a concession to the group of nine African countries, which wanted to make clear that the sovereign right to exploit resources was accompanied by the right to control them.

Louis Sohn, above, at 491 (footnotes omitted). Is this tantamount to saying, "we don't really know what it means, but if everyone else can accept it we will"?

6. *The final form of Principle 21.* Professor Sohn explains Principle 21 in its final form as follows:

> The final text does not merely reiterate the generally accepted principle that a state has the sovereign right to exploit its own resources, but gives the blessing of the Charter and of the principles of international law to the right of a state to exploit these resources pursuant to its own environmental policies. While this provision does not go as far as to assert that a state has unlimited sovereignty over its environment, it comes quite close to such an assertion. An over-broad interpretation of this sovereign right would be inconsistent with the rest of the Declaration which emphasizes the fact that no part of the global environment can be separated from the rest and that it has to be preserved and improved for the benefit of all the people of both the present and future generations. No state can claim an absolute right to ruin its environment in order to obtain some transient benefits. It should think not only of the effect on other peoples but also about the future of its own people. It should not ruin the soil of its country in order to get a few extra crops or to sell more wood or pulp. Destruction and depletion of irreplaceable resources are clearly condemned by the Declaration, even when there is no effect abroad, and a state cannot engage in such activities behind the shield of misconceived sovereignty. It would have been better, therefore, if some clearer guideline had been inserted in the first part of Principle 21. It is unfortunate that the Conference did not consider the proposal by the Holy See that in the exploitation of national resources states should follow "a just environmental policy." There is clearly need here for some standard referring to the common good rather than to states' own policies, however inadequate.
>
> The second part of Principle 21 was considered by many so important that they were willing to pay the price of the imperfections of the first part in order to nail down a crucial rule of general importance. The Canadian delegation, for instance, later commented that this principle reflects existing rules of international law, the first element in it stressing the rights of states, "while the second element made it clear that those rights must be limited or balanced by the responsibility to ensure that the exercise of rights did not result in damage to others." This balancing of rights and responsibility was essential "to reconcile national interests and those of the international community."[8] While the principle of responsibility of one state for damage caused in another is generally recognized, . . . Principle 21 makes clear that the rule of responsibility applies not only to damage caused to the environment of other states but also to any injury inflicted on the environment of "areas beyond the limits of national jurisdiction," such as the high seas or Antarctica.

8. . . . Principles 21 and 22 have been accepted by the Governments of the United States and Canada, in a joint communiqué of July 13, 1972, as the basis for "the development of law and procedures for settlement of disputes of an environmental nature." . . . [Footnote in original—Eds.]

Sohn, above, at 492-493 (some footnotes omitted).

7. *A principle at odds with itself?* Is the "responsibility to ensure . . ." stated in Principle 21 absolute? If not, how should that responsibility be balanced against the state's "sovereign right to exploit [its] own resources pursuant to [its] own environmental policies"?

8. *Jurisdiction and control.* Principle 21 refers to the responsibility of states for activities "within their jurisdiction or control . . ." This phrase clearly covers activities within the territory of a state, but how much farther does it go? The answer to this question is not entirely clear, since the precise juridical content of the term "control" is uncertain and the outer limits of a state's "jurisdiction" are determined by applying a reasonableness test. *See* Restatement (Third) of the Foreign Relations Law of the United States §403 (1987). Professor Sohn explores the ramifications of a state's responsibility for activities under its "control":

> Within the ambit of the principle are not only damage-causing activities within the area under a state's jurisdiction, including its territorial waters, but also activities conducted by persons or ships under its "control," wherever they may act. This extension of the principle applies clearly to citizens of a state, to ships flying its flag, and perhaps even to corporations incorporated in its territory. It is more doubtful whether it applies to residents of a state, to ships owned by its nationals but flying other countries' flags, or to foreign subsidiaries controlled by corporations incorporated in the state. Even if broad application of this principle should result in concurrent responsibility of several states, it may be hoped that states would be willing to interpret this provision in a manner which would best ensure an adequate preservation of the human environment.

Sohn, above, at 493. In light of the possibility of "concurrent responsibility" you should begin considering a question we will revisit later, namely, whether a state such as the United States would be responsible under Principle 21 for harm caused in another state, such as India, by a subsidiary of a company incorporated under the laws of the first state, such as in the case of the Bhopal disaster.

9. *The ILA weighs in.* The 1986 Seoul Declaration of the International Law Association contains an article that tracks, in part, Principle 21:

> The protection, preservation and enhancement of the natural environment for the present and future generations is the responsibility of all States. *All States have the responsibility to ensure that activities within their jurisdiction or control do not cause damage to the environment of other States or of areas beyond the limits of national jurisdiction.* All states should co-operate in evolving international norms and regulations in the field.

International Law Association, Declaration of the Progressive Development of Principles of Public International Law Relating to a New International Economic Order, 29 Aug. 1986, art. 7.5 (emphasis added). The last sentence of the article parallels Principle 22 of the Stockholm Declaration, discussed in the following note.

10. *Liability?* While Principle 21 makes a strong statement on the responsibility of states to prevent transfrontier environmental harm, it does not specify what the legal consequences would be if a state failed to do so. The Stockholm Declaration addresses the latter question only obliquely, in Principle 22, which provides as follows:

> **Principle 22**
>
> States shall co-operate to develop further the international law regarding liability and compensation for the victims of pollution and other environmental damage caused by activities within the jurisdiction or control of such States to areas beyond their jurisdiction.

Unfortunately, the principle stops short of expressly affirming the liability of a state for transfrontier harm caused by activities within its jurisdiction or control. However, by using the word "further," it does appear to recognize implicitly that "some law on the subject already exists." Sohn, above, at 495. During the preparations for the Stockholm Conference, some states "accepted the idea of liability of a state for damage caused to areas beyond that state's jurisdiction, [while] others expressed doubts about it." *Id.* at 494 (footnotes omitted). In fact, even the following straightforward proposal of Canada proved unacceptable:

> Each state has the responsibility to compensate for damage to the environment caused by activities carried on within its territory.

U.N. Doc. A/CONF.48/PC.12, Annex I, at 3 (1971). Also rejected was the following proposal by China:

> The victim state has the right to demand compensation from the polluter-country which has discharged or dumped at will toxic substances, thereby seriously polluting and poisoning the environment of other states.

U.N. Doc. A/CONF.48/WG.1/CRP.23, at 3 (1972). The language finally adopted was the most that could be agreed upon. In light of the various proposals that were rejected, can Principle 22 be taken as embodying any principle at all concerning liability?

Professor Sohn argues that, in addition to its recognition, implicit in the word "further," that some law on the subject already exists, Principle 22

> also makes clear that liability is not limited to pollution but also extends to other environmental damage, for instance, that caused by "environmental ag[g]ression," such as weather and climate modification, changing the flow of ocean currents, melting the polar icecaps, etc. Principle 22 follows Principle 21 in broadening liability; it applies not only to activities within the jurisdiction of states, but also to those under their control.

Sohn, above, at 495-496.

Unfortunately, the cooperation called for in Principle 22 has been slow in materializing. That even states themselves recognize and are evidently frustrated by this is clear from Principle 13 of the Rio Declaration, note 3 above, adopted 20 years after the Stockholm Conference:

Principle 13

> States shall develop national law regarding liability and compensation for the victims of pollution and other environmental damage. States shall also cooperate in an expeditious and more determined manner to develop further international law regarding liability and compensation for adverse effects of environmental damage caused by activities within their jurisdiction or control to areas beyond their jurisdiction.

Does Principle 13 of Rio add anything to, or subtract anything from, Principle 22 of Stockholm? Is its rather frustrated and impatient tone significant?

11. *More from Stockholm on prevention.* Another principle of the Stockholm Declaration dealing generally with the prevention of environmental harm is Principle 6, which provides as follows:

> The discharge of toxic substances or of other substances and the release of heat, in such quantities or concentrations as to exceed the capacity of the environment to render them harmless, must be halted in order to ensure that serious or irreversible damage is not inflicted upon ecosystems. The just struggle of the peoples of all countries against pollution should be supported.

Does this principle employ language of legal obligation concerning the discharge of toxic substances? Or is it merely hortatory? What is the legal effect of the second sentence? Professor Sohn comments as follows:

> [T]he Conference added [to the text of the Preparatory Committee], as a result of a Chinese proposal, the rousing second sentence. . . . It might have been more useful if the Conference instead, or in addition, had in the first sentence imposed an obligation on states to take all practicable steps to halt the discharges of toxic and other harmful substances.

Sohn, above, at 462 (footnote omitted). The following principle, Principle 7, applies Principle 6 to the subject of marine pollution. However, Principle 7 employs normative language ("States *shall* take all possible steps to prevent pollution of the seas. . . ."). Why would the conference use such language in the specific context of marine pollution but not with regard to the discharge of toxic substances in general?

■ RESTATEMENT (THIRD) OF THE FOREIGN RELATIONS LAW OF THE UNITED STATES

American Law Institute
§601 (1987)

§601. State Obligations with Respect to Environment of Other States and the Common Environment

(1) A state is obligated to take such measures as may be necessary, to the extent practicable under the circumstances, to ensure that activities within its jurisdiction or control

(a) conform to generally accepted international rules and standards for the prevention, reduction, and control of injury to the environment of another state or of areas beyond the limits of national jurisdiction; and

(b) are conducted so as not to cause significant injury to the environment of another state or of areas beyond the limits of national jurisdiction.

Notes and Questions

1. *The ALI and the significance of the Restatement.* The American Law Institute

> is a nonprofit membership association whose members are selected on the basis of professional standing. Its members include judges, legal academicians, and lawyers in independent private practice, in government, and in law departments of business and other enterprises. The Institute's purpose, since its organization in 1923, has been the "clarification and simplification of the law and its better adaptation to social needs." The work products of the Institute, particularly the Restatements of the Law, receive recognition on the basis of the scholarly and professional care and responsibility with which they are carried out.

American Law Institute (ALI), Restatement (Third) of the Foreign Relations Law of the United States XI (1987) (hereinafter Restatement (Third)). Thus, despite what its title might imply, the Restatement (Third) does not represent the official position of the United States government. In fact, the ALI states in the foreword that "[i]n a number of particulars the formulations in this Restatement are at variance with positions that have been taken by the United States Government." Restatement (Third) at IX. The authoritative value of Restatement (Third) derives from the reputation of the ALI. But the reduction of entire fields or subfields into one or two "black-letter" sections (identified using symbols [§], which in some legal systems connote a paragraph of a statute) may tend to induce unduly heavy reliance upon the ALI's "restatement" of the law in those fields. Indeed, "[l]ike the previous Restatement [of U.S. Foreign Relations Law[9]], its impact may be even greater than that of the Restatements of other subjects, due to the relative lack of familiarity of the American bench and bar with international law. The likelihood that lawyers in the United States will rely heavily upon the Restatement (Third), coupled with the increasing frequency with which practice in this country assumes a transnational dimension, makes this a particularly important Restatement." S. McCaffrey, The Restatement's Treatment of Sources and Evidence of International Law, 25 Intl. Law. 311, 312 (1991).

2. *Muddied water?* Reflecting the increasing importance of international environmental problems, Restatement (Third) devotes an entire chapter (Part VI) to "The Law of the Environment," a subject that is dealt with in two reporters' notes in the previous Restatement of Foreign Relations Law.[10] However, the chapter consists of only four sections: one deals with "Remedies for Violations of Environmental Obligations" and two with marine pollution, leaving only §601 to deal with the obligations of states with regard to the environment. Commendable as it is that the ALI has expanded its treatment of the subject, it is perhaps not surprising that its effort to condense the entire field of international environmental law into four sections has drawn criticism. Professor David Caron has commented that

> the resulting product constitutes only a modest step toward presenting the foreign relations law of the United States pertaining to the environment. Part VI takes a narrow view of the law of the environment, limiting itself to transfrontier pollution and, even then, relegates most of the discussion of conventional law to reporters' notes. . . . As a symbolic step, Part VI is to be applauded. As a restatement of the foreign relations law of the United States pertaining to the environment, it oversimplifies and sometimes muddies the waterways of the law.

9. American Law Institute, Restatement (Second) of the Foreign Relations Law of the United States (1965).

10. *Id.* at §§18, Reporters' Note 3, and 23, Reporters' Note 3.

David Caron, The Law of the Environment: A Symbolic Step of Modest Value, 14 Yale J. Intl. L. 528 (1989).

3. *Parsing §601.* Focusing on the language of §601, what is the effect of the phrase, "to the extent practicable under the circumstances"? Does the word "practicable" refer to factual practicability? Economic practicability? Could a State A, under §601, successfully defend a claim for transfrontier pollution damage in State B on the ground that preventing the harm would mean a loss of jobs in State A? What is meant by the term "circumstances"? Economic circumstances? Circumstances relating to the availability of technology? Natural phenomena such as topography or weather? Professor Caron comments as follows on the effect of the phrase "to the extent practicable under the circumstances":

> Although this qualification points to a standard defined by customary practice, the comments and reporters' notes do little to explain the phrase. The phrase renders the obligation contextual; that is, the obligation is not absolute but rather is dependent upon the circumstances present and the limits of practicality. . . . Whether measures practicable under the circumstances are more or less exacting than reasonable measures is unclear. To the extent that the phrase "practicable under the circumstances" leads subsection 601(1) in effect to require a standard of care akin to due diligence, the section adopts a conservative view of the environmental obligation of States. Indeed, the black letter provisions make no mention of the possibility of strict liability for certain ultrahazardous activities such as nuclear power generation.

Caron, above, at 535, 536 (footnotes omitted).

4. *"Generally accepted international rules": clear injunction or easy way out?* What are the "generally accepted international rules and standards" to which states must conform under subparagraph (1)(a)? Comment *b* to §601 states: "This phrase is adopted from the law of the sea. . . . The obligation under Subsection (1)(a) refers to both general rules of customary international law (see, *e.g.*, the *Trail Smelter* case. . . .) and those derived from international conventions, and from standards adopted by international organizations pursuant to such conventions, that deal with a specific subject, such as oil pollution or radioactive wastes." Restatement (Third), above, §601, Comment *b*. Professor Caron comments in part as follows on the Restatement's use of this phrase: "Discussions regarding this phrase on the floor of the American Law Institute only confirm the language's lack of precision. The suggestion that a State should be bound by rules and standards that are neither customarily nor conventionally applicable is unusual to say the least." Caron, above, at 538 (footnote omitted). The phrase is discussed more fully in *id.* at 537-539.

5. *Evaluating the Restatement.* Professor Caron concludes that, "[o]verall," the Restatement's treatment of international environmental law "is

too general for the specialist and too confusing for the novice." Caron, above, at 540. Is he right?

■ FINAL REPORT OF THE EXPERTS GROUP ON ENVIRONMENTAL LAW ON LEGAL PRINCIPLES FOR ENVIRONMENTAL PROTECTION AND SUSTAINABLE DEVELOPMENT, ARTICLE 10

in *Experts Group on Environmental Law of the World Commission on Environment and Development (Brundtland Commission), Environmental Protection and Sustainable Development 75 (1987)*

PRINCIPLES SPECIFICALLY CONCERNING TRANSBOUNDARY NATURAL RESOURCES AND ENVIRONMENTAL INTERFERENCES

Article 10
Prevention and Abatement of a Transboundary Environmental Interference

States shall, without prejudice to the principles laid down in Articles 11 and 12,[11] prevent or abate any transboundary environmental interference or a significant risk thereof which causes substantial harm—i.e. harm which is not minor or insignificant.

Notes and Questions

1. *About the Experts Group.* "The Experts Group on Environmental Law was established in 1985 to prepare a report on legal principles for environmental protection and sustainable development, and proposals for accelerating the development of relevant international law, for consideration by the World Commission on Environment and Development." Environmental Protection and Sustainable Development 1 (1987) (hereinafter referred to as "Experts Group Report"). Certain of the provisions contained in the report of the Experts Group probably reflect existing law; others constitute proposals for the progressive development of the law—in particular, "legal principles which *ought to be in place now or before the year 2000* to support environmental protection and sustainable development within and among all States." Experts Group Report, above, at 7 (emphasis in original). The Experts Group was chaired by Robert Munro of Canada; Johan Lammers of the Netherlands served as Rapporteur. The 13-member

11. Articles 11 and 12 are entitled, respectively, "Liability for transboundary environmental interferences resulting from lawful activities," and "Transboundary environmental interferences involving substantial harm far less than cost of prevention." These articles will be considered in section B of this chapter on Procedural Norms and in Chapter 9, Accountability and Compliance.

Group included lawyers from Belgium, France, Japan, Kenya, Mexico, the Philippines, Saudi Arabia, the Soviet Union, and the United States. The genesis of the World Commission on Environment and Development, also known as the Brundtland Commission, is described in its highly influential report as follows:

> The World Commission on Environment and Development was created as a consequence of General Assembly resolution 38/161 adopted . . . in the fall of 1983. That resolution called upon the Secretary-General to appoint the Chairman and Vice-Chairman of the Commission and in turn directed them to jointly appoint the remaining members, at least half of whom were to be selected from the developing world. The Secretary General appointed Mrs. Gro Harlem Brundtland of Norway, then leader of the Norwegian Labour Party [and later Prime Minister], as Chairman and Dr. Mansour Khalid, the former Minister of Foreign Affairs from Sudan, as Vice-Chairman.[12] . . . The Commission . . . functioned as an independent body. All its [22] members . . . served the Commission in their individual capacities, not as representatives of their governments.

World Commission on Environment and Development, Our Common Future 352 (1987). The Commission's Report was submitted to the U.N. General Assembly as U.N. Doc. A/42/427 of August 4, 1987, and "[w]elcom[ed]" by the General Assembly in resolution 42/187, adopted without a vote on December 11, 1987.

2. *Article 10 under a microscope.* With regard to Article 10, can this be said to embody an existing international legal obligation? In its commentary, the Experts Group cites in support of the article the "classic statement" of the *Trail Smelter* tribunal, i.e., that "no State has the right to use or permit the use of its territory in such a manner as to cause injury by fumes in or to the territory of another . . ." Can this principle really be generalized? What about chronic problems such as long-distance transfrontier air pollution and pollution of major international watercourses such as the Rhine? Doesn't the very existence—and persistence—of these problems demonstrate that states have not actually accepted such a general legal obligation?

3. *Preventing "risk."* What is the justification for Article 10's requirement that a state "prevent. . . . a significant *risk* [of a transboundary environmental interference]"? If such a risk were created, would a neighboring state have a right of action if the risk did not materialize in actual harm? How would this aspect of the article apply, for example, to the French practice of locating nuclear power plants in border areas? Or to dams on large international watercourses, upstream of at least one riparian country?

12. William Ruckelshaus was the American member.

INTERNATIONAL LAW ASSOCIATION (ILA), RULES OF INTERNATIONAL LAW APPLICABLE TO TRANSFRONTIER POLLUTION, ARTICLES 3 AND 4

ILA, Report of the Sixtieth Conference, Montreal, 1982 158, at 160, 167 (1982)

Article 3 (Prevention and Abatement)

(1) Notwithstanding the rule of Article 5 concerning competing uses of shared natural resources[13] States are in their legitimate activities under an obligation to prevent, abate and control transfrontier pollution to such an extent that no substantial injury is caused in the territory of another State.

(2) Furthermore States shall limit new and increased transfrontier pollution to the lowest level that may be reached by measures practicable and reasonable under the circumstances.

(3) States should endeavour to reduce existing transfrontier pollution, below the requirements of paragraph 1 of this Article, to the lowest level that may be reached by measures practicable and reasonable under the circumstances.

Article 4 (Highly Dangerous Substances)

Notwithstanding the provisions in Art. 3 and 5 States shall refrain from causing transfrontier pollution by discharging into the environment substances generally considered as being highly dangerous to human health. If such substances are already being discharged, States shall eliminate the polluting discharge within a reasonable time.

Notes and Questions

1. *About the ILA.* The International Law Association (ILA), a non-governmental organization, was founded in 1873 and has a membership of approximately 4,000 lawyers from a broad spectrum of countries. At its biennial meetings, the ILA adopts resolutions setting forth rules and recommendations on different subjects of international law. The resolutions may be looked to as an indication of the view of a cross-section of international lawyers as to what the law is, and where it should be going, on a given subject.

13. Article 5 is entitled "Shared Natural Resources" and provides that in cases where uses of such resources conflict, each state is entitled to a reasonable and equitable share. ILA, Report of the Sixtieth Conference, Montreal, 1982, 158, at 168 (1982).

2. *Everybody loves* Trail Smelter. Like the Brundtland Commission's Experts Group, the ILA relies heavily upon the *Trail Smelter* award. The commentary to Article 3 states that the duty to avoid transfrontier pollution harm "was expressly stated in the *Trail Smelter* decision, according to which it was Canada's duty to see that in future the *Trail Smelter* refrain from causing damages in the State of Washington. . . ." ILA, Report of the Sixtieth Conference, Montreal, 1982, 158, at 163 (1982) (hereinafter ILA Report). Do you agree with that characterization of the decision?

3. *Where's the risk?* Is it significant that the ILA's Article 3 does not cover the *risk* of transfrontier pollution harm, while risk is covered by article 10 of the Brundtland Commission's Experts Group?

4. *The basis of the rule in state practice.* In support of the rule stated in Article 3, paragraph 1, the commentary cites the following instances of state practice:

> (a) The quality of the water of the River Espierre flowing from the highly industrialized and urbanized Roubaix-Tourcing area in France to the more rural area around Tournai and Courtrai in Belgium was totally destroyed by pollution. After continuous Belgian complaints in 1970 the French communal authorities took measures to improve the situation. . . .
>
> (b) In 1956 several Austrian hydro-electric facilities caused heavy pollution of the Mur River by a [failed] attempt to clean discharged sludge. Yugoslavian fisheries were injured and two Yugoslavian paper mills had to stop operation. Austria accepted its responsibility and signed in 1959 an agreement with Yugoslavia whereby Austria had to pay [Austrian] Sch. 300.000 and handed over 20 tons of high grade paper. . . .
>
> (c) As a result of expanding industrial and other activities the vicinities of Detroit-Windsor and Port Huron-Sarnia were subjected to substantial quantities of air pollution crossing the boundary in the middle of the sixties (1966). The Governments of the USA and Canada agreed to refer this matter to the IJC [International Joint Commission], (pursuant to Art. IX of the Boundary Waters Treaty of 1909). In 1972 the Commission recommended a number of measures. . . .
>
> (d) In 1978 a hazardous environmental and public health situation existed at the Mexican-US American border which resulted from the improper disposal of untreated sewage and other wastes, including those from a slaughterhouse, into the New River by the [Mexican] City of Mexicali, Baja California. By this time the construction of sewage collection and purification facilities is underway and is expected to be completed soon. . . .[14]
>
> (e) Fumes containing a high degree of SO_2, emanating from the thermal power plant of Hoffmann-La Roche on the Swiss side of the border, seriously [disturbed] the inhabitants of the bordering German villages. On complaint of the German communities the Swiss authorities decreed that the power

14. [What the commentary does not indicate is that the sewage treatment plant was funded by the United States government. —EDS.]

> plant had to be fuelled in the future only by gas or sulphur-free oil. Since then the odour has ceased. . . .
>
> (f) In consequence of Swiss complaints the [disturbing] odours emanating from the refuse dump of Waldshut [Germany] were considerably reduced. The complaints of communities in Lorraine [France] concerning emissions emanating from the refuse dump of Saarbrucken [Germany], [and the] German complaints about the refuse dump near Lothringian Kreuzwald were equally successful. . . .
>
> (g) A serious case of transfrontier air pollution in the Upper Rhine Valley was the contamination of Swiss and German pastures by emissions of a chemical plant at Huningen (France); milk and cattle had to be eliminated. The French authorities forbade the dumping of the poisonous by-products of the insecticides produced on open waste heaps and ordered the covering of the existing heap. . . .

ILA Report, above, at 163-164. Do these examples of state practice support the rule in paragraph 1? Do they reveal anything about how strict states regard the obligation to be?

5. *Prohibited vs. equitable pollution.* While the opening phrase of Article 3, paragraph 1, might suggest otherwise ("*Notwithstanding* the rule of Article 5 . . ."), the commentary to that article states that if "the damage consists merely in the reduction of the potential use of a shared natural resource the special rule of article 5 on equitable sharing of the resource is applicable and supersedes the general rule of article 3, para. 1." ILA Report, above, at 160. Thus, if state A's use of a shared resource caused substantial pollution injury to state B, the rights of the two states would be governed by the rule of equitable sharing rather than by the duty not to cause transfrontier pollution injury to other states—wouldn't they? Much obviously depends upon what is meant by "reduction of the potential use." But if the above interpretation is correct, state A's activity may prove to be lawful as an "equitable use" of the shared natural resource, even though it harms state B. Is this a good rule? Is the notion of an equitable share of the assimilative capacity of a common river or airshed a sound one as a matter of policy? Does paragraph 3 of Article 3 make that notion easier to accept? Who determines when A has exceeded its equitable share? We will explore many of these questions further in Chapter 16 on international water resources.

6. *Existing vs. new pollution.* Note that paragraph 2 of Article 3 imposes a higher standard with regard to new and increased transfrontier pollution than that laid down for existing pollution in paragraph 1. What is the basis for this difference in treatment? A second difference between paragraphs 1 and 2 is that there is no requirement of injury under paragraph 2. Should a state have to take the measures required by paragraph 2 if no injury is caused to other states? Why?

7. *A special rule for dangerous substances?* If your answer to the question

in the preceding note was no, would you make an exception for "highly dangerous substances" of the kind dealt with in Article 4? Like paragraph 2 of Article 3, Article 4 contains no injury requirement. Nor is it limited to *transfrontier* pollution. Do you believe this rule represents existing state practice? Does it represent wise policy? Why?

■ OVERVIEW OF THE EXISTING CUSTOMARY LEGAL REGIME REGARDING INTERNATIONAL POLLUTION

P.-M. Dupuy
International Law and Pollution 61-67, 80-82 (D. Magraw ed. 1991)

The existing customary international legal regime regarding international pollution consists of principles and rules of which a large number have been defined in the last two decades by the progressive gathering of recurrent treaty provisions, recommendations made by international organizations, resolutions adopted at the end of international conferences, and other texts that can be said to have influenced State practice. From a strict point of view, this legal regime should consist only of those principles that receive a concrete application in the usual conduct and behavior of States, so that they materialize the general opinio juris and can then be considered as part of customary international law.

Nevertheless, everybody knows that it has become more difficult than in the past to define very precisely the contents of present customary rules, given the rapid evolution of modern general international law. In the field of international environmental law in particular, international institutions, both intergovernmental and, at a lower stage, non-governmental (e.g., the Institut de Droit Internationale, the International Law Association, and the International Union for Conservation of Nature) have played an important role.

A number of guidelines emitted by these bodies have penetrated gradually into contemporary State practice. In certain cases, these guidelines bring an important contribution to the definition of international standards on the basis of which the due diligence to be expected from "well-governed" modern States can be established. "Soft law"—by which I mean international directives or undertakings that are not, strictly speaking, binding in themselves—thus is a phenomenon of real importance in this branch of international law. Soft law must be taken into account in the tentative analysis and interpretation of what is certainly already "hard law," that is, international directives or undertakings that are binding of their own accord under international law. Examples of this process will be encountered later in this chapter.

Obligation to Prevent Transfrontier Pollution

The basic principle governing transfrontier environmental pollution is that States shall prevent or abate any such damaging interference that causes or entails a significant risk of causing substantial harm. On the basis of a broad comparison of treaty law, international resolutions, and regional practice, it seems possible to define this well-established rule as follows:

> In the exercise of their sovereign rights to exploit and use, pursuant to their development policies, their natural resources, States shall take into account the impact of actual or anticipated activities in areas placed under their jurisdiction on the environment situated beyond their national frontiers. They shall take, in good faith and with all due diligence, appropriate measures to prevent transfrontier pollution by elaborating, in particular, rules and procedures adapted to the requirements of the protection of the environment, and see to it that these are effectively applied.

Let us examine the origin and legal basis of the principle and its implications as well as some of the best ways of implementing it.

ORIGIN AND LEGAL BASIS OF THE PRINCIPLE

Support for the obligation not to cause substantial harm by transfrontier pollution is to be found in the classic statement in the international arbitral award of the Trail Smelter case. . . .

Confirmation of this ruling may be found in the attitude taken by the International Court of Justice in the Corfu Channel case. . . . These cases emphasize the interdependence of States and the requirement to take other States' interests into account.

It would be a mistake to think that this principle could be applied only to the relations established between neighboring States and not in a wider geographical context. This question is of definite importance in view of the behavior of certain kinds of transfrontier pollution. For example, air pollution caused by some gaseous substances often reaches places very far from the place where the toxic emissions originated. One can normally impose the above obligation in such situations of long-distance pollution because the rule regarding the harmless use of territory can quite well dispense with arguments based on actual contiguity; the rule is a natural corollary of a sovereign State's exclusive jurisdiction over its territory, as pointed out, for example, in the Island of Palmas arbitration (United States v. Netherlands) delivered by Max Huber in 1928.

This fundamental principle seems to have been accepted by the actual world community of States. It is one case in which international declarations and institutional resolutions support the expression of a universal opinio juris. The duty not to cause substantial harm through transfrontier pollution in the area under the jurisdiction of another State may be deemed to have been explicitly accepted in many collective statements of States, among which Principle 21 of the Declaration on the Human Environment, adopted nearly twenty years ago during the 1972 United Nations Conference, is no doubt one of the most important. . . . This formulation is of paramount importance, in particular for developing countries, because it is made of two balancing elements: on the one hand, the right of a State to develop its economy and, on the other hand, the duty not to cause transfrontier environmental damage.

The substance of Principle 21 has been reaffirmed by several international bodies and in particular the U.N. General Assembly, in Resolution 3129 of December 1973 on Co-operation in the Field of Environment Concerning Natural Resources Shared by Two or More States, and Resolution 3281 of December 1974 proclaiming the Charter of Economic Rights and Duties. . . .

Numerous treaty provisions formulate the same general obligation. . . .

One should note the somewhat stricter formulation in the 1982 U.N. Convention on the Law of the Sea, article 194(2) of which reads as follows:

> States shall take all measures necessary to ensure that activities under their jurisdiction or control are so conducted as not to cause damage by pollution to other States and their environment, and that pollution arising from incidents or activities under their jurisdiction or control does not spread beyond the areas where they exercise sovereign rights in accordance with this Convention.

As easily observed, this multilateral codification treaty provision is a faithful retaking of the declaratory Principle 21 of Stockholm . . . although it does not balance the obligation not to cause transfrontier pollution with a right to develop economically.

A confirmation of the customary value of the obligation to prevent transfrontier pollution is to be found, without being paradoxical, in the argumentation developed by States in concrete cases, when they seem partly to ignore this general rule of law. In fact, they take due care to refer expressly to the legal value of this principle, explaining that their precise behavior in the case does not violate it. The attitude both of Brazil in relation with Argentina in the Itaipu barrage affair and, even more, of India in the context of its difficulties with Bangladesh relating to the diversion of a part of the Ganges waters is interesting in this regard.

This general obligation cannot be considered as an absolute one, however. States cannot be deemed to have violated international law every time they have not been able to prevent the occurrence of transfrontier pollution. This obligation of prevention exists only to the extent that the risk of causing international environmental damage is reasonably foreseeable. It can be strengthened in regard to special areas that require particular ecological protection, such as areas the 1980 World Conservation Strategy refers to as "life-support systems," such as ecosystems of plants, animals, and microorganisms together with the nonliving components of their environment and related ecological processes essential for the functioning of the biosphere in all its diversity. . . .

IMPLICATIONS AND MEANS OF IMPLEMENTING THE PRINCIPLE

The first implication of the principle delineated above seems clearly to be the death of the Harmon Doctrine—if, indeed, it was still extant. According to that doctrine regarding international watercourses, which [Attorney General] Harmon . . . expressed more than one hundred years ago, every State is free, within the frontiers delimiting its area of jurisdiction, to undertake or let develop any action that it considers beneficial for the national interest, without taking into account the material consequences of such decision outside the national territory.[15] The demise of the Harmon Doctrine has occurred even though, case by case, there can always be temptations for States engaged in concrete development projects to forget part of their actual duties in this area.

This general obligation of prevention implies that the State must consider what can or could be the eventual interferences of present and anticipated activities on the environment situated in the territory of other States. This idea has inspired procedures generally designated as "environmental impact assessments" in several countries, for example the United States, Canada, France, the Federal Republic of Germany, and Ireland. . . .

In any event, international customary law has not developed sufficiently to define precisely what kind of procedures should be enforced by States to apply their general obligation to prevent transfrontier pollution. One can certainly take into consideration the level of development of the concerned States in assessing what kind of procedure they should enforce. International impact statements probably already constitute part of the implementation of "due diligence," as far as industrialized countries are concerned. Is it absolutely possible, however, to reach the same conclusion as far as developing countries are concerned?

As far as the legal basis of State responsibility for transfrontier pollution is concerned, one can revisit what has been said earlier about the legal ground of the obligation to prevent such pollution: there is a "primary obligation" (in the sense laid down by Roberto Ago in his reports to the [U.N. International Law Commission] on State Responsibility) which is the obligation of harmless use of territory. Its content, as mentioned above, has been quite precise in the past twenty years, as determined both by the

15. The Harmon Doctrine is discussed further in Chapter 16, below.

practice of States (including treaty practice) and by the soft law resolutions which, in the medium term, can be considered as expressing progressively what is or, in certain cases, will be soon, the common opinio juris inside the world community.

These resolutions also make it easier to define what should be the average behavior of a "well-governed State" in regard to transfrontier pollution problems. Accordingly, the standards of international "due diligence" can be expected to become more and more definite with the progress of international cooperation. Due diligence appears here as the measure of international responsibility. It is both the counterpart to the exclusive exercise of territorial jurisdiction and the limiting factor on international responsibility flowing from failure to act in accordance with international norms.

But one must see that there is also a place for special regimes defining [standards] *rationae materiae* (i.e., for some kinds of damages by pollution, for instance chemical ones) or *rationae loci.* Here we meet again the actual and potential importance of regional cooperation inside or even outside international standing bodies. We are confronted again with the efficiency of agreements of cooperation. . . . And the definition of special ecological quality standards by such treaties will make it easy to strengthen the regime of liability by giving to it the advantages for the victims that usually are found in regimes of strict liability. All, in this matter, is a question of burden of proof and standard of proof.

International ecostandards are essentially divided in two categories. The first is composed of what one could call qualitative ecostandards. They are basically parameters to be taken into account because respecting them has an influence on the quality of the environment and the ecological equilibrium of a given natural resource (for instance, the elements referred to earlier in regard to the definition of what should be, in a concrete case, the equitable apportionment of a shared natural resource). They are useful, but nevertheless still open to discussion.

The second category, that of quantitative ecostandards, is adopted on the basis of an agreement between technicians and experts in the matter concerned. This kind of ecostandard is frequently encountered in technical annexes or, more seldom, in the text of conventions for the protection of the environment. One can give many illustrations of this technique: the 1972 United States-Canada Agreement on the Water Quality of the Great Lakes; the 1973 Agreement concerning the Permanent and Definitive Solution to the International Problem of the Salinity of the Colorado River concluded between Mexico and the United States; . . . .

From the point of view of international responsibility, what is interesting about these quantitative ecostandards, adopted by way of treaty law, is that they can be precisely controlled by technical measures and accomplished by technicians, even if one must not overevaluate the objectivity of technical criteria and evaluations. They are not susceptible to determination by lawyers, arbitrators, or judges on the ground of personal convictions. A concrete and official statement that the standard has been exceeded will then suffice to establish prima facie that the State from which the water flows, for instance, is liable to repair the damages caused by such a violation of the internationally agreed norm. [The 1973 agreement between Mexico and the United States on the Salinity of the Colorado River, for example, contains precise quantitative requirements that constitute] a definition of legality which leaves almost no room for approximate evaluation and later discussions. Even if not possible in all cases, the recourse to such a form of international ecostandards could . . . greatly help in the efficiency of international responsibility, which stays otherwise, as it is daily shown, practically unemployed. . . .

Notes and Questions

1. *The Dupuy formulation.* On the basis of the materials you have examined thus far, do you agree with Professor Dupuy's formulation of the "well-established rule" of customary international law concerning the prevention of transfrontier pollution? How stringent is this formulation of the rule? Is it more or less stringent than the rule stated by the *Trail Smelter* tribunal? Principle 21 of the Stockholm Declaration? Section 601 of the Restatement?

2. *LDCs and EIAs.* How would you answer Professor Dupuy's question whether developing countries should be (are) required to enact and enforce a requirement to prepare environmental impact statements for planned activities with potential transfrontier impacts? If they are not obligated to do this, what is the basis for the exception? Do they become obligated when they attain a certain level of development? If so, how should this level be defined? Who should have the burden of proving that a given country is or is not "developed" for this purpose?

3. *The meaning of "due diligence."* Professor Dupuy observes that "[d]ue diligence . . . [is] the measure of international responsibility" in this field. What is the meaning of "due diligence"? Who has the burden of proving that it has or has not been exercised? Is due diligence a "subjective" standard that varies with the country concerned, or is an "objective" one that requires all states to observe the same standard of conduct? If the former, what would it take for a country that had in the past been subject to a lower standard to be held to a higher one? Do other states, or the international community as a whole, have any responsibility for assisting such a state in meeting higher standards? We will encounter these issues again when we consider the accountability of a state for international environmental harm in Chapter 9.

2. *Conservation and Use of the Environment and Natural Resources*

■ FINAL REPORT OF THE EXPERTS GROUP ON ENVIRONMENTAL LAW ON LEGAL PRINCIPLES FOR ENVIRONMENTAL PROTECTION AND SUSTAINABLE DEVELOPMENT, ARTICLE 2

Experts Group on Environmental Law of the World Commission on Environment and Development (Brundtland Commission)
Environmental Protection and Sustainable Development 42 (1987)

General Principles Concerning Natural Resources and Environmental Interferences

Article 2
Conservation for Present and Future Generations

States shall ensure that the environment and natural resources are conserved and used for the benefit of present and future generations.

Notes and Questions

1. *It sounds nice, but on closer examination* . . . As a practical matter, how are states to fulfil their obligation under Article 2 to "ensure" that "the environment and natural resources are conserved and used for the benefit of present and future generations"? Is it enough that they exercise their best efforts toward these ends? Or is the obligation an absolute one, as the word "ensure" implies?

2. *The Experts Group explains.* The Experts Group's commentary to Article 2 contains, inter alia, the following explanation of the article's requirement that the environment and natural resources be conserved and used for the benefit of present and future generations:

> This implies, in the first place, a basic obligation for States to conserve options for future generations by maintaining to the maximum extent possible the diversity of the natural resource base. It requires a management of natural resources or the environment in such a manner that they may yield the greatest sustainable benefit to present generations while maintaining their potential to meet the needs and aspirations of future generations. Conservation of the diversity of the natural resource base for the benefit of future generations is warranted as the possibilities to develop substitute products or to improve production and/or extraction technologies are not unlimited. Or else because future generations may otherwise only be able to obtain the same benefits at considerably higher costs.
>
> The second basic obligation for States following from the duty to hold

> the natural heritage of mankind in trust for future generations, concerns the prevention or abatement of pollution or other forms of degradation of natural resources or the environment, which would reduce the range of uses to which the natural resources or environment could be put or which would confront future generations with enormous financial burdens to clean up the environment.

Experts Group Report, above, at 43. What does the Experts Group mean when it says that states must maintain "*to the maximum extent possible* the diversity of the natural resource base"? Does this mean old-growth forests have to be preserved in the face of claims that doing so would mean loss of jobs and perhaps closing of lumber mills? How does a state know what environmental quality or resource quantity or quality will be necessary to "meet the needs and aspirations of future generations"? Might it actually have to *improve* existing environmental quality or the quality of certain natural resources?

3. *Article 2 and international law.* Is it likely that Article 2 would be acceptable to countries of the North and South alike? If not, what does that say about its status as a rule of international law? If Article 2 does embody an international legal obligation, who could enforce it? Citizens of the state in question? Other states, acting individually or collectively? The "organized international community," i.e., the international community acting through the United Nations? In particular, who could enforce a state's obligations to future generations, assuming it were possible to tell when they had been violated?

4. *International watercourses.* Article 20 of the United Nations Convention on International Watercourses provides as follows:

> **Protection and Preservation of Ecosystems**
>
> Watercourse States shall, individually and, where appropriate, jointly, protect and preserve the ecosystems of international watercourses.

United Nations Convention on the Non-Navigational Uses of International Watercourses, May 21, 1977, article 20, U.N. Doc. A/RES/51/229, July 8, 1997, *reprinted in* 36 I.L.M 700 (1997). How would you define the "ecosystem" of an international watercourse? Would it include: (1) fish in the water? (2) a river's banks and adjacent areas? (3) birds whose habitat is in riverine areas? Suppose upstream logging has caused erosion that has deposited a significant amount of silt into the channel of an international watercourse. Would this violate article 20? Suppose dams on an international watercourse prevent fish migration and spawning upstream. Would this violate article 20?

3. The "Precautionary Principle"

We have considered the precautionary "principle" or "approach" earlier as a method of dealing with scientific uncertainty (*see* Chapter 4). We now focus upon its normative status in international relations. The following materials should help you to answer the question whether international law requires states to adopt a precautionary approach and, if so, what that would entail.

■ RIO DECLARATION ON ENVIRONMENT AND DEVELOPMENT, PRINCIPLE 15

Adopted by the United Nations Conference on Environment and Development, June 14, 1992
U.N. Doc. A/CONF.151/5/Rev.1, June 13, 1992,* reprinted in *31 I.L.M. 874 (1992)

Principle 15

In order to protect the environment, the precautionary approach shall be widely applied by States according to their capabilities. Where there are threats of serious or irreversible damage, lack of full scientific certainty shall not be used as a reason for postponing cost-effective measures to prevent environmental degradation.

■ NORTH AMERICAN FREE TRADE AGREEMENT, ARTICLES 715(4) AND 907(3) (1992)

House Doc. No. 103-149 (vols. 1 & 2), 103d Cong., 1st Sess.

Article 715 [Sanitary and Phytosanitary Measures]
Risk Assessment and Appropriate Level of Protection

4. Notwithstanding paragraphs (1) through (3) and Article 712(3)(c), where a Party conducting a risk assessment determines that available relevant scientific evidence or other information is insufficient to complete the assessment, it may adopt a provisional sanitary or phytosanitary measure on the basis of available relevant information, including from international or North American standardizing organizations and from sanitary or phytosanitary measures of other Parties. The Party shall, within a reasonable period after information sufficient to complete the assessment is presented to it, complete its assessment, review and, where appropriate, revise the provisional measure in the light of the assessment.

Article 907 [Standards-Related Methods]
Assessment of Risk

3. Where a Party conducting an assessment of risk determines that available scientific evidence or other information is insufficient to complete the assessment, it may adopt a provisional technical regulation on the basis of available relevant information. The Party shall, within a reasonable period

after information sufficient to complete the assessment of risk is presented to it, complete its assessment, review and, where appropriate, revise the provisional technical regulation in the light of that assessment.

THE STATUS IN INTERNATIONAL LAW OF THE PRINCIPLE OF PRECAUTIONARY ACTION

Lothar Gündling
5 Intl. J. Estuarine & Coastal L. 23, 23-24, 25-30 (1990)

Recognition at the North Sea Conferences of the principle of precautionary action was a major negotiation goal of the Federal Republic of Germany. In the Federal Republic the principle of precautionary action ("Vorsorgeprinzip") is considered one of the most important principles of environmental policy, some even consider it the primary one. And there is no doubt that the principle of precautionary action is also a principle of law although there is considerable disagreement as to the scope and the limits of the principle.

The Final Declaration of the Second INSC [International North Sea Conference] . . . [mentions the] principle of precautionary action . . . several times. The first reference might even be considered a definition:

> Accepting that, in order to protect the North Sea from possibly damaging effects of the most dangerous substances, a precautionary approach is necessary which may require action to control inputs of such substances even before a causal link has been established by absolutely clear scientific evidence.

"Precautionary Action": An Elusive Concept

The principle of precautionary action has a variety of aspects which makes it difficult to develop a common understanding. . . . There is controversy at least with regard to the following questions:

- What is the specific content of the principle of precautionary action?
- What are the functions of the principle of precautionary action?
- Does the principle of precautionary action require specific instruments or regulatory approaches, and, if yes, what are these?

Both the status and the content of the principle of precautionary action are still surrounded by uncertainties. . . .

■ REMARKS, PANEL ON NEW DEVELOPMENTS IN INTERNATIONAL ENVIRONMENTAL LAW

Daniel Bodansky

American Society of International Law, Proceedings of the 85th Annual Meeting 413, 414-417 (1991)

. . . First endorsed by the International North Sea Conference in 1987, the precautionary principle is playing an increasingly prominent role in international environmental negotiations. Various versions of the principle have been included in resolutions of the UN Environment Programme, the Paris and Oslo Commissions, the London Dumping Convention, the Caribbean and Mediterranean Regional Seas Programmes, and the Commission for the Conservation of Antarctic Marine Living Resources (CCAMLR), among others. Indeed, so frequent is its invocation that some commentators are even beginning to suggest that the precautionary principle is ripening into a norm of customary international law. . . .

While originating in the context of the marine environment, the precautionary principle is applicable to environmental problems more generally, since all involve uncertainty to some degree. Indeed, the problems of ozone depletion and climate change illustrate that we may have even less scientific knowledge of atmospheric than marine ecosystems, and therefore less ability to predict the effects of discharges into the air than into the water. For this reason, the precautionary principle is now being applied to nonmarine issues such as global warming and is beginning to be framed in general terms. A recent example was the Declaration of the Economic Commission for Europe (ECE) Bergen Conference on Sustainable Development, which stated, "Environmental measures must anticipate, prevent and attack the causes of environmental degradation. Where there are threats of serious or irreversible damage, lack of full scientific certainty should not be used as a reason for postponing measures to prevent environmental degradation."

Although the precautionary principle is often espoused, its parameters and meaning are not altogether clear. In my talk today, I want to explore some of the different meanings of the precautionary principle. I will draw to some extent on examples from U.S. domestic law, since we have a longer and more substantial experience with environmental regulation at the national than at the international level.

The first thing to note is that the precautionary principle is not new. Proponents of the principle often seem to assume it is, and claim, for example, that the United States opposes it. But while the United States may take a dim view of the precautionary principle in international negotiations, it has in fact been utilized extensively in U.S. domestic environmental legislation. The "no discharge" requirement of the 1972 Federal Water Pollution Control Act is one example. It reflects congressional rejection of the assimilative capacity approach. Rather than limit emissions based on their predicted effects on water quality—predictions that have significant and perhaps inherent uncertainties—the Federal Water Pollution Control Act presumes that discharges of pollutants are bad and requires that they be reduced to the limits of available technology.

Even at the international level, the precautionary principle has a longer history than is sometimes realized. Proposals in the 1970s for a moratorium on commercial whaling, for example, reflected a precautionary approach. The moratorium was based not on scientific evidence that continued whaling would endanger whale species, but on uncertainty about whether whaling could safely continue.

The precautionary principle is perhaps a useful corrective to the environmentally reckless policies of some countries. In essence, it says that some types of risks are worse than others, and we should bias our actions to avoid them. The precautionary principle thus represents a rejection of risk-neutrality, which measures risk purely as the product of the magnitude and probability of harm. A risk-neutral person would be indifferent between a 50 percent risk that two dolphins will die and a one-in-a-million risk that a million dolphins will die. Both have an expected average outcome of one dolphin death and both are worth the same level of expenditures to avoid. The precautionary principle, in contrast, says that we should do more—that is, we should take extra precautions—to avoid some types of risks than others.

One variant of the precautionary principle focuses on environmental risks generally. It says that environmental risks are worse than other types of risk and we should bias our actions to prevent them—we should err on the side of the environment. For example, consider the question: How much should we spend to avoid a 10 percent risk of environmental harm that we value at $1 million? A risk-neutral person would simply multiply the $1 million of potential harm by the 10 percent probability and answer: $100,000. But if we are particularly risk-averse with respect to environmental harms, we might be willing to spend far more. This principle that we should err on the side of the environment becomes particularly important if our knowledge is so limited that we cannot even quantify uncertainty, and thus cannot establish a probability distribution of possible outcomes. In such a situation, since we cannot quantify costs and benefits, we must necessarily make a value choice about where to place the risk of error.

A second variant of the precautionary principle focuses not on environmental harms per se, but on the size of the downside risk. According to this view, a small likelihood of catastrophic harm is worse than a substantial likelihood of moderate harm, and we should err on the side of caution by trying to minimize the risk of these catastrophic harms. Thus, the Second World Climate Conference calls for application of the precautionary principle to situations posing a threat of "serious and irreversible harm"—for example, depletion of the ozone layer due to chlorofluorocarbon (CFC) emissions or global warming.

The precautionary principle says that we should err on the side of the environment, or caution, or both. But how should we do so? Generally, the law uses two techniques to resolve uncertainties. First, the burden of proof can be used to allocate the risk of uncertainty. Second, evidentiary presumptions can bridge gaps in our knowledge.

In some cases, our knowledge, though uncertain, defines a probability distribution of possible environmental effects. There may be a 10 percent likelihood, for example, of 5 degrees of global warming over the next 50 years, a 20 percent likelihood of 4 degrees of global warming, and so forth. The burden of proof can then be used to establish the appropriate level of precaution. Do we need a reasonable certainty of global warming before taking regulatory action, or merely a better than 50 percent probability, or only a plausible possibility? If our normal nonprecautionary approach is to use a "more likely than not" standard, we can bias our decision making to avoid environmental or catastrophic harms by easing that burden of proof, or reversing it altogether.

Alternatively, we can deal with uncertainty through evidentiary presumptions, which bridge gaps in our knowledge. This is particularly appropriate when our knowledge is so limited that we cannot even meaningfully quantify uncertainties. In such circumstances, evidentiary presumptions allow us to make qualitative judgments. One example is the presumption that substances that are dangerous in the laboratory are also dangerous in nature. This overcomes all the uncertainties about the actual environmental effects of chemical discharges—uncertainties about their pathways, interactions with other chemicals, and so forth. Or we can make the presumption that correlations imply causality, or that animal tests are indicative of human health effects. These are all means of operationalizing the precautionary principle by building conservative assumptions into our calculations and predictions.

The precautionary principle provides a general orientation to environmental issues. In my view, however, it is far too vague to serve as a regulatory standard. It either does not address—or addresses only in the most general terms—two key questions: First, what level of risk warrants precautionary action? And, second, what level of precaution is warranted and at what price? Indeed, the answers to these questions given by different formulations of the precautionary principle are so varied that it is difficult to speak of a single precautionary principle at all.

Consider the first question: When is it appropriate to take a precautionary approach? As a general matter, this is a function of the level of both risk and uncertainty associated with an activity. We are willing to tolerate less uncertainty about large risks than small. But where do we draw the line between acceptable and unacceptable risks and how certain must we be that that line has been crossed? Thus far, formulations of the precautionary principle have addressed these questions in only a superficial way. The Paris Commission, for example, has adopted the view that "it may be necessary to act upon the scientifically based presumption of a causal link between emissions and effects even if no *definitive* evidence of such a link has been established." Similarly, the Second North Sea Conference Declaration called for controls even before there is "absolutely clear scientific evidence." This shift in the burden of proof is essentially trivial, since "definitive" or "absolutely clear" scientific evidence is rarely if ever available—except, of course for death or taxes. Scientists speak in terms of probabilities not certainties. To say that definitive scientific evidence is not required thus does not represent a true shift in the burden of proof.

Formulations of the precautionary principle that establish evidentiary presumptions have somewhat greater content. The North Sea Conference Declarations, for example, call for application of the precautionary principle to all emissions of substances that are persistent, toxic, and liable bioaccumulate, even when there is no scientific evidence to prove a causal link between emissions of such substances and adverse environmental effects. Under this test, evidence is required only that a substance is persistent, toxic and bioaccumulative, not that actual environmental harm has resulted, since substances with these characteristics are presumed to cause environmental harm. Even making this presumption, however, considerable questions remain—for example, about the necessary levels of persistence and toxicity.

If we were to determine that precautionary action is warranted, we would still have to answer the second question I posed earlier: *What* precautionary measures are warranted? How much should we err on the side of caution? Should we prohibit an activity altogether—should we ban, for example, all use of CFCs, or high seas driftnets, or whaling? Or should we merely take abatement measures and, if so, how do we determine the appropriate amount of abatement? Should we look only at the magnitude and likelihood of the environmental hazards posed by an activity? Or should we also take into account the costs of prevention or abatement? Even if we were to accept the precautionary principle fully, its regulatory implications for such complex problems as acid rain or global warming are by no means clear.

Formulations of the precautionary principle by international organizations have addressed these regulatory questions in only a cursory way. Some commentators have suggested that the precautionary principle implies adoption of a "best available technology" or "clean production" standard. But this is not self-evident.

Moreover, as the last twenty-odd years of experience with the Federal Water Pollution Control Act has shown, it is one thing to establish "no discharge" or "best available technology" standards; it is quite another to determine what these mean in practice. As critics of the act never tire of noting, there is no logical stopping point to the process of defining the "best available technology"; we can always improve technology to remove a little more pollutants if we are willing to pay enough.

All of this is to say that even if we adopt the precautionary principle, we are still left with the problem: *What is* the cautious course of action? In many situations it is not simply a matter of erring on the side of caution; we must decide *which is* the cautious side. For example, U.S. law adopts what is often thought to be a precautionary approach to drug licensing; drugs are presumed to be dangerous and manufacturers must produce substantial evidence about safety before a new drug can be marketed. This may minimize the risks posed by the use of drugs—it may help prevent tragedies such as thalidomide. But it may increase other risks—the risk, for example, that people will die from a disease that is curable by a new but still insufficiently tested drug. In the pollution realm, a precautionary approach to discharges into the marine environment—as advocates of the precautionary principle have urged—may simply transfer those risks to other media. Rather than incinerate hazardous wastes at sea—which has now been banned by the parties to the London Dumping Convention—states may increase incineration on land. Rather than spray with DDT—which causes chronic harms but has a low toxicity—farmers may use other more acutely toxic pesticides. Rather than use CFCs for refrigeration and as solvents, other substances will be used whose environmental consequences are still unknown. The precautionary principle seems to suggest that the choice is between risk and caution; but in fact, often the choice is between one risk and another.

Finally, even if we adopt the precautionary principle—or a policy of risk minimization—this may not achieve the intended result. Many of our most serious current problems were totally unanticipated and would probably not have been prevented even if we had erred on the side of caution. CFCs and DDT, for example, were viewed as environmentally benign when they were developed. The problem was not that states permitted their use in the face of uncertainties, but rather that people were not even focusing on and did not test for the right types of harms. Extensive studies were done of the acute toxicity of DDT, but not of its chronic effects; and the very features that make CFCs so destructive—their persistence and stability—were originally seen as minimizing environmental impacts. To paraphrase an aphorism of Lord Rothschild, "There is no point taking precautionary action until we have compared the risks that worry us with those that don't but should."

It is therefore perhaps appropriate to take a cautious attitude toward the precautionary principle. We may wish to adopt it as a general goal. But it would be a mistake to believe it will resolve the difficult problems of international environmental regulation or prevent new hazards from emerging in the future.

Notes and Questions

1. *Precaution and the Climate Change Convention.* Article 3, paragraph 3 of the United Nations Framework Convention on Climate Change provides in part as follows:

> 3. The Parties should take precautionary measures to anticipate, prevent or minimise the causes of climate change and mitigate its adverse effects. Where there are threats of serious or irreversible damage, lack of full scientific certainty should not be used as a reason for postponing such measures, taking into account that policies and measures to deal with climate change should be cost-effective so as to ensure global benefits at the lowest possible cost. . . .

United Nations Framework Convention on Climate Change, New York, May 9, 1992, *reprinted in* 31 I.L.M. 849 (1992). Is the use of "should" throughout this provision legally significant? Why did the drafters not use "shall"? Do you find it ironic that the Rio Declaration—a nonbinding instrument—uses "shall" in its formulation of the precautionary principle (which is, in pertinent part, nearly identical to that of the Climate Change Convention) while the Convention uses "should"?

In light of Professor Bodansky's observations, is the reference to "full scientific certainty" in the Climate Change Convention appropriate?

2. *Precaution and the Biodiversity Convention.* The Biodiversity Convention does not set forth the precautionary principle in one of its substantive provisions but in its preamble: "*Noting also* that where there is a threat of significant reduction or loss of biological diversity, lack of full scientific certainty should not be used as a reason for postponing measures to avoid or minimize such a threat." Do you believe this point should have been dealt with in one of the articles of the convention rather than its preamble? What is the significance of its treatment in the preamble? How could or should such a preambular provision be used? What are the similarities and differences between this formulation and those of the Rio Declaration and Climate Change Convention?

3. *Other instruments.* The precautionary principle, in one form or another, has been included in a number of other recent instruments. These include Articles 5(c) and 6 of the 1995 Agreement for the Implementation of the Provisions of the United Nations Convention on the Law of the Sea of December 10, 1982 Relating to the Conservation and Management of Straddling Fish Stocks and Highly Migratory Fish Stocks, U.N. Doc. A/CONF.164/37 (1995) (*see also* Annex II to that agreement); Annex II, Article 3(3)(c) of the 1992 Convention for the Protection of the Marine Environment of the North-East Atlantic, 32 I.L.M. 1069 (1992); Article 3, General Obligations, paragraph 1, of the 1996 Protocol to the 1972 IMO London Dumping Convention;[16] paragraph 5 of the Washington Declaration on Protection of the Marine Environment from Land-Based Activities (1995); paragraph 10 of the 1996 Istanbul Declaration; and the 1995 Pan-European Biological and Landscape Diversity Strategy.

4. *Precaution in the World Court.* The precautionary principle was re-

16. Convention on the Prevention of Marine Pollution by Dumping of Wastes and Other Matter, 29 December 1972, 1046 U.N.T.S. 120, 26 UST 2403, 11 I.L.M. 1294 (1973); 1996 Protocol, adopted November 7, 1996, IMO Doc. LC/SM 1/6, November 14, 1996.

cently invoked by New Zealand in its appeal to the International Court of Justice to halt French underground nuclear testing in the South Pacific. *Nuclear Tests Case* (New Zealand v. France), request by New Zealand for an Examination of the Situation, August 21, 1995, at paragraphs 105-108. France responded that the legal status of the principle was "uncertain." ICJ, Verbatim Record, CR 95/20, September 12, 1995, at 71. In his opinion dissenting from the Court's order of September 22, 1995 (declining to reopen the case and thus to consider halting the tests), Judge Weeramantry concluded that the precautionary principle is "gaining increasing support as part of the international law of the environment."

5. *Different precautionary approaches.* The effect of the NAFTA provisions quoted above is to allow a country to take precautionary action in the situation of scientific uncertainty. The Bamako Convention on Hazardous Wastes (Africa), 30 J.L.M 775 (1991), in contrast, requires a country to take action if there is scientific uncertainty. Rio Principle 15 refers only to cost-effective measures and states that lack of certainty shall not be used as a reason for postponing such measures. Can these three be reconciled? Is there a core attribute common to all of them?

6. *The precautionary principle and international law.* Is the precautionary principle a principle of international law? If so, what is its content? Professors Birnie and Boyle conclude as follows:

> Despite its attractions, the great variety of interpretations given to the precautionary principle, and the novel and far-reaching effects of some applications suggest that it is not yet a principle of international law. Difficult questions concerning the point at which it becomes applicable to any given activity remain unanswered and seriously undermine its normative character and practical utility, although support for it does indicate a policy of greater prudence on the part of those states willing to accept it.

Patricia W. Birnie & Alan E. Boyle, International Law and the Environment 98 (1992). Contrast these views with those of Professor Sands, who is more sanguine, although guardedly so, about the status of the principle:

> The legal status of the precautionary principle is evolving. At a minimum, however, there is sufficient evidence of state practice to justify the conclusion that the principle, as elaborated in the Rio Declaration and the Climate Change and Biodiversity Conventions, has now received sufficiently broad support to allow a good argument to be made that it reflects a principle of customary law. That said, the consequences of its application in any potential situation will be influenced by the circumstances of each case.

Philippe Sands, Principles of International Environmental Law 212-213 (1995).

7. *Is it a "principle" or an "approach"?* In Chapter 4 we asked whether it makes any difference whether the precautionary principle is regarded

as a "principle" or an "approach." Is your answer now the same as it was then?

8. *Implementation.* What is the preferable method of implementing the precautionary principle? Some approaches that have been used include requiring use of the best available technology, setting environmental quality objectives, and outright bans on the use or release of specified substances. How do these approaches differ in terms of their effectiveness in promoting environmental quality? In terms of their economic impact? Does the appropriateness of a particular method depend upon how the precautionary principle is stated (e.g., "serious" vs. "irreversible" or "catastrophic" harm; "absolutely clear" scientific evidence vs. likelihood that harm will result).

9. *General principles and regulatory standards.* Do you agree with Professor Bodansky that the precautionary principle "is far too vague to serve as a regulatory standard"? If so, what is its use? Is there value to general principles in international agreements? Should they be avoided, except perhaps in preambles?

10. *The same standards for developing countries?* While the subject is treated separately in section C, below, it is important to bear in mind when considering the foregoing materials the way in which substantive norms of prevention apply or should apply to developing countries. Should these states be given some leeway in complying with their environmental obligations? That is, for example, however "strict" the obligation to prevent harm is in general, should it be less strict when applied to developing countries? Is a "double-standard" a good or a bad thing in this context? What arguments can you think of at this stage for and against applying substantive norms of prevention differently to developing countries than to developed ones?

After having studied the basic decisions bearing upon international environmental problems and the selection of authorities set forth in this section, you should have a good grasp of the fundamental substantive norms guiding the behavior of states in the field. We turn next to an examination of the most fundamental *procedural* norms of international environmental law. Some of these were foreshadowed in the case law, particularly in the *Lake Lanoux* award. While we present substantive and procedural norms separately, there are important links between them. Do you see how the two categories of norms are interlinked?

B. PROCEDURAL NORMS

In the preceding section we examined fundamental substantive norms of international environmental law. In this section we turn to rules intended to establish procedures to implement, or ensure the efficacy of, the substantive norms. These rules take a variety of forms, such as requirements of environmental impact assessment, prior notification of planned activities posing a risk of transfrontier environmental harm, sharing of data and information, consultations, negotiations, and fact-finding. It is sometimes said that these requirements are implicit in substantive norms of prevention—for example, that a state cannot fulfil its obligation to prevent transfrontier environmental harm unless it conducts an environmental impact assessment to determine whether a planned activity will cause such harm, and provides prior notification of its plans to potentially affected states so that they may determine for themselves whether such harm is likely to occur. Procedural norms are also said to be specific applications of the general obligation of states to cooperate with each other. Forms of cooperation may range from providing notice of planned activities, or data on air or water quality, to the establishment of joint institutional mechanisms for the management of shared natural resources.

In this section we deal principally with the most fundamental procedural norms. Procedural norms applicable to environmental emergencies are treated in the following chapter. You will note that although the rules dealt with in the present section are of a fundamental nature, some of them are quite detailed. You should ask yourself throughout the section which of the norms can be said to be binding upon states, either as treaty provisions or as expressions of norms of customary international law. In fact, you might ask yourself initially whether customary international law contains any procedural norms at all. It may surprise you that, as illustrated in the first excerpt, procedural norms are sometimes considerably more controversial than those of substantive law. What is the reason for this? Is it because some of these rules are more concrete than substantive norms, in the sense that they possess a higher degree of "determinacy"?[17] Because they are perceived as placing greater restrictions on a state's sovereignty than substantive norms? Consider these questions as you study the following materials.

1. *Prior Notification and Consultation*

■ THE STOCKHOLM DECLARATION ON THE HUMAN ENVIRONMENT

Louis Sohn
14 Harv. Intl. L.J. 423, 496-502 (1973)

During the preparatory stage of the Conference, Principles 21 and 22 relating to possible damage to the environment and to liability for it were

17. *See* T. Franck, Legitimacy in the International System, 82 Am. J. Intl. L. 705, 713 (1988). Norms lacking in determinacy may not be taken seriously by states and are sometimes "so vague, so uncompelling, that *A*'s obligation and *B*'s right all but elude the mind." P. Weil, Towards Relative Normativity in International Law?, 77 Am. J. Intl. L. 413, 414 (1983).

accompanied by a third principle relating to the duty to provide a proper warning to other states. The Working Group of the Preparatory Committee originally proposed that:

> Relevant information must be supplied by States on activities or developments within their jurisdiction or under their control whenever they believe, or have reason to believe, that such information is needed to avoid the risk of significant adverse effects on the environment in areas beyond their national jurisdiction.

This so-called Principle 20 was the subject of lengthy debates at Stockholm and was forwarded by the Conference to the 27th session of the General Assembly, which incorporated a modified version of it in a separate resolution. . . .

Since the Working Group could not agree on a proper formulation, it presented two complementary texts, one emphasizing the duty to consult and the other empowering a state to demand consultation if another state's activities threaten damage. They read as follows:

> Each State has the duty to undertake international consultations before proceeding with activities which may cause damage to the environment of another State or to the environment of areas beyond the limits of national jurisdiction.
>
> A State having reason to believe that the activities of another State may cause damage to its environment or to the environment of areas beyond the limits of national jurisdiction may request international consultations concerning the envisaged activities.

Some delegations contended that these provisions were not suitable for inclusion in the Declaration because they were either "inherent in the obligations undertaken by Member States in the Charter of the United Nations, and thus redundant," or "were an extension of these obligations which would be outside the scope of a declaratory and inspirational instrument." It would be more appropriate to deal with them through international treaties, which would require, however, detailed negotiations. Others opposed these provisions on substantive grounds, arguing that they "neither had a sound juridical basis nor could be considered politically desirable, at least at the present stage of scientific knowledge of the problems of the environment."

At the second session of the Working Group the Netherlands suggested forthrightly that:

> States shall inform other States directly concerned or appropriate international organizations on any envisaged activity which may cause damage to the environment of those States or of areas beyond the limits of national

> jurisdiction; in appropriate cases States shall enter into international consultations.

A more limited proposal was made by Australia, which, however, contained the additional obligation to engage in a "collaborative investigation." Brazil, Egypt, and Yugoslavia proposed an even vaguer statement, stressing the need to "supply the relevant information on facts that, in the view of those responsible for them, may provide serious environmental damage beyond national jurisdiction." As revised later, in cooperation with Costa Rica and Zambia, this proposal was accepted by the Working Group and became Principle 20 of the Preparatory Committee draft.

At Stockholm a group of African countries suggested a strengthening of the obligation by deleting the words "they believe, or have reason to believe that" and by omitting the word "significant." Argentina would also have strengthened the obligation by adding the following additional sentence:

> This information must also be supplied at the request of any of the Parties concerned, within appropriate time, and with such data as may be available and as would enable the above-mentioned Parties to inform and judge by themselves of the nature and probable effects of such activities.

On the other hand, Brazil suggested the following limitation:

> No State is obliged to supply information under conditions that, in its founded judgment, may jeopardize its national security, economic development or its national efforts to improve environment.

The Conference decided to refer the text and the proposed amendments for the consideration of the General Assembly in the hope that a consensus would emerge by the time the General Assembly discussed that principle.

Brazil, which was the main opponent in Stockholm of adopting a principle which might be misused for placing obstacles in the path of development, took the lead at the General Assembly in presenting a draft resolution which was co-sponsored by a large group of developing countries and a few developed countries. It was proposed that the General Assembly adopt the following resolution:

> The General Assembly, . . .
>
> Bearing in mind that, in exercising their sovereignty over their natural resources, States must seek, through effective bilateral and multilateral cooperation or through regional machinery, to preserve and improve the environment,

> 1. Emphasizes that, in the exploration, exploitation and development of their natural resources, States must not produce significant harmful effects in zones situated outside their national jurisdiction;
>
> 2. Recognizes that co-operation between States in the field of the environment, including co-operation towards the implementation of principles 21 and 22 of the Declaration of the United Nations Conference on the Human Environment, will be effectively achieved if official and public knowledge is provided of the technical data relating to the work to be carried out by States within their national jurisdiction with a view to avoiding significant harm that may occur in the human environment of the adjacent area;
>
> 3. Recognizes further that the technical data referred to in the preceding paragraph will be given and received in the best spirit of co-operation and good neighbourliness, without this being construed as enabling each State to delay or impede the programmes and projects of exploration, exploitation and development of the natural resources of the States in whose territories such programmes and projects are carried out.

Some states were, however, opposed to the revival of Principle 20, arguing, inter alia, that it was for each state to decide the kind of information it wished to transmit. Canada attempted to revise the proposed resolution, because it believed that the proposal made an attempt to reinterpret Principles 21 and 22 of the Stockholm Declaration.

. . . The Mexican representative also objected to the draft, as it could be interpreted to mean that "the responsibility to ensure protection of the environment, embodied in principles 21 and 22, could be met by merely informing neighbouring countries," while Mexico's view was that "it was the responsibility of all States to avoid activities within their jurisdiction or control which might cause damage to the environment beyond their national frontiers and to repair any damage caused." The New Zealand representative thought that the draft severely weakened Principles 21 and 22, because the words "significant harmful effects" and "significant harm" might give rise to endless debates about what was harmful and what was significant. There was also the implication that the duty to cooperate can be effectively fulfilled by merely exchanging information. The Netherlands representative did not consider the draft satisfactory since "a State whose activities had harmful effects on the environment outside its national jurisdiction was responsible for providing the other States concerned with as much advance information as possible." The draft was also restricted to harm to "adjacent areas," though damage sometimes might occur in other areas as well.

After the delegates of Brazil, Argentina, and the United States made clear that the draft was not intended to derogate from, modify, weaken, or limit Principles 21 and 22, Canada agreed to withdraw her two amendments. Nevertheless, to make doubly sure, Australia, Canada, Mexico, New Zealand, and Panama introduced a supplementary resolution declaring that "no resolution adopted at the twenty-seventh session of the General

Assembly can affect principles 21 and 22 of the Declaration." When it came to voting, the spirit of compromise prevailed; the first resolution was adopted by 114 votes to none, with 10 abstentions, and the supplementary resolution was accepted by 111 votes to none, with 11 abstentions.

The General Assembly, having informally agreed not to examine the substance of the Declaration and not to entertain any amendments to it, did not even contemplate the possibility of adding the principle embodied in the first resolution to the Declaration. Nevertheless one might consider, for all practical purposes, the new principle has become Principle 22A (or 22 bis, should the European nomenclature be used). It balances neatly the desire of some states to be informed in time of any activities within the territory of a state so that steps might be taken to avoid significant harm in adjacent areas, with the firm conviction of other states that such information should not be used by a state to delay or impede the development of natural resources in another state. As to whether this line can be drawn in practice, only future experience in applying this resolution will tell. Nevertheless, however vaguely stated, this principle provides the legal basis for a state which feels threatened to require the state in which a dangerous activity is conducted to provide the other state with the relevant technical data. This is certainly a step in the right direction. Like the requirement for an environmental impact statement in some national legal systems, the fact that there is a requirement to provide the technical data might result in the abandonment of some marginal projects.

Notes and Questions

1. *A Darwinian dynamic?* Professor Sohn's account provides a dramatic illustration of the dynamics of international negotiations. Why was the original proposal of the Working Group so controversial? What, specifically, would it have called for? Was that proposal consistent with the statements of the *Lake Lanoux* tribunal concerning prior notification?

2. *You go first.* Is there any real difference between requiring a state planning new activities to consult with other potentially affected states and permitting the latter to request consultations concerning such activities? If not, why did the Working Group find it necessary to present "two complementary texts?" You are counsel to the state planning the activities: Which version would you advise that state to support?

Why did the resolution embodying "Principle 22A" not require the planning and potentially affected states to enter into consultations? Do you think the reasons were substantive (e.g., there is no need for consultations so long as the planning state provides prior notification) or more political (e.g., requiring the planning state to enter into consultations concerning planned activities within its borders would constitute an infringement of its sovereignty)?

3. *Case study: The Itaipú project.* The effect that a controversy between two states can have on the shaping of international law is starkly illustrated by the background of the negotiations over "Principle 20." In the early 1970s, Brazil and Argentina became involved in a controversy concerning their respective plans to construct separate dams on the Paraná River.[18] The Paraná forms the border between Brazil and Paraguay and, farther downstream, between Paraguay and Argentina; thus, Brazil is an upper riparian state on the river. Argentina was concerned that Brazil's dam (at Itaipú) would impair the effectiveness of the Argentine project and took the position that Brazil was required under international law to provide it with technical information concerning the plans and to enter into consultations so that Argentina's concerns could be taken into account.

> Brazil refused, however, to acknowledge the existence of such an obligation and the dispute between Argentina and Brazil on this question even made it impossible during the 1972 UN Conference on the Human Environment to reach consensus on Principle 20 of the Draft Declaration on the Human Environment, which referred to the obligation of States to supply information on activities within their territory which could have significant adverse effects on the environment of other States.

J. Lammers, Pollution of International Watercourses 295 (1984). It was only because Brazil and Argentina were able to reach agreement after the Stockholm Conference on the principle of prior notification that the General Assembly was able to adopt "Principle 22A." *Id.* While the agreement later came unraveled, Argentina and Brazil ultimately resolved their differences. Today, Brazil's Itaipú dam is one of the largest in the world.

4. *The steamroller gambit.* What if the planning state provides prior notification but ultimately decides to proceed with the project over the objections of the potentially affected state? Would this constitute a "breach" of the planning state's "obligations" under "Principle 22A," principles of general international law reflected in the *Lake Lanoux* award, or other principles of international law? Would it matter how long the planning state waited after the notification? Assume it waited a year; would the legal position of either of the parties be affected if it could be shown that the planning state always intended to go forward with the project as originally planned? Is this what the Mexican representative was worried about?

5. *The approach of the UN Convention on International Watercourses.* The recently adopted United Nations Convention on International Watercourses, considered later in this section, takes a somewhat different approach to the problem of prior notification. It provides that a riparian state

18. For a fuller account of the controversy, *see* J. Lammers, Pollution of International Watercourses 294-295 (1984).

must provide prior notification of planned activities that may adversely affect other riparian states. It then lays down specific requirements concerning, inter alia, the reply to the notification, the effect of a failure to reply within six months, consultations, and the period during which the planning state must suspend the implementation of the project. Which approach is preferable? That of "Principle 22A" is more general and flexible, allowing it to be adapted to suit a variety of circumstances, but that of the convention is considerably more concrete. What are some of the other strengths and weaknesses of each? If you were advising the potentially affected state, which approach would you prefer?

6. *"Damage" vs. "harm."* While Principles 21 and 22 of the Stockholm Declaration refer only to "damage to the environment" and "environmental damage," respectively, "Principle 22A" employs the expressions "significant harmful effects" and "significant harm." Was the New Zealand representative right that the latter terms "severely weaken[] Principles 21 and 22?" Incidentally, is it factual or legal harm that's prohibited? Is there any difference?

■ RIO DECLARATION ON ENVIRONMENT AND DEVELOPMENT, PRINCIPLE 19

Adopted by the United Nations Conference on Environment and Development, June 14, 1992
U.N. Doc. A/CONF.151/5/Rev.1, June 13, 1992,* reprinted in *31 I.L.M. 874 (1992)

Principle 19

States shall provide prior and timely notification and relevant information to potentially affected States on activities that may have a significant adverse transboundary environmental effect and shall consult with those States at an early stage and in good faith.

Notes and Questions

1. *Parsing the principles.* Compare Principle 19 with "Principle 22A." Is one more stringent than the other?

2. *The benefit of hindsight.* Does the fact that Principle 19 forms an integral part of the Rio Declaration confirm that "Principle 22A" was in fact accepted by the world community as a principle that was on a par with those contained in the Stockholm Declaration?

3. *Improvement with age?* The straightforward manner in which Principle 19 is formulated suggests that the requirements of prior notification

and consultation it embodies were either uncontroversial or at least not nearly so problematic as they had been at Stockholm. Why might this be?

4. *Problem.* State A is planning a project that may have an adverse effect on State B. What if State A provides prior notification and enters into consultations with State B, but ultimately decides to proceed with the project over the objections of State B? Would this constitute a "breach" of State A's "obligations" under Principle 19, principles of general international law reflected in the *Lake Lanoux* award or other principles of international law? Would it matter how long the consultations lasted? Assume the consultations lasted a year; would the legal position of either of the parties be affected if it could be shown that the planning state always intended to go forward with the project as originally planned? Is this what the Mexican representative was worried about in the discussions relating to what eventually became "Principle 22A" of the Stockholm Declaration? Compare your answers to these questions to the ones you gave to the questions posed in note 4 following the excerpts from the Sohn article, above.

■ GENERAL PRINCIPLES CONCERNING NATURAL RESOURCES AND ENVIRONMENTAL INTERFERENCES, ARTICLES 15, 16, AND 17

Final Report of the Experts Group on Environmental Law on Legal Principles for Environmental Protection and Sustainable Development Experts Group on Environmental Law of the World Commission on Environment and Development (Brundtland Commission), Environmental Protection and Sustainable Development 29-30 (1987)

Article 15
Exchange of Information

States shall provide the other States concerned upon their request and in a timely manner with all relevant and reasonably available data concerning a transboundary natural resource, including the uses made of such a resource and transboundary interferences with them, or concerning a transboundary environmental interference.

Article 16
Prior Notice of Planned Activities, Environmental Impact Assessments

1. States planning to carry out or permit activities which may entail a transboundary interference or a significant risk thereof with the reasonable and equitable use of a transboundary natural resource or which may entail a transboundary environmental interference or a significant risk thereof causing substantial harm in an area under national jurisdiction of another State or in an area beyond the limits of national jurisdiction shall give timely notice to the States concerned. In particular, they shall on their own initiative

or upon request of the other States concerned provide such relevant information as will permit those other States to make an assessment of the probable effects of the planned activities.

2. When a State has reasonable grounds for believing that planned activities may have the effects referred to in Paragraph 1, it shall make an assessment of those effects before carrying out or permitting the planned activities.

Article 17
Consultations

Consultations shall be held in good faith, upon request, at an early stage between, on the one hand, States whose reasonable and equitable use of a transboundary natural resource is or may be affected by a transboundary interference or whose environmental interests are or may be affected by a transboundary environmental interference and, on the other hand, States in whose area under national jurisdiction or under whose jurisdiction such a transboundary interference originates or may originate in connection with activities carried on or contemplated therein or thereunder.

Notes and Questions

1. *Considering congruence.* Article 16 deals with prior notification of planned activities that may harm other states and environmental impact assessment. How does the provision on prior notification (paragraph 1) differ, if at all, from "Principle 22A" discussed in the Sohn excerpts, above? From Principle 19 of the Rio Declaration?

2. *Considering consultations.* Article 17 addresses the subject of consultations. Does this article apply only to the situations addressed in Article 16, paragraph 1, or does it apply to other situations as well? If the latter, what other situations? Should a requirement of consultations have been included in Article 16, as was done in the case of Principle 19 of the Rio Declaration? Finally, are there sound reasons of policy for requiring the planning state to enter into consultations only "upon request"? Are there activities that could fall through the cracks of the system established by Articles 16 and 17? For example, are there activities as to which the situs state need provide no notification, yet which pose a risk of causing transfrontier environmental harm, a risk that is unknown to the potentially harmed state? Does Article 17 cover such a situation?

3. *Data sharing.* Why is the obligation to provide data under Article 15 only triggered by another state's request? Should states not be obligated to share data and information concerning transboundary natural resources even in the absence of such a request? What are the difficulties with each of these approaches? The 1997 UN Convention on International Watercourses, excerpted below, requires in Article 9 that data and information

relating to shared watercourses be exchanged on a *regular* basis. Can you see why this might be appropriate for watercourses but perhaps not so important in other situations?

■ RULES OF INTERNATIONAL LAW APPLICABLE TO TRANSFRONTIER POLLUTION, ARTICLES 7 AND 8

International Law Association (ILA)
Report of the Sixtieth Conference, Montreal, 1982, 158, at 171, 175 (1982)

Article 7 (Prior Notice)

(1) States planning to carry out activities which might entail significant risk of transfrontier pollution shall give early notice to States likely to be affected. In particular they shall on their own initiative or upon request of the potentially affected States, communicate such pertinent information as will permit the recipient to make an assessment of the probable effects of the planned activities.

(2) In order to appraise whether a planned activity implies a significant risk of transfrontier pollution, States should make environmental assessments before carrying out such activities.

Article 8 (Consultations)

(1) Upon request of a potentially affected State, the State furnishing the information should enter into consultations on transfrontier pollution problems connected with the planned activities and pursue such consultations in good faith and over a reasonable period of time.

(2) States are under an obligation to enter into consultations whenever transfrontier pollution problems arise in connection with the equitable utilization of a shared natural resource as envisaged in Art. 5.

Notes and Questions

1. *Pursuing the "hobgoblin of little minds"*[19]*(?)* Are the ILA's procedural rules consistent with the others set forth in this chapter?

2. *Parsing the paragraphs.* Is it significant that paragraph 2 of Article 7 uses the term "should" in relation to environmental impact assessments, while paragraph 1 of that article provides that states "shall" give early notice of planned activities? Notice also that Article 8 provides in paragraph

19. [With apologies to Ralph Waldo Emerson, who said "A foolish consistency is the hobgoblin of little minds. . . ."—Eds.]

1 that states "should" enter into consultations "on transfrontier pollution problems connected with the planned activities," but that under paragraph 2 of that article they "are under an obligation to" (i.e., "shall") enter into consultations "whenever transfrontier pollution problems arise in connection with the equitable utilization of a shared natural resource. . . ." Why the difference in treatment? Article 5 provides as follows:

Article 5 (Shared Natural Resources)

> If the utilization of a shared natural resource in the territory of a State causes transfrontier pollution and conflicts with the competing utilization of this resource in the territory of another State, each State sharing the natural resource is entitled within its territory to a reasonable and equitable share of the utilization.

ILA, Report of the 60th Conference, at 168. This article would presumably apply, e.g., to cases in which two or more states utilize a common airshed or watershed.

Problem. Can you think of a good reason why there should be a legal obligation to enter into consultations where pollution of a river flowing from state A into state B interferes with B's use of the water for domestic purposes, but not where sulphur dioxide fumes from a planned copper smelter in state A would cause personal injury and property damage in state B? Does the distinction simply lie in the difference between actual and threatened harm? If so, is such a distinction a sound one? What about the case where the smelter in state A commences operation and causes harm of the kind described in state B: Is A obligated to consult with B about the pollution damage under the ILA's articles?

3. *Trees don't "use" air but people do—?* The commentary to Article 8 states as follows:

> As for cases of air pollution, . . . it is not possible to affirm the existence of an international duty to enter into consultations, due to the lack of sufficient State practice on the basis of a legal conviction. . . . Whenever transfrontier pollution can be categorized as a use of a transfrontier medium, to which the rule of equitable apportionment . . . applies, States are under an obligation to enter into consultation.

No authority is cited for this proposition. Is the proposition itself tenable? Is it something any good lawyer could plead around? The commentary to Article 5 states: "it cannot be said that air is, e.g., used for growing forests, so that the destroying of forests by sulfuric fumes like in the Trail Smelter Case is to be regulated according to the rule of Article 3, para. 1 [which prohibits the causing of transfrontier pollution harm]." Does this explanation strengthen the case for a distinction between transfrontier air pollution causing harm (no duty to consult) and transfrontier air pollution interfering with the use of air in the neighboring state?

■ UNITED NATIONS CONVENTION ON THE LAW OF THE NON-NAVIGATIONAL USES OF INTERNATIONAL WATERCOURSES

U.N. Doc. A/RES/51/229, July 8, 1997, **reprinted in** *36 I.L.M 700 (1997), selected provisions*

Part III. Planned Measures

Article 11
Information Concerning Planned Measures

Watercourse States shall exchange information and consult each other and, if necessary, negotiate on the possible effects of planned measures on the condition of an international watercourse.

Article 12
Notification Concerning Planned Measures with Possible Adverse Effects

Before a watercourse State implements or permits the implementation of planned measures which may have a significant adverse effect upon other watercourse States, it shall provide those States with timely notification thereof. Such notification shall be accompanied by available technical data and information, including the results of any environmental impact assessment, in order to enable the notified States to evaluate the possible effects of the planned measures.

Article 13
Period for Reply to Notification

Unless otherwise agreed:

(a) A watercourse State providing a notification under article 12 shall allow the notified States a period of six months within which to study and evaluate the possible effects of the planned measures and to communicate the findings to it;

(b) This period shall, at the request of a notified State for which the evaluation of the planned measures poses special difficulty, be extended for a period of six months.

Article 14
Obligations of the Notifying State During the Period for Reply

During the period referred to in article 13, the notifying State:

(a) Shall cooperate with the notified States by providing them, on request, with any additional data and information that is available and necessary for an accurate evaluation; and

(b) Shall not implement or permit the implementation of the planned measures without the consent of the notified States.

Article 15
Reply to Notification

The notified States shall communicate their findings to the notifying State as early as possible within the period applicable pursuant to article 13. If a notified State finds that implementation of the planned measures would be inconsistent with the provisions of articles 5 or 7, it shall attach to its finding a documented explanation setting forth the reasons for the finding.

Article 16
Absence of Reply to Notification

1. If, within the period applicable pursuant to article 13, the notifying State receives no communication under article 15, it may, subject to its obligations under articles 5 and 7, proceed with the implementation of the planned measures, in accordance with the notification and any other data and information provided to the notified States.

2. Any claim to compensation by a notified State which has failed to reply within the period applicable pursuant to article 13 may be offset by the costs incurred by the notifying State for action undertaken after the expiration of the time for a reply which would not have been undertaken if the notified State had objected within that period.

Article 17
Consultations and Negotiations Concerning Planned Measures

1. If a communication is made under article 15 that implementation of the planned measures would be inconsistent with the provisions of articles 5 or 7, the notifying State and the State making the communication shall enter into consultations and, if necessary, negotiations with a view to arriving at an equitable resolution of the situation.

2. The consultations and negotiations shall be conducted on the basis that each State must in good faith pay reasonable regard to the rights and legitimate interests of the other State.

3. During the course of the consultations and negotiations, the notifying State shall, if so requested by the notified State at the time it makes the communication, refrain from implementing or permitting the implementation of the planned measures for a period of six months unless otherwise agreed.

Article 18
Procedures in the Absence of Notification

1. If a watercourse State has reasonable grounds to believe that another watercourse State is planning measures that may have a significant adverse

effect upon it, the former State may request the latter to apply the provisions of article 12. The request shall be accompanied by a documented explanation setting forth its grounds.

2. In the event that the State planning the measures nevertheless finds that it is not under an obligation to provide a notification under article 12, it shall so inform the other State, providing a documented explanation setting forth the reasons for such finding. If this finding does not satisfy the other State, the two States shall, at the request of that other State, promptly enter into consultations and negotiations in the manner indicated in paragraphs 1 and 2 of article 17.

3. During the course of the consultations and negotiations, the State planning the measures shall, if so requested by the other State at the time it requests the initiation of consultations and negotiations, refrain from implementing or permitting the implementation of those measures for a period of six months unless otherwise agreed.

Article 19
Urgent Implementation of Planned Measures

1. In the event that the implementation of planned measures is of the utmost urgency in order to protect public health, public safety or other equally important interests, the State planning the measures may, subject to articles 5 and 7, immediately proceed to implementation, notwithstanding the provisions of article 14 and paragraph 3 of article 17.

2. In such case, a formal declaration of the urgency of the measures shall be communicated without delay to the other watercourse States referred to in article 12 together with the relevant data and information.

3. The State planning the measures shall, at the request of any of the States referred to in paragraph 2, promptly enter into consultations and negotiations with it in the manner indicated in paragraphs 1 and 2 of article 17.

Notes and Questions

1. *The UN Convention on International Watercourses.* The Convention on the Law of the Non-Navigational Uses of International Watercourses was adopted by the United Nations General Assembly on May 21, 1997. The convention was negotiated by government delegations to the UN on the basis of a set of draft articles prepared over more than 20 years by the International Law Commission of the United Nations (ILC). Additional background information on the convention and references to further relevant material are provided in Chapter 16. The convention is the only universal agreement on the subject of the non-navigational uses of international watercourses. While not yet in force, it is nonetheless an important instrument. Many of the provisions of the convention reflect existing international law. The convention will almost certainly influence future bilateral and regional treaties on the subject; the ILC's articles on which the Convention is based already have done so.

2. *The status of the prior notification principle.* With the inclusion in the convention by the ILC and the General Assembly of a regime of prior notification of planned projects, can this procedure now be said to be part of international law, if it wasn't already? Or should any normative force of the principle be confined to the field of international watercourses?

3. *The devil was not in the details.* Why do you suppose the procedures in Part III of the convention are so detailed? Why not just stop with Article 11? (This had been the proposal of the then-Soviet member of the International Law Commission, who drafted the original version of Article 11.) Could the level of detail of Part III provide some comfort to planning or potentially affected states, or both?

4. *The balancing act.* Do the provisions of Part III strike an even balance between the interests of notifying (usually upstream) and notified (usually downstream) states?

5. *The Rolling Stones gambit.* Can the notifying state simply go through the motions of complying with Part III's procedures, singing "Time Is On My Side," and go ahead with its project after all applicable time periods have expired? If so, how would you draft a provision or set of provisions that would check such a temptation?

2. *Environmental Impact Assessment and Planning*

■ FINAL REPORT OF THE EXPERTS GROUP ON ENVIRONMENTAL LAW ON LEGAL PRINCIPLES FOR ENVIRONMENTAL PROTECTION AND SUSTAINABLE DEVELOPMENT, ARTICLES 5, 7, 16, AND 18

Experts Group on Environmental Law of the World Commission on Environment and Development (Brundtland Commission), Environmental Protection and Sustainable Development (1987)

Article 5
Assessment of Planned Activities

States planning to carry out or permit activities which may significantly affect a natural resource or the environment shall make or require an assessment of their effects before carrying out or permitting the planned activities.

Article 7
Planning and Implementation of Development Activities

1. States shall ensure that the conservation of natural resources and the environment is treated as an integral part of the planning and implementation of development activities. Particular attention shall be paid to environmental

problems arising in developing countries and to the need to incorporate environmental considerations in all development assistance programmes.

2. States shall make available to other States, and especially to developing countries, upon their request and under agreed terms scientific and technical information and expertise, results of research programmes, training opportunities and specialized equipment and facilities which are needed by such other States to promote rational use of natural resources, and the environment or to prevent or abate interference with natural resources or the environment, in particular in cases of environmental emergencies.

Article 16
Prior Notice of Planned Activities, Environmental Impact Assessments

[This article is set forth under section 1, Prior Notification and Consultation, above.]

Article 18
Co-operative Arrangements for Environmental Assessment and Protection

In order to maintain or attain a reasonable and equitable use of a transboundary natural resource or to prevent or abate transboundary environmental interferences or significant risks thereof the States concerned shall, inter alia:

(a) establish co-ordinated or unified systems for the collection and dissemination of data relating to the transboundary natural resource or for regular observation of transboundary environmental interferences;

(b) co-ordinate and, where appropriate, jointly undertake scientific or technical studies to that effect;

(c) establish by common agreement specific environmental standards, in particular environmental quality standards and emission standards;

(d) jointly establish or resort to an institutional mechanism or other appropriate arrangements.

RIO DECLARATION ON ENVIRONMENT AND DEVELOPMENT, PRINCIPLE 17

Adopted by the United Nations Conference on Environment and Development, June 14, 1992

PRINCIPLE 17

Environmental impact assessment, as a national instrument, shall be undertaken for proposed activities that are likely to have a significant adverse impact on the environment and are subject to a decision of a competent national authority.

■ UN ECE CONVENTION ON ENVIRONMENTAL IMPACT ASSESSMENT IN A TRANSBOUNDARY CONTEXT (ESPOO CONVENTION)

Feb. 25, 1991, U.N. Doc. E/ECE/1250,* reprinted in *30 I.L.M. 800 (1991)

[Review this convention as reprinted in I.L.M., available in law libraries, or in any set of documents required by your professor.]

■ RULES OF INTERNATIONAL LAW APPLICABLE TO TRANSFRONTIER POLLUTION, ARTICLE 7(2)

International Law Association (ILA)
Report of the Sixtieth Conference, Montreal, 1982

[This provision is set forth under section 1, Prior Notification and Consultation, above.]

Notes and Questions

1. *The impact assessment requirement.* Article 5 of the Experts Group Report deals with environmental impact assessment. Compare Article 5 with Principle 17 of the Rio Declaration on Environment and Development. Which formulation of the requirement of environmental impact assessment is preferable? With regard to both formulations, how does a state know in advance whether a proposed activity "may significantly affect a natural resource or the environment," or is "likely to have a significant adverse impact on the environment"? Isn't one of the main purposes of impact assessment precisely to make these determinations? How would you formulate the requirement?

2. *The Espoo Convention.* The Espoo Convention was adopted and signed by 26 states and the European Community. (Under Article 16, it is open for signature only by member states of the Economic Commission for Europe (ECE), states having consultative status with the ECE and the European Union.) It entered into force on September 10, 1997, in accordance with its Article 18(1).

3. *Espoo vs. other instruments.* What do you believe to be the most significant differences between the approach of the Espoo Convention and the systems embodied in the other instruments we have considered? Which is preferable? Why?

4. *Public participation or meddling by aliens?* Consider the requirement of Espoo's Article 2, paragraph 6 that "the public in areas likely to be affected" be provided an opportunity "to participate in relevant environmental impact assessment procedures" on an equal footing with the public of the state of origin. Is this a realistic requirement? Why would a state of origin want to allow members of the public in another state to participate in its environmental impact assessment (EIA) procedures? What if a state of origin makes no provision for the participation of *its* citizens and residents in such procedures?

5. *A query re inquiries.* What is the "inquiry commission" envisioned in Article 3, paragraph 7 and Appendix IV of the Espoo Convention? What are the advantages and disadvantages of such bodies? Why not just require that any difference be submitted to binding arbitration or adjudication?

6. *Whose side is time on?* The final paragraph of Espoo's Article 5 makes the time frame within which consultations are to take place—and, implicitly, the period during which the state of origin must suspend initiation of the proposed activity—dependent upon the agreement of the parties. How do you believe this will work in practice? Would it have been preferable to provide expressly that the State of origin must wait (1) a "reasonable" period of time, or (2) a fixed period, such as six months, before implementing the proposed activity?

7. *Objectors and steamrollers.* What happens under Espoo when the affected state objects to the implementation of the proposed activity? Is this situation adequately provided for? If you were representing the affected state, would you believe Article 6, paragraph 1, provided sufficient protection for that state? What recourse does the affected state have under the convention if the state of origin proceeds with the project over its objections?

8. *Transboundary assessments under NEPA.* A contentious issue for many years has been whether assessments of transboundary impacts should be conducted as part of the EIA process under the National Environmental Policy Act (NEPA) of 1969. On July 1, 1997, the Council on Environmental Quality, the presidential body charged with overseeing the implementation of NEPA, issued Guidance on NEPA Analyses for Transboundary Impacts. In this guidance, CEQ states that NEPA requires analysis and disclosure of transboundary impacts of proposed federal actions taking place within the United States. United States courts had already assumed that NEPA requires analysis of transboundary impacts. Swinomish Tribal Community v. Federal Energy Regulatory Commission, 627 F.2d 499 (D.C. Cir. 1980) (allowing Canadian intervenors to challenge the adequacy of an environmental impact statement (EIS) relating to raising the height of the Ross Dam in Washington State); and Wilderness Society v. Morton, 463 F.2d 1261 (D.C. Cir. 1972) (granting intervenor status to Canadian environmental organizations challenging the adequacy of the trans-Alaska pipeline EIS). In the

guidance CEQ refers, inter alia, to the *Trail Smelter* Arbitration, Principle 21 of the Stockholm Declaration, and Principle 2 of the Rio Declaration as reflecting binding customary international law. It also refers to the "duty to give notice to others to avoid or avert such harm" and states that transboundary EIAs are an appropriate means of implementing these principles.

9. *A North American Agreement on TEIA?* Article 10(7) of the North American Agreement on Environmental Cooperation, the NAFTA environmental side agreement, provides for conclusion of an agreement on transboundary environmental impact assessment by the three parties to the NAFTA (Canada, Mexico, and the United States). At this writing, negotiations on such an agreement are under way.

3. Cooperation

■ GENERAL PRINCIPLES CONCERNING NATURAL RESOURCES AND ENVIRONMENTAL INTERFERENCES, ARTICLES 8, 14, AND 18

Final Report of the Experts Group on Environmental Law on Legal Principles for Environmental Protection and Sustainable Development, above, at 27, 29, 31

Article 8
General Obligation to Co-Operate

States shall co-operate in good faith with other States or through competent international organizations in the implementation of the provisions of the preceding articles.

Article 14
General Obligation to Co-Operate on Transboundary Environmental Problems

1. States shall co-operate in good faith with the other States concerned in maintaining or attaining for each of them a reasonable and equitable use of a transboundary natural resource or in preventing or abating a transboundary environmental interference or significant risk thereof.

2. The co-operation shall, as much as possible, be aimed at arriving at an optimal use of the transboundary natural resource or at maximizing the effectiveness of measures to prevent or abate a transboundary environmental interference.

Article 18
Co-operative Arrangements for Environmental Assessment and Protection

[This article is set forth under section 2, Environmental Impact Assessment and Planning, above.]

■ UNITED NATIONS CONVENTION ON THE NON-NAVIGATIONAL USES OF INTERNATIONAL WATERCOURSES, ARTICLE 8

U.N. Doc. A/RES/51/229, July 8, 1997, **reprinted in** *36 I.L.M. 700 (1997)*

Article 8
General Obligation to Co-operate

1. Watercourse States shall cooperate on the basis of sovereign equality, territorial integrity, mutual benefit and good faith in order to attain optimal utilization and adequate protection of an international watercourse.

2. In determining the manner of such cooperation, watercourse States may consider the establishment of joint mechanisms or commissions, as deemed necessary by them, to facilitate cooperation on relevant measures and procedures in the light of experience gained through cooperation in existing joint mechanisms and commissions in various regions.

Notes and Questions

1. *The meaning of "cooperation."* How is it possible to determine when a state has breached its obligation to "cooperate"? Can international law really force states to cooperate? Is Israel obligated to cooperate with Jordan concerning allocation of Jordan River waters or with Syria concerning the headwaters of the Jordan? The United States with Canada concerning acid rain? If so, what form should that cooperation take? Is it possible to define the meaning of "cooperation" in the context of international environmental problems in general, or does the definition vary according to the problem and the states concerned?

Principle 24 of the 1972 Stockholm Declaration on the Human Environment provides as follows:

> International matters concerning the protection and improvement of the environment should be handled in a co-operative spirit by all countries, big or small, on an equal footing. Co-operation through multilateral or bilateral arrangements or other appropriate means is essential to effectively control, prevent, reduce and eliminate adverse environmental effects resulting from activities conducted in all spheres, in such a way that due account is taken of the sovereignty and interests of all States.

International cooperation also figures prominently in the Rio Declaration, above, especially Principle 7:

> States shall cooperate in a spirit of global partnership to conserve, protect and restore the health and integrity of the Earth's ecosystem. In view of

> the different contributions to global environmental degradation, States have common but differentiated responsibilities. The developed countries acknowledge the responsibility that they bear in the international pursuit of sustainable development in view of the pressures their societies place on the global environment and of the technologies and financial resources they command.

We will take up the concept of "common but differentiated responsibility" in section C, below. For now we may note that other United Nations instruments stressing the importance of cooperation in this area include: General Assembly (UNGA) Resolution 2995 of December 15, 1972 on Cooperation between States in the Field of the Environment; and UNGA Resolution 37/7 of October 28, 1982 on the World Charter for Nature, para. 21. Is the "obligation" to cooperate a real obligation or simply a way for states to make it appear that they are accepting certain very fundamental and important obligations when in fact they are not, and will not? If it is a real obligation, we must return to the question asked at the beginning of this note.

2. *The transplantability of "cooperative arrangements."* The Experts Group's Article 18 requires states to establish "cooperative arrangements." In Article 8 of the Watercourse Convention this is, in effect, recommended. A highly successful example of such an arrangement is the International Joint Commission (IJC) established by the United States and Canada under their 1909 Boundary Waters Treaty. The IJC is discussed in the note following the *Trail Smelter* award in Chapter 6, above. The United States and Canada have a long history of good and peaceful relations. But how frequently is this the case in other parts of the world? How often do conditions prevail that would necessitate, or even permit, the establishment of such "arrangements"? Is it realistic to expect states the world over to follow the examples of successful arrangements of this kind in other regions, such as that of the IJC? But perhaps this is a short-sighted perspective on the issue. Perhaps what the Experts Group has in mind is that escalating competition for increasingly scarce natural resources will *necessitate* the establishment of cooperative arrangements in order to preserve environmental security and avoid outbreaks of violence. Or perhaps cooperative arrangements are—or soon will be—necessary to the effective implementation of states' obligations to avoid transboundary harm, to use shared resources in an equitable and reasonable manner, and the like. Which of these explanations for, or justifications of, Article 18, if any, seems most plausible to you?

3. *Modalities of cooperation.* Interestingly, the second paragraph of Article 8 of the Watercourses Convention was added to the ILC's one-paragraph text by government delegates during the negotiation of the Convention. Why do you suppose the ILC had not included a similar paragraph? Why might it have been added by governments?

4. Environmental Legislation

RIO DECLARATION ON ENVIRONMENT AND DEVELOPMENT, PRINCIPLE 11

Adopted by the United Nations Conference on Environment and Development, June 14, 1992

PRINCIPLE 11

States shall enact effective environmental legislation. Environmental standards, management objectives and priorities should reflect the environmental and developmental context to which they apply. Standards applied by some countries may be inappropriate and of unwarranted economic and social cost to other countries, in particular developing countries.

GENERAL PRINCIPLES CONCERNING NATURAL RESOURCES AND ENVIRONMENTAL INTERFERENCES, ARTICLE 4

Final Report of the Experts Group on Environmental Law on Legal Principles for Environmental Protection and Sustainable Development, above, at 26

Article 4
Environmental Standards and Monitoring

States shall:

(a) establish specific environmental standards, in particular environmental quality standards, emission standards, technological standards and product standards, aimed at preventing or abating interferences with natural resources or the environment;

(b) establish systems for the collection and dissemination of data and regular observation of natural resources and the environment in order to permit adequate planning of the use of natural resources and the environment, to permit early detection of interferences with natural resources or the environment and ensure timely intervention, and to facilitate the evaluation of conservation policies and methods.

Notes and Questions

1. The Experts Group addresses environmental protection on the domestic level in a number of articles (*see* Articles 4, 5, and 7(1)), and the Rio Declaration devotes several principles to these matters (e.g., Principles 8, 11, 15, 16, 17). Is it appropriate for international law to require states to provide for certain matters in their domestic legislation? Might it be

more appropriate in some fields than in others? Why can't it be left to each country to decide how it will implement its international obligations? Or are these international obligations at all?

2. *Exclusive "domestic jurisdiction."* Article 2, paragraph 7 of the United Nations Charter provides in part as follows:

> Nothing contained in the present Charter shall authorize the United Nations to intervene in matters which are essentially within the domestic jurisdiction of any state or shall require the Members to submit such matters to settlement under the present Charter. . . .[20]

How would the phrase "matters which are essentially within the domestic jurisdiction of [a] state" be defined in the context of environmental problems? For purposes of comparison consider that a state's observance of the human rights of individuals subject to its jurisdiction—including its citizens—is regarded as a matter of international concern and not exclusively within its "domestic jurisdiction." It is therefore subject to international law. *See, e.g.,* 2 Restatement (Third) of the Foreign Relations Law of the United States, Part VI, Protection of Persons (Natural and Juridical), Introductory Note, at 144-145 (1987); and section D, below. Should the same be true of environmental protection, even if the problem in question has no direct international ramifications?

3. *Substance vs. procedure.* Should an obligation to enact domestic legislation be regarded as a substantive or a procedural obligation? Does it matter?

4. What if state A dutifully enacts all the kinds of legislation provided for in the above excerpts but then does not implement any of it? Has it fulfilled its obligations under the above provisions?

5. Summary

■ ACID RAIN AND OZONE LAYER DEPLETION: INTERNATIONAL LAW AND REGULATION

J. Brunnée
103-111 (1988)

2. Procedural Rules

A) TERMINOLOGY

Multiple links between the different "natural environments" not only require rules delineating the terms of international coexistence, they also

20. Paragraph 7 continues: "but this principle shall not prejudice the application of the enforcement measures under Chapter VII." Chapter VII, entitled Action with Respect to Threats to the Peace, Breaches of the Peace, and Acts of Aggression, confers powers upon the UN Security Council to deal with threats to or breaches of international peace and security.

necessitate rules structuring some degree of cooperation without which coexistence would not be possible. The "good neighborliness" of nations sharing natural resources thus gives rise to some procedural rules to which the countries concerned must submit their conduct.

Cooperation with regard to potential or existing transfrontier pollution can consist of a number of modes of conduct, or can refer to a basic attitude in which states deal with each other. A unilateral form of cooperation is the providing of information on environmentally relevant activities to a (potential) victim state. Building on the exchange of information, the neighboring countries concerned can enter into consultations. This bi- or multilateral form of cooperation consists of an exchange of views on the environmental situation in question. Finally, by making use of both information and consultation, states can negotiate the relevant environmental issues. Negotiations require the basic readiness of the polluting state to consider and accommodate the other country's concern. The decision to act itself remains reserved to the polluting country, which is not obliged to actually enter into an agreement. However, the difference between consultations and negotiations is one of degree only and it is not always possible to distinguish the two forms of cooperation. Literature and international documents often do not draw a sharp line between the two. Therefore, they will be discussed jointly in the following paragraphs on the assumption that consultations are a preliminary stage to negotiations.

B) THE DUTY TO COOPERATE

International environmental law imposes a general duty on states to cooperate in their use of transboundary natural resources. General Assembly Resolution 2995 (XXVII) stresses that ". . . in exercising their sovereignty over their natural resources, States must seek, through effective bilateral and multilateral co-operation or through regional machinery to preserve and improve the environment. . . ." A similar duty is stipulated in the General Assembly Resolution 3129 (XXVIII): ". . . the duty of the international community to adopt measures to protect and improve the environment and particularly the need for continuous international collaboration . . . to this end. . . ." Further evidence of a general duty to cooperate can be found in, for example, the OECD Recommendation C(74) 224 of November 14, 1974 on Principles Concerning Transfrontier Pollution, Principles 1, 7, 9, 12 of the UNEP Draft Principles of Conduct, Articles 3-5, 7-10 of the 1979 ECE Convention, Articles 1 ff. of the 1980 Memorandum of Intent between Canada and the United States [MOI], the Mexican-United States Agreement on Cooperation in the Border Area, Articles 18, 19 of the ASEAN Convention, and Articles 2, 4 of the Vienna Convention on the Ozone Layer. Whether states are obliged to make use of the aforementioned more specific means of cooperation, is subject to some dispute. . . .

C) DUTY TO NOTIFY AND INFORM

It is generally accepted that states, if they intend to use areas under their jurisdiction or control in a way that may cause significant transfrontier environmental damage, are under a duty to give prior notification to the potential victim. They are also obliged to supply and exchange further information. The duty of states to notify other states of potential danger had already been pronounced in the *Corfu Channel* case. The rule evolved in the context of shared water resources and was formulated in Article XXX of the Helsinki Rules.

> 1. With a view to preventing disputes from arising between basin States as to their legal rights or other interests, it is recommended that each basin State furnish relevant and *reasonably available information* to the other basin States concerning the waters of a drainage basin within its territory and its use of, and activities with respect to such waters. (Emphasis added.)
>
> 2. A State . . . should in particular furnish any other basin State, *the interests of which may be substantially affected, notice* of a proposed construction on installation which would alter the regime of the basin. . . . (Emphasis added.)

Until recently there was disagreement as to the existence of a generally applicable rule of international law obliging states to inform neighboring countries of potential transfrontier pollution. Some still contend that, in spite of extensive treaty practice, states exchange information or consult each other on an ad hoc basis.

The 1972 Stockholm Declaration limits itself to a very broad reference to information exchange in Principle 20. . . .

Outside the United Nations context, the most authoritative formulations of the principle of information exchange are to be found in the OECD Recommendation C(74) 224 and especially under Title C of the OECD Recommendation C(77) 28:

> (a) *The country of origin,* on its own initiative or at the request of an exposed country, *should communicate* to the latter *appropriate information* concerning it *in matters of transfrontier pollution or significant risk of such pollution* and enter into consultations with it. (Emphasis added.)
>
> (b) In order to enable a country of origin to implement adequately the principles set out in Title A of this Recommendation, *each exposed country should,* on its own initiative or at the request of the country of origin, *supply appropriate information of mutual concern.* (Emphasis added.)

Further confirmation of the principle of information can be found in several bilateral and multilateral agreements. In its Article 3 the MOI between Canada and the United States refers to prior notification of environmental risks or potential risk as "long standing practice." . . . References to the exchange of information can also be found in Article 6 of the Mexico-United States Border Agreement, Article 3, 4 and 8 of the 1979 ECE Convention, Articles 18-20 of the ASEAN Conservation Agreement, and Article 4 as well as Annex II of the Vienna Ozone Layer Convention. . . .

Examples from European experience illustrate that states are usually willing to supply the relevant information. In the case of the construction of a nuclear power plant in Fessenheim (Alsace) the French Commissariat à l'Energie Atomique in 1971 eventually agreed to let German authorities participate in measuring radioactive propagation. Through a French-German Commission on the safety of nuclear power plants in the border area, the French government subsequently provided information on the facilities in Fessenheim and in Cattenom.

In other cases of nuclear power plant projects, prior information was supplied to the neighboring countries. In 1977 the government of Luxembourg supplied the German Saarland with information about planned nuclear power plants in the border area. Germany and Switzerland set up an Area Planning Commission and the German delegation furnished detailed information on projected locations for nuclear power plants to be built close to the Swiss border by 1990. A similar Commission, through which information on two plants was supplied to the Dutch government, exists between Germany and the Netherlands.

In summary, the duty to exchange information on (potentially) harmful transboundary (air) pollution can be considered a rule of international law. The difficulty lies in the delineation of the rule's extent. It is not clear what degree of harm or risk is necessary to actually "activate" the duty. State practice points at a relatively high threshold.

. . .

D) THE DUTY TO CONSULT AND NEGOTIATE

It is less clear whether, beyond the duty of notification or information, states are also obliged to consult with potentially harmed neighboring states. Some authors contend that there is a general duty of consultation in transfrontier pollution cases. Others claim that the existing evidence of confirming *opinio iuris* and state practice is, especially regarding air pollution, not sufficient.

With respect to water resources, the principle of consultation is widely accepted as a rule of customary international law. The 1909 Boundary Waters Treaty between the United States and the United Kingdom/Canada provides an early example. With the International Joint Commission (IJC) the parties set up a body which, as one of its major tasks, offered a forum for consultations. Further support for the existence of the principle can be derived from the *Lac Lanoux* case. . . .

The principle of consultation has as well been recognized by the International Court of Justice in the *North Sea Continental Shelf* cases and the *Fisheries Jurisdiction* Case.

In support of a broader applicability of the principle it can be argued that it emanates from the obligation of peaceful settlement of disputes underlying the United Nations Charter and laid down in Chapter IV. Although duty to engage in consultations or negotiations on transboundary air pollution can certainly not be derived directly from the peaceful settlement principle, the latter does provide a guideline for the conduct of states in the case of a dispute arising because of unlawful transfrontier pollution. A duty to consult or to negotiate would arise under the Charter mainly, perhaps only, if the continuation of the dispute threatened international peace and security (Article 33 United Nations Charter). Thus far disputes about transfrontier air pollution have not represented such a threat.

. . . [T]he OECD recommendations of 1974 and 1977 provide indications of a duty to engage in consultations. In Principle 7 the 1974 Recommendation says that: "Countries should enter into consultation on an existing or foreseeable transfrontier pollution problem at the request of a country which is or may be directly affected and should diligently pursue such consultations on this particular problem over a reasonable period of time." The other documents mentioned with regard to a duty to inform equally lend support to the existence of an obligation to consult. General Assembly Resolution 3129, Article 3 of the Charter of Economic Rights and Duties of States, and the UNEP Draft Principles of Conduct all make reference to consultations to be engaged in by states sharing a natural resource. . . .

It could be asked whether States actually consider themselves obligated to consult with concerned countries or whether they only do so at their convenience. One would expect that the large number of countries that support the consultation principle feel an obligation to consult in relevant cases. States may, of course, argue that a significant danger of transfrontier air pollution does not exist, but this in itself indicates that in principle they recognize the duty to consult. The above-mentioned examples of European state practice, particularly those involving border area commissions, support this view. The International Boundary and Water Commission (IBWC) established between Mexico and the United States, and the United States-Canada IJC point in the same direction. However, it should be remembered that the IBWC is primarily concerned with technical issues; consultations on other matters appear to take place on a rather ad hoc basis. Although not displaying a regular pattern, the transfrontier pollution cases between the United States and Canada indicate that both countries are willing to engage in consultations.

In summary, I am concluding that state practice is too scattered to lend support to the existence of a general rule of prior consultation or even negotiations. In many cases the existing practice has evolved around particularly significant risks of harm.

For cases of air pollution causing or threatening to cause *significant* transboundary harm it can therefore be concluded that a rule of customary international law obliges states to consult with concerned neighboring states. But it must be stressed once again that the obligation is only one to consult or to negotiate in good faith and not one to actually reach an agreement. States have thus far not been ready to agree on such a caveat to their sovereignty.

Notes and Questions

1. *That attractive but elusive concept, "cooperation."* In the introductory paragraphs of this section, it was noted that some view procedural norms as specific applications of the general obligation of states to cooperate with each other. In light of your examination of the foregoing materials, do you believe there is a general obligation to cooperate under international law? If so, what is its content? For example, what do Israel and Syria have to do to fulfil their respective obligations to cooperate with each other? In the case of activities that threaten or may cause transboundary pollution harm, such as a proposed nuclear plant or pulp mill that is to be located on an international watercourse, what specifically does the obligation to cooperate require? Did France fulfil the obligation in the case of the Fessenheim and Cattenom facilities discussed by Brunnée? More generally, how can states be *made* to cooperate? If the essence of "cooperation" is "working together," how can two neighboring countries that do not have diplomatic relations with each other be required to cooperate? Would it not be simpler, more realistic and, in view of the sovereign rights of the state concerned, more sound legally to dispense with "obligations" of notification, consultation, and negotiation? Would it not be more realistic to require simply that the two states not harm each other? Is there anything wrong with the latter approach, particularly in the field of the environment?

2. *The obligation to negotiate.* On the basis of your study of the materials in sections A and B of this chapter, do you believe that the tribunal in the *Lake Lanoux* case was correct in holding that France was under an obligation to negotiate with Spain? Would France's obligations vis-a-vis Spain be any different today than they were in the 1950s?

3. *Problem.* Should the causing of substantial transfrontier pollution harm be proscribed under all circumstances? Consider the following hypothetical case: Pollution from irrigation of farmland in state A, upstream on the Red River, enters the Red and causes substantial harm in state B, a lower riparian on the Red. B complains to A, citing serious adverse human health problems and property damage due to the pollution. A responds

that it must continue the irrigation at present levels to be able to feed its people; any less would cause starvation, and A cannot afford to import food. How should this case be resolved? We will study possible legal responses to this kind of case in more detail in Chapter 16.

4. *Implementation of procedural norms.* Do you believe procedural norms can ever "work" in the absence of some joint mechanism such as a joint commission? If so, why are there so many such commissions? If not, why have them?

5. *Remedies.* If a state does breach its obligation to prevent transfrontier pollution harm, what is the harmed state's remedy? Compensation? What if the harm is purely "environmental"—that is, it involves no personal injury or property damage, in the sense of economic loss but, for example, kills wildlife or fouls a pristine river? Should a symbolic payment of a nominal amount of money be a sufficient remedy? Or should the state of origin be required to restore the damaged river or wildlife (assuming this were possible) or pay the cost of such restoration? What if the harm is not to another state but to the commons? If compensation is the appropriate remedy, whom does the state of origin pay? If restoration is required, who should monitor the restoration efforts to ensure that they are adequate? We will consider many of these questions in the following chapter.

Additional Reading

For further discussions of procedural norms *see, e.g.,* Aida Luisa Levin, Protecting the Human Environment: Procedures and Principles for Preventing and Resolving International Controversies, especially pp. 1-13 (UNITAR 1977); G. Handl & B. Simma, Granzüberschreitendes Nukleares Risiko und Völkerrechtlicher Schutzanspruch (1989); and P.-M. Dupuy, Overview of the Existing Customary Legal Regime Regarding International Pollution, in International Law and Pollution 61, 69-78 (D. Magraw ed. 1991).

C. APPLICATION OF ENVIRONMENTAL NORMS TO DEVELOPING COUNTRIES

Earlier in this chapter we asked you to consider preliminarily the way in which environmental norms apply or should apply to developing countries. This is an issue to which increasing attention has been given since the 1972 Stockholm Conference on the Human Environment. It is a thread that runs through the entire fabric of international environmental law. Anyone who has participated in a recent multilateral diplomatic negotiation in the field can attest that the issue will be raised in one way or another in virtually any such discussions. If the instrument finally agreed upon does not make special provision for developing countries, it is likely that its provisions will have been drafted in such a way as to take their circumstances into account. Is the same true of norms of general, or customary international law? In what ways *are* the needs, interests, and special situation of developing countries taken into account in normative prescriptions? Is it appropriate to establish or recognize such a double standard? On what grounds can special—and therefore different—treatment of developing countries be justified? Practical ones (these countries are not in a position to comply with some obligations anyway, so why not recognize that and help them so that their noncompliance does not hurt us)? Political ones (it is important for developed countries to maintain good relations with developing countries—which have around three-quarters of the world's population—for a host of reasons, many of which do not concern the environment)? Moral ones (the developed countries should help developing countries, especially the least developed ones, in any way possible, including by allowing them to devote their resources to the provision of food and water and to the alleviation of absolute poverty)?

In the pages that follow we present, first, the relevant principles of the Stockholm and Rio Declarations, then, as an illustration of how the issue is dealt with in treaties, a provision of the Climate Change Convention. Finally we reproduce an analysis of the different ways in which international law takes the special situation of developing countries into account.

DECLARATION OF THE UNITED NATIONS CONFERENCE ON THE HUMAN ENVIRONMENT ("STOCKHOLM DECLARATION"), PRINCIPLE 23

Stockholm, 16 June 1972, Report of the United Nations Conference on the Human Environment, U.N. Doc. A/CONF.48/14/Rev.1, at 3 (1973), U.N. Doc. A/CONF.48/14, at 2-65, and Corr.1 (1972),* reprinted in *11 I.L.M. 1416 (1972)

PRINCIPLE 23

Without prejudice to such criteria as may be agreed upon by the international community, or to such standards which will have to be determined nationally, it will be essential in all cases to consider the systems of values prevailing in each country, and the extent of the applicability of standards which are valid for the most advanced countries but which may be inappropriate and of unwarranted social cost for the developing countries.

■ RIO DECLARATION ON ENVIRONMENT AND DEVELOPMENT, PRINCIPLES 6 AND 7

Adopted by the United Nations Conference on Environment and Development, June 14, 1992

PRINCIPLE 6

The special situation and needs of developing countries, particularly the least developed and those most environmentally vulnerable, shall be given special priority. International actions in the field of environment and development should also address the interests and needs of all countries.

PRINCIPLE 7

States shall cooperate in a spirit of global partnership to conserve, protect and restore the health and integrity of the Earth's ecosystem. In view of the different contributions to global environmental degradation, States have common but differentiated responsibilities. The developed countries acknowledge the responsibility that they bear in the international pursuit of sustainable development in view of the pressures their societies place on the global environment and of the technologies and financial resources they command.

Notes and Questions

1. *Principle 6.* What are the practical implications of Principle 6? Does it mean that developed countries and international financial institutions are to give special priority to providing financial and technical assistance to developing countries? Does it imply that international environmental obligations should be applied less strictly or perhaps sometimes not at all to developing countries?

2. *Principle 7.* Again, what are the practical implications of this principle? That developed countries have a special obligation to assist developing countries in meeting their environmental obligations? That developed countries can continue to pollute, for example, if they are able to induce developing countries to refrain from polluting? Or that developed countries have "used up" most of their "pollution quota" whereas developing countries have much leeway left to engage in such environmentally harmful—but economically productive—practices as polluting and deforestation? Do you believe your conclusions are borne out by Article 3, paragraph 1 of the Climate Change Convention, reproduced below?

3. Two other principles of the Rio Declaration are also relevant in this connection: Principles 11 and 15.

a. *Principle 11* deals with domestic legislation rather than international law. It provides as follows:

> States shall enact effective environmental legislation. Environmental standards, management objectives and priorities should reflect the environmental and developmental context to which they apply. Standards applied by some countries may be inappropriate and of unwarranted economic and social cost to other countries, in particular developing countries.

This principle thus calls for states to enact "effective environmental legislation" but recognizes that such laws should be tailored to the conditions of the country concerned. Would it not have been enough to say only that—for example, to stop at the end of the second sentence? Why do you think the third sentence was felt to be necessary? If all developed countries regulate air pollution from automobiles and factories strictly, does this mean that developing countries should be expected to so as well? For that matter, why did the Rio Declaration deal with domestic legislation at all? Is this not a matter within the domestic jurisdiction of states and therefore within their unfettered discretion?

b. *Principle 15,* which deals with the "precautionary approach," provides that this concept is to be "widely applied by States according to their capabilities." Does this mean that where developing countries "lack . . . full scientific certainty," they may "postpon[e] cost-effective measures to prevent environmental degradation" even "[w]here there are threats of serious or irreversible damage"?

■ UNITED NATIONS FRAMEWORK CONVENTION ON CLIMATE CHANGE, ARTICLE 3, PARAGRAPHS 1 AND 2

Article 3
Principles

> 1. The Parties should protect the climate system for the benefit of present and future generations of humankind, on the basis of equity and in accordance with their common but differentiated responsibilities and respective capabilities. Accordingly, the developed country Parties should take the lead in combating climate change and the adverse effects thereof.
>
> 2. The specific needs and special circumstances of developing country Parties, especially those that are particularly vulnerable to the adverse effects of climate change, and of those Parties, especially developing country Parties, that would have to bear a disproportionate or abnormal burden under the Convention, should be given full consideration.

Notes and Questions

1. *The rationale for differential treatment.* There are various possible rationales for treating developing countries differently, and they are not necessarily mutually exclusive. As noted at the outset of this section and as explored more fully in the Magraw excerpt below, differential treatment of developing countries might be justified on practical, political, or moral grounds. Is there any counterpart to the notion of "common but differentiated responsibility" on the domestic level? That is, are some individuals treated differently than others under domestic legal systems? If so, are the justifications similar to those supporting differential treatment of developing countries under international law?

2. *Article 3 and Principle 7.* To rephrase a question asked above, what does Principle 7 of the Rio Declaration mean when it states that "developed countries acknowledge the responsibility that they bear in the international pursuit of sustainable development"? Is it saying that in view of their greater contribution to global environmental problems, developed countries "acknowledge responsibility" to remedy those problems? To what extent is this interpretation supported in the case of climate change by Article 3(1) of the Climate Change Convention? In accepting this formula, are developed countries agreeing to reduce "the pressures their societies place on the global environment" (e.g., by changing production and consumption patterns)? Or are they agreeing to provide financial and technological assistance to developing countries so that they might develop in a sustainable manner?

3. *The Humpty-Dumpty gambit.*[21] In its "Interpretive Statements for the Record," the United States declared that it "does not accept any interpretation of Principle 7 that would imply a recognition or acceptance by the United States of any international obligations or liabilities, or any diminution of the responsibilities of developing countries." U.N. Doc. A/CONF.151/26/Rev.1 (Vol. II), at 18 (1993). Assume you are the Legal Adviser to the Foreign Ministry of the United Kingdom and that the United Kingdom made no such interpretive statement. Would it thereby be regarded as having accepted "international obligations or liabilities" in this regard? Does the fact that the United States made this statement while the United Kingdom did not make a difference?

4. *Translating principles into provisions.* The notions of "global partnership" and "common but differentiated responsibilities" contained in Principle 7 have been given concrete expression in other instruments in the form of different standards, delayed compliance timetables, and less stringent commitments. Apart from other possible justifications, use of these techniques often assists in encouraging universal participation in instru-

21. Quoth Humpty Dumpty: "When *I* use a word, . . . it means just what I choose it to mean—neither more nor less." Lewis Carroll, Through the Looking Glass, ch. 7.

ments dealing with such important problems as stratospheric ozone depletion (the Montreal Protocol) and global climate change (the Framework Convention on Climate Change). For example, in the view of some knowledgeable observers the Montreal Protocol's combination of inducements and trade restrictions presumably led countries such as China and India, which alone could have undermined the protective regime, to join the agreement.[22] Examples of these techniques may be found, inter alia, in the following instruments.

a. Article 5 of the *Montreal Protocol,* entitled Special Situation of Developing Countries, entitles a developing country party "to delay its compliance with the control measures set out in [the Protocol] by ten years after that specified in [the relevant provisions]." The article also provides that parties are to "facilitate access to environmentally safe alternative substances and technology" for developing country parties and to facilitate "the provision of subsidies, aid, credits, guarantees or insurance programmes" to assist developing country parties in acquiring alternative technology and substitute products.

b. The *Climate Change Convention* takes the special circumstances and needs of developing countries into account in a number of ways, including the structuring of the parties' obligations (Article 4(1)) and allowing differences in reporting requirements (Article 12). That agreement's innovative notion of "joint implementation" (Article 4(2)(a) and (b)) permits a developed country party to meet a portion of its commitment to limit greenhouse gas emissions by assisting a developing country party in the implementation of its obligations to maintain its tropical forests, which provide a sink for those gasses.

c. The *Biological Diversity Convention,* which is replete with references to the special situation of developing countries, provides in Article 20(1) that developed country parties are to "provide new and additional financial resources to enable developing country Parties to meet the agreed full incremental costs to them of implementing measures which fulfil the obligations of this Convention. . . ." Paragraph 4 of that article then provides:

> The extent to which developing country Parties will effectively implement their commitments under this Convention will depend on the effective implementation by developed country Parties of their commitments . . . related to financial resources and transfer of technology and will take fully into account the fact that economic and social development and eradication of

22. *See, e.g.,* Winfried Lang, Trade Restrictions as a Means of Enforcing Compliance with International Environmental Law, in Enforcing Environmental Standards: Economic Mechanisms as Viable Means? 265, at 282 (Rüdiger Wolfrum ed., 1996).

> poverty are the first and overriding priorities of the developing country Parties.

Does this provision make the provision of financial and technological resources by developed country parties a condition precedent to the obligations of developing countries? Or is it simply a statement of fact? Does it matter? Why or why not?

d. After listing "General obligations" in Article 4, the 1994 *Desertification Convention*[23] provides in Article 5 for additional "Obligations of affected country Parties" and then, separately, in Article 6 for additional "Obligations of developed country Parties." Among the latter are obligations to "provide substantial financial resources and other forms of support to assist affected developing country Parties" in undertaking relevant activities (Article 6(b)) and to "promote the mobilization of new and additional funding pursuant to Article 20 [on Financial resources]."

e. Article 26 of the *1996 Protocol to the 1972 IMO London Dumping Convention*[24] allows states joining the agreement within certain time limits to notify the secretary-general of the IMO that they "will not be able to comply with specific provisions" of the protocol, other than those concerning incineration at sea or dumping of radioactive wastes or other radioactive matter, during a transitional period.

f. Finally, the principle of common but differentiated responsibilities is also reflected, expressly or by implication, in declarations adopted at recent universal conferences held under United Nations auspices. *See, e.g.*, the 1995 Copenhagen Declaration on Social Development, para. 28;[25] and the 1996 Istanbul Declaration on Human Settlements and the Habitat Agenda,[26] para. 10.

5. *Special treatment of former communist states?* "Countries with economies in transition"—an expression used to refer to the former Soviet bloc countries of Central and Eastern Europe—are also given beneficial treatment in certain recent instruments, including the Conventions on Biological Diversity and Climate Change. The Biodiversity Convention allows these countries to "voluntarily assume the obligations of the developed country Parties," thereby implicitly exempting them from developed country obliga-

23. U.N. Doc. A/AC.241/15/Rev.7, 33 I.L.M. 1328 (1994).

24. Convention on the Prevention of Marine Pollution by Dumping of Wastes and Other Matter, 29 December 1972, 1046 U.N.T.S. 120, 26 U.S.T. 2403, 11 I.L.M. 1294 (1973); 1996 Protocol, adopted 7 November 1996, I.M.O. Doc. LC/SM 1/6, November 14, 1996.

25. United Nations, World Summit for Social Development, March 6-12, 1995, The Copenhagen Declaration and Programme of Action 1, at 12 (1995).

26. The Habitat Agenda: Goals and Principles, Commitments and Global Plan of Action, United Nations Conference on Human Settlements (Habitat II), Istanbul, Turkey, June 3-14, 1996; noted in 35 I.L.M. 1568 (1996).

tions under the treaty. The Climate Change Convention approaches the subject of classifying countries by in effect listing all nondeveloping country parties in Annex I, and listing only developed countries—members of the OECD, excluding countries with economies in transition—in Annex II. It then differentiates between countries listed in Annexes I and II, providing more stringent obligations for the OECD countries listed in Annex II. Finally, special consideration is urged for these countries in instruments adopted at universal conferences held under United Nations auspices, such as the World Summit for Social Development, Copenhagen, 1995. Paragraph 18 of the Copenhagen Declaration adopted at that meeting states that: "Countries with economies in transition, which are also [i.e., in addition to developing countries] undergoing fundamental political, economic and social transformation, require the support of the international community as well."[27] It should further be recalled in this connection that the Montreal Protocol, concluded during the Soviet era, also makes special allowances for communist bloc countries. Article 2(6) of the Montreal Protocol in effect "grandfathers" the relevant facilities of these countries that were under construction or contracted for prior to a specified date, taking into account that the economies of these countries operated under five-year plans. More recently, certain Central and Eastern European countries requested, and in December 1995 were granted, special treatment with respect to their obligations under the Protocol.

In the following excerpt, Daniel Magraw proposes three different categories of international environmental norms that may be applied to developing countries. Consider whether you believe that a single category should be applied to all developing countries with regard to all environmental problems; whether different categories should be applied to all developing countries depending upon the problem being addressed; or whether different categories should be applied to different developing countries (developing countries that are at different levels of development).

■ LEGAL TREATMENT OF DEVELOPING COUNTRIES: DIFFERENTIAL, CONTEXTUAL, AND ABSOLUTE NORMS

Daniel Barstow Magraw
1 Colo. J. Intl. Envtl. L. & Poly. 69, 69-76 (1990)

I. INTRODUCTION

The treatment of developing countries arises in virtually every discussion of international environmental protection and resource management.

27. United Nations, World Summit for Social Development, March 6-12, 1995, The Copenhagen Declaration and Programme of Action 1, at 7 (1995).

This serious and difficult issue must be confronted successfully in order to realize effective solutions to international environmental problems.

From a practical (nonpolitical) perspective, developing countries are the source of much of the world's pollution and contain much of the world's population and natural resources. That population demands improved standards of living, and those resources are a tempting target for uncontrolled exploitation. Moreover, most of the staggering increase in world population projected for the next thirty years—from five billion now to eight-to-nine billion by 2025—will occur in developing countries, leading to further pressures on the environment. International environmental protection measures thus must involve the continuous participation of developing countries in order to be viable.

Achieving effective participation by developing countries in international environmental protection, however, is complicated by the fact that developing countries face greater difficulties than do developed countries with respect to managing environmental problems. Developing countries often do not have sufficient technical expertise to evaluate complex technological proposals or to monitor ongoing performance, especially (as is often the case) where control of the day-to-day operations is effectively in the hands of foreigners. Similarly, developing countries may not have sufficient information to predict the potential for transboundary harm created by activities of foreign or foreign-owned entities within their territory because they may not receive full information from such entities. Developing countries frequently lack regulatory and administrative skills necessary to effectuate pollution control laws, and they may not have the legislation drafting skills and experience necessary to draft adequate laws. Moreover, developing countries face an unusually high risk of suffering transboundary harm from ill-planned or hazardous activities of neighbors, because the neighboring countries are typically developing countries—which themselves are subject to the relative disabilities just mentioned—and because the governments and people of the affected developing country are typically not as aware of the potential harm, or as able to detect, monitor, or remedy such harm. The foregoing difficulties are aspects of the overarching reality that developing countries have relatively few resources to devote to environmental protection—domestic or international—and relatively low technical and regulatory capabilities for use in that effort.

From a political perspective, there are two points to note. First, at the international level, developing countries comprise more than a majority of the world's approximately 165 countries, and they contain approximately three-quarters of the world's population. Developing countries are significant to developed countries such as the United States in many arenas not expressly involving the environment. It is obvious that developing countries' claims cannot simply be ignored.

The second political consideration concerns the domestic level. Political leaders in developing countries face tremendous pressures to accomplish short-term economic growth, even if that involves sacrificing the environment. The importance of "sustainable development," as that term is used in *Our Common Future* (the Brundtland Commission's Report), and the dependence of long-term economic development on environmental protection are increasingly accepted by developing-country leaders. But that recognition has not yet spread to the masses (or to many policymakers). Until it does (and perhaps even thereafter), impatience and resultant political pressure will be the rule. In the absence of special incentives, expecting that developing countries' political leaders will surmount that pressure in the interests of the global environment, or even to pursue their own countries' sustainable development, is naive. That is especially true because even developed countries often do not adhere domestically to the environmental advice they dispense internationally, as evidenced by current exploitation of Hawaiian rain forests.

From a moral perspective, an urgent and undeniable imperative exists that the standard of living of the world's poorest people be improved. Roughly one billion people live in "absolute poverty," that is, in a form of existence so characterized by malnutrition, exposure to the elements, disease, and illiteracy that it is below any reasonable standard of human decency. The moral imperative to alleviate absolute poverty has profound implications for international environmental law. On the one hand, it means that the situation with which international law must deal is more complicated and threatening: Improving the absolute poor's standard of living will inevitably place greater demands on natural resources and will probably—though not necessarily—require increased energy use. On the other hand, the moral imperative places a constraint on the means international law can use to deal with the worsening situation: Environmental norms must be structured so as to minimize interference with the effort to lift people from absolute poverty.

Moral philosophy may also have implications regarding the extent to which developing and developed countries should be subject to the same international environmental standards. One might make an argument based on the philosophy of John Locke (1632-1704) that developing countries are not entitled to any differential treatment. The Lockean principle of acquisition from a commons permits one to appropriate or use a resource provided that one does not take more than one can use without waste and that after one's acquisition there is "enough, and as good left in common for others." How much it is permissible to take depends on how many others want to use the resource and how much they are likely to need or want. Presumably, the Lockean principle covers using an area such as the sea as a disposal site. If there are only a few other polluters bordering, for example, the Mediterranean Sea, and if they want to only put small amounts of pollutants into the Sea, then State A may be able to put in a large amount of pollutant (call this amount N) without violating the Lockean condition. Later, when there are many more States putting pollutants into the Mediterranean, another State, B, may not be able to dispose of an amount as large as N without running afoul of the Lockean proviso. State B then has no complaint that A used to be able to dispose of the greater amount N, or that A was able to dispose of a greater aggregate amount over time by having an earlier need for disposal.

The Lockean proviso, however, cuts in the other direction as well. Suppose that A continues to dispose of amount N every year even while new polluters, in order to avoid violating the Lockean proviso, have to dispose of less than N per year. Here, the newer polluters have grounds to complain that there is no longer any basis for A's claim that it is entitled to dispose of amount N. State A, like the other polluters, is entitled to contribute only an amount that takes into account the number of parties wanting to make use of the commons.

Consider this problem in a real case. Many scientists think that uncontrolled burning of rain forests in western Brazil contributes significantly to climatic change. States that industrialized earlier than Brazil and whose fossil fuel use contributes much of the rest of the problem, might complain that Brazil cannot make this large deposition of carbon dioxide into the atmosphere without violating the Lockean proviso. Surely, this would be correct. But Brazil would also be correct in responding that other States can no longer put as much carbon dioxide into the atmosphere as they were once free to do. Brazil would be correct, that is, in appealing to the Lockean proviso in demanding that cuts be multilateral rather than limited to Brazil alone.

But might Brazil be able to use Locke to argue further that developed States should cut back more than Brazil should, on the grounds that the need to develop economically (or to benefit Brazil's absolute poor) should be considered in determining what is "enough"? Such an argument would be buttressed by moral conclusions drawn from the imperative to improve the standard of living of those living in absolute poverty, from a philosophical approach that generally favors access to resources based on need (Brazil's needs are presumably greater than those of developed States), from a philosophical approach centered on ability (developed States generally have more resources and technical capacity to combat international environmental degradation than Brazil has), and from a philosophical approach that emphasizes who caused the problem in question (anthropogenic activities in developed countries have historically contributed more to global warming than have anthropogenic activities in Brazil).

It is beyond the scope of this article to explore fully the problems of fairness between developing and developed countries in distributing the burdens of dealing with international environmental protection and resource management. It is clear, however, that these fairness issues will have to be taken seriously. Moreover, it will not be plausible either for developed countries to insist that they should be allowed to continue contributing as much pollution as they did just because they started doing it first, or for developing countries to claim that they can determine their level of pollution without reference to the condition of the biosphere as a whole.

One hopes, of course, for a consonançe between the international legal regime—as it presently exists and as it evolves in the future—and the political, practical, and moral considerations just mentioned. In the remainder of this article, I examine the existing international legal regime with respect to three types of norms—differential, contextual, and absolute—and conclude that international environmental norms should be fashioned to take into account in appropriate situations the specific capabilities and needs of developing countries.

II. Analytic Framework: Types of Norms

For purposes of this article, there are three general types of international norms. These types delimit the treatment that international law can and does provide developing countries.

A. DIFFERENTIAL NORMS

The first type of norm is what I call a "differential" norm, by which I mean a norm that on its face provides different, presumably more advantageous, standards for one set of States than for another set. In theory, the sets of States can be distinguished on any ground (other than simply that one set is composed of States that are acting and the other set consists of the States that are affected by the action). The differential norms of greatest interest here are those that distinguish between developing countries and developed countries. An example of a differential environmental norm is contained in the 1987 Montreal Protocol on Substances that Deplete the Ozone Layer, which allows developed countries five years to decrease pollution to a specified level, but developing countries—defined in terms of annual per capita consumption of ozone-depleting substances—an additional ten years to reach the same level.

The Montreal Protocol is highly unusual, perhaps unique, because it defines "developing countries." The other conventions and instruments (such as UN General Assembly declarations) that provide differential treatment to "developing countries" may be relying on a common sense definition of the term or on the treatment of countries within the UN system (the United Nations, for example, maintains a list of "least-developed" developing countries). In the absence of a specific definition, countries as different as Burundi and Brazil are presumably treated the same—i.e., as "developing countries"—and disputes may arise regarding whether or not a country qualifies as "developing."

By singling out one set of countries for different treatment, differential norms effectively take into account more than one type of interest. In the case of the Montreal Protocol, for example, the interests in not unduly interfering with improving standards of living in developing countries and in preserving the ozone layer are concurrently protected. That protection can be provided more or less flexibly. The Montreal Protocol provides very specific rules. In contrast, the earliest example of a different norm distinguishing between developing and developed countries is very general: It allows each developing country to decide for itself how far it will provide economic rights to nonnationals.

B. CONTEXTUAL NORMS

The second type of norm is what I call a "contextual" norm, by which I mean a norm on its face provides identical treatment to all States affected by the norm but the application of which requires (or at least permits) consideration of characteristics that might vary from country to country. Applying a contextual norm thus typically involves balancing multiple interests and characteristics.

Contextual norms, e.g., "reasonable" or "equitable," thus usually are indeterminate (that is also the case with differential norms that contain contextual elements). Depending on what factors may be considered, contextual norms allow disputing States wide latitude for arguing compliance or noncompliance. They also provide little, if any, certainty in predicting the outcome of the few international disputes settled by third parties such as courts and arbitral tribunals. Moreover, they permit such third parties to manipulate results within a broad range. Obviously, these effects can interfere with public order.

On the other hand, the indeterminacy of contextual norms or, in some cases, the flexibility of contextual norms that arises from the attributes that give rise to indeterminacy, can be advantageous in four types of situations. First, it is often easier to reach agreement on a contextual norm than on a more definite and precise norm, because of indeterminacy; and the fact that a contextual norm exists indicates, at the least, a recognition that the situation in question is of legitimate concern to all or part of the international community. Thus, although the existence of a contextual norm can, in some circumstances, give a false impression of progress and serve to distract attention from achieving a fully effective solution, in other circumstances a contextual norm can focus attention on a problem and lead to the subsequent formulation and acceptance of appropriate, definite norms. Moreover, the indeterminacy of contextual norms is not infinite: A contextual norm specifies the terms for discourse about the issue to which it applies and provides some bounds of acceptable behavior—bounds which, although not exact, usually are sufficiently precise that some conduct commonly will be seen as exceeding them. Even though a contextual norm might be less desirable in a given situation than a norm with clear meaning, therefore, a contextual norm might be preferable to having no applicable standard at all, which might be the only realistic alternative.

The second type of situation in which indeterminacy of contextual norms—or, more precisely, the attributes of contextual norms that create indeterminacy—is desirable involves problems that are clouded by uncertainty, either about scientific knowledge or about the range of factual situations to be covered by the norm, with the result that the precise contours of the optimal (or even suboptimal but still desirable) solution are unknowable, even by States otherwise willing to agree to an applicable norm. In such a case, an indeterminate norm is sometimes preferable to having no norm, for the reasons described in the immediately preceding paragraph. More importantly, the attributes of a contextual norm that give rise to indeterminacy also typically lead to flexibility in interpreting and applying the norm. That flexibility allows coverage of and sensitivity to a range of factual situations and of causes and effects, and it thus is desirable in dealing with the type of problem being discussed here, i.e., those so clouded by current uncertainty that a precise optimal solution is unknowable.

A related set of issues regarding which flexibility is desirable is that in which the costs of determining all the possible factual situations to be covered by a norm (or group of norms) and of articulating and agreeing on a precise norm are so high that they outweigh the benefits that would be gained from having a precise norm. A flexible contextual norm may be the most efficient means of providing a standard to deal with these issues.

Fourth, flexibility can be advantageous even with respect to issues whose current solution is clear, if significant changes in the relevant milieu are likely to occur. Examples of such changes include advances in scientific understanding about the environmental (or other) effects of particular behavior, developments in the technology applicable to solving a given pollution problem, or changes in pressures on the ecosystem at risk. Flexibility enables a contextual norm to adapt to changed circumstances and thus eliminates the need to negotiate and agree upon a new standard—a process that can be time-consuming, expensive, or impossible.

Contextual norms are either general, in which case the terms of the norm do not place a limit on the characteristics that may be considered, or limited, in which case the norm is phrased such that the set of relevant characteristics is defined (more or less precisely). Restricting the factors that may be considered in applying a contextual norm limits the indeterminacy (and flexibility) of the norm. The 1972 Convention on International Liability for Damage Caused by Space Objects, which provides for absolute liability on the part of the State from whose territory the space object was launched, contains general contextual norms: The injured State is allowed to make a claim until one year after that State "could *reasonably* be expected to have learned the facts," and compensation to be determined according to "principles of *justice* and *equity*." In contrast, an example of a limited contextual norm in the environmental area is the 1972 World Heritage Convention's requirement that a country, in protecting natural and cultural heritage, "*do all it can* to this end, to the *utmost of its own resources*."

The use of contextual norms has a long history. Consider, for example, the requirement that efforts taken in self-defense must be proportional. The limited contextual norms of greatest interest here are those that permit or require consideration of factors corresponding typically, but not necessarily unvaryingly, to the economic developmental level of a country, such as the World Heritage Convention's reference to States' "resources."

C. ABSOLUTE NORMS

The third type of norm is what I call an "absolute" norm, by which I mean a norm that provides identical treatment to all countries and does not require or permit consideration of factors that vary between countries. An example of an absolute norm is the 1987 Nuclear Accident Notification Convention's requirement of "immediate" notification of pending transboundary harm.[28] Applying an absolute norm often involves inquiring into the facts of the specific case (e.g., one must determine when a nuclear accident occurred and when notification occurred in order to ascertain whether notification was "immediate"); and reasonable people differ about what facts are relevant to such inquiries. No bright line thus exists between absolute and contextual norms. It is usually clear, however, on which side of the line a rule or principle falls.

Absolute norms have the capacity for being very precise (as do differential norms that do not contain contextual elements). In the area of environmental protection, precision is frequently desirable because the behavior or effect at issue is normally described specifically. Examples include emissions of hydrocarbons and exposure to ionizing radiation; it is usual to speak of these in terms of specific numbers of parts per million and rems, respectively.

Absolute norms are not necessarily precise, however. Sometimes they are ambiguous or undefined. An example would be an agreement providing that damages must be paid for transboundary harm, without defining the terms "damages" or "harm." Such a lack of clarity can, but does not automatically, result in disadvantages and advantages of flexible contextual norms.

Notes and Questions

1. *Making the categories fit the facts.* In what circumstances do you believe it would be appropriate to use each of the types of norms identified by Professor Magraw? For example, should developing country A be excused for depositing toxic waste into a river that flows into developing country B solely on the ground that A is a developing country?

28. Convention on Early Notification of a Nuclear Accident, Sept. 26, 1986, *reprinted in* 25 I.L.M. 1369 (1986). By using the term "absolute," I do not mean to imply that an absolute norm is impervious to excuses for nonperformance, such as necessity and self-defense.

2. *Role-playing I.* If you were legal adviser to the United States Department of State would you prefer any of these types of norms over any other? Would you instruct your delegate to the negotiation of an international agreement to try to use one type of norm or another?

3. *Role-playing II.* Imagine now you are a judge on the International Court of Justice. Would you have any preference?

4. *The United States and developing countries.* Is it in the interest of the United States to give differential treatment to developing countries? Why, or why not?

D. HUMAN RIGHTS

The relationship between the environment and international human rights law has received much attention. Commentators have urged recognition of a "right to a clean environment," a "right to a healthy environment," or simply a "right to environment." Whatever it is called, recognition of such a human right may lead to a more expansive view of environmental protections than an international environmental law reliant solely upon the rights and obligations of states vis-à-vis each other. Ideally, a human rights approach would ensure protections for individuals and/or groups as against their governments, as well as procedural rights for the implementation of the substantive guarantees.

This chapter examines the relationship between human rights and environmental protection by first introducing the subject of international human rights law (section 1), then looking at the relationship between that field and the environment (sections 2 and 3), and examining the basis (section 4) and nature (section 5) of an "environmental" human right.

1. Introduction to Human Rights Law

■ THE NEW INTERNATIONAL LAW: PROTECTION OF THE RIGHTS OF INDIVIDUALS RATHER THAN STATES

Louis B. Sohn
32 Am. U.L. Rev. 1, 1, 17-21 (1982)

THE DYNAMIC CHANGES IN INTERNATIONAL LAW SINCE THE SECOND WORLD WAR

The modern rules of international law concerning human rights are the result of a silent revolution of the 1940's, a revolution that was almost unnoticed at the time. Its effects have now spread around the world, destroying idols to which humanity paid obeisance for centuries. Just as the French Revolution ended the divine rights of kings, the human rights revolution that began at the 1945 San Francisco Conference of the United Nations has deprived the sovereign states of the lordly privilege of being the sole possessors of rights under international law. States have had to concede to ordinary human beings the status of subjects of international law, to concede that individuals are no longer mere objects, mere pawns in the hands of states.

Before dwelling on the various aspects of this revolution, however, it is useful to turn first to its prehistory, to the various strands of international law from which this new tapestry was woven. The human rights revolution did not appear suddenly full-grown, like Minerva springing from Jupiter's head. Its main substantive rules and its procedural safeguards can be traced back many centuries, to the origin of international law itself. . . .

The Promotion and Protection of Civil and Political Rights of Individuals

The Nature of "Human Rights"

Up to this point it has been assumed that "human rights" is a well-known concept and does not require detailed explanation. That assumption is, however, confronted by two problems. First, the theoretical nature of human rights has been debated fiercely, without resolution, since ancient time. In the play *Antigone,* Sophocles described Antigone's dilemma when King Creon prohibited the burial of her brother, who had been killed while rebelling against the King. When she was arrested for violating that order, she defended her action by claiming that the King could not override the "immutable, unwritten laws of heaven." The King replied that traitors must be punished; a state must have laws and they must be obeyed in all things, just and unjust alike; otherwise, there will be anarchy, and there is no evil worse than anarchy.

Similarly, when rebelling against the English King, the American revolutionaries in 1776 relied in their Declaration of Independence on the concept of "inalienable rights" endowed by their Creator. In the same spirit, the French National Assembly in 1789 set forth in the Declaration of the Rights of Man and of the Citizen "the natural and imprescriptible rights of man." More recently, Jacques Maritain pointed out:

> [The] human person possess[es] rights because of the very fact that it is a person, a whole, a master of itself and of its acts . . . by virtue of natural law, the human person has the right to be respected, is the subject of rights, possesses rights. These are things which are owed to a man because of the very fact that he is a man.

The United Nations' concept of human rights embraces this natural law concept of rights, rights to which all human beings have been entitled since time immemorial and to which they will continue to be entitled as long as humanity survives. Thus, both the Universal Declaration of Human Rights and the two Covenants assert in the first paragraphs of their preambles that "recognition of the inherent dignity and of the equal and inalienable rights of all members of the human family is the foundation of freedom, justice and peace in the world." More recently, in specifying the guiding concepts for future human rights work within the United Nations' system, the General Assembly listed among those concepts the natural law idea that "[a]ll human rights and fundamental freedoms of the human person and of peoples are inalienable."

These "inalienable" rights, both permanent and universal, differ from rights, bestowed by positive law, that a state can give and take away. The distinction between these two categories of rights becomes evident when a state attempts to limit human rights in the interest of the community during an emergency. Thus, the International Covenant on Civil and Political Rights permits states to derogate from certain of its provisions when a public emergency threatens the life of the nation; in contrast, the Covenant does not permit derogation from certain inalienable rights, including the right to life, freedom from torture or cruel, inhuman, or degrading treatment or punishment, freedom from slavery and servitude, nonapplicability of retroactive laws, right to recognition as a person before the law, and the right to freedom of thought, conscience, and religion. No state is allowed to deprive individuals of these inalienable rights; such rights are part of a higher law that no positive law can overrule.

There are two other categories of rights: first, those which a state can limit in times of emergency, such as freedom from compulsory labor, right to liberty and security of person, right to humane treatment in prison, right to certain minimum guarantees in criminal proceedings, and freedom from interference with privacy, family, home, or correspondence; and, second, those which the state can limit in order to protect national security, public order (*ordre public*), and public health or morals. The second category includes the following rights listed in the Covenant on Civil and Political Rights: the right to liberty of movement; the freedom to choose one's residence; the right to a public hearing; freedom to manifest one's religion or beliefs in public; freedom of expression and to seek, receive, and impart information and ideas, orally or in print; right of peaceful assembly; and freedom of association. Of the rights listed in the International Covenant on Economic, Social and Cultural Rights, only the rights relating to trade unions are subject to similar restrictions. Other rights arising under the Covenant can be limited solely "for the purpose of promoting the general welfare in a democratic society."

Some scholars may find these differentiations petty. Nevertheless, they show the marriage of positivist and natural law doctrines, the positive law helping to enforce natural law distinctions.

THE INTERNATIONAL COVENANTS: OVERVIEW

When the Commission on Human Rights finished the Universal Declaration, it began preparing the other part of the International Bill of Rights, a convention containing precise obligations that would be binding on the States Parties. There were initial fears that the various rights would drown in a sea of limitations and exceptions, but this danger was avoided by careful delineation of the conditions under which rights could be limited, and identification of those rights that could not be limited under any circumstances. Another difficulty did, however, arise. It proved impossible to formulate in a parallel manner all the rights listed in the Universal Declaration; it became necessary to divide the materials into two categories: civil and political rights; and economic, social, and cultural rights. These two categories were embodied in two separate Covenants—a name that was preferred to the less solemn "convention"—each differing from the other in several respects. The main difference was in their treatment after coming into force. States Parties were to give the Covenant on Civil and Political Rights immediate effect through appropriate legislative or other measures and by making available an effective remedy to any person whose rights have been violated. In contrast, each State Party to the Covenant on Economic, Social and Cultural Rights agreed only to take steps, to the maximum of its available resources, toward a progressive realization of the rights recognized in that Covenant. The Covenant thus contained a loophole: because a state's obligation was limited to the resources available to it, a poor state could proceed slowly, progressing only as fast as its resources permitted. If its resources should diminish, for example, during an economic crisis, its progress could wane. In contrast, the Covenant on Civil and Political Rights permits no such excuses; a state must guarantee civil and political rights fully on ratification, subject only to the limitations previously discussed.

Although doubts have been expressed about the legal force of the Declaration, the Covenants are now binding on more than seventy states, almost half of the members of the world community. Among the parties to the Covenants are states from all regions: Africa, Asia, the Americas, Western Europe, and Eastern Europe. Among members of the European Community, Denmark, France, the Federal Republic of Germany, Italy, the Netherlands, and the United Kingdom have ratified the Covenants. These states are also parties to the 1950 European Convention on Human Rights, which contains provisions parallel to those in the Covenant on Civil and Political Rights. Two special institutions, the European Commission of Human Rights and the European Court of Human Rights, have developed considerable jurisprudence with respect to the European Convention. There are almost daily press releases about cases submitted or decided. In

Europe, international decisions on human rights issues thus have become routine; they are no longer extraordinary occurrences.

This European jurisprudence throws light not only on the provisions of the European Convention, but also on the similar provisions in the Covenant on Civil and Political Rights. In a discussion of the Covenant, therefore, it might be useful to refer occasionally to the European experience under the Convention. There is also a well-developed inter-American system of human rights, based on the American Convention on Human Rights, which entered into force in 1978. The most recent addition to the family of regional human rights instruments is the African Charter on Human and Peoples' Rights, approved in 1981.

Another general point must be made. Although the rights protected by the Covenants are stated with greater precision than those listed in the Universal Declaration, the former are broad enough in scope to surmount differences among various political, economic, and social systems, as well as among widely differing cultures and stages of development. Consequently, only the last factor—differences in stages of development, especially economic development—need be taken into account in applying the Covenant on Economic, Social and Cultural Rights. In contrast, even that factor does not excuse nonimplementation of the Covenant on Civil and Political Rights.

The Covenants and national constitutions or laws are meant to coexist. The Covenants do not supersede any constitutions or laws that provide more protection to individuals. Where the Covenants go beyond a domestic law in protecting a particular right, the state concerned has the duty to adopt any additional legislative or other measures that may be necessary to give effect to the right recognized in the Covenants.

2. *Human Rights and Environmental Objectives*

■ HUMAN RIGHTS, ENVIRONMENTAL RIGHTS, AND THE RIGHT TO ENVIRONMENT

Dinah Shelton
28 Stan. J. Intl. L. 103, 106-107 (1991)

Laws often respond to perceived social problems by restraining the exercise of power and establishing agreed norms of public conduct. Viewed from this perspective, laws protecting human rights respond to threats to human dignity and existence by upholding the fundamental, immutable foundations of human rights as recognized in international instruments. In addition, formulations of rights reflect emerging social values. For example, although slavery was once widespread, nations now universally repudiate it, and international law recognizes freedom from slavery as a non-derogable human right. More recently, a right to privacy has been recognized in response to technological advances spawning increasing intrusion into home and family.

The goal of international human rights law, as expressed in the Universal Declaration of Human Rights and the International Covenants, is "freedom, justice and peace in the world." The means of achieving this goal begin with legal recognition of the equal and inalienable rights of all members of the human family and of the inherent dignity possessed by each individual.

An immediate, practical objective of international human rights law is to gain international recognition of specific human rights. Successfully placing personal entitlements within the category of individual human rights preserves them from the ordinary political process. Individual rights may thus significantly limit the political will of a democratic majority, as well as a dictatorial minority. For example, in attempting to attain a widely accepted policy goal, even a representative democracy may not produce legislation that limits or abolishes the individual right to be free from cruel, inhuman, or degrading treatment or punishment. This absolute limitation on domestic political decisions is potentially an important consequence of elaborating a right to environment, particularly given the high short-term costs involved in many environmental protection measures and the resulting political disfavor.

■ MAKING SPACE FOR NEW HUMAN RIGHTS: THE CASE OF THE RIGHT TO DEVELOPMENT

Philip Alston
1 Harv. Human Rights J. 3, 3-4 (1988)

In the 1980's, the language of human rights has come steadily to occupy almost as prominent a position in international discourse as rights language does in American municipal law discourse. It is now widely accepted that the characterization of a specific goal as a human right elevates it above the rank and file of competing societal goals, gives it a degree of immunity from challenge and generally endows it with an aura of timelessness, absoluteness and universal validity. It has recently been suggested, for example, that in the United States context "the assertion . . . of rights can express political vision, affirm a group's humanity, contribute to an individual's development as a whole person, and assist in the collective political development of a social or political movement, particularly at its early stages."

Given such perceptions of the potential power of rights rhetoric, it is hardly surprising that claims for the recognition of new human rights have proliferated dramatically in recent years. In the international arena the most enduring claims have been put forward under the rubric of "third generation solidarity rights." Although the generational terminology is considered misleading and unhelpful by many commentators, several of the "new" human rights have prospered well beyond the expectations of their proponents (and certainly beyond those of their detractors). The right to development, for example, has been recognized in the African Charter of Human and Peoples' Rights which entered into force, for over half of the African States, in October 1986; and in December 1986, the United Nations General Assembly adopted a Declaration on the Right to Development. The right to a clean environment is also recognized in the African Charter and is contained in the most recent draft of a proposed Additional Protocol to the American Convention on Human Rights. The "Right of Peoples to Peace" was the subject of a Declaration adopted by the UN General Assembly in 1984, the implementation of which continues to be a controversial item on the Assembly's agenda. The right to humanitarian assistance has also received considerable attention.

This proliferation has given rise to widely divergent reactions both among governments and scholars. Proponents of the "new" human rights contend that the excessively individualistic bias of the UN's approach has at last been corrected; that the human rights tradition has proven itself to be capable of responding to new needs and challenges; that the values, aspirations and traditions of the developing countries (most of which were not independent at the time of the adoption of the Universal Declaration of Human Rights) have finally been taken into account; and that human rights is no longer an area artificially divorced from the most urgent issues of the day such as peace, development and environmental protection.

■ CONJURING UP NEW HUMAN RIGHTS: A PROPOSAL FOR QUALITY CONTROL

Philip Alston
78 Am. J. Intl. L. 607, 607-617 (1984)

Writing in 1968, the year of the 20th anniversary of the adoption of the Universal Declaration of Human Rights, Richard Bilder concluded that "in practice, a claim is an international human right if the United Nations General Assembly says it is." Fifteen years later, as the 35th anniversary is celebrated, the authoritative role that Bilder correctly attributed to the General Assembly is in serious danger of being undermined.

The problem has manifested itself in three ways. First, the General Assembly has, on several occasions in recent years, proclaimed new rights (i.e. rights which do not find explicit recognition in the Human Rights Covenants) without explicitly acknowledging its intention of doing so and without insisting that the claims in question should satisfy any particular criteria before qualifying as human rights. Second, there has been a growing tendency on the part of a range of United Nations and other international bodies, including in particular the UN Commission on Human Rights, to proceed to the proclamation of new human rights without reference to the Assembly. Third, the ease with which such innovation has been accomplished in these bodies has in turn encouraged or provoked the nomination of additional candidates, ranging from the right to tourism to the right to disarmament, at such a rate that the integrity of the entire process of recognizing human rights is threatened.

In principle, both the validity and the necessity of a dynamic approach to human rights, as well as the expansion, where appropriate, of the list of recognized human rights, cannot reasonably be disputed. However, reason for serious concern with respect to current trends arises not so much from the proliferation of new rights but rather from the haphazard, almost anarchic manner in which this expansion is being achieved. Indeed, some such rights seem to have been literally conjured up, in the dictionary sense of being, "brought into existence as if by magic."

The absence of any established procedure by which candidates for new rights are scrutinized has resulted in an unfortunate situation: bodies at a lower level in the international organizational hierarchy than the General Assembly have tended to proclaim the existence of new rights without adequate consideration of the basis for, let alone the advisability or implications of, such action and without leaving the Assembly with an adequate opportunity to determine whether or not the giving of its imprimatur is warranted.

. . .

In one sense, the authority vested in the Assembly to proclaim human rights is based on firm legal foundations. It is a logical and direct outcome of the Assembly's mandate, contained in Article 13 of the United Nations Charter, to "initiate studies and make recommendations for the purpose of . . . assisting in the realization of human rights and fundamental freedoms for all without distinction as to race, sex, language, or religion." . . .

Recognition of the essential dynamism of the notion of human rights inevitably requires a willingness to consider the need to proclaim additional human rights. The challenge is to achieve an appropriate balance between, on the one hand, the need to maintain the integrity and credibility of the human rights tradition, and on the other hand, the need to adopt a dynamic approach that fully reflects changing needs and perspectives and responds to the emergence of new threats to human dignity and well-being. . . .

If we were to establish a list of criteria a given claim must satisfy in order to qualify as a human right in terms of international law, it might look something like this. The proposed new human right should:

- reflect a fundamentally important social value;
- be relevant, inevitably to varying degrees, throughout a world of diverse value systems;

- be eligible for recognition on the grounds that it is an interpretation of UN Charter obligations, a reflection of customary law rules or a formulation that is declaratory of general principles of law;
- be consistent with, but not merely repetitive of, the existing body of international human rights law;
- be capable of achieving a very high degree of international consensus;
- be compatible or at least not clearly incompatible with the general practice of states; and
- be sufficiently precise as to give rise to identifiable rights and obligations.

The question to be answered then is how to apply these or comparable criteria in practice. The possible options are to establish substantive or procedural requirements, either or both of which would have to be satisfied before a given claim could be recognized as a new right.

At first glance, the laying down of specific substantive requirements such as those listed above is appealing, and it has in fact been advocated . . . by a number of commentators.

The difficulty of devising and applying universally acceptable substantive criteria must not be permitted to obscure the fact that procedural requirements may be used as an indirect means to achieve many of the same objectives. Indeed, "conformity with minimum procedural standards relating to the decision process" is, as Professor Schachter has recently written, "an essential requirement for legitimizing international decisions." It is significant that most of the shortcomings identified above with respect to the present approach to new human rights concern the procedure followed rather than the outcome sought to be achieved. . . .

Notes and Questions

1. *Development, environment and human rights.*

> [T]here is the obvious relationship among the environment, economic development and human rights that occurs with global problems involving the shared concerns of health, safety and individual well-being. It is certainly reasonable to claim that development is about improving the quality of life and, therefore, inappropriate development is development inconsistent with basic human rights. It is further reasonable to claim that development at the expense of environmental quality is detrimental to our human condition.
>
> The study of the relationship among these three subject areas is a complex and multidimensional one that today is certainly embryonic. Nevertheless, many of the legal issues raised by the global problems of technology develop-

> ment, population growth, desertification, famine, global warming, ozone depletion, deforestation, nuclear proliferation, and the miserable poverty besetting a large percentage of our world are arguably at the intersection of the more legally developed areas of environment, economic development and human rights.

Robert E. Lutz, *Environment, Economic Development and Human Rights: A Triangular Relationship?*, 1988 Proc. of ASIL Ann. Meeting 40, 40-41. Do you agree?

2. *A human right to tourism?* A wide range of special interest groups perceive the usefulness of attaching the "human rights" label to further their cause. For example, the World Tourism Organization has proclaimed "tourism has become increasingly a basic need, a social necessity, a human right." Although the right to a clean environment is not a frivolous claim, does declaring it a human right without support at the highest international levels threaten the integrity of the entire process of human rights recognition? *See* Noralee Gibson, *The Right to a Clean Environment*, 54 Sask. L. Rev. 5, 9 (1990); Philip Alston, *Conjuring Up New Human Rights: A Proposal for Quality Control*, 78 Am. J. Intl. L. 607 (1984).

3. The Interrelationship between Human Rights and Environmental Protection

How a human right to the environment might be classified affects how it is recognized and how its scope is defined.

■ HUMAN RIGHTS, ENVIRONMENTAL RIGHTS, AND THE RIGHT TO THE ENVIRONMENT

Dinah Shelton
28 Stan. J. Intl. L. 103, 103-105 (1991)

A growing number of global and regional human rights instruments and national constitutions include a right to environment among their guarantees. The United Nations Commission on Human Rights also has asserted a link between preservation of the environment and the promotion of human rights. The Commission recently supported a decision of the Sub-Commission on Prevention of Discrimination and Protection of Minorities to study the relations between the two subjects.

There is no doubt that the global environment is deteriorating and that failure to alleviate current environmental degradation may threaten human health and human life. However, the necessary and appropriate international legal response remains unclear. These problems generate a host of questions and public policy alternatives. A fundamental question is whether human rights and environmental protection are premised upon fundamentally different social values, such that efforts to implement both simultaneously will produce more conflict than improvement, or, on the other hand, whether human rights and environmental protection are complementary, each furthering the aims of the other.

Some theorists suggest that environmental issues belong within the human rights category, because the goal of environmental protection is to enhance the quality of human life. Opponents argue, however, that human beings are merely one element of a complex, global ecosystem, which should be preserved for its own sake. Under this approach, human rights are subsumed under the primary objective of protecting nature as a whole.

A third view, which seems to best reflect current law and policy sees human rights and environmental protection as each representing different, but overlapping, societal values. The two fields share a core of common interests and objectives, although obviously not all human rights violations are necessarily linked to environmental degradation. Likewise, environmental issues cannot always be addressed effectively within the human rights framework, and any attempt to force all such issues into a human rights rubric may fundamentally distort the concept of human rights. This approach recognizes the potential conflicts between environmental protection and other human rights, but also the contribution each field can make to achieving their common objectives.

In order to contribute to environmental protection using a human rights approach—or vice versa—this third view suggests several alternatives. First, environmental problems may be combated through the assertion of existing human rights, such as the rights to life, personal security, health, and food. In this regard, a safe and healthy environment may be viewed either as a pre-condition to the exercise of existing rights or as inextricably intertwined with the enjoyment of these rights. A second, intermediate position proposes a set of "environmental rights" (rights *of* the environment as well as *to* the environment) based upon existing rights to information about and involvement in the political design-making process. Third, and most ambitiously, a specific "right to the environment" could be formulated and added to the current catalogue of human rights. . . .

. . . The fundamental issue is whether international human rights law can contribute to environmental protection, or conversely, whether international environmental policies can serve human rights concerns. . . .

Notes and Questions

1. *Nature for humans?* The article by Professor Shelton alludes to the controversial assertion that some environmentalists fear may be the out-

come of a "human-centered" (anthropocentric) view of environmental law. The problem arises from the concept of "human rights" as a species-chauvinistic approach that reduces the protection of nature to its value to humans. *See* Dinah Shelton, *Human Rights, Environmental Rights, and the Right to the Environment,* 28 Stan. J. Intl. L. 103, 108-109 (1991); Edith Brown Weiss, *Our Rights and Obligations to Future Generations for the Environment,* 84 Am. J. Intl. L. 198 (1990).

2. *Humans for nature?* Approaching environmental protection from a natural (biocentric) perspective poses the question of whether and to what extent humans have a moral obligation to preserve nature for its own sake and to what extent humans should sacrifice for this preservation. For example, assume the spotted owl has no direct or indirect economic value. Should it be preserved even though this would hurt the timber industry economically?

4. Emergence of a Right to a Clean Environment

Supporters of the contention that there is a right to a clean environment must show evidence that it is a prevailing legal principle before claiming protections for victims. The strongest proposition for the right lies in establishing it as an international legal standard binding on nations and found in treaties or in customary international law. If it is an emerging right, it is not clearly defined in scope and context, and advocates cannot contend that the right exists, as widely recognized in international law. Alternatively, there are some who might argue that the right is inferred from other rights already recognized. How do you think such a human right should be described? Is it a "human" right at all?

a. A New Human Right

■ INTERNATIONAL LEGAL PROTECTION FOR VICTIMS OF ENVIRONMENTAL ABUSE

Michelle Leighton Schwartz
18 Yale J. Intl. L. 355, 359-361 (1993)

Several theories support the contention that government action violates international human rights law if it causes environmental damage that results in harm to an individual or group. One theory holds that environmental damage is actionable whenever a victim can link it to an established or fundamental human right, such as the right to life. A more expansive theory holds that environmental damage, at some as yet undefined threshold, is actionable because everyone has the right to live in a healthy environment. The existence *vel non* of this latter right and its precise content and nature have stirred much debate. A third theory argues for intergenerational equity, based on the notion that each generation has a moral obligation to protect the environment for immediate benefit and for the benefit of future generations. It is unclear whether this concept conveys an enforceable *right.*

All three theories yield the conclusion that states have a fundamental duty to refrain from environmentally destructive acts which could injure human beings (again, the threshold for violation is uncertain), and to take affirmative action to prevent environmental harm where possible. Some proponents of these theories argue that, in fulfilling their human rights obligations, states may be obliged to promulgate standards to regulate environmental quality, especially to prevent and control pollution to the air, water, and soil.

These theories are undergoing analysis by the Sub-commission on the Prevention of Discrimination and Protection of Minorities under the mandate of the U.N. Commission on Human Rights. The Sub-commission's investigation has found that international, regional, and national bodies have adopted many instruments that could be used to strengthen environmental protection. Still, whether potential victims can use these documents to prevent an environmental threat to their lives, health, livelihood, and culture or to seek redress for injuries, remains uncertain.

Other U.N. bodies have only begun to consider the relationship between human rights and the environment. Although state participants at the U.N. Conference on Environment and Development (UNCED) ["Earth Summit" in Rio de Janeiro in June 1992] agreed on the need to protect victims of environmental destruction, the UNCED failed to address environmental human rights in any meaningful way, to develop any programs for the U.N. or for regional bodies, or to set a future agenda on the issue.

■ HUMAN RIGHTS AND PROTECTION OF THE ENVIRONMENT: A MILDLY "REVISIONIST" VIEW

Günther Handl
Human Rights, Sustainable Development and the Environment 117, 120-122 (Antonio Augusto Cancado Trindade ed. 1992)

At the outset it might be advisable to point out that the international human rights discourse continues to suffer from an unresolved "contradiction between conceptions of human rights as either inherent in human beings by virtue of their humanity or as benevolently granted by the state." This affects not just the perception of the burden of proof but the very nature of the argument regarding the existence of such rights in general international law. For example, some adherents of a natural law theory of human rights might be apt to view any "just claim" as an existing human right. Most international lawyers, however, are likely to agree that the process of international recognition of human rights evinces overlapping positive and natural law conceptions. They are also likely to insist, notwithstanding the relative dearth of traditional state practice in the sense of international claims and counterclaims involving human rights, [that] evidence of actual supportive state practice remains an essential element of any persuasive argument that a given human rights claim is recognized by general international law.

This evidentiary requirement applies firstly, even if we assume that by now states implicitly recognize the United Nations General Assembly's special declaratory authority to determine the human rights nature of claims, and secondly, notwithstanding the possibility that with respect to human rights claims, actual state practice may be less of an essential underpinning of international normativity than would be the case in other contexts. After all, from the perspective of assessing allegedly new customary international legal norms, including human rights norms, deeds speak louder than words: only actual practice endorsing a claimed entitlement may provide a realistic measure of states' determination to render the prescriptive standard effective. Absent a "credible communication" to that effect, the alleged human rights standard is a mere paper right.

In any event, a diminished evidentiary standard regarding actual practice might be applicable only to human rights that are fundamental or inalienable ones. What can be said with confidence, therefore, is that the more attenuated the natural law basis of an alleged human right, the more important will be support of evidence of its reflection in positive international law, i.e., the practice of states and other relevant transnational actors.

Leaving aside for the moment the problem of its intrinsic relativity, the so-called "right to environment," or the right to a "clean," even to a "healthy environment" should be difficult to conceptualize as an inalienable one, notwithstanding the important objectives it purports to serve. If "inalienability" implies the impermissibility of derogations from the human right concerned, it should be evident why any meaningful environmental entitlement would not qualify: The evolution of environmental protection measures has involved a constant re-ordering of socio-economic priorities, of accommodating, adjusting, or off-setting mutually restrictive, if not exclusive, public policy objectives. Environmental entitlements have been and will continue to be susceptible to restrictions for the sake of other, socio-economic objectives, such as ensuring continued "development" or "saving jobs." In short, since a generic environmental entitlement would not be inalienable, it would not therefore share either a characteristic that is traditionally viewed as a hallmark of "natural" rights. Conceptually, it is instead squarely rooted in positive law.

Those who attempt to make the case for an existing or emerging generic environmental human right, therefore, would have to back up their claims by solid positive legal evidence. Alas, when analyzed in light of this evidentiary standard, the claims concerned are unpersuasive: Thus far, the idea of a generic entitlement—as against "sectoral" environmental rights of individuals—has not found express affirmation in any binding or effective international legal instrument.

b. Theoretical Bases

Traditionally, human rights have been considered to be based on the protection of universal values that relate to human dignity. Other theories suggest that the universality characteristic of human rights derives from a basis other than the inherent dignity of the human person.

If the right to a clean environment is a human right, it must fall within an acceptable theory of human rights. Three theories have been advanced as to the basis of the right to a clean environment. Consider the following:

■ THE RIGHT TO A CLEAN ENVIRONMENT

Noralee Gibson
54 Sask. L. Rev. 5, 12, 16-17 (1990)

1. Cultural Legitimacy Theory

The first theory asserts the right to a clean environment derives from cultural legitimacy. Cultural legitimacy is defined as "the quality or state of being in conformity with recognized principles or accepted rules and standards of a given culture." If the theoretical basis of the right to a clean environment is a value or norm accepted by a wide range of cultural traditions, it may be recognized as a human right.

2. Indispensability Theory

The threat to human existence and survival provides a second basis for the right to a clean environment. The right to a clean environment is indispensable to the exercise of other human rights. A clean and healthy environment is a prerequisite for the enjoyment of other human rights. Under the indispensability theory, the right to a clean environment is an essential condition for the fulfillment of all human rights.

3. Survival Need Theory

In conjunction with the broader international goal of saving the ecosystem, one can formulate an international right to a clean environment. This right would be extended to all members of the ecosystem including humans. It is a right based on need. This right would be viewed as the most basic need of all living organisms. It is even more fundamentally important than individual human rights; it is concerned with the collective survival of all human beings. It is this most important objective to which the right to a clean environment should be linked and not to individual human rights. Granting the rights to the environment as a whole is a recognition of its value, not to us as consumers of environmental amenities, but as an integral part of life itself. . . .

Also, if the right to a clean environment can be viewed as a survival need, it is truly a "universal" right since the cultural aspect of legitimization is not a factor. The need for survival is universal due to every organism's inherent need and desire to survive.

Notes and Questions

1. *Direct or indirect protection?* As a rule, an individual's environment is indirectly protected when the environment in general is protected. However, an individual's particular environment could also be legally protected in a direct manner through recognition of an individual's right to a clean and healthy environment. *See* Heinhard Steiger et al., *The Fundamental Right to a Decent Environment,* in Trends in Environmental Policy and Law 1, 2 (Michael Bothe ed. 1980).

2. *The nature of human rights.* There is substantial disagreement as to the precise nature of human rights, their sources and their practical implications. International human rights law is developing in ways which attempt to balance diverse ideologies and garner allegiances of widely varying cultural traditions. *See* Philip Alston, *Making Space for New Human Rights: The Case for the Right to Development,* 1 Harv. Hum. Rts. J. 3, 29 (1988); Kamenka & Tay, *Philosophy and Human Rights: A Survey and Select Annotated Bibliography of Recent English Language Literature,* 70 Archiv Fur Rechts-und Sozialphilosphie, 291, 297 (1984).

Proponents of new human rights such as the right to a clean environment contend that these rights have already become part of customary international law. Opponents argue that these rights are not legal rights but are either political or social principles. Is the right to a clean environment a "moral" right, without any legal force? *See* Louis B. Sohn, *The New International Law: Protection of the Rights of Individuals Rather Than States,* 32 Am. U.L. Rev. 1, 61 (1982); Noralee Gibson, *The Right to a Clean Environment,* 54 Sask. L. Rev. 5, 15 (1990).

c. Articulations of a Human Right

(i) International Instruments

DECLARATION OF THE UNITED NATIONS CONFERENCE ON THE HUMAN ENVIRONMENT

***June 1972*, reprinted in *11 I.L.M. 1416 (1972)*.**

PRINCIPLE 1

Man has the fundamental right to freedom, equality, and adequate conditions of life, in an environment of a quality that permits a life of dignity and well-being, and he bears a solemn responsibility to protect and improve the environment for present and future generations. . . .

Notes and Questions

1. *The Stockholm Declaration and the right to environment.* At the international level, the Stockholm Declaration in 1972 formulated the first evidence of a right to a clean environment. Although the text does not explicitly state that there is a right to a clean environment, it does express the issue in human rights terms. The General Assembly subsequently adopted the declaration. However, the General Assembly has not specifically proclaimed the existence of a right to a clean environment, despite proposals that it do so.

2. *The Stockholm Declaration: additional provisions.* Article 2 of the Stockholm Declaration is also read as being a source of environmental protection. It declares that protection of the human environment is a precondition for the well-being of present and future generations and "the duty of all Governments." Iveta Hodkova, *Is There a Right to a Healthy Environment in the International Legal Order?*, 7 Conn. J. Intl. L. 65, 66 (1991).

3. *The General Assembly and a right to environment.* In December 1989, the UN General Assembly considered a resolution that would have recognized a "healthy environment" as a human right. The resolution was blocked by the government of Brazil under former President Jose Sarney, who was sensitive to criticism of Brazil's environmental practices.

4. *The Brundtland Commission and a right to environment.* The Legal Experts Group of the World Commission on Environment and Development (WCED or the Brundtland Commission) explicitly incorporated into its report, General Principles Concerning Natural Resources and Environmental Interferences, the provision that "[a]ll human beings have the fundamental right to an environment adequate for their health and well-being." (Principle 1) Although the term "adequate" is vague and may

have many different meanings according to the socio-economic situation of a country, one author argues this provision does provide the basis for "an international obligation on the part of the State vis-à-vis another State . . . to protect the environment for all individuals. . . ." Iveta Hodkova, above, at 67 (1991) (citing Experts Group on Environmental Law of the World Commission on Environment and Development, Environmental Protection and Sustainable Development: Legal Principles and Recommendations 40 (1986)).

5. *The Hague Declaration.* The Conference on the Environment drafted the Hague Declaration of 1989 following WCED's efforts. This document's relevant provision states "[b]ecause of the nature of the dangers involved, remedies to be sought involve not only the fundamental duty to preserve the ecosystem, but also the right to live in dignity in a viable global environment. . . ." Declaration on the Hague Environment, March 11, 1989, 28 I.L.M. 1308, 1309 (1989). Is there a correlation between the right to live and the global environment?

The declaration also ties the implementation of a human right to live (which includes environment protection obligations) to the development of a UN organization to create and enforce international agreements to control pollution. Although the document does not have the force of law, it demonstrates states' recognition that cooperation on such issues is essential. Twenty-four states have adopted the Hague Declaration.

6. *An international court for the environment?* The 1989 International Congress on "A More Efficient International Law on the Environment and Establishing an International Court for the Environment within the United Nations System" stressed in its Final Statement the need for "obligatory and legal procedures for preventing and regulating any conflicts" at the international level. The Final Statement called for a body that would plan and manage the world environment, establish an international court for the environment accessible to states, United Nations organs, and private citizens. *See* Final Statement, International Congress on a More Efficient International Law on the Environment and Establishing an International Court for the Environment within the United Nations System (1989), *reprinted in* 19 Envtl. Poly. & L. 138 (1989).

■ INTERNATIONAL ASSOCIATION OF DEMOCRATIC LAWYERS DRAFT DECLARATION OF HUMAN RIGHTS AND THE RIGHTS OF PEOPLES TO PEACE AND DISARMAMENT

- the right of all individuals and peoples to an environment of such quality as to enable them to live with dignity and enjoy a state of well-being.

Notes and Questions

1. *The World Charter.* The World Charter for Nature, adopted by the UN General Assembly in 1982 by a vote of 111 to 1, with 18 abstentions, sets out General Principles that include: "Nature shall be respected . . . ;" the genetic viability of life forms shall be protected; all areas of the earth shall be subject to principles of conservation with special protection being given to habitats of rare or endangered species; and ecosystems, organisms and land, marine and atmospheric resources shall be managed in a way to achieve "optimum sustainable productivity." 1982 U.N.Y.B. 1023; World Charter for Nature, G.A. Res. 27/7, 37 U.N. GAOR Supp. (No. 51) at 17, U.N. Doc. A/37/51 (1982), *reprinted in* 22 I.L.M. 455 (1983). At least one commentator has argued that while the World Charter lacks an explicit pronouncement of a human right to environment, its General Principles—along with other similarly worded international statements—can be used to infer such a right. *See* Melissa Thorme, *Establishing Environment As a Human Right,* 19 Denv. J. Intl. L. & Poly. 301, 317 (1991). Can you see how one might make such an argument?

The United States cast the lone dissenting vote on the World Charter. Why do you suppose the United States cast that vote?

2. *UNESCO's contribution.* An additional source for the right to a clean environment can be found in a 1980 UNESCO colloquium on new human rights. The colloquium discussed "the right to a healthy and ecologically balanced environment." *See* UNESCO, Symposium on New Human Rights: The Rights of Solidarity, Mexico City, 1980, at 1, UNESCO Doc. 55 81/CONF 806/4 (1981).

(ii) Regional Instruments

Regional instruments are able to promote the right to a clean environment in a unique way that global treaties cannot. Regional bodies are comprised of fewer states, which have closer ties to each other geographically, culturally, historically, and politically. How can these commonalities aid in reaching regional agreements to recognize the right to environment? Do they have a role in the progressive development of universal norms?

■ THE AFRICAN CHARTER OF HUMAN AND PEOPLES' RIGHTS

June 26, 1981, Article 24, 21 I.L.M. 59

All peoples shall have the right to a general satisfactory environment favorable to their development.

Notes and Questions

1. *The African Charter.* The African Charter became effective in 1986 making it the first international document to delineate the right "to a general satisfactory environment." (African Charter on Human and Peoples' Rights, entered into force Oct. 21, 1986). The charter differs from other documents stipulating this general right by recognizing that social and economic rights are a precondition for the recognition of civil and political rights and in that it defines the right as a collective right to "peoples" rather than individuals. The charter lacks specific legal obligations, providing only that: "[s]tate parties . . . shall allow the establishment and improvement of appropriate national institutions entrusted with the promotion and protection of the rights and freedoms guaranteed by the present Charter." (Article 26). The charter has been characterized as a "philosophic document with weak or non-existent means of implementation." *See* Hodkova, above, at 76 (1991); W. Paul Gormely, *The Right to a Safe Environment,* 28 Indian J. Intl. L. 1, 16 (1988).

2. *The OAS.* The Organization of American States has expressed the human right to a clean environment in the Additional Protocol to the American Convention on Human Rights, approved in 1988. The right is delineated in Article 11 as:

> 1. Everyone shall have the right to live in a healthy environment and to have access to basic public services.
>
> 2. The States Parties shall promote the protection, preservation and improvement of the environment.

Additional Protocol to the American Convention on Human Rights, *approved* Nov. 14, 1988, 28 I.L.M. 161 (1989). This expresses an explicit right to environmental protection, and the rights adopted in the Protocol are "promised the protection of the inter-American human rights system." *See* Dinah Shelton, *Improving Human Rights Protections: Recommendations for Enhancing the Effectiveness of the Inter-American Commission and Inter-American Court of Human Rights,* 3 Am. U.J. Intl. L. & Poly. 323, 323-325 (1988). On the other hand, Article 12 proclaims: "[e]veryone shall have the right to live in an environment free of pollution and to have access to basic urban services, especially a safe water supply and sewerage services." Does this mean that the preceding provision is merely a general declarative provision without the force of law until another specific provision delineates the exact type of environmental protection? *See* Günther Handl, above, at 120-122.

One commentator notes that the OAS system "does not provide efficient means of protecting rights. . . . Very few cases have been referred to the Inter-American Court by the Inter-American Commission and few have been addressed by the Commission itself. The system is primarily geared to large-scale violations of human rights. . . ." Hodkova, above, at 74.

One major impediment to actions by individuals may be Article 1. It requires states to cooperate on an international level and to adopt all necessary measures "to the extent allowed by their available resources, and taking into account their degree of development" to protect the guaranteed rights. The parties must also adopt domestic legislation to realize the rights. Do these provisions swallow up the right and render the protocol's protection to individuals useless? Further, the protocol does not grant individuals the right to petition for violations of the right to the environment, but allows the Inter-American Commission on Human Rights to conduct investigations and make recommendations on the status of the rights enunciated in the protocol. (Article 19(7)). Is this a political way to restrict by procedural requirements the individual right to a healthy environment?

3. *The Council of Europe.* The Council of Europe is dedicated to "the maintenance and further realization of human rights and fundamental freedoms." In light of this purpose, it adopted the European Convention on Human Rights (European Convention for the Protection of Human Rights and Fundamental Freedoms, Nov. 4, 1950, 213 U.N.T.S. 221) and the European Social Charter (*opened for signature,* Oct. 18, 1961, 529 U.N.T.S. 89) which together implement civil, political, economic, social, and environmental human rights. Since the 1970s the Council of Europe has strived to create a human right to a healthy environment, but objections have prohibited its adoption. One effort initiated was the Draft Protocol to the European Convention on Human Rights providing that

> Article 1: (1) No one should be exposed to intolerable damage or threats to his health or to intolerable impairment of his well-being as a result of adverse changes in the natural conditions of life.
>
> (2) An impairment of well-being may, however, be deemed to be tolerable if it is necessary for the maintenance and development of the economic conditions of the community and if there is no alternative way of making it possible to avoid this impairment.
>
> Article 2: (1) If adverse changes in the natural conditions are likely to occur in his vital sphere as a result of the actions of other parties, any individual is entitled to demand that the competent agencies examine the situation in all cases where Article 1 applies.
>
> (2) Any individual acting under paragraph 1 shall, within a reasonable time, receive detailed information stating what measures—if any—have been taken to prevent those adverse changes.

Draft Protocol to the European Convention on Human Rights and Fundamental Freedoms, *reprinted in* Human Rights in a Changing East-West Perspective 216, 229 (1990).

Although the draft is stated in general terms and does not obligate payment of damages for prior injuries, it was not adopted. Professor Shelton has opined that the European member states lacked the political will to accept these proposals due to: "(1) a fear of watering down the European Convention with a series of newly claimed human rights; (2) the belief that the right to environment lacks justiciability; and (3) the fact that each state has serious environmental problems which could be the subject of complaint if the right gained acceptance." Dinah Shelton, *Human Rights, Environmental Rights, and the Right to Environment,* above, 28 Stan. J. Intl. L., —, 103, 133 (1991).

In 1990, the Assembly of the Council of Europe adopted the Recommendation to the Parliamentary Assembly on the Formulation of a European Charter and a European Convention on Environmental Protection containing not only an individual's definitive right to a healthy environment but also a respective legal duty:

> 1. Every person has the fundamental right to an environment and living conditions conducive to his good health, well-being and full development of the human personality.
> 2. Every Contracting European State has a duty to preserve and protect the environment in the interests of the health and well-being of all people inside and outside of Europe, for the benefit of present and future generations.

Eur. Parl. Assem., 42d Sess., Recommendation 1130, at 2 (1990).

The draft of the ECE Charter on Environmental Rights and Obligations is also a recent document espousing the right to an adequate environment and the responsibility of everyone to contribute to the environment's protection and conservation. In addition, it contains the right to information on environmental issues and access to decision making. (Draft ECE, at 2).

4. *Mini-case study: The European Convention on Human Rights.* Gregoria López Ostra lived with her family in the vicinity of Lorca, in the region of Murcia, Spain. In 1988 she suffered health problems from a waste treatment plant located on government property twelve meters from her home. The facility was being operated without a required permit. Despite a temporary evacuation of people in the area by the municipality, they continued to experience health problems. Doctors confirmed that living in this highly polluted area caused López Ostra's daughter to suffer from nausea, vomiting, allergic reactions, bronchitis, and anorexia. López Ostra sought relief in Spain without success. She therefore applied to the European Commission of Human Rights, established by Article 19 of the European Convention for the Protection of Human Rights and Fundamental Freedoms, Nov. 4, 1950, 213 U.N.T.S. 222. López Ostra claimed that the problems caused by the plant violated her rights under Articles 3 and 8 of the European Convention, which provide as follows:

Article 3

No one shall be subjected to torture or to inhuman or degrading treatment or punishment.

Article 8

(1) Everyone has the right to respect for his private and family life, his home and his correspondence.

(2) There shall be no interference by a public authority with the exercise of this right except such as is in accordance with the law and is necessary in a democratic society in the interests of national security, public safety or the economic well-being of the country, for the prevention of disorder or crime, for the protection of health or morals, or for the protection of the rights and freedoms of others.

The commission rejected the Article 3 claim but found a violation of Article 8. The European Court of Human Rights, in its decision of December 9, 1994,[29] held unanimously that Spain's failure to prevent harmful pollution from the plant violated Article 8 of the European Convention. The court stated:

> despite the margin of appreciation left to the respondent State, the Court considers that the State did not succeed in striking a fair balance between the interest of the town's economic well-being—that of having a waste-treatment plant—and the applicant's effective enjoyment of her right to respect for her home and her private and family life.

The court held Spain liable for four million pesetas in damages and more than one million pesetas for costs and expenses. The decision is significant because the European Convention contains no provision on "environmental rights" per se.

Do you see any danger in relying on Article 8 for protection such as that sought by López Ostra? Why do you suppose she did not base her case on the right to life (Article 2) or the right to physical integrity and health (Article 3), neither of which is subject to broad exceptions?

(iii) National Laws

A diverse number of states are beginning to recognize and articulate these rights in national legislation and constitutions.

Both developed and developing countries, in the last couple of decades, have incorporated a right to the environment into their constitutions. For example, in the United States individual state constitutions began in 1960

29. Series A: Judgments and Decisions, vol. 303, C, Case of López Ostra v. Spain.

to recognize the right. Five states explicitly, and perhaps 11 states implicitly, recognize the right to the environment. The constitutions of Illinois and Hawaii explicitly guarantee the right to a clean environment, providing that "[e]ach person has the right to a clean and healthful environment." *See* Haw. Const. art. XI, §9; and Ill. Const. art IX, §2. *See also* the constitutions of California, Florida, Massachusetts, Montana, Pennsylvania, Rhode Island, and Virginia.

Furthermore, the Constitution of Peru (1979) in Article 123 states: "[e]veryone has the right to live in a healthy environment, ecologically balanced and adequate for the development of life and preservation of the countryside and nature. Everyone has the duty to conserve the said environment." Constitutions of the Countries of the World, vols. I-XV (Albert P. Blaustein & Gisbert H. Flanz, eds. 1990). The Portuguese Constitution (1975) claims: "[a]ll have the right to a human, healthy and ecologically balanced human environment and the duty to protect it." The now former Yugoslavian Constitution of 1974 in Article 192 proclaimed: "[m]an shall have the right to a healthy environment. Conditions for realization of this right shall be ensured by the social community."

Generally no rules were adopted to guarantee or enforce any human rights in the former Communist countries. These rights were considered effectuated by the interests of the socialist community. *See* Hodkova, above, at 77. Since the collapse of the Communist regime, the Czechoslovak Federal Assembly adopted in 1991 a new constitution entitled Charter of Fundamental Rights and Freedoms. *See* The Charter of Fundamental Rights and Freedoms of the Czech and Slovak Federative Republic, A Constitutional Law, *adopted* Jan. 9, 1991, Prague. Article 35 of the Charter contains an explicit right to a healthy environment:

1. Everyone has the right to live in a favorable environment;
2. Everyone is entitled to timely and complete information about the state of the environment and natural resources;
3. In exercising his or her rights nobody may endanger or cause damage to the environment, natural resources, the wealth of natural species, and cultural monuments beyond limits set by law.

The charter attests that international agreements on human rights ratified by the state are obligatory and supersede national law. (Article 2 at 1). Still, many of the environmental rights contained in the charter may remain merely declarative for some time given the economic conditions and the outdated industrial and power facilities that produce great amounts of ground, water, and air pollution.

Due to the enormous amount of deforestation of the Amazon, the Brazilian government enacted the 1988 constitution implementing Chapter VI as a safeguard for the region. It states: "[e]veryone is entitled to an ecologically balanced environment, which is an asset of everyday use to the common man and essential to a healthy quality of life; this imposes a duty on the government and the community to protect and preserve it for the present and future generations." Albert P. Blaustein, Federative Republic of Brazil (1988), *reprinted in* 3 Constitutions of the Countries of the World (Albert P. Blaustein & Gisbert H. Flanz, eds. 1990). Chapter VII imposes responsibility on the Brazilian government to preserve and restore ecosystems, and biological diversity, and protect the flora and fauna, and for practices that place them at risk of extinction. The effectiveness of this bold step will remain to be seen given the country's high foreign debt and reliance on the timber and cattle ranching industries.

The 1990 Constitution of the Republic of Namibia in Article 91(c) delegates authority to an "Ombudsman" to "investigate complaints concerning the over-utilization of living natural resources, the irrational exploitation of non-renewable resources, the degradation and destruction of ecosystems and failure to protect the beauty of Namibia." This authority may be the most extensive in that it provides a specific body power with respect to certain actions.

Other constitutions tend to be more restrictive and allow only citizens to be beneficiaries of the right. The constitution of the Republic of Korea (1978) in Article 34 proclaims: "[a]ll citizens shall be entitled to live in a clean environment." What restrictions does this mean for foreigners harmed by a neighboring government's actions? Does such a right have any force if an action against the polluting government is prevented by the act of state doctrine in the victim state's court and the polluter's domestic law does not recognize foreign citizen actions?

Yet, in other cases the right to the environment is inferred from other obligations imposed on individuals, governments, and states. The 1982 Netherlands Constitution, Article 21, proclaims: "It shall be the concern of the authorities to keep the country habitable and to protect and improve the environment." Furthermore, the Indian Constitution (1974), in Article 48A, declares: "The states shall endeavor to protect and improve the environment and to safeguard the forests and wildlife of the country."

Questions

What is the probative value of these national constitutions that include a right to environment? Do they mean that these states automatically recognize and respect the right domestically and/or internationally and that they consider themselves legally responsible for their actions? What amount of state practice would be sufficient to show a firm commitment to be bound? Is any quantum of state practice sufficient, or does there need to be a formal recognition of the right through a treaty?

d. Application of Existing Human Rights

The case for a human right to the environment does not necessarily have to rest on general propositions stated in instruments espousing the right. Some supporters of such a human right argue that the protections and obligations afforded by other "related" and recognized human rights achieve a similar result. For the most part, rights that may incorporate the right to a clean environment are contained in the Universal Declaration of Human Rights. Most commonly, the right to the environment is seen as incorporated within the right to life. Consider the following and reflect on whether applying existing human rights to preserve and protect the environmental condition is an effective way to proceed.

■ HUMAN RIGHTS, ENVIRONMENTAL RIGHTS, AND THE RIGHT TO ENVIRONMENT

Dinah Shelton
28 Stan. J. Intl. L. 103, 112-113, 116 (1991)

The relationship between existing human rights and environmental protection has been described several ways. One view sees environmental protection as a prerequisite or precondition to the exercise of fundamental human rights. This formulation has inherent risks, however, because governments can and have used "preconditions" as a pretext to deny the enjoyment of guaranteed rights. For example, some developing countries have used economic development as a precondition to the enjoyment of civil and political rights, turning the latter into a "luxury" beyond their means.

Another perspective views environmental protection not as a precondition for human rights, but rather as an integral part of their enjoyment. For example, individuals have brought petitions to international human rights tribunals alleging violations of guaranteed rights as a result of environmental damage. The United Nations Human Rights Committee, established by the International Covenant on Civil and Political Rights, recently decided such a case and recognized environmental harm as a valid cause of action. . . .

[I]nternational cases of the European Commission and Court [also] indicate that existing human rights standards can afford some limited environmental protection. In particular, international tribunals have accepted that environmental harm may violate the right to privacy, the right to life, and the right to property. In addition, European cases demonstrate that human rights protections will not necessarily prevent a state from adopting and enforcing environmental norms, even though the European Convention does not explicitly include environmental protection as one of the permissible grounds for limiting human rights guarantees. However, the scope of protection for the environment based on existing human rights norms remains narrow because environmental degradation is not itself a cause for complaint, but rather must be linked to an existing right. As a result, efforts have arisen to enumerate more specific environmental rights.

Notes and Questions

1. *The right to life.* The right to life is a fundamental, non-derogable human right. The right is guaranteed in the Universal Declaration of Human Rights in Article 3, "[e]veryone has the right to life, liberty, and security of person." Other instruments further define the right. The International Covenant on Civil and Political Rights, Article 6(1), the African Charter on Human and Peoples Rights, Article 4, and the American Convention on Human Rights, Article 4(1), prohibit the "arbitrary" deprivation of life, while the European Convention for the Protection of Human Rights and Fundamental Freedoms, Article 2(1), prohibits the "intentional" deprivation of life.

2. *Clarification of the right to life.* International and regional institutions and tribunals have further clarified these instruments in the context of the right to life by suggesting that states have a positive obligation to protect the lives of people within their jurisdiction. For instance, the UN Human Rights Committee has pronounced that the right to life is deprived by a state's failure to take appropriate measures to prevent or investigate the disappearance and killing under the International Convention on Civil and Political Rights, Article 6. Communication No. 161/1983, CCPR/C/31/D/159/1983. In the *Velasquez Rodriguez* case, the Inter-American Court of Human Rights declared that states have the affirmative duty to "prevent, investigate and punish any violation of the rights recognized by the Convention . . . and provide compensation . . . for damages." Thus, the Court held that the failure to prevent, investigate or punish the people responsible for the disappearance of citizens violated the victims' human rights. Velasquez Rodriguez Case, Inter-Am. Ct. H.R. 1988, App. VI at 70-71, OAS/Ser. L/V/III.19, doc. 13 (Aug. 31, 1988). The European Court of Human Rights held, in Soering v. United Kingdom, that a human rights violation existed if a state extradited a defendant when it was foreseeable that he could suffer inhumane and degrading treatment in the extradited state. Soering v. United Kingdom, 161 Eur. Ct. H.R. (ser. 1) (1989). Could the families of victims of deadly environmental disasters bring the same type of action due to the government's sponsorship of a development project, its failure to prevent a disaster due to lack of mandatory planning procedures, or a failure to investigate or force a cleanup?

3. *The right to life and the environment.* A few judicial pronouncements support the contention that the right to life may be deprived by a state's

activities posing life-threatening environmental risks. In the case of the Yanomami Indians, an indigenous group, the Inter-American Commission on Human Rights stated that the Brazilian government violated the right to life and other human rights including liberty and personal security, residence, movement, and the preservation of health and well-being. The government did not pursue appropriate measures to prevent environmental harm caused by a government-approved development project in the Amazon region. Case No. 7615, Inter-Am. C.H.R. 24, 28, 33, OEA/ser.L/V/11.66, doc. 10 rev. 1 (1985). The Yanomamis have specifically claimed the loss of life, cultural identity, and property. Should the scope of other human rights be interpreted to include an affirmative duty to prevent these types of losses, or should there be a specific right to a clean environment which encompasses these protections? *See* Petition for the Huaorani People, the Huaorani People v. Ecuador, Inter-Am. C.H.R. (June 1, 1990).

4. *The right to health.* In E.H.P. v. Canada, residents alleged that 200,000 tons of radioactive waste remaining in Port Hope posed serious health risks in violation of Article 6(1) of the International Covenant of Civil and Political Human Rights. The International Human Rights Committee abstained from determining the merits of the case due to jurisdictional defects, but it observed that the case "raised serious issues with regard to the obligation of States parties to protect human life." E.H.P. v. Canada, No. 67/1980 at 27, 2 Selected Decisions of the Hum. Rts. Comm. Under the Optional Protocol 20 (1990).

5. *The right to privacy.* Environmental threats may also violate other human rights. Courts have not had the opportunity to define the scope of all of these rights including their duties and limits, except that the European Court of Human Rights has arguably determined the right of privacy in the environmental context. In *Powell and Rayner,* the court recognized that noise pollution can prevent the realization of this right when it affects the quality of one's family and home life. The court left open the possibility that a state may have a duty under certain circumstances to prevent harm from activities by infringing on privacy, yet it determined that these interests must be balanced against broader community interests. Powell and Rayner Case, 172 Eur. Ct. H.R. (ser. A) at 18-19 (1990).

e. Procedural Guarantees

Experience indicates that in order for a human right to the environment to be fully realized and to obligate states to an affirmative duty to protect against environmental destruction or harm to people, the ultimate rights must have corresponding procedural guarantees. The substantive right maybe of little use if an individual or group cannot exercise the right by being made aware of potential harms, participating in decisionmaking processes, and petitioning courts or organizations with respect to violations.

INTERNATIONAL LEGAL PROTECTION FOR VICTIMS OF ENVIRONMENTAL ABUSE

Michelle Leighton Schwartz
18 Yale J. Intl. L. 355, 368 (1993)

Rights to information and political participation are fundamental to the exercise of traditional human rights, because one's survival and well-being depend upon knowledge of environmental risks and the ability to minimize or avoid them. Uninformed communities cannot adequately protect their lives, livelihood, property, cultural heritage, and natural resources; nor can they call for reforms in their government's environmental management policies. States should be held to an affirmative duty to assess the environmental and public health risks associated with activities under their jurisdiction or control, and to inform those persons potentially affected.

The recognition of such an obligation under human rights doctrine would guarantee a type of due process for persons affected by government-sanctioned harm to the environment. An informed public can prevent the execution of an ill-conceived development project, lobby for the regulation of hazardous facilities, and take similar steps to protect itself from harm. Moreover, public involvement in environmental management can reduce the risk of political, economic, and cultural conflict that can lead to widespread human rights violations. Open public discussions would help build broader consensus and overcome group differences.

Notes and Questions

1. *A right to environmental information?* The right to free expression is considered a fundamental human right in many international documents. It is recognized in Article 19 of the Declaration of Human Rights as the right of individuals "to seek, receive and impart information and ideas through any media regardless of frontiers." The scope of the right traditionally entailed a duty of governments to reveal information only when the public made a request. Recently, however, the European Court of Human Rights has expanded this entitlement to include the "right of the public to be properly informed," especially when public health and safety is at issue. *See* Sunday Times v. United Kingdom, Judgment No. 30, 2 Eur. H.R. Rep. 245 para. 66. Schwartz advocates expanding the right "to include a 'right of access' to government-held information . . . [that would] affect the health of a specific individual or group of individuals" and when a fundamental right is involved, "governments should take the initiative to disclose relevant information in a manner reasonably calculated to put the potentially affected parties on actual notice so that those parties may take steps to protect their interests." Schwartz, *International Legal Protection for Victims of Environmental Abuse,* 18 Yale J. Intl. L. 355, 370 (1993).

2. *National security and other exceptions.* One potential problem with expanding the scope of access to government-held information is the issue involving a reasonable derogation due to "national security interests" or an objection that the expense of providing information outweighs the benefits. The Universal Declaration legitimatizes these concerns by restricting the right of information when prescribed by law and necessary for national security, public safety, and the protection of the reputation, confidentiality, and the rights of others. (Article 19(3).) Furthermore, who should be able to make a determination that there is no right to information under these decisions: the government claiming the restriction; a domestic court or agency; or an international court or agency? Furthermore, can the right to information be effective without the right of individuals to participate or be represented before government agencies making decisions about what information to make publicly available? Without the right of access to decisionmaking, what are the restraints on government decisionmaking?

3. *A right to be warned of transboundary disasters?* Does international environmental law provide rules about communication when a disaster occurs and there is transboundary environmental harm? What is the extent to which a state is obliged to warn other states affected or potentially affected? These questions are dealt with in Chapter 9. But of present interest is whether threatened or harmed individuals in affected countries have a right to be warned and to other relevant information from the source state. Although states have entered into bilateral and multilateral information exchange agreements, should the right be directly given to individuals whether or not there is an agreement? Does the evidence of numerous existing agreements to provide information reflect an emerging or customary international norm to which individuals or states can assent? Suppose the transboundary harm arises from an ongoing activity: same result?

5. The Nature of the Right

a. Form and Substance

■ HUMAN RIGHTS, ENVIRONMENTAL RIGHTS, AND THE RIGHT TO ENVIRONMENT

Dinah Shelton
28 Stan. J. Intl. L. 103, 122-124 (1991)

Generations of Rights

A few authors have proposed classifying existing and evolving rights into "generations" according to perceived historical evolution and theoretical differences. Under this framework, civil and political rights are "first generation" rights and define a sphere of personal liberties into which the government cannot enter. For example, freedom of speech simply requires the government to abstain from interference. Economic and social rights, the "second generation" of rights, require government action. The right to a certain standard of living necessitates the involvement of the state. New rights, established under the rubric "third generation,"

> may both be *invoked against* the State and *demanded* of it; but above all (and herein lies their essential characteristic) they can be realized only through the concerted efforts of all the actors on the social scene: the individual, the State, public and private bodies and the international community.

This formulation presents several difficulties. First, in the domestic law of some countries and to a certain extent in international law, economic and social rights and their corresponding imposition of duties were the "first generation," preceding the recognition of civil and political rights. Second, the concept of "generations," and whether or not a right fits into a particular generation, gives no guidance as to whether or not a claim should be recognized as a human right.

Third, the claimed "generational" distinctions between positive and negative state obligations and those rights which encompass both do not exist in practice. As recent case law has clarified, the obligations generally imposed upon states in human rights instruments demand both abstention from violation and positive action to ensure the rights guaranteed. In a case concerning the rights contained in the American Convention on Human Rights—most of which are civil and political rights—the Inter-American Court of Human Rights sets a significant precedent by concluding that article 1 of the Convention, which requires states to respect and ensure the rights guaranteed, imposes on each state

> a legal duty to take reasonable steps to prevent human rights violations and to use the means at its disposal to carry out a serious investigation of violations committed within its jurisdiction, to identify those responsible, to impose the appropriate punishment and to ensure the victim adequate compensation.

Therefore, the Court has declared that states have affirmative duties with respect to civil and political rights, as well as with respect to economic and social rights. A state may become responsible for violations by private actors if it fails to exercise due diligence to prevent the violations or to respond to them. If a government does not seriously investigate human rights violations committed by private parties, "those parties are aided in a sense by the government, thereby making the State responsible on the international plane." In the case before it, the Court held Honduras responsible either for causing disappearances of citizens or for failing to take affirmative action to prevent or remedy the disappearances. "Rights" imposing affirmative duties on states are sometimes held not to be rights because courts cannot enforce such duties. However, the Inter-American Court found a way to impose liability on the Honduran government for malfeasance and, in the alternative, for nonfeasance by measuring the damage caused to the victims and their families.

b. Content of the Right

■ THE HUMAN RIGHT TO A CLEAN, BALANCED AND PROTECTED ENVIRONMENT

Janusz Symonides
20 Intl. J. Legal Info. 24, 28-29 (1992)

The main beneficiary is an individual who receives a right to enjoy and to use the environment, understood broadly as embracing not only physical or natural but also social and cultural elements. Nobody can be discriminated in his/her access to environment, though equal limitations and duties may be imposed on all in the name of its preservation.

The main debtor is the state which is obliged to organize protection, conservation, and improvement of the environment, to ensure that it will be clean, healthy and ecologically balanced. The state's obligation to act is not only determined by this right and by domestic laws, but also arises from binding international norms concerning various aspects of environmental protection.

The right to a clean, balanced and protected environment is a fundamental one because it is vital for the exercise of other individual rights and duties, including the right to life. Because of this, it cannot be qualified as an exclusively economic and social right, though in its implementation, there might be some analogy with other social rights—for example, the right to health.

The right to the environment assumes solidarity with other human beings and mankind. Everyone is simultaneously the creditor and debtor, has the right to a protected environment but also has the duty to protect and improve it. Each person may enjoy his/her right alone or in association with others. Therefore, this right is a collective right, enjoyed by communities. This solidarity extends to future generations and goes beyond the limits of national jurisdiction. Environmental protection, because of its subregional, regional, and global aspects, has an international dimension; therefore the right and duty to the environment has to be seen also in this perspective.

IS THERE A RIGHT TO A HEALTHY ENVIRONMENT IN THE INTERNATIONAL LEGAL ORDER?

Iveta Hodkova
7 Conn. J. Intl. L. 65, 80 (1991)

The existing international system of traditional human rights protection has a longer tradition than that of implementation and enforcement of environmental law. Further, the right to a healthy environment is not a human right in the strict sense; for example, it is frequently referred to as a collective right; in other words its collective dimension is considered more significant. In light of these difficulties, the integration of the right to a healthy environment within the traditional system which views human rights as wholly individual has been slow and uncertain.

HUMAN RIGHTS AND PROTECTION OF THE ENVIRONMENT: A MILDLY "REVISIONIST" VIEW

Günther Handl
Human Rights, Sustainable Development and the Environment 117, 133-134 (Antonio Augusto Cancado Trindade ed. 1992)

Support for international environmental human rights . . . cuts across a wide spectrum of international public opinion. We are witnessing not only a growing advocacy of environmental concerns as human rights issues. Increasingly, it is also being claimed that there exists already, or there is about to emerge, a broad generic entitlement to a healthy, decent or otherwise qualified environment. Indeed, often this entitlement is referred to simply as a "human right to the environment"—unqualified.

The assumption that inspires a significant portion of the public discourse namely that today the cause of environmental protection is furthered by the postulation of a generic human right to a decent or healthy environment, however, is a problematic one. While it should be self-evident that there is a direct functional relationship between protection of the environment and the promotion of human rights, it is much less obvious that environmental protection ought to be conceptualized in terms of a generic human right. Indeed, the emphasis on such a perspective on the interrelationship of human rights and environmental protection carries significant costs; it reflects a maximalist position that offers little prospect of becoming reality in the near term while its propagation diverts attention and efforts from other more pressing and promising environmental and human rights objectives. In short, a generic international environmental entitlement, both as an already existing and an emerging human rights concept, is a highly questionable proposition.

Notes and Questions

1. *Who/what benefits?* Is the proposition that the individual is the true beneficiary of a human right to a healthy environment practical? Should individual rights be subordinated to, or somehow balanced with, the interests of society at large?

2. *General vs. specific "environmental" rights.* Should environmentalists and human rights advocates concentrate their efforts on the recognition of specific rights that would eventually lead to the full realization of a healthy environment? One such specific delineation may be the right to water, considered below.

3. *Is immediate implementation required?* Even if a right such as a right to water were derived from other rights, what guarantees do claimants have that the right should be immediately satisfied due to the urgency of the situation? What if the state responds that it can only implement the protections in question progressively and to the extent its resources will allow? *See* International Covenant on Economic, Social and Cultural Rights, Article 11. Should this apply to drinking water? Water for agriculture (food)? If one state deprives residents of another state of sufficient water for basic human needs, would the deprived individuals have a human rights claim against the government of the first state?

c. Context of the Right

Environmentalists and human rights advocates seek a workable human right to the environment to rescue victims whose lives have been or are being threatened because of a serious environmental disaster, the lack of a government's action to correct or prevent the overall effects of environmental depletion, and the lack of necessities of food and water due to shortages due to contamination or depletion. The relationship between the right and the persons or groups depending on it brings to the surface the realities of how the right should be defined, its scope and limits.

Several contexts in which a human right to environment seems applicable include the plights of indigenous peoples and environmental refugees. Concerns for economic development, sustainable development, and future generations also generate questions of how the protection of such rights might operate.

(i) Indigenous Peoples

HUMAN RIGHTS AND THE ENVIRONMENT: PRELIMINARY REPORT

U.N. ESCOR, United Nations Human Rights Commission, Sub-Commission on Prevention of Discrimination and Protection of Minorities, 43rd Sess., Agenda Item 4, at 3-7, U.N. Doc. E/CN.4/Sub.2/1991/8 (Fatna Zhora Ksentini, Special Rapporteur)

Indigenous peoples are the descendants of the original inhabitants of territories since colonized by foreigners; they have distinct cultures which set them apart from the dominant society; many have until comparatively recently, had a high degree of control over their development; indigenous peoples have a strong sense of self-identity.

INTERNATIONAL LABOUR ORGANISATION: CONVENTION CONCERNING INDIGENOUS AND TRIBAL PEOPLES IN INDEPENDENT COUNTRIES

Opened for signature ***June 27, 1989, art. 1, 28 I.L.M. 1382, 1384-1385 (1989)***

Article 1

1. This Convention applies to:

(a) tribal peoples in independent countries whose social, cultural and economic conditions distinguish them from other sections of the national community, and whose status is regulated wholly or partially by their own customs or traditions or by special laws or regulations;

(b) peoples in independent countries who are regarded as indigenous on account of their descent from the populations which inhabited the country, or a geographical region to which the country belongs, at the time of conquest or colonization or the establishment of present state boundaries and who, irrespective of their legal status, retain some or all of their own social, economic, cultural and political institutions.

2. Self-identification as indigenous or tribal shall be regarded as a fundamental criterion for determining the groups to which the provisions of this Convention apply.

3. The use of the term "peoples" in this Convention shall not be construed as having any implications as regards the rights which may attach to the term under international law.

■ INTERNATIONAL LEGAL PROTECTION FOR VICTIMS OF ENVIRONMENTAL ABUSE

Michelle Leighton Schwartz
18 Yale J. Intl. L. 355, 364-366 (1993)

From time immemorial, indigenous peoples judiciously managed their natural resources for food, shelter, medicine, and cultural enrichment. They lived in productive harmony with the land. Today, "there are over 200 million indigenous people and many of them live in some of the world's most vulnerable ecosystems." Oil exploration, mining, deforestation, dam construction, and pollution degrade their environment, placing their cultural heritage—and sometimes their very survival—in peril. Often, indigenous communities are forced to leave their lands and either relocate to impoverished areas on the outskirts of the cities or shantytowns, or leave their friends and family to become migrant laborers. . . .

[T]he special relationship between indigenous people and their environment is not yet formally recognized in a human rights instrument. Advocates of indigenous peoples should therefore seek to broaden established rights, such as the rights to self-determination and to freedom from apartheid and cultural genocide.

The right to self-determination is the right of peoples under colonial and alien domination to choose their political status freely and to pursue their economic, social, and cultural development without discrimination. In its broadest sense, the right to self-determination encompasses the rights of indigenous peoples to regain, enjoy, and enrich their cultural heritage; "to maintain and develop their identities, languages and religions"; and "to maintain, protect and have access to sacred sites."

■ NEW DEVELOPMENTS IN INDIGENOUS RIGHTS

Hurst Hannum
28 Va. J. Intl. L. 649, 666-668 (1988)

Indigenous peoples unanimously emphasize the spiritual nature of their relationship with the land or earth, which is basic to their existence and to their beliefs, customs, traditions, and culture. Although the economic benefits that may be obtained from exploitation of natural resources is of increasing importance to many indigenous communities, land is not merely a possession or means of production.

. . .

The direct genocide of the nineteenth century has largely given way to continuing assaults by governments and private parties on indigenous lands and their sub-soil mineral and oil deposits. These conflicts almost invariably arise in the context of national development plans, and they will undoubtedly remain the major concern of many indigenous groups. For example, even though ILO Convention No. 107 recognizes indigenous rights to collective ownership of land and compensation for land expropriated by government, its provisions regarding forcible relocation are weak. In addition, many states assert ownership of all rights to subsoil resources, even if indigenous or private ownership of the land itself is recognized. Finally, many states commonly maintain that incursions onto traditional indigenous land are necessary to ensure national security, especially where such lands are border areas.

DISREGARDING ENVIRONMENTAL LAW: PETROLEUM DEVELOPMENT IN PROTECTED NATURAL AREAS AND INDIGENOUS HOMELANDS IN THE ECUADORIAN AMAZON

Judith Kimerling
14 Hastings Intl. & Comp. L. Rev. 849, 849-855 (1991)

Ecuador, a small nation on the Pacific coast of South America, is home to some of the earth's most biologically diverse rain forests. The eastern half of Ecuador, sloping down from the Andes mountains, forms part of the western Amazon basin, encompassing over thirteen million hectares of tropical rain forest. Known in Ecuador as the *Oriente,* this area is the home of 350,000 to 500,000 people, including 8 groups of indigenous people, as well as recent colonists from Ecuador's coastal and highland region.

The *Oriente* is also home to a thriving and environmentally destructive oil industry. Over the past 2 decades, foreign oil companies . . . together with Ecuador's national oil company, have extracted almost 1.5 billion barrels of oil from the Ecuadorian Amazon. In the process, oil company roads have opened an estimated one million hectares of rain forests to colonization by incoming settlers. Accidental oil spills from the Trans-Ecuadorian Pipeline alone have dumped an estimated 400,000 barrels (16.8 million gallons) of oil, most of it in the *Oriente.* Hundreds of oil wells generate more than 4.3 million gallons of toxic wastes every day, virtually all of which are spilled or discharged into the environment without treatment. This process contaminates countless streams and rivers, often the only sources of water for surrounding communities. Additionally, burning oil and gas contaminate the air, along with volatile organics that enter the air and form oil-covered waste pits, roads, and unremediated spills.

Despite provisions in the Ecuadorian Law of Forestry and Conservation of Natural Areas and Wildlife that require that protected natural areas be preserved in an "unaltered state," national parks and other protected areas have not been off-limits to the oil industry. Oil development is currently underway or contemplated for every protected area in the *Oriente.* These areas are also the homelands of indigenous peoples who are seriously threatened by oil development activities, despite their constitutional "right to an environment free of contamination [Constitucion Politica de la Republica del Ecuador, tit. II, sec. 1, art. 19, cl.2]. . . ." Although Ecuadorian law unambiguously recognizes the public interest in a clean and healthy environment, and charges the government with environmental protection responsibilities, the national government has shown little or no willingness to comply with the law and establish meaningful environmental controls over the nation's most powerful industry. . . .

[The plight of the indigenous does not only stem from a pacifist government, but also from direct government action further harming them.] The national government of Ecuador, however, continues to view the frontier as a frontier to be conquered. As a result, the *Oriente* people are increasingly threatened by aggressive government policies that seek to develop and colonize their lands, and assimilate them into the dominant Ecuadorian culture. In theory, the Ecuadorian national culture is homogenous; in reality, it is ethnically diverse, with extremes of wealth and poverty. According to one noted anthropologist, "racism in Ecuador is institutionalized to a degree that would shock even black Americans," and "enthnocide" is a strategy of the national government to conquer Amazonia. For Amazonian people, assimilation means rejecting their traditional beliefs and ways of life, lowering their standard of living, and entering the lowest social and economic levels of Ecuadorian society. The loss of ancestral lands means they cannot and will not survive.

Notes and Questions

1. *Environmental apartheid?* The environmental rights of indigenous peoples may be inferred from other rights designed to protect them. For example, Schwartz argues that, "the destruction of tribal heritage and culture may implicate the international crime of apartheid when a government pursues development strategies that intentionally disenfranchise members of indigenous groups on the basis of cultural heritage or that prevent them from participating in decisions regarding their own displacement." Schwartz, above, at 366. The International Convention on the Suppression and Punishment of the Crime of Apartheid defines the crime of apartheid as the taking of any, "measures calculated to prevent a racial group or groups from participation in the political, social, economic and cultural life of the country and the deliberate creation of conditions preventing the full development of such a group or groups, in particular by denying to members of a racial group or groups basic human rights and freedoms. . . ." Based on this definition, could indigenous peoples claim that aggressive government practices depriving them of their land or a

clean environment is a deprivation of the human right to the environment, resulting in a crime of apartheid?

2. *A human right to ownership?* The fundamental economic issue facing indigenous peoples is the right of ownership of traditional land and resources. (This issue has implications that go beyond economics, of course.) For example, in 1988, tribal groups blocked logging operations in Canada and Malaysia, claiming tribal ownership of the lands in dispute. *See* Sanders, *The UN Working Group on Indigenous Populations,* 11 Hum. Rts. Q. 406, 428 (1989). What specific entitlements in international human rights law could be used as the basis of such a claim?

3. *The role of IFIs.* Advocates claim that international financial institutions add to the destitute position of indigenous people. For example, large scale development projects often require involuntary relocation of indigenous peoples. The World Bank has policy guidelines for its projects that require resettlement. However, failure to follow these guidelines has threatened the rights of indigenous peoples and caused numerous problems. For example, 39 dams financed by the World Bank from 1979 to 1985 required relocation of 750,000 people. *See* Dixon, Talbot, & Lemoigne, *Dams and the Environment: Consideration in World Bank Projects,* World Bank Technical Paper No. 110, Washington, D.C.; Kane, *Human Rights and the Environment* 12 (1990).

4. *Development of indigenous homelands, continued.* Many developing countries, strapped for cash, turn to development projects that can damage the environment but bring in needed foreign exchange. Although environmental safeguards are written into loans, enforcement is difficult. In 1985, Brazil received a loan for a road-paving project in tropical forest states, opening up formerly isolated regions to colonization and development. The loan included a plan to set aside lands for indigenous peoples, conduct ecological monitoring, and use improved construction techniques. Two years into the project, however, all environmental aspects of the project were delayed or unimplemented. *See* Aeppel, *Rain Forest Misuse Prompts Ultimatum,* The Christian Sci. Monitor, Aug. 14, 1987. For a general description of the cause of indigenous peoples, *see* Alan Thein Durning, *Guardians of the Land: Indigenous Peoples and the Health of the Earth,* World Watch Paper 112 (Dec. 1992).

5. *Development of indigenous homelands III.* The experience of indigenous peoples from the mid-1940s through the mid-1980s was such that international development programs were seen as a means of depriving them of their homelands and natural resources. This was particularly true of hydro-electric programs, agricultural projects, and mining and petroleum extraction activities. Many indigenous peoples saw themselves as victims of progress because development projects seemed to be in the interests of governments, international agencies, and nonlocal people. Indigenous leaders began to press for recognition of their social, economic, and cultural rights and particularly for the right of self-determination in government

and use of resources. Discussions between indigenous peoples and UN agencies culminated in the adoption of the International Labour Organisation Convention Concerning the Protection and Integration of Indigenous and Other Tribal and Semi-Tribal Populations in Independent Countries (Convention 169) on June 27, 1989 (28 I.L.M. 1382), which addresses the rights of indigenous peoples to control and maintain their own economic development, religion, and ways of life. Some of the principles of Convention 169 were incorporated into the draft Universal Declaration of the Rights of Indigenous Peoples, which is a farther reaching document with respect to both collective and individual rights of indigenous peoples. *See* Robert K. Hitchcock, *International Human Rights, the Environment, and Indigenous Peoples*, 5 Colo. J. Intl. Envtl. L & Poly. 1 (1994).

■ DRAFT DECLARATION ON THE RIGHTS OF INDIGENOUS PEOPLES

In 1987, the Working Group on Indigenous Populations (WGIP) began an intensive effort to draft a new human rights instrument specifically directed at the plight of indigenous peoples. A discussion text was prepared for a 1988 meeting. That text was revised over the next several years through the process of debates and inter-sessional consultations with various governments, indigenous representatives, and human rights specialists. Between 1991 and 1993, the process of refinement continued as consensus language emerged among the WGIP members on some of the more controversial issues concerning political and territorial rights.

The WGIP had concluded that implementation of existing human rights standards and instruments would not be adequate to ensure protection for the survival of indigenous peoples as a distinct group. The existing human rights system was structured around the relationship between the individual and the state which does not address issues unique to indigenous peoples such as dispossession of land and resources and disregard of political and social institutions. The Draft Declaration (United Nations Commission on Human Rights Sub-Commission on Prevention of Discrimination and Protection of Minorities: Draft United Nations Declaration on the Rights of Indigenous Peoples, Adopted, August 26, 1994, 34 I.L.M. 541), addresses those issues unique to indigenous peoples by underscoring the importance of collective human rights which supplements individual rights norms.

The Draft Declaration is substantively groundbreaking in its recognition of collective rights for indigenous peoples. It addresses human rights, self-determination, territorial and resource rights, cultural genocide, environment, development, and dispute resolution. The Draft Declaration also reflects existing standards in a rapidly evolving area of international law by demonstrating the merging of human rights and environmental law in an integrated way.

The purpose and philosophy of the Draft Declaration are set forth in the preamble, emphasizing the urgent need to respect and promote the inherent rights and characteristics of indigenous peoples, especially their rights to their land, territories, and resources, which derive from their political, economic and social structures and from their cultures, spiritual traditions, histories and philosophies and recognizing also that respect for indigenous knowledge, cultures and traditional practices contributes to sustainable and equitable development and proper management of the environment.

The Draft Declaration consists of forty-five articles concerning relationships between indigenous peoples and the natural environment. Some of these articles emphasize the rights of indigenous peoples to the possession and use of their traditional territories, some emphasize the importance of the natural world in indigenous cultural practices, and others emphasize the rights of indigenous peoples to exercise self-government within their territories. Articles 7, 25, 26, and 30, which are particularly relevant to environmental protection, read as follows:

Article 7

Indigenous peoples have the collective and individual right not to be subjected to ethnocide and cultural genocide, including prevention of and redress for: Any action which has the aim or effect of depriving them of their integrity as distinct peoples, or of their cultural values or ethnic identities;

(a) An action which has the aim or effect of dispossessing them of their lands, territories or resources;

(b) Any form of population transfer which has the aim or effect of violating or undermining any of their rights;

(c) Any form of assimilation or integration by other cultures or ways of life imposed on them by legislative, administrative or other measures; Any form of propaganda directed at them.

Article 25

Indigenous peoples have the right to maintain and strengthen their distinctive spiritual and material relationships with the lands, territories, waters and coastal seas and other resources which they have traditionally owned or otherwise occupied or used, and to uphold their responsibilities to future generations in this regard.

Article 26

Indigenous peoples have the right to own, develop, control and use lands and territories, including the total environment of the lands, air, waters, coastal seas, sea-ice, flora and fauna and other resources which they have traditionally owned or otherwise used. This includes the right to the full recognition of their laws, traditions and customs, land-tenure systems and institutions for the development and management of resources, and the right to effective measures by states to prevent any interference with, alienation of or encroachment upon these rights.

Article 30

Indigenous peoples have the right to determine and develop priorities and strategies for the development or use of their lands, territories and other resources, including the right to require that States obtain their free and informed consent prior to the approval of any project affecting their lands, territories and other resources, particularly in connection with the development, utilization or exploitation of mineral, water or other resources. Pursuant to agreement with the indigenous peoples concerned, just and fair compensation shall be provided for any such activities and measures shall be taken to mitigate and adverse environmental, economic, social, cultural or spiritual impact.

Note

Indigenous rights and environmental justice. A parallel has been drawn between the rights of indigenous peoples on the international law front and the "environmental justice" movement occurring in the United States. Environmental justice links two social problems unconnected in the minds of many: environmental hazards and racism. Several studies suggest that members of racial and ethnic minority groups in the United States suffer from disproportionate exposure to environmental hazards due to environmentally noxious land uses, resulting from inadequate political and financial power to combat potentially unsound environmental projects implemented by governments, corporations, and development agencies with vast resources. As in the case of indigenous peoples around the world, minority communities in the United States, specifically Latinos, African Americans, and Native Americans, may suffer from exclusion, political power imbalances, and institutionalized racial and class discrimination, which may influence environmental project siting and policy implementation. *See* Eileen Gauna, *Federal Environmental Citizen Provisions: Obstacles and Incentives On the Road to Environmental Justice,* 22 Ecology L.Q. 1 (1995).

The following case illustrates an effort to use human rights and international environmental norms to protect indigenous people and their environment.

TOM BEANAL, ON BEHALF OF HIMSELF AND ALL OTHERS SIMILARLY SITUATED v. FREEPORT-MCMORAN, INC.

United States District Court for the Eastern District of Louisiana
969 F. Supp. 362 (1997)

STANWOOD R. DUVAL, JR., District Judge

Before the court is a motion to dismiss Plaintiff Tom Beanal's ("Beanal") claims against Freeport-McMoRan, Inc. and Freeport-McMoRan Copper & Gold, Inc. (collectively "Freeport"). . . .

THE PARTIES

Plaintiff Tom Beanal ("Beanal") is a resident of Tamika, Irian Jaya within the Republic of Indonesia. He is a leader of the Amungme Tribal Counsel of Lambaga Adat Suku Amungme (LEMASA). He filed suit against Freeport on April 29, 1996, individually and on behalf of all other similarly situated. . . . Since no class has been certified, Beanal is the lone plaintiff at this stage.

Defendants Freeport-McMoRan, Inc. and Freeport-McMoRan Copper & Gold, Inc. are Delaware corporations headquartered in New Orleans, Louisiana. Freeport owns an Indonesia-based subsidiary named P.T. Freeport Indonesia ("PT-FI").

Freeport operates the "Grasberg Mine," an open pit copper, gold and silver mine situated in the Jayawijaya Mountains in Irian Jaya, Indonesia. The mine allegedly encompasses approximately 26,400 square kilometers.

THE COMPLAINT

Beanal's first amended complaint alleges that Freeport has committed environmental torts, human rights abuses, and cultural genocide. Beanal states that the court has jurisdiction over this case based on diversity jurisdiction, . . . the Alien Tort Statute, 28 U.S.C. §1350 ("§1350"), and the Torture Victim Protection Act of 1991, SEC. 1, et. seq., 28 U.S.C. 1350 note. . . .

The court reviews the claims made pursuant to §1350 to determine if a cause of action exists.[30] The current view of §1350 is that it grants a federal cause of action as well as a federal forum in which to assert the claim. Xuncax v. Gramajo, 886 F. Supp. 162, 179 (D. Mass. 1995) (citations

30. To satisfy the jurisdictional threshold under §1350, a plaintiff must state a tort in violation of the law of nations. Courts have, accordingly, engaged in a more searching preliminary review of the merits than is required, for example, under the more flexible "arising under" formulation. Filartiga v. Pena-Irala, 630 F.2d 876, 887 (2d Cir. 1980).

omitted). The Fifth Circuit has acknowledged the generally held view that section 1350 is appropriately used by individuals asserting claims for violation of international law of human rights. De Sanchez v. Banco Central de Nicaragua, 770 F.2d 1385, 1396, n. 16 (5th Cir. 1985). Freeport appropriately moved to dismiss for failure to state a cause of action . . . rather than for lack of subject matter jurisdiction. . . .

Summary of Freeport's Bases for Dismissal

Freeport asserts numerous reasons for the court to dismiss the claims for human rights violations and the environmental claims. . . . As to the human rights claims asserted pursuant to the Alien Tort Statute, Freeport argues: (1) The Alien Tort Statute does not provide a private right of action; (2) Freeport is not a state actor; and (3) The TVPA supersedes the Alien Tort Statute for claims of torture and extrajudicial killings. As to the human rights violations asserted under the Torture Victim Protection Act ("TVPA"), Freeport argues that Beanal has failed to state a claim because: (1) The TVPA does not apply to corporations; (2) Beanal has not alleged that Freeport acted under color of foreign law; (3) Plaintiff failed to exhaust local remedies.

Freeport asserts five bases for dismissal of claims for international environmental torts brought under section 1350: (1) Beanal lacks standing to bring the environmental claims; (2) Plaintiff has failed to state a claim because environmental practices do not violate the law of nations; (3) The act of state doctrine bars Plaintiff's claims; (4) The local action doctrine mandates dismissal; and (5) The claims should be dismissed for failure to join an indispensable party, namely, the Republic of Indonesia.

The court discusses each issue in turn. . . .

A. STANDING

. . .

In light of Beanal's status as the sole named plaintiff, the court finds that he has standing to bring claims on his own behalf for certain human rights violations, genocide and environmental torts. Beanal alleges in his complaint that he has been personally injured by certain human rights abuses and environmental practices. The court finds that Beanal has standing to assert those claims for which he alleges an individualized injury. Beanal requests a judgment for money damages as well as specific relief, either of which would redress the harm caused by Freeport for its alleged wrongdoing, if any.

Disregarding those allegations which appear to have been made on behalf of other putative class members,[31] the following specific injuries shall be regarded as have been asserted by Plaintiff individually:

31. The following claims are made on behalf of others and disregarded for purposes of this motion: (1) Wendy Tambuni was stabbed and shot to death while being transported

(1) Torture, detention, surveillance, destruction of property. Amended Complaint P 12. Plaintiff may have experienced such practices personally and claims damages for associated injuries. Id. P 46.

(2) Purposeful, deliberate, contrived and planned cultural demise of the Amungme culture due to various human rights and environmental violations. Id. PP 41-45. The court permits Beanal to make his claim for "cultural genocide" as a member of the Amungme tribe only.

(3) All alleged environmental violations from various mining practices carried out in and nearby the locality where Plaintiff resides, including: destruction, pollution, alteration, and contamination of natural waterways, as well as surface and ground water sources; deforestation; destruction and alteration of physical surroundings. Id. PP 24-40.

Plaintiff alleges that he is a resident of Tamika, Irian Jaya, Indonesia, where the Grasberg mine is located, and is a member of an indigenous tribe that inhabits the area. As a local inhabitant, Plaintiff has a palpable interest in the damage Freeport allegedly causes to nearby waterways and water source, soil, and forests, as well as any aesthetic injuries.

B. HUMAN RIGHTS VIOLATIONS

Beanal seeks to redress human rights violations under the Alien Tort Statute and the Torture Victim Protection Act. As noted above, Beanal complains individually of (1) arbitrary arrest and detention, (2) torture, (3) surveillance, (4) destruction of property, and (5) severe physical pain and suffering. Id. P 12. Beanal alleges that Freeport engaged in these abuses through its security guards "in conjunction with third parties."

. . .

The court must determine whether Beanal has stated a cause of action under the Alien Tort Statute or the Torture Victim Protection Act for any of these alleged injuries.

1. §1350: The Alien Tort Statute

The Alien Tort Statute provides:

> The district courts shall have original jurisdiction of any civil action by an alien for a tort only, committed in violation of the law of nations [or a treaty of the United States].

on Freeport bus, Amended Complaint P 13; (2) Three unnamed civilians were killed after being tortured, Id. P 14; (3) Four unnamed civilians were arbitrarily arrested at their homes, imprisoned in Freeport containers and then disappeared, Id. P 15.

28 U.S.C. §1350. Beanal has not pled nor argued that a treaty applies. Rather, Beanal asserts that Freeport's conduct violated the law of nations.

Though mostly ignored since its enactment in 1789, §1350 has more recently been used in connection with international human rights litigation. Filartiga v. Pena-Irala, 630 F.2d 876, 887 (2d Cir. 1980). Courts have recognized important precepts which relate to this case, namely, where a private individual asserts a claim against a private actor for violation of the law of nations. First, §1350 provides a private right of action. . . . Second, an individual found to have violated the law of nations may be held liable under §1350. . . .

To make out a claim under §1350, three elements must be satisfied: (1) an alien sues (2) for a tort (3) committed in violation of the law of nations. . . . The first two requirements are satisfied here: Beanal is an alien and has alleged tortious conduct.

The issue before the court, therefore, is to determine whether the alleged conduct sets forth a violation of the law of nations. To do so, the court must determine, first, whether there is an applicable norm of international law and, second, whether it has been violated. . . . To be recognized as an international tort under §1350, the alleged violation must be definable, obligatory (rather than hortatory), and universally condemned. Filartiga, 630 F.2d at 881. In making its determination, a court is guided by the sources from which customary international law is derived, including the usage of nations, judicial opinions and the works of jurists. . . . Filartiga instructed that the law of nations is dynamic, rather than static: "Courts must interpret international law not as it was in 1789, but as it has evolved and exists among the nations of the world today." Filartiga, 630 F.2d at 881. In sum, an international tort, i.e. one that violates the law of nations, should satisfy the following requirements:

(1) no state condones the act in question and there is a recognizable "universal" consensus of prohibition against it;
(2) there are sufficient criteria to determine whether a given action amounts to the prohibited act and thus violates the norm;
(3) the prohibition against it is non-derogable and therefore binding at all times upon all actors.

. . . Restatement (Third) of Foreign Relations Law of the United States §§701-702 ("Restatement").

2. §1350 Claim Not Requiring State Action: Genocide

Beanal's complaint of genocide is less than crystal clear. One portion of the first amended complaint is entitled "Cultural Genocide," but the word "genocide" does not otherwise appear. Beanal essentially complains that the alleged human rights abuses and environmental violations have resulted in the demise of the culture of the indigenous tribal people.

The court reviews the facts Beanal alleges under the caption "Cultural Genocide": . . .

The egregious human rights and environmental violations, which have terrorized the tribal communities of the Amungme and other Indigenous tribal people, destroyed their natural habitats and caused dislocation of the populations have resulted in the purposeful, deliberate, contrived and planned demise of a culture of indigenous people whose rights were never considered, whose heritage and culture were disregarded and the result of which is ultimately to lead to the cultural demise of unique pristine heritage which is socially, culturally and anthropologically irreplaceable.

. . . The problem is that Beanal has failed to make the core allegation that Freeport is committing genocide on a group of people. If Beanal in fact means that Freeport is destroying the Amungme culture, then he has failed to state a claim for genocide. On the other hand, if Beanal intended to state that Freeport is committing acts with the intent to destroy the Amungme group, i.e. its members, then he has failed to make this allegation sufficiently explicit. The court finds that a claim for genocide is not sufficiently clear and Beanal shall be given the opportunity to make a more definite statement, pursuant to Rule 12(e).

[The Court concluded that] Beanal has failed to allege state action. Beanal has failed to allege what role, if any, that Indonesian military personnel played in committing the alleged conduct. More importantly, Beanal has failed to allege facts which would convert Freeport's alleged conduct into official action. State action is required to state a claim for violation of the international law of human rights. The court therefore dismisses without prejudice Beanal's claim for human rights violations under the Alien Tort Statute for failure to state a claim, and grants Plaintiff leave to amend his complaint. . . .

[The court found that the Torture Victim Protection Act (TVPA) does not supersede or curtail the scope of §1350 but concluded that because Freeport is a corporation and not an "individual" for purposes of the TVPA, Freeport cannot be held liable under that law.]

C. ENVIRONMENTAL CLAIMS

Freeport contends that Plaintiff's environmental claims should be dismissed on at least five different grounds; the court reaches only the first. Plaintiff has failed to state a claim for environmental violations upon which relief can be granted under §1350 because Freeport's alleged environmental practices do not appear to have violated the law of nations.

As set forth in the complaint, Plaintiff alleges that Freeport's mining operations and drainage practices have resulted in environmental destruction with human costs to the indigenous people. The mine itself has hollowed several mountains, re-routed rivers, stripped forest and increased toxic and non-toxic materials and metals in the river system. Amended Complaint P 29. Another culprit is discharged water containing tailings from Freeport's mining operations, for it is from this discharge that a stream of environmental and human problems flow, including:

1) pollution, disruption and alteration of natural waterways leading to deforestation, Id. P 26;
2) health safety hazards and starvation, Id. P 27;
3) degradation of surface and ground water from tailings and solid hazardous waste, Id. P 28).

Beanal alleges that the tailings drainage is mismanaged. Beanal further alleges that acid mine drainage is equally devastating, due to resulting sulfide oxidation and leaching, and also inadequately managed. In summary, Plaintiff complains:

> Plaintiffs specifically allege that defendant corporations have failed to engage in a zero waste policy, unacceptable enclosed waste management system, have failed to maximize environmental rehabilitation, have failed to engage in an appropriate acid leachate control policy, have failed to adequately monitor the destruction of the natural resources of Irian Jaya and have disregarded and breached its international duty to protect one of the last great natural rain forests and alpine areas in the world. Id. P 40.

The court next determines whether any of these allegations, if true, amount to a violation of the law of nations. Plaintiff has not alleged that Freeport violated a specific treaty provision. As discussed above, in order to state a claim for violation of the law of nations under §1350, plaintiff must establish the existence of a cognizable international tort. "These international torts, violations of current customary international law, are characterized by universal consensus in the international community as to their binding status and their content. That is, they are universal, definable, and obligatory international norms." [Forti v. Suarez-Mason, 672 F. Supp. 1531, at 1540 (D.C. Cal. 1987), reconsidered on other grounds, 694 F. Supp. 707 (N.D. Cal. 1988).] To determine whether such a norm exists, the court may consider the works of jurists, general usage and practice of nations and judicial decisions recognizing and enforcing that law. In this instance, the court reviewed case law, the Restatement, and a recent treatise on international environmental law. Having done so, the court discerns no claim of action against Freeport based on an international tort.

As a preliminary matter, courts have recognized that §1350 may be applicable to international environmental torts. See Aquinda v. Texaco, Inc., 1994 WL 142006 (S.D.N.Y. 1994); Amlon Metals, Inc. v. FMC Corp., 775 F. Supp. 668, 670 (S.D.N.Y. 1991). Neither of these cases, however, found a cause of action for environmental torts in violation of the law of nations. Aquinda referenced the possible application of §1350 for environmental practices "which might violate international law." Aquinda, 1994

WL 142006, *7. That suit was subsequently dismissed on grounds of comity, forum non-conveniens, and failure to join a necessary party. Aquinda v. Texaco, Inc., 945 F. Supp. 625, 627 (S.D.N.Y. 1996). Amlon involved the shipment of allegedly hazardous copper residue to a purchaser in England for metallic reclamation purposes. Among its claims, the purchaser sought recovery in tort under the Alien Tort Statute. The court rejected plaintiff's reliance on the Stockholm principles to support a cause of action under the §1350 because "those Principles do not set forth any specific proscriptions, but rather refer only in a general sense to the responsibility of nations to insure that activities within their jurisdiction do not cause damage to the environment beyond their borders." Amlon, 775 F. Supp. at 671. This point is well taken with respect to Beanal's complaint.

Beanal has failed to articulate a violation of the international law. Plaintiff states that the allegations support a cause of action based on three international environmental law principles: (1) the Polluter Pays Principle; (2) the Precautionary Principle; and (3) the Proximity Principle. None of the three rises to the level of an international tort. Principles of International Environmental Law I: Frameworks, Standards and Implementation 183-18 (Phillipe Sands ed., 1995) (hereinafter "Sands"). Sands includes the three principles mentioned by Plaintiff in a list of general rules and principles "which have broad, if not necessarily universal, support and are frequently endorsed in practice." Id. at 183. Also listed are (1) the good-neighborliness and international co-operation principle and (2) the following rule, regarded the cornerstone of international environmental law: "The obligation reflected in Principle 21 of the Stockholm Declaration and Principle 2 of the Rio Declaration, namely that states have sovereignty over their natural resources and the responsibility not to cause environmental damage." Id. Sands concludes:

> Of these general principles and rules only Principle 21/Principle 2 and the good neighborliness/international co-operation principle are sufficiently substantive at this time to be capable of establishing the basis of an international cause of action; that is to say, to give rise to an international customary legal obligation the violation of which would give rise to a legal remedy. The status and effect of the others remains inconclusive, although they may bind as treaty obligations or, in limited circumstances, as customary obligations. Id.

The three principles relied on by Plaintiff, standing alone, do not constitute international torts for which there is universal consensus in the international community as to their binding status and their content. Xuncax, 886 F. Supp. at 186. More to the point, those principles apply to "members of the international community" rather than non-state corporations. 945 F. Supp. at 629-630, 652. Plaintiff alleges that Freeport's environmental practices reflect corporate decisions, rather than state practices. A non-state corporation could be bound to such principles by treaty, but not as a matter of international customary law. See Id. Consistent with this conclusion, the Restatement mentions only state obligations and liability in the area of environmental law. Restatement §§601-602.

In sum, Beanal has failed to allege an international environmental tort. The court dismisses Beanal's environmental claims for failure to state a cause of action for violation of international environmental law. Beanal has failed to articulate a substantive claim. In addition, Beanal alleged no facts that would establish, if proven, that Freeport's environmental practices constitute state action. Even assuming for the purposes of this motion that Beanal's allegations are true, Freeport's alleged policies are corporate policies only and, however destructive, do not constitute torts in violation of the law of nations. Having so concluded, the court finds it unnecessary to rule on Freeport's remaining defenses to the environmental allegations lodged against it.

CONCLUSION

For the reasons stated, Beanal's claims brought under §1350 for cultural genocide, human rights violations and international environmental torts are dismissed without prejudice. Plaintiff is granted leave to amend his complaint in order to more specifically allege his claims for genocide and human rights violation. . . .

Notes and Questions

1. *An appropriate vehicle?* Do you believe the Alien Tort Statute is an appropriate vehicle for the righting of alleged environmental wrongs such as the ones involved in this case? For a case finding subject matter jurisdiction under the Alien Tort Statute in a class action by residents of Burma (Myanmar) against, inter alia, various oil companies, *see John Doe I, et al. v. Unocal Corp.,* ____ F. supp. ____ (D.D.C. 1997), Lexis 5094. The court there found that the "state action" requirement was satisfied because: "[a] private individual acts under color of law . . . when he acts together with state officials or with significant state aid."

2. *The court's application of the law.* Do you believe the court applied correctly the principles of international environmental law that were drawn to its attention? Should the plaintiff have cited other principles?

3. *The* Filartiga *fountainhead.* As may have been apparent from your reading of *Beanal,* the now-famous *Filartiga* case was the first one in which the Alien Tort Statute was used to vindicate human rights claims in United States courts. In *Filartiga,* the Second Circuit held that deliberate torture perpetrated under color of official authority violates universally accepted norms of human rights law. The suit had been brought by citizens of Paraguay against another Paraguayan for the wrongful death, by torture, of the son of one of the plaintiffs. The defendant, then Inspector General

of Police in Asuncion, Paraguay, later came to the United States, where he was served with process in this action. He fled before a subsequent judgment for compensatory and punitive damages could be enforced. 557 F. Supp. 860 (E.D.N.Y. 1984).

4. *The* Aguinda *case.* A case that is in many respects similar to *Beanal* is Aguinda v. Texaco, 1994 WL 142006 (S.D.N.Y. 1994). In that case plaintiffs, citizens of Ecuador, contended that Texaco's operations in that country caused harm to indigenous peoples living in the rain forest and to their property, as well as to the stability of Amazon basin habitats. Plaintiffs claimed that defendant had engaged in "environmental abuse during a period ending in 1990, including large-scale disposal of inadequately treated hazardous wastes and destruction of tropical rain forest habitats involving a substantial portion of Ecuadoran territory in the Amazon basin." *Id.* The court reserved decision on Texaco's motions to dismiss, specified limits on discovery, and encouraged the parties to settle the matter out of court, perhaps with the assistance of an impartial third party.

(ii) Environmental Refugees

(1) Introduction

INTERNATIONAL LEGAL PROTECTION FOR VICTIMS OF ENVIRONMENTAL ABUSE

Michelle Leighton Schwartz
18 Yale J. Intl. L. 335, 375-376 (1993)

The exploitation and degradation of natural resources has led to the creation of a new refugee phenomenon: "environmental refugees." These are people fleeing natural disasters, such as radical land transformations, the construction of dams and irrigation works, or toxic contamination. Environmental refugees now comprise the largest, as well as the fastest growing, group of displaced persons in the world. Over 135 million people may be at risk of being displaced by severe desertification alone. Although the problem has reached critical proportions, these refugees do not fall within the traditional legal definition of "refugee" and, thus, generally do not qualify for international assistance and protection. Existing laws and institutions must be modified to protect and assist environmental refugees.

Notes and Questions

1. *What is an "environmental refugee"?* Scholars have defined the term "environmental refugees" as people "forced to leave their traditional habitat, temporarily or permanently, because of a marked environmental disruption (natural and/or triggered by people) that jeopardized their existence and/or seriously affected the quality of their life." *See* Essam Elhinnawi, U.N. Env't Programme, Environmental Refugees 4 (1985). Three types of

environmental refugees are recognized: those displaced temporarily by a natural disaster; those permanently displaced by changes to their subsistence base such as development projects; and those who migrate temporarily or permanently because of environmental degradation affecting their quality of life. Environmental factors cause these persons to migrate both within and across national boundaries. *Id.* at 4-5.

2. *Contributing factors.* The environmental disruption which causes the people's flight refers to "any physical, chemical and/or biological changes in the ecosystem (or the resource base) that renders it temporarily or permanently unsuitable to support human life." *Id.* at 4. The following is a profile of case studies conducted on environmental refugees and the triggering force of destruction that caused their plight.

(2) Causes of Environmental Migration

■ INTERNATIONAL LEGAL PROTECTION FOR VICTIMS OF ENVIRONMENTAL ABUSE

Michelle Leighton Schwartz
18 Yale J. Intl. L. 335, 376-378

1. Irrigation and Flood Control Projects

Large-scale irrigation projects share many of the environmental and human impact problems of the hydro-power dams. . . . For example, the Narmada Project in India, one of the biggest water development and resettlement projects ever planned, will displace more than one million people in the states of Maharashta and Madhya Pradesh. Nearly two hundred thousand of these people are members of indigenous groups. Although the Maharashta government has promised two hectares of land to all displaced persons over eighteen years of age, insufficient land and infrastructure makes fulfillment of this pledge unlikely. In fact, only five to ten percent of those displaced by this project have received compensation under the rehabilitation program since its institution six years ago. Furthermore, no reliable mechanism exists in India to involve the affected people in project planning or to redress their injuries.

The Volta River dam in Ghana is another example. Resettlement proposals tied to the project changed significantly over the years. Approximately 80,000 people were displaced by the dam. Of these, 17,000 immediately opted for a cash settlement and left the area. Another 64,000 moved to new villages; however, a large number soon moved on when they were faced with shortages of housing, cleared land, money and food.

2. Desertification

Unsustainable farming practices stemming from overpopulation, poverty, drought, and economic pressures have led to widespread land degradation in various Third World countries. Desertification, for example, affects about 3.6 billion hectares, or about one quarter of the world's total land area. About half of the people most threatened by desertification live in the Sahel, a semi-arid zone stretching across the entire continent of Africa, from Mauritania in the West to the Horn of Africa in the East. Droughts in the area can last for years, or even decades. Over the past few decades, intensive farming and rapid deforestation have led to massive soil depletion and erosion. Ground cover not cleared for cultivation is harvested for cooking fuel, frequently in violation of local laws. A recent study by the World Conservation Union (IUCN) concluded that, "[a]lternative fuel and building supplies could reduce the pressure on the shrinking forests. But unless those alternatives are available, people in the Horn will not stop cutting wood until the entire region is totally deforested." This study estimated that "by the year 2010 some 38,000 square kilometers of the Ethiopian highlands will be down to bare rock and a further area of 60,000 square kilometers will have less than 10 centimeters of soil remaining on it." This degradation of land forces the people dependent on it to abandon their agricultural subsistence and relocate to already overpopulated cities nearby, where the influx of additional people will contribute to further land degradation.

Notes and Questions

1. *Environmental refugees and climate change.* The plight of people forced to migrate because of deteriorating ecosystems has the potential to worsen in the coming years because of the threat of global warming. Some scientists estimate that the greenhouse effect could cause average global temperatures to rise 2.2 degrees in the next 40 years. (*See* Chapter 12.) This could lead to a three-foot (approximately one meter) rise in sea levels. Paul Kennedy catalogues the potential catastrophes of a one-meter rise in sea levels and estimates somewhere between 15 and 20 million environmental refugees. According to Kennedy, a two-meter rise in sea level would render 177,000 inhabitants of the Maldive Islands inundated. A one-meter rise in sea levels would cause Bangladesh to lose 11.5 percent of its land where 8.5 million people currently live and would have devastating effects on countries such as Egypt and China, where populations reside in low-lying deltas. Other areas would also be affected by an increased likelihood of monsoons and devastating storm floods. *See* Paul Kennedy, Preparing for the Twenty-First Century 109-110 (1993).

2. *Classifying the causes.* There are at least four circumstances that indirectly result in displacement: (1) systematic human rights violations, (2) war, armed conflict, communal violence, and aggression, (3) development-induced relocation and (4) damage to the environment. Presently, displacement is not viewed as a human rights violation and does not trigger international concern in a workable manner. In 1980, the World Bank began

regulation of development induced displacement by issuing guidelines to establish appropriate international standards for development projects. However, in view of the fact that plans are prepared by government borrowers who may give priority to the concept of eminent domain rather than the rights of its citizens not to be displaced, the potential for flawed development projects and serious human rights violations is immense. Addressing these concerns by first recognizing a person's right not to be displaced shifts the burden to the relocator and gives primacy to the human rights aspect rather than the developmental one, or at a minimum puts the two on equal footing. Maria Stavroupoulou, *The Right Not to Be Displaced,* 9 Am. U. J. Intl. L. & Poly. 689, 701, 728-732 (1994). Envision how a discourse would transpire about a proposed project that would cause dislocation if the human rights concerns received such recognition.

(iii) A Human Right to Water?

■ A HUMAN RIGHT TO WATER: DOMESTIC AND INTERNATIONAL IMPLICATIONS

Stephen C. McCaffrey
5 Geo. Intl. Envtl. L. Rev. 1, 5-12 (1992)

II. The Right to Water as a Human Right

A. THE NECESSITY OF ESTABLISHING THE RIGHT

Water is essential to human, as well as other forms of life. It is consumed directly and used for such basic needs as sanitation, cleansing and growing food. In fact, some three-quarters of the water consumed by humans is used in agriculture. Thus, water shortages or contamination can lead to famine, disease and even death. The situation is summed up by the United Nations Department of Technical Cooperation for Development as follows:

> No resource is more basic than water. Water is essential for life, crucial for relieving poverty, hunger and disease and critical for economic development. Despite enormous improvements over the past 15 years, hundreds of millions of men, women and children still do not have proper water for drinking and sanitation. Many remain unemployed because water resources cannot support agricultural or industrial growth. Water problems ultimately end up as "people" problems.
>
> As world population increases and development efforts expand, water needs can only increase. By the end of the [twentieth] century, global water use is expected to reach twice the level of 1980.

In a number of countries—including Burma (Myanmar), Indonesia, Haiti and Kenya—less than half the population has access to safe drinking water. Such water shortages may result from natural phenomena and poor management, but often political factors are involved as well. According to recent reports, for example, the Sudanese government is currently forcing some 400,000 squatters in Khartoum to relocate to camps with inadequate water supplies and other services. The United States government has characterized the relocation program as a virtual "death sentence" for many of those being resettled, most of whom are Christians and animists from the southern part of the country. The largest relocation camp holds more than 80,000 individuals yet was served by only one functioning well when a reporter visited the site.

A somewhat more subtle form of forced relocation, this time involving more overt water deprivations, is alleged to be occurring in Israel and the Occupied Territories. In a case brought before the International Water Tribunal,[32] the complainants charge that at least half of some seventy Arab communities in the center and north of Israel are not recognized by the state and are not connected to national drinking water networks. This situation is said to have led to serious health problems as well as environmental distress. The plaintiffs charge that Israel is using "water as a means to pressure certain Arab communities to evacuate their places of residence and relocate against their will." In the West Bank, it has been reported that Israel is controlling supplies of groundwater—the region's only significant water source—by permitting its settlers to drill many deep wells while restricting the number and depth of Arab wells. This practice has caused Arab wells to dry up, forcing some Arabs to relocate.

The cases reviewed above illustrate how water can be used as a political weapon. But individuals can also be deprived of an adequate supply of safe drinking water through mere governmental neglect or mismanagement. For example, the Libyan government has pursued what have been described as "grandiose" projects, such as "an effort to build a $25 billion artificial river," while "many Libyans live without basic services like water and sewer systems." And much of the agricultural land in Chile is irrigated with water from the same rivers into which most domestic and industrial waste is dumped. This resulted in an outbreak of cholera in 1991, largely because Santiago, Chile's capital city, has no water treatment plants.

Natural phenomena, government mismanagement, and political maneuverings may all contribute to water shortages. Depriving individuals of fresh water can force them to relocate or, worse, result in disease and even death. The severity of the effects of water deprivation mandates a serious response from the international community. Access to adequate amounts of safe, useable fresh water should be recognized as a human right. The

32. The Second International Water Tribunal was initiated by non-governmental organizations (NGOs) and held from 17 to 21 February, 1992, in Amsterdam, where the Tribunal is headquartered. Cases are presented by NGOs to an independent and impartial "jury," or panel, of scientific and legal experts. The panel heard twelve cases that were brought by NGOs from different regions of the world. *See* Ellen Hey & André Nollkaemper, *The Second International Water Tribunal,* 22 Envtl. Pol'y & L. 82 (1992).

following section explores the legal framework for treating this "right to water" as a human right.

B. STATUS OF THE RIGHT UNDER UNIVERSAL HUMAN RIGHTS INSTRUMENTS

Given the potential for its use by governments for improper purposes and, more fundamentally, its importance to human life and civilization, it is surprising that water is not mentioned at all in either of the 1966 United Nations covenants on human rights or in the Universal Declaration of Human Rights. If there is a right to water under the basic instruments of international human rights law, therefore, it must be inferred.

1. The Universal Declaration of Human Rights

[A]rticle 25 of the Declaration proclaims that "[e]veryone has the right to a standard of living adequate for the health and well-being of himself and of his family, including food. . . ." It seems obvious that such a standard of living could not exist without an adequate supply of water suitable for drinking. Further, unless food were imported from other states, the "right" to an adequate standard of living *presumes* an adequate supply of water to sustain agriculture to the extent necessary to feed a state's population.

As a General Assembly resolution, the Declaration is not binding per se. However, its most fundamental provisions are generally thought either to have passed into customary international law, or to constitute an authoritative interpretation of relevant U.N. Charter provisions, or both. However, while the provisions of the Declaration which are now considered binding include many so-called "liberty rights"—that is, "rights not to be treated in certain ways, or not to be interfered with"—it is by no means clear that they would include what have been referred to as "welfare rights"—"rights to be assured the provision of certain goods or services considered necessary for human well-being." Article 25's right to an adequate standard of living falls into the "welfare rights" category, thus casting doubt upon its status as a binding obligation. Even if it were binding, a right to water would still have to be inferred from that provision. That is, it would have to be established that a right to water is implicit in the right to an adequate standard of living to which the article explicitly refers.

2. The 1966 Covenants

Even if such an implicit right were established, it is likely that states would not be required to guarantee the right immediately, but would only have to implement it progressively, and to the extent permitted by their resources. This seems to follow from the fact that the right would derive from the article of the Declaration whose counterpart is article 11 of the Covenant on Economic, Social and Cultural Rights (E.S.C. Covenant). While the Covenant on Civil and Political Rights (C.P. Covenant) "imposes an immediate obligation 'to respect and to ensure' the rights it proclaims," States Parties to the E.S.C. Covenant need only implement the obligations under that agreement progressively. Let us then turn to the C.P. Covenant to see whether it would support a right to water.

Article 6, paragraph 1, of the C.P. Covenant provides: "Every human being has the inherent right to life. This right shall be protected by law. No one shall be arbitrarily deprived of his life." Can this right be interpreted to embrace a right to water sufficient to sustain life? An affirmative answer to this question would place a significant obligation on states since, as noted above, the C.P. Covenant "imposes an immediate obligation 'to respect and to ensure' the rights it proclaims and to take whatever other measures are necessary to bring about that result."

Unfortunately, respected commentators have taken the view that "[t]he human right to life per se . . . is a civil right, and it 'does not guarantee any person against death from famine or cold or lack of medical attention.' " Rather, the right to life, according to this view, is a guarantee against the arbitrary deprivation of life by the state. Therefore, "the mere toleration of malnutrition by a state will not be regarded as a violation of the human right to life, whereas purposeful denial of access to food, e.g., to a prisoner, is a different matter." There is thus a line of thought according to which Article 6 does not require the state to take affirmative actions to ensure that its citizens have access to adequate sustenance, but only obliges it to refrain from practicing or tolerating arbitrary deprivations of life. It would therefore be difficult to infer a right to water under this interpretation of Article 6.

The recent trend, however, seems to be toward a more expansive interpretation of Article 6. Most notably, the Human Rights Committee, established by the C.P. Covenant, has declared that the right to life, as the most fundamental human right, may not be understood in a restrictive sense and, further, that its protection requires that states adopt *positive* measures. According to this view, a restrictive interpretation of the right to life is out of place in today's world. Professor [now Judge] Rosalyn Higgins, [formerly] member of the Human Rights Committee, has written that "virtually all states have accepted that this broader reading of Article 6 is possible." Thus "under the right to life, in its modern and proper sense, not only is protection against any arbitrary deprivation of life upheld, but furthermore States are under the duty 'to pursue policies which are designed to ensure access to the means of survival' for all individuals and all peoples."

The General Comments adopted by the Human Rights Committee under Article 40, paragraph 4 of the C.P. Covenant state:

> [The Committee] has noted that the right to life has been too often narrowly interpreted. The expression 'inherent right to life' cannot properly be understood in a restrictive manner, and the protection of this right requires that States adopt positive measures. In this connection, the Committee considers

> that it would be desirable for States parties [to the C.P. Covenant] to take all possible measures to reduce infant mortality and to increase life expectancy, especially in adopting measures to eliminate malnutrition and epidemics.

Thus, this modern view would interpret the right to life broadly, so that it "comprises the right of every human being not to be deprived of his life (*right to life*) and the right of every human being to have the appropriate means of subsistence and a decent standard of life (preservation of life, *right of living*)." Construed as including the right to appropriate means of subsistence, the right to life would clearly encompass the right to sanitary drinking water.

But even those adhering to a wider view of Article 6 seem to believe that it is not that the right to life *encompasses* the other rights (e.g., right to subsistence) but rather that the "safeguarding of this foremost right is an essential condition for the enjoyment of the entire range of civil and political, as well as economic, social and cultural rights." While this interpretation undoubtedly strengthens the right to life, it does not create a right to sustenance within the C.P. Covenant. This is unfortunate, since the Covenant on Economic, Social and Cultural Rights imposes significantly lower burdens on governments to affirmatively meet its obligations.

Article 11 of the E.S.C. Covenant provides in part that the Parties "recognize the right of everyone to an adequate standard of living for himself and his family, including adequate food, clothing and housing, and to the continuous improvement of living conditions." It will be taken as self-evident for the purposes of this analysis that the right to an adequate standard of living defined in article 11 includes a supply of water that is at least adequate to meet basic human needs.

While the right proclaimed in article 11 is potentially quite far-reaching, a state party to the E.S.C. Covenant undertakes only "to take steps . . . to the maximum of its available resources, with a view to achieving progressively the full realization of the rights recognized in the Covenant." Thus, in contrast to the C.P. Covenant, there is no obligation on parties to the E.S.C. Covenant to implement its provisions immediately. This follows from the vast disparity of resources and capabilities among existing and potential parties to the E.S.C. Covenant. The "rights" enumerated and defined in the E.S.C. Covenant are thus more in the nature of goals than of presently existing entitlements. Therefore, while it seems clear that a right to water may be derived from the provisions of the E.S.C. Covenant, such a right would not necessarily have to be given immediate effect by the state concerned. States Parties to the E.S.C. Covenant would, however, be under an obligation to work toward "achieving progressively the full realization" of the right, within the framework of the right to an adequate standard of living under article 11. The acceptance of this proposition would in itself be an important and positive step forward.

Thus, while significant obstacles to the establishment of the human right to water as an immediately binding obligation persist, it is clear that, at least in some form, the right may be inferred under the basic instruments of international human rights law. Given the often devastating results when individuals are denied fresh water, the relevant provisions of existing human rights instruments ought to be interpreted broadly, so as to facilitate the implementation of the right to water as quickly and comprehensively as possible. . . .

Notes and Questions

1. *Implementing the right.* How would the government of a country experiencing water shortages guarantee a "human right to water" (assuming one existed)? Would it matter whether the right had its basis in the C.P. Covenant or the E.S.C. Covenant?

2. *Problem: The interplay with interstate relations.* If upstream state A diverts so much of the water of the River Blue, flowing into state B, that the inhabitants of state B do not have sufficient water for their domestic needs, can state A be said to have violated the human rights of those individuals in state B? What remedies might be available: (a) to the citizens of state B? (b) to state B vis-à-vis state A?

3. *Mini-case study: The Southern Peru Copper Corporation.* This case involved a complaint brought before the International Water Tribunal by citizens' groups and a local municipality against Southern Peru Copper Corporation (SPCC), a United States company operating in Peru. The Tribunal's jury found, inter alia, that SPCC's use of water for copper production "seriously decreased the water resources previously available for the use of the local population for agricultural, grazing and household needs. This reverses the order of priority of water uses established by national laws and the Declaration of Amsterdam and has resulted in the displacement of people and in desertification of the area." International Water Tribunal, case of Associación Civil "Labor", et al., v. Southern Peru Copper Corporation, USA, February 18, 1992, Amsterdam. *See* McCaffrey, above, note 24. This case illustrates the potential for conflict between development efforts and the needs of the local population. Assuming a human right to water, would the government of Peru be found to have violated its obligations to the affected individuals flowing from such a right?

VIII

Environmental Disasters

Environmental disasters such as oil spills, industrial accidents, and floods often cause grave human and ecological harm. Partly for this reason and partly because, by definition, they strike without warning, these situations frequently capture the attention of the public and are prominently reported in the news media. This often serves to galvanize the political will of states, resulting in legal action on the national or international level aimed at preventing or mitigating future incidents of the kind in question. It is thus not surprising that lawmaking in the field of the environment—especially on the international plane—has been characterized as "legislation by disaster."[1] Two well-known cases illustrate the point: The *Torrey Canyon* spill off the English coast of 1967, and the British response of destroying the tanker without the consent of the flag state in order to protect its coastline, was followed by the conclusion of the Convention Relating to Intervention on the High Seas in Cases of Oil Pollution Casualties of November 29, 1969, 26 U.S.T. 765, 970 U.N.T.S. 211. And the international community responded to the Chernobyl accident of April 26, 1986, by concluding two agreements the following September: the Convention

1. *See, e.g.*, Tammy Alcock, "Ecology Tankers" and the Oil Pollution Act of 1990: A History of Efforts to Require Double Hulls on Oil Tankers, 19 Ecology L.Q. 97 (1992) (hereinafter Alcock), stating with regard to the history of the controversy over requiring double hulls on oil tankers: "Ultimately, it is a story of a system which seems to require a disaster to force change." *Id.* at 100 (footnote omitted).

on Early Notification of a Nuclear Accident of September 26, 1986, *reprinted in* 25 I.L.M. 1370, and the Convention on Assistance in the Case of a Nuclear Accident or Radiological Emergency of the same date, U.N.T.S. Reg. no. 24643, *reprinted in* 25 I.L.M. 1377.

But surely no one would seriously argue that we should wait for accidents to happen before concluding agreements or enacting legislation to prevent them or minimize their effects. Or would they? The more unlikely the accident, the more expensive the preventive measures, the more powerful the forces resisting preventive measures, the less politically important the people or environment likely to be affected, and the stronger will be the argument against measures of prevention. The debate over whether to require double hulls on oil tankers[2]—initially sparked by the *Torrey Canyon* spill but only resolved in the United States as a result of the *Exxon Valdez* disaster[3]—is but one of the many illustrations of this point.

In this chapter, we examine the international legal framework governing environmental emergencies. You should evaluate the various sources included in sections B and E of the chapter to determine, as nearly as you can, (1) their authoritative value, and (2) whether they adequately take into account the forces identified in the preceding paragraph. We have chosen the term "disasters" to describe unplanned phenomena that cause or threaten damage. These events have also been referred to as "emergencies," "incidents," "emergency situations," and "accidents." They may be of human (e.g., chemical spills and industrial plant explosions) or natural (e.g., floods and ice floes) origin. You should ask yourself whether the rules expressed in a given document are appropriate to both kinds of emergency situations (for example, would rules concerning notification and responsibility apply equally to chemical spills and floods?). We will generally concentrate upon environmental emergencies that cause or threaten transfrontier harm—for example, a chemical spill in one country carried by an international watercourse into another country. But we will also touch upon other situations whose "transfrontier" character is more subtle. For example, the plant involved in the Bhopal disaster could be said to have been "exported" to India from the United States by Union Carbide, whose subsidiary operated the plant. Are these situations covered at all by the rules governing emergencies in one state causing or threatening harmful effects in another? Another example of a national disaster having international though not transfrontier repercussions is one that affects a world heritage site wholly within the state. The present chapter can only touch upon the important problem of marine oil spills. Marine pollution is dealth with in Chapter 13.

2. *See, e.g.,* Alcock, *id.* (noting at 108 that the *Exxon Valdez* spill of approximately 11 million gallons of crude oil would most likely have been prevented had that tanker been double-hulled).

3. *See* Oil Pollution Act of 1990, Pub. L. No. 101-380, 104 Stat. 484, requiring that double-hulled ships be phased in over a period of 25 years.

A. CASE STUDIES

The following case studies describe major and well-known industrial accidents of a non-nuclear nature. Nuclear accidents will be covered in section E of this chapter.

1. Seveso

■ NATURE AND SCOPE OF THE PROBLEM

Ved Nanda and Bruce Bailey
in Transferring Hazardous Technologies and Substances 3, 3-7
(G. Handl & R. Lutz eds. 1989)

On July 10, 1976, an explosion occurred in Meda, Italy at the Icmesa plant owned by Givaudan, a subsidiary of the Swiss-controlled Hoffmann-LaRoche chemical combine. A thick whitish cloud of trichlorophenol gas with a pungent, medicinal odour containing approximately four and one-half pounds of the substance 2, 3, 7, 8 dibenzo-paradioxin, known as TCDD or dioxin, was released into the atmosphere surrounding the plant. A northerly wind moved the cloud to the south over an area some four and one-half miles long and one-third of a mile wide before dispersing about half an hour after the initial release. The cloud eventually dispersed as droplets over parts of seven towns, the three most affected being Meda, Seveso and Cesano Maderno.

The Icmesa plant, located about 13 miles north of Milan, produced mainly trichlorophenol gas, a chemical used primarily to make hexachlorophene, an ingredient in cleansers and germicides, and 2-4-5, a defoliant employed by the American armed forces during the Vietnam war. On July 10, 1976, for an unknown reason, temperatures within the plant's system rose, causing pressure to build up. Production at the plant usually took place at a temperature of 180 degrees centigrade, while temperatures of 230 degrees centigrade could cause the process to go out of control. On that Saturday in 1976, the temperature in the system rose to 300 degrees centigrade, even though the controls were set for cooling. As a consequence of the pressure build-up, a safety valve burst, and the cloud of trichlorophenol gas was released into the atmosphere.

The head of Givaudan at that time, Guy Waldvogel, stated that the plant had two cooling plants built into its security systems, although these may not have been put into action soon enough. As would be the case at Bhopal, the Icmesa plant had been the subject of safety complaints prior to the accident, including assertions by workers at the plant that security measures for handling toxic substances were inadequate and that the plant lacked a dump tank or vapour recovery system. This latter defect meant that once the safety valve burst, the vapours were released directly into the atmosphere. A medical survey of workers at the plant also indicated that many had in the past suffered from nausea and vomiting, burns, blisters, intoxication and vertigo.

The pattern of company management failing to inform local authorities as to the type of products being in the chemical production processes, the exact nature of the production processes and the high-risk potential involved which eight years later would characterize the Bhopal context were present at the Icmesa plant. Initially, plant officials kept quiet about the release, hoping that rain would wash away the pollution, before finally informing local authorities twenty-seven hours after the explosion took place. It then took the plant managers seven days to inform local authorities that dioxins were present in the vapour cloud which had been released by the explosion. This delay was with regard to a substance three ounces of which could injure or kill most of New York City's population. Local authorities magnified these errors of delay by taking five days to place some of the areas contaminated by the dioxin off-limits to workers and residents. In addition, the superhighway through the area remained open, and clean-up crews wore their contaminated protective clothing into non-contaminated neighbouring areas.

Once the magnitude and nature of the accident were realized by the local authorities, three zones were established around the plant, with the most contaminated zone designated as Zone A. Inside this zone, which initially encompassed about 285 acres, the 730 inhabitants were evacuated, and the area was sealed off. The 175 children of the residents living in this zone were sent to state-subsidized summer camps. All agricultural, industrial, and commercial activity in Zone A was halted, including the sale and consumption of locally produced foodstuffs. Zone B, which included about 451 acres, was classified as slightly polluted, and the 4,280 residents were allowed to remain at home, although they were urged to send their children away and pregnant women were asked to submit to medical examinations. A larger area, Zone C, was designated as a safeguard zone where the residents were advised not to eat produce grown in the area.

The immediate human medical effects of the accident were primarily in the form of more than 500 cases of chloracne and other forms of skin disease. Some of these cases persisted for more than two years from the time of the accident. The most severe biological impact came in the form of the loss of produce and domestic animals raised in the contaminated zones, all of which either died or had to be destroyed.

The indirect and more long-term effects of the accident went beyond the physical impacts upon the inhabitants of the three zones. Immediately following the accident, orders for furniture and clothes sold by local merchants were either canceled or large discounts were demanded. The plant itself was permanently closed a little more than a month after the accident.

As a consequence of the forced evacuation and relocation of the residents of the contaminated area, many families and businesses were disrupted. Houses in the most contaminated areas were demolished, while structures left standing had to be decontaminated. Initially, the Italian government allocated $48.4 million to carry out these measures, with most of that money earmarked for decontamination and health projects for affected residents.

The magnitude of the problem can be seen by the fact that for months after the accident, officials were not sure how to clean up the affected area. Demonstrations by former residents occurred, protesting at the slow pace of the government's decontamination programme. The basic reclamation plan finally approved by the regional government provided that all vegetation and soil to a depth of one foot from the directly affected areas were to be removed and incinerated at 1,000 degrees centigrade. Once an area had been sufficiently decontaminated to allow human activity again, a research and experimental laboratory to study techniques for neutralizing or reducing the effects of dioxin was constructed. Nearly three years after the accident, data supplied by the laboratory indicated that there was no sign that the toxicity of remaining dioxin-contaminated areas was diminishing.

By the time the decontamination efforts had been largely completed, more than two tons of chemical waste containing dioxin had been removed from the total of 4,400 acres of land which had been contaminated by the Icmesa plant. Even the disposal of this waste was not without mishap, as the 41 drums containing the waste disappeared during their transport out of Italy. The drums were eventually located in a storehouse in northern France after considerable public furor. Finally, more than six years after the accident, the Italian government oversaw the dismantling of the Icmesa reactor and the burial of the remaining rubble from the reactor in lead barrels in a 160,000 cubic metre ditch situated in a corner of the once highly contaminated sector. A committee of independent scientists reported that eight years after the accident, no chemical traces of the explosion were visible, except for occasional continuing cases of chloracne. The committee reported that Hoffmann-LaRoche was planning to landscape the affected area into a 40-hectare park.

Hoffmann-LaRoche indicated fairly early on that it intended to accept responsibility for the consequences of the explosion and to compensate those damaged by the accident, perhaps partly as a result of the findings of a special parliamentary investigating commission set up by the Italian government. The commission's report, issued one year after the accident, accused the Hoffmann-LaRoche subsidiary, Givaudan, of not only failing to inform the local and regional Italian authorities about the nature of the Icmesa operations, but also of failing to install automatic control and warning devices.

The Italian government and the Lombardy region reached a settlement with Givaudan with regard to compensation for the Seveso accident. Givaudan agreed to pay the two governments a total of $80 million as payment for expenses incurred by various Italian ministries, land reclamation, health work, rebuilding in the area, lost crops and decontamination.

The commune of Seveso filed suit in Geneva, Switzerland against Givaudan in early 1979 for damages to the community and its inhabitants. The suit accused Givaudan of failing to take adequate safety precautions, failing to correct those inadequacies after becoming aware of them, and attempting to cover up after the explosion. Seveso and Givaudan reached a settlement of the suit in late 1983 when Givaudan agreed to pay about $7.2 million to Seveso as payment for damages.

Five Icmesa executives, including the plant's managing director, technical director, plant designer, company chairman, and plant engineer, were brought to trial as a result of the Seveso explosion. The five men were charged with negligence leading to a disaster, causing contamination of a vast inhabited area that had to be evacuated, and failure to have adequate safety systems. The Italian court found the five guilty and assessed sentences ranging from two and one-half to five years in prison. Four of the convictions were overturned on appeal, while the fifth sentence was suspended. Charges against the mayor of Meda and local health officials were initially filed and then later dropped. The charges had been based upon the officials' failure to apply existing legislation which could have avoided the disaster.

Two and one-half years after the Seveso accident, Italy, which had virtually no environmental legislation in force during 1976, enacted legislation which reformed its national health-care system. Provisions within the new law which had a bearing on environmental hazards caused by harmful substances included standards for the production, registration, sale and use of chemical substances capable of upsetting the biological and ecological balance; the establishment and maintenance of a national inventory of chemical substances; and the creation of "risk maps" based on requirement that all factories provide data on the toxicological characteristics of the products they use and their possible effects on humans and the environment.

Note

The *Seveso Directive.* In connection with your consideration of the Seveso accident, you may wish to consult the "Seveso Directive" (Council Directive on Major Accident Hazards of Certain Industrial Activities, Doc. 82/501/EEC, O.J. No. L 230/1, Aug. 5, 1982) adopted by the Council of the European Communities June 24, 1982, as amended March 19, 1987, which is discussed in the Brown Weiss excerpt below and is available in many international environmental law document collections.

2. *Bhopal*

■ NATURE AND SCOPE OF THE PROBLEM

Ved Nanda & Bruce Bailey
in Transferring Hazardous Technologies and Substances 7-11
(G. Handl & R. Lutz eds. 1989)

On the night of December 2-3, 1984, toxic methyl isocyanate (MIC) gas escaped from an underground storage tank at a Union Carbide chemical manufacturing plant in Bhopal, India, and leaked into the atmosphere. The leaked gas covered an area of 25 square miles, and resulted in an unparalleled catastrophe, causing the death of over 1,600 people and injuring over 200,000 people as a direct result of the leak; several hundred more died in the next few months due to the fatal effects of the lethal gas. Livestock were killed, crops damaged, and business interrupted.

In the aftermath of the world's worst industrial accident, medical authorities were uncertain about the long-term effects of exposure to the deadly gas. Two years after the disaster, it was reported that lingering effects on many Bhopal residents included: "shortness of breath, eye irritation, and depression." The Indian government reported that the death toll has risen to 2,347 people, that 30,000 to 40,000 people had suffered serious injuries in the incident, and that it had received 500,000 leak-related claims.

The accident occurred at the Bhopal plant of Union Carbide India, Ltd. (UCIL), a subsidiary of the Union Carbide Corp., a New York Corporation with headquarters in Danbury, Connecticut, which owns 50.9% of its Indian subsidiary. The Indian government blamed Union Carbide for errors in the design, management, and oversight of the Bhopal plant, and specifically asserted that "unreasonable and highly dangerous and defective plant conditions" caused the catastrophe. It cited inadequate safety measures, faulty alarm systems, storage of huge quantities of toxic chemicals, lack of cooling facilities, and poor maintenance at the factory. The company, on the other hand, contended that the responsibility must lie with its subsidiary along with the state of Madhya Pradesh where the plant was located and the central government of India; it also alleged sabotage by a disgruntled worker at the plant.

In the Bhopal district court where the case is pending, Union Carbide contended that although it owned 50.9% of the stock in its subsidiary, the government of India has barred it from running the plant. Instead, it said that "it sold general design drawings to its Indian subsidiary, which then hired companies to do detailed design and construction. The parent trained some of the plant managers, but was unable to dictate the plant's daily operations." It added that the 1973 agreement for the sale of the design, approved by the Indian government, stipulated that the parent "shall not, in any way, be liable for any loss, damage, personal injury or death" resulting from the use of the design specifications by the UCIL. The company also contended that "the Indian government had approved and inspected the plant, knew about the dangers of MIC and refused to allow American employees from Carbide to remain in India to provide technical assistance requested by its subsidiary to the Indians running the plant . . . (T)he state government in Bhopal had allowed people to move close to the plant, hence knowing the dangers they would face in an accident." Earlier, in a federal district court in New York, similar charges and counter charges regarding the responsibility for the design of the plant, overall control and training of the personnel were exchanged by the government of India and Union Carbide.

Questions have been raised about the safety of the plant design in Bhopal, which went into production in 1980, and the adequacy of safety equipment and operating systems. None of the safety devices worked. Because of instrumentation errors, monitoring gauges did not work and hence there was no early warning of impending disaster. The mechanical valves which were supposed to act as a backstop measure were dysfunctional. Also, the vent gas scrubber (VGS) intended to neutralize any leaking gas by automatically "washing" the toxic gas with caustic soap, thereby rendering it harmless, was shut off when the leak occurred. The flair tower designed to burn leaking gas had also been shut down. However, according to one report, "because of faulty design, both the VGS and flair tower together also could not have prevented the MIC from escaping into the atmosphere." As evidence of the faults in the plant design, it was reported that there was no backup system to prevent this kind of gas escape. Safety measures used elsewhere by Union Carbide were lacking; for example, the UCIL lacked the computerized pressure/temperature sensing system, and there were no effective alternatives. A study of the design analysis of the storage area for MIC led one reporter to two conclusions:

> First, that the short-sighted design modifications made in the pipeline connections, less than a year ago, along with the dysfunctioning of some valves, were primarily responsible for water ingress in the MIC tank. And second, the original design of the MIC storage area did not provide even a single safe route for a toxic gas at a very high temperature and pressure to be neutralized before escaping into the atmosphere. In other words, the safety features were greatly under designed.

Following the Bhopal disaster, several claims on behalf of the victims were filed in India as well as in the United States, raising questions about the possible violations of Indian Law which prohibits solicitation of clients and contingency fees. Meanwhile, on February 20, the Indian government adopted the Bhopal Gas Leak Disaster Ordinance, and on March 29, 1985, enacted the Bhopal Gas Leak Disaster (Processing of Claims) Act, under which the government of India assumed responsibility as the sole representative of all the victims of the gas leak to bring a single action against Union Carbide. Subsequently, in April 1985, the Indian government, on behalf of the victims, filed as *parens patriae* a lawsuit against Union Carbide in the federal district court for the Southern District of New York, seeking both compensatory and punitive damages in an unspecified amount. Before filing the suit, which invoked six separate theories of liability on the part of Union Carbide—absolute liability, strict liability, negligence, breach of warranty, misrepresentation and the multinational enterprise liability theory—the government of India had rejected a Union Carbide offer to settle the controversy for $200 million dollars.

Two U.S. lawyers challenged the Indian government's action of filing a lawsuit on behalf of all the victims by in turn filing a suit in India. The challenge to block the Indian suit in the United States was based on the alleged violations by the Indian government's legislation of the right of Indian citizens under the Constitution of India to choose their own counsel and, on the contention that if the Indian government also shared the responsibility for the disaster by failing to enforce safety regulations, it could not represent the victims because of a conflict of interest.

The Judicial Panel on Multidistrict Litigation consolidated all the lawsuits brought in the United States in federal district court in the Southern District of New York. A year after the suit was brought, District Judge Keenan dismissed the case on the grounds of forum non conveniens under three conditions: one, that Union Carbide consent to submit to the jurisdiction of the courts of India and continue to waive defenses based on the statute of limitations; two, that Union Carbide agree to satisfy any judgment rendered against it by an Indian court, provided that the minimal requirements of due process are met; and three, that Union Carbide comply with U.S. rules on discovery under the federal rules of civil procedure.

Earlier efforts for a negotiated settlement were unsuccessful when the Indian government rejected a Union Carbide offer of $350 million dollars, which with interest would have accrued to $500-$600 million, and which was accepted by lawyers representing private plaintiffs in litigation. Union Carbide appealed the Judge's ruling contending that the Indian government must also be bound by U.S.-style discovery rules. Attorneys for the individual plaintiffs in the Bhopal case also appealed the ruling by Judge Keenan that sent the proceedings to India. Subsequently, on September 5, 1986, the Indian government sued Union Carbide in the Bhopal district court in India for damages arising out of the gas leak. The Indian government is seeking at least $3 billion from Union Carbide Corp. in claims arising from the disaster. In January 1987, the Second Circuit Court of Appeals [affirmed the judgment of] the Federal District Court [but deleted the second and third conditions]. At the end of November 1987, all ongoing efforts to reach a negotiated settlement between the government of India and Union Carbide had stalled, and the Indian government filed criminal charges to culpable homicide in Bhopal against Union Carbide.

Subsequently, on December 17, 1987, Judge M. W. Deo of the Bhopal District court ordered Union Carbide to pay $270 million in interim relief to the victims of the accident. On review, the State high court ruled that an interim payment of $193 million be paid.

The Bhopal tragedy created a momentum to seek appropriate international, regional and national action to provide proper expert safeguards for hazardous substances and technologies, and effective international assistance in establishing standards and in providing guidance to developing countries.

Note

The Supreme Court of India approved a settlement in the Bhopal case in February, 1989, under which Union Carbide and Union Carbide of India Ltd. agreed to pay $470 million to the Indian Government for the benefit of the victims of the disaster.

3. Basel

■ NATURE AND SCOPE OF THE PROBLEM

Ved Nanda & Bruce Bailey
in Transferring Hazardous Technologies and Substances
supra, *at 16-19*

Ten years after the Seveso accident, a major toxic chemical spill occurred in Europe when efforts to put out a fire at a chemical storage warehouse of Sandoz, a major Swiss chemical multinational, in Basel, on November 1, 1986, resulted in a huge discharge of toxic chemicals into the Rhine. While Swiss authorities initially reported that 30 tons of chemicals, including herbicides, pesticides and poisonous mercury, leaked into the Rhine, some French reports put the figure of the spilled chemicals as high as 1,000 tons. Eventually, Sandoz announced that much of the 1,246 tons of material inside the warehouse, including 824 tons of insecticide, 71 tons of herbicide, 39 tons of fungicide, 4 tons of solvents, and 12 tons of organic compounds containing mercury, was washed into the river by the water used by the firemen in putting out the fire.

The worst accident of this kind since Seveso caused ecological disaster, adversely affecting France, Germany and the Netherlands, in addition to Switzerland. Subsequent reports said that Basel escaped a major environmental disaster "by a whisker," for the city could have suffered toxic fumes if the fire had burned longer. Former West German Chancellor, Willy Brandt, referred to Basel as "Bhopal on the Rhine," and some political parties started calling it "Baselpal," while the French and West German press renamed the city "Chernobasel," or "Chernobale." On the evening of November 1, 2,000 demonstrators marched through the streets of Basel carrying banners which read, "Seveso-Bhopal-Schweizerhalle." Schweizerhalle is the Basel suburb where the Sandoz plant is located. Subsequently, it was revealed that several more incidents of chemical spills in the Rhine immediately preceding and in the few weeks following the Basel spill had occurred, which also involved other Swiss chemical giants such as CIBA-Geigy, though reportedly none was as serious as the Sandoz spill.

The Sandoz spill and those other incidents of chemical spills in the Rhine caused a great deal of concern in Europe. Questions raised included those of adequate notification, safety standards, violation of pollution control laws, and liability and compensation. Calls were made for European community action and for international cooperation to prevent such pollution. The Netherlands representative told a special meeting of environment ministers from the states bordering the Rhine, convened in Zurich November 12, 1986, that, following the accident, it had already spent a quarter of a million dollars on pollution control.

On December 19, 1986, the French Environment Minister presented the Swiss government with a bill for $38 million for damages to French interests arising from the spill. The figure of $38 million was estimated by an independent commission of French experts based upon short-term damages to the fishing and boating industries; medium-term damages, including the cost to restore the ecosystem; and potential damages, including the cost of building dams and other facilities linked to the Rhine, such as a water pumping system, assuming that no significant pollution of the groundwater aquifer had occurred. The Swiss government and the Sandoz and CIBA-Geigy officials showed their willingness to settle claims for damages, although it was not clear who was to assume responsibility for how much of the claimed damages. Subsequently, Sandoz paid damages to French fishermen and to the French government. Among other developments at Sandoz, safety rules related to the storage of toxic and flammable substances in the Sandoz group of companies were strengthened; Sandoz also set up the "Sandoz Rhine Fund" to help repair ecological damage from the November 1986 disaster and announced its donation of $7.3 million to the World Wildlife Fund for a three-year project to restore the flora and fauna of the Rhine River.

Among the multilateral responses to the accident, noteworthy attempts include the establishment of a working group among French, Swiss, and German representatives to update the proper functioning of the information exchange systems and emergency contacts. Also, an agreement was reached on December 19, 1986, regarding the necessary measures to prevent industrial accidents and to limit their consequences, at a ministerial conference on Rhine Pollution, and a proposal was made by the executive director of UNEP, Mostafa K. Tolba, that for the prevention of transboundary toxic pollution, treaties similar to the ones earlier adopted on international notification and mutual assistance in the event of a nuclear accident under the auspices of IAEA, be negotiated.

Tolba said at a press conference of December 15, 1986, that UNEP's existing International Register of Potentially Toxic Chemicals (IRPTC) could act as a framework for administering the two treaties. He said that as there are no existing agreements requiring international notification in the case of an accident involving toxic chemicals, a new convention on the subject is desirable. Commenting on the Sandoz incident, Tolba said that the chemical spill at Basel "shows the ecological and economic folly of assuming that if we ignore safety standards in the chemical industry somehow the problems will go away." He added that "(t)he accident reveals the full extent of the apathy, confusion and general unpreparedness of the world's most advanced nations and the deplorable inadequacy of international legislation." The notification requirement would obligate governments to provide instant information on the chemicals involved and their predicted behaviour, the location of the plant, and the safety measures undertaken. The second convention would call for prompt assistance among states parties after an accident to minimize damage and harm.

Earlier, on November 20, 1986, Tolba had suggested that "a legal package should be drafted to prevent another Bhopal or another Basel." As part of that package, he outlined the need for "instituting a programme for governments, in cooperation with industry, to work with local leaders, identify acutely toxic chemicals, help prepare control measures to limit accidental releases and deal with such accidents."

Note and Question

Lessons from the Sandoz Incident. In *The Sandoz Spill: The Failure of International Law to Protect the Rhine from Pollution*, 16 Ecology L.Q. 443, 480 (1989), Aaron Schwabach concludes as follows: "If there is anything to be gained from the Sandoz disaster, it is a realization that the existing treaty regime is inadequate to protect the Rhine from chemical pollution, and that new measures are urgently needed if the river's ecology is to be saved from complete destruction." Recalling that the Rhine basin lies in one of the most highly integrated and developed regions in the world, what lessons would you draw from this experience for developing countries sharing an international watercourse?

B. GENERAL NORMS APPLICABLE TO ENVIRONMENTAL EMERGENCIES

1. *Overview*

■ ENVIRONMENTAL DISASTERS IN INTERNATIONAL LAW

Edith Brown Weiss
in **Anuario Juridico Interamericano 1986** ***141 (1988)***

INTRODUCTION

With the rapid industrialization of countries there are more accidents causing environmental disasters which affect many people and often many countries. Sandoz, Chernobyl, Bhopal, Seveso and Amoco-Cadiz are only the most recent and vivid examples.[4] Some of these accidents occur in factories producing toxic chemicals, others in nuclear reactors. Some involve marine pollution, while others affect shared natural resources such as lakes and airsheds. Still other natural disasters destroy natural or cultural resources of importance to the world, such as the massive forest fire in Borneo a few years ago.[5]

This article is concerned with the status of international law regarding environmental disasters. It covers man-induced environmental disasters having significant transboundary effects, natural disasters affecting shared natural resources, and disasters which affect important natural and cultural resources impressed with elements of common patrimony. The last includes world natural and cultural heritages, international gene banks, and similar resources.[6] While international law regarding environmental accidents has traditionally focused on those causing significant transboundary damage, it is now timely to extend it to those disasters which threaten natural and cultural resources regarded by the international community as having elements of common patrimony.

There are three primary aspects to the management of environmental

4. . . . On March 16, 1978, the oil tanker Amoco-Cadiz ran aground and broke up, spilling 220,000 tons of crude oil which reached 245 miles of coastline in Brittany, France. See: Current Reports, 6 *Int'l. Env't Rep.* (BNA) 471 (1983).

5. The Borneo fire of early 1984 lasted several months and destroyed over 13,000 square miles of plant and animal life. Such destruction affects timber resources, soil quality, and reservoir and canal siltation levels. See: "Wound in the World," *Asiaweek* 34 (July 13, 1984); "Devastated Forest Offers a Rare View of Rebirth," *New York Times*, April 24, 1984, p. 61.

6. See Convention for the Protection of the World Cultural and Natural Heritage, Nov. 16, 1972, 27 UST 37, T.I.A.S. Nol 8226, 11 *I.L.M.* 1358 (1972), by which parties designate certain sites as World Cultural Heritages. Parties are obliged to set up services to protect natural and cultural heritages (Art. 5), to assist one another in these measures if so requested, and to avoid actions which may injure these heritages either directly or indirectly (Art. 6).

disasters: preventing the disaster, minimizing the damage, and compensating for damage. The duty to compensate for damage represents the traditional approach. It is also the least effective in protecting the environment against disasters. The duty to minimize damage and provide emergency assistance, which is potentially more effective, appears in an increasing number of international agreements, and has emerged as a principle of customary international law. The duty to prevent accidents has been somewhat overlooked in international law, although international agreements increasingly include it in general terms.

I. PREVENTING ENVIRONMENTAL DISASTERS

The duty to prevent environmental disasters obligates States to enact safety measures and procedures to minimize the likelihood of major environmental accidents, such as nuclear reactor accidents, toxic chemical spills, oil spills or forest fires.

Its premise is the factual awareness that it is far more effective protection for the human environment to prevent accidents than to try to compensate for the injuries caused. This is particularly true for the protection of future generations and for protection against long-term damage to the environment, which may be irreversible or reversible only at staggering costs.

The recent accidents at Chernobyl and at Sandoz illustrate this. While the immediate effects of the accident at Chernobyl on people in the vicinity of the accident were identified, the damage to crops, vegetation, and animal life in the European countries was less clear. Several countries initiated costly measures banning the sale of domestic products, such as milk, artichokes, and other produce, and banning certain food imports in the belief that these items were contaminated by radiation. Long-term damage to people, particularly children, from exposure to radiation and long-term damage to the soils and ecological systems remains unclear and will never be fully compensated.[7]

Similarly in the Sandoz chemical spill on the Rhine, it is impossible to compensate fully for the short- and long-term damage to the fish and ecosystem of the river and for the as yet unclear health effects from exposure to contaminated water supplies. Moreover, the massive forest fires in Borneo in 1984 caused large-scale destruction of tropical forests rich in biological

7. The long-term radioactive contamination of flora and soils comes from caesium-137 and caesium-134, with half-lives of 30 and 2 years, respectively. Mathematical models which predicted that rain would wash radioactive particles into the soil have proven inaccurate, as vegetation remains contaminated in some areas. Even after radionuclides are washed off, grasses and other vegetation can take up the radioactivity from the soil. This is especially true in areas where the soil is low in clays and micas, soil types which bind caesium effectively. HOWARD and LIVENS, "May Sheep Safely Graze?", *New Scientist* 46 (April 23, 1987). For the uncertainty in health and environmental effects, see: 43 *Bull. Atomic Scientists* 10 (1986). The issue contains several relevant articles.

diversity, a treasure for both present and future generations. The loss of species by the fire can never be compensated.[8]

Even if it were possible to compensate for all the damages caused by environmental disasters, which it is not, the costs of doing so would far outweigh the costs of prevention. Thus, imposing a duty upon States to prevent environmental accidents is far more efficient than relying on compensatory measures after the accident occurs. It ensures that those who can prevent the damage, at least cost, are required to do so. Moreover, it is equitable, because those who benefit from the activity assume the costs of it, rather than shifting them to another community, such as future generations.

The duty to prevent environmental disasters is part of the principle of State responsibility, as reflected in Principle 21 of the Stockholm Declaration of the Human Environment. It is confirmed in other texts. The U.S. Restatement of Foreign Relations Law, for example, provides in Sec. 601 that "A state is obligated to take such measures as may be necessary, to the extent practicable under the circumstances, to ensure that activities within its jurisdiction or control (a) conform to generally accepted international rules and standards for the *prevention,* reduction and control of injury to the environment of another state or of areas beyond the limits of national jurisdiction." (Emphasis added.) If a State breaches the obligation, it is responsible for injury to the environment of another State resulting from the violation.

The duty to prevent environmental disasters posits that there are standards and procedures which States can follow to reduce the likelihood and magnitude of accidents. The specific content of these measures must, of course, be negotiated by the States themselves. Several essential elements can be identified. These include: 1) adoption of safety standards for the location and operation of industrial and nuclear plants and vehicles; 2) maintenance of equipment and facilities to ensure ongoing compliance with safety measures; 3) monitoring of facilities, vehicles, or conditions to detect dangers; and 4) training of workers and monitoring of their performance to ensure compliance with safety standards.

These safety measures will have different specific applications depending upon whether the protection is for an industrial source, a nuclear source, an important natural resources reserve, or a cultural heritage.

To date, the duty to prevent environmental disasters is found in relatively few international documents and agreements. One of the pioneering efforts to develop this duty is a 1983 resolution of the European Council

8. Early observations after the fire showed that small plants, vines, and soft wood trees were growing quickly, while the large hardwood trees were not regenerating. Many bird and animal species are no longer found because the fire destroyed nut and fruit bearing trees upon which they depend. See: *Asiaweek* 34 (July 13, 1984) supra note 5; *New York Times* (April 24, 1984) p. 4, supra note 5.

on Environmental Law, "Principles Concerning International Cooperation in Environmental Emergencies Linked to Technological Development." This resolution expressly calls for limits on siting of all hazardous installations, for the adoption of safety standards to reduce the risk of emergencies, and for monitoring and emergency planning.

The duty has been implemented primarily in those conventions governing transport of oil and hazardous substances by sea and by rail and inland waterways, in the 1982 Directive of the European Economic Community on Major Accident Hazards of Certain Industrial Activities, and in several agreements governing shared natural resources between Canada and the United States. Increasingly, the general duty is included in agreements governing emergency assistance for other potential environmental disasters. In 1975, the IAEA adopted nuclear safety standards to minimize the differences in safety standards between countries, but these were not binding. The IAEA is now working to establish more stringent, binding safety standards.[9]

As the World Commission on Environment and Development has asserted in its Report, it is now time to make safety measures mandatory. The Report recommends that international agreement be reached on codes of practice for nuclear reactor operations, including minimum safety standards, agreed site selection criteria, as well as "consultation and notification prior to the siting of all major civil nuclear related installations," and standards for operator training and international licensing. For industrial operations the Commission recommended countries "strengthen national capabilities and the framework for bilateral and regional cooperation" by enforcing regulations or guidelines for the safe operation of industrial plants, locating plants away from population centers, and training workers adequately in safe operational procedures and emergency preparedness. If a State has a hazardous facility located on its territory in which an accident could affect one or more neighboring States, it should provide information to the potentially affected States about the plant and establish mutually agreed criteria for the location of hazardous new plants. The recommendations are important for they recognize that certain decisions about hazardous facilities which are within the sovereign domain of States should nevertheless be subject to certain international duties, if an accident at them would have transnational effects.

Since many of the relevant hazardous industrial plants are privately operated, the question arises whether the State is or should be responsible for the actions of private actors within its jurisdiction or control. As discussed

9. [The Convention on Nuclear Safety was adopted on June 17, 1994 by a diplomatic conference convened by the International Atomic Energy Agency. IAEA Doc. INFCIRC/449, July 5, 1994, Annex; 33 I.L.M. 1514 (1994). For the historial background of the Convention *see* IAEA Doc. GOV/INF/723, paras. 5-21, and Paul C. Szasz, Introductory Note, 33 I.L.M. 1514 (1994). —EDS.]

above, the duty to prevent environmental disasters is appropriately viewed as a principle of State responsibility. Sec. 207 of the Restatement of Foreign Relations Law of the United States provides that "A state is responsible for any violation of its obligations under international law resulting from action or inaction by the government of the State . . . or any organ . . . or other agent." While a State is not ordinarily responsible for acts of individuals, it is responsible for its own failure to control or regulate.

To protect against environmental disasters, it is important for States to agree to a suite of safety measures which the State has responsibility for ensuring that private parties within its jurisdiction or control implement. This is the approach adopted in the 1982 EEC Directive, on industrial accident hazards, commonly known as the Seveso Directive. Article 3 provides that States "shall adopt the provisions necessary to ensure that, in the case of industrial activities specified in Article 1, the manufacturer is obliged to take all the measures necessary to prevent major accidents and to limit their consequences for man and the environment." The Directive appropriately focuses on requiring States to enact procedures to ensure that their private operators implement the safety measures necessary to prevent environmental disasters.

II. MINIMIZING DAMAGE AND PROVIDING EMERGENCY ASSISTANCE

The duty to minimize damage and to provide emergency assistance applies both to the State in which the accident occurs and to those States that are in a position to help alleviate the damage. Many bilateral and multilateral agreements contain these obligations. Certain obligations of States in responding to major environmental disasters exist as customary international law.

A State in which a major environmental disaster occurs has the duty to minimize the damage to the human environment. At a minimum this requires that a State promptly notify countries that may be affected, provide available information about the course of the accident, and inform affected States of measures it is taking to reduce the damage. States must also take necessary and practicable steps to prevent or reduce injury to other States from the accident. They must to do so for both natural and man-induced disasters, although the State may bear no responsibility for injury caused by the natural disaster. Those States potentially affected by an environmental disaster have an obligation to cooperate in minimizing the damage. The failure to do so on their own territory may be a defense available to the State in which the accident occurred, if claims for reparation are made against it. With respect to marine pollution disasters, States are obligated to develop contingency plans for responding to such incidents in their area. States have been extending this obligation to other kinds of environmental disasters.

The duty to minimize damage from environmental disasters derives from the principle of State responsibility. Principle 21 of the Stockholm Declaration . . . reflects customary international law. Support for it is contained in the resolution of earlier disputes, such as the Trail Smelter Arbitration, and in the multitude of international agreements which implement it. The U.S. Restatement on Foreign Relations Law confirms this obligation of States to "reduce and control" injury to the environment of other States and areas beyond national jurisdiction.

There are four aspects to the duty to minimize damage: the duty to notify promptly; the duty to provide information to potentially affected States; the duty to develop contingency plans; and the duty to cooperate in minimizing damage, as by providing emergency assistance.

1. The Obligation to Notify

As early as 1949, the International Court of Justice in the Corfu Channel case affirmed the obligation of a State to warn other countries exposed to dangers in its territory which could cause serious injury or death. The Court cited a State's duty not to permit knowingly the use of its territory in such a way as to violate the rights of others and "elementary considerations of humanity" as bases for this duty. The same considerations underlie the extension of the duty to notify other States of major environmental disasters which may affect them.

The duty to notify appears in many treaties concerned with environmental disasters and in Sec. 601 of the Restatement of Foreign Relations Law on the Law of Environment, Article 9 of the Montreal Rules of the International Law Association, and Article 19 of the Legal Principles proposed in the report of the World Commissions on Environment and Development.

Treaties concerned with international waterways, marine pollution, nuclear accidents, forest fires, and other environmental catastrophes embody this duty. The provisions normally call for immediate notification when the State becomes aware that an emergency exists which could affect other countries or territories. Those regional marine pollution agreements which establish a regional organization call for giving notice to that body as well as to the potentially affected States. Several agreements for forest fires and nuclear emergencies call for parties to designate national authorities to receive the notification. The duty to notify promptly and in good faith is firmly established in international law.

2. The Obligation to Provide Information

There is also an obligation in international law to provide timely and relevant information to the potentially affected States. This has several aspects. The first is the need to provide relevant information about the accident to enable States to take their own measures to minimize the damage; the second is to inform States of measures that the host State is taking to prevent or reduce damage. Both aspects of this obligation appear in the Montreal Rules of the ILA and in the Legal Principles proposed by the World Commission on Environment and Development. Many of the international agreements which provide for notification specifically refer to one or both aspects. The 1986 IAEA Convention on Nuclear Disasters provides in Article 5 a detailed list of information to be provided, if available, which includes information relevant to forecasting the scope and effects of the accident and the off-site protective measures planned. It is important for States in which an environmental disaster occurs to provide both kinds of information to enable a potentially affected State to take appropriate preventive or mitigating measures. If notice is to be effective, it must include relevant and appropriate information.

3. The Obligation to Develop Contingency Plans

There is arguably a duty in customary international law to develop contingency plans for responding to marine pollution disasters in nearby areas, which may soon extend to other kinds of disasters. The multilateral agreements addressing marine pollution emergencies contain such provisions. The Law of the Sea Convention in Article 199 requires States to develop such plans. The U.S. Restatement of Foreign Relations Law on the Law of the Environment in Sec. 605.(2) on marine pollution sets forth a State's responsibility to develop contingency plans to the extent necessary and practicable. The comments note that "neighboring states are obligated to develop and be ready to put into operation contingency plans for responding to pollution incidents affecting the marine environment in their vicinity."

The obligation to develop contingency plans is also found in certain bilateral and multilateral agreements concerned with forest fires, nuclear accidents, and other environmental catastrophes. The 1986 Convention for the Protection of the Natural Resources and Environment of the South Pacific Region provides in Article 15 that the "Parties shall develop and promote individual contingency plans and joint contingency plans for responding to incidents . . ." Certainly the development of contingency plans is essential for effective responses to environmental disasters and should be part of customary international law applicable to major environmental disasters, particularly those that may be ultrahazardous. It is, however, doubtful that international law as yet requires States in the absence of an international agreement to develop such national contingency plans for disasters other than marine pollution.

4. The Obligation to Cooperate in Minimizing Damage

As part of the duty to minimize damage from environmental disasters, there is an emerging duty in international law which requires States to cooperate with each other in combating environmental disasters and preventing damage. This duty is reflected in the increasingly large number of bilateral and multilateral agreements which provide for emergency assistance and for mutual cooperation in mitigating damage. The details of this obligation are, however, by no means clear. For example, do all States have a duty to provide emergency assistance if requested? Must they be potentially affected by the disaster or is it sufficient that they have the capability to render assistance? What kinds of assistance must be provided? Who is responsible for paying the cost of the emergency assistance? The existing agreements address these issues in different ways.

There are an increasing number of global, regional and bilateral agreements which set forth the duty to provide emergency assistance. . . . The earliest international agreements were negotiated to facilitate assistance in the event of oil pollution spills or nuclear accidents: the Nordic Mutual Emergency Assistance Agreement in Connection with Radiation Accidents (1963), the International Convention Relating to Intervention on the High Seas in Case of Oil Pollution Casualties (1969) and the Agreement for Cooperation in Dealing with Pollution of the North Sea by Oil (1969, revised 1983). More recently, under the auspices of the IAEA, States have concluded two international agreements governing nuclear accidents, one of which addresses emergency assistance. The Director of the United Nations Environment Programme, M. Tolba, has proposed that two similar conventions be negotiated for transboundary toxic pollution. Many regional agreements provide for emergency assistance in case of marine pollution.

There are also many bilateral agreements that provide for emergency assistance to extinguish forest fires, to combat threats to international rivers such as from pollution or floods, and to contain other environmental disasters. These include agreements between France and the Federal Republic of Germany (1977), between Germany and Luxembourg (1978), between Czechoslovakia and the German Democratic Republic (1956), between France and Spain (1959), between Chile and Argentina (1961) and between Switzerland and France (for water pollution accidents) (1977). A 1986 bilateral agreement between Argentina and Brazil provides for mutual assistance in the event of nuclear accidents. In addition, there are numerous agreements in North America between Canada and the United States, between Mexico and the United States, and between States within the United States and provinces in Canada, which provide for emergency assistance for environmental catastrophes such as forest fires and accidents contaminating waters. . . .

The actions required by these agreements vary from notification and exchange of information to the development of joint contingency plans and a regional center to coordinate mutual assistance efforts. The regional seas conventions are at the forefront of using multilateral bodies to coordinate emergency assistance for environmental disasters. Some of the bilateral agreements, particularly for fire, include provisions for monitoring that accident. Almost all of the agreements provide for easing the national barriers, such as custom controls, for parties providing assistance. Indeed the easing of these barriers is a primary rationale for the agreements. Relatively few of the agreements address the difficult issue of who must bear the costs of the emergency assistance.

One of the most difficult issues in providing emergency assistance is that of assigning responsibility for the costs of the assistance. There are three basic approaches for bearing the costs: the party receiving the assistance, the party giving the assistance, or both on the basis of some mutually agreed principles for sharing the costs of accidents. The OECD has adopted the last approach to sharing the cost of oil spills. This approach may be appropriate for large-scale operations, which could affect many countries. If the party providing the assistance were to bear the full costs of doing so, there would be little incentive to provide adequate assistance. The political gains that come from providing assistance can be satisfied by only minimal assistance. On the other hand, if the party receiving the assistance must bear the full cost of compensating those who provide it, they may be unable to pay for it. If the affected government were to be responsible for the costs of assistance, this should be coupled with an obligation on other parties to provide full-scale assistance upon request.

The most effective method of allocating the costs of assistance is likely to be agreement in advance upon procedures for sharing the costs, which should be incorporated into the arrangements for providing emergency assistance. The Nordic Convention on Nuclear Disasters requires each party to pay all expenses incurred within its territory, with the assisting State having the right to reimbursement for such expenses (salaries, equipment costs, transport, etc.) from the State assisted unless otherwise agreed. The 1986 IAEA Convention offers parties a choice: to offer assistance without payment for costs or to provide it on a wholly or partly reimbursable basis. Several of the agreements regarding forest fires and other disasters between Canada and the United States and between Mexico and the United States include provisions for allocating costs as do the European bilateral agreements concerning environmental catastrophes.

If States are to be willing to offer effective emergency assistance promptly, it will generally be important to develop in advance agreed principles for the sharing of the costs. Whether this takes the form of agreement to invoke certain model guidelines offered by the international community or of [a] mutually agreed formula must be left to the States concerned. While the issue is controversial, the failure to address it may impair effective emergency assistance.

III. COMPENSATING FOR INJURIES FROM ENVIRONMENTAL DISASTERS

When accidents occur and damage results, someone must bear the costs. International law is not entirely clear on who must bear the costs under which circumstances. There appears to be a consensus that under international law breaches of obligations of State responsibility to prevent accidents and minimize damage incur responsibility for resulting injuries and that even if no breaches occur, States may be liable for injuries resulting from ultrahazardous activities or the release of highly dangerous substances. Whether they may be liable under international law for injuries resulting from other kinds of accidents is not settled.

If the State has certain duties under the principle of State responsibility to prevent accidents and to reduce or minimize damage, violation of these obligations incurs the responsibility of the State for the resulting injuries. Sec. 602 of the U.S. Restatement on Foreign Relations Law on the Law of the Environment provides, for example, that "A State is responsible for any significant injury, resulting from a violation of obligations under subsection (1) (on preventing harm to the environment and minimizing damage), to the environment of another state or to its property, or to persons or property within that state's territory or under its jurisdiction or control." Principle 21 of the legal principles proposed by the World Commission on Environment and Development similarly provides that a State is responsible under international law for a breach of an obligation regarding the environment and must "provide compensation for the harm caused." State responsibility for harm is incurred when a State fails to comply with binding rules of international law.

Even if a State complies with its obligations under the principle of State responsibility, it may nevertheless be liable for injuries resulting from environmental disasters if the activity was ultrahazardous or involved the release of highly dangerous substances, such as radiation and toxic chemicals. In these cases, States are liable for the injury under the principle of strict liability. Some commentators have contended that strict liability should apply whenever States cause environmental harm to other States or areas outside their jurisdiction and control. States would then be liable for serious environmental injury from accidents, whether or not they had complied with their obligations under the principle of State responsibility.

The International Law Commission has created a separate body to address questions of liability for environmental injuries resulting from activities that are lawful in international law. The draft principles encourage States to establish their own liability regime, and if they do not to balance a number of factors in determining liability. There is no agreement yet within the Commission on the principles.

The conceptual question of whether a State can be liable for damage if it has complied with generally accepted standards and procedures for preventing injury has been addressed in the context of national environmental legislation, which may offer useful insights for international law. Under the U.S. Clean Air Act and the U.S. Clean Water Act, compliance with the permits and standards set forth in the Acts and associated regulations precludes liability for damage under federal common law doctrines. It does not foreclose remedies that may be available under the common law as developed within each State. This provides an incentive to comply with federal regulations but recognizes the rights of States to maintain their own standards and remedies for environmental damage. In international law, this would mean that compliance with internationally accepted safety standards and procedures could preclude liability for damage in international law (except for abnormally dangerous activities or toxic releases), but it would not foreclose the application of a country's remedies under domestic law.

Even when there is no liability in international law for injuries caused by certain environmental disasters, parties may be liable under the domestic laws of States. Such issues have traditionally been addressed by national courts, as in the litigation following the Amoco Cadiz oil spill off the coast of France, where French parties sued in United States courts invoking, in part, U.S. marine tort law. States can also enact domestic legislation to compensate their own nationals for damage received from accidents elsewhere. Several countries in Europe have passed legislation compensating environmental injury caused by the Chernobyl nuclear accident. Their reticence in seeking compensation from the Soviet Union may reveal in part a reluctance to implement strict liability for injuries from environmental disasters which could be applied to them in case of accidents on their soil.

Conclusions

International law regarding environmental disasters has developed significantly in the last two decades. Today there are many agreements addressing this question, which cover not only marine pollution disasters but nuclear disasters, forest fires, international water pollution accidents, and other environmental catastrophes. The duty to minimize environmental injury by giving prompt notification, providing information, and cooperating in minimizing injury is now part of customary international law and is encompassed within the principle of State responsibility. Attention must now be given to the duty to prevent environmental disasters, which also comes within the principle of State responsibility and constitutes customary international law. However, efforts to define acceptable safety standards and practices have been lagging in many important areas. It is time for States to turn their attention to this aspect of international law relating to environmental disasters. Prevention of accidents is the most effective way to protect our natural and cultural resources for present and future generations.

2. *Principle 18, Rio Declaration*

■ PRINCIPLE 18, RIO DECLARATION ON ENVIRONMENT AND DEVELOPMENT

adopted at Rio de Janeiro by the United Nations Conference on Environment and Development, June 14, 1992, U.N. Doc. A/ CONF.151/5/Rev.1, June 13, 1992,* reprinted in *31 I.L.M. 874 (1992)

PRINCIPLE 18

States shall immediately notify other States of any natural disasters or other emergencies that are likely to produce sudden harmful effects on the environment of those States. Every effort shall be made by the international community to help States so afflicted.

Notes and Questions

1. *Problem.* Suppose the headwaters of the River Blue are located in a remote, mountainous region of country A. Suppose further that this region experienced unusually heavy rainfall one week and that in the past rainfall of this nature had caused flooding in downstream country B (but not in country A). Does Principle 18 indicate that country A should notify country B? Of what?

2. *Is Principle 18 binding?* What is the authoritative value of Principle 18? Is it binding on states? If not, how could it be used by a state that has been the victim of an environmental disaster?

3. *Principle 18 and the Nuclear Accident Conventions.* You should compare Principle 18 with the more specific obligations contained in the two conventions adopted under the auspices of the International Atomic Energy Agency (IAEA) following the Chernobyl accident, considered below.

3. *Article 9, Montreal Rules*

■ INTERNATIONAL LAW ASSOCIATION, RULES OF INTERNATIONAL LAW APPLICABLE TO TRANSFRONTIER POLLUTION, ARTICLE 9, EMERGENCY SITUATIONS

ILA,* Report of the Sixtieth Conference Held at Montreal, Aug. 29, 1982, to Sept. 4, 1982 *176 (1983)

Article 9
Emergency Situations

When as a result of an emergency situation or of other circumstances activities already carried out in the territory of a State cause or might cause a sudden increase in the existing level of transfrontier pollution the State of origin is under a duty:

(a) to promptly warn the affected or potentially affected States;

(b) to provide them with such pertinent information as will enable them to minimize the transfrontier pollution damage;

(c) to inform them of the steps taken to abate the cause of the increased transfrontier pollution level.

Comment

1. Notice to potentially affected States is to be furnished not only when the risk of transfrontier pollution results from planned activities, but also whenever as a consequence of an emergency situation, activities already carried out are likely to cause an increase in the existing level of transfrontier pollution. In this case the duty to warn the neighbouring States arises from a concrete situation, as for example from the uncontrolled emission of chlorine gases from a chemical plant. Therefore it is out of the question for the polluting State to argue that the operation of the said plant does not represent a danger of transfrontier pollution, as it usually happens when States are requested to furnish prior information. On the other hand, it seems obvious that States will not be as reluctant to warn potentially affected neighbours of emergency situations as they are in giving them in advance notice of projects likely to cause transfrontier pollution. In fact, in this latter case they always risk to get massive opposition from the public authorities and from individuals in the potentially affected country, which often leads to a standstill of the project and to the imposition of additional and costly safety measures.

2. A duty to warn potentially affected States in cases of emergency has been laid down in several international conventions which, however, mostly relate to the utilization of international rivers, as the Draft European Convention for the protection of international watercourses against pollution, the Agreement between the United States and Canada concerning the Great Lakes water quality of 1972 and the Agreement between the Federal Republic of Germany and the German Democratic Republic on principles concerning damage control at the border of 1973. Such a duty is also foreseen in some conventions for the protection of the marine environment, for example in the Helsinki Convention of 1974 and in the Barcelona Convention of 1976.

3. Significantly, Principle 9 of the UNEP's draft rules on shared natural resources (UNEP/1b. 12/2) also formulates the duty to warn in the mandatory language "States have a duty urgently to inform" and does not use the expression "it is necessary for States" adopted for the duty of prior information. On the contrary, the O.E.C.D. prefers only to recommend the warning of potentially affected States in Title F of its Recommendation C (74) 224.

4. In addition to the duty to warn, the States on whose territory the emergency situation arises have the duty to provide potentially polluted States such

pertinent information on the matter as will enable them to take appropriate steps in order to eliminate, reduce or combat the effects of such a situation. This implies the furnishing of details about the activity at the origin of the increased transfrontier pollution danger, the circumstances which lead to the creation of the emergency and the measures already taken by the polluting State to abate the transfrontier pollution.

Note

Emergencies on international watercourses. Compare the approach taken by the ILA to the problem of transfrontier harm caused by emergencies in general to that of the 1977 United Nations Convention on the Law of the Non-Navigational Uses of International Watercourses, U.N. Doc. A/RES/51/229:

Article 28
Emergency Situations

1. For the purposes of this article, "emergency" means a situation that causes, or poses an imminent threat of causing, serious harm to watercourse States or other States and that results suddenly from natural causes, such as floods, the breaking up of ice, landslides or earthquakes, or from human conduct, such as industrial accidents.

2. A watercourse State shall, without delay and by the most expeditious means available, notify other potentially affected States and competent international organizations of any emergency originating within its territory.

3. A watercourse State within whose territory an emergency originates shall, in cooperation with potentially affected States and, where appropriate, competent international organizations, immediately take all practicable measures necessitated by the circumstances to prevent, mitigate and eliminate harmful effects of the emergency.

4. When necessary, watercourse States shall jointly develop contingency plans for responding to emergencies, in cooperation, where appropriate, with other potentially affected States and competent international organizations.

4. *Article 19, Brundtland Commission Experts Group Report*

■ FINAL REPORT OF THE EXPERTS GROUP ON ENVIRONMENTAL LAW ON LEGAL PRINCIPLES FOR ENVIRONMENTAL PROTECTION AND SUSTAINABLE DEVELOPMENT, ARTICLE 19, EMERGENCY SITUATIONS (1987)

Article 19
Emergency Situations

1. In the case of an emergency situation or other change of circumstances suddenly giving rise to a transboundary interference or a significant risk

thereof with the reasonable and equitable use of a transboundary natural resource or to a transboundary environmental interference or a significant risk thereof, causing substantial harm in an area under national jurisdiction of another State or in an area beyond the limits of national jurisdiction, the State in whose area under national jurisdiction or under whose jurisdiction the interference originates shall promptly warn the other States concerned, provide them with such pertinent information as will enable them to minimize the transboundary environmental interference, inform them of steps taken to abate the cause of the transboundary environmental interference, and cooperate with those States in order to prevent or minimize the harmful effects of such an emergency situation or other change of circumstances.

2. States shall develop contingency plans in order to prevent or minimize the harmful effects of an emergency situation or other change of circumstances referred to in Paragraph 1.

Notes

1. *Other instruments. See also* the United Nations Convention on the Transboundary Effects of Industrial Accidents, Helsinki, March 17, 1992, *reprinted in* 31 I.L.M. 1330 (1992), and the document discussed in the following note.

2. *The OECD weighs in.* An international effort to assign responsibility for the costs of accident prevention and mitigation is the Recommendation of the Council of the Organization for Economic Co-Operation and Development (OECD) on the Application of the Polluter-Pays Principle to Accidental Pollution, OECD Doc. C(89)88(Final), July 25, 1989, *reprinted in* 28 I.L.M. 1320 (1989). The recommendation contains a set of "Guiding Principles Relating to Accidental Pollution." According to their terms, the principles "concern some aspects of the application of the Polluter-Pays Principle to hazardous installations." (Para. 1.) They provide, inter alia, that: "the operator of a hazardous installation should bear the cost of reasonable measures to prevent and control accidental pollution from that installation which are introduced by public authorities in Member countries . . . prior to the occurrence of an accident in order to protect human health or the environment" (Para. 4); and that "(d)omestic law which provides that the cost of reasonable measures to control accidental pollution after an accident should be collected as expeditiously as possible from the legal or natural person who is at the origin of the accident, is consistent with the Polluter-Pays Principle." (Para. 5.) The principles state that while the cost of the measures referred to "is as a general rule met by the general budget, public authorities may with a view to achieving a more economically efficient resource allocation, introduce specific fees or taxes payable by certain installations on account of their hazardous nature (e.g., licensing fees), the proceeds of which to be allocated to accidental pollution prevention and control." (Para. 9.) This would not affect the recovery by public

authorities of the cost of reasonable measures to control or otherwise respond to accidental pollution. (Para. 16.)

C. CONTINGENCY PLANNING AND HAZARD MANAGEMENT

■ INTERNATIONALIZATION OF HAZARD MANAGEMENT IN RECIPIENT COUNTRIES: ACCIDENT PREPAREDNESS AND RESPONSE

Günther Handl
in Transferring Hazardous Technologies and Substances: The International Legal Challenge 106, 106-107, 111-117 (G. Handl & R. Lutz eds. 1989)

INTRODUCTION

Recent large-scale industrial accidents have sharply increased latent public unease about hazardous technology and substances and prompted concerted efforts by governments, industry, and international organizations to improve hazard management worldwide. While global industrial accident experience demonstrates that hazard management has been seriously deficient in both developed and developing countries, shortcomings appear greatly accentuated when hazardous technology and substances are non-indigenous or transferred, and particularly so when the recipient nation falls into the developing country category.

The reasons for this are well known. Transboundary transfers of hazardous technology or substances often imply inter-cultural transfers of alien values and concepts. The technological, scientific, and organizational demands of any given hazardous transfer can severely tax, if not overwhelm, local hazard management abilities. For example, a recent authoritative survey of radiation protection capabilities concludes that

> many developing countries simply lack the necessary infrastructure to implement a radiation protection policy based on international standards. . . . They lack the basic legislation and supporting regulations, as well as effective national authorities, qualified manpower, and necessary equipment.

Against the yardstick of management practices in industrialized countries, much of industrial hazard management in the Third World might have to be described in similarly negative terms.

. . .

Local "Risk Communication"

For present purposes local "risk communication" might be termed the routine, i.e., non-emergency, flow of information about risks of hazardous installations or processes, either from industry to government, from government to public, or from industry to the public. As an element of public policy for both minimizing the consequences of accidents and preventing them in the first place, its importance can hardly be exaggerated.

Many of the major industrial accidents of the last few years provide dramatic illustrations of the negative consequences of risk communication failures. Apart from possibly considerable political penalties, such as loss of public trust in risk management processes and institutions, failure to communicate information about risk is likely to translate into greater environmental, public health, and thus economic costs. For example, during the Flixborough[10] and Seveso accidents, counter-measures to reduce the severity of local impacts were severely hampered by the fact that local authorities, quite apart from the public, had been kept in the dark about the nature and quantity of chemicals utilized in the struck facilities. Similarly, at Bhopal, the apparent lack of public knowledge about the general hazard characteristics of methyl isocyanate—a fact that, amongst other things, points to failure by the plant operator properly to communicate risk information—may have been a major factor in the virtual absence of off-site emergency preparations for a disaster of the kind experienced. . . .

First steps towards international regulation of local dissemination of hazard information were taken in Europe. In the aftermath of the accident in Seveso, in 1982 the EC Council adopted a directive on major-accident hazards, the so-called "Seveso-Directive." To tighten risk communication obligations and, in particular, to counter a trend in national implementing legislation that would have rendered risk communication less than effective, the Directive was substantially amended in 1988. It now calls for communication of very detailed risk information—on an "active basis"—to any person liable to be affected by a major accident. If a most recent Proposal for an EC Council Directive on the freedom of access to information on the environment should be approved, the result could be a highly effective hazard management system within the European Communities.

In the summer of 1988, the OECD Council adopted a Decision-Recommendation on the subject matter of local risk-communication. As a result, member states are now under an obligation to ensure that specific risk information relating to hazardous installations be provided to the public as well as information on appropriate behaviour to reduce risk in the event of accidents. In terms of its normative quality, the OECD measure does not, however, match the revised Seveso-Directive. While EC countries are

10. In 1974, an explosion at a chemical plant in Flixborough, England, killed 29 and wounded dozens of people. *See 29 Workers Dead, More than 40 Injured and Huge Area of Surrounding Land Devastated, The Times,* June 3, 1974, 1, col. 1.

legally obliged actively to communicate detailed hazard information, active communication of comparable information is merely recommended under the OECD document.

So far, the application of formally binding international prescriptions on local risk communication has been limited to mostly Western industrialized nations. Indeed, the 1985 World Bank Guidelines for Identifying, Analyzing, and Controlling Major Hazard Installations in Developing Countries steer clear of the issue, even though the Guidelines were directly inspired by the Seveso Directive which specifically focused on local risk communication. However, recently, risk communication has begun occupying a central place in international efforts to enhance accident preparedness and response planning worldwide, and especially in developing countries.

In 1986, the United Nations Environment Programme (UNEP) started work on practical measures to help governments, particularly in developing countries, to minimize the risk of hazardous industrial accidents, especially accident consequences. To date, the result has been a formal document detailing specific elements of a process for responding to technological accidents at local level, called "APELL" (Awareness and Preparedness for Emergencies at Local Level). A key objective of APELL is to increase local awareness of industrial hazards by encouraging communication of risk information to local community members and involving them in all aspects of emergency response planning. APELL provisions on risk communication are couched in terms of mere recommendations and do not convey any particular order of priority as to the steps to be taken. There is no mistaking, however, of the importance ascribed to the basic information process, the necessity to assure a two-way flow of communication. Since its formal introduction several developing countries with widely differing political systems have indicated their willingness to apply APELL.

APELL in turn is closely modelled on an industry-wide campaign that was launched by the United States Chemical Manufacturers Association (CMA) after the Bhopal tragedy and a chemical leak at a similar plant at Institute, West Virginia, the Community Awareness and Emergency [Response] (CAER) Program. Indeed, CMA and its European counterpart, the Conseil Européen des Fédérations de l' Industrie Chimique (CEFIC), have worked hand-in-glove with UNEP in adapting CAER for worldwide use. Clearly, the chemical industry has on its own accepted local risk communication as a globally applicable policy objective, one that industry should support in developing countries as well as in Western industrialized societies.

Against this background of international/transnational initiatives and growing domestic pressure for better risk information for local communities, it would seem that the concept of risk communication is rapidly gaining in status as a standard against which the adequacy of local hazard management might be reviewed internationally.

Transboundary "Risk Communication"

Effects of accidents at hazardous installations may not respect international boundary lines. Hazard management in recipient countries therefore must extend to exchanges of pertinent information with neighbouring countries on any significant transboundary risks associated with the use of hazardous technology or substances. On the international level, such exchanges serve accident prevention and mitigation functions similar to those assumed by local risk communication for the benefit of local host communities.

Today there can be no doubt that states are legally required to initiate such information exchanges as soon as they have reason to believe that any proposed or ongoing activity within their territory or subject to their jurisdiction carries a risk of significant transboundary harm. This international obligation to provide prior information and engage in consultations is an essential procedural counterpart to the state's substantive customary obligation to prevent significant transboundary harm.

If internationally the basic informational entitlement must be deemed non-controversial, threshold questions regarding the activation as well as the scope of the transboundary risk communication process can pose significant problems. A recent OECD Council Decision on the Exchange of Information Concerning Accidents Capable of Causing Transfrontier Damage,[11] which is aimed at hazardous industrial installations, seeks to refine the operational parameters of the obligations concerned. The Decision's significance thus lies in specifying in compulsory fashion the contents of information to be exchanged and offering a legal definition of what constitutes a "hazardous installation." For member-states of the European Community, the Seveso Directive had already established a similarly well-defined duty to provide transboundary risk information to exposed neighbouring countries.

Although formally these international standards apply only regionally, they establish guideposts of broad international significance. In other words, they are likely to be used as general yardsticks for evaluating any recipient country's performance in the internationally mandatory process of transboundary risk communication.

As presently conceived, transboundary risk communication is an intergovernmental dialogue on transboundary risk management. Rights and obligations are those of states. However, state practice points towards the emergence of at least a regional standard pursuant to which private individuals would be owed a corresponding obligation to be included in the transboundary risk communication process. Thus the notion of "equal rights of access," the idea that states ought to open their administrative and judicial proceedings to potentially affected residents of risk-exposed

11. OECD Doc. C(88) 84 (Final) (1988), *reproduced in* 28 I.L.M. 249 (1989).

neighbouring countries, has found particularly strong support within the OECD. Principle 14 of the 1978 UNEP Principles of Conduct in the Field of the Environment,"[12] recommends "equal access and treatment" as a generally applicable concept, albeit with some qualifications. A recommendation of similar import was approved by the International Law Association. More recently, the "Expert Group on Environmental Law" of the World Commission on Environment and Development (WCED) proposed legal principles for environmental protection and sustainable development which—much like an earlier resolution on water pollution adopted by the Institute of International Law—advocates implementation of the principle as an international legal obligation of states.

Notwithstanding these strong endorsements that come on top of some supportive state practice, presently it would be difficult to characterize "equal right of access" as embodying a universal customary international legal standard applicable to national environmental resource management. On the other hand, in Western Europe as well as North America, "equal right of access" can be said to have evolved into an internationally normative concept. . . .

D. PROVISION OF RELIEF TO ACCIDENT VICTIMS

■ THE BHOPAL DISASTER: STRUCTURING A SOLUTION

Daniel Magraw
57 U. Colo. L. Rev. 835, 838, 840-847 (1986)

II. Background Legal Issues

The Bhopal litigation has raised a myriad of significant legal issues, many of which will recur if mass injuries involving United States multinational corporations occur abroad in the future. I will briefly allude to some of those issues in order to provide a background for the discussion regarding structuring a settlement to the various litigation. . . .

A final issue relates to who should bear the responsibility for the disaster. There are four possible repositories of liability: (1) Carbide (India), the immediate owner of the facility from which the gas escaped; (2) the shareholders of Carbide (India), including Carbide (U.S.); (3) the victims; and

12. Draft Principles of Conduct in the Field of the Environment for the Guidance of States in the Conservation and Harmonious Utilization of Natural Resources Shared by Two or More States, *text in* 19 I.L.M. 1097 (1978).

(4) the regulatory authorities, possibly including the Government of India, the Government of the State of Madhya Pradesh, the Government of Bhopal, and the United States Government. Without endorsing any of the allegations, some of the arguments for allocating liability are as follows.

It has been alleged that Carbide (India) should be liable either on a strict-liability theory or because it was negligent in operating the plant and in failing to provide sufficient warning to the potentially affected population.

It has been alleged that Carbide (U.S.) should be liable on the theory that it was negligent with respect to training persons to operate the plant, designing the plant, or controlling its subsidiary. In addition, it has been argued that a multinational enterprise as a whole should bear financial responsibility for all of its activities, regardless of corporate form and, alternately, that traditional doctrine regarding piercing the corporate veil indicates liability on the part of Carbide (U.S.). It might also be argued that Carbide (U.S.) is directly liable by analogy to the "entrustment" doctrine, i.e., that a bailor is liable to an insured third party if the bailor knew or should have known that its bailee was likely to harm the third party and failed to take reasonable precautions to protect the third party. Finally, as an alternative to holding Carbide (U.S.) directly liable, it might be argued that Carbide (India) has a right of contribution or indemnification against Carbide (U.S.), either on the basis of the entrustment doctrine argument just described or on the basis of a contractual or common-law duty on the part of Carbide (U.S.) to supply Carbide (India) with safe and up-to-date technology and assistance.

It has been argued that some of the victims are at fault, and thus should be wholly or partly liable, because they knew or should have known that there existed danger in living close to the plant and nevertheless moved onto vacant land surrounding the plant. That argument is obviously extremely harsh; it flies in the face of economic realities in India and is contrary to the usual United States law (and presumably the Indian law) of nuisance.

With respect to the regulatory authorities, it has been argued that the Government of India and the state and local governments were negligent and thus should be liable for allowing the shantytown to develop so close to the plant (possibly in violation of an Indian ordinance mandating a vacant zone around such a plant), for regulating the safety conditions in the plant in a faulty manner, or for applying pressure with respect to hiring personnel who were more qualified by their political affiliation than by their professional competence. The Government of India, however, appears to be shielded by sovereign immunity under Indian law and probably also would have been under the United States Foreign Sovereign Immunities Act if it had not brought suit itself in United States courts, and thus opened the way to counterclaims arising out of the same occurrence. It has been alleged that the United States should be liable for not adequately regulating Carbide (U.S.), an allegation that probably is not persuasive but which has potentially far-reaching ramifications.

III. Structuring a Solution

A. Salient Characteristics of the Solution

It is appropriate to begin by identifying some of the salient characteristics of a desirable solution. First, the solution should occur relatively rapidly—a goal that may already have become unattainable due to the fact that 24 months have, as of the time this article goes to press, already passed since the disaster—because of the personal suffering of victims that will occur otherwise. Speed may also be in the interest of Carbide (India) and Carbide (U.S.) because the threat of massive liability may be more harmful than the actual liability turns out to be (e.g., in terms of lost good will, depressed stock prices, and increased credit terms). In addition, the continued existence of the litigation may strain to some degree—probably small—the relationship between the United States and India, and may be detrimental to other United States interests because, for example, perceived misbehavior abroad by United States corporations tends to discredit the foreign image of the United States and may adversely affect the availability of foreign business opportunities to other United States corporations.

Second, the solution should be reached without incurring unnecessary transaction costs. The primary issue here would appear to be the desirability of avoiding excessive legal fees, but other expenses can also soar astronomically in complex tort litigation involving complicated issues (such as forum non conveniens), disputes regarding settlement proposals, and extensive and sometimes duplicative (because of the participation of separately represented plaintiffs in different courts) discovery. For example, it has been reported that an average of 63% of the recoveries in the early asbestos litigation was consumed by expenses and legal fees; that figure has reportedly dropped to 41% on more recent claims.

Third, the solution should resolve all potential claims in India and in the United States, both because of the need for speed described above and because, if it does not, the likelihood of defendants agreeing to a settlement would be greatly decreased or the amount of such a settlement would be greatly decreased. This is typically an issue in mass torts; it is complicated here by the international aspect, i.e., that the courts of at least two countries need to recognize the settlement as final and binding.

Fourth, individual claims should be determined in an impartial and reasonable manner. That goal, which is not extraordinary in itself, is particularly difficult to achieve here because of the presence of United States and Indian claimants, the vast economic disparity between the two countries (a United States judge or jury might arguably have difficulty assessing injuries suffered by shantytown inhabitants and their families in India), and the difficulty in verifying claims brought by poor residents of a country with a relatively low documentation level.

Fifth, the total amount of the settlement should be adequate to compensate injured persons in a reasonable and fair manner. Two questions must be resolved in this regard: whether the standard should reflect the realities of life in India as opposed to the greater wealth of the United States, and whether punitive damages should be awarded. The former question should be resolved by limiting damages for residents of India to the Indian realities; any greater award would be a windfall and would distort the risks of doing business in India (thus discouraging non-Indian, and particularly United States, persons from doing business in India and, as a result, hindering India's development efforts). The latter question could be answered either way, depending on what law applies and how egregious the relevant behavior turns out to have been.

Sixth, in allocating liability through a settlement, the conduct-guidance effect of that allocation must be kept in mind: how important is it to provide incentives to the various actors to behave more carefully? In addition, it should be remembered that the allocation of liability may have a significant effect in discouraging or changing the nature of foreign investment in, and technology transfer to, developing countries. For example, allocating liability to the nation in which the parent corporation is headquartered (or is incorporated or is the nation of the residence of the majority shareholders) would presumably cause that nation to regulate more strictly all foreign investment and technology export. This result could increase safety levels, but could also easily lead to decreasing those types of activities and could thus hamper developing countries' efforts to create employment opportunities, increase standards of living, and decrease dependency on imports. Alternatively, capital and technology exporting states might insist on bilateral or multilateral investment treaties to allocate liability. Although hardly objectionable in theory, such treaties might inevitably allocate liability in a manner unfavorable to developing countries, because those countries most probably would have less bargaining power. Also, there would be an undesirable disruption in international trade during those negotiations, and the transaction costs of the negotiations would be high. Finally, placing liability on the "exporting" state (here, the United States) might cause a dangerous laxity on the part of the "importing" state (here, India).

Similarly, although on a different level, holding the parent corporation liable could be expected to decrease the total amount of foreign investment by increasing the risk of such investment. Such an allocation of liability might lead to the exercise of greater care in supervising the operations of foreign branches or subsidiaries, but it might also result in either exporting only simpler or older and more thoroughly tested technology—a result that presumably would increase safety but that also could leave the developing countries' products unable to compete in export markets—or in a restructuring of foreign activities, e.g., toward licensing instead of direct investment. These and other policy considerations affect the calculus of allocating liability.

B. A PROPOSED STRUCTURE

Taking into account the foregoing considerations, and acknowledging that the proposal outlined below raises a number of novel legal questions whose outcomes are uncertain, a solution to the Bhopal litigation might be structured as follows, to be accomplished in part via a self-executing executive agreement between the United States and India, and accompanied by any implementing legislation that may be constitutionally required by either of the two countries.

First, India and the United States should agree that India will expropriate all claims arising from the Bhopal disaster. (The March 29, 1985 Indian Act may already have accomplished such an expropriation, but that result is not obvious.) Such an agreement would remove any uncertainty with respect to India's ability to act as *parens patriae* in United States courts. The same result might be achieved in the absence of an executive agreement on this point if India expropriated the claims and President Reagan, in accord with the Second Hickenlooper Amendment, filed a statement in United States courts that the foreign policy interests of the United States require application of the Act of State doctrine (i.e., that the courts of one country will not challenge the acts of another country taken within that country's territory).

In either event, United States involvement in effectuating the expropriation (and the solution more broadly) would not imply any fault on the part of the United States. Rather, active United States involvement in fostering a solution is indicated by the international complexion of the problem and the fact that the Bhopal situation implicates a variety of United States interests which would be furthered by settling it fairly and expeditiously. It might be argued by United States citizens and residents that either United States action, and especially direct agreement by the United States to the Indian Government's expropriation, was a "taking" requiring just compensation under the fifth amendment and that the amount ultimately received from the claims settlement tribunal (described below) did not constitute just compensation. The United States Claims Court should have jurisdiction over such a claim, notwithstanding the so-called "treaty exception" to that court's jurisdiction, but this issue is not clear.

Second, India and the United States should agree that the amount of every claim will be determined expeditiously by a claims settlement tribunal to be established in India, by India and the United States jointly, the judges of which would be appointed by India and the United States. The cost of such tribunal would be borne equally by India and the United States. The agreement should also provide that any lump-sum amount received in settlement of the Bhopal claims shall be distributed in toto (pro rata if necessary), without deduction for any tribunal expenses, by India to the claimants whose claims had been expropriated, in accordance with the determination of the tribunal. Any amounts received, concurrently with the lump-sum payment, settling specified individual claims would be passed on by India to those claimants in full, and such claimants would be barred from bringing their claims before the claims settlement tribunal. Attorneys' fees would be limited to 10% of the amount actually received by each claimant.

The provisions just described (which are similar in some respects to those leading to the currently operating United States-Iran Claims Tribunal in the Hague), would remove cases from the court systems of both India and the United States to a specialized and presumably more expeditious forum. The likelihood of reduced delay would be furthered by having tribunal expenses paid by the two countries; they would have an incentive to facilitate the efficient operation of the tribunal. Such cost sharing would also reflect the two countries' interests in fairly resolving the disputes and the savings in costs that would otherwise be incurred by their judicial systems in processing the claims, and provide an incentive—albeit modest—to those countries to regulate more vigorously in the future.

The scheme would also enable and encourage the settlement of all claims related to the Bhopal disaster at one time. Moreover, it would permit the United States and other claimants to settle individually at that time if they so desired.

The specialized tribunal, whose decisions would be limited to determining the extent of injury and the corresponding measure of damages, would presumably apply consistent standards and operate fairly. United States participation in choosing tribunal members would presumably lead to reasonable evaluation of United States residents' claims (assuming such claims were not settled separately).

Use of a tribunal located in India would also lower transaction costs for claimants overall. (Disregarding attorneys' fees for the moment, Indian claimants' costs would presumably decrease because of the tribunal; United States claimants' costs would presumably increase.) The limitation on attorneys' fees would further reduce transaction costs (the United States successfully used such a 10% limitation with respect to United States nationals' claims against the German Democratic Republic).

Finally, Carbide (U.S.) and Carbide (India) should, simultaneously with the signing of the United States-India executive agreement described above, pay to India a lump sum in full and final settlement of all claims against the Union Carbide group of companies related to the Bhopal disaster, with the exception of any specified individual claims that are settled as part of the same arrangement and for which payment is made at the same time. The amount of that settlement should reflect a reasonably informed estimate of the numbers and types of injuries suffered and should be based principally on the actual damages suffered (thus, for example, loss of livelihood of an Indian resident would be measured by his or her expected income in India). Punitive damages would not be included unless investigation revealed that particularly egregious behavior had occurred and the applicable law would allow punitive damages. Such a settlement would liquidate the Union Carbide corporate group's Bhopal-related liability and would presumably lead to a generous amount for distribution among claimants.

IV. Conclusion

This article proposes a structure for settling the Bhopal litigation that seeks to protect, in a balanced manner, the interests of the parties—including India—to the various litigation as well as of the United States. That structure could also serve as a starting point for resolving future occurrences similar to the Bhopal disaster. The proposal outlined herein obviously depends in large part on cooperation, statesmanship and, perhaps, leadership by the United States. Given the various considerations involved, including the fact that the Bhopal disaster is likely to recur in other forms, such involvement comports with the interests of the United States in particular and is in the interest of justice generally.

Note

See also Stephen C. McCaffrey, Expediting the Provision of Compensation to Accident Victims, in Transferring Hazardous Technologies and Substances 199 (G. Handl & R. Lutz eds. 1989).

E. NORMS APPLICABLE TO NUCLEAR ACCIDENTS

1. Case Study: Chernobyl

At approximately 1:23 A.M. on Saturday, April 26, 1986, an accident occurred in nuclear power Reactor No. 4 at Chernobyl, USSR. The processes leading to the accident commenced the day before, when operators began to prepare for a test of one of the reactor's two turbogenerators. The test was essentially intended to determine whether the generator could be used, in the event of a local electricity failure, to power the reactor's emergency cooling system until emergency electricity reserves could take over. In the many hours of preparing for the test, the operators disengaged the emergency cooling system from the reactor, disconnected both generators from external electricity, and neutralized a number of automatic safety systems from both generators. These steps violated crucial provisions of the operating regulations. As the reactor's power was decreased before the test, the reactor became unstable, which ultimately caused the operators to increase and then reduce the flow rate of cooling water through the reactor.

The reactor in which the experiment was being conducted was one of 73 nuclear power reactors in the Soviet Union. Those nuclear reactors, like all nuclear power reactors, generate electricity by using controlled nuclear reactions, caused by the inherent instability of radioactive elements in the reactor core, to heat water into steam, which then turns turbines in turbogenerators that generate electricity. In the case of Reactor No. 4, the radioactive element used was uranium enriched with uranium 235. Neutrons (which are particles within atoms) emitted by the core's uranium collide with other uranium, thus causing energy in the form of heat to be released. Under proper circumstances, a chain reaction occurs leading to the continuous supply of energy.

Perhaps counterintuitively, reactors produce more energy if the neutrons emitted by the core's uranium are slowed down, at least within certain limits. In most United States nuclear power reactors, the material—called the "moderator"—used to slow down the neutrons is water. Chernobyl, however, used graphite (1,700 tons of it) as the moderator; water was used only as a coolant. The moderation occurred by moving 1,659 fuel rods containing the uranium in or out of the massive graphite block.

The use of graphite as the moderator has a number of worrisome consequences, as contrasted with the use of water. Perhaps the most problematic consequence is that the reactor becomes more unstable. Either or both of a temperature increase or a loss of water (for example, from the cooling system) causes the nuclear reaction to increase and thus more energy and heat to be released. The opposite is true regarding water-moderated reactors. Also, graphite (which is soft luminous carbon) burns, but water does not, so if there is a problem, graphite poses more of a risk than water does.

The reason that graphite was used as the moderator at Chernobyl is that the use of graphite increases the amount of plutonium that is produced as a byproduct. Plutonium, which is another radioactive element, is used in the production of nuclear weapons. The reactors at Chernobyl were part of the Soviet Union's backup system for manufacturing plutonium for military purposes. Plutonium-producing nuclear facilities in the United States also use graphite as a moderator.

When the test at Chernobyl finally began in the early hours of April 26—to quote from an English translation of the Soviet Union's official report on the accident—a "continuing decrease in the water flow rate through the channels of the reactor under conditions of an increase in power led to intense steam formation and then to a crisis," which included overheating of the fuel and its disintegration. Ensuing chemical reactions led to a massive steam explosion, followed by a thermal explosion. Those explosions—neither of which was a nuclear explosion—blasted a hole in the roof, casting aside in that process a 1,000-ton concrete shield. The explosions started at least 30 individual fires, including in the graphite core itself, and led to the immediate release of large amounts of radioactive material from the reactor.

A column of radioactive particles rose over one-half mile into the atmosphere above the plant, thus raising the likelihood of long-distance pollution from the accident. Moreover, because much of the radioactivity was carried by smoke from the burning graphite and because graphite particles are so fine, the radioactive material was not prone to fall to the earth very quickly, thus further increasing the danger of transboundary radioactive pollution.

Altogether, it is estimated that approximately 18 million curies—which is a measure of radiation—were released into the atmosphere by the Chernobyl accident. About one-quarter of that, over 4 million curies, were released the day of the explosions. By way of comparison, the accident at Three Mile Island released a total of approximately 18 curies—that is, about one-millionth as many as were released at Chernobyl.

A top Ukrainian official reached the plant 90 minutes after the first explosion. He found injured and stunned people stumbling or lying around, flames and smoke everywhere, and invisible lethal radioactivity lurking anywhere. Soviet leaders in Moscow were alerted shortly thereafter, and crisis-management teams dispatched by Moscow arrived in Chernobyl later that day. According to a member of the first team to arrive, it was only as they approached Chernobyl and saw the glowing red from the graphite core that they really appreciated the magnitude of the disaster. By that time, many severe injuries had occurred, especially among fire fighters and medical personnel, many of whom displayed extraordinary bravery. The first physicians to arrive at the reactor tried to practice triage, but with no accurate sense of how much exposure anyone had had. One hundred and twenty-nine of the most seriously injured persons were airlifted to a Moscow hospital, which had much earlier been designated as the national medical center for nuclear injuries, for longer-term medical care.

Over the next week or so, the Soviet Union engaged in a concentrated effort to try to put out the graphite fire and reduce and eliminate the release of radioactive materials. Those efforts primarily consisted of dumping from helicopters 5,000 tons of a theretofore untested mixture onto the smoldering reactor. The mixture consisted of boron (to absorb neutrons), dolomite (to create carbon dioxide to smother the fire), clay and sand (to act as a filter to trap radioactive particles), and lead (to melt into a smooth cover to absorb radiation and transfer heat).

This blanketing technique was intended to block the release of radioactive particles into the atmosphere. But it also had the unfortunate effect of increasing the temperature inside the already red-hot graphite pile, which in turn raised the possibilities of a reactor-core meltdown or the collapse of the reactor's cement foundation. Either of those events would have allowed massive amounts of radioactive material to contaminate the water table 50 feet below. An intense debate occurred within the crisis-management team regarding whether the blanketing approach should be used at all. By Sunday, April 27, the decision was made to begin, but serious doubts remained.

For five days, the blanketing technique resulted in decreasing radiation emissions but increasing core temperatures. On May 2, however, a frightening development occurred: radiation emissions also began to rise. On May 5, they reached the highest level since the explosions. Tension and doubt were intense. The blanketing continued, but new alternative steps, involving a tunnel, were also initiated. Then, unexpectantly, the radiation emissions virtually ceased the next day. The immediate crisis was over.

As a result of the emission of radioactive materials, 31 people died in the days and months immediately following the accident, most of them from radiation burns. Approximately 30 more remained hospitalized six months after the accident. About 20 countries, including the United States, volunteered to assist, or responded quickly to requests for assistance, by sending medical supplies, equipment, and personnel. Estimates vary widely regarding medical difficulties that will arise in the future as a result of exposure. Everyone agrees that cancer, leukemia, and genetic mutation rates will increase, but it is not clear by how much. Estimates of the rise in the death toll over the next 70 years range from a few thousand to tens of thousands. That figure does not include the many people who will experience painful and debilitating illnesses that fall short of death.

Approximately 1,000 square kilometers in the Soviet Union, in which 135,000 people formerly resided, were evacuated as uninhabitable soon after the accident, and they remain unpopulated. That area includes the town of Pripyat, where reactor workers and their families lived. On the day of the accident, the Soviet Union ordered the 49,000 inhabitants of Pripyat to stay indoors. Only a few disobeyed to sneak a look at the burning reactor, and they were among the casualties, "victims of curiosity." On Sunday morning, 1,100 buses, in a column 12 miles long, drove from Kiev and elsewhere into the radioactive danger zone to evacuate the residents of Pripyat. The town was evacuated, reportedly with almost no panic. Persons in other nearby areas were not evacuated for several more days and thus suffered greater exposure to radiation. The damage in the Soviet Union was officially stated as about $3 billion, though Western observers put the figure much higher.

Damage also occurred outside the Soviet Union. During the first two days after the accident, radioactive clouds drifted in a northwestern direction to Sweden and Finland, turned southeast across Polish territory, Czechoslovakia, southern Germany, and north again to the Netherlands.

On the following days, the pollutants went directly southeastward, thus affecting Austria and northern Italy (as well as Kiev and other portions of the Soviet Union that had theretofore been relatively untouched). After several days, the radioactive pollutants reached the western United States and Japan.

Because of the nearly incomprehensible speed at which nuclear reactions occur, once prompt criticality was reached, the operators had less than one second to rectify the situation. Obviously, no warning was possible that the accident was occurring. Even after the accident, however, neither the existence of the accident nor the drift of the clouds was communicated to potentially affected countries by the Soviet Union. The first public indication of danger came from Sweden. The Soviet Union did not even acknowledge the existence of the accident until two and one-half days after it occurred, and the information disclosed after that was scanty until August, when a comprehensive report was issued to the International Atomic Energy Agency (IAEA). Affected states were essentially left to their own devices to detect the pollutants, including both their nature and amount, during the critical period during which precautionary measures were possible.

It is likely that early notification and information would have made a difference. For example, radioactive materials can affect people via a number of routes, including direct skin contact from and inhalation of materials falling from the sky, direct skin contact from and inhalation of materials lying on the ground and kicked up as dust by activities such as walking, and by ingesting food or water that has been contaminated by radioactive materials. A state that has been warned of the imminent arrival of airborne radioactive materials can instruct its residents to stay indoors and to avoid ingesting certain types of food that are likely to be contaminated, such as milk or leafy vegetables. In addition, more aggressive steps can be taken, such as providing Iodine pills to a population to minimize the intake of radioactive Iodine 131, which has a half life of only eight days and which, together with Cesium 137 and Strontium 90, is one of the three most common and dangerous radioactive elements emitted by Chernobyl.

Many countries took efforts to minimize the harmful effects of the radiation, once they learned of the accident. Poland, for example, prohibited children in some regions from drinking milk, prohibited the pasturing of cattle, and provided children doses of Iodine. Bavaria, in the Federal Republic of Germany, removed 3,000 tons of powdered milk from circulation and paid the dairy that produced it approximately $2,000,000 in compensation; and the sale of other foodstuffs was banned in West Germany—foodstuffs that were freely available across the border in France. The contaminated powdered milk was subsequently sold to Egypt (it was intercepted and impounded before it left Germany); similar sales occurred from European countries to other developing countries.

Non-Soviet news coverage during the period immediately following the accident was extensive and, in many cases, sensationalistic and inaccurate.

In at least one instance, a newspaper disregarded an explicit denial by its Moscow correspondent and reported inaccurately that 2,000 persons had died at Chernobyl and were buried in a mass grave. Western news media, as well as some others outside the Soviet Union, seemed to derive what the Germans call Schadenfreude, or joy in the suffering of others, from the Chernobyl tragedy. In any event, the inaccurate reporting gave the Soviet Union a means by which to deflect some of the criticism and doubts directed at it. If such exaggerated accounts were to appear widely in the United States following a nuclear accident here, the results might well be panic and increased casualties.

In the aftermath of Chernobyl, the Soviet Union reaffirmed its dedication to nuclear energy. Globally, 378 nuclear power plants now operate, providing 15 percent of the world's electricity. Ninety-seven of these plants are in the United States. Another 175 are scheduled for operation worldwide.

An IAEA delegation visited the Soviet Union soon after the accident and thereafter served as a channel of communication about the accident. In addition, the IAEA formed an expert working group on nuclear safety standards and convened an international conference to review the accident and to draft conventions on two of the important issues raised by it: emergency notification and assistance. Those conventions were negotiated and finalized unusually expeditiously, being opened for signature on September 26, 1986, five months after the accident. The Convention on Early Notification of a Nuclear Accident entered into force just one month later, on October 27, 1987. The Convention on Assistance in the Case of a Nuclear Accident or Radiological Emergency entered into force on February 26, 1987. (Thse conventions are reprinted in 25 I.L.M. 1391 & 1377 (1986)).

The Soviet Union denied, in the period immediately after the accident, liability for damage in other states. Among other points, Soviet diplomats reportedly objected on the ground that other states' preventive measures were extreme and unnecessary. As far as is known, no states have made diplomatic claims to the Soviet Union for compensation for harm from the accident, although the United Kingdom reportedly reserved its right to make such a claim.

Notes and Questions

1. *A Soviet nuclear sub accident.*

> On 4 and 6 October, [1986,] the Soviet Union notified the [International Atomic Energy Agency] of the fire on, and the subsequent sinking of, one of its nuclear-powered and nuclear-armed submarines, indicating that there was no danger of nuclear explosion or radioactive contamination of the environment. Though it was not specified that this notification was

> made in accordance with the Early Notification Convention, it may be noted that such notification would be consistent with the undertakings by the USSR to apply the Convention provisionally and also to apply it to *all* nuclear activities.

Introductory Note, 25 I.L.M. 1391-1392 (1986).

2. *Applying the general principles.* How would the general principles contained in the drafts of the ILA and the WCED Legal Experts Group in section B of this chapter apply to a Chernobyl-like situation? To what extent do they differ from the obligations laid down in the Convention on Early Notification, discussed in the following excerpt?

3. *Chernobyl's conventional fallout.* The two agreements adopted in the aftermath of the Chernobyl disaster are the Convention on Early Notification of a Nuclear Accident, September 26, 1986, *reprinted in* 25 I.L.M. 1391 (1986) and the Convention on Assistance in the Case of a Nuclear Accident or Radiological Emergency, September 26, 1986, *reprinted in* 25 I.L.M. 1377 (1986).

2. The Legal Response

■ OVERVIEW OF LEGAL AND TECHNICAL ASPECTS OF NUCLEAR ACCIDENT POLLUTION

Andronico O. Adede
in International Law and Pollution 129, 129-132, 136-138 (D. Magraw ed. 1991)

INTRODUCTION

The concern with the adequacy of international legal regimes for dealing with pollution problems arising from nuclear accidents and the need to strengthen international technical standards for enhancing nuclear safety received a notable impetus following the 1986 Chernobyl nuclear accident in the U.S.S.R. Governments seemed more ready to consider specific international measures in response to the Chernobyl nuclear accident with its transboundary effects than they were following the 1979 Three Mile Island nuclear accident (TMI) in the U.S.A.

TMI, let it be observed briefly, encouraged the preparation by the International Atomic Energy Agency (IAEA) of two sets of nonlegally binding instruments, namely, the Guidelines on Emergency Assistance Arrangements in Connection with a Nuclear Accident or Radiological Emergency, and the Guidelines on Reportable Events, Integrated Planning and Information Exchange in a Transboundary Release of Radioactive Materials. As is well known, TMI also resulted in a large number of measures and programs to improve nuclear safety through improved engineering devices and more competent operation of nuclear plants. It prompted federal supervision and redesign of nuclear plants leading to more diligent evaluation of safety aspects of nuclear installations both by the U.S. government, through the National Regulatory Commission (NRC), and by the industry itself, through the Atlanta-based Institute of Nuclear Power Operations (INPO).

The Chernobyl accident, in contrast, resulted in the immediate elaboration of two legally binding international instruments by the IAEA, namely, the Convention on Early Notification of a Nuclear Accident (IAEA Notification Convention) and the Convention on Assistance in the Case of a Nuclear Accident or Radiological Emergency (IAEA Assistance Convention). Both of these have been acknowledged as landmarks in the history of the treaty-making process. It also resulted directly in the expanded program on nuclear safety and improvements by the IAEA and additional activities for the IAEA support missions in the field of nuclear safety and radiological protection. Such support missions, which are usually undertaken only upon request by a member State of the IAEA, include the Operational Safety Review Team (OSART), the Assessment of Significant Safety Event Team (ASSET), the Operational Safety Indicator Program (OSIP), the program of Integrated Safety Assessment of Research Reactor (INSARR), and the Radiation Protection Advisory Team (RAPAR). Apart from an increased demand for these support missions, at the request of member States, there was also an increased awareness of the role played by the IAEA Incident Reporting System (IAWA-IRIS) and the International Nuclear Information System (INIS). There also emerged a concern with finding ways to make legally binding the IAEA Nuclear Safety Standards (NUSS) and the evolution of the equally important questions of nuclear waste disposal through the IAEA Waste Management Advisory Program (WAMAP).

[I]t is important to note at once that, while the efforts to find appropriate remedies for the victims of nuclear-accident pollution have resulted in international measures through the elaboration of international legal instruments, international technical standards for enhancing nuclear safety have not been amendable to formulation into internationally binding legal instruments. As will be noted further, nuclear safety remains a primary responsibility of individual States enforcing their national regulations and is still the subject of the non-legally binding guidelines such as those developed by the IAEA under its NUSS program. [*See* footnote 9, above, concerning the 1994 Nuclear Safety Convention.—Eds.]

Treaty Law on Nuclear Accident Before and After TMI and Chernobyl

Before TMI and Chernobyl, several multilateral treaties were concluded to deal specifically with the question of civil liability for nuclear accidents in land-based nuclear installations, thus providing remedies for victims of nuclear-accident pollution. Other treaties were aimed at ensuring physical protection of nuclear material especially from theft or acts of sabotage, which could lead to exposure of the public to ionizing radiation, and treaties establishing liability for accidents arising from transportation of nuclear material and operation of nuclear ships. A checklist of these treaties, focusing on the instruments dealing specifically with the problems of pollution damage from nuclear accidents, includes:

1. the Paris Convention on Third-Party Liability in the Field of Nuclear Energy, July 29, 1960, as amended in 1964 and 1982 (adopted within the framework of Organization for Economic Co-operation and Development [OECD] and therefore regional in character);
2. the Vienna Convention on Civil Liability for Nuclear Damage, May 21, 1963 (adopted within the framework of the IAEA and therefore global in character);
3. the Brussels Convention on the Liability of Operations of Nuclear Ships, May 25, 1962;
4. the Nordic Mutual Emergency Assistance Agreement in Connection with Radiological Accidents, 1963;
5. the Brussels Convention Relating to Civil Liability in the Field of Maritime Carriage of Nuclear Material, December 17, 1971 (adopted within the framework of the International Maritime Organization [IMO]);
6. the Vienna Convention on the Physical Protection of Nuclear Material, March 3, 1980;
7. the IAEA Convention on Early Notification of a Nuclear Accident, 1986; and
8. the IAEA Convention on Assistance in the Case of a Nuclear Accident or Radiological Emergency, 1986.

There have also been a number of bilateral agreements dealing specifically with cooperation in nuclear safety matters such as exchange of information and consultation. The usefulness of these bilateral agreements was endorsed in the IAEA Assistance Convention, which regards bilateral arrangements as additional means of giving effect to the broad framework of the multilateral convention. . . .

Recognizing the Focus of the IAEA Notification and Assistance Conventions

As noted briefly earlier, the IAEA already succeeded in producing two conventions in direct response to Chernobyl, focusing on the matter clearly signaled in the title of each convention: the Convention on *Early Notification* of a Nuclear Accident; and the Convention on *Assistance* in the Case of a Nuclear Accident or Radiological Emergency.

These two conventions were tailored to address the specific issues among those exposed by the Chernobyl accident and with respect to which the IAEA member States believed international legal instruments were achievable as a matter of urgency. The member States singled out the need to establish a treaty obligation to notify a nuclear accident with potential transboundary effects: whom to notify, how to notify, and the information to be notified. The emphasis was on the early warning following a nuclear accident that might have transboundary consequences, alerting States likely to be affected and thus enabling them to take some precautionary measures addressing, in that connection, the special needs of the developing countries. Whether or not the notification would include nuclear accidents arising from military activities of a State became a make-or-break conference issue and was indeed settled in a subtle way, as explained in the drafting history of the relevant articles of the Convention.

The IAEA also singled out the need to establish a multilateral legal framework for providing emergency assistance promptly: how to request the assistance; how to render it, the modalities for undertaking an assistance mission itself, having regard to the applicable bilateral arrangements; the question of equipment and personnel; and also the financial aspects of assistance. The financial aspects of assistance, it may be noted, also became another make-or-break conference issue, which defied solution until the last hours of negotiations of the conventions, as indicated in the drafting history of the relevant article.

The two conventions are already in force. Through the continued collaborative efforts between the IAEA, the World Meteorological Organization (WMO), and the Global Telecommunication System (GTS), the machinery established for early warning of the nuclear accident under the Notification Convention has now been successfully tested to evaluate its efficacy. It may also be observed that assistance in an actual radiological emergency has been rendered through the IAEA to a member State (Brazil) in the framework of the Assistance Convention in connection with the radiological emergency caused by the disused cesium-137 source in that member State.

The work on these two conventions clearly demonstrated the vital role played by the IAEA as an organization respected by its member States as a forum in which they could consult and cooperate in solving a specific international problem. It is expected that such cooperation will continue to be maintained with other relevant international organizations, such as the World Health Organization (WHO), the International Labour Organisation (ILO), and other United Nations bodies, including United Nations Environment Programme (UNEP) and the United Nations Scientific Committee on the Effects of Atomic Radiation (UNSCEAR).

The basic approach of the IAEA with respect to the Notification and Assistance Conventions was to stay close to what was evidently achievable and to avoid the temptation of trying to solve, at once, all conceivable problems which might flow from a transboundary nuclear accident and radiological emergency. Thus, certain issues were deliberately left out of consideration of the two conventions in order to focus upon the obligation to notify a transboundary nuclear accident and on the framework for providing prompt assistance in the event of a nuclear accident or radiological emergency.

Commentators unfamiliar with the drafting history of the two conventions will always wonder why (and some of those who took part in the negotiations will continue to lament the fact that) the two IAEA conventions did not:

1. define the term "radiological safety significance";
2. contain provisions on intervention level which may be a trigger factor for notification of accidents; and
3. address the question of State responsibility and compensation for nuclear damage.

Apart from the last point, on which the IAEA has commenced a study toward an appropriate solution, . . . the issues were, in fact, considered during the drafting process of the two conventions. One of them—intervention level—has been singled out for subsequent scientific study under the auspices of the IAEA. Recognizing the focus chosen for the two conventions, it was necessary to limit the scope of the two instruments, in the course of their elaboration, to the specific concern articulated by the member States while leaving open the consideration of other related questions to treatment elsewhere. The two conventions clearly achieved the purpose for which they were intended and thus should be acknowledged as such. . . .

Further reading: For a discussion of treaty measures needed to prevent nuclear accidents and their transboundary effects, *see* Günther Handl, Transboundary Nuclear Accidents: The Post-Chernobyl Multilateral Legislative Agenda, 15 Ecology L.Q. 203 (1988).

Note

The explosion of a nuclear power plant is everyone's worst nightmare. Yet not only are nuclear power plants perfectly legal under international law, until the conclusion of the 1994 Nuclear Safety Convention[13] there were no internationally mandated safety standards governing their design

13. *See* footnote 9, above.

and construction.[14] Even the Nuclear Safety Convention is based on the principle that "responsibility for nuclear safety rests with the State having jurisdiction over a nuclear installation. . . ."[15] In other words, any country that can get its hands on the technology necessary to construct a nuclear power plant may do so.[16] The rules of international law reviewed in this chapter would certainly apply to such plants, as they would to any other activity whose operation entails a risk of harm. Yet where the harm that might be caused is so potentially catastrophic, should the international community not take a more active role in the regulation of these facilities? What form might such involvement take? Would "legislation" on the international plane be sufficient? What about liability for damage caused? If there is no international legal prohibition of such activities, and if harm results from the non-negligent operation of one of them, how could the situs state be liable? This is one of the questions we will grapple with in the following chapter.

14. *See generally* the article by Günther Handl cited in the immediately preceding Further reading recommendation, especially at p. 205.

15. Convention on Nuclear Safety, footnote 9, above, preambular paragraph (iii). The convention relies for implementation upon the submission of reports on legislative, regulatory, and administrative measures taken by states parties to carry out their obligations under the convention. The reports are submitted to periodic review meetings of the parties to the Convention, which are to be convened at least every three years.

16. *See,* in this connection, Anthony D'Amato & Kirsten Engel, State Responsibility for the Exportation of Nuclear Power Technology, 74 Va. L. Rev. 1011 (1988).

IX

Accountability and Compliance

In previous chapters we have considered the international legal system (Chapter 5) and general norms of international law concerning environmental harm (Chapter 7). In this chapter we will explore mechanisms for holding states accountable for violating norms of international environmental law and for ensuring, or encouraging, compliance with those norms. We will also consider the availability of national courts and administrative agencies to persons seeking redress for transfrontier environmental harm. Thus, the present chapter examines how the general principles reviewed in Chapter 7 apply in the specific context of environment-related obligations and injuries. Not dealt with in this chapter is the possibility of enforcing international environmental obligations through the use of trade sanctions, which are considered in Chapter 20. After briefly reviewing general principles of responsibility, the chapter surveys general principles of accountability and compensation for international environmental harm, then examines how those principles apply to developing countries. The next section concerns innovative approaches of several recent treaties to the problem of compliance. We then deal with the question of private remedies for international environmental harm and conclude with a look at criminal responsibility for such harm.

A. BACKGROUND: BASIC PRINCIPLES OF STATE RESPONSIBILITY

Lest disproportionate importance be ascribed to this chapter, it might be well to pause for a moment to reflect again on the nature of international law. It is sometimes thought that international law is not really "law" because it is a decentralized system with no police force and no set of courts with compulsory jurisdiction to enforce it. Thus the reader might—mistakenly, in our view—look to this chapter for proof as to whether rules of international environmental law are "enforceable" and thus whether there really is any "law" in this field at all. It is worth recalling in this connection Professor Henkin's observation that "[I]t is probably the case that *almost all nations observe almost all principles of international law and almost all of their obligations almost all of the time.*" Louis Henkin, How Nations Behave 47 (2d ed. 1979). (Emphasis Added.) This, even though,

> in international society, there is no one to compel nations to obey the law. . . . [P]hysical coercion is not the sole or even principal force ensuring compliance with law. Important law is observed by the most powerful, even in domestic societies, although there is no one to compel them. In the United States, the President, Congress, and the mighty armed forces obey orders of a Supreme Court whose single marshal is unarmed.

Henkin, *id.*, at 92.

Against this background, let us briefly review the basic principles of international responsibility examined in Chapter 5. A state incurs responsibility when it breaches an international obligation, also referred to as a "primary rule" of international law. An example of such a primary rule is the obligation not to cause transfrontier pollution harm to another state. Breach of a primary rule entails the responsibility of the state that has committed the breach (the author state) and engages "secondary" rules that deal, inter alia, with the legal consequences of the breach of an international obligation.[1] These secondary rules specify the content, forms, and degrees of international responsibility.[2] Analytically, the legal consequences of breaching an international obligation are new obligations of the author state that arise by virtue of the breach of the primary rule.

These new obligations of a state that has breached an international obligation are aspects of the fundamental obligation of that state to make "reparation" for the injury caused to the other state or states. As the term

1. Secondary rules also concern whether an internationally wrongful act has been committed in the first place. *See* Part 1 of the draft articles on State Responsibility adopted by the International Law Commission on first reading in 1980, entitled The Origin of International Responsibility, [1980] Y.B. Intl. L. Commn., vol. 2, pt. 1, p. 30 (1981). *See, e.g.,* Articles 1, 3, and 16, reproduced in Chapter 8, above, at p. [2].

2. *See, e.g.,* Willem Riphagen, Special Rapporteur, Preliminary Report on the Content, Forms and Degrees of International Responsibility (Part 2 of the Draft Articles on State Responsibility), [1980] Y.B. Intl. L. Commn., vol. 2, pt. 1, 107 (1982).

implies, the duty to make reparation requires the author state to "repair" the harm ("restitution") or, when that is not possible, to provide monetary compensation ("indemnity") to the injured state. In certain cases, a form of reparation known as "satisfaction" may be the appropriate remedy for "moral" (i.e., nonmaterial) injury to a state's dignity, honor, or prestige. Satisfaction may take such forms as presentation of official regrets, punishing minor officials, or formally acknowledging the unlawful nature of the act. In sum, "[r]eparation is the generic term which describes the various methods available to a State for discharging or releasing itself from [international] responsibility. The forms of reparation may consist in restitution, indemnity or satisfaction." E. Jiménez de Aréchaga, International Law in the Past Third of a Century, 159 Rec. des Cours 9, 285 (1978-I).

Of particular interest in the case of international environmental harm is the notion of restitution. Formally known as "restitution in kind" or "*restitutio in integrum,*" the purpose of this remedy is, as far as possible, to "wipe out all the consequences of the illegal act and re-establish the situation which would, in all probability, have existed if that act had not been committed." *Chorzow Factory* case, P.C.I.J. Series A, No. 17, at 47 (1928). Technically, only if and to the extent that restitution in kind is not possible, need compensation be paid. In fact, however, the payment of compensation is the most common form of reparation. E. Jiménez de Aréchaga, above, at 286.

But in environmental cases should restorative measures not be preferred, when they would be appropriate? For example, shouldn't State A be required to clean up hazardous waste that one of its corporations dumped in State B? What special problems does the obligation to remediate present in international environmental cases? Some of them are illustrated by the *Cosmos 954* incident, in which Canada was reluctant to allow the Soviet Union to come onto Canadian territory to clean up the radioactive debris left when a Soviet nuclear-powered satellite crashed in Canada.[3]

Another example is the case concerning *Certain Phosphate Lands in Nauru* (Nauru v. Australia), in which the Republic of Nauru claimed that Australia was responsible for the rehabilitation of Nauruan phosphate lands mined during administration of Australia prior to the island's independence in 1968. Nauru's Application instituting proceedings against Australia before the International Court of Justice states that "[a]s a result of this mining process, there remained on the mined-out lands nothing but a forest of limestone pinnacles, varying between 5 and 15 metres in height. The land was thus rendered completely useless for habitation, agriculture, or any other purpose unless and until rehabilitation was carried out." Application of the Republic of Nauru, filed May 19, 1989, p. 14. Australia admitted, in a report to the United Nations Trusteeship Council filed in

3. *See generally* Carl Christol, International Liability for Damage Caused by Space Objects, 74 A.J.I.L. 346 (1980).

1948, that once the phosphate deposits were exhausted, "all but the coastal strip of Nauru will be worthless." Application, above, at 18. Nauru claimed, inter alia, that Australia had failed to comply with its trusteeship obligations, engaged in a denial of justice, and abused its rights over the Territory of Nauru, and thus had a "duty of restitution [which] . . . extends to the restoration of those parts of the island, mined [during the relevant period], to a reasonable condition for habitation by the Nauruan people as a sovereign nation." Application, above, at 30. Nauru therefore claimed that Australia was "bound to make restitution or other appropriate reparation to Nauru," and reserved the right to request "an award of aggravated or moral damages. . . ." The case was settled by the two states by agreement concluded August 10, 1993, before the court could rule on Nauru's claims. The case was accordingly removed from the court's docket. The settlement, which included a cash payment of $A107 million, was "without prejudice to Australia's long-standing position that it bears no responsibility for the rehabilitation of the phosphate lands. . . ." Article 1(1). The settlement documents are reprinted in 32 I.L.M. 1471 (1993).

In such cases should the author of the damage be required to pay the cost of restorative measures taken by countries in the position of Canada or Nauru? What if the *status quo ante* cannot be reestablished? You should bear these questions in mind as you work through the material in this chapter.

The foregoing recapitulation covers the basic forms of state responsibility under traditional international law, yet it by no means exhausts the ways in which a state may be held accountable for causing international environmental harm. For example, an injured state may resort to self-help by taking countermeasures against the author state. The application of countermeasures—which have been referred to as "an indispensable means of implementation of State responsibility"[4]—is perhaps the most common method of "enforcing" international law. Countermeasures may consist of actions that would be lawful whether or not the target state had violated international law (retorsion), or of actions that would be unlawful but for the fact that they are taken in response to a wrongful act by another state (reprisals[5]). But even in the latter case, an otherwise unlawful response will be legitimate only if it is (1) necessary and (2) proportional to the breach and injury.[6] Countermeasures involving otherwise unlawful acts (in particular, reprisals) typically have the most bite and are therefore resorted

4. Gaetano Arangio-Ruiz, Special Rapporteur, Fifth Report on State Responsibility, U.N. Doc. A/CN.4/453 at 5 (1993).

5. As used in the field of international responsibility, the term "reprisal" is not confined to responses involving the use of force. In fact, since the use of force is sharply curtailed by the United Nations Charter (*in fine* Article 2(4) and Article 51), the great majority of reprisals today are of a nonforcible character.

6. On the requirements of necessity and proportionality, *see generally* Restatement (Third) of the Foreign Relations Law of the United States §905 (1987). For a study of proportionality, *see* Judith Gail Gardam, Proportionality and Force in International Law, 87 A.J.I.L. 391 (1993).

to frequently to enforce international law. However, their use often results in an escalating spiral of action and response by the states involved. They are imperfect as a method of enforcing international law because they rely on unilateral determinations by the *allegedly* injured state that (1) the "author" state has in fact committed a breach, and (2) the conditions for a lawful response—necessity and proportionality—are satisfied. However, since there is no generally applicable international enforcement mechanism, and in the absence of a system of dispute resolution that has been accepted by the states involved, such unilateral enforcement may be the only course of action available. The International Law Commission of the United Nations has considered whether a state that believes it has been injured by an internationally wrongful act of another state must seek a third-party determination of whether a breach was in fact committed before resorting to countermeasures. *See* Gaetano Arangio-Ruiz, Special Rapporteur, Fifth Report on State Responsibility, U.N. Doc. A/CN.4/453 at 39, *et seq.* (1993); and 1994 I.L.C. Rep. 364-366. The commission ultimately decided not to include such a requirement in the complete set of draft articles on state responsibility adopted on first reading in 1996, but only to require prior fulfillment of the obligation to negotiate. Article 48, 1996 I.L.C. Rep. 144-145.

Another question not addressed by the basic principles of state responsibility reviewed above is that of "strict liability," also known as "objective responsibility" or "liability without fault." Specifically, is a state internationally responsible, in the sense outlined above, only if it has failed to measure up to a certain standard of conduct, (i.e., if it has somehow acted culpably or has been at "fault")?[7] Or may a state be held accountable even if its conduct has been beyond reproach, but when one of its activities (such as a space object) causes environmental or other harm to another state?

A final question not specifically addressed by the traditional rules of state responsibility is whether a state may be held criminally responsible for at least certain violations of international law. This notion was introduced in Chapter 2 and will be explored further in the present chapter.

Consideration of the following paradigms of international environmental harm may help you to focus upon some of the issues presented by application of rules of international responsibility to environmental cases.

> *Paradigm 1.* A smelter in State A emits sulphur dioxide fumes that cause damage to the environment, including private property, in neighboring State B.
>
> Issues include whether State A must stop the harmful pollution; whether State A must pay State B, or the injured parties, compensation for the damage;

7. For discussions of the role of fault in the field of state responsibility, *see, e.g.*, Gaetano Arangio-Ruiz, Special Rapporteur, Second Report on State Responsibility, [1989] Y.B. Intl. L. Commn., vol. 2, pt. 1, 1, 47 (1992); and Ian Brownlie, Principles of Public International Law 436-440 (3d ed. 1979).

whether it would make any difference if State A were a developing country; whether, and the extent to which, purely environmental damage must be halted or is compensable; whether injured private parties can gain legal redress directly from the source state or activity; and what standards apply where injured private parties seek redress from the harmful activity.

Paradigm 2. The *Gusher,* a ship registered in State A, spills a large quantity of oil on the high seas—i.e., beyond the limits of national jurisdiction. The spill causes severe harm to the marine environment but does not result in direct damage to any individual state.

Issues include whether State A is responsible for the damage to the marine environment and, if so, to whom; whether an individual state or a group of states, though not directly injured, would have standing to assert A's responsibility and claim appropriate relief; and whether the international community could hold State A responsible for the spill and, if so, how the response of the community should be organized. Similar issues would be presented by other forms of pollution of the commons (such as nuclear weapons tests in the atmosphere, resulting in fallout into the high seas; or dumping of hazardous waste in Antarctica) and by destruction of common resource (e.g., taking of dolphins, whales, or highly migratory fish species in an unsustainable way; or extermination of a species located wholly within national borders).

Paradigm 3. Company X, incorporated under the laws of State A, establishes a chemical manufacturing subsidiary in State B. The subsidiary's plant explodes, causing deaths, widespread injuries and property damage in State B.

Issues include whether State A is responsible to State B; and whether individuals having suffered legal injuries in State B can bring actions against State A or Company X and, if so, where.

Note and Questions

The importance of the location of the act and the harm. Professor Christopher Stone observes that the

> division of the planet into regions of separate political significance has enormous significance for the global environment. . . . Given the prevailing framework of international law, the legal and diplomatic response available [to environmental harm] depends to a considerable extent upon the location of the hazarding actions and of the threatened injury, with reference to [the] twofold division into national territory and common areas.

Christopher Stone, The Gnat Is Older Than Man: Global Environment and Human Agenda 36 (1993). Professor Stone illustrates "five possible combinations of (1) where the harm-threatening activity occurs, and (2) where the harm is concentrated" in the following table.

Combinations of Act and Harm Sites

Site of act	*Site of harm*	*Example*
(1) Nation A	Nation A	A destroys a wholly internal critical habitat
(2) Nation A	Nation B	A's radioactive debris blows across the boundary into neighboring B
(3) Nation A	Commons	A's sewage invades the high seas
(4) Commons	Commons	A overfishes the high seas
(5) Commons	Nation B	A's tankers discharge wastes on the high seas, which invade B's beaches

Stone, above, at 37.

As you study the foregoing matrix, consider which states or other international actors must participate in the solution to the environmental problem in question. For example, do other states have an interest in (or any rights concerning) situation number (1)? What if the "wholly internal critical habitat" is a national park that has been designated by UNESCO as a World Heritage Site? What about situation (3)? Do any states have a right to protest against A? Must all states participate in the protest in order to obtain relief from A? How could the responses of all (or even some) of the states seeking relief be organized? Need they be organized? That is, could (should) each state wishing to defend the commons take unilateral measures against A? You should consider these questions as you study the materials in this chapter, as well as the related materials in chapter 20.

B. GENERAL PRINCIPLES OF INTERNATIONAL RESPONSIBILITY FOR ENVIRONMENTAL HARM

■ FORMS OF INTERNATIONAL RESPONSIBILITY FOR ENVIRONMENTAL HARM

Riccardo Pisillo-Mazzeschi
in International Responsibility for Environmental Harm 15, 15, 16-17, 29, 34-35 (Francesco Francioni & Tullio Scovazzi eds. 1991)

. . . [W]e must first clarify what forms, theoretically and generally, the international responsibility of States may take. In this regard, we can basically identify three different regimes of responsibility for a wrongful act and one regime of liability without a wrongful act.

The first regime of responsibility for a wrongful act is the one of fault responsibility. According to the traditional view, such regime is characterized by the fact that it is up to the victim State to prove, in addition to the breach of the international obligation, the psychological fault (wilful or negligent conduct) of the organs of the State accused of the wrongful act. According, instead, to a different thesis, and one which I prefer, emphasis must be placed on the content of a particular category of primary obligations of the State and therefore one must speak of a regime of responsibility for breach of due diligence obligations (considering due diligence as an objective and international standard of behaviour).

Fault responsibility is in contrast to objective responsibility (or responsibility without fault). In the traditional view, the latter is characterized by the fact that responsibility does not require fault, but arises from the mere breach of an international obligation. We can identify two different regimes of objective responsibility: objective and relative responsibility (or strict responsibility), when the State accused of the wrongful act may invoke one of the circumstances precluding wrongfulness allowed by international law; and objective and absolute responsibility, when no circumstance precluding wrongfulness is allowed. Instead, in the view which I prefer, which looks at the problem from the perspective of primary rules, one should not speak of objective (relative or absolute) responsibility, but of responsibility for breach of obligations of result (relative or absolute), understood as obligations in contrast with due diligence obligations.

Lastly, as we mentioned at the outset, alongside these three different forms of responsibility for a wrongful act, there must also be allowed the possibility of a regime of liability without a wrongful act. Such regime is characterized by the fact that the obligation to pay compensation, or, more generally, liability, arises from lawful activities, on the basis of the mere causal link between these activities and the damage done. For this reason, such form of liability is, by its own nature, objective and absolute.

Liability without a wrongful act must be clearly contrasted to responsibility for a wrongful act, in the three possible forms we have described. Instead, in the doctrine there is often conceptual and terminological confusion. Indeed, many authors, in referring to liability without a wrongful act, speak of objective responsibility or of strict responsibility. In this way, they erroneously assume that the distinction between responsibility for a wrongful act and liability without a wrongful act corresponds to the distinction between fault responsibility and responsibility without fault. . . .

[State] Practice

In short, we can say that there exists today a general rule of international law that binds the States to oversee activities within their jurisdiction or control, so that such activities do not cause significant environmental harm either to the territory or resources of other States or to common spaces and resources. The breach of this rule may occur either "directly" owing to wrongful behaviour of State organs, or of dependent agencies and bodies of the State, or "indirectly" owing to the State's breach of the obligation to prevent and repress the polluting activities of private persons. However, in both cases the obligations of the State appear limited by the rule of due diligence. . . .

Conclusions

In the first place, the practice shows that there now exist, in general international law, real and binding primary obligations of the States on the protection of the environment, whose breach involves responsibility for a wrongful act.

Secondly, the practice shows that such obligations are limited by the due diligence rule. This is particularly evident in the most common situation, regarding environmental harm, which concerns State responsibility in relation to acts of private persons. In this area, State obligations appear as typical obligations of protection, which require active behaviour by the State which materializes in activities of prevention and repression; and whose breach determines responsibility for omission. It is therefore not surprising that such obligations are limited by the due diligence rule, as is true for obligations of protection also in other areas of international law, such as those concerning the protection of aliens and representatives of foreign States or the protection of the security of foreign States.

However, even in the more uncommon situation of responsibility of the State for its own conduct, that is to say, for wrongful acts "directly" committed by State organs, or by agencies and bodies dependent on the State, responsibility occurs for breach of due diligence obligations. This happens because, as far as protection of the environment is concerned, general international law does *not* require the State to refrain from carrying out technological or industrial activities that might cause [transboundary] environmental harm, since such activities are considered, in themselves, lawful; on the contrary it requires the State only to take the necessary measures to ensure that such activities do not create significant environmental harm. In other words, international law does *not* assume that State activities causing transnational damage are thereby to be considered unlawful.

In short, in both the above situations, international law does *not* place on the States a negative obligation to refrain, but rather a positive obligation to protect. But the active measures that the State must adopt cannot, obviously, in this matter guarantee a certain result, seeing that the result depends also on objective elements that are strongly unpredictable. Therefore it is logical that international law may place on the State only the obligation to "make every effort" to reach this result[, i.e.,] a due diligence obligation. . . .

To conclude, we should make a final consideration regarding the degree of due diligence required for ultra-hazardous activities. With regard to these activities, the general rule on the flexibility of diligence regarding possible damage requires the State to exercise a particularly high degree of diligence in prevention. In this case, the due diligence obligation strongly tends to approach an obligation of result: that is, to create a situation of presumption unfavourable to the damaging State. In other words, the high degree of due diligence required of the State leads to an inversion of the burden of proof; that is, unless there is proof to the contrary, the damaging State is considered as having breached its own due diligence obligations.

Further reading: For further discussions of general rules of international responsibility for environmental harm, *see, e.g.,* International Responsibility for Environmental Harm (Francesco Francioni & Tullio Scovazzi, eds. 1991); Jutta Brunnée, Acid Rain and Ozone Layer Depletion: International Law and Regulation 112-121 (1988); Lothar Gündling, Verantwortlichkeit der Staaten für grenzüberschreitende Umweltbeeinträchtigungen, 45 Zeitschrift für Ausländisches Öffentliches Recht und Völkerrecht 264 (1985); Alfred Rest, Responsibility and Liability for Transboundary Pollution Damage, in eds., Transboundary Air Pollution 299 (C. Flinterman, B. Kwiatkowska, & J. Lammers 1986); Alfred Rest, Ecological Damage in Public International Law, 22 Environmental Policy and Law 31 (1992); Günther Handl, State Liability for Accidental Transnational Environmental Damage by Private Persons, 74 Am. J. Intl. L. 525 (1980); K.R. Hoffman, State Responsibility in International Law and Transboundary Pollution Injuries, 25 Intl. & Comp. L.Q. 509 (1976); and OECD, Responsibilities and Liability of States in Relation to Transfrontier Pollution (1979).

■ FINAL REPORT OF THE EXPERTS GROUP ON ENVIRONMENTAL LAW ON LEGAL PRINCIPLES FOR ENVIRONMENTAL PROTECTION AND SUSTAINABLE DEVELOPMENT, ARTICLES 11, 12, AND 21

with excerpts from commentaries,* in *Experts Group on Environmental Law of the World Commission on Environment and Development (Brundtland Commission), Environmental Protection and Sustainable Development 80-82, 85-88, 119-120, 127-130 (1987)

Article 11
Liability for Transboundary Environmental Interferences Resulting from Lawful Activities

1. If one or more activities create a significant risk of substantial harm as a result of a transboundary environmental interference, and if the overall technical and socio-economic cost or loss of benefits involved in preventing or reducing such risk far exceeds in the long run the advantage which such

prevention or reduction would entail, the State which carried out or permitted the activities shall ensure that compensation is provided should substantial harm occur in an area under national jurisdiction of another State or in an area beyond the limits of national jurisdiction.

2. A state shall ensure that compensation is provided for substantial harm caused by transboundary environmental interferences resulting from activities carried out or permitted by that State notwithstanding that the activities were not initially known to cause such interferences.

Comment

The provisions contained in this article constitute an exception to the basic principle laid down in Article 10.[8]

Paragraph 1 provides that the duty of a State to prevent or abate activities which create a significant risk of substantial harm as a result of a transboundary environmental interference does not exist if the overall technical and socio-economic cost or loss of benefits involved in preventing or reducing such risk far exceeds in the long run the advantage which such prevention or reduction would entail. However, the State which carried out or permitted the activities shall ensure that compensation is provided should substantial harm occur in . . . another State or . . . beyond the limits of national jurisdiction. . . .

It may be that the cost or loss of benefits involved so far exceeds in the long run the advantage which the prevention or reduction of the risk of substantial harm would entail that it is not warranted to make such cost or sustain such loss of benefits. The price to be paid for the right to continue with or undertake the activity, however, is a duty for the State of origin . . . to ensure that compensation is provided for the substantial harm which is actually caused in . . . another State or . . . beyond the limits of national jurisdiction.

This obligation to ensure that compensation is provided constitutes an instance of strict liability *under international law,* to the extent that the State of origin is financially liable vis-à-vis the victim State for the harmful consequences of an act not prohibited under international law. . . .

Such liability may arise for activities which involve a risk of causing extraterritorial harm of a possibly exceptionally serious dimension, i.e. for so-called ultrahazardous activities.

Strict liability of States under international law in respect of ultrahazardous activities has been accepted in a few treaties, viz., the well-known 1972 Convention on Liability for Damage Caused by Objects Launched into Outer Space, and, the less well-known, 1973 Treaty between Argentina and

8. [It will be recalled that Article 10, *supra,* provides in its entirety that: "States shall, without prejudice to the principles laid down in Articles 11 and 12, prevent or abate any transboundary environmental interference or a significant risk thereof which causes substantial harm—i.e. harm which is not minor or insignificant." Experts Group Report at p. 75.]

Uruguay concerning the La Plata River and its Maritime Limits (Article 51 concerning water pollution). . . .

. . . [S]trict liability *under national law* has been accepted by many States in various treaties and in their national legislation or judicial decisions for certain ultrahazardous activities. In these cases strict liability is imposed on operators or owners of installations, aircraft[] or vessels, that create the risk. . . .

Note

Evaluating Article 11. Professor Sanford E. Gaines, in an article entitled Taking Responsibility for Transboundary Environmental Effects, 14 Hastings Intl. & Comp. L. Rev. 781 (1991), offers a critique of the legal principles elaborated by the Legal Experts Group of the Brundtland Commission. He has the following comments on Article 11:[9]

> Article 11 addresses the matter of liability for transboundary environmental harms within the context established by article 10 [reproduced in Chapter 7.A]. . . . Article 10 . . . must be read as creating a perfectly symmetrical system in which the following occur: (1) all activities that create substantial harm are by definition unlawful, and compensation is therefore owed for the resulting harms; and (2) activities creating less than substantial harm are lawful, and there is no independent obligation to compensate for insubstantial harm. . . .
>
> Article 11 should be interpreted, therefore, as providing two limited exceptions in which compensation should be provided even though the harm-causing activity was lawful under the terms of article 10. . . .
>
> The second limited exception created by article 11 allows one state to create a significant risk of substantial harm to another when the "overall technical and socio-economic cost" of preventing or abating the risk "far exceeds in the long run the advantage which such prevention or reduction would entail." This allowance to create transboundary risk of harm is subject to the condition that the state ensure that compensation is provided should substantial harm in fact occur.
>
> Although this bespeaks a doctrine of strict liability for all foreseeable harms from environmental interferences, the commentary illustrates strict liability through references to generally recognized international law precedents and selected national law principles, all of which limit strict liability to ultrahazardous activities. The commentary thus raises a substantial . . . doubt whether the experts intended an obligation to provide compensation for nonultrahazardous activities that might create a significant risk of substantial harm that is costly to prevent, such as sulfur dioxide emissions from power plants.
>
> The traditional international law concept of strict liability has become

9. 14 Hastings Intl. & Comp. L. Rev. 781, 801, 802-805 (1991) (footnotes omitted).

an obstructive anachronism in the environmental field and should be discarded in favor of the emerging principle in state practice of strict polluter liability for all remediation costs and natural resource damages. In U.S. environmental law, concepts of strict liability extend far beyond ultrahazardous activities, and cost-benefit analyses are not favored as defenses to liability where the risks were known and preventable. . . .

Even if article 11 is read broadly to invoke strict liability for any substantial harm resulting from any activity creating a significant risk of harm from environmental interference, it is still shackled by its built-in cost-benefit test. One can only hope that the Experts Group['s] use of a cost-benefit test represents a deviation from the main trend of international law, induced perhaps by the political and scholarly fascination with cost-benefit and risk-benefit analysis in the early 1980s. Such a test should have no reserved seat in the house of international liability law, though it might be applied as part of a balance of interests evaluation in appropriate cases. Particularly with respect to transboundary interferences that involve nations in different circumstances [i.e., activities in one country affecting a neighboring country of different development level], a cost-benefit approach will almost always favor the wealthy nation at the expense of the impoverished nation because of the higher value of every economic activity in a highly developed economy.

Even in scenarios involving roughly equivalent parties on both sides, cost-benefit analysis has profound flaws that make it unsuitable for environmental liability analysis. First, it continues to be much easier to count costs or benefits associated with commercial and industrial activities (which typically have very precise accounting systems) than it is to count the costs (or benefits) associated with human health, ecological values, or aesthetic values.

Second, cost-benefit analysis of long-term activities and effects, which is what article 11 explicitly calls for, relies on discount rates to reduce all factors to constant dollars. Discount rates effectively shorten the time horizon of the analysis because costs and benefits more than fifteen or twenty years in the future have a negligible effect on the calculation. Thus, the technique does not fully account for effects on the current generation, and future generations do not enter into the calculation at all. Eminent ecologists and some economists have raised a strong protest against the cost-benefit approach because of the inherent bias of the analysis in favor of the short-term consequences.[10]

10. The most influential group to speak out on this issue is the Science Advisory Board of the U.S. Environmental Protection Agency. In their provocative report on setting priorities and strategies for environmental protection, delivered in September 1990 . . . , the science advisors made improvements in methods for valuing natural resources and long-term effects one of their top ten priorities. As they summarized the problem:

> Traditional forms of economic analysis, as applied to the costs and benefits of economic development and environmental protection, have systematically undervalued natural resources. This practice threatens the world's natural resources—like estuaries and rainforests—without which the lives of future generations will be impoverished. The failure of current analytical techniques to estimate properly either the full benefits of natural ecosystems or the full costs of activities that degrade them too often has allowed the justification of long-term ecological degradation for the sake of present gain.

U.S. Envtl. Protection Agency Science Advisory Board, Reducing Risk: Setting Priorities and Strategies for Environmental Protection 25 (1990).

Third, the whole notion of cost-benefit compromises has the semblance of betrayal. The experts declare the paramount environmental protection principles, and then propose the cost-benefit test. The time has come, as the WCED itself has said, "to break out of past patterns." Our past patterns have included an overwhelming emphasis on technical and socioeconomic costs and benefits to the neglect of the ecological infrastructure. To allow those same technical and socioeconomic considerations to become the justification for imposing, albeit with monetary compensation, substantial environmental harm on other countries is to perpetuate, not to break with, the past patterns that have brought us to our current juncture. Every legal principle, including principles granting opportunities to take risks and principles defining the permissible depletion or degradation of nonrenewable resources, must reflect and express a full integration of economic desires with the imperative need to maintain and, if at all possible, revitalize, local and global ecosystems.

While the fact that an activity creates merely a risk of harm rather than an immediate harm should not be allowed to become an excuse for ignoring the basic responsibility to respect the environmental integrity of other nations, neither should countries be liable for engaging in risky activities as if they were sure to cause the worst potential injury. . . . [A]n orientation of liability toward risk might detract from, or even supplant entirely, liability's principal focus on legal responsibility for manifest harms.

■ FINAL REPORT OF THE EXPERTS GROUP ON ENVIRONMENTAL LAW ON LEGAL PRINCIPLES FOR ENVIRONMENTAL PROTECTION AND SUSTAINABLE DEVELOPMENT

with excerpts from commentaries,* in *Experts Group on Environmental Law of the World Commission on Environment and Development (Brundtland Commission), Environmental protection and Sustainable Development 80-82, 85-88, 119-120, 127-130 (1987)

Article 12
Transboundary Environmental Interferences Involving Substantial Harm Far Less Than Cost of Prevention

1. If a State is planning to carry out or permit an activity which will entail a transboundary environmental interference causing harm which is substantial but far less than the overall technical and socioeconomic cost or loss of benefits involved in preventing or reducing such interference, such State shall enter into negotiations with the affected State on the equitable conditions, both technical and financial, under which the activity could be carried out.

2. In the event of a failure to reach a solution on the basis of equitable principles within a period of 18 months after the beginning of the negotiations or within any other period of time agreed upon by the States concerned, the dispute shall at the request of any of the States concerned, and under the

> conditions set forth in . . . Article 22, be submitted to conciliation or thereafter to arbitration or judicial settlement in order to reach a solution on the basis of equitable principles.

Comment

Article 12 deals with the case that a State is planning to carry out or permit an activity which will entail a transboundary environmental interference which causes harm which is substantial but far less than the overall technical and socio-economic cost or loss of benefits involved in preventing or reducing such interference. The activity envisaged here differs from those dealt with in Paragraph 1 of Article 11 in that it concerns an activity of which it is foreseeable [that] it will *definitely* cause substantial harm in an area under the national jurisdiction of another State or in an area beyond the limits of national jurisdiction, while the activities dealt with in Paragraph 1 of Article 11 "merely" involve a risk of causing extraterritorial harm of a possibly exceptionally serious dimension, i.e. concern of so-called ultrahazardous activities. . . .

. . . As we have . . . seen, the State who carries out or permits . . . ultrahazardous activities must ensure that compensation is provided should substantial extraterritorial harm occur. This is, in fact, nothing else than the fair and equitable price which ought to be paid for the lawful continuation of an ultrahazardous activity which, on balance, must still be regarded as predominantly beneficial. It may be wondered whether the same principle should not apply to the type of activity envisaged in the present article, i.e. that it could invariably be lawfully undertaken provided payment of compensation is ensured.

Little support can be found for this in the international practice of States, possibly because situations calling for the application of that principle have so far occurred only rarely. . . .

However, the application of the principle of strict liability—and the idea of balancing of interests which it implies—to activities *definitely* causing substantial extraterritorial harm, is generally regarded as considerably more revolutionary than the application of that principle to activities which "merely" involve a significant risk of harm as envisaged in Paragraph 1 of Article 11.

. . . Article 12 . . . exempts the activity dealt with in that article from the operation of Article 10, which would otherwise apply to it. Thus, in spite of the fact that the activity would cause substantial extraterritorial harm, it is not regarded either as clearly unlawful, or as clearly lawful. Instead a duty to negotiate on the equitable conditions under which the activity could take place has been provided for.

Article 12 implies that, if the activity concerned is in fact to be carried out, the State who carries out or permits the activity must ensure that compensation—financial or in kind—is provided for as indemnification for the substantial harm caused. . . .

Note

Evaluating Article 12. Professor Gaines has the following comments on Article 12:[11]

> Article 12, if implemented, might emerge as the most powerful of all the principles in the Experts Group's report. Although it legitimizes one nation's plan to authorize the otherwise unlawful imposition of substantial transboundary harm, it compels a process through which the potentially affected countries have an opportunity to influence the planning, siting, design, emergency response, and financial assurances aspects of the project. It is difficult to gauge the true import of article 12, however, because it leaves many critical issues unresolved.
>
> The most fundamental question unresolved by article 12 is whether the requirement for the acting state to negotiate gives the receiving state the power to veto the project.[12] Although the commentary does not allude to this question at all, the legitimacy that the article gives to the planned activity suggests that the article intends the acting state's right to engage in the activity to take precedence over any right in the affected state to be free of interference. [I]t seems better to reverse the ranking of these rights and establish the right to be free of environmental interferences imposed by others as a paramount right subject to curtailment only in compelling circumstances.
>
> Another matter left open is whether compensation must be paid or is simply a topic for negotiation. The commentary, observing that the article implies an obligation to ensure compensation, goes on to conclude that compensation "must always be provided for if the activity . . . is to be carried out or permitted." Would it be sufficient for the acting state to create an insurance fund to compensate for possible injuries? Why should the principle restrict the affected state's option to trade away some or all of the compensation in return for other benefits, such as risk abatement measures?
>
> The article itself gives no clue as to what equitable conditions should shape the course of negotiations or arbitration, and the commentary sheds no additional light on this critical phrase. Is facility location, for example, entirely at the acting state's discretion, or is it an appropriate equitable factor for the affected state to bargain over? Suppose that from the affected state's point of view the whole project looks like a pork barrel project with no real economic justification; who gets to judge the merits of the planned activity, and by what information? Is linkage with other projects on either side of the boundary acceptable as part of the broader equity between the two states?
>
> Another intriguing open question arises [in the case of] long-range environmental interferences. How far does the obligation to negotiate extend? One presumes, for example, that article 12 would require France to negotiate with Germany if France wanted to build a dam on the Rhine River near Strasbourg. Would article 12 require France to negotiate with the Netherlands as well? If we count acid rain as a substantial harm, does the

11. Gaines, above, at 805-807.
12. [You will recall that this question was addressed in the *Lake Lanoux* Award.—EDS.]

United States have to negotiate with Canada before issuing permits for a coal-burning power plant in Kentucky? Does Brazil need to negotiate with the Maldives if it plans to clearcut a section of the Amazon because the forest loss will enhance global warming that threatens, quite literally, the national security of the Maldives?

■ FINAL REPORT OF THE EXPERTS GROUP ON ENVIRONMENTAL LAW ON LEGAL PRINCIPLES FOR ENVIRONMENTAL PROTECTION AND SUSTAINABLE DEVELOPMENT

with excerpts from commentaries,* in *Experts Group on Environmental law of the World Commission on Environment and Development (Brundtland Commission), Environmental protection and Sustainable Development 80-82, 85-88, 119-120, 127-130 (1987)

Article 21
[State Responsibility][13]

1. A State is responsible under international law for a breach of an international obligation relating to the use of a natural resource or the prevention or abatement of an environmental interference.

2. In particular, it shall:

(a) cease the internationally wrongful act;

(b) as far as possible, re-establish the situation which would have existed if the internationally wrongful act had not taken place;

(c) provide compensation for the harm which results from the internationally wrongful act;

(d) where appropriate, give satisfaction for the internationally wrongful act.

Comment

. . . [Article 21] provides that in the event of a breach of [the mentioned] obligations, the State will incur so-called State responsibility, i.e. become answerable for the consequences which international law attaches to breaches of international law. . . .

Restitution in kind, specific restitution or *restitutio in integrum* purports to re-establish the situation which would have existed if the wrongful conduct had not taken place. It is this form of reparation to which the victim State appears to be primarily entitled. . . . "[R]eparation must, in so far as possible, wipe out all the consequences of the illegal act."[14] Thus, restitution may, e.g. require measures to restore a depleted fish population or to clean the bed and banks of a watercourse. However, restitution is often

13. Article 21 is untitled but is the only article contained in the section of the Report entitled "State Responsibility."

14. [The quotation is from the well-known decision of the Permanent Court of International Justice in the *Chorzow Factory* Case (Merits), P.C.I.J., Ser. A, No. 17, at 47 (1928).—Eds.]

not, or only partially, possible, or, when possible, is not requested by the injured State or is only capable of being effected by public authorities or persons in the injured State. In those cases compensation will be a proper remedy.

. . . Well known is the payment of compensation by Canada for the injury inflicted in the state of Washington in the United States by air pollution caused by a zinc and lead smelter in *Trail* (Canada). . . .

Another instance of a duty to pay compensation is to be found in the decision of the District Court of Rotterdam of December 1983 in the *Mines Domaniales de Potasse d'Alsace case.* Here the defendant was not [a] State but state-owned potassium mines which were ordered to pay compensation for the transboundary harm caused to Dutch market gardeners as a result of the discharge by the defendant of waste salts into the Rhine in France. It is noteworthy that the court based its decision, inter alia, on an established breach of international law by the potassium mines.

A brief observation may finally be made on the third form of reparation besides *restitutio in integrum* and compensation, i.e. satisfaction. This constitutes a remedy for moral or political injury caused to another State. In contemporary international law and practice, satisfaction usually takes the form of a presentation of official regrets or apologies, of penal or disciplinary measures against guilty minor officials, or of a declaration by an international court or arbitral tribunal that an internationally wrongful act has been committed.

■ RESTATEMENT (THIRD) OF THE FOREIGN RELATIONS LAW OF THE UNITED STATES, §601(2), (3) (1987)

§601. State Obligations with Respect to Environment of Other Sates and the Common Environment

. . .

(2) A state is responsible to all other states

(a) for any violation of its obligations under Subsection (1)(a), and

(b) for any significant injury, resulting from such violation, to the environment of areas beyond the limits of national jurisdiction.

(3) A state is responsible for any significant injury, resulting from a violation of its obligations under Subsection (1), to the environment of another state or to its property, or to persons or property within that state's territory or under its jurisdiction or control.

Notes and Questions

1. *Responsibility to everyone?* With regard to §601(2), would a state really be "responsible to *all* other states" for every kind of breach of the

obligations under subsection (1)(a) (reproduced in Chapter 7, above)? For example, would the United States be responsible to the entire international community for causing transfrontier water pollution damage to the environment of Mexico in violation of subsection (1)(a)?

2. *To whom does the right run (continued)?* Comment *b* to §601 states that: "Where an international rule or standard has been violated, *any state* can object to the violation; where a state has been injured in consequence of such violation, it is entitled to damages or other appropriate relief from the responsible state. . . ." Restatement Third, above, §601, comment *b*(emphasis added). This would seem to mean that according to the Restatement, the "international rules and standards" referred to in §601 constitute obligations *erga omnes*—obligations owed to the entire international community. Such a position would stand in sharp contrast to the way in which obligations *erga omnes* were characterized by the International Court of Justice in the *Barcelona Traction* case, 1970 I.C.J. Rep. 3. The examples of such obligations cited by the court in that case include those deriving "from the outlawing of acts of aggression, and of genocide, as also from the principles and rules concerning the basic rights of the human person, including protection from slavery and racial discrimination." *Id.*, para. 34. These examples indicate that obligations *erga omnes* are only those that are of essential importance to the international community, something that cannot be said about every violation of every "international rule and standard." The Restatement itself, in a comment to §902, Interstate Claims and Remedies, states that "any state may call on the violating state to terminate a significant injury *to the general environment*. . . ." Restatement Third, above, §902, comment *a*. Is a state's responsibility to "all other states" limited by the terms of §601 to injuries to "the general environment," whatever that term may mean?

■ RESTATEMENT (THIRD) OF THE FOREIGN RELATIONS LAW OF THE UNITED STATES, §602 (1) (1987)

§602. Remedies for Violation of Environmental Obligations

(1) A state responsible to another state for violation of §601 is subject to general interstate remedies (§902) to prevent, reduce, or terminate the activity threatening or causing the violation, and to pay reparation for injury caused. . . .

Comment

a. *International law remedies.* The remedies referred to in Subsection (1) usually begin with a protest against the violation, accompanied by a demand that the offending state terminate the violation, desist from further violations, and make reparation for past violations. If the matter is not resolved by diplomatic negotiations, the aggrieved state may resort to agreed third-party procedures, such as conciliation, mediation, arbitration, or adjudication. Some neighboring states have established international joint commissions to deal with transboundary problems, including pollution, but usually such commissions can only make recommendations. Strictly limited and reasonable measures of "self help" may be permitted in special circumstances. . . . Remedies under international law are to the injured state; whether that state is obligated to pay any reparation received over to any injured person in its territory is a matter of its domestic law. . . .

Remedies under this section are available for injury to a state's environmental interests within its territory as well as to interests beyond its territory, such as injury to its fishing interests on the high seas; it may pursue remedies, not only for injury to state interests but also to those of its political subdivisions or of its inhabitants or nationals. A state may also pursue appropriate remedies for injury to the common interest in the global commons, such as the high seas.

Even where reparations for past injuries are not appropriate or feasible, a state may demand that violations be discontinued.

b. *Local remedies.* A state responsible for transfrontier pollution can fulfill its obligation to inhabitants of other states who suffered injuries by giving them access to its tribunals for adjudication of their claims. If such local remedies are available, the person who suffered injuries must exhaust these remedies before the state of which he is a national can bring an international claim on his behalf under Subsection (1). . . . The two states, however, may agree at any time to settle the claim or include it in a lump-sum settlement. . . .

■ INTERNATIONAL LAW AND THE ENVIRONMENT

Patricia W. Birnie & Alan E. Boyle
136-137 (1992)

There are various disadvantages to enforcing international environmental law [through the traditional approach of interstate claims based on the principle of state responsibility], particularly if it involves compulsory resort to judicial institutions. These disadvantages include the adverse effect on relations between the states concerned; the complexity, length, and expense of many international proceedings; the technical character of environmental problems and the difficulties of proof which legal proceedings may entail; and the unpredictable outcome of litigation, a consequence of the unsettled character of much of the law on this subject. Perhaps the most significant objection is that the traditional model exemplified by the *Trail Smelter* case is concerned largely with affording reparation or other remedies as a response to violations of international law. Such a system is inherently bilateral and confrontational in character: it assumes that "injured states" whose rights are affected are the primary actors in seeking compliance with legal standards of environmental protection. Its closest analogy in national legal systems is the law of tort, and adjudication is the method of dispute settlement to which it is most suited.

Claims for transboundary pollution damage are thus the most obvious application for this approach, yet in practice even here the obstacles are such that states have preferred to avoid the law of state responsibility and to rely on other methods of establishing liability using national law. . . . No modern pollution disaster, including Chernobyl, Sandoz, or the *Amoco Cadiz* has resulted in the adjudication of an international claim against the state concerned; the case law is thus sparse and increasingly old. Efforts by the [International Law Commission of the United Nations (ILC)] to develop and reform the law relating to state liability for environmental injury are controversial and of little appeal. The main reason for discussing the subject at all . . . is thus not its immediate practical utility but because an understanding of what it can and cannot offer is essential to an explanation of other developments in the international legal system which have largely taken its place. Moreover, as environmental problems worsen, the possibility that states might have recourse to international claims against their neighbours may itself exercise an influence on the negotiation of environmental agreements and the settlement of disputes. It is thus not to be entirely discounted.

The "Polluter Pays Principle (PPP)." In 1972 the Council of the Organisation for Economic Cooperation and Development (OECD)—whose members include Western industrialized countries—adopted the "Polluter Pays Principle," or PPP, which concerns the internalization of pollution-control costs. OECD, Guiding Principles Concerning International Economic Aspects of Environmental Policies, Recommendation C(72) 128, para. 4, adopted May 26, 1972, *reprinted in* 11 I.L.M. 1172 (1972). It provides as follows:

> The principle to be used for allocating costs of pollution prevention and control measures to encourage rational use of scarce environmental resources and to avoid distortions in international trade and investment is the so-called "Polluter-Pays-Principle." This Principle means that the polluter should bear the expenses of carrying out the [pollution control] measures decided by public authorities to ensure that the environment is in an acceptable state. In other words, the cost of these measures should be reflected in the cost of goods and services which cause pollution in the production and/or consumption. Such measures should not be accompanied by subsidies that would create significant distortions in international trade and investment.

Notes and Questions

1. *A principle of prevention or liability?* It is evident that this principle concerns accountability *ex ante* rather than *ex post.* That is, the PPP is not a rule of law requiring a polluter to pay compensation to one who has been harmed by its pollution. The PPP is instead intended as a principle of economic policy to be implemented on the domestic level to insure that what would otherwise be "externalities" of economic activities are internalized, so that the cost of pollution control measures are reflected in the price of the item produced by the activity. Thus, rather than dumping waste into a river or sending it through a smokestack into the air—imposing external costs on society and the environment—the PPP calls for an activity to treat the waste before discharging it, to install scrubbers on its smokestacks, and the like. These may be expensive measures and may well cut into the profits of the activity. But the OECD takes the position that if the consumers of the product are not willing to pay for *all* of its costs (i.e., cost of production + profit + cleanup costs), the activity should not be considered economically viable. The seminal discussion of how the law should deal with the social costs of economic activities is Ronald Coase, The Problem of Social Cost, 3 J. Law & Econ. 1 (1960).

2. *Who really pays?* Is it really the "polluter" who pays under the PPP? In German the PPP is translated as the "Verursacherprinzip," the "Verursacher" being the one who *causes* the pollution. Who *does* cause the pollution generated by economic activities? Is it acceptable for a firm to pass the costs of pollution prevention through to the consumers of its product? *See* OECD, Note on the Implementation of the Polluter-Pays Principle, OECD Doc. Env. (73)32, adopted Jan. 21 1974, *reprinted in* 14 I.L.M. 238, 239 (1975), which states: "From the point of view of conformity with the PPP, it does not matter whether the polluter passes on [to consumers] some or all of the environment costs or absorbs them."

3. *The transmogrification of the PPP.* There is, understandably, considerable confusion about the meaning of the PPP. It is taken by some as an *ex post* principle of liability, requiring that compensation be paid to pollution victims. While this was not the original intent of the PPP, it has evolved considerably, especially in Europe. For a discussion of the evolution of the PPP, *see* Sanford E. Gaines, The Polluter-Pays Principle: From Economic Equity to Environmental Ethos, 26 Tex. Intl. L.J. 463, 471-487 (1991). For example, Principle 5 of the European Community's Principles of a Community Environment Policy, adopted in 1973, provides: "The cost of preventing and eliminating nuisances must in principle be borne by the polluter." 16 O.J. Eur. Comm. (No. C 112) 6 (1973). And Article 25 of the Single European Act provides:

> Action by the Community relating to the environment shall be based on the principles that preventive action should be taken, that environmental

damage should as a priority be rectified at source, and that the polluter should pay.

Cmnd. 9758 (1986). This provision establishes a legal basis for environmental action by the European Union, thus taking the PPP a step beyond the nonbinding measures pioneered by the OECD. For a discussion of how the OECD and the European Community began in the late 1980s to apply the PPP to liability for environmental harm, *see* Gaines, above, in this note, 481-487.

4. *The PPP, the OECD and liability.* The OECD has itself applied the PPP to the post-event costs of accidental pollution. On July 25, 1989, the OECD Council adopted a Recommendation on the Application of the Polluter-Pays Principle to Accidental Pollution, O.E.C.D. Doc. C(89) 88 (Final), July 25, 1989, *reprinted in* 28 I.L.M. 1320 (1989). According to the Guiding Principles Relating to Accidental Pollution annexed to that Recommendation, "[d]omestic law which provides that the cost of reasonable measures to control accidental pollution after an accident should be collected as expeditiously as possible from the legal or natural person who is at the origin of the accident, is consistent with the Polluter-Pays Principle." *Id.*, para. 5. But "[i]f the accidental pollution is caused solely by an event for which the operator clearly cannot be considered liable under national law, such as a serious natural disaster that the operator cannot reasonably have foreseen, it is consistent with the Polluter-Pays Principle that public authorities do not charge the cost of control measures to the operator." *Id.*, para. 7.

5. *The PPP and transboundary harm.* The PPP has been applied in transboundary contexts. For example, in the Preamble of the 1992 United Nations Convention on the Transboundary Effects of Industrial Accidents, the parties "Tak[e] into account . . . the polluter-pays principle as a general principle of international environmental law. . . ." Done at Helsinki, March 17, 1992, *reprinted in* 31 I.L.M. 1330 (1992). But it is often the case that, in transboundary pollution contexts, it is the *victim* that pays the polluter to abate pollution. For example, the United States has provided assistance to Mexico to treat sewage in Tijuana that would otherwise be carried north across the border via the Tijuana River to foul beaches in the Southern California city of San Diego. Could these be illustrations of the Coase Theorem?

6. *The PPP at Rio.* A version of the PPP is contained in the Rio Declaration, adopted at the Earth Summit in 1992:

Principle 16

National authorities should endeavour to promote the internalization of environmental costs and the use of economic instruments, taking into account the approach that the polluter should, in principle, bear the cost of pollution, with due regard to the public interest and without distorting international trade and investment.

Rio Declaration on Environment and Development, adopted June 14, 1992, U.N. Doc. A/CONF.151/5/Rev. 1, *reprinted in* 31 I.L.M. 874 (1992). Does this sound to you like a formulation of a "general principle of international environmental law," as the PPP is characterized in the convention referred to in the previous note?

7. *The PPP and climate change.* Would the PPP apply in the context of climate change? If so, how? Professor Gaines in effect suggests that it could, but that it should in that case be based "on notions of moral responsibility, fairness, effectiveness, and international solidarity, rather than on any exaggerated doctrine of a legally enforceable liability." He cites the Multilateral Fund under the Montreal Protocol on Substances That Deplete the Ozone Layer as an example of how such an approach might work. Gaines, above, at 493.

C. APPLICABILITY OF GENERAL PRINCIPLES OF ACCOUNTABILITY TO DEVELOPING COUNTRIES

In section C of Chapter 7 we saw that international environmental obligations often take into account the special situation of developing countries. The question we deal with here is whether similar allowances are made for developing countries in rules of accountability and compliance. To a certain extent this question is addressed by the same sources we considered in the context of norms of prevention. For example, Principle 23 of the Stockholm Declaration speaks in general terms of the need to "consider . . . the extent of the applicability of standards which are valid for the most advanced countries but which may be inappropriate and of unwarranted social cost for the developing countries." And Principle 7 of the Rio Declaration embodies the concept of "common but differentiated responsibilities." Neither of these provisions is confined, by its terms, to the primary obligations of states—obligations to reduce greenhouse gas emissions, to prevent specified levels of bycatch of sea turtles in tuna fishing or to prevent harmful transboundary water pollution, for example. They could apply as well to the issue of whether and to what extent a developing country is legally responsible or accountable for certain conduct. It may even be the case that a question of responsibility or accountability of a developing country would not arise in respect of a given norm simply because the norm is so flexible that it could not be said to have been "breached" in the formal sense. This point may in effect be raised by a country as a defense to a diplomatic claim that the country had breached a particular obligation—for example, a norm providing that states are to "exercise their best efforts," use "all appropriate means," or "the best practicable means at their disposal and in accordance with their capabilities,"[15] or "exercise due diligence"[16] to bring about a certain state of affairs. A developing country accused of having breached such an obligation could simply respond that it had in fact exercised its best efforts, and the like, and that it had therefore not breached the obligation.

A separate but increasingly important aspect of the treatment of developing countries relates specifically to compliance. Its essence is captured in the phrase, "common but differentiated responsibilities" (e.g., Principle 7 of the Rio Declaration), a concept intended to contribute to the formation of the "new and equitable global partnership" that it is the goal of the Rio Declaration to establish.[17] The "common but differentiated responsibilities" of developing and developed states may be implemented, for example, through delayed compliance timetables, or grace periods, such as those provided for in the Montreal Protocol.[18] Similarly, Article 26 of the 1996 Protocol to the 1972 IMO London Dumping Convention[19] allows states joining the agreement within certain time limits to notify the secretary-general of the IMO that they "will not be able to comply with specific provisions" of the protocol, other than those concerning incineration at sea or dumping of radioactive wastes or other radioactive matter, during a transitional period. Examples of other ways in which this principle is implemented, in respect of compliance, may be found in such instruments as the following: The Climate Change Convention permits a developing country party to fulfil part of its obligation to limit anthropogenic emissions of greenhouse gasses by, inter alia, assisting a developing country party in the implementation of—for example, in complying with—its obligations to maintain its tropical forests.[20] The Convention on Biological Diversity makes the obligations undertaken by developing country parties dependent upon the provision by developed country parties of new and additional financial resources as well as access to and transfer of technology on fair and most favorable terms (e.g., Articles 8(m), 20(2), and especially 20(4)). These actions by developed country parties might be regarded analytically

15. 1982 United Nations Convention on the Law of the Sea, art. 194(1), 21 I.L.M. 1261 (1982).

16. International Law Commission, Draft Articles on the Law of the Non-Navigational Uses of International Watercourses, art. 7(1), 1994 I.L.C. Rep. 236, U.N. Doc. A/49/10 (1994).

17. Rio Declaration, Preamble.

18. *See* the discussion in the excerpt from Daniel Magraw's article in section C of the chapter on Norms of Prevention, above.

19. Convention on the Prevention of Marine Pollution by Dumping of Wastes and Other Matter, 29 December 1972, 1046 U.N.T.S. 120, 26 U.S.T. 2403, 11 I.L.M. 1294 (1973); 1996 Protocol, adopted Nov. 7, 1996, I.M.O. Doc. LC/SM 1/6, Nov. 14, 1996.

20. 1992 U.N. Framework Convention on Climate Change, art. 4(2)(a) and (b).

as conditions precedent to the obligations of developing countries, especially those provided for in the Biodiversity Convention. But they might also be viewed as means by which developed states may assist developing states in complying with those obligations. Some provisions expressly provide for such assistance. For example, under Article 4(5) of the Climate Change Convention, developed countries are to "take all practicable steps to promote, facilitate and finance, as appropriate, the transfer of, or access to, environmentally sound technologies and know-how to other Parties, particularly developing country Parties, to enable them to implement the provisions of the Convention."

Questions

1. *From each according to its ability . . . ?* If developing country A breaches an obligation to country B, resulting in damage to country B, should A's obligations to cease the wrongful conduct and repair the damage (i.e., restore the *status quo ante* or, to the extent that that is not possible, compensate B for its loss) be in any way lessened solely by virtue of the fact that A is a developing country? What would the policy and legal justifications be for such a result?

2. *Environmental assistance.* Why might developed country A consider it to be in its interest to assist developing country B to comply with B's international environmental obligations? Can you think of specific examples of situations in which A's interest might be especially acute?

3. *The case of "economies in transition."* As we have seen above in relation to norms of prevention, the countries with economies in transition (chiefly those in Central and Eastern Europe) have made claims of entitlement to special treatment, akin to that which has been accorded developing countries. Do the same considerations that might support such treatment for these countries in relation to norms of prevention also apply to norms of accountability?

D. THE GLOBAL COMMONS

In section A of this chapter we asked you to consider three paradigms of international environmental harm. The second of these dealt with pollution of the commons—in that case, the sea beyond the limits of national jurisdiction. You were also asked to reflect upon a matrix developed by Professor Christopher Stone, situations two and three of which concern harm to the commons. In this section, we take up those situations.

1. *Case Study: The Wreck of the* Bahia Paraiso[21]

On January 28, 1989, an Argentine ship grounded off the Antarctic Peninsula and began to leak oil into the waters and the coastline of Antarctica, causing that continent's "first major environmental crisis." The 435-foot ship *Bahia Paraiso* was on her way to deliver supplies to the Argentine government's Esperanza research station in Antarctica when rocks in the Bismark Strait tore a 30-foot gash in her hull. She later capsized and sank, spreading a ten-mile slick. The *Bahia Paraiso* carried 250,000 gallons of diesel oil. One week after the accident, an estimated two-thirds of the fuel had leaked into the surrounding sea.

Oil from the wreckage of the *Bahia Paraiso* soon washed ashore, affecting wildlife at the nearby United States research base Palmer Station. Scientists' initial reports were grim. Thousands of krill (small crustaceans that form an essential link in the Antarctic food chain) were found dead along the coast near Palmer Station. Half of the adult skua population had abandoned their nesting grounds, leaving chicks vulnerable to predators. Penguin rookeries near Palmer Station, home to some 24,000 birds, were surrounded by oil. An early survey of 40 penguins found 38 had been "oil dipped." The oil affects the birds' natural insulation and may be deadly if swallowed.

The United States and Argentina both assisted in the cleanup of the oil spill. Immediately following the grounding, the United States dispatched a Navy transport aircraft carrying cleanup equipment. The gear was flown to Chile, where it was rerouted to a supply ship operated by the United States National Science Foundation. The Argentine government sent navy ships to assist in the cleanup effort.

2. *Remedies for Harm to the Commons*

■ THIRD STATE REMEDIES FOR ENVIRONMENTAL DAMAGE TO THE WORLD'S COMMON SPACES

Jonathan I. Charney

in *Francioni & Scovazzi eds.*, supra, *149, 175-177.*

International law imposes on all States certain rights and duties with respect to the environment in the world's common spaces. General customary international law requires that all States behave in a manner so as not to cause harm to the environment of areas beyond the jurisdiction of any state including, *a fortiori*, the high seas, outer space, and the Antarctic.

21. From Jonathan I. Charney, Third State Remedies for Environmental Damage to the World's Common Spaces, in Francioni & Scovazzi eds., below 529–531.

. . . Under some interpretations of traditional international law when no State has suffered a particular injury, no State may seek an international remedy. In the case of the world's common spaces restrictive remedy rules may permit grave injuries to be unredressed. [Professor Charney] argues that a particular injury to a State is not always necessary before a State may pursue an international remedy. In some circumstances international law finds a constructive or theoretical injury to be sufficient for standing. These occasions arise when there is no reasonable alternative to third-State[22] remedies and substantial interests of the international community are at stake. Because there is no particular injury, a third State cannot expect that the full panoply of rights and remedies would be available. The third-State remedy is a measure born of necessity and given no more leeway than that necessity requires.

The notion of third-State remedies is especially important for [common spaces]. Because no State may suffer a particular injury upon the violation of a norm applicable to the world's common spaces, there must exist a third-State remedy or none at all. International law appears to permit all States to remedy violations of legal duties designed to protect the environment of the world's common spaces. A violation of these norms, therefore, provides standing to assert a third-State remedy against the polluting State.

That is not to say that all States are therefore competent to mount against a State accused of harming the environment of a common space the full range of remedies and pretend, as it were, to have suffered a particular injury. Third States may take some steps to protect their interest in the environment of the world's common spaces. A [S]tate certainly may exercise its *droit de regard,* or file diplomatic protests with the responsible [S]tate. These somewhat circumspect measures would doubtless comport with the limited competence possessed by third States. Other, more formidable remedies may or may not be appropriate, depending upon the circumstances.

In the case of the *Bahia Paraiso,* . . . or for that matter in any similar circumstance involving an injury to the environment of the world's common spaces, a careful application of third-State remedies may be appropriate. Indeed, if there ever were a case to be made for third-State remedies, it is present in matters like the *Bahia Paraiso* tragedy. Here, international law has imposed certain obligations on all States with respect to the Antarctic and the marine environments. A breach of these obligations affects the interests of the entire community of States. The exercise of third-State remedies in this context is especially appropriate given their necessity. No other form of remedy is available due to the absence of a particularly injured State. Furthermore, the subject-matter is of distinctly universal concern—Antarctica has been called the common heritage of mankind. . . . In sum, the resort to limited third-State remedies in situations

22. [A "third State" is a State that has suffered no direct, particular injury.—Eds.]

where the damage to the environment of the world's common spaces had taken place in violation of international law is not only appropriate under the eye of international law, but necessary for the maintenance of good order among States.

Notes and Questions

1. *The standing problem.* For a discussion of the idea that states' obligations in the area of climate change run *erga omnes, i.e.,* to all states, *see* Frederic L. Kirgis, Jr., Standing to Challenge Human Endeavors That Could Change the Climate, 84 A.J.I.L. 525 (1990).

2. *Is the international community capable of responding?* Aside from third state remedies, should the international community itself not respond in some way to grave environmental injuries in the global commons? How could such a response be organized? Presumably through the United Nations, but how could or should this be done within the existing organizational framework of the UN? Would the passage of a resolution by the General Assembly concerning each case be sufficient? Would the Security Council have a role to play in such situations? What about such organs of the UN as the International Court of Justice or even the Trusteeship Council?

3. *Defining the "commons."* How should the "commons" be defined? There is probably general agreement that the concept includes the high seas, the global atmosphere, Antarctica, and outer space. But what about endangered species? Is there not an important community interest in the preservation of biological diversity in general and certain species (like the whale and the elephant, for example), in particular? What if the state of Biodiva decides to allow the unrestricted hunting, to extinction, of the Rarabong, a species that is especially valued by the international community but which is found only in Biodiva? Who (i.e., what state or states, the international community, etc.) could respond, and how?

E. NONCONFRONTATIONAL APPROACHES TO COMPLIANCE

Are there approaches other than rules of responsibility and liability for encouraging compliance with norms of international environmental law? As the international community becomes increasingly organized, both through universal institutions (of which the United Nations is the foremost example) and through sectoral treaty regimes (such as those relating to climate change, biodiversity, protection of the ozone layer, and the like), it becomes possible to ever greater degrees to monitor and foster compliance with international standards of behavior, both customary and conventional. In this section we look briefly at the role of international institutions in achieving compliance, and at new treaty-based approaches to that objective.

1. The Role of International Institutions

■ INTERNATIONAL LAW AND THE ENVIRONMENT

Patricia W. Birnie & Alan E. Boyle
160-163 (1992)

[The following considers] the role of international institutions, particularly those of an intergovernmental character, as mechanisms which facilitate [the] implementation and enforcement [of international environmental law]. The key tasks which such bodies perform in this context are those of information and data collection, receiving reports on treaty implementation by states, facilitating independent monitoring and inspection and acting as a forum for reviewing the performance of states or the negotiation of further measures and regulations. Such bodies may thus acquire law enforcement, lawmaking, and dispute settlement functions. In some cases they are also responsible for the allocation or management of natural resources.

International institutions are useful for law enforcement purposes in so far as they enable states to be held accountable to other member states, exercising a form of collective or community supervision. To the extent that such bodies are open to participation of other interested bodies or NGOs with observer status this accountability may also extend to a wider public, although none of the environmental treaties goes as far as the ILO [International Labour Organisation] Convention, under which employers and trade union organizations participate directly in the process of scrutiny. Accountability is exercised mainly by techniques of general supervision or control of states in the performance of their international obligations, or of other agreed standards of conduct. These obligations or standards will usually have a treaty basis, partly because institutional supervision has proved to be a widely acceptable method of treaty enforcement, but the technique is also capable of application to rules of customary law. It is, for example, one method by which the principle of equitable utilization of shared resources can be implemented, or by which preferential or shared rights to common resources such as high seas fisheries can be allocated. . . .

Supervision of this kind generally also entails the negotiation and elaboration of detailed rules, standards, or practices, usually as a means of giving effect to the more general provisions of framework treaties. Not only does this form of lawmaking or international regulation facilitate treaty implementation, it also gives treaties a dynamic character and enables the parties to respond to new problems or priorities. . . .

Thus the combination of regulatory and supervisory functions in the hands of international institutions is first of importance in making international agreements more effective in their operation. The absence of any provision for institutional supervision or regulation is, by contrast, often a sign that the treaty in question is ineffective and leads to obsolescence. . . . Regulation and supervision by international institutions has been identified as part of a general trend away from the solution of problems by strictly judicial means and towards the resolution of conflicts through an equitable balancing of interests and *ad hoc* political compromise. Used in this way international institutions become a forum for dispute settlement and treaty compliance through discussion and negotiation, rather than by adjudication of questions of law or interpretation. Moreover, community pressure and the scrutiny of other states in an intergovernmental forum may often be more effective than other more confrontational methods. The International Whaling Commission and the consultative meeting of the London Dumping Convention afford particularly good examples of this form of conflict resolution.

Secondly, . . . individual states may lack standing to bring international claims relating to the protection of global common areas, such as the high seas. In such cases accountability through international institutions may be the only practical remedy available. This problem can only partly be circumvented by resorting to other methods of enforcing environmental cooperation and protection treaties. Compliance with the MARPOL Convention, the London Dumping Convention, or the CITES Convention, to take three examples, cannot readily be secured by suspension or termination of the treaty in case of material breach, as envisaged by Article 60 of the Vienna Convention on Treaties, since that would primarily harm the international community, not the defaulting state, and would run counter to a policy of ensuring the widest possible participation in such agreements. Moreover, it is possible for international institutions to give a more flexible interpretation to treaties of this kind and to apply to this process a specialized expertise based on experience and knowledge of the issues concerned, and aimed at securing compliance, rather than adjudicating on breach. Thus it is not surprising that provision for institutional supervision and regulation is now common in environmental treaties. It is certainly a more significant basis for dispute settlement in an environmental context than state responsibility.

Professors Birnie and Boyle go on to discuss, inter alia, Supervisory Techniques (reporting, fact-finding, research, and inspection), Standard-

Setting and International Regulation, International Management, and Dispute Settlement by Intergovernmental Institutions. Some of these techniques are illustrated in the following subsection.

2. New Treaty Approaches to the Problem of Compliance

■ NONCOMPLIANCE PROCEDURES UNDER THE MONTREAL PROTOCOL AND AMENDMENTS THERETO

(*See* Chapter 11, section D, on Implementation of the Montreal Protocol.)

■ STRENGTHENING NATIONAL COMPLIANCE WITH INTERNATIONAL ENVIRONMENTAL AGREEMENTS

Edith Brown Weiss
27 Envtl. Poly. & L. 297 (1997)[23]

[The following excerpt is based on research by Harold K. Jacobson and Edith Brown Weiss with more than 30 scholars, which focused on nine countries and five international agreements.[24]]

In 1972, when the United Nations Conference on the Human Environment was held in Stockholm, there were only about three dozen multilateral environmental agreements. Today there are more than 900 international legal instruments (mostly binding) that are either focused on environment or contain one or more important provisions concerned with environment. These instruments are viewed as primary means for affecting the behavior of states and the many other actors today: subnational governments, industries, nongovernmental organizations and individuals. They involve substantial costs to states and to the targeted and interested actors, whether in the negotiations for the agreements or their implementation. Until recently little attention has been given to the extent to which states and other actors comply with these agreements. In this brief article, I argue that compliance is a complex process involving both the intent and the capacity of states, that the three alternative compliance strategies embodied in international

23. This article is adapted from that presented to the 25th Anniversary of the Elizabeth Haub Prize winners in Wiesbaden, Germany, April 1997.

24. Harold K. Jacobson and Edith Brown Weiss, Strengthening Compliance with International Environmental Accords: Preliminary Observations from a Collaborative Project, 2 Global Governance 1 (1995). The research will be published as Engaging Countries: Strengthening Compliance with International Environmental Accords (Edith Brown Weiss & Harold K. Jacobson eds. 1998).

agreements—sunshine, incentives, and sanctions—and the institutional design of agreements affects intent and capacity, and that the choice of strategies must be targeted to individual countries' intent and capacity. Moreover, the preferred strategy choices vary across different areas of international agreements: trade, labor, human rights, arms control, and environment.

I. The Conceptual Framework

The traditional stylized model of compliance assumes that countries accept international agreements only when their governments regard them as in their interest. Because of this, countries generally comply with the obligations they have assumed. If they do [not], sanctions are used to punish offenders and deter violations.

But the reality is different. While countries join agreements that are in their self-interest, there are many reasons why countries may find them to be in their self-interest. And these reasons affect their willingness and their capacity to comply. In the best of worlds, countries may join to show leadership in addressing a problem. But they also may join because others are doing so, or because governments with leverage over them are pressing them to do so, or because of domestic interests. Countries may join because the obligations require no changes in their present behavior, or they may join with no intention of immediately complying and may even lack the capacity to comply.

The traditional framework for analyzing compliance is hierarchic, static and focused on states. Governments negotiate international agreements, which are then usually put into force through implementing legislation or regulations at the national level. States ensure that other actors comply with the domestic measures. This approach is hierarchic because it moves from the international agreement and member states downward to the subgovernmental units and to the nongovernmental organizations and individual actors. It is static because it assumes a snapshot at some point in time accurately captures compliance with the agreement.

A more realistic framework for understanding compliance is non-hierarchic, includes many actors other than states and treats compliance as a process that changes over time. The agreements themselves evolve over time, both as to the obligations they contain and the implementing measures. In this framework, states continue as central and essential actors, but others actors are also very important. These include intergovernmental organizations, secretariats servicing the agreements, nongovernmental organizations, private industrial and commercial enterprises, and individual actors. These nonstate actors interact dynamically in complex ways in patterns that vary among agreements and within countries.

The international study of national compliance found, based on empirical research, that in general national compliance increases over time, with countries frequently devoting more resources to compliance over time. But compliance also declines during certain periods for certain countries and particular agreements. Economic chaos, political instability and sudden decentralization have caused compliance to decrease, especially for agreements for which there is no strongly vested interest in securing compliance.

Two critical factors explaining national compliance are a country's intent and a country's capacity to comply. Both may change over time. In designing international agreements and implementing measures, states should consider the appropriate mix of strategies to encourage member countries to have both the intent and the capacity to comply with the agreements.

II. Intent and Capacity

The study on national compliance revealed that when countries join agreements they are in quite different positions with regard to their intent to comply and their capacity to do so, and that both factors change over time.

Intent is difficult to determine. It can be generally discerned from analyzing the behavior of countries. It is not to be confused with the formal votes or positions countries may assert in international meetings. Some countries intend to comply with the obligations they assume at the time they join the agreement. Implementing legislation that fully satisfies the treaty obligations may be already in effect; the country's past practice may already be in compliance with at least the substantive obligations of the treaty. In some cases, countries may join treaties without having carefully considered the obligations; they may even be unaware of them. Others may join with no intention to comply, as in the case of certain central and east European countries becoming parties to the Protocols on Sulphur Dioxide and Nitrogen Oxide to the UN ECE Long Range Transboundary Air Pollution Convention. They may bend to international pressure, or may respond to "bribes" by other states, or they may join to foster international cooperation in general in anticipation of other returns. There may be conflicts in intent within a country which reflect internal divisions. "[A] government may be divided, the foreign ministry may intend to comply while other branches of government may have no intention of abandoning practices that contravene the accord."[25] The national government may even intend to comply, but relevant provincial governments do not. In many cases, countries may intend to comply in the abstract, but the agreements have too low priority in the country to receive the attention and resources needed for compliance.

25. Harold K. Jacobson and Edith Brown Weiss, Compliance with International Environmental Accords: Achievements and Strategies (1996).

Countries must also have the capacity to comply. Many assets are important: an effective and honest bureaucracy, economic resources, public support, and technical expertise and know-how. These assets differ among states when they join an agreement, and the assets change over time in response to domestic and international events. International environmental agreements, in particular, have targeted financial and technical assistance to states to help them develop the capacity to comply. In many cases, the acute issue for member states is one of prioritization: how much resources to devote to compliance with particular obligations contained in the agreements. This issue is particularly difficult when it involves coordination among several ministries and with provincial and local governments, which may be recalcitrant.

While the only effective strategy to increase the political intent and the capacity to comply is to engage countries in the agreement, countries can facilitate this through the strategies they adopt in designing and implementing international agreements and the institutional structure that they create with the agreement.

III. Strategies for Compliance

International legal strategies to encourage compliance may be grouped into three categories: negative incentives in the form of penalties, sanctions and withdrawal of privileges; sunshine methods such as monitoring, reporting, transparency and NGO participation; and positive incentives, such as special funds for financial or technical assistance, access to technology or training programs. In addition there are traditional public international law remedies for breach of an agreement, as set forth in the Vienna Convention on Treaties and customary international law. The question is which methods work best under what set of circumstances. In part, this can only be answered through empirical research. . . .

A. Sanctions

Under the traditional framework for compliance, parties rely on sanctions, penalties, and such measures as withdrawal of privileges under the convention to enforce treaty commitments. In trade law, sanctions have been regarded as essential to achieving compliance. In international environmental law, sanctions are rarely used. When used, individual parties ban trade in certain products with violators of the agreement or deny certain status accorded under the agreement to the violating party.

Trade sanctions have been threatened to enforce CITES. For example, the CITES Standing Committee recommended that parties ban trade in wildlife products with China [and Taiwan] for violating prohibitions on trade in rhinoceros horns and tiger parts. Not long before, the Standing

Committee considered a trade ban on CITES products with Italy. Using trade sanctions to enforce multilateral environmental agreements raises problems of consistency with the General Agreement on Tariffs and Trade as incorporated in the new World Trade Organization. The World Trade Organization prohibits import quotas, requires national treatment between imported and domestic products, and requires most favored nation treatment among countries—that is, the most favorable treatment offered to one exporting country must be granted to all, but provides relevant exceptions in Article XX(b) and (g). These issues are considered in Chapter 20.

Withdrawing the privileges of membership in a convention is another traditional enforcement measure. The World Heritage Convention provides for a variation of this. While the text of the convention provides only for countries to list sites on the World Heritage List, the guidelines provide for delisting a World Heritage site if the country is in violation of its obligations to conserve the site. The language is ambiguous as to whether the host country must consent to the delisting. The sanction has not been used; no site has been removed from the World Heritage List, although the integrity of several sites is severely threatened.

There are instances in which sanctions in the form of withdrawal of some of the privileges of membership in the convention apply. In the Montreal Protocol, for example, countries qualifying as Article V developing countries qualified to receive assistance from the Montreal Protocol Fund can lose that status if they do not provide baseline data on consumption levels of controlled substances within a certain time after joining the agreement.

Public international law provides remedies for breaches of treaty obligations and of rules of customary international law. The Vienna Convention on Treaties indicates under what circumstances parties may withdraw from an agreement because of a breach of an obligation by a member party. Rules of customary international law set forth rights of retorsion and counter measures. They have not been invoked generally for international environmental problems. Nonetheless, such remedies are always available to states, providing that the legal requirements have been satisfied.

In international environmental law, sanctions are a "last resort" after other methods have failed. It is not clear the extent to which sanctions are needed as a latent threat in order to make other methods of achieving compliance effective. This issue is discussed below.

B. THE SUNSHINE APPROACH

The key way of insuring compliance is through what I have labeled the "sunshine strategy." This approach relies on monitoring behavior of various actors through regular reports, site visits, and international review procedures, on transparency and access to information, on media access and coverage to provide public awareness, on nongovernmental organization participation in monitoring compliance, and on informal pressures by parties and by secretariats to comply. It relies on what has been termed the "reputation" factor to induce compliance.

Monitoring is essential to any effective program to increase implementation and compliance with treaty obligations. Monitoring may take many forms: off site monitoring through advanced technologies of scientific baselines or other criteria; reports by parties or nongovernmental organizations; on site monitoring by parties, secretariat officials or consultants; and international review of materials submitted by parties or gathered from other sources.

Of late, reporting has become a primary monitoring instrument. Nearly all of the most recent UNEP conventions require regular reports from parties on implementation of the agreements. Indeed there is almost a "bandwagon" effect among countries to include a provision on reporting in new agreements.

A reporting requirement is useful in that it engages countries in implementing the agreement. Some official(s) in the country must be responsible for filing the report. Moreover, reports are an important tool for educating countries about their commitments under the agreement and potentially a means to build local capacity to comply with the agreement.

But there are also problems with relying on reporting as the key monitoring tool. Officials required to file reports under the burgeoning number of international agreements may find that their time is mostly occupied by preparing reports rather than by taking the actions called for under the convention, or addressing other high priority environmental actions. Indeed, in countries with a scarcity of skilled labor, the government may need to devote much of its time to meeting reporting requirements. This is a problem of "congestion in treaty reporting." Moreover, unless the reporting requirements are standardized, the data may be difficult to compare and evaluate. Great variations in content in national reports for a given agreement may occur. In other cases, national reports may begin to look alike across different issue areas as information technology makes for easy transfer of written material.

Reports are useful monitoring tools if they convey information that others can review and verify. This requires an international process of review, and means to draw violations to the attention of parties for actions. However, both secretariats and parties can be reluctant to call particular countries to account for inaccurate reports.

Some studies have found low rates of compliance by parties generally with reporting requirements. Many countries do not report or do not report on a timely basis. The reports may be incomplete or may be inaccurate, as when the same data is reported for several years. It may be difficult to determine whether the data is reliable. However, the preoccupation with the relatively low rates of compliance with reporting obligations in international environmental agreements may be slightly misplaced. It is arguably much less important that all countries comply with the obligation to file regular reports than that the countries that are major players in a particular agreement comply. Here the record of compliance with reporting obligations is much stronger.

Reporting is linked with transparency—to states, to non-state actors and to individuals. Nongovernmental organizations rely upon this transparency to monitor and encourage compliance with the convention, although admittedly the information might also be used to circumvent the obligations in some circumstances. Providing other member states and non-state actors with access to information makes it generally more likely that unreliable reports and inaccurate data will be detected.

The sunshine strategy relies on nongovernmental organizations, expert communities, and corporate actors to make possible parties' compliance with international agreements. Nongovernmental organizations bring violations to the attention of governments and of Secretariats servicing the convention. International nongovernmental organizations, such as Greenpeace International and Friends of the Earth, may work with local nongovernmental organizations to pressure countries to comply or may exert pressure directly on governments or on corporate actors. Non-state actors (and individuals) bring suspected violations to the attention of the secretariats servicing the agreements, to the parties and to the media. While these organizations have been much more active in industrialized countries than in developing countries, their numbers are growing worldwide.

Under some agreements NGOs are explicitly asked to monitor the agreement. For example, the World Conservation Monitoring Unit tracks national country reports of imports and exports of listed species for CITES. Other nongovernmental organizations systematically monitor state behavior on their own initiative, as in TRAFFIC's monitoring of trade in endangered species and tropical timber.

Sometimes the most effective monitoring of compliance takes place in the private sector. Corporations have a keen interest in maintaining a "level playing field." Under the Montreal Protocol, for example, a handful of large companies that produce CFC's and other controlled substances have an important financial stake in insuring that competitors abide by the agreement. They also have the resources to monitor compliance, albeit quietly.

Finally, the sunshine strategy relies on consultation and informal pressures such as jawboning to induce compliance. Secretariats consult with governments and with nongovernmental organizations, industry, and individuals. Governments consult with secretariats, nongovernmental organizations and industry. Secretariats often play an important but quiet role in bringing informal pressure to bear upon noncomplying actors.

The sunshine strategy builds upon the culture which surrounds the politics of environmental issues in many, but not all, countries. Publics see environment as an issue in which they ought to have access to information and an opportunity to participate in decisions affecting them. Governments are becoming accustomed to non-state actors as influential participants in the policy process, whether formally or informally. Thus, in contrast to areas such as trade and national security, the sunshine strategy finds fertile ground.

C. INCENTIVES

International agreements increasingly rely on positive incentives to induce compliance. The incentive approach is based on the belief that many problems of compliance are problems of the lack of capacity to comply. If countries have the intent to comply but lack capacity, incentives can be an effective strategy for securing compliance. They may also be effective in shaping the interests and hence the intent of the country in complying.

Incentives may take the form of training materials and seminars, special funds for financial or technical assistance, access to technology, or bilateral assistance outside the framework of the convention.

Many international environmental agreements provide for the establishment of special funds to assist parties in complying with the convention. The 1972 World Heritage Convention established a special fund, which although small, has regularly assisted countries in conserving sites on the World Heritage List. Similarly, parties to the Montreal Protocol established in 1990 the Montreal Protocol Fund to assist Article V developing countries to comply with their Protocol obligations. The two Rio conventions, the Framework Convention on Climate Change and the Biological Diversity Convention, provide for funding to countries to meet the global incremental costs of complying with the conventions, although they do not establish separate funds to do so.

The Global Environmental Facility, created in 1990 initially as a $1.2 billion, 3-year fund, provides grants and loans to developing countries for specific environmental problems: ozone depletion, biological diversity, climate change, and marine pollution. It has been restructured and become permanent. The scope now encompasses desertification. The GEF potentially provides an additional source of financial incentives to countries to build local capacity to comply with international commitments.

Developing countries have increasingly viewed provision for financial and technical assistance as prerequisites for joining international environmental conventions. India, for example, insisted that the Montreal Protocol Fund be in place before joining the Protocol. During negotiations for the Desertification Convention, countries insisted on having access to funds as a prerequisite to concluding the convention.

Financial incentives build local capacity to comply with treaty obligations. But access to funds can also be used as a "stick" to ensure compliance with treaty obligations. For example, in 1995, the GEF linked fulfillment of obligations under the Montreal Protocol to receipt of GEF funds.

Training is an important component of the incentive strategy. Generally the funds devoted to training and the numbers of people trained annually have increased for international environmental conventions. For example, funds devoted to training under the Convention on International Trade in Endangered Species have increased sharply since 1994.

Training programs build local capacity to comply with treaty obligations and engage local actors in the agreement. However, care must be taken to ensure that the proper people are trained and at least some of those who are trained will continue working with the agreements beyond six months. Various strategies can be employed: moving training to the regions or within countries, training slightly larger numbers of people than might be needed so that some may still be on the job in a year. Other techniques include: training the "trainers" who can then conduct regular seminars, providing clear training manuals, and scrutinizing training applicants for quality.

Of the three compliance strategies, only two are in frequent use: the sunshine and the positive incentive strategies. Sanctions and other enforcement measures are rarely resorted to, and then only for items in international trade. Sanctions are a blunt instrument. By contrast the sunshine and positive incentive approaches are more flexible and rather more subtle instruments to encourage compliance.

D. INSTITUTIONAL MEASURES

The institutional structure of the regime surrounding each international agreement affects compliance. Features intended to encourage compliance include the establishment of an implementation committee and noncompliance procedures, which have been unusually effective for the Montreal Protocol, engagement of an enforcement officer (as in CITES), publication of violations (as in CITES and Basel), providing a formal role for NGOs (as in UNESCO's World Heritage Convention and in CITES), developing a formal link with industry (as in the Montreal Protocol and OzonAction) and establishing scientific and technical assessment and advice bodies to ensure that the convention keeps pace with scientific advances (as in the Montreal Protocol).

The role of the institutional features in facilitating compliance often evolves over time. The implementation committee and noncompliance procedures of the Montreal Protocol were used initially to help noncomplying Article V developing countries come into compliance with reporting obligations. However, in 1995 parties were using the procedures to exert strong pressure upon several countries, such as the Russian Federation, to come into compliance with procedural and substantive obligations. In the World Heritage Convention, the role of the IUCN and organizations concerned with cultural heritage has shifted from an almost exclusive early emphasis on evaluating sites for whether they were suitable for the World Heritage List to a substantial focus on monitoring member state conservation of the listed sites. Similar changes have taken place in the functions assumed by institutions established for other international agreements. Thus, in designing international agreements, it is important to consider whether the parties will be able to use the institutional features to respond flexibly over time to new needs and demands.

Secretariats to international agreements play important roles in securing compliance by member countries and targeted nonstate actors. They have substantial influence in part because they may be the only body with comprehensive knowledge of the extent to which parties are complying. They are uniquely situated to respond to questions and to jawbone actors into compliance. One of the most important measures for securing compliance is to ensure that secretariats for the agreements have secure funding and long-term personnel contracts. In light of the financial crisis in the United Nations system, some secretariats have moved largely to short-term contracts of one to three months, and funds provided by the parties to the agreement, even if in separate bank accounts, have become subject to general restrictions on use. Secretariats need to attract and retain high quality personnel and to be able to implement long-range planning for implementing the convention and ensuring compliance by member countries.

IV. Linking Compliance Strategies with Intent and Capacity

With respect to each international agreement, it is possible to create a figure of four boxes joining intent and capacity: countries with intent to comply and high capacity; countries with low intent to comply but with capacity; countries with intent to comply but lacking in capacity; and countries with no intent to comply and with no capacity. In each of these four categories, member countries will always have varying degrees of intent to comply and varying degrees of capacity to comply. Strategies for compliance must be targeted to move countries toward having both the intent and the capacity to comply. Different strategies need to be emphasized for different categories of countries, although a mix of strategies should be available.

For those countries having both the intent and the capacity, the sunshine strategy may be especially important, for it facilitates monitoring by both governments and nonstate actors. Sanctions are of secondary importance, primarily to ensure that countries are not tempted to change their intent to comply. When countries have the intent to comply, but lack the capacity, incentives are especially important, although sunshine strategies may have an important secondary role in mobilizing nonstate actor support and in monitoring progress in building capacity. This category includes many developing countries. Countries that lack intent but have the capacity may be particularly susceptible to some form of sanction, but the sunshine approach may be important in reshaping intent. Incentives may also help. For those countries lacking intent and capacity, all three strategies may be essential.

One of the complications of linking intent, capacity and compliance strategies is that both the intent and the capacity of countries to comply may change over time. National compliance changes over time in response to many factors. This suggests that the suite of measures needed to promote or to ensure compliance by member countries may also change over time.

V. Compliance Strategies Compared Across Areas of International Law

In international environmental law, countries have relied primarily upon the sunshine and the incentive approaches to secure compliance. Sanctions have been rarely used. Nor have formal dispute resolution mechanisms been employed. Patterns of strategies used, however, vary across the fields of international law.

In general, compliance strategies have focused heavily on elements of the sunshine approach in both the human rights and the labor areas. By contrast, trade agreements and arms control instruments have relied more on sanctions and other enforcement measures. Formal dispute resolution is an integral part of international trade law, much less so in environmental law.

While one can speculate on the reasons for the differences in emphasis among the areas of international law, the issue is appropriately explored in a subsequent article. However, since international environmental issues have from the beginning been of public concern and since all states share a common interest in a healthy global environment, the emphasis on sunshine and incentive strategies for compliance seems understandable and appropriate. . . .

Note

Consider also the following observations by Antonia and Abram Chayes:

> All international regimes face problems with free-riders, holdouts, and defectors. In the environmental field, these difficulties are intensified. Regulation seems to entail large and visible short-term costs to entrenched business interests. It may be seen as discriminating between rich and poor nations. The benefits are widely diffused in space and time, and it is often fairly easy for an actor to extract them without accepting the burdens of compliance. . . .
>
> Still, although quantitative measures may be hard to find, there is no reason to think that fulfillment by states of their international obligations

compares unfavorably to compliance with domestic legal rules—certainly not with those covering the distribution and use of narcotic drugs or even the payment of taxes. . . .

[In determining why states comply with their international obligations, a] point of departure is to recognize that in efforts to induce compliance with international regulation, the prime concern is not to identify and punish "violators." Compliance systems in international regulatory regimes are instruments for maintaining a dynamic equilibrium among strongly backed competing interests, so that the regime continues to be viable in a constantly changing international setting.

A. Chayes & A. Chayes, Adjustment and Compliance Processes in International Regulatory Regimes, in Preserving the Global Environment 290 (1991).

LESSONS LEARNED IN GLOBAL ENVIRONMENTAL GOVERNANCE

Peter Sand
31-34 (1990)

Complaints and Custodial Action

As an alternative to legal action against the responsible party, recourse to a non-judicial international institution may provide a first-choice remedy when environmental agreements are infringed. [Sand discusses the non-compliance procedures then being developed for the Montreal Protocol, which are examined in Chapter 11.]

A much bolder step toward collective compliance control was taken by the 1957 Rome Treaty establishing the *European Economic Community* (EEC). Article 155 made the EEC Commission the guardian of the treaty's implementation, and article 169 empowered it to initiate proceedings against any member state in case of infringements, sanctioned if necessary by formal action in the European Court of Justice at Luxembourg. Over the past ten years, this "custodial" procedure has become one of the most important means of enforcing EEC environmental standards.

The EEC infringement proceedings comprise three stages: As a first step, the Commission sends "letters of formal notice" to member states that fail to enact or apply a Community directive, or to report on its enactment or application. After giving the member state an opportunity to respond, the Commission can next render a "reasoned opinion" confirming the infringement in light of all the facts gathered. If the member state still doesn't comply, the Commission may then refer the matter to the European Court of Justice. During 1988, the Commission issued 93 letters of formal notice, 71 reasoned opinions, and 11 references to the court concerning infringements of EEC environmental directives (some 70 of which were in force at that time). . . .

What may be the most significant feature of this procedure is mentioned nowhere in the treaty and evolved only gradually during its implementation. More than half of the infringement proceedings initiated against member states were based not on the Commission's own monitoring of compliance but on citizen complaints—from private individuals, associations (such as Greenpeace and Friends of the Earth), or municipalities. As a result of public information on the complaints procedure and the establishment of a "complaints registry" within the Commission secretariat in Brussels, the number of environmental complaints rose dramatically—from 10 in 1982 to 190 in 1988 and to 460 in 1989. While complaints are usually based on local non-compliance with EEC standards, some have wider effects: a single complaint by a resident in one of the United Kingdom's two non-attainment areas with regard to the 1980 EEC *Directive on Air Quality Limit Values and Guide Values for Sulphur Dioxide and Suspended Particulates* thus triggered a Commission investigation that led to infringement proceedings against seven member states.

Significantly, the EEC has no powers of physical enforcement comparable to those of a national government. Although virtually all of the more than 30 judgments rendered by the European Court of Justice in environmental infringement proceedings since 1982 went against the defendant member states and upheld the Commission's opinion, not all led to compliance. In the 1988 case of *Commission vs. Kingdom of Belgium*, for instance, the court noted that Belgium had failed to fulfill its obligations under article 171 of the treaty by refusing, in defiance of earlier (1982) judgments of the court, to adopt the measures necessary to implement four EEC directives on waste disposal. The mere opening of EEC action can, however, have internal political and economic consequences in member states. In the United Kingdom, the government's plans for privatization of local water management agencies were stalled in part because of pending EEC infringement proceedings, when it turned out that some areas scheduled for privatization did not meet EEC water quality standards. As a result of this growing impact on local environmental quality, the "custodial action" procedure of the EEC commission has evolved from a three-stage to a four-stage process: the optional first stage in most cases is now a citizen complaint.

Environmental Audits

Besides judicial review, international organizations have developed other forms of compliance control. Probably the body with the most such experience is the *International Labour Organization* (ILO), which has enacted and monitored a long line of multilateral conventions since the 1920s—ranging from bans on white lead paint and other occupational health hazards, to work-place protection from air pollution, radiation, and toxic chemicals. All these conventions contain provisions on dispute settlement that allow states to initiate complaints and *ad hoc* inquiries against other states for not observing the treaty. However, a detailed study of ILO's enforcement record over more than sixty years shows that this adversarial procedure was used only rarely and then mostly for political potshots. Instead, ILO member states developed an entirely different procedure that turned out to be far more effective in enforcing compliance: annual or biennial reporting by governments, combined with regular auditing by an independent technical Committee of Experts to ascertain compliance in each member state, followed by public debate of these audited reports by the Conference Committee on the Application of Conventions and Recommendations.

Over the years, the ILO "auditing" system—with the active participation of both trade unions and employers' associations—has turned into a worldwide public hearing that clearly induces more compliance by governments than the threat of any intergovernmental legal action would. The *U.N. Commission on Human Rights* applies a similar procedure of country reports and public hearings, in which non-governmental organizations . . . play an active role.

In the environmental field, the biennial Conference of the Parties to the *Convention on International Trade in Endangered Species of Wild Fauna and Flora* (CITES) has become a forum for international review of compliance with the treaty, again with massive NGO support. Similarly, reviews of treaty implementation by parties to the *Convention on Long-Range Transboundary Air Pollution* and its protocols are carried out and published regularly by the Executive Body for the Convention.

In all these cases, periodic audits of compliance with agreed-upon international standards are well established. Essential to this process is publicity. It facilitates collective review and mutual accountability by all member states and, even more important, exposes governmental compliance reports to scrutiny by non-governmental groups and, through them, by the public. . . .

One strong point of environmental audits is timing. Audits can make a difference *before* things have gone seriously wrong—unlike traditional judicial review mechanisms based on liability, which can only intervene after the fact. Considering the clear need to make environmental controls preventive rather than corrective, now may be the time to envisage a global auditing body that would periodically evaluate the performance of states and organizations in complying with their international obligations. Rather than relying on *ad hoc* review by a tribunal, where "action" would inevitably turn into confrontation, it may be preferable to assign this function to a permanent intergovernmental body—such as the *United Nations Trusteeship Council,* as recently suggested by Maurice Strong, Secretary General of the U.N. Conference on Environment and Development. As in the field of standard-setting and regulation, more imaginative approaches to compliance control are needed today than those drawn from outdated legal textbooks. An obvious and largely untapped source is the rich procedural experience of existing international institutions.

Note

The role of citizens in enforcement of environmental obligations on the international level is also provided for in the 1993 North American Agreement on Environmental Cooperation (NAAEC), the environmental side agreement to the North American Free Trade Agreement (NAFTA). Article 14 of the NAAEC, entitled Submissions on Enforcement Matters, provides in paragraph 1 that the NAAEC Secretariat "may consider a submission from any non-governmental organization or person asserting that a Party is *failing to effectively enforce its environmental law*, if the Secretariat finds that the submission [satisfies six conditions]" (emphasis added). Under paragraph 2 of the article, if the Secretariat determines that a submission satisfies the requirements set forth in paragraph 1 it is to "determine whether the submission merits requesting a response from the Party." Article 15 of the agreement provides that the secretariat is to inform the Commission's Council (composed of cabinet-level representatives of the three parties (Article 9(1)) if it "considers that the submission, in the light of any response provided by the Party, warrants developing a factual record. . . ." If the council by a two-thirds vote instructs it to do so, the secretariat is then to prepare a factual record; this record may be made public if the council, again by a two-thirds vote, decides to do so. As of September 1997, 12 submissions had been received by the Commission's Secretariat in Montreal. One of these led to a factual record by that time, which the council decided whether to make public.

■ PROMOTING COMPLIANCE WITH INTERNATIONAL ENVIRONMENTAL LEGAL STANDARDS: REFLECTIONS ON MONITORING AND REPORTING MECHANISMS

Kamen Sachariew
[1991] Y.B. Intl. Envtl. L. 31 (1992)

. . . A variety of legal instruments and institutional mechanisms designed to review and enhance the implementation of global and regional agreements have evolved within the international system. They include procedures for the regular exchange of scientific information; for notification in cases of accidents threatening appreciable environmental injury;

and for prior consultation and environmental impact assessment of activities within one state which are capable of causing damage to the environment in areas beyond that state's national jurisdiction. They also include international networks for monitoring the state of the environment within the scope of the agreement concerned and reporting systems and review procedures to monitor and assess states' performance in implementing treaty obligations. To a more limited extent, such techniques also include enforcement measures such as inspections, sanctions, state responsibility and liability.

. . . Two [of the techniques and mechanisms of supervision in international environmental law], monitoring and reporting, . . . are in many respects typical of the techniques of supervision used in legal instruments designed to protect the environment. . . . [T]he analysis of monitoring and reporting systems also highlights some general trends in international environmental law as a specific field of legal regulation. These trends include the strong emphasis on prevention and on management-oriented institutionalized action.

As far as prevention is concerned, it should be noted at the outset that states have developed monitoring and reporting systems to review the process of treaty implementation and detect potential compliance problems at an early stage. This inherently preventative bias is of particular importance in the field of international environmental law where the traditional "enforcement" oriented approach—being centered on claims for reparation, sanctions, reprisals and compulsory jurisdiction—has proved too narrow. Harm caused to the natural environment by human activities is often irreversible, making it impossible to restore the *status quo ante* through a claim for *restitutio in integrum.* It is also difficult to assess damage to the environment or to ecosystems in terms of monetary compensation and to establish the causal link between a given activity and its transboundary effects.

Monitoring and reporting systems developed for the purpose of reviewing the overall process of treaty implementation and assessing the effectiveness of control measures thus serve the dual objectives of tracking compliance and of furnishing information necessary for adjusting the standards set by the international legal instrument. This duality of function is indicative of a general trend in international environmental law; the shift from so-called "secondary rules" of state responsibility towards "primary" substantive and procedural rules of supervision. As a consequence, the processes of applying and of making international environmental law become almost indistinguishable; assessment of compliance may well merge into legislative action to adjust—by reinterpretation or reformulation—a standard or rule that has given rise to a compliance issue. By their very nature, monitoring and reporting systems perform on either a continuing or a periodic basis and within an institutional setting. The trend towards institutionalism is one of the most prominent features of international environmental law. Out of some two hundred international legal instruments in the field of environmental protection, more than forty create new international bodies, or entrust existing ones with secretarial, review or co-ordination functions. Among the instruments agreed to in the last decade, the share of those providing for institutional co-operation is even higher. This trend is inspired by the need for permanent arrrangements for constant monitoring and scientific evaluation of the state of a given environmental medium or ecosystem, for the updating of international standards, for the establishment and implementation of joint management schemes and for the facilitation of information exchange among the parties. This trend towards institutionalism is also a reflection of the need to monitor domestic implementation of international rules for the protection of the environment which, due to the very nature of the processes involved, may require repeated implementing efforts over a relatively long period of time. Furthermore, it is a trend that is encouraged by the fact that an institutional setting assures both a more objective and public review of implementation.

Another feature of monitoring and reporting systems that is typical of general developments in international environmental law is the involvement of non-governmental organizations (NGOs). While states and state-controlled inter-governmental organs are the two principal types of actors involved in reviewing the implementation of international environmental rules, individuals and national as well as international NGOs are playing an ever increasing role in that process. This is occurring despite the fact that they do not possess the full status of subjects of international law. The form of NGO participation ranges from domestic action and application of local remedies in cases with a transboundary element, to filing petitions and initiating individual complaint procedures in international organizations, and includes the preparation of independent reports on state compliance with international environmental obligations. At this stage it is important to stress that NGOs introduce an often critical element of external and independent assessment of state compliance which is otherwise difficult to obtain. This is especially true of reporting systems which normally rely on "self-assessment" by the controlled state and of supervision procedures taking place within international organizations that are stymied by unanimity requirements, "opting out" clauses or other loopholes contained in international agreements.

Questions

Why do you suppose these compliance mechanisms and techniques have been developed? What's wrong with traditional liability rules? Do you see analogues on the domestic level to the compliance techniques and mechanisms discussed in the foregoing excerpts?

F. PRIVATE REMEDIES

1. *General Principles, International Instruments, and National Legislation*

■ FINAL REPORT OF THE EXPERTS GROUP ON ENVIRONMENTAL LAW ON LEGAL PRINCIPLES FOR ENVIRONMENTAL PROTECTION AND SUSTAINABLE DEVELOPMENT

above, ***at 119-122***

Article 20
Non-intergovernmental Proceedings

States shall provide remedies for persons who have been or may be detrimentally affected by a transboundary interference with their use of a transboundary natural resource or by a transboundary environmental interference. In particular, States of origin shall grant those persons equal access as well as due process and equal treatment in the same administrative and judicial proceedings as are available to persons within their own jurisdiction who have been or may be similarly affected.

COMMENT

. . . The first sentence of the principle formulated above implies a duty for both the State of origin and the (possibly) affected State to provide, where necessary by agreement or otherwise, for such matters as the jurisdiction of courts, the applicable law and the enforcement of administrative and judicial decisions. The second sentence of the principle relates more particularly to the State of origin urging it to avoid discrimination by granting (potentially) affected foreign victims equivalent access to and treatment in the same administrative and judicial proceedings as are available to persons within their own jurisdiction who have been or may be similarly affected. . . .

PROCEEDINGS IN THE STATE OF ORIGIN

There are various reasons why (potentially) affected foreign persons should be given access to, and adequate treatment by, the administrative and judicial authorities in the State of origin of a transboundary interference.

It allows the (potential) victims to take action *proprio motu* for the protection of their interests instead of waiting until action is taken by their government. This government may not be willing to hold the State of origin responsible, e.g., out of fear of being itself confronted with counterclaims by the other State concerning transboundary interferences which it may in its turn cause in the area of national jurisdiction of the other State or simply because it does not wish to burden the perhaps already delicate relation with the State of origin. It may also be that the (potentially) affected State may not be successful for various reasons in having the interference abolished or reduced at the interstate level, e.g., because the State of origin cannot be deemed to have breached an international duty of due diligence to prevent transboundary pollution. From the viewpoint of the State of origin domestic proceedings may well be preferred as such proceedings may prevent the State of origin from being held responsible at the intergovernmental level by the (potentially) affected State.

However, while there are good reasons why in certain cases resort to domestic proceedings in the State of origin is to be preferred over the intergovernmental approach, such proceedings will not always be possible.

In some countries (potentially) affected foreign persons will have *locus standi* before administrative authorities or courts, e.g., in France (see: the decision rendered by the Judicial Division of the *Conseil d'Etat* on 23 December 1981 concerning objections raised, inter alia, by certain German and Luxembourg municipalities, nature conservation associations and citizens against the Decree of 11 October 1978 recognizing the public utility of the nuclear power station at Cattenom (France), in Rev. Jur. de l'Environnement 1982 p. 295; see also: the decision of 27 July 1983 of the *Tribunal Administratif* of Strasbourg concerning a request of French potassium mines for a licence to continue to discharge waste salts into the Rhine, in *La Province de la Hollande septentriomale et autres v. Etat-Ministre de l'Environnement (Commissaire de la République du Haut-Rhin)* TA 227/81, 700/81 to 232/81, and 1197/81 and the decision rendered by the Judicial Division of the Conseil d'Etat on 18 April 1986, in *Société les Mines de Potasse d'Alsace v. La Province de la Hollande septentrionale et autres,* Case No. 53/934), or in the Netherlands (see: the decision of 3 October 1978 of the Chairman of the Judicial Division of the Dutch Council of State concerning objections raised by the German town of Borkum against a licence issued by the Dutch Ministry of Transport and Water Management provisionally allowing certain waste water discharges in the Ems-Dollard estuary, in Administratieve Beslissingen 1979 p. 353), or in Switzerland (see: the decision of the Swiss *Bundesrat* of 22 August 1979 explicitly recognizing the right of certain private persons living in Germany to lodge an administrative appeal against the licences for the construction of a nuclear power station in Leibstadt, in 44 Verwaltungspraxis der Bundesbehörden 1980 p. 86).

In other countries the administrative authorities and/or courts take the view that the scope of the applicable administrative law is strictly territorial, so that foreign interests are not considered to be legally affected nor protected by that law with the consequence that the foreign complainants are denied *locus standi.* This is the case in Austria (see, e.g. the 1913 decision of the Austrian Imperial and Royal Administrative Court concerning the diversion of water from the Leithe River, in 7 AJIL 1913 pp. 653-665, or the decision of 30 May 1969 of the Austrian Administrative Court in the *Salzburg Airport case* in Erkentnisse und Beschlüsse des Verwaltungsgerichtshofs No. 7582(A) p. 264 (1964)), or in the Federal Republic of Germany (see the 1985 decision of the *Verwaltungsgericht* Oldenburg, 3rd Chamber Osnabrück in *Hamers v. den Niedersächsischen Minister für Bundesangelegenbeiten* (Case 3 OS VG A 259/82/Mi)).

In some States of origin civil proceedings may be brought only before the courts of the place of the injury (see, e.g. English, Canadian and other Commonwealth case law concerning injury to foreign real property in the House of Lords decision *British South Africa Company v. Companbia de Mocambique* [1983] AC 602; or Article 20 of the Italian Code of Civil Procedure).

While in the case of proceedings before administrative authorities or courts the administrative policy or law of the State of origin will be determinative, in civil proceedings problems concerning the choice of the applicable law may rise.

Questions concerning the competence of, or the policy or law to be applied by, the administrative or judicial (whether administrative, civil or criminal) authorities of the State of origin have to some extent become the subject of treaties or recommendations by intergovernmental organizations.

Thus the 1968 European Community Convention on Jurisdiction and Enforcement of Judgments in Civil and Commercial Matters . . . allows, in the interpretation given by the court of Justice of the European Community to Article 5(3) of that Convention, civil torts to be brought before the courts of the State of origin or before those of the affected State (see Judgment of 30 November 1976, in *Report of Cases before the Court* 1976-8 (Case 21/76)). . . .

RESTATEMENT (THIRD) OF THE FOREIGN RELATIONS LAW OF THE UNITED STATES, §602(2) (1987)

§602. Remedies for Violation of Environmental Obligations

. . . (2) Where pollution originating in a state has caused significant injury to persons outside that state, or has created a significant risk of such injury, the state of origin is obligated to accord to the person injured or exposed to such risk access to the same judicial or administrative remedies as are available in similar circumstances to persons within the state.

Comment

B. ***Local Remedies.*** . . .

Subsection (2) applies the principle of non-discrimination against foreign nationals (§711, Comment *f*). This principle requires that a state in which pollution originates avoid discrimination in the enforcement of applicable international rules and standards, as well as give to foreign victims the benefit of its own rules and standards for the protection of the environment, even if they are stricter than the international rules or standards. Subsection (2) applies the principle of nondiscrimination also to remedies. A state must provide the same procedures, and apply the same substantive law and the same measures of compensation, to persons outside its territory as are available to persons injured within its territory. Thus, a state applying the "polluter-pays" principle should apply it to all pollution originating within the state, whether it causes injury at home or abroad. If a state applies the principle of strict liability, a victim of transfrontier pollution will be entitled to the benefit of that principle. On the other hand, if the state makes liability conditional on fault or negligence, the foreign victim can be required to meet that condition even if in the place of injury fault or negligence is not a necessary element for liability. Similarly, if a state's law imposes an obligation to reduce pollution to the lowest level that is attainable by the application of the most advanced technology that is economically feasible, this requirement applies equally to pollution at home and abroad.

When environmental injury in one state results from private activity in another state, a remedy may sometimes be available in the courts of the victim state, or even of a third state, and if the victim has received satisfaction by such a remedy the interstate remedy would abate.

C. AVAILABILITY OF PRIVATE REMEDIES UNDER STATE LAW

Under the law of many states, pollution damage is considered a local tort; suit for damages lies only in the state where the injury occurred, not in the state where the pollution originated. If personal jurisdiction over the person responsible for the pollution can be obtained in the state where the injury occurred, a suit for compensation or for an injunction would lie, but such suit might not be possible if the alleged polluter has no business or property in that state. Even if a suit there is brought under a long-arm statute and results in a default judgment, the judgment might not be enforceable in the polluter's home state. . . .

■ UNITED NATIONS CONVENTION ON THE LAW OF THE SEA, ARTICLE 235(2) AND (3)

Article 235
Responsibility and Liability

2. States shall ensure that recourse is available in accordance with their legal systems for prompt and adequate compensation or other relief in respect

of damage caused by pollution of the marine environment by natural or juridical persons under their jurisdiction.

3. With the objective of assuring prompt and adequate compensation in respect of all damage caused by pollution of the marine environment, States shall co-operate in the implementation of existing international law and the further development of international law relating to responsibility and liability for the assessment of and compensation for damage and the settlement of related disputes, as well as, where appropriate, development of criteria and procedures for payment of adequate compensation, such as compulsory insurance or compensation funds.

Notes and Questions

1. *The meaning of Article 235(2).* What does paragraph 2 of Article 235 really require states to do? Must they enact new legislation if existing provisions are inadequate? What is the significance of the phrase "in accordance with their legal systems" in this regard? Does it mean they only have to offer what is already available, but on a nondiscriminatory basis? Or does it mean that they must enact new measures if none are presently in place?

2. *"Ensuring" recourse.* How can a state "*ensure* that recourse is available"? Might there not be cases in which damage was caused, but because of proof or procedural problems courts would not grant relief?

3. *The approach of the Watercourses Convention.* These and other problems led the International Law Commission to reject a proposal to include a provision in its draft articles on international watercourses similar to Article 235(2). Instead, the commission adopted a draft article that formed the basis for Article 32 of the UN Convention on International Watercourses:

Article 32
Non-discrimination

Unless the watercourse States concerned have agreed otherwise for the protection of the interests of persons, natural or juridical, who have suffered or are under a serious threat of suffering significant transboundary harm as a result of activities related to an international watercourse, a watercourse State shall not discriminate on the basis of nationality or residence or place where the injury occurred, in granting to such persons, in accordance with its legal system, access to judicial or other procedures, or a right to claim compensation or other relief in respect of significant harm caused by such activities carried on in its territory.

United Nations Convention on the Law of the Non-Navigational Uses of International Watercourses, U.N. Doc. A/RES/51/229, July 8, 1997. Again, does the phrase "in accordance with its legal system" offer an escape route for the state that does not wish to accord access, equal or otherwise, to individuals from other countries? If you were representing such an individual, what argument(s) would you make against using that phrase as justification for not granting equal access?

■ INTERNATIONAL LAW AND THE ENVIRONMENT

Birnie & Boyle
above, *pp. 189-190, 201-205*

[B]y addressing the position of individuals and other legally significant entities directly, international law facilitates a more effective approach to the enforcement and implementation of environmental law, primarily through the use of national legal systems. The importance of national law can be observed at three levels, and involves not only the attribution of rights, but also of obligations.

First, national law is the medium through which states will usually implement their international obligations and regulate the conduct of their own nationals and companies both inside their borders and beyond. In this sense it enables the notion of individual responsibility to become part of the system of enforcement. Moreover, for the purpose of making international regimes more effective, international law may afford states an extended or extraterritorial protective jurisdiction to act against non-nationals, as in the exclusive economic zone, or to treat certain offences as crimes against international law over which all states have jurisdiction.

Secondly, national law may be used as a means of reallocating transboundary environmental costs. In this sense it represents an alternative to reliance on interstate claims, over which its main advantage is that it gives individuals control over the proceedings and places liability directly on the polluter concerned. The role of international law in this context is to ensure that obstacles to transboundary litigation are removed and in certain cases to ensure also that liability standards are harmonized and an effective remedy guaranteed.

Finally, national law may give individuals a means of securing protection from transboundary harm without resort to the intervention of their own government, and may in some cases also allow them to compel governments to abide by their international obligations. This possibility depends on the character of the legal system in question, but it can be facilitated by international recognition of a right to a decent environment or of a right of equal access to transboundary remedies. In this broader sense, individuals and NGOs can be empowered to act as part of the enforcement structure of international environmental law. In general, making national remedies available is consistent with the view that there are significant advantages in avoiding resort to interstate remedies for the resolution of transboundary environmental disputes wherever possible. . . .

(3) Civil Liability for Environmental Damage in Transboundary Proceedings

(a) Advantages

For the individual victim of transboundary environmental damage, the main advantage of recourse to civil liability proceedings is that this affords a direct and immediate remedy without resort to interstate claims or the complexities of the law of state responsibility. Crucially, any proceedings will be wholly at the plaintiff's discretion.

A second advantage is that recourse to civil liability helps implement the "polluter pays" principle referred to in Chapter 3. This principle provides an important justification for harmonization of national environmental liability laws, and for affording transboundary access to appropriate remedies. In essence, it favours directing the primary liability for damage away from states under international law, and instead passes transboundary costs directly to the operator or owner of the installation, industry, or activity in question. The extent to which this approach actually results in the ultimate polluter paying the full costs will then depend not on procedural obstacles but on whether liability is strict or dependent on proof of negligence, on whether it is limited in amount and on whether environmental clean-up and reinstatement costs are included.

These advantages are such that international policy and state practice have shown a strong preference for the direct accountability of the polluter in national law as the best means of facilitating recovery of compensation for pollution damage. This can be observed in OECD's principle of equal access, in certain UNEP guidelines, and in several significant treaties, including Article 235(2) of the 1982 UNCLOS and the 1988 Convention for the Regulation of Antarctic Mineral Resource Activities. The former requires states to ensure that recourse is available within their legal systems for prompt and adequate compensation for marine pollution damage caused by persons under their jurisdiction. The latter requires the operator of any Antarctic mineral undertakings to be held strictly liable for any damage to the environment or ecosystem. Other treaties, including those dealing with oil pollution from ships or with nuclear accidents, establish more complex schemes, considered below. These precedents have influenced negotiations concerning liability for dangerous activities harmful to the environment, and for the carriage of hazardous and noxious substances and wastes. Moreover, as part of his regime of liability for hazardous activities, ILC rapporteur Barboza has proposed that states should be required to give their courts jurisdiction to deal with transboundary claims in accordance with national law without discrimination based on nationality, domicile, or residence.

Principle 22 of the Stockholm Declaration, which called on states to cooperate in the development of international law concerning liability and compensation for environmental damage, did not specify that it should take the form of civil liability, but in practice what has begun to emerge is a dual system, in which civil liability will generally represent the most efficient means of securing redress, save where its disadvantages leave state responsibility as a subsidiary remedy of last resort.

(B) DISADVANTAGES

Without international cooperation and agreement, transboundary civil proceedings encounter several serious obstacles in many jurisdictions. The most important is the rule applied by some legal systems which denies courts jurisdiction over actions concerning foreign land. This rule may bar plaintiffs from bringing proceedings in the courts of the state from which the harm has originated. Its existence explains why the *Trail Smelter* case was referred not to the Canadian courts but to arbitration.

A plaintiff who seeks to avoid this jurisdictional problem by resorting to courts in his own state, where the damage has occurred, faces other difficulties. These may include a defence of sovereign immunity, if the foreign enterprise is governmental in character. Some states now deny such immunity where the tort is deemed to have taken place within their territory, or where it is not committed "in the exercise of sovereign authority." The latter point could be relied on to exclude immunity for most industrial activities on the ground that they are *iure gestionis*, which is the view taken by German courts when the Soviet Union was sued in respect of the Chernobyl disaster. Schreuer notes that a rigid requirement that the tort take place entirely within the territory of the forum would continue to allow immunity in cases of transboundary pollution, but international judicial decisions and state practice generally give territoriality a more extended definition under which it is sufficient if the effects are present in the forum state. In any event, international law does not require states to grant immunity in these circumstances, it merely permits them to do so, and the rules applied by any one jurisdiction should not be given undue weight.

Other problems will relate to the choice of applicable law, the enforcement of any judgment against a foreign defendant, who may have no assets within the jurisdiction of the court, and the possible use of a *forum non conveniens* defence. These difficulties are exacerbated in the case of ships or nuclear installations where the defendant's main or only asset may have been lost in the accident giving rise to proceedings. There is also likely to be difficulty obtaining injunctions relating to activities in the territory of other states.

The plaintiff may thus prefer the foreign forum, if available, in order to be sure of an effective remedy. Much will then depend on how satisfactorily the legal system of that forum deals with polluting activities. If it is unduly favourable to local industry, the transboundary plaintiff may be left with no redress, or with rights of a very limited character only. Thus, determining where to bring the proceedings may be critical to their success.

These are essentially issues of private international law, but they are sufficiently important for the intervention of public international law to have become necessary in order to remove some or all of the obstacles. There are two ways in which this can be done; by requiring adequate provision for equal access, or by securing a harmonization of civil liability laws on an agreed basis. Both techniques have been used to make civil liability more widely available to transboundary plaintiffs, and to guarantee an effective remedy.

(C) EQUAL ACCESS AND CIVIL LIABILITY

The positive impact of OECD's principle of equal access is best observed in the provision which now exists in Western Europe for transboundary civil liability. The effect of the 1974 Nordic Convention, and of the Brussels and Lugano Conventions on Civil Jurisdiction and the Enforcement of Judgments is that civil remedies are now available to transboundary claimants throughout Scandinavia, the EEC, and EFTA. In North America, legislation of some US states and Canadian provinces follows the pattern of the 1982 Uniform Transboundary Reciprocal Access Act, a model law drafted by national bar associations. In some cases existing law, particularly in the US, already permits access for foreign claimants. Civil actions have become the accepted method for recovering damages in respect of transboundary air and water pollution in all these jurisdictions. Some bilateral agreements also apply equal access to liability for nuclear accidents, although this is uncommon.

There is less evidence of support for the principle of equal access to civil liability proceedings in other regions. As we have seen, the principle was not referred to in Principle 22 of the Stockholm Declaration, nor is it found in UNEP's regional seas treaties, or in others concerned with dumping and land-based sources of marine pollution. At best, with a few exceptions, UNEP has mostly followed the position taken in the Stockholm Declaration. Moreover, an altogether different approach has been adopted in regional and global treaties dealing with ultrahazardous activities, including oil tankers and nuclear installations. Thus, in so far as Article 235(2) of the 1982 UNCLOS and the ILC's articles on international liability incorporate equal access, they do not yet represent a clear international consensus on the general principle of facilitating equal access, nor do they necessarily rest on widespread state practice in the developing world.

Moreover, equal access is not necessarily the best way to deal with civil liability, unless, as we have seen, the law of the state where the harm originates makes adequate provision, or its choice of law rules allows reference to the law of the place where the injury occurs. The criticism that where this is not the case, equal access may prove more favourable to the polluter can be overcome, however, by giving the plaintiff the choice of venue in which to bring proceedings. The European Court of Justice has interpreted Article 2 of the 1968 Brussels Convention on Jurisdiction and Enforcement of Judgments in this sense in its decision in *Handelswerkerij Bier v. Mines de Potasse d'Alsace.* This convention facilitates choice of forum by making judgments obtained in one jurisdiction enforceable in another, but it does not solve the problem of choice of applicable law. The Dutch district court which heard the liability proceedings in the *Handelswerkerij* case tried unsuccessfully to do so by applying international law to determine the liability of the defendants. Alternatively, some legal systems are willing to apply whichever national law is most favourable to the plaintiff in transboundary claims. Neither enforceability of judgments nor choice of law is regulated by OECD's scheme of "equal access," however.

■ LESSONS LEARNED IN GLOBAL ENVIRONMENTAL GOVERNANCE

Peter Sand
30-31 (1990)

. . . The *Trail Smelter* case developed into an international arbitration only because a deadlock arose between local legal rules. . . . Had these domestic procedural obstacles been removed by more flexible rules governing foreign parties, the case would probably never have moved to intergovernmental arbitration.

More recent environmental case law demonstrates that numerous local legal remedies are available to defuse transboundary problems and to resolve the apparent conflicts between divergent legal systems. For example, in the [*Poro* decision, summarized in the Case Study below], a German appeal court chose to determine damages "in accordance with the law most favorable to the plaintiff"—in this instance, the French Civil Code. Significantly, the bulk of disputes over transboundary pollution damage along the Rhine River since 1975 were resolved by local remedies, either through national courts or by out-of-court settlements and insurance.

Of course, this approach also requires a degree of mutual recognition to be given to foreign decisions—as, for instance, under the Brussels (1968) and Lugano (1988) Conventions on jurisdiction and enforcement of judgments in civil and commercial matters in Europe. There must be certain guarantees for the status of foreign parties in local judicial and administrative proceedings, as under the 1974 *Nordic Environmental Protection Convention.* . . . The *Recommendations on Equal Right of Access and Non-discrimination in Relation to Transfrontier Pollution,* adopted in 1976 and 1977 by the Organization for Economic Cooperation and Development, played a pilot role in this field. . . . Opening local remedies to foreign parties can go a long way toward de-escalating transboundary disputes to their ordinary neighborhood level.

■ THE UNIFORM TRANSBOUNDARY POLLUTION RECIPROCAL ACCESS ACT

Armin Rosencranz
15 Envtl. Poly. & L. 105 (1985)

When the Nordic Convention on the Protection of the Environment was [concluded in 1974], granting citizens in Denmark, Norway, Sweden and Finland equal access in environmental disputes to the courts and administrative proceedings of all four countries, few North American lawyers supposed that a comparable measure would ever be adopted to help resolve environmental disputes in North America. Canadian provinces had always been unreceptive to the use of their courts by non-residents. . . .

It now appears that the steady and painstaking efforts of the Uniform Law Conference of Canada and the (U.S.) National Conference of Commissioners on Uniform State Laws, working cooperatively, have brought about several historic adoptions of the "equal access" principle on the North American continent.

Building on the 1977 OECD recommendation for "Implementation of a Regime of Equal Right of Access and Non-Discrimination in Relation to Transfrontier Pollution," and the work of the American and Canadian Bar Associations in their joint 1979 report, "Settlement of International Disputes Between Canada and the USA," the two uniform law conferences in 1982 drafted the Transboundary Pollution Reciprocal Access Act (TBPRAA).[26]

[As of May 1997, the TBPRAA had been adopted by seven American states—Colorado, Connecticut, Michigan, Montana, New Jersey, Oregon, and Wisconsin, and by three Canadian provinces—Manitoba, Ontario, and Prince Edward Island.[27]]

The TBPRAA guarantees equal access for the victims of transboundary pollution to the courts or tribunals where the pollution originated. Residents of any state or province that has adopted the TBPRAA may sue polluters in other jurisdictions that have adopted similar legislation. The act removes a jurisdictional rule of private international law first articulated by the English courts in *British South Africa Co. v. Companhia de Mozambique* (1893). This case, which still represents the law in Canada, requires that all actions for trespass, nuisance or negligent injury to land must be brought

26. [This law was discussed briefly following the *Trail Smelter* case in Chapter 6. eds.]
27. [Uniform Laws Ann., Matrimonial, Family and Health Laws (1987), 1997 Supp. (Pocket Part)—Eds.]

in the jurisdiction where the land is located rather than where the nuisance or injury originated.

Under existing law, courts and tribunals in Canada may not take full account of the environmental impact of a polluting activity. Pollution victims are often left without recourse if the damaging activity happens to be carried on in a neighboring jurisdiction. American courts do not follow the *British South Africa* case, and have occasionally been creative in fashioning remedies to victims of transboundary pollution damage. But transboundary pollution problems may be too complex and important to be left to the vagaries of judge-made law.

The TBPRAA provides that when suit is brought in the province or state where the alleged pollution originated, the local substantive and procedural law of that jurisdiction governs the case. The rights and remedies of non-residents under the Act simply become equal to those of residents.

In Europe, only the Netherlands formally grants equal access to its courts and tribunals to citizens of all nations. As noted earlier, Denmark, Norway, Sweden and Finland subscribe among themselves to the equal access principle through the Nordic Convention on the Protection of the Environment. The principle evidently has a way to go before being broadly accepted in both Europe and North America.

Notes and Questions

1. *The effectiveness of private remedies.* The Rosencranz excerpt demonstrates that it is not only the nationality or residence of the victim that may cause problems of access; procedural rules, sometimes arcane ones like that of the *British South Africa* case, can do the job just as effectively. When these obstacles are added up, is the conclusion that private remedies are not an effective form of relief from transboundary pollution?

2. *The effectiveness of the Reciprocal Act.* Does the slow pace of adoption of the Reciprocal Act, and the failure of some border states and provinces to adopt it at all, suggest that it is not an effective way of dealing with the problem of procedural obstacles to private redress for transboundary environmental harm?

Additional Reading

For a discussion of procedural and related obstacles to private litigation in transnational environmental cases, *see* Stephen C. McCaffrey, Expediting the Provision of Compensation to Accident Victims, *in* Transferring Hazardous Technologies and Substances: The International Legal Challenge 199, 204-217 (G. Handl & R. Lutz, eds. 1989).

2. *Case Study:* Poro v. Houillières du Bassin du Lorraine (HBL)[28]

A power plant on the French side of the Saar River, which commenced operation in 1954 as a subsidiary of the state-owned Lorraine Basin Mining Company, emitted smoke and coal dust which affected the neighboring part of the Saar Valley, including the plaintiff's community of Kleinblittersdorf on the German side of the Saar. Plaintiff owned and operated a resort consisting of several vacation cabins and a restaurant with an adjoining garden. He claimed that [emissions] from the plant had destroyed various fruit and garden crops, and had rendered his cabins unrentable and garden terrace unusable. As a result, he claimed money damages for loss of earnings in the amount of 1,521,580 French francs for both the years 1954 and 1955. Plaintiff alleged that before the plant's establishment the region on both sides of the Saar was purely agricultural, that defendant's activity was the only one in the area which emitted pollutants, and that therefore the disturbances caused by the plant were not usual for the locality. It was further contended that the defendant had acted wrongfully in that the plant's emission control devices were insufficient and defective: While modern devices attain 99% efficiency, the defendant had only required an efficiency of 97% and actually achieved a level of 88%. It was therefore alleged that defendant had committed a delict, the constituent elements of which occurred in France and Germany, and that the law of the place of the wrong would be both the law of France and that of Germany. The plaintiff claimed that under the German choice of law rule, referring to the law most favorable to the plaintiff, French law (Art. 1384 Code Civil) should govern the case since it did not require proof of fault. But it was asserted that the result would be the same if German law (sec. 823 BGB) were applied since the action was also well founded under its provisions.

For its part, the defendant claimed that the suit was inadmissible because it was actually directed against the French government: The power plant was operated for the benefit of the French State and the latter was therefore a necessary party to the action; but a foreign state . . . cannot be sued before a German court. It was further alleged that the plaintiff's loss of business was due to the unusually bad weather conditions in 1954 and 1955 and to plaintiff's mismanagement. The defendant disputed plaintiff's claim that the use of its property was unusual for the vicinity, arguing that the whole Saarland is an industrial area in which a substantial degree of air pollution is normal. Furthermore, the defendant pointed out that it

28. Oberlandesgericht Saarbrücken, judgment of Oct. 22, 1957, No. 2 U 45/47, 11 NJW 752 (1958); 2 JBl Saar. 69 (1958); IPRspr. No. 42, p. 151 (1956-57). This summary of the case is from Stephen McCaffrey, Private Remedies for Transfrontier Environmental Disturbances 40-44 (IUCN 1975) (footnotes omitted).

had been granted a permit to operate its facility by the competent French agency, and therefore maintained that it was entitled to emit the allegedly offensive matter. To the plaintiff's claim that it had acted negligently in failing to provide proper emission control devices, defendant replied that the plant was built after careful study according to the most current state of technology and that the emission control system was constructed by two reliable firms with experience in this area. In short, defendant claimed that no more could be done to prevent its plant from affecting property in its vicinity. With respect to the applicable law, defendant argued that the dispute should be decided according to German law, since the latter refers to the whole law of France, including French conflict of laws rules, and these rules refer back to the law of the place of injury.

The court began by taking up defendant's contention that its status as a quasi-public corporation exempted it from suit before a German court. It held that while foreign states are exempt . . . , commercial enterprises of foreign states in the form of legal entities are subject to German legal process.

The court next considered which law to apply to plaintiff's claim. . . . Following the German choice of law rule, which refers to the law most favorable to the plaintiff, the court determined that Article 1384 of the French Civil Code [CC] should be applied since it required no proof of fault in contrast to section 823 of the German Civil Code. The court noted that plaintiff could establish a right to recovery under Article 1384 CC simply by showing that the defendant's power plant unlawfully caused him damage. Under section 823 BGB, on the other hand, plaintiff must not only demonstrate that his property or business was unlawfully injured by defendant, and that he suffered damage thereby, but he also must prove fault on the part of the defendant. . . .

Finally, on the choice of law issue, the court dealt with the question whether to apply only the substantive delictual provision of French law, or whether to look to the "whole law" of France, including its choice of law rules. It concluded that the principle referring to the law most favorable to the plaintiff excluded a reference back to German law. Moreover, the court reasoned, even if the whole [law of France] were applied, the same result would follow since French private international law refers to the law of the place of the act in tort cases, not to that of the place of the injury as contended by defendant. . . .

The court next turned to defendant's contention that it should not be liable for any injury suffered by plaintiff because its emission control devices were constructed in accordance with the latest state of technology. It held that this fact was inconsequential since under Art. 1384 CC the fault of the party causing the injury is irrefutably presumed. The only defenses to liability are (1) proof by defendant that the damage was brought about by an act of God, by accident or through the fault of the plaintiff, or (2) that the defendant was entitled to cause the damage. The court found that a right of the latter nature was not included in the plant's permit and could not be implied from the French "neighborhood law," which obliges a neighboring landowner to bear only such disturbances as would be present in a normal neighborhood relationship. The court found that the plant's emissions of soot and coal dust considerably exceeded the amount usually present in the locality before the plant's construction. It was further considered evident that an industrial use of property such as defendant's was not usual in that portion of the Saar Valley, in the contemplation of [the applicable provision of German law], and that plaintiff's community of Kleinblittersdorf had a rural character prior to the establishment of the power plant.

Since the trial court had determined that the plaintiff had suffered injury due to the operation of the defendant's plant, the court of appeals held that from the standpoint of defendant's liability it was irrelevant that there may have been other reasons (e.g., poor weather conditions or plaintiff's mismanagement) for plaintiff's loss of earnings. So long as these other possible causes would lead only to a reduction in the amount of defendant's liability, and not to an elimination thereof, they could be reserved for consideration in the subsequent proceedings on the amount of damage for which defendant would be liable.

Notes and Questions

1. *Defining the "neighborhood."* How did the court define the relevant "locality" or "neighborhood" for purposes of determining whether the defendant's activity was unusual? Did it consider areas on both sides of the border? If so, was that proper?

2. *The French permit.* Why wasn't the plant's permit an absolute defense? Should it have been?

3. *The applicable law.* Suppose the German court had found that German rather than French law would be more favorable to the plaintiff. Would it be fair to the French plant to hold it to German standards?

4. *Mini-case study:* The Salzburg Airport case:[29]

> The German municipality of Freilassing, which lies directly across the border from the airport [at Salzburg, Austria], and a private property owner from Freilassing sought to challenge an order by the Austrian Supreme Civil Aviation Authority . . . permitting the expansion of the scope of operation of the Salzburg airport, apparently on the ground that such would cause

29. Decision of May 30, 1969 (No. 233/69 and 314/69), amtliche Sammlung (1969) No. 7528 (A) 1969, p. 264. *See* the comment on this case by Christoph Schreuer, *Zur verwaltungs- und völkerrechtlichen Problematik des Salzburger Flughafenfalles*, 26 Österreichische Juristenzeitung 542 (1971). This summary of the case is from Stephen McCaffrey, Private Remedies for Transfrontier Environmental Disturbances 74-75 (IUCN 1975) (footnotes omitted).

> them increased aircraft noise disturbance. The Supreme Administrative Court of Austria dismissed the claims for the following reasons: The challenged permit was granted pursuant to . . . the Austrian Aviation Act which, the court reasoned, is applicable only in the territory of the Republic of Austria. [T]his statute grants affected state and local governmental bodies and "statutory interest groups" the opportunity to comment upon proposed modifications of an airport's scope of operation. The court held that because of the essentially territorial character of this administrative legal norm, the right granted extends only to Austrian governmental bodies and interest groups, and not to those in a foreign country. The German municipality therefore had no right, or legal capacity, to challenge the permit under the Aviation Act. It followed that the private citizen complainant, as an owner of foreign property, was likewise accorded no right by the Aviation Act to challenge the Austrian administrative order.

Do you agree with the Austrian court's rationale? Compare and contrast the approaches of the German court in the *Poro* case and that of the Austrian court in the *Salzburg Airport* case. Why did the latter court not consider itself able to take into account the concerns of those on the other side of the border? If in *Poro* the plant had been in Germany and the injured resort owner in France, do you believe the court would have taken the injuries into account in a suit for damages against the German plant?

In the United States, individuals residing in other countries are often permitted to participate in administrative proceedings concerning possible effects in their countries of planned activities in the United States. This is true, for example, of proceedings in the state of California concerning a sewage outflow in San Diego affecting Mexican nationals from the state of Baja California. Interview with officials at California State Water Resources Control Board. *See also* Clean Air Act §115, 42 U.S.C. §7415.

G. CRIMINAL RESPONSIBILITY

■ CRIMES AGAINST THE ENVIRONMENT

Stephen McCaffrey
in 1 International Criminal Law 541 (M. Cherif Bassiouni, ed. 1986)[30]

. . . [V]arious international instruments, principles and theories . . . attach penal consequences to conduct resulting in serious harm to vital or scarce natural resources; and a number of states have enacted legislation, often pursuant to international instruments, making it a crime under their municipal law to cause harm to internationally shared resources. . . .

30. [Portions of this excerpt have been updated by the author for the purposes of this book.—EDS.]

[T]here are sound reasons for criminalizing environmentally harmful conduct. And it is submitted that these reasons apply with equal vigor to resources that are shared on the domestic and international levels. In fact, the considerations which support and explain criminalization on the domestic level may apply with even greater force to internationally shared resources. It is not necessary here to enter the debate about whether such resources are *res nullius* or *res communis* because many of them are, by their very nature, simply not capable of appropriation and reduction to ownership. They may, however, be used in a manner which forecloses certain uses by others or even leads to their complete destruction: air and water may be polluted, species may be extinguished.

Because it is thus likely that internationally shared resources will often be protected even less by private vigilance than their domestic counterparts, the argument for their protection by penal sanctions would seem to be stronger than that applicable to resources shared domestically. Furthermore, some internationally shared resources—such as certain species of flora and fauna—may be entirely and forever extinguished because of the "commons" effect, which may be more pronounced when the commons in question overlaps jurisdictions or is beyond the limits of national jurisdiction: to the extent that (a) national laws do not reach the conduct in question, and (b) the conduct is not governed by a relevant international regime, it will operate free of both private, and any existing public, regulatory constraints.

These considerations have led states, both individually and collectively, to attach penal sanctions to certain kinds of conduct and activities that threaten, damage or destroy those natural resources which represent internationally shared values. . . .

II. International Instruments That Envisage Criminal Responsibility of Private Persons

PENAL CHARACTERISTICS

There are a number of types of provisions found in international instruments relating to nature and the environment which might be considered to be penal in nature, or to be of such a character as to be part of the field of international criminal law. Our editor has proposed the following list of characteristics, the presence of any one of which would qualify an instrument as belonging to the field of international criminal law: (1) explicit or implicit declaration of certain conduct as a crime under international law; (2) criminalization of the conduct under national law; (3) providing for the prosecution or extradition of the alleged perpetrator; (4) providing for punishment of the person found guilty; (5) cooperation through the various modalities of judicial assistance in the enforcement of the agreement; (6) establishment of a priority in theories of jurisdiction and perhaps recognition of the applicability of universal jurisdiction; (7) reference to an international criminal jurisdiction; and (8) exclusion of the defense of superior orders. These criteria have provided guidance in the identification of instruments to be included in the present study.

CONVENTIONS

The vast majority of the instruments surveyed for this study contain a blend of items (2) through (4) on the list set out above. Most commonly, these instruments require the contracting parties to take "appropriate measures to ensure the application of the provisions of the [agreement in question] and the punishment of infractions against [those] provisions." Other approaches include requiring the parties to "enact and enforce such legislation as may be necessary to make effective the . . . provisions [of the agreement] with appropriate penalties for violations thereof," providing that violations "shall be an offence punishable under the laws of the territory in which the ship is registered," and providing that the parties "shall enact and enforce such legislation and other measures as may be necessary for the purpose of giving effect to [the] Agreement," which agreement includes various prohibitions. These types of provisions are found in some fifteen multilateral agreements relating to the environment. Some agreements expressly recognize their deterrent function in provisions to the effect that "the penalties specified under the law of a party shall be adequate in severity to discourage violations of the present Convention. . . ."

A number of conventions contain what might be referred to as "policing provisions" which allow parties to take action on the spot to enforce the rules of the agreement. This is true, for example, of the 1911 Convention for the Preservation of Fur Seals in the North Pacific, which provides in article 1 that persons offending against the Convention's prohibition against pelagic sealing "may be seized" by the authorities of the territory in which the violation occurs. The same convention, in article 7, provides that each party "will maintain a guard or patrol in the waters frequented by the seal herd in the protection of which it is especially interested, so far as may be necessary for the enforcement of the [Convention]." Similarly, the 1937 International Agreement for the Regulation of Whaling provides in article 1 that the parties "will maintain at least one inspector of whaling on each factory ship under their jurisdiction." The Interim Convention on Conservation of North Pacific Fur Seals of 1957 goes further, allowing a "duly authorized official of any of the Parties" to board and search "any vessel . . . subject to the jurisdiction of any of the Parties" which he "has reasonable cause to believe . . . is offending against the prohibition of pelagic sealing. . . ." The Convention goes on to provide that if after searching the vessel the official "continues to have reasonable cause to believe that the vessel or any person on board thereof is offending against the prohibition, he may seize or arrest such vessel or person." Finally, what might be referred to as a "self-policing provision" is found in the Agreement between Canada and the United States on Great Lakes Water Quality of 1978. An annex to that agreement provides as follows:

> As soon as any person in charge [of a vessel] has knowledge of any discharge of harmful quantities of oil or hazardous polluting substances, immediate notice of such discharge shall be given to the appropriate agency in the jurisdiction where the discharge occurs; failure to give this notice shall be made subject to appropriate penalties.

RECOMMENDATIONS AND RESOLUTIONS

Various international or intergovernmental bodies have produced instruments that call for the use of penal sanctions to safeguard nature and the environment. . . . [The author discusses draft articles adopted by the UN International Law Commission in the context of its work on the Draft Code of Crimes Against the Peace and Security of Mankind. These articles are examined in Chapter 15.]

The United Nations Educational, Scientific and Cultural Organization in 1962 adopted a "Recommendation concerning the safeguarding of the beauty and character of landscapes and sites" which contains the following provisions:

> The General Conference recommends that Member States should apply the following provisions by adopting, in the form of a national law or in some other way, measures designed to give effect in the territories under their jurisdiction to the norms and principles embodied in this recommendation. . . .
>
> 35. Violation of the rules governing the protection of landscapes and sites should involve payment of damages or the obligation to restore the site to its former condition, as far as possible.
>
> 36. Administrative or criminal prosecutions should be provided for in the case of deliberate damage to protected landscapes and sites.

In 1994, the United Nations Economic and Social Council called on the secretary general of the United Nations Commission on Crime and Criminal Justice to include environmental crime in the Commission's crime control program. At its meeting from April 26 to May 6, 1994, the U.N. Commission on Crime and Criminal Justice adopted a German proposal calling for increased use of criminal law to prosecute environmental crimes. And in 1995, at the 9th U.N. Congress on the Prevention of Crime and the Treatment of Offenders, the plenary session adopted a workshop's conclusions that corporations should be held accountable for environmental crimes.

The Consultative Assembly of the Council of Europe in 1972 adopted a recommendation on "environment policy in Europe" which included, as one of its "principles of a national environmental policy," that of "introduc[ing] into the penal code the concepts and description of crimes or offenses against the environment which would entail severe sanctions." And in 1977 the Committee of Ministers of the Council of Europe adopted a resolution dealing specifically with the subject of "The Contribution of Criminal Law to the Protection of the Environment." This resolution states that "while recourse to the criminal law in this field should be a last resort, nevertheless use must be made of it when other measures are not observed or are ineffective or inadequate. . . ."

VALUES PROTECTED

[I]nternational criminal law has as its principal *raison d'être* the protection of certain shared values the international community has come to recognize as being so important that penal sanctions must be imposed on those who threaten or impair them. A survey of international instruments relating to the global environment reveals that a wide variety of values fall into this category, ranging from natural beauty and the integrity of the environment in general to specific species of flora and fauna. The following examples of these values illustrate their wide diversity.

A number of conventions with penal features include provisions on the protection of particular species or of flora and fauna in general. For example, the preamble of CITES provides that the contracting states:

> RECOGNIZ[E] that wild fauna and flora in their many beautiful and varied forms are an irreplaceable part of the natural systems of the earth which must be protected for this and the generations to come; [and are]
>
> CONSCIOUS of the ever-growing value of wild fauna and flora from aesthetic, scientific, cultural, recreational and economic points of view. . . .

Perhaps more common are instruments with penal characteristics that are directed toward the protection of a specific species.

The international community has for some time now recognized the importance of protecting the ocean from pollution and has produced a number of instruments providing for the prosecution by municipal authorities of individual polluters. Interestingly, however, the same cannot yet be said of the atmosphere.

A number of instruments having penal characteristics emphasize the importance of safeguarding the beauty of nature, and aesthetic considerations in general. This is true, for example, of CITES. . . . Another example is the 1940 Convention on Nature Protection and Wildlife Preservation in the Western Hemisphere, which declares the intent of the parties "to protect and preserve scenery of extraordinary beauty, unusual and striking geologic formations, regions and natural objects of aesthetic historic or scientific value. . . ."

The importance of aesthetic considerations is also recognized by intergovernmental organizations. The Committee of Ministers of the Council of Europe has declared that "the beauty of landscapes must be protected by all possible means . . . ," and the General Conference of UNESCO in 1962 adopted a recommendation, containing penal provisions, specifically addressed to "the safeguarding of the beauty and character of landscapes and sites." . . .

Finally, some instruments expressly recognize the responsibility of present generations to protect and preserve the earth's resources for future generations. Examples of this type of provision may be found both in CITES, and in the 1946 Convention for the Regulation of Whaling. The latter agreement recognizes "the interest of the nations of the world in safeguarding for future generations the great natural resources represented by the whale stocks. . . ."

III. State Responsibility

The breach of an international legal obligation is an internationally wrongful act that gives rise to state responsibility. The question arises whether some breaches may be so serious—because of both the gravity of the breach and the importance of the obligation involved—that they result in a form of state responsibility that may be termed "criminal." The International Law Commission in 1976[31] tentatively answered this very controversial question in the affirmative by provisionally adopting article 19 of its draft articles on State Responsibility. Entitled "International Crimes and International Delicts," article 19 provides in pertinent part as follows:

> 1. An act of a State which constitutes a breach of an international obligation is an internationally wrongful act, regardless of the subject matter of the obligation breached.
>
> 2. An internationally wrongful act which results from the breach by a State of an international obligation so essential for the protection of fundamental interests of the international community that its breach is recognized as a crime by that community as a whole, constitutes an international crime.
>
> 3. Subject to paragraph 2, and on the basis of the rules of international law in force, an international crime may result, inter alia, from:
>
> . . .
>
> (d) a serious breach of an international obligation of essential importance for the safe-guarding and preservation of the human environment, such as those prohibiting massive pollution of the atmosphere or of the seas.

The Commission's stated rationale for distinguishing between international "delicts" and "crimes" was, in essence, that "general international

31. [Article 19 was maintained in the complete set of draft articles on State Responsibility adopted by the International Law Commission on first reading in 1996. 1996 I.L.C. Rep. 131.—Eds.]

law now differentiates between various types of internationally wrongful acts, and consequently, between different regimes of state responsibility." Those internationally wrongful acts which (a) are particularly serious, and (b) violate an obligation essential for the safeguarding of the fundamental interests of the international community as a whole are denominated "international crimes" by article 19.

This draft article has been, and continues to be, accorded a mixed reception by states, commentators, and members of the Commission itself.[32] The doubts that have been expressed about the notion of state "criminal" responsibility seem to be due in large measure to the fact that the nature of the "regime" of such a form of responsibility is, at present, not at all clear. In particular, concern has been expressed about what kinds of consequences would ensue from an "international crime" for the acting state, the "victim" state (if there was one in particular) and third states. For example, questions have been raised as to the validity of the concept that a state, as opposed to an individual leader of a state, is capable of committing a crime. Similarly, it has been asked whether an entire population of a nation should be treated as international criminals because of the actions of their leaders. Strong doubts have also been expressed as to whether there is any solid evidence that the concept of international criminal responsibility is actually recognized in the practice of states. This would presumably be necessary in light of the definition of the concept of an "international crime" in article 19(2), which requires that the "international community as a whole" recognize the act or practice in question as a crime. According to the commentary to article 19, this means that "a given internationally wrongful act shall be recognized as an 'international crime,' not only by some particular group of states, even if it constitutes a majority, but by all the essential components of the international community." One might wonder whether "all the essential components of the international community" could ever agree that a given type of environmentally harmful act would constitute an "international crime" in view of the broad exposure this would entail, as well as the fact that there presently exists no agreement which could serve as the basis for such an offense.

The fact that the notion of state criminal responsibility is controversial, however, does not diminish the force of the following statement in the commentary to article 19:

> [T]he astounding progress of modern science, although it has produced and continues to produce marvelous achievements of great benefit to mankind, nevertheless imparts a capacity to inflict kinds of damage which would be

32. For an excellent review of the historical background of article 19, the reactions of states and Commission members to it, and the main problems raised by the notion of state criminal responsibility, see International Crimes of States: A Critical Analysis of the ILC's Draft Article 19 on State Responsibility (Joseph H.H. Weiler, *et al.* eds., 1989), a collection of documents prepared for the Conference on State Responsibility and the Concept of Crimes of States, held in Florence, 27 and 28 October 1984. . . .

> fearfully destructive not only of man's potential for economic and social development but also of his health and of the very possibility of survival for the present and future generations.

This language is redolent of the suggestion that the Commission was particularly concerned about environmental damage caused by nuclear explosions.[33] Indeed, a number of conventions dealing with the subject of nuclear weapons possess penal characteristics, such as prohibition of the conduct in question by private parties. For example, article 1 of the Treaty Banning Nuclear Weapon Tests in the Atmosphere, in Outer Space and Under Water provides that the parties undertake "to prohibit, to prevent, and not to carry out any nuclear weapon test explosion, or any other nuclear explosion, at any place under its jurisdiction or control," in the areas covered by the convention." While the killing of all life on Earth may be viewed as the ultimate environmental offense, however, such conduct must be considered to be beyond the scope of this chapter.

IV. Generally Recognized Principles of Law

Article 38 of the Statute of the International Court of Justice lists as one of the sources of international law to be applied by the Court "the general principles of law recognized by civilized nations." The theory here is essentially that if a norm is generally recognized by states on the municipal level, it is also one which may, in appropriate circumstances, be drawn upon in regulating their relations *inter se.*

An increasing number of states have enacted legislation providing for punishment of environment-related offenses. This trend has been given a significant boost by CITES, to which [approximately] 130 countries are parties. . . .

INTERNATIONAL LAW AND THE ENVIRONMENT

Birnie & Boyle
above, *pp. 208-210*

(3) Universal Jurisdiction and Crimes Against International Law

Universal jurisdiction entitles a state to prosecute an offence even in the absence of any connection based on nationality, territory, or the protective principle. Piracy is the clearest and least controversial example of this much

33. [Cf. the advisory opinion of the International Court of Justice on the question of the legality of the threat or use of nuclear weapons, discussed in the notes following the *Nuclear Tests* case in Chapter 6.—Eds.]

disputed form of jurisdiction, which rests on the assumption that the crimes in question are contrary to international public order. Thus it is the interest of every state in suppressing such offences which justifies their status as crimes which any state may prosecute. . . . The basis of the [UN International Law Commission's, or ILC's] proposed "Code of [Crimes] Against the Peace and Security of Mankind," and of conventions dealing with torture and hijacking, is that every state in whose territory the alleged perpetrator is present shall either try or extradite. . . .

It is the ILC's version of the universality principle with which the concept of port state jurisdiction employed in article 218 of the 1982 [United Nations Convention on the Law of the Sea] is broadly comparable. The crucial feature of this article is that it gives the state in whose port the vessel is present the right to prosecute for pollution offences committed on the high seas or in the maritime zones of other states, subject to a right of pre-emption by the flag state. But, unlike other applications of the principle, this article represents an extension so far not reflected in state practice. It is also the only application relevant to the enforcement of environmental law.

[The authors discuss earlier provisions of the ILC's draft Code of Crimes relating to the environment. They argue that a] preferable approach would limit the category [of offenses] to violations of applicable international rules intended to cause serious harm to the natural environment; a possible example would be the conduct of Iraq in setting fire to Kuwaiti oil wells in 1991.

Nevertheless it is by no means clear that such a rule in whatever form [is] at present part of international law. States have generally been reluctant to allow broad claims of universal jurisdiction. . . . Moreover, although the 1977 Additional Protocol I to the Geneva Conventions includes provisions on protection of the environment in time of armed conflict, which some writers see as representing customary law, it falls short of including these articles in the category whose grave breach constitutes war crimes. . . . The inclusion of environmental offenses may prove a significant development if adopted in practice, however, because of its potential utility in protecting the global commons. Here there is a case for treating very serious and deliberate pollution as equivalent to piracy, since the public interest of all states is affected and effective enforcement may otherwise be lacking. In this respect the argument for universal jurisdiction over individuals mirrors the argument for an *actio popularis* covering "international crimes" under Article 19 of the ILC's articles on state responsibility, in so far as it enables states to take unilateral action to protect community concerns.

Notes and Questions

1. *Why criminalize?* What are the reasons for criminalizing certain conduct? Do they apply on the international level? Do you believe the

available enforcement mechanisms are adequate to deter the conduct that is criminalized?

2. *Individual versus state crimes.* Do you see the difference between criminalizing conduct by individuals, on the one hand, and states, on the other? What are the advantages and disadvantages of each form of criminal responsibility? How do you punish a state? Does history offer any lessons on the advisability of punishing countries?

3. *The Basel Convention.* The Basel Convention on the control of Transboundary Movements of Hazardous Wastes and Their Disposal of March 22, 1989, provides in Article 4, paragraphs 3 and 4, that

> 3. The Parties consider that illegal traffic in hazardous wastes or other wastes is criminal.
>
> 4. Each Party shall take appropriate legal, administrative and other measures to implement and enforce the provisions of this Convention, including measures to prevent and punish conduct in contravention of the Convention.

Additional Reading

For an earlier description of criminal law of the environment in the United States, *see* Jaro Mayda, Penal Protection of the Environment, 26 Am. J. Comp. L. 471 (Supp. 1978). For a description of the recent work of the United Nations Commission on Crime Prevention and Criminal Justice concerning environmental protection, *see* Gerhard Loibl & Markus Reiterer, Criminal Law and the Protection of the Environment, 27 Envtl. Poly. & L. 400 (1997).

Concluding Questions

Are you satisfied with the current state of the international system, or systems, concerning accountability and compliance in the field of the environment? If not, what would you change? Are your suggestions practical or utopian? On the intergovernmental level, do you believe the new, non-confrontational approaches hold promise? Should they be viewed as complementary to or as a replacement for intergovernmental litigation or arbitration? On the private level, is the current state of the law adequate? That is, do you believe more should be done to ensure the availability of private recourse for transfrontier pollution damage? What about criminalization of environmental insults? Does this approach hold promise? How do these techniques relate to the alternative environmental protection strategies considered in the next chapter?

X

Regional Transboundary Pollution

Transboundary pollution might be said to have catalyzed the development of international environmental law. As we will see in section B of this chapter, pollution of international watercourses has been the subject of treaty provisions for well over a century. While air pollution has been known since ancient times, it has been recognized as an international problem only relatively recently. The case that many regard as the fountainhead of international environmental law, the *Trail Smelter Arbitration,* was decided in 1941. It took another 30 years for governments to begin to appreciate the seriousness of the problem of the long-distance transport of air pollution.

In this chapter we look at the way in which states have tackled the problem of regional transboundary pollution. We deal first with transboundary air pollution and, specifically, the phenomenon commonly known as "acid rain," both in North America and in Europe. We then move to water pollution. After considering efforts to codify general principles in this field, we focus on the efforts of Canada and the United States to protect the Great Lakes ecosystem. You should read these materials in light of the cases in Chapter 6—in particular *Trail Smelter*—and the fundamental norms or prevention considered in Chapter 7. To what extent have the solutions suggested by the cases and the norms of prevention influenced or been carried over into the regimes considered in this chapter?

A. CASE STUDY: ACID RAIN

Air pollution respects no national boundaries; it may easily flow from one country to another. Thus, transboundary air pollution forms a major issue in international environmental relations. For present purposes, "transboundary air pollution" will be defined as "air pollution whose physical origin is situated wholly or in part within the area under the national jurisdiction of one State and which has adverse effects in the area under the jurisdiction of another State."[1] Two major international agreements have been concluded on transboundary air pollution: the 1991 United States-Canada Air Quality Agreement and the 1979 ECE Convention on Long-Range Transboundary Air Pollution.

1. Canada-United States Acid Rain

a. Background

By the early 1970s, it was known that air pollution could damage human health, natural resources such as soils, plants, and trees, aesthetic interests such as views, and historical and cultural assets such as statues and monuments.

As a result of these concerns, Canada and the United States enacted Clean Air Acts intended to improve ambient air quality through the control of sulphur dioxide, nitrogen oxides, particulates, and carbon monoxide. By 1984, Canada had reduced its sulphur dioxide emissions by approximately 41 percent and the United States had reduced its emissions by approximately 24 percent. Although these reductions improved air quality in the vicinity of the emissions, they had the opposite effect regarding long-range air pollution because the Acts effectively encouraged the construction of tall stacks that dispersed pollution over a greater geographic area. One of the results of the long-range pollution was acid deposition, more commonly referred to as acid rain, which involves the deposition (e.g., via rain, snow, mist, and fog) of acids from the atmosphere to Earth's surface. Acid rain is mainly caused by sulfur oxides and nitrogen oxides; these gases are oxidized to form sulfuric acid and nitric acid when they come into contact with water.[2] The vast majority of sulfur dioxide emissions come from industrial facilities, with the main culprits being electric utilities in the United States and metal smelters in Canada. Nitrogen oxides are primarily caused

1. Convention on Long-Range Transboundary Air Pollution, Nov. 13, 1979, T.I.A.S. No. 10541.

2. The National Acid Precipitation Assessment Program, Interim Assessment: The Causes and Effects of Acidic Deposition 1-4 (1987). Scientists assign approximately two-thirds of the blame for causing acid rain to sulphur oxides and one-third to nitrogen oxide. *Id.*

by electric utilities, transportation, and industry.[3] In the early 1980s, the United States was emitting approximately 25.7 million tons of sulphur dioxide and 23 million tons of nitrogen dioxide annually, while Canada's annual emissions totalled 5.2 million tons and 2 million tons, respectively.

By 1977, it became evident that emissions in Canada were leading to acid deposition in northeastern United States, and that emissions in the United States were leading to acid deposition in eastern Canada, thus causing significant damage to surface waters and aquatic life. A study by the International Joint Commission (Canada-United States) showed that large amounts of pollutants in the Great Lakes resulted from atmospheric deposition.[4] Negotiations between the two countries led to the formation in 1978 of a Bilateral Research Consultation Group (BRCG) on the long-range transport of airborne pollutants. The BRCG's mandate was to facilitate information exchange, to coordinate research activities, and to develop an agreed scientific database for developing solutions to the problem. Also in 1978, the United States Congress passed a resolution calling upon the president to initiate discussions with Canada in order to negotiate a cooperative agreement to protect the air quality of North America. In July 1979, Canada and the United States jointly announced their intention to develop such an agreement. On August 5, 1980, the two countries signed the Memorandum of Intent on Transboundary Air Pollution, which stated the two countries' intention of working towards developing a bilateral agreement on air quality and established five joint work groups to investigate various aspects of acid deposition. The technical and scientific work groups released their final reports in February 1983 and referred them for peer review. Later in 1983, the United States peer review panel issued its report calling for reductions in emissions and rejecting the argument that more research was needed before regulatory action could be taken. Canada's peer review panel reached the same conclusion.

On January 25, 1984, President Ronald Reagan stated that the United States would intensify research into the causes and effects of acid rain rather than taking action to reduce emissions. This position caused considerable consternation in Canada. Two months later, Prime Minister Brian Mulroney and President Reagan each appointed a Special Envoy on Acid Rain to study the issue further.

Between 1977 and 1985, Canada's claim was essentially that it was taking unilateral action to reduce sulphur dioxide emissions in eastern Canada by approximately 50 percent and to reduce the transboundary flux from Canada to the United States by at least 50 percent and that the flux of sulphur dioxide from the United States to Canada was injuring lakes and streams in eastern Canada, among other natural resources, and should be

3. Acid Rain and Friendly Neighbors: The Policy Dispute Between Canada and the United States (Jurgen Schmandt & Hillary Roderick, eds. 1988).

4. *Id.* at 65.

reduced by 50 percent. (Throughout the negotiations, Canada focused on sulphur dioxide because it believed that the acid deposition problem in Canada is a sulphur-driven phenomenon due to the fact that the soil in eastern Canada tends to be nitrogen deficient.) During this period, negotiations regarding acid rain occurred at non-national levels: Canada and Quebec negotiated, as did Ontario and New York.

The special envoys released their report in January 1986 and concluded that acid rain is a serious transboundary problem that creates environmental hazards in both countries. In March of that year, the two leaders endorsed the special envoys' report.

The two countries took several steps to implement the special envoys' recommendations, including the formation of a Bilateral Advisory and Consultative Group and, in the United States, the establishment of a five-year, $5 billion program to develop alternative technologies to remove sulphur from coal.

By 1988, Canada claimed that 14,000 lakes and at least nine salmon-bearing rivers were dead (i.e., they could no longer support aquatic life) due to acid rain, that 150,000 other lakes were being acidified (i.e., they had a pH level less than 6.0, the acidity level at which detrimental biological effects begin to occur), and that several hundred thousand more were vulnerable to acidification. Canada also raised fears about the large percentages of the best agricultural land (85 percent) and forests (50 percent) in eastern Canada receiving high levels of acid rain.

During acid-rain discussions with the United States, Canada expressed its view that the United States is bound by international law to reduce the transboundary flow of sulphur dioxide emissions to the point where they do not cause significant damage in Canada. Canada based its view on, inter alia, the *Trail Smelter*,[5] *Corfu Channel*,[6] and *Lake Lanoux*[7] cases and on Principle 21 of the Stockholm Declaration on the Human Environment[8] (these were considered in Chapters 6 and 7). The United States, relying on the same authorities, was of the view that it was doing all that is required by international law. Canada did not request that the dispute be submitted to a binding dispute-settlement mechanism (despite the fact that other environmental disputes between the two countries have been so decided), preferring instead a negotiated solution.

Litigation to prompt United States action was attempted by the state of New York and environmental groups in United States courts, pursuant to section 115 of the Clean Air Act,[9] which requires the administrator of

5. *Trail Smelter* (U.S. v. Can.), 3 R. Intl. Arb. Awards 1905 (1938 & 1941).

6. *Corfu Channel* (U.K. v. Alb.), 1949 I.C.J. 4 (Judgment of 9 Apr.)

7. *Lac Lanoux* (Fr. v. Spain), 24 I.L.R. 101 (1957) (English), 12 R. Intl. Arb. Awards 281 (1957) (French).

8. Stockholm Declaration on the Human Environment, Sept. 16, 1972, U.N. Doc. A/CONF. 48/14/Rev. 1, at 3 (1973), *reprinted in* 11 I.L.M. 1416 (1972).

9. 38 U.S.C. §7415(a) (1982).

the United States Environmental Protection Agency (EPA) to give, under specified circumstances, formal notification to a state in which emissions originate that the administrator "has reason to believe . . . cause or contribute to air pollution which may reasonably be anticipated to endanger public health or welfare in a foreign country. . . ." (Formal notification would require a state to revise its implementation plan to prevent or eliminate the danger.) Those cases were not successful.[10]

During the last four years of President Reagan's administration (1985 to 1989), the United States position was dominated by the claim that the United States needed more information before it would commit to reduce the transboundary flux. The governors of New York and Ohio also negotiated during this period and suggested an emissions-reduction program that would be funded by the two states and by the United States federal government.

The United States's insistence on the need for more information focused on perceived uncertainties regarding acid rain's causes (e.g., the role of compounds such as nitrogen oxides and volatile organic compounds), effects (e.g., the importance of naturally occurring neutralizers), and control costs. Canada argued that enough certainty existed. The debate intensified with the release in 1987 of the Interim Report of the United States National Acid Precipitation Assessment Program (NAPAP), a ten-year program established by act of Congress in 1980 to study acid rain in the United States. The Interim Report was highly controversial, especially the 67-page Executive Summary. Canada objected that the Executive Summary did not consider evidence in Canada, used a threshold pH level of 5.0 (which is 10 times more acidic than the 6.0 pH level at which biological damage begins), excluded lakes smaller than ten acres and waterways, assumed a 300 percent increase in United States nuclear power generation in forecasting emissions reductions, and was not peer reviewed.

After George Bush became president in January 1989, he proposed major changes in the United States Clean Air Act, which eventually were enacted in October 1990.[11] Those changes, which require utilities to reduce emissions of sulphur by ten million tons by the year 2000, apparently will meet Canada's demands for a 50 percent decrease in the transboundary flux of sulphur dioxide.

b. The 1991 Agreement

In July 1990, Prime Minister Mulroney and President Bush announced that the two countries "have agreed to begin negotiations for a practical

10. *See, e.g.,* Thomas v. New York, 802 F.2d 1443 (D.C. Cir. 1986), *cert. denied,* 482 U.S. 919 (1987); Ontario v. EPA, 912 F.2d 1525 (D.C. Cir. 1990).

11. 1990 Clean Air Act Amendments, Pub. L. No. 101-549, 104 Stat. 2399.

and effective air quality accord."[12] Negotiations on that accord resulted in the Agreement on Air Quality between the two countries of March 13, 1991, 30 I.L.M. 676 (1991). Article IV of the agreement is entitled "Specific Air Quality Objectives." Paragraph 2 of that article provides in part that "[e]ach Party's specific objectives for emissions limitations or reductions of sulphur dioxide and nitrogen oxides, which will reduce transboundary flows of these acidic deposition precursors, are set forth in Annex 1." The agreement also establishes a bilateral Air Quality Committee to assist the parties with its implementation and assigns specific responsibilities to the International Joint Commission established by the 1909 Boundary Waters Treaty between the two countries.[13] Selected provisions follow.

■ AGREEMENT BETWEEN THE GOVERNMENT OF THE UNITED STATES OF AMERICA AND THE GOVERNMENT OF CANADA ON AIR QUALITY

The Government of the United States of America and the Government of Canada, hereinafter referred to as "the Parties,"

Convinced that transboundary air pollution can cause significant harm to natural resources of vital environmental, cultural and economic importance, and to human health in both countries;

Desiring that emissions of air pollutants from sources within their countries not result in significant transboundary air pollution;

Convinced that transboundary air pollution can effectively be reduced through cooperative or coordinated action providing for controlling emissions of air pollutants in both countries;

Recalling the efforts they have made to control air pollution and the improved air quality that has resulted from such efforts in both countries;

Intending to address air-related issues of a global nature, such as climate change and stratospheric ozone depletion, in other fora;

Reaffirming Principle 21 of the Stockholm Declaration . . . ;

Noting their tradition of environmental cooperation as reflected in the Boundary Waters Treaty of 1909, the Trail Smelter Arbitration of 1941, the Great Lakes Water Quality Agreement of 1978, as amended, the Memorandum of Intent Concerning Transboundary Air Pollution of 1980, the 1986 Joint Report of the Special Envoys on Acid Rain, as well as the ECE Convention on Long-Range Transboundary Air Pollution of 1979;

Convinced that a healthy environment is essential to assure the well-

12. Joint Statement, July 8, 1990, in Public Papers of the Presidents of the United States, George Bush, 1990, bk. II, p. 977 (1991).

13. 36 Stat. 2448 (1910).

being of present and future generations in the United States and Canada, as well as of the global community;

Have agreed as follows:

. . .

Article III
General Air Quality Objective

1. The general objective of the Parties is to control transboundary air pollution between the two countries.

2. To this end, the Parties shall:

(a) in accordance with Article IV, establish specific objectives for emissions limitations or reductions of air pollutants and adopt the necessary programs and other measures to implement such specific objectives;

(b) in accordance with Article V, undertake environmental impact assessment, prior notification, and, as appropriate, mitigation measures;

(c) carry out coordinated or cooperative scientific and technical activities, and economic research, in accordance with Article VI, and exchange information, in accordance with Article VII;

(d) establish institutional arrangements, in accordance with Articles VIII and IX; and

(e) review and assess progress, consult, address issues of concern, and settle disputes, in accordance with Articles X, XI, XII and XIII.

Article IV
Specific Air Quality Objectives

1. Each Party shall establish specific objectives, which it undertakes to achieve, for emissions limitations or reductions of such air pollutants as the Parties agree to address. Such specific objectives will be set forth in annexes to this Agreement.

2. Each Party's specific objectives for emissions limitations or reductions of sulphur dioxide and nitrogen oxides, which will reduce transboundary flows of these acidic deposition precursors, are set forth in Annex 1. Specific objectives for such other air pollutants as the Parties agree to address should take into account, as appropriate, the activities undertaken pursuant to Article VI.

3. Each Party shall adopt the programs and other measures necessary to implement its specific objectives set forth in any annexes.

4. If either Party has concerns about the programs or other measures of the other Party referred to in paragraph 3, it may request consultations in accordance with Article XI.

. . .

Article IX
Responsibilities of the International Joint Commission

1. The International Joint Commission is hereby given, by a Reference pursuant to Article IX of the Boundary Waters Treaty, the following responsi-

bilities for the sole purpose of assisting the Parties in the implementation of this Agreement:

(a) to invite comments, including through public hearings as appropriate, on each progress report prepared by the Air Quality Committee pursuant to Article VIII;

(b) to submit to the Parties a synthesis of the views presented pursuant to sub-paragraph (a), as well as the record of such views if either Party so requests; and

(c) to release the synthesis of views to the public after its submission to the Parties.

2. In addition, the Parties shall consider such other joint references to the International Joint Commission as may be appropriate for the effective implementation of this Agreement.

Article X
Review and Assessment

1. Following the receipt of each progress report submitted to them by the Air Quality Committee in accordance with Article VIII and the views presented to the International Joint Commission on that report in accordance with Article IX, the Parties shall consult on the contents of the progress report, including any recommendations therein.

2. The Parties shall conduct a comprehensive review and assessment of this Agreement, and its implementation, during the fifth year after its entry into force and every five years thereafter, unless otherwise agreed.

3. Following the consultations referred to in paragraph 1, as well as the review and assessment referred to in paragraph 2, the Parties shall consider such action as may be appropriate, including:

(a) the modification of this Agreement;

(b) the modification of existing policies, programs or measures.

. . .

c. The First Five-Year Review of the 1991 Agreement

On October 25, 1996, Environment Canada and the United States Environmental Protection Agency released the third biennial progress report under the 1991 United States-Canada Air Quality Agreement.[14] This report is the first five-year review of the Air Quality Agreement. Overall, the report drew a positive conclusion to the first five years of the pact. According to the report, U.S. sulphur dioxide emissions in 1995 were 5.3 million tons at 263 targeted first-stage facilities, which is a 51 percent decline

14. International Joint Commission, United States-Canada Air Quality Agreement, Progress Report (1996).

since 1980.[15] The reduction in sulphur dioxide emissions led to a decrease in water sulfates, which improved water quality in both countries.[16] As a result, "substantial progress" has been made in decreasing acid rain and the damage in forests has been slowed.[17]

The report did not give the air quality policies of Canada and the United States a completely favorable review. While sulfur dioxide emissions have decreased, other atmospheric pollutants, such as acidic aerosols, have increased in both countries. Accordingly, commentators have suggested that the scope of the Air Quality Agreement should be expanded to cover regional smog, ground-level ozone, toxic air contaminants, inhalable particulate matter, and acid aerosols.[18] Moreover, current levels of nitrogen deposition may offset the benefits of acid rain reduction achieved by the agreement. Finally, the effectiveness of the Air Quality Agreement may be impeded by reluctance of the parties to submit disagreements to the governments under the agreement. For example, Adele Hurley, the Canadian cochairman of the International Joint Commission, resigned in September 1996 because of Canada's refusal to submit United States plans concerning the use of coal-fired power generating facilities in the Midwest to the parties under the agreement.[19] If the disagreement had been submitted to the parties, the United States would have been required to act under the Clean Air Act.

Questions

1. *Applying the principles.* Which country was right about how the great precedents, *Trail Smelter, Corfu Channel, Lac Lanoux,* and Principle 21, apply to the United States-Canada acid rain problem?

15. *Id.* at 1. Sulphur dioxide emissions at these facilities (most of which are utilities) were also 3.4 million tons lower than requirements established by the Clean Air Act. *Id.* Including Canada, total sulphur dioxides decreased from 31.4 million tons in 1980 to 24.1 million tons in 1994, a 23 percent decrease. This decrease is expected to continue, with predicted emissions in the United States of 19.1 million tons in 2000 and 17.3 million tons in 2010. Emissions in Canada will be 3 million tons in 2000 and 3.1 million tons in 2010, for an aggregate of 22.1 million tons in 2000 and 20.4 million tons in 2010 in both countries.

16. *Id.* at 3. In addition, lake nitrate levels in some regions, such as the Adirondack Mountains, have also decreased. Nitrous dioxide levels, which totaled 25.3 million tons for both countries in 1980 are expected to decline to 22.8 million tons in 2000 before increasing to 23.8 million tons in 2010. Canadian NOx levels should remain constant at two million tons per year. *Id.*

17. *Id.* The report found "no evidence" of widespread forest decline from acid rain, but it did note that there were exceptions in "especially sensitive" regions.

18. International Joint Commission, Media Release, The International Joint Commission Releases Report on Canada-United States Air Quality Agreement, Feb. 2, 1996.

19. The facilities would have allegedly harmed air quality in southern Ontario, New Hampshire, and Vermont. The International Joint Commission is composed of six commissioners, three each from the United States and Canada. Since all of the United States commissioners and one of the Canadian commissioners voted against submission to the parties, the motion for submission was defeated. Official Quits over Cross-Border Pollution, Chicago Tribune, Sept. 11, 1996.

2. *Problem.* You are the United States Legal Adviser. What is your legal argument supporting the view that the United States "was doing all that is required by international law"?

3. *Negotiation vs. binding third-party settlement.* Why would Canada prefer a negotiated solution to some form of binding third-party settlement, such as arbitration or submission of the case to the International Court of Justice?

4. *The precautionary principle.* Is this a case in which the precautionary principle should be applied? Review the manner in which the principle was stated in the Rio Declaration (Chapter 7.A). Would that version require abatement of the transboundary fluxes?

5. *Acid rain and the dismal science.* Assuming that there was a greater flow of air pollution from the United States to Canada than vice versa, can you state in very general terms the economic effects of this phenomenon? Can the United States be said to be imposing an "externality" on Canada?

2. *Acid Rain Within the European Union Region*

■ THE EUROPEAN APPROACH TO ACID RAIN

Johan Lammers
in International Law and Pollution 265, 267-282 (Daniel Magraw ed. 1991)

THE 1979 LONG-RANGE TRANSBOUNDARY AIR POLLUTION CONVENTION

The 1979 LRTAP Convention[20] was concluded by 32 European States (including the Byelorussian SSR and the Ukrainian SSR), the European Economic Community, Canada, and the United States during a High Level Meeting concerning protection of the environment held from November 13-16, 1979, in Geneva within the framework of the UN ECE. It entered into force on March 16, 1983. In spite of the official title of the Convention, which refers to "transboundary" air pollution only, many of its provisions deal with "air pollution, including transboundary air pollution." While this category may not be restricted to acid rain, it can be safely said that the wish to cope with long-distance acid rain constituted the main reason for concluding the Convention. Because practically all European States—whether State of origin of acid rain or victim thereof (if not both) and whether located in East or West Europe—took part in the negotiations for the Convention and eventually ratified the Convention, the Convention

20. [Convention on Long-Range Transboundary Air Pollution, Nov. 13, 1979, T.I.A.S. No. 10541, *reprinted in* 18 I.L.M. 1442 (1979).—EDS.]

gives a clear indication of what written international obligations for preventing and abating acid rain appeared to be generally acceptable for European States in 1979.

Substantive obligations—or rather obligations prescribing the development of policies and strategies—are to be found in articles 2, 3, and 6 of the 1979 LRTAP Convention. Articles 2 and 3 contain fundamental principles of the Convention. Article 2 provides:

> The Contracting Parties, taking due account of the facts and problems involved, are determined to protect man and his environment against air pollution and shall endeavour to limit, and, as far as possible, gradually reduce and prevent air pollution, including long-range transboundary air pollution.

Article 3 provides:

> The Contracting Parties, within the framework of the present convention, shall by means of exchanges of information, consultation, research and monitoring, develop without undue delay policies and strategies which shall serve as a means of combating the discharge of air pollutants taking into account efforts already made at national and international levels.

Article 6, concerning air quality management, provides:

> Taking into account Articles 2 to 5, the ongoing research, exchange of information and monitoring and the results thereof, the cost and effectiveness of local and other remedies and, in order to combat air pollution, in particular that originating from new or rebuilt installations, each Contracting Party undertakes to develop the best policies and strategies including air quality management systems and, as part of them, control measures compatible with balanced development, in particular by using the best available technology which is economically feasible and low- and non-waste technology.

An important feature of the quoted provisions is their very comprehensive scope. They do not purport to protect merely certain specific interests against air pollution, but in fact all interests which could possibly be detrimentally affected by such pollution. Moreover, the provisions apply to "air pollution, including long-range transboundary air pollution," "air pollutants," or "air pollution"; that is, they do not apply to *transboundary* air pollution *only*, so that their application is not made dependent on proof of such pollution. As far as transboundary air pollution is concerned, this may be of a short- or a long-range nature. Moreover, as has already been noted, the quoted provisions cannot be deemed to apply to acid rain only, even though acid rain has beyond any doubt been the major *ratio concludendi* of the Convention. It is further noteworthy that the quoted provisions apply in principle to air pollution as defined in the Convention without any qualification as to the seriousness of the harm caused, so that, strictly speaking, proof of substantial harm is not required to be able to invoke the provisions.

The scope of the quoted provisions of the 1979 LRTAP Convention is thus extremely broad, a welcome feature from an environmentalist point of view. A close reading of the quoted provisions, however, makes clear that there is in fact very little reason for satisfaction.

Because of the many qualifications to which the obligation to prevent or abate air pollution has been subjected, the quoted provisions are characterized by a considerable lack of real commitment on the part of the parties to prevent or abate air pollution. The term in article 2 "taking due account of the facts and problems involved" is singularly vague and ambiguous; depending on the circumstances, it may serve to strengthen or weaken the obligation to prevent or abate air pollution. Apart from that, the parties shall only "*endeavour* to limit, and, *as far as possible, gradually* reduce and prevent" air pollution. The verb "endeavour" implies that there is not even a firm obligation on the part of the parties to prevent an *increase* in the amount of air pollution originating in their territory. More stringent verbs, however, such as "make every effort" or "undertake," were not generally acceptable to the negotiating States. Also, as has been noted, there is an obligation only to "gradually reduce" the air pollution. Given the cost and the technical problems involved in such an effort, this limitation is understandable. But even that obligation is weakened because there is an obligation only to reduce air pollution gradually "as far as possible."

The lack of real commitment to control air pollution is also apparent from articles 3 and 6. Those articles, in fact, only impose on the parties a duty to *develop* air quality management policies and strategies, not to *implement* such policies and strategies. As to the *means* to develop those policies and strategies at the *international* level, the parties have committed themselves in article 3 only to "exchanges of information, consultation, research and monitoring." The obligation in article 6 is further circumscribed by the general reference to article 2 with its noted weak elements and by its permitting the parties to take into account "the cost and effectiveness of local and other remedies" and speaking of "control measures compatible with *balanced development*, in particular by using the best available technology which is *economically feasible*." The restriction that the control measures must be "compatible with balanced development" was inserted to cover the situation of certain less-developed European countries—for example, Romania, Spain, and Ireland—which feared that their industrial development would be unduly hampered in the future. The insertion of the restriction was a condition for those countries in order to be able to accept article 6.

The previously mentioned restrictive elements in article 6 may be deemed, in fact, to give a more specific meaning to the verb "endeavour" in article 2. Although it is true that article 6 puts some additional emphasis on the prevention of pollution from *new* or *rebuilt* installations, one should not lose sight of the fact that the qualifications mentioned earlier apply in principle also to pollution originating from such installations. In fact, this point only confirms that the Convention does not even contain a firm commitment of the parties to prevent an *increase* of the existing air pollution originating in their territory.

A proposal made by the Nordic countries during the negotiations to the effect that the parties would agree in the Convention to give highest priority to the conclusion in 1981 of an annex on sulphur compounds containing strategies and policies for the prevention of an increase in, and subsequently a progressive reduction of, long-range transboundary air pollution according to a timetable to be agreed on, appeared unacceptable to the pollution-exporting countries. The non-committal provisions in articles 2, 3, and 6 as eventually adopted reflect the reluctance, at least in 1979, by the COMECON countries and such other pollution-exporting West European countries as the United Kingdom and the Federal Republic of Germany to accept legally binding obligations to make meaningful air pollution control measures.

As has already been noted, the 1979 LRTAP Convention entered into force on March 16, 1983. In a resolution adopted on the occasion of the opening of the Convention for signature, however, the signatories declared that they would initiate as soon as possible and on an interim basis the *provisional* implementation of the Convention and carry out the obligations arising from it to the maximum extent possible pending its entry into force. This resolution had been proposed by the Nordic countries after it had become clear that the Convention would contain obligations which were considerably less stringent than those proposed by the Nordic countries. Adoption of the resolution was, in fact, considered by the Nordic countries as a sine qua non for their signing of the Convention.

It is evident that the 1979 LRTAP Convention constitutes above all a vehicle for promoting exchange of information, consultation, research, and monitoring necessary for the development of policies and strategies to combat air pollution. The task of promoting and reviewing the implementation of the Convention has been entrusted to the so-called Executive Body for the Convention, which consists of representatives of the parties operating within the framework of the UN ECE and the Senior Advisers to ECE Governments on Environmental Problems. The provisional implementation of the Convention pending its entry into force was promoted and reviewed by an Interim Executive Body, which met for the first time in November 1980.

The 1985 Sulphur Protocol

As aptly stated by Hendrick Vygen, the 1979 LRTAP Convention "can only be judged fairly if it is not seen as a static event but as a point of departure for a dynamic negotiating process in pursuit of a better air quality in the ECE region." This process was to take place through the establishment of an Executive Body for the Convention that would meet at least once a year.

During the Ministerial Conference on Acidification of the Environment, which took place from June 28-30, 1982, in Stockholm following two expert meetings on the effects of acidification and on control strategies, it was agreed that

> The acidification problem is serious and, even if deposition remains stable, deterioration of soil and water will continue and may increase unless additional control measures are implemented and existing control policies are strengthened.

The Conference henceforth agreed that further concrete action was needed within the framework of the 1979 LRTAP Convention. Noteworthy in 1982 was also the new strong involvement of the Federal Republic of Germany after reports had shown considerable damage to the German forests as a result of acid rain.

During the first session of the Executive Body for the LRTAP Convention in June 1983, Sweden, Norway, and Finland proposed that the parties to the Convention agree to a 30% reduction of their national sulphur emissions by 1993, using 1980 as a basis for calculation. This proposal was supported by Switzerland, Austria, the Federal Republic of Germany, Canada, Denmark, and the Netherlands. Agreement (with the exception of the United States) in the Executive Body, however, could only be reached on "the *need* to decrease effectively [without quantitative specification] the total annual emissions of sulphur compounds or their transboundary fluxes by 1993-*1995*, using 1980 emission levels as the basis for calculations of reductions." At the Canada-Europe Ministerial Conference on Acid Rain held in Ottawa on March 21, 1984, the 30% club was enlarged by the addition of France. A further step was taken during the Multilateral Conference on the Causes and Prevention of Damage to Forests and Waters held in Munich from June 24-27, 1984, when a total of 18 countries—now including the U.S.S.R. and a number of other East European countries—agreed to reduce their annual sulphur emissions *or other transboundary fluxes* by at least 30% as soon as possible and at the latest by 1993, using 1980 as the base year. It was then also recognized that the contribution to air pollution by certain countries, in particular some of the smaller South European countries and Ireland, was of little significance.

At the request of the Munich Conference, the text of a formal international agreement embodying the political agreement reached at the Ottawa and Munich Conferences was elaborated within the Executive Body for the 1979 LRTAP Convention, resulting eventually in the adoption on July 9, 1985, in Helsinki of the Protocol to the 1979 Convention on Long-Range Transboundary Air Pollution on the Reduction of Sulphur Emissions or their Transboundary Fluxes by at Least 30 Per Cent (the Sulphur Protocol).[21] Article 2 of the Protocol contains the basic substantive provision: "The parties shall reduce their national annual sulphur emissions or their transboundary fluxes by at least 30 per cent as soon as possible and at the latest by 1993, using 1980 levels as the basis for calculation of reductions." Article 10(3) contains a special arrangement for States that accede to the Protocol after its entry into force. Such a State shall nevertheless implement article 2 at the latest by 1993. If the Protocol is acceded to after 1990, however, article 2 may be implemented later than 1993, but not later than 1995. The possibility of accession enables States that were not willing to sign the Protocol—for example, the United Kingdom, the United States, Spain, and Poland—to become parties to the Protocol at some appropriate moment in the future after the closing of the very short period reserved for signing it (i.e., July 5-12, 1985).

For a number of the signatories, it was clear that the Protocol constituted only a first step toward the abatement of acidification of the environment by sulphur compounds and that a much bigger reduction in emissions would be needed in the long run if a suitable decrease in acid deposition were to be achieved. This realization was expressed as follows by the Netherlands on the occasion of the signing of the Protocol: "based on a number of assumptions . . . only a reduction of SO_2 emissions by a factor of 3.5 and a reduction of NOx emissions by a factor of 1.5 would result in an acceptable level of deposition in Western Europe."

Yet, as to further reductions, the parties were able to agree in the Protocol only on a very noncommittal text. Instead of providing that "The parties shall study at the national level the necessity for further reductions," or even better "shall endeavour to effect further reductions," article 3 of the Protocol merely provided:

> The Parties recognize the *need* for each of them to *study* at the national level the necessity for further reductions, beyond those referred to in Article 2, of sulphur emissions or their transboundary fluxes *when environmental conditions warrant.*

On the opening day for signature, the Sulphur Protocol was signed by 21 out of the then 30 parties to the 1979 LRTAP Convention. On September 2, 1987, following ratification by 16 States, the Sulphur Protocol entered into force. For Luxembourg, Switzerland, and Belgium, the Sulphur Protocol entered into force later.

Notable absentees are Greece, Iceland, Ireland, Poland, Portugal, Romania, Spain, Turkey, the United Kingdom, the United States, and Yugoslavia. Of these, Romania (as of December 31, 1987) had not yet become a

21. [Protocol on the Reduction of Sulphur Emissions or Their Transboundary Fluxes by at Least 30%, *reprinted in* [1 Ref. File] Intl. Envtl. Rep. (BNA) 21:3021 (1989).—EDS.]

party to the 1979 LRTAP Convention. Among the other countries, the absence of Poland, Spain, the United Kingdom, and the United States is to be especially deplored because of the very substantial amount of SO_2 emissions caused by those countries.

Poland refused to become a party to the Sulphur Protocol because it did not have adequate modern technology to reduce its SO_2 emissions. The United States stated that since 1970 it had already considerably reduced its SO_2 emissions, and in its view these pre-1980 reductions should have been taken into account in the Protocol. Moreover, according to the United States, further SO_2 emission reductions should only be undertaken after new scientific information had been acquired indicating the need to make such reductions and if such reductions appeared to be justified by cost-benefit analyses. Also, the United Kingdom pointed to the fact that it had already considerably reduced its SO_2 emissions since 1970. It intended to reduce its emissions further after 1980, but uncertainty in the development of its (nuclear) means of energy supply made it uncertain whether the timetable imposed by the Sulphur Protocol could be met. As stated more specifically in a major speech on U.K. environmental policy by William Waldgrave, the U.K. Minister of State at the Department of Environment:

> The decision not to join the "30% Club" was not an easy one: we realise how important the 30% protocol is as a symbol of nations' concern to act on acid rain, and we thought about the issue extremely carefully before we took the position we did at the recent Helsinki meeting. To explain that position, I must mention . . . a specific difficulty. . . .
>
> The specific difficulty arose from domestic circumstances in the past twelve months in the UK and our projection of energy requirements towards the end of the century. I mentioned earlier the enormous improvements in air quality that we have achieved in the United Kingdom. Our emissions of sulphur dioxide have been declining steadily since 1970: they now stand some 42% below the level in that peak year. Since 1980, they have fallen by about 25%.
>
> This trend began before a number of our European partners began to move on the downward path, and has been caused by a combination of factors, some of which I have already mentioned. The use of lower sulphur fuels, more efficient use of energy and industrial modernization have also played a substantial part.
>
> We expect that the further development of nuclear power; continued improvements in energy efficiency; and, in the longer term, the development of new and cleaner combustion technologies will all help to ensure that this downward trend continues.
>
> However, we currently face an unusual degree of uncertainty. Our figures for 1984, in particular, are not a reliable guide, because last year industrial action compelled us to burn an atypical mix of fuels in our power stations and elsewhere. We also await the outcome of a major public inquiry into a new nuclear power station. While the Government's long-term plans indicate an increasing proportion of nuclear as a source of electricity, this depends

> on decisions which may have to be the subject of further detailed public enquiries.
>
> For all these reasons we cannot be absolutely certain about the change in our sulphur dioxide emissions over the next decade, and we decided that we should not sign the protocol unless we were sure that we would meet its conditions in all respects. However, it *is* my government's policy to achieve further reductions in the emission of sulphur dioxide—we are aiming to get these down to 30% of 1980 levels, by the end of the 1990s. We have little reason to doubt that we shall achieve our aim, although possibly in a slightly longer timescale than envisaged in the protocol; but we do not believe that we would be justified in taking specific and costly action to meet the timetable laid down in the protocol.

Unlike the 1979 LRTAP Convention, the Sulphur Protocol entailed for the parties a highly definitive and concrete commitment to reduce their national sulphur emissions: "*shall* reduce . . . 30 *per cent* . . . at the latest by *1993*, using *1980* levels as the basis for calculation." The sources from which and the measures by which the 30% reduction was to be achieved were not specified in the Protocol, however. Apart from a very general obligation in article 6 to the effect that "the parties shall . . . develop without undue delay national programmes, policies and strategies which shall serve as a means of reducing sulphur emissions or their transboundary fluxes," freedom of choice of sources and measures was in fact left to the parties in achieving the required reduction of sulphur emission. Another important aspect of the Sulphur Protocol was that by accepting 1980 as the base year for calculation of the reduction of the sulphur emissions, the parties to the Protocol implicitly also accepted a ceiling for sulphur emissions. As is noted above, such a ceiling was neither explicitly nor implicitly provided for in the 1979 LRTAP Convention.

While the obligation laid down in article 2 of the Protocol is clear and straightforward and for that reason must be preferred over the vague and noncommittal obligations contained in the 1979 LRTAP Convention, a few critical observations should nevertheless be made. Why was the year 1980 and not another year chosen as the base year for calculating the 30% reduction in sulphur emissions? A quick look at the survey of national SO_2 emissions compiled by the Secretariat of the UN ECE shows that for most of the parties to the Sulphur Protocol the total national emission of sulphur dioxide in 1984 or 1985 (July 9, 1985, being the date of adoption of the Protocol) was already lower—for some countries, considerably lower—than in the agreed base year 1980. For example, for France the total SO_2 emission was 3,558,000 tons in 1980 and 1,845,000 tons in 1985; for the Federal Republic of Germany these figures were 3,200,000 tons in 1980 and 2,400,000 tons in 1985; for Italy 3,800,000 tons in 1980 and 3,150,000 tons in 1983; for the United Kingdom (not a party to the Protocol) 4,670,000 tons in 1980 and 3,540,00 tons in 1984; and for the U.S.S.R. 12,800,000 tons in 1980 and 11,100,000 tons in 1985. Thus, even before the Sulfur

Protocol had become binding on the parties, a clear downward trend in the total emission of SO_2 was already taking place and was perceivable in most of the major SO_2-emission-producing countries.

To a large extent, this downward trend may probably be attributed to a shift in the use from relatively high SO_2-emission-producing fuels to less- or non-SO_2-emission-producing fuels (such as, for example, the use of hydropower, geothermal energy, and nuclear energy). . . .

While the downward trend in SO_2 emissions has greatly facilitated the conclusion of the Sulphur Protocol, this does not mean that the Protocol is only of minor relevance. The Sulphur Protocol will remain important, among other reasons, in that it constitutes a legal bar against a reversal of the SO_2-emission trend when economic conditions or energy consumption patterns tend to lead again to an increasing use of relatively high-SO_2-emission-producing fuels.

Apart from the question whether there is an upward or downward trend in the use of fossil fuels after the selected base year—and this may not be the same for all countries—there also is the fact that certain countries may have already effected considerable cuts in SO_2 emissions *before* the base year, while others have not. Accordingly, a 30% cut as provided for in the Sulphur Protocol will have the result that country A that already undertook considerable cuts in SO_2 emissions before the base year will in the end be obliged to reduce its sulphur emissions to a considerably larger extent than country B that only started to take control measures after the base year. This finding follows clearly from the following example in which it is assumed that countries A and B emitted the same amount of sulphur dioxide in 1970 (100 units), but country A reduced its emissions by 30% before 1980, whereas country B did not.

	1970	*1980*	*1993*
Country A:	100	70	49
Country B:	100	100	70

Another aspect of the 30% cut in the Sulphur Protocol is that it applies to all parties regardless of the size of the population and the level of industrial development. Consider the following hypothetical situation: a less developed country L having a population of, for instance, 1,000,000 inhabitants will have to reduce its SO_2 emissions, for example, from 20 to 14 units, while a more developed country M having the same population but a much higher level of economic development will have to reduce its SO_2 emissions, for example, from 100 to 70 units. Although the reduction for country M is considerably greater than for country L, it is also true that country M may still continue to emit considerably more sulphur dioxide than country L should no further control measures be taken in the future. Given the need for drastic SO_2 emission reductions from an environmental point of view, equity would seem to require that country M be obliged to achieve a considerably higher percentage of SO_2 emission reductions than country L. It is further clear that if country M had already achieved considerable SO_2 emission reductions before the base year it would not be entitled, or in any event would be entitled much less, to invoke that fact vis-à-vis country L. As the Sulphur Protocol did not take account of considerable differences in industrial development and the resulting considerable differences in amounts of SO_2 emissions caused, this aspect could in fact be dealt with only by not putting pressure on less developed countries to become a party to the Sulphur Protocol. This solution is not an ideal one, of course, because at present no SO_2-emission limits are imposed on less developed countries that are not parties to the Sulphur Protocol. In light of this situation, the following statement by the U.K. Minister for Environment in his speech to the German Foreign Policy Society is critical:

> This brings me to the more fundamental difficulty which my government also faced—the arbitrary nature of the protocol itself. If the proposition had been a 40% reduction from the year of peak emissions, the UK would have already met that condition. If the protocol had been based on a figure for emissions per head of population, its impact on the countries concerned would also have been quite different. And if the protocol had been designed as a first step toward reducing deposition to a level tolerable by the environment in the most vulnerable areas, it would have gained in logic and, again, been different in format.
>
> In short, my government sees the protocol as arbitrary in its approach, and only one of several ways in which a common will to reduce emissions can be demonstrated. But I stress here that, even though we were not able to sign the protocol, we believe that our actual performance will be equal to—or better than—that of a number of countries who did. The Swedish Government, amongst others, recognizes this; in a recent assessment of the efforts being made in a number of European countries to reduce sulphur emissions, they estimated that the UK would achieve a cut of 50% between 1970 and 1995; a figure which is not dissimilar from the 55% they recorded for the Federal Republic.

A major factor to be kept in mind, of course, is the fact that in spite of the considerable reduction in SO_2 emissions already achieved before 1980, the United Kingdom was in 1980—as it was in 1985—still the greatest SO_2 emitter in Western Europe. In that year it emitted 4,670,000 tons per year compared with 3,558,000 tons for France; 3,200,000 tons for the Federal Republic of Germany; 3,800,000 tons for Italy; and 3,200,000 for Spain (not a party to the Protocol).

What has been said above amply illustrates that the 30% reduction clause in article 2 of the Sulphur Protocol was a substantive provision of a very general, simple, and straightforward nature that did not take account of any special conditions possibly existing in the member States of the UN ECE. Among the other special conditions that were not taken into account are the nature and the extent of the harm caused by sulphur compounds in each State.

As has already been noted, the Sulphur Protocol formed in the eyes of a number of its signatories only a first step toward the abatement of the acidification of the environment by sulphur compounds. Nevertheless, pleas made by the Nordic countries, Austria, Switzerland, the Federal Republic of Germany, and the Netherlands to develop a second stage to the Sulphur Protocol that would lead to a further tightening of the sulphur emission abatement goals remain so far without success.

The NOx Protocol

At its fourth session in November 1986, the Executive Body for the LRTAP Convention expanded the mandate of its Working Group on Nitrogen Oxides, allowing it to elaborate a draft protocol to the LRTAP Convention concerning control of emissions of nitrogen oxides or their transboundary fluxes. The resistance on the part of the East European countries to elaborating such a protocol—which still existed during the third session of the Executive Body in July 1985—had ceased. The East European countries, however, made their cooperation dependent on the willingness of the Western countries to agree on provisions in the future NOx Protocol obliging the parties to facilitate the transfer of technology to reduce emissions of nitrogen oxides.

The NOx Protocol eventually concluded on November 1, 1988, at Sofia, envisages a two-stage approach with regard to the substantive or basic obligations of the parties "to control and/or reduce national annual emissions of nitrogen oxides or their transboundary fluxes." As a first step, the parties shall arrive at a *stabilization* of the levels of NOx emissions or the transboundary fluxes thereof. In particular, they shall as soon as possible take effective measures to control and/or reduce their NOx emissions or transboundary fluxes so that these—at the latest by December 31, 1994—do not exceed the level of emissions or transboundary fluxes in the year 1987 or in any previous year to be specified by a State upon signature of, or accession to, the Protocol, provided that in addition with respect to any Party specifying such a previous year, its national average transboundary fluxes or national annual average emissions of nitrogen oxides for the period from January 1, 1987, to January 1, 1996, do not exceed its transboundary fluxes or national emissions for the year 1987.

Contrary to the 1985 Sulphur Protocol, the NOx Protocol thus does not oblige the parties to achieve certain quantified reductions of the NOx emissions or transboundary fluxes from the 1987 level or level of a previous year of such emissions or transboundary fluxes. Reductions or NOx emissions or transboundary fluxes are only required to the extent that such emissions or transboundary fluxes have increased after 1987 or after a selected previous base year. It follows that the stabilization provision envisaged in the Protocol does not preclude increases in NOx emissions or transboundary fluxes over present levels, provided that at the target date the level of emissions or transboundary fluxes does not exceed the level in 1987 or in a selected previous base year.

The fact that the NOx Protocol entitles the parties to select the year 1987 *or any previous year* as the year of reference for their duty to stabilize their NOx emissions or transboundary fluxes thereof, allows a party to select a year in which the level of its national annual NOx emissions or transboundary fluxes thereof was higher than in the year 1987. The possibility for each party to the Protocol to select the base year most suitable to it introduces in the basic obligations of the parties a flexible element that is not to be found in the 1985 Sulphur Protocol. Moreover, this possibility permits taking into account NOx emission reductions resulting from anti-pollution measures taken by a State before 1987 or to ignore possible reductions resulting from decreasing economic activities. However, as has been indicated above, the right to select a previous year is not unqualified. A State selecting such a previous year will be obliged to make sure that its national *average* annual transboundary fluxes or national *average* annual emissions for a period from January 1, 1987, to January 1, 1996, do not exceed its transboundary fluxes or national emissions for the year 1987. It was hoped that by means of this flexible element certain States, such as the United States, which were not able to adhere to the 1985 Sulphur Protocol, would be able to sign and ratify the NOx Protocol.

The NOx Protocol envisages the stabilization of NOx emissions or transboundary fluxes only as one, albeit very important, *part* of the measures to be taken in the short term. The parties shall *furthermore* (i.e., not *merely* with a view to achieve the *stabilization* of NOx emissions or transboundary fluxes at the agreed target date and thus involving in certain countries the possibility of NOx emission *reductions*), at the latest two years after the date of entry into force of the protocol, apply *national emission standards to major new or substantially modified stationary* sources and *new mobile* sources based on *the best available technologies which are economically feasible*, taking into account the Technical Annex and, in respect of mobile sources, also the relevant decisions taken within the framework of the Inland Transport Committee of the UN ECE. With regard to major *existing stationary* sources, the parties are obliged to introduce gradually and without a final deadline control measures, taking into consideration the Technical Annex mentioned earlier, the characteristics of the plant, its age, its rate of utilization, and the need to avoid operational disruption. The Technical Annex is of recommendatory nature only; its purpose is to provide guidance for the parties in identifying economically feasible technologies they can use to effect the obligations of the Protocol.

While the measures discussed above are all short-term and first-stage, the NOx Protocol also contains provisions on measures to be taken in its second stage. Those provisions, however, are only programmatic and cooperative. No later than six months after the date of entry into force of the Protocol, the parties shall commence negotiations on further steps to reduce NOx emissions taking into account, among other factors, the best available scientific and technical developments and internationally accepted critical loads. To that end the parties shall cooperate to establish (1) critical loads, (2) NOx emission reductions required to achieve agreed objectives based on critical loads, and (3) measures and a timetable commencing no later than January 1, 1996, for achieving such reductions.

The critical loads approach plays an important role in the second stage of the NOx Protocol. By a "critical load" is meant a quantitative estimate of an exposure to one or more pollutants (i.e., nitrogen oxides in the case of the NOx Protocol) below which significant harmful long-term effects on specified sensitive elements of the environment do not occur according to present knowledge. The development and application of the critical loads approach is hence an effect-related approach designed to determine on a scientific basis necessary reductions of NOx emissions taking account of the sensitivity of the receptor and the impact of the pollutant on the receptor.

It follows from the foregoing that, according to the present Protocol, *major* reductions of NOx emissions or transboundary fluxes from the level in 1987 or a selected previous year will in all probability be realized only in the second half of the 1990s. In this connection, it is important that the NOx Protocol explicitly leaves open the possibility for parties to take more stringent measures than provided for in the Protocol. Indeed, a number of European States—in particular Austria, Belgium, Denmark, the Federal Republic of Germany, Finland, France, Italy, Liechtenstein, the Netherlands, Norway, Sweden, and Switzerland—consider the obligations envisaged in the Protocol as too weak and declared themselves prepared to accept an obligation to reduce NOx emissions by at least 30% by the year 1998 at the latest, using the levels of any year between 1980 and 1986 as the basis for calculating the reduction. The refusal of other States to commit themselves already in the first stage of the Protocol to substantial NOx emission reductions is mainly based on the grounds that, in their view, the necessary scientific, ecological, geophysical, and economic substantiation for such reductions is still lacking as the critical load approach referred to above has not yet been sufficiently developed and that, in their view, the causal relationship between NOx emissions and damage has not yet sufficiently been demonstrated. According to those States, the first stage of the Protocol should be used not only to stabilize NOx emissions but also to develop scientifically substantiated targets for NOx emission reductions.

In addition to the substantive or basic obligations to control NOx emissions, the Protocol also includes a provision specifically dealing with unleaded fuel. The parties shall as soon as possible, and no later than two years after the date of entry into force of the Protocol, make unleaded fuel sufficiently available, in particular cases as a minimum along main international transit routes, to facilitate the circulation of vehicles equipped with catalytic converters. The attenuating qualification, "in particular cases as a minimum along main international transit routes," was inserted to meet the concern of the Soviet Union, where unleaded fuel is expected not to be generally available for a long time. . . .

Notes and Questions

1. *Comparing the approaches.* How do the approaches to the acid rain problem taken by the United States and Canada, on the one hand, and the ECE countries, on the other, differ? Which one is preferable?

2. *LRTAP and North America.* Why did the LRTAP Convention not solve the problem between the United States and Canada, both of which are parties to it?

3. *The LRTAP Convention as a model.* Do you believe the LRTAP Convention could serve as a model for a general, framework agreement on transfrontier air pollution that would include both developed and developing countries? What specific provisions mentioned by Lammers would or would not be suitable for such an agreement?

4. *A substantial harm requirement.* Lammers notes that "proof of substantial harm is not required to be able to invoke the provisions" of the convention. What are the advantages and disadvantages of this approach? How does this feature of the convention bear, if at all, upon your answer to question 3, above?

5. *A license to pollute?* Does the LRTAP Convention require parties to prevent increases in existing air pollution? If not, was the conclusion of the convention just a waste of time and effort?

6. *Inequitable reductions?* Why did the ECE countries agree in the 1985 Sulphur Dioxide Protocol to an approach that would allow a more developed country to emit considerably more SO_2 than a less developed country? Should less developed countries have been given more incentive to join the protocol, (e.g., by requiring a lower percentage of reductions or by granting them a grace period)?

7. *Comparing the protocols.* Which approach is preferable, the stricter one of the Sulphur Protocol or the more flexible one of the Nitrogen Protocol? (The United States *is* a party to the Nitrogen Protocol.)

8. *Critical loads.* What are the advantages and disadvantages of the "critical loads" approach, as compared with the other approaches taken in the protocols?

9. *The VOC Protocol.* A Protocol to the LRTAP Convention on Volatile

Organic Compounds (VOCs) was adopted on November 18, 1991. Protocol on the Control of Emissions of Volatile Organic Compounds or Their Transboundary Fluxes, 31 I.L.M. 568 (1992). A member of the United States negotiating team describes VOCs as follows:

> VOCs are emitted by a wide variety of stationary sources of air pollution, as well as by motor vehicles and many commercial and consumer products. In the presence of sunlight, they react with by-products of combustion known as oxides of nitrogen (NOx) to form tropospheric (ground-level) ozone, an important component of "smog." This tropospheric ozone is often formed far downwind from the precursor VOC and NOx emissions. Thus, VOC emissions may lead to ozone formation in a neighboring country. Once formed, ozone also drifts across international borders.

David P. Novello, Introductory Note, 31 I.L.M. 568 (1992). Mr. Novello offers the following brief description of the Protocol itself:

> The VOC Protocol aims to limit emissions of VOCs and the formation of ozone and other "photo-chemical oxidants" through two principal mechanisms. . . . The first . . . provides several options from which countries may choose in order to freeze or reduce their VOC emissions. The second . . . requires the adoption of technology-based controls for stationary sources, motor vehicles, and products that emit VOCs. . . . This represents a compromise between the position advocated by Nordic and other European countries, which favored a fixed percentage reduction in emissions, and the position advanced by the U.S., which favored a "best available technology" approach.

Id. at 569. The VOC protocol provides for three different options for meeting emission reduction requirements: a 30 percent reduction between 1988 (or other base year between 1984 and 1990 selected by a party); reduction of emissions by 30 percent only within areas within which transboundary pollution actually occurs (tropospheric ozone management areas, or TOMAs); and, for countries with economies in transition (those of the former Eastern European bloc), freezing emissions by 1999, provided they emitted less than specified amounts in 1988. The TOMA option had been proposed by Canada on the ground that emissions from only a small part of its territory cross the border into the United States. TOMAs must be agreed to by all parties to the protocol and, in any event, by 1999 total nationwide VOC emissions from a party adopting this approach must not exceed 1988 levels.

10. *The 1994 Sulphur Protocol.* On June 14, 1994, a new Sulphur Protocol to the LRTAP Convention was adopted at Oslo. Protocol on Further Reduction of Sulphur Emissions, *reprinted in* 33 I.L.M. 1540 (1994). This agreement concerns the further reduction of sulphur emissions and, for the parties, replaces the original 1985 agreement. The parties to 1994 protocol agree to reduce sulphur emissions to the lesser of their 1990

emissions or their obligation under the 1985 protocol. Article 2(5) contains specific obligations to limit emissions from new and existing sources. "Parties subject to the United States/Canada Air Quality Agreement of 1991" are exempted from the requirements of that paragraph. Annex I consists of a map setting forth critical loads ("critical sulphur depositions"). Annex II establishes a detailed list of the sulphur dioxide emission ceilings. Annex IV lists a variety of methods by which parties may control sulphur dioxide emissions. Annex V contains emission and sulphur content limit values for major stationary combustion sources and for motor vehicle fuel ("gas oil").

11. *The 1998 Protocols.* On March 31, 1998, states members of the United Nations Economic Commission for Europe concluded two new protocols, which were opened for signature on June 24, in Aarhus, Denmark: The Protocol on Persistent Organic Pollutants (POPs) and the Protocol on Heavy Metals. These are addressed in Chapter 14 on Hazardous Wastes and Heavy Metals. In addition, negotiations of another protocol on Nitrogen Oxides began in earnest that year.

12. *Circumventing the Senate?* The LRTAP Convention and all of its protocols are executive agreements of the United States, rather than "treaties," and therefore do not require the advice and consent of the Senate. Do you believe the Executive Branch should have involved the Senate in the approval process of these instruments? Is their subject matter appropriate for executive agreements?

Additional Reading

See generally Peter H. Sand, Regional Approaches to Transboundary Air Pollution, in Energy: Production, Consumption, and Consequences 246 (1990).

3. *Transboundary Pollution in ASEAN: Cooperative Approaches*

■ NOTE

Simon SC Tay, National University of Singapore, 1997

The ASEAN Cooperation Plan on Transboundary Pollution ("ASEAN Plan") was adopted at the ASEAN Environment Ministers Meeting held in Kuala Lumpur, Malaysia on 21 October 1994. It covers three "programme areas" of transboundary pollution, covering atmospheric pollution, the transboundary movement of hazardous wastes, and transboundary shipborne pollution.

The immediate catalyst for the ASEAN Plan may be traced to the problem of transboundary haze which, between August and October 1994, covered Malaysia, Singapore and parts of Indonesia. Caused by land clearing activities in the Indonesian islands of Kalimantan and Sumatra, the haze caused unhealthy atmospheric pollution levels in the three countries, resulting in a number of asthma-related hospitalizations and delayed air flights.

Despite the identification of the cause of the haze and evidence of transboundary harm, there are no express references in the ASEAN Plan to Principle 21 of the Stockholm Declaration and issues of state responsibility. Instead, it emphasizes the need for inter-state cooperation and lays out a framework for shared strategies, coordinated activities and the adoption of common standards and training.

In this, different roles are envisaged for laws and institutions at the national level and at the regional level. Differences can also be discerned in the roles of the state from which the haze originates, and those states affected, although no states are named and obligations of the different state parties are not clearly defined.

Details in respect of atmospheric pollution exemplify the approach taken. The ASEAN Plan sets objectives of cooperation to assess the origins and causes, nature and extent of local and regional haze incidents; to prevent and control the sources of haze by applying sound technologies and strengthening both national and regional capabilities; and to develop national and regional emergency response plans. To meet those objectives, short and longer term strategies are identified, as are more specific activities.

Short-term strategies emphasize the need to prevent the forest fires by timely detection, the deployment of ground forces and the involvement of local communities. It is also agreed that the burning of biomass during dry weather periods should be prohibited. Longer term strategies aim for "zero-burning" practices and technologies, with efforts to create awareness to eliminate the use of fire in clearing land. Economically sound and environmentally friendly methods in agriculture are instead to be introduced.

The ASEAN Plan sets a long list of agreed activities. Some of these are to be undertaken by each country, at the national level. These include establishing "National Focal Points" to inventorize existing resources, establish mechanisms to provide and disseminate information; and establishing procedures for reporting by Forestry and other relevant agencies. Others require inter-state cooperation, like developing a common air quality index; sharing knowledge and technology in the prevention of forest fires; and establishing a mechanism for forest fire-fighting.

Consistent with the framework of the ASEAN Plan, some cooperative efforts have been noticeable, including the supply of satellite imaging from Singapore to the Indonesian authorities, to better detect the location of fires.

Existing ASEAN institutions are also incorporated. The ASEAN Specialized Meteorological Centre, for example, is to develop a model to predict the spread of haze. The ASEAN Institute of Forest Management is asked to expand its role in strengthening national capacity in forest fire management.

The ASEAN Plan takes a similar, but less detailed, approach to the other sectors concerning the transboundary movement of hazardous waste and shipborne pollution.

In contrast to treaties in other regions that deal with transboundary pollution, the ASEAN Plan is notable for the absence of concrete standards and binding obligations. It instead emphasizes more general cooperative efforts. This may be interpreted as being in line with the general ASEAN preference for avoiding legalistic approaches. The approach in the ASEAN Plan might also be lauded for recognizing the region as one eco-system and, therefore, that each state owes a duty to assist the other in dealing with common problems. The ASEAN Plan may also be interpreted as a pragmatic approach that recognizes the different interests and strengths of the states involved and, as such, applies the principle of a common but differentiated responsibility.

The ASEAN Plan, however, may also be criticized as a departure from the norm of state responsibility, enshrined in Principle 21. While the ASEAN Plan creates a commendable framework, it is weak in terms of establishing thresholds for action, identifying the specific obligation of each member state and allowing for monitoring and compliance of cooperative and coordinated actions that are needed to fill in that framework.

An early comment on the ASEAN Plan suggested that it "symbolizes ASEAN's promise to the people in South East Asia that their governments will strive to protect the environment from pollution." (Tookey, The ASEAN Cooperation Plan, [1996] Env. Liability, p. 36.) In the light of subsequent events that promise has yet to be fulfilled. August 1997 witnessed a return of the haze problem in the region. The causes were again fires in Indonesia used for land-clearing. Pollution levels in 1997 were higher than those in 1994, with the Pollution Standards Index reaching dangerous levels above 500 and 600 in East Malaysia, and above 200 in Singapore.

The ASEAN Environment Ministers' Meeting in September 1997, held in Indonesia, witnessed three notable events. The first was the acknowledgment of "moral responsibility" by Indonesia and a rare public apology from its head of government, President Suharto, to ASEAN countries affected by the haze. The second was the action taken at the national level, with new Indonesian laws threatening heavier fines and the cancellation of licenses for those companies which carried on clearing land by fire. The third was a continuation of ASEAN efforts towards cooperation, with Malaysia initiating discussions of a regional fire-fighting force.

Despite these developments, the emphasis of the ASEAN Plan on modes of cooperation over the attribution of state responsibility remains to be vindicated by effective implementation and an abatement of the haze.

B. POLLUTION OF INTERNATIONAL WATERCOURSES

1. Introduction to the Problem

■ FOURTH REPORT ON THE LAW OF THE NON-NAVIGATIONAL USES OF INTERNATIONAL WATERCOURSES

Stephen McCaffrey
[1988] Y.B. ILC, vol. 2, pt. 1, 205, 218-219 (1992)

. . . [T]he pollution of fresh water has been a concomitant of human civilization since the dawn of history.

> The sewage of human societies, all the waste and refuse of agrarian communities, have been discharged throughout the years into the waters of rivers, since there were no other means of disposal. . . . Since the earliest civilizations flourishing along the Nile, the Tigris, the Euphrates, the Indus, the Ganges, the Yang-tze, etc., one of the oldest uses of river waters was the irrigation of arid lands. . . . It is well known that irrigation is one of the most common sources of pollution through the process of increase in the salinity of the waters which percolate through the soil before the water is returned to the mainstream.[22]

Of course, the concentration of people in cities meant increased potential for pollution of the rivers on which urban areas often developed. "In the days of ancient Rome the water of the Tiber river was already seriously polluted by the filth of the city."

Even by the Middle Ages, the capacity of humans to pollute fresh water had reached such proportions that water pollution has been linked to the "frequent outbreaks of terrible epidemics, such as the black plague of the 14th century which killed one-third of mankind. . . ." Cholera epidemics, as recently as the 19th century, have also been laid to water pollution.

The advent of industrialization, along with increased urbanization and the accompanying development of sewage disposal systems (originally, simply means of conveying untreated sewage to a river) exacerbated the problem tremendously. "In light of these developments it is not surprising that this pollution, which had originally often only a local or regional character, increasingly came to transcend interstate frontiers and even began to affect adversely the quality of marine waters."

Unfortunately, despite the development over the years of sophisticated technology for the monitoring and control of fresh water pollution,

22. J. Sette-Camara, "Pollution of international rivers", *Recueil des cours de l'Académie de droit international de La Haye, 1983-III* (The Hague, Martinus Nijhoff, 1985), vol. 186, p. 139.

recent studies have confirmed that the outlook for the future is not encouraging. . . .

The "Global 2000 Report" prepared by the United States Council on Environmental Quality, presented the following scenario concerning [human] use of water . . . :

> By the year 2000, worldwide urban and industrial water withdrawals are projected to increase by a factor of about 5, reaching 1.8-2.3 trillion cubic meters. . . .
>
> Urban and industrial effluent will be concentrated in the rivers, bays, and coastal zones near the world's largest urban-industrial agglomerations. In the developing world—where 2 billion additional persons are projected to be living by the year 2000 and where rapid rates of urbanization continue—urban and industrial water pollution will become ever more serious because many developing economies will be unable or unwilling to afford the additional cost of water treatment.

This sobering forecast is reinforced by the ["Environmental Perspective to the Year 2000 and Beyond" prepared by the United Nations Environment Programme (UNEP)[23]], which adds important information concerning the use and pollution of fresh water:

> 16. There have been significant changes in weather patterns partly as a result of loss of forests and vegetation cover. This has reduced river flows and lake levels and also lowered agricultural productivity. Irrigation has greatly improved arability . . . [and] has also been playing a vital role in the Green Revolution. Inappropriate irrigation, however, has wasted water, washed out nutrients and, through salinization and alkalinization, damaged the productivity of millions of hectares. Globally, salinization alone may be removing as much land from production as the land being irrigated. . . .
>
> . . .
>
> 20. Overuse of pesticides has polluted water and soil, damaging the ecology of agriculture and has created hazards for human health and animals. . . .
>
> 21. Use of chemical fertilizers *per capita* has increased five-fold between 1950 and 1983. In some countries excessive use of fertilizers, along with household and industrial effluents, has caused eutrophication of lakes, canals and irrigation reservoirs, and even coastal seas through run-offs of nitrogen compounds and phosphates. Ground water has also been polluted by nitrates in many places, and nitrate levels in rivers have risen steadily over the last two decades. Degradation of the quality of surface and ground water, caused

23. . . . [S]tudy adopted by the UNEP Governing [Council] at its fourteenth session (decision 14/13 of 19 June 1987); see *Official Records of the General Assembly, Fortysecond Session, Supplement No. 25* (A/42/25), annex II. The study was adopted by the [United Nations] General Assembly [in 1987] "as a broad framework to guide national action and international co-operation on policies and programmes aimed at achieving environmentally sound development," and annexed to its resolution 42/186 of 11 December 1987.

by chemicals including nitrates, has been a significant problem in developed and developing countries alike.

Of course, increased use and pollution of fresh water brings with it increased possibilities of disputes between watercourse States, not to mention spiralling environmental harm. Of specific relevance to the present inquiry in this connection is the following "shared perception of Governments" identified in the UNEP ["Environmental Perspective"]:

> Environmental degradation can be controlled and reversed only by ensuring that the parties causing the damage will be accountable for their action, and that they will participate, on the basis of full access to available knowledge, in improving environmental conditions. . . .

. . .

i. International Agreements

International agreements are a particularly rich source of evidence of State practice in relation to the pollution of international watercourses. [Professor Johan] Lammers lists eighty-eight international agreements "containing substantive provisions concerning pollution of international watercourses."[24] Provisions relating to pollution have been discovered in international agreements concluded as early as the 1860s. The approach States have taken to the pollution of international watercourses, as reflected in their agreements, has evolved considerably. The early agreements often ban such pollution outright. An example is the 1868 Final Act of the delimitation of the international frontier of the Pyrenees between France and Spain, which provides:

> . . . The discharge of foul or harmful water into the bed of the said river by riparian or other proprietors shall also be prohibited.

The object of many of the early provisions was to protect fisheries. Again, they were usually quite strict. For example, [Article 17 of] the 1904 Convention between France and Switzerland for the regulation of fishing in their frontier waters provides:

> Factories, plants or establishments of any kind situated near the Doubs shall be prohibited from discharging into the water any waste or substances that may be harmful to fish.

24. [Johan Lammers, Pollution of International Watercourses 124, *et seq.* (1984). —Eds.]

A characteristic of these early fishery agreements, which is quite common in modern pollution-control instruments, is that they set what amounts to a water quality standard. In the case of the 1904 Convention just referred to, the standard is very general (as is typical of these agreements)—avoidance of harm to fish. Similarly, the 1909 Boundary Waters Treaty between Canada and the United States, rather than prohibiting all pollution of boundary waters, proscribes only that which causes certain transfrontier damage:

Article IV

> It is further agreed that the waters herein defined as boundary waters and waters flowing across the boundary shall not be polluted on either side to the injury of health or property on the other. . . .

A different approach, but one that still provides a standard for determining the degree of permissible pollution, is that of the 1960 Indus Waters Treaty between India and Pakistan. Article 4, paragraph 10 of that agreement provides:

> Each Party declares its intention to prevent, as far as practicable, undue pollution of the waters of the Rivers which might affect adversely uses similar in nature to those to which the waters were put on the Effective Date, and agrees to take all reasonable measures to ensure that, before any sewage or industrial waste is allowed to flow into the Rivers, it will be treated, where necessary, in such manner as not materially to affect those uses: Provided that the criterion of reasonableness shall be the customary practice in similar situations on the Rivers.

Thus, rather than focusing on harm to, e.g. fish, health or property, this provision employs the standard of adverse effects upon certain uses of the waters in question. . . .

The more recent agreements concerning the pollution of international watercourses are typically more precise in defining water quality standards to be met or maintained, in setting water quality objectives, or in regulating the discharge into watercourses of different kinds of pollutants. The 1978 Agreement between Canada and the United States on Great Lakes Water Quality exemplifies this approach. . . .

Another example of a recent agreement which classifies pollutants with regard to their character and regulates their discharge accordingly is the 1976 Convention on the protection of the Rhine against chemical pollution. Annex I of this agreement contains a so-called "black list" of dangerous substances, whose discharge into the Rhine the parties are to take appropriate steps to eliminate. Under article 3 of the Convention, "any discharge . . . that may contain one of the Annex I substances" is to be "subject to prior authorization from the competent authority of the government concerned." Annex II contains a "grey list" of less dangerous substances, whose discharge is to be reduced. The Convention also provides for national inventories of pollution discharges, which are to be reported to the International Commission for the Protection of the Rhine against Pollution. If a party to the agreement notes a "sudden and sizeable increase" in any of the substances listed in the annexes, or becomes aware of an accident that may seriously endanger the quality of the waters, Article 11 of the agreement requires that party to inform the Commission and the parties likely to be affected "without delay". . . .

Other agreements require consultation with or approval of the parties, or a joint commission, before action is taken which would alter water quality. For example, Article 4 of the 1972 Convention on the status of the River Senegal provides that no plan that may appreciably modify, *inter alia,* the sanitary condition of the waters, may be executed without prior approval of the contracting parties. . . . An analogous approach, reflected in a number of agreements, is to lay down only a general principle on pollution, leaving its elaboration and implementation to a joint commission. This approach is, for example, envisaged in the 1974 Draft European Convention [for the Protection of International Watercourses Against Pollution] elaborated under the auspices of the Council of Europe, as well as in other European agreements. It is also adopted in the 1964 Convention and Statutes relating to the development of the Chad Basin.

2. *General Principles*

■ RESOLUTION ON THE POLLUTION OF RIVERS AND LAKES AND INTERNATIONAL LAW ("ATHENS RESOLUTION")

Institute of International Law, Athens, September 12, 1979, Annuaire de l'Institut de droit international, vol. 58-I, Athens Session, Sept. 1979, at 197 (1980)[25]

THE INSTITUTE OF INTERNATIONAL LAW

Recalling its Resolutions of Madrid in 1911 and of Salzbourg in 1961;

Conscious of the multiple potential uses of international rivers and lakes and of the common interest in a rational and equitable utilization of such resources through the achievement of a reasonable balance between the various interests;

Considering that pollution spread by rivers and lakes to the territories of more than one State is assuming increasingly alarming and diversified

25. Translation of authentic French text.

proportions whilst protection and improvement of the environment are duties incumbent upon States;

Recalling the obligation to respect the sovereignty of every State over its territory, as a result of which each State has the obligation to avoid any use of its own territory that causes injury in the territory of another State,

Hereby adopts the following articles:

Article I

1. For the purpose of this Resolution, "pollution" means any physical, chemical or biological alteration in the composition or quality of waters which results directly or indirectly from human action and affects the legitimate uses of such waters, thereby causing injury.

2. In specific cases, the existence of pollution and the characteristics thereof shall, to the extent possible, be determined by referring to environmental norms established through agreements or by the competent international organizations and commissions.

3. This Resolution shall apply to international rivers and lakes and to their basins.

Article II

In the exercise of their sovereign right to exploit their own resources pursuant to their own environmental policies, and without prejudice to their contractual obligations, States shall be under a duty to ensure that their activities or those conducted within their jurisdiction or under their control cause no pollution in the waters of international rivers and lakes beyond their boundaries.

Article III

1. For the purpose of fulfilling their obligation under Article II, States shall take, and adapt to the circumstances, all measures required to:

(a) prevent any new form of pollution or any increase in the existing degree of pollution; and

(b) abate existing pollution within the best possible time limits.

2. Such measures shall be particularly strict in the case of ultra-hazardous activities or activities which pose a danger to highly exposed areas or environments.

Article IV

In order to comply with the obligations set forth in Articles II and III, States shall in particular use the following means:

(a) at national level, enactment of all necessary laws and regulations and adoption of efficient and adequate administrative measures and judicial procedures for the enforcement of such laws and regulations;

(b) at international level, cooperation in good faith with the other States concerned.

Article V

States shall insure international liability under international law for any breach of their international obligations with respect to pollution of rivers and lakes.

Article VI

With a view to ensuring an effective system of prevention and of compensation for victims of transboundary pollution, States should conclude international conventions concerning in particular:

(a) the jurisdiction of courts, the applicable law and the enforcement of judgements;

(b) the procedure for special arrangements providing in particular for objective liability systems and compensation funds with regard to pollution brought about by ultra-hazardous activities.

Article VII

1. In carrying out their duty to cooperate, States bordering the same hydrographic basin shall, as far as practicable, especially through agreements, resort to the following ways of cooperation:

(a) inform co-riparian States regularly of all appropriate data on the pollution of the basin, its causes, its nature, the damage resulting from it and the preventive procedures;

(b) notify the States concerned in due time of any activities envisaged in their own territories which may involve the basin in a significant threat of transboundary pollution;

(c) promptly inform States that might be affected by a sudden increase in the level of transboundary pollution in the basin and take all appropriate steps to reduce the effects of any such increase;

(d) consult with each other on actual or potential problems of transboundary pollution of the basin so as to reach, by methods of their own choice, a solution consistent with the interests of the States concerned and with the protection of the environment;

(e) coordinate or pool their scientific and technical research programs to combat pollution of the basin;

(f) establish by common agreement environmental norms, in particular quality norms for the whole or part of the basin;

(g) set up international commissions with the largest terms of reference for the entire basin, providing for the participation of local authorities if this proves useful, or strengthen the powers or coordination of existing institutions;

(h) establish harmonized, coordinated or unified networks for permanent observation and pollution control;

(i) develop safeguards for individuals who may be affected by polluting activities, both at the stages of prevention and compensation, by granting on a non-discriminatory basis the greatest access to judicial and administrative procedures in States in which such activities originate and by setting up compensation funds for ecological damage the origin of which cannot be clearly determined or which is of exceptional magnitude.

Article VIII

In order to assist developing States in the fulfillment of the obligations and in the implementation of the recommendation referred to in this Resolution, it is desirable that developed State and competent international organizations provide such States with technical assistance or any other assistance as may be appropriate in this field.

Article IX

This Resolution is without prejudice to the obligations which fundamental human rights impose upon State with regard to pollution occurring in their own territories.

HELSINKI RULES ON THE USES OF WATERS OF INTERNATIONAL RIVERS

adopted by the International Law Association (ILA) at its Fifty-second Conference, held in Helsinki in 1966, ILA, Report of the Fifty-second Conference, Helsinki, Aug. 14-20, 1966, at 484 (1967).[26]

CHAPTER 3—POLLUTION

Article IX

As used in this Chapter, the term "water pollution" refers to any detrimental change resulting from human conduct in the natural composition, content, or quality of the waters of an international drainage basin.

Article X

1. Consistent with the principle of equitable utilization of the waters of an international drainage basin, a State:

(a) must prevent any new form of water pollution or any increase in the degree of existing water pollution in an international drainage basin which would cause substantial injury in the territory of a co-basin State, and

26. The Helsinki Rules and commentary are also published separately in pamphlet form. ILA, *Helsinki Rules on the Uses of the Waters of International Rivers* (1967).

(b) should take all reasonable measures to abate existing water pollution in an international drainage basin to such an extent that no substantial damage is caused in the territory of a co-basin State.

2. The rule stated in paragraph (1) of this Article applies to water pollution originating:

(a) within a territory of the State, or

(b) outside the territory of the State, if it is caused by the State's conduct.

Article XI

1. In the case of a violation of the rule stated in paragraph (1)(a) of Article X of this Chapter, the State responsible shall be required to cease the wrongful conduct and compensate the injured co-basin State for the injury that has been caused to it.

2. In a case falling under the rule stated in paragraph (1)(b) of Article X, if a State fails to take reasonable measures, it shall be required promptly to enter into negotiations with the injured State with a view toward reaching a settlement equitable under the circumstances.

Notes and Questions

1. *The Institute of International Law.* Like the ILA,[27] the Institut de Droit International (Institute of International Law (IIL)) was established in 1873. It is also a nonofficial body, but is composed of only some 120 members elected on the basis of their high repute in the field of international law. The institute has adopted a number of resolutions on subjects of international law. What is the meaning of the "no pollution" requirement of the IIL's Article II, in view of Articles III and IV?

2. *Other codifications.* Other efforts to codify principles of international law concerning pollution of transboundary waters are contained in drafts that deal comprehensively with the law of international watercourses, notably those of the International Law Association (ILA) and the International Law Commission of the United Nations (ILC). Relevant provisions of the ILA's Helsinki Rules are set out above. The ILC's draft articles on the Law of the Non-Navigational Uses of International Watercourses were adopted in 1994. Report of the International Law Commission on the Work of its Forty-sixth Session 197, 49 U.N. GAOR Supp. (No. 10), U.N. Doc. A/49/10 (1994). They formed the basis of the negotiations under United Nations auspices leading to the adoption by the General Assembly of the 1997 Convention, relevant provisions of which are set forth below.

27. *See* Chapter 8.A, note 1 following the ILA's Rules of International Law Applicable to Transfrontier Pollution, for a brief description of the ILA.

UNITED NATIONS CONVENTION ON THE LAW OF THE NON-NAVIGATIONAL USES OF INTERNATIONAL WATERCOURSES

U.N. Doc. A/RES/51/229, July 8, 1997, **reprinted in** *36 I.L.M 700 (1997)*

PART IV. PROTECTION, PRESERVATION AND MANAGEMENT . . . .

Article 21
Prevention, reduction and control of pollution

1. For the purpose of this article, "pollution of an international watercourse" means any detrimental alteration in the composition or quality of the waters of an international watercourse which results directly or indirectly from human conduct.

2. Watercourse States shall, individually and, where appropriate, jointly, prevent, reduce and control the pollution of an international watercourse that may cause significant harm to other watercourse States or to their environment, including harm to human health or safety, to the use of the waters for any beneficial purpose or to the living resources of the watercourse. Watercourse States shall take steps to harmonize their policies in this connection.

3. Watercourse States shall, at the request of any of them, consult with a view to arriving at mutually agreeable measures and methods to prevent, reduce and control pollution of an international watercourse, such as:

(*a*) Setting joint water quality objectives and criteria;

(*b*) Establishing techniques and practices to address pollution from point and non-point sources;

(*c*) Establishing lists of substances the introduction of which into the waters of an international watercourse is to be prohibited, limited, investigated or monitored.

Article 22
Introduction of alien or new species

Watercourse States shall take all measures necessary to prevent the introduction of species, alien or new, into an international watercourse which may have effects detrimental to the ecosystem of the watercourse resulting in significant harm to other watercourse States.

Article 23
Protection and preservation of the marine environment

Watercourse States shall, individually and, where appropriate, in cooperation with other States, take all measures with respect to an international watercourse that are necessary to protect and preserve the marine environment, including estuaries, taking into account generally accepted international rules and standards.

■ UNITED NATIONS ECONOMIC COMMISSION FOR EUROPE (ECE), CONVENTION ON THE PROTECTION AND USE OF TRANSBOUNDARY WATERCOURSES AND INTERNATIONAL LAKES

done at Helsinki, March 17, 1992 (Helsinki Convention),* reprinted in *31 I.L.M. 1312 (1992)

Article 1
Definitions

For the purposes of this Convention, . . .

2. "Transboundary impact" means any significant adverse effect on the environment resulting from a change in the conditions of transboundary waters caused by a human activity, the physical origin of which is situated wholly or in part within an area under the jurisdiction of a Party, within an area under the jurisdiction of another Party. Such effects on the environment include effects on human health and safety, flora, fauna, soil, air, water, climate, landscape and historical monuments or other physical structures or the interaction among these factors; they also include effects on the cultural heritage or socio-economic conditions resulting from alterations to those factors; . . .

Article 2
General Provisions

1. The Parties shall take all appropriate measures to prevent, control and reduce any transboundary impact.

2. The Parties shall, in particular, take all appropriate measures:

(a) To prevent, control and reduce pollution of waters causing or likely to cause transboundary impact;

(b) To ensure that transboundary waters are used with the aim of ecologically sound and rational water management, conservation of water resources and environmental protection;

(c) To ensure that transboundary waters are used in a reasonable and equitable way, taking into particular account their transboundary character, in the case of activities which cause or are likely to cause transboundary impact;

(d) To ensure conservation and, where necessary, restoration of ecosystems.

3. Measures for the prevention, control and reduction of water pollution shall be taken, where possible, at source.

4. These measures shall not directly or indirectly result in a transfer of pollution to other parts of the environment.

5. In taking the measures referred to in paragraphs 1 and 2 of this article, the Parties shall be guided by the following principles:

(a) The precautionary principle, by virtue of which action to avoid the potential transboundary impact of the release of hazardous substances shall not be postponed on the ground that scientific research has not fully proved a causal link between those substances, on the one hand, and the potential transboundary impact, on the other hand;

(b) The polluter-pays principle, by virtue of which costs of pollution prevention, control and reduction measures shall be borne by the polluter;

(c) Water resources shall be managed so that the needs of the present generation are met without compromising the ability of future generations to meet their own needs.

6. The Riparian Parties shall cooperate on the basis of equality and reciprocity, in particular through bilateral and multilateral agreements, in order to develop harmonized policies, programmes and strategies covering the relevant catchment areas, or parts thereof, aimed at the prevention, control and reduction of transboundary impact and aimed at the protection of the environment of transboundary waters or the environment influenced by such waters, including the marine environment.

7. The application of this Convention shall not lead to the deterioration of environmental conditions nor lead to increased transboundary impact.

8. The provisions of this Convention shall not affect the right of Parties individually or jointly to adopt and implement more stringent measures than those set down in this Convention.

Article 3
Prevention, Control and Reduction

1. To prevent, control and reduce transboundary impact, the Parties shall develop, adopt, implement and, as far as possible, render compatible relevant legal, administrative, economic, financial and technical measures, in order to ensure, inter alia, that:

(a) The emission of pollutants is prevented, controlled and reduced at source through the application of, inter alia, low- and non-waste technology;

(b) Transboundary waters are protected against pollution from point sources through the prior licensing of waste-water discharges by the competent national authorities, and that the authorized discharges are monitored and controlled;

(c) Limits for waste-water discharges stated in permits are based on the best available technology for discharges of hazardous substances;

(d) Stricter requirements, even leading to prohibition in individual cases, are imposed when the quality of the receiving water or the ecosystem so requires;

(e) At least biological treatment or equivalent processes are applied to municipal waste water, where necessary in a step-by-step approach;

(f) Appropriate measures are taken, such as the application of the best available technology, in order to reduce nutrient inputs from industrial and municipal sources;

(g) Appropriate measures and best environmental practices are developed and implemented for the reduction of inputs of nutrients and hazardous substances from diffuse sources, especially where the main sources are from agriculture (guidelines for developing best environmental practices are given in annex II to this Convention);

(h) Environmental impact assessment and other means of assessment are applied;

(i) Sustainable water-resources management, including the application of the ecosystems approach, is promoted;

(j) Contingency planning is developed;

(k) Additional specific measures are taken to prevent the pollution of groundwaters;

(l) The risk of accidental pollution is minimized.

2. To this end, each Party shall set emission limits for discharges from point sources into surface waters based on the best available technology, which are specifically applicable to individual industrial sectors or industries from which hazardous substances derive. The appropriate measures mentioned in paragraph 1 of this article to prevent, control and reduce the input of hazardous substances from point and diffuse sources into waters, may, inter alia, include total or partial prohibition of the production or use of such substances. Existing lists of such industrial sectors or industries and of such hazardous substances in international conventions or regulations, which are applicable in the area covered by this Convention, shall be taken into account.

3. In addition, each Party shall define, where appropriate, water-quality objectives and adopt water-quality criteria for the purpose of preventing, controlling and reducing transboundary impact. General guidance for developing such objectives and criteria is given in annex III to this Convention. When necessary, the Parties shall endeavour to update this annex.

Notes and Questions

1. *The approach of the 1997 United Nations Convention.* The United Nations Convention contains only one article on pollution, and of the three paragraphs in that article, one is devoted to defining that term. It is true that these articles should be read together with Article 20 (set forth in note 4 following Article 2 of the Brundtland Commission's Experts Group in Chapter 7.A.2). But do they reflect a current and sophisticated approach to the control of pollution? How do they compare with the provisions of the ECE Helsinki Convention? Can you see any reason or reasons for the differences in approach?

2. *The United Nations Convention's rules on pollution, harm, and equitable utilization.* The provisions of the United Nations Convention requiring equitable utilization (Article 5) and prohibiting harm to other states (Article 7) are set forth in Chapter 16, section C, below. As we will see in that chapter, the equitable utilization and "no-harm" rules may come into conflict and if they do, it is not obvious how that conflict should be resolved. How do the convention's provisions on pollution fit in with those on equitable utilization and "no harm?" Does Article 21(2) take a "no-harm" approach? If so, why does it not flatly prohibit harmful transboundary pollution? If you believe it takes an equitable utilization approach, is this sound as a matter of policy? That is, can we speak of an "equitable right" to pollute?

3. *The regional nature of the Helsinki Convention.* As we have noted earlier, the ECE is a regional organization including Europe (Western and Eastern), Canada and the United States. The Helsinki Convention, per Articles 23 and 25, is for practical purposes open only to states in the ECE region and "regional economic integration organisations constituted by . . . States members of the [ECE]. . . . " It entered into force on October 6, 1996. Should an effort have been made to broaden participation in this agreement? Are the principles it contains somehow peculiarly applicable to watercourses in Europe and North America?

4. *The Helsinki Convention and norms of allocation and use.* You should revisit the Helsinki Convention when studying the materials in Chapter 16 on the allocation and use of international watercourses. Compare it to the instruments examined in that chapter. How does it differ from them? What explanations can you think of for any differences you identify?

5. *Mini-case study: The* Rhine Chlorides *Case.* Mines de Potasse d'Alsace (MDPA), a French state-owned potash mine near Mulhouse, has for many years been disposing of its waste salts by dumping them into the Rhine River. It alone was responsible for 54 percent of the total chloride content of the Rhine. The resulting salinity of Rhine water has caused various problems for downstream users. Horticulturists in the Netherlands, the lowest riparian on the Rhine, have found it necessary to treat the river's water before using it for their plants.

Three Dutch horticulturists and the Reinwater (literally, "clean water") Foundation brought suit against the MDPA in Rotterdam, seeking compensation for the damage they had suffered. After the jurisdiction of the Dutch court was confirmed by the European Court of Justice,[28] and long delays, the suit ultimately resulted in a judgment of the Netherlands Supreme Court in 1988 holding MDPA liable to compensate the plaintiffs for a share of the damage they had suffered, proportionate to MDPA's contribution to the Rhine's total chloride pollution load.[29]

In 1976 the Rhine Basin countries concluded the Rhine Chlorides Convention to address this problem. Bonn Convention on the Protection of the Rhine River Against Pollution by Chlorides, Dec. 3, 1976, *reprinted in* 16 I.L.M. 265 (1977) (France, Germany, Luxembourg, the Netherlands, and Switzerland). Under the convention, the cost of reducing the discharge of salts is shared among France (30 percent), Germany (30 percent), the Netherlands (34 percent) and Switzerland (6 percent). The convention was not an immediate success, principally due to public protests in France against the alternative means of disposal it envisioned, namely, injection of the wastes underground. Protesters feared the injection could pollute groundwater used locally as a source of drinking water. Members of the

28. Handelskwekerij G.J. Bier B.V. v. Mines de Potasse d'Alsace S.A., Judgment of Nov. 30, 1976, Case 21/76.

29. Judgment of Sept. 23, 1988, HR, 13,303 Rechtspraak van de Week 1988, at 150.

French Parliament accordingly refused to ratify the Bonn Convention. The Netherlands was so angered by this refusal that it took the extraordinary step—especially for one EU member state vis-à-vis another—of recalling its ambassador to France. The agreement eventually entered into force in July 1985, after it had been modified on the basis of new scientific studies. In September 1991 the parties signed an additional protocol that eliminated injection as an alternative means of disposal, providing instead for discharge reductions when certain chloride levels are reached in the Rhine and for temporary storage on land. The protocol allows France to dispose of the stored chlorides by dumping them into the Rhine when the river reaches high flow levels. The costs of storage are shared by the parties on the basis of the formula indicated above. On this case, *see generally* Carel H.V. De Villeneuve, Western Europe's Artery: The Rhine, 36 Nat. Res. J. 441, 445-448 (1996).

How does this attempted resolution of the Rhine salt problem square with the general principles contained in the above excerpts? Can you explain, in economic terms, why the Netherlands would have agreed to the arrangement contained in the Rhine Chlorides Convention? Will this arrangement result in market distortions? Do you believe private lawsuits such as the one described above can play a positive role in overall efforts to reduce Rhine pollution?

3. Case Study: Protection of the Great Lakes Ecosystem

■ CONTROLLING GREAT LAKES POLLUTION: A STUDY IN UNITED STATES-CANADIAN ENVIRONMENTAL COOPERATION

Richard Bilder

70 Mich. L. Rev. 469, 473-475, 480-484 (1972)

I. Background

United States-Canadian cooperation regarding Great Lakes pollution problems has developed within a special geographical, economic, legal, and political context. A brief description of this setting may suggest the significance of these pollution problems and some of the reasons for the particular form this cooperation has taken.

The United States-Canadian boundary is one of the longest in the world, extending for about 3,500 miles from Passamaquoddy Bay on the Atlantic to the Fuca Straits of Vancouver on the Pacific, and along the Alaskan-Canadian boundary, for another 1,500 miles from the Pacific to the Arctic Ocean. About 2,000 miles of this boundary is water; it passes along rivers such as the St. Croix, St. John, and the St. Lawrence, through Lake Ontario, the Niagara River, Lake Erie, the Detroit River, Lake St.

Clair, the St. Clair River, Lake Huron, the St. Marys River, and Lake Superior, and on to Rainy Lake and Lake of the Woods. In addition, a number of rivers, such as the Red, the Columbia, and the Yukon, flow across the boundary.

The Great Lakes constitute the largest fresh-water system in the world, representing about a quarter of the world's total fresh-water supply. Of the total Great Lakes' water area of 95,000 square miles, about two-thirds is within United States jurisdiction and one-third in Canadian jurisdiction. Of the total Great Lakes drainage basin area of some 3000,000 square miles, about 59 percent is in the United States and 41 percent in Canada. Eight states, Illinois, Indiana, Michigan, Minnesota, New York, Ohio, Pennsylvania, and Wisconsin, border on the Great Lakes, and a number of others have close economic links with the region. In Canada, only the Province of Ontario borders on the Lakes, although the Province of Quebec also has considerable concern with Great Lakes problems.

In 1966 some 30 million people lived on or near the Great Lakes, comprising about one out of every three Canadians and one out of every eight Americans. All indications are that the Great Lakes' population is rapidly expanding; projections for the year 2000 suggest the emergence of a Great Lakes megalopolis with a population approaching 60 million people.

In view of the length of this common boundary and the substantial clustering of people and industry along certain portions of it, it is not surprising that problems of boundary waters and transboundary pollution have assumed a growing importance in United States-Canadian relations. While the concern of the two governments with boundary pollution problems dates back at least to the early years of the twentieth century, these problems have assumed a new dimension and importance as a result of rapid industrial and population development during and after the Second World War. . . .

II. The Development of Great Lakes Environmental Cooperation: Framework, Institutions, and History

A. The 1909 Treaty

The basic framework for American-Canadian cooperation respecting boundary waters problems is the [Boundary Waters Treaty of 1909 (1909 Treaty)],[30] which establishes the International Joint Commission between

30. [Treaty with Great Britain Relating to Boundary Waters and Question Arising Between the United States and Canada, Jan. 11, 1909, 36 Stat. 2448 (1910), T.S. No. 548, 12 Bevans 319, entered into force May 5, 1910. Professor Bilder explains in footnote 34: "The 1909 Treaty was signed by Great Britain on behalf of Canada, which did not acquire full powers in treaty-making until 1923. However, the Treaty has been implemented completely by Canada."—Eds.]

the United and Canada. The Treaty, which developed out of earlier ad hoc efforts to deal with boundary waters questions, was designed primarily to protect the levels and navigability of the Great Lakes and other boundary waters against unilateral diversion or obstruction, but it has provided the basis for an increasing involvement by the Commission in pollution and other problems as well. . . .

The Treaty distinguishes (1) "boundary waters," which are defined as those waters along which the international boundary runs; (2) "tributary waters," which are defined as the waters flowing into boundary waters; (3) waters flowing from boundary waters; and (4) the waters of rivers flowing across the boundary. For example, since the International Boundary does not run through Lake Michigan, that Lake is considered a tributary water rather than a boundary water.

The rights and obligations of the countries under the Treaty differ among these various categories of waters. Thus, the Treaty provides that navigation of all boundary waters shall be free and open to the inhabitants and vessels of each country without discrimination; this same right shall apply to the waters of Lake Michigan and to canals connecting boundary waters. On the other hand, the Treaty provides that each country retains exclusive jurisdiction and control over the use and diversion of all waters on its own side of the boundary that in their natural channels would flow across the boundary or into boundary waters. However, if through interference with or diversion of such waters injury is caused on the other side of the boundary, any injured party is entitled to the same legal remedies as if that injury had taken place in the country where the diversion or interference occurred. Moreover, neither party surrenders rights it may have to object to interference with or diversion of waters on the other side of the boundary that would have the effect of materially injuring navigation on its own side of the boundary.

A principal purpose of the 1909 Treaty is the regulation of uses, obstructions, or diversions of the boundary waters, and the Commission is given broad powers in this respect, which again are stated with reference to particular categories of waters. Unless otherwise provided by special agreement, the Commission's approval is required for any uses, obstructions, or diversions of boundary waters on either side of the boundary that affect the natural level or flow of boundary waters on the other side of the boundary. Moreover, the Commission's approval is required for the construction or maintenance "of any remedial or protective works or any dams or other obstructions in waters flowing from boundary waters or in waters at a lower level than the boundary in rivers flowing across the boundary, the effect of which is to raise the natural level of waters on the other side of the boundary." In passing upon such cases, the Commission is to be guided by certain rules and principles. One of these is that each party shall have, on its own side of the boundary, equal and similar rights in the use of the boundary waters. Another is that an order of precedence is established among various uses of the waters, namely: (1) uses for domestic and sanitary purposes; (2) uses for navigation; and (3) uses for power and irrigation purposes. No use shall be permitted by the Commission that tends materially to conflict with or restrain a preferred use.

Article IV of the Treaty includes a provision that "boundary waters and water flowing across the boundary shall not be polluted on either side to the injury of health or property on the other." Neither the term "pollution" nor the term "injury" is defined, and the Treaty is silent with respect to any procedures for enforcement of this obligation.

Finally, the Treaty establishes broad and flexible provisions concerning the handling of disputes and other questions between the governments. Article IX authorizes the Commission to render advisory reports to the governments at their request. It provides that "any other questions or matters of difference arising between (the two countries) involving the rights, obligations, or interests of either in relation to the other or to the inhabitants of the other, along the common frontier . . . shall be referred from time to time to the . . . Commission for examination and report" whenever either government requests such reference. The Commission is authorized in each case so referred to examine and report upon the facts and circumstances of the particular questions, together with such conclusions and recommendations as may be appropriate, subject, however, to any restrictions that may be imposed by the terms of the reference. "Such reports of the Commission shall not be regarded as decisions of the questions or matters so submitted either on the facts or the law, and shall in no way have the character of an arbitral award." Procedures are set forth governing such advisory references. In addition, Article X provides detailed procedures under which questions or matters of difference may be referred to the Commission, by the consent of the two governments, for a binding arbitral decision or finding. To date, however, the provisions of Article X have never been utilized.

THE GREAT LAKES WATER QUALITY AGREEMENT

National Research Council of the United States and Royal Society of Canada

The Great Lakes Water Quality Agreement: An Evolving Instrument for Ecosystem Management *2, 4, 7-9, 77-78, 80, 83-84, 85-86, 91-92, 93 (1985)*

[Editors' Note: The following is excerpted from a report of a group of experts appointed by the United States National Research Council and the Royal Society of Canada to review the Great Lakes Water Quality Agreement.

The subsequent protocol to the agreement reflected certain findings of the report.]

THE GREAT LAKES BASIN AND THE 1978 AGREEMENT

The Great Lakes basin's waters include the five Great Lakes (Figure [10]-1 above) and four major connecting channels, with most of the outflow eventually entering the Gulf of St. Lawrence. The relatively small land area of the basin has many urban areas and centers of industrial activity, most of which are expanding. Significant areas of the basin are devoted to agriculture and forestry in which industrialized practices predominate. There is also a hinterland that is sparsely settled but used for recreational purposes. The industrial, commercial, and residential life of some 37 million humans in the basin, and many more millions living outside of it, have the potential to produce intense impacts on the basin ecosystem.

One unique characteristic of the basin, apart from holding a great proportion of the world's surface fresh water (perhaps 20 percent) is the fact that two of the lakes, Michigan and Superior, have a water renewal

Figure 10-1
The Great Lakes

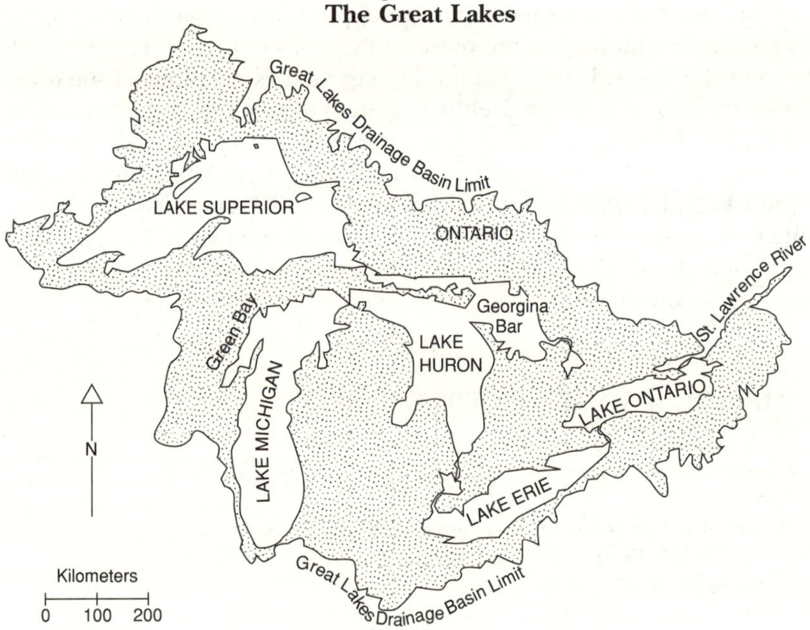

(*Source:* National Research Council of the United States and Royal Society of Canada, The Great Lakes Water Quality Agreement: An Evolving Instrument for Ecosystem Management 3 (1985)).

time of 100 years or more (water renewal time is a relative indication of the time required to flush out contaminants). The two lower lakes, Erie and Ontario, can be flushed more quickly, but their inflowing water comes predominantly from the upper lakes, which, if contaminated, exert a profound influence on the lower lakes.

Both the 1972 and 1978 Great Lakes Water Quality Agreements (GLWQA) are widely recognized as among the world's pioneering international instruments designed to foster intergovernmental cooperation to correct pollution in a large river basin. As such, the committee believes that the two governments should continue and strengthen the 1978 GLWQA. These Agreements were undertaken in the context of the 1909 Boundary Waters Treaty between the United States and Canada, also a pioneering initiative for the time. That Treaty is concerned largely with water levels and flows but also with transboundary pollution. Several binational assessments of transboundary pollution problems were undertaken by the IJC within the framework of the Treaty between 1916 and 1968. The 1972 and 1978 Agreements are a continuing (albeit atypical) reference under the Treaty, recognizing that periodic attempts to correct damages from pollution had been unsuccessful. By 1972, management capabilities had been developed with respect to water levels and flows, but water-quality actions were mostly reactive to events after they had reached crises.

Over the past century, several different types of action by human activities within the basin have led to deleterious effects on the water and aquatic biota. The problems have gradually expanded from local, to lake-wide, to a basin-wide scale. Some of these actions have caused relatively benign influences and some have been quite harmful; some have had relatively short-term consequences and others have affected the ecosystem for long periods of time. Some problems are readily apparent to laymen and some can be documented only by using advanced scientific methods. . . .

Toxic Contaminants[31]

The parties made numerous commitments in the 1978 Agreement . . . concerning objectives and programs to control the amounts of "persistent toxic substances" and "hazardous polluting substances" entering the Great Lakes basin ecosystem. In retrospect, these goals were ambitious but probably appropriate for the time especially with respect to zero discharge. The "zero discharge" of persistent toxic substances for which no lower threshold of safety is apparent is consistent with Article IV in the 1909 Boundary Waters Treaty stating that the two countries should not pollute the boundary waters to the injury of the other.

31. [The U.S.-Canada Strategy for Virtual Elimination of Toxics in Great Lakes was released by the two countries April 7, 1997. 20 Intl. Envt. Rep. 401 (1997).—Eds.]

Some progress has been made toward reduction of industrial discharges of toxic substances, although some problems remain. At the same time, toxics originating from contaminated groundwater or from atmospheric deposition are more important sources to the Great Lakes than originally thought. Although tightly regulated, certain persistent compounds such as DDT, PCBs, and dioxins apparently continue to enter Great Lakes waters. Toxic substances in sediments continue to be a source for bioaccumulation through food chains into harvestable fish, especially in areas of concern in all the state and provincial jurisdictions. Leakage of contaminants from landfill sites into the Niagara River and into the St. Clair River are of great concern. Therefore, the committee strongly endorses the 1985 Great Lakes Science Advisory Board recommendation for mapping of groundwater conditions around and under the Great Lakes basin for the necessity of data on geology and hydrology, soils, and depth to water tables. Toxic substances are carried into Great Lakes waters by vaporization from treatment plants, combustion of fossil fuels, and incineration of waste products from all parts of the basin and beyond it. Toxic substances are also transported to the lakes through the atmosphere from far outside the basin.

In this regard, the committee finds that the toxic substances control programs that were relatively easy for governments to act on have progressed furthest (e.g., controls on use of pesticides and on emissions from certain industrial point sources). However, most of the progress on these sources had been made before the 1978 Agreement without reference to the Great Lakes. The more difficult programs, such as controls on diffuse sources, remediation of contamination from landfill sites, development and implementation of measures to control in-place pollutants, and a more general comprehensive strategy to control atmospheric deposition of toxic substances, have been slow in advancing. For these difficult issues, researchers are still seeking to define and quantify the magnitude of the risks, and program managers and engineers are still considering various corrective measures. Funding for such research, which would result in the needed technological innovation, has been both limited and uncertain.

The committee concludes that the current programs for controlling persistent toxic substances in the Great Lakes Ecosystem are inadequate. Of concern are the lipophilic character of many of the chemicals (such as PCBs and dioxins), the hydrologic residence times of some of the contaminants in the lakes, the ability of the chemicals to biomagnify in the food chains, the evidence of effects on the ecosystem, and possible subtle effects on humans exposed to the chemicals. The lack of effective control measures seems likely to affect many generations to come. Thus, there is an urgency to achieve a reduction of toxic pollutants in the Great Lakes and thereby to reduce the risks to the human population using the resources of the basin.

The committee therefore recommends that measures be taken to increase the awareness of the public (including industry and politicians) as to the extent and implications of the toxic chemical problems in the Great Lakes basin.

Despite the general goal of zero discharge from known point sources, the jurisdictions on both sides of the border seem not to consider the goal practicable and are accepting moderate levels of contaminant releases from industrial and other sources. The committee finds that significant sources of contamination have remained relatively uncontrolled in the Great Lakes for many years. While the Water Quality Board in 1984 began to develop plans for remedial action in the areas of concern, significant revisions of the relevant sections of the Agreement are still essential. *The committee recommends that the Agreement encourage action on the major sources of contamination at the areas of concern, that effective solutions be implemented, and that rigorous valuative case studies be undertaken and published.* Overall, the committee finds that the sources of toxic substances in the Great Lakes basin are larger and more diverse than was anticipated in 1978, and that control programs need to be much more comprehensive than anticipated.

In view of the above, the committee strongly recommends that, as part of a comprehensive toxic substances management strategy, there should be components that deal fully with the diverse sources of contamination. This will require:

- *An inventory of all sources of toxic chemicals found at potentially significant levels in the Great Lakes ecosystem and, within the limits of data availability, those that are not responding to present control actions. This inventory would include extra-basin and intra-basin gaseous and particulate emissions, land-based inputs, resuspension from sediments, and inputs from contaminated groundwater.*
- *Actions toward an effective long-term solution to leaking toxic waste dumps recognizing that although expensive in the short run, the result can be expected to be of benefit to the health of the Great Lakes ecosystem and human population.*
- *Control actions against all identifiable sources of toxic chemicals to the Great Lakes basin. Studies on the cost-effectiveness of action programs should include the long-term benefits of such programs.*
- *Siting and operation of modern toxic-waste treatment centers in all regions of the basin. An annex should be added to the Agreement to provide for strict management of toxic wastes, both those disposed of carelessly in the past and those in prospect for the future.*

Existing toxic-waste dumps as sources of contaminants to Great Lakes water are an especially difficult problem. Removal and treatment of these toxic wastes are difficult because they are mixed with earth, debris, and other solid wastes. The nature of the chemicals in these sites are often unknown, and the groundwater may be contaminated. Although action plans are being developed for the most serious sites, the committee recommends that the Agreement recognize this issue as an area of priority action. . . .

Institutional Arrangements Under the Agreement

INTRODUCTION

The Great Lakes Water Quality Agreement of 1978 is part of a broad, complex, and changing set of institutional arrangements existing within and between the United States and Canada.

These arrangements and organizations may be cast into three distinct settings:

(a) The joint institutions established by the 1972 and 1978 Agreements that facilitate their (the Agreements) implementation;
(b) Other bi-national governmental and non-governmental institutions concerned with Great Lakes resources; and
(c) The federal, state, provincial, and local governments within Canada and the United States governing environmental quality and resource allocations in the Great Lakes basin.

These institutions are important because it is through them that policies and programs relating to Great Lakes water quality are implemented. In spite of their importance, there is a "historical absence of a systematic analysis of the Great Lakes institutional system and its components" (Donahue, 1984). For some issues and concerns, this absence has hampered the committee's review of institutions.

The 1978 Agreement outlines a broad spectrum of organizational forms and program functions designed to achieve certain water-quality objectives. In effect, the Agreement may be interpreted as specifying a particular management system with interconnections between the various forms and functions for the purpose of achieving the objectives. Formalists emphasize the importance of the organizational and legal forms while functionalists affirm the preeminence of pragmatic functions within the system. In examining the current institutions under the 1978 Agreement, the committee recognized that it was dealing with an evolving system which should not be criticized merely because the system's features, as manifested in 1985, differ in some ways from what may be inferred from the language of 1978.

In general, the recommendations set forth in this chapter arise from two basic concerns of the committee. One is the need for a clearer delineation of the responsibilities of the various institutions involved in managing Great Lakes water quality. Such clarification should lead to a better functioning of the various institutions as well as greater accountability for their actions.

The second concern is based on the committee's desire to see Great

Lakes water quality managed more from an ecosystem approach. This means, for example, that Great Lakes water-quality-related programs and policies, and the institutions that implement them, should be guided by the two basic ecosystem goals set forth in the 1978 Agreement to "restore and maintain the integrity of the waters of the Great Lakes basin ecosystem". . . .

JOINT INSTITUTIONS UNDER THE AGREEMENT

PRESENT RESPONSIBILITIES

Overall, the record of the IJC and the associated joint institutions, as the record for the implementation of the Agreement, is one of substantial success at least with respect to their responsibilities that most closely resemble those of a traditional reference. For this, they deserve much credit. However, the joint institutions have lagged in executing certain responsibilities, and in others improvements could still be made.

Data Collection, Analysis and Distribution

Under Article VII 1 (a) and (b) of the 1978 Agreement, the IJC is directed to (a) collate, analyze and disseminate data and information supplied by the parties and provincial and state governments relating to water quality and pollution loading to the boundary waters and (b) collect, analyze, and disseminate data and information concerning the objectives and programs established under the Agreement. The Commission does not collect data in its own right but relies on that provided by others. In addition, Article VII provides that the IJC "shall have authority to verify independently the data and other information submitted by the parties

Figure [10]-2
International Joint Commission and its advisory bodies including offices in Canada and the United States.

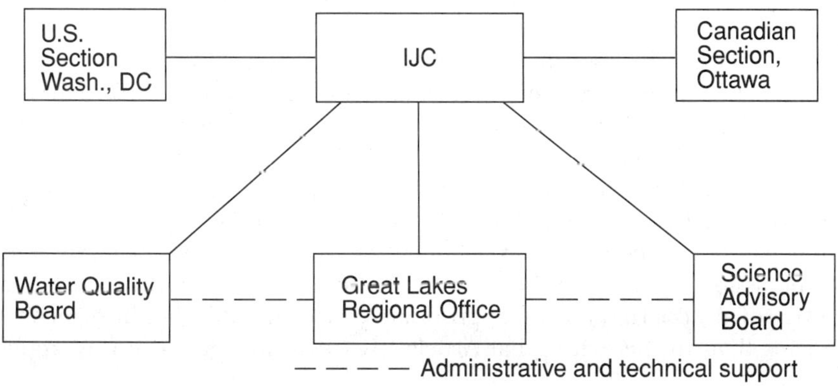

and by the state and provincial governments through such tests or other means as appear appropriate to it, consistent with the Boundary Water Treaty and with applicable legislation." . . .

The Water Quality Board has assumed primary responsibility for the functions related to data collection under the Agreement. Most of its programs have emphasized nutrient loading objectives (especially those relating to phosphorus), topics related to pollution from land-use activities (PLUARG), and toxic chemicals. The Science Advisory Board (or the Research Advisory Board prior to 1978) has directly or indirectly recommended or endorsed specific data-gathering projects such as International Field Year of the Great Lakes, project "HYPO," atmospheric contaminants in the Upper Lakes reference, and lake-wide review of agency surveillance. The Regional Office has played the role of review coordinator and has published findings related to specific objectives.

Individual governmental agencies, however, actually obtain the data and have exercised primary responsibility for their synthesis and summary; there has been little synthesis of information sets submitted by different agencies. Usually, the Water Quality Board collates the agencies' summaries of results that cover near-shore studies conducted by states, the U.S. Environmental Protection Agency (EPA), and the Ontario Ministry of the Environment. Offshore data gathering has been the responsibility mostly of EPA, the U.S. National Oceanic and Atmospheric Administration and Environment Canada.

More often than not, state, federal, and provincial agencies appear to carry out their programs with little effective interagency coordination, even in cases where coordination was explicitly intended, as in the studies of the Niagara River Toxics Committee, where a group was established outside the IJC framework. . . .

An additional problem relating to data collection and analysis arises in the information provided by the Water Quality Board to the IJC. As noted above, the Board is dependent on the parties, states, and provinces to collect and transmit the data to the Board. In addition, the Board is composed of senior officials who represent these governments. While these representatives may be willing to share sensitive information among themselves, they may be less willing to share it with the Commission or to release it publicly. There is a two-step reporting process: (1) the Boards report to the IJC, and (2) the IJC then reports to the parties. At present, the Commission does not exercise independent verification and peer review of the reports that the Water Quality Board issues to the Commission. Since, as noted in the Commission's first Biennial Report, the Commission on occasion has questioned the completeness of its "institutions" reports, the Commission should exercise its authority to arrange for an independent review of any Board report, as appropriate. The committee therefore recommends that, to the extent that Article VII (5) is interpreted not to apply to information submitted to the IJC by a board, the Agreement authorizes that the Commission undertake as necessary to verify independently information submitted to it by any board.

Advice and Recommendations by the Joint Institutions

The 1978 Agreement sets forth the following responsibilities of the IJC that define this role:

1. Tendering advice and recommendations on "problems of, and matters related to, the quality of the boundary waters of the Great Lakes system." These matters include not only objectives, programs, and measures called for in the Agreement but also, in general, relevant legislation, standards, and other regulations [Articles VII (1), (d) and (e)];
2. Preparing a "full report" to these governments no less frequently than biennially "concerning progress towards the achievement of the General and Specific Objectives." This report is to include (a) as appropriate, matters related to programs set forth in the Agreement Annexes, (b) "an assessment of the effectiveness of the programs and other measures undertaken pursuant to this Agreement," and (c) advice and recommendations [Article VII (3)].
3. Tendering advice and recommendations and providing assistance in the Great Lakes basin ecosystem [Article VII (1) (f)].

To implement these responsibilities, the IJC relies on the joint institutions established in the 1978 Agreement; the Water Quality Board, the Science Advisory Board, and the Regional Office. As an initial impression, the IJC has been successful in providing policy advice relating to Great Lakes water quality to the two parties and to state and provincial governments. The two Biennial Reports prepared under the Agreement by the IJC contain numerous specific program assessments and recommendations, as do the many reports issued by the IJC and its boards. For example, in 1982, the Science Advisory Board conducted a review of Great Lakes research activities to determine where gaps existed. The Board found that there was minimal research that examined the role of groundwater in contaminating the Great Lakes and subsequently created a Groundwater Contamination Task Force to review this question. As a result, recommendations were made in the Board's 1983 Annual Report regarding research needs on groundwater contamination (Science Advisory Board, 1983). This recommendation was transmitted to the parties in the IJC's 1984 Biennial report (International Joint Commission, 1984).

On further examination, the committee has concluded that this assessment of the IJC, being successful in providing policy advice, must be tempered. Although the IJC and its boards produce a considerable number of recommendations, information submitted to the committee indicates that only a fraction of them are formally recognized and responded to by the parties. This happens even though the parties, through the Agreement, originally solicited the advice. . . .

Investigations

The 1978 Agreement assigns two specific responsibilities for investigations to the IJC. Under Article VII 1 (g), the Commission is to investigate subjects related to the Great Lakes basin ecosystem, "as the parties may from time to time refer to it." Article VII 3 in the Agreement establishes that the IJC may "at any time make special reports to the parties, to the state and provincial governments and to the public concerning any problem of water quality in the Great Lakes system." In addition, the Water Quality Board and the Science Advisory Board may conduct investigations pursuant to their general terms of reference.

Since the signing of the 1978 Agreement, the parties have not asked the IJC to conduct any investigations. Rather, all investigation activities have been initiated by the Water Quality Board and the Science Advisory Board. Within the two Boards, investigations are assigned to various committees or ad hoc task forces. The Regional Office should provide technical and financial assistance to task forces.

The 1983 Report of the Water Quality Board does not explicitly identify its investigational activities, but they appear to be oriented to the responsibilities of program coordination and the collation and dissemination of data.

The investigations of the Science Advisory Board are tied to its evaluation of research needs in the Great Lakes. During 1982, for example, the Board identified eight areas of significant gaps in scientific knowledge. These gaps were then addressed by task forces and committees created by the Board (Scientific Advisory Board, 1983).

These positive aspects of the investigative function, however, belie a lack of coordination within the IJC. The Boards' investigative initiatives seem to be self-initiated rather than responses to specific problems or issues raised by the Commission. Furthermore, the standing committees within the Science Advisory Board structure (e.g., Aquatic Ecosystems Objective Committee) appear to be largely autonomous units, their agenda and membership being determined by the task force chairperson. This situation runs counter to the Agreement, which establishes these Boards as advisors to the IJC and not as independent entities.

The committee believes it would be useful for the IJC to assert itself more and initiate specific investigations, as needed. The Agreement allows such studies as special reports (i.e., the special report on Niagara River Pollution, International Joint Commission, 1981c), and at least one Commissioner has noted that the IJC should conduct these types of studies without waiting for a reference (Seaborn, 1984). . . .

NEW RESPONSIBILITY—DISPUTE RESOLUTION

One important issue in implementing any Agreement is the resolution of disputes concerning alleged violations of the Agreement. To date, disputes over the implementation of the 1978 Agreement have been few. Indeed, there has been only one important dispute over an alleged violation of the Agreement, the Niagara River controversy. At issue was whether the United States was in violation of the 1978 Agreement because of seepage of pollutants from landfills into the Niagara River and, hence, into Lake Ontario. This dispute was addressed outside the framework of the Agreement and the IJC in the ad hoc intergovernmental Niagara River Toxics Committee.

The committee is concerned that these disputes will increase. [T]he 1978 Agreement sets forth highly detailed obligations of the parties relating to the control of water pollution in the Great Lakes. Moreover, as scientific knowledge advances, there may be more specific standards incorporated into the Agreement. Also, the inclusion into the Agreement of implementation deadlines may become more necessary and frequent.

■ 1978 GREAT LAKES WATER QUALITY AGREEMENT BETWEEN THE UNITED STATES AND CANADA

as amended by *the 1983 and 1987 Protocols, done at Ottawa Nov. 22, 1978, 30 U.S.T. 1383, T.I.A.S. 9257,* as amended *Oct. 16, 1983, T.I.A.S. 10798 and Nov. 18, 1987, T.I.A.S. 11551, consolidated in International Joint Commission, Revised Great Lakes Water Quality Agreement of 1978 (1988)*

Article I
Definitions

As used in this Agreement:

. . .

(g) "Great Lakes Basin Ecosystem" means the interacting components of air, land, water and living organisms, including *humans*, within the drainage basin of the St. Lawrence River at, or upstream from, the point at which this river becomes the international boundary between Canada and the United States.

. . .

Article II
Purpose

The purpose of the Parties is to restore and maintain the chemical, physical, and biological integrity of the waters of the Great Lakes Basin Ecosystem. In order to achieve this purpose, the Parties agree to make a maximum effort to develop programs, practices and technology necessary for a better understanding of the Great Lakes Basin Ecosystem and to eliminate or reduce to the maximum extent practicable the discharge of pollutants into the Great Lakes System.

Consistent with the provisions of this Agreement, it is the policy of the Parties that:

(a) The discharge of toxic substances in toxic amounts be prohibited and the discharge of any or all persistent toxic substances be virtually eliminated;

(b) Financial assistance to construct publicly owned waste treatment works be provided by a combination of local, state, provincial, and federal participation; and

(c) Coordinated planning processes and best management practices be developed and implemented by the respective jurisdictions to ensure adequate control of all sources of pollutants.

Article III
General Objectives

The Parties adopt the following General Objectives for the Great Lakes System. These waters should be:

(a) Free from substances that directly or indirectly enter the waters as a result of human activity and that will settle to form putrescent or otherwise objectionable sludge deposits or that will adversely affect aquatic life or waterfowl;

(b) Free from floating materials such as debris, oil, scum, and other immiscible substances resulting from human activities in amounts that are unsightly or deleterious;

(c) Free from materials and heat directly or indirectly entering the water as a result of human activity that alone, or in combination with other materials, will produce color, odor, taste, or other conditions in such a degree as to interfere with beneficial uses;

(d) Free from materials and heat directly or indirectly entering the water as a result of human activity that alone, or in combination with other materials, will produce conditions that are toxic or harmful to human, animal, or aquatic life; and

(e) Free from nutrients directly or indirectly entering the waters as a result of human activity in amounts that create growths of aquatic life that interfere with beneficial uses.

Article IV
Specific Objectives

1. The Parties adopt the Specific Objectives for the boundary waters of the Great Lakes System as set forth in Annex 1, subject to the following:

(a) The Specific Objectives adopted pursuant to this Article represent the minimum levels of water quality desired in the boundary waters of the Great Lakes System and are not intended to preclude the establishment of more stringent requirements.

(b) The determination of the achievement of Specific Objectives shall be based on statistically valid sampling data.

(c) Notwithstanding the adoption of Specific Objectives, all reasonable and practicable measures shall be taken to maintain or improve the existing water quality in those areas of the boundary waters of the Great Lakes System where such water quality is better than that prescribed by the Specific Objectives, and in those areas having outstanding natural resource value.

(d) The responsible regulatory agencies shall not consider flow augmentation as a substitute for adequate treatment to meet the Specific Objectives.

(e) The Parties recognize that, in certain areas of inshore waters, natural phenomena exist which, despite the best efforts of the Parties, will prevent the achievement of some of the Specific Objectives. As early as possible, these areas should be identified explicitly by the appropriate jurisdictions and reported to the International Joint Commission.

(f) The Parties recognize that there are areas in the boundary waters of the Great Lakes System where, due to human activity, one or more of the General or Specific Objectives of that Agreement are not being met. Pending virtual elimination of persistent toxic substances in the Great Lakes System, the Parties, in cooperation with State and Provincial Governments and the Commission, shall identify and work toward the elimination of:

(i) Areas of Concern pursuant to Annex 2;
(ii) Critical Pollutants pursuant to Annex 2; and
(iii) Point Source Impact Zones pursuant to Annex 2.

2. The Specific Objectives for the boundary waters of the Great Lakes System or for particular portions thereof shall be kept under review by the Parties and the International Joint Commission, which shall make appropriate recommendations.

3. The Parties shall consult on:

(a) The establishment of Specific Objectives to protect beneficial uses from the combined effects of pollutants; and

(b) The control of pollutant loading rates for each lake basin to protect the integrity of the ecosystem over the long term. . . .

■ BINATIONAL COOPERATION FOR GREAT LAKES WATER QUALITY: A FRAMEWORK FOR THE GROUNDWATER CONNECTION

George Francis
65 Chi.-Kent L. Rev. 359, 361-368 (1989)

III. The Great Lakes Water Quality Agreement

. . . Under the terms of the Boundary Waters Treaty, the [International Joint Commission (IJC)] serves as a commission of inquiry on transboundary water issues referred to it by the parties to the Treaty. In 1970, the IJC reported on a 1964 Reference to investigate the pollution problems of the lower Great Lakes. Its recommendations laid the foundation for the first Great Lakes Water Quality Agreement, signed in 1972. The Agreement was renewed and expanded considerably in 1978 and was amended in 1987. The IJC has, in effect, been given a continuing Reference to oversee the implementation of the Agreement and recommend to the parties particular measures to be taken. Since 1978, the IJC reports biennially, following a public meeting at which its two main Advisory Boards present their reports, and statements are heard from various interest groups.

The Agreement has five main provisions, many of which have been considerably elaborated since 1972. They call for:

1. The establishment of general and specific water quality objectives. The 1987 Protocol expanded this to call for "lake ecosystem objectives" for each Lake or portion thereof and for "ecosystem health indicators" to assess progress towards reaching these objectives;

2. Programs and measures to be taken by federal, state and provincial jurisdictions to meet these objectives. Each jurisdiction would develop its own regulatory and administrative programs to do this;

3. Cooperation through IJC in a joint monitoring of the measures being taken and of their effectiveness in achieving the objectives as determined by environmental monitoring. IJC was originally to have been given an independent verification capability for doing this evaluation;

4. Additional studies to be conducted, as necessary, to determine the extent and nature of problems being confronted. Initially, the studies were directed toward assessing the water quality of the upper Lakes and the extent to which pollution associated with land-use activities was impacting the Lakes; and

5. The establishment of a Great Lakes Water Quality Board, a Science (formerly Research) Advisory Board to advise the Commission, and a Great Lakes Regional Office. The office is located in Windsor, Ontario, and it works with Commission staff in Washington and Ottawa on various program matters.

The purpose of the Agreement was made quite explicit in 1978, namely: "to restore and maintain the physical, chemical and biological integrity of the waters of the Great Lakes Basin Ecosystem." This purpose reflected an emerging view from within some research and academic circles that much more was involved in defining water quality than physical and chemical terms. Experience gained from years of effort at "cleaning up" the Great Lakes showed that a much more systemic perspective was required to understand the problems and what might be done about them. A brief synopsis of this experience is presented below with reference to the first three of the main provisions of the Agreement. . . .

A. SETTING THE OBJECTIVES

Until 1987, a technical working group reporting to both Boards and through the Boards to the Commission undertook detailed reviews of the scientific and technical literature for particular contaminants. Using the "most sensitive beneficial use" as the standard for water quality, the group recommended specific quality objectives in terms of safe levels that should not be exceeded anywhere in the Lakes. Some forty-one specific objectives have been recommended, and at least thirty-five of them have been incorporated into the 1987 Protocol. The parties to the Agreement have now taken it upon themselves to determine the new ecosystem objectives.

Several difficulties have arisen from the approach taken by the technical working group to fulfill its task of deciding upon contaminant-specific objectives. First, the scientific knowledge required to decide upon an objective was sufficient for only a relatively small number of contaminants. By 1985, the number of contaminants reported from the water, the sediment, the fish, and the fish-eating birds in the Great Lakes exceeded 1,000. This list is presently being scrutinized very critically, but it appears that the knowledge needed to set objectives may be sufficient for less than ten percent of the confirmed contaminants. Second, contaminants for which there is sufficient knowledge to propose objectives may not pose serious problems compared with others that are less well known and for which objectives cannot be proposed. Regulatory agencies were faced with expectations that they would monitor for the presence of certain contaminants in the Lakes only when scientists could agree on safe levels for them. Regulatory agencies, however, had their own priorities for monitoring.

Third, laboratory work confirmed the view that different contaminants do not always act independently of one another in the environment. Instead, the contaminants may interact in the water or the biota and give rise to synergistic or antagonistic effects. Some contaminants bioaccumulate and biomagnify such that safe levels in fish for human consumption may require water-quality objectives to be set at levels below those at which they could be detected. From the mid-1970s, higher incidences of cancers and birth defects were found in fish, turtles, and fish-eating birds in the more heavily contaminated near-shore areas around the Lakes. Human health concerns were raised by these findings but, with a few exceptions, these concerns have not been addressed.

These findings gave rise to debates about the use of multi-chemical objectives based on ecotoxicological tests under field rather than laboratory conditions and about the search for ecosystem objectives that would rely heavily on biomonitoring. The 1987 Protocol reflects this thinking.

B. PROGRAMS AND MEASURES

Especially during the first five years of the Agreement, priority was given to the reduction of phosphorus entering the Lakes. The purpose was to reduce eutrophication and the associated problems of nuisance algae growth and oxygen depletion of the bottom waters, especially in the central basin of Lake Erie. Five strategies have been used to achieve this:

1. Set legal limits on phosphorus in detergents while searching for

substitute compounds. Ontario had a limit of 2.2 percent phosphorus set by federal legislation in 1973. From 1972 through 1988, the eight states have set limits of 0.5 percent phosphorus in detergents, and the soap and detergent industry has apparently found acceptable substitutes for phosphorus;

2. Construct or upgrade municipal sewage treatment plants and maintain effluent concentrations of one milligram per liter total phosphorus maximum for all treatment plants discharging more than one million gallons per day directly into the Lakes. This has been the major thrust of attention and expenditure during the Agreement, especially in the earlier years. About three-quarters of the forty or so municipal sewage treatment plants subject to this measure are reported to be complying with this requirement;

3. Regulate phosphorus from industrial discharges "to the maximum practicable extent." This is part of the overall industrial pollution control programs within each jurisdiction, and quantitative information on the extent to which phosphorus discharges have been reduced does not seem to be available;

4. Agree on "targets" for reducing the total loadings of phosphorus in the lower Lakes. This was called for by the 1978 Agreement to be in place by 1980, but the "Phosphorus Load Reduction Supplement" did not get signed until October 1983. The load reductions for Lakes Erie and Ontario were deemed to require additional measures besides the ones being implemented, and target reductions were allocated between the two countries; and

5. Introduce strategies to reduce non-point sources of phosphorus entering the Lakes from agricultural and other land-use practices. These are required to meet load reductions agreed to in 1983. Pilot projects to promote conservation tillage systems which minimize sediment and nutrient losses from cultivated land are underway in the Lake Erie basin in both countries. If widely adopted by farmers, they are expected to reduce the losses of fertilizers and, at the same time, reduce loadings to rivers and the Lake.

By the time of the 1978 Agreement, toxic contaminants had become the central issue to be addressed. This focus resulted from the apparently sudden discoveries of substances such as methylated mercury, PCBs, and mirex at certain localities in the Lakes over the preceding ten years. This led to more systematic surveys of the extent of the problems. The 1978 Agreement declared that "[t]he intent . . . is to virtually eliminate the input of persistent toxic substances in order to protect human health and ensure the continued health and productivity of living aquatic resources and man's use thereof," and that the philosophy adopted to achieve this "shall be zero discharge." Four strategies are being pursued:

1. Develop effective controls for the eleven first priority persistent toxic contaminants, the "critical pollutants." As the number of reported

contaminants in the Great Lakes increased, so did the debate over how to select the top priority contaminants for regulatory control. Technical committees in various jurisdictions were convened to select the critical pollutants and, using somewhat different criteria, they each derived different but often overlapping lists. The Water Quality Board finally chose eleven based on the fact that they:

- are known to be present in the Great Lakes,
- are highly toxic and persistent,
- can bioaccumulate to levels that threaten human health and biota in the aquatic ecosystem,
- have had abatement or other corrective actions taken but are still present in unacceptable levels,
- represent a variety of sources, pathways and uses, and
- may also be members of larger chemical families so that actions taken for one could be expected to concurrently control or apply to other substances with similar properties.

Data are being sought to create a "mass balance" accounting for the quantity of each substance entering the ecosystem, the quantity stored, transferred, or degraded within the ecosystem, and the quantity leaving the ecosystem. Sources are to be identified and the goal is to eliminate these sources within five years;

2. Analyze the "quantitative structure-activity relationships" of all other reported contaminants to determine priorities for further research, testing, and/or control measures. The list of reported contaminants is being scrutinized as a first step;

3. Prepare remedial action plans (RAPs) for forty-two designated "areas of concern" identified by the Water Quality Board. These are badly polluted near-shore areas and rivers connecting the Lakes. The RAPs have become a major focal point of interest in the Water Quality Agreement, mainly because they require the cooperation of a range of governmental agencies, industries, non-governmental organizations and local citizen groups, many of which had not previously been associated with Great Lakes issues. The Water Quality Board has specified the range of topics to be addressed in each RAP, and they review drafts of them. Few have been completed as of mid-1989, and the ones that have, such as that for Green Bay, Wisconsin, will have to develop effective cooperation over a number of years to implement what is required by the approved Plan; and

4. Prepare "lake wide management plans for critical pollutants." The first of these, for Lake Ontario, was completed in 1989. They raise issues similar to those of the RAPs in terms of public involvement and interagency cooperation to implement what has to be done.

C. THE GREAT LAKES INTERNATIONAL SURVEILLANCE PLAN

Surveillance and monitoring activities are carried out under the terms of the Agreement to determine the degree to which jurisdictional control requirements are being met: to assess progress towards achieving the water quality and ecosystemic objectives, to evaluate trends in variables being monitored, and to identify emerging problems. The Great Lakes Quality Board first developed the International Surveillance Plan (GLISP) in 1975. It is subject to periodic modifications in the light of changing information requirement and the most recent version was prepared in 1986. Under GLISP, the Board strived to incorporate data needed for enforcement actions by regulatory agencies with information useful for understanding aquatic ecosystems, a combination which lead to periodic criticisms from those who seek more comprehensive data sets to serve one or the other of these two purposes.

The data are gathered by state and provincial agencies for the near-shore areas of the Lakes and by federal agencies for the offshore areas through to the international boundary. Samples are analyzed by government and private laboratories, and quality checks are required from time to time. The data are compiled and reviewed by the Water Quality Board which prepares reports every two years for the IJC. Special intensive surveys are conducted for each of the Lakes every five years or so.

This monitoring has shown a gradual decline in the amounts of phosphorus in the lower Lakes in the spring, before algae growth occurs, and to a lesser extent, during the summer months. Biomonitoring of gull eggs and fish has also shown a sharp decline over ten years in the concentrations of DDT and PCBs, related to the cessation of use of these chemicals in the Basin. Monitoring has also revealed the extent to which many other contaminants are present. Particular problem areas have been identified repeatedly over the years and have led the Water Quality Board in 1985 to designate forty-two of them as special "areas of concern" for which remedial action plans are being prepared. With the effects of water pollution control measures starting to appear, the importance of controlling airborne pollutants and non-point source pollutants running off the lands and from combined sewage and storm water overflows has become more evident.

Notes and Questions

1. *The legal implications of the ecosystem approach.* The 1978 Protocol differs from the 1972 Agreement in that it incorporates the concept of basin ecosystem management to indicate that parties are not concerned solely with contamination of the lakes themselves or direct discharges into

them. What difference does this concept make in the parties' legal obligations? In implementation of the agreement?

2. *Legal obligations under the 1987 Protocol.* We have seen that as a result of the 1985 report Canada and the United States adopted the 1987 Protocol to the 1978 Agreement, which addressed groundwater contamination and atmospheric transport of toxic chemicals. Does the protocol obligate the parties to undertake any specific activities? What problems do you foresee for the parties in implementing obligations to control groundwater contamination?

3. *The role of the IJC.* The 1978 Great Lakes Water Quality Agreement and its predecessor in 1972 were negotiated as a result of a Reference to the International Joint Commission under Article IX of the 1909 Boundary Waters Treaty. Given this, could Canada or the United States use the reference procedures of Article IX for issues that arise under the Great Lakes Agreement?

4. *The Virtual Elimination Strategy.* In 1997, Canada and the United States signed the Binational Strategy for the Virtual Elimination of Persistent Toxic Substances from the Great Lakes Basin. Inter alia, the Strategy identifies quantitative targets for reduction of anthropogenic use, discharge, and release of certain compounds of serieous concern, including, PCBs, mercury, dioxin, and furans.

5. *The Great Lakes regime as a model.* On the basis of your reading of the materials in Part B of this Chapter, to what extent do you believe the treaty regime for the control of Great Lakes Pollution can serve as a model for other international watercourses? Is it sui generis? Why or why not? In determining whether a particular water pollution control regime is applicable to other watercourses, what is most important: the characteristics (i.e., levels of development, etc.) of the countries involved and the relations between them, or the nature of the watercourses governed by the regime?

Additional Reading

GREAT LAKES POLLUTION PROBLEMS

R. Bilder, Controlling Great Lakes Pollution: A Study in United States-Canadian Environmental Cooperation, 70 Mich. L. Rev. 469 (1972).

Symposium on Prevention of Groundwater Contamination in the Great Lakes Region, 65 (No. 2) Chicago-Kent L. Rev. 345 (1989).

18 J. Intl. L. 1 (1986) (Papers produced for a Great Lakes Seminar on the diversion and consumptive use of waters in the Great Lakes.).

Council on Environmental Quality, *Environmental Quality,* The Great Lakes, Ch 8, at 325 (1990).

Daniel DeWitt, Great Words Needed for the Great Lakes: Reasons to Rewrite the Boundary Waters Treaty of 1909, 69 Indiana L.J. 299 (1993).

Mark Dinsmore, Like a Mirage in the Desert: Great Lakes Water Quality Preservation Efforts and Their Punitive Effects, 24 Tol. L. Rev. 449 (1993).

Anthony Earl, Protecting the Great Lakes: The Case for a Regional Approach, 24 Tol. L. Rev. 271 (1993).

POLLUTION OF INTERNATIONAL FRESHWATER IN GENERAL

J. Sette-Camara, Pollution of international rivers, Recueil des cours de l'Académie de droit international de La Haye, 1983-III (1985), vol. 186, p. 139.

Johan Lammers, Pollution of International Watercourses (1984).

André Nollkaemper, The Legal Regime for Transboundary Water Pollution: Between Discretion and Constraint (1993).

XI

Controlling Ozone Depletion

In the stratosphere, high above Earth, a layer of ozone filters ultraviolet radiation from sunlight, protecting Earth and its inhabitants. In recent years the ozone layer has been threatened by human-made chemicals, such as chlorofluorocarbons, which are used in air conditioners and refrigerators. As described in detail below, these chemicals can migrate into the stratosphere and destroy the ozone layer. In the Antarctic, a large hole has developed in the ozone layer, and most recently very significant thinning of the ozone layer over the Arctic has developed. Holes in the ozone layer or even depletion of the density of the ozone layer means more ultraviolet radiation reaches Earth. This can cause skin cancer and cataracts in humans and damage flora and fauna.

The depletion of the stratospheric ozone layer must be distinguished from the problem of ozone pollution in the lower atmosphere (the troposphere). In the air we breathe, large quantities of ozone—emitted by cars, for example—damage human health. Thus, ozone is an air pollutant that the United States and other countries regulate. This problem must not be confused with the problem of depletion of the stratospheric ozone layer that protects Earth from ultraviolet radiation.

Depletion of the ozone layer is an inherently long-term, intergenerational issue. Chlorine chemicals we produce today drift up to the stratosphere over time and remain there to deplete the ozone layer. They dissipate only over time. Chlorine chemical emissions today cause damage decades in the future.

Concern about the health of the ozone layer led to a historic agreement in 1985, the Vienna Convention for the Protection of the Ozone Layer, negotiated under the auspices of the United Nations Environment Programme. The agreement provided a framework for monitoring and learning about the ozone layer but did not provide specific controls on substances believed to deplete the ozone layer. In 1987 countries adopted a protocol to the agreement that does provide such controls: the Montreal Protocol on Substances That Deplete the Ozone Layer. Since it is a protocol, countries wishing to join the agreement must become parties to the Vienna Convention as well as to the Protocol.

Since 1987, scientific evidence has suggested that the problem of ozone depletion may be more serious than had been believed, and additional chemicals are reducing the ozone layer. This has led to amendments to the Protocol in June 1990 and in November 1992, which have added chemicals to the list of controlled substances, and to adjustments in 1990, 1992, 1994, 1995, and 1997 such that some chemicals are now to be phased out even well before the year 2000.

As you read these materials, consider what general norms of international environmental law might apply in the absence of an agreement, the reasons the Protocol could be negotiated and then amended so quickly despite the economic disruptions its controls threatened, whether the provisions in the agreement are adequate to cope with rapidly changing scientific knowledge about the ozone layer, and the problem of compliance with the agreement.

A. THE SCIENTIFIC BACKGROUND

1. The Ozone Layer

The following excerpt by Richard Benedick, the chief United States negotiator for the Montreal Protocol, discusses the historical evolution of scientific understanding of the problem of ozone depletion and the role that science played in reaching an agreement.

■ OZONE DIPLOMACY

Richard E. Benedick
(ch. 2, excerpt) (1991)

The Montreal Protocol was the result of research at the frontiers of science combined with a unique collaboration between scientists and policy makers. Unlike any previous diplomatic endeavor, it is based on continually evolving theories, on state-of-the-art computer models simulating the results of intricate chemical and physical reactions for decades into the future, and on satellite-, land-, and rocket-based monitoring of remote gases measured in parts per trillion. An international agreement of this nature could not, in fact, have occurred at any earlier point in history.

Disturbing Theories

The existence of ozone was unknown before 1839. An unstable form of oxygen composed of three, rather than the customary two, atoms of oxygen, ozone has been characterized as "the single most important chemically active trace gas in the earth's atmosphere." This significance derives from two singular properties. First, certain wavelengths of ultraviolet radiation are absorbed by the very thin "layer" of ozone molecules surrounding Earth, particularly in the upper part of the atmosphere known as the stratosphere, approximately 6 to 30 miles above the surface. If these biologically active ultraviolet (UV-B) lightwaves were to reach the planet's surface in excessive quantities, they could damage and cause mutations in human, animal, and plant cells. Second, the distribution of ozone throughout different altitudes could influence the temperature structure and circulation patterns of the stratosphere and thus have major implications for climate around the world. It is no exaggeration to conclude that the ozone layer, as currently constituted, is essential to life as it has evolved on Earth.

In 1973 two University of Michigan scientists, Richard Stolarski and Ralph Cicerone, were exploring the effects of possible chemical emissions from National Aeronautics and Space Administration rockets. Their research, published in 1974, indicated that chlorine released in the stratosphere could unleash a complicated chemical process that would continually destroy ozone for several decades. A single chlorine atom, through a catalytic chain reaction, could eliminate tens of thousands of the ozone molecules. This theory, though interesting, did not at first seem alarming, because the potential release of chlorine from space rocketry would be inconsequential.

In 1974 Mario Molina and Sherwood Rowland at the University of California, Irvine, became intrigued with some peculiar properties of a family of widely used anthropogenic chemicals, the chlorofluorocarbons [CFCs]. Molina and Rowland discovered that, unlike most other gases, CFCs are not chemically broken down or rained out quickly in the lower atmosphere but rather, because of their exceptionally stable chemical structure, persist and migrate slowly up to the stratosphere. Depending on their individual structure, different CFCs can remain intact from many decades to several centuries. The two researchers concluded that CFCs are eventually broken down by solar radiation and in the process release large quantities of chlorine into the stratosphere. The combined implications of these two independently-arrived-at hypotheses were deeply disturbing. The researchers had not anticipated any link between CFCs and ozone depletion. There had been no prior suspicion that CFCs were harmful to the environment. Indeed, following their invention in the 1930s, CFCs had seemed an ideal chemical. They had been thoroughly tested by customary standards and found to be safe. The possibility that dangers could originate many miles above Earth's surface was never considered.

CFCs are unusually stable, nonflammable, nontoxic, and noncorrosive—qualities that make them extremely useful in many industries, where they often replaced other chemicals, such as ammonia in refrigerators and air conditioners, as well as effective propellants in spray containers for cosmetics, household products, pharmaceuticals, and cleaners. They are also excellent insulators and are standard ingredients in the manufacture of a wide range of rigid and flexible plastic-foam materials. Their nonreactive properties make them seemingly perfect solvents for cleaning microchips and telecommunications equipment and for use in a myriad of their industrial applications. And, as an added bonus, CFCs are inexpensive to produce.

The 1974 theories came, therefore, as an economic as well as environmental bombshell. Because new uses had continually been found for CFCs, their production had soared from 150,000 metric tons in 1960 to over 800,000 metric tons by 1974. Because of their long lifetimes, as much as nine-tenths of all CFCs ever emitted was still in the atmosphere. Millions of tons of prior-year CFC production were thus already en route, so to speak, to their fatal stratospheric rendezvous with ozone. Even if CFC emissions were to level off or decline, chlorine would continue to accumulate in the stratosphere for decades. If the chlorine-ozone break-down process actually occurred in the stratosphere, as indicated by the laboratory results, some future depletion of the vitally important ozone layer seemed inescapable.

2. *The Antarctic Ozone Hole*

■ OZONE DIPLOMACY

Richard E. Benedick
(ch. 2 excerpt) (1991)

British scientists in 1985 published astonishing findings based on a review of land-based measurements of stratospheric ozone made at their Halley Bay station in the Antarctic. So unbelievable at first were these measurements that the scientists had delayed publication for nearly three years while they painstakingly rechecked and reviewed their data and the accuracy of their instruments. They finally concluded that ozone levels recorded during the Antarctic springtime (September-November) had fallen to about 50 percent lower than they had been in the 1960s. Although concentrations recovered by mid-November, the amount of the seasonal ozone loss had apparently accelerated sharply beginning in 1979. The "ozone hole" (that is, a portion of the stratosphere in which greatly diminished ozone levels were measured) had also expanded by 1985 to cover an area greater in size than the United States.

This unexpected revelation was quickly confirmed by Japanese and U.S. scientists rechecking their own data sets. . . .

The ozone hole did not, however, provide any clear signal for policymakers at that time. Scientists in 1986 and 1987 were far from certain that CFCs were involved in Antarctica. Nor could they confirm whether the hole was a localized phenomenon peculiar to unusual polar conditions or an ominous precursor of future ozone losses elsewhere over the planet. Since ozone concentrations over Antarctica did recover after each springtime collapse, the phenomenon was contrary to known theory and did not conform to the global model predictions of gradual and pervasive long-term depletion. To add to the confusion, the downward trend was broken in late 1986—just before the start of the diplomatic negotiations—when Antarctic ozone concentrations actually improved over the previous year.

There were several credible theories, besides the role of CFCs, to account for the ozone hole, including polar winds, volcanic activity, and sunspots. Even Rowland, writing in 1986 just before the treaty negotiations began, admitted that "the causes of the massive seasonal loss of ozone over Antarctica are not yet fully understood, and its implications for the ozone layer above the rest of the earth are also uncertain."

A year later Rowland appeared to believe that the Antarctic revelation was the "driving force" behind the negotiations. Other observers have also ascribed the success at Montreal to the "dread factor" of Antarctica. But for those closest to the process, these judgments seem more a product of hindsight, overlooking how little was known about this phenomenon during the negotiations. Disturbing new evidence from a major Antarctic expedition of September-November 1987 was not, in actuality, completely analyzed and released until six months after the treaty was signed. . . .

The hole over Antarctica did attract additional public attention to the ozone issue (though more in the United States than in Europe and Japan, where greater public pressure on governments was most needed). It may also have influenced some participants in the negotiations as evidence of the fragility of Earth's atmosphere. Significantly, however, Antarctica was never discussed at the negotiations, which were based solely on the global models. Even two months after Montreal, the U.S. Environmental Protection Agency had to conclude that "the Antarctic ozone hole cannot yet serve as a guide for policy decisions."

3. Depletion of the Ozone Layer over the Northern Hemisphere

On February 4, 1992, NASA scientists first reported finding severely increased levels of chlorine monoxide in the atmosphere above the Northern Hemisphere. Besides the ozone-depleting chemicals, the scientists measured lower-than-usual levels of nitrogen oxides, which are considered ozone-protectors. The nitrogen combines with the free chlorine atoms and in that way prevents the chlorine from breaking down the ozone molecule.

By December 1992, the researchers had announced that the chlorine was destroying the stratospheric ozone and that it had already caused a 10 percent loss in some areas. In April 1993, research revealed that there was 10 percent less ozone in the Northern Hemisphere than in 1992 and that all of the chlorine molecules present in the stratosphere changed into ozone-depleting forms. Martyn Chipperfield, Satellite Maps Ozone Destroyer, Nature, at 592, Apr. 15, 1993.

Although there is no "hole" like the one over the South Pole, the increased chlorine levels have caused a thinning of the ozone layer over an area extending from the North Pole down as far as New England and France. One NASA researcher, Dr. Joseph Waters, stated that the amount of ozone in the Arctic is decreasing by 0.7 percent per day in a season when it should be increasing. Satellite Finds Growing Threat to Ozone, N.Y. Times, Apr. 15, 1993, B7.

The threat of the phenomenon causes great concern among those studying atmospheric conditions, since the reduced ozone in the Northern Hemisphere will be affecting densely populated areas. While the ozone hole over the South Pole covered over 9 million square miles in 1992, the area was mainly uninhabited. The Northern thinning, though, will directly affect thousands of human lives. Not only is the increased ultraviolet radiation that reaches earth killing the phytoplankton in the ocean, but also it is changing agriculture and causing damage to humans.

4. The Chemicals That Cause Ozone Depletion

As you read in Benedick's article, ozone molecules are broken apart by a chemical reaction of chlorine atoms pulling the oxygen atoms and binding with them. The problematic chemicals are found in many household products, such as refrigerators and aerosol spray cans, and in auto air conditioners. They also have a variety of other uses, such as cleaning solvents for superconductors and, in the case of halons, as fire suppressants.

As a CFC- or halon-containing product is produced and used, the chemicals escape into the air and begin to move up through the lower layer of the atmosphere and into the stratosphere. The release itself takes up to 30 years, depending on the product, and the traveling time usually lasts between seven and ten years. Once in the stratosphere, the stable chemical structure of the molecules allows them to remain there for long periods of time. These so-called residency times, combined with the release and travel times, result in a delay in both the depletion of ozone after the use of the CFC and in the "fixing" of the ozone after the use is stopped.

According to UNEP data from 1989, CFCs are produced mainly by industries making refrigerators, air-conditioning units, and heat pumps (30 percent of world use); by foams (28 percent of world use); by aerosol pumps (27 percent of world use); by the cleaning of electronic parts; by degreasing; and by dry-cleaning. Halons are mainly found in fire extinguishers. As a result, both production and consumption are concentrated in the major developed industrial countries. Alice Enders and Amelia Porges reported 30 percent of world CFC consumption for both the United States and the European Community, and 13 percent for Japan. The developing countries accounted for only 10 percent of the total world consumption.

While consumption of the chemicals has been widely dispersed, the group of producers has been highly concentrated. When the Montreal Protocol was negotiated, DuPont was the largest of only five producers in the United States and supplied a large share of the market for the chemicals. In Europe, Imperial Chemical Industries was the leader of the nine producers. Including Japan, there were only 19 companies producing almost 80 percent of the world's CFCs.

This small number of producers played a key role in making the limiting of CFC releases possible. Not only were the corporations active in negotiating the protocol, but they continue to be active in working to develop recovery methods and substitutes that are affordable alternatives to CFCs.

So far, hydrochlorofluorocarbons and hydrofluorocarbons are the most widely used substitutes worldwide. Unfortunately, these products are still more expensive than the CFCs they replace, due to more complex production processes and the need to redesign the final product itself. In addition, the HCFCs and HFCs are also suspected of contributing to the greenhouse effect and so are targets of international efforts to prevent harm to the global climate (*see* chapter 12, below). The 1992 amendment to the Montreal Protocol set a phaseout schedule for HCFCs starting in 1996, to reach zero by 2030 (Fourth Meeting of the Parties to the Montreal Protocol, Nov. 1992, Annex III G, adding article 2F).

The meeting of the parties in June 1990, called the London Meetings, amended the protocol to include carbon tetrachloride and methyl chloroform as regulated chemicals, speeded up the phaseout times, and lowered the allowed consumption and production of CFCs and halons.

The Fourth Meeting of the Parties in 1992 continued this trend, adding HCFCs and HBCBs, as well as methyl bromide, to the list of controlled chemicals. The latter chemical is known to be highly efficient at depleting ozone, but since there are no substitutes yet, protests against its ban were great enough to prevent action beyond a freeze in amounts produced.

B. INTERNATIONAL LEGAL PRINCIPLES

1. The Historical Perspective

The following excerpt outlines principles of international law that may apply to the depletion of the ozone layer in the absence of a controlling treaty.

■ A HISTORICAL BACKGROUND ON THE CHLOROFLUOROCARBON OZONE DEPLETION THEORY AND ITS LEGAL IMPLICATIONS

Sylvia Maureen Williams
Transboundary Air Pollution (Flinterman, Kwiatkowska & Lammers eds., 1986)

A number of principles of international law are applicable, *ab initio,* to the problem in question. First and foremost, mention should be made of the principle of international responsibility of states which has kept appearing over the years in the decisions of international courts and tribunals and has been the subject of lengthy debates at the doctrinal level.

The well-known principle underlying the *Trail Smelter* arbitration and, later, the *Corfu Channel* judgment, that no state has the right to allow its territory to be used for acts contrary to the rights of other states is, without doubt, applicable to the ozone depletion problem except that conditions are somewhat different. Whereas in the *Trail Smelter* and *Corfu Channel* cases the responsibility of the state causing the damage arises *vis à vis* another specific country and, therefore, indemnities are more easily determined, in the present instance, the damage affecting the ozone layer—perhaps irreversible and, certainly, retarded—would be reaching the whole international community. The state would, therefore, be responsible *erga omnes* for environmental damage. It necessarily follows that the assessment of the damage and the obligation to restore to the *status quo ante* become far more complex. . . .

Of no small importance in the discussion of the legal aspects of ozone depletion is, next to the principle of state responsibility, the role played by the principles relating to the abuse of rights and good neighborliness with, of course, the limitations pointed out earlier concerning the global nature of the ozone protection issue. We should be equally aware, however, of the difficulty of drawing a clear line between an abuse as distinct from a harsh but justified use of a right under international law. It is sometimes extremely difficult to determine when a legitimate right is overstepped. Similarly, one ought to bear in mind that, in this assumption, the concept of good neighborliness would include all nations of the world irrespective of their geographic proximity.

The United Nations Stockholm Declaration on the Human Environment of 1972 has, conversely, provided a number of principles concerning damage to the environment in general and not only damage from one state to another. Principle 6 is of special significance: it calls for the halting of the release of toxic substances in quantities to exceed the capacity of the environment to render them harmless. Principle 21 recognizes the rights of states to exploit their resources under international law provided they ensure that these activities do not cause damage to the environment of other states or to areas beyond national jurisdiction. Principle 22 stresses the need for progressive development of international law in connection with liability and compensation for the victim of pollution or other environmental damage.

Notes and Questions

1. *Applying international legal principles to ozone damage.* These general principles of international law applicable to damage due to the depletion of the stratospheric ozone layer are becoming of less interest since most countries have joined the Montreal Protocol. However, some states are still not parties to it. What problems do you foresee in applying the international legal principles set forth to these countries?

2. *Applying transfrontier principles to global pollution.* The principles discussed above were developed in the context of transfrontier pollution damage. Can they be readily applied to global pollution problems such as depletion of the ozone layer?

3. *Liability and compensation for injuries resulting from ozone damage.* The Montreal Protocol does not address liability. Apart from the protocol, how would liability apply? If an abnormal number of skin cancers appeared in people living in areas of countries near Antarctica, would a principle of liability apply? Who would be liable? How would you determine liability? What would be the measure of compensation?

4. *Apportioning liability.* Could you apportion liability for damage among countries on the basis of a country's percentage of global production or consumption of ozone-depleting chemicals? Is the analogy apt to the "market-share" approach of United States tort law in apportioning liability?

5. *Conditions for successful negotiations.* The author of the above excerpt wrote that at that time she did not expect countries to be able to reach an

international agreement to control the chemicals that deplete the ozone layer. This was only shortly before the Vienna Convention on the ozone layer and the Montreal Protocol were successfully concluded. Why would the successful negotiation of an agreement be so difficult to anticipate on this subject? Consider carefully the background to the negotiation outlined previously by Benedick.

2. *More Recent Principles*

We have previously discussed the precautionary principle (or approach), one version of which is that countries should not decline to take measures to respond to a serious environmental threat because of the lack of scientific certainty. (*See* chapters 4 and 7 on risk assessment and on general principles.) Does the Montreal Protocol represent a successful application of this principle? What difference does the existence of such a principle make?

The Rio Declaration speaks of "common but differentiated" responsibilities in Principle. As you read the Montreal Protocol, consider whether the protocol reflects this principle. Consider also the extent to which the protocol implements a principle of intergenerational equity.

C. THE MONTREAL PROTOCOL

In March 1985, the Vienna Convention for the Protection of the Ozone Layer established a framework system for addressing the multilateral environmental problems of ozone depletion. Division between representatives wanting a phaseout of CFCs and those wanting production caps prevented the adoption of any formal commitments to limit the substances, but the groundwork was laid for further work.

By 1987, the two groups were able to reach a compromise, and the Montreal Protocol placed quantitative limits on both the production and the consumption of CFCs and halons. As of July 1, 1998, the Vienna Convention on the Ozone Layer had 166 parties. The Montreal Protocol had 165 parties. The 1990 London Amendment to the protocol had 121 parties; the 1992 Copenhagen Amendment had 76 parties.

The Montreal Protocol is based on consumption levels of countries. Consumption is determined by calculating production of the chemicals minus exports plus imports. Exports to nonmember countries may not be included in the calculation. Thus, there is an incentive not only to limit production but also to trade only with states party to the agreement.

The Protocol makes special provision in Article V for developing countries: a ten-year delay in required compliance with targets and timetables, a separate consumption limit of 0.3 kilograms per capita, access to a Multilateral Fund (1990 Amendment) to assist with the costs of compliance, and the promotion of bilateral technical assistance programs. The classification of a country as qualifying under Article V(1) to deserve special treatment is not permanent but is subject to the recommendations of an Open-Ended Working Group of the Parties. Some countries have been declassified, such as Singapore and Saudi Arabia; others have been reclassified to become Article V countries, such as Georgia.

The Protocol gives certain countries flexibility in meeting their obligations. To attract the former Soviet Union, the Protocol provides in Article 2(6) that any country that already has facilities under construction or contracted for prior to September 1987 to produce the controlled chemicals may add this production to its 1986 base year level in determining its compliance with base year production. The Protocol also includes "industrial rationalization" among countries. Under this policy, a country can transfer part of its calculated level of production of controlled chemicals to another country. While industrial rationalization can take place between developed member countries, or between developing member countries, it is not intended for transfer between developed and developing countries.

The Protocol prohibits exports and imports of controlled subtances with countries that are not party to the treaty (although an exception for nonparties that are determined to be in full compliance with the control measures in Article 2 of the Protocol). In a second phase, the trade ban with nonparties would extend to products containing the controlled substances and upon agreement of the parties in five years to products produced with the controlled chemicals. However, in 1992 parties accepted the recommendation of the Technology and Economic Assessment Panels and decided not to implement the ban based on process.

While trade in bulk CFCs is small in value relative to world merchandise trade, trade in CFC-containing products (heating and cooling equipment, passenger cars, airplanes, ships and boats with air conditioners and/or heat pumps) amounts to approximately 12 percent of world trade. Products currently produced with, but not containing, CFCs (semiconductors and products with electronic components) amount to an additional 16 percent of world trade.

Since the 1980s, the producers and users of CFCs have been seeking means to recover, reuse, and substitute for CFCs. The recycling of CFCs is an important issue. Unless managed appropriately, it could lead to stockpiling of CFCs and undermine the effectiveness of the regime.

Besides the quantitative limits on chemicals that deplete the ozone layer, the protocol contains an innovative financial assistance mechanism to allow developing countries to pursue environmentally sound policies and comply with the protocol. Under the protocol, countries have established a general multilateral fund administered by the World Bank, the United Nations Environment Programme (UNEP), the United Nations Development Programme (UNDP), and, since 1993, the United Nations Industrial Development Organization (UNIDO). Initiated in the 1990 London meeting (*see* Amendment X of the London Meeting Report), the "Interim Multinational Fund" was made permanent by an amendment passed in Copenhagen. *See* Annex IX, Fourth Meeting of the Parties. The most notable characteristic of this fund is that it is specifically not for economic development. Instead, countries contribute to help offset the costs of Article V countries complying with the protocol. The fund "shall meet all agreed incremental costs of Parties in order to enable their compliance with the control measures of the Protocol." As of November 1996, agreed contributions had reached $152 million.

The fund secretariat has worked with OZONAction, a UNEP-industry group in Paris, France, to help develop and review country programs and proposed projects under the fund. By 1996, most but not all Article V countries had developed country programs or were in the process of doing so. The review process for the programs and projects is stringent.

As part of the country program, each country must designate an ozone action officer. These officers meet regularly on a regional basis to discuss implementation problems and to exchange views.

Note

Read the text of the Montreal Protocol, together with the 1990 London Adjustments and Amendments and the Copenhagen Adjustments and Amendments of 1992, as outlined in Table 11-1. (In Table 1, "ADJ" made in accordance with Article 2.9 of the Protocol.)

Table 11-1[1]
Montreal Protocol on Ozone Depleting Substances

A: London 1990 Conference of the Parties

Substance	*Adjustments and Amendments*	
CFCs	ADJ:	After the first day of the 7th month following entry into force of MP, annual consumption or product levels will not exceed 1986 levels.
	ADJ:	After January 1, 1995, annual consumption or production will not exceed 50% of 1986 levels.
	ADJ:	After January 1, 1997, annual consumption and production levels will not exceed 15% of 1986 levels.
	ADJ:	After January 1, 2000, annual consumption and production levels will not exceed zero.

Table 11-1[1]
Continued

Halons	ADJ:	After January 1, 1992, annual consumption or production levels will not exceed 1986 levels.
	ADJ:	After January 1, 1995, annual consumption or production levels will not exceed 50% of 1986 levels.
	ADJ:	After January 1, 2000, annual consumption and production levels will not exceed zero.
Other Fully Halogenated CFCs	AMEND:	After January 1, 1993, annual consumption or production will not exceed 80% of 1989 levels.
	AMEND:	After January 1, 1997, annual consumption or production will not exceed 15% of 1989 levels.
	AMEND:	After January 1, 2000, annual consumption or production will not exceed zero.
Carbon Tetrachloride	AMEND:	After January 1, 1995, annual consumption or production will not exceed 15% of 1989 levels.
	AMEND:	After January 1, 2000, annual consumption or production will not exceed zero.
Trichlorethane (Methyl Chloroform)	AMEND:	After January 1, 1993, annual consumption or production will not exceed 1989 levels.
	AMEND:	After January 1, 1995, annual consumption or production will not exceed 70% of 1989 levels.
	AMEND:	After January 1, 2000, annual consumption or production will not exceed 30% of 1989 levels.
	AMEND:	After January 1, 2005, annual consumption or production will not exceed zero.

B: Copenhagen 1992 Conference of the Parties

Substance	Adjustments and Amendments	
CFCs	ADJ:	After January 1, 1994, annual

Table 11-1[1]
Continued

		consumption or production will not exceed 25% of 1986 levels.
	ADJ:	After January 1, 1996, annual consumption or production will not exceed zero.
Halons	ADJ:	After January 1, 1994, annual consumption or production will not exceed 25% of 1989 levels.
	ADJ:	After January 1, 1996, annual consumption or production will not exceed zero.
Other Fully Halogenated CFCs	ADJ:	After January 1, 1994, annual consumption or production will not exceed 1989 levels.
	ADJ:	After January 1, 1996, annual consumption or production will not exceed zero.
Carbon tetrachloride	ADJ:	After January 1, 1996, annual consumption or production will not exceed zero.
Trichlorethane (Methyl Chloroform)	ADJ:	After January 1, 1996, annual consumption or production will not exceed zero.
Hydrochloro-fluorocarbons	AMEND:	After January 1, 1996, annual consumption or production will not exceed the sum of 3.1% of calculated level of consumption in 1989 of the controlled substances in Group 1 of Annex A and the calculated level of consumption in 1989 of the controlled substances in Group 1 of Annex C.
	AMEND:	After January 1, 2004, annual consumption will not exceed 65% of the sum above.
	AMEND:	After January 1, 2010, annual consumption will not exceed 35% of the sum above.
	AMEND:	After January 1, 2015, annual consumption will not exceed 10% of the sum above.
	AMEND:	After January 1, 2020, annual consumption will not exceed 0.5% of the sum above.

Table 11-1[1]
Continued

	AMEND:	After January 1, 2030, annual consumption will not exceed zero.
Hydrobromo-fluorocarbons	AMEND:	After January 1, 1996, annual consumption will not exceed zero.
Methyl Bromide	AMEND:	After January 1, 1995, annual consumption will not exceed 1991 levels.

C: Vienna 1995 7th Meeting of the Parties

Substance		*Adjustments to Non-Article V Countries and to Article V Countries*
Trichlorethane (Methyl Chloroform)	ADJ:	After January 1, 1993, annual consumption and production will be frozen.
	ADJ:	After January 1, 1994, annual consumption and production will be reduced by 50% of 1993 levels.
	ADJ:	After January 1, 1996, annual consumption or production will not exceed zero.
	ADJ:	**After January 1, 2003, annual consumption and production will be frozen at 1998-2000 average levels (base).**[a]
	ADJ:	**After January 1, 2005, annual consumption and production will be reduced by 30% from base levels.**
	ADJ:	**After January 1, 2010, annual consumption and production will be reduced by 70% from base levels.**
	ADJ:	**After January 1, 2015, annual consumption and production will not exceed zero.**
Hydrochloro-fluorocarbons[a]	ADJ:	After January 1, 1996, annual consumption or production will be frozen at 1989 levels plus 2.8% of 1989 consumption of CFCs (base).
	ADJ:	After January 1, 2004, annual consumption or production will be reduced by 35% from base levels.

Table 11-1[1]
Continued

C: Vienna 1995 7th Meeting of the Parties

Substance		*Adjustments to Non-Article V Countries and to Article V Countries*
	ADJ:	After January 1, 2010, annual consumption or production will be reduced by 65% from base levels.
	ADJ:	After January 1, 2015, annual consumption or production will be reduced by 90% from base levels.
	ADJ:	**After January 1, 2016, annual consumption and production will be frozen at 2015 levels.**
	ADJ:	After January 1, 2020, annual consumption or production will be phased out, allowing for a service tail of up to 0.5% until 2030 for existing refrigeration and air-conditioning equipment.
	ADJ:	**After January 1, 2040, annual consumption and production will not exceed zero.**
Hydrobromo-fluorocarbons[b]	ADJ:	After January 1, 1996, annual consumption and production levels will not exceed zero.
Methyl Bromide	ADJ:	After January 1, 1995, annual consumption and production will be frozen at 1991 levels.
	ADJ:	After January 1, 2001, annual consumption and production will be reduced by 25% from 1991 levels.
	ADJ:	After January 1, 2005, annual consumption and production will be reduced by 50% from 1991 levels.
	ADJ:	After January 1, 2010, annual consumption and production will not exceed zero.

Table 11-1[1]
Continued

D: Montreal 1997 9th Meeting of the Parties		
Substance		*Adjustments to Non-Article V Countries and to Article V Countries*
CFCs[c]	**ADJ:**	**The lower of the average of annual calculated level of production for the period 1995 to 1997 or a calculated level of production of 0.3 kg/capita will be used for determining compliance levels of Annex A CFCs.**
	ADJ:	**The lower of the average of annual calculated level of production for the period 1998 to 2000 or a calculated level of production of 0.2 kg/capita will be used for determining compliance levels of Annex B CFCs.**
Methyl Bromide	ADJ:	After January 1, 1999, annual consumption or production will not exceed 75% of 1991 levels.
	ADJ:	**After January 1, 1999, annual consumption or production will not exceed 85% of 1991 levels.**
	ADJ:	After January 1, 2001, annual consumption or production will not exceed 50% of 1991 levels.
	ADJ:	**After January 1, 2001, annual consumption or production will not exceed 60% of 1991 levels.**
	ADJ:	After January 1, 2003, annual consumption or production will not exceed 30% of 1991 levels.
	ADJ:	**After January 1, 2003, annual consumption or production will not exceed 40% of 1991 levels.**
	ADJ:	After January 1, 2005, annual consumption or production will not exceed zero.

Table 11-1[1]
Continued

D: Montreal 1997 9th Meeting of the Parties

Substance	*Adjustments to Non-Article V Countries and to Article V Countries*
	ADJ: After January 1, 2005, annual consumption and production will not exceed 15% of 1991 levels.[d] Annual consumption or production will also not exceed 80% of the average of its annual calculated levels of consumption and production for the period of 1995 to 1998 inclusive.
	ADJ: After January 1, 2015, annual consumption or production will not exceed zero.

[1]Revised and updated from table in *Engaging Countries: Strengthening Compliance with International Environmental Accords* ch. 5 (Edith Brown Weiss & Harold K. Jacobson, ed. MIT Press, forthcoming). Note: Entries in **bold** apply to Article V countries.

[a]34 hydrochlorofluorocarbons.

[b]34 hydrobromofluorocarbons.

[c]Annex A CFCs are CFCs 11, 12, 113, 114, and 115. Annex B CFS are CFCs 13, 111, 112, 211, 212, 213, 214, 215, 216, and 217.

[d]Will apply save to the extent that the parties decide to permit the level of production or consumption that is necessary to satisfy uses agreed by them to be critical uses.

1. Negotiation of the Protocol

As discussed, the first convention concerned with the high level ozone layer was the Vienna Convention on the Protection of the Ozone Layer, concluded in March 1985. At the time countries discussed including measures to control emissions of chemicals that deplete the ozone layer, but there was no agreement to do so. For the next 21 months, some countries discussed the issue informally. Several influential international workshops addressing the scientific and regulatory aspects were held. Finally, negotiations for a protocol opened in December 1986. A chronology of major events through 1992 is given here so that the reader can appreciate the chronology of the international legislative process to that date; additional important events have occurred since then, as described below.

■ CHRONOLOGY: INTERNATIONAL REGIME ON THE OZONE LAYER

Paul C. Szasz, International Norm-making, in Environmental Change and International Law 76-78 (Edith Brown Weiss, ed. 1992).

	*Protection of the ozone layer**
1973-1974	*Richard Stolarski and Ralph Cicerone, studies of release of chlorine in the atmosphere*
1974	*Mario Molina and Sherwood Rowland, studies of CFCs in the atmosphere and stratosphere*
8 Mar. 1977	**UNEP's World Plan of Action on the Ozone Layer, Washington**
Apr. 1980	**UNEP Governing Council resolution on restriction of CFC usage**
May 1981	**UNEP Governing Council resolution initiating negotiations towards an ozone agreement**
1981	**Meeting of legal experts convened by UNEP, Montevideo**
Jan. 1982	First session of Ad Hoc Working Group of Legal and Technical Experts for the Preparation of a Global Framework Convention for the Protection of the Ozone Layer, convened by UNEP, Stockholm (NB: there were seven sessions, until 1985)
1983	**Establishment of the "Toronto Group"**
22 Mar. 1985	VIENNA CONVENTION ON THE PROTECTION OF THE OZONE LAYER
1986	*WMO/UNEP Report on Atmospheric Ozone*
May 1986	*Workshop on CFC production and consumption trends, convened by EEC and UNEP, Rome*
Sep. 1986	*Workshop on alternative regulatory strategies on protection of ozone, convened by USA and UNEP, Leesburg (USA)*
Dec. 1986	First negotiating session on a protocol to the Vienna Convention, convened by UNEP, Geneva
Feb. 1987	Second negotiating session on a protocol to the Vienna Convention, convened by UNEP, Vienna
Apr. 1987	Third negotiating session on a protocol to the Vienna Convention, convened by UNEP, Geneva
Jun. 1987	Meeting of heads of key delegations, convened by UNEP, Brussels
8-13 Sep. 1987	Preliminary meetings preceding the Montreal Conference, convened by UNEP, Montreal
16 Sep. 1987	MONTREAL PROTOCOL ON SUBSTANCES THAT DEPLETE THE OZONE LAYER

*Protection of the ozone layer**

Apr.-May 1989	First Meeting of the Parties to the Vienna Convention and the Montreal Protocol, Helsinki
27-29 Jun. 1990	Second Meeting of the Parties to the Vienna Convention and the Montreal Protocol, London (adoption of ADJUSTMENTS AND AMENDMENTS TO MONTREAL PROTOCOL)
Jun. 1991	Third Meeting of the Parties to the Vienna Convention and the Montreal Protocol, Nairobi (also Executive Committee of Interim Multi-lateral Fund)
Oct. 1992	Fourth Meeting of the Parties to the Vienna Convention and the Montreal Protocol, Copenhagen

*Code: Typeface indicates the following:

Scientific Developments and Meetings Not Part of International Legislative Process

Legal and Political Meetings and Statements Not Part of Non-Regional International Legislative Process

Meetings Relating to the International Legislative Process

LEGAL INSTRUMENTS ADOPTED

As you read the following materials, consider the different interests involved in the negotiations for the Protocol. Also consider the importance of the structure of the private industries affected. Note that the CFC industry is highly concentrated, with five producers each in the United States and Japan and nine producers in the European Community (EC). DuPont is the largest American producer, estimated to account for 25 percent of world production, and Imperial Chemical Industries (ICI) is the largest European producer. The CFC-consuming industry, by contrast, is much less concentrated because of the multiple uses of CFCs. What effects did the structure of the CFC industry have on the negotiations?

■ SUCCESSFUL CONVENTIONS AND CONVENTIONAL SUCCESS: SAVING THE OZONE LAYER

Alice Enders & Amelia Porges
in *The Greening of World Trade Issues (K. Anderson and R. Blackhurst eds., 1991)*

WHY AN INTERNATIONAL AGREEMENT ON THE OZONE LAYER WAS POSSIBLE

The "tragedy of the commons," as popularized by Hardin (1968), is a classic problem. Individuals using a scarce common property resource engage in behavior that is individually incentive-compatible, but this leads to over-exploitation of the resource. The problem has been identified as a form of Prisoner's Dilemma. The Nash equilibrium of this non-cooperative, static, non-zero sum game leads to excessive pollution. Olson's (1965) description of free-riding in the production of a public good has also been used to describe the problem of solving global commons issues—an individual who cannot be excluded from the benefits of a collective good once it is produced has little incentive to voluntarily contribute to providing it. In Olson's problem, free-riding is inherent when the production of the collective good does not require the participation of all players.

The Prisoner's Dilemma in international pollution problems has been given a generic functional form by Barrett (1990) and by Low and Safadi (1991). Barrett's model is a symmetric Prisoner's Dilemma game where a sub-group of players have solved the cooperation problem between themselves (leaders), and they seek the cooperation of the remaining potential players (followers). Leaders may offer compensation to free riders to induce them to join but, for certain parameter values, compensation exceeds the collective benefits and an equilibrium to the leader-follower game does not exist. Note that in a symmetric Prisoner's Dilemma game where leadership is not exogenous, this division between leaders and followers is never a Nash or best-reply equilibrium.

The two leading world consumers of CFCs, the United States and the EC, each accounted for about 30 per cent of world consumption in 1986, and their shares of world production of CFCs were 30 and 45 per cent, respectively. For each entity, the impact on the ozone layer of reducing its own CFC consumption and production depends on the CFC consumption and production decisions of the other. The cost of abatement will increase as production of CFCs is reduced and their prices rise. Thus, on either the production or consumption side, the Prisoner's Dilemma can be reduced to a game played between the EC and the United States.

The United States and the European Community are the principal players in the Prisoner's Dilemma game—they constitute both the major part of the problem and its solution. Low-consuming countries are a very minor element in the game but, as discussed below, they may become more important players in the future. This is why, in our view, the leader-follower model with symmetric costs and benefits is not appropriate to the ozone layer problem.

The model we prefer to describe agreement on ozone layer depletion is the repeated Prisoner's Dilemma, where many cooperative solutions are possible provided that commitments are enforced. Two problems must be solved: (i) the problem of making credible commitments; and (ii) the problem of mutual monitoring and enforcement without an external authority.

Viewed from this perspective, the outcome of this non-cooperative game is unrelated to "the polluter pays principle." With a non-binding agreement, cooperation evolves from incentives for present and future actions. A notion of entitlement based on harm wrought by past actions is not relevant. Thus, the dominant role of high-income countries in emissions of ozone-depleting substances and the pollution of the ozone layer, compared to the insignificant contribution of low-income countries, will not shape an agreement. This does not mean that compensation will be absent from all multilateral nonbinding agreements, but simply that its basis comes from incentives of potential signatories to an agreement.

The scope for an international agreement on ozone layer depletion in a repeated game also depends on the future potential for action. Currently, there are no low-income countries that are significant consumers of CFCs. Even China, the leading low-income consumer, accounts for only 1.5 per cent of the world total. According to UNEP (1989), the U.S. Environmental Protection Agency projects annual demand growth for China, India and other developing regions in the range of 5 to 15 per cent for the period 1992-2000. Applying these growth rates to low per capita consumption figures ensures that the overall level of CFC consumption in low-income countries will still be very low by the turn of the century, but rising incomes and populations will cause demand for CFCs in low-income non-Parties to rise over time.

In the Prisoner's Dilemma described above for global CFC production and consumption, the game between the EC and the United States has two levels—the national level and the industry level. Their CFC industries are highly concentrated, and may be described by the familiar quantity-setting Cournot duopoly with restricted entry, which also has the structure of a Prisoner's Dilemma. For many years, the industry resisted any form of regulation of CFCs. Unilateral government regulation of CFCs in one entity led to the capture of market share by producers of the other entity—as the domestic industry argued after the United States' aerosol ban in 1978. Once regulation was inevitable by the mid-1980s, only coordinated regulatory actions taken simultaneously by the governments where major consuming markets are located was acceptable to producers. While *ex post* profits might be reduced, there are clear advantages to the industry as a whole to collusion with respect to restricting the entry of new producers in target markets. As (higher-price) substitutes looked like they were becoming available, existing producers sought an agreement that regulated CFC production in a closed "competition area."

Quantitative limits on CFC production are a form of regulation preferred by the industry. Regulation through a limit on consumption would have led to competition between producers with excess capacity, reducing profits of all. And regulation by imposing taxes would have reduced profits. According to Benedick (1991), the "adjusted production" approach of the Montreal Protocol was chosen purely for commercial reasons. (A consumption limit was included as a result of pressure from net importing countries (such as the Nordic) who were concerned that as production limits came into effect, CFC producers in the United States and the EC would favor domestic consuming industries.)

Notes and Questions

1. *A pathbreaking agreement.* The Montreal Protocol is a pathbreaking example of countries' willingness to address a problem in which the harmful consequences of our activities today will be felt primarily by our children and their descendants. Why were countries able to reach an agreement?

2. *Developing countries and the Montreal Protocol.* Why would developing countries be reluctant to join the Montreal Protocol? What incentives does the protocol provide to attract them?

One of the major achievements of the meeting of the parties at Copenhagen was the establishment of a Multilateral Fund to help offset the costs of Article V countries in complying with the protocol. The Indian government was not satisfied with the mere promise of the establishment of the fund; the actual fund had to be set up before India would join the protocol.

The Montreal Protocol now has all of the major industrialized developing countries as parties. Since these are the ones with large internal and, potentially, external markets, the potential for restricting widespread usage of ozone-depleting chemicals is significantly increased.

3. *Equity and the structure of the protocol.* Are there other equity issues embedded in the structure of the protocol?

4. *Ozone protection and international trade.* The Montreal Protocol prohibits trade in controlled substances (and eventually in products produced with controlled substances) with nonparties. Is this consistent with the General Agreement on Tariffs and Trade? How would you go about analyzing this question? Does it matter that there is an exception for nonparties that are determined by the Conference of the Parties to be in compliance with Article 2 (Control Measures) of the Protocol? Thses issues are considered in detail in chapter 20, on environment and trade.

5. *Dispute resolution.* Note that the Montreal Protocol does not contain formal dispute resolution procedures in the text. However, the formal dispute resolution provisions in the Vienna Convention on the Protection of the Ozone Layer do apply. To date they have never been used. Why do you think that may be? (When responding, consider the material on the noncompliance procedures that have been developed under the Protocol, as outlined below.) If the dispute resolution procedures are never used, do they nonetheless serve a useful function for the parties? How?

6. *More on the Montreal Protocol.* Many articles have been written about the Montreal Protocol and its annexes. *See, e.g.*, Edward A. Parson, Pro-

tecting the Ozone Layer, Institutions for the Earth 27-74 (Peter M. Haas, Robert O. Keohane, Marc A. Levy, eds. 1993); Anne Gallagher, The New Montreal Protocol and the Future of International Law for the Protection of the Environment, 14 Houston J. Intl. L. 267 (1992) (discussing the history and structuring of the Vienna Convention, Montreal Protocol, and the 1990 Meeting, as well as suggesting ways to improve implementation of the protocol).

7. *Developments in environmental diplomacy.* Richard Benedick has analyzed the Montreal Protocol and written on what he finds to be the most important developments in environmental agreement-making as a result of the negotiations. In the following excerpt, from Ozone Diplomacy chapter on Lessons for a New Diplomacy (19__), notice Benedick's emphasis on the concepts of scientific uncertainty, the role of nongovernmental actors, and equity issues as integral parts of the negotiating process.

> The international community was successful in its approach to the problem of protecting the stratospheric ozone layer. The experience gained from this process suggests several elements of a new kind of diplomacy for addressing such similar global ecological threats as greenhouse warming.
>
> *Scientists must play an unaccustomed but critical role in international environmental negotiations.* Without modern science and technology, the world would have remained unaware of the danger to ozone until it was too late. Science became the driving force behind ozone policy. The formation of a commonly accepted body of data and analyses and the narrowing of ranges of uncertainty were prerequisites to a political solution among negotiating parties far apart. . . .
>
> *Governments may have to act while there is still scientific uncertainty, responsibly balancing the risks and costs of acting or not acting.* By the time the evidence on such issues as the ozone layer and climate change is beyond all dispute, the damage may be irreversible, and it may be too late to forestall serious harm to human life and draconian costs to society. Politicians must therefore resist a tendency to lend too much credence to self-serving economic interests that demand scientific certainty, maintain that dangers are remote and unlikely, and insist that the costs of changing their ways are astronomical. The signatories at Montreal knowingly imposed substantial short-run economic dislocations even though the evidence was incomplete; the prudence of their decision was demonstrated when the scientific models turned out to have underestimated the effects of CFC's on ozone. . . .
>
> *Educating and mobilizing public opinion are essential to generate pressure on hesitant governments and private companies.* . . .

2. *Scientific Uncertainty and the Precautionary Approach*

As you remember from the chapter on scientific uncertainty, new scientific information changes the way countries approach their environmental problems. The more certain and serious the harm, the more willing a country is to act and spend money to prevent that harm.

The negotiators of the Montreal Protocol provided three mechanisms for adapting the substantive requirements to new scientific findings. First, the protocol calls for a regular meeting of the parties to monitor progress and consult on necessary modifications. Article XI (1).

Secondly, the protocol has provided for technical assessments prior to the meetings. Article VI of the protocol requires that the parties set up expert panels to report progress and help in the assessment of progress which is to take place at least once every four years. The Technical and Economic Assessment Panels have been critical in enabling the parties to move more quickly to phase out ozone-depleting chemicals and to add new chemicals to the list.

Unlike many international agreements, the protocol does not require formal amendments to change the phaseout dates for the listed chemicals. Instead, it allows for "adjustments". *See* Article II (9) (". . . the Parties may decide whether: (i) adjustments to the one depleting potentials . . . should be made and, if so, what the adjustments should be; and (ii) further adjustments and reductions of production or consumption of the controlled substances from the 1986 levels should be undertaken and, if so, what the scope, amount and timing of any such adjustments and reductions should be").

To add new chemicals to the list, however, requires an amendment. *See* Article II (10).

The major benefit of an adjustment rather than an amendment process is that there is no need to have the parties get the changes approved by the national legislatures. Instead, the expert committee proposes the changes, the parties vote, and if passed, the adjustment becomes a binding modification of the protocol.

The London meeting of the parties in June 1990 resulted in both adjustments to the protocol and amendments to the protocol. The adjustments became effective in March 1991; the amendments not until August 1992. Why the difference? Do you understand why parties to the protocol may have assumed different sets of obligations?

Accelerating CFC phase-out. On April 15, 1992, 56 countries agreed to speed up the phaseout of chlorofluorocarbons. The timetable adopted by the working group of parties to the Protocol required a complete phaseout by January 1, 1996, four years earlier than that provided in the 1990 London Amendments. The Protocol originally only called for 50 percent reduction of 1986 consumption levels by the year 2000. A ministerial meeting of the parties in Copenhagen in November 1992 approved the new timetable (*see* Fourth Agreement, Annex I). Note how countries agreed to phaseout chlorofluorocarbons much more quickly than anticipated when the Protocol was negotiated.

Consider the provisions of the Protocol. Are they adequate to let countries respond effectively to the rapid changes in our scientific knowledge of the seriousness of the problem?

The adjustment process has been used several times since its development: 1990, 1992, 1994, 1995. The Protocol has been amended in 1990, 1992, and 1997.

Consider the devices that were included in the Montreal Protocol to adjust to changes in scientific understanding of the problem. How would these work if countries want to agree at the next meeting of the parties to (1) speed up the rate of phasing out methyl bromide and (2) add new chemicals to the list of controlled substances?

The Special Case of Methyl Bromide. The precautionary principle or approach is raised by recent problems between the United States and the European Community in negotiating the phaseout of methyl bromide.

Methyl bromide is a chemical used widely in both agricultural and urban areas as a pesticide. Although once the chemical is sprayed on fields the dusted crops should be covered to prevent release of the bromide into the air, there have been occasions when the pesticide leaked or was incorrectly applied and escaped. *See* Pesticide Peril to Ozone May Lead to Ban, L.A. Times, July 26, 1992, A1.

Once in the air, methyl bromide destroys ozone very efficiently. The scientific panel for the Montreal Protocol that reviewed bromide's effects estimated that methyl bromide has an ozone depleting potential 40 times greater than that of CFCs. *See* L.A. Times, above. However, the destructive potential lasts for only two years. Unlike a ban on CFCs, which will continue destroying ozone for up to 30 years after production ends, a ban on methyl bromide could have very quick benefits for the ozone layer.

As a result, at the November 1992 meeting of the parties to the Montreal Protocol, the United States wanted a ban on the production of methyl bromide. However, the European Community argued that the phaseout date be held off until more findings verified the degenerative impacts of human-made methyl bromide upon ozone.

While the National Oceanic and Atmospheric Administration estimates that 25 percent of the methyl bromide in the stratosphere comes from industrially produced bromide, not everyone agrees. Further, there is a huge demand for the chemical as a pesticide and there is reportedly no substitute. A USDA official set the potential losses from crops at $500 million per year if a ban on its use went into effect immediately. *See* L.A. Times, above.

In the end, the 1992 proposal for a ban failed. At the Ninth Meeting of the Parties in 1997, member countries agreed to phase out consumption of methyl bromide by the year 2005, except that to meet basic needs, countries may consume up to 15 percent of their calculated levels in 1991. Article V developing countries must reach zero consumption by the year 2015, except for uses agreed to be "critical."

3. *Compliance*

At the 1992 Rio Conference on Environment and Development, countries agreed that compliance with international agreements was one of the most important legal issues on the agenda for the next few decades. Consider how the Montreal Protocol handles the problem of compliance. What problems do you foresee with monitoring compliance and with obtaining compliance with the protocol?

■ SUCCESSFUL CONVENTIONS AND CONVENTIONAL SUCCESS: SAVING THE OZONE LAYER

Alice Enders & Amelia Porges
in *The Greening of World Trade Issues (K. Anderson & R. Blackhurst eds., 1991)*

COMPLIANCE WITH THE MONTREAL PROTOCOL . . .

Two separate procedures apply with regard to possible non-complying acts: dispute settlement under the dispute settlement provisions in Article 11 of the Vienna Convention, and a compliance procedure established at the Second Meeting of the Parties. The Third Meeting has confirmed that these procedures are coexisting and mutually independent. . . .

In response to a mandate in the Protocol, a non-compliance procedure was developed and adopted in 1990 at the Second Meeting of the parties. As of 1991, the most severe sanction that may be applied under the Protocol in the event of non-compliance is to withdraw the benefit of inclusion within the trade provisions and access to the financial mechanism that Parties enjoy. Thus, a ban on the export to and import from the Party in question goes into effect for CFCs, as well as a ban on the importation of CFC-containing products. Note that these are not *trade sanctions,* since they are not penalties or restrictions on products other than ozone-depleting chemicals or products containing CFCs. These measures simply convert the non-complying Party to a non-Party for the purposes of the trade relations between Parties and non-Parties.

In any case it would be difficult to establish trade sanctions for use against non-complying Parties because an exchange of concessions does not lie at the heart of the Protocol. A Party to the Protocol is obligated to phase out CFCs, and the benefit of a diminished rate of stratospheric ozone layer depletion is a collective one. For most countries, this benefit cannot be withdrawn in response to non-compliance; only non-compliance by the United States or EC would imperil the attainment of this benefit over the short-term. In this manner, a non-complying Party to the Protocol (and indeed a non-Party) may be a true free-rider in the medium-term—it cannot be excluded from the benefits of producing a public good in which its participation is not required.

While non-compliance is a classic difficulty in international agreements, meeting Protocol commitments is unlikely to be a problem in high-income countries, where a preference for ozone-safe products expressed through consumer preference and through government regulation is present. In the EC and the United States, the primary risk might be that producers would cheat on their commitment to phase out CFCs. But this is unimportant because those producers are in a position to pass through cost increases, and are interested in strict regulation of substances so as to capture scarcity rents during the phaseout period, to maintain barriers to entry and to commercialize substitute chemicals. The economic pressures for deviation are more intense downstream among industrial consumers, many of whom are in less-concentrated industries. Yet even they are subject to national regulation and to the Protocol's cutoff of imports from non-Parties.

For developing-country Parties to the Protocol, the full economic costs of foregoing CFC consumption are as yet uncertain, but they are certainly greater relative total income than in high-income Parties. Furthermore, the consumer preference for ozone-safe products may not be as well established in poorer countries due to the lack of widely circulating information on ozone layer depletion. However, the various trade provisions of the Protocol make eventual non-compliance an economic proposition only in a country with a large internal or external non-Party market for CFC consumption. Once phaseout must begin after 1999, problems with compliance at the governmental level are likely to emerge only in the most populated developing-country Parties.

Notes and Questions

1. *Establishing a procedure for noncompliance.* At the Copenhagen meeting of the parties, the member countries agreed to adopt a procedure for noncompliance with the provision of the protocol and set out possible measures to be taken. *See* Fourth Meeting, Annexes IV and V.

Procedurally, the amendment in Annex IV provides for the creation of an Implementation Committee whose task is to take and evaluate complaints against members who are accused of not fulfilling their treaty obligations. The committee is to report to the Meeting of the Parties, which will then decide whether action should be taken or whether there is a valid excuse.

Annex V setting out possible measures to be taken in the case of unexcused noncompliance contains only three subsections. The first is a provision of "appropriate assistance." The second and third are negative sanctions, "issuing cautions" (Annex V (B)) and suspension of rights and privileges, "including those concerned with industrial rationalization, production, consumption, trade, transfer of technology, financial mechanism, and institutional arrangements" (Annex V (C)).

Other authors have asserted the need for more stringent measures to ensure compliance with the Protocol. *See, e.g.*, Michael David Ehrenstein, A Moralistic Approach to the Ozone Depletion Crisis, 21 Inter-American L. Rev. 611 (1990) (suggesting that fostering a strong sense of moral duty to protect the ozone layer would allow for making destroying it a crime).

2. *The requirement to submit national reports.* The main instrument that parties have to monitor compliance with the obligations to limit or phase out consumption of controlled ozone-depleting substances is through the submission of annual reports. These are sent to the secretariat in Nairobi to be compiled and reviewed. The Implementation Committee under the Protocol reviews cases of noncompliance with the reporting requirement and with the substantive obligations. Soon after the Protocol came into effect, many countries either did not provide the annual reports or failed to provide complete reports on time. In 1991, of the 48 countries required to report 1989 data, only 20 had fully complied as of March 1991. But in November 1996, 104 of the 141 parties that should have reported data for 1994 had done so. This is a substantial improvement over 1991.

Some have questioned the value of reporting in international environmental agreements. What problems do you foresee with reporting? If a country did not file a report, what options would be open to the Implementation Committee? What factors would influence their decision on the appropriate action? How could countries make reporting an effective tool for monitoring compliance? Some have suggested that for some agreements on-site monitoring is preferable to reporting. Would this be feasible for the Montreal Protocol?

3. *Smuggling of controlled chemicals.* One of the most serious problems in enforcing the Protocol is that CFCs that are newly produced are being smuggled into certain countries as recycled CFCs. Smuggling of CFCs from Mexico into the United States has been perceived as a serious problem and has resulted in arrests, for example, in January 1997, under United States law. In response to concerns about smuggling, the parties adopted an amendment in 1997 that requires countries to establish a licensing system by the year 2000 for the export and import of controlled chemicals listed in annexes A, B, C, and E. What problems do you foresee in implementing a licensing system?

4. *Criminal penalties.* While there is precedent for making environmentally damaging activity criminal nationally, there is no international

agreement containing such types of provisions. Should the Protocol require that countries treat smuggling of controlled chemicals as a crime?

D. IMPLEMENTATION OF THE MONTREAL PROTOCOL

Different countries use different approaches in implementing international commitments within their countries, as described in chapter 5, sec. A.7. In terms of the United States, the Montreal Protocol is not a self-executing treaty (*see* chapter 5, sec. A.7, note 2). Thus, for the United States (and many other countries)national legislation or regulations are needed to make it domestically enforceable.

1. The United States

The United States Clean Air Act was already in place when the United States signed the Montreal Protocol in September 1987. Because the Clean Air Act already required limited uses of CFCs nationally, the substantive requirements of the Montreal Protocol could simply be implemented under the authority granted under the act in section 602(c) (which allows the administrator to add chemicals to the lists of controlled substances to the extent consistent with the Montreal Protocol).

The original United States regulations implementing the Montreal Protocol, contained in Title VI of the Clean Air Act, were published in 1988, with minor revisions thereafter. The regulations restrict the production and consumption of controlled substances. Allowances are apportioned among companies based on their market share of national production and import levels during the baseline year. For chemicals listed before the London Amendments the baseline year is 1986. For chemicals listed later, the baseline varies. Section 606 of the act allows for accelerated phaseouts of chemicals consistent with the Montreal Protocol as long as the change is announced to the public and subject to debate (606(a)(3)). Accordingly, the Copenhagen Adjustments and Amendments, which set out baselines of 1989 levels for HCFCs, 1991 levels for methyl bromide, and for the elimination of hydrobromofluorocarbons by 1996, became part of the national law. Trading of production rights is allowed. The timetable for phasing out methyl bromide in the Clean Air Act is shorter than that allowed by the 1997 adjustment, should the Clean Air Act be "adjusted" to fit the longer timetable?

On January 1, 1990, taxes on ozone-depleting substances went into effect, as called for in the Omnibus Reconciliation Act of 1989. On January

1, 1993, the excise tax was raised under the Energy Policy Act of 1992. This increase is consistent with the plan to annually raise the tax as an additional disincentive to produce or consume the chemicals. *See* 58 Fed. Reg. 4768.

STRATOSPHERIC OZONE: UNITED STATES REGULATION OF CHLOROFLUOROCARBONS

Orval E. Nangle
16 B.C. Envtl. Affairs L. Rev. 531 (1989)

The Montreal Protocol does not specify how its production and consumption limitations are to be met. Each party to the Protocol has discretion to choose its own method. EPA has published two rules in order to implement the Protocol in the United States: one rule for collection of the United States 1986 production and consumption data and a second rule that would implement the Protocol's substantive requirements.

Congress did not enact any special enabling legislation for these regulations. Both rules are issued under statutory authority granted in the Clean Air Act. EPA's authority to require information on 1986 production, consumption, imports, and exports of CFCs and halons is contained in section 114 of the Clean Air Act. The Act empowers the Administrator to "require any person who owns or operates an emission source or is subject to any requirement of this chapter . . . to . . . provide such other information as he may reasonably require." Likewise, authority to regulate CFCs and halons is contained in section 157(b) of the Clean Air Act. . . .

The regulations replicate the requirements of the Montreal Protocol. They regulate the same controlled substances over specified control periods, specify the same staged freezes and reductions, and restrict trade to comply with the Protocol. Moreover, the regulations become effective only after the Protocol enters into force.

A. 1986 Calculated Levels

EPA has required producers, importers, and exporters of the controlled substances listed in Annex A of the Protocol to report the amount (in kilograms) of each controlled substance: (1) produced in the United States of its territories in 1986, (2) used and entirely consumed as a chemical intermediary in the production of other chemicals in 1986, (3) imported into the United States or its territories in 1986 (including the date, port of entry, and country of origin), and (4) exported from the United States or its territories (including the date, port of exit, country of destination, and date of arrival at destination). This information was required by January 13, 1988. The information obtained provided the basis for determining the calculated levels of production and consumption in the United States for 1986, an essential part of the regulatory scheme.

B. Regulatory Approach

Before settling on a regulatory approach, EPA considered three economic incentive approaches as well as several engineering controls and product bans. The economic incentive approaches use higher CFC and halon prices to provide incentive for firms to reduce their use of those chemicals. Higher prices should cause firms that can make relatively low-cost reductions to do so.

One of these economic incentive approaches provided for the auction of CFC permits to any interested party. The permit would allow a firm to produce a specified amount of CFCs during a specified control period, the number of permits auctioned determined by the permissible calculated levels for each group of controlled substances. Revenues from the auctions would go to the United States Treasury. It would not be permissible to hold permits for use in a later control period because such use could result in a violation of the Protocol in a future year. The trading of permits, however, would be permissible.

Another economic incentive approach involved setting production quotas based on regulatory goals. The quotas would be allocated to the five domestic CFC producers and the approximately ten United States importers based on their share of the market in 1986. Quotas could not be saved for use in a future year but could be traded among producers and importers for use in the same control year.

The third economic incentives approach considered by EPA involved the use of regulatory fees. EPA would assess fees against the regulated chemicals to encourage reduced usage, basing the amount of those fees on the chemical's ozone depletion potential and the permitted calculated levels of CFCs. A margin for error would be included to assure the target goal is met. Revenues would go to the United States Treasury.

EPA also considered developing specific engineering control measures requiring targeted CFC-user industries to reduce their consumption. EPA could, for example, ban the use of CFC-blown packaging, require additional recovery and recycling from solvent users of CFCs, and require recycling of CFCs used in sterilization. EPA could select control options based on pertinent societal considerations such as available technologies, cost of reductions, and quantity of reductions. A hybrid of these engineering controls/bans and of allocated quotas made up a fifth approach that EPA considered.

Because concerns over environmental protection and legality could undermine the program and administrative costs of controls and bans could be high, EPA chose the allocated quota approach. The sole identified drawback to the allocated quota approach was that CFC and halon producers and importers might realize substantial profits as a result of the scarcity created by regulation. Moreover, the allocated quota approach provides economically efficient reductions, involves minimal administrative costs, does not raise potential legal issues, and is the most easily enforced option.

C. Production and Consumption Levels

. . .

Because the regulations ensure compliance with the Protocol provisions limiting both production and consumption, they create separate production allowances and consumption allowances. The regulations apportion calculated levels of baseline production allowances to any person who produced one or more controlled substances in the United States during 1986. The apportionment is equal to that person's calculated level of production of Group I and Group II controlled substances during 1986. The regulations allocate baseline consumption allowances to persons who produced and/or imported one or more controlled substances into the United States in 1986. The apportionment is equal to the calculated level of Group I and Group II controlled substances produced and/or imported in 1986 minus the amount of each controlled substance exported in 1986. . . .

Importers of controlled substances must maintain records showing the quantity of each controlled substance imported, the date imported, the port of exit and entry, the country from which each substance was imported, the commodity code, the importer number for the shipment, a copy of the bill of loading, an invoice, and the United States Customs Services Entry Summary Form. On a quarterly basis, importers must provide EPA with a report summarizing the information in their daily records, including the total quantity (kilograms) of each controlled substance imported during the previous quarter, the calculated level of Group I and Group II controlled substances imported during the quarter and since the beginning of the control period, and the importer's total expended and unexpended consumption allowances at the end of the month. . . .

F. Users

It is important to note that no consumption allowances are required to use CFC's or halons. In fact, users of controlled substances are not involved with production allowances, consumption allowances, record keeping, or reporting. . . .

G. Enforcement

EPA will monitor compliance by reviewing the submitted reports and by inspecting sites. The Clean Air Act authorizes EPA to pursue injunctive relief, criminal prosecutions, or civil penalties of up to $25,000 per day for each violation. The regulations provide added bite to civil penalties by narrowly defining what constitutes a violation. Each kilogram of a controlled substance produced in excess of production allowances or in excess of consumption allowances constitutes a separate violation. Likewise, each kilogram imported from a non-party also constitutes a separate violation. Furthermore, the regulations provide that any producer who fails to maintain the required records and reports may be assumed to have been producing at full capacity during the period for which records or reports were not kept. The result of this approach is to allow EPA to impose substantially greater civil penalties, thus discouraging violations.

Note

EPA prohibition on nonessential uses (from 58 Federal Register 4768). On January 15, 1993, the EPA issued a final ruling under section 610 of the Clean Air Act prohibiting the sale or distribution of "Non-Essential Products" that release CFCs.

The ban took effect on February 16, 1993, and resulted in the prohibition of CFC-propelled party streamers and noise horns, cleaning fluids for noncommercial photographic equipment, and flexible foams, among other things.

In determining "nonessentiality," the EPA is to take into account the availability and cost of substitutes, "health and safety" of both the product and the available substitutes, and "other relevant factors," which include the economic impact of a ban. *See* Clean Air Act, §602 and 58 Fed. Reg. 4768.

2. The European Community

The European Community has implemented the Montreal Protocol through a regulation, which means it is immediately binding upon states. Generally the EC uses the form of a directive in adopting environmental legislation, in order to give member countries flexibility in bringing their legislation into conformity with the EC legislation. By contrast, a regulation is directly applicable to countries and comes into effect immediately. According to Jachtenfuchs, in the article excerpted below, the EC chose to use a regulation to avoid trade distortions from nonsimultaneous application of the legislation and to underline the urgency of the issue.

■ THE EUROPEAN COMMUNITY AND THE PROTECTION OF THE OZONE LAYER

Markus Jachtenfuchs
J. Comm. Mkt. Studies 261 (Mar. 1990)

The Montreal Protocol, signed on 16 September 1987, had to be implemented by Community legislation. This was necessary because the CFC producers are not bound by the international treaty, but only by Community or national laws. . . .

After the Commission had published its proposals for implementation of the Montreal Protocol in February 1987, the Parliament had to deliberate on the issue for a second time, this time in the framework of a formal consultation procedure according to Art. 130s of the EEC Treaty, as amended by the Single European Act. A majority, comprised of the communist, the socialist, and the rainbow group approved amendments urging the Council to use Art. 2 (11) of the Protocol which opened up the possibility of adopting stricter national standards (European Parliament, 1988). On 14 October 1988, the regulation was adopted by the Council as proposed by the Commission. In drafting the regulation . . . the Commission endeavored to transform every detail of the Montreal Protocol into Community legislation, including all possible exceptions (Commission 1988b: 2-3).

It is worth noting that the Commission chose the legal form of a regulation for the implementation of the Protocol. Usually, environmental legislation is adopted in the form of Directives, in order to leave the Member States more room to adopt the necessary measures according to their own legal traditions. However, in order to avoid trade distortions resulting from non-simultaneous application of the proposed legislation, and also to underline the urgency of the matter, the Commission chose to propose a regulation which was directly applicable to Member States and could come into force immediately.

3. *Other Countries*

1. DuPont Corporation, one of the most active members in achieving the mandatory reductions in the Montreal Protocol, is also one of the most vigorous developers of substitutes for the banned CFCs. DuPont agreed to assist China with complying with the limits by supplying the chemical industry ministry with CFC substitutes, new technology, and expert advice. World Environment Report, July 2, 1993, at 19.

China's position as the world's most populous nation and its complex administrative network make implementation of environmental regulations especially challenging. It is hoped that the involvement of private industry will ease some of the burden on the government and reduce the demand for CFCs from the projected 70,000-80,000 tons by 1996. World Environment Report, February 2, 1993, at 26. For a summary of China's approach to implementing the Montreal Protocol, *see* Daniel Magraw, International Environmental Legal Issues, in International Occupational and Environmental Medicine 130, 134-35 (Box 13-1, by Zhao Ying) (Jessica A. Herzstein et al. eds., 1998).

2. In Singapore, Exxon Chemical Asia became the second producer of a CFC substitute used by electronics producers for cleaning circuit boards. *See* A Cleaner, The Straits Times, October 7, 1992. As of October 1992, Actrel ED, an ozone-safe product, posed a challenge to DuPont's Axarel in Southeast Asia's computer and electronics industry.

The computer and electronics industry is the largest user of CFCs in Singapore, accounting for 65 percent of the total CFCs used in 1991.

The development of substitutes for ozone-depleting chemicals is hoped to continue the lowering of the annual CFC consumption, which has gone from 4,000 tons in 1986 to 1,600 tons in 1991.

3. One of the most important concerns is whether large developing countries such as India and China will meet their obligations after the ten-year period of delay provided in the Protocol. To the extent that many new producers of the controlled substances are being established in developing countries, it may be difficult suddenly to curtail production of the controlled substances within a decade. Substitutes may still be more expensive. Will the Protocol fund be sufficient?

4. India, an Article V country, is producing ozone-depleting substances for the export market as well as for internal consumption. Is this consistent with the obligations of the protocol? What legal arguments would you make on behalf of India? On behalf of an industrialized country?

5. There are increasing reports of CFCs being smuggled into the United States. The chemicals come in as recycled CFCs when in fact they are original production. Why do you think that this is occurring? Does the tax Congress levied on CFC producers in the United States affect the smuggling problem? How would you recommend that the United States address this problem in its regulations? What could other parties do under the protocol? Recall that the 1997 Amendment to the Montreal Protocol calls upon parties to put in place by the year 2000 a licensing system for imports and exports of new, used, recycled, and reclaimed controlled substances listed in annexes A, B, C, and E to the protocol.

6. *Source Materials.* For a very useful compilation of official documents and decisions relating to the international regime protecting the ozone layer, correlated to specific articles of the Protocol, as well as other information, *see* UNEP Ozone Secretariat, Handbook for the International Treaties for the Protection of Ozone Layer (4th ed. 1996).

XII

Global Climate Change

In June 1992, at the United Nations Conference on Environment and Development, countries opened for signature the United Nations Framework Convention on Climate Change (FCCC). The FCCC sets forth a framework for addressing climate change, although it does not contain binding targets and timetables for controlling emissions of gases that cause global warming. Ten years—even five years—earlier, most people thought it would be impossible for countries ever to agree on such an international convention. In 1997, the Kyoto Protocol to the FCCC was finalized and adopted. It contains binding targets and timetables for industrialized countries.

"Climate" is the general term for the seasonal interactions of air and water in the atmosphere. Climate consists of the elements of temperature, precipitation, wind, and cloud cover, and it affects every substance on the planet, whether organic or inorganic. In turn, any substance that affects the climate has other affects on the globe.

Climate change offers a useful case study of many of the issues raised in general terms earlier in this book. Climate change is an inherently intergenerational problem. The actions we take today will cause effects for several decades or more. Climate change, by its very nature, is a common global concern of all countries, for climate respects no political boundaries. The climate system involves interactions among the land, air, freshwater and oceans, and humans, wherever they may be. While there is agreement on the scientific theory of the greenhouse effect and climate change (also referred to as "global warming" and "greenhouse warming"). There is significant scientific uncertainty about whether global warming will occur, how much global warming will occur, and what the local and regional distributions of the effects of global warming will be. Moreover, there is uncertainty about the benefits and costs of actions to prevent global warming and about the sufficiency of adaptive responses to global warming. However, there is emerging agreement that the average rate of global warming will be greater than any seen in the last 10,000 years. IPCC, IPCC Second Assessment: Climate Change 1995: The Science of Climate Change, Working Group I, at 39 (1995).

Climate change differs considerably from other global environmental concerns, such as ozone depletion, because it involves complex interactions between air, land, and water; the human-induced causes go to the heart of countries' economies; and there are large economic costs associated both with the effects of climate change and measures to prevent and mitigate it. Internationally there is still considerable disagreement about what to do about the threat of global warming.

As you read this chapter, ask yourself what role the level of uncertainty plays, or should play, in the development of legal instruments and regimes designed to minimize the harmful impacts of global warming. Will the FCCC and the Kyoto Protocol be as effective in the context of climate change as the Montreal Protocol (addressed in Chapter 11, above) was for ozone? What type of policies would a precautionary approach require?

For early analyses of the legal issues surrounding climate change, *see* Edith Brown Weiss, A Resource Management Approach to Carbon Dioxide During the Century of Transition, 10 Denver J. Intl. L. & Poly. 487 (1981); World Climate Change: The Role of International Law and Institutions (Ved P. Nanda, ed., 1983). For a view of international law and global warming, *see* Daniel Bodansky, May We Engineer the Climate?, 33 Climatic Change no. 3, 309 (July 1996); Geoffrey Palmer, The Implications of Climate Change for International Law and Institutions, 2 Transnatl. L. & Contemp. Probs. 205 (1992); Ray Jay Davis, Climatic Change and Apocalypse and Law, 6 BYU J. Pub. L. 213 (1992); Prue Taylor, International Legal Control of the Greenhouse Effect, 20 Victoria U. of Wellington L. Rev. 45 (1990); Alan E. Boyle, International Law and the Protection of the Global Atmosphere: Concepts, Categories, and Principles, in International Law and Global Climate Change 7-19 (Robin Churchill & David Freestone eds., 1991).

Several symposia on the broad topic of climate change have been sponsored by law journals in the United States, and the papers presented have been published in special collections. Among these are: Special Issue: Global Warming, 14 S. Ill. U. L. J. (Winter 1990); Energy and the Environment: Intersecting Global Issues, 9 Ariz. J. Intl. & Comp. L. (Spring 1992); Doman Colloquium on Global Change and International Law, 1 Colo. J.

Intl. Envtl. L. & Poly. (Summer 1990); Symposium: Confronting Global Warming, 2 Transnatl. L. & Contemp. Probs. (Spring 1992).

A. UNCERTAINTY AS TO WHETHER HUMAN-INDUCED CLIMATE CHANGE IS OCCURRING

Until recently, there has been a great deal of scientific uncertainty surrounding the questions of whether, to what degree, when, and with what effects in what regions our human activities are inducing global warming. However, with the Second Assessment Report of the Intergovernmental Panel on Climate Change (IPCC), broad consensus in the scientific community appears to have emerged that human-induced climate change is a reality. *See* IPCC, IPCC Second Assessment Report: Climate Change 1995 (1995); *see also* IPCC, Climate Change (1991).

In 1989, the United States National Academy of Sciences, the National Academy of Engineering, and the Institute of Medicine jointly formed a high-level panel of experts with two subpanels to address the scientific basis of global warming and to evaluate alternative strategies for addressing it. A portion of this panel's report is given below. Compare this early report with the much more recent report that follows it, the Second Assessment Report of the IPCC. Note in particular the greater level of confidence as to the effects of climate change in the language of the IPCC Second Assessment Report. At the same time, though, attention should be paid to the Second Assessment Report's conclusion that earlier reports appear to overstate the amount of global warming.

1. Assessing Climate Change

■ POLICY IMPLICATIONS OF GREENHOUSE WARMING

Committee on Science, Engineering and Public Policy
National Academy of Sciences, National Academy of Engineering,
Institute of Medicine (1991)

BACKGROUND

THE GLOBAL NATURE OF GREENHOUSE WARMING

Greenhouse warming is global in at least two respects. First, greenhouse gases released anywhere in the world disperse rapidly in the global atmosphere. Neither the location of release nor the activity resulting in a release makes much difference. A molecule of CO_2 from a cooking fire in Yellowstone or India is subject to the same laws of chemistry and physics in the atmosphere as a molecule from the exhaust pipe of a high performance auto in Indiana or Europe. Second, the anticipated climatic effects include changes in the global circulation of air and water. Global average temperature is often used as an indicator of the various climatic effects. Climate change, however, has many facets: seasonal cycles and annual fluctuations of temperature and precipitation, wind speed and direction, and strength and direction of ocean currents. Although the results of climate change will differ from place to place, they derive from global processes.

GREENHOUSE GAS EMISSIONS FROM HUMAN ACTIVITIES

Greenhouse warming is complicated in another, more fundamental way. The amounts released vary, of course, but virtually every form of human activity contributes some amount of greenhouse gas to the atmosphere or removes some from the atmosphere. Subsistence agriculture contributes its bit, as does modern industry and the consumption and use of modern goods and services. Growing trees remove CO_2 from the atmosphere, but burning wood for heating and cooking releases CO_2 into the atmosphere. Rice paddies and cattle contribute CH_4. Industrial activities include releases of all the greenhouse gases to varying extents. In most societies the burning of fossil fuels for electricity and transportation is a major contributor.

Since releases of greenhouse gases are connected to most economic activity, significant reductions in their emission may affect the economic competitiveness of individuals, firms, and nations. Avoiding additional greenhouse warming may be costly, it may create economic winners and losers, and it may alter trade balances. . . .

The climate is extremely variable. Temperature, humidity, precipitation and wind vary markedly from week to week and season to season. These natural variations are commonly much larger than the changes associated with greenhouse warming. There are also patterns to these natural variations, and it is these patterns that we think of as "climate."

The importance of greenhouse warming will be determined by the magnitude and abruptness of the associated climatic changes. Useful prediction requires credible quantitative estimates of those changes. Numerical computer simulations using general circulation models (GCMs) are generally considered the best available tools for anticipating climatic changes. Data from previous interglacial periods can be compared to results from computer models. Past conditions, however, are inexact metaphors for current increases in atmospheric concentrations of trace gases.

In order to simulate the intricate climatic system, GCMs themselves are complicated. A typical GCM involves hundreds of thousands of equations and dozens of variables. About half a dozen different model types exist, and others are being developed.

General circulation models most commonly simulate the equilibrium climatic conditions associated with doubling atmospheric concentrations of CO_2 compared to preindustrial levels. Current GCM simulations based on these assumptions show a range of global average equilibrium temperature increases of 1.9° to 5.2°C (3.4° to 9.4°F). The GCM results have been interpreted in slightly different ways by groups with differing perspectives. The Intergovernmental Panel on Climate Change (IPCC) used a range of 2° to 4°C (3.6° to 7.2°F) accompanying an equivalent doubling of preindustrial CO_2. The National Research Council's Board on Atmospheric Sciences and Climate used a range of 1.5° to 4.5°C (2.7° to 8.1°F), numbers receiving slightly greater usage among atmospheric scientists.

For the purposes of informed policy choice, it is crucial to acknowledge the limited capability of the GCMs. This is especially true because there is no clear connection between temperature records of the last century and the atmospheric accumulation of greenhouse gases. The temperature record for the northern hemisphere, for example, shows some rise until about 1940, a slight decrease from 1940 until the mid-1970s, followed by another rise. There currently is no persuasive evidence that these variations were driven by growing atmospheric concentrations of greenhouse gases. The 100-year temperature record is not inconsistent with the range of climate sensitivity predicted by the GCMs, but neither is it inconsistent with the natural variability of the earth's atmosphere.

There is another key limitation on the knowledge acquired from GCMs. In essence there are fewer than two dozen GCM simulation runs with five independent models on which to base conclusions. Every one incorporates untested and invalidated hypotheses. . . . The limited number of GCM simulations has two important consequences. First, there are too few runs to scientifically determine "most likely" values within the range. Second, it is not strictly possible to eliminate temperature changes of less than 1°C (1.8°F) or greater than 5°C (9°F). . . .

The panel believes that prudent policy choices should be based on conservative assumptions in the face of large uncertainty. The panel uses as range of 1° to 5°C (1.8° to 9°F) and notes that it is broader than ranges adopted by other groups. In the panel's view, this range expresses much less unwarranted faith in the numbers produced by GCMs than does a narrower range.

INTERGOVERNMENTAL PANEL ON CLIMATE CHANGE, IPCC SECOND ASSESSMENT REPORT: CLIMATE CHANGE 1995 (UNEP 1995)

IPCC Second Assessment Synthesis of Scientific-Technical Information Relevant to Interpreting Article 2[1] of the 1992 UN Framework Convention on Climate Change

Climate change presents the decision maker with a set of formidable complications: considerable remaining uncertainties inherent in the com-

1. Article 2 of the Framework Convention ("UNFCCC") describes the ultimate goal of the UNFCCC as:

plexity of the problem, the potential for irreversible damages or costs, a very long planning horizon, long time lags between emissions and effects, wide regional variations in causes and effects, an irreducibly global problem, and a multiple of greenhouse gases and aerosols to consider. Yet another complication is that effective protection of the climate system requires international cooperation in the context of wide variations in income levels, flexibility and expectations of the future; this raises issues of efficiency and intra-national, international and intergenerational equity.

Global mean surface temperature has increased by between about 0.3 and 0.6° since the late 19th century, a change that is unlikely to be entirely natural in origin. The balance of evidence from changes in global mean surface air temperature and from changes in geographical, seasonal and vertical patterns of atmospheric temperature, suggests a discernible human influence on global climate. Global sea level has risen by between 10 and 25 cm over the past 100 years and much of the rise may be related to the increase in global mean temperature.

There are inadequate data to determine whether consistent global changes in climate variability or weather extremes have occurred over the 20th century. On regional scales there is clear evidence of change in some extremes and climate variability indicators. Some of these changes have been toward greater variability, some have been toward lower variability. However, to date it has not been possible to firmly establish a clear connection between these regional changes and human activities.

Assuming the "best estimate" value of climate sensitivity[2] and including the effects of future increases in aerosol concentrations, models project an increase in global mean surface temperature relative to 1990 of about 2°C by 2100. This estimate is approximately one-third lower than the "best estimate" in 1990. This is due primarily to lower emission scenarios (paricularly for CO_2 and CFCs), the inclusion of the cooling effect of sulphate aerosols, and improvements in the treatment of the carbon cycle. Combining the lowest IPCC emission scenario with a "low" value of climate sensitivity and including the effects of future changes in aerosol concentrations leads to a projected increase of about 1°C by 2100. The corresponding projection for the highest IPCC scenario combined with a "high" value of climate sensitivity gives a warming of about 3.5°C.

> stabilization of greenhouse gas concentrations in the atmosphere at a level that would prevent dangerous anthropogenic interference with the climate system. Such a level should be achieved within a timeframe sufficient to all ecosystems to adapt naturally to climate change, to ensure that food production is not threatened and to enable economic development to proceed in a sustainable manner.

Id.

2. In IPCC reports, climate sensitivity usually refers to long-term (equilibrium) change in global mean surface temperature following a doubling of atmospheric equivalent CO_2 concentration.

All model simulations . . . show the following features: greater surface warming of the land than of the sea in winter; a maximum surface warming in high northern latitudes in winter, little surface warming over the Arctic in summer; an enhanced global mean hydrological cycle, and increased precipitation and soil moisture in high latitudes in winter. Warmer temperatures will lead to a more vigorous hydrological cycle; this translates into prospects for more severe droughts and/or floods in some places and/or less severe droughts and/or floods in other places. . . . Future climate changes may also involve "surprises." In particular, these arise from the non-linear nature of the climate system. When rapidly forced, non-linear systems are especially subject to unexpected behavior.

Human-induced climate change represents an important additional stress, particularly to the many ecological and socio-economic systems already affected by pollution, increasing resource demands, and non-sustainable management practices. The vulnerability of human health and socio-economic systems—and to a lesser extent, ecological systems—depends upon economic circumstances and institutional infrastructure. This implies that systems typically are more vulnerable in developing countries where economic and institutional circumstances are less favorable. . . . The composition and geographic distribution of many ecosystems (e.g., forests, rangelands, deserts, mountain systems, lakes, wetlands and oceans) will shift as individual species respond to changes in climate; there will likely be reductions in biological diversity and in the goods and services that ecosystems provide society. Some ecological systems may not reach a new equilibrium for several centuries after the climate achieves a new balance.

Crop yields and changes in productivity due to climate change will vary considerably across regions and among localities, thus changing the patterns of production. Productivity is projected to increase in some areas and decrease in others, especially the tropics and subtropics. Existing studies show that on the whole, global agricultural production could be maintained relative to baseline production in the face of climate change projected under doubled equivalent CO_2 equilibrium conditions. . . . However, focusing on global agricultural production does not address the potentially serious consequences of large differences at local and regional scales, even at mid-latitudes. There may be increased risk of hunger and famine in some locations; many of the world's poorest people—particularly those living in subtropical and tropical areas and dependent on isolated agricultural systems in semi-arid and arid regions—are most at risk of increased hunger.

Climate change clearly will increase the vulnerability of some coastal populations to flooding and erosional land loss. Estimates put about 46 million people per year currently at risk of flooding due to storm surges. In the absence of adaption measures, and not taking into account anticipated population growth, 50-cm sea-level rise would increase this number to about 92 million; a 1-meter sea-level rise would raise it to about 118 million. . . .

Estimated land losses range from 0.05% in Uruguay, 1.0% for Egypt, 6% for the Netherlands and 17.5% for Bangladesh to about 80% for the Majuro Atoll in the Marshall Isalnds, given the present state of protection systems.

Notes

1. There are a few scientists who have vigorously questioned whether global warming will occur. *See, e.g.,* Boyce Rensberger, "Greenhouse Effect" Seems Benign So Far, The Washington Post, June 8, 1993, at A1 (reporting the findings of Patrick J. Michaels, state climatologist for Virginia and author of a report in Research & Exploration, June 1993). For a provocative assessment of the scientific evidence, *see* Patrick J. Michaels & David E. Stocksbury, The Failure of the Popular Vision of Global Warming, 9 Ariz. J. Intl. Comp. L. 53 (1992). *See also* Patrick J. Michaels & Robert C. Balling, Climate History During the Recent Greenhouse Enhancement, in A Global Warming Forum 297, at 298 (A. Geyer ed., 1993) ("However, within certain broad limits, how much the world will warm is irrelevant. Rather, the critical policy question is how will the world warm, because the real effect will be expressed by its regionality, seasonality, and distribution within the day-night cycle. Viewed in light of these factors, there are now several compelling lines of evidence that indicate the chance of an ecologically or economically disastrous global warming is becoming more remote.").

The disbelief is partly due to the historical fluctuations in temperature. These differences vary regionally as well as temporally, introducing even more ambiguity into the question of global warming. Climatic Change and the Mediterranean 17 (L. Jeftic, J.D. Milliman & G. Sestini eds., 1992). The public, therefore, is faced with a dispute in the scientific community and has to decide what to believe or not believe.

2. For more on scientific uncertainty surrounding climate change, *see* Center for Environmental Information, Inc., General Interest and Policy, 5 Global Climate Change Digest 196 (1992) (citing a study of midwestern climate scientists that shows that half of those questioned believed climate change was occurring and half did not, as compared to a 20 percent believer rate in 1982); Jeremy Leggett, Global Warming: the Scientific Evidence and Its Implications, 2 Transnatl. L. & Contemp. Probs. 1 (1992); Stephen Schneider, The Global Warming Debate: Are We Ready for International Action? *id.* at 61; William R. Moomaw, Assessing the Greenhouse Challenge, 14 S. Ill. U. L.J. 169 (1990); Climate Change: Science, Impacts and Policy (J. Jaeger & H.L. Ferguson eds., 1991).

3. There has been considerable disagreement about the extent to which governments should impose economically painful measures to reduce the threat of global climate change. Economists disagree about both the immediate costs of proposed measures as well as on the long-term costs

and benefits. Governments, in turn, are wary of imposing economically painful measures to combat so precarious a threat. Some argue that the costs of lowering consumption may be quite high in the short term and could pose a threat of economic recession if not managed carefully. *See, e.g.,* Andrew R. Solow & James M. Broadus, Global Warming: Quo Vadis? (It's Not Easy Being Green: Ecopolitics in the 90s), 14 The Fletcher Forum of World Affairs 262 (1990); David Pearce, Evaluating the Socio-Economic Impacts of Climate Change: An Introduction, in Climate Change: Evaluating the Socio-Economic Impacts 9 (1991); T.C. Schelling, International Burden Sharing and Cooperation, in Economic Policy Responses to Global Warming 2 (R. Dornbusch & J. Poterba eds., 1991) ("no nation will find it in the purely national interest to engage on its own substantial abatement"). *See also* William R. Cline, The Economics of Global Warming (1992) (admonishing that the long-term possibility of significant climate change cannot be ignored in looking at the costs and benefits of actions to prevent human-induced climate change and estimating an 18°F rise in temperature in 300 years with a cost to the United States economy of 6 percent of GDP annually or $350 billion). The IPCC Second Assessment Report notes that delaying action might reduce overall costs of mitigation because of potential technological advances, but that delay might also increase costs because it would increase the rate and magnitude of climate change and any adaption required to meet that change. *See* Summary for Policymakers: Scientific-Technical Analyses of Impacts, Adaptions and Mitigation of Climate Change, in IPCC Second Assessment Report: Climate Change 1995 (1995). For an excellent analysis of the issues from various perspectives, *see* Climatic Change: Integrating Science, Economics, and Policy (N. Nakienovi, W.D. Nordhaus, R. Richels & F.L. Toth eds., 1996).

4. As the IPCC Second Assessment Report noted, greenhouse gases (GHG) not only increase global temperatures but also disrupt weather patterns, resulting in more widely varying hydrological phenomena. When added to other meteorological occurrences such as El Niño, the results can be devastating. The El Niño phenomenon reverses the direction of winds and ocean currents and alters ocean temperature between Indonesia and the Pacific coast of the Americas, resulting, for example, in torrential rain and floods in South America. Reversal of ocean currents also alters fish migratory patterns, devastating local fishing communities. Globally, El Niño may lead to famine in Africa, floods in North America, and widespread forest fires in Indonesia. Current understanding suggests El Niño is caused by a weakening of the trade winds near Indonesia; once the trade winds weaken, warm water surges eastward across the Pacific and El Niño begins. Global warming caused by greenhouse gases may either alter trade winds off Indonesia, leading to increased occurrences of El Niño in the future, or when combined with El Niño, may create even more devastating floods and torrential rainfall in some regions and famines in others. *See* UNEP,

The El Niño Phenomenon (UNEP/GEMS Environment Library No. 8, 1992); Summary for Policymakers: The Science of Climate Change, in IPCC Second Assessment: Climate Change 1995 (1995).

5. The Second Conference of the Parties to the Framework Convention, which met in Geneva in July 1996, issued the Geneva Declaration, which endorsed the IPCC Second Assessment Report conclusions and called for legally binding objectives and significant reductions in greenhouse gas emissions. The Geneva Declaration declared the Second Assessment Report to be "currently the most comprehensive and authoritative assessment of the science of climate change, its impacts, and response options now available." However, a group of other parties, including Australia and OPEC countries, continued to doubt the validity of the Second Assessment report. Australia stated that "it would be premature for this meeting to identify a particular point at which greenhouse gas concentrations might constitute human interference. . . . We believe that neither the science nor the assessment of impacts are as yet sufficiently advanced to nominate a specific level."

6. As the effects of climate change have become clearer, the insurance industry (principally European and Japanese insurers) has taken the lead in pushing for early and significant reductions in GHG to head off possible increased claims resulting from property damage. Insurance industry representatives are particularly worried about a series of "billion dollar" storms since 1987. *See* Stephen Schmidheiny & Frederico J.L. Zorraquin, Financing Change: The Financial Community, Eco-Efficiency, and Sustainable Development (1996) (arguing that the insurance industry should push for increased environmental protection); Charles Weiss, Can Market Mechanisms Ameliorate the Effects of Long-Term Climate Change? 15 Climatic Change No. 1-2, at 299 (1989).

7. One reason it is so difficult to assess climate change is that individual countries often submit data to the Secretariat of the Framework Convention on Climate Change on their emission levels that is incomplete, unreliable, and inconsistent. In 1995, reporting requirements were adopted, but it is still too early to tell whether these requirements will produce more accurate information. *See* GAO, Global Warming: Difficulties Assessing Countries' Progress Stabilizing Emissions of Greenhouse Gases (1996).

8. In January 1997, the President's Committee of Advisors on Science and Technology issued a report stating that the United States is "underinvesting" in the research and development necessary to understand, anticipate, adapt to, and mitigate climate change. The report called for increasing the emphasis on regional changes in the United States Global Change Research Program, improving monitoring technology and networks so that more complete data on climate change could be developed, increasing funding and improving interagency coordination for studying the socioeconomic aspects of climate change, and demonstrating world leadership in future climate change negotiations. *See* President's Committee of Advisors on Science and Technology, Report on Sustainable Development (1997).

9. Finally, there is the problem of potential benefits from greenhouse warming. Though there is virtual unanimity of opinion that depletion of ozone will harm all life on Earth, this agreement does not exist for climate change.

If the effects of increased temperatures are as predicted, coastal cities will be flooded, tropical forests will dry out, and temperate zones will become deserts. *See* IPCC, Second Assessment Report: Climate Change 1995, at 31 (1995) (providing a full color chart showing possible climatic changes throughout the world). On the other hand, the northern countries will become warmer, with a corresponding lengthening of growing seasons and emergence of new tourism destinations. For example, scientists recently reported that the growing season in the Northern Hemisphere is now starting a week earlier than it did in 1975, as a result of increased carbon dioxide in the atmosphere. These possibilities would help local economies in those areas, perhaps to the extent of outweighing the costs. *See also* John S. Hoffman, Contingency Planning for a Hotter Earth: Will Rising CO_2 Levels Bring Economic Catastrophe or Simply Create New Investment Opportunities?, 7 Directors & Boards 34 (1982); *but see* William R. Cline, The Economics of Global Warming 43-77, 277-311 (1992) (arguing that unless viewed from a time frame of 300 years, cost-benefit analysis of the greenhouse effect does not adequately account for the externality costs).

Additional Reading

On various aspects of the general topic of global climate change, *see* A Global Warming Forum: Scientific, Economic, and Legal Overview (Richard A. Geyer ed., 1993); WMO/UNEP Intergovernmental Panel on Climate Change, Climate Change: The IPCC Response Strategies (1991); WMO/UNEP Intergovernmental Panel on Climate Change, IPCC Second Assessment: Climate Change 1995 (1995); Edith Brown Weiss, In Fairness to Future Generations 345-351 (1989); John Firor, The Heating Up of the Climate, 1 Colo. J. Intl. Envtl. L. & Poly. 29 (1990); American Society of International Law, World Climate Change—Greenhouse Effect, in Proceedings of the Eighty-Fourth Annual Meeting of the American Society of International Law (1990). For a regional focus, *see* Climatic Change and the Mediterranean (L. Jeftic, J.D. Milliman, & G. Sestini eds., 1992); Rogelio Gonzalez Garcia et al., Climate Change and Environmental Policies in Mexico, 9 Ariz. J. Intl. & Comp. L. 217 (1992). For an introduction to the scientific mechanisms controlling the greenhouse effect, *see* Arthur N. Strahler & Alan H. Strahler, Environmental Geoscience (1975).

For an economic perspective on the possible global warming, *see* William R. Cline, The Economics of Global Warming (1992) (arguing that the scientific uncertainty must be approached with a very long-term view of economic damages that may result when using cost-benefit analysis); Samuel Fankhauser & David W. Pierce, The Social Costs of Greenhouse

Gas Emissions, in The Economics of Climate Change 71 (1994) (finding that many of the differences between various economic models of climate change can be accounted for by the varying assumptions embodied in the discount rate).

2. *The Science of Greenhouse Gases*

Greenhouse gases are those chemicals that, when released into the atmosphere, absorb infrared radiation. In this way, GHGs trap heat energy in reradiated from Earth's surface in the troposphere that initially was radiated by the sun in short-wave form and was subsequently to a long-wave form. The "warming," therefore, is actually a noncooling, which has the cumulative result of increased temperatures. The actual chemistry is much more complex. For further study, *see* Robert M. Garrels et al., Chemical Cycles and the Global Environment (1975).

Since the chemical reaction for trapping heat is not specific to a particular molecular structure, there are many potential sources of warming. By far the most prominent greenhouse gas is carbon dioxide. Other gases, however, are much more efficient heat traps.

The system used to denote the relative efficiency of a gas's heat-trapping characteristics is the Global Warming Potential (GWP). The GWP can be used as a basis for comparing the severity of the effects of various gases on the climate.

a. Carbon Dioxide (CO_2)

Carbon dioxide is the gas humans and animals emit when we breathe. In contrast to the chlorofluorocarbons which deplete the ozone layer, carbon dioxide is found naturally in the atmosphere. The main sources of carbon dioxide emissions are the burning of fossil fuels: coal, oil, and natural gas. The use of coal causes higher emissions of carbon dioxide than oil and far higher than natural gas. Trees take in and use up carbon dioxide in photosynthesis, but when they are cut down and burned, the stored carbon is released. Therefore, even the earliest human populations must have contributed a certain amount of carbon dioxide to the atmosphere. However, in the past, carbon dioxide levels remained relatively constant, as the amount produced was about equal to the amount stored. IPCC, Climate Change xxx (1991) (200 billion tons/yr. natural input of CO_2).

Since industrialization, the balance has shifted. Within the last century, scientists estimate that the amount of GHGs that have been added to the atmosphere have caused a 0.3-0.6°C rise in the average temperature. IPCC, IPCC Second Assessment: Climate Change 1995: The Science of Climate Change, Working Group I, at 4, 26 (1995). According to the IPCC in 1995, carbon dioxide accounts for about 60 percent of the additional climate warming due to GHGs since preindustrial times, about four times that of the next largest gas (by volume), methane (CH_4). Over time though, the relative importance of carbon dioxide is expected to grow. The length of time that the various gases remain in the atmosphere before removal also differs, with carbon dioxide often remaining in the atmosphere for 100 years or more, methane lasting for nine to 15 years, and nitrous oxide lasting for around 120 years. IPCC, above, at 15, 22.

Commercial energy use is now by far the greatest anthropogenic source of carbon dioxide in the atmosphere, accounting for 18.8 of the 21.8 billion metric tons of carbon dioxide produced in 1985. By 1990, global energy use accounted for the production of 20 billion metric tons of carbon dioxide. Deforestation is the second largest source of carbon dioxide emissions, contributing 2.6 billion tons, but only if the forest or wood is burned, rots, or is consumed by termites. Otherwise the carbon remains stored in the wood.

The IPCC Second Assessment reported that 10 to 30 percent gains in energy efficiency could be produced at little or no cost through conservation measures and improved management practices. Increased energy efficiency would mean that less energy is needed, with a corresponding decrease in carbon emissions. With implementation of current best available technology, efficiency gains of 50 to 60 percent could be achieved. For example, the use of new technology could increase the efficiency of conversion of fossil fuels in electrical power generation. Alternatively, coal-powered energy generation facilities could be converted to oil or natural gas, while oil-powered facilities could be converted to natural gas. Further reductions in emissions could be made by switching to renewable sources of energy such as solar, biomass, wind, hydro, and geothermal energy. For an excellent summary of the sources and impacts of the major greenhouse gases, *see* Greenhouse Gas Trends, in Policy Options for Stabilizing Global Climate (1990). For reading on the regulation of CO_2 emissions, *see generally* Richard Cooper, Toward a Real Global Warming Treaty, 77 For. Aff. 66 (1998); Christopher D. Stone, Beyond Rio: "Insuring" Against Global Warming, 86 Am. J. Intl. L. 445 (1992).

b. Other Gases

There are many other GHGs besides carbon dioxide. Slightly more than one-third of the estimated greenhouse gas emissions in 1985 were from three major types of non-CO_2 compounds: methane (CH_4); nitrous oxide (N_2O) chlorofluorocarbons (CFC-11, CFC-12); and human-made alternatives to CFCs (i.e., hydroflourochlonide (HFC), perflurochloride (PFC), and sulfur hexaflouride (SF_6)). Mehtane and nitrous oxide are sometimes emitted as the waste products of agricultural activities. Rice cultivation, enteric fermentation, and fuel production produced the majority of the methane emissions; use of fertilizers and nylon production were the main sources of N_2O release (*see* Table 12.1, below).

The Intergovernmental Panel on Climate Change has developed a global warming potential index that attempts to relate different GHG to carbon dioxide. In this index, one ton of CH_4 and N_2O is equal to 11 and 270 tons of carbon dioxide, respectively. IPCC, Climate Change 1992: The Supplementary Report to the IPCC Scientific Assessment (1992); IPCC, Climate Change 1994: Radiative Forcing of Climate Change (1995) (the non-naturally occurring GHGs (e.g., CFC and HFC) even higher GUPs). (This index imperfectly reflects the extra harm by CH_4 and N_2O because it measures only the relative radiative forcing capability of the gases, which in the case of CH_4 and N_2O is not equal to the damage they cause and which varies over time. Samuel Fankhauser & David W. Pierce, The Social Costs of Greenhouse Gas Emissions, in The Economics of Climate Change 71, 78 (1994).) Stated differently, these gases hold heat more efficiently, so that while emitted in smaller quantities, they nevertheless do great damage to the environment. For example, the 0.6 metrictons (Mt) of CFCs produced in 1985 had the equivalent effect on the atmosphere of 3200 Mt of CO_2.

Thus any effort to control global warming must consider the global warming potential for each of the gases, not just CO_2, and the potential effects of policy instruments in causing shifts to emitting more of one gas and less of another. For a good summary of the sources and impacts of the major GHGs, *see* Greenhouse Gas Trends, in Policy Options for Stabilizing Global Climate (1990). *See also* Table 12-2, below, indicating Co_2 emissions from 20 countries.

3. Greenhouse Gases, Population, and Developing Countries

■ POLICY IMPLICATIONS OF GREENHOUSE WARMING

Committee on Science, Engineering and Public Policy
National Academy of Sciences, National Academy of Engineering, Institute of Medicine (1991)

THE EFFECTS OF WORLD POPULATION AND ECONOMIC GROWTH

The world's population today is 5.3 billion, and it is expected to continue to grow at about 1.7 percent per year at current rates of fertility. . . . This increasing population is one of the major factors affecting trends in greenhouse gas emissions. More people create greater demands for food, energy, clothing, and shelter. Producing such products emits greenhouse gases.

Table 12-1
Estimated 1985 Global Greenhouse Gas Emissions from Human Activities

	Greenhouse Gas Emissions (Mt/yr)	*CO_2-Equivalent Emissions (Mt/yr)*	*%*
CO_2 Emissions			
Commercial energy	18,800	18,800	(57)
Tropical deforestation	2,600	2,600	(8)
Other	400	400	(1)
TOTAL	21,800	21,800	(66)
CH_4 Emissions			
Fuel production	60	1,300	(4)
Enteric fermentation	70	1,500	(5)
Rice cultivation	110	2,300	(7)
Landfills	30	600	(2)
Tropical deforestation	20	400	(1)
Other	30	600	(2)
TOTAL	320	6,700	(20)[c]
CFC-11 and CFC-12 emissions			
TOTAL	0.6	3,200	(10)
N_2O Emissions			
Coal combustion	1	290	(>1)
Fertilizer use	1.5	440	(1)
Gain of cultivated land	0.4	120	(>1)
Tropical deforestation	0.5	150	(>1)
Fuel wood and industrial biomass	0.2	60	(>1)
Agricultural wastes	0.4	120	(>1)
TOTAL	4	1,180	(4)
TOTAL		32,880	(100)

Note: CO_2-equivalent emissions are calculated from the Greenhouse Gas Emissions column by using the following multipliers:

CO_2	1
CH_4	21
CFC-11 and -12	5,400
N_2O	290

Numbers in parentheses are percentages of total.

Total does not sum due to rounding errors.

Source: Adapted from U.S. Department of Energy (1990). The Economics of Long-Term Global Climate Change: A Preliminary Assessment—Report of an Interagency Task Force (National Technical Information Service).

Table 12-2
Carbon Dioxide Emission Estimates

	1960		*1970*		*1980*		*1988*	
	Total	*Per Capita*	*Total*	*Per Capita*	*Total*	*Per Capita*	*Total*	*Per Capita*
East Germany	263.6	15.4	160.6	15.8	306.9	18.3	327.4	19.8
United States	2858.2	16.1	4273.5	20.9	4617.4	20.2	4804.1	19.4
Canada	193.2	10.6	333.3	15.4	424.6	17.6	437.8	16.9
Czechoslovakia	129.8	9.5	199.1	13.9	242.4	15.8	233.6	15.0
Australia	88.4	8.4	142.6	11.4	202.8	13.9	241.3	14.7
USSR	1452.4	6.6	2303.4	9.5	3282.0	12.5	3982.0	13.9
Poland	201.7	7.0	303.6	9.2	459.8	12.8	459.4	12.1
West Germany	544.9	9.9	736.6	12.1	762.7	12.5	669.9	11.0
United Kingdom	589.6	11.4	643.1	11.4	588.9	10.3	559.2	9.9
Romania	53.5	2.9	119.5	5.9	199.8	9.2	220.7	9.5
South Africa	98.6	5.5	149.6	6.6	213.4	7.7	284.2	8.4
Japan	234.3	2.6	742.1	7.3	934.6	8.1	989.3	8.1
Italy	110.4	2.2	286.0	5.5	372.5	6.6	359.7	6.2
France	274.3	5.9	426.1	8.4	484.4	9.2	320.1	5.9
Korea	49.1	0.4	52.1	1.5	125.8	3.3	204.6	4.8
Spain	12.8	1.5	110.7	3.3	198.7	5.5	187.7	4.8
Mexico	63.1	1.8	106.0	1.8	260.3	3.7	306.9	3.7
People's Republic of China	789.4	1.2	775.9	1.0	1490.1	1.5	2236.3	2.1
Brazil	46.9	0.7	86.5	0.7	176.7	1.5	202.4	1.5
India	121.7	0.4	195.4	0.4	350.2	0.4	600.6	0.7

NOTE: Emission estimates are rounded and expressed in million tons of CO_2; per capita estimates are rounded and expressed in tons of CO_2. All tons are metric.

Source: Adapted from Thomas A. Boden, Paul Kaniciruk & Michael P. Farrell. Trends '90: A Compendium of Data on Global Change. (Oak Ridge, Tenn.: Oak Ridge National Laboratory 1990).

Economic growth also produces more greenhouse gas emissions. If population grows with constant per capita income, more resources are used for food, clothing, and shelter. If per capita income grows in a constant population, the demand for goods also grows, particularly for health and education services, transportation, and housing. Most nations in the world have policies to reduce population growth rates, but all nations seek to achieve rapid growth in per capita income. The reduction of greenhouse gas emissions is well served by the first objective (reducing population growth) but, depending on the means used, can be in conflict with the second (growth in per capita income).

The detailed links between population growth and greenhouse gas emissions are complex and not well understood. The developing countries that have reduced their population growth rates within the last 30 years did so only after rapidly increasing their standards of living. This often was accompanied by environmental degradation. Perhaps it will be possible to rapidly raise living standards without resulting in traditional patterns of pollution. Unfortunately, there are few examples to guide us. What is needed is a breakthrough in strategies for development, especially with respect to energy supply and demand. Developing countries experiencing rapid economic growth will need effective mitigation programs if they are to avoid substantial increases in their greenhouse gas emissions. Implementing new strategies will require funds that will probably be scarce if populations grow rapidly. Nevertheless, at any given per capita rate of greenhouse gas emissions, a smaller population means fewer emissions, as well as less stress on the environment in general. . . .

Since the 1970s the trend of increasing emissions has been reversed for most of the developed countries. . . .

. . . Unfortunately, this trend is limited to the developed nations. As the developing countries continue to industrialize, their emission levels increase. Between 1970 to 1988, for example, India's per capita CO_2 emission levels rose from 0.4 Mt to 0.7 Mt; Brazil's from 0.7 Mt to 1.5 Mt; and the People's Republic of China from 1.2 Mt to 2.1 Mt.

Related to this increase is the high population growth rate. . . .

However, the population issue is more complex than "more people means more energy consumption and more greenhouse gas emissions." Rather, the specific populations which are growing affect the possibilities of environmental successes. Developing countries have had growth rates far above those of most developed countries over the last decade. This means that in the near future, large young populations will be living in economies which are still struggling to industrialize as well as provide their citizens with basic resources.

An easily identifiable result of having large populations is the probability of increased energy consumption. Additionally, higher population densities in rural areas will lead to greater deforestation and depletion of natural landscapes as fuel and crop needs put increased pressure on the land. This, in turn, can result not only in losses of biodiversity, but also in greater release of greenhouse gases. . . .

As the populations of the developing countries often live in monoproduction countries, the detrimental effects of climate changes may be intensified. A fragile economy is much more likely to be severely harmed than one with numerous products. *See also* Peter Usher, Climate Change and the Developing World, 14 S. Ill. U. L.J. 257 (1990); Rogelio Gonzalez Garcia et al., Climate Change and Environmental Policies in Mexico, 9 Ariz. J. Intl. Comp. L. 217 (1992).

Notes and Questions

1. *Developing countries.* Numerous reports suggest that the role of developing countries is central to a climate convention, mainly because of their large and growing populations and increasing greenhouse gas emission levels. Some proposals call for developing countries to assume greater responsibility in curbing domestic greenhouse gas emissions as their economies develop. However, this proposal is fiercely opposed by some, who argue that developed countries that produce the vast majority of greenhouse gas emissions should do more to cut their own emissions before asking developing countries to cut their emissions. *See* section B.4.e, below. Another issue is whether industrialized countries should be able to sponsor GHG emission reduction programs in developing nations, with the industrialized state and developing state sharing credit for the reduction in emissions. While supporters of this idea argue that it would attract capital toward more climate-beneficial projects, critics argue that it would allow industrialized nations to escape having to take any domestic emissions cuts. *See* section B, below, for a discussion of the Framework Convention on Climate Change and the Kyoto Protocol. *See generally* Peter Hayes, The Global Greenhouse Regime: Who Pays? Science, Economics and North-South Politics, in The Climate Change Convention (1993).

2. *Industrialized countries.* Do developed states have an obligation to help finance developing states' efforts to reduce CO_2 or to transfer technology that extends beyond self-preservation? Do the developing states have a right to monetary help? Consider the statement that industrialized countries have a responsibility "to cooperate with developing countries in international action, without standing in the way of the latter's development, by contributing additional financial resources, by appropriate transfer of technology, by engaging in close cooperation concerning scientific observation, by analysis and research, and finally by means of technical cooperation geared to forestalling and managing environmental problems" (Climate

Change: The IPCC Response Strategies, Executive Summary (3) (b), p. xxvi (1991)). As you read the following materials, consider whether the FCCC and the Kyoto Protocol adequately address this issue.

3. *The E-8.* The Worldwatch Institute's 1997 State of the World report coined a term, the "E-8," to describe eight countries that will have a greater effect on the future of the world than the Group of Seven (G-7) industrialized countries (which became the G-8 with the addition of Russia around 1997). According to this view, four of the E-8, Germany, Japan, Russia, and the United States, shape global trends through economic strength, high consumption rates, technological prowess, and social trend setting. The other four E-8 countries, Brazil, China, India, and Indonesia, have large populations, rapid economic growth, and richness of biodiversity. Worldwatch Institute, State of the World: 1997 (1997).

B. RESPONDING TO CLIMATE CHANGE

1. *Adapting to Climate Change*

Most of the policy discussion has focused on whether, and if so, to what extent, to prevent or control human-induced climate change. But there is also a substantial body of opinion that says the best response to human-induced climate change is to focus on adaptation.

Because our present way of life and economic system revolve around activities that emit greenhouse gases, solving the climate change problem will not be possible by simply prohibiting consumption of one product or by requiring special devices on production facilities. Rather, a more systematic approach may be called for, encompassing a range of activities from reduction of fossil fuel consumption, substitution of cleaner sources of energy, and increased efficiency to the reduction of deforestation, better management of resource consumption, improved methods of agricultural production, and increased efforts of population control. *See generally* IPCC, Second Assessment Report: Climate Change 1995 (1995); *See also* Lakshman Guruswamy, Integrated Environmental Control: Expanding Matrix, 22 Envtl. L. 77, 80 (1992).

Throughout history, communities have adapted to modest changes in climate. Sometimes this has been accomplished through governmental interventions, but most often it has been the result of gradual changes in patterns of behavior. Some have argued that there is no reason to adopt measures to prevent or mitigate climate change, because communities will be able to adapt readily to the changes. But poor communities are often the ones least able to adapt to change. In adapting to changes, the efforts must again be diverse, targeting the multiple areas of life that climate affects. This includes development of food crop strains that can withstand new temperatures and moisture levels, as well as changes in engineering designs to handle natural emergencies of floods and storms.

As you read the following excerpt from the report of the United States National Academy of Sciences, consider how you would respond to the arguments both of the panel and of the dissenting voice of Jessica Matthews, which is contained in a lengthy footnote.

■ POLICY IMPLICATIONS OF GREENHOUSE WARMING

Committee on Science, Engineering and Public Policy
National Academy of Sciences, National Academy of Engineering, and National Institute of Medicine (1991)

Just as strategic planning requires ranking greenhouse warming with all the other changes ahead, it also demands sorting human activities and nature into classes of sensitivity and adaptability to greenhouse warming alone. [See Table 5.1, with respect to the United States. The panel then discusses the different classifications.]

Table 5.1
The Sensitivity and Adaptability of Human Activities and Nature

	Low Sensitivity	*Sensitive, but Adaptation at Some Cost*	*Sensitive, Adaptation Problematic*
Industry and energy	X		
Health	X		
Farming		X	
Manages forests and grasslands		X	
Water resources			
Tourism and recreation		X	
Settlements and coastal structures		X	
Human migration		X	
Political tranquility		X	
Natural landscapes			X
Marine ecosystems			X

Source: Chapter 5 of the report of the Adaptation Panel.

ACTIVITIES WITH LOW SENSITIVITY

Fortunately, several human activities have low sensitivity, allowing us to concentrate on others. Machinery and buildings are renewed faster than the projected pace of greenhouse warming, and so industry should have little trouble adapting. In general, the decision-making horizons in industry are shorter than the time at which most climatic impacts would emerge. Most industries in countries like the United States can thus be expected to adapt as the climate changes.

The expected climatic changes are within the range people now experience where they live and to which those who move usually learn to adapt. In industrial countries, public health should be less at risk than it is elsewhere. The pace of improvements in health from better technology and public measures can and likely will exceed any deterioration from greenhouse warming. Epidemics from causes already known, failure to control population, and chemical pollution are more serious threats to health than greenhouse warming.

Activities That Are Sensitive But Can Be Adapted at a Cost

As the most valuable outdoor human activity, farming would have the greatest impact on national income due to greenhouse warming. Average warming would not greatly affect yields, but seasonal variations in precipitation and evaporation would. Experience shows, however, that farming must continually adapt to cope with, and even exploit, the stresses and fickle nature of climate. Adaptations to climate change would be required in both rich and poor countries to protect crops, substitute new ones, and protect their foundations of soil and water.

Should climate warm, most cities would try to adapt rather than abandon their sites. Although the adaptation might be costly, the costs would in most cases be lower than the cost of moving the city. By far the highest costs would be in coastal cities, where added protection would be needed in response to storms if the sea rises. Where the coast is thinly settled, protective zoning or even retreat may be sensible.

For the nation as a whole, tourism and recreation seem adaptable to greenhouse warming at little net cost.

Activities That Are Sensitive with Questionable Adjustment or Adaptation

In the unmanaged systems of plants and animals that occupy much of our landscape and oceans, however, the rate of change of some key processes may be slower than the pace of greenhouse warming, making their future questionable. Unmanaged ecosystems respond relatively slowly, and hence their adaptability to greenhouse warming is more questionable than that of the managed systems of crops on a farm or timber in a plantation. Response is slow because the replacement of plants and animals on an acre of wild land or in an estuary can take decades or centuries and because evolution takes centuries or millennia.

Greenhouse warming would not likely make land barren except at the arid extremes of existing climates if the climate became drier. What *is* likely are changes in the composition of ecological communities in favor of those species that are able to move rapidly and the disappearance of some species that move slowly. Marine plants and animals inhabiting intertidal regions of rocky shores undoubtedly would be affected by rising sea levels. Coral reefs, which are breeding and feeding areas for many of the world's tropical fisheries, could suffer because they appear to be particularly sensitive to water temperature changes.

Conclusions

. . . [A] rise in global average temperatures in the next century above those of any period in the last 200,000 years cannot be excluded. Unfortunately, there currently is no way to reliably determine the effects of such global changes for particular regions. These changes will probably be gradual. People in the United States likely will have no more difficulty adapting to such future changes than to the most severe conditions in the past, such as the Dust Bowl.[3] Other countries may have more

3. Jessica Matthews, a member of the Synthesis Panel, disagrees with this conclusion with the following statement:

> The analysis does not support the conclusion that greenhouse warming will be no more demanding than past climatic changes. If the change is unprecedented in the experience of the human species, how can it be claimed that people will have no more difficulty adapting to future changes than to those of the past?
>
> The reasoning used here is that human economic activities are largely divorced from nature and that modern technology effectively buffers us from climate. Combined with assumptions of gradual change, no surprises, and an olympian perspective on national costs, the result is an unduly sanguine outlook. Even as a portrayal of a best case scenario (rather than a most likely one), this is a flawed analysis.
>
> First, it underestimates the extent to which human societies, even affluent ones, depend on the underpinning of natural systems. While recognizing that the pace of greenhouse warming will most likely exceed the rate at which species and ecosystems can adapt, the study does not go on to examine the resulting impacts of severe ecosystem disruption on human societies.
>
> Also, the impacts of climate change on economic activities are considered separately, sector by sector (farming, industry, transportation, etc.). This is understandable given the great difficulty of analyzing the interactions, but here the compartmentalization of impacts in both the natural and economic spheres seems to have led to the distorted view that people, economic activity, infrastructure, and natural context can be disassociated. The finding that "expected climatic changes are within the range people now experience . . . and to which those who move usually learn to adapt," means nothing about adaptation to greenhouse-induced change. The fact that one can move with ease from Vermont to Miami has nothing to say about the consequences of Vermont acquiring Miami's climate.
>
> Reasoning from the experience of past adaptations is risky given that in the past societies could usually expect that climate fifty years hence would be reasonably like that of the present. This will probably not be the case during a greenhouse warming, because of the difficulties of forecasting regional impacts, the rate of expected change,

difficulty, especially poor countries or those with fewer climate zones. Some natural systems of plants and animals would be stressed beyond sustainability in their current form, a prospect some people may find unacceptable. The stronger the concern about these various changes, the greater the motivation to slow greenhouse warming.

In addition, the panel has not found it possible to rule out or rule in such major disturbances as sudden and major changes in regional climates, ocean currents, atmospheric circulations, or other natural or social phenomena. At present, it is not possible to analyze their likelihood or consequences.

Human societies and natural systems of plants and animals change over time and react to changing climate just as they react to other forces. It would be fruitless to try to maintain all human and natural communities in their current forms. There are actions that can be undertaken now, however, to help people and natural systems adjust to some of the anticipated impacts of greenhouse warming. The panel recommends action now . . . based on gradual climate change. Such action would be more important if climate change proved to be sudden and unanticipated rather than smooth and predictable.

Notes and Questions

1. *Adaptability of developing countries.* The IPCC also explicitly recognized that developing countries will have more difficulty adapting to changes in climate than will developed countries and implementing adaptions. This is due in large part to limited funds for research. However, the geographic considerations of large coastal populations and possible negative agriculture effects worsen the potential problems considerably. For additional reading, *see* IPCC, Coastal Zone Management, Climate Change 133, 144-146 (1991) (reporting that high population densities combined with the productivity of the coastal areas make the socio-economic effects of sea level rise associated with global warming particularly harmful).

2. *Adaptability of ecosystems.* Adaptability of natural ecosystems is expected to vary, according to the IPCC. Forested areas are expected to shift, as are growth rates and species composition found in any given

---

and because we may be operating under conditions with which mankind has no past experience.

Finally, it may be strictly accurate that regional "pluses and minuses" will combine to produce "small net change for a nation of our size." But the distribution of impacts in time and space matters more than this treatment suggests. Costs that are indisputably enormous (including human suffering) begin to appear deceptively manageable when viewed solely from the perspective of their impacts on a multitrillion dollar economy. For example, in the case of cities, the study finds that while "adaptation might be costly, the costs would in most cases be lower than the cost of moving the city."

area. Rangelands will generally remain the same. Perhaps the greatest effects will be found in coastal areas, where climate change and resulting rising sea levels may lead to erosion of shores, increased salinity of estuaries and freshwater aquifers, changed sediment and nutrient transport, altered chemical and microbiological contamination, and increased flooding. Summary for Policymakers: Scientific-Technical Analyses of Impacts, Adaptions and Mitigation of Climate Change, in IPCC Second Assessment Report: Climate Change 1995, at 29-32 (1995).

3. *Sea level rise and rivers.* One of the most talked-about impacts of global warming is the rise in sea level that would occur due to melting of the polar ice caps. Less discussed, but still important, is the role of rivers in the climate change scenario. How will the international law of rivers and waterways adapt to the differences global warming would impose? Does the Climate Convention adequately address this problem? For reading on this topic, *see* Ludwik A. Teclaff, The River Basin Concept and Global Climate Change, 8 Pace Envtl. L. Rev. 355 (1991); Gretta Goldenman, Adapting to Climate Change: A Study of International Rivers and Their Legal Arrangements, 17 Ecol. L.Q. 741 (1990).

Additional Reading

For additional reading on the scientific and social science aspects of global climate change, *see* WMO/UNEP Intergovernmental Panel on Climate Change, Climate Change: The IPCC Response Strategies, (1991); John Firor, The Heating Up of the Climate, 1 Colo. J. Intl. Envtl. L. & Poly. 29 (1990); Stephen H. Schneider, The Genesis Strategy: Climate and Global Survival (1976). For a regional focus, *see* Climatic Change and the Mediterranean (L. Jeftic, J.D. Milliman, & G. Sestini eds., 1992); Rogelio Gonzalez Garcia et al., Climate Change and Environmental Policies in Mexico, 9 Ariz. J. Intl. & Comp. L. 217 (1992). For early suggestions for United States policies for dealing with the greenhouse effect internationally, *see* Policy Options for Stabilizing Global Climate: Report to Congress (1990); Committee on Science, Engineering, and Public Policy, Policy Implications of Greenhouse Warming: Mitigation, Adaptation, and the Science Base (1992). For views on greenhouse policy from Germany and the EC, *see* A Regime to Control Greenhouse Gases (J.C. di Primio & G. Stein eds., 1991) (proceedings from a workshop in Bad Neuenahr on possible responses to the threat of a greenhouse warming). *See also* E. Donald Elliott Jr., Global Climate Change and Regulatory Uncertainty, 9 Ariz. J. Intl. Comp. L. 259 (1992); Daniel Bodansky, May We Engineer the Climate, 33 Climatic Change no. 3, at 309 (July 1996) (suggesting that if it eventually becomes possible to engineer the climate, difficulties associated with international decisionmaking would make it more efficient to put a flat ban on climatic engineering than to decide where and how much to engineer the climate).

2. *Responding to the Threat: The Framework Convention on Climate Change*

a. Background

The realization of the potential destructiveness of our accustomed means of achieving our standard of living resulted in states moving toward a multilateral Climate Change Convention. A chronology of events leading up to the conclusion of the negotiations of the Convention appears below (adapted from Paul C. Szasz, International Norm-making, in Environmental Change and International Law 78-80 (Edith Brown Weiss ed., 1992)).

In June 1992, less than 18 months after the initiation of negotiations, the Framework Convention on Climate Change opened for signature. But while the formal negotiations were speedy despite the complexity of climate change, the period building up to the opening of the negotiations was longer. In 1979, a cooperative effort by UNEP, WMO, and the ICSU brought together the First World Climate Conference. This was followed by several further meetings on the carbon dioxide problem, culminating in the global warming meeting of 1985 in Villach, Austria, where international consensus on the importance of the problem was achieved.

In Geneva, in November 1988, 35 nations founded the Intergovernmental Panel on Climate Change (IPCC) to assess the effects of human activities on climate change and to analyze science, policy implications, and response strategies to the greenhouse effect in three working groups. This body met periodically over the next 20 months and produced a consensus document indicating that the global temperature could be expected to rise significantly in response to human activities. This was technically a scientific panel, but governments sent other officials as well as scientists. Many have called the result "negotiated science"; in the end the process was essential for providing the international consensus necessary to open negotiations on a convention on climate change.

The call for a framework convention on the global climate started in March 1989, with the Declaration of the Hague. It continued in the same year at international meetings in Helsinki, Nairobi, and Noordwijk, the Netherlands. The Second World Climate Conference in 1990 created task groups to conduct more research and to prepare a draft convention for the Rio de Janeiro Conference.

The convention was negotiated under the umbrella of the Intergovernmental Negotiating Committee (INC), a free-standing body established by the United Nations General Assembly. The INC continued to meet until the convention went into effect and was replaced by a meeting of the parties. The IPCC also continued to meet, even though there is no explicit mention of it in the text of the Climate Convention.

In 1992, the Framework Convention on Climate Change was opened for signature in Rio at the UN Conference on Environment and Development. It went into effect on March 21, 1993. As of January 23, 1998, 174 countries were party to the convention.

CHRONOLOGY OF EVENTS LEADING UP TO FRAMEWORK CONVENTION*

12-23 Feb. 1979	**First World Climate Conference, convened by WMO**
9-15 Oct. 1985	**International Conference on the Assessment of the Role of Carbon Dioxide and Other Greenhouse Gases in Climate Variations and Associated Impacts, Villach (Austria), sponsored by UNEP, WMO, and ICSU**
28 Sep.-2 Oct. 1986	**Conference on Developing Policies for Responding to Future Climatic Change, Villach (Austria)**
1986	**Establishment of the UN system interagency Advisory Group on Greenhouse Gases (AGGE)**
Nov. 1987	**Policies Issues Workshop on Developing Policies for Responding to Climatic Change, Bellagio (Italy)**
27-30 Jun. 1988	**Conference on the Changing Atmosphere: Implications for Global Security, convened by the Canadian Department of External Affairs, Toronto**
Nov. 1988	First session of the Intergovernmental Panel on Climate Change (IPCC), Geneva, established by UNEP and WMO
6 Dec. 1988	**UNGA Resolution: Protection of Global Climate for Present and Future Generations of Mankind (A/RES/43/53)**
20-22 Feb. 1989	**Meeting of Legal and Policy Experts on the Changing Atmosphere, convened by the Canadian Department of External Affairs, Ottawa**
11 Mar. 1989	**Declaration of the Hague**
28-30 Jun. 1989	Second session of IPCC, Nairobi
7 Nov. 1989	**Noordwijk Declaration of the Ministerial Conference on Atmospheric Pollution and Climate Change**
1990	Third session of IPCC
27-31 Aug. 1990	Fourth session of IPCC, Sundsvall (Sweden)

29 Oct.-7 Nov. 1990	**Second World Climate Conference, convened by WMO, Geneva, and Ministerial Declaration**
21 Dec. 1990	Establishment of Intergovernmental Negotiating Committee for a Framework Convention on Climate Change (A/RES/45/212)
4-14 Feb. 1991	First session of the Intergovernmental Negotiating Committee for a Framework Convention on Climate Change, Washington
13-15 Mar. 1991	Fifth session of IPCC, Geneva
19-28 Jun. 1991	Second session of the Intergovernmental Negotiating Committee for a Framework Convention on Climate Change
9-20 Sep. 1991	Third session of the Intergovernmental Negotiating Committee for a Framework Convention on Climate Change
29-31 Oct. 1991	Sixth session of IPCC
9-20 Dec. 1991	Fourth session of the Intergovernmental Negotiating Committee for a Framework Convention on Climate Change
10-12 Feb. 1992	Seventh session of IPCC, Geneva
18-28 Feb. 1992	Fifth session of the Intergovernmental Negotiating Committee for a Framework Convention on Climate Change, New York
Apr. 1992	Informal consultations among principal delegations, Paris
30 Apr.- 8 May 1992	Sixth session of the Intergovernmental Negotiating Committee for a Framework Convention on Climate Change

*Code: Typeface indicates the following:

Scientific Developments and Meetings Not Part of Non-Regional International Legislative Process

Legal and Political Statements Not Part of Non-Regional International Legislative Process

Meetings Relating to the International Legislative Process

LEGAL INSTRUMENTS ADOPTED

Source: Paul C. Szasz, International Norm-making, in Environmental Change and International Law (Edith Brown Weiss ed., 1992).

Notes and Questions

1. *Precautionary approach.* Did the precautionary approach require countries to try to draft a formal convention to limit the emission of greenhouse gases?

2. *Focussed or comprehensive?* Before the climate change negotiations began there was considerable scholarly debate as to whether the negotiations ought to include only those countries that were major emitters of greenhouse gases or whether they should include all countries. What arguments do you see for either position?

3. *The FCCC.* The Framework Convention has 174 member states as of January 1998. A list of the countries that have signed the convention is available online at the Framework Convention's Secretariat at http://www.unfcc.de/index.html. This site also lists countries that are included in Annex I and II, the importance of which is described below. For a comprehensive analysis of the negotiations for the climate framework convention and of the provisions in the Convention text, *see* Daniel Bodansky, The United Nations Framework Convention on Climate Change: A Commentary, 18 Yale J. Intl. L. 451 (1993); *see also* Negotiating Climate Change: The Inside Story of the Rio Convention (Irving M. Mintzer & J. Amber Leonard eds., 1994).

For early views regarding a global climate convention, *see* Michael Grubb, Options for an International Agreement, in Combating Global Warming: Study on a Global System of Trade 11 (1992) (suggesting what issues and possibilities should be determined in an international agreement to limit greenhouse gases); Abram Chayes, Managing Transition to a Global Warming Regime or What to do til the Treaty Comes, in Greenhouse Warming (1991); Stephen Schneider, The Global Warming Debate: Are We Ready for International Action?, 2 Transnatl. L. & Contemp. Probs. 61 (1992); Robert E. Dickinson, Do We Know Enough About Climate Change to Justify Action?, 9 Ariz. J. Intl. & Comp. L. 47 (1992); David A. Wirth & Daniel A. Lashof, Beyond Vienna and Montreal: A Global Framework Convention on Greenhouse Gases, 2 Transnatl. L. & Contemp. Probs. 79 (1992). For possible problems with legal arrangements to lower the threat of global warming, *see* International Environment: Strengthening the Implementation of Environmental Agreements (1992); J.H. Ausubel, T.F. Malone et al., International Environmental Research and Assessment: Proposals for Better Organization and Decision Making (1992). *See also* Christopher D. Stone, Beyond Rio: "Insuring" Against Global Warming, 86 Am. J. Intl. L. 445 (1992) (advocating development of insurance to protect against the damaging effects of climate change, in addition to an international convention).

b. The Climate Change Convention

The 1992 Framework convention on climate change covers all greenhouse gases. Under the Convention, parties are to provide national inventories of sources and sinks of greenhouse gases, and regular national reports on policies and measures that limit emissions of these gases and enhance the sinks for them. These inventories and reports are subject to international review by the parties. While the Convention sets up a very important process by which parties can monitor and control greenhouse gas emissions, it does not contain explicit targets and timetables for stabilizing atmospheric concentrations of the gases.

Much of the focus in the policy debate on climate change has been on preventing significant climate change induced by human activities ("anthropogenic change"). The FCCC incorporates in Article 3 (Principles) a number of legal principles that we have discussed; other legal principles are omitted. The following material highlights some of these principles and omissions. As you consider these materials, ask yourself whether you understand what they mean. If you were a government official or a lawyer advising a business entity or a nongovernmental organization, how would you describe what is required by the principles?

In Article 4, the Convention sets forth the commitments of the parties, including the commitments of developed country parties (so-called Annex I countries) regarding limiting GHG emissions. Note that the commitments do not cover GHGs controlled by the Montreal Protocol (the subject of chapter 11, above). Why is that? Note also that the parties who will actually be subject to the latter obligations are developed countries and other countries that are listed in Annex I. In particular, pay close attention to the content and structure of Article 4(2), which sets forth a timetable for developed countries to reduce greenhouse gases in section (a), but the goal of returning emissions to 1990 levels in section (b). Why might a lay reader conclude that the Convention sets forth targets and timetables? What should a lawyer conclude?

■ EXCERPT FROM THE UNITED NATIONS FRAMEWORK CONVENTION ON CLIMATE CHANGE

Reprinted in full at *31 I.L.M. 849 (1992)*

Acknowledging that change in the Earth's climate and its adverse effects are a common concern of humankind,

Concerned that human activities have been substantially increasing the atmospheric concentrations of greenhouse gases, that these increases enhance the natural greenhouse effect, and that this will result on average in additional warming of the Earth's surface and atmosphere and may adversely affect natural ecosystems and humankind, . . .

Acknowledging that the global nature of climate change calls for the widest possible cooperation by all countries and their participation in an effective and appropriate international response, in accordance with their common but differentiated responsibilities and respective capabilities and their social and economic conditions, . . .

Recalling also that States have, in accordance with the Charter of the United Nations and the principles of international law, the sovereign right to exploit their own resources pursuant to their own environmental and developmental policies, and the responsibility to ensure that activities within their jurisdiction or control do not cause damage to the environment of other States or of areas beyond the limits of national jurisdiction, . . .

Article 1

For the purposes of this Convention:

. . .

2. "Climate change" means a change of climate which is attributed directly or indirectly to human activity that alters the composition of the global atmosphere and which is in addition to natural climate variability observed over comparable time periods. . . .

Article 2

The ultimate objective of this Convention and any related legal instruments that the Conference of the Parties may adopt is to achieve, in accordance with the relevant provisions of the Convention, stabilization of greenhouse gas concentrations in the atmosphere at a level that would prevent dangerous anthropogenic interference with the climate system. Such a level should be achieved within a time-frame sufficient to allow ecosystems to adopt naturally to climate change, to ensure that food production is not threatened and to enable economic development to proceed in a sustainable manner.

Article 3

In their actions to achieve the objective of the Convention and to implement its provisions, the Parties shall be guided, *inter alia*, by the following:

1. The Parties should protect the climate system for the benefit of present and future generations of humankind, on the basis of equity and in accordance with their common but differentiated responsibilities and respective capabilities. Accordingly, the developed country Parties should take the lead in combatting climate change and the adverse effects thereof.

2. The specific needs and special circumstances of developing country Parties, especially those that are particularly vulnerable to the adverse effects of climate change, and of those Parties, especially developing country Parties, that would have to bear a disproportionate or abnormal burden under the Convention, should be given full consideration.

3. The Parties should take precautionary measures to anticipate, prevent or minimize the causes of climate change and mitigate its adverse effects. Where there are threats of serious or irreversible damage, lack of full scientific certainty should not be used as a reason for postponing such measures, taking into account that policies and measures to deal with

climate change should be cost-effective so as to ensure global benefits at the lowest possible cost. To achieve this, such policies and measures should take into account different socio-economic contexts, be comprehensive, cover all relevant sources, sinks and reservoirs of greenhouse gases and adaption, and comprise all economic sectors. Efforts to address climate change may be carried out cooperatively by interested Parties. . . .

Article 4

1. All Parties, taking into account their common but differentiated responsibilities and their specific national and regional development priorities, objectives and circumstances, shall:

(a) Develop, periodically update, publish and make available to the Conference of the Parties . . . national inventories of anthropogenic emissions by sources and removals by sinks of all greenhouse gases not controlled by the Montreal Protocol, using comparable methodologies to be agreed upon . . .

(b) Formulate, implement, publish and regularly update national, and where appropriate, regional programmes containing measures to mitigate climate change . . . and measures to facilitate adequate adaption to climate change;

(c) Promote and cooperate in the development, application and diffusion, including transfer, of technologies, practices and processes that control, reduce or prevent anthropogenic emissions of greenhouse gases . . . including the energy, transport, industry, agriculture, forestry and waste management sectors; . . .

2. The developed country Parties and other Parties included in annex I commit themselves specifically as provided for in the following:

(a) Each of these Parties shall adopt national policies and take corresponding measures on the mitigation of climate change, by limiting its anthropogenic emissions of greenhouse gases and protecting and enhancing its greenhouse gas sinks and reservoirs. These policies and measures will demonstrate that developed countries are taking the lead in modifying longer-term trends in anthropogenic emissions consistent with the objective of the Convention, recognizing that the return by the end of the present decade to earlier levels of anthropogenic emissions of carbon dioxide and other greenhouse gases not controlled by the Montreal Protocol would contribute to such modification, and taking into account the differences in these Parties' starting points and approaches, economic structures and resources bases, the need to maintain strong and sustainable economic growth, available technologies and other individual circumstances, as well as the need for equitable and appropriate contributions by each of these Parties to the global effort regarding that objective. These Parties may implement such policies and measures jointly with other Parties and may assist other Parties in contributing to the achievement of the objective of the Convention and, in particular, that of this subparagraph;

(b) In order to promote progress to this end, each of these Parties shall communicate, within six months of the entry into force of the Convention for it and periodically thereafter . . . detailed information on its policies and measures referred to in subparagraph (a) above, as well as on its resulting projected anthropogenic emissions by sources and removals of greenhouse gases not controlled by the Montreal Protocol . . . with the aim of returning individually or jointly to their 1990 levels these anthropogenic emissions of carbon dioxide and other greenhouse gases not controlled by the Montreal Protocol. . . .

3. The developed country Parties and other developed Parties included in annex II shall provide new and additional financial resources to meet the agreed full costs incurred by developing country Parties in complying with their obligations under Article 12, paragraph 1. They shall also provide such financial resources, including for the transfer of technology, needed by the developing country Parties to meet the agreed full incremental costs of implementing measures that are covered by paragraph 1 of this Article and that are agreed between a developing country Party and the international entity or entities referred to in Aricle 11, in accordance with that Article. The implementation of these commitments shall take into account the need for adequacy and predictability in the flow of funds and the importance of appropriate burden sharing among the developed country Parties. . . .

5. The developed country Parties and other developed Parties included in annex II shall take all practicable steps to promote, facilitate and finance, as appropriate, the transfer of, or access to, environmentally sound technolgies and know-how to other Parties, in particular developing country Parties, to enable them to implement the provisions of the Convention. . . .

7. The extent to which developing country Parties will effectively implement their commitments under the Convention will depend upon the effective implementation by developed country Parties of their commitments under the Convention related to financial resources and transfer of technology and will take into account that economic and social development and poverty eradication are the first and overriding priorities of the developing country Parties. . . .

Article 7

1. A Conference of the Parties is hereby established.

2. The Conference of the Parties, as the supreme body of this Convention, shall keep under regular review the implementation of the Convention and any related legal instruments that the Conference of the Parties may adopt, and shall make, within its mandate, the decisions necessary to promote the effective implementation of the Convention. To this end, it shall:

(a) Periodically examine the obligations of the Parties and the institutional arrangements under the Convention, in light of the objective of the Convention, the experience gained in its implementation and the evolution of scientific and technological knowledge; . . .

6. The United Nations, its specialized agencies and . . . any State member thereof or observers thereto not Party to the Convention, may be represented at sessions of the Conference of the Parties as observers. Any body or agency, whether national or international, governmental or non-governmental, which is qualified in matters covered by the Convention, and which has informed the secretariat of its wish to be represented at a session of the Conference

of the Parties as an observer, may be so admitted unless at least one-third of the Parties present object. . . .

Article 9

1. A subsidiary body for scientific and technological advice is hereby established to provide the Conference of the Parties and, as appropriate, its other subsidiary bodies with timely information and advice on scientific and technological matters relating to the Convention. This body shall be open to participation by all Parties and shall be multidisciplinary. It shall comprise government representatives competent in the relevant field of expertise. It shall report regularly to the Conference of the Parties on all aspects of its work. . . .

Article 10

1. A subsidiary body for implementation is hereby established to assist the Conference of the Parties in the assessment and review of the effective implementation of the Convention. . . .

Article 11

1. A mechanism for the provision of financial resources on a grant or concessional basis, including for the transfer of technology, is hereby defined. It shall function under the guidance of and be accountable to the Conference of the Parties, which shall decide on its policies, programme priorities and eligibility criteria related to this Convention. . . .

Article 12

1. In accordance with Article 4, paragraph 1, each Party shall communicate to the Conference of the Parties, through the secretariat, the following elements of information:

(a) A national inventory of anthropogenic emissions by sources and removals by sinks of all greenhouse gases not controlled by the Montreal Protocol, to the extent its capacities permit, using comparable methodologies to be promoted and agreed upon by the Conference of the Parties;

(b) A general description of steps taken or envisaged by the Party to implement the Convention; and

(c) Any other information that the Party considers relevant. . . .

Article 14

1. In the event of a dispute between any two or more Parties concerning the interpretation or application of the Convention, the Parties concerned shall seek a settlement of the dispute through negotiation or any other peaceful means of their own choice. . . .

Notes and Questions

1. *Precautionary measures.* The Climate Convention notes in Article 3 that "[t]he parties should take precautionary measures to anticipate, prevent, or minimize the causes of climate change and mitigate its adverse effects. Where there are threats of serious or irreversible damage, lack of full scientific certainty should not be used as a reason for postponing such measures, taking into account that policies and measures to deal with climate change should be cost-effective so as to ensure global benefits at the lowest possible cost." Note that the article refers to "precautionary measures" and not to the precautionary principle. What legal difference does this make? Do you see any significant differences in the definition of "precautionary measures" from those discussed in other chapters of this book? Could a country use this language to justify a carbon tax? Could an environmentally conscious non-governmental organization use this language effectively to argue that a carbon tax is required?

2. *Equity.* Article 3(1) provides that the "[p]arties should protect the climate system for the benefit of present and future generations of humankind, on the basis of equity and in accordance with their common but differentiated responsibilities and respective capabilities. Accordingly, the developed country Parties should take the lead in combating climate change and the adverse effects thereof." How would you define "equity" here? What does "intergenerational equity" mean in the context of climate change? *See* Edith Brown Weiss, In Fairness to Future Generations: International Law, Common Patrimony, and Intergenerational Equity 345 (1989). *See* James C. Wood, Intergenerational Equity and Climate Change, 8 Geo. Intl. Envtl. L. Rev. 293 (1996).

3. *"Common but differentiated."* The reference to "common but differentiated responsibilities" may be a newly emerging principle. *See* Principle 8 of the Rio Declaration on Environment and Development. Is it clear to you what it means? *See also* Daniel Magraw, Legal Treatment of Developing Countries: Differential, Contextual, and Absolute Norms, 1 Colo. J. Intl. Envtl. L. & Poly. 69 (1990) (arguing there is a customary international law requirement to take developing countries' interests into account; excerpted in chapter 7, above).

4. *Stockholm Principle 21.* The Convention neither explicitly obligates countries to respect Principle 21 of the Stockholm Declaration on the Human Environment nor includes the language of the principle in the obligations of the Convention. Why would countries be reluctant to include it? What would be the legal implications of doing so? When the principle was drafted in 1972, countries were concerned largely with transfrontier pollution. Do you see any problems with applying the principle to problems such as climate change or ozone depletion? Principle 21 is stated verbatim in the Convention's preeamble.

5. *Liability.* The convention also does not mention liability. Are coun-

tries liable for damage from climate change? Consider the following hypothetical case. Suppose that one of the island countries, such as the Maldives, is substantially inundated or even disappears as a result of rising sea levels from climate change. Is there any legal redress for the Maldives? Against whom could the country bring a claim? In what forum? On the basis of what theory of liability?

Some have argued that traditional notions of liability in international law are not applicable to climate change. Rather there can only be a general notion of accountability between states. During the Climate Change Convention negotiations, the small island states were sufficiently concerned about this issue that they pressed for countries to establish a special trust fund for them to compensate for measures to adjust to future climate change. They were unsuccessful in this effort, but the issue remained before the international community and arose again during negotiations of the Kyoto Protocol (described below), as did the claim by oil-producing countries that they should be compensated because some efforts to decrease GHG emissions could hurt their economies. Are there any principles in international law that may be useful to the island countries in pressing their concerns?

6. *Transfrontier pollution.* Many of the principles you have read about relate directly to transfrontier pollution. Can they be applied to problems of climate change?

7. *"Common concerns of mankind."* The Framework Convention on Climate Change acknowledges in its preamble that "Earth's climate and its adverse effects are a common concern of mankind." How would you define a "common concern of mankind"? What legal obligations may flow from this? UNEP sponsored two meetings of legal experts in an effort to define this proposed principle more fully, but no formal definition has yet been adopted by the international community. For a thought-provoking economic analysis of the implications of the concept, *see* William D. Nordhaus, Locational Competition and the Environment (mimeo, May 31, 1994, available from author).

8. *"New and Additional resources."* As mentioned above, many believe that the participation of developing countries is central to a regime for controlling climate change because of their large and growing populations and increasing greenhouse gas emission levels. What obligation do the developed states have under the Convention to help finance the developing states' efforts at reducing and controlling greenhouse gas emissions? There was considerable debate over whether the developed countries would provide new and additional funding to developing countries under the Climate Convention. Note the formula that was agreed upon. If you were advising a government in implementing the Convention, how would you calculate the amount of financial assistance?

There was also considerable debate as to whether the fund for the Convention would come under the umbrella of the Global Environmental

Facility of the World Bank, UNDP, and UNEP or whether it would be a separate fund to be executed by states parties to the Convention. Note the agreed formulation. Since the Biological Diversity Convention does not incorporate this formulation, the United States initially withheld its signature.

9. *Problems in implementation.* What problems do you foresee in implementing the convention? Note that Articles 9 and 10 establish a Subsidiary Body for Scientific and Technical Advice and a Subsidiary Body for Implementation. What role will the Intergovernmental Panel on Climate Change (IPCC), which set the scientific stage for countries to agree on the FCCC, have in light of these provisions? What role should it have?

10. *"Joint implementation."* One of the innovations under the FCCC is the proposal for "joint implementation" by countries party to the convention. Article 2 of the Convention provides that the "ultimate objective" of the convention is to achieve "stabilization of greenhouse gas concentrations in the atmosphere at a level that would prevent dangerous anthropogenic interference with the climate system." Joint implementation (also referred to as JI) is a proposed strategy for achieving this; as its name suggests, it would permit parties to implement policies and measures for reducing greenhouse gas emissions jointly with other parties. Norway introduced the concept in the negotiations in 1991; and efforts were undertaken to develop criteria for joint implementation. In theory, it could permit developed countries to focus on reducing emissions of greenhouse gases in developing countries by financing new control technologies there, rather than taking more costly measures at home to control greenhouse gases. The intent is that joint implementation will lead to measures that will provide the global benefit of stabilizing atmospheric concentrations of greenhouse gases at the lowest cost. In the negotiations of the Kyoto Protocol to the Framework Convention (discussed below), parties took a range of positions on joint implementation, from prohibiting it to encouraging it. *See* Report of the Ad Hoc Group on the Berlin Mandate on the Work of its Sixth Session, Bonn, Mar. 3-7, 1997, FCCC/AGBM/1997/3/Add.1 (1997). For analysis of the many legal and policy issues associated with Joint Implementation, *see* Criteria for Joint Implementation under the Framework Convention on Climate Change (1994); Onno Kuik, Paul Peters & Nico Schrijiver, Joint Implementation to Curb Climate Change: Legal and Economic Aspects (1994). Glenn Wiser, Joint Implementation: Incentives for Private Sector Mitigation of Global Climate Change, 9 Geo. Intl. Envtl. L. Rev. 747 (1997) (exploring incentives for private sector participation in a joint implementation system and the adoption of instruments for a joint implementation market).

11. *Environmental NGOs.* Article 7(6), which establishes the Conference of the Parties, also provides that "qualified" NGOs can obtain observer status at the conference meetings, unless one-third of the parties present object. What difference will the presence of environmental groups at these meetings have? Compare the willingness of drafters of the Framework

Convention to include NGOs to the reluctance of international trade forums such as the WTO to include environmental NGOs.

12. *Article 4(2)(b).* What precisely does Article 4(2)(b) require as a legal matter? What does it say about emissions after the year 2000?

c. Developments Leading to the Kyoto Protocol to the FCCC (1997)

At the first meeting of the Conference of the Parties (COP) in Berlin, Germany, in March 1995, countries agreed to a mandate to negotiate a new, legally binding international instrument to apply to the period beyond the year 2000. That instrument was to consider quantified targets and timetables for controlling greenhouse gas emissions by Annex I (developed) countries. The parties established an Ad Hoc Group on the Berlin Mandate for considering a future protocol. The target date for the instrument was 1997. *See also* B. Arts & W. Rudig, Negotiating the "Berlin Mandate": Reflections on the First "COP" to the UN Framework Convention on Climate Change, 4 Envtl. Polit. 481 (1995).

The second meeting of the Conference of the Parties, in Geneva in 1996, endorsed the conclusions of the IPCC Second Assessment Report reproduced above in section A.1. Perhaps the most significant event at the conference was the shift in position by the United States to support for a protocol or other instrument that would include a binding target for reducing GHG emissions, if such an instrument used an emissions trading scheme (as described below). However, the conference also saw increased conflict emerge over climate change, with OPEC countries fearful that adaption measures would involve reducing the use of petroleum products. The meeting also reached agreement on contents of the "national communications" that developing countries were scheduled to begin submiting in April 1997, specifying what steps they are taking to reduce GHG emissions. (Annex I countries were already required to submit "national communications.")

The third meeting of the Conference of the Parties, in Kyoto, Japan, in December 1997, was projected to adopt a legal instrument that would include binding targets and timetables for reductions in GHG emissions. Various proposals were floated on how these reductions should be accomplished. The United States proposed to establish a "budget" for GHG emissions that would last up to ten years and cap each country's total emissions of all GHGs not covered by the Montreal Protocol —i.e., carbon dioxide (CO_2), methane (CH_4), nitrous oxide (NO_2), hydrogen-flourochride (HFC), perflourochloride (PFC), and sulfur hexaflouride (SF_6)— during this period at 1990 levels. A country could exceed this cap by "borrowing" emissions from the next budget period but would have to repay the "borrowings" with additional reductions. Developed nations could "jointly implement" GHG reduction projects with developing nations and split the emissions credits equally. The United States also proposed an international system of GHG emissions trading between industrialized nations. Finally, developing countries would be required to take "no regrets" measures—measures that make sense for other reasons, such as saving money. By contrast to the United States plan, the European Community (EC) proposed that industrialized nations reduce emissions of only three GHGs (carbon dioxide, methane, and nitrous oxide), but by a larger percentage: 15 percent from 1990 levels. Japan proposed that emissions of the same three GHGs be reduced by 5 percent. Japan also proposed an afforestation project of 5 million hectares by 2020. *See* Government Reportedly Set to Launch Global Afforestation Scheme, Yomiuri Shinbum, Apr. 20, 1997, at 25. A list of some proposals is available in Report of the Ad Hoc Group on the Berlin Mandate on the Work of Its Sixth Session, Bonn, Mar. 3-7, 1997, at 49-55, FCCC/AGBM/1997/3/Add.1 (1997). None of these proposals contained a legally binding limit on the ultimately important issue of the actual concentration of GHGs in the atmosphere, though some of them had specific goals in mind in this respect.

Notes and Questions

1. What problems do you foresee in implementing precise targets and timetables? What difference does it make whether the protocol addresses only CO_2 or includes other greenhouse gases?

2. Do you agree that the form of a convention to limit greenhouse gases should be a framework convention with protocols rather than a single treaty or agreement? What are the advantages and disadvantages of each?

3. Strategies for ensuring compliance by parties with targets and timetables are discussed below. What issues can you foresee?

4. What procedures might be made available to update the targets and timetables to keep pace with scientific knowledge?

3. Emissions Trading to Control Greenhouse Gas Emissions

In an earlier chapter, we discussed the idea of pollution of the environment as an example of a tragedy of the commons. In the context of climate change, the similarities remain valid. Limitations on the amount of GHGs emitted can be adopted, but it would be impossible to set a complete ban on production.

The United States and other countries have argued that the problem of controlling GHG emissions can be best handled through a trading scheme. That is, allocate the right to emit GHGs to specific entities within an economy and allow potential emitters to use or sell their right to emit or to buy rights to emit from others. In theory, this would keep the total emissions at the desired level, while taking advantage of the creativity spurred by profit-making. There has been considerable discussion that the emissions trading scheme developed under the United States Clean Air Act, and in order to implement the Canada-United States Air Quality Agreement, might be appropriate internationally to control GHG emissions in a more efficient manner.

What are the advantages and disadvantages of letting the market implement environmental policy? How would the initial allocation(s) of emissions rights be accomplished? What should be the extent of the government's supervisory role? In thinking about this, it may be helpful to bear in mind that at least two different levels of trading are possible in a climate change emission trading system—within a country and between countries. With respect to the latter, should only countries be able to trade, or should private entities also be able to?

■ EMISSIONS TRADING AND CLIMATE CHANGE

Edith Brown Weiss & M.P.A. Kindall
(mimeo 1992)

In the past the United States has actively promoted the use of emissions trading if any system for limiting greenhouse gas emissions were to be agreed upon at the global level.

An emissions trading program is a system that allocates—on some basis—rights to emit a given substance or substances—among various sources or potential sources. Any entity that is allocated such a right can either use it or transfer it to another entity. The entity that is able to reduce emissions below the level of its allocation thus has a valuable commodity which can be sold to someone else—presumably another entity that cannot reduce emissions to the level of its allocation without incurring a very high cost. Society achieves the same level of emissions reductions that it would have achieved if each entity had emitted no less, and no more, than its allocated amount, but the overall cost is reduced: the company that can achieve reduced emissions at least cost will have an incentive to do so.

Promising as emissions trading is, it does not solve every problem, nor does it eliminate all administrative tasks. Emissions trading is a mechanism for accomplishing environmental goals efficiently; it cannot determine what those environmental goals should be or how much society should be willing to pay collectively to achieve those goals. Nor does emissions trading necessarily produce an equitable distribution of the burden of meeting society's environmental goals. That issue can only be addressed through the way in which emissions rights are allocated at the outset.

The U.S. experience with emissions trading indicates that an effective emissions trading program requires certain important elements: market participants with easy access to good information about the emissions credit market; a regulatory system that creates emissions rights that are relatively easy to calculate and are dependable; and regulatory agencies that are capable of approving applications quickly and monitoring compliance effectively. Thus, an emissions trading system has certain infrastructure requirements.

An emissions trading system would only be necessary if a protocol to the Climate Convention required states parties to reduce net emissions of greenhouse gases by a given amount.

The climate change issue is complicated by the fact that many gases contribute to the enhanced greenhouse effect. . . . Reductions in anthropogenic emissions for any one greenhouse gas might not produce sufficient reductions in overall GHG emissions to mitigate potential effects of the enhanced greenhouse effect. This is particularly true where reductions in emissions of one gas could lead to increases in emissions of other gases. Shifting from oil and coal consumption to natural gas, for example, would result in reduced CO_2 emissions, but the positive effects of this reduction could be completely offset by increases in methane emissions that occur from leaks in natural gas transmission pipelines.

The U.S. advocated a comprehensive approach that would permit countries to control net greenhouse emissions as they saw fit, rather than mandating a specific set of reductions for each greenhouse gas. Thus, one country could reduce its net emissions by concentrating on reduced net CO_2 emissions—it could encourage greater energy efficiency in the transportation and energy sectors and conduct vigorous afforestation and reforestation efforts, thus increasing its carbon dioxide "sinks." Or, if it preferred, it could concentrate on reducing methane emissions from natural gas transmissions, coal beds, and rice paddies.

This, in effect, is emissions trading between gases. It can be accomplished only if there is a scientifically sound basis for comparing the effect of one greenhouse gas to another in terms of its global warming potential. The Intergovernmental Panel on Climate Change produced such a "global warming potential" index, and it is undergoing revision as our knowledge of the science improves. The use of such an index would permit countries to allocate their global warming potential "budgets" among those activities that they determined to be most important.

The possibilities for emissions trading in a climate regime do not end there, however. The system could also be designed to allow international trading of emissions allowances. Thus, a country that did not use all of its allocated GHG emissions allowances could sell them to another country, thereby giving countries an incentive to go beyond their reduction targets. Additionally, countries could receive emissions credits for actions that they took to reduce emissions in other countries as well as in their own. This would provide added incentives for the transfer of environmentally sound technology, which all recognize to be a key component in the control of greenhouse gas emissions worldwide.

The details for designing such a system would not be trivial. Allocation of greenhouse gas emissions rights likely would be an extremely contentious issue; one could present equity arguments for allocations based on per capita emissions, historical emissions, or capacity for emitting greenhouse gases. Equally difficult would be designing an effective system for monitoring emissions and ensuring compliance. . . . The potential problems are enormous.

EMMISSIONS BUDGETS: Building An Effective International Greenhouse Gas Control System

Daniel J. Dudek
Environmental Defense Fund
(February 1997)

This report . . . proposes an emissions budget and trading system for greenhouse gases that includes the following: national budgets; covering all sources and sinks; expressed as total GHG [greenhouse gas] emissions over a decade-long period; and in terms of carbon equivalent units (CEUs).

Nations could meet their decadal budget obligations by trading CEUs with each other and by "saving" CEUs whenever their decadal GHG emissions total was less than their total budget. Such CEUs could be used to offset GHG emissions in subsequent decadal periods and even earn "premiums" in the form of increases in their emissions value.

To ensure compliance, countries would be obligated to furnish detailed annual reports of their current and cumulative emissions and of the acquisition and/or sale of their CEUs. Countries exceeding their budgets would be subject to a two-pronged automatic sanction. The emissions value of any CEUs such countries had exported would be discounted upon their use by those holding such CEUs. In addition, cumulative GHG emissions in excess of a country's decadal budget—adjusted to reflect CEUs acquired or exported by the country—would be deducted—again automatically—from the country's budget for the decadal period immediately following.

Finally, each decade's emissions budget for affected nations would be established during the course of an ongoing review process undertaken by the Secretariat. Emissions budgets for upcomming decades would be announced at the 5-year point of the current decadal period after asessments of the atmospheric and climate science and of technology developments as well as of the performance to date of the overall regime. . . .

Mechanics of Reporting, Accounting and Trading

One of the innovations introduced by the SO2 emissions trading program under the U.S. Clean Air Act was that the SO2 emissions "allowance" served—all at the same time—as i) the currency of trading, ii) the instrument of compliance for affected sources and iii) the regulatory mechanism applied by the U.S. EPA for ensuring sources' accountability and for "tracking" emissions trades. Similarly, the protocol can establish a single, simple sovereign accounting system that performs the same multiplicity of functions for an international GHG emissions budget and trading regime.

At the same time, this system would be able to succeed without relying on the allocation of emissions "allowances" or marketable permits. . . .

Trading

Through this approach, which is, in effect, one of double-entry record-keeping, the international emission trading system can accommodate GHG emissions trading between and among private firms in different nations while ensuring both the integration of private and sovereign trading and the full GHG emissions budget accountability of all nations. In addition, it does not presuppose any particular set of policy approaches that participating nations may use on a domestic level, nor does it rely on developing extensive new institutional authorities internationally.

In fact, under this system, virtually any firm operating virtually any domestic policy regime can transact the international sale of purportedly suplus GHG emissions reductions. Meanwhile, the integrity of the system of accountability remains assured. This approach achieves this by requiring nations to report annually all emissions exports, whether initiated by the sovereign itself or any private firms operating within sovereign borders. Even private firm sales transactions, therefore, of necessity will have to be effectuated through both their being reported to the government of the selling firm and a coresponding deduction being taken from the sovereign's budget. . . .

Joint Implementation and Participation

. . . GHG emissions from the developing world are rapidly reaching or exceeding par with those generated by the industrialized and Eastern bloc nations. Their emissions trajectory corresponds to their economies increasing importance and activity in the global marketplace. . . .

. . . Ostensibly, the most effective way of using the emissions trading market to create incentivies for developing countries to participate in an international GHG regime is to condition their ability to engage in transactions in the emissions trading market on their agreement to subject themselves to a GHG emissions budget. . . .

Erecting such a barrier to developing nations' participation in trading may prove to be too crude and risky a strategy, however, while also denying opportunities for achieving environmental and economic gains. In contrast, permitting international GHG emissions trading for and with nations prior to their accepting GHG emissions budget—that is, joint implementation—may offer a smoother path by which developing countries can "graduate" to full participation in the emissions budget regime. . . .

Typically, the kinds of international transaction that would result in the transfer of GHG emissions reduction credits would have the mutual economic benefits to buyer and seller characteristic of trading: sellers would gain a new, additional sources of revenue and buyers would be able to achieve compliance at lower cost. Moreover, these transactions would bring a host of benefits crucial to the credibility, durability and environmental performance of a GHG protocol. First, the very opportunity afforded firms and sovereigns in the industrialized world to meet their GHG emissions budgets at reduced cost and with greater flexibility would enhannce the acceptance and credibility of an international GHG regime.

At the same time, those developing economies experiencing the greatest growth in the current economic time horizon are making substantial infrastructure investments whose environmental consequences, including GHG emissions, could have long-lasting effects for good or ill. Investments of the sort that yielded transactable GHG reductions for the host economy or the foreign investor simultaneously would help direct the host countries' economic growth along paths that were less, rather than more, GHG emissions-intensive. In addition to the environmental benefits that would result directly from this outcome, achieving growth in this way would make it that much easier for these countries to accept, eventually, a GHG emissions budget. As a result, the implicit gradualism in this strategy could speed and facilitate thse countries' graduation to more rigorous international GHG obligations. . . .

Notes and Questions

1. In January 1992, the *Wall Street Journal* reported that research conducted by the United Nations Conference on Trade and Development had determined that trading of pollution rights futures and options would be the most effective way to stop global warming. *See* Jeffrey Taylor, Global Market In Pollution Rights Proposed by U.N., Wall St. J. Jan. 31, 1992, C1. Combating Global Warming: Study on a Global System of Tradeable Carbon Emissions Entitlements (1992) (a cooperative effort containing chapters by various authors outlining a possible system of carbon emission trading, proposed first in Bergen, Norway, in 1990). In early 1997, a group of 2,000 economists, including six Nobel laureates, announced its support for either reducing carbon emissions by tradeable emissions or through a carbon tax. Action to Curb Greenhouse Emissions Wins Endorsement from 2,000 Economists, 20 Intl. Envtl. Rep. 152 (Feb. 19, 1997).

A recommendation paper in the 1992 UNCTAD study entitled "Trading Entitlements to Control Carbon Emissions: A Practical Way to Combat Global Warming" proposed that an International Environmental Protection Agency be formed to issue pollution permits that could be traded on private exchange markets.

Permits would be allocated to participating countries, which would decide for themselves how to regulate the sale to companies. Each permit would allow a producer to emit one ton of CO_2 per year, so that a company producing more than this amount would have to buy extra allowances from another. Like the United States Clean Air Act system of tradeable SO_2 permits, the CO_2 allowances could be traded in lots of 100 on stock exchanges. The global authority would reduce the total number of permits issued over time, spurring incentives to develop cleaner technologies and lessen the threat of global warming.

2. Although emissions trading is mentioned in the Berlin Mandate, in the negotiations leading to the proposed Kyoto Protocol, parties adopted a wide range of positions over emissions trading, ranging from prohibiting it to allowing it, subject to countries implementing national mechanisms for certification and verification of trades. Under some proposals, emissions trading would be available for gases besides carbon dioxide, provided that those gases were first translated into their carbon dioxide equivalents. However, it was also proposed that emissions trading should not be considered until it had been more fully discussed and its principles outlined so that it can be determined whether emissions trading offers environmental benefits. *See* Report of the Ad Hoc Group on the Berlin Mandate on the Work of Its Sixth Session, Bonn, Mar. 3-7, 1997, at 48-49, FCCC/AGBM/1997/3/Add.1 (1997).

3. For a review of lessons from the use of tradeable permit schemes in other areas for climate change, *see* OECD, Climate Change: Designing a Tradeable Permit System (1992). For the implementation of the sulphur dioxide emissions trading system under United States law and a comparison of United States law with the global trading plan, *see* Acid Rain Allowance Allocation and Reserves, 40 C.F.R. 72, 73, 75 (1993); *see also,* Edith Brown Weiss, Environmentally Sustainable Competitiveness: A Comment, 102 Yale L.J. 2123, 2139-2141 (1993); National Academy of Public Administration, The Environment Goes to Market (1994) (discussing experience with tradeable emission permits in California); Bernard S. Black & Richard J. Pierce, Jr., The Choice Between Markets and Central Planning in Regulating the U.S. Electricity Industry, 93 Colum. L. Rev. 1339 (1993) (describing United States experience with emissions trading under the Clean Air Act); Tom H. Tietenberg, Economic Instruments for Environmental Regulation, in Economic Policy Toward the Environment 86 (Dieter Helm, ed. 1991).

For further reading on carbon trading proposals, *see* Combating Global Warming: Study on a Global System of Tradeable Carbon Emissions Entitlements (1992) (a cooperative effort containing chapters by various authors outlining a possible system of carbon emission trading, proposed first in Bergen, Norway, in 1990); Christopher D. Stone, Beyond Rio: "Insuring" Against Global Warming, 86 Am. J. Intl. L. 445 (1992) ("The tradeable permit system provides the least-cost way to achieve that politically agreed-upon target, inasmuch as the emissions that do take place represent the social optimum . . ." at 462); J.I. Liebermann, To Market, To Market, 8 Issues Sci. Technol. 25 (1992). For a comparison to past attempts at pollution trading, Tom Tietenberg, Relevant Experience with Tradeable Entitlements, Combating Global Warming, above (explaining the United States systems of transferable permits for SO_2 and water pollutants and of lead banking, as well as the use of pollution permits in Germany, Canada, the United Kingdom, and limited fish catch permits in New Zealand).

4. Analytically, emissions trading has similarities to a carbon tax. A

major difference is who receives the benefits. The government receives revenues generated by a carbon tax, which it may use to reduce other taxes, such as the income tax, that have distortionary effects on the economy. Under an emissions trading regime, by contrast, entities that possess emissions rights can sell or trade those rights they do not need. The entities that possess those rights will thus enjoy windfall profits while other entities that must acquire rights to emit will have additional costs, which may be passed on to consumers. Thus, under emissions trading, consumers may face additional costs without the benefit of having other taxes reduced by the government. *See* Stephen Smith, Who Pays for Climate Change Policies? Distributional Side-Effects and Policy Responses, in The Economics of Climate Change 277 (1994). However, emissions trading is often thought to be more politically palatable than a carbon tax. For example, President Clinton proposed an energy tax in 1993, only to see the proposal soundly defeated.

5. One of the major issues under an emission trading regime is allocation of the emissions rights. Allocation—which involves distributing trillions of dollars of assets (in the form of emissions rights), perhaps for eternity—offers many opportunities for corruption and political influence (both domestically and internationally) as some entities might be willing to pay political actors for scarce emission rights that they could then resell to other entities at a higher price. Concerns over potential corruption might thus lead one to favor a carbon tax. On the other hand, under a carbon tax, one of the major issues would be determining the proper level of the tax, with it being very likely that some entities would claim that the price was too high. With emissions trading, the market clearing price of emission rights would determine the amount of the charge, so there would probably be less criticism that the tax was too high. Instead, criticism would be focused over the amount of emissions permitted, as higher levels of permitted emissions would increase the supply of emissions available for trading and thus reduce the price of emissions in the event entities needed to purchase additional rights to emit. *See* OECD, Global Warming: Economic Dimensions and Policy Responses 49-51 (1995). Criticism might also be expected with respect to who is allocated the emission rights, including questions about distributive equity, political influence, and concentration of economic power.

4. *The Kyoto Protocol to the Framework Convention on Climate Change (1997)*

a. Introduction: Basic Characteristics

The Kyoto Protocol to the FCCC was adopted in 1977 after intense negotiations spanning two years and culminating in a high-level negotiation in Kyoto, Japan, at the Third Conference of the parties to the FCCC. The Protocol is an unusually complicated instrument, perhaps unavoidably so given the unusual degree of scientific uncertainty and importance of its subject matter. Not only must the Protocol be read with a close eye on the FCCC, but the Protocol's wording is occasionally unusually obtuse, and substantively related provisions are often found in different parts of the Protocol. Moreover, because details of some contentious issues were left to be decided in the future by the Conference of the Parties of the FCCC or by the Meeting of the Parties of the Protocol, it will be necessary to track future developments in those fora in order to understand the implications of certain provisions.

Generally speaking, some of the defining features of the Kyoto Protocol are as follows. The Protocol takes a comprehensive approach by covering both actual emissions of GHGs and sinks that sequester carbon and by covering all six GHGs not covered by the Montreal Protocol. It provides legally binding, individualized emissions targets for countries listed in Annex I of the FCCC (so-called Annex I countries, which are primarily OECD members, some Eastern European countries, and some former republics of the Soviet Union). These targets—which are specified in Annex B to the Protocol—are to be met over a five-year budget period, running from 2008 to 2012. The Protocol allows countries flexibility in meeting their targets, domestically, as well as internationally via a set of innovative mechanisms. These mechanisms include not only emissions trading but also joint implementation between industrialized countries—note the change in the use of the term "joint implementation" from the FCCC context—and cooperation among industrialized and developing countries via a Clean Development Mechanism. Details regarding some of these aspects of the Protocol are provided below. For a more thorough discussion, *see* Clare Breidenich, Daniel Magraw, Anne Rowley & James Rubin, Current Development: The Kyoto Protocol to the Framework Convention on Climate Change, 92 Am. J. Intl. L. 322 (1998).

Some of the critical provisions from the Kyoto Protocol are reproduced below. Following those provisions is an excerpt from the decision, taken by the FCCC Conference of the Parties at Kyoto, that adopted the Protocol and specified issues to be taken up at the next Conference of the Parties (November 1998).

■ KYOTO PROTOCOL TO THE UNITED NATIONS FRAMEWORK CONVENTION ON CLIMATE CHANGE, ARTICLES 3-8, 11-12, 17-19 & ANNEX B

Kyoto Protocol to the FCCC, FCCC Conference of the Parties, 3d Sess., UN Doc. FCCC/CP/1997/L7/Add. 1 (Dec. 10, 1997).

Article 3

1. The Parties included in Annex I shall, individually or jointly, ensure that their aggregate anthropogenic carbon dioxide equivalent emissions of

the greenhouse gases listed in Annex A do not exceed their assigned amounts, calculated pursuant to their quantified emission limitation and reduction commitments inscribed in Annex B and in accordance with the provisions of this Article, with view to reducing their overall emissions of such gases by at least 5 per cent below 1990 levels in the commitment period 2008 to 2012.

2. Each Party included in Annex I shall, by 2005, have made demonstrable progress in achieving its commitments under this Protocol.

3. The net changes in greenhouse gas emissions from sources and removals by sinks resulting from direct human-induced land-use change and forestry activities, limited to afforestation, reforestation and deforestation since 1990, measured as verifiable changes in carbon stocks in each commitment period, shall be used to meet the commitments under this Article of each Party included in Annex I. The greenhouse gas emissions by sources and removals by sinks associated with those activities shall be reported in a transparent and verifiable manner and reviewed in accordance with Articles 7 and 8.

4. Prior to the first session of the Conference of the Parties serving as the meeting of the Parties to this Protocol, each Party included in Annex I shall provide, for consideration by the Subsidiary Body of Scientific and Technological Advice, data to establish its level of carbon stocks in 1990 and to enable an estimate to be made of its changes in carbon stocks in subsequent years. The Conference of the Parties serving as the meeting of the Parties to this Protocol shall, at its first session or as soon as practicable thereafter, decide upon modalities, rules and guidelines as to how, and which, additional human-induced activities related to changes in greenhouse gas emissions by sources and removals by sinks in the agricultural soils and the land-use change and forestry categories shall be added to, or subtracted from, the assigned amounts for Parties included in Annex I, taking into account uncertainties, transparency in reporting, verifiability, the methodological work of the Intergovernmental Panel on Climate Change, the advice provided by the Subsidiary Body for Scientific and Technological Advice in accordance with Article 5 and the decisions of the Conference of the Parties. Such a decision shall apply in the second and subsequent commitment periods. A Party may choose to apply such a decision on these additional human-induced activities for its first commitment period, provided that these activities have taken place since 1990.

5. The Parties included in Annex I undergoing the process of transition to a market whose base year or period was established pursuant to decision 9/CP.2 of the Conference of the Parties at its second session shall use that base year or period for the implementation of their commitments under this Article. Any other Party included in Annex I undergoing the process of transition to a market economy which has not yet submitted its first national communication under Article 12 of the Convention may also notify the Conference of the Parties serving as the meeting of the Parties to this Protocol that it intends to use an historical base year or period other than 1990 for the implementation of its commitments under this Article. The Conference of the Parties serving as the meeting of the Parties to this Protocol shall decide on the acceptance of such notification.

6. Taking into account Article 4, paragraph 6, of the Convention, in the implementation of their commitments under this Protocol other than those under this Article, a certain degree of flexibility shall be allowed by the

Conference of the Parties serving as the meeting of the Parties to this Protocol to the Parties included in Annex I undergoing the process of transition to a market economy.

7. In the first quantified emission limitation and reduction commitment period, from 2008 to 2012, the assigned amount for each Party included in Annex I shall be equal to the percentage inscribed for it in Annex B of its aggregate anthropogenic carbon dioxide equivalent emissions of the greenhouse gases listed in Annex A in 1990, or the base year or period determined in accordance with paragraph 5 above, multiplied by 5. Those parties included in Annex I for whom land-use change and forestry constituted a net source of greenhouse gas emissions in 1990 shall include in their 1990 emissions base year or period the aggregate anthropogenic carbon dioxide equivalent emissions by sources minus removals by sinks in 1990 from land-use change for purposes of calculating their assigned amount.

8. Any Party included in Annex I may use 1995 as its base year for hydrofluorocarbons, perfluorocarbons and sulphur hexafluoride, for the purposes of the calculation referred to in paragraph 7 above.

9. Commitments for subsequent periods for Parties included in Annex I shall be established in amendments to Annex B to this Protocol, which shall be adopted in accordance with the provisions of Article 21, paragraph 7. The Conference of the Parties serving as the meeting of the Parties to this Protocol shall initiate the consideration of such commitments at least seven years before the end of the first commitment period referred to in paragraph 1 above.

10. Any emission reduction units, or any part of an assigned amount, which a Party acquires from another Party in accordance with the provisions of Article 6 or of Article 17 shall be added to the assigned amount for the acquiring Party.

11. Any emission reduction units, or any part of an assigned amount, which a Party acquires from another Party in accordance with the provisions of Article 6 of Article 17 shall be subtracted from the assigned amount for the transferring Party.

12. Any certified emission reductions which a Party acquired from another Party in accordance with the provisions in Article 12 shall be added to the assigned amount for the acquiring Party.

13. If the emissions of a Party included in Annex I in a commitment period are less than its assigned amount under this Article, this difference shall, on request of that Party, be added to the assigned amount for that Party for subsequent commitment periods.

14. Each Party included in Annex I shall strive to implement the commitments mentioned in paragraph 1 above in such a way as to minimize adverse social, environmental and economic impacts on developing country Parties, particularly those identified in Article 4, paragraphs 8 and 9, of the Convention. In line with relevant decisions of the Conference of the Parties on the implementation of those paragraphs, the Conference of the Parties serving as the meeting of the Parties to this Protocol shall, at its first session, consider what actions are necessary to minimize the adverse effects of climate change and/or the impacts of response measures on Parties referred to in those paragraphs. Among the issues to be considered shall be the establishment of funding, insurance and transfer of technology.

Article 4

1. Any Parties included in Annex I that have reached an agreement to fulfill their commitments under Article 3 jointly, shall be deemed to have met those commitments provided that their total combined aggregate anthropogenic carbon dioxide equivalent emissions of the greenhouse gases listed in Annex A do not exceed their assigned amounts calculated pursuant to their quantified emission limitation and reduction commitments inscribed in Annex B and in accordance with the provisions of Article 3. The respective emission level allocated to each of the Parties to the agreement shall be set out in that agreement.

2. The Parties to any such agreement shall notify the secretariat of the terms of the agreement on the date of deposit of their instruments of ratification, acceptance or approval of this Protocol, or accession thereto. The secretariat shall in turn inform the Parties and signatories to the Convention of the terms of the agreement.

3. Any such agreement shall remain in operation for the duration of the commitment period specified in Article 3, paragraph 7.

4. If Parties acting jointly do so in the framework of, and together with, a regional economic integration organization, any alteration in the composition of the organization after adoption of this Protocol shall not affect existing commitments under this Protocol. Any alteration in the composition of the organization shall only apply for the purposes of those commitments under Article 3 that are adopted subsequent to that alteration.

5. In the event of failure by the Parties to such an agreement to achieve their total combined level of emission reductions, each Party to that agreement shall be responsible for its own level of emissions set out in the agreement.

6. If Parties acting jointly do so in the framework of, and together with, a regional economic integration organization which is itself a Party to this Protocol, each member State of that regional economic integration organization individually, and together with the regional economic integration organization acting in accordance with Article 24, shall, in the event of failure to achieve the total combined level of emission reductions, be responsible for its level of emissions as notified in accordance with this Article.

Article 5

1. Each Party included in Annex I shall have in place, no later than one year prior to the start of the first commitment period, a national system for the estimation of anthropogenic emissions by sources and removals by sinks of all greenhouse gases not controlled by the Montreal Protocol. Guidelines for such national systems, which shall incorporate the methodologies specified in paragraph 2 below, shall be decided upon by the Conference of the Parties serving as the meeting of the Parties to this Protocol at its first session.

2. Methodologies for estimating anthropogenic emissions by sources and removals by sinks of all greenhouse gases not controlled by the Montreal Protocol shall be those accepted by the Intergovernmental Panel on Climate Change and agreed upon by the Conference of the Parties at its third session.

Where such methodologies are not used, appropriate adjustments shall be applied according to methodologies agreed upon by the Conference of the Parties serving as the meeting of the Parties to this Protocol at its first session. Based on the work of, *inter alia* the Intergovernmental Panel on Climate Change and advice provided by the Subsidiary Body for Scientific and Technological Advice, the Conference of the Parties serving as the meeting of the Parties to this Protocol shall regularly review and, as appropriate, revise such methodologies and adjustments, taking fully into account any relevant decisions by the Conference of the Parties. Any revision to methodologies or adjustments shall be used only for the purposes of ascertaining compliance with commitments under Article 3 in respect of any commitment period adopted subsequent to that revision.

3. The global warming potentials used to calculate the carbon dioxide equivalence of anthropogenic emissions by sources and removals by sinks of greenhouse gases listed in Annex A shall be those accepted by the Intergovernmental Panel on Climate Change and agreed upon by the Conference of the Parties at its third session. Based on the work of, *inter alia* the Intergovernmental Panel on Climate Change and advice provided by the Subsidiary Body for Scientific and Technological Advice, the Conference of the Parties serving as the meeting of the Parties to this Protocol shall regularly review and, as appropriate, revise the global warming potential of each greenhouse gas, taking fully into account any relevant decisions by the Conference of the Parties. Any revision to a global warming potential shall apply only to commitments under Article 3 in respect of any commitment period adopted subsequent to that revision.

Article 6

1. For the purpose of meeting its commitments under Article 3, any Party included in Annex I may transfer to, or acquire from, any other such Party emission reduction units resulting from projects aimed at reducing anthropogenic emissions by sources or enhancing anthropogenic removals by sinks of greenhouse gases in any sector of the economy, provided that:

(a) Any such project has the approval of the Parties involved;

(b) Any such project provides a reduction in emissions by sources, or an enhancement of removals by sinks, that is additional to any that would otherwise occur;

(c) It does not acquire any emission reduction units if it is not in compliance with its obligations under Article 5 and 7; and

(d) The acquisition of emission reduction units shall be supplemental to domestic actions for the purposes of meeting commitments under Article 3.

2. The Conference of the Parties serving as the meeting of the Parties to this Protocol may, at its first session or as soon as practicable thereafter, further elaborate guidelines for the implementation of this Article, including for verification and reporting.

3. A Party included in Annex I may authorize legal entities to participate, under its responsibility, in actions leading to the generation, transfer or acquisition under this Article of emission reduction units.

4. If a question of implementation by a Party included in Annex I of the requirements referred to in this Article is identified in accordance with the relevant provisions of Article 8, transfers and acquisitions of emission reduction units may continue to be made after the question has been identified, provided that any such units may not be used by a Party to meet its commitments under Article 3 until any issue of compliance is resolved.

Article 7

1. Each Party included in Annex I shall incorporate in its annual inventory of anthropogenic emissions by sources and removals by sinks of greenhouse gases not controlled by the Montreal Protocol, submitted in accordance with the relevant decisions of the Conference of the Parties, the necessary supplementary information for the purposes of ensuring compliance with Article 3, to be determined in accordance with paragraph 4 below.

2. Each Party included in Annex I shall incorporate in its national communication, submitted under Article 12 of the Convention, the supplementary information necessary to demonstrate compliance with its commitments under this Protocol, to be determined in accordance with paragraph 4 below.

3. Each Party included in Annex I shall submit the information required under paragraph 1 above annually, beginning with the first inventory due under the Convention for the first year of the commitment period after this Protocol has entered into force for that Party. Each such Party shall submit the information required under paragraph 2 above as part of the first national communication due under the Convention after this Protocol has entered into force for it and after the adoption of guidelines as provided for in paragraph 4 below. The frequency of subsequent submission of information required under this Article shall be determined by the Conference of the Parties serving as the meeting of the Parties to this Protocol, taking into account any timetable for the submission of national communications decided upon by the Conference of the Parties.

4. The Conference of the Parties serving as the meeting of the Parties to this Protocol shall adopt at its first session, and review periodically thereafter, guidelines for the preparation of the information required under this Article, taking into account guidelines for the preparation of national communications by Parties included in Annex I adopted by the Conference of the Parties. The Conference of the Parties serving as the meeting of the Parties to this Protocol shall also, prior to the first commitment period, decide upon modalities for the accounting of assigned amounts.

Article 8

1. The information submitted under Article 7 by each Party included in Annex I shall be reviewed by expert review teams pursuant to the relevant decisions of the Conference of the Parties and in accordance with guidelines adopted for this purpose by the Conference of the Parties serving as the meeting of the Parties to this Protocol under paragraph 4 below. The information submitted under Article 7, paragraph 1, by each Party included in Annex I shall be reviewed as part of the annual

compilation and accounting of emissions inventories and assigned amounts. Additionally, the information submitted under Article 7, paragraph 2, by each Party included in Annex I shall be reviewed as part of the review of communications.

2. Expert review teams shall be coordinated by the secretariat and shall be composed of experts selected from those nominated by Parties to the Convention and, as appropriate, by intergovernmental organizations, in accordance with guidance provided for this purpose by the Conference of the Parties.

3. The review process shall provide a thorough and comprehensive technical assessment of all aspects of the implementation by a Party of this Protocol. The expert review teams shall prepare a report to the Conference of the Parties serving as the meeting of the Parties to this Protocol, assessing the implementation of the commitments of the Party and identifying any potential problems in, and factors influencing, the fulfillment of commitments. Such reports shall be circulated by the secretariat to all Parties to the Convention. The secretariat shall list those questions of implementation indicated in such reports for further consideration by the Conference of the Parties serving as the meeting of the Parties to this Protocol.

4. The Conference of the Parties serving as the meeting of the Parties to this Protocol shall at its first session, and review periodically thereafter, guidelines for the review of implementation of this Protocol by expert review teams taking into account the relevant decisions of the Conference of the Parties.

5. The Conference of the Parties serving as the meeting of the Parties to this Protocol shall, with the assistance of the Subsidiary Body for Implementation and, as appropriate, the Subsidiary Body for Scientific and Technological Advice, consider:

(a) The information submitted by Parties under Article 7 and the reports of the expert reviews thereon conducted under this Article; and

(b) Those questions of implementation listed by the secretariat under paragraph 3 above, as well as any questions raised by Parties.

6. Pursuant to its consideration of the information referred to in paragraph 5 above, the Conference of the Parties serving as the meeting of the Parties to this Protocol shall take decisions on any matter required for the implementation of this Protocol.

Article 11

1. In the implementation of Article 10, Parties shall take into account the provisions of Article 4, paragraphs 4, 5, 7, 8 and 9, of the Convention.

2. In the context of the implementation of Article 4, paragraph 1, of the Convention, in accordance with the provisions of Article 4, paragraph 3, and Article 11 of the Convention, and through the entity or entities entrusted with the operation of the financial mechanism of the Convention, the developed country Parties and other developed Parties included in Annex II to the Convention shall:

(a) Provide new and additional financial resources to meet the agreed full costs incurred by developing country Parties in advancing the implementation of existing commitments under Article 4, paragraph 1(a), of the Convention that are covered in Article 10, subparagraph (a); and

(b) Also provide such financial resources, including for the transfer of technology, needed by the developing country Parties to meet the agreed full incremental costs of advancing the implementation of existing commitments under Article 4, paragraph 1, of the Convention that are covered by Article 10 and that are agreed between a developing country Party and the international entity or entities referred to in Article 11 of the Convention, in accordance with that Article.

The implementation of these existing commitments shall take into account the need for adequacy and predictability in the flow of funds and the importance of appropriate burden sharing among developed country Parties. The guidance to the entity or entities entrusted with the operation of the financial mechanism of the Convention in relevant decisions of the Conference of the Parties, including those agreed before the adoption of this Protocol, shall apply *mutatis mutandis* to the provisions of this paragraph.

3. The developed country Parties and other developed Parties in Annex II to the Convention may also provide, and developing country Parties avail themselves of, financial resources for the implementation of Article 10, through bilateral, regional and other multilateral channels.

Article 12

1. A clean development mechanism is hereby defined.

2. The purpose of the clean development mechanism shall be to assist Parties not included in Annex I in achieving sustainable development and in contributing to the ultimate objective of the Convention, and to assist Parties included in Annex I in achieving compliance with their quantified emission limitation and reduction commitments under Article 3.

3. Under the clean development mechanism:

(a) Parties not included in Annex I will benefit from project activities resulting in certified emission reductions; and

(b) Parties included in Annex I may use the certified emission reductions accruing from such project activities to contribute to compliance with part of their quantified emission limitation and reduction commitments under Article 3, as determined by the Conference of the Parties serving as the meeting of the Parties to this Protocol.

4. The clean development mechanism shall be subject to the authority and guidance of the Conference of the Parties serving as the meeting of the Parties to this Protocol and be supervised by an executive board of the clean development mechanism.

5. Emission reductions resulting from each project activity shall be certified by operational entities to be designated by the Conference of the Parties serving as the meeting of the Parties to this Protocol, on the basis of:

(a) Voluntary participation approved by each Party involved;

(b) Real, measurable, and long-term benefits related to the mitigation of climate change; and

(c) Reductions in emissions that are additional to any that would occur in the absence of the certified project activity.

6. The clean development mechanism shall assist in arranging funding of certified project activities as necessary.

7. The Conference of the Parties serving as the meeting of the Parties to this Protocol shall, at its first session, elaborate modalities and procedures with the objective of ensuring transparency, efficiency and accountability through independent auditing and verification of project activities.

8. The Conference of the Parties serving as the meeting of the Parties to this Protocol shall ensure that a share of the proceeds from certified project activities is used to cover administrative expenses as well as to assist developing country Parties that are particularly vulnerable to the adverse effects of climate change to meet the costs of adaptation.

9. Participation under the clean development mechanism, including in activities mentioned in paragraph 3(a) above and in the acquisition of certified emission reductions, may involve private and/or public entities, and is to be subject to whatever guidance may be provided by the executive board of the clean development mechanism.

10. Certified emission reductions obtained during the period from the year 2000 up to the beginning of the first commitment period can be used to assist in achieving compliance in the first commitment period.

Article 17

The Conference of the Parties shall define the relevant principles, modalities, rules and guideline, in particular for verification, reporting and accountability for emissions trading. The Parties included in Annex B may participate in emissions trading for the purposes of fulfilling their commitments under Article 3. Any such trading shall be supplemental to domestic actions for the purpose of meeting quantified emission limitation and reduction commitments under that Article.

Article 18

The Conference of the Parties serving as the meeting of the Parties to this Protocol shall, at its first session, approve appropriate and effective procedures and mechanisms to determine and to address cases of non-compliance with the provisions of this Protocol, including through the development of an indicative list of consequences, taking into account the cause, type, degree and frequency of non-compliance. Any procedures and mechanisms under this Article entailing binding consequences shall be adopted by means of an amendment to this Protocol.

Article 19

The provisions of Article 14 of the Convention on settlement of disputes shall apply *mutatis mutandis* to this Protocol.

Annex B

Party	*Quantified emission limitation or reduction commitment* (percentage of base year or period)
Australia	108
Austria	92
Belgium	92
Bulgaria*	92
Canada	94
Croatia*	95
Czech Republic*	92
Denmark	92
Estonia*	92
European Community	92
Finland	92
France	92
Germany	92
Greece	92
Hungary*	94
Iceland	110
Ireland	92
Italy	92
Japan	94
Latvia*	92
Liechtenstein	92
Lithuania*	92
Luxembourg	92
Monaco	92
Netherlands	92
New Zealand	100
Norway	101
Poland*	94
Portugal	92
Romania*	92
Russian Federation*	100
Slovakia*	92
Slovenia*	92
Spain	92
Sweden	92
Switzerland	92
Ukraine*	100
United Kingdom of Great Britain and Northern Ireland	92
United States of America	93

*Countries that are undergoing the process of transition to a market economy.

■ DECISION 1/CP.3 OF THE FCCC THIRD CONFERENCE OF THE PARTIES, ADOPTION OF THE KYOTO PROTOCOL TO THE FCCC

FCCC Conference of the Parties, 3d Sess., UN Doc. FCCC/CP/1997/L.7/Add.1 (Dec. 10, 1997), art. 5

THE CONFERENCE OF THE PARTIES, . . .

5. *Requests* the Chairman of the [FCCC] Subsidiary Body for Scientific and Technological Advice and the Chairman of the [FCCC] Subsidiary Body for Implementation, taking into account the approved programme budget for the biennium 1998-1999 and the related programme of work of the secretariat (FCCC/CP/1997/INF.1), to give guidance to the secretariat on preparatory work needed for the consideration by fourth session of the Conference of the Parties of the following matters, and to allocate work on these matters to the respective subsidiary bodies as appropriate:

(a) Determination of modalities, rules and guidelines as to how and which additional human induced activities related to changes in greenhouse gas emissions and removals in the agricultural soil and land-use change and forestry categories shall be added to, or subtracted from, the assigned amount for Parties included in Annex I, as provided for under Article 3, paragraph 4, of the Protocol;

(b) Definition of relevant principles, modalities, rules and guidelines, in particular for verification, reporting and accountability of emissions trading, pursuant to Article 17 of the Protocol;

(c) Elaboration of guidelines for any Party included in Annex I to transfer to, or acquire from, any other such Party any emission reduction units resulting from projects aimed at reducing anthropogenic emissions by sources or enhancing anthropogenic removals by sinks of greenhouse gases in any sector of the economy, as provided for under Article 6 of the Protocol; and

(d) Consideration of and, as appropriate, action on suitable methodologies to address the situation of Parties listed in Annex B of the Protocol for whom single projects would have a significant proportional impact on emissions in the commitment period;

b. Quantified Emissions Limitation and Reduction Objectives (QELROs or "Targets"): Emissions and Sinks

Determining the legally binding targets for industrialized countries established by the Kyoto Protocol can be somewhat complex. Essentially, these limitations are based on individualized percentage changes—usually reductions, but sometimes increases—in emissions from a base year (often referred to as 1990, but which can in fact be other years depending on the country and the particular GHG), augmented or decreased by voluntary participation in emissions trading, joint implementation, or the Clean Development Fund. Both actual emissions of GHGs and the effect of sequestering carbon in "sinks" such as forests are taken into account, although the exact procedure for doing that for sinks is not clear on the face of the Protocol and may give rise to substantial and significant debate in future years. The following excerpt describes the process of determining emissions reduction targets and of taking sinks into account.

■ CURRENT DEVELOPMENT: THE KYOTO PROTOCOL TO THE UNITED NATIONS FRAMEWORK CONVENTION ON CLIMATE CHANGE

Clare Breidenich, Daniel Magraw, Anny Rowley & James Rubin
92 Am. J. Intl. L. 317, 322-325 (1998)(some footnotes omitted and others edited)

EMISSION REDUCTION TARGETS

[A]rticle 3 of the Protocol establishes QELROs [quantified emissions limitation and reduction objectives] or emission targets for FCCC Annex I countries, with the exception of Turkey. The Protocol sets targets against base year emission levels. For most parties, 1990 is the official base year. However, certain countries with economies in transition[4] are authorized by a decision of the Conference of the Parties to use a different base year,[5] and other countries with economies in transition may apply to use a different base year.[6] Also, as described in greater detail below, any Annex I country may select 1995 as the base year for the three synthetic GHGs (HFCs, PFCs and SF6). The negotiated emission targets for each Annex I

4. The FCCC, United Nations Framework Convention on Climate Change, *opened for signature* June 4, 1992, S. Treaty Doc. No. 102-38 (1992), 31 I.L.M. 849 (1992) (entered into force Mar. 21, 1994) [hereinafter FCCC], in Annex I identifies the following countries as "countries that are undergoing the process of transition to a market economy": Belarus, Bulgaria, Czechoslovakia, Estonia, Hungary, Latvia, Lithuania, Poland, Romania, the Russian Federation and Ukraine. Similarly, Annex B of the Kyoto Protocol to the FCCC, FCCC Conference of the Parties, 3d Sess., UN Doc. FCCC/CP/1997/L.7/ Add.1 (Dec. 10, 1997), identifies Bulgaria, Croatia, the Czech Republic, Estonia, Hungary, Latvia, Lithuania, Poland, Romania, the Russian Federation, Slovakia, Slovenia and Ukraine as countries that are undergoing the process of transition to a market economy.

5. *See* FCCC Conference of the Parties, 2d Sess., UN Doc. FCCC/CP/1996/15/Add.1, Decision 9/CP.2, at 16 (Oct. 29, 1996).

6. As of this writing, four parties—Bulgaria, Hungary, Poland and Romania—have chosen alternative base years.

country are contained in Annex B to the Protocol,[7] and are listed as percentages of base year emission levels. For example, the target for the United States, which is listed as 93, corresponds to a 7 percent reduction from 1990 levels (or from 1995 levels for the three synthetic GHGs, as explained below). The targets range from an 8 percent reduction (i.e., 92) in the base year emissions level for the European Community (Community or EC) to a 10 percent increase (i.e., 110) in the base year emissions level for Iceland. Overall, the emission reduction among countries listed in Annex B is equivalent to about 5.2 percent of their emissions, if one does not take into account the possible use of 1995 as a base year for synthetic GHGs and the possible use of the Clean Development Mechanism by industrialized countries, both of which are discussed in more detail below.

The difference in parties' individual targets is the outcome of contentious negotiations. Several parties, notably EC member states and the United States (until the last stages of the negotiations), called for a uniform target for all industrialized-country parties (although the Community envisioned differentiation among its own member states). Other parties, led strongly by Australia, and including Japan, Norway and Iceland, argued that differentiated targets, rather than a uniform target, were appropriate, owing to the vast differences in countries' national circumstances, particularly natural resources and energy production and consumption profiles. In the final negotiations, parties were not able to reach agreement on a uniform target and opted for individual, differentiated targets.

The uniform 8 percent reduction target for the EC member states is also noteworthy. With respect to the FCCC's aim of returning emissions of Annex I countries to 1990 levels by the year 2000, parties are allowed to achieve that aim individually or jointly.[8] Consequently, the Community developed an arrangement, often referred to as the "EC bubble," to share emission reductions among its member states. This arrangement was fundamental to the Community's ability to gain member state support for a reduction target in the Protocol. Under the EC internal burden-sharing agreement, certain member states such as Portugal and Ireland will be allowed to increase their emissions from 1990 levels. Thus, for the Community as a whole to reach the 8 percent reduction target, other member states will be required to reduce emissions by more than 8 percent. Originally, the

7. The Annex B countries are Australia, Austria, Belgium, Canada, Croatia, the Czech Republic, Denmark, Estonia, the European Community, Finland, France, Germany, Greece, Hungary, Iceland, Ireland, Italy, Japan, Latvia, Liechtenstein, Lithuania, Luxembourg, Monaco, the Netherlands, New Zealand, Norway, Poland, Portugal, Romania, the Russian Federation, Slovakia, Slovenia, Spain, Sweden, Switzerland, Ukraine, the United Kingdom and the United States. There are some differences between this list and the original list of countries in FCCC Annex I. These differences are due mainly to the dissolution of former Eastern European countries such as Czechoslovakia and Yugoslavia. Hence the Czech Republic, the Slovak Republic, Slovenia and Croatia are all listed in Annex B but were not listed in Annex I. In addition, Turkey, which was listed in Annex I, has not ratified the FCCC and is not currently listed in Annex B.

8. FCCC, *supra* note 4, Art. 4(2)(a), (b).

Community based its burden-sharing arrangement on an overall 10 percent reduction.[9] Although the FCCC allows for internal burden sharing among Annex I countries with respect to its aim of reducing GHG emissions from those countries to 1990 levels, such burden sharing was not automatically a part of the Kyoto Protocol and had to be negotiated. Under Article 4 of the Protocol, Annex B countries may jointly fulfill their commitments under its Article 3. It is possible that the internal EC arrangement may be renegotiated in light of the Kyoto Protocol's requirements. At least until the internal EC arrangement is renegotiated and the FCCC Secretariat is notified of it under Article 4, the individual targets for the member states set forth in Annex B reflect a common EC target, not in the internal burden-sharing arrangements.

Rather than a single-year, fixed-target, the Protocol establishes a cumulative target that applies to a multiyear "commitment period." Each Annex I country must ensure that its aggregate emissions during the commitment period do not exceed its "assigned amount."[10] The first commitment period is established by the Protocol as 2008-2012.[11] This multiyear formulation was devised to give parties greater flexibility in meeting their emission reduction commitments and to take into account annual fluctuations, for example, from business cycles. Article 3 implies that there will be subsequent commitment periods of unspecified duration.[12] Each party's initial "assigned amount" is calculated by multiplying its base year emissions by its individual target in Annex B and then multiplying the result by five—the number of years in the first commitment period.[13] However, the assigned amount may increase or decrease, depending on the party's participation in market-based mechanisms authorized by the Protocol. . . .

SINKS

. . . The Protocol also takes emissions and sequestration from the land use change and forestry (LUCF) sector into account. The FCCC broadly directs countries to mitigate climate change by addressing "anthropogenic emissions by sources and removals by sinks"[14] but does not specify how parties are to take account of carbon sequestration (and corresponding emissions) in the forestry sector. This vagueness led to inconsistencies in how parties account for and credit emissions from LUCF. Some parties have failed to provide any data on this sector, while those which have done

9. The Community proposed an overall decrease in emissions of 15% but had reached internal agreement only on how to allocate a 10% reduction.

10. Kyoto Protocol, *supra* note 4, Art. 3(1).

11. *Id.*, Art. 3(7).

12. *E.g.*, *id.*, Art. 3(7), (9)

13. *Id.*

14. FCCC, *supra* note 4, Art. 4(2)(a), (b).

so differ, some reporting the information separately and others combining it with other categories of emissions to generate a net total.

Perhaps more problematic, most countries calculate emissions from LUCF as an annual flow rate of carbon sequestered or emitted. Since the ability of trees to sequester carbon declines over time, a country with a large proportion of forested area, hence a high rate of carbon sequestration in the base year, will not be able to maintain the same rate of carbon sequestration in later years as its forestry resources age. The declining rate of carbon sequestration in these countries makes an emission target more difficult to attain. Conversely, countries that had net emissions from LUCF in their base year, due to deforestation, can ease the difficulty in attaining their target simply by decreasing the rate of deforestation. Thus, the system under the FCCC rewarded countries that historically had been deforesters and penalized countries that historically had been afforesters.

Because of these factors and the complexity of measuring emissions from LUCF, the negotiations on the sinks language in the Kyoto Protocol were some of the most difficult of the negotiations. The parties finally agreed to a compromise solution. As a general matter, sinks are not included in calculating base year emissions; however, they do play a role during the commitment period. Under the Protocol, Annex I countries must give an accounting of the net changes in LUCF emissions and removals by sinks during the commitment period that are due to human-induced activities and that began after 1990.[15] This new accounting system will reward countries that are increasing their forestry sinks, and penalize those whose sinks are decreasing. Recognizing the difficulty that this new accounting system will create for a few parties, the Protocol requires Annex I countries with net emissions from LUCF in 1990 (i.e., those Annex I countries which were deforesting in 1990) to include those emissions in their base year which has the effect of correspondingly raising their assigned amount and allowed emissions.[16] The meeting of the parties to the Protocol (MOP) is to provide further guidance on LUCF activities that may be counted toward emission targets. . . .

c. Market-Based Mechanisms

Article 4(2) of the FCCC states that parties may "individually or jointly" implement policies and measures aimed at reducing GHG emissions to 1990 levels by 2000. The convention does not provide any further guidance as to how such cooperation might occur, in particular as to whether the FCCC allows emissions reduction credit for joint implementation (JI) between industrialized and developing countries. Some countries argued that

15. Kyoto Protocol, *supra* note 4, Art. 3(3).
16. *Id.*, Art. 3(7).

such JI would be efficient for Annex I countries and encourage the transfer of climate-friendly technology. Other countries countered that JI and other such mechanisms would allow rich countries to buy their way into compliance without taking any domestic corrective measures of their own and that these countries would buy up relatively cheap emissions credits, leaving developing countries to bear heavier costs later.

This debate ultimately led to the establishment at the first Conference of the Parties (COP-1) of a pilot program, referred to as "Activities Implemented Jointly" (AIJ), to gain experience in cooperative activities to reduce emissions. The parties agreed to decide by 2000 whether to continue the pilot phase or to allow countries to get emissions reduction credit for such projects.

The debate continued into the negotiations leading up to the meeting in Kyoto, encompassing not only JI and emissions trading but also the question of whether the European Community could share its emissions reduction among community members in an arrangement that came to be known as the "EU bubble." The following excerpt describes the outcome at Kyoto.

■ CURRENT DEVELOPMENT: THE KYOTO PROTOCOL TO THE UNITED NATIONS FRAMEWORK CONVENTION ON CLIMATE CHANGE

Clare Breidenich, Daniel Magraw, Anne Rowley & James Rubin
92 Am. J. Intl. L. 317, 326-327 (1998) (some footnotes edited)

[U]ltimately, four distinct mechanisms reflecting the competing proposals on transboundary emission reduction cooperation were incorporated in the Protocol. Project-based transfer credits, or JI among Annex I countries, is authorized by Article 6 and accounted for in Article 3(10) and 3(11). Through these provisions the Annex I countries and private-sector participants will be able to invest in emission reduction projects in the territory of any other Annex I country and to apply emission reduction credits for those projects toward their national emission targets. As a precondition for acquiring credit for an emission reduction through such project-based JI, parties must be in compliance with the measurement and reporting requirements of the Protocol.[17] Article 6 does not contain rules or guidelines for the certification and tracking of projects or for attaining credit for emission reductions generated by any such projects, but these may be further developed by the MOP.[18]

17. Kyoto Protocol to the FCCC, FCCC Conference of the Parties, 3d Sess., UN Doc. FCCC/CP/1997/L.7/Add.1 (Dec. 10, 1997), Art. 6(1)(c).
18. *Id.*, Art. 6(2)

In comparison to project-based trading under Article 6, a target-based emissions tradition system is authorized by Article 17 and accounted for in Article 3(10) and 3(11). Despite difficult, lengthy debate, the parties were not able to agree in Kyoto on the specific mechanism or rules for target-based emissions tradition; therefore, these articles do not provide much detail on the type of system contemplated by the parties. Instead, the Protocol simply authorizes Annex B countries to participate in emissions trading with each other and to use such trading to meet emission target commitments under Article 3. It also directs the COP (under the FCCC) to develop the rules and modalities for emissions trading (e.g., concerning accounting, verification and reporting of trades). If the COP does not agree on modalities and guidelines for emissions tradition, Annex I countries may be able to do that on a bilateral or multilateral basis with respect to emissions trading inter se. Finally, the Protocol specifies that such trading shall be "supplemental to domestic actions" to meet emission target commitments.[19] The COP, rather than the MOP, was tasked with the duty of defining the rules and modalities of trading prior to entry into force of the Protocol.[20]

Authorization of the EC burden-sharing arrangement is contained in Article 4. Early in the negotiations, as a concession to other Annex I countries that viewed this arrangement as conferring a special advantage on EC member states, the Community proposed language that would allow other Annex I parties the option of "bubbling" (i.e., meeting their commitments individually or jointly). Article 4 allows Annex I parties, including those acting within the framework of regional economic integration organizations, to agree to fulfill their Article 3 commitments jointly.

A fourth mechanism for international cooperation on emission reductions is authorized by Article 12 and accounted for in Article 3(12). This mechanism reflects the evolution of a concept first proposed by Brazil to deal with noncompliance—the "Clean Development Mechanism" (CDM). Under the CDM, Annex I parties may invest in emission reduction projects in developing countries and may apply some portion of the reductions generated by these projects toward meeting their emission target under Article 3.[21] In return, a share of the proceeds of these projects will be used to finance adaptation to climate change in particularly vulnerable developing countries, as well as to cover the administrative expenses of the mechanism.[22] The CDM will be supervised by an executive board and subject to the guidance of the MOP,[23] which will develop rules and guide-

19. *Id.*, Art. 17. JI under Article 6 is also subject to the requirement that it be supplemental to domestic actions to reduce GHG emissions. *Id.*, Art. 6(2)(d).

20. *Id.*, Art. 17.

21. *Id.*, Art. 12(3)(b).

22. *Id.*, Art. 12(8).

23. *Id.*, Art. 12(4).

lines for operating the mechanism,[24] and will designate operational entities to certify and track projects.[25] Certified emissions reductions obtained as early as the year 2000 may be used to assist in achieving compliance in the first commitment period.[26] Hence, under the CDM, Annex I countries may be able to generate emission reduction credits applicable to their QELROs by investing in projects in developing countries that meet certain requirements.

d. Implementation and Compliance

Implementation of and compliance with the Kyoto Protocol are obviously of great importance. Consider the following excerpts.

■ ELEMENTS OF A SUPERVISORY PROCEDURE FOR THE CLIMATE REGIME

Hermann E. Ott
39 Heidelberg J. Intl. L. 732, 744 (1997)

[T]here is still a broad consensus that the [non-compliance] procedure should be non-confrontational, non-punitive and rather facilitative in nature. These characteristics are reasonable in light of the experiences with the non-compliance procedure of the Montreal Protocol (1987) and they are also in line with academic thinking on this subject. A punitive approach does not offer much success in bringing about compliance if the reasons for non-compliance are, in general, not a wilful disregard for legal obligations, but rather the incapacity of Governments, the ambiguity of norms or changing circumstances between the adoption of a treaty and its entry into force.

■ CURRENT DEVELOPMENT: THE KYOTO PROTOCOL TO THE UNITED NATIONS FRAMEWORK CONVENTION ON CLIMATE CHANGE

Clare Breidenich, Daniel Magraw, Anne Rowley & James Rubin
92 Am. J. Intl. L. 317, 329-332 (1998)

[C]ritics of the Protocol have argued that it has no effective compliance regime. Actually, the Protocol contains several elements designed to pro-

24. *Id.*, Art. 12(7).
25. *Id.*, Art. 12(5).
26. *Id.*, Art. 12(10).

mote compliance by the parties. Most of these elements build on the existing structural and institutional components of the FCCC. The Protocol, however, expands on and improves the Convention's mechanisms in several ways. These improvements take the form of (1) strengthening the nature of the commitments to be legally binding, (2) requiring more rigorous reporting, (3) establishing a more critical review process, and (4) mandating the development of procedures and mechanisms to address cases of noncompliance. In addition, the Protocol elaborates the FCCC's approach in allowing each party flexibility with respect to how it implements its obligations and in encouraging cooperation among parties. Overall, the compliance provisions are designed to work together to form a logical progression of steps, beginning with reporting and review requirements and potentially culminating in consequences for noncompliance. Various compliance components of the Protocol and their relationship to provisions of the FCCC are described in more detail below.

Legally Binding Targets

A fundamental difference between the Convention and the Protocol is the nature of emissions reduction commitments. The FCCC established an aspirational commitment: each Annex I party does not actually commit itself to return to 1990 emissions levels, but rather to undertake policies and measures to mitigate climate change, and to "communicate . . . detailed information on its policies and measures . . . as well as on its resulting projected anthropogenic emissions by sources and removals by sinks of greenhouse gases not controlled by the Montreal Protocol . . . , with the aim of returning" its anthropogenic emissions of those GHGs to their 1990 levels. Verification and assessment of compliance with this obligation thus necessarily involves a subjective assessment of whether the party communicated detailed information with the aim of returning its GHG emissions to their 1990 levels, and there are no binding consequences for failure to comply with this aim. Indeed, parties do not violate the FCCC by exceeding their 1990 emissions. In contrast, the Kyoto Protocol establishes a clear, mandatory set of targets. The operative language of Article 3(1) commits parties to ensure that their emissions do not exceed their assigned amounts. Because the obligation is clear and precise, objective assessment of compliance with targets is greatly facilitated and there is a legal consequence for exceeding the targets—noncompliance with the Protocol.

Flexibility in Implementing

The Protocol allows flexibility at both the national and international levels with respect to how parties may implement their obligations. At the national level, each party may select its own policies and measures. At the international level, the market-based mechanisms described above provide parties with several possible choices. For example, the ability of a party to increase its assigned amount by acquiring tons through the international flexibility mechanisms provides an opportunity for parties, which might otherwise be in noncompliance at the end of a compliance period, to come into compliance. This flexibility will enhance implementation and compliance because it allows each party to design its own approach in light of its unique environmental, economic, social and political situation.

MEASUREMENT OF EMISSIONS

Under the FCCC, parties are directed to use the standard methodologies recommended by the IPCC to measure and estimate their national GHG emissions. The Protocol further defines this directive and mandates that parties have a national system for the estimation of GHG emissions from sources and the removal of such emissions by sinks in place at least one year prior to the beginning of the first commitment period (i.e., by 2007). The Protocol also requires that parties use the standardized IPCC methodologies for the preparation of national GHG inventories. While this requirement was already applicable under the FCCC, it was set forth in a Decision by the Parties, and not in the text of the Convention itself. The Kyoto Protocol goes a step further by requiring that the inventories of parties that fail to use these methods must be adjusted to account for uncertainty, which encourages parties to adopt the most current methodologies—those used by the IPCC. These new provisions on measurement will greatly enhance the accuracy, transparency and comparability of parties' national emissions inventories—features that are essential to verifying attainment of emission targets.

REPORTING

The FCCC established two basic reporting requirements: (1) annual inventories and accounts of GHG emission budgets, and (2) periodic national communications that provide detailed information on all aspects of parties' implementation of the Protocol. Under the Protocol, reporting requirements are expanded to incorporate additional information to enable the annual accounting of cumulative emission targets and international GHG trading. Article 7 of the Protocol contains the expanded reporting requirements. Article 7(1) requires each party, as part of its annual inventory, to provide the information necessary to ensure that it is in compliance with the budgetary and other commitments of Article 3. Article 7(2) requires each party to provide, in this periodic national communication, information necessary to ensure its compliance with all of its obligations under the Protocol. Guidelines to specify the additional information required and the reporting format must be adopted by the MOP at its first session. Furthermore, the parties must determine modalities for centralized accounting of emission targets and trades. The FCCC Secretariat, which also serves as the Protocol Secretariat, is responsible for collecting, compiling and publishing national GHG inventory data. Accounting for emission targets and transactions could be a natural extension of this function.

Review of Implementation

The FCCC established a process for the review of information submitted by Annex I parties in national communications. Decision 3/CP.1 calls for secretariat-led expert teams to conduct in-country technical reviews of individual party communications. Although acceptance of the country visits is voluntary on the part of each party, to date all Annex I parties have undergone in-depth review of their first national communication. Reviews of the second national communications are scheduled for 1998 and 1999.

The Protocol builds upon and strengthens the in-depth review process established by the FCCC in two ways. First, under the FCCC, inventory information is collected annually, but has been published and reviewed only in conjunction with periodic national communications. Article 8(1) of the Protocol requires an annual review of national inventory and emissions target information as part of the centralized accounting of assigned amounts. Second, the review of parties' implementation under the Protocol will be conducted more thoroughly and critically than under the FCCC. Under the Protocol, teams of experts, coordinated by the secretariat and nominated by the parties to the Protocol with assistance as appropriate from intergovernmental organizations, are directed to conduct a comprehensive technical assessment of the full range of a party's implementation of the Protocol, and to identify any potential problems that a party might have in fulfilling its commitments. The secretariat will forward any problems identified in the expert teams' reports for consideration by the MOP. The MOP is authorized to take decisions on any matter required for implementation of the Protocol. In addressing potential compliance problems, the MOP is required to consider: information provided by the party in question in its relevant inventories and national communications; the reports of, and compliance issues raised by, the expert review teams; and questions raised by parties to the Protocol. Guidelines governing review of implementation by the expert review teams are to be adopted by the MOP at its first session.

Consequences of Noncompliance

Whereas the Convention called for consideration of the establishment of a multilateral consultative process to deal with implementation issues, the Protocol established two automatic consequences for compliance and, more generally, in Article 18, requires the parties to establish appropriate and effective procedures and mechanisms to determine and address cases of noncompliance, including development of an indicative list of consequences for noncompliance. The parties, in developing the indicative list of consequences must take into consideration the cause, type, degree and frequency of noncompliance, as those factors relate to individual cases of potential noncompliance. The Protocol also requires that any procedures or mechanisms that involve binding consequences for noncompliance may be adopted by parties only by amending the Protocol. This language in Article 18 was adopted as a compromise between those parties that wanted binding, but unspecified consequences, on the one hand, and those that were not willing to commit themselves to binding but unspecified consequences, on the other hand. Essentially, the parties agreed to defer consideration of specific, binding consequences to a later date, but also agreed that they would adopt a list of indicative measures that could be implemented sooner, although they would not be legally binding.

---

e. Developing Countries

By its terms, the Berlin Mandate precluded the introduction of new commitments for developing countries in the Protocol at Kyoto. The Berlin Mandate, however, did call for parties to "advance the implementation" of existing commitments under FCCC Article 4.1; those commitments apply to all parties.

The Protocol does allow developing countries to voluntarily assume binding emissions reductions obligations through amending Annex B, in order to be able to engage in emissions reduction trading. Either through this or some other means, it is essential over the long term to include developing countries in emissions reduction efforts. From a scientific perspective, GHG emissions from developing countries are expected to surpass those of industrialized countries sometime early in the 21st century, so the cooperation of developing countries is necessary in order to control anthropogenic climate change. From a political perspective, some countries—notably the United States—do not want to risk putting their industries at a competitive disadvantage by incurring Kyoto Protocol-related costs that facilities in other (developing) countries are not required to incur. These countries are unlikely to become parties to the protocol unless there is some sort of "meaningful participation"—a term used by President Clinton—by developing countries (although it is not obvious how much and what type of participation is needed to be "meaningful"). Developing countries, on the other hand, tend to view the climate change problem as having been caused by the economic development activities of the industrialized countries and thus believe those countries should take the first steps to alleviate it, before developing countries are asked to take steps that might slow their economic development. *See, e.g.,* Cheng Zheng Kang,

Equity, Special Considerations, and the Third World, 1 Colo. J. Intl. Envtl. L. & Poly. 57, 61-63 (1990). Some commentators are skeptical that the Kyoto Protocol's approach has a meaningful opportunity for success, as indicated by the following excerpt.

■ TOWARD A REAL GLOBAL WARMING TREATY

Richard Cooper
77 For. Aff. 66 (1998)

. . . Stabilizing the amount of greenhouse gases in the atmosphere will eventually require reducing carbon emissions to levels that cannot be reached without the engagement of the developing countries, but the framework of the proposed treaty is unacceptable to them. There is unlikely to be any generally acceptable principle for allocating valuable emission rights between rich and poor countries, making the success of the Kyoto approach a probable impossibility. . . .

The currently preferred appoach to a treaty limiting greenhouse gas emissions centers around imposing agreed national targets on emissions—possibly permitting some of the allowed emissions to be sold from one nation to another. . . . A second approach, which has received less emphasis, stresses agreement on a set of actions that countries would undertake with a view toward reducing emissions. The latter option has been unwisely marginalized. Mutually agreed-on actions have better prospects of success than national targets.

. . . For problems such as reducing emissions, the favorite instrument of economists is to tax the offending activity. All countries could agree to impose a common carbon emissions tax, which would increase the price of fossil fuels in proportion to their carbon content, with possible tax exemptions for uses that do not emit carbon dioxide, such as production of some plastics.

. . . In principle, it should be possible to extend the idea of a common carbon tax to methane as well, covering wetland rice production, decomposable refuse, gas pipeline losses, and cattle raising. That more difficult step could be phased in later.

Notes and Questions

1. *The "assigned amount"*. In order to better understand how emissions targets actually work under the Kyoto Protocol, it might be useful to diagram the steps in determining what exactly a country's assigned amount is. At what point will a country know whether it is in compliance with its target? Will it matter if many emission trades have occurred in the private sector?

When an emission trade occurs, on whom should the risk of nonperformance of Kyoto Protocol obligations fall—the buyer or the seller?

2. *Measuring sources and sinks.* What measurement problems are likely to be encountered in implementing the Kyoto Protocol? How should sinks be calculated? Does it make sense to ignore carbon stored in soil or sinks operating in marine areas?

3. *Noncompliance mechanisms.* Are Hermann Ott's ideas at odds with implementation and compliance provisions in the Kyoto Protocol? What additional implementation/compliance mechanisms or binding consequences for noncompliance should be adopted to strengthen the Protocol?

4. *Carbon taxes.* Do you agree with Richard Cooper's analysis? How easy would it be to get the United States (which sometimes seems allergic to new taxes), China (with its vast reserves of coal), and Saudi Arabia (with its reserves of oil and gas) to agree on a carbon tax? What about countries that do not become parties to such an agreement—would parties have to impose a border tax adjustment to avoid inequity and competitive disadvantage with such nonparties? Keep this in mind when covering the materials on international trade in chapter 20, below: Would the WTO agreements impose any restraints on the ability to utilize border tax adjustments?

5. *The Byrd resolution.* On July 21, 1997, the United States Senate passed a nonbinding resolution sponsored by Senator Byrd (the Byrd Resolution) stating:

> . . . Whereas the exemption for Developing Countries is inconsistent with the need for global action on climate change and is environmentally flawed; . . .
>
> *Resolved,* That it is the sense of the Senate that—
>
> (1) the United States should not be a signatory to any protocol to, or other agreement regarding, the United Nations Framework Convention on Climate Change . . . which would—
>
> (A) mandate new commitments to limit or reduce greenhouse gas emissions for the Annex I Parties, unless the protocol or other agreement also mandates new specific scheduled commitments to limit or reduce greenhouse gas emissions for Developing Country Parties within the same compliance period, or
>
> (B) would result in serious harm to the economy of the United States; . . . .

What would it take to satisfy this requirement? Would it suffice if Brazil, China, India, and Indonesia agreed to emission reduction targets, even if not as stringent as those applicable to the United States? As indicated above, President Clinton said there must be "meaningful participation" by developing countries. Are the two standards necessarily different?

6. How would you go about trying to convince developing countries voluntarily to undertake binding emission reduction commitments? How

does your approach square with the polluter pays principle and other principles you have studied in this course?

7. For analysis of developing country concerns, *see, e.g.*, Joyeeta Gupta, The Climate Change Convention and Developing Countries: From Conflict to Consensus? 1997; J. K. Parikh, Joint Implementation and North-South Cooperation for Climate Change, 7 Intl. Envtl. Aff. 22 (1995) (addressing North-South equity concerns with joint implementation between developed and developing countries).

XIII

Protection of the Marine Environment

Protection of the marine environment is regulated generally by Part XII of the 1982 United Nations Convention on the Law of the Sea (UNCLOS).[1] In addition, a number of agreements deal with regional seas, and other instruments address specific problems, such as vessel-source pollution and land-based source pollution. This chapter will provide a brief overview of this regulatory system. Efforts to protect marine mammals are dealt with in section C of Chapter 19, which focuses on whales, fur seals, polar bears, and dolphins.

While major oil spills capture public attention, more serious degradation of marine ecosystems occurs through over-exploitation of marine resources, such as fish stocks, and the cumulative effect of pollution carried into the sea by rivers and discharged directly into it by coastal facilities. It is therefore important to view the problem of protection of the marine environment from a holistic perspective, one that is not limited to any one problem or class of problems, such as marine pollution. Article 192 of UNCLOS, the first provision in Part XII, captures the essence of this approach. That article provides in its entirety as follows:

1. Dec. 10, 1982, U.N. Doc. A/CONF/62/122, *reprinted in* United Nations, The Law of the Seas: Official Text of the United Nations Convention on the Law of the Sea with Annexes and Index (UNCLOS), U.N. Sales No. E.83 V.5 (1983).

Article 192
General Obligation

States have the obligation to protect and preserve the marine environment.

This provision is striking in both its generality and lack of qualification. But what does it mean as a practical matter? What do states actually have to do, or refrain from doing, to comply with this obligation? What precisely is meant by the expression "marine environment" (the term is not defined in the convention)? Some light is shed on these questions by the historical development of the law concerning the protection of the marine environment, the more specific provisions of UNCLOS bearing on this problem, and other related instruments. This chapter is devoted to these matters. We begin with a brief look at the factual context in which the legal rules operate.

A. THE SEA AND ITS USE BY HUMANS

Oceans cover approximately 71 percent of Earth's surface and comprise the great preponderance of its hydrosphere. The average depth of the sea is estimated to be 3,790 meters (12,430 feet). For purposes of comparison, the average elevation of land above sea level is only 840 meters (2,760 feet). While all the seas of the world share certain obvious characteristics, many have unique attributes. For example, shipping lanes and straits are used more intensively than other parts of the ocean for navigation, making accidents and spills there more likely; some areas of the sea are more ecologically fragile than others; some seas, such as the Mediterranean and the Baltic, are semi-enclosed, inhibiting the exchange of their waters with those of the rest of the ocean and thus slowing the process of self-purification; and some parts of the ocean are utilized more intensively by humans than others, resulting in more pollution, both chronic and accidental.

Human uses of the seas have changed and intensified over time. Originally a convenient highway—for travel, trade, exploration, and the like—and a source of food, the sea today is also used for the extraction of oil and other minerals (from the subsoil and the seabed, respectively), the laying of cables and pipelines, the placement (on the seabed) of antisubmarine warfare devices, tourism, and waste disposal. Over half of the global population lives within 60 kilometers of the coast, and by 2020 this percentage could increase to three quarters.[2] The concentration of human settle-

2. Agenda 21, para. 17.3, Report of the United Nations Conference on Environment and Development, vol. 1, p. 239, U.N. Doc. A/CONF.151/26/Rev.1 (Vol. I) (1993).

ments and activities near coastal areas and in river basins results in massive pollution of the marine environment from land-based sources. Over 70 percent of marine pollution comes from these sources, while maritime transport and dumping at sea contribute only 10 percent each.[3] Yet, as we will see, while the two latter sources are governed by international agreements, land-based sources have thus far eluded global legal regulation beyond the general provisions of UNCLOS. However, regional seas agreements address land-based sources, and under UNEP auspices states have negotiated global guidelines and a global action program.

But it is not only pollution that threatens the integrity of marine ecosystems. For centuries humans have engaged both in fishing and hunting of marine mammals (including, e.g., whales, fur seals, and sea otters), with results that have sometimes been disastrous for the species in question. Let us take fishing as an example of the potential effects of human exploitation of marine living resources. Technological advances have enabled humans to catch fish in vast quantities to feed the growing human population, as well as animals and even plants (as fertilizer), and to reach areas of the ocean that were until recently too remote or inhospitable for significant fishing activities. What was once done with rod and small net is now accomplished with sonar, satellites, spotter planes, factory processing ships, and enormous nets. The latter include driftnets, which may be 30 miles long and may, as "ghost nets," go on catching fish, marine mammals, and birds for months or even years after they have been lost or abandoned.[4] The result of this greatly enhanced capacity has been overfishing and the collapse of a number of fish stocks. While the average catch rose steadily following World War II at a rate of 6 to 7 percent annually, "after 1970, as more and more stocks were depleted, the average annual growth . . . fell to only about 1 per cent."[5] Still, the total world fish catch rose from 28 million tons in 1958 to 80 million tons in 1986 and is expected to reach 100 million tons by 2000.[6] According to the Food and Agriculture Organization of the UN (FAO), 70 percent of the world's fish stocks are today either fully exploited, overexploited, or depleted.

These problems present enormous challenges. Is the existing legal framework equipped to deal with them? Has it kept pace with the capacity of humans to develop new technologies that hold the potential for both great good and great harm? Consider these overarching questions as you read through the following materials.

3. *Id.*, para. 17.18, at 243.

4. On driftnets *see, e.g.*, FAO Fisheries Report No. 4349; and Large-Scale Pelagic Driftnet Fishing, FAO Doc. COFI/91/5, Jan. 1991, and Supp. 1, Apr. 1991. For a good, brief discussion, *see* Patricia W. Birnie & Alan E. Boyle, International Law & the Environment 490-491 (1992).

5. World Commission on Environment and Development, Our Common Future 266 (1987).

6. Review of the State of the World Fishery Resources, FAO Doc. COFI/91/Inf.3, Apr. 1991.

B. THE LAW OF THE MARINE ENVIRONMENT[7]

1. Historical Development

It was not until the latter half of the present century that humans began to inflict wide-ranging harm on the marine environment. It was therefore not until well after World War II that humans, and thus states, began to recognize the need to protect the marine environment. Thus the law of the marine environment is of relatively recent vintage. The law of the sea itself, however, is quite venerable.[8]

What D.P. O'Connell has described as the "central and persistent theme" of the history of the law of the sea is "the competition between the exercise of governmental authority over the sea and the idea of the freedom of the seas."[9] This tension is captured eloquently in the so-called battle of the books of the seventeenth century, between Hugo Grotius's *Mare Liberum* (1609) and John Selden's *Mare Clausum* (1635). As their titles indicate, these works argued, respectively, that "states may not individually or collectively acquire the high seas areas by occupation since they are *res communis omnium* or *res extra commercium*"; and that the sea "is as capable of private dominion as land, and the king of Great Britain is lord of all the sea inseparably and perpetually appendant to the British Empire."[10] By the end of the eighteenth century most claims to large areas of the sea had effectively been abandoned, and in the twentieth century, "the freedom of the seas has come to be accepted as a 'general', 'basic', or 'fundamental' principle of international law: some are even prepared to treat it as *jus cogens.*"[11] But even this principle has been effectively eroded in the latter decades of this century as the "high seas," to which the concept of the freedom of the seas applies, have been steadily shrinking with the expansion of coastal state jurisdiction, in particular the recognition in the 1982 Convention of the 200-mile exclusive economic zone.[12] Is this a positive or a negative development with regard to the marine environment? You should consider this question in relation to such specific problems as the control

7. *See generally* 2 D.P. O'Connell, The International Law of the Sea, ch. 25 (I.A. Shearer ed. 1984); Johnston, ed., The Environmental Law of the Sea (1981); Birnie & Boyle, footnote 4, above, ch. 7 (marine pollution), at 251, et seq., ch. 8 (marine pollution from land-based sources), at 304-320, and ch. 13 (marine living resources), at 490, et seq.; and Jonathan I. Charney, The Marine Environment and the 1982 United Nations Convention on the Law of the Sea, 28 Intl. L. 879 (1994).

8. *See generally, e.g.,* 1 D.P. O'Connell, supra footnote 7, ch. 1, 1-29 (1982); R.P. Anand, Origin and Development of the Law of the Sea (1983); and W.E. Butler, Grotius and the Law of the Sea, in Grotius and International Relations 209 (H. Bull, B. Kingsbury & A. Roberts, eds. 1990).

9. O'Connell, supra footnote 7, at 1.

10. Butler, supra footnote 8, at 211.

11. *Id.* at 212.

12. *See* UNCLOS, supra footnote 1, Part V, arts. 55, et seq. *See generally* 1 D.P. O'Connell, supra footnote 8, ch. 15, at 553, et seq.

of vessel-source pollution, the protection of marine mammals, and the protection and management of fish stocks.

Reflecting the relative intensity of different uses of the seas during the first half of the twentieth century, early efforts to protect the marine environment for the most part addressed living resources rather than pollution. Among the agreements concluded during this period were treaties for the protection of fur seals (1911),[13] fisheries (1923, 1930),[14] and whales (1931).[15] The pace picked up considerably after World War II, with the conclusion of additional agreements on marine living resources[16] and, in 1954, the Convention for the Prevention of Pollution of the Sea by Oil.[17] This treaty, which addressed discharges of oil from ships, was followed four years later by the Geneva Convention on the High Seas—one of four agreements on the law of the sea adopted under United Nations auspices in 1958.[18] Article 24 of the High Seas Convention required parties to adopt rules for the prevention of marine pollution from "the discharge of oil from ships or pipelines or resulting from the exploitation and exploration of the seabed and its subsoil. . . ." The widely publicized *Torrey Canyon* disaster of March 1967—together with the United Kingdom's response[19]—highlighted the threat to the marine environment from accidental oil spills by tankers, as well as the legal issues raised by such incidents.[20] Agreements were concluded shortly thereafter to confirm the right of the coastal state to respond to threats posed by such incidents[21] and to provide for civil

13. Convention for the Preservation and Protection of Fur Seals, July 7, 1911, 37 Stat. 1542, T.S. 564, 104 B.S.F.P. 175.

14. Convention between Canada and the United States for the Preservation of the Halibut Fishery of the Northern Pacific Ocean, Mar. 2, 1923, 32 L.N.T.S. 93; Convention Establishing an International Pacific Salmon Fisheries Commission, 1930, 184 L.N.T.S. 306.

15. Convention for the Regulation of Whaling, Sept. 24, 1931, 155 L.N.T.S. 349, 49 Stat. 3079, T.S. 880.

16. Among the agreements concluded shortly after World War II were the London Convention for the Regulation of the Meshes of Fishing Nets and the Size Limits of Fish, Apr. 5, 1946, 231 U.N.T.S. 199; the Washington International Convention for the Regulation of Whaling, Dec. 2, 1946, 161 U.N.T.S. 72, 62 Stat. 1716, TIAS 1849, U.K.T.S. No. 5 (1949); and the FAO Agreement for the Establishment of the Indo-Pacific Fisheries Commission, Feb. 26, 1948, 120 U.N.T.S. 59, 62 Stat. 3711, T.I.A.S. 1895.

17. May 12, 1954, 327 U.N.T.S. 3, 12 U.S.T. 2989, T.I.A.S. 4900.

18. Convention on the Territorial Sea and the Contiguous Zone, Apr. 29, 1958, 516 U.N.T.S. 205, 15 U.S.T. 1606; Convention on the Continental Shelf, Apr. 29, 1958, 499 U.N.T.S. 311, 15 U.S.T. 471; Convention on the High Seas, Apr. 29, 1958, 450 U.N.T.S. 82, 13 U.S.T. 2312, TIAS 5200; and Convention on Fishing and Conservation of the Living Resources of the High Seas, Apr. 29, 1958, 559 U.N.T.S. 285, 17 U.S.T. 138, T.I.A.S. 5969. All four agreements, done at Geneva, are known as the 1958 "Geneva Conventions" on the law of the sea.

19. The UK responded to the threat to its coastline posed by the breakup of the *Torrey Canyon* by destroying the tanker without the consent of the flag state. This incident was followed by the conclusion of the Convention Relating to Intervention on the High Seas in Cases of Oil Pollution Casualties of Nov. 29, 1969, 26 U.S.T. 765, 970 U.N.T.S. 211.

20. *See generally* R. Michael M'Gonigle & Mark W. Zacher, Pollution, Politics, and International Law: Tankers at Sea (1979).

21. *See* Convention, 1996 Oil Pollution Casualties, supra footnote 19.

liability for marine oil pollution damage.[22] The 1970s saw the conclusion of several regional treaties[23] and two global agreements for the protection of the marine environment. The latter—the 1972 London Dumping Convention[24] and the 1973/1978 MARPOL Convention[25]—continue to be among the most important global instruments in force concerning the prevention of marine pollution. During this same decade, however, a major international effort was underway to negotiate an agreement covering all aspects of the law of the sea: The Third United Nations Conference on the Law of the Sea (1973-1982).

2. *The Approach of the United Nations Convention on the Law of the Sea (UNCLOS)*

The Law of the Sea Conference, "the largest and most complex international negotiation ever held,"[26] produced the 1982 United Nations Convention on the Law of the Sea (UNCLOS).[27] This agreement has been said to be, "after the United Nations charter itself, . . . the most far-reaching and potentially influential agreement on the peacetime conduct of nations ever

22. Brussels International Convention on Civil Liability for Oil Pollution Damage, Nov. 29, 1973, 973 U.N.T.S. 3, U.K.T.S. No. 106 (1975), 9 I.L.M. 45 (1970), establishing strict liability of the shipowner, which may be limited under specified conditions; Brussels International Convention on the Establishment of an International Fund for Compensation for Oil Pollution Damage, Dec. 18, 1971, 1110 U.N.T.S. 57, U.K.T.S. No. 95 (1978), 11 I.L.M. 284 (1972), supplementing the compensation available under the Civil Liability Convention.

23. Oslo Convention for the Prevention of Marine Pollution by Dumping from Ships and Aircraft, Feb. 15, 1972, 932 U.N.T.S. 3, U.K.T.S. No. 119 (1975), 9 I.L.M. 359 (1970); Copenhagen (Nordic) Agreement on Cooperation in Oil Pollution, Sept. 16, 1971, 2 International Protection of the Environment: Treaties and Related Documents 502 (B. Rüster, B. Simma & M. Bock eds.); and Barcelona Convention for the Protection of the Mediterranean Sea against Pollution, Feb. 16, 1976, U.N.T.S. Reg. No. 16908, 15 I.L.M. 290 (1976); *See also* the Bonn Agreement for Cooperation in Dealing with Pollution of the North Sea by Oil, June 9, 1969, 704 U.N.T.S. 3, 9 I.L.M. 359 (1970).

24. IMO Convention on the Prevention of Marine Pollution by Dumping of Wastes and Other Matter, Dec. 29, 1972 (as amended Oct. 12, 1978), 1046 U.N.T.S. 120, 26 U.S.T. 2403, T.I.A.S. 8165, 11 I.L.M. 1294 (1972).

25. London International Convention for the Prevention of Pollution from Ships (MARPOL), Nov. 2, 1973, 12 I.L.M. 1319 (1973), as amended by the London Protocol of 17 Feb. 1978, T.I.A.S., 17 I.L.M. 546 (1978).

26. William Wertenbaker, The Law of the Sea—I & II, The New Yorker, Aug. 1 and Aug. 8, 1983. This article contains an excellent description of the negotiations and their dynamics, as well as of the personalities involved.

27. UNCLOS, supra footnote 1. The convention entered into force on Nov. 16, 1994, in accordance with its Article 308. The United States has not become a party as of this writing, even though the principal objections of the United States to the treaty had been eliminated through the adoption by the UN General Assembly, on June 28, 1994, of the Agreement relating to the Implementation of Part XI of the United Nations Convention on the Law of the Sea of Dec. 10, 1982, 33 I.L.M. 1309 (1994). The vote was 121 in favor, none against, and 7 abstentions. GA Res. 48/263 (July 28, 1994). The agreement in effect amends Part XI, which contains the proposed regime for mining in the deep seabed. *See* Law of the Sea Forum: The 1994 Agreement on Implementation of the Seabed Provisions of the Convention on the Law of the Sea, 88 Am. J. Intl. L. 687 (1994).

attempted."[28] It is also the only global treaty dealing, albeit in a general way, with all aspects of the protection of the marine environment. Furthermore, UNCLOS "clarifies the extent of coastal States' authority in the various maritime areas [e.g., the territorial sea and the exclusive economic zone], thus contributing also to the clarification of the scope of the other existing Conventions."[29]

The convention devotes one entire chapter, Part XII, to the "[p]rotection and [p]reservation of the [m]arine [e]nvironment." However, other provisions on the subject are scattered throughout the treaty. This is true not only of the definition of "pollution of the marine environment," to which we will return, but also of environmental provisions in sections of the convention dealing with, inter alia, the territorial sea (Part II), straits (Part III), archipelagic waters (Part IV), the exclusive economic zone (Part V), the high seas (Part VII), enclosed or semienclosed seas (Part IX), the exploration and exploitation of the seabed (Part XI), and marine scientific research (Part XIII). Part XII itself consists of 11 sections,[30] which contain Articles 192-237 of the convention. These provisions "serve as a framework for existing and future conventions of a specialized kind as well as for State cooperation within International Organizations and through their law-making and enforcement activity."[31]

Birnie and Boyle observe that UNCLOS reflects a number of fundamental changes in the law concerning the protection of the marine environment. "Of these perhaps the most important is that pollution can no longer be regarded as an implicit freedom of the seas; rather, its diligent control from all sources is now a matter of comprehensive legal obligation affecting the marine environment as a whole, and not simply the interests of other states."[32] (What are the implications of this change? If interests of other states are not affected, are these true "obligations"? Why or why not?)

Part XII begins by laying down the all-important "general obligation" to protect and preserve the marine environment in Article 192, set forth above. It then recognizes, in Article 193, the "sovereign right of States to exploit their natural resources," but provides that states must exercise this right "in accordance with their duty to protect and preserve the marine environment." (You should compare this formulation with that of Principle 21 of the Stockholm Declaration/Principle 2 of the Rio Declaration: Which

28. Wertenbaker, supra footnote 26.

29. Tullio Treves, Oceans, in World Treaties for the Protection of the Environment 149, 150 (1992).

30. Those are: Section 1, General Provisions; Section 2, Global and Regional Cooperation; Section 3, Technical Assistance; Section 4, Monitoring and Environmental Assessment; Section 5, International Rules and National Legislation to Prevent, Reduce and Control Pollution of the Marine Environment; Section 6, Enforcement; Section 7, Safeguards; Section 8, Ice Covered Areas; Section 9, Responsibility and Liability; Section 10, Sovereign Immunity; and Section 11, Obligations under Other Conventions on the Protection and Preservation of the Marine Environment.

31. Treves, above footnote 29, at 150.

32. Birnie & Boyle, above footnote 4, at 253.

do you consider preferable from an environmental protection point of view?) Article 194 is entitled "Measures to prevent, reduce and control pollution of the marine environment." "Pollution of the marine environment" is broadly defined in Article 1(1)(4) as

> the introduction by man, directly or indirectly, of substances or energy into the marine environment, including estuaries, which results or is likely to result in such deleterious effects as harm to living resources and marine life, hazards to human health, hindrance to marine activities, including fishing and other legitimate uses of the sea, impairment of quality for use of sea water and reduction of amenities.[33]

Article 194 lays down general obligations concerning marine pollution and sets forth a nonexhaustive catalogue of sources of pollution that states are required to address. As the article encapsulates well the approach of the convention to the control of marine pollution, we set it forth here in full:

Article 194
Measures to prevent, reduce and control pollution of the marine environment

1. States shall take, individually or jointly as appropriate, all measures consistent with this Convention that are necessary to prevent, reduce and control pollution of the marine environment from any source, using for this purpose the best practicable means at their disposal and in accordance with their capabilities, and they shall endeavor to harmonize their policies in this connection.

2. States shall take all measures necessary to ensure that activities under their jurisdiction and control are so conducted as not to cause damage by pollution to other states and their environment, and that pollution arising from incidents or activities under their jurisdiction or control does not spread beyond the areas where they exercise sovereign rights in accordance with this Convention.

3. The measures taken pursuant to this Part shall deal with all sources of pollution of the marine environment. These measures shall include, *inter alia,* those designed to minimize to the fullest possible extent:

(a) the release of toxic, harmful or noxious substances, especially those which are persistent, from land-based sources, from or through the atmosphere or by dumping;

(b) pollution from vessels, in particular measures for preventing accidents and dealing with emergencies, ensuring the safety of operations at sea, preventing intentional and unintentional discharges, and regulating the design, construction, equipment, operation and manning of vessels;

(c) pollution from installations and devices used in exploration or exploitation of the natural resources of the sea-bed and subsoil, in particular measures for preventing accidents and dealing with emergencies, ensuring

33. UNCLOS, supra footnote 1, Article 1(1)(4).

> the safety of operations at sea, and regulating the design, construction, equipment, operation and manning of such installations or devices;
>
> (d) pollution from other installations and devices operating in the marine environment, in particular measures for preventing accidents and dealing with emergencies, ensuring the safety of operations at sea, and regulating the design, construction, equipment, operation and manning of such installations or devices.
>
> 4. In taking measures to prevent, reduce or control pollution of the marine environment, States shall refrain from unjustifiable interference with activities carried out by other States in the exercise of their rights and in pursuance of their duties in conformity with this Convention.
>
> 5. The measures taken in accordance with this Part shall include those necessary to protect and preserve rare or fragile ecosystems as well as the habitat of depleted, threatened or endangered species and other forms of marine life.

Subsequent provisions of Part XII elaborate on the measures to be taken with regard to each of the sources enumerated in paragraph 3 of Article 194. They also specify in detail the authority of states to enforce obligations concerning marine pollution in the different maritime zones. The convention strikes a delicate balance between the traditional authority of flag states over pollution from ships and the authority of coastal and port states, which has developed more recently in response to threats to their marine environment. The subject of jurisdiction to enforce these obligations is a complex one, since more than one state may have jurisdiction over a vessel under international law at the same time. The convention also permits especially stringent measures to be applied with regard to areas as to which there is a particular risk due to oceanographic, ecological, or traffic conditions.[34]

Notes and Questions

1. *The status of UNCLOS.* The Convention on the Law of the Sea entered into force on November 16, 1994. As of March 1998, there were 124 parties. The United States is not, however, a party. But in March 1983, President Reagan issued a Statement on United States Oceans Policy in which he noted the United States decision not to sign the Convention because of its deep seabed mining provisions, but went on to state that the convention "contains provisions with respect to traditional uses of the oceans [i.e., uses other than deep seabed mining] which generally confirm

34. UNCLOS, supra footnote 1, Article 211(6)(a).

existing maritime law and practice and fairly balance the interests of all states" and that "the United States is prepared to accept and act in accordance with the balance of interests relating to traditional uses of the ocean. . . ."[35] He also proclaimed a 200-nautical-mile exclusive economic zone for the United States—a jurisdictional zone that did not exist prior to the convention. As you might expect, this infuriated some states because of the understanding during the negotiation of the convention that the text as finally adopted was a "package deal"—a state had to accept all of it or could take advantage of none of it (other than provisions reflecting existing customary international law, of course). Does the position of the United States vis-à-vis the convention affect its right to assert violations of provisions of Part XII?

2. *Examining Article 194.* Article 194 is commendable in its coverage of sources of marine pollution. But is it sufficiently strict with regard to the "measures" to be taken as to those sources? What is the meaning of the phrases "the best practicable means at their disposal" and "in accordance with their capabilities"? Are these loopholes that may undermine the convention's entire regime concerning marine pollution? Why do you suppose they were included in the article? Do these phrases make Article 194 consistent or inconsistent with the norms of prevention we examined in Chapter 7?

3. *Vessel-source pollution.* Article 211, "Pollution from vessels," provides for the "prevention, reduction and control" of marine pollution from vessels by the flag state (para. 2), the port state (para. 3) and the coastal state (paras. 4-6). Not surprisingly, a coastal state's authority over foreign vessels increases as they near its shore. In the 200-mile exclusive economic zone the laws and regulations it adopts must conform to "generally accepted international rules and standards established through the competent international organization or general diplomatic conference." This formula is used frequently in the convention, referring to widely accepted obligations adopted under the auspices of the International Maritime Organization (IMO—formerly the International Maritime Consultative Organization, IMCO) or by a diplomatic conference that prepared an international agreement. In a coastal state's 12-mile territorial sea, on the other hand, its right to adopt such laws and regulations is unrestricted, except that these measures may not hamper the innocent passage of foreign vessels through those waters. (Innocent passage is regulated by Part II, Section 3 of UNCLOS, Articles 17-32.) Finally, the convention permits a state to "establish particular requirements . . . as a condition for the entry of foreign vessels into their ports or internal waters or for a call at their offshore terminals," requiring such a state to "give due publicity to such

35. 19 Weekly Comp. Pres. Docs. 383 (1983), 83 Dept. State Bull., No. 2075, at 70-71 (1983), 22 I.L.M. 464 (1983).

requirements" and to "communicate them to the competent international organization"—generally the IMO. This gives states importing large quantities of oil, such as the United States and Japan, considerable authority over the standards governing foreign oil tankers. However, the fact that many tankers are also registered in such states or owned by their nationals acts as a practical check on the stringency of the regulations they are prepared to adopt. Enforcement of laws and regulations concerning marine pollution is governed by Section 6 of Part XII. Broad authority is given to port states to enforce "applicable international rules and standards" concerning a discharge occurring on the high seas or to investigate a discharge violation at the request of another state within whose jurisdiction the discharge occurred or where it caused or threatened damage (Article 218). Coastal states are also granted significant enforcement powers (Article 220).

4. *Problem.* The good ship *MV Leaky,* a large oil tanker registered in state A, strikes a reef in the exclusive economic zone (EEZ) of state B, causing it to spill a large quantity of oil. The oil slick spread both into the territorial sea of state C and into the high seas. Which states have authority with regard to this incident? Which states' laws apply? Which states have enforcement authority? How should action on the public (state-to-state) and private (e.g., lawsuits against the ship owner seeking redress for damage) levels be coordinated in such cases, if at all?

C. OCEAN DUMPING

Marine pollution emerged as a serious global problem in the period between 1950 and 1970. Just as there were more oil spills, discharges from ships, and dumping of wastes into the ocean, so also there was a growing awareness that the oceans did not have an unlimited capacity to absorb wastes without harming the marine environment. States negotiated agreements to control the dumping and discharge of wastes into oceans long before they negotiated agreements governing air pollution or, with the notable exception of the United States-Canada Boundary Waters Agreement, fresh water.

The London Convention of 1972 (informally known previously as the London Dumping Convention) was a product of the 1972 Stockholm Conference preparations. The London Convention was concluded in December 1972, six months after Stockholm, and became effective in August 1975. As of June 1997, 75 countries were party to the agreement. In 1996 countries negotiated a Protocol to the Convention, which replaces the 1972 agreement for those countries that ratify the protocol. The following reading provides a concise overview of the 1972 Convention.

1. The London Convention of 1972

■ SEA CHANGES? OCEAN DUMPING AND INTERNATIONAL REGULATION

Alan B. Sielen
1 Geo. Intl. Envtl. L. Rev. 2 (1988)

Many governments today face substantial pressure to open up the oceans to greater use as a waste disposal medium. This pressure stems primarily from a growing inventory of wastes and the difficulty of finding technically suitable and politically acceptable waste-disposal sites on land. The wastes involved range from the very toxic, such as high-level radioactive wastes, to the relatively benign, such as garbage. Some parts of the scientific community have also taken greater interest lately in the oceans' potential for receiving wastes. This scientific debate results from the large strides made in recent years in understanding the scientific aspects of marine pollution, as well as the development of new analytic tools for assessing risks to humans and the environment and for monitoring the effects of pollution over time.

An important manifestation of this growing interest in the oceans as a place for waste disposal is the emergence of major global and regional marine protection treaties. To date one of the most significant agreements has been the London Dumping Convention. . . .

I. THE LONDON DUMPING CONVENTION

The Convention has provided the basic global framework for the control of the deliberate disposal (ocean dumping) of all wastes at sea since its entry into force in 1975. Ocean dumping operations usually consist of collecting wastes generated on land, loading them on a ship or barge, and then taking them out to sea for the express purpose of disposal. Although most wastes are dumped from vessels, the London Convention's definition of dumping also includes deliberate disposal from "aircraft, platforms or other manmade structures. . . ." The incineration of hazardous chemicals at sea is also regulated as a form of ocean dumping under the United States Marine Protection, Research, and Sanctuaries Act (MPRSA) and the London Convention.

Dumping does not include discharges from what are usually referred to as "land-based sources" of marine pollution: rivers, pipelines, outfalls, and runoff. Nor does it include operational discharges from vessels, offshore drilling operations, or disposal arising from or related to the exploration, exploitation, and associated offshore processing of seabed mineral resources. In the United States, these activities are regulated under separate laws and, in the case of vessel pollution, are also subject to a broad array of international conventions on vessel design, construction, operation, manning, and liability for damage from tanker spills.

Ocean dumping accounts for only about ten percent of all pollution of the seas; its impact, however, if left uncontrolled, can result in significant damage to the marine environment. For example, most dumping, for reasons of economy, takes place relatively close to shore. Thus, the waste may be deposited in or near biologically productive continental shelf areas. Moreover, the cumulative impacts of ocean dumping may significantly increase as more countries begin to look towards the oceans as a repository for industrial, chemical, agricultural, and radioactive wastes, as well as contaminated dredged material and sewage sludge.

A. APPLICATION

Under the London Convention, national authorities in contracting states must control dumping consistently with the provisions of the Convention. Accordingly, regardless of whether the waste is actually to be dumped in the Contracting Party's territorial waters, a Contracting Party will require that all vessels loading in its ports or territorial seas for the purpose of dumping must first obtain a permit from the Contracting Party's designated agency. Any of the Contracting Party's own vessels planning to dump anywhere in the world must also obtain a permit. In addition, a Contracting Party will require foreign vessels to obtain permits before dumping in offshore areas subject to the Party's jurisdiction—usually 200-mile exclusive economic zones (EEZs). Enforcement is left for the most part to the flag states, although coastal states may apply the Convention to foreign vessels dumping in their EEZ. As in most international environmental agreements, individual countries are free to apply standards stricter than the London Convention's to their own activities. . . .

The International Maritime Organization (IMO) in London, a specialized agency of the United Nations, serves as Secretariat for the Convention. In this capacity, the IMO receives notifications from governments of dumping permits issued, distributes documents, holds regular consultative and scientific group meetings, and carries out all other administrative tasks necessary to the Convention's operation. The Contracting Parties have been rather fortunate in this respect as the IMO continues to be one of the most efficient bureaucracies on the international scene.

B. REGULATORY STRUCTURE: BLACKLIST/GRAYLIST

The London Convention's basic approach to regulation is embodied in its three technical Annexes, and is relatively simple. Annex I lists those substances that may not be dumped because of their potential to harm the marine environment. These "blacklisted" substances include such highly toxic or persistent substances as high-level radioactive wastes, organohalogens, mercury, cadmium, oil, and persistent plastics. Certain of these Annex

I substances, however, may be incinerated at sea in accordance with regulations set by the London Convention.

Exceptions to the Annex I prohibitions are made in cases of "emergencies, posing unacceptable risks relating to human health and admitting no other feasible solution." In addition, and most significantly, the Annex I prohibitions do not include substances that are "rapidly rendered harmless by physical, chemical, or biological processes in the seas," or apply to cases where blacklisted substances are found only as "trace contaminants" in other wastes such as sewage sludge or dredged spoils.

Annex II identifies wastes containing significant amounts of substances posing less danger to the environment. These "graylist" substances may be dumped so long as special care is taken with regard to factors such as site selection, monitoring, packaging of the wastes, and disposal methods intended to mitigate environmental contamination.

Materials not found in either Annex I or II may be dumped under a general permit issued in compliance with the requirements of Annex III. Annex III contains environmental protection criteria which national authorities must carefully consider before issuing any dumping permit. These criteria include consideration of possible effects on marine life, amenities, and other uses of the sea along with factors pertaining to the suitability of any particular disposal operation such as the characteristics and composition of the waste, description of the disposal site, method of disposal, and the practical availability of land-based alternatives.

Over the years, Contracting Parties have supplemented the Convention with additional guidance relating to the implementation of the Convention. These additions have ranged from amendments to the Convention and its Annexes to guidelines that define and interpret key technical terms used in the Annexes including "rapidly rendered harmless," "trace contaminants," and "significant amounts."

In this way, member countries have been able to both apply their practical experience gained in the disposal of common wastes, such as contaminated dredged material, and establish new controls for emerging technologies, such as ocean incineration. Some of the more significant initiatives undertaken pursuant to the Convention include regulations and technical guidelines for ocean incineration, arbitration procedures for the peaceful settlement of disputes arising under the Convention, criteria for allocating substances to the Convention's Annexes, and guidance on the application of the Annexes to dredged material.

2. *The 1996 Protocol to the London Convention*

In the fall of 1996, parties to the London Convention adopted the 1996 Protocol, which supersedes the 1972 Convention for all member states that join the protocol. The new agreement essentially updates the 1972 treaty to keep pace with changes in our understanding of marine pollution and with measures needed to protect the oceans. It adopts the "precautionary approach" and permits dumping of wastes in the ocean only if the wastes fall into those categories listed in an annex and a permit has been obtained. It prohibits the incineration of wastes at sea, bans the export of wastes to other countries for dumping or incineration at sea, provides for setting up procedures to handle complaints, obligates countries to promote technical cooperation and assistance (although it does not establish a fund for such assistance), establishes formal dispute resolution procedures, and provides in an annex for waste audits, which include alternative forms of waste disposal. The protocol opened for signature on April 1, 1997, and must be ratified by 26 states, including 15 contracting parties to the London Convention, to go into effect. As of December 1997, seven contracting parties had signed the protocol, with all but Denmark subject to ratification. As you read the excerpts from the 1996 Protocol, consider how it differs from the 1972 Convention.

■ 1996 PROTOCOL TO THE CONVENTION ON THE PREVENTION OF MARINE POLLUTION BY DUMPING OF WASTES AND OTHER MATTER, 1972 AND RESOLUTIONS ADOPTED BY THE SPECIAL MEETING

As adopted by the Special Meeting of Contracting Parties to the London Convention 1972 on Nov. 7, 1996

THE CONTRACTING PARTIES TO THIS PROTOCOL,

STRESSING the need to protect the marine environment and to promote the sustainable use and conservation of marine resources,

NOTING in this regard the achievements within the framework of the Convention on the Prevention of Marine Pollution by Dumping of Wastes and Other Matter, 1972 and especially the evolution towards approaches based on precaution and prevention . . .

TAKING INTO ACCOUNT relevant international agreements and actions, especially the United Nations Convention on the Law of the Sea, 1982, the Rio Declaration on Environment and Development and Agenda 21,

RECOGNIZING ALSO the interests and capacities of developing States and in particular small island developing States, BEING CONVINCED that further international action to prevent, reduce and where practicable eliminate pollution of the sea caused by dumping can and must be taken without delay to protect and preserve the marine environment and to manage human activities in such a manner that the marine ecosystem will continue to sustain the legitimate uses of the sea and will continue to meet the needs of present and future generations,

HAVE AGREED as follows: . . .

Article 2
Objectives

Contracting Parties shall individually and collectively protect and preserve the marine environment from all sources of pollution and take effective measures, according to their scientific, technical and economic capabilities, to prevent, reduce and where practicable eliminate pollution caused by dumping or incineration at sea of wastes or other matter. Where appropriate, they shall harmonize their policies in this regard.

Article 3
General Obligations

1 In implementing this Protocol, Contracting Parties shall apply a precautionary approach to environmental protection from dumping of wastes or other matter whereby appropriate preventative measures are taken when there is reason to believe that wastes or other matter introduced into the marine environment are likely to cause harm even when there is no conclusive evidence to prove a causal relation between inputs and their effects.

2 Taking into account the approach that the polluter should, in principle, bear the cost of pollution, each Contracting Party shall endeavour to promote practices whereby those it has authorized to engage in dumping or incineration at sea bear the cost of meeting the pollution prevention and control requirements for the authorized activities, having due regard to the public interest.

3 In implementing the provisions of this Protocol, Contracting Parties shall act so as not to transfer, directly or indirectly, damage or likelihood of damage from one part of the environment to another or transform one type of pollution into another.

4 No provision of this Protocol shall be interpreted as preventing Contracting Parties from taking, individually or jointly, more stringent measures in accordance with international law with respect to the prevention, reduction and where practicable elimination of pollution.

Article 4
Dumping of Wastes or Other Matter

1 .1 Contracting Parties shall prohibit the dumping of any wastes or other matter with the exception of those listed in Annex 1.

.2 The dumping of wastes or other matter listed in Annex I shall require a permit. Contracting Parties shall adopt administrative or legislative measures to ensure that issuance of permits and permit conditions comply with provisions of Annex 2. Particular attention shall be paid to opportunities to avoid dumping in favour of environmentally preferable alternatives.

2 No provision of this Protocol shall be interpreted as preventing a Contracting Party from prohibiting, insofar as that Contracting Party is con-

cerned, the dumping of wastes or other matter mentioned in Annex 1. That Contracting Party shall notify the Organization of such measures.

Article 5
Incineration at Sea

Contracting Parties shall prohibit incineration at sea of wastes or other matter.

Article 6
Export of Wastes or Other Matter

Contracting Parties shall not allow the export of wastes or other matter to other countries for dumping or incineration at sea. . . .

Article 9
Issuance of Permits and Reporting

1 Each Contracting Party shall designate an appropriate authority or authorities to:

.1 issue permits in accordance with this Protocol;

.2 keep records of the nature and quantities of all wastes or other matter for which dumping permits have been issued and where practicable the quantities actually dumped and the location, time and method of dumping; and

.3 monitor individually, or in collaboration with other Contracting Parties and competent international organizations, the condition of the sea for the purposes of this Protocol.

2 The appropriate authority or authorities of a Contracting Party shall issue permits in accordance with this Protocol in respect of wastes or other matter intended for dumping or, as provided for in article 8.2, incineration at sea:

.1 loaded in its territory; and

.2 loaded onto a vessel or aircraft registered in its territory or flying its flag, when the loading occurs in the territory of a State not a Contracting Party to this Protocol . . .

Article 10
Application and Enforcement

1 Each Contracting Party shall apply the measures required to implement this Protocol to all:

.1 vessels and aircraft registered in its territory or flying its flag;

.2 vessels and aircraft loading in its territory the wastes or other matter which are to be dumped or incinerated at sea; and

.3 vessels, aircraft and platforms or other man-made structures believed to be engaged in dumping or incineration at sea in areas within which it is entitled to exercise jurisdiction in accordance with international law.

2 Each Contracting Party shall taken appropriate measures in accordance

with international law to prevent and if necessary punish acts contrary to the provisions of this Protocol.

3 Contracting Parties agree to co-operate in the development of procedures for the effective application of this Protocol in areas beyond the jurisdiction of any State, including procedures for the reporting of vessels and aircraft observed dumping or incinerating at sea in contravention of this Protocol.

4 This Protocol shall not apply to those vessels and aircraft entitled to sovereign immunity under international law. However, each Contracting Party shall ensure by the adoption of appropriate measures that such vessels and aircraft owned or operated by it act in a manner consistent with the object and purpose of this Protocol and shall inform the Organization accordingly.

5 A State may, at the time it expresses its consent to be bound by this Protocol, or at any time thereafter, declare that it shall apply the provisions of this Protocol to its vessels and aircraft referred to in paragraph 4, recognising that only that State may enforce those provisions against such vessels and aircraft.

Article 11
Compliance Procedures

1 No later than two years after the entry into force of this Protocol, the Meeting of Contracting Parties shall establish those procedures and mechanisms necessary to assess and promote compliance with this Protocol. Such procedures and mechanisms shall be developed with a view to allowing for the full and open exchange of information, in a constructive manner.

2 After full consideration of any information submitted pursuant to this Protocol and any recommendations made through procedures or mechanisms established under paragraph 1, the Meeting of Contracting Parties may offer advice, assistance or co-operation to Contracting Parties and non-Contracting Parties. . . .

Article 16
Settlement of Disputes

1 Any disputes regarding the interpretation or application of this Protocol shall be resolved in the first instance through negotiation, mediation or conciliation, or other peaceful means chosen by parties to the dispute.

2 If no resolution is possible within twelve months after one Contracting Party has notified another that a dispute exists between them the dispute shall be settled at the request of a party to the dispute, by means of the Arbitral Procedure set forth in Annex 3 unless the parties to the dispute agree to use one of the procedures listed in paragraph I of Article 287 of the 1982 United Nations Convention on the Law of the Sea. The parties to the dispute may so agree, whether or not they are also States Parties to the 1982 United Nations Convention on the Law of the Sea.

3 In the event an agreement to use one of the procedures listed in paragraph I of Article 287 of the 1982 United Nations Convention on the Law of the Sea is reached, the provisions set forth in Part XV of that Conven-

tion that are related to the chosen procedure would also apply, mutatis mutandis.

4 The twelve month period referred to in paragraph 2 may be extended for another twelve months by mutual consent of the parties concerned.

5 Notwithstanding paragraph 2, any State may, at the time it expresses its consent to be bound by this Protocol, notify the Secretary-General that, when it is a party to a dispute about the interpretation or application of article 3.1 or 3.2, its consent will be required before the dispute may be settled by means of the Arbitral Procedure set forth in Annex 3. . . .

Annex 1
Wastes or Other Matter That May be Considered for Dumping

1 The following wastes or other matter are those that may be considered for dumping being mindful of the Objectives and General Obligations of this Protocol set out in articles 2 and 3:

.1 dredged material;

.2 sewage sludge;

.3 fish waste, or material resulting from industrial fish processing operations;

.4 vessels and platforms or other man-made structures at sea;

.5 inert, inorganic geological material;

.6 organic material of natural origin; and

.7 bulky items primarily comprising iron, steel, concrete and similarly unharmful materials for which the concern is physical impact, and limited to those circumstances where such wastes are generated at locations, such as small islands with isolated communities, having no practicable access to disposal options other than dumping. . . .

3 Notwithstanding the above, materials listed in paragraphs 1.1 to 1.7 containing levels of radioactivity greater than de minimis (exempt) concentrations as defined by the IAEA and adopted by Contracting Parties, shall not be considered eligible for dumping; provided further that within 25 years of 20 February 1994, and at each 25 year interval thereafter, Contracting Parties shall complete a scientific study relating to all radioactive wastes and other radioactive matter other than high level wastes or matter, taking into account such other factors as Contracting Parties consider appropriate and shall review the prohibition on dumping of such substances in accordance with the procedures set forth in article 22.

Annex 2
Assessment of Wastes or Other Matter That May be Considered for Dumping

GENERAL

1 The acceptance of dumping under certain circumstances shall not remove the obligations under this Annex to make further attempts to reduce the necessity for dumping.

CONSIDERATION OF WASTE MANAGEMENT OPTIONS

5 Applications to dump wastes or other matter shall demonstrate that

appropriate consideration has been given to the following hierarchy of waste management options, which implies an order of increasing environmental impact:

.1 reuse;
.2 off-site recycling;
.3 destruction of hazardous constituents:
.4 treatment to reduce or remove the hazardous constituents; and
.5 disposal on land, into air and in water.

6 A permit to dump wastes or other matter shall be refused if the permitting authority determines that appropriate opportunities exist to re-use, recycle or treat the waste without undue risks to human health or the environment or disproportionate costs. The practical availability of other means of disposal should be considered in the light of a comparative risk assessment involving both dumping and the alternatives.

Notes and Questions

1. When the 1996 Protocol goes into effect, it will replace the original convention for those countries party to the 1972 Convention who have ratified the protocol. What problems do you foresee if some but not all of the countries party to the 1972 Convention ratify the 1996 Protocol?

2. During the 1980s the former Soviet Union's Navy disposed of high-level radioactive materials in the northern seas, which led to an international furor in 1991. The Soviet foreign ministry argued that the dumping did not violate the 1972 Convention because Article VII exempted vessels and aircraft entitled to sovereign immunity under international law. What does the 1996 Protocol provide? Do you agree that there is no violation of international law? For excellent coverage of the Soviet dumping, *see* William Zimmerman, Elena Nikitina, and James Clem, The Soviet Union and the Russian Federation: A Natural Experiment in Environmental Compliance, chapter 9 in Engaging Countries: Strengthening Compliance with International Accords, eds. Edith Brown Weiss and Harold K. Jacobson, 1998.

3. Suppose that a country wishes to dump low-level nuclear wastes in the oceans. May it do so under the London Convention of 1972 or the 1996 Protocol?

4. Suppose that a country wishes to incinerate its wastes at sea. May it do so under the 1996 Protocol? Note that in 1993, parties to the London Convention decided to prohibit incineration at sea; the modification entered into force 100 days after it was adopted by the parties except for countries that filed a declaration indicating they did not accept the change. If a country ratified the 1996 Protocol and had filed a declaration under the 1972 Convention refusing to accept the ban on incineration, is it obligated to abide by the provision in the 1996 Protocol? Supposing the country had not yet ratified the protocol?

5. Suppose that country wishes to dispose of sewage sludge at sea.

What would be required for a country to do so under the 1972 Convention? Under the 1996 Protocol?

6. Note the provision in the 1996 Protocol relating to dispute settlement. The 1972 Convention does not provide for dispute settlement, but an amendment was proposed that dealt with it. The amendment was never ratified by the requisite number of countries. Note how the 1996 Protocol provision addresses the dispute settlement mechanisms available under the Law of the Sea Treaty. Does the provision solve the hypothetical problem of "forum shopping" to settle international disputes?

7. Other parts of this book have discussed the use of incentives as a means to induce compliance with an international agreement. Compare the 1972 and 1996 agreements in this regard. Are countries required to provide assistance under the 1996 Protocol?

8. The secretariat for the London Convention is housed in the International Maritime Organization in London, England. What branch of government in the member states do you think normally represents the countries at the IMO?

D. LAND-BASED SOURCES OF MARINE POLLUTION

1. *The United Nations Convention on the Law*

> The major threats to the health and productivity and biodiversity of the marine environment result from human activities on land—in coastal areas and further inland. Most of the pollution load of the oceans, including municipal, industrial and agricultural wastes and run-off, as well as atmospheric deposition, emanates from such land-based activities and affects the most productive areas of the marine environment, including estuaries and near-shore waters. These areas are likewise threatened by physical alteration of the coastal environment, including destruction of habitats of vital importance for ecosystem health.[36]

As indicated earlier, land-based sources contribute over 70 percent of marine pollution.[37] These substances are carried into the sea by rivers but can also be discharged directly into it from coastal facilities and sewage pipes.[38] According to Agenda 21: "Many of the polluting substances origi-

36. Global Programme of Action for the Protection of the Marine Environment from Land-Based Activities, Nov. 3, 1995, at 7, U.N. Doc. UNEP (OCA) /LBA/IG.2/7, Dec. 5, 1995.

37. Agenda 21, para. 17.18, Report of the United Nations Conference on Environment and Development, vol. 1, at 243, U.N. Doc. A/CONF.151/26/Rev.1 (Vol. I) (1993).

38. Many of these pipes extend considerable distances out to sea. Examples may be found in southern California and in Vancouver, British Columbia. The latter has given rise to concern in Washington State, across the Strait of Juan de Fuca.

nating from land-based sources are of particular concern to the marine environment since they exhibit at the same time toxicity, persistence and bioaccumulation in the food chain."[39] In fact, most of the contaminants Agenda 21 identifies as posing "the greatest threat to the marine environment" derive from land-based sources. These include sewage, nutrients (largely from agricultural runoff), sediments, litter and plastics, and metals.[40] But since much of this pollution originates from so-called nonpoint sources (e.g., agricultural runoff, oil washed off of roadways and parking lots by precipitation) it is difficult to regulate on the national level and hence on the international plane. The result is that to date, there is no global agreement devoted exclusively to marine pollution from land-based sources. It is, however, the subject of regional treaties and nonbinding instruments. In addition, as we have seen, land-based marine pollution is addressed in the United Nations Convention on the Law of the Sea. Building on the requirements of Article 194(3)(a), set forth above, Article 207 of UNCLOS provides in part as follows:

Article 207
Pollution from Land-Based Sources

> 1. States shall adopt laws and regulations to prevent, reduce and control pollution of the marine environment from land-based sources, including rivers, estuaries, pipelines and outfall structures, taking into account internationally agreed rules, standards and recommended practices and procedures.

Article 207 goes on to provide for action by states on the regional and global levels with regard to land-based sources. In fact, a number of protocols have already been concluded under the Regional Seas Programmes of UNEP. These include the 1980 Protocol for the Protection of the Mediterranean Sea Against Pollution from Land-based Sources, the 1990 Protocol to the Kuwait Regional Convention for the Protection of the Marine Environment Against Pollution from Land-based Sources, the 1983 Protocol for the Protection of the South-East Pacific Against Pollution from Land-based Sources, and the 1992 Protocol on Protection of the Black Sea Marine Environment Against Pollution from Land-based Sources. A draft protocol on the protection of the marine environment from land-based activities is being developed under the Wider Caribbean Action Plan. *See* United Nations Environment Programme (UNEP), Second Meeting of the Experts on Land-based Sources of Pollution in the Wider Caribbean Region, San Juan (March 1994).

Article 213 of UNCLOS provides for enforcement on the national level of the Convention's rules on land-based marine pollution:

39. Agenda 21, supra footnote 37.
40. *Id.*

Article 213
Enforcement with Respect to Pollution from Land-Based Sources

> States shall enforce their laws and regulations adopted in accordance with article 207 and shall adopt laws and regulations and take other measures necessary to implement applicable international rules and standards established through competent international organizations or diplomatic conference[s] to prevent, reduce and control pollution of the marine environment from land-based sources.

Chapter 17 of Agenda 21 recommends that states "[c]onsider updating, strengthening and extending the Montreal Guidelines [for the Protection of the Marine Environment from Land-Based Sources[41]], as appropriate," and that they "[i]nitiate and promote the development of new regional agreements, where appropriate."[42] On November 3, 1995, the Global Programme of Action for the Protection of the Marine Environment from Land-based Activities was adopted by the High-level Segment of the Intergovernmental Conference to Adopt a Global Programme of Action for the Protection of the Marine Environment from Land-based Activities.[43] Also adopted at that meeting was the Washington Declaration on Protection of the Marine Environment from Land-Based Activities.[44] The Global Programme of Action contains detailed recommendations for action at the national, regional and international levels. In addition, it recommends specific actions for different categories of pollution sources and other threats, including sewage, persistent organic pollutants (POPs),[45] radioactive substances, heavy metals, oils (hydrocarbons), nutrients, sediments, litter, and physical alteration and destruction of habitats.

Notes and Questions

1. *A customary norm?* Birnie and Boyle are of the view that relevant treaty provisions "support the conclusion that the diligent control of land-based sources of marine pollution required by Articles 194, 207, and 213 of the 1982 UNCLOS constitutes a rule of customary international law." Patricia W. Birnie & Alan E. Boyle, International Law and the Environment

41. [UNEP Governing Council Decision, May 24, 1985, U.N. Doc. UNEP/GC.13/9/Add.3, UNEP/GC/DEC/13/18II, UNEP Environmental Law Guidelines and Principles No. 7. —Eds.]

42. Agenda 21, footnote 2, above, at 245.

43. Document UNEP (OCA)/LBA/IG.2/6, Dec. 5, 1995, Annex II, at 16.

44. Document UNEP (OCA)/LBA/IG.2/7, Dec. 5, 1995.

45. "Persistent organic pollutants (POPs) are a set of organic compounds that: (i) possess toxic characteristics; (ii) are persistent; (iii) are liable to bioaccumulate; (iv) are prone to long-range transport and deposition; and (v) can result in adverse environmental and human health effects at locations near and far from their source." Global Programme of Action, footnote 48, above, at 37.

at 305 (1992). In light of the requirements for the formation of a rule of customary international law we studied in Chapter 5, do you agree?

2. *Enforcement by other states?* Could another state assert a violation of the obligation referred to in note 1? If so, would that other state have to have suffered a direct injury as a result of the violation? If not, how can the obligation be enforced? Is it an obligation *erga omnes?* If so, how could it be enforced?

■ SAVING THE MEDITERRANEAN

Peter M. Haas
6-68, 107-116 (1990)

The Mediterranean states confronted evidence of pollution in the 1960s. In 1972 Lord Peter Ritchie-Calder alerted the world that:

> The Mediterranean Sea is sick. It needs intensive care, day and night nursing. By nature it has always been delicate but its condition has grievously deteriorated in recent years. The short term prognosis is obvious: on present trends, things will get worse because the effects will be multiplied and magnified by the increase in industrial activity. Recreational beaches will be tarred and ordured. The sea will be out of bounds for bathers. Seafood will be a health hazard. In terms of epidemic diseases, the Mediterranean can become a biological time bomb. The trees will be dying around the coasts, suffocated or poisoned by polluted sea winds.

The coastal area and harbors had always been polluted by industrial growth, but the increasing tanker use of the sea in the 1960s greatly exacerbated the problems. There were now tactile tar balls on many Mediterranean beaches. Lacking any real information about the extent of pollution, the Mediterranean states requested the United Nations Environment Programme (UNEP) to develop a program for evaluating the extent of the problem, determining its sources, and controlling them. In 1975 sixteen Mediterranean governments approved the Mediterranean Action Plan (Med Plan). Twelve years later a greatly expanded program is in place "to take all appropriate measures . . . to prevent, abate, and combat pollution . . . and to protect and enhance the marine environment."

The Med Plan consists of an interconnected set of four components: regional treaties; coordinated research and monitoring; integrated planning; and administrative and budgetary support. Beginning in 1976 with seven pilot monitoring and research projects, a protocol banning marine dumping, another protocol urging cooperation in case of oil spills, and a framework convention, the participating states have now developed a far more comprehensive program. They completed the first phase of studying pollution in the region, and established the monitoring program as a

Sources of Pollution in the Mediterranean

Land-Based Sources of Marine Pollution: The Mediterranean

Peter M. Haas, Saving the Mediterranean, Columbia University Press, 1990.

continuing institution supported by governments rather than by international organizations. They established regional centers to coordinate oil spill management actions, the preservation of species, integrated development planning, and studies of development projects of specific interest to developing states. A coordinating headquarters unit was established in Athens, with a Mediterranean staff supported by annual contributions from all the Mediterranean countries. Governments meet biannually to review the program. The parties adopted legal agreements that establish marine parks to preserve endangered marine species and to ban pollution from land-based sources.

The Land-Based Sources Protocol, which was signed in 1980 and entered into force in 1983, is the most important part of the Med Plan, as it sets limits on industrial, municipal, and agricultural emissions into the Mediterranean, as well as controlling wastes transmitted by rivers and through the atmosphere. Politically, the adoption of this protocol is the capstone of the Med Plan, as it was the most contentious issue negotiated between the developing (LDCs) and developed states (DCs). Controlling land-based sources directly influences industrialization policies, about which the LDCs are extremely sensitive. The protocol's adoption without significant alteration, and its subsequent ratification by Algeria and Egypt, who initially opposed it, demonstrates a dramatic change from considering environmental protection and economic development as incompatible goals to accepting an uneasy balance between them.

These Med Plan efforts at marine pollution control have become more comprehensive over time. By 1982 many more pollutants were covered by the protocols than were included initially. The sources of pollution that were regulated grew from oil pollution from tankers to land-based emissions from industry, municipal sewers, and agricultural spraying. Initially treating only pollutants that were dumped directly into the sea and transmitted by Mediterranean currents, the Med Plan came to cover pollution that is transmitted by major rivers to the sea and blown through the atmosphere. Its strength grew from an exhortatory framework convention in 1976 to a set of controls over specific substances by 1983. . . .

Legal Component

The legal component of the Med Plan was underway by February 1976 in Barcelona, as twelve states signed the umbrella Convention for the Protection of the Mediterranean Sea Against Pollution (the Barcelona convention), the Protocol for the Prevention of Pollution of the Mediterranean Sea by Dumping from Ships and Aircraft. . . .

THE BARCELONA CONVENTION AND PROTOCOLS

The Barcelona convention laid out states' general commitment to protect the Mediterranean from pollution and specified forms of pollution that countries would seek to control. It commits states to a continuing program encompassing the development of future legal agreements to control pollution by dumping from ships and aircraft, from discharges from ships, and from land-based sources; to cooperate in dealing with oil spill emergencies; and to control pollution from the exploration and exploitation of the continental shelf and the seabed and its topsoil. It further provides for scientific monitoring and research and scientific and technological cooperation. . . .

The states quickly ratified the Barcelona convention and protocols, which entered into force in February 1978. By this time work was underway on the monitoring and research projects, providing an input of accepted scientific knowledge that stimulated action on protocols to control more sources of pollution. UNEP played a minor role in the Barcelona discussions, as states were dealing with relatively uncontentious forms of pollution. As they came to deal with the more difficult land-based sources, UNEP's influence in the form of agreements grew as it authorized the drafting of the protocol and supplied information to delegates in order to persuade them to support it.

THE LAND-BASED SOURCES PROTOCOL

With the Land-Based Sources Protocol, the Mediterranean countries directed their attention to controlling a new and important source of pollution. The treaty came to cover the entire gamut of land-based pollutants, banning a number of agricultural compounds used as fungicides, biocides, and pesticides (organohalogens, organophosphorous compounds, and organotins); it also covered some industries (various heavy metals and industrial compounds), thermal pollutants from energy generation, and municipal wastes. The protocol also came to include pollutants transmitted by rivers and through the atmosphere, and added many pollutants to the ones already regulated on the grey list of the dumping protocol. By supporting this new treaty countries agreed to adopt new industrial and agricultural practices, as well as building sewage systems.

UNEP was largely responsible for determining the range of pollutants covered by the protocol and the channels by which they are transmitted. Allocation of the cost of their control was accomplished through political compromise, although UNEP also played a significant role in suggesting the specifics of such compromises. . . .

Negotiations took three years. Countries first considered the draft protocol at a meeting in Athens in February 1977. Delegates were initially very leery about the principles, and, without the attention generated by the Med X report, would have been unlikely to continue the exercise. Legal discussions occurred in October 1977 in Venice, in January 1978 in Monaco, in June 1979 in Geneva, and at the final May 1980 Conference of Plenipotentiaries in Athens.

LDCs and DCs had recurring disagreements. Disputes revolved around the question of which channels of transmission would be covered; whether the protocol would cover new or existing installations; and whether pollution would be regulated by ambient or emission standards. . . .

The biggest point of dissension involved how the substances should be controlled: by emission controls, as preferred by the Europeans, or through the ambient standards advocated by the South. The crux of the protocol lies in Articles 5 and 6, which committed the parties to "eliminate pollution" by the substances listed in Annex I (the black list) and to "strictly limit pollution" by the substances listed in Annex 2 (the grey list). The LDCs, sensitive to the possible economic effects of banning the emission of a number of substances from their industries, argued that their coasts, because they historically had experienced less industrial pollution, were better able to assimilate emissions; hence the protocol should make reference to the capacity of the receiving environment to assimilate wastes. The industrialized countries, with greater coastal pollution, advocated the adoption of emission standards rather than the ambient standards supported by the LDCs. France and Italy were already committed to following emission standards under the EEC Directive on Pollution Caused by Certain Dangerous Substances Discharged Into the Aquatic Environment of the Community. . . .

LDC delegates were generally unaware of the actual chemical content of their industrial waste or of the health effects of these substances, but were afraid that these restrictions would impose unknown costs on them. For instance, Tunisia opposed placing fluorides and phosphorous on the grey list, because it thought that they were associated with phosphate mining, which Tunisia conducts along the Mediterranean coast. In 1978 UNEP had presented a comprehensive two-volume profile of the substances listed in the technical annexes (IRPTC 1978). In the face of such overwhelming technical support for the potential harm from such substances, LDC scientists accepted the need for their control, and convinced their foreign ministry counterparts to accept their inclusion in the protocol. . . .

The parties finally included the atmospheric transport of pollutants as an area of control, but deferred specific action on it until an unspecified point in the future "under conditions to be defined in an additional annex" (Bliss-Guest 1981). . . .

The emission/ambient disagreement was finally resolved at the Conference of Plenipotentiaries. Both sides had been adamant in adhering to their positions; the industrialized states were already committed to emission standards, and the LDCs staunchly refused to accept emission standards. The secretariat preferred emission standards because of their ease of application. Finally, at the Conference of Plenipotentiaries, the countries finally agreed to compromise by applying emission standards for the black list and ambient standards for the gray list, based on suggestions by the UNEP secretariat. The LDCs also insisted on reference to "the economic capacity of the Parties and their need for development, the level of existing pollution and the real absorptive capacity of the marine environment" in connection with the guidelines for the development of standards regulating the emission of the covered materials.

LDCs, who in 1977 were concerned that the protocol would be used to retard their economic development, were appeased by the differentiation between ambient and emission standards. These concessions by the Europeans effectively gave LDC industries a comparative advantage over their European competitors. Because the North African coast is not as polluted as the southern European coast, the application of ambient standards means that the LDC factories do not have to introduce pollution controls immediately for gray-listed materials, whereas European factories will.

The protocol was quickly ratified or acceded to by Algeria, Egypt, France, Monaco, Tunisia, Turkey, and the EEC. It entered into force in June 1983. . . .

The substance of the treaty—the actual pollutants that are controlled—was adopted by scientific consensus. Its conclusion was eased by political compromise, in which UNEP also had a hand.

In the case of the technical annexes, foreign ministry officials deferred to the authority of the region's marine scientists, who were responsible for its negotiation. Convinced by data provided by UNEP's epistemic community, these scientists accepted the urgency of managing a wide variety of pollutants. . . .

Within these parameters, the Land-Based Sources Protocol was completed by political compromise. The LDCs were assured that atmospheric transport and river transport of pollution, radioactive wastes, and technology transfer would be covered by the protocol, and that some ambient standards would be included. The DCs were satisfied by a full list of substances in the annexes that were largely consistent with EEC obligations, even though France had to accept some ambient standards and some controls exceeding those laid out in the EEC directive.

2. *The Montreal Guildines*

Consider the provisions of the 1985 Montreal Guidelines, which are nonbinding except to the extent that they may represent customary international law. What legal effect do they have in the Mediterranean? Do they adequately address the problems of land-based sources of marine pollution?

■ PROTECTION OF THE MARINE ENVIRONMENT AGAINST POLLUTION FROM LAND-BASED SOURCES: MONTREAL GUIDELINES

reprinted in *14 Environmental Policy and the Law No. 2/3, at 77 (1985)*

1. Definitions

For the purposes of these guidelines:

. . .

(b) "Land-based sources" means:

(I) Municipal, industrial or agricultural sources, both fixed and mobile, on land, discharges from which reach the marine environment, in particular:

From the coast, including from outfalls discharging directly into the marine environment and through run-off;

Through rivers, canals or other watercourses, including underground watercourses; and

Via the atmosphere.

. . .

2. Basic Obligation

States have the obligation to protect and preserve the marine environment. In exercising their sovereign right to exploit their natural resources, all States have the duty to prevent, reduce and control pollution of the marine environment.

3. Discharges Affecting Other States or Areas Beyond the Limits of National Jurisdiction

States have the duty to ensure that discharges from land-based sources within their territories do not cause pollution to the marine environment of other States or of areas beyond the limit of national jurisdiction.

4. Adoption of Measures Against Pollution from Land-Based Sources

1. States should adopt, individually or jointly, and in accordance with their capabilities, all measures necessary to prevent, reduce and control pollution from land-based sources, including those designed to minimize to the fullest possible extent the release of toxic, harmful or noxious substances, especially those which are persistent, into the marine environment. States should ensure that such measures take into account internationally agreed rules, criteria, standards and recommended practices and procedures.

2. In taking measures to prevent, reduce and control pollution from land-based sources, States should refrain, in accordance with international law, from unjustifiable interference with activities carried out by other States in the exercise of their sovereign rights and in pursuance of their duties in conformity with internationally agreed rules, criteria, standards and recommended practices and procedures.

5. Co-operation on a Global, Regional or Bilateral Basis

1. States should undertake, as appropriate, to establish internationally agreed rules, criteria, standards and recommended practices and procedures to prevent, reduce and control pollution from land-based sources, with a view to co-ordinating their policies in this connection, particularly at the local and regional level. Such rules, criteria, standards and recommended practices and procedures should take into account local ecological, geographical and physical characteristics, the economic capacity of States and their need for sustainable development and environmental protection, and the assimilative capacity of the marine environment, and should be reviewed from time to time as necessary. . . .

6. Duty Not to Transfer or Transform Pollution from Land-Based Sources

In taking measures to prevent, reduce and control pollution from land-based sources, States have the duty to act so as not to transfer directly or indirectly, damage or hazards from one area to another or transform such pollution into another type of pollution.[46]

Notes and Questions

1. If you were designing a convention to control land-based sources of marine pollution in the Caribbean, what lessons can be learned from

46. Guideline 6 does not prevent the transfer or transformation of pollution in order to prevent, reduce and control pollution of the environment as a whole.

experience with the protocol in the Mediterranean? What would the guidelines dictate?

2. Review the materials on the Great Lakes Water Quality Agreement and the changes in the agreement that have occurred from 1972 to the present. (*See* chapter 10). Does the Great Lakes experience suggest any issues and approaches for the Caribbean in addressing land-based sources of marine pollution?

3. The regional seas program of the United Nations Environment Programme was one of the most important outputs from the 1972 Stockholm Conference on the Human Environment. There are now UNEP conventions for most regional seas. The pattern has always been to require that one or more protocols to the framework agreement be ratified at the same time as the convention. Thus, the Noumea Convention for the Protection of the Natural Resources and Environment of the South Pacific Region (SPREP) has protocols on dumping and on pollution emergencies that countries consider as part of the package in ratifying the agreement. What advantages and disadvantages do you see in this approach? Why is a protocol on land-based sources normally not included in the initial tranche of protocols for a new regional seas agreement?

XIV

Hazardous Substances: Wastes, Toxic Chemicals, Heavy Metals

Since 1980, there has been growing international concern about materials that are hazardous when stored or used within countries: hazardous wastes, nuclear wastes, toxic chemicals, heavy metals, and pesticides. They are of international environmental concern both because they move in trade across national borders and because their release and use may have harmful transboundary consequences. The issues are of special concern to developing countries, many of whom see themselves as the dumping ground for hazardous wastes and toxic chemicals. This chapter focuses on the international legal regime for hazardous wastes and the emerging regimes for toxic chemicals, particularly persistent organic chemicals.

A. HAZARDOUS WASTES

■ CLAMPING DOWN ON THE INTERNATIONAL WASTE TRADE

Judy Christrup
13 Greenpeace 8 (Nov./Dec. 1988)

Last March, a Norwegian freighter arrived on Africa's west coast to deliver its cargo. The manifest said "raw materials for bricks," and the

Guinean concrete manufacturer who received the shipment planned to use the dark ash for road building and cinder blocks.

The material proved less than adequate; newly-made bricks crumbled in the hands of the laborers. But there was another problem. Nearby, where the rest of the ash was piled, the trees were dying. The reason: the "raw material for bricks" was actually Philadelphia's burned municipal trash, incinerator ash laced with a host of heavy metals and dioxins.

How did contaminated ash from Philadelphia find its way into West Africa's bricks? The story is a parable for the toxics age. A Norwegian company, Bulkhandling, contracted with Philadelphia to dispose of a total of 250,000 tons of its municipal incinerator ash. Bulkhandling's original plan was to dump the lot in the Panamanian wetlands of Bocas de Toro as roadfill.

But Panama backed out of the deal after learning from Greenpeace that the toxic ash would pose a serious threat to their beautiful marshland, the last remaining Panamanian habitat for the endangered manatee and home to a variety of other wildlife, including sea turtles, ducks and jaguars. When the contract fell through, Bulkhandling had possession of 30,000 tons of the ash, 15,000 tons ended up in an Ohio landfill. The other half was routed to Guinea.[1]

. . . This is the international waste trade, a business that sends everything from household trash to PCBs [polychlorinated biphenyls] circling the globe. . . . Roughly 275 million tons of hazardous effluent are generated [in the United States] each year . . . a figure based on what one U.S. law, the Resource Conservation and Recovery Act (RCRA), classifies as hazardous waste. It doesn't include the thousands of tons that go undetected by the Environmental Protection Agency's (EPA) regulatory system. Nor does it include de facto hazardous wastes, such as the municipal incinerator ash that traveled from Philadelphia to Panama to Guinea, that isn't defined as hazardous by the law.

The rationale behind transboundary movements of hazardous waste is economic. The costs of disposing of wastes in compliance with domestic regulations in industrialized countries may be significantly higher than the costs of disposal outside the country. Developing countries may find the payments enormously attractive, especially when they exceed or nearly exceed a country's GNP. In other cases, countries simply need the hard currency that disposal of hazardous wastes provides, as in the former German Democratic Republic.

There are three basic approaches to addressing the growing international trade in wastes: to prohibit export and import of wastes; to regulate

1. Eventually Bulkhandling's agent (the Norwegian consul) and twelve government officials were arrested. Bulkhandling retrieved the ash to bring back to Philadelphia.

the trade in wastes, as by requiring prior informed consent; and to facilitate the trade in waste by eschewing international regulation. Countries have moved from the third approach, essentially a laissez-faire approach, relying on the second one, consisting of multilateral and bilateral regulatory agreements, and have been flirting with the first by agreeing to ban shipments of hazardous wastes from OECD (Organisation for Economic Cooperation and Development) countries to non-OECD countries. As you read the materials below, consider the legal implications of each approach from the perspective of industrialized, industrializing, and developing states.

1. The Prevailing Legal Regime

The 1989 UNEP Basel Convention on the Transboundary Movement of Hazardous Wastes, *reprinted in* 28 ILM 657 (1989) is the central multilateral agreement. We advise that you read the text of this treaty. The agreement provides that hazardous wastes can only be exported to a country with its prior informed written consent. Prior informed consent is also needed from each transit country. Importing countries have the right to prohibit the import of such wastes. In addition, each state must take "appropriate measures" to "[p]revent the import of hazardous wastes and other wastes if it has reason to believe that the wastes in question will not be managed in an environmentally sound manner." Article 4 (2)(g). If an importing state has given its consent, but disposal cannot be done in an environmentally sound manner, the exporting state has the duty to make alternative arrangements, including, if necessary, to reimport the waste. Trade in hazardous wastes is prohibited between parties and nonparties unless there is an agreement or arrangement in place between the two countries that is consistent with the Convention. Article 11.

■ INTERNATIONAL MANAGEMENT OF HAZARDOUS WASTES

Katharina Kummer, 47-48 (1995)
Reprinted by permission of Oxford University Press

Taking into account Decision II/12 of the Conference of the Parties, the fundamental principles of the Basel Convention, as it stands, can be summarized as follows:

(1) The generation of hazardous wastes should be reduced to a minimum (principle of waste minimization).
(2) Where it is unavoidable, the wastes should be disposed of as close as possible to the source of generation (principle of proximity of disposal).

(3) In a number of instances, the export of hazardous wastes is prohibited absolutely; hazardous wastes may not be exported from OECD to non-OECD countries, or from any party state to Antarctica, or to a state not party to either the Basel Convention or a treaty establishing equivalent standards, or to parties which have banned the import of hazardous wastes.

(4) In all other cases, transboundary hazardous waste movements must conform to the provisions of the Convention or a treaty establishing equivalent standards, or to parties which have banned the import of hazardous wastes.

(5) The cornerstone of this regulatory system is the prior informed consent (PIC) of the prospective states of import and transit.

(6) Hazardous wastes that have been exported illegally, as well as legally exported hazardous wastes that cannot be safely disposed of in the state of destination, must be re-imported into the state of origin.

Because of disagreements during the negotiations, the principles outlined above have not been consistently followed throughout the Convention. Sometimes they have been weakened or modified. *See* Katharina Kummer, International Management of Hazardous Wastes, quoted above; *see also* Elli Louka, Overcoming National Barriers to International Waste Trade (1994). After the Convention went into effect, parties have further refined some aspects of the regime.

Notes and Questions

1. *Basic references.* For reference materials, *see* Transboundary Movements and Disposal of Hazardous Wastes in International Law: Basic Documents (Barbara Kwiatkowska & Alfred H.A. Soons, eds. 1993).

2. *The OECD-nonOECD ban.* The second meeting of the Conference of the Parties to the Basel Convention in March 1994 adopted a decision "to prohibit immediately all transboundary movements of hazardous wastes which are destined for final disposal from OECD to non-OECD countries" and "to phase out by 31 December 1997, and prohibit as of that date, all transboundary movements of hazardous wastes which are destined for recycling or recovering operations from OECD to non-OECD States." The decision permits a non-OECD state that does not have a national ban on importing hazardous wastes to inform the Basel Convention Secretariat that it would allow the import of specific categories of hazardous wastes from an OECD State, but only until December 31, 1997. Second Meeting of Conference of parties to Basel Treaty on Control of Transboundary Movements of Hazardous Wastes, adopted March 25, 1994. The United States strongly opposed the decision, and the process of adopting it was unusually bitter and devisive. What prompted this decision? Does it promote

efficient waste management? Equitable waste management? In November 1995 at the Third Meeting of the Conference of the parties, member states decided to amend the Basel Convention to prohibit all transboundary movements of hazardous wastes from states who are members of the OECD and the European Community (EC) and from Lichtenstein to all other states. The United States opposed this amendment, as it had the earlier decision. Decision III, 1, Nov. 28, 1995, UNEP/CHW.3/35. As of March 1998, only 16 countries had ratified the ban, and the amendment was thus not in effect. Can you argue that the ban is environmentally unsound decision? In thinking about that question, consider the excerpt from Theo Colburn, Dianne Dumonoski & John Peterson Myers, in section B.1, below. Note that the United States Supreme Court has forbidden states to prohibit the import of wastes from other states as a burden on interstate commerce. City of Philadelphia v. New Jersey, 437 U.S. 617 (1977).

3. *The United States and Basel.* While the Basel Agreement has been in effect since 1991, the United States is not yet a party as of mid-1998. The Senate has given its advice and consent, but the United States has not deposited its instrument of ratification on the grounds that the necessary implementing legislation to bring the United States into compliance with the agreement has not yet been passed by the Congress. The Resource Conservation and Recovery Act (RCRA) needs to be amended to give the United States the authority to prohibit export of hazardous wastes if they will not be disposed of in an environmentally sound manner abroad and to reimport the wastes that have been sent abroad for disposal in violation of the Convention. The Toxic Substances Act (TSCA), which regulates PLBs, is also implicated.

4. *The Amlon Metals* case. The case of Amlon Metals, Inc. v. FMC Corp., 775 F. Supp. 668 (S.D.N.Y. 1991) illustrates the difference that implementing legislation could make. While the United States corporation FMC contracted with the United Kingdom corporation Amlon to recycle nonhazardous wastes, the wastes that arrived in the U.K. contained xylene and other hazardous chemicals. British authorities ordered that the wastes be stored at Amlon's facilities, and Amlon sued unsuccessfully in both British and United States courts, with the latter finding no basis for jurisdiction under existing statutes. Amlon was stuck with the waste. If the United States' implementing legislation for the Basel Convention had been in effect then, the results may have been different because the United States district court would have been able to exercise jurisdiction over the contractual claims. *See* Sean D. Murphy, Prospective Liability Regimes for the Transboundary Movement of Hazardous Wastes, 88 Am. J. Intl. L. 24 (1994).

2. *Definition of Hazardous Wastes*

The question of which wastes should be included in the scope of the Basel Convention generated considerable debate during the negotiations and is subject to ongoing controversy. The convention adopts the concept of the 1985 OECD draft agreement on hazardous wastes (never finalized), which defines the wastes to be covered by reference to a set of technical annexes, supplemented by a provision that allows every party to determine, by national legislation, additional wastes that are hazardous. The relevant annexes to the Basel Convention are closely modelled on the corresponding annexes to the relevant legislation of the European Union and the OECD.

Notes and Questions

1. *Problems in defining hazardous wastes.* What problems do you foresee in defining hazardous wastes? How should a country treat wastes that are regarded domestically as nonhazardous but contain material that is covered by the Basel Convention? Suppose the exporting country considers a material as a hazardous waste, but the importing country does not, or vice versa?

2. *Distinction between recyclables and nonrecyclables?* One of the most controversial issues has been the absence of a distinction between "recyclable" and "nonrecyclable" wastes in the text of the convention. The Basel Convention defines "wastes" as substances subject to disposal. It applies to both wastes subject to final disposal as well as wastes exported for recycling. It does not distinguish between wastes based on the purpose of the export. This issue is particularly controversial for the recycling of scrap metal and other recoverable materials, much of which is shipped to other countries such as China, India, and Pakistan for recycling and recovery. A technical working group was established under the Convention to consider this issue.

■ OECD COUNCIL DECISION CONCERNING THE CONTROL OF TRANSFRONTIER MOVEMENTS OF WASTES DESTINED FOR RECOVERY OPERATIONS

(C(92) 39, March 30, 1992)

THE COUNCIL,

Having regard to Article 5(a) of the Convention on the Organisation for Economic Co-operation and Development of 14 December 1960;

Having regard to the Decision and Recommendation of the Council of 1 February 1984 on Transfrontier Movements of Hazardous Waste [c(83)180(Final)] which requires Member countries to control transfrontier movements of hazardous wastes;

Having regard to the Decision of the Council of 27 May 1988 on Transfrontier Movements of Hazardous Wastes [C(88)90(Final)] which defines "wastes," identifies those wastes referred to as hazardous wastes in relevant Council Acts, and sets out a classification system for wastes subject to transfrontier movements;

Having regard to the Decision-Recommendation of the Council of 31 January 1991 on the Reduction of Transfrontier Movements of Wastes [C(90)178/Final] which, inter alia, calls for delineation of such controls as may be appropriate for the transfrontier movement of wastes destined for recovery operations, clarification of the definition of such wastes and characterization of those wastes which may require differing levels of control;

Having regard to the Basel Convention on the Control of Transboundary Movements of Hazardous Wastes and their Disposal, adopted on 22 March 1989, and noting that most Member countries and the European Economic Community have become signatories to this Convention;

Desiring to conclude an arrangement or agreement under Article 11 of that Convention;

Noting that recovery of valuable raw materials from wastes has been an integral part of the international economic system and that well established international markets exist for the collection and processing of such wastes;

Noting further that many industrial sectors are already implementing waste recovery techniques in an economically and environmentally satisfactory manner, thus protecting limited virgin sources of raw materials, and convinced that further efforts in this direction are necessary and should be encouraged;

Recognising that efficient and environmentally sound management of wastes may justify some transfrontier movements of such wastes in order to make use of adequate recovery facilities in other countries;

Convinced however that, pursuant to the obligations set forth in the relevant Council Acts and compatible with the provisions of the Basel Convention, an appropriate system should be implemented to control transfrontier movements of those wastes destined for recovery operations;

Convinced that all persons involved in any contracts or arrangements for transfrontier movements of wastes destined for recovery operations must have the appropriate legal status to ensure environmentally sound management of these wastes; and

Recognising that work is now in progress within the United Nations Environmental Programme concerning the environmentally sound management of hazardous wastes.

On the proposal of the Environmental Committee:

I. DECIDES that Member countries shall control transfrontier movements of wastes destined for recovery operations within the OECD area as specified in Annex 1 which is an integral part of this Decision.

II. INSTRUCTS the Environmental Committee in co-operation with other relevant OECD bodies, in particular the Trade Committee, to review periodically the control system and the lists of wastes set out in Annex 1, taking into account the criteria listed in Annex 2, and to make any proposals it deems necessary for revisions of Annex 1.

III. INSTRUCTS the Environment Committee in co-operation with other relevant OECD bodies to review annually action taken by Member countries in pursuance of this Decision.

IV. REQUESTS the Secretary General to transmit this Decision to the Executive Director of the United Nations Environment Programme and the Interim Secretariat of the Basel Convention.

Annex 1

I. Definitions

For the purposes of this Decision:

WASTES are as defined OECD Council Decision C(88)90(Final) of 27 May 1988.

RECOVERY OPERATIONS means activities leading to resource recovery, recycling, reclamation, direct re-use or alternative uses as listed in Table 2B of the Annex of OECD Council Decision C(88)90(Final) of 27 May 1988.

TRANSFRONTIER MOVEMENT means any shipment of wastes destined for recovery operations from an area under the national jurisdiction of one OECD Member country to an area under the national jurisdiction of another OECD Member country.

RECOVERY FACILITY means an entity which, under applicable domestic law, is operating or is authorized to operate in the importing country to receive wastes and to perform recovery operations on them.

INTERNATIONAL WASTE IDENTIFICATION CODE ("IWIC") is the classification system specified and described in OECD Council Decision C(88)90(Final) of 17 May 1988.

EXPORTING COUNTRY means any OECD Member country from which a transfrontier movement of wastes is planned or has commenced.

IMPORTING COUNTRY means any OECD Member country to which a transfrontier movement of wastes is planned or takes place for the purpose of submitting the wastes to recovery operations therein.

COUNTRY OF TRANSIT means any OECD Member country other than the exporting or importing country across which a transfrontier movement of wastes is planned or takes place.

Notes and Questions

1. *Basel Article 11.* OECD Council Decision C(92)39, which is legally binding, qualifies as a Basel-consistent agreement under Article of the

Convention, thus allowing trade in hazardous wastes between a party and a nonparty (such as the United States), if both are OECD members.

2. A technical working group was established to consider the extent to which scrap metal and other materials destined for recovery are covered by the Basel Convention and the ban on shipments from OECD countries to non-OECD countries. At the fourth conference of the parties in Malaysia in February 1998, the working group presented two lists of wastes: those that are hazardous and those that are nonhazardous, with the first list defining those wastes that cannot be shipped from an OECD country to a non-OECD country under the convention. The lists did not define all scrap metals, most plastics, or paper as hazardous. The lists would thus allow most shipments of wastes for recycling in developing countries to continue.

Question: Why should scrap metal from OECD countries destined for recovery in developing countries be exempt from the the Basel Convention and thus from the OECD-nonOECD ban?

3. The Prior Informed Consent Regime

■ INTERNATIONAL MANAGEMENT OF HAZARDOUS WASTES

Katharina Kummer, 65-66, (1995)

As noted above, any transboundary movement of hazardous wastes which is not, in principle, prohibited, and which is in conformity with the general obligations, must be carried out in accordance with the Convention's regulatory system (Article 4(1.c) and (2.f)). This system, generally referred to as the PIC procedure, is regulated in Articles 6 and 7 and in Annex VA of the Convention. Party states must designate at least one competent authority responsible for administering the PIC procedure (see para. 18 below). The duties of the states involved, as outlined below, are to be carried out by their competent authorities.

. . .

The Position of the States of Export and Import

The state of export has the duty to notify the prospective states of import and transit of any intended transboundary movement of hazardous wastes. The state of export can either provide this information itself or require the generator or exporter to do so, through the channel of its competent authority. The information to be provided must be sufficiently detailed to enable the authorities of the states of import and transit to assess the nature and the risks of the intended movement; the content of the information is specified in Annex VA. Among other things, the reason for the export; the exporter and the generator; the site and process of generation; the nature of the wastes and their packaging; the intended itinerary; the site of disposal; the disposer; and the method of disposal as per Annex IV must be specified (Article 6(1)). In accordance with Article 6(6)-(8), the exporting state may, with the prior approval of the states of import and transit, allow the use of a general notification for shipments of wastes having the same characteristics and the same transport route, for a maximum period of 12 months.

In order to promote uniformity in this regard, the (then) Interim Secretariat of the Basel Convention prepared a form to be used for the notification of transboundary movements of hazardous wastes, which is based on the above requirements. Following a consideration of this form by the open-ended Ad Hoc Committee on Implementation, the Conference of the Parties provisionally adopted it, and recommended that states use it and provide comments to the Secretariat.

The state of import must respond to the notifier in writing, consenting to the movement with or without conditions, denying permission for the movement, or requesting further information. In its reply, the state of import must also confirm the existence of a contract between the exporter and the disposer, which specifies the environmentally sound disposal of the wastes. Copies of the importing state's final response must be sent to the competent authorities of all states involved in the transaction (Article 6(2) and (3.b)). The state of export may not allow the movement to commence until the notifier has received the importing state's written consent, along with the confirmation of the existence of the contract (Article 4(1.c), Article 6(2) and (3)). The Convention gives no time limit for the response by the importing state. Since the consent of the importing state has to be explicit and unconditional, a movement may not be permitted to commence if *no* response is given by that state. After the completion of the disposal operation, the exporter and the exporting state must be informed accordingly (Article 6(9)).

This regulation is very detailed; however, some points are again left open. For example, there is no requirement for the state of export to verify the contents of the contract concluded between the exporter and the disposer; the transaction may commence on the basis of mere confirmation of its existence.

Questions

Foreseeable problems with the informed consent regime. What problems do you foresee in implementing the prior informed consent regime for transboundary movements of hazardous wastes? Would it make a difference whether the shipments were between industrialized countries, such as Canada and the United States, or between an industrialized country, such as Italy, and a developing one?

4. Disposal in an Environmentally Sound Manner

■ INTERNATIONAL MANAGEMENT OF HAZARDOUS WASTES

Katharina Kummer, 56-58, (1995)

Parties must require that hazardous wastes subject to transboundary movement are managed in an environmentally sound manner, whatever the place of their disposal (Article 4(8)). Thus, in accordance with the principle of nondiscrimination, the same rules and standards must be applied to hazardous wastes moved out of the state of generation as to those disposed of domestically. Article 4(10) prohibits the transfer, "under any circumstances," of the generating state's obligation to ensure environmentally sound management of hazardous wastes to the states of import or transit. By implication, the duty to ensure environmentally sound management is thus allocated primarily to the generating state. That state may not allow the export of hazardous wastes if is has "reason to believe" that their environmentally sound management and disposal would not be guaranteed in the prospective state of import (Article 4(2.e)). The Basel Convention does not specify the manner or the extent to which the state of export must verify this. It does not give the exporting state the right of active verification, e.g., by means of prior EIA of a disposal facility, nor is this right recognized by customary law, as we saw in Chapter I(F) above. Any such initiative might thus come up against claims to sovereignty by the importing state. Therefore, except where the lack of proper facilities is notorious, the term "reason to believe" must be interpreted to refer to the exporting state's conclusion based on relevant information received from the importing state. The prospective state of import has the parallel obligation to prohibit the import of hazardous wastes into its territory if it has reason to believe that they would not be managed in an environmentally sound manner (Article 4(2.g)).

The Basel Convention itself defines the crucial notion of "environmentally sound management" only in very general terms (Article 2(2) and (8)), a fact that has been criticized extensively. For the purposes of the Convention, this term means "taking all practicable steps to ensure that hazardous wastes or other wastes are managed in a manner which will protect human health and the environment against the adverse effects which may result from such wastes."

After the adoption of the Convention, additional efforts were made to give more concrete content to the notion of environmentally sound management of hazardous wastes. In accordance with Article 4(8) and Resolution 8 of the Basel Conference, work on a set of technical guidelines for the environmentally sound management of hazardous wastes has made significant progress over the past years. An informal consultative meeting of experts in October 1991 developed a set of principles, parameters and matrices intended to help states with the assessment of the environmental soundness of disposal options, and with decisions on intended transboundary movements of hazardous wastes. Subsequently, the Executive Director of UNEP convened a Technical Working Group, which now forms part of the infrastructure established under the Convention (see para. 18 below). Based on the work of the informal consultative meeting, and with input from the Convention Secretariat, the Technical Working Group has to date prepared two sets of Technical Guidelines. The first covers the four following waste streams, accorded priority by the Group: wastes from the production and use of organic solvents (Y6 in Annex I of the Convention); waste oils from petroleum origins and sources (Y8); wastes comprising or containing PCBs, PCTs and PBBs (Y10); and wastes collected from households (Y46 in Annex II). The second set addresses one recycling and two disposal operations, i.e., specially engineered landfill (D5 in Annex IVA); incineration on land (D10); and used oil re-refining (R9 in Annex IVB). The sets of guidelines form a part of the Framework Document on the Preparation of Technical Guidelines, which also provides guidance on their preparation. The main purpose of the Technical Guidelines is to provide governments and organizations with elements, criteria and principles which, applied together, constitute environmentally sound management of hazardous wastes.

Questions

Environmentally sound disposal standards. What standards should apply to determine whether the disposal might be in an environmentally unsound manner? Should United States standards for disposal of hazardous wastes in the United States be applied in this context to disposal abroad by United States waste generators?

5. Reimportation of Wastes

Under the Basel Convention it is important to distinguish between wastes that have been legally exported and those that have been illegally exported. In the case of the illegal export of wastes, the states of export shall ensure that the wastes are "(a) taken back by the exporter or the generator or, if necessary, by itself into the State of export, or, if impracticable, (b) are otherwise disposed of in accordance with the provisions of this Convention." (Article 9.) In the case of legally exported wastes in which disposal cannot be completed in accordance with the terms of the contract, "the State of export shall ensure that the wastes in question are taken back into the State of export, by the exporter, if alternative arrangements cannot be made for their disposal in an environmentally sound manner, within 90 days from the time that the importing State informed the State of export and the Secretariat. . . . To this end, the State of export and any Party of transit shall not oppose, hinder or prevent the return of those wastes to the State of export." (Article 8.)

Who has the primary responsibility for reimporting the wastes? If the wastes were legally exported, does the exporting state have the affirmative obligation to take back the wastes? Kommers comments that "Article 8 . . . constitutes an innovative approach which does not as yet seem to be supported by customary law, or have precedents in treaty provisions." Suppose the wastes were illegally exported, would the exporting state have a duty to take them back? If the exporting country has such a duty, at what point in the country of disposal does the obligation begin—from the waste disposal site or only from the port of entry? Why does the answer to this question matter?

The United States and Mexico reached an understanding on the return of hazardous wastes under the bilateral Agreement of Cooperation Between the United States of America and the United Mexican States Regarding the Transboundary Shipments of Hazardous Waste and Hazardous Substances, which is memorialized in a letter of November 12, 1986, from the Deputy Legal Advisor to the United States Department of State to the Legal Adviser to the Secretariat of Foreign Relations of Mexico. The relevant portion provides:

> In accordance with Articles 4 and 9 of the Annex, the United States will allow reentry of shipments of hazardous waste and hazardous substances in compliance with domestic law where the exporter is responsible for the shipment. Further, under Article 9, the United States will readmit any shipment of hazardous substances that was not lawfully imported into Mexico when appropriate arrangements have been made with the U.S. exporter for return of the shipment and for its proper use or disposal in the United States or reexport to another country.

Does this language fully answer the legal issues raised above?

6. *Agreements and Arrangements*

There are regional and bilateral agreements that also address the transboundary movements of hazardous wastes, primarily the Bamako Convention governing movements in Africa, OECD Decision C(92)39 (*See* above), and the bilateral agreements between the United States and Canada and between the United States and Mexico. Some of the provisions in these agreements differ from those of the Basel Convention, and an important legal issue is the extent to which they are consistent with the provisions of the convention. Article 11 provides that

> Parties may enter into bilateral, multilateral, or regional agreements with Parties of non-Parties provided that such agreements or arrangements do not derogate from the environmentally sound management of hazardous wastes and other wastes as required by this Convention. These agreements or arrangements shall stipulate provisions which are not less environmentally sound than those provided for by this Convention in particular taking into account the interests of developing countries.

Notes and Questions

1. *Arrangements.* What form and context must an agreement have to satisfy Article 11 and thus to allow trade between a party and nonparty? What will be the relationship between Article 11 and the OECD-nonOECD ban if the latter becomes effective.

2. For reference materials, *see generally* OECD, Transfrontier Movements of Hazardous Wastes (1985); Katharina Kummer, International Management of Hazardous Wastes (1995); Eli Louka, Overcoming National Barriers to International Waste Trade (1995) (covers hazardous and radioactive wastes); Transferring Hazardous Technologies and Substances: The International Legal Challenge (Günther Handl & Robert Lutz eds., 1989).

B. HAZARDOUS CHEMICALS

Increasing attention has been paid in recent years to the threats to human, animal, and plant health posed by hazardous chemicals, including industrial chemicals, pesticides, and heavy metals. These chemicals include heavy metals, such as lead and mercury; industrial chemicals, such as PCBs (polychlorinated biphenyls, a family of chemicals used to insulate electrical equipment) and methyl isocyanate (which resulted in thousands of deaths in Bhopal, India); pesticides, such as DDT and chlordane; and herbicides, such as paraquat. There is a thriving international market in many hazardous chemicals, involving both developed and developing countries.

Hazardous chemicals play major roles in industry and agriculture and often have beneficial effects. The risks their use creates vary widely, depending not only on the attributes of the chemicals themselves but also on how they are used, the pathways through which people, animals, or plants are exposed to them, the characteristics of the exposed population, and the behavior patterns of members of those populations.

Concerns about hazardous chemicals have increased for several reasons. The Bhopal disaster in 1984, referred to above and described in detail in chapter 8, focused concern on single-event tragedies. Increased experience with chemicals such as leaded gasoline and some carcinogens focused attention on risks from longer-term exposure. Better understanding of bioaccumulation (the accumulation of a substance in the tissue of an organism over time), bioconcentration (the increased concentration of a substance in organisms as one progresses up the food chain, such as the concentration of DDT in bald eagles and peregrine falcons), the persistence over time of some chemicals (e.g., DDT and PCBs), and the wide geographic dispersion of chemicals (e.g., polar bears and humans in the Arctic have high levels of PCBs in their bodies) raised the level of concern about the potentially widespread effect of chemicals, even those used in low amounts. Improved research allowed moving beyond risk assessments based primarily on cancer risks to include other risks, such as interference with the endocrine system and developmental and reproductive damage.[2] Examining risks to different segments of society revealed differential risks that depend on inherent susceptibility or different behavior patterns. For example, children may have increased susceptibility, women and men may have different susceptibilities, and people who subsist primarily on locally caught fish may have higher than normal exposure rates to certain chemicals that bioaccumulate in those fish. Although our understanding of these and other aspects of chemical use has improved, much remains to be learned about these questions.

1. *The Problem*

The following excerpt addresses many of the effects identified above.

■ OUR STOLEN FUTURE

Theo Colborn, Dianne Dumanoski & John Peterson Myers
91-104 (1996)

[R]esearch over the past two decades has given scientists a good understanding of how PCBs travel through ecosystems and migrate over long

2. *See, e.g.,* Theo Colburn, Dianne Dumanoski & John Peterson Myers, Our Stolen Future (1996).

distances. Based on this knowledge, it is possible to imagine the journey of an individual PCB molecule. Though the specific route and events in the journey we are about to describe are hypothetical, the plot is a plausible scenario built from historical accounts and a myriad of scientific studies.

Our imaginary PCB molecule—a chemical known among scientists as PCB-153 because of the arrangement of its chlorine atoms—had already been around for some time before it set off on its global wanderings just after World War II ended. As the market for PCBs began to grow in the 1930s, the Monsanto Chemical Works expanded production at its plant in Anniston, Alabama, where it heated a mixture of the chemical biphenyl, a particular form of chlorine, and iron filings to create PCBs. During the spring of 1947, the workers at the Anniston factory made up a batch of PCBs containing fifty-four percent chlorine. As the chlorine gas bubbled through the heated biphenyl, six atoms of chorine bonded to one of the biphenyls in the tank, and PCB-153 came into being. After an alkali wash and some distillation to purify the newly formed PCBs Monsanto often sold the compound—which contained not only PCB-153 but dozens of other members of the large PCB family—under its brand name Aroclor-1254.

Almost half a century later, the PCBs made on that spring day might be found virtually anywhere imaginable: in the sperm of a man tested at a fertility clinic in upstate New York, in the finest caviar, in the face of a newborn baby in Michigan, in penguins in Antarctica, in the bluefin tuna served at a sushi bar in Tokyo, in the monsoon rains falling on Calcutta, in the milk of a nursing mother in France, in the blubber of a sperm whale cruising the South Pacific, in a wheel of ripe brie cheese, in a handsome striped bass landed off Martha's Vineyard on a summer weekend. Like most persistent synthetic chemicals, PCBs are world travelers.

Our imaginary molecule of PCB-153 that would end up in a polar bear in the high Arctic might have made its first trip by train. A few weeks after the manufacture of this molecule, the freight train carrying a shipment of Aroclor-1254 rumbled over the rails in New York State headed for a plant in western Massachusetts where General Electric manufactured electrical transformers.

These ubiquitous metal cans attached to electrical poles were an essential component in the growing grid that sent electricity from generating systems over high voltage power lines and into homes to power lights, radios, vacuum cleaners, and refrigerators—the wonderful new twentieth-century electric conveniences. The transformers made at GE's Pittsfield, Massachusetts, plant reduced the high-voltage current from the transmission lines into the lower voltage required by lights and appliances.

From General Electric's perspective, the PCBs were an ideal insulating coolant for their capacitors and for transformers used in situations where flammability was a concern. Because PCBs did not catch fire and burn, they offered a safer alternative to the flammable oil used in transformers before this new synthetic product was developed. The company had developed its own custom formula for transformers called Pyranol, containing Aroclor and oils which it blended at the Pittsfield plant.

With the postwar economic boom, the demand for transformers and other electrical equipment seemed insatiable. America was building new houses for returning GIs as fast as it could—houses that needed new appliances and increased electrical service. While it would be very difficult to retrace the precise sequence of events that led to the escape of our PCB molecule into the environment, we can imagine that the next step in its journey took place at Pittsfield and from interviews with a former plant employee and public records, we can reconstruct what might have taken place on a typical summer day. That summer the production line in Pittsfield was working at full tilt, and the Pyranol in the factory storage tanks did not sit around for long. On a steamy day in June, a worker reached for a hose at his workstation that was connected through underground pipes to storage tanks. After making a final check on the transformer he had been finishing, he opened the valve and filled it to the top with Pyranol. In a few days, our molecule of PCB-153, sealed tightly inside that new transformer, was heading back south by train.

The oil refineries in the west Texas city of Big Spring were also scrambling that summer to keep up with the postwar economic boom, for the explosive growth of suburbs was creating a new class of commuters who needed new cars and gasoline to power them. One of the city's smaller oil and chemical companies, now no longer in business, was moving as quickly as possible to build a new refinery complex, but the project had stalled for several months while the contractors awaited the arrival of back-ordered electrical equipment. The shipment of transformers from GE to the refinery finally arrived in July. Within a week, the distribution transformer containing the molecule of PCB 153 was installed and in service in a building that housed the control room for the new installation.

Not even a month had passed before a fierce August thunderstorm tore through Big Spring, filling the air with exploding thunder and leaping lightning that struck at several places during the short, violent storm, including the power lines supplying the refinery. As the power surge hit the transformer near the control room, it responded with a metallic thump and the building went dark.

The following morning, the refinery's maintenance supervisor lifted the cover of the transformer to inspect the damage. Seeing twisted, crumbled coils, he decided that the unit was beyond repair, so he asked one of his men to empty the unit and send it off to the dump. The maintenance worker complied, hauling the transformer to the parking lot. As he tilted the transformer, its oily contents oozed out onto the red dirt of the parking lot, and PCB-153 slipped into the greasy puddle. The worker reckoned the oil might help keep down the insufferable dust. Since PCBs have an affinity for organic matter, the molecule quickly attached itself to a dust particle.

But with the roaring winds of west Texas, dust never stays put long.

Four months later, a winter storm roared through and swept the molecule aloft. Stampeding curtains of dust drove toward the town of Tarzan, where they beat against barns and houses as the winds howled. The dust particle with PCB-153 rode the whirlwind, bouncing with the turbulence like a cowboy on a bronco. The wild ride ended when the dust particle sifted through the fine cracks around a doorsill and settled in a drift on the kitchen floor.

When the windstorm passed, the woman of the house surveyed her kitchen with a sigh. The fine red dust coated the windowsills and lay two inches deep before the door. With a weary efficiency, she took up her corn-straw broom and whisked the dust particle with our itinerant molecule into a dustpan. As it fell into the wastebasket, the dust particle sifted down into a crumpled, grease-stained newspaper page that the housewife had used to drain her bacon that morning.

By the end of the week, PCB-153 was buried under trash in a local dump, an informal affair in a ravine with a parched creek bed. Despite the rivulets that flowed down through the growing mountain of trash during summer thunderstorms, the molecule stayed put for more than two years, for unlike many chemicals, PCBs don't dissolve readily in water.

The late winter of 1948 brought a spell of heavy rains to west Texas. After intermittent downpours, the creek surged to life in the beginning of March and roared toward the trash that tumbled down the side of the ravine. The rolling waters took a bite out of one edge of the trash mound, exposing a cross section of the town's recent history and sweeping the greasy newspaper and the molecule from the transformer spill downstream. The floodwaters subsided the following morning, leaving the soggy newspaper sheet stranded on a sandbar five miles away. PCB-153 was clinging to a greasy blotch on the page, shielded from the light but exposed to warm spring air.

As the sun climbed higher and winter turned to spring, the lump of paper dried and slowly warmed. With the sun beating down on the paper in early April, PCBs suddenly began disengaging from the dust particle moving upward, floating into the air as a vapor. The PCB-153 was suddenly free. The journey that would end in the rump fat of a Norwegian polar bear had begun.

The molecule caught a warm gentle breeze from the southwest, wafting north and east over the shrub-covered expanse of east Texas toward the fragrant pine forests of Arkansas. . . .

During three weeks of unusually cool and cloudy weather, the molecule clung to a rotting leaf in a hollow on a rocky outcropping, but as soon as the sun reemerged and the temperature climbed, the molecule floated off again. It lingered over St. Louis for several days and sloshed about in a stagnant air mass. Then, as a Bermuda high developed off the southern Atlantic coast, a torrent of air rushed through from the south and swept the PCB molecule northward over the radiant green cornfields of southern Illinois toward the Great Lakes.

The air flow generated by the Bermuda high pushed north with the speed of a freight train. The molecule tumbled onward in a great white bank of cumulus clouds. But as the warm winds rushed through Chicago and out over Lake Michigan, they met a wall of cooler air because the Great Lakes, like any large body of water, warmed more slowly in spring than the surrounding land. In the night chill, the PCB-153 suddenly condensed back into a liquid state for the first time since it had left Missouri.

The breeze died just before midnight and the molecule settled on the dark water near the lakeshore city of Racine, Wisconsin. Like all PCBs, the molecule had a predilection for surfaces, so it lingered about on the boundary between the air and water, bumping now and again into other wandering members of its extended family. The molecule found it hard, however, to remain unattached for very long. Its strong attraction to organic matter drew it to a patch of algae, rootless plants that floated like a gauzy green veil near the water's surface. When the opportunity presented itself, the molecule grabbed on to one of the tiny plants and, clinging to its waxy surface, washed back and forth along the shoreline near the mouth of the Root River, moving with the vagaries of the wind and waves.

Plant-eaters, such as the water flea, nibbled around the edges of the green veil, and some of the plants ended up as their salad course, but the tiny plant PCB-153 was riding managed to escape and live its full life span—which lasted three weeks. The alga began to yellow and grow tattered around the edges. The dead plant grew water-logged and sank, carrying PCB-153 with it.

The dead alga settled on the bottom and was quickly covered by soil washing into the lake from a city dump at the water's edge. Accumulating sediment buried the molecule even deeper in the lake muds, and with each passing year, its chances of getting back into circulation seemed to grow slimmer. PCB-153 might be impervious to the attack of the bacteria that broke down most chemicals, but it could be entombed.

Persistence is viewed as a virtue in people. In chemicals, it is the mark of a troublemaker. The synthetic chemical industry helped bring convenience and comfort to American homes, but at the same time, it unleashed dozens of chemicals, including PCBs, that became notorious for combining the devilish properties of extreme stability, volatility, and a particular affinity for fat.

Besides PCBs, this lot includes the pesticides DDT, chlordane, lindane, aldrin, dieldrin, endrin, toxaphene, heptachlor, and the ubiquitous contaminant dioxin, which is produced in many chemical processes and during the burning of fossil fuels and trash. They ride through the food web on particles of fat or vanish into vapors that gallop on the winds to distant lands. In *Silent Spring,* Rachel Carson put the persistent pesticides at the top of her most-wanted list. It didn't occur to her to include compounds such as PCBs that may not be particularly poisonous (in the usual sense of causing immediate death or cancer) but are persistent—a fact scientists did not recognize until 1966, four years after *Silent Spring* was published.

The members of the PCB family that contain fewer chlorine atoms do have a few enemies, including two bacteria from the Achomobacter genus. But chlorine heavies like PCB-153 are impervious to almost everything save ultraviolet B radiation from the sun. Because of the way PCBs move through the environment, hidden in soil, sediments, animal tissue, and other places, these deadly rays only rarely encounter them. . . .

On a spring day in 1956, a monstrous rock came hurtling down into the stretch of sediment where the PCB-153 lay buried. As the shock rippled through the buried mud, the molecule sprang free in a burst of hydrogen sulfide gas that filled the water with bubbles. The molecule rode one of the tiny glistening spheres upward toward the light and air.

Within hours, the PCB-153 was lodged in the fat of a water flea that had gobbled it up while grazing along the surface. This was a fat-loving molecule's dream, a ticket to ride, and it would take PCB-153 to the top of the food chain.

The water flea acted like a filter, sifting tiny plants and the PCBs clinging to them out of the water while it fed, so as the days passed more and more PCBs accumulated in the body fat of the tiny animal. Less persistent contaminants do not build up in this way because animals can break them down into water-soluble substances and excrete them. Many PCBs, on the other hand, resist breakdown, and once ingested, they are drawn by their chemical structure to the animal's fat, where they remain indefinitely. Over its short ten-day life, the flea's PCB concentrations grew to four hundred times the levels in the water. When it was finally eaten by a small shrimp called a mysid, the water flea passed on this legacy of fat-loving persistent chemicals to its predator, and the PCB-153 moved a rung higher on the Lake Michigan food web.

In its life, the mysid would eat hundreds of water fleas and inherit a bundle of persistent chemicals with each bite. The PCBs riding in its fat, like PCB-153, found themselves in growing company that included not only their own chemical family but other persistent compounds as well, such as DDT and toxaphene, a pesticide used heavily then in cotton fields in the south. For a time, agricultural specialists thought toxaphene was an improvement over DDT because it disappeared quickly from the fields where it was sprayed. It was some time before anybody realized that it did not disappear at all; it vaporized and moved on. Much of it came sailing on the winds to the Great Lakes.

The mysid eventually became a meal for a smelt—a small, tasty fish that darts about in offshore waters in flashing silver schools. As the smelt gorged on mysids and other smaller critters, the persistent chemical concentrations multiplied seventeen more times.

Smelt were a particular favorite with the families that crowded into local eateries in Racine for the Friday-night fish fry, and over time, their body fat would also bear witness to the nights when they had popped down dozens of the succulent little fish with a side order of potato pancakes or dined grandly on lake trout or coho salmon.

The smelt containing our PCB-153 molecule cruised Lake Michigan for two years before it was ambushed by a lake trout. Now the molecule moved to the trout and rested in its fat for another five years until an angler hooked the trophy-size fish on the last day of vacation at a family cottage in Door County, Wisconsin.

The following morning, the trout, packed on ice in a cooler in the back of a station wagon, was heading eastward on the interstate toward upstate New York. . . .

Three days later, however, the fish ended up in the family's trash barrel rather than on a platter at the dinner table. . . .

A blizzard of gulls swirled around the trash collection truck when it arrived at a landfill outside Rochester. As the rank fish carrying the molecule tumbled onto the growing trash mountain, the gulls dove at it like shoppers at a half-price sale, squawking and jostling each other to grab a bite. In a matter of minutes, they had picked the carcass clean.

PCB-153 wound up in the fat of a female gull, which had spent more than a dozen years feeding on the fish in Lake Ontario, so the molecule simply added to her already substantial store of contaminants. In the Great Lakes food chain, the herring gulls occupy a spot just below the bald eagles, which sometimes nab a herring gull or two. By the time PCBs have moved this high on the food chain, the concentrations have multiplied to 25 million times the levels found in the water.

The following spring, the female herring gull headed for Scotch Bonnet Island, roughly one hundred miles east of Toronto on the Canadian shore of Lake Ontario. The gull and her mate quickly set their stake on a good patch of sand in the middle of the gull colony, a location considered preferable to the edges, where the chicks might be more vulnerable to predators. The pair courted and mated. Afterward, the female scraped a hollow in the sand and laid two large lightly speckled eggs that she dutifully set about incubating.

A tiny beak broke through one shell six weeks later, but the chick could only muster feeble pecks and it died, seemingly from exhaustion. The other egg showed no signs of life at all, but the pair stayed on the nest for another week. The mother finally abandoned the nest without fledging a single offspring.

PCB-153 and its relatives had passed from the mother gull into the yolk of the lifeless egg and had contributed to its death, along with DDT, dioxin, and other contaminants. A skunk carted off the rotting egg five days later but then thought better of eating it and dropped it on a rock near the shore, where it smashed. Some of the yolk spattered into the water, and PCB-153 was off on another trip up the food chain, this time via a crayfish—a small bottom-feeding scavenger that vacuumed up the bits of fatty yolk sloshing in the shallows near shore.

Before long, the crayfish that had dined on the egg yolk became dinner for one of the American eels that hunted at night in the weedy shallows. The eel is something of a contrarian when it comes to spawning. Many species, such as salmon and herring, spend their maturity at sea and then return upriver to their birthplace to spawn. American eels, on the other hand, frequent freshwater rivers and lakes most of their lives before finally making a long pilgrimage out to the Sargasso Sea—an area in the Atlantic Ocean between the West Indies and the Azores—to spawn before dying. Curiously, the eels migrating from the Great Lakes and other northern waters are all female, while those migrating from southern rivers tend to be males.

. . . The eel carrying PCB-153 swam onward for more than six months with a mystifying urgency before finally reaching the floating raft of sargasso seaweed that give this region of warm, salty waters its name. There beneath the clear tropical waters east of the Bahamas and south of Bermuda, a rolling congregation of eels, gathered from the Gulf Coast to Newfoundland, spawned and then expired from exhaustion—their long journey ended, their compelling mission accomplished.

The eel's flesh disintegrated quickly in the warm tropical waters, and PCB-153 sloughed off in a shred of fat that floated up to the surface of the Sargasso Sea under the intense tropical sun. In the heat, the molecule suddenly vaporized once more and, carried on prevailing winds, began hopscotching north. At any cold spot it encountered, the molecule condensed and settled on any available surface, only to be off again as soon as the summer sun warmed the surface. Alternating between liquid and gas, it rode the winds farther and farther north. The waters grew colder, making it increasingly difficult for the molecule to become airborne. Instead it hitchhiked on one of the small floating plants at the bottom of the North Atlantic food web, sweeping into the Gulf Stream and from then on north and east toward Iceland.

Two hundred miles east of Iceland, a small shrimplike creature called a copepod finally nabbed the plant and PCB-153 as it filtered a meal out of the rich waters of the North Atlantic. Five days later, a cloud of copepods was swept into a swift current that carried it quickly north and east like a giant conveyer belt toward the edge of the solid pack ice in the Greenland Sea, where a large school of Arctic cod had gathered to feast on the incoming bounty.

The gray green water boiled with the feeding cod, one of the most abundant species in high Arctic waters. As one of the small fish digested its stomachful of copepods, PCB-153 migrated to the fatty tissue near its tail, which already had a considerable store of persistent chemicals. The

Arctic food web, which includes the cod, is quite simple, but it includes many long-lived animals that accumulate significant amounts of contamination over a lifetime. For this reason, the Arctic food web concentrates and magnifies persistent chemicals to an even greater degree than that of the Great Lakes. Though far from a top predator, this cod carried PCBs at 48 million times the concentration found in the surrounding waters. Even so, the cod are still less contaminated than Great Lakes salmon because the ocean waters they inhabit are far cleaner.

Arctic cod spend the greater part of their lives feeding beneath the solid vault of ice that closes over high Arctic waters for most of the year. That season, the cod carrying PCB-153 followed the shifting food supply, and on the trail of a particularly abundant crop of copepods, it gradually swam toward the eastern part of the Greenland Sea. During the icebound period, ringed seals depend exclusively upon the schools of cod that wander beneath the ice.

It was only a matter of time before the cod carrying PCB-153 became a meal for a hungry adolescent seal that shot through the water, propelled by its powerful hind flippers. Like many seals searching for food, the youngster had wandered along a fracture in the sea ice west of the Svalbard Islands. The hunting had been good that winter, and the seal had added significantly to its ample blubber, which, despite its short life, contained not only PCB-153 but a high concentration of chlordane, DDT, toxaphene, and other persistent chemicals that were finding their way to the Arctic from all over the world. A seal eats hundreds of fish, ingesting and storing all the PCBs that had accumulated in them. For this reason, the PCB levels in the seals are eight times greater than in the cod, or 384 million times the concentrations in the ocean water.

Once the sea closes over with ice, the seals breathe through holes that they keep open by punching through at regular intervals with their noses. The great white bears can sniff out these holes from a remarkable distance, and they often hunt by waiting in ambush.

The young seal had just surfaced to breathe when a bear that had been waiting on its stomach near the breathing hole lunged out and, in a single continuous movement, flipped the 150-pound animal out of the water and onto the ice. The ringed seal died instantly in the attack by the five-year-old female bear, who had learned the hunting technique from her mother before going off on her own two and a half years earlier.

In thirty minutes, she had consumed the best parts of the seal—its skin and succulent blubber—and acquired PCB-153 along with considerable synthetic chemical legacy. The bear was quickly gaining weight because of the good hunting, so as she laid on more fat the molecule moved into her well-insulated rump.

. . . As she settled in for the winter, the fertilized eggs implanted in her womb and began to grow. In the dead of winter, two tiny pink cubs, weighing only a pound and a half each, slipped into the world unnoticed by their sleeping mother. Crawling across her creamy expanse, they found their way to her nipples and began nursing on her rich, fatty milk.

Throughout the winter, the mother and cubs all lived on the ample layers of fat she had laid down the previous year. As the fat melted away, PCB-153 was on the move again, this time into the breast milk of the female bear. The cubs were nursing greedily and growing rapidly. As one of the female cubs tugged at the nipple, the molecule shot into her from her mother with a blast of warm, thick milk.

No one yet knows how persistent chemicals like PCBs harm polar bears or how much it takes to cause damage. But given experience with other wildlife species, it seems certain that PCB-153 and other persistent hormone-disrupting chemicals pose a greater hazard to the developing cubs than to the mother who ingested the chemicals from the seal blubber.

The polar bear twins topped twenty pounds by the time the new mother emerged from her den into the honey light of the Arctic spring. They would continue to nurse for more than two years and grow to roughly four hundred pounds each on the rich diet of polar bear milk. With each meal, they would take in more of the persistent chemicals that had traveled thousands of miles to the remote Arctic. The concentrations of PCBs had multiplied 3 billion times as they moved up the Arctic food chain to the polar bear, the top predator and largest land carnivore.

A decade later, one of the twins may have been among the pregnant females who emerged from a den in Svalbard without any cubs of her own.

Question

Local or global threat. On the basis of the preceding excerpt, does it matter where a persistent organic pollutant is emitted in terms of its effect on health and the environment in a particular place?

For some harmful chemicals or harmful uses of chemicals, less harmful alternatives exist. Societies and individuals have already taken some steps to minimize the use of harmful chemicals. For example, leaded gasoline is banned in many countries because of the developmental and other health risks, especially to children, of lead; and there is a movement toward integrated pest management (IPM) to reduce the use of pesticides, herbicides, and fungicides in agriculture. Nevertheless, international efforts are underway at the global, regional, and bilateral levels to confront risks from hazardous chemicals cooperatively and to increase our understanding of them.

The following excerpt discusses some of the pathways by which exposure to hazardous chemicals occurs and international efforts to address this set of issues.

INTERNATIONAL COOPERATION TO ADDRESS RISKS FROM PESTICIDES AND HAZARDOUS CHEMICALS

Peter Lallas & Steve Wolfson
mimeo (1997)

B. Sources and Routes of Exposure

. . . The probability of exposure to harmful levels of pesticides and dangerous chemicals varies with each chemical and with each stage of the life-cycle of the product or substance. The discussion below reviews several different sources and routes of exposure, and some of the consequences of these exposures, in both developed and developing countries.

Transport of these substances can occur through air or by water, and often is helped along by human action such as transport, trade in dangerous or contaminated products (e.g., foods with pesticide residues), dredging of contaminated areas, and disposal activities. This long-range transport can occur as a result of a release in any of the life-cycle stages described below.

1. ACCIDENTS AND UNINTENDED RELEASES (ALL STAGES OF LIFE-CYCLE)

The adage "accidents will happen" certainly is true in the case of pesticides and dangerous chemicals. Some of the most serious incidents associated with these products result from accidents—whether in manufacture, handling/transport, use, or disposal.

The Bhopal disaster, noted above, involving a U.S.-controlled pesticide formulation facility in India, illustrates the extreme consequences of accidents involving dangerous pesticides. A number of other well-known incidents have captured headlines in recent years. These include:

- the 1986 fire at a chemical warehouse in Basel, Switzerland that sent toxic fumes into France and Germany and released toxic chemicals into the Rhine river, damaging riverine ecosystems and polluting water supplies downstream;
- the 1990 pesticide spill from a train into the Sacramento River in California, illustrating the potential risks during transport; and
- the poisoning of 20,000 Swainson's Hawks, about five percent of the world's population, in the Argentine pampas in 1995, linked to applications of the pesticide monocrotophos.

Concerns over the possibility of accidental releases are magnified by data indicating that production, transport and use of many pesticides and dangerous chemicals continue to rise. In the case of pesticides, EPA estimates that about 4 billion pounds of pesticide (by volume of active ingredient) are produced annually wordwide. The U.S. produces about 1 billion pounds, while other countries produce 3 billion pounds. More than 1400 active ingredients in over 60,000 formulations are in use around the world.

The production figures are even higher with respect to chemicals more broadly. As of 1990, there were more than eight million known chemicals. Approximately 70,000 of these are in common use, and as many as 1,000 new chemicals may come onto the market each year.

The data show a large increase in recent years in the volume of manufacturing of pesticides, for example, in developing countries such as India and China and certain countries in South America. Some of these new production facilities are owned by multinational companies. . . . At the same time, locally-owned production of pesticides in developing countries has grown in response to lively and profitable markets, including export markets.

Absent improved safety practices, increases in production, transport, storage, and use may translate into more accidental releases and more adverse impacts, both to humans and to the environment.

2. EXTRACTION OF MATERIALS: MINING

In some cases, dangerous substances are released at the first stage in the life-cycle of many products or substances: i.e., the extraction of raw materials. Most notable in this regard, perhaps, is mining for heavy metals, such as lead, silver, cadmium, zinc and others. Many countries throughout the world have active mine operations. In the case of many developing countries, these mines often are operated by large foreign companies (e.g., U.S., Canadian, Australian).

The mining process is a potential source of release of heavy metals or pollutants into the environment. Rain or floodwaters can quickly carry contaminant-laden tailings from mining operations into lakes or other waterways. Because these contaminants tend to be heavy and persistent, they often collect in sediments at the bottom of waterways. They can pose a risk to fish and birds that feed in contaminated areas, as well as to drinking water supplies. For many developing countries, mining can be a greater source of pollution than manufacturing or processing.

3. PRODUCTION AND PROCESSING ACTIVITIES

[Another] potential source of release of pesticides or hazardous substances comes during the production or formulation process.

A recent study of hazards in the workplace in Canada, for example, identifies a number of serious workplace health concerns posed by chemicals. . . . As with accidents, these occupational risks seem likely only to rise as rates of manufacture and use rise also.

Other data documents the serious occupational hazards posed by the use of lead in production activities. . . .

Manufacturing operations also release a wide range of chemicals directly into the environment outside the workplace. A particularly important concern in this regard is the release of dioxins and furans as unintended by-products of certain industrial operations. Operations which release these two substances as by-products include hazardous, industrial, medical and sewage sludge incineration, municipal waste combustion, combustion of fossil fuels and organic materials containing chlorine, certain metals recovery processes, pulp and paper production, and others.

More generally, according to data gathered by the U.S. Environmental Protection Agency as part of its Toxic Release Inventory, there were more than 300 toxic materials totalling approximately 2.2 million metric tons released by industrial activity in the U.S. in 1990. . . . While data for other countries is not readily available, recent figures indicate that Japan has larger emissions of heavy-metals than the U.S., and that China and India have larger estimated emissions than several countries of the OECD.

4. HANDLING AND USE (INCLUDING SPECIAL RISKS FOR FARMERS)

Pesticides, in particular, are released into contact with people and the environment at the stage of handling and use. Farmers who handle and use pesticides face particularly high risks of harmful exposures. Recent data cited by the World Resources Institute, in collaboration with the United Nations Environment Programme (UNEP) and the United Nations Development Programme (UNDP), indicates that pesticide poisoning "is disconcertingly common in developing nations, representing a major occupational hazard for farmers and their families."

Harmful exposures also occur in developed countries; however, the extent of harm appears to be much higher in developing countries. A 1990 study of the World Health Organization estimated that as many as 25 million workers in developing countries, or three percent of the entire agricultural workforce, suffer occupational pesticide poisoning each year. . . .

Pesticides extend their sphere of influence well beyond farmworkers to a much larger population. Studies in developing countries, in particular, indicate dangerously high levels of contamination in fish and on locally grown vegetables. Pesticide run-off from farming operations can pollute waterways, affecting aquatic life, birds and drinking water supplies.

The use or handling of certain other products or substances, besides pesticides, also can create serious risks of exposure and harm. This is true, for example, of products containing lead, asbestos, phosphates and other harmful substances.

5. RISKS FROM UNSAFE STORAGE AND DISPOSAL

Releases also occur at the stage of storage and disposal of products or substances. An important example of this is the case of obsolete pesticide stocks. In Kenya, for example, obsolete pesticide stocks total approximately 100 million tons and are left over from previous locust control campaigns.

More generally, the FAO recently identified more than 7 million kilograms of unusable and outdated pesticides in thirty-five countries in need of safe disposal. In many cases, the containers are corroded, leaking or unlabelled.

The problem also applies to developed countries. In the U.S., for example, dangerous discarded chemicals and pesticides are found in a number of hazardous waste sites throughout the country.

C. The Circle of Poison

In recent years, special attention has been given to one particular pathway for risks from pesticides: the so-called "circle of poison." This refers to the phenomenon where domestically prohibited pesticides which are exported can return in the form of dangerous residues on food items grown in other countries and imported for domestic consumption. Some have suggested this concern as a rationale for banning the export of domestically prohibited pesticides.

The extent to which such a risk exists is subject to debate. Under the Federal Food, Drug and Cosmetic Act (FFDCA), EPA sets, and the Food and Drug Administration (FDA) enforces, tolerance levels for the amount of residues of specific pesticides permitted on various food items imported for domestic consumption. If a pesticide is prohibited domestically on the basis of health risks to those who consume treated food items, the tolerance for that pesticide can be revoked. Thus, imports of food items with residues of such domestically prohibited pesticides would be subject to enforcement action by FDA, which monitors pesticide residues on food imports.

To the extent that exported pesticides do end up as residues on products that then move into international markets, approaches other than export controls could be employed. For example, . . . improved monitoring might be a more effective means of addressing any such problem than bans by individual countries on export of domestically prohibited pesticides. One reason for this is that even where unilateral export bans exist, food producers in other countries could obtain many domestically banned pesticides from producers in countries other than the U.S. This latter concern could be addressed at least in part, however, by "internationalizing" the bans so that other sources of supply would be similarly closed off.

. . . Perhaps a stronger basis for concern about exports is the evidence concerning the potential for exported pesticides to adversely effect health or the environment in other countries where they are used. . . .

Other types of transboundary impacts and concerns also can result from the production, transport, trade, use and disposal of pesticides or chemicals. Indeed, the discharge of chemicals used in production activities into international waterways or airsheds, whether by accident or not, has created a large number of bilateral or regional environmental issues and problems.

D. Regulatory Safeguards in Developing Countries

Third World importers have no way to effectively control trade in chemicals that have been banned or severely restricted in exporting countries.

The effects of pesticides and hazardous chemicals are felt in all countries where they are available (and beyond). The degree of impact, however, varies significantly according to a variety of factors. One major factor is the level of law, regulation and implementation capacity within an individual country where these products are available and used.

The nature and degree of regulatory control over pesticides and hazardous chemicals in developing countries varies significantly, as does the level of resources available for implementation and enforcement. In many cases developing countries have not yet developed rigorous controls and procedures to guard against the risks of these products, and/or do not have the resources to implement such controls. In some cases, regulatory systems are virtually non-existent. . . .

Many developing countries have not implemented systems to generate and analyze the information needed to assess the relative dangers of a particular pesticide or chemical. As noted by UNEP:

> It is not just a question of numbers. In most cases the problem is of information: how to get it, how to spread it, and how to make sure it is used properly. The greatest obstacle to our safe use and disposal of chemicals is ignorance.

. . . The lack of regulatory infrastructure is accompanied by poor handling and storage practices, and high-risk use techniques. Risks during transport, for example, are heightened in many developing countries by improper or merely careless storage and handling and improper labeling and packaging.

For example, labels that should contain warnings and directions for safe use may not contain complete information, or may not be read or understood by the workers who handle the pesticides. Workers often fail to wear protective clothing to minimize exposure in the handling and application of pesticides, even though many pesticides readily are absorbed through the skin or the lungs, particularly in the humid and hot conditions of the tropics. Extremely dangerous situations arise due to handling by careless, illiterate or workers, distribution of pesticides in inadequately protective containers, such as empty beverage bottles where they might be mistaken for a soft-drink, application by users unfamiliar with the necessary protective procedures in the mixing and application process, and inadequate warnings to people who live in areas where pesticides are applied.

Many pesticide operators do not have access to running water and are unable to clean up after appliciation, resulting in pesticide-contaminated clothing entering the home. Households often store drinking water and food in "recycled" pesticide containers. Many developing countries also lack the infrastructure (medical and otherwise) to respond to pesticide poisonings.

Accordingly, while health and environmental problems from pesticides and dangerous chemicals also arise in developed countries, they often pale in comparison to problems facing those developing countries that have not yet developed rigorous controls and procedures to guard against the risks of these products.

E. Trade in Toxic Products

The very large volumes of international trade in toxic and hazardous products is another key element of the global situation with respect to these products, and raises a variety of issues and concerns. In 1992, the global market for pesticides was valued at $25.2 billion. Global sales of pesticides increased at an average annual rate of 11.2 percent between 1960 and 1992. In terms of volume, it is estimated that approximately .4 billion pounds of domestically manufactured pesticides are exported annually. NACA estimates that about 9 percent of those exports are unregistered, or approximately 36 million tons.

. . . Developing countries, for their part, have dramatically increased their use of pesticides. In the 1940's and 1950's, developing countries accounted for only a small fraction of total global use of pesticides. Between 1972 and 1985, pesticide imports increased 48 percent in Latin America, 95 percent in Africa and 261 percent in Asia.

At present, developing countries purchase approximately 31 percent of global pesticide exports, in an amount exceeding $21 billion per year. In recent years, some analysts projected that by the year 2000 the market for pesticides will double in developing countries.

These increases in import and use are essentially the result of the adoption, by many developing countries, of the chemical-intensive, high-yield farming methods of the so-called "green revolution" of the 1960's and 1970's. This style of farming emphasizes, among other things, the development of large plantations to produce export crops, such as coffee, bananas, cocoa, cotton, pineapples, coconuts and sugar cane. The development of large, monocultural plantations with year round plantings of a single crop made crops more vulnerable to pest attacks, and led to increased demand for pesticides as an integral part of the new approach to farming. In addition, until recently many developing countries encouraged broader use of pesticides through domestic subsidies, agriculture extension programs, and tax incentives.

This style of farming essentially follows the patterns of farming adopted in many parts of the United States and, to some extent, Europe. Indeed, WRI/UNEP/UNDP, refer to

> [t]he galloping spread of Western-style intensive agriculture, coupled with the movement toward commodity agriculture and away from traditional subsistence farming, [that] has fueled pesticide use in developing countries.

These large commodity plantations provide export products and, accordingly, sources of foreign currency for many developing countries—often needed to repay large foreign debts.

A substantial number of pesticides exported to developing countries are banned for domestic use in the country of export. These include pesticides that have not been registered for use (rather than affirmatively banned), sometimes as a result of a withdrawal of the application for registration by the manufacturer.

The export of domestically banned pesticides is illustrated by the . . . exports of [a] domestically prohibited pesticide, chlordane, one of the most persistent and toxic pesticides ever made. Following cancellation of agricultural uses in the 1970s and cancellation of use for structural pest control in the 1980s, U.S. customs records show a ten-fold increase in exports, to over 3.6 tons *per day* between 1987 and 1990. A new study by the Foundation for the Advancements in Science and Education (FASE) compiled evidence of a significant volume of shipment of hazardous pesticides from U.S. ports between 1992 and 1994, including at least 25 million pounds of pesticides whose use is forbidden in the U.S.

. . . The situation in Africa is of particular concern. [A U.S. AID-sponsored study by Winrock International Environmental Alliance found] that many countries in Africa lack the capabilities or resources to control or even monitor imports of pesticides in the first place. Notwithstanding the existence of the United Nations voluntary program calling for Prior Informed Consent (PIC) by national authorities of the importing country prior to shipment, the study finds that many of the formally listed PIC materials (not locally produced) remain in sub-Saharan Africa. Evidence suggests patterns of illegal shipment and use of banned products, as well as misuse and overdosing. It also concludes that there is insufficient knowledge of international guidelines and codes of conduct, and that enforcement is a chronic problem.

2. *International Legal Initiatives*

There have been several important international legal initiatives in the 1990s to address problems of hazardous chemicals, persistent organic pollutants (POPS), and heavy metals.

In March 1998, states concluded three agreements: on the application of prior informed consent to international trade in hazardous chemicals and pesticides, on persistent organic pollutants, and on heavy metals. The first was negotiated under the auspices of the Food and Agricultural Organization at the United Nations and UNEP; the latter two were negotiated as protocols to the UN ECE Long-Range Transboundary Air Pollution Convention. All were opened for signature by states in June 1998. Together they carry out part of the mandate that states agreed to in Agenda 21 at the 1992 United Nations Conference on the Human Environment in Rio de Janeiro, Brazil.

a. The Historical Context and the Issues

The following excerpt provides historical background to the international efforts to address hazardous chemicals and pesticides, persistent organic chemicals, and heavy metals. Note the authors' discussion of the issues that were central in the negotiation of the 1998 agreements.

■ INTERNATIONAL COOPERATION TO ADDRESS RISKS FROM PESTICIDES AND HAZARDOUS CHEMICALS

Peter Lallas & Steve Wolfson
mimeo (1997)

A. Overview: The Evolution of an International Agenda

The problem of dangerous pesticides and chemicals is now prominent on the international environmental agenda. The adoption of Chapter 19 of Agenda 21 at Rio de Janeiro in 1992 marked a key moment in the defining the issue. Chapter 19 of Agenda 21 identifies six programme areas for action:

- expanding and accelerating international assessment of chemical risks;
- harmonization of classification and labelling of chemicals;
- information exchange on toxic chemicals and chemical risks;
- establishment of risk reduction programmes;
- strengthening of national capabilities and capacities for management of chemicals; and
- prevention of illegal international traffic in toxic and dangerous products.

Under the third programme area, Chapter 19 calls for implementation of existing voluntary Prior Informed Consent (PIC) procedures and consideration of expeditious work toward legally binding instruments in this area. Under the fourth programme area, it calls for "concerted activities to reduce risks for toxic chemicals . . . [that could include] . . . the phasing out or banning of toxic chemicals that pose an unreasonable or otherwise unmanageable risk to the environment or human health and those that are toxic, persistent and bio-accumulative and whose use cannot be adequately controlled."

The international community has been strengthening its institutional capacity to achieve sound management of chemicals. In 1994, the International Conference on Chemical Safety established the Intergovernmental Forum on Chemical Safety (IFCS), and adopted a set of Priorities for Action to indicate priorities for immediate actions and goals to be achieved over the longer term. These included a call to move forward on the possible development of a legally binding instrument on PIC.

The IFCS is now an ongoing forum for high level environmental policymakers from national governments to meet to maintain dialogue on international chemicals issues, and to help chart new courses to implement commitments in this area, including those under Agenda 21. The IFCS has placed special emphasis on including interested members of the public, both from environmental organizations and the affected industry. To date, its emphasis on open dialogue among key policymakers and the public is providing a unique forum to advance this agenda (i.e., DDT, aldrin, dieldrin, endrin, chlordone, heptachlor, hexachlorobenzene, mirex, toxaphene, PCBs, dioxins and furans).

In May 1994, the UN Commission on Sustainable Development directly addressed these issues, and endorsed the initial IFCS priorities for action. The Commission noted that efforts to control the risks of chemicals to human health and the environment "have not kept pace with the widespread and growing use of chemicals in all sectors worldwide." The Commission urged governments, international organizations and relevant nongovernmental organizations to increase efforts to ensure that chemicals are managed and used in a sustainable way.

In parallel to these events, UNEP and FAO established a "Task Force" on strengthening the legal basis of the Amended London Guidelines on Prior Informed Consent in January 1993. This Task Force was established under the existing Ad Hoc Working Group of Experts on the Implementation of the London Guidelines. The Task Force first met in September 1993 to discuss elements of a possible PIC convention.

Also in parallel to these discussions, parties to the 1979 UN ECE Convention on Long-Range Transboundary Air Pollution (LRTAP) commenced discussions on the development of new protocols to LRTAP to address POPs and heavy metals. A number of studies were developed to guide this work, which led among other things to the initial listing of 12 POPs that were subsequently endorsed by UNEP at the multilateral level.

These various discussions and meetings laid the groundwork for negotiation of what might be considered the two "flagship" initiatives in the near-term global chemicals agenda: a multilateral legally binding instrument on PIC, and a legally binding instrument on POPs. The formal decision to negotiate a legally binding PIC instrument was made at a meeting of the UNEP Governing Council in January 1995. In June 1996, an IFCS experts meeting issued a formal recommendation to the next meeting of the UNEP Governing Council to launch negotiations of a legally binding instrument on POPs, beginning with the UNEP list of 12 POPs.

B. A Legally Binding Instrument for Prior Informed Consent (PIC)

1. Overview of the PIC

The development of a PIC instrument is emerging as a major international initiative focused specifically on trade in dangerous chemicals as an important piece of the emerging international chemicals regime.

The PIC approach is based on the notion that exporting countries should ensure that importing countries have the opportunity to make informed decisions on whether or not to receive a pesticide that has been banned or severely restricted elsewhere prior to receiving shipments of those pesticides. If the importing country decides to refuse to receive a particular PIC-list pesticide, the exporting country's government is responsible for taking the necessary steps under its own laws to prohibit the export of the unwanted pesticide.

While actions by individual countries which are major exporters, such as the U.S., are clearly significant, the efforts of one country alone will not be sufficient to address this problem. Exports of hazardous chemicals from other countries can be just as harmful as U.S. exports. Therefore, the effectiveness of any policy that limits pesticide exports would be enhanced to the extent that other nations adopt parallel policies. Negotiation of a legally binding multilateral agreement to require Prior Informed Consent before export of certain dangerous chemicals presents itself as a means to achieve this goal.

2. Basis for the PIC Instrument

The current PIC negotiations build upon existing procedures of the FAO and UNEP for information exchange and notification regarding pesticides and chemicals that evolved during the 1980s. These include: a provisional notification scheme adopted for banned and severely restricted chemicals (1984); the FAO Code of Conduct on the Distribution and Use of Pesticides (1985) and the UNEP London Guidelines for the Exchange on Information in International Trade (1987, amended in 1989). The PIC concept was developed and incorporated into both the FAO Code and the UNEP London Guidelines in 1987. These instruments make the PIC procedures (and related provisions) voluntary, not mandatory.

The voluntary PIC procedure has been administered jointly by UNEP and FAO under the 1989 London Guidelines. To oversee the implementation of the Amended London Guidelines, which include provisions establishing the PIC procedure, UNEP and FAO set up an "Ad Hoc Working Group of Experts."

Under the voluntary procedures, participating countries identify chemicals that have been "banned or severely restricted" and submit a "notification of control action" to the International Register of Potentially Toxic Chemicals (IRPTC). IRPTC prepares a "decision guidance document" on the banned or severely restricted chemical and distributes it to the participating countries. The Guidelines define "banned or severely restricted" as covering chemicals for which all or virtually all uses have been prohibited by government action.

Once the decision guidance document has been approved and the chemical added to the PIC list, countries notify IRPTC whether they wish to accept shipment of the chemical, or wish that the chemical not be exported to their country. Any decision not to accept a chemical must apply equally to domestic production as well as import from other countries. IRPTC collects the decisions of importing countries and provides them to all participants. Exporting countries are expected to respect the decisions of importing countries within the limits of their national authorities.

The Guidelines include a number of responsibilities relating to trade in covered chemicals in addition to provisions for prior informed consent *per se.* These include provisions covering actions by importing and exporting countries, and technical assistance.

The voluntary system lacks a strong mechanism for monitoring compliance or for enforcing the commitments of the parties. Indeed, in the absence of any binding obligation for exporting countries to mandate compliance by exporters with the decisions of importing countries, the degree to which importing countries can be reasonably expected to undertake the expense necessary to implement the PIC system is questionable.

3. THE EMERGING LEGALLY BINDING PIC INSTRUMENT

Negotiations have commenced to transform this existing system into a legally binding instrument. . . .

[A] significant issue is determining what will be the criteria for including chemicals or other substances on the PIC list. In the past, listing on the PIC list is triggered by a threshold number of domestic measures that ban or severely restrict a particular chemical. The negotiators of the Convention will give close consideration to this issue.

The Convention should also improve on the voluntary system by including a mechanism for monitoring compliance and for encouraging adherence by the parties to the commitments embodied in the convention. Governments should examine carefully the various options to promote compliance, including, *inter alia,* the development of reporting obligations, a non-compliance procedure, and other provisions.

The question of how often consent needs to be obtained also deserves examination. Under current PIC procedures, once a country consents to import a particular PIC-listed product, it is not necessary for the exporter to seek or obtain consent for subsequent shipments of the same product. Some might argue, however, in certain cases, this could be inadequate to ensure full consideration of health and environmental risks. One such case might be where subsequent shipments are of a significantly larger scale than that for which consent was given previously.

Governments should also explore mechanisms to promote improved technical cooperation and assistance in the context of a PIC Convention, with a particular focus on enhancing the regulatory capacities of developing countries. Strengthened efforts in this regard will, over the long run, be an essential component to addressing environmental harms linked with trade in PIC-covered pesticides/chemicals, as described above.

Another major issue that remains to be addressed is how the convention will address non-parties. One commonly stated reason why other agreements have included special provisions for non-parties is to address the concern over "free-riders": countries that receive the benefits of a global agreement to address an environmental problem without being bound to comply with obligations in the agreement. Another concern is that the activities of these non-parties could undercut the parties' efforts to achieve the goals of the agreement.

In some cases, non-parties can also undermine the regime by putting parties at a serious economic or competitive disadvantage. For these and other related reasons, a number of other international environmental agreements, such as CITES, the Basel Convention, and the Montreal Protocol, contain trade restrictions against (non-complying) non-parties.

On the other hand, it might be argued that countries that import chemicals covered under a PIC convention are not "free-riding" if they simply decide not to avail themselves of the protection of the agreement. Moreover, impacts from shipments of chemicals to such countries might be primarily felt by their own citizens. In these circumstances, the rationale for imposing trade restrictions against non-parties might not apply.

Non-party exporters might pose a different set of concerns. These non-parties stand to potentially gain in trade terms from the restraint excercised by other exporters who comply with the Convention. Therefore, development of appropriate measures to discourage this type of behavior may advance the effectiveness of the Convention.

A related issue is the relationship between provisions in the PIC and the WTO/GATT trade rules. Countries certainly have the option of including provisions in the PIC that would supersede earlier obligations, as between those same parties. This "later in time prevails" rule would not apply, however, to countries that choose not to become party to the PIC instrument.

Alternatively, countries could seek to negotiate provisions that are not inconsistent with previous obligations. Finally, they could also choose to include a "savings clause" in the PIC that explicitly preserves some or all existing rights and obligations, including those under the WTO/GATT.

This latter course of action could be controversial in some quarters from an environmental policy perspective. There remains significant concern that the rules of the international trade system could be applied in an overly restrictive way that would hamper the ability to achieve environmental objectives. This concern would be amplified if the WTO would, in effect, sit in judgment on actions relating to the implementation of an MEA. Related to this, WTO dispute settlement bodies might not possess the technical and environmental expertise and perspective to make such determinations.

C. A Mulitateral Instrument on POPs

As described above, the essence of a PIC regime is to restrict the export of covered products where the country of import withholds consent for such export. A PIC system does not explicitly require that certain substances not be traded at all; nor does it establish controls on production or use of such substances.

Theoretically, one approach to address this concern is to expand the PIC to include provisions to ban the export of certain pesticides or chemicals that pose exceptionally high risks to health and the environment. This approach could take the form of an annexed "ban list," with specified procedures for including particular products or substances.

This possibility, however, has essentially been overtaken by the fact that the international community is now well along the path to developing a separate legal instrument on persistent organic pollutants, or POPs.

. . . The IFCS experts recommended specific international actions at the global level on POPs. Most prominently, the experts called for ". . . expeditious development of a legally binding instrument . . . initially beginning with the 12 specified POPs."

In this context, the experts recommended the rapid phase-out of production and subsequent remaining use of listed pesticides, subject to narrow provision for remaining "recognized uses" where alternatives are not yet available. In parallel, they recommended phase-out over time on a global scale of the listed industrial chemicals, with provisions to manage remaining use, storage and disposal in the transition to complete elimination.

With regard to those POPs that are generated as unwanted by-products (e.g., dioxins and furans), the experts recommended that currently available measures that can achieve a meaningful and realistic level of release reduction and/or source elimination should be pursued expeditiously. They also recommended that realistic action be taken to destroy obsolete stocks of listed POPs and to remediate environmental reservoirs, calling upon manufacturers and importing countries to work together to solve this problem on a priority basis.

These provisions will need to be designed in light of the particular issues presented by each substance, and with a view to facilitating implementation. As recognized by the IFCS experts, provisions will be needed to address special concerns of developing countries. In keeping with recent practice, major considerations are likely to include funding, technology transfer and division of responsibility in implementing commitments.

The task will be difficult. In some cases, substitutes will be more expensive in the short-term, or difficult to obtain. Recent experience in the U.S. suggests some of the difficulties in tackling emissions of dioxins and furans—difficulties which may be magnified in other countries with less access to needed technologies and pollution prevention techniques. Producers, traders, users, and others with specific economic interests will certainly be engaged. Some issues, such as destruction of stockpiles and remediation of contaminated sites, involve complex technical, legal and financial consideration.

. . . There will also be challenging issues of how to translate existing international principles into concrete approaches under a POPs instrument. For example, the Rio Declaration identifies the precautionary principle and the notion of common but differentiated responsibility for global environmental problems between developed and developing countries.

With respect to the precautionary principle, Rio states that where there are threats of serious or irreversible damage to the environment, lack of full scientific certainty shall not be used as a reason to postpone cost-effective action to prevent degradation. In the case of POPs, it might be argued that this principle should be invoked, for example, to support action in response to evidence of endocrine disruption effects of POPs, even though uncertainty remains regarding the health and environmental consequences of endocrine disruption.

Rio Principle 7, for its part, states that:

> States shall cooperate in a spirit of global partnership to conserve, protect and restore the health and integrity of the Earth's ecosystem. In view of the different contributions to global environmental degradation, States have common but differentiated responsibilities. The developed countries acknowledge the responsibility that they bear in the international pursuit of sustainable development in view of the pressures their societies place on the global environment and of the technologies and financial resources they command.

There is likely to be extensive discussion as to how this priciple is relevant to POPs, taking into account global patterns of production, use and release (which have evolved significantly over time) as well as questions of capacity and resources. One important issue will be whether commitments under the POPs regime should be "differentiated" among groups of countries. A related question will be how otherwise to structure the agreement so that countries that lack capacity are better able to implement its commitments: for example, through provisions on funding, technical cooperation, technology, and non-compliance procedures. Recent agreements such as the Montreal Protocol on Substances that Deplete the Ozone Layer and the Framework Convention on Climate Change, offer important references for this debate.

D. Regional Initiatives on POPs

. . . Under the North American Agreement on Environmental Cooperation, the U.S., Mexico and Canada in October 1995 adopted a Resolution for the Sound Management of Chemicals. The Resolution now calls upon the parties to complete regional action plans on PCBs, DDT, Chlordane, and Mercury by December 1996. In keeping with commitments of Chapter 19 of Agenda 21, noted above, the action plans should identify regulatory and non-regulatory measures to minimize exposure to these substances, and ultimately phase out those that pose unreasonable and otherwise unmanageable risks.

In parallel, the U.S. and Canada are nearing completion of a new, Binational Strategy for the Virtual Elimination of Persistent Toxic Substances from the Great Lakes Basin. This Strategy has gone through several stages of drafting, and was placed in the U.S. Federal Register for public comment in October 1996. The Strategy is designed to help implement commitments under the Great Lakes Water Quality Agreement relating to persistent toxic substances, and builds upon a number of bilateral initiatives in this regard in recent years between the U.S. and Canada. Among other things, the Strategy identifies quantitative targets for reduction of the use, discharge and release, as a result of human activities, of a number of substances of greatest concern, including PCBs, mercury, dioxins and furans, and others.

There have also been important commitments to strengthen regulatory capacity at the regional level. At the December 1994 Summit of the Americas in Miami, Florida, for example, thirty-four leaders of the Western Hemisphere joined in the adoption of a new, regional initiative and action plan on Pollution Prevention in the hemisphere. Among other things, the action plan calls for governments to strengthen technical and institutional capacity to address environmental priorities such as pesticides and lead, to further develop environmental laws and enforcement in these and other areas. In parallel, the U.S. joined with the leaders of Central American countries to make a separate, and similar set of commitments focused specifically upon the U.S. and Central America.

These commitments are generating new momentum for cooperative action to strengthen environmental laws, build capacity, and improve efforts to address priority environmental issues in a regional context within the Americas. They provide a major ongoing opportunity for work at the local and regional level to promote the international agenda on POPs and chemicals. . . .

Questions

1. *The precautionary principle/approach.* Is the statement of the precautionary principle (or precautionary approach) given in this excerpt adequate? Is it the only one that is possible? *See* Chapter 4, above.

2. *Silence as acceptance?* In a prior informed consent regime, should consent have to be express, or should silence on the part of the importing state be deemed to be consent? Should the answer depend on whether the importing state is a developing country or not? In Basel, does consent have to be express? In the UNEP PIC Guidelines?

b. The 1998 Agreements

As noted previously, three international agreements were concluded in March 1998, as this book went to press. They address hazardous chemicals and pesticides, persistent organic pollutants, and heavy metals, respectively.

(i) The Prior Informed Consent (PIC) Agreement

The Convention for the Application of the Prior Informed Consent Procedure for Certain Hazardous Chemicals and Pesticides in International Trade (PIC Convention) builds upon the nonbinding Amended London Guidelines for the Exchange of Information and Chemicals in International Trade of UNEP and the FAO's International Code of Conduct on the Distribution and the Use of Pesticides, which is also nonbinding.

Article 1 provides that the objective of the agreement is "to promote shared responsibility and cooperative efforts among Parties in the international trade of certain hazardous chemicals. . . . by promoting and facilitating information and exchange about their characteristics and by providing for a national decision-making process on their import and by disseminating these decisions to Parties." The Convention applies to banned or severely restricted chemicals and to hazardous pesticide formulations.

The Convention covers those chemicals that were already listed as part of the voluntary procedures preceding the treaty. As of June 1998, the Prior Informed Consent (PIC) list under the Convention included five industrial chemicals and seventeen pesticides that are banned or severely restricted. It also included five pesticides categorized as "severely hazardous pesticides formulations."

Under the Convention, states notify the Convention's secretariat of final regulatory actions regarding those chemicals that are banned or severely restricted for use in its territory, and the secretariat in turn notifies the parties. The parties decide whether to list the chemical in Annex III. All parties have to consent to the import of Annex III chemicals. Countries wishing to export chemicals banned or severely restricted by the territory of the exporting country, but not yet listed on Annex III, must notify the country of import and provide specific information, including safety data, with the export. No reservations to the agreement are permitted.

Questions

1. *Domestically prohibited goods.* Why is prior informed consent not required for the export of all chemicals that have been banned or severely restricted for use within the territory of the exporting country?

2. How does the agreement address the concerns raised in the Lallas and Wolfson excerpt?

3. *Effectiveness.* What problems do you foresee in making the Convention effective? Suppose you are exporting a banned chemical or pesticide to another country and want to be sure that the farmer who applies the pesticide knows of the dangers in its use. Would a legal obligation of the exporting country to notify the importing country be sufficient? What additional measures might be taken?

(ii) The LRTAP Protocols on Persistent Organic Pollutants and on Heavy Metals

On March 31, 1998, states who were members of the United Nations Economic Commission for Europe concluded two new protocols to the Convention on Long-Range Transboundry Air Pollution (LRTAP, discussed in chapter 9 above), which were opened for signature on June 24, 1998, in Aarhus, Denmark: the Protocol on Persistent Organic Pollutants (POPs) and the Protocol on Heavy Metals.

The first protocol (POPs Protocol) addresses the problem of persistent organic pollutants that resist natural degradation and cause serious harm to human health and the environment. As the excerpt from *Our Stolen*

Future indicated, the Arctic ecosystem and indigeous people who live on fish and mammals are particularly vulnerable to harm from persistent organic chemicals. Under the POPS Protocol parties agree to take effective measures "to eliminate the production and use of the substances" listed in Annex I (Article 3 (1)(a)) to ensure that the destruction and disposal of these substances and the transboundary movement of the substances are done in an "environmentally sound manner,"(Article 3 (1)(b)), to reduce the total annual emissions of each substance listed in Annex III from a base line year to be determined individually, and to use best available techniques to reduce emission for new stationary sources or alternative strategies that achieve comparable reductions. There are exemptions to the controls, including for laboratory-scale research.

Notably the POPs Protocol looks to public awareness and participation as a means to implement the agreement and encourage compliance. Article 6, Public Awareness, provides that the parties must "promote the provision of information to the general public, including individuals who are direct users of persistent organic pollutants" and notes that the information may cover risk assessment, ways to eliminate the use of POPs (as through integrated pest management), alternatives to POPs, and the economic and social impacts of the alternatives.

The Protocol on Heavy Metals obligates countries to reduce their total annual emissions into the atmosphere of the heavy metals listed in Annex I with reference to a base year of 1990 or an alternative base year from 1985 to 1995 as set by the country when it joins the agreement. The three heavy metals listed in Annex I are cadmium, lead, and mercury. Other heavy metals may be added by amendment. In addition, the protocol obligates parties to adopt the best available techniques for reducing emissions of the heavy metals for new and existing stationary sources or, in some cases, to adopt strategies to reduce emissions that achieve equivalent overall emission reductions. Annex III provides detailed guidance on determining the best available techniques for 11 categories of stationary sources of heavy metals.

Questions

1. *Implementation.* What problems do you foresee in implementing technology-based obligations to control POPs and heavy metals?

2. *The VOC Protocol.* Compare these protcols with the VOC Protocol discussed in Chapter 9. Note that the VOC Protocol had not yet gone into effect as of July 1998. Why might states hesitate in joining these protocols?

3. *Compliance review.* Both protocols contain a separate identical article (Article 11—POPs, Article 9—Heavy Metals) addressed to issues of

compliance. The articles provide that "[c]ompliance by each Party with its obligations under the present Protocol shall be reviewed regularly. The Implementation Committee . . . shall carry out such reviews and report to the Parties." What specific measures might be suggested to increase compliance with these protocols? (Review the materials in Chapter 9 on accountability and compliance.)

General Notes and Questions on Hazardous Chemicals

1. *Parallels.* In what ways do the problems encountered with hazardous chemicals parallel those of hazardous wastes?

2. *Developing countries and domestically prohibited goods.* What attributes of developing countries might make them more (or less) vulnerable than developed countries to risks associated with hazardous chemicals? Should countries ban the export of goods whose use is banned or severely restricted domestically?

3. International activities at different levels can reinforce each other. The issue of eliminating lead in gasoline is one example.This issue was not new, of course. Several NGOs, for example the National Resources Defense Counsil and Alliance to End Childhood Lead Poisoning, as well as governments and other organizations had been taking or pressing for action for years. In May 1994, the United Nations Commission on Sustainable Development (CSD) recognized the severe health impacts of human exposure to lead and encouraged further efforts to reduce human exposure to lead. In November 1994, the seven Central American countries and the United States reached agreement on working to eliminate the use of lead in gasoline, an agreement that was based on a joint statement to the same effect a month earlier by the heads of state of the Central American countries. Later that month, language was agreed to among all the countries in the Western Hemisphere (except Cuba) to do the same thing. These non-legally binding agreements—the CONCAUSA and the Summit of the Americas Plan of Action, respectively—were formally adopted by heads of state at the Summit of the Americas in Miami in December 1994. Dangers from lead exposure were considered by the Organisation for Economic Co-operation and Development in 1995 and led to a declaration to phase out the use of lead in gasoline except for narrow and specialized uses (e.g., race car fuel). The CSD further discussed lead issues in 1995.

In 1996, at the Second United Nations Conference on Human Settlements (Habitat II),[3] the entire world community agreed to "eliminate as soon as possible the use of lead in gasoline." The World Bank has become very active in lead abatement and elimination efforts; and its

3. Article 42(bb) of the Habitat Agenda.

statement that lead is the single most dangerous pollutant for developing countries was influential in getting the international community to commit at Habitat II to eliminate the use of lead in gasoline.

The 1997 Special Session of the United Nations General Assembly also adopted non-legally binding language regarding lead in its five-year review of Agenda 21 and UNCED.

What guidance does this provide regarding how to approach dealing with hazardous chemicals at the international level?

4. In 1997, the International Forum on Chemical Safety undertook a major study of chemicals that disrupt the endocrine (hormone) system—so called endocrine disruptors—which, among other things, threaten developmental and reproductive damage. Early scientific knowledge indicates that these synthetic chemicals pose unusual challenges to policymakers and regulators, not only because the chemicals (which include PCBs, dioxin, and furans, just to name a few) are so widespread but also for several other reasons: effects are often noncarcinogenic; effects may not be felt directly by the person exposed but rather by that person's offspring, sometimes several decades later; effects may be caused by a single hit at a particular time in development; effects may occur at extremely low concentrations (e.g., parts per trillion); and some of the chemicals may be more dangerous at low concentrations than at high ones. *See generally* Theo Colburn, Dianne Dumanoski & John Peterson Myers, Our Stolen Future (1996).

XV

Military Activities

Before and during all of recorded history, and sadly continuing through present times and for at least the foreseeable future, armed conflicts—whether international or civil—have been, are, and will be with us. They are among the characteristic endeavors of our species. Inevitably such conflicts disturb and damage the environment: sometimes merely incidentally or collaterally, such as the devastation wrought by a battle; sometimes purposefully, when one party seeks to destroy the other's means of livelihood; and sometimes perhaps even manipulatively, when changes in the environment *per se* are sought to injure the enemy.[1]

But as we will see, even in ancient times concern was occasionally shown to lessen the destructive effects of military activities on the environment, and with the recent surge in environmental consciousness, this concern has become a noticeable though probably rarely a determining factor in military planning and operations. While the considerations driving this concern are clear, two countervailing points of view should also be borne in mind: First, efforts to protect the environment, while people are strug-

1. *See* A.H. Westing, Warfare in a Fragile World: Military Impact on the Human Environment, Stockholm International Peace Research Institute (SIPRI) 1 (1980). *See also* J.P. Robinson, The Effects of Weapons on Ecosystems (1979); Protection of the Environment During Armed Conflict and Other Military Operations 69 International Law Studies—U.S. Naval War College (R.J. Grunawalt, J.E. King & R.S. McClain, eds. 1996); M.N. Schmitt, Green War: An Assessment of the Environmental Law of International Armed Conflict, 22 Yale J. of Intl. Law 1 (1977).

gling for their very lives or for the preservation of ideals that they value even more highly than life, must necessarily be futile. And second, the only way to stop or at least discourage wars is to make them as terrible as possible (e.g., the strategy of "mutually assured destruction"), rather than to regulate and tame them so as to make them "acceptable."

As will be evident from the material that follows, measures or rules to protect the environment during armed conflict are closely related and often derive from endeavors to protect other values threatened by military conflicts. These include: (1) the protection of people (e.g., civilians, disabled soldiers), which is the province of "humanitarian" law; (2) the protection of facilities (e.g., waterworks) required to preserve the lives of people or whose destruction would directly threaten such lives (e.g., a nuclear power plant); (3) the protection of private and public property in general from wanton destruction; and (4) the protection of cultural heritage, which falls at the intersection of humanitarian and environmental law.

Finally, while in a sense all combat at least temporarily creates an environment inimical to human and other life, as well as to precious objects, it is useful to try to distinguish between the dangers of the battlefield and genuine environmental degradation. Thus while flying bullets or even poison gases may make an area temporarily uninhabitable or at least inhospitable, nuclear pollution or even widely dispersed non-self-destructing mines may inhibit the utilization of that area for generations. In between these extremes are defoliants or other poisons, whose effects linger but fade within a matter of years. It will be seen that one of the complications of making warfare less destructive on the environment is the need to decide what types of effects are to be taken into consideration for this purpose. Where would you draw the line? The materials in this chapter may be of assistance to you in answering this question.

A. CASE STUDY: THE GULF WAR

■ WAR IN THE GULF: THE ENVIRONMENT; OIL THREATENS FISHING AND WATER SUPPLY

Robert D. McFadden

Copyright 1991 The New York Times Company

The New York Times

January 26, 1991

Section 1; Page 1; Column 3

Millions of gallons of crude oil spilling from a Kuwaiti offshore terminal could wreak major, lasting environmental damage in the Persian Gulf and could cripple fishing and desalting plants that supply much of the region's fresh water, environmental experts said yesterday. . . .

It is unclear how much oil has gushed from the Sea Island Terminal 10 miles off Kuwait, although Defense Department estimates ranged up to several million barrels, which at 42 gallons to the barrel would be more than 125 million gallons. If it is that large, it already rivals history's largest oil spill and has dwarfed the 1989 Exxon Valdez tanker disaster, which dumped some 11 million gallons of heavy crude into Prince William Sound, fouling thousands of miles of Alaskan shoreline and killing large numbers of birds and marine life.

The size of a spill is not always a gauge of its potential harm. The world's largest spill, a 1979 oil well blowout in the Gulf of Mexico, released 140 million gallons but had almost no impact because currents and winds kept it at sea. In contrast, the 1979 Amoco Cadiz spill of 68 million gallons in the English Channel wiped out whole species and communities of marine life along the coast of Brittany. The Persian Gulf, being all but landlocked, appears to be highly vulnerable. . . .

■ WAR IN THE GULF: THE FOULED SEA; RELENTLESS TIDE OF OIL FOULS SHORES OF EMPTY SAUDI CITY

R. W. Apple Jr., Special to The New York Times

The New York Times
January 28, 1991
Section A; Page 1; Column 3

KHAFJI, Saudi Arabia, Jan. 27—The cormorants, usually among nature's more elegant creatures, with their long necks and alert faces, looked like despondent hobos in their coats of thick, black sludge.

They could no longer fly. They could no longer even hop over a foot-high concrete curb. Near death, they teetered along in the lee of a pier, glancing frantically about. These two were the last pair alive on this particular stretch of beach, three miles south of the Kuwaiti border.

Seven other cormorants lay dead nearby, their feathers matted with oil and sand. A little farther down the strand, a pair of ducks sat as immobile as hunters' decoys, unable even to turn their heads, their eyes glassy.

"A preview of much worse things to come," said a Saudi official named Ibrahim, who asked that the rest of his name not be used, as he surveyed the stark seaside scene. "The oil will kill everything in its path."

"Scorched Ocean Policy"

A ranking American officer based here spoke bitterly of "Saddam's scorched-ocean policy." . . .

■ AFTER THE WAR: THE ENVIRONMENT; BURNING WELLS TURN KUWAIT INTO LAND OF OILY BLACKNESS

Donatella Lorch, Special to The New York Times

The New York Times
March 6, 1991
Section A; Page 1; Column 4

KUWAIT CITY, March 5—Barely 10 miles south of Kuwait City, the sun disappears and black oily soot settles on passing cars and coats the flat desert scrub.

Vast reaches of flame shoot into layered billows of pitch black smoke. Even the black and white cows that graze on the brush have turned gray and blend into the darkness.

If the wind blows north, Kuwait City gets buried in a cloud so dark that even at midday, motorists must turn on their headlights.

Desert Around Wells is Mined

This scene of eerie devastation is the Greater Burgan oil field, the largest oil field in Kuwait, that holds 684 out of 950 oil wells in the country. Kuwaiti Oil Company officials say all of them were dynamited by the Iraqi military forces the week before the ground war began. Most of the desert around the wells has been mined.

As four American concerns and a Canadian consulting company arrive in Kuwait to help put out the fires, the prognosis is dim. Kuwaiti oil officials say it will take at least 2 years before most of the fires can be put out and 5 to 10 years before Kuwaiti oil production is back to prewar levels. . . .

■ AFTER THE WAR: ANOTHER WAR BEGINS AS KUWAITI OIL-WELL FIRES THREATEN REGION'S ECOLOGY; BEYOND MIDEAST, BLACK RAIN AND ACID-FILLED CLOUDS

Marlise Simons, Special to The New York Times

The New York Times
March 16, 1991
Section 1; Page 4; Column 4

PARIS, March 15—Satellite images show that heavy pollution from Kuwait's burning oil wells is extending for hundreds of miles to the north and east of the sabotaged fields, and scientists say they have found traces of the soot throughout the Northern Hemisphere.

The enormous volume of gases and soot particles shooting into the air from hundreds of fires has caused acid rain in a region stretching from Bulgaria to Afghanistan and Pakistan, European weather specialists say.

But after watching the smoke and dirty clouds for three weeks, specialists have concluded that the pollution will inflict most of its damage in a 500-mile range, mostly above Iran and Iraq. Despite warnings of worldwide consequences, atmospheric specialists said the pollution was not likely to have a serious impact on the global climate.

OIL FIRE POLLUTION ASSESSED; WIND SAID TO DISPERSE MOST TOXIC SUBSTANCES

Michael Weisskopf, Washington Post Staff Writer

The Washington Post
April 4, 1991
Section A; Page 25

Burning oil wells in Kuwait are releasing up to 500,000 tons of air pollution a week, but brisk winds are dispersing the most toxic substances so quickly that all but the frailest residents appear to be spared any immediate danger, a U.S. government task force reported yesterday.

Levels of airborne particulates were measured at concentrations that, at least for brief periods, were more than 400 times higher than are permitted in the United States under standards enforced by the Environmental Protection Agency.

In the first official assessment of environmental damage caused by the six-week Persian Gulf War, the task force cautioned that health risks could increase dramatically with the onset of atmospheric inversions in the summer. Such a phenomenon would clamp a dome of stagnant air over the region, trapping pollutants now rising from raging wells of the tiny gulf nation at roughly 10 times the rate of emissions from all U.S. industrial and utility power plants combined.

The principal victims of such a meterological shift would be young children whose lungs are still developing and people with breathing problems who react adversely to pollutants, according to officials at the EPA.

"You never want to use another nation's misfortune as an opportunity for gain, but there's so much smoke from the wells that there are lessons to learn," said Jim Makris, the EPA's director of emergency preparedness who headed the eight-member task force that sampled the gulf's air during a recent 11-day visit.

With more than 500 oil wells set afire and millions of gallons of oil dumped into the gulf during the war, the region is considered a unique laboratory to study the environmental consequences.

According to a briefing paper obtained yesterday from the EPA, the oil spill caused "extensive damage" to coral reefs, sea turtles, marine mammals, sea grasses and large populations of migratory birds.

But the focus of the U.S. task force was on air pollution. Officials took 14 samples of the air over the oil fields, the U.S. Embassy in Kuwait City and residential areas immediately downwind of the conflagration. Special monitoring devices were used to measure levels of the three most common and feared byproducts of an oil fire—hydrogen sulfide and sulfur dioxide gases and particulate matter.

Unexpectedly, the researchers did not find high concentrations of the gases that can attack the respiratory system. Makris said they probably were diluted by very strong winds from the northwest.

But levels of particulates, including the smallest particles that can penetrate deep into the lungs, were much higher than the EPA's maximum allowable standard. Some levels in Kuwait reached 935 particles per cubic meter of air over a 20-minute period, Makris said. The EPA's standard for the smallest particles allows a maximum of 150 particles per cubic meter over a 24-hour period.

Local residents and U.S. troops stationed in Kuwait City have complained of headaches and eye irritation, Makris said. And a brief report issued by the task force noted that asthma and chronic lung disease patients "may experience exacerbation of their symptoms," warranting special advisories and precautions for them.

But "the situation does not appear to be life-threatening under current exposure conditions," the task force concluded, adding that "if meteorological conditions change . . . there would be adverse effects for those susceptible individuals."

Separate materials prepared by the EPA noted that about 15,000 U.S. troops in Kuwait are subject to "episodic exposure" to pollution from the oil fires. But none are stationed in the fields where the threat is greatest.

The task force said it was too early to predict the long-term effects. But in the EPA material, officials said that continuous exposure to high levels of pollution can cause irreversible lung tissue damage in children under the age of 12.

Makris played down the danger of the pollutants to neighboring countries. Particulates are now hovering less than 10,000 feet above the ground, far short of the 35,000-foot altitude where the jet stream could pick up the pollutants.

The EPA paper belittled fears of a long-term cooling from the pollution blotting out sunlight, a hypothetical phenomenon known as nuclear winter. But officials predicted a "significant change" in short-term weather, including a small intensification of monsoons.

The thick plume of smoke also is expected to reduce the amount of sunlight over farms, lowering crop production, the EPA paper predicted.

"Very near the source, the plume is dense enough that solar radiation is virtually cut off, so that plant photosynthesis is terminated while the area is shaded."

As you read the materials that follow, consider how they would apply to the actions reported above. Would these acts have been unlawful in the nineteenth century? In the early twentieth century? Are they unlawful today? If so, are they—or should they be considered—"ordinary" internationally wrongful acts (international "delicts") or are they more in the nature of crimes? If the former, what form would reparation take? Compensation? Punitive damages? Cleanup obligations? If the latter, are they crimes of the state of Iraq? Of Saddam Hussein? Both? How could any delictual or criminal responsibility be enforced or implemented? In your response consider that Iraq has suggested that smoke from the burning oilfields formed a protective cover that prevented airstrikes against Iraqi ground forces and that the oil spill discouraged attacks by sea.

It should, however, be noted that most of the dire predictions of environmental disasters turned out to be wrong or exaggerated—as already suggested by the last of the accounts, dated April 4, 1991. There was no detectable or in any event long-range effect on the global climate. Though the Persian Gulf remains somewhat polluted, there appears to have been no permanent destruction of significant marine life. The oil fires were put out—albeit at great expense—within a year. How do these subsequent facts affect your responses to the queries in the previous paragraph?

B. HISTORICAL BACKGROUND

1. *Pre-Modern Times*

Concern for at least certain kinds of flora during hostilities is not new. Among the many laws and rules Moses communicated to the people of Israel was the following:

> When you are trying to capture a city, do not cut down its fruit trees, even though the siege lasts a long time. Eat the fruit, but do not destroy the trees; the trees are not your enemies. You may cut down the other trees and use them in the siege mounds until the city is captured.[2]

2. Deuteronomy 20:19-20 (Good News Bible, American Bible Society, 1976).

Is this an "environmental" rule or one focusing on human sustenance? Is there a difference? Why did Moses draw a distinction between different kinds of trees?

Other leaders were not as careful to protect elements of the environment during warfare, and indeed sometimes ordered deliberate environmental destruction. Thus at the end of the Third Punic War, Rome not only had Carthage destroyed, but spread its fields with salt so as to prevent crops from growing and thus the revival of its historic enemy. More proximate both temporally and geographically, General Sherman's march to the sea towards the end of the American Civil War constitutes an example of purposeful environmental destruction designed to break the economic strength and the will of the adversary, in that case, the Confederacy.

2. *Mid-Nineteenth to Mid-Twentieth Century*

The beginnings of humanitarian law are often traced to the 1868 St. Petersburg Declaration prohibiting the use of explosive bullets, which, in spite of its narrow objective, introduced, in its preamble, the important concept:

> That the only legitimate object which States should endeavor to accomplish during war is to weaken the military forces of the enemy; . . .[3]

Though the historical and verbal context indicates that this rule was meant to apply to human lives and thus was the first general expression of the basic principle of humanitarian law, it is formulated broadly enough so that it was later recognized as also providing a basis for proscribing any purposeful long-term environmental destruction.

The next steps in creating a substantial body of humanitarian law were giant ones. They were taken at the 1899 and 1907 Hague Peace Conferences, which inter alia promulgated the 1899 Hague Convention II Respecting the Laws and Customs of War on Land and the almost identical 1907 Hague Convention IV on the same subject. Both these instruments were concerned primarily with the protection of human lives and only secondarily with that of private and public property. Nevertheless they set out the important Martens Clause (quoted in section C.3, below) which was formulated broadly enough to encompass environmental concerns once these entered the public consciousness; furthermore, they also contained important provisions protecting enemy property (quoted in section C.4 below), which can have the effect—though it was originally unintended—of proscribing

3. [St. Petersburg] Declaration Renouncing the Use, in Times of War, of Explosive Projectiles Under 400 grammes Weight, 138 C.T.S. 297-299; *reproduced in* Documents on the Laws of War 30-31 (A. Roberts and R. Guelff, eds. (1982)).

many attacks on the environment insofar as such attacks would damage and destroy protected property.

Finally, soon after World War II and as a consequence of that conflict—to date the most destructive one in human history—the four 1949 Geneva Conventions on Protecting the Victims of War were adopted, which recodified essentially the entire body of international humanitarian law, including rules proscribing the wanton destruction of property (*see* section C.4, below). Again, though there was still no overt reference to the environment, these provisions may be used, if there are no more explicit provisions binding the belligerent, to indirectly protect environmental values.

3. Post-Stockholm Conference and Post-Viet Nam War

As we have seen, it might be said that the dawning of environmental consciousness in the field of international law began only after the 1972 Stockholm United Nations Conference on the Human Environment. In relation to the development of the laws of war there was still a slight further delay, in that the most important military power in the world, the United States, was not interested in further developing that body of law until the Viet Nam conflict had been closed. Quite soon thereafter, however, a series of treaties were concluded that either were entirely devoted to the protection of the environment in warfare or were humanitarian law treaties that now for the first time specifically addressed environmental concerns: the 1976 Convention on the Prohibition of Military or Any Other Hostile Use of Environmental Modification Techniques ("ENMOD Convention");[4] the 1977 Additional Protocols I[5] & II[6] to the 1949 Geneva Conventions; and the 1980 Convention on Prohibitions or Restrictions on the Use of Certain Conventional Weapons Which May Be Deemed to Be Excessively Injurious or to Have Indiscriminate Effects ("Inhumane Weapons Convention").[7]

In addition, a number of nontreaty instruments, such as the 1982 World Charter for Nature,[8] promulgated by the UN General Assembly, contain provisions relevant to the protection of the environment in relation to warfare.

As a counterpoint to these efforts to provide protection of the environment even during warfare, there occurred a short but violent war that seemed designed to provide textbook examples of environmental warfare,

4. 1108 U.N.T.S. 151, 31 U.S.T. 333, T.I.A.S. 9614, 16 I.L.M. 88 (1977); Documents on the Laws of War, footnote 3, above, at 377.

5. 1125 U.N.T.S. 3; 16 I.L.M. 1391 (1977); Documents on the Laws of War, footnote 3, above, at 387.

6. 1125 U.N.T.S. 609; 16 I.L.M. 1442 (1977); Documents on the Laws of War, footnote 3, above, at 447.

7. 1342 U.N.T.S. 7; 19 I.L.M. 1529 (1980); Documents on the Laws of War, footnote 3, above, at 467.

8. A/RES/37/7 of Oct. 28, 1982, 22 I.L.M. 455 (1983); *see* section C.1 below.

consisting of efforts to wreak environmental destruction of higher magnitude than previous similar activities. This, of course, was the Gulf War. This conflict featured deliberate release of massive oil flows into the sea; the torching of hundreds of oil wells; the large-scale laying and abandonment of landmines; and the bombing of a nuclear reactor and of facilities for manufacturing or storing chemical and biological weapons—some of which were described in the Case Study.

Unsurprisingly, therefore, as soon as that war was concluded, and even before all the oil fires burning in Kuwait were extinguished or an assessment could be made of the long- and short-range environmental damage caused, numerous domestic and international studies[9] were conducted and meetings[10] convened to determine, first of all, to what extent the relevant rules of international law were adequate—obviously not to prevent what had occurred, but at least clearly to condemn it—and what supplementary measures should be considered. Although initially there appeared to be considerable enthusiasm for a major new treaty to consolidate, solidify, and advance all aspects of the protection of the environment in military conflicts (e.g., a so-called Fifth Geneva Convention), or at least for considerable improvements in the existing instruments, it soon enough became apparent that it was not easy to design new measures that were likely to provide significantly more protection to the environment and that there was actually little support among governments (and particularly their military establishments) for extensive new regulations of this type. As a result, the 1992 Rio Conference on Environment and Development passed up the opportunity to launch relevant new initiatives. Only at the Second ENMOD Review Conference in 1992 and at the First Review Conference of the Inhumane Weapons Convention in 1995-96 were a few modest advances made;[11] furthermore, 1995 saw the initiation of some major efforts to grapple with the growing problem of the spread of landmines—an incident of the many current low-scale, largely civil conflicts around the world.

9. *See, e.g.,* in 15:2 Disarmament: A Periodical Review by the United Nations (1992), three studies on Environmental Destruction as a Method of Warfare, by M. Bothe, Do We Need New Law?, at 101; A.W. Dahl, Environmental Destruction in War, at 113; P.C. Szasz, International Law Applicable to the Gulf War, at 128. *See also* the Report of the Senate Committee on Environment and Public Works: Gulf Pollution Task Force, The Environmental Aftermath of the Gulf War, Section 6 International Law and Iraqi Well Fires and Oil Spill, at 49-83 (March 4, 1992).

10. In particular, International Council of Environmental Law, Munich Consultations on Law Concerning the Protection of the Environment in Times of Armed Conflict, Munich, Dec. 13-15, 1991; Roundtable conference organized jointly by the Centre for Defense Studies, Kings College, Greenpeace International and the London School of Economics, June 3, 1991; Canadian Department of External Affairs and International Trade/United Nations, Conference of Experts on the Use of the Environment as a Tool of Conventional Warfare, Ottawa, July 10-12, 1991.

11. *See* section C.9 below.

Questions

1. *Are we making progress?* On the basis of what you have read up to this point, how far has the international community come from Moses's day in developing legal norms for the protection of the environment in times of armed conflict?

2. *Why the hesitancy?* Why would countries be reluctant to develop new, stronger regimes for the protection of the environment from such deliberately destructive acts as occurred during the Gulf War?

In the following section we will review the present state of the relevant rules of international law consequent on both the pre- and the post-1972 legal instruments, including some currently under consideration.

C. CURRENT INTERNATIONAL LAW ON THE PROTECTION OF THE ENVIRONMENT IN WARFARE

1. General Principles Relating to War and the Environment

In the absence of any general treaty or even declaration providing for the protection of the environment in warfare, there are only a few relatively scattered provisions that deal directly with this subject.

Additional Protocol I to the 1949 Geneva Conventions was adopted in 1977 after extensive negotiations under the aegis of the International Committee of the Red Cross (ICRC) and is—as explained above—basically of a humanitarian nature, as are the four 1949 treaties that it supplements. Nevertheless, reflecting the spirit of these times, it also sets out a number of explicitly environmental provisions, which constitute at present the strongest expression of an obligation to protect nature in warfare:

Part III—Methods and Means of Warfare
Combatant and Prisoner-of-War Status

SECTION I—METHODS AND MEANS OF WARFARE

Article 35 Basic rules

. . .

3. It is prohibited to employ methods or means of warfare which are intended, or may be expected, to cause widespread, long-term and severe damage to the natural environment.

. . .

Part IV—Civilian Population

SECTION I—GENERAL PROTECTION AGAINST EFFECTS OF HOSTILITIES

Chapter III Civilian Objects

. . .

Article 55—Protection of the natural environment

1. Care shall be taken in warfare to protect the natural environment against widespread, long-term and severe damage. This protection includes a prohibition of the use of methods or means of warfare which are intended or may be expected to cause such damage to the natural environment and thereby to prejudice the health or survival of the population.

2. Attacks against the natural environment by way of reprisals are prohibited.

Unfortunately, a number of important states, including the United States, have not yet become parties to Protocol I—in the case of the latter, probably in part because of these very provisions. For this reason, and also because of the relative recency of its adoption and the little practice in implementing it, these cannot be said yet to have become customary law.

In 1982, the UN General Assembly adopted, by an all but unanimous vote (opposed only by the United States, for several reasons that are here irrelevant), the World Charter for Nature, which contains the following two here-pertinent provisions:

5. Nature shall be secured against degradation caused by warfare or other hostile activities.

. . .

20. Military activities damaging to nature shall be avoided.

Though not a formally binding instrument, the World Charter, because of its extensive and careful negotiation and the large support it received on adoption, does constitute a soft-law instrument of importance for the development of international environmental law.

Unlike the 1972 Stockholm Declaration, which is silent on this subject, the 1992 Rio Declaration on Environment and Development adopted by UNCED contains the following provision:

Principle 24

Warfare is inherently destructive of sustainable development. States shall therefore respect international law providing protection for the environment in times of armed conflict and cooperate in its further development, as necessary.

Again, though not yet having achieved the status of customary law, this is a weighty instrument of which account must be taken.

Questions

The substance of Principle 24. How much real substance does this principle contain? Does it add anything new? If not, do you believe it was worth including it in the Rio Declaration? Why or why not?

Later in 1992, the UN General Assembly, reacting to the experiences of the Gulf War, adopted a resolution on "[p]rotection of the environment in times of armed conflict,"[12] the preamble of which recited that the Assembly:

> *Recognizing* that the use of certain means and methods of warfare may have dire effects on the environment,
>
> *Recognizing also* the importance of the provisions of international law applicable to the protection of the environment in times of armed conflict and, in particular, both the rules of universal applicability laid down in the Hague Convention respecting the Laws and Customs of War on Land, of 18 October 1907, with the Regulations attached thereto, and the Geneva Convention relative to the Protection of Civilian Persons in Time of War, of 12 August 1949, and the applicable rules of the Protocol Additional to the Geneva Conventions of 12 August 1949, and relating to the Protection of Victims of International Armed Conflicts (Protocol I), of 1977, and of the Convention on the Prohibition of Military or any Other Hostile Uses of Environmental Modification Techniques, of 1976,
>
> *Expressing its deep concern* about environmental damage and depletion of natural resources, including the destruction of hundreds of oil-well heads and release and waste of crude oil into the sea, during recent conflicts,
>
> *Noting* that existing provisions of international law prohibit such acts,
>
> *Stressing* that destruction of the environment, not justified by military necessity and carried out wantonly, is clearly contrary to existing international law,
>
> . . .

Questions

1. *The value of the resolution.* What is the effect of these statements? To put it another way, what is their authoritative value?

2. *Problem.* You represent an environmental NGO. If the governments sponsoring the resolution had asked for your organization's endorsement

12. A/RES/47/37 of Nov. 25, 1992.

of these paragraphs prior to its presentation to the General Assembly, would you have given it? Why or why not?

■ LEGALITY OF THE USE BY A STATE OF NUCLEAR WEAPONS

Advisory Opinion of July 8, 1996, International Court of Justice
1996 I.C.J. 66; 35 I.L.M. 809, 1343 (1996)[13]

[On July 8, 1996, the International Court of Justice issued its Advisory Opinion on the question contained in UN General Assembly Resolution 49/75 K of December 15, 1994:[14] "Is the threat or use of nuclear weapons in any circumstance permitted under international law?" In the opinion the court referred to several of the above-mentioned instruments and went on to state:]

> 29. The Court recognizes that the environment is under daily threat and that the use of nuclear weapons could constitute a catastrophe for the environment. The Court also recognizes that the environment is not an abstraction but represents the living space, the quality of life and the very health of human beings, including generations unborn. The existence of the general obligation of States to ensure that activities within their jurisdiction and control respect the environment of other States or of areas beyond national control is now part of the corpus of international law relating to the environment.
>
> 30. . . .
>
> The Court does not consider that the treaties in question could have intended to deprive a State of the exercise of its right of self-defence under international law because of its obligations to protect the environment. Nonetheless, States must take environmental considerations into account when assessing what is necessary and proportionate in the pursuit of legitimate military objectives. Respect for the environment is one of the elements that go to assessing whether an action is in conformity with the principles of necessity and proportionality.
>
> This approach is supported, indeed, by the terms of Principle 24 of the Rio Declaration, ...
>
> 31. The Court notes further that Articles 35, paragraph 3, and 55 of Additional Protocol I provide additional protection for the environment. Taken together, these provisions embody a general obligation to protect the natural environment against widespread, long-term and severe environmental damage; the prohibition of methods and means of warfare which are in-

13. *See also* section C.8, below.

14. Article 96 of the United Nations Charter provides that the General Assembly and Security Council may request the ICJ "to give an advisory opinion on any legal question." In addition, other UN organs and specialized agencies that are authorized by the General Assembly may request such opinions "on legal questions arising within the scope of their activities."

tended, or may be expected, to cause such damage; and the prohibition of attacks against the natural environment by way of reprisal.

These are powerful constraints for all States having subscribed to these provisions. . . .

33. The Court thus finds that while the existing international law relating to the protection and safeguarding of the environment does not specifically prohibit the use of nuclear weapons, it indicates important environmental factors that are properly to be taken into account in the context of the implementation of the principles and rules of the law applicable to armed conflict.

Notes and Questions

1. *The Court's contribution.* What is the legal effect of the Court's statements, set forth above? Are they merely quintessential examples of *obiter dicta,* in light of the fact that this is, of course, an "advisory" opinion? Could these statements be cited by one state against another in a subsequent dispute?

2. *The irrepressible Principle 21.* There is a modified version of Principle 21 in the above passages of the Court's opinion. Can you find it? Does the Court's version strengthen or weaken the original? What is the effect of the Court's having "restated" it?

3. *The environment and self-defense.* The Court is clearly of the view that the right of self-defense can trump environmental obligations. But it indicates that "environmental considerations" may impose significant constraints on a country's freedom to take measures of self-defense. Are these statements by the Court restricted to the use of nuclear weapons? Or do they have broader applicability?

4. *Other decisions of the Court concerning nuclear weapons.* You should recall in this connection the Court's decisions in the *Nuclear Tests* cases and concerning New Zealand's 1995 "request for an examination of the situation" as a result of France's underground tests beginning in that year. These cases are treated in Chapter 6.

2. *Environmental Warfare*

The so-called ENMOD Convention was negotiated in the Conference of the Committee on Disarmament (CCD) and adopted by the UN General Assembly on December 10, 1976, but so far has attracted only 64 parties, including the United States, Russia, and the United Kingdom, but not China or France or—and this was relevant in respect of the Gulf War—Iraq, which signed, but has not yet ratified the convention. Its principal provisions are the following:

The States Parties to this Convention,

. . .

Realizing that the use of environmental modification techniques for peaceful purposes could improve the interrelationship of man and nature and contribute to the preservation and improvement of the environment for the benefit of present and future generations,

Recognizing, however, that military or any other hostile use of such techniques could have effects extremely harmful to human welfare,

. . .

Article I

1. Each State Party to this Convention undertakes not to engage in military or any other hostile use of environmental modification techniques having widespread, long-lasting or severe effects[15] as the means of destruction, damage or injury to any other State Party. . . .

Article II

As used in article I, the term "environmental modification techniques" refers to any technique for changing—through the deliberate manipulation of natural processes—the dynamics, composition or structure of the Earth, including its biota, lithosphere, hydrosphere and atmosphere, or of outer space.[16]

In addition, ENMOD contains procedural provisions for consultations among the parties, including with the assistance of a Consultative Commit-

15. Though these terms are not defined in the ENMOD Convention itself, the General Assembly was informed of an understanding formally recorded by CCD as to the meaning of certain of these, as follows:

It is the understanding of the Committee that, for the purpose of this Convention, the terms "widespread," "long-lasting" and "severe" shall be interpreted as follows:

(a) "widespread": encompassing an area on the scale of several hundred square kilometers;
(b) "long-lasting": lasting for a period of months, or approximately a season;
(c) "severe": involving serious or significant disruption or harm to human life, natural and economic resources or other assets.

It is further understood that the interpretation set forth above is intended exclusively for this Convention and is not intended to prejudice the interpretation of the same or similar terms if used in connexion with any other international agreement.

See Understanding Relating to Article I [of ENMOD], 31 GAOR Suppl. No. 27 (A/31/27), Annex I, Annex.

16. The Second Review Conference of the Parties to ENMOD (Geneva, Sept. 14-18, 1992) determined that the military or any other hostile use of herbicides as an environmental modification technique within the meaning of Article II of the Convention, is a method of warfare prohibited by Article I, "if such use of herbicides upsets the ecological balance of a region, thus causing widespread, long-lasting or severe effects as a means of destruction, damage or injury to any other State party" (UN Docs. ENMOD/CONF/II/12, part II; and A/47/550 (1992)).

tee of Experts (*see* section D.1, below), as well as for periodic Review Conferences of the parties. These mechanism are all designed to operate under the aegis and with the assistance of the United Nations.

Note

The scope of ENMOD. It should be noted that this treaty refers not to just collateral or even purposeful destruction of the environment, but only to those instances when the environment itself is being manipulated to gain a military advantage—for example, by seeding clouds for rain at an inopportune time for the enemy, or perhaps causing a drought. Fortunately, in this respect, humankind's powers are still rather limited, though this may not always be so in the future. However, at present, this sole treaty that is entirely addressed to the environmental aspects of warfare has only most limited application.

3. *General Principles of Humanitarian Law*

Article 22 of the Hague Regulations, in both the versions attached to the 1899 Hague Convention II and the 1907 Hague Convention IV, proclaims: "The right of belligerents to adopt means of injuring the enemy is not unlimited." The 1977 Additional Protocol I broadened this principle slightly in Article 35(1): "In any armed conflict, the right of the Parties to the conflict to choose methods or means of warfare is not unlimited."

Note

The scope of the provisions. It is clear that these provisions are designed to prohibit unreasonable injuries or destructions (i.e., ones that do not bear any rational relation to the military advantage that they might promise to the party concerned). But do they cover the environment? Although originally intended to apply to human lives and to property, they are expressed so broadly that other interests, such as the environment, can also be presumed to fall under their protection. In this connection it might be noted that immediately following this general rule in Protocol I is Article 35(3), set forth above, relating to the environment.

As already mentioned, the preamble to the 1899 Hague Convention II introduced the "Martens Clause," which in the form in which it appeared in the preamble to the 1907 Hague Convention (IV) Respecting the Laws and Customs of War on Land reads as follows:

> Until a more complete code of the laws of war has been issued, the high contracting Parties deem it expedient to declare that in cases not included in the Regulations adopted by them, the inhabitants and the belligerent remain under the protection and the rule of the principles of the law of nations, as they result from the usages established among civilized peoples, from the laws of humanity, and the dictates of the public conscience.[17]

Notes

1. *The "dictates of public conscience."* It should be noted that whatever the "dictates of public conscience" may have required in 1899 or 1907, at the end of the twentieth century they almost certainly condemn wanton environmental destruction.[18]

2. *The provisions' legal status.* It is important to note that all these provisions, except those stated solely in Additional Protocol I, are firmly part of universal customary law, binding on all states whether or not they have become parties to the Hague Conventions.

4. Protection of Property

The Regulations Respecting the Laws and Customs of War on Land (the "Hague Regulations"), Annexed both to the 1899 Hague Convention II and the 1907 Hague Convention IV, proclaim in Article 23(g):

> . . . it is forbidden:
> (g) To destroy or seize the enemy's property, unless such destruction or seizure be imperatively demanded by the necessities of war;

Article 55 of the Hague Regulations provides:

> The occupying State shall be regarded only as administrator and usufructuary of public buildings, real estate, forests, and agricultural estates belonging to the hostile State, and situated in the occupied country. It must safeguard the capital of these properties, and administer them in accordance with the rules of usufruct.

17. 205 C.T.S. 277, at 279; *reproduced in* Documents on the Laws of War, footnote 3, above, at 45. For the form in which it appeared in the 1899 Convention (187 C.T.S. 429, at 421), *see id.*, at 4.

18. At the 1991 Canadian Conference of Experts referred to in footnote 10, above, the Chairman's Conclusions included a statement that: "The customary laws of war, in reflecting the dictates of public conscience, now include a requirement to avoid unnecessary damage to the environment." *See also* the extracts from A/RES/47/37, quoted in section C.1, above.

Although these provisions were, when drafted, only intended to protect private and public property rights, it was discovered after the 1990-1991 Gulf War that actions such as the Iraqi torching of hundreds of Kuwaiti oil wells could most persuasively be condemned on the basis of these general, nearly century-old provisions. This was because all the parties to that war were bound by the provisions as either customary[19] or conventional (i.e., treaty-based) international law, while the specifically environment-protecting provisions of the recent instruments described below had not yet clearly attained the status of customary law nor had Iraq or certain other participating states become parties to the relevant treaties.

Article 53 of the 1949 Geneva Convention IV (Protection of Civilian Persons in Time of War)[20] somewhat strengthened Article 23(g) of the Hague Regulations, as follows:

> Any destruction by the Occupying Power of real or personal property belonging individually or collectively to private persons, or to the State, or to other public authorities, or to social or cooperative organizations, is prohibited, except where such destruction is rendered absolutely necessary by military operations.

Question

Defining "destruction." What is meant by "destruction," in relation to environmental values? If complete annihilation is intended, would the environment be better protected by Article 53 of Geneva Convention IV or Article 55 of the Hague Regulations?

5. *Prohibitions Against the Unleashing of Dangerous Forces*

In 1976 the International Law Association adopted its Madrid Resolution on the Protection of Water Resources and Water Installations in Times of Armed Conflict, which, inter alia, provides in Article IV that:

> The destruction of water installations containing dangerous forces, such as dams and dykes, should be prohibited when such destruction may involve grave dangers to the civilian population or substantial damage to the basic ecological balance.

19. It should be noted that the customary nature of the Hague Regulations has been acknowledged by the post-World War II Nuremberg Tribunal, as well as by many other authoritative statements about humanitarian law.

20. 75 U.N.T.S. 287; 6 U.S.T. 3516; T.I.A.S. 3365; Documents on the Laws of War, footnote 3, above, at 271.

1977 Additional Protocol I provides:

Article 56
Protection of Works and Installations Containing Dangerous Forces

1. Works or installations containing dangerous forces, namely dams, dykes . . . , shall not be made the object of attack, even where these objects are military objectives, if such attack may cause the release of dangerous forces and consequent severe losses among the civilian population. . . .

2. The special protection against attack provided by paragraph 1 shall cease:

. . .

(a) for a dam or dyke only if it is used for other than its normal function and in a regular, significant and direct support of military operations and if such attack is the only feasible way to terminate such support; . . .

Article 29 of the 1997 UN Convention on the Law of the Non-Navigational Uses of International Watercourses (U.N. Doc. A/Res/51/229, Annex) provides as follows:

Article 29
International Watercourses and Installations In Time of Armed Conflict

International watercourses and related installations, facilities and other works shall enjoy the protection accorded by the principles and rules of international law applicable in international and non-international armed conflict and shall not be used in violation of those principles and rules.

Question

Would this article prohibit the bombing of a dam? Do you need more facts to answer this question? If dams are protected during hostilities by international law, could the state in which a dam is situated place a missile battery next to the dam?

In December 1990, coincidentally just toward the end of the quiescent period of the Gulf War, the UN General Assembly, basing itself on a number of earlier resolutions by the General Conference of the International Atomic Energy Agency (IAEA), adopted a resolution on Prohibition of attacks on nuclear facilities[21] in which it stated, inter alia, that it is

Aware of the fact that an armed attack on a nuclear installation could result in radioactive releases with grave consequences within and beyond the boundaries of the State which has been attacked, and

21. A/RES/45/58 J of Dec. 4, 1990.

Convinced of the need to prohibit armed attacks on nuclear installations from which such releases could occur and of the urgency of concluding an international agreement in this respect, . . .

4. *Calls upon* all States that have not done so to become parties to Additional Protocol I of 1977 to the Geneva Conventions of 12 August 1949 and upon all States parties to that Protocol to consider, in the context of a possible diplomatic conference, how to improve the present regime with regard to the protection of nuclear facilities; . . .

6. *Appeals* to all States to take into account, when reviewing their military policies, the danger of radioactive releases potentially resulting from an attack on a nuclear facility; . . .

6. *Protection of Cultural Property*

The 1954 Hague Convention for the Protection of Cultural Property in the Event of Armed Conflict[22] provides:

Article 4
Respect for Cultural Property

1. The High Contracting Parties undertake to respect cultural property . . . by refraining from any use of the property and its immediate surroundings or of the appliances in use for its protection for purposes which are likely to expose it to destruction or damage in the event of armed conflict; and by refraining from any act of hostility directed against such property.

Article 9
Immunity of Cultural Property under Special Protection

The High Contracting Parties undertake to ensure the immunity of cultural property under special protection by refraining, from the time of entry in the International Register, from any act of hostility directed against such property and, except for the cases provided for in paragraph 5 of Article 8, from any use of such property or its surroundings for military purposes.

These provisions are referred to and reinforced by 1977 Additional Protocol I, which provides:

Article 53
Protection of Cultural Objects and of Places of Worship

Without prejudice to the provisions of the Hague Convention for the Protection of Cultural Property in the Event of Armed Conflict of 14 May 1954, and of other relevant international instruments, it is prohibited:

(a) to commit any acts of hostility directed against the historic monu-

22. 249 U.N.T.S. 215.

ments, works of art or places of worship which constitute the cultural or spiritual heritage of peoples;

(b) to use such object in support of the military efforts;

(c) to make such objects the object of reprisals.

Question

Applying the provisions. Would these provisions prevent a state from using as a weapons testing area a natural site—such as a forest, mesa, or canyon—that had religious or spiritual significance to a particular ethnic group? What about using it as a military staging area?

7. Protection of Particular Environments

Protocol (III) on Prohibitions or Restrictions on the Use of Incendiary Weapons[23] of the 1980 Inhumane Weapons Convention provides in Article 2, paragraph 4:

> It is prohibited to make forests or other types of plant cover the object of attack by incendiary weapons except when such natural elements are used to cover, conceal or camouflage combatants or other military objectives, or are themselves military objectives.

Question

Would this article prohibit acts such as the United States's defoliation of forests in Viet Nam through the use of napalm bombs and Agent Orange?

8. Prohibition or Restriction of Certain Weapons

From 1961 to 1991 the UN General Assembly adopted a series of resolutions[24] declaring that the use of nuclear weapons would violate the UN Charter and be a crime against humanity. Given the limited powers of the General Assembly, these resolutions constitute mere nonbinding recommendations to member states made pursuant to Articles 10 and 11(1) of the UN Charter.

23. 1342 U.N.T.S. 171, at 172.

24. *E.g.*, A/RES/1653 (XVI) of Nov. 24, 1961, and A/RES/46/37 D of Dec. 6, 1991.

■ LEGALITY OF THE USE BY A STATE OF NUCLEAR WEAPONS

Advisory Opinion of July 8, 1996, International Court of Justice
1996 I.C.J. 66; 35 I.L.M. 809, 1343 (1996)

[Recall that the General Assembly asked the Court to render an advisory opinion on the question whether "the threat or use of nuclear weapons [is] in any circumstance permitted by international law." The Court gave the following answers with regard to the legality of the use of such weapons:[25]]

A. There is in neither customary nor conventional international law any specific authorization of the threat or use of nuclear weapons; [Unanimously]
B. There is in neither customary nor conventional international law any comprehensive and universal prohibition of the threat or use of nuclear weapons as such; [By 11 votes to 3] . . .
D. A threat or use of nuclear weapons should also be compatible with the requirements of international law applicable in armed conflict, particularly those of the principles and rules of international humanitarian law, as well as with specific obligations under treaties and other undertakings which expressly deal with nuclear weapons; [Unanimously]
E. It follows from the above-mentioned requirements that the threat or use of nuclear weapons would generally be contrary to the rules of international law applicable in armed conflict, and in particular the principles and rules of humanitarian law;

   However, in view of the current state of international law, and of the elements of fact at its disposal, the Court cannot conclude definitively whether the threat or use of nuclear weapons would be lawful or unlawful in an extreme circumstance of self-defence, in which the very survival of a State would be at stake; [By 7 votes to 7, by the President's casting vote]
F. There exists an obligation to pursue in good faith and to bring to a conclusion negotiations leading to nuclear disarmament in all its aspects under strict and effective international control. [Unanimously]

Note

The General Assembly took note of this Advisory Opinion and called upon states to comply immediately with paragraph F above.[26]

---

25. The portions of the opinion that relate directly to the environment are quoted in section C.1, above.
26. A/RES/51/45 M of Dec. 10, 1996; *see also* A/RES/51/45 G of the same date.

The UN General Assembly has also in each recent year adopted a resolution[27] always entitled "Prohibition of the dumping of radioactive wastes," in which it "[e]xpresses grave concern regarding any use of nuclear wastes that would constitute radiological warfare and have grave implications for the national security of all states." The resolutions further request the standing Conference on Disarmament to intensify efforts towards the early conclusion of a convention on the prohibition of radiological weapons, and to take into account radioactive wastes as part of the scope of such conventions. Again, these resolutions constitute mere recommendations to member states, and the principles expressed therein will not become binding except through the adoption and entry into force of a convention along the lines called for by these resolutions, or acceptance as law through state practice. In spite of the persistent urging of the Assembly and of many states, little progress is being made on this subject in the Conference on Disarmament.

The International Conference on the Control of the International Trade in Arms, Munitions, and Implements of War convened by the League of Nations adopted the 1925 Geneva Protocol for the Prohibition of the Use in War of Asphyxiating, Poisonous and Other Gases, and of Bacteriological Methods of Warfare.[28] More recently this treaty, which only prohibited the *use* of certain weapons against other parties, has been greatly strengthened by the 1972 Convention on the Prohibition of the Development, Production and Stockpiling of Bacteriological (Biological) and Toxin Weapons and on Their Destruction[29] and the 1993 Convention on the Prohibition of the Development, Production, Stockpiling and Use of Chemical Weapons and on Their Destruction,[30] whose terms, as indicated by their respective titles, go far beyond mere prohibitions on use.

Question

Offensive to humans but not the environment? It can, of course, be argued that as these biological and chemical weapons, while potentially horrendous if used (as designed) against humans, generally do not—unlike nuclear or radiological weapons—constitute a long-term threat, they should not be considered as offensive to the environment. Do you agree? That is, if a state used such weapons but affected only the natural environment, should it be regarded as having violated these agreements?

27. *E.g.*, A/RES/46/36 K of Dec. 6, 1991, A/RES/49/75 A of Dec. 15, 1994, and A/RES/51/45 J of Dec. 10, 1996.

28. 154 L.N.T.S. 65; Documents on the Laws of War, footnote 3, above, at 137.

29. 1015 U.N.T.S. 163; 26 U.S.T. 583; T.I.A.S. 8062; 11 I.L.M. 309 (1972).

30. U.N. Doc. CD/CW/WP.400/Rev.1; 32 I.L.M. 800 (1993).

9. *Mines and Other Remnants of War*

The 1907 Hague Convention VIII (relative to the Laying of Automatic Contact Mines)[31] contains regulations designed to minimize the possibility that naval mines laid in a particular location in wartime should continue to endanger peaceful shipping after the occasion for using them has passed and outside of the area of intended use.

In recent years increasingly greater attention has been paid to the persistent danger posed by the tens of millions of landmines scattered throughout many countries, some from older conflicts and many more of quite recent vintage; because of the long-term nature of this hazard, it is frequently characterized as an environmental one.

One of the first legal instruments to address this problem was Protocol II (On Prohibitions or Restrictions on the Use of Mines, Booby Traps and Other Devices) to the 1980 Convention on Prohibitions and Restrictions on the Use of Certain Conventional Weapons Which May Be Deemed to Be Excessively Injurious or to Have Indiscriminate Effects (Inhumane Weapons Convention), which requires that minefields either be carefully mapped to facilitate removal after the period of active hostilities or consist of mines that will self-destruct reasonably rapidly so as not to constitute a long-lasting hazard. It also calls for international co-operation in the removal of minefields, mines, and booby-traps. At the recent first Review Conference of Parties to the Inhumane Weapons Convention (1995-1996) this protocol was strengthened.[32]

In 1982 the UN General Assembly, after having received reports on several studies concerning the dangers and other problems caused to civilian users of land that had formerly served as battlefields, as testing areas for new weapons or as training grounds for troops, adopted a resolution on Remnants of War,[33] in which the Assembly states that it is:

> *Convinced* that the responsibility for the removal of the remnants of war should be borne by the countries that planted them,
>
> *Recognizing* that the presence of the material remnants of war, particularly mines, on the lands of developing countries seriously impedes their development efforts and causes loss of life and property,
>
> . . .
>
> 2. *Regrets* that no real measures have been taken to solve the problem of remnants of war despite the various resolutions and decisions adopted thereon by the General Assembly and the Governing Council of the United Nations Environment Programme;
>
> 3. *Reiterates* its support of the just demands of the States affected by

31. 205 C.T.S. 331; Documents on the Laws of War, footnote 3, above, at 85.
32. 35 I.L.M. 1206 (1996).
33. A/RES/37/215 of Dec. 20, 1982.

> the implantation of mines and the presence of the remnants of war on their lands for compensation from the States responsible for those remnants;

There has been no follow-up on that resolution, and thus the sentiments expressed by the General Assembly remain at best hortatory. At this stage it would seem difficult to characterize them even as *de lege ferenda.* However, it might be noted that this resolution is fully compatible with the above-mentioned provisions of Protocol II to the Inhumane Weapons Convention and is reinforced by the Security Council resolution mentioned immediately below.

The limited legal force of the above provisions was reinforced by the fact that at the conclusion of the Gulf War, Iraq was required to agree to assist in locating its mines, first by the temporary cease-fire agreement of March 2, 1991 and then by a resolution adopted by the Security Council later on the same day,[34] by which the Council

> 3. *Further demands* that Iraq:
>
> (d) Provide all information and assistance in identifying Iraqi mines, booby traps and other explosives as well as any chemical and biological weapons and material in Kuwait, in areas of Iraq where forces of Member States cooperating with Kuwait pursuant to resolution 678 (1990) are present temporarily, and in adjacent waters; . . .

In 1995 and 1996 the UN General Assembly adopted resolutions on mine clearance, and also in 1996 a conference was held on that subject.

On September 18, 1997, some 90 countries, having met for three weeks in Oslo, adopted the Convention on the Prohibition of the Use, Stockpiling, Production and Transfer of Anti-Personnel Mines and on Their Destruction,[35] which is addressed to antipersonnel landmines and, inter alia, requires the destruction within four years of those in storage and generally within ten years of those already emplaced. Having been endorsed by the General Assembly,[36] the treaty was opened for signature in Ottawa on December 3, 1997, following which it will be subject to ratification or accession. The United States refused to participate in the adoption of the treaty because several conditions it insisted on, including an exemption for the Korean peninsula, were not met. Though the treaty is likely to be brought into force relatively soon, its ultimate significance is uncertain, as the participation of other important countries such as China, India, Pakistan, and Russia is also doubtful.

34. S/RES/686 (1991) of Mar. 2, 1991.
35. 36 I.L.M. 1507 (1997).
36. A/RES/52/38A of Dec. 9, 1997, *see also* A/RES/52138H of Dec. 9, 1997.

10. Prohibition of War and of Preparations Therefor

Evidently, the most effective means of eliminating the environmental damage caused by warfare would be to eliminate war itself. However, considering that even the more immediate horrors of this persistent human activity have been insufficient to motivate mankind to put a stop to it, environment-based arguments can at best add a make-weight to what should be, but never have been, sufficient arguments for perpetual peace. Nevertheless, note should be taken of several recent nonbinding expressions of the world community that establish a direct link between warfare and the threat of environmental destruction.

In 1980 the UN General Assembly adopted a resolution[37] on the Historical Responsibility of States for the Preservation of Nature for Present and Future Generations, in which it stated:

> *Conscious* of the disastrous consequences which a war involving the use of nuclear weapons and other weapons of mass destruction would have on man and his environment,
>
> *Noting* that the continuation of the arms race, including the testing of various types of weapons, especially nuclear weapons, and the accumulation of toxic chemicals are adversely affecting the human environment and damaging the vegetable and animal world,
>
> *Bearing in mind* that the arms race is diverting material and intellectual resources from the solution of the urgent problems of preserving nature,
>
> . . .
>
> 1. *Proclaims* the historical responsibility of States for the preservation of nature for present and future generations;
> 2. *Draws the attention* of States to the fact that the continuing arms race has pernicious effects on the environment and reduces the prospects for the necessary international co-operation in preserving nature on our planet;

Principle 25 of the Rio Declaration puts it simply: "Peace, development and environmental protection are independent and indivisible."

This having been said, it should be noted that even if preparations for war are condemned, it is in the course of these preparations that steps can be taken that are of great importance for the protection of the environment before, during, and after actual armed conflicts. This is so in part because the preparations for war are normally carried out during periods of peace, when states are fully subject to their normal international legal obligations, while during a conflict special rules may apply and some normal rules may be suspended (*see* the following section). Furthermore, in many respects the course of a war is set during the preceding period of peace, and once a conflict is inflamed it may be too late to change such course significantly.

37. A/RES/35/80 of Oct. 30, 1980.

In this connection Article 36 of 1977 Additional Protocol I is particularly relevant:

> In the study, development, acquisition or adoption of a new weapon, means or method of warfare, a High Contracting Party is under an obligation to determine whether its employment would, in some or all circumstances, be prohibited by this Protocol or by any other rule of international law applicable to the High Contracting Party.

Recall that Protocol I contains the important environmental obligations quoted in section 1 above, and thus presumably a state party to the Protocol would have to determine whether, for example, the use of a proposed new weapon would be compatible with these obligations and with others that arise from other instruments to which it is a party, or even from customary law.

Paragraph 2 of the General Assembly resolution set out immediately above, to the effect that the arms race itself has pernicious effects on the environment, also has interesting implications. What was evidently on the Assembly's mind was the major environmental damage done in many countries from maneuvers and other military exercises, from the testing of new weapons and particularly from target practice with old ones, and even from the process of manufacturing certain weapons, particularly nuclear ones. Indeed, recently the Assembly also became aware of the fact that even the process of disarmament can have deleterious effects on the environment, for example, in the destruction of stockpiles of certain weapons, such as chemical ones.[38]

11. The Status of General Environmental Protection Treaties in Time of War

As appears from other chapters of this book, over the years numerous treaties have been concluded, including worldwide ones with substantial participation and regional ones with complete participation of the states concerned, that when complied with provide important protection to many aspects of the environment (e.g., the many treaties prohibiting pollution of the high seas or of regional seas and the UN Convention on the Law of the Sea with its important environmental provisions). The question is to what extent do these treaties continue to apply during times of war, and in particular to what extent are belligerents bound by treaty obligations (whether deriving from bilateral or from multilateral instruments) vis-à-vis hostile belligerents, and vis-à-vis nonbelligerents? If these environmental

38. *See* A/RES/50/70 M of Dec. 12, 1995, on Observance of environmental norms in the drafting and implementation of agreements on disarmament and arms control.

treaties continued to apply in spite of a state of war, at least the *legal* protection of the environment would be greatly advanced.

Interestingly enough, there are no clear answers to these questions. Indeed, only most recently, in the course of the post-Gulf War studies, has their importance been recognized. The ICRC in a study[39] it prepared at the behest of the UN General Assembly,[40] recommended as one measure to be taken (instead of formulating a comprehensive new treaty on the protection of the environment during warfare), the review of the applicability in armed conflict of international environmental law. These studies, in which (as of mid-199) a number of official and academic institutions are engaged, will evidently take some time, and more time will be necessary to achieve any substantial consensus. Some considerations that will presumably be taken into account in these studies are:

(a) The 1969 Vienna Convention on the Law of Treaties[41] provides:

(i) In Article 73:

> The provisions of the present Convention shall not prejudge any question that may arise in regard to a treaty . . . from the outbreak of hostilities between states.

(ii) In Article 75:

> The provisions of the present Convention are without prejudice to any obligation in relation to a treaty which may arise for an aggressor State in consequence of measures taken in conformity with the Charter of the United Nations with reference to that State's aggression.

This suggests that the Security Council might specify, in a decision taken under Chapter VII of the UN Charter ("Action with respect to Threats to the Peace, Breaches of the Peace, and Acts of Aggression") that a state it characterizes as an aggressor in a given conflict, remains bound by all or some (e.g., environmental) treaty obligations, even if it would normally be relieved of such obligations in the course of a war.

(b) That while in many treaties, including some environmental ones, the obligations of the parties are in effect reciprocal—and thus can conveniently be suspended or perhaps even terminated between parties that are at war—many environmental treaties might be said to create *erga omnes*

39. U.N. Doc. A/48/269, July 29, 1993, part II.
40. *See* A/DEC/46/417 of Dec. 9, 1991, on the agenda item: "Exploitation of the environment as a weapon in times of armed conflict and the taking of practical measures to prevent such exploitation."
41. 1155 U.N.T.S. 331; 8 I.L.M. 679 (1969).

obligations (i.e., such as run to all other parties or perhaps even to the world community as a whole). This, for example, would be true of a treaty that forbids pollution of an international "commons," such as the high seas, certain regional seas, Antarctica, the atmosphere, and outer space. Since two or more parties cannot, by an agreement inter se, reduce their obligations under such a treaty, should they be able to do so merely because they are engaged in a war with each other?

(c) It may be necessary to examine each relevant treaty, and perhaps even individual provisions, in order to determine whether it could have been the intention of the parties that such instrument continue in force during a period of armed conflict. Except for the few treaties that contain an explicit statement on this subject, or where a clear answer can be found in its history, this may be a very complicated and controversial exercise, unless some general rules can be developed.

(d) In its above-mentioned Advisory Opinion on the Legality of the Use by a State of Nuclear Weapons,[42] the World Court merely stated:

> 30. However, the Court is of the view that the issue is not whether the treaties relating to the protection of the environment are or are not applicable during an armed conflict, but rather whether the obligations stemming from these treaties were intended to be obligations of total restraint during military conflict.[43]

Questions

1. *All's fair in . . . war?* Do you believe environmental treaties should be regarded as being suspended during armed conflict? Does it depend on the treaty's subject matter and the specific obligations it contains? Should states involved in hostilities be permitted to place nuclear weapons on the ocean floor despite treaty obligations to the contrary?

2. *Treaties and third states.* Can or should a treaty be construed to create obligations on parties to it that run in favor of nonparties—even where the obligations concern something as important as pollution of an international "commons"? How would this work, legally? Technically, would the obligations (assuming they run to anyone other than other parties to the treaty) run in favor of nonparty states, or the international community as a whole? If the latter, how could they be enforced? For example, who could file a protest in the event one of the obligations was violated?

42. *See* sections 1 and 8, above.
43. 1996 I.C.J. 66, at 83, para. 30; 35 I.L.M. 821 (1996).

D. ENFORCEMENT

It is notorious that international law is difficult to enforce—indeed is rarely enforced directly, but relies largely on the experience that most states, albeit for diverse reasons, most of the time conform to their international obligations (*see* Chapter 5, section C.1). This appears to be generally true also of international environmental law, although innovative compliance mechanisms have been developed in this field, as we have seen in Chapter 9. However, in the area explored in the present chapter, that is the law applicable to armed conflicts, it would not be surprising if voluntary compliance might be relatively low.

For this reason, the present section explores various devices that bear on improving state compliance with obligations relevant to the protection of the environment during warfare.

1. Settlement of Disputes

This subject is dealt with generally in Chapter 5, section B. However, it should be noted that certain of the treaties discussed in the present chapter have their own special disputes resolution provisions.

Thus Article V of the ENMOD Convention provides:

> 1. The States Parties to this Convention undertake to consult one another and to co-operate in solving any problems which may arise in relation to the objectives of, or in the application of the provisions of, the Convention. Consultations and co-operation pursuant to this article may also be undertaken through appropriate international procedures within the framework of the United Nations and in accordance with its Charter. These international procedures may include the services of appropriate international organizations, as well as of a Consultative Committee of Experts as provided for in paragraph 2 of this article.
>
> 2. For the purposes set forth in paragraph 1 of this article, the Depositary shall, within one month of the receipt of a request from any State Party to this Convention, convene a Consultative Committee of Experts. Any State Party may appoint an expert to the Committee whose functions and rules of procedure are set out in the annex, which constitutes an integral part of this Convention. The Committee shall transmit to the Depositary a summary of its findings of fact, incorporating all views and information presented to the Committee during its proceedings. The Depositary shall distribute the summary to all States Parties.
>
> 3. Any State party to this Convention which has reason to believe that any other State Party is acting in breach of obligations deriving from provisions of the Convention may lodge a complaint with the Security Council of the United Nations. Such a complaint should include all relevant information as well as all possible evidence supporting its validity.

> 4. Each State Party to this Convention undertakes to co-operate in carrying out any investigations which the Security Council may initiate, in accordance with the provisions of the Charter of the United Nations, on the basis of the complaint received by the Council. The Security Council shall inform the States Parties of the results of the investigation.
>
> 5. Each State Party to this Convention undertakes to provide or support assistance in accordance with the provisions of the Charter of the United Nations, to any State Party which so requests, if the Security Council decides that such party has been harmed or is likely to be harmed as a result of violation of the Convention.

Article 90 of the 1977 Additional Protocol I provides for the establishment of an "International Fact-Finding Commission" of 15 persons elected by the states parties to the Protocol that have especially consented to the procedure provided by this article. When such a party brings an allegation of a "grave breach" (i.e., one of a number of defined serious violations of the Protocol or of the 1949 Geneva Conventions—*see* section D.4, below), then a chamber is formed consisting of five members of the commission and of one representative each (who may not be a national) of the accused and the accuser party. After due investigation the chamber is to prepare a report of the facts found and of any recommendations made and present this confidentially to the parties. There is no requirement that such recommendations be complied with.

2. *Preparation of Military Manuals*

One of the most promising practical measures proposed by the ICRC in its 1993 report to the UN General Assembly[44] was the preparation, dissemination, and use of military manuals and instructions that would set out, in language and forms understandable and usable by subordinate military commanders, the practical rules for protecting the environment during warfare. The ICRC annexed to its report a draft of guidelines for the preparation of such manuals, and in 1994 submitted a revised version,[45] which the General Assembly in effect endorsed.[46]

3. *Civil Liability*

In a potentially precedent-setting provision the Security Council in the resolution it adopted at the end of the Gulf War[47] required

44. Footnote 39, above.
45. A/49/323, Annex (1994).
46. A/RES/49/50 of Dec. 9, 1994, para. 11.
47. S/RES/687 (1991) of Mar. 3, 1991.

> 16. . . . that Iraq, without prejudice to the debts and obligations of Iraq arising prior to 2 August 1990, which will be addressed through the normal mechanisms, is liable under international law for any direct loss, damage, including environmental damage and the depletion of natural resources, or injury to foreign Governments, nationals and corporations, as a result of Iraq's unlawful invasion and occupation of Kuwait;

To determine the extent of these damages the Security Council, by other provisions of the same resolution as well as by subsequent ones, established a Claims Commission. That commission has established procedures for considering environmental claims, which were required to be submitted by February 1997. To assist the commission, UNEP established a Working Group of Experts on Liability and Compensation for Environmental Damage arising from Military Activities, which submitted its report in 1996,[48] covering questions such as the law to be applied, the extent of the rights of states and international organizations to bring claims, the definition of environmental damage and depletion of natural resources, and the valuation of such damage and depletion.

For a number of years, the UN International Law Commission (ILC) has been working to formulate a set of provisions on "International Liability for Injurious Consequences Arising out of Acts Not Prohibited by International Law." One of its successive Rapporteurs on this subject had suggested the adoption of the following draft Articles:[49]

Article 24
Harm to the Environment and Resulting Harm to Persons or Property

> If the transboundary harm proves detrimental to the environment of the affected State:
>
> (a) The State of origin shall bear the costs of any reasonable operation to restore, as far as possible, the conditions that existed prior to the occurrence of the harm. If it is impossible to restore these conditions in full, agreement may be reached on compensation, monetary or otherwise, by the State of origin for the deterioration suffered; . . .

Article 26
Exceptions

> 1. There shall be no liability on the part of the State of origin or the operator, as the case may be:
>
> (a) If the harm was directly due to an act of war, hostilities, civil war, insurrection. . . .

48. U.N. Doc. UNEP/Env.Law/3/Inf.1 (1996).

49. Report of the ILC on its 42d session, 45 GAOR Suppl. No. 10 (A/45/10), ch. VII, paras. 515-516, at 274-277 (1990). In his report to the 43d (1991) session of the commission, the rapporteur proposed some restructuring of the provisions quoted below, but without any substantive changes (A/CN.4/437, paras. 59 and 61).

However, as of its 1997 session, the ILC had not yet taken any action with respect to these proposals.[50]

4. *Criminal Responsibility*

Article 147 of the Geneva Convention relative to the Protection of Civilian Persons in Time of War provides in pertinent part as follows:

> Grave breaches . . . shall be those involving any of the following acts, if committed against persons or property protected by the present Convention: . . . extensive destruction and appropriation of property, not justified by military necessity and carried out unlawfully and wantonly.

Article 85 of Additional Protocol I to the 1949 Conventions provides in relevant part as follows:

> 3. . . . the following acts shall be regarded as grave breaches of this Protocol, when committed wilfully, in violation of the relevant provisions of this Protocol, and causing death or serious injury to body or health:
>
> . . .
>
> (c) launching an attack against works or installations containing dangerous forces in the knowledge that such attack will cause excessive loss of life, injury to civilians or damage to civilian objects . . . ;
>
> . . .
>
> 5. Without prejudice to the application of the Conventions and of this Protocol, grave breaches of these instruments shall be regarded as war crimes.

It should, however, be noted that violations of Articles 35(3) and 55 of Protocol I (section C.1, above) are not characterized as grave breaches.

The ILC has indicated in Article 19 of its Draft Articles on "State Responsibility," provisionally adopted in 1996, that an international crime [of a state] may result, inter alia, from:

> (d) a serious breach of an international obligation of essential importance for the safeguarding and preservation of the human environment, such as those prohibiting massive pollution of the atmosphere or of the seas.[51]

50. The report of the ILC's Working Group on International Liability for Injurious Consequences Arising Out of Acts Not Prohibited by International Law, which the Commission submitted to the General Assembly (Report of the ILC on its 48th session, 51 GAOR Suppl. No. 10 (A/51/10), Annex I), does not deal with this matter.

51. Report of the ILC on its 48th session, 51 GAOR Suppl. No. 10 (A/51/10), Ch. III.D.1 (Article 19), para. 65 at 131 (1996).

Question

Was Iraq a criminal? Would the actions taken by Iraq during the Gulf War, described in the Case Study, qualify as an international crime under the ILC's Article 19?

Under another topic long on its agenda, the ILC recently completed and reported to the General Assembly a Draft Code of Crimes Against the Peace and Security of Mankind, which contains the following provision of present interest:[52]

Article 20

> Any of the following war crimes constitute a crime against the peace and security of mankind when committed in a systematic manner or on a large scale:
>
> . . .
>
> (g) In the case of armed conflict, using methods or means of warfare not justified by military necessity with the intent to cause widespread, long-term and severe damage to the natural environment and thereby gravely prejudice the health and survival of the population and such damage occurs.

It is now for the General Assembly to decide whether and how to provide for giving legal effect to the Draft Code.

On July 17, 1998 a conference convened by the UN General Assembly adopted the Rome Statue of the International Criminal Court. Among the "most serious crimes of concern to the international community as a whole", over which the new Court is to have jurisdiction, are "war crimes" defined by Article 8, sub-paragraph 2(b), to include:

> (iv) Intentionally launching an attack in the knowledge that such attack will cause . . . widespread, long-term and severe damage to the natural environment which would be clearly excessive in relation to the concrete and overall military advantage anticipated;[53]

The draft articles on State Responsibility are meant to deal with crimes of states—a concept whose precise meaning and implications are not as yet entirely clear. On the other hand, the Draft Code of Crimes as well as the International Criminal Court, are designed to deal with crimes under international law by individuals—on the *Nuremberg* model—though Article

52. Report of the ILC on its 48th session, 51 GAOR Suppl. No. 10 (A/51/10), Ch. II.D, Article 20 and Commentary para. (15), at 110, 112, 119-120 ___.

53. A/CONF.183/9 (1998); 37 I.L.M. ___ (1998).

4 of the Draft Code makes it clear that this fact "is without prejudice to any question of the responsibility of States under international law."

Summary

Although incidental and sometimes even purposeful environmental destruction has been a feature of warfare throughout recorded history, and even though systematic efforts to diminish the cruelties of warfare by the creation of international humanitarian law can be traced back to the middle of the nineteenth century, explicit provisions concerning the protection of the environment during warfare were first formulated only in the mid-1970s. Considerable progress had been made in promulgating relevant treaty instruments (as well as a number of solemn but at best imperfectly binding international declarations) by the time of the Gulf War. However, many important participants in that conflict had not yet become parties to these relatively new treaties; consequently, intensive post-Gulf War legal reviews determined that to the extent that the environmental outrages committed during that conflict clearly violated international law, the only violations were of rules of humanitarian law that proscribe the wanton destruction of private and public property.

The initial reactions to this discouraging state of affairs were unofficial efforts to codify and develop this area of the law into a comprehensive new treaty instrument. However, enthusiasm for such a project soon faded, for both technical and legal reasons. The objectives currently being addressed are more modest but also stand a greater chance of being attained. Most of these are summarized in a report that the ICRC submitted to the UN General Assembly in 1993. These include: (1) the preparation and use of military manuals along the lines proposed in a set of guidelines submitted by the ICRC in 1994, on which the training of military units and commanders and the preparation of combat operations could then be based; (2) the clarification of some uncertainties in the relevant treaties, and in particular of the terms "widespread," "long-lasting," and "severe" used in different senses in the ENMOD Convention and in the 1977 Additional Protocol I; (3) encouragement of wider participation in the relevant treaties, and in particular the ENMOD Convention and 1977 Additional Protocol I; and (4) a study of and possibly decisions concerning the continuing applicability in time of war of general environmental treaties, as between belligerents and between belligerents and nonbelligerents.

Concluding Questions

1. *The conjunctive or the disjunctive?* The ENMOD Convention forbids actions that have "widespread, long-lasting *or* severe effects" on the environ-

ment. The 1977 Protocol I to the 1949 Geneva Conventions prohibits causing "widespread, long-term *and* severe" damage to the natural environment. The ILC's draft Code of Crimes against the Peace and Security of Mankind might consider criminal the causing of "widespread, long-term *and* severe damage" to the natural environment and the statute of the International Criminal Court actually does so.

(1) Are military authorities likely to favor the conjunctive or the disjunctive use of the three terms in the quotes above?
(2) What are the likely views of environmental activists?
(3) Which do you consider more reasonable?

2. *The legality of Iraq's attacks on the environment.* After the Gulf War, most legal experts concluded that the extensive Iraqi offenses against the environment may not have violated any environmental obligations binding on Iraq, but probably did violate the 1907 Hague Convention prohibitions against the wanton destruction of private and public property.

(1) On the basis of the materials in this chapter, or any others of which you are aware, do you agree with these conclusions?
(2) Are there circumstances under which it could make a difference (i.e., that clear offenses against the environment might not violate Hague Convention obligations)?

3. *A new treaty?*

(1) Do you consider whether it would be desirable to draw up at this stage a comprehensive treaty prohibiting various types of offenses against the environment in:
   (a) Preparations for war;
   (b) During warfare?
(2) Could such a treaty sensibly relate to civil wars?

4. *Is a legalistic approach realistic?* It is sometimes asserted that a military commander will never forego taking an action in order to protect the environment if doing so would endanger the lives of soldiers under his or her command. If this is accurate, does it mean that international law to protect the environment during hostilities is doomed to fail? Are there choices made by field commanders that affect the environment that do not involve that stark trade-off or any significant trade-off between environmental protection and tactical advantage? What about how toxic substances are handled and disposed of? Are there choices made before hostilities begin and before troops are deployed that affect the environment during hostilities? For example, might the United States military have developed a defoliant that was less damaging to health than Agent Orange was? What about the life-cycle effects on the environment of military material? Are these better approached via domestic law or international law?

5. *The applicability of environmental treaties in wartime.*

(1) Do you consider that general environmental treaties should be deemed to continue to apply during warfare:
   (a) Between opposing belligerents;

(b) Between belligerents and neutrals?

(2) Whether or not such treaties are deemed to continue to apply during warfare, should international forces (e.g., UN, NATO) be bound by them:

(a) Absolutely;

(b) Only if the opposing forces are so bound?

6. *Problem:* You are the legal adviser on international environmental questions to a government that has nuclear weapons. What response would you advise should be given to another government that is threatening to use nuclear weapons in a conflict with your state?

7. *War and the environment.* Do you believe that nature should no longer be fair game in mankind's conflicts? If so, is this because of nature's importance to humans or because of its importance for its own sake?

PART THREE

NATURAL RESOURCES MANAGEMENT

INTRODUCTION

International environmental law covers both pollution control and natural resource conservation. Both are components of one problem—the protection of the environment. Natural resources[1] encompass all living resources, both fauna and flora, other renewable resources such as freshwater and soils, and nonrenewable resources.[2] For purposes of this book, it also includes the conservation of biological diversity. The following material focuses on water, fauna, flora, and other renewable resources.

Renewable natural resources are part of the natural system and do not respect political boundaries. Yet the international system that we have developed to manage our natural resources starts from the point of division of the globally shared environmental system into essentially "privatized" units of national sovereign states that have sovereign control over the resources within their borders. This principle has been repeated frequently

1. We recognize that the term "resource" is an economic one and that it is anthropocentric, which may not appeal to some readers. But it is widely used in the environmental field, and there are no widely accepted substitutes.

2. Such resources may never be technically exhausted, because as they become less plentiful the price will rise, providing incentives for the development of substitutes or alternative technologies that do not require the nonrenewable resource in question. In other cases, the real price of the resource may rise (at least theoretically), thus making it effectively unavailable.

in United Nations General Assembly resolutions and in international agreements.

Increasingly states have agreed to constrain what they can do with their resources if their activities affect global commons such as the ozone layer, high seas, or outer space; or cause harm to neighboring areas; or damage resources within countries that are impressed with elements of common patrimony for Earth. Thus, states have negotiated conventions to control marine pollution; to control freshwater allocations and pollution; to conserve wetlands, biologically diverse areas, and world heritages within their borders; and to control international trade in endangered species.

The distinction between pollution control and natural resource conservation is an artificial one. Forests are destroyed both by clearing them through unsustainable practices and by pollution that causes them slowly to die. Supplies of freshwater on an international river can become scarce, both because an upstream state is diverting the flow or because salt water is intruding upriver when there is insufficient freshwater flowing downriver. Similarly, the flow of water determines whether a given amount of nontoxic pollutants will exceed pollution standards.

The distinction is also artificial in the sense that both pollution control and natural resource conservation are faced with the same underlying allocation system: namely a first-come, first-served system. The country that pollutes a common airshed or stream may encounter no problem until another country joins in polluting the area. Often it is difficult to dislodge or control the party that was there first polluting the air or water. Similarly, the country that first captures natural resources—initially through settling the country and claiming national sovereignty—has as the first claimant the right to use the resources in whatever way desired unless the country agrees to controls on use. (Issues of allocation of freshwater are addressed in Chapter 16.) Nonetheless, for purposes of clarity, this book treats pollution control and natural resource conservation separately.

Regimes for natural resource conservation may be divided as follows: regimes for shared natural resources, such as airsheds or international watercourse systems (including both surface and ground water); regimes for living resources that at least in part occupy internationally common areas such as the high seas; and regimes for resources that are located within national boundaries but are of interest to the international community. Different rules of allocation and use and different institutional means for managing these resources have emerged.

Nonrenewable Resources

Before embarking on a detailed look at these resources, nonrenewable resources merit some attention. These include oil, natural gas, coal, and other minerals. While technically hydrocarbons are renewable, the time scale of hundreds of thousands of years makes them nonrenewable for our purposes. Technically some ground water aquifers (fossil waters or confined aquifers) are also nonrenewable in the sense that they have existed for thousands of years and cannot be recharged from the natural flow of water.

For these resources, several legal issues arise. The first is whether there are any normative obligations to future generations that affect our use today. As indicated in Chapter 2 on the philosophical framework, there may be a duty to conserve options for future generations, which would include the diversity of nonrenewable resources. This does not mean that these resources cannot be used, but rather research to develop acceptable substitutes for them and to extract and use them more efficiently must accompany uses that deplete the supply. Moreover, it is arguable that at least some small part of the resource must always be maintained, since history shows that there are always uses that have not yet been discovered for the resources. To eliminate the resource would deprive future generations of important options for addressing their own problems.

Moreover, the use of nonrenewable resources generates important pollution problems. Using coal, for example, generates the precursors of acid rain and emits carbon dioxide, affecting global temperature and thereby climate. These issues have been addressed in the previous chapters on pollution control.

The Economic Framework for Natural Resource Conservation

From the perspective of a lawyer, several economic issues are important. The first relates to the conditions that affect decisions about the use of natural resources. Here international legal instruments play a crucial role, for they may set the terms upon which these decisions take place. In the marketplace such decisions would theoretically be governed by benefit-cost ratios and the intergenerational component of that—the discount rate. For discussion of these, *see* chapter 3 on the economic context. Unfortunately, the discount rate has been a poor instrument for measuring the long-term environmental consequences of retaining natural resources rather than using them immediately. For example, hardwood forests, which require decades to grow, may have important environmental functions such as controlling soil erosion, which may in turn protect against the filling of dams downstream; buffering climate, which may protect against hotter temperatures; may harbor wildlife; and may provide recreational, aesthetic, and other benefits. But the contemporary economic instruments for considering whether to save or cut the forest are not good at considering these benefits. We do not yet have good techniques for quantifying these benefits, and the discount rate normally considers investments only in a ten-year time frame.

Moreover, legal instruments that result in distortions of the real price of the resource, such as instruments that promote subsidized and inefficient uses, may cause rapid depletion of valuable natural resources, often in environmentally unsound ways. For example, tax incentives to cut down biologically diverse tropical forests may lead not only to the loss of biological diversity but to barren, unproductive soils for the future.

One of the most difficult problems in international environmental law is the calculation in economic terms of damage to the environmental system. If hazardous chemicals spill into an international river, and contaminate water supplies, kill fish, and pollute ecosystems, how do we calculate the costs? The Exxon Valdez oil spill provided a vivid example of the difficulty of pricing wildlife that is not hunted or pricing the health of ecosystems. These issues were addressed in Chapter 3 on economic resources, which discusses alternative methods of calculating natural resource damage, and you will want to reconsider them as you read the materials on natural resources.

XVI

Norms of Allocation and Use: Fresh Water

The growing scarcity of the world's fresh water supplies on a per capita basis portends increasing competition and conflict in the coming century between countries sharing rivers, lakes, and aquifers. After briefly introducing the problem, this chapter looks at one of the most infamous theories in natural resources law, the "Harmon Doctrine." It then offers a case study of the Tigris-Euphrates Basin and presents an overview of the general principles governing the allocation and use of international watercourses.

THE EVOLUTION OF THE LAW OF INTERNATIONAL WATERCOURSES

Stephen McCaffrey
45 Austrian J. Pub. Intl. L. 87, 88-89 (1993)

Two ominous phenomena relating to fresh water confront humanity at the close of the twentieth century: the dramatic and continuing increase in the use of water, and the growing pressure that is placed on the Earth's finite and constant water resources by the world's ever-expanding population. Professor H.A. Smith in his classic work "The Economic Uses of International Rivers" made the following observation more than a half century ago concerning the demand for water: "One of the most noteworthy features of the last hundred years has been the immense increase in the use of water." Professor Smith ascribed this trend to a combination of changes in personal habits and scientific progress, factors which continually interact: "The demand for water stimulates invention, and the facility of obtaining it is forever increasing the demand." This observation explains why those who consume the most water *per capita* live in the most technologically sophisticated countries. In the United States, for example, the average person consumes over 70 times as much water as the average resident in Ghana.

But it is the Earth's mushrooming population, which is increasingly concentrated in urban areas, that is placing inexorable strains on fresh water supplies. Professor Smith was prophetic on this point, as well. He remarked that the "immense consumption [of water *per capita* in the world's growing urban areas] now compels nearly all great cities to draw their water supply from distant sources by complicated methods, and this development has had its own international consequences." And, of particular relevance to the present inquiry, Smith noted that development pressures can lead political units "to divert water which in its natural course would flow into other states, and these latter regard such diversion as a violation of their rights." It is these changes in the nature of human society and the ways in which it uses water that have prompted corresponding changes in the law governing transboundary water resources. For international drainage basins constitute approximately 47 per cent of the Earth's land area; they cover about 60 per cent of both Africa and Latin America.

Notes and Questions

Spaceballs to the rescue? The possibility that "space snowballs" have been bombarding our planet for millennia (N.Y. Times, May 29, 1997, p. 1, col. 5) may be thought to provide some comfort to the water-stressed regions of the world. But Dr. Thomas M. Donahue, who hypothesized these small, comet-like balls of ice, estimates that they add only one inch of water to the Earth's surface every 10,000 to 20,000 years. While this is not an insignificant amount, especially in the history of the globe, it probably does not hold out much hope for humans in the coming century. Would these snowballs from space constitute a part of the "global commons"? A "shared natural resource"? If so, what legal and policy consequences should follow therefrom? Could water-stressed countries claim a percentage of the amount of water contributed by the space snowballs from countries with a water surplus? How would you calculate the percentage? On what legal ground(s) could such a claim be made? Could the same or similar arguments be made for the icebergs that are "calved" by Antarctica? Can you think of any existing legal analogues?

Additional Reading

On water scarcity issues in general, *see, e.g.*, Water in Crisis (Peter Gleick, ed. 1993); La Rivière, Threats to the World's Water, 261 Scientific American

80 (Sept. 1989); Sandra Postel, Last Oasis: Facing Water Scarcity (1997); The Scarcity of Water: Emerging Legal and Policy Responses (Edward H.P. Brans, Esther J. de Haan, André Nollkaemper & Jan Rinzema, eds. 1997). On legal issues raised by water scarcity, *see, e.g.*, Stephen McCaffrey, Water Scarcity: Institutional and Legal Responses, in *id.* at 43.

A. THE "HARMON DOCTRINE"

■ WATER, POLITICS, AND INTERNATIONAL LAW

Stephen McCaffrey
in Water in Crisis 92, 96 (Peter Gleick, ed. 1993)

[A] dispute [between Mexico and the United States] gave rise to what is perhaps the most infamous legal view yet espoused publicly by a state concerning international riparian rights. The controversy stemmed from diversions of water from the Rio Grande in the late 19th century by farmers and ranchers in the U.S. states of Colorado and New Mexico. According to Mexico, these diversions reduced the supply of water to Mexican communities in the vicinity of Ciudad Juarez. The Rio Grande rises in Colorado, flows through New Mexico, then forms the border between the United States state of Texas and Mexico before emptying into the Gulf of Mexico. Mexico protested the diversions in October, 1895, declaring that the legal claim of those living on its side of the Rio Grande "to the use of the water of that river is incontestable, being prior to that of the inhabitants of Colorado by hundreds of years."

The U.S. Secretary of State responded that the United States was not obligated to halt the diversions. He relied on a legal opinion prepared by Attorney General Judson Harmon, which has since become known as the "Harmon Doctrine." According to the opinion:

> The fundamental principle of international law is the absolute sovereignty of every nation, as against all others, within its own territory. . . .
>
> > All exceptions . . . to the full and complete power of a nation within its own territories must be traced up to the consent of the nation itself. They can flow from no other legitimate source.[1]

While nothing in the opinion denied a duty to avoid causing harm to other countries, it has been taken as standing for the proposition that international law allows a state complete freedom of action with regard to international watercourses within its territory, irrespective of any conse-

1. [This quotation is from The Schooner Exchange v. McFadden, 11 U.S. (7 Cranch) 116, 3 L. Ed. 287 (1812), a sovereign immunity case involving the question of whether a foreign vessel was immune from suit in United States courts, decided by the United States Supreme Court in an opinion by Chief Justice Marshall.—EDS.]

quence that might ensue in other countries. In fact, the response of the State Department to Mexico on the basis of Harmon's opinion took precisely this position. It declared that

> the rules of international law imposed upon the United States no duty to deny to its inhabitants the use of the water of that part of the Rio Grande lying wholly within the United States, although such use resulted in reducing the volume of water in the river below the point where it ceased to be entirely within the United States, the supposition of the existence of such a duty being inconsistent with the sovereign jurisdiction of the United States over the national domain.

The United States nonetheless joined Mexico in instructing the International Boundary Commission, which the two countries had established in 1889, to investigate and report on the Rio Grande question.

> The Commissioners' report stated that Mexico had been wrongfully deprived for many years of its equitable rights and they recommended that the matter be settled by a treaty dividing the use of the waters equally, Mexico to waive all claims for indemnity for the past unlawful use of water.[2]

The United States and Mexico substantially followed the recommendations of the report in their agreed resolution of the dispute, which was embodied in the 1906 Convention concerning the Equitable Distribution of the Waters of the Rio Grande for Irrigation Purposes.

Notes and Question

1. *Harmon's folly.* The doctrine of "absolute territorial sovereignty" epitomized by the Harmon Doctrine enjoyed a certain amount of popularity, principally among upstream states, during the nineteenth century. Its downstream-country counterpart was the idea of "absolute territorial integrity," according to which a downstream state had the right to receive the same quantity (and presumably quality) of water it had always received. Many specialists in the field of the law of international watercourses believe both doctrines have now given way to a more flexible principle of equitable utilization, which would accommodate inevitable changes in the use made of an international watercourse by the riparian states. This principle is explored below. You should ask yourself as you read through the materials in this chapter whether you believe that the Harmon Doctrine is still "alive." For a study of the practice of the United States and other countries concluding that it is not, *see* Stephen McCaffrey, The Harmon Doctrine One Hundred Years Later: Buried, Not Praised, 36 Nat. Res. J. 549 (1996).

2. United States of America, Memorandum of the State Department of Apr. 21, 1958, Legal Aspects of the Use of Systems of International Waters with reference to Columbia-Kootenay River System under Customary International Law and the Treaty of 1909, 85th Cong., 2d Sess., Senate doc. No. 118 (Washington, D.C., 1958), p. 64. [Renumbered footnote.]

2. *Any port in a storm?* As a matter of legal analysis, are there any problems with basing an opinion concerning international water rights on a decision in a sovereign immunity case involving a foreign vessel? (*See* footnote 1, above and accompanying text.)

3. *Problem.* You are the United States Secretary of State's Legal Adviser. You are informed that the United States is downstream of Canada on the Columbia River and that Canada plans certain works in its territory that would have adverse effects on American plans to develop the river. The only precedent you have is that described in the above excerpt—the "Harmon Doctrine" and the subsequent resolution of the dispute that gave rise to it. What legal position can you expect Canada to take in the Columbia River case, and how will you respond to it?

4. *United States government lawyer-contortionists.* Because it did not serve United States interests in cases in which the United States would be on the *receiving* end of pollution or other actions in upstream states, United States government lawyers have been bending over backwards to repudiate the Harmon Doctrine almost from the time it was articulated. *See* McCaffrey, note/question 1, above; *and see* the State Department memorandum cited in footnote 2, above.

5. *Harmon redivivus?* During the negotiation of the recently adopted UN Convention on the Law of the Non-Navigational Uses of International Watercourses, discussed below, and in their explanations of vote on the Convention, several countries lamented what in their view was the failure of the Convention to take due account of "sovereignty." Most, if not all of these countries were upstream states. But does this necessarily mean they were embracing the Harmon Doctrine?

B. CASE STUDY: THE TIGRIS-EUPHRATES BASIN

■ WATER, POLITICS, AND INTERNATIONAL LAW

Stephen McCaffrey
in Water in Crisis 92, 93 (Peter Gleick, ed. 1993)[3]

The Tigris and Euphrates River systems are often treated as one basin because they unite in the Shatt-al-Arab waterway shortly before emptying into the Persian Gulf. Both rivers rise in Turkey and flow through or along Syrian territory before entering Iraq. While the Euphrates flows through Syria for a considerable distance, the Tigris never enters Syria entirely but only forms the border of that country with Turkey briefly before flowing into Iraq. Tributaries flowing from the Zagros Mountains in Iran also contribute importantly to the Tigris. The Euphrates is currently the subject of the

3. [Footnotes deleted—EDS.]

greatest development efforts, especially in Turkey, but the flow of the Tigris system is approximately 65 percent greater than that of the Euphrates. Iraq is more heavily dependent upon water from the Tigris and Euphrates than Syria or Turkey, with a majority of the Iraqi population relying upon those rivers for all of their water needs.

Turkey is currently constructing a US$21 billion water project on the Euphrates in southeast Anatolia, called the Greater Anatolia Project (GAP), which has given rise to considerable concern on the part of Syria and Iraq. The GAP project will ultimately consist of 21 dams which will be used for the production of hydroelectric power and for the irrigation of up to 1,500,000 hectares. It has been estimated that when completed in the late 1990's, the project could cause Syria to lose up to 40 percent of its water from the Euphrates and Iraq as much as 90 percent. The largest dam in the project, the Ataturk dam, was completed in 1990. In order to begin filling the reservoir behind the dam, Turkey stopped the flow of the Euphrates entirely for one month, from mid-January to mid-February of 1990.

Needless to say, this action disturbed the two lower riparians greatly. Turkey has stated that it will guarantee a flow of 500 cubic meters per second (CMS) below the project and maintains that increased releases before the January, 1990 stoppage of the Euphrates kept the average flow at that level. Iraq, however, is not satisfied with that amount. At a ministerial level meeting of the three states in June of 1990, Iraq requested 700 CMS, basing its claim on what it termed its "acquired rights" to the use of Euphrates waters for irrigation. According to Iraq, these rights derived from use of the waters for that purpose for thousands of years. Indeed, the waters of the Tigris and Euphrates have been used for irrigation in what is now Iraq since the time of ancient Mesopotamia, some 6,000 years ago.

Unlike the situation in the Jordan basin, the relations between the countries in the Tigris-Euphrates basin have not been marked by military conflict over water. There are, in fact, bilateral agreements between Turkey and Iraq and between Syria and Iraq concerning certain aspects of their water relations. Furthermore, since 1983 Syria has been participating in the work of a Joint Technical Regional Rivers Committee that had been established by Iraq and Turkey in 1980, at the invitation of those two countries. Yet water is undeniably a source of tension in the region and a crucial element in the overall political relations between the three countries.

Turkey has accused both Syria and Iraq of providing sanctuary to the Marxist Kurdish Workers' Party (PKK), which is waging a violent and bloody independence campaign against the Turkish government. In October, 1989, then prime minister Turgut Ozal, later became Turkey's president, declared that Euphrates water would be cut off unless activities of the PKK were curtailed. But after assuming the presidency, Ozal . . . stated that Turkey "will never use the control of water to coerce or threaten [our neighbors]." While this should be of some comfort to Turkey's neighbors, Turkish officials have denied any obligation to provide water to downstream countries. For example, Turkey's Minister of State, Kamran Inan, has been reported to have stated that "We have no international obligations" concerning the Tigris and Euphrates.

Even if coercion or pressure is not an objective, however, the GAP project poses a significant threat to downstream water users. Syria, for example, depends heavily upon the Euphrates for drinking water, irrigation and industrial uses, and to a lesser extent for electricity. According to one account, "With its population growing at 3.7% per year, Syria would be running short of water by the end of the century even without the GAP. With it, Syria faces a water catastrophe." While Iraq may look to the Tigris as an alternative source of supply, it is sufficiently concerned with the flow of the Euphrates that in 1974 it threatened to bomb the al-Thawra dam in Syria and massed troops along the border, alleging that the dam reduced the river's flow. It is not only water quantity, but also water quality that is at stake. Return flows from the massive irrigation projects contemplated as part of GAP will carry salts as well as fertilizer and pesticide residues back into the Euphrates. This may render the water unfit for drinking, unless treated, and reduce its suitability for irrigation and some industrial uses.

C. GENERAL PRINCIPLES OF INTERNATIONAL LAW CONCERNING THE ALLOCATION AND USE OF INTERNATIONAL WATERCOURSES

1. The United Nations Convention

■ UNITED NATIONS CONVENTION ON THE LAW OF THE NON-NAVIGATIONAL USES OF INTERNATIONAL WATERCOURSES

U.N. Doc. A/RES/51/229, July 8, 1997*, reprinted in *36 I.L.M 700 (1997)

PART I. INTRODUCTION

Article 1
Scope of the Present Convention

1. The present Convention applies to uses of international watercourses and of their waters for purposes other than navigation and to measures of protection, preservation and management related to the uses of those watercourses and their waters.

2. The use[s] of international watercourses for navigation is not within the scope of the present Convention except insofar as other uses affect navigation or are affected by navigation.

Article 2
Use of Terms

For the purposes of the present Convention:

(a) "Watercourse" means a system of surface waters and groundwaters constituting by virtue of their physical relationship a unitary whole and normally flowing into a common terminus;

(b) "International watercourse" means a watercourse, parts of which are situated in different States;

(c) "Watercourse State" means a State Party to the present Convention in whose territory part of an international watercourse is situated, or a Party that is a regional economic integration organization, in the territory of one or more of whose Member States part of an international watercourse is situated;

. . .

Part II. General Principles

Article 5
Equitable and Reasonable Utilization and Participation

1. Watercourse States shall in their respective territories utilize an international watercourse in an equitable and reasonable manner. In particular, an international watercourse shall be used and developed by watercourse States with a view to attaining optimal and sustainable utilization thereof and benefits therefrom, taking into account the interests of the watercourse States concerned, consistent with adequate protection of the watercourse.

2. Watercourse States shall participate in the use, development and protection of an international watercourse in an equitable and reasonable manner. Such participation includes both the right to utilize the watercourse and the duty to cooperate in the protection and development thereof, as provided in the present Convention.

Article 6
Factors Relevant to Equitable and Reasonable Utilization

1. Utilization of an international watercourse in an equitable and reasonable manner within the meaning of article 5 requires taking into account all relevant factors and circumstances, including:

(a) Geographic, hydrographic, hydrological, climatic, ecological and other factors of a natural character;

(b) The social and economic needs of the watercourse States concerned;

(c) The population dependent on the watercourse in each watercourse State;

(d) The effects of the use or uses of the watercourses in one watercourse State on other watercourse States;

(e) Existing and potential uses of the watercourse;

(f) Conservation, protection, development and economy of use of the water resources of the watercourse and the costs of measures taken to that effect;

(g) The availability of alternatives, of comparable value, to a particular planned or existing use.

2. In the application of article 5 or paragraph 1 of this article, watercourse States concerned shall, when the need arises, enter into consultations in a spirit of cooperation.

3. The weight to be given to each factor is to be determined by its importance in comparison with that of other relevant factors. In determining what is a reasonable and equitable use, all relevant factors are to be considered together and a conclusion reached on the basis of the whole.

Article 7
Obligation Not to Cause Significant Harm

1. Watercourse States shall, in utilizing an international watercourse in their territories, take all appropriate measures to prevent the causing of significant harm to other watercourse States.

2. Where significant harm nevertheless is caused to another watercourse State, the States whose use causes such harm shall, in the absence of agreement to such use, take all appropriate measures, having due regard for the provisions of articles 5 and 6, in consultation with the affected State, to eliminate or mitigate such harm and, where appropriate, to discuss the question of compensation.

Article 8
General Obligation to Cooperate

1. Watercourse States shall cooperate on the basis of sovereign equality, territorial integrity, mutual benefit and good faith in order to attain optimal utilization and adequate protection of an international watercourse.

2. In determining the manner of such cooperation, watercourse States may consider the establishment of joint mechanisms or commissions, as deemed necessary by them, to facilitate cooperation on relevant measures and procedures in the light of experience gained through cooperation in existing joint mechanisms and commissions in various regions.

Article 9
Regular Exchange of Data and Information

1. Pursuant to article 8, watercourse States shall on a regular basis exchange readily available data and information on the condition of the watercourse, in particular that of a hydrological, meteorological, hydrogeological and ecological nature and related to the water quality as well as related forecasts.

2. If a watercourse State is requested by another watercourse State to provide data or information that is not readily available, it shall employ its best efforts to comply with the request but may condition its compliance

upon payment by the requesting State of the reasonable costs of collecting and, where appropriate, processing such data or information.

3. Watercourse States shall employ their best efforts to collect and, where appropriate, to process data and information in a manner which facilitates its utilization by the other watercourse States to which it is communicated.

Article 10
Relationship Between Different Kinds of Uses

1. In the absence of agreement or custom to the contrary, no use of an international watercourse enjoys inherent priority over other uses.

2. In the event of a conflict between uses of an international watercourse, it shall be resolved with reference to articles 5 to 7, with special regard being given to the requirements of vital human needs.

PART III. PLANNED MEASURES

Article 11
Information Concerning Planned Measures

Watercourse States shall exchange information and consult each other and, if necessary, negotiate on the possible effects of planned measures on the condition of an international watercourse.

. . .[4]

Article 32
Non-Discrimination

Unless the watercourse States concerned have agreed otherwise for the protection of the interests of persons, natural or juridical, who have suffered or are under a serious threat of suffering significant transboundary harm as a result of activities related to an international watercourse, a watercourse State shall not discriminate on the basis of nationality or residence or place where the injury occurred, in granting to such persons, in accordance with its legal system, access to judicial or other procedures, or a right to claim compensation or other relief in respect of significant harm caused by such activities carried on in its territory.

Article 33
Settlement of Disputes

1. In the event of a dispute between two or more Parties concerning the interpretation or application of the present Convention, the Parties concerned shall, in the absence of an applicable agreement between them, seek a settlement of the dispute by peaceful means in accordance with the following provisions.

2. If the Parties concerned cannot reach agreement by negotiation re-

4. [The remaining articles in Part III are set forth in Chapter 8, section B.—EDS.]

> quested by one of them, they may jointly seek the good offices of, or request mediation or conciliation by, a third party, or make use, as appropriate, of any joint watercourse institutions that may have been established by them or agree to submit the dispute to arbitration or to the International Court of Justice.
>
> 3. Subject to the operation of paragraph 10 of the present article, if after six months from the time of the request for negotiations referred to in paragraph 2, the Parties concerned have not been able to settle their dispute through negotiation or any other means referred to in paragraph 2, the dispute shall be submitted, at the request of any of the parties to the dispute, to impartial fact-finding in accordance with paragraphs 4 to 9, unless the Parties otherwise agree. . . .

Notes and Questions

1. *What's in a name?* The UN "Convention" is a multilateral treaty (*see* Chapter 5, above), and thus is a legally binding instrument. Or is it? When does it become binding? Whom does it bind? Could it ever "bind" countries that were not parties to it? How? Or, to put it another way, in what sense? In this connection, a short excursion into the Convention's history may be enlightening.

2. *Provenance.* The UN Convention is based on a draft prepared by the International Law Commission of the United Nations (ILC). *See* Report of the International Law Commission on the Work of Its Forty-sixth Session, 1994 I.L.C. Rep. 197, 49 UN GAOR Supp. (No. 10), UN Doc. A/49/10 (1994). The ILC was established by the UN General Assembly in 1947 to promote "the progressive development of international law and its codification." Statute of the I.L.C., Article 1, para. 1, UN Doc. A/CN.4/4/Rev.2 (1982). It is composed of 34 experts on international law, from as many countries, who are elected by the UN General Assembly and serve in their individual capacities rather than as representatives of governments. In furtherance of its purpose, the ILC prepares drafts on general subjects of international law that are ultimately referred to the General Assembly for its action. The Assembly has often called conferences of UN member states for the purpose of elaborating conventions, or multilateral treaties, on the basis of ILC drafts. This has occurred, for example, with regard to the 1958 UN Conventions on the Law of the Sea, the 1961 Vienna Convention on the Law of Diplomatic Relations and the 1969 Vienna Convention on the Law of Treaties. The commission is currently considering another subject relating to the environment, "International Liability for Injurious Consequences of Acts Not Prohibited by International Law." The latter subject is dealt with in Chapter 9, above.

The ILC began work on international watercourses in 1974, pursuant to a request from the General Assembly in 1970. It completed the "first reading," or provisional adoption, of the draft articles on international watercourses at its 1991 session. As is the usual practice, the articles were then transmitted by the UN Secretary General to governments for their comments, which were due in January 1993. For an evaluation of the draft articles as adopted on first reading, *see* Doman Colloquium on the Law of International Watercourses: Review of the ILC's Draft Rules on the Non-Navigational Uses of International Watercourses, 3 Colo. J. Intl. Envtl. L. & Poly. 197-334 (1992). After receiving comments from governments (fewer than 30 states submitted observations) the commission gave the draft a "second reading" which it completed in 1994. *See* Stephen McCaffrey, The International Law Commission Adopts Draft Articles on International Watercourses, 89 Am. J. Intl. L. 395 (1995). The ILC transmitted the draft to the General Assembly with a recommendation that a convention be elaborated on the basis of the articles. 1994 I.L.C. Rep. 196-197. The General Assembly decided, in Resolution 49/52 of December 9, 1994, to "convene a Working Group of the Whole, open to States Members of the United Nations or members of specialized agencies, . . . to elaborate a framework convention" on the subject, based on the draft adopted by the ILC. (*Id.*, operative para. 3.)

What is the significance of all of this? That the international lawmaking process is painfully slow? What are some possible reasons for the torpidity of the process? As to the effect of the Convention on nonparties, would it help to know how much of it was a "codification" and how much "progressive development" of international law? How could you find this out?

3. *Arbitral antecedents.* Recall the award in the *Lake Lanoux* arbitration, reproduced in Chapter 6, above. Are the principles enunciated there consistent with those contained in the Convention?

4. *The Convention's cornerstone: equitable utilization.* The principle of equitable utilization, set forth in Article 5, has the advantage of permitting changes in the legal regime of a river in a manner that corresponds to changes in hydrological conditions and the needs of the states concerned. It is also a useful tool in situations where there is insufficient water, qualitatively or quantitatively, to satisfy the demands of all riparian states. *See also* Articles IV and V of the pathbreaking Helsinki Rules on the Uses of Waters of International Rivers, and accompanying commentary, adopted by the International Law Association (ILA) in 1966, reproduced below (hereinafter referred to as ILA, *Helsinki Rules*). As stated in the commentary to Article IV of the Helsinki Rules, "[t]he idea of equitable sharing is to provide the maximum benefit to each basin State from the uses of the waters with the minimum detriment to each." ILA, *Helsinki Rules,* at 10.

As a preliminary matter, what constitutes "use" or "utilization" of an international watercourse system? Would either expression include activities such as deforestation that do not directly involve use of the water but may have far-reaching impacts on the watercourse system (e.g., through increased siltation and pollution)? *See generally* S. McCaffrey, Fifth Report on the Law of the Non-Navigational Uses of International Watercourses, part I, Water-Related Hazards and Dangers, [1989] Y.B. Intl. L. Commn., vol. 2, pt. 1, at 91, 93 (1992).

Secondly, how does environmental protection fit in with the ideas of "maximum benefit" and "minimum detriment"? Does it have a place within the doctrine of equitable utilization?

5. *Equitable pollution?* Pollution of international watercourses was dealt with in Chapter 10, above. Is pollution a form of "utiliz[ation]" of a watercourse for the purposes of Article 5? If so, is there/should there be an equitable right to pollute? How would you define such a right? What about withdrawal of water from a watercourse: Is that a form of utilization? Swimming or boating? Is recreational boating a "non-navigational" use of a watercourse? Is this just another highly theoretical law professor's question, or might it actually be significant in some circumstances?

6. *The Convention's other (!?) cornerstone: The "no-harm" principle.* Article 7 as adopted by the ILC on first reading in 1991 read simply as follows:

> Watercourse States shall utilize an international watercourse in such a way as not to cause appreciable harm to other watercourse States.

The International Law Commission's Commentary to this version states:

> Article 7 sets forth the fundamental rule that a State utilizing an international watercourse shall do so in a manner that does not cause appreciable harm to other watercourse States. This well-established rule is a specific application of the principle of the harmless use of territory expressed in the maxim *sic utere tuo ut alienum non laedas,* which is itself a reflection of the sovereign equality of States. In other words, the exclusive competence that a watercourse State enjoys within its territory is not to be exercised in such a way as to cause damage to other watercourse States. To cause such damage would be to interfere with the competence of those other watercourse States over matters within their territories.

International Law Commission, Draft Articles on the Law of the Non-Navigational Uses of International Watercourses, Report of the International Law Commission on the Work of Its Fortieth Session, 43 U.N. GAOR Supp. (No. 10), U.N. Doc. A/44/10 (1988), at 83, 85 (as amended upon adoption of the Draft Articles on first reading in 1991) (footnotes omitted). How much of this is applicable to the version of Article 7 now contained in the convention? What is the key language?

7. *Problem.* Suppose the Blue River rises in state A and flows into state B and that state A permits its nationals to pollute the river in such a way as to make it unsuitable for swimming in state B. In all other respects, the river is still usable by state B. Has A breached the 1991 version of Article 7, set forth in note/question 6, above?

8. *Can harm be equitable? The dilemma of the duelling cornerstones.* Could

Article 5 of the convention and the version of Article 7 adopted on first reading (set forth in note/question 6 above) be potentially inconsistent with each other? Assume for example that state B is a lower riparian country, located in relatively flat terrain, that has developed an agricultural economy. Assume further that state A is an upper riparian on the same river and begins to develop its water resources after state B has established its agricultural water uses and in a way that causes "significant harm" to state B. Assume, finally, that an "equitable and reasonable" allocation of the water could be arrived at, but not without requiring state B to tolerate some harm. Which principle should prevail: "equitable utilization" or "no harm"?

9. *A first cut at the Gordian knot.* The ILC in 1991 answered the question put at the end of the foregoing note in the following way:

> *[P]rima facie,* at least[,] utilization of an international watercourse . . . is not equitable if it causes other watercourse States appreciable harm. . . . The Commission recognizes, however, that in some instances the achievement of equitable and reasonable utilization will depend upon the toleration by one or more watercourse States of a measure of harm. In these cases, the necessary accommodations would be arrived at through specific agreements.

Report of the International Law Commission on the Work of Its Fortieth Session, above, at 84. Is this answer satisfactory? Specifically, is it the principle of "equitable utilization" or that of "no harm" that should prevail in the event of conflict? How can it be said that "utilization of an international watercourse . . . is not equitable if it causes other . . . States . . . harm"? Is it not one of the primary purposes of the equitable utilization doctrine to distribute burdens equitably when there simply is not enough water to go around? Could the ILC's initial solution not have the effect, in some cases, of freezing the development of those riparian states (like state A in the above hypothetical) that lose the race to the river? On the other hand, how could giving precedence to equitable utilization be reconciled with the *sic utere tuo* maxim, to which the International Court of Justice has given its imprimatur in the *Corfu Channel* case, and which is enshrined in the *Trail Smelter* award as well as Principle 21 of the Stockholm Declaration (below)? *See generally* Stephen McCaffrey, The Law of International Watercourses: Some Recent Developments and Unanswered Questions, 17 Denver J. Intl. L. & Poly. 505, 508-510 (1989).

10. *The Gordian knot II.* The controversy surrounding the relationship between the rules of "equitable utilization" and "no-harm" prompted the ILC to revise Article 7. The version finally adopted by the ILC in 1994 provides as follows:

> 1. Watercourse States shall exercise due diligence to utilize an international watercourse in such a way as not to cause significant harm to other watercourse States.

> 2. Where, despite the exercise of due diligence, significant harm is caused to another watercourse State, the State whose use causes the harm shall, in the absence of agreement to such use, consult with the State suffering such harm over:
>
> (a) the extent to which such use is equitable and reasonable taking into account the factors listed in article 6;
>
> (b) the question of ad hoc adjustments to its utilization, designed to eliminate or mitigate any such harm caused and, where appropriate, the question of compensation.

1994 ILC Rep., above, at 236. The commission's Commentary offers the following explanation of the new article:

> The Commission in this article is setting forth a process aimed at avoiding significant harm as far as possible while reaching an equitable result in each concrete case. Optimal use of finite water resources of an international watercourse is considered in light of the interests of each watercourse State concerned. This is in accord with emphasis throughout the articles . . . on consultations and negotiations concerning planned measures.

1994 I.L.C. Rep., above, at 236. Do you prefer this approach to the "bright-line" test in the 1991 version of the article? Which standard won out ultimately in the commission: equitable utilization or "no-harm"? Do you agree with this result?

11. *The Gordian knot III.* Of course, the UN General Assembly had the last word on the matter. What do you think of the version of Article 7 that finally emerged in the Convention? Did the governments negotiating the Convention bollix up the article? Is the final version in the Convention closer to the ILC's 1991 or 1994 text? Does the version in the Convention still set forth a "process"? If so, what is it? Can you tell from the face of the article which of the two rules, "equitable utilization" or "no-harm," prevails in the event of a conflict? If you can't tell, what would you draw upon in interpreting the article? *See generally* the 1969 Vienna Convention on the Law of Treaties, itself a treaty prepared on the basis of an ILC draft, Articles 31 and 32. U.N. Doc. A/CONF. 39/27, at 289 (1969), *reprinted in* 8 I.L.M. 679 (1969). The basic rule of the 1969 Convention is that "[a] treaty shall be interpreted in good faith in accordance with the ordinary meaning to be given to the terms of the treaty in their context and in the light of its object and purpose." *Id.*, art. 31(1). Does this help? What is the "object and purpose" of the Watercourse Convention?

12. *Which "cornerstone" for the Euphrates?* Would it make any difference whether the "equitable utilization" or the "no harm" rule were applied in the dispute over the Euphrates River described earlier in this chapter?

13. *The significance of "significant harm."* Does the expression "significant harm" as used in Article 7 embody a factual or a legal standard? Does

this question in any way hold the seeds of a solution to the problem of reconciling the equitable utilization and "no-harm" doctrines?

14. *The role of "vital needs."* Re-read Article 10(2) of the Convention. What role, if any, might the concept of "vital human needs" play in reconciling the principles of "equitable utilization" and "no-harm"?

15. *The Bank's conundrum.* In the hypothetical in note 7, if the development of state A's water resources is being financed by the World Bank, what criterion or criteria should the Bank employ to decide whether it should fund projects proposed by state A (e.g., dams and other works)? Equitable allocation of the uses and benefits of the international watercourse? Avoidance of significant harm to state B?

16. *A perspective from the dismal science.* Continuing with the line of inquiry we began in the previous note, what about the harm that state A will suffer if it is not allowed to proceed with its plans? Consider the following excerpts from Ronald Coase, The Problem of Social Cost, 3 J.L. & Econ. 1 (1960):

> The traditional approach has tended to obscure the nature of the choice that has to be made. The question is commonly thought of as one in which A inflicts harm on B and what has to be decided is: how should we restrain A? But this is wrong. We are dealing with a problem of a reciprocal nature. To avoid the harm to B would inflict harm on A. The real question that has to be decided is: should A be allowed to harm B or should B be allowed to harm A? The problem is to avoid the more serious harm. . . .
>
> . . . If we are to discuss the problem in terms of causation, both parties caused the damage. If we are to attain an optimum allocation of resources, it is therefore desirable that both parties should take the harmful effect . . . into account in deciding on their course of action.
>
> . . . What has to be decided is whether the gain from preventing the harm [to state B] is greater than the loss which would be suffered elsewhere [*viz.*, by state A] as a result of stopping the action which produces the harm.

Should this analytical framework be utilized by the Bank in deciding whether, or under what conditions, to fund state A's proposals? Even if it were found that the gain to state A from the projects would exceed the harm they would cause to state B, would it be consistent with international law to permit state A to proceed? Does it make a difference whether the rule of decision is (a) "equitable utilization" or (b) "no significant harm"? Does Coase's analysis take environmental factors into account? Under what circumstances would it? Must a price tag be placed on natural systems and living organisms that would be harmed in order to factor them into Coase's analysis?

17. *Borders and Coasean transactions.* In the above-cited article, Coase points out that high transaction costs may mean that an assignment of rights by law (e.g., under the "no-harm" rule) is impossible to change through the bargaining process. International boundaries and political factors may indeed give rise to transaction costs that are so high as to make

it virtually impossible for the states concerned to arrive at a bargain (e.g., one in which state B agrees to tolerate a certain measure of harm in exchange for some of the electrical power generated by state A's dam). Advise the World Bank as to how this consideration should be taken into account in deciding on whether to fund state A's proposal.

18. *Wars as transaction costs.* In some regions of the world, political and other factors produce added barriers to agreement on apportionment of the uses and benefits of shared water resources:

> Water rather than oil could cause the next Middle East war, according to national leaders and political observers in the region.
>
> Jordan's King Hussein has repeatedly warned Western visitors that a water shortage could induce Jordan to wage war against Israel, and a massive dam project in Turkey has sparked military threats from Syria and Iraq.

International Environment Reporter, Current Report 413 (Oct. 10, 1990).

You are a senior adviser to the United States Secretary of State, who has asked you for a memorandum concerning possible solutions to Middle East water problems. Would you advise the secretary that rules of international law, such as that contained in the Convention's Articles 5 and 7, are an effective means of dealing with such problems? If a law-based approach would not, in your view, be effective, what sort of approach would?

See generally J. Starr & D. Stoll, U.S. Foreign Policy on Water Resources in the Middle East (1987); Cooley, The War Over Water, 54 For. Poly. 3 (1984); Water in the Middle East: Conflict or Cooperation? (T. Naff & R. Matson, eds. 1984); Water Resources in the Middle East: Impact on Economics and Politics, Proceedings, Eightieth Ann. Mtng, Am. Socy. Intl. L. 249 (1986); Thomas Naff, Water: An Emerging Issue in the Middle East?, The Annals of the American Academy of Political Scientists 68 (Nov. 1985); and J. Waterbury, Hydropolitics of the Nile Valley (1979).

2. *Comments on the International Law Commission's Draft Articles*

In the following two excerpts the authors comment upon the version of the ILC's draft articles adopted on first reading in 1991.

■ THE INTERNATIONAL LAW COMMISSION'S DRAFT ARTICLES ON THE LAW OF INTERNATIONAL WATERCOURSES: PRINCIPLES AND PLANNED MEASURES

Charles Bourne

3 Colo. J. Intl. Envtl. L. & Poly. 65, 89-91 (1992)

The real contradiction that exists between Draft Articles 5 and 7, that is to say, between the principle of equitable utilization and the no appreciable harm rule, may be illustrated by considering the *Flathead River* case. The Flathead River flows from south-eastern British Columbia into north-western Montana. When a company proposed to establish a coal mine on Cabin Creek, a tributary of the Flathead River in British Columbia, there were objections to the project, and the Canadian and US governments referred the matter to the International Joint Commission (IJC), under article IV of the Boundary Waters Treaty for study. In December 1988 the IJC submitted its report and recommendations to the governments.

Relying on the technical assessment of a Study Board established by it, the IJC recommended that the governments not approve the projected mine. While noting that the available data were incomplete, it felt confident in holding that the operation of the mine would violate the no injurious pollution rule of article IV of the Boundary Waters Treaty, or at least that it carried the risk of that violation. In particular, the IJC concluded that damage would inevitably occur to the habitat, which would cause a significant loss of fish population. And this loss, it said, "would be such as to cause a reduction in the quantity and quality of the sport fishing activity in the United States and create a negative impact on the associated economic infrastructure since the affected fish population migrate for much of their adult lives to United States waters." The IJC, however, indicated that its conclusion was "not based on the dollar losses . . . , although . . . there will be demonstrable and sustained economic loss to a number of interests dependent on this fishery," but on the ground that "a reduction of the fish population . . . would undoubtedly be an injury of most serious consequence to the integrity of the fishery itself, and thus to that property interest in the public domain on the other side of the border."

This conclusion was dictated by the strict no injury rule of article IV. Would the same conclusion have been reached if the governing rule were that of equitable utilization? The IJC itself perhaps indicated otherwise, for its final recommendation to the governments was that they "consider, with the appropriate jurisdictions, opportunities for defining and implementing compatible, equitable and sustainable development activities and management strategies in the upper Flathead River basin." The fact of the matter is that the IJC was precluded by the no injury rule of article IV from itself attempting to reach an equitable and reasonable balancing of the conflicting interests of the parties. If it had been free to do so, it might well have found in favour of the project; for, while the evidence established that the fish population would be reduced, it did not show that the fishery would suffer any long-term or irreversible damage. Furthermore, while the negative impact of the project on sport fishing and on the associated economic infrastructure was remarked on, there was no mention of the impact of a rejection of the project on the economy of British Columbia and Canada. Even under the ILC's Draft Article 6, these are relevant factors that must be taken into account in determining the equitable and reasonable manner of utilization of an international watercourse.

5. Summary

Flathead River demonstrates the weakness of a no harm rule in watercourse cases; in the last analysis, those called upon to apply it cannot ensure that their decision or recommendation, as the case may be, is equitable and reasonable. This so even if the rule is qualified by words such as *appreciable*, unless one is prepared to give them such a meaning that the rule becomes equivalent to that of equitable utilization.

Although, as seen above, there was some suggestion in the proceedings of the ILC that the apparent conflict between the two rules in Draft Articles 5 and 7 was not real, in its commentary to article 7 the ILC did acknowledge that in some instances the application of the no appreciable harm rule might not achieve an equitable and reasonable utilization. In that case, it wrote, the necessary accommodations would be arrived at through specific agreements. It added: "Thus, a watercourse State may not justify a use that causes appreciable harm to another watercourse State on the ground that the use is 'equitable', in the absence of agreement between the watercourse States concerned." This is a frank admission of the existence of a real conflict between the two articles. . . .

In its Draft Articles 11 to 19 on planned measures, the ILC has elaborated the customary international law applicable to States in their utilization of the waters of an international watercourse. In doing so, it has developed this law progressively, and the result should prove to be acceptable to States.

On the other hand, the ILC has not been so successful in defining the general principles of law applicable to international watercourses. Its formulation of the principles dealing with equitable utilization (articles 5 and 6), the duty to cooperate (article 8) and exchange data and information regularly (article 9), and the relationship between uses (article 10) reflect current law. The novelty comes in article 7, which effectively makes no appreciable harm the primary rule of international water resources law, relegating the principle of equitable utilization to a subordinate role. This change in the law is profound.

Notes and Questions

1. *A flat prohibition of harm on the Flathead vs. an equitable right to pollute.* What do you think of Professor Bourne's analysis of the Flathead River case? Do you agree that it was unfortunate that the IJC was compelled by the "strict no injury rule of article IV" of the 1909 Boundary Waters Treaty to recommend against approval of the Cabin Creek coal mine? Is protection of the environment despite (assumed) economic loss in British Columbia realistic? Do you agree with Professor Bourne that it would have been better for the two countries to strike an appropriate balance between environmental protection and economic development rather than flatly to prohibit development?

2. *Where's the transboundary pollution?* The relevant portion of Article IV of the 1909 Boundary Waters Treaty provides simply as follows: "It is . . . agreed that . . . boundary waters and waters flowing across the boundary shall not be polluted on either side to the injury of health or property on the other." Is this a prohibition of transboundary pollution? If not, can you see how the IJC could have concluded that pollution strictly confined to Canada would violate this provision?

■ BACKGROUND AND OVERVIEW OF THE INTERNATIONAL LAW COMMISSION'S STUDY OF THE NON-NAVIGATIONAL USES OF INTERNATIONAL WATERCOURSES

Stephen McCaffrey

3 Colo. J. Intl. Envtl. L. & Poly. 17, 22-23, 25-27, 28-29 (1992)

Two fundamental questions concerning the draft articles persisted until the very end of the Commission's work on the provisionally adopted text. They concerned, respectively, the physical scope of the draft articles and the utility of a set of general principles concerning the non-navigational uses of international watercourses.

The question of the physical scope of applicability of the draft articles (which is another way of referring to the question of how to define the term *international watercourse*) proved controversial from the outset of the Commission's work on the topic and was ultimately not resolved until work on the draft was otherwise complete. Thus the Commission did not face this issue squarely until its 1991 session. It ultimately decided that the rules of the draft articles should apply to the entire "system" of surface and underground waters constituting by virtue of their physical relationship a unitary whole, and flowing into a common terminus. This decision is reflected in article 2 on use of terms.

The second question is even more fundamental in nature. It is whether it is possible to draft a single set of articles whose provisions will be appropriate for all of the many different international watercourses in the world, particularly in view of the widely differing circumstances of the States making use of them. This problem was addressed early in the Commission's work on the topic, and in 1980 the ILC, in adopting the first set of articles, decided to employ what has become known in the field of international environmental law as a "framework agreement" approach. This approach was carried over into the present set of draft articles in the form of article 3 on watercourse agreements. Thus the draft articles set forth general principles and rules that States can apply and adjust through specific watercourse agreements to suit the conditions of individual watercourses and the needs of the States concerned. . . .

This survey should not be concluded without noting that two additional parts that had been proposed to the Commission were not included in the draft articles as finally approved. One of these chapters was titled "Implementation," and contained a set of articles on the following subjects: private remedies, provision of information to the public, jurisdictional immunity, a conference of the parties, and amendment of the draft articles. The other part was titled "Fact-Finding and Settlement of Disputes." It contained an article on fact-finding, as a means of implementation of the provisions of the draft and of dispute avoidance, and four articles on the settlement of disputes (viz., obligation to settle disputes by peaceful means; consultations and negotiations; conciliation; and arbitration).

All that remains in these two chapters at this stage of the Commission's work is article 32, "Non-discrimination," which is based on article 4, "Equal Right of Access," of the proposed chapter on implementation. The Commission's Drafting Committee had, in fact, forwarded to the full Commission for its consideration an article titled "Recourse under Domestic Law," which provided as follows: "A watercourse State shall ensure that recourse is available in accordance with its legal system for compensation or other relief in respect of appreciable harm caused in other States by activities related to an international watercourse carried on by natural or juridical persons under its jurisdiction."

This article, which was a slightly modified version of article 3, paragraph 1 of the chapter on implementation proposed in the sixth report, had originally been modeled upon article 235, paragraph 2 of the 1982 United Nations Convention on the Law of the Sea (UNCLOS). Despite the striking similarity of the article to that provision of UNCLOS, which had been generally acceptable to States, the Commission was unable to reach consensus on the acceptability of such a provision in the context of international watercourses. While some members supported the provision, and even argued that it together with article 32 as finally adopted did not go far enough, others feared that it might result in interference by private individuals in matters that primarily concerned relations between States. That the article on recourse under domestic law gave rise to such controversy is somewhat puzzling in light of both the similar provision in the Law of the Sea Convention and the acceptance by the Commission of article 32 on non-discrimination, which could prove to be more onerous in some circumstances than a requirement to ensure the availability of recourse under domestic law.

As reported to the Commission in plenary session, the article concerned only the elimination of any substantive or procedural obstacles to obtaining relief for extraterritorial harm. It did not deal with the question of access to the applicable procedures, the subject of article 32. The possibility that recourse may be available for domestic, but not extraterritorial, harm is a real one, as demonstrated by the facts leading up to the well-known *Trail Smelter* arbitration. There the injured citizens in the US state of Washington could not bring an action directly against the smelter in the Canadian city of Trail, British Columbia because of a common law doctrine known as the "local action rule," which required that actions to recover for injury to land be brought in the jurisdiction where the land is located. Since jurisdiction could not be obtained over the smelter in the state of Washington, the plaintiffs were compelled to request that the US Government take up their claims. The continuing vigor of this doctrine has prompted the respective uniform law organizations in Canada and the United States to promulgate draft provisions dealing with the problem. It is unfortunate that the Commission was not prepared to do the same.

. . . I would like to suggest a few issues that I believe are particularly deserving of attention. . . .

1. Equitable utilization versus the obligation not to cause harm: which of these rules prevails in the event that they conflict?

2. What is the standard of responsibility for a breach of the draft articles—for example, article 7, which prohibits causing harm to other watercourse States?

3. Is the "framework agreement" approach viable in the field of international watercourses?

4. Is the "system" concept, as presently formulated in article 2, the soundest way of defining the physical scope of applicability of the draft articles (for example, should unrelated/confined groundwater have been included? Should the "common-terminus requirement be retained, and if so, should cases in which basins are connected by means of canals or otherwise somehow be taken into account)?

3. The Helsinki Rules

■ HELSINKI RULES ON THE USES OF WATERS OF INTERNATIONAL RIVERS, WITH EXCERPTS FROM COMMENTARY

adopted by the International Law Association (ILA) at its Fifty-second Conference held in Helsinki in 1966, ILA, Report of the Fifty-second Conference, Helsinki, Aug. 14-20, 1966, at 484 (1967).[5]

CHAPTER 1—GENERAL

ARTICLE I

The general rules of international law as set forth in these chapters are applicable to the use of the waters of an international drainage basin

5. The Helsinki Rules and commentary are also published separately in pamphlet form. ILA, Helsinki Rules on the Uses of the Waters of International Rivers (1967).

except as may be provided otherwise by convention, agreement or binding custom among the basin States.

ARTICLE II

An international drainage basin is a geographical area extending over two or more States determined by the watershed limits of the system of waters, including surface and underground waters, flowing into a common terminus.

ARTICLE III

A "basin State" is a state the territory of which includes a portion of an international drainage basin.

Comment

General. Traditionally, those States territorially concerned with an international drainage basin have been referred to as "riparian," "coriparian," "upper riparian," "lower riparian." These terms are based upon the view that the territory of the State so described touches a river flowing on the surface of the drainage basin.

Recognition of the fact that underground waters may flow from a State without reaching the surface in its territory into the territory of other States in an international drainage basin where they contribute substantially to the surface flow, demonstrates that the terms based upon the word "riparian" are inadequate to describe all States included within the international drainage basin.

These chapters therefore adopt the term "basin State" as a comprehensive one to include all States whose territories contribute waters to the international drainage basin, whether or not "riparian."

Illustration

The International River Meander flows on the surface through States A, B, and C. An underground spring in State D contributes water to an underground stream that flows into the Meander in the territory of B. All of these States are basin States although only A, B, and C are riparian States.

Chapter 2
Equitable Utilization of the Waters of an International Drainage Basin

ARTICLE IV

Each basin State is entitled, within its territory, to a reasonable and equitable share in the beneficial uses of the waters of an international drainage basin.

Comment

(a) General. This Article reflects the key principle of international law in this area that every basin State in an international drainage basin has the right to the reasonable use of the waters of the drainage basin. It rejects the unlimited sovereignty position, exemplified by the "Harmon Doctrine," which has been cited as supporting the proposition that a State has the unqualified right to utili[z]e and dispose of the waters of an international river flowing through its territory; such a position imports its logical corollary, that a State has no right to demand continued flow from co-basin States.

The Harmon Doctrine has never had a wide following among States and has been rejected by virtually all States which have had occasion to speak out on the point. It is noteworthy that, in the recent international rivers dispute between Bolivia and Chile over the Lauca River, Chile, the upper basin State, despite the heat of the controversy, did not assert the Harmon Doctrine in an attempt to justify its conduct; on the contrary it recognized that Bolivia has certain rights in the waters. [*See* note from Bolivian Ambassador to the Chairman of the Council of the O.A.S., OEA/Serv. B/VI, April 15, 1962.] Similarly in the Jordan Basin dispute between Israel and certain Arab States both sides have adhered to the position that each is entitled to a reasonable share of the basin waters [31 Dept. State Bull. 132 (1954); *see* U.S. Security Council Off. Rec., Supp. January-March, 1962, at 87-88 (S/5084) (1962)].

This Article recognizes that each basin State has rights equal in kind and correlative with those of each co-basin State. Of course, equal and correlative rights of use among the co-basin States does not mean that each such State will receive an identical share in the uses of the waters. Those will depend upon the weighing of factors considered in Article V of this Chapter.

A use of a basin State must take into consideration the economic and social needs of its co-basin States for use of the waters, and *vice-versa.* This consideration may result in one co-basin State receiving the right to use water in quantitatively greater amounts than its neighbours in the basin. The idea of equitable sharing is to provide the maximum benefit to each basin State from the uses of the waters with the minimum detriment to each.

(b) Beneficial Use. To be worthy of protection a use must be "beneficial," that is to say, it must be economically or socially valuable, as opposed, for example, to a diversion of waters by one State merely for the purpose of harassing another.

A "beneficial use" need not be *the* most productive use to which the water may be put, nor need it utilize the most efficient methods known in order to avoid waste and insure maximum utili[z]ation. As to the former, to provide otherwise would dislocate numerous productive and, indeed, essential portions of natural economies; the latter, while a patently imperfect solution, reflects the financial limitations of many States; in its application, the present rule is not designed to foster waste but to hold States to a duty of efficiency which is commensurate with their financial resources. Of course, the ability of a State to obtain international financing will be considered in this context. Thus, State A, an economically advanced and prosperous State which utilizes the inundation method or irrigation, might be required to develop a more efficient and less wasteful system forthwith, while State B, an underdeveloped State using the same method might be permitted additional time to obtain the means to make the required improvements.

ARTICLE V

(1) What is a reasonable and equitable share within the meaning of Article IV is to be determine in the light of all the relevant factors in each particular case.

(2) Relevant factors which are to be considered include, but are not limited to:

(a) the geography of the basin, including in particular the extent of the drainage area in the territory of each basin State;

(b) the hydrology of the basin, including in particular the contribution of water by each basin State;

(c) the climate affecting the basin;

(d) the past utilization of the waters of the basin, including in particular existing utilization;

(e) the economic and social needs of each basin State;

(f) the population dependent on the waters of the basin in each basin State;

(g) the comparative costs of alternative means of satisfying the economic and social needs of each basin State;

(h) the availability of other resources;

(i) the avoidance of unnecessary waste in the utilization of waters of the basin;

(j) the practicability of compensation to one or more of the co-basin States as a means of adjusting conflicts among uses; and

(k) the degree to which the needs of a basin state may be satisfied, without causing substantial injury to a co-basin State;

(3) The weight to be given to each factor is to be determined by its importance in comparison with that of other relevant factors. In determining what is a reasonable and equitable share, all relevant factors are to be considered together and a conclusion reached on the basis of the whole.

Comment

General. This Article provides the express, but flexible guidelines essential to insuring the protection of the "equal right" of all basin States to share the waters. Under the rules set forth "all the relevant factors" must be considered. An exhaustive list of factors cannot readily be compiled, for there would likely be others applicable to particular cases.

This Article states some of the factors to be considered in determining what is a reasonable and equitable share.

Stated somewhat more generally, the factor-analysis approach seeks primarily to determine whether (i) the various uses are compatible, (ii) any of the uses is essential to human life, (iii) the uses are socially and economically valuable, (iv) other resources are available, (v) any of the uses is "existing" within the meaning of Article VIII, (vi) it is feasible to modify competing uses in order to accommodate all to some degree, (vii) financial contributions by one or more of the interested basin States for the construction of works could result in the accommodation of competing uses, (viii) the burden could be adjusted by the payment of compensation to one or more of the co-basin States, and (ix) overall efficiency of water utilization could be improved in order to increase the amount of available water.

In short, no factor has a fixed weight nor will all factors be relevant in all cases. Each factor is given such weight as it merits relative to all the other factors. And no factor occupies a position of preeminence *per se* with respect to any other factor. Further, to be relevant, a factor must aid in the determination or satisfaction of the social and economic needs of the co-basin states.

By way of example, suppose that State A, a lower co-basin State, has, for many years, used the waters of an international river for irrigation purposes. State B upstream now wishes to utilize the waters for hydro-electric power production. The uses for hydro-electric power and irrigation purposes are in partial conflict because the storage period for the hydroelectric use overlaps the growing season. Neither State uses, or wishes to use, the water for any other purpose at this point in time. State A, while having made substantial economic progress and enjoying prosperity, continues, as it always has, to use the inundation method of irrigation. A study of the basin indicates that the hydroelectric use would be more valuable than irrigation and the resulting dam would permit the introduction of conservation measures through the control of seasonal flooding, thus providing incidental benefit to all users. Study indicates that change to modern agricultural irrigation coupled with flow control afforded by the dam would permit, after some period of adjustment, reasonable agricultural productivity in State A, although probably less than that prevailing before. Moreover, while at one time several million people in State A depended upon the agricultural products produced in the basin area for survival, there are now alternative sources for obtaining food, at approximately the same cost, although not sufficient to satisfy fully all needs. A recent geological survey indicates the presence of substantial underground waters in the territory of State A. The contemplated uses in State B would benefit a new community of several hundred thousand people. Power could be obtained from other resources but at greater cost. On these facts the following factors are relevant to a determination of an equitable sharing: an existing reasonable use; dependence upon the waters; population; geographic, climatic and weather conditions; the existence of alternative sources of food supply; inefficient utilization; and the financial status of the respective co-basin states.

An existing reasonable use is entitled to significant weight as a factor and, as indicated in Article V, consideration must be given to protecting it. However, it is but one factor. In the foregoing illustration, there are other important factors: irrigation is not the more valuable of the competing uses in this instance; there are, moreover, alternative sources of food available; the availability of sources of underground water indicate that the need for water by State A may be satisfied from them, while State A has nevertheless continued to draw off the same amount of water from the international river utilizing an outmoded and wasteful process; the economic climate in State A favours growth. As regards State B, a key factor is that there are alternative sources of power.

A careful analysis shows that, despite the usual desirability of protecting existing reasonable uses, the competing factors indicate that some modification of the existing use is called for. The existence of alternative sources of agricultural products, the conservation benefits to the co-basin States, the employment of a wasteful and antiquated method of utili[z]ation and its potential for replacement by a less wasteful method within the financial ability of State A and the potential value of the proposed use—all dictate modification and accommodation.

Armed with this information, it may be possible to reconcile the conflicting uses. For example, reduction in appropriation for irrigation to the extent of the availability of usable water from the underground sources, or the abandonment of inundation in favour of a more efficient method, or the utilization of alternative sources of food supply (to the extent that it can reasonably do so) or any combination of these may be required of State A. On the other hand, State B may be required to bear some of the cost necessary to develop a modern irrigation system in State A, or in obtaining alternative food or water supplies for State A. If State A were required to abandon any portion of a permanent installation, some compensation by State B might be appropriate.

The employment of any one or some combination of the above measures may suffice to reconcile the conflict. If no other solution can be found, however, one of the uses may necessarily have to prevail to the impairment of the other use; the amount and kind of compensation, if any, to the State deprived of its use would then be determined. Irrigation, although an existing use, may nevertheless be required to give way since the weight of the factors favours the hydroelectric use. Under these facts, State B would, in all likelihood, be required to pay State A in part for discontinuance or impairment of the use.

There are alternative sources of electricity available to State B, but at a higher cost. State A may be required to compensate State B for all or a part of the cost differential, if the use of the waters for the production of power is precluded or limited.

This illustration shows how the several factors relevant to the particular case are to be considered and how the principle of equitable utili[z]ation is applied in order to achieve a fair and just settlement.

ARTICLE VI

A use or category of uses is not entitled to any inherent preference over any other use or category of uses.

ARTICLE VII

A basin State may not be denied the present reasonable use of the waters of an international drainage basin to reserve for a co-basin State a future use of such waters.

ARTICLE VIII

1. An existing reasonable use may continue in operation unless the factors justifying its continuance are outweighed by other factors leading to the conclusion that it be modified or terminated so as to accommodate a competing incompatible use.

2. (a) A use that is in fact in operation is deemed to have been an existing use from the time of the initiation of construction directly related to the use or, where such construction is not required, the undertaking of comparable acts of actual implementation.

(b) Such a use continues to be an existing use until such time as it is discontinued with the intention that it be abandoned.

3. A use will not be deemed an existing use if at the time of becoming operational it is incompatible with an already existing reasonable use. . . .[6]

Chapter 6—Procedures For the Prevention and Settlement of Disputes

ARTICLE XXVI

This Chapter relates to procedures for the prevention and settlement of international disputes as to the legal rights or other interests of basin States and of other States in the waters of an international drainage basin.

. . .

ARTICLE XXIX

1. With a view to preventing disputes from a rising between basin States as to their legal rights or other interest, it is recommended that each basin

6. [The Helsinki Rules' provisions on pollution are set forth in Chapter 10.—Eds.]

State furnish relevant and reasonably available information to the other basin States concerning the waters of a drainage basin within its territory and its use of, and activities with respect to such waters.

2. A State, regardless of its location in a drainage basin, should in particular furnish to any other basin State, the interests of which may be substantially affected, notice of any proposed construction or installation which would alter the regime of the basin in a way which might give rise to a dispute as defined in Article XXVI. The notice should include such essential facts as will permit the recipient to make an assessment of the probable effect of the proposed alteration.

3. A State providing the notice referred to in paragraph (2) of this Article should afford to the recipient a reasonable period of time to make an assessment of the probable effect of the proposed construction or installation and to submit its views thereon to the State furnishing the notice.

4. If a State has failed to give notice referred to in paragraph (2) of this Article, the alteration by the State in the regime of the drainage basin shall not be given the weight normally accorded to temporal priority in use in the event of a determination of what is a reasonable and equitable share of the waters of the basin.

ARTICLE XXX

In case of a dispute between States as to their legal rights or other interests, as defined in Article XXVI, they should seek a solution by negotiation.

ARTICLE XXXI

1. If a question or dispute arises which relates to the present or future utilization of the waters of an international drainable basin, it is recommended that the basin States refer the question or dispute to a joint agency and that they request the agency to survey the international drainage basin and to formulate plans or recommendations for the fullest and most efficient use thereof in the interests of all such States.

2. It is recommended that the joint agency be instructed to submit reports on all matters within its competence to the appropriate authorities of the member States concerned.

3. It is recommended that the member States of the joint agency in appropriate cases invite non-basin States which by treaty enjoy a right in the use of the waters of an international drainage basin to associate themselves with the work of the joint agency or that they be permitted to appear before the agency.

. . .

ARTICLE XXXIII

1. If the States concerned have not been able to resolve their dispute through negotiations or have been unable to agree on the measures de-

scribed in Article XXXI and XXXII, it is recommended that they form a commission of inquiry or an ad hoc conciliation commission, which shall endeavour to find a solution, likely to be accepted by the States concerned, of any dispute as to their legal rights.

2. It is recommended that the conciliation commission be constituted in the manner set forth in the Annex.

Notes and Questions

1. *The ILA.* It will be recalled[7] that the ILA is a non-governmental organization that adopts resolutions on subjects of international law at its biennial meetings.

2. *The Helsinki Rules.* The Helsinki Rules, as they are universally known, are a landmark effort and are still referred to today as being an authoritative statement of the law of international watercourses. Not only do they cover all phases of the subject but, perhaps most importantly, they represent the first attempt at a detailed codification of the doctrine of equitable utilization.

3. *The Helsinki Rules vs. the 1997 UN Convention.* What are the principal differences between the approaches of the UN Convention and the Helsinki Rules? Are the two approaches reconcilable?

4. *Equitable utilization meets (and trumps?) no-harm.* Re-read Article X, set forth in chapter 10. How does it resolve the potential conflict between equitable utilization and the prohibition of significant harm (in this case, of "substantial [pollution] injury")? Can the problem really be solved simply by saying, "consistent with the principle of equitable utilization," thou shalt not cause substantial injury to thy neighbor through new forms of or increases in the degree of existing water pollution?

5. *Dispute avoidance and settlement.* Read Article XXIX again, carefully. Does it *require* provision of information (para. 1), the giving of prior notification of planned measures (para. 2), etc.? How does this compare or contrast with the UN Convention? (The Convention's provisions on prior notification, beyond Article 11, which appears above, are set forth in section B of Chapter 7.) If not, why not? Are such provisions properly placed in a chapter on disputes? Or should they be treated as substantive obligations, as the UN Convention does?

The recommendation that a joint agency be used to help resolve disputes is well founded in state practice. The International Joint Commission between the United States and Canada, referred to in the Bourne excerpt above, is perhaps the best example of how effective such a body can be in avoiding and resolving disputes.

7. *See* Chapter 7.A, note 1 following the ILA's Rules of International Law Applicable to Transfrontier Pollution.

Since facts are often at the root of international water controversies, impartial fact-finding is often indispensable. Compare Article XXXIII of the Helsinki Rules with Article 33 of the UN Convention. In what way(s) are the two similar or different?

6. *The Helsinki Rules vs. the Salzburg Rules.* As you read the following excerpt, ask yourself how the approach of that set of articles, adopted by a different organization, differs from the one taken by the Helsinki Rules.

4. *The Salzburg Rules*

■ INSTITUTE OF INTERNATIONAL LAW RESOLUTION ON THE USE OF INTERNATIONAL NON-MARITIME WATERS

Annuaire de l'Institut de droit international, vol. 49-II, Salzburg Session, September 1961, at 381 (1961)

THE INSTITUTE OF INTERNATIONAL LAW

Considering that the economic value of the use of waters has been modified by modern techniques and that the application of said techniques to the waters of a river basin extending upon the territory of several States generally affects the whole of these States, and that this evolution requires an adjustment in the legal field;

Considering that there is a common interest in maximizing the use of available natural resources;

Considering that the obligation not to cause an unlawful prejudice to a third party is one of the basic principles governing general relations between neighboring countries;

Considering that, for the use of waters involving several States, each of the above-mentioned States may obtain, through consultations, joint planning and reciprocal concessions, the benefits of a more efficient development of natural resources;

Notes the existence of the following rules in international law and makes the following recommendations:

Article I

The present rules and recommendations apply to the use of waters which are part of a river or of a watershed extending upon the territory of two or more States.

Article II

Every State has the right to make use of the waters flowing across or bordering its territory subject to the limitations imposed by international law and in particular those which result from the following legal dispositions. That right is limited by the right to use by the other States concerned with the same river or watershed.

Article III

If the various States disagree upon the extent of their rights of use, the disagreement shall be settled on the basis of equity, taking into consideration the respective needs of the States, as well as any other circumstances relevant to any particular case.

Article IV

Each State may only proceed with works or to use the waters of a river or watershed that may affect the possibilities of use of the same waters by other States on condition of preserving for those States the benefit of the advantages to which they are entitled by virtue of Article III, as well as adequate compensation for any losses or damages incurred.

Article V

The works or uses referred to in the abovementioned article may only be initiated after due advance notice has been given to the States concerned.

Article VI

If objections are raised, the States shall enter in negotiations in view of reaching an agreement within a reasonable time. To this end, it is desirable that the States involved make use of technical expertises and if need be of appropriate commissions and organizations to reach solutions ensuring maximum benefits for all concerned.

Article VII

During the negotiations, every State should, according to the principle of good faith, refrain from proceeding with the works or uses in dispute, or from any other measures likely to aggravate the conflict or to make a settlement more difficult.

Article VIII

If the States involved cannot reach an agreement within a reasonable time, it is recommended to submit to judicial or arbitral settlement the question whether the intended development runs counter to the abovementioned rules. If the State raising objections to the projected works or uses is opposed to any judicial or arbitral settlement, the other State remains free, under its own responsibility, to proceed with said works or uses, while remaining obligated by the provisions of Articles II to IV.

Article IX

It is recommended to the States concerned by particular watersheds to consider whether it would not be appropriate to set up joint organizations for the preparation of water utilization plans to facilitate their economic development, as well as to prevent or settle any disputes that might occur.

Notes and Questions

1. *A "Sixties" mentality?* Do the rules set forth in the Institute's 1961 "Salzburg Resolution" reflect current international standards and values? Can it be said that there is today a "common interest in maximizing the use of available natural resources"? Is "maximizing" the same as "optimizing"? Can "maximum use" be squared with the concept of "sustainable development" (discussed in chapter 1)?

2. *ILA vs. IIL.* Are the Institute's articles simply another way of stating the doctrine of equitable utilization? If so, do they differ at all from the Helsinki Rules? How? Would any distinctions you identify make any difference in actual cases? In the Euphrates case? Can you reconcile the third preambular paragraph of the Salzburg Resolution with its Article III?

5. The Gabčíkovo-Nagymaros Case

■ CASE CONCERNING THE GABČÍKOVO-NAGYMAROS PROJECT (HUNGARY/SLOVAKIA)

International Court of Justice
Judgment of Sept. 25, 1997

[Hungary and Slovakia brought this case to the Court on July 2, 1993, by Special Agreement signed on April 7, 1993, which entered into force on June 28 of that year. The case concerned a project on the Danube River, provided for by a 1977 treaty between Hungary and Czechoslovakia, consisting of a series of dams and barrages on a stretch of approximately 200 kilometers of the Danube between Bratislava, the capital of Slovakia, and Budapest, the capital of Hungary. For most of the length of this stretch the Danube forms the border between the two countries. Upstream of the point at which it begins to form the border it is for a short distance wholly within what is now Slovak territory; downstream of the border sector it passes into Hungary. According to the treaty, its purposes were chiefly to improve navigation, provide flood protection, and produce electricity. The treaty provided for the construction of two series of locks, one at Gabčíkovo, on a 31-kilometer bypass canal in Czechoslovak (now Slovak) territory, and the other at Nagymaros, in Hungarian territory. In order to fill the bypass canal and thus operate the hydroelectric power plant and ship locks at Gabčíkovo, the treaty called for the Danube to be dammed at Dunakiliti, an installation which was Hungary's responsibility under the agreement.

[Citing environmental concerns, Hungary stopped work on both the Nagymaros and the Dunakiliti portions of the project in 1989 and purported to terminate the treaty unilaterally in May 1992. Czechoslovakia decided to put the upper part of the project into operation by damming the Danube, beginning on October 24, 1994, at Cunovo, a point at which the river is solely in Czechoslovak (now Slovak) territory. This created a reservoir (although a smaller one than foreseen under the treaty) and diverted most of the flow of the Danube (80 to 90 percent) into the bypass canal until the point at which that canal rejoins the bed of the Danube. The Cunovo dam and related structures are known as "Variant C"—the title given one of the possible "provisional solutions" considered by Czechoslovakia after Hungary's abandonment of the project. On January 1, 1993, Slovakia became an independent state.

[As indicated below, the court essentially held that both parties had breached their international obligations, Hungary by stopping work on the project and Slovakia, as successor to Czechoslovakia, by putting into operation Variant C. It also held that Hungary's purported termination of the 1977 treaty was ineffective, that the project—including Cunovo—would have to be placed under a joint operational regime, and that—unless the parties agree otherwise—they must compensate each other for the injurious consequences of their respective breaches.

[The court's opinion and some of the separate and dissenting opinions contain a wealth of material pertaining to the field of international environmental law. The following passages of the court's opinion are relevant to the field in general and to the subject of allocation and use of shared natural resources.]

17. The Danube has always played a vital part in the commercial and economic development of its riparian States, and has underlined and reinforced their interdependence, making international co-operation essential. Improvements to the navigation channel have enabled the Danube, now linked by canal to the Main and thence to the Rhine, to become an important navigational artery connecting the North Sea to the Black Sea. In the stretch of river to which the case relates, flood protection measures have been constructed over the centuries, farming and forestry practised, and, more recently, there has been an increase in population and industrial activity in the area. The cumulative effects on the river and on the environment of various human activities over the years have not all been favourable, particularly for the water régime.

Only by international co-operation could action be taken to alleviate these problems. Water management projects along the Danube have frequently sought to combine navigational improvements and flood protection with the production of electricity through hydroelectric power plants. The potential of the Danube for the production of hydroelectric power has been extensively exploited by some riparian States. The history of attempts to harness the potential of the particular stretch of the river at issue in these proceedings extends over a 25-year period culminating in the signature of the 1977 Treaty.

18. . . . Article 15 [of the 1977 treaty] specified that the contracting parties "shall ensure, by the means specified in the joint contractual plan, that the quality of the water in the Danube is not impaired as a result of the construction and operation of the System of Locks." . . .

It was stipulated in Article 19 that:

> The Contracting Parties shall, through the means specified in the joint contractual plan, ensure compliance with the obligations for the protection of nature arising in connection with the construction and operation of the System of Locks.

Article 20 provided for the contracting parties to take appropriate measures, within the framework of their national investments, for the protection of fishing interests in conformity with the Convention concerning Fishing in the Waters of the Danube, signed at Bucharest on 29 January 1958. . . .

[Hungary had contended that even though its stoppage of work was in breach of the 1977 treaty, it was justified by a "state of ecological necessity" to which the implementation of the project might have given rise.]

49. The Court will now consider the question of whether there was, in 1989, a state of necessity which would have permitted Hungary, without incurring international responsibility, to suspend and abandon works that it was committed to perform in accordance with the 1977 Treaty and related instruments.

50. In the present case, the Parties are in agreement in considering that the existence of a state of necessity must be evaluated in the light of the criteria laid down by the International Law Commission in Article 33 of the Draft Articles on the International Responsibility of States ["State Responsibility"] that it adopted on first reading. That provision is worded as follows:

> **Article 33. State of Necessity**
>
> 1. A state of necessity may not be invoked by a State as a ground for precluding the wrongfulness of an act of that State not in conformity with an international obligation of the State unless:
>
> (a) the act was the only means of safeguarding an essential interest of the State against a grave and imminent peril; and

(b) the act did not seriously impair an essential interest of the State towards which the obligation existed.

2. In any case, a state of necessity may not be invoked by a State as a ground for precluding wrongfulness: . . .

(c) if the State in question has contributed to the occurrence of the state of necessity.

(*Yearbook of the International Law Commission*, 1980, Vol. II, Part 2, p. 34.)

In its Commentary, the Commission defined the "state of necessity" as being

> the situation of a State whose sole means of safeguarding an essential interest threatened by a grave and imminent peril is to adopt conduct not in conformity with what is required of it by an international obligation to another State" (ibid., para. 1). . . .

51. The Court . . . observes . . . that [the state of necessity] can only be accepted on an exceptional basis. . . .

[A]ccording to the Commission, the state of necessity can only be invoked under certain strictly defined conditions which must be cumulatively satisfied; and the State concerned is not the sole judge of whether those conditions have been met.

52. In the present case, the following basic conditions set forth in Draft Article 33 are relevant: it must have been occasioned by an "essential interest" of the State which is the author of the act conflicting with one of its international obligations; that interest must have been threatened by a "grave and imminent peril"; the act being challenged must have been the "only means" of safeguarding that interest; that act must not have "seriously impair[ed] an essential interest" of the State towards which the obligation existed; and the State which is the author of that act must not have "contributed to the occurrence of the state of necessity." Those conditions reflect customary international law.

The Court will now endeavour to ascertain whether those conditions had been met at the time of the suspension and abandonment, by Hungary, of the works that it was to carry out in accordance with the 1977 Treaty.

53. The Court has no difficulty in acknowledging that the concerns expressed by Hungary for its natural environment in the region affected by the Gabcíkovo-Nagymaros Project related to an "essential interest" of that State, within the meaning given to that expression in Article 33 of the Draft of the International Law Commission.

The Commission, in its Commentary, indicated that one should not, in that context, reduce an "essential interest" to a matter only of the "existence" of the State, and that the whole question was, ultimately, to be judged in the light of the particular case (see Yearbook of the International Law Commission, 1980, Vol. II, Part 2, p. 49, para. 32); at the same time, it included among the situations that could occasion a state of necessity, "a grave danger to . . . the ecological preservation of all or some of [the] territory [of a State]" (ibid., p. 35, para. 3); and specified, with reference to State practice, that "It is primarily in the last two decades that safeguarding the ecological balance has come to be considered an 'essential interest' of all States." (Ibid., p. 39, para. 14.)

The Court recalls that it has recently had occasion to stress, in the following terms, the great significance that it attaches to respect for the environment, not only for States but also for the whole of mankind:

> the environment is not an abstraction but represents the living space, the quality of life and the very health of human beings, including generations unborn. The existence of the general obligation of States to ensure that activities within their jurisdiction and control respect the environment of other States or of areas beyond national control is now part of the corpus of international law relating to the environment.

Legality of the Threat or Use of Nuclear Weapons, Advisory Opinion, I.C.J. Reports 1996, pp. 241-242, para. 29.

54. The verification of the existence, in 1989, of the "peril" invoked by Hungary, of its "grave and imminent" nature, as well as of the absence of any "means" to respond to it, other than the measures taken by Hungary to suspend and abandon the works, are all complex processes.

As the Court has already indicated . . . , Hungary on several occasions expressed, in 1989, its "uncertainties" as to the ecological impact of putting in place the Gabcíkovo-Nagymaros barrage system, which is why it asked insistently for new scientific studies to be carried out.

The Court considers, however, that, serious though these uncertainties might have been they could not, alone, establish the objective existence of a "peril" in the sense of a component element of a state of necessity. The word "peril" certainly evokes the idea of "risk"; that is precisely what distinguishes "peril" from material damage. But a state of necessity could not exist without a "peril" duly established at the relevant point in time; the mere apprehension of a possible "peril" could not suffice in that respect. It could moreover hardly be otherwise, when the "peril" constituting the state of necessity has at the same time to be "grave" and "imminent." "Imminence" is synonymous with "immediacy" or "proximity" and goes far beyond the concept of "possibility." As the International Law Commission emphasized in its commentary, the "extremely grave and imminent" peril must "have been a threat to the interest at the actual time" (Yearbook of the International Law Commission, 1980, Vol. II, Part 2, p. 49, para. 33). That does not exclude, in the view of the Court, that a "peril" appearing in the long term might be held to be "imminent" as soon as it is established, at the relevant point in time, that the realization of that peril, however far off it might be, is not thereby any less certain and inevitable.

The Hungarian argument on the state of necessity could not convince the Court unless it was at least proven that a real, "grave" and "imminent" "peril" existed in 1989 and that the measures taken by Hungary were the only possible response to it. . . .

57. The Court concludes . . . that, with respect to both Nagymaros and Gabcíkovo, the perils invoked by Hungary, without prejudging their possible gravity, were not sufficiently established in 1989, nor were they "imminent"; and that Hungary had available to it at that time means of responding to these perceived perils other than the suspension and abandonment of works with which it had been entrusted. What is more, negotiations were under way which might have led to a review of the Project and the extension of some of its time-limits, without there being need to abandon it. The Court infers from this that the respect by Hungary, in 1989, of its obligations under the terms of the 1977 Treaty would not have resulted in a situation "characterized so aptly by the maxim *summum jus summa injuria*". . . .

. . . [A]lthough the principal object of the 1977 Treaty was the construction of a System of Locks for the production of electricity, improvement of navigation on the Danube and protection against flooding, the need to ensure the protection of the environment had not escaped the parties, as can be seen from Articles 15, 19 and 20 of the Treaty. . . .

The Court infers from all these elements that, in the present case, even if it had been established that there was, in 1989, a state of necessity linked to the performance of the 1977 Treaty, Hungary would not have been permitted to rely upon that state of necessity in order to justify its failure to comply with its treaty obligations, as it had helped, by act or omission to bring it about. . . .

[The Court then turned to the legality of "Variant C."]

78. [I]n practice, the operation of Variant C led Czechoslovakia to appropriate, essentially for its use and benefit, between 80 and 90 per cent of the waters of the Danube before returning them to the main bed of the river, despite the fact that the Danube is not only a shared international watercourse but also an international boundary river.

Czechoslovakia submitted that Variant C was essentially no more than what Hungary had already agreed to and that the only modifications made were those which had become necessary by virtue of Hungary's decision not to implement its treaty obligations. It is true that Hungary, in concluding the 1977 Treaty, had agreed to the damming of the Danube and the diversion of its waters into the bypass canal. But it was only in the context of a joint operation and a sharing of its benefits that Hungary had given its consent. The suspension and withdrawal of that consent constituted a violation of Hungary's legal obligations, demonstrating, as it did, the refusal by Hungary of joint operation; but that cannot mean that Hungary forfeited its basic right to an equitable and reasonable sharing of the resources of an international watercourse. . . .

[In discussing whether Czechoslovakia's putting into operation of Variant C could be justified as a countermeasure,[8] the Court stated, inter alia, as follows:]

85. In the view of the Court, an important consideration is that the effects of a countermeasure must be commensurate with the injury suffered, taking account of the rights in question.

In 1929, the Permanent Court of International Justice, with regard to navigation on the River Oder, stated as follows:

> [the] community of interest in a navigable river becomes the basis of a common legal right, the essential features of which are the perfect equality of all riparian States in the user of the whole course of the river and the exclusion of any preferential privilege of any one riparian State in relation to the others.

Territorial Jurisdiction of the International Commission of the River Oder, Judgment No. 16, 1929, P.C.I.J., Series A, No. 23, p. 27.

Modern development of international law has strengthened this principle for non-navigational uses of international watercourses as well, as evidenced by the adoption of the Convention of 21 May 1997 on the Law of the Non-Navigational Uses of International Watercourses by the United Nations General Assembly.

The Court considers that Czechoslovakia, by unilaterally assuming control of a shared resource, and thereby depriving Hungary of its right to an equitable and reasonable share of the natural resources of the Danube—with the continuing effects of the diversion of these waters on the ecology of the riparian area of the Szigetköz—failed to respect the proportionality which is required by international law.

86. Moreover, . . . the fact that Hungary had agreed in the context of the original Project to the diversion of the Danube (and, in the Joint Contractual Plan, to a provisional measure of withdrawal of water from the Danube) cannot be understood as having authorized Czechoslovakia to proceed with a unilateral diversion of this magnitude without Hungary's consent. . . .

97. Finally, Hungary argued that subsequently imposed requirements of international law in relation to the protection of the environment precluded performance of the Treaty. The previously existing obligation not to cause substantive damage to the territory of another State had, Hungary

8. [That is, a measure that would be unlawful but for the fact that it was a legitimate response to the prior wrongful act of another state.—Eds.]

claimed, evolved into an erga omnes obligation of prevention of damage pursuant to the "precautionary principle." On this basis, Hungary argued, its termination was "forced by the other party's refusal to suspend work on Variant C.". . .

112. Neither of the Parties contended that new peremptory norms of environmental law had emerged since the conclusion of the 1977 Treaty, and the Court will consequently not be required to examine the scope of Article 64 of the Vienna Convention on the Law of Treaties [providing for termination of a treaty through the emergence of a peremptory norm of international law (*jus cogens*) with which the treaty is in conflict]. On the other hand, the Court wishes to point out that newly developed norms of environmental law are relevant for of the Treaty and that the parties could, by agreement, incorporate them through the application of Articles 15, 19 and 20 of the Treaty. These articles do not contain specific obligations of performance but require the parties, in carrying out their obligations to ensure that the quality of water in the Danube is not impaired and that nature is protected, to take new environmental norms into consideration when agreeing upon the means to be specified in the Joint Contractual Plan.

By inserting these evolving provisions in the Treaty, the parties recognized the potential necessity to adapt the Project. Consequently, the Treaty is not static, and is open to adapt to emerging norms of international law. By means of Articles 15 and 19, new environmental norms can be incorporated in the Joint Contractual Plan.

The responsibility to do this was a joint responsibility. The obligations contained in Articles 15, 19 and 20 are, by definition, general and have to be transformed into specific obligations of performance through a process of consultation and negotiation. Their implementation thus requires a mutual willingness to discuss in good faith actual and potential environmental risks.

It is all the more important to do this because as the Court recalled in its Advisory Opinion on the *Legality of the Threat or Use of Nuclear Weapons*, "the environment is not an abstraction but represents the living space, the quality of life and the very health of human beings, including generations unborn" (I.C.J. Reports 1996, para. 29; see also paragraph 53 above).

The awareness of the vulnerability of the environment and the recognition that environmental risks have to be assessed on a continuous basis have become much stronger in the years since the Treaty's conclusion. These new concerns have enhanced the relevance of Articles 15, 19 and 20.

113. The Court recognizes that both Parties agree on the need to take environmental concerns seriously and to take the required precautionary measures, but they fundamentally disagree on the consequences this has for the joint Project. In such a case, third-party involvement may be helpful

and instrumental in finding a solution, provided each of the Parties is flexible in its position. . . .

[In discussing the legal consequences of its judgment, the court stated in part as follows:]

140. It is clear that the Project's impact upon, and its implications for, the environment are of necessity a key issue. The numerous scientific reports which have been presented to the Court by the Parties—even if their conclusions are often contradictory—provide abundant evidence that this impact and these implications are considerable.

In order to evaluate the environmental risks, current standards must be taken into consideration. This is not only allowed by the wording of Articles 15 and 19, but even prescribed, to the extent that these articles impose a continuing—and thus necessarily evolving—obligation on the parties to maintain the quality of the water of the Danube and to protect nature.

The Court is mindful that, in the field of environmental protection, vigilance and prevention are required on account of the often irreversible character of damage to the environment and of the limitations inherent in the very mechanism of reparation of this type of damage.

Throughout the ages, mankind has, for economic and other reasons, constantly interfered with nature. In the past, this was often done without consideration of the effects upon the environment. Owing to new scientific insights and to a growing awareness of the risks for mankind—for present and future generations—of pursuit of such interventions at an unconsidered and unabated pace, new norms and standards have been developed, set forth in a great number of instruments during the last two decades. Such new norms have to be taken into consideration, and such new standards given proper weight, not only when States contemplate new activities but also when continuing with activities begun in the past. This need to reconcile economic development with protection of the environment is aptly expressed in the concept of sustainable development.

For the purposes of the present case, this means that the Parties together should look afresh at the effects on the environment of the operation of the Gabčíkovo power plant. In particular they must find a satisfactory solution for the volume of water to be released into the old bed of the Danube and into the side-arms on both sides of the river.

141. It is not for the Court to determine what shall be the final result of these negotiations to be conducted by the Parties. It is for the Parties themselves to find an agreed solution that takes account of the objectives of the Treaty, which must be pursued in a joint and integrated way, as well as the norms of international environmental law and the principles of the

law of international watercourses. The Court will recall in this context that, as it said in the *North Sea Continental Shelf* cases:

> [the Parties] are under an obligation so to conduct themselves that the negotiations are meaningful, which will not be the case when either of them insists upon its own position without contemplating any modification of it.

I.C.J. Reports 1969, p. 47, para. 85. . . .

147. Re-establishment of the joint régime will . . . reflect in an optimal way the concept of common utilization of shared water resources for the achievement of the several objectives mentioned in the Treaty, in concordance with Article 5, paragraph 2, of the Convention on the Law of the Non-Navigational Uses of International Watercourses, according to which:

> Watercourse States shall participate in the use, development and protection of an international watercourse in an equitable and reasonable manner. Such participation includes both the right to utilize the watercourse and the duty to cooperate in the protection and development thereof, as provided in the present Convention.". . .

148. . . . Now the Court will turn to the legal consequences of the internationally wrongful acts committed by the Parties.

149. The Permanent Court of International Justice stated in its Judgment . . . in the case concerning the *Factory at Chorzów:*

> reparation must, as far as possible, wipe out all the consequences of the illegal act and reestablish the situation which would, in all probability, have existed if that act had not been committed.

P.C.I.J., Series A, No. 17, p. 47.

150. Reparation must, "as far as possible," wipe out all the consequences of the illegal act. In this case, the consequences of the wrongful acts of both Parties will be wiped out "as far as possible" if they resume their co-operation in the utilization of the shared water resources of the Danube, and if the multi-purpose programme, in the form of a co-ordinated single unit, for the use, development and protection of the watercourse is implemented in an equitable and reasonable manner. . . .

155. For these reasons,

THE COURT,

(1) . . .

A. Finds, by fourteen votes to one, that Hungary was not entitled to suspend and subsequently abandon, in 1989, the works on the Nagymaros Project and on the part of the Gabčíkovo Project for which the Treaty of 16 September 1977 and related instruments attributed responsibility to it;

IN FAVOUR: President Schwebel; Vice-President Weeramantry; Judges Oda, Bedjaoui, Guillaume, Ranjeva, Shi, Fleischhauer, Koroma, Vereshchetin, Parra-Aranguren, Kooijmans, Rezek; Judge ad hoc Skubiszewski;

AGAINST: Judge Herczegh;

B. Finds, by nine votes to six, that Czechoslovakia was entitled to proceed, in November 1991, to the "provisional solution" as described in the terms of the Special Agreement;

IN FAVOUR: Vice-President Weeramantry; Judges Oda, Guillaume, Shi, Koroma, Vereshchetin, Parra-Aranguren, Kooijmans; Judge ad hoc Skubiszewski;

AGAINST: President Schwebel; Judges Bedjaoui, Ranjeva, Herczegh, Fleischhauer, Rezek;

C. Finds, by ten votes to five, that Czechoslovakia was not entitled to put into operation, from October 1992, this "provisional solution";

IN FAVOUR: President Schwebel; Vice-President Weeramantry; Judges Bedjaoui, Guillaume, Ranjeva, Herczegh, Shi, Fleischhauer, Kooijmans, Rezek;

AGAINST: Judges Oda, Koroma, Vereshchetin, Parra-Aranguren; Judge ad hoc Skubiszewski;

D. Finds, by eleven votes to four, that the notification, on 19 May 1992, of the termination of the Treaty of 16 September 1977 and related instruments by Hungary did not have the legal effect of terminating them;

IN FAVOUR: Vice-President Weeramantry; Judges Oda, Bedjaoui, Guillaume, Ranjeva, Shi, Koroma, Vereshchetin, Parra-Aranguren, Kooijmans; Judge ad hoc Skubiszewski;

AGAINST: President Schwebel; Judges Herczegh, Fleischhauer, Rezek;

(2) . . .

B. Finds, by thirteen votes to two, that Hungary and Slovakia must negotiate in good faith in the light of the prevailing situation, and must take all necessary measures to ensure the achievement of the objectives of the Treaty of 16 September 1977, in accordance with such modalities as they may agree upon;

IN FAVOUR: President Schwebel; Vice-President Weeramantry; Judges Oda, Bedjaoui, Guillaume, Ranjeva, Shi, Koroma, Vereshchetin, Parra-Aranguren, Kooijmans, Rezek; Judge ad hoc Skubiszewski;

AGAINST: Judges Herczegh, Fleischhauer;

C. Finds, by thirteen votes to two, that, unless the Parties otherwise agree, a joint operational régime must be established in accordance with the Treaty of 16 September 1977;

IN FAVOUR: President Schwebel; Vice-President Weeramantry; Judges

Oda, Bedjaoui, Guillaume, Ranjeva, Shi, Koroma, Vereshchetin, Parra-Aranguren, Kooijmans, Rezek; Judge ad hoc Skubiszewski;

AGAINST: Judges Herczegh, Fleischhauer;

D. Finds, by twelve votes to three, that, unless the Parties otherwise agree, Hungary shall compensate Slovakia for the damage sustained by Czechoslovakia and by Slovakia on account of the suspension and abandonment by Hungary of works for which it was responsible; and Slovakia shall compensate Hungary for the damage it has sustained on account of the putting into operation of the "provisional solution" by Czechoslovakia and its maintenance in service by Slovakia;

IN FAVOUR: President Schwebel; Vice-President Weeramantry; Judges Bedjaoui, Guillaume, Ranjeva, Herczegh, Shi, Fleischhauer, Parra-Aranguren, Kooijmans, Rezek; Judge ad hoc Skubiszewski;

AGAINST: Judges Oda, Koroma, Vereshchetin; . . .

PRESIDENT SCHWEBEL and JUDGE REZEK append declarations to the Judgment of the Court.

VICE-PRESIDENT WEERAMANTRY, JUDGES BEDJAOUI and KOROMA append separate opinions to the Judgment of the Court.

JUDGES ODA, RANJEVA, HERCZEGH, FLEISCHHAUER, VERESHCHETIN and PARRA-ARANGUREN, and JUDGE AD HOC SKUBISZEWSKI append dissenting opinions to the Judgment of the Court.

Notes and Questions

1. *The effect of uncertainty.* Do you believe the court handled correctly the question of "scientific uncertainty" as to the possible effects of the project? Of the "precautionary principle"? If so, see if you can restate what in the court's view a state in the position of Hungary in 1989 should do. If not, how would you strike the balance between the values of the stability of treaty regimes, on the one hand, and environmental protection, on the other?

2. *Sustainable development.* Did the outcome of the case give effect to the "concept" of sustainable development, as the court called it? (Judge Weeramantry, in his separate opinion, maintains it is a "principle.") If you do not believe so, how would you strike *that* balance?

3. *Treaties and custom.* This case provides a rather dramatic illustration of the interplay between treaties and customary international law. There was a treaty, but the parties had an obligation to negotiate to implement its general terms (in particular, those of Articles 15, 19, and 20); and a party that breached the treaty had to conform its conduct to the requirements of the customary international law of international watercourses.

Concluding Questions

1. *Increasing demand, constant supply.* We began this chapter by noting that fresh water is becoming increasingly scarce on a per capita basis, especially in areas of the world where it is most needed, such as Africa and the Middle East. Since much of the world's fresh water is contained in international drainage basins—and this is particularly true in the regions just referred to—it seems inevitable that disputes between states over water will increase in number and intensity. On the basis of the foregoing readings, do you believe the existing legal rules are up to the task of preventing and resolving these disputes?

2. *Problem.* Assume you have been appointed sole arbitrator in the Euphrates case outlined earlier in this chapter. How would you decide the case? Would you emphasize the doctrine of "equitable utilization" or the "no-harm" principle?

3. *Quantity and quality.* While the instruments in this chapter generally deal with both allocation and pollution, we have chosen to treat the two problems separately for analytical reasons (Chapter 10, section B focuses on pollution of international watercourses). It is worth emphasizing, however, that problems of quantity and quality are often interrelated. For example, a quantitatively adequate supply may be of no use because of its poor quality. Similarly, water of the purest quality may be quantitatively insufficient to meet the needs of the recipient country. This highlights the need for a holistic approach to the management of international fresh water resources. Such an approach would also advance goals of conservation, which are dealt with in the following chapter.

XVII

International Protection of National Sites: World Heritage and Wetlands

This chapter focuses on the general category of international agreement in which states agree to controls and other measures on the use of resources located within their borders. Both the World Heritage Convention and the Wetlands Convention, negotiated in the early 1970s, exemplify this category. The 1992 Convention on Biological Diversity and the Rio Non-Binding Forrest Principles, which will be studied later, also address this theme.

A. THE WORLD HERITAGE CONVENTION

The 1972 Convention for the Protection of the World Cultural and Natural Heritage provides that certain natural and cultural sites can be designated as world heritages and conserved for present and future generations. The Convention was arranged in parallel with the preparations for the historic 1972 United Nations Conference on the Human Environment in Stockholm, Sweden. As of January 1998, 153 countries were party to the Convention, and 552 properties in more than 100 countries were included on the World Heritage List. This list included 418 cultural sites, 114 natural sites, and 20 mixed cultural and natural sites.

The Convention derives from two separate initiatives: to conserve cultural properties and natural properties. After World War II, countries were determined to conserve important cultural properties for the future. The subsequent initiatives were centered in the United Nations Education, Scientific and Cultural Organization (UNESCO). In 1954 countries negotiated the Hague Convention on the Protection of Cultural Property in the Event of Armed Conflict. This was followed by campaigns under the auspices of UNESCO to save specific cultural sites and three years later by the establishment of an international nongovernmental organization dedicated to conserving cultural properties—the International Council on Monuments and Sites (ICOMOS). UNESCO adopted a series of resolutions that authorized the negotiation of a new international agreement to protect cultural properties, and by spring 1971 draft text was ready.

At the same time the International Union for the Conservation of Nature and Natural Resources (IUCN) prepared a draft convention to protect national parks, some historic structures, certain natural sites, and important wildlife areas. The sites were to become part of a World Heritage Trust. The United States, and especially Russell Train, was instrumental in encouraging the creation of a trust and a new convention.

Eventually in 1972 the two drafts were combined into a single convention, which was opened for signature in November of that year and went into effect in 1977.

The Convention tries to conserve important national and cultural sites through the use of a World Heritage List. Individual countries nominate national and cultural sites for inclusion on the World Heritage List. As provided in the convention, non-governmental organizations prepare the background investigations and reports as to whether the proposed sites merit inclusion on the World Heritage List, and parties to the convention decide whether to approve the listing. Only a small portion of the sites nominated are approved.

Under the Convention states that have natural and cultural properties on the list are obligated to protect them, and other states are also obligated to refrain from actions that would endanger them. If they are put on the List of World Heritage Sites in Danger, the sites will be afforded such protections. As of December 1997, there were 25 world heritage sites on the danger list.

The Convention provides for a World Heritage Fund to assist developing countries in maintaining world heritage sites. Countries with a site on the endangered list are eligible for special funds to protect the site. The secretariat has also tried to enlist the support of the Global Environmental Facility to fund natural heritage conservation projects, with limited success to date.

There are three new institutions created by the treaty: the general assembly, the committee, and the bureau. The general assembly, which meets biannually, has very limited powers. Its main task is to elect members of the World Heritage Committee, which is comprised of 21 member states serving six-year terms. The committee, which meets annually (usually in December), approves the listing of sites on the World Heritage List, changes in the Operational Guidelines, changes in listing criteria, and programmatic developments, such as monitoring and conservation of sites. It has always operated by consensus. The bureau, composed of the chairman of the committee, five vice-chairs, and the rapporteur, are elected members of the committee. The bureau, which meets twice a year, prepares the agenda for the upcoming committee meetings, deals with emergency assistance requests and other problems, and serves as an important forum for considering new initiatives, such as the Strategic Plan in 1992. The secretariat for the Convention is located at UNESCO headquarters in Paris, France. Until May 1992, administration of the natural and the cultural sites were handled within separate divisions of UNESCO. In 1992, a separate secretariat unifying administration of the Convention for both natural and cultural sites was created.

Since the Convention came into effect, states have expanded its scope and assumed new powers in implementing it. All of this has been accomplished not through amendment, but through the development of Operational Guidelines and alterations to the Guidelines. In December 1992, the World Heritage Committee adopted for the first time "Strategic Guidelines" to chart priorities in the future implementation of the Convention.

For the most of the life of the Convention, parties have been concerned with whether to put nominated sites on the World Heritage List. As of January 1998, there are over 500 sites on the World Heritage List. In 1993 the parties added landscapes to the categories of properties that could be listed as world heritage sites.

While countries have always had the capacity to indicate that a world heritage site within the country should be placed on the List of World Heritage Sites in Danger, it is only within the last few years that member states have taken it upon themselves to put a site on the danger list in the absence of a request from the host country. Members voted to inscribe Dubrovnik in Croatia and Manas National Park in India on the endangered list without the consent of the host countries. In 1993, the World Heritage Committee placed the Everglades National Park on the danger list, even though the United States had not requested this and abstained in the voting. Since this assertion of authority by the parties is controversial, it is unclear whether the practice will become permanent.

The outbreak of the hostilities in the former Yugoslavia brought new attention to the problem of protecting world heritage properties during civil war or strife. In 1991 and 1992, the secretariat and bureau members devoted considerable time to this problem. Consultant visits to Dubrovnik to try to preserve the heritage site intact were unsuccessful.

In the 1990s the issue of whether and how to delist a site already on the World Heritage List has arisen. No site has ever been taken off the World Heritage List, although in December 1993 Germany, Thailand, and the United States indicated that the step should be considered for Manas National Park. Mount Nimba Nature Reserve in Guinea, which was put on the danger list in 1992, poses the issue dramatically, because it has become a promising source of minerals since its inscription on the World Heritage List. The World Heritage Convention does not address the issue, but the Operational Guidelines provide detailed delisting procedures that are intended to ensure that all possible measures are taken to prevent deletion but to authorize the World Heritage Committee to delist if these fail. Since there has been no case of delisting, there is controversy over whether delisting can take place over the host state's opposition and whether a site must be delisted at a host country's request.

In June 1992, the bureau considered for the first time a strategic plan for implementing the Convention, which placed greater emphasis upon monitoring and compliance, and recommended that the meeting of the parties devote significant time to the issue. The Strategic Guidelines adopted in December 1992 set forth the new agenda, which also includes promoting greater public awareness of the Convention. Since then, more attention has been given to monitoring the state of the natural and cultural properties on the World Heritage List and to reviewing implementation of the convention. This is reflected in the agenda of the World Heritage Committee meetings, which in 1993 devoted significant attention to monitoring reports of the International Council on Monuments and Sites (ICOMOS) and the International Union for the Conservation of Natural Resources (IUCN) for 60 sites.

The World Heritage Convention is an early and outstanding example of an international agreement that explicitly provides for non-governmental organizations to assist in its implementation. Articles 13 and 14 explicitly reference three intergovernmental and non-governmental organizations: the International Centre for the Study of the Preservation and Restoration of Cultural Property (the Rome Centre), ICOMOS, and IUCN.

ICOMOS and IUCN, in particular, have played important roles. They evaluate requests to put cultural properties and natural sites, respectively, on the World Heritage List; review requests from countries for financial and technical assistance; and, more recently, monitor at least some of the sites. They have routinely participated in the meetings of the bureau and of all the parties. However, few non-governmental organizations, other than those specified in the Convention, have been closely involved with the convention.

As you read the following excerpts, consider whether the World Heritage Convention offers a useful legal framework for conserving unique sites located within national borders. What are the incentives to list sites on the World Heritage List or to maintain them in the face of local threats? Consider also the content of member countries' obligations under the Convention. How specific are the obligations? How does this affect countries' implementation of the convention? Can you argue that the generality or specificity of the obligations makes Countries more or less willing to join the World Heritage Convention? For detail on the World Heritage Convention, *see* Edith Brown Weiss, The Five International Treaties: A Living History, ch. 5, in Engaging Countries: Strenghthening Compliance with Inernational Environmental Accrods (1998).

INTERNATIONAL WILDLIFE LAW: AN INTERNATIONAL TREATIES CONCERNED WITH THE CONSERVATION OF WILDLIFE

Simon Lyster
222-226 (1985)

5. The Nature of the Parties' Obligations to Protect World Heritage Sites

A) CONSERVATION OF SITES IN THE WORLD HERITAGE LIST

Articles 4 and 5 of the Convention set out the obligations on Parties to conserve sites in the World Heritage List which are situated in their territories.

Article 4 states:

> Each State Party to this Convention recognizes that the duty of ensuring the identification, protection, conservation, presentation and transmission to future generations of the cultural and natural heritage referred to in Articles 1 and 2 and situated on its territory belongs primarily to that State. It will do all it can to this end, to the utmost of its own resources and, where appropriate, with any international assistance and cooperation, in particular, financial, artistic, scientific and technical, which it may be able to obtain.

Article 5 states:

> To ensure that effective and active measures are taken to the protection, conservation and presentation of the cultural and natural heritage situated on its territory, each State Party to this Convention shall endeavor, in so far as possible, and as appropriate for each country: a) to adopt a general policy which aims to give the cultural and natural heritage a function in the life of the community and to integrate the protection of that heritage into comprehensive planning progammes; b) to set up within its territories, where such services do not exist, one or more services to the protection, conservation and presentation of the cultural and natural heritage with an appropriate staff and possessing the means to discharge their functions; c) to develop scientific and technical studies and research and to work out such operating methods as will make the State capable of counteracting the dangers that threaten its cultural or natural heritage; d) to take the appropriate legal, scientific, technical, administrative and financial measures necessary for the

> identification, protection, conservation, presentation and rehabilitation of this heritage; and e) to foster the establishment or development of national or regional centres for training in the protection, conservation and presentation of the cultural and natural heritage and to encourage scientific research in this field.

The only Court to have considered the nature of the obligations imposed on Parties by Articles 4 and 5 is the High Court of Australia in the recent case of *The Commonwealth of Australia v. The State of Tasmania.* The case arose because of plans by the State of Tasmania to construct a dam on the Gordon River, downstream of its junction with the Franklin River in an area known as the Western Tasmania Wilderness National Parks which the Commonwealth of Australia (i.e. the federal Australian government) nominated for inclusion in the World Heritage List on 13 November 1981. The World Heritage Committee accepted the nomination in December 1982 although, aware of Tasmania's plans, it expressed "serious concern" at the likely effect of the proposed dam and recommended that "the Australian authorities take all possible measures to protect the integrity of the property." The Commonwealth of Australia then took two steps to protect the site. The Governor-General exercising his authority under Section 69 of National Parks and Wildlife Conservation Act of 1975 issued the World Heritage (Western Tasmania Wilderness) Regulations (S.R. Nos. 31 and 66 of 1983) and the Australian Parliament adopted the World Heritage Properties Conservation Act of 1983. Both the Regulations and the Act made construction of the dam illegal. The State of Tasmania challenged the constitutional authority of the Commonwealth of Australia to make a law or to adopt regulations prohibiting construction of the dam and the Commonwealth sought a ruling from the High Court that the measures taken to protect the Western Tasmania Wilderness National Parks were valid. A key question in the argument before the Court was whether the World Heritage Convention imposes a legal duty on each Party to protect a site in the World Heritage List which is situated on its territory. The Commonwealth of Australia contended that the Convention does impose such a duty while the State of Tasmania argued that the Convention imposed no real obligation but is merely a statement of aspiration or political accord.

Since it is the only case in which this issue has been considered, the findings of the Court bear consideration in some detail. By a 4-3 majority decision the Court upheld the authority of the Commonwealth to stop the dam, and the opinions of the four Justices who formed the majority all state categorically that the Convention imposes a legal duty on Australia to protect Western Tasmania Wilderness National Parks. The Court recognized that the key sections of the Convention are Articles 4 and 5. Asking himself the question "does the Convention impose an obligation on Australia to protect the area which has been entered on the World Heritage List and, if so, what kind of obligation?", Justice Mason stated in *The Commonwealth of Australia v. The State of Tasmania* that Article 5

> . . . imposes obligations on each state with the object set out in the opening words of the article "[t]o ensure that effective and active measures are taken for the protection, conservation" etc. of the heritage in the discharge of the responsibility acknowledged by Article 4. Article 5 cannot be read as a mere statement of intention. It is expressed in the form of a command . . . Indeed, there would be little point in adding the qualifications "in so far as possible" and "as appropriate for each country" unless the Article imposed an obligation. The first qualification means "in so far as is practicable" and the second takes account of the difference in legal systems. Neither the qualifications nor the existence of an element of discretion is inconsistent with the existence of an obligation. There is a distinction between a discretion as to the manner of performance and a discretion as to performance or non-performance. The latter, but not the former, is inconsistent with a binding obligation to perform. (*see Thorby v. Goldberg* (1964) 112 C.L.R. 597, at pp. 604-605, 613, 614-615.)

Justice Brennan stated that the last part of Article 4 and the first part and (d) of Article 5 are critical. In considering whether the want of specificity in Articles 4 and 5 and the discretion they leave to each Party as to how it will protect World Heritage sites makes them merely hortatory, he concluded that the Articles are not merely hortatory and

> that there is a clear obligation on Australia to act under Articles 4 and 5, though the extent of that obligation may be affected by decisions taken by Australia in good faith.

Justice Brennan went on to say that

> the obligation under Article 4 of the Convention leaves no discretion in a Party as to whether it will abstain from taking steps in discharge of the "duty" referred to in that Article. Each Party is bound to "do all it can . . . to the utmost of its own resources," and the question whether it is unable to take a particular step within the limits of its resources is a justifiable question. No doubt the allocation of resources is a matter for each Party to decide, and the allocation of resources for the discharge of the obligation may thus be said to be discretionary, but the discretion is not large. It must be exercised "in good faith," as Article 26 of the Vienna Convention requires. If a Party sought exemption from the obligation on the ground that it had allocated its available resources to other purposes, the question whether it had done so in good faith would be justiciable.

In a strongly worded dissenting opinion the Chief Justice, Sir Harry Gibbs, disagreed with the Court's decision, stating that

> it is unnecessary to consider whether if the words of Arts. 4 and 5 which purport to impose an obligation had appeared in, for example, a commercial contract, they would in an appropriate context have imposed a duty to do what was reasonably possible and fitting in the circumstances. It is however

impossible to conclude that Arts. 4 and 5 were intended to impose a legal duty of that kind on the States Parties to the Convention. If the conduct which those articles purport to prescribe was intended to be legally enforceable, the obligations thereby created would be of the most onerous and far reaching kind. The obligations would extend to any property which might reasonably be regarded as cultural or natural heritage within the meaning of Arts. 1 and 2 of the Convention, whether or not it was included on the World Heritage List, and would require a State Party to the convention to take all legal measures within its constitutional power that might reasonably be regarded as appropriate for the identification and protection of such property, and to apply all of its financial resources that it could possibly make available for the same purpose; there would of course be further obligations, but what I have said suffices to indicate the nature of the burden which the articles would impose. The very nature of these obligations is such as to indicate that the State Parties to the Convention did not intend to assume a legal obligation to perform them.

The Commonwealth of Australia v. The State of Tasmania is a landmark decision both because it is the first test of the scope of the Convention in a court of law and because the majority of judges stated so clearly that each Party has a legal duty to do all it can to protect sites in the World Heritage List which are situated within its own territorial boundaries. Although decisions of the High Court of Australia are not binding on other parties, the case is certain to be of considerable influence as and when other parties to the Convention are faced with a similar problem.

B) CONSERVATION OF SITES NOT IN THE WORLD HERITAGE LIST BUT WHICH ARE PART OF THE CULTURAL AND NATURAL HERITAGE REFERRED TO IN ARTICLES 1 AND 2

The conservation obligations imposed on Parties by Articles 4 and 5 are not limited to sites in the World Heritage List. Also included are sites which are part of the cultural and natural heritage as defined by Articles 1 and 2 of the Convention.

Article 4 states that

> [e]ach State Party to this Convention recognizes that the duty of ensuring the identification, protection, conservation, presentation and transmission to future generations of *the cultural and natural heritage referred to in Articles 1 and 2 and situated on its territory,* belongs primarily to the State. . . . (emphasis added).

Article 5 starts with the words:

> [t]o ensure that effective and active measures are taken for the protection, conservation and presentation of *the cultural and natural heritage situated on its territory,* each State Party shall endeavor . . . (emphasis added).

This is an important point since the cultural and natural heritage within the meaning of Articles 1 and 2 may include substantially more sites than those in the World Heritage List. As was pointed out earlier in this chapter, it is up to each Party to identify sites on its territory which it deems to be part of the cultural and natural heritage within the meaning of Articles 1 and 2, while the compilation of the World Heritage List is the responsibility of the World Heritage Committee. It is quite conceivable, therefore, that a Party might decide that a site in its territory is part of the cultural and natural heritage as defined by Articles 1 and 2, notwithstanding that it is not on the World Heritage List. Australia, for example, has declared a 780 hectare area and numerous cultural sites in Tasmania, which are outside the Western Tasmania Wilderness National Parks and not on the World Heritage List, to be part of the natural and cultural heritage as defined by Articles 1 and 2 of the Convention. Furthermore, Section 3(2) of Australia's World Heritage Properties Conservation Act states that the provisions of the Act apply to sites submitted to the World Heritage Committee for listing and to sites "declared by the regulations to form part of the cultural and natural heritage" as well as to sites that the World Heritage Committee has actually agreed to include on the World Heritage List.

INTERNATIONAL LAW AND PARK PROTECTION: A GLOBAL RESPONSIBILITY

Daniel Magraw,
in *Our Common Lands: Defending the National Parks*
113, 118-50, 162-163 (David J. Simon ed., 1988)

I. Introduction

National parks and other areas administered by the National Park Service (hereinafter referred to jointly as "national parklands") currently face a variety of threats from outside their borders. Such threats are commonly referred to as "external threats." Many, probably most, external threats are domestic threats, that is threats to national parklands originating in the United States.

Others, however, are international threats to national parklands that originate outside the United States. International threats can be either continuous and long-term, such as acid rain resulting from ongoing industrial activity, or instantaneous or short term, such as radioactive fallout from the accident at the Soviet Union's Chernobyl nuclear power reactor. Some national parklands adjoin a U.S. boundary with another nation and are threatened by sources in that nation. Glacier National Park, which is threatened by water pollution from the proposed Cabin Creek coal mine in British Columbia, Canada, and by logging in Canada, is one example.

Approximately twenty-four national parklands immediately adjacent to U.S. borders with Canada and Mexico may be so affected. Four of those national parklands and sixty other national parklands are on U.S. seacoasts and thus face possible threats from pollution occurring in international or foreign waters. . . .

The legal effect and meaning of the World Heritage Convention is not entirely clear. The only case to analyze the Convention is an Australian case, *Australia v. Tasmania.* It is beyond cavil that the Convention is binding (on the United States, Canada, and the other states that are parties to it) as international law. Nevertheless, there is no international forum that automatically has jurisdiction to hear disputes arising under the Convention, and none appears likely. Thus, it might be impossible for a nation alleging that another nation is violating the Convention to be able to obtain an international adjudicatory determination of that allegation.

With respect to enforceability in U.S. domestic courts, a crucial question is whether the Convention requires implementing legislation in order to be effective, that is, whether the Convention is "self-executing." The *Tasmania* case did not address that question because under Australian law, treaties cannot be self-executing. If it is not self-executing, it will not be effective as domestic law within the United States (although it remains in force as international law and binding on the countries that are parties to it) unless implementing legislation is passed. The Solicitor of the Department of the Interior has concluded that the World Heritage Convention is not self-executing. That result is not free from doubt, however. The Secretary of the Interior has been designated to direct and coordinate U.S. participation in the Convention, and the Secretary has issued rules setting forth policies and procedures in that regard, which may give rise to enforceable domestic legal rights.

As discussed in greater detail in Part II, below, Articles 4 and 5 of the Convention place obligations for protecting cultural and natural heritage sites on the nation in which those sites are located. In addition, Article 6.2 imposes an obligation on parties to the Convention to aid in "the identification, protection, conservation and preservation of the cultural and natural heritage" identified in the World Heritage List, if the nation in which the site is located so requests. The extent of the obligation is not clear from the face of the Convention, and research has revealed no source that analyzes that question. Nevertheless, vis-à-vis other nations that are parties to the Convention, Article 6.2 offers protection of some sort to national parklands that are on the World Heritage List.

Article 6.3 of the Convention imposes an obligation on parties "not to take any deliberate measures which might damage directly or indirectly the cultural and natural heritage referred to in Articles 1 and 2 situated on the territory of other" parties to the Convention. The meaning of Article 6.3 is subject to debate. For instance, the important term "damage directly or indirectly" is subject to widely differing interpretations. Further,

Article 6.3 applies by its terms regardless of whether the heritage site has been placed on the World Heritage List, an interpretation that is supported by the structure of the Convention as a whole and by several opinions in the *Tasmania* case. If that interpretation is correct, Canada may be obligated to prevent British Columbian approval of the Cabin Creek coal mine, even though Glacier National Park, which would seem to qualify easily as a natural area of "outstanding value from the point of view of science, conservation, or natural beauty," has not yet been approved at the international level for placement on the World Heritage List. The constitutional powers of the Canadian provinces complicate the analysis, however. Article 34 of the Convention provides that if the federal government has the authority to prevent the prohibited action, it must do so; but if the federal government does not have that authority, it is obligated only to inform the competent authorities at the provincial level with its recommendations. . . .

Another possible source of international obligations is the Man and the Biosphere Program, which operates under the auspices of UNESCO (the United Nations Educational, Scientific and Cultural Organization). Perhaps the primary component of that program is the biosphere reserve project, which began in the early 1970s and is not based on an international agreement per se. Each participating country, of which there are now 104, voluntarily establishes its own national autonomous committee. The activities of those committees are coordinated to some degree by UNESCO, but UNESCO does not control their operations. Two hundred fifty-two biosphere reserve sites now exist in sixty-six nations.

The United States, which continues to participate in the Man and the Biosphere Program even though it has withdrawn from membership in UNESCO, has designated all or part of twenty-six national parklands as biosphere reserves. Preliminary research has not revealed any basis for concluding that the biosphere reserve project creates binding legal obligations for the participating nations with respect to biosphere reserves in other nations. Nevertheless, the project may give rise to expectations that warrant some legal protection and contains, at the very least, an element of moral suasion. That result might particularly follow where two adjacent parks are both biosphere reserves, as is the case with the United States' Glacier National Park and Canada's Waterton Lakes National Park. Recently proposed legislation would direct the Secretary of the Interior to give priority attention to biosphere reserves.

The Solicitor of the U.S. Department of the Interior reportedly is, at the time of this writing, preparing a legal memorandum analyzing the Cabin Creek situation in light of international law, including the World Heritage Convention and the biosphere reserve program. That analysis will be highly important not only with respect to Cabin Creek, but also as it will, for the first time, establish official U.S. positions on these international law issues. . . .

The World Heritage Convention obligates participatory nations in which outstanding natural or cultural resources are located to engage in some activities, although the extent of that obligation is uncertain. Article 4, for example, states that each party to the Convention:

> recognizes that the duty of insuring the identification, protection, conservation, presentation and transmission to future generations of the cultural and natural heritage referred to in Articles 1 and 2 and situated on its territory, belongs primarily to that State. It will do all it can to this end, to the utmost of its own resources and, where appropriate, with any international assistance and cooperation.

The inclusion of the word "duty" is reassuring; the qualification implied by the terms "do all it can," "to the utmost of its own resources," and "where appropriate," reduce the strength of that obligation considerably.

Similarly, Article 5 provides that each party to the Convention "shall endeavor, insofar as possible, and as appropriate for each country" to take a number of enumerated measures, including "the appropriate legal, scientific, technical, administrative and financial measures necessary for the identification, protection, conservation, presentation and rehabilitation of [the cultural and natural heritage situated on its territory]." It is not obvious that the promise to "endeavor, insofar as possible, and as appropriate for each country" entails any obligation other than one of good faith. The judges in the *Tasmania* case disagreed on that issue. A 1981 Interior Department legal memorandum (summarizing a 1980 memorandum) states that "the Convention . . . established a general good faith responsibility for each signatory to protect heritage properties, but left latitude for implementation to each country." (The 1981 memorandum further says that 16 U.S.C. §470a-1 "implements these provisions . . . and [restricts] that latitude" in such a way that "the Secretary [of the Interior] must be satisfied that each nominated site has adequate legal protection to ensure its preservation.") There does not appear to be a definitive answer at present regarding the extent of the obligations imposed by Articles 4 and 5 of the Convention, but it is clear that the obligations exist and that they at least require good faith efforts.

B. THE UNITED STATES AND THE WORLD HERITAGE CONVENTION

The United States has more than 20 sites on the World Heritage List. Parties to the World Heritage Convention also placed two World Heritage Sites in the United States on the Endangered List of Sites: the Everglades (nominated as a World Heritage Site in 1979) and, most recently, Yellowstone National Park (nominated in 1978). The United States abstained in voting to put the Everglades on the endangered list and requested that Yellowstone National Park be put on the list.

Yellowstone National Park is currently the focus of considerable controversy because of private efforts to develop mineral resources just outside the park. What legal effect does the listing of Yellowstone National Park on the World Heritage List have in controlling private mining activity near the site? Does it make any difference that the site has been put on the endangered list?

The Department of Interior has primary responsibility for implementing the convention. In practice, the Secretary of the Department of the Interior has delegated authority to the National Park Service, which is part of the Interior Department, to implement the agreement. A representative from the National Park Service usually heads the United States delegation to meetings of the parties to the convention.

For additional references, *see* International Union for the Conservation of Nature/United Nations Education, Scientific, and Cultural Organization's World Heritage Committee, The World Heritage Twenty Years Later (1992); J.G. Nelson & E.A. Alder, Toward Greater Understanding and Use of the World Heritage Convention (1992).

Notes and Questions

1. *The international community's interest.* Does the international community have an interest in natural or cultural resources that are located within the borders of one country?

2. *Outside pressure.* Would a government resent or welcome pressure from the international community, an international organization, or another country to protect one of its natural or cultural resources? What if the pressuring organization were a non-governmental organization?

3. *Compliance.* How would you measure compliance with the World Heritage Convention?

4. *A hypothetical.* Consider a hypothetical in which Queensland permits a foreign oil company to explore for oil in an area adjacent to the Great Barrier Reef. Could the United Kingdom, for example, bring a claim against Australia to the International Court of Justice to try to stop the exploration from continuing? What procedural and substantive problems do you foresee? From what you have read about the *Tasmania* case, could a case be brought by the federal government against Queensland?

C. THE WETLANDS CONVENTION

Wetlands, which include marshes, fens, peatlands, and marine waters less than six meters deep, are one of Earth's most important systems for protecting wildlife habitats and controlling floods. The health of wetlands depends on both the quantity and the quality of water available to them. In some cases, human activities that affect wetlands occur only within the borders of states. In other cases, offending activities occur beyond national borders and cause transnational air and water pollution, which jeopardize wetlands.

In response to concern about the alarming rate of wetlands loss throughout the world, 18 countries in 1971 concluded the Convention on Wetlands of International Importance Especially as Waterfowl Habitat, popularly known as "the Ramsar Convention" after the city (in Iraq) in which it is was adopted. The convention has been amended once, in 1982. As of June 1998, 110 countries are parties to the convention. The Ramsar Convention is intended to protect wetlands from human destruction, as from pollution and water drainage. Parties are obligated to designate suitable wetlands in their territory for inclusion in the List of Wetlands of International Importance (with special attention to migratory waterfowl), to promote conservation of wetlands on the list, and to promote the conservation of all wetlands (whether or not on the list), and to promote and maintain nature reserves. In contrast to the World Heritage Convention, listing under the Ramsar Convention is unilateral. Parties do not screen any wetland proposed for inclusion on the list. Each state is required to list a wetland at the time it consents to be a party. It may of its own volition substitute one wetland for another wetland if the matter raises "urgent national interest," but the overall area of protected wetlands insofar as possible must not decrease. As of June 1990, 480 wetlands were listed covering more than 30 million hectares; as of June 1998, there were over 900 Ramsar sites. The Convention is funded by annual contributions from the contracting parties. As in the World Heritage Convention, there is a special Wetlands Conservation Fund attached to the Convention to assist developing countries to comply with the treaty. IUCN, a hybrid nongovernmental/intergovernmental organization, is home to the secretariat of the Convention in Switzerland.

Parties to the Ramsar Convention meet every three years to review policies and activities and to set new initiatives. Each member country reports to the conference on its national protection of wetlands. The 1996 Conference was held in Brisbane, Australia, at which time parties adopted a strategic plan, to be in effect from 1997-2002. The plan, among other things, noted the need to build the capacity of governments, non-governmental organizations, local communities, and the private sector to conserve wetlands and to use them wisely, and the need to integrate protection of wetlands into decisionmaking. Parties also favorably considered the Organization for Economic Co-operation and Development's (OECD) new guidelines on policies to protect wetlands as appropriate for all member countries. *See* OECD Development Assistance Committee, Guidelines No.

9 for Aid Agencies for Improved Conservation and Sustainable Use of Tropical and Sub-Tropical Wetlands (1995).

The Convention has been criticized because it does not impose stringent binding obligations on the parties. It speaks in terms of an obligation to "promote" the conservation of listed sites and to "promote" establishment of nature reserves. Frequently a country, particularly a developing country, that has put a particular wetland on the Ramsar Wetlands List will have a plaque prominently displayed at the entrance to the wetland indicating that it is a protected site. Whether this effort to enlist effective public support for the wetland is successful, however, is doubtful, particularly when there are no effective environmental laws in place or local officials can be easily corrupted so as to ignore threatening pollution or pillaging of migratory waterfowl. Nonetheless countries seem pleased to be able to cite to wetlands that are listed as important under the Ramsar Convention, and international monitoring of protected sites by on-site visits of secretariat officials and their consultants can be important compliance measures.

Notes and Questions

1. What leverage does the Convention provide to national officials interested in protecting their country's wetlands? Consider the following: In 1995, the Colombia Superintendence of Notaries denied property rights over lands that serve to protect the environment or conserve natural resources. Its instructions said that wetlands are inalienable, that they serve vital regulatory functions in the environment, and that for these reasons they must be considered as goods for public use. The existence of acquired rights over wetlands was therefore not permissible and the granting of any such contract illegal. Most of the 50,000 hectares of wetlands in the savannah region around Bogota, the primary target of the ruling, were already destroyed in the last 50 years.

2. The Convention permits a country to delete one wetland that is listed and substitute wetlands elsewhere. Can one wetland really be substituted for another without thwarting the purposes of wetland protection? Many scientists are very skeptical of this approach. Why is this provision then included in the Convention? Would countries simply refuse to comply with the agreement when it became seriously inconvenient for them if such a provision were not included?

3. What measures would you recommend to increase compliance with the Convention and why?

4. Consider the following problem: Brazil, Argentina, Uruguay, Bolivia, and Paraguay want to construct a controversial waterway (the Hidrovia waterway) along the borders of the countries from a Uruguayan port to

the remote interior of Brazil. The last fifth of the waterway would be through the Pantanal swamp. Environmentalists contend that as much as 40 percent of the Pantanal wetlands, which encompasses 56,000-80,000 square miles, could be destroyed. They also predict alteration of the hydrological regime, water quality deterioration, increased flooding in the area, loss of biodiversity, decline in bioproductivity, and loss of landscape complexity. Read the text of the Wetlands Convention. If the four countries were parties to the Ramsar Convention, could it affect the outcome of the proposal? How? (Note that Latin American countries have been slow to join the Convention, with the exception of Chile, Uruguay, and Venezuela.)

Additional Readings

Simon Lyster, International Wildlife Law ch. 10 (1985); Daniel Navid, The International Law of Migratory Species: The Ramsar Convention, 29 Nat. Res. J. 1001 (1989); Cyril de Klemm, La Convention de Ramsar et la conservation des zones humides cotieres, particulierment en Mediterranee, Revue-Juridique de l'Environnement 577 (1990).

XVIII

Biological Diversity

Countries have long been concerned with protecting particular species of fauna and flora. Today the concern has turned to conserving the biological diversity of natural systems. This means that the focus is no longer on protecting only endangered species but rather on the health of ecosystems.

Legal concern with species is ancient. Wildlife laws have existed since at least the time of the Romans. However, older laws were used mainly to define what constituted private ownership of wildlife. Today, there are more than 100 international agreements protecting wildlife. For a thorough discussion of the history of wildlife laws, *see* Michael J. Bean, The Evolution of National Wildlife Law (1977); William F. Sigler, Wildlife Law Enforcement 1-9, 29-31 (1980).

Concern with protecting the health of ecosystems as a way to conserve biological diversity is relatively recent. While the 1940 Western Hemisphere Convention recognized the importance of ecosystem protection, little was done to implement it. Other regional conventions negotiated some 28 years later have given increasing attention to ecosystem protection. In 1992, countries concluded the Convention on Biological Diversity which—for the first time—obligates countries to establish a monitoring network for biological diversity.

The Council on Environmental Quality's Eleventh Annual Report (1985) defines "biological diversity" as "a broad catchall term including the interconnected and related concepts of genetic diversity, . . . ; species or ecological diversity . . . ; and habitat or natural diversity . . ." (at 273). It goes on to assert that "[t]he issue of biological diversity, in its broadest sense, has become one of the most important and pressing environmental concerns of the 1980's. . . . Increasing numbers of biologists, taxonomists, [and] ecologists . . . have quickly come to agreement that the preservation of biological diversity is arguably the most serious problem facing the nations of the Earth. . . ." *Id.; see also* Fred P. Bosselman, Extinction and the Law: Protection of Religiously-Motivated Behavior, 68 Chi-Kent L. Rev. 15 (1992) (discussing United States laws enacted to prevent the extinction of species and cultures).

For sources containing introductory as well as in-depth information about the issues surrounding biodiversity, *see* Vandana Shiva et al., Biodiversity: Social and Ecological Perspectives (1991); Office of Technology Assessment, Technologies to Maintain Biological Diversity, Summary (1987) (setting out OTA's results of a presentation to Congress on the problems and policy options for maintaining biological diversity); Jeffrey McNeely et al., Conserving the World's Biological Diversity (1990) (including a bibliography of sources); WRI/IUCN/UNEP, Global Biodiversity Strategy: Guidelines for Action to Save, Study, and Use Earth's Biotic Wealth Sustainably and Equitably (1992) (creating an action plan for conserving biodiversity); Bryan G. Norton, Why Preserve Natural Variety? (1987) (discussing the economic and intrinsic values of biodiversity); Walter V. Reid & Kenton R. Miller, World Resources Institute, Keeping Options Alive: The Scientific Basis for Conserving Biodiversity (1989); UNEP, Genetic Resources: An Overview (1980); Norman Myers, The Sinking Ark: A New Look at the Problem of Disappearing Species (1979); L. Kaufman, Why the Ark Is Sinking (1981); Norman Myers, For Dear Life, The Guardian, June 10, 1993, at 12; Special Issue: Biodiversity and Ecological Management, 22 Envtl. L. (1992); Dan L. Perlman and Glenn Adelson, Biodiversity: Exploring Values and Priorities in Conservation (1997). For charts and statistics on United States biological diversity conservation work in developing countries, *see* Janet N. Abramovitz, A Survey of U.S.-Based Efforts to Research and Conserve Biological Diversity in Developing Countries (World Resources Institute, 1989); National Research Council, A Biological Survey for the Nation (1993).

A. THE PROBLEM

■ BIOLOGICAL RESOURCES

Edith Brown Weiss
In Fairness to Future Generations 193 (1989)

Loss of the world's diversity would be worse than "energy depletion, economic collapse, limited nuclear war or conquest by a totalitarian government. As terrible as those catastrophes would be for us, they could be repaired in a few generations. The one process ongoing in the 1980's that will take millions of years to correct is the loss of genetic and species diversity by the destruction of natural habitats. This is the folly our descendants are least likely to forgive us."[1]

Biological resources are an invaluable patrimony. They have provided us with important crops, medicines, industrial products, and basic commodities such as shelter and clothing. Yet the diversity of our biological resources, including fauna and flora, is declining at an ever-increasing rate. The tropical forests, which contain much of our biological diversity, are being rapidly diminished. The annual net loss of tropical humid forests is between ten and twenty million hectares. If these trends continue, 25 to 40 percent of the tropical forests will disappear with them. Estuaries and wetlands, which also harbor many species, are being rapidly filled or polluted. These degradations will mean that plant and animal species will become extinct at an unprecedented rate. As many as one million species are likely to become extinct by the end of the century. While new species are constantly emerging, the rate of extinction far exceeds that of creation.

THE CURRENT STATE OF BIOLOGICAL DIVERSITY

E.O. Wilson
Biodiversity 3, 8, 10-12 (E.O. Wilson, ed. 1988)

Biological diversity must be treated more seriously as a global resource, to be indexed, used, and above all, preserved. Three circumstances conspire to give this matter an unprecedented urgency. First, exploding human populations are degrading the environment at an accelerating rate, especially in tropical countries. Second, science is discovering new uses for biological diversity in ways that can relieve both human suffering and environmental destruction. Third, much of the diversity is being irreversibly lost through extinction caused by the destruction of natural habitats, again especially in the tropics. Overall, we are locked into a race. We must hurry to acquire the knowledge on which a wise policy of conservation and development can be based for centuries to come. . . .

RAIN FORESTS AS CENTERS OF DIVERSITY

In recent years, evolutionary biologists and conservationists have focused increasing attention on tropical rain forests, for two principal reasons. First, although these habitats cover only 7% of the Earth's land surface, they contain more than half the species in the entire world biota. Second,

1. E.O. Wilson, *quoted in* R. Goodland, C. Watson & G. Ledec, Environmental Management in Tropical Agriculture 207 (1984).

the forests are being destroyed so rapidly that they will mostly disappear within the next century, taking with them hundreds of thousands of species into extinction. Other species-rich biomes are in danger, most notably the tropical coral reefs, geologically ancient lakes, and coastal wetlands. Each deserves special attention on its own, but for the moment the rain forests serve as the ideal paradigm of the larger global crisis. . . .

How Much Diversity Is Being Lost?

No precise estimate can be made of the numbers of species being extinguished in the rain forests or in other major habitats, for the simple reason that we do not know the numbers of species originally present. However, there can be no doubt that extinction is proceeding far faster than it did prior to 1800. The basis for this statement is not the direct observation of extinction. To witness the death of the last member of a parrot or orchid species is a near impossibility. With the exception of the showiest birds, mammals, or flowering plants, biologists are reluctant to say with finality when a species has finally come to an end. There is always the chance (and hope) that a few more individuals will turn up in some remote forest remnant or other. But the vast majority are not monitored at all. Like the dead of Gray's "Elegy Written in a Country Churchyard," they pass from the Earth without notice. . . .

In general, the tropical world is clearly headed toward an extreme reduction and fragmentation of tropical forests, which will be accompanied by a massive extinction of species. At the present time, less than 5% of the forests are protected within parks and reserves, and even these are vulnerable to political and economic pressures. For example, 4% of the forests are protected in Africa, 2% in Latin America, and 4% in Asia (Brown, 1985). Thus in a simple system as envisioned by the basic models of island biogeography, the number of species of all kinds of organisms can be expected to be reduced by at least one-half—in other words, by hundreds of thousands or even (if the insects are as diverse as the canopy studies suggest) by millions of species. . . .

The current reduction of diversity seems destined to approach that of the great natural catastrophes at the end of the Paleozoic and Mesozoic eras—in other words, the most extreme in the past 65 million years. In at least one important respect, the modern episode exceeds anything in the geological past. In the earlier mass extinctions, which some scientists believe were caused by large meteorite strikes, most of the plants survived even though animal diversity was severely reduced. Now, for the first time, plant diversity is declining sharply (Knoll, 1984). . . .

Biological Diversity

Biological diversity usually refers to three elements: (1) the number of different ecosystems (communities of plants and animals and the environments that sustain them) and their relative frequencies in a country or in the world; (2) the number of species of animals and plants and their relative frequencies; and (3) the genetic variation within each species.

The variability we see in the life forms on Earth is primarily a result of variations in DNA (deoxyribonucleic acid), as expressed in genes—the blueprints for life. Genetic variability is greatest among species, but variability among isolated populations of a species or among individuals in a population is also important. A rare species is a genetically vulnerable species. If the number of individuals is small, the probability of advantageous genetic variations occurring is reduced, and inbreeding may perpetuate disadvantageous characteristics. Preserving biological diversity, then, entails preserving not only species but also different populations of species and the largest feasible number of individuals within those populations. . . .

The Modern Loss of Biological Diversity

Human activities in the last quarter of the twentieth century are reducing biological diversity at a rate that may be unprecedented in the history of life on Earth. It is impossible to assess, with our limited knowledge, the consequences of the disappearance of species for the stability of Earth's environment or the economic value lost because of extinctions. The best available estimates indicate that if current trends continue, some 15-20 percent of the estimated 10 million to 30 million species of plants and animals alive in 1980 may become extinct by 2000 (see Wolf 1987), and many more species could be lost in the early decades of the twenty-first century. Development activities can be modified to help reduce these disturbing trends. As is shown below, the irreversible large-scale loss of biological diversity is not an unavoidable aspect of modern human survival or of economic development; it is a by-product of conducting human affairs without sufficient regard for the long-term human needs or sufficient awareness of the needs of other aspects.

The most striking difference between natural and human-induced extinction is in the rates. Over the millennia the rate of natural extinction of species has usually been slightly less than the rate of formation of new species through evolutionary processes (Myers 1979). Human activity is greatly accelerating the extinction rate; several hundred species *a day* may become extinct over the next twenty to thirty years. . . .

Another difference is that whereas in the course of evolution a species that becomes extinct is often replaced by a better-adapted successor or group of successors, human induced extinctions are evolutionary dead-ends. Furthermore, although human beings are not the first species to have caused the extinction of other species, they are the first to be aware of the implications of their actions and to be capable of controlling them.

The reduction of wildland habitats to less than the critical amount necessary for the survival of a species is by far the greatest cause of modern extinctions. Although many endangered species live in temperate areas, the problem is most severe in tropical regions, where at least two-thirds of the world's species of plants and animals are found. . . .

Although elimination of wildland habitats accounts for most present-day extinctions, direct overexploitation and the introduction of nonnative species that become pests or weeds are also important causes. To minimize these extinction risks, development projects must adhere to sustained-yield harvesting of forests and fisheries and must avoid introducing potential pests or weeds in agricultural and fishery projects.

The Case for Preserving Biological Diversity

There are compelling economic, scientific, aesthetic, and ethical reasons for preserving biological diversity. All of them are grounded in the view that because species extinctions are completely irreversible, preserving biological diversity keeps open important options for the future.

The *economic* justification for preserving biological diversity is that many species of wild plants and animals are undeveloped resources—that is, they have significant economic potential that is currently undiscovered, undervalued, or underutilized. Biological resources are essential to human existence, and the preservation of biological diversity is important to the maintenance and improvement of agriculture, forestry, ranching, fisheries, medicine, industry, and tourism.

The importance of genetic diversity for sustaining and increasing agricultural production is increasingly acknowledged. Without a diverse genetic base for plant breeding, the development of high-yielding crop varieties probably could not be sustained. The disappearance of many domesticated crop varieties and their wild relatives has made many of the world's productive farming areas increasingly susceptible to catastrophic attacks by pests and diseases. . . .

Wild plants and animals are also fundamentally important for modern medicine and offer even greater future applications. Over 40 percent of all prescriptions written in the United States contain one or more drugs that originate from wild species (fungi, bacteria, higher plants, and animals); annual sales of such drugs in this one country are over $8 billion (Farnsworth 1982). In many cases it is still impossible to synthesize these compounds or more costly to synthesize them than to obtain them from living sources; in any case it would not have been possible to know what compound to synthesize without first having the natural model.

Wild plant and animal species are of great and increasing importance to industry as sources of tannins, resins, gums, oils, dyes, and other commercially useful compounds. Until about 1850 even the rubber tree (*Hevea brasiliensis*) was just another Amazonian tree species of unknown economic value. The potential for new industrial products from currently unknown or poorly known plant and animal species is significant but impossible to quantify. Such products may even include hydrocarbons for an oil-short world. . . .

These examples illustrate the range of economic uses of many wild plants and animals. But probably less than 5 percent of all the world's species have been inventoried and scientifically named, and even fewer have been assessed for possible human use. Moreover, now that genetic engineering techniques increasingly permit the transfer of genes from one species to another, the extinction of any one species means a lost opportunity for transferring potentially useful genes to other species. Biological resources, unlike petroleum and other fossil fuels, are completely renewable, but only if care is taken to keep them alive and able to reproduce. The protection of biological diversity is relatively low cost . . . and helps to preserve the means available for addressing unpredictable future problems.

The *scientific* reason for species preservation is that we cannot understand the interactions of life forms and their environments unless we can observe how they function in the absence of significant human intervention. It is therefore necessary to conserve comprehensive samples of ecological systems in an undisturbed state. Moreover, each species has unique psychological, biochemical, and population characteristics, the study of which can help us to understand basic life processes. In addition to the direct economic applications of research on poorly known species, eventual economic payoffs are likely to emerge from more basic scientific research.

Wild animals are critically valuable in medical research. To meet the needs of researching without depleting native stocks, captive breeding of those animals that are being taken from wild at unsustainable rates should be encouraged. In malaria research there is no substitute for the rare and dwindling northern Columbian subspecies of the owl monkey (*Aotus trivirgatus*). . . .

The *aesthetic* justification is that many wild species of plants and animals are an irreplaceable source of wonder, inspiration, and joy to human beings because of their beauty, intriguing appearance, variety, or fascinating behavior. The French anthropologist Claude Levi-Strauss described wild species as "an irreplaceable marvel, equal to the works of art which we religiously preserve in museums." Millions of people who may never actually encounter many wild species derive enrichment and vicarious satisfaction from reading and learning about them; are our descendants to be denied these pleasures?

The *ethical*, or moral, justification espoused by a significant and growing number of people, is that human beings should not exercise their power to obliterate other species at will—even species not known to have any practical value to humankind. From this perspective nonhuman species have their own intrinsic value independent of any practical or utilitarian value they may have for human beings. This ethical viewpoint has been called the "Noah principle" (Ehrenfeld 1981). A related, perhaps more traditional, view is that to eradicate other species is to deprive future generations of options and thus to fail in the duty of stewardship. For a couple of generations of human beings to eliminate unnecessarily a sizable proportion of the diversity of life on Earth can be construed as an act of considerable arrogance.

B. OPTIONS FOR CONSERVING BIOLOGICAL DIVERSITY

There are two basic ways to conserve biological diversity: in situ, which means conservation of habitats, and ex situ, through gene banks and zoos or botanical gardens. The latter is a stop gap measure at best, although it is an attractive approach for educating people about animals and plants and enlisting their support in conservation efforts.

In situ conservation involves keeping a species in its natural environment and protecting that environment from anthropogenic damage. Consistent with the predominating preference for in situ over ex situ conservation, Walter V. Reid and Kenton R. Miller explain that "[i]n situ conservation maintains not only a variety's genetic diversity but also the evolutionary interactions that allow it to adapt continually to shifting environmental conditions, such as changes in pest populations or climate." Walter V. Reid and Kenton R. Miller, Keeping Options Alive: The Specific Basis for Conserving Biodiversity (1989). Areas such as wildlife reserves, national parks, and protected landscapes offer the opportunity to maintain not only the targeted endangered species, but also to keep the entire local ecosystem intact. *See generally* Craig A. Arnold, Conserving Habitats and Building Habitats: The Emerging Impact of the Endangered Species Act on Land Use Development, 10 Stan. Envtl. L.J. 1 (1991); George Cameron Coggins & Irma S. Russell, Beyond Shooting Snail Darters in Pork Barrels: Endangered Species and Land Use in America, 70 Geo. L.J. 1433 (1982).

Wildland management is the least costly—and in many cases the only—means available for effectively maintaining biological diversity. For certain groups of plants and animals, off-site (ex situ) preservation techniques can be useful supplements to the in situ preservation provided by wildlands. But ex situ techniques—zoos and other captive breeding facilities; botanical gardens; arboreta; cryogenic storage of embryos, eggs, and sperm; seed and pollen banks; and tissue cultures—cannot be expected to meet most biological conservation needs.

1. National Parks and Wildlife Reserves

National parks exist in most nations of the world, and are among the most prominent ways for a government to show support for the environment.

Parks and wildlife reserves are examples of in situ conservation techniques, as the entire ecosystem (or at least a substantial part of it) is kept intact, and species coexist as in nature. In 1969, the International Union for the Conservation of Nature and Natural Resources suggested that "national park" should be a term exclusively used for areas "where (a) ecosystems are not materially altered by human exploitation, and plant and animal species, geomorphological sites, and habitats are of special interest, (b) authority has prevented exploitation or occupation in the whole area and ecological, geomorphological, or aesthetic features are respected, and (c) visitors are allowed to enter under special conditions for inspirational, educative, cultural, and recreational purposes. N.C. Pollock & B. Litt, Animals, Environment and Man in Africa 90-91 (1975) (this book also gives a brief overview of the history of national parks, starting with Yellowstone National Park's founding in 1872).

As they allow in situ conservation, national parks can maintain a fuller diversity than can ex situ methods. *But see* Kyla Seligsohn-Bennett, Mismanaging Endangered and "Exotic" Species in the National Parks, 20 Envtl. L. 415 (1990) (criticizing the way the national parks in the United States handle endangered species, focusing on grizzly bears in Yellowstone National Park and feral horses in Assateague National Seashore).

Further, reserves that are open to the public can increase interest in the environment and also bring in much needed currency to fund conservation efforts. *See, e.g.*, N.C. Pollock & B. Litt, Animals, Environment and Man in Africa 96 (1975); *but see* Raymond Bonner, Peril and Hope for Africa's Wildlife (arguing that the maintenance of national parks often infringes on the native populations' way of life); Trouble in Paradise: The Exhausted Earth, Boston Globe, May 30, 1993, at 8 (reporting the complaints of relief workers that environmentalists concerned about saving the biodiversity of Madagascar ignore the needs of the people who live there).

Because parks and wildlife reserves have been treated as areas of sovereign national interest, the legal regimes controlling land usage within the boundaries of the park are overwhelmingly national or local. For a good discussion of the legal structure of the Canadian national park system, *see* H. Ian Rounthwaite, The National Parks of Canada: An Endangered Species?, 46 Saskatchewan L. Rev. 43 (1981); for an historical view of the development of some of the state parks in the western United States, *see* Thomas R. Cox, The Park Builders: A History of State Parks in the Pacific Northwest (1988).

In February 1992, the World Congress on National Parks, Protected Areas and the Human Future took place in Venezuela. The Congress adopted the Caracas Declaration, which stresses the importance of "well-managed national parks and protected areas." The declaration views the park system as necessary for the maintenance of biological diversity, and crucial for the support of human and nonhuman life. For humankind, the protected areas have "immense scientific, educational, cultural, recreational and spiritual value," in addition to being necessary for agriculture and medicine.

The declaration urges national and international bodies to "consolidate and enlarge national systems of well-managed protected areas with buffer zones and corridors, so that by the year 2000 they safeguard the full representative range of land, fresh water, coastal and marine ecosystems of each country." It asks governments to be sensitive to the interests of the indigenous people, women, and children of the present and future generations. The declaration stresses the need for education, professional training, and scientific research. Towards this end, it encourages public funding and adequate financial allocations. Lastly, it seeks international technical and financial cooperation and regional participation in regard to ecosystems that cross national borders. *See* The Conservation Foundation, Managing National Park System Resources: A Handbook on Legal Duties, Opportunities, and Tools (Michael A. Mantell, ed. 1990); *See also* Graham A. Yapp, Wilderness in Kakadu National Park: Aboriginal and Other Interests, 29 Nat. Resources J. 171 (1989); R. Michael Wright, Morne Trois Pitons National Park in Dominica: A Case Study in Park Establishment in the Developing World, 12 Ecology L.Q. 747 (1985); Joseph L. Sax, Is Anyone Minding Stonehenge? The Origins of Cultural Property Protection in England, 78 Cal. L. Rev. 1543 (1990) (focusing on the development of cultural preservation policies in England).

2. *Alternative Approaches to Habitat Conservation*

The following two excerpts focus on clarifying property rights to biological resources as a key to successful conservation and management. What legal issues do you foresee with each approach? What are the advantages and limitations of each approach in conserving biological diversity?

In the first article, the French scholar Cyril de Klemm argues that the property of species should be vested in the world community, and a system should be developed to ascribe a value to species with payment of royalties for their use.

■ CONSERVATION OF SPECIES: THE NEED FOR A NEW APPROACH

Cyril de Klemm
9 Envtl. Poly. & L. 122-127 (1982)
(numbering of paragraphs omitted)

A) INTRODUCTION

The present deficiencies can and must be corrected if species and their genetic resources are to survive and contribute to man's well-being in the future. For that purpose, a new three-fold approach seems essential:

- a system should be developed to ascribe a value to species;
- the property of species should be vested in the world community;
- a global conservation treaty based on reciprocal obligations and providing for sustainable financing of conservation action should be concluded at world level.

B) ASCRIBING A VALUE TO SPECIES

To establish the value of species, a methodology will have to be developed. In this process, four major components of species value could be taken into consideration.

Species are valuable because of the market value of their individual members which, in turn, derives from certain qualities and attributes which are characteristic of a species. If a species is lost so also will the qualities and attributes that made its individual members valuable be lost.

The value of species is for economists to determine with the assistance of scientists. So far, it would seem that very little work, if any, has been carried out to that end. This may be due to the alleged unimportance of the matter or, perhaps, because the conventional tools and techniques of economic analysis are inadequate to deal with this new subject. . . .

Many species have, for the time being, no recognized use and, as we say, many more are probably still undiscovered and undescribed. Any one of them may, however, acquire suddenly, a considerable economic or scientific value. Species which have for the time being no actual value will need, therefore, to be assigned a potential one based on the probability of the discovery of important uses in the future. Such a probability could be determined on the basis of the past rate of discoveries and on the expected acceleration of that rate in the future as the investigation of species develops, especially if a world conservation organization is set up.

Many difficulties will undoubtedly arise and a considerable degree of arbitrariness will have to be accepted. One must be confident, however, that, with time and experience, a satisfactory method can be developed. A possible approach could consist in ascribing a basic value to all species belonging to a certain group, which could be a taxonomic group such as a class or a family or a functional group such as forest trees, wild fruit trees, or wild relatives of crops and to use coefficients to take care of such factors as genetic distinctness, probable potential uses unknown role in the ecosystem.

Far-ranging, abundant species are not very numerous and assigning them a value may not, therefore, be overly difficult. Most species are closely linked to a specialized habitat such as a particular species of tree. In such a case, the tree could be assigned an aggregate value and the individual value of the aggregated species be neglected until a specific usage is discovered for any of them.

The same method could be applied to species which are presumed to exist but are still unknown to science. A large majority of them are insects or other invertebrates and epiphitic, parasitic, or saprophytic plants of tropical rain forests. Most are probably also ecologically specialized and linked to one species of tree and could therefore be aggregated, albeit in unknown numbers, to the value of known species.

The assignment of a value to species will have important consequences for their conservation. It will indeed become possible to assign a value to individuals. The simplest method could consist in dividing the species value by the number of individuals in that species. Admittedly, this figure is generally unknown, but the rarer a species is known to be, the better generally the knowledge of its numbers. For common species, a reasonable approximation, based perhaps on biomass, will probably be enough. Thus, animals and plants belonging to rare species will have much higher value than those belonging to abundant ones, although the value of the species themselves may be the same.

Knowing the value of individual plants and animals, it will be possible to calculate the value of the wildlife contained in a given area. This, together with other factors such as uniqueness, rarity, or representativeness should lead to the development of a method to assess the value of natural ecosystems or protected areas. . . .

C) VESTING THE OWNERSHIP OF SPECIES IN THE WORLD COMMUNITY

It must be recognized that the concept of value as applied to species will be necessarily of a particular nature. Species, although their members are and should remain things susceptible of private ownership, are in themselves abstract concepts. A species is the sum of its individual members as long as they are alive. All have a share in the value of the species. But dead specimens have no more than a market value. The value of a species, as defined, derives essentially from the benefits that it can bring to mankind. This value is obviously universal and should not benefit solely individual countries or groups. So far, problems or disputes relating to the legal status of species have never really arisen. This may well be due to the fact that no specific value had been ascribed to species, as distinct from individuals. If this situation changes, as we believe it must, there will be strong incentives for states or entities to proclaim themselves owners of certain species. The usefulness to mankind of the gene pool of wild species may then very well be diverted from the advancement of the well being of the world society to the promotion of particular interests. There must be, therefore, a recognition of the right for mankind to enjoy the benefits derived from the natural capital constituted by the species of fauna and flora of the Earth.

As we saw earlier, it would be impossible for legal and practical reasons to instore private or state monopolies on the use of genetic resources and even if such monopolies were established, they would be impossible to enforce abroad. Moreover, for moral reasons, it would seem that no state should have the right to deny other states the benefits deriving from these resources. The owner of species should therefore be the world community as a whole. . . .

This would have far-reaching consequences: the world community would be legally protected against infringements; would have legal standing to sue for the protection of its right; would be entitled to collect royalties for the use of the genetic resources of the species which it owns. . . .

V. A World Treaty

b) Principles

To become an accepted rule of international law upon which an appropriate machinery could be established, the principle of the ownership (or trusteeship) of species by the world community should be embodied in a new world convention on the conservation of the natural genetic heritage of mankind. Three further principles, which follow directly from the first, should at the same time be laid down:

1. The benefits derived from species should be accessible to all nations;
2. All states have the duty to conserve species under their jurisdiction;
3. States should, at least, receive compensation from the world community for the expenses and loss of earning thus incurred.

1) The Principle of Accessibility

Genetic processes should be accessible to all nations for research, development, or propagation. This means essentially that there should be no restriction on the export of genetic material other than those which may be imposed by world agreement and that no state should be denied access to such material. Nothing would be changed, however, in respect of the present jurisdiction of states over individual animals and plants as the principle of accessibility should not mean that there should be no restrictions on taking. Quite to the contrary, strict restrictions on taking will often be a prerequisite if long-term accessibility is to be ensured. Similarly, restrictions on national and international trade in wild species and products will continue to apply. But states should not be able to deny to any legitimate and bona fide research body, including other states and certain international organizations, access to the gene pools under their jurisdiction, neither should they be entitled to make claims against the use of these genetic resources by other parties. . . .

2) The Principle of Stewardship

If the natural genetic heritage is a valuable resource owned by the world community, there is obviously a requirement to conserve it. This, clearly, is a task that must be carried out by range states and should include an adequate inventory of species and natural areas, monitoring of their status, and the adoption of conservation measures including, but not necessarily limited to, appropriate land use planning, establishment of protected areas, control of over-exploitation and of exotic species and the abatement of certain forms of pollution. Active management measures will also be required for certain areas or species of special concern. Priorities will have to be set reflecting world requirements and criteria for their determination established. Technical assistance should, if necessary, be made available on request.

3) The Principle of Compensation

As a counterpart of the duties taken upon by states, on behalf of the world community, to allow access to genetic conservation, fairness requires that such states receive at least appropriate compensation from the world community to assist them in meeting the cost of research, monitoring, conservation and management and to make up for the loss of earning incurred as a result of the establishment of protected areas closed to exploitation and development. The source of the funds required to provide for this compensation could be royalties paid for the use of genetic resources by their very users. The laying down of reciprocal obligations would, for the first time, introduce a quid pro quo in a conservation treaty and would, at the same time, provide for financial resources commensurate with the needs. Indeed, as it becomes possible to assess the value of protected natural areas, the amounts paid could be proportionate to that value. Thus, instead of being considered as a loss to the economy, protected areas would actually be contributing to the Gross National Product. . . .

2) Scope of the Royalty System

As we have seen, the value of species derives from different forms of actual or potential uses. The question, therefore, arises as to which of these forms will lend themselves best to a royalty system.

First and foremost comes the use of wild species for the development of new crops (as for instance the Jojoba . . .), or by appropriate crossing or other gene transfer techniques, for the incorporation of wild germplasm into already domesticated races of animals or plants (as with perennial maize . . .). The production of natural substances through modern genetic engineering techniques also falls into this category. All these uses can be considered as directly gene dependent.

Another gene dependent use is the production of chemical substances such as drugs from wild or cultivated plant populations or by synthesis after the presence of a new molecule has been identified by chemical analysis in a wild species. Furthermore, it often happens that molecules thus discovered are used as models for the synthesis of whole families of related molecules which could otherwise never be developed in the absence of the natural model. Finally, substances such as vaccines, obtained from non-domestic laboratory animals such as monkeys and perhaps, in the future, armadillos . . . also belong to this class. In all these cases, the royalties would seem to be fully justified and should not pose insuperable practical problems.

A further category of uses relates to the introduction into an ecosystem, generally man-made, of animals or plants for the purpose of filling a vacant ecological niche, thereby restoring the balance of nature. Examples are the introduction of predators or parasitoids for biological control or the release of pollinators. These organisms are generally mass reared in laboratories from specimens initially collected in the wild. The production of certain species is now undertaken by commercial companies and royalties could here also be envisaged.

There remains the case of individual members of species, which are taken directly from the wild and consumed, used or processed for their flesh, fibers, skin, oil, wool or any other feature. Admittedly, this is a category which relates only to the use of individual specimens and not of genetic processes. It would seem, however, that even in this case, the collection of royalties on the use of wild species would be required if the financial means to ensure their conservation and sustainable utilization are to be secured. Care should, however, be taken not to provide, in so doing, an incentive to over-exploitation. This could well be the case if a large fraction of the sums collected was merely fed back into the country of origin of the species concerned. This can be resolved by the conclusion of agreements between the organization and recipient countries providing for the maintenance of the genetic diversity of the resource and its sustainable payment of royalties. In some cases such as, for instance, that of pharmaceuticals obtained directly from wild populations or of animals and plants with a high market value in international trade, royalties would have to be set at a high level to deter collection from the wild and encourage the development of synthetic substitutes or propagation in capacity. This will have, naturally, to be fully coordinated with the governing body of the CITES Convention. In all cases, royalties will have to be collected from importers.

To sum up, the system should cover, in principle, all substances, products and propagative material, such as seeds, obtained by the artificial propagation of wild species or by the transfer of germplasm from wild to domesticated or cultivated species. It should also include at least certain substances such as drugs obtained directly from wild specimens or synthesized or initiated on the basis of models provided by molecules available in wild species. Commercial sales of biologically active organisms, including pollinators and biological control agents should also be covered. . . .

Decisions will also have to be made as to the coverage of genetic resources deriving from cultivated or domesticated plants or animals. As far as the use of their genetic potential is concerned, there is obviously not much difference between wild and cultivated species. On the other hand, legal problems could arise in connection with the difficulty of identifying countries of origin.

Finally, there remains to determine whether the system should only apply to new uses or to existing uses as well. There again, case by case decisions seem to be the only practical answer. It will, therefore, be necessary to establish a flexible machinery and procedure to allow the governing body of the organization to extend the provisions of the convention to any type of genetic resources use as it may deem appropriate.

3) The User Pays Principle

Royalties should be paid by the users of genetic resources for commercial purposes and should be used to finance conservation action just as polluters must contribute financially to pollution control on the basis of the now widely accepted "polluter pays principle."

Users should be understood as meaning the manufacturers of industrial, pharmaceutical and other products which derive any or all of their characters from the use of genetic resources, the multipliers of seeds or other propagative material marketed to farmers and possibly the growers or processors of certain major industrial or food crops such as cocoa, coffee, oil-palm, rubber or sugarbeet. Obviously, a thorough analysis of the market situation will have to be made before all categories of users are clearly identified. Problems relating to the stage in the production process (e.g., production of the raw material, processing, marketing) at which royalties should be paid, and as to whether or not payments should be shared among two or more of the actors in the process, will also have to be considered.

It may also be worthwhile to investigate whether a system of concessions could not have some advantages. Under such a system, prospective users would apply to the organization to obtain from the world community a concession to use certain genetic resources against the payment of royalties. . . .

5) Enforcement

Enforcement will be centered around two basic questions: the payment of royalties by users and compliance with the principles of accessibility and stewardship on the part of member states.

The establishment of the obligation to pay royalties and the subsequent payment of these amounts should in principle be relatively easy, provided necessary links and procedures are developed between the organization and international and national bodies entrusted with the administration of patents. Indeed, in most cases, the user of a genetic resource will also be the holder of a patent or of a plant breeder's right. Obviously, even though genes and natural processes deriving from species cannot be patented, the techniques used to transfer genes to synthesize chemical compounds or to process natural substances, can be. To protect themselves against competitors and to secure their rights to receive royalties, users will, therefore, generally file for a patent. Since in their application, they will have to disclose the nature of their invention and establish its novelty, its link with the natural heritage will become public knowledge. As a consequence, a condition to the granting of a patent could well be that payments be subsequently made to the world conservation fund. Thus, if payments are not made, an easy sanction could be the suspension of the patent until payments are resumed.

After a patent has expired, the invention falls into the public domain for anyone to use. Steps should therefore be taken to ensure that royalties be paid by any new user of the invention. A possible solution could be the establishment of a public register of species-related inventions in the public domain. The use of listed inventions would remain unrestricted but subject to the payment of the corresponding royalty. If payments are not made, the right of use could be denied. . . .

With regard to compliance by states with the principles of accessibility and stewardship, enforcement will be greatly facilitated by the existence of reciprocal obligations. Thus, a state that would be refusing access to some of the species under its jurisdiction could be denied access to other species in other countries. The absence of adequate conservation measures could be considered as a form of denial and result in the same effect. It would also be considered as a violation of the duty of stewardship and could be sanctioned by suspension or reduction of payments made by the world conservation fund to the country concerned.

In the next excerpt, the economist Roger Sedjo argues for the importance of property rights as a way to conserve biological resources.

■ PROPERTY RIGHTS FOR PLANTS

Roger A. Sedjo
97 Resources Magazine 1-4 (1989)

All too often, the resources that civilizations take most for granted are those that require diligent attention in order to be cared for well. Plant genetic material is one of them. Also called germplasm, it is a valuable economic resource that is often in limited supply and is sometimes threatened with destruction. . . .

Protection against destruction is difficult to achieve under current law and management systems. Naturally occurring plant genetic resources are treated as a common property resource, owned by no one. This absence of property rights opens up the possibility of excessive exploitation of the resource, a variation on the "tragedy of the commons." The absence of ownership denies individuals and countries the possibility of benefiting commercially from the presence of unique genetic resources within their jurisdictional boundaries. There is little incentive, other than altruism, to incur costs to safeguard the habitat of unique and endangered wild species.

Nor can this situation be easily changed by the introduction of national management and regulation. Public management usually cannot internalize to the country the benefits of genetic resources to which it has no internationally recognized property rights (although this is not the case for many common-pool resources that are under public management). Absence of property rights means, for example, that the recently discovered Mexican species of perennial maize is likely to provide Mexico with only negligible benefits, even if the desired genetic traits of the species prove to be of enormous economic value worldwide. Mexico therefore has little economic incentive to preserve undisturbed any vegetation in which this and similarly valuable (but as yet unknown) plant genetic material may be hidden.

Systemic Limitations

The existing management system provides property rights for improved and genetically engineered plants, as well as government protection of selected habitat. Such an approach appears to do an excellent job of generating investments for the development of technology to improve seed strains and for the distribution of technically improved genetic material to users throughout the world. However, the system is doing a poor job of protecting the wild genetic resources and the habitat in which these valuable resources reside. Furthermore, there is little in the system that addresses the question of the sharing of financial gains with the Third World.

Since property rights are not now assignable to natural species, the Third World countries in which the majority of these species reside have no means to derive financial benefits from the utilization of "their" species in commercial application. By contrast, since property rights in improved species are available, breeders can capture the commercial gains through improvements in resources without making payments to the countries from which the basic genetic materials derive.

Moreover, although many wild genetic resources are believed to be threatened with extinction, the existing system provides few incentives for their protection. Pharmaceutical firms and other users of genetic resources have little control over habitat maintenance in sovereign Third World countries. These countries, for their part, lack recognized property rights to genetic resources and cannot capture the rents—that is, the financial benefit of these resources. Thus the current term relies almost exclusively upon governments for protection of habitat in a context where governments themselves have few direct incentives to undertake protection and where their actual performance in protection has been mixed at best.

An Alternative System . . .

One alternative system that may have merit is based on viewing genetic resources as the property of the state in which it resides. Under this system, property rights would be assigned in order to provide incentives for protection and wise management. Property rights for plant species could be expanded and extended to cover newly discovered natural species, whereas under current legal interpretations only special genetic stock, current breeder lines, and genetically engineered organisms are recognized as having ownership. Such an approach would allow the genetically rich Third World countries an opportunity to profit directly from the ownership of genetic resources. Property rights to species would also provide a direct financial incentive to protect and maintain the natural habitat in which rare and as yet unknown species may reside, since their discovery and development at some time could generate direct financial returns to the owner.

Under a system in which the concept of property rights was extended to include species not now known or utilized, newly discovered natural genetic resources would become the property of the political state in which those resources reside. In principle, the state would be free to declare all such resources as the property of the state, or it could grant private property rights to individuals or corporations that discover the genetic resources. Having ownership of the resources, the owners—public or private—could be expected to have an interest in their longterm preservation and development.

Alternatively, the state might decide that the rights be defined in terms of the ownership of land upon which the species resides, and that such rights be treated no differently than rights to other natural resources and property in that political entity. With the state controlling the rights, it could voluntarily sell or distribute those rights in any way it deemed appropriate. A domestic corporation or governmental department could be created to manage the system, or the rights could be transferred to private interests.

Markets for Genetic Material

The transfer of a wild genetic resource to private interests might be accomplished by having the private interest make an initial payment and subsequently pay royalties based upon the commercial earnings of products that utilize the resource. The country where the resource resides could negotiate an exclusive agreement with a firm, or allow a number of firms to utilize the resource under a set of mutually agreed-upon conditions. Agreement might be reached as part of bilateral negotiations or as the result of a competitive bidding process. Should a particular germplasm be discovered in several countries simultaneously, the potential users would be free to negotiate the best deal possible with the country of their choice. A necessary condition for such a system is the possibility of describing a plant with sufficient specificity so that the property right could be clearly and unambiguously assigned. Only under such a condition could those rights be enforced.

Markets for genetic material could function just as markets do for other resources. A country with sole ownership of certain germplasm, for example, might choose to behave like a monopolist in regard to a particular germplasm, demanding high prices in return for rights to utilize the resource. These conditions might be so onerous as to have no takers. Such market behavior is unlikely, however, because it runs at least two risks. First, the same natural germplasm might be discovered in another country. In this case a monopolist's bargaining power would be seriously compromised and the strategy of withholding the germplasm from development would backfire, resulting in loss of the monopoly position. Second, biotechnology may develop in such a fashion as to bypass the usefulness of the particular germplasm. Hence, by withholding the germplasm from development the monopoly would lose its opportunity for negotiating favorable conditions.

In both cases, the longer a monopolist withholds the germplasm from the market, the greater is the possibility that events will compromise the favorable initial bargaining situation. Where several countries have the same unique germplasm resource, the possibility for collusion and the formation of a cartel exists. However, cartels have been historically unstable, and the possibilities for finding alternative germplasm resources are likely to be substantial.

It might be deemed desirable to restrict the period of property rights for natural germplasm to some limited period—say seventeen years, as it is for patents. The period could begin when the property right is assigned, presumably sometime close to the discovery of a new germplasm. However, this restriction need not compromise the incentive effects of the proposed system. The very possibility of discovering a previously unknown genetic resource with commercial potential provides some incentive to preserve habitat.

In most respects the system proposed would be similar to that which currently exists for handling other resources. For example, if a country believes that it has a valuable petroleum deposit, it may choose to develop the resource itself, negotiate drilling rights with a major petroleum company, or sell some or all of the drilling rights (together with a royalty provision) to the highest bidder, who could then proceed with development. For a resource that is not commercially viable given current technology and markets, the country may choose a fourth option: set the resource aside for possible development at a more auspicious time. In principle, there is no reason why such a system of property rights could not be devised for unused genetic resources.

Advantages

The major socially desirable feature of the proposed system is that it would provide nonaltruistic incentives for the preservation of rare species and germplasm—no small matter, since the pressure on genetic resources is growing as the result of changing demands for land use. Such a system need not preclude existing governmental efforts to preserve habitat; nor should it be viewed as a substitute for existing efforts to preserve areas of wide or unique biodiversity. The two approaches are not mutually exclusive. Under the property rights system, national governments would also have economic incentives to protect regions of rich biological diversity. Thus the future value of currently unknown genetic resources could be captured. The destruction of unique genetic resource would not only represent a global social loss, but this loss would be translated into a direct economic opportunity foregone for the country in which the resource resides.

A system that provides property rights for owners of natural plant germplasm also would provide a mechanism for the restoration of balance in the gene trade between the gene-rich Third World and the gene-poor industrial world. Just as plant-breeding countries would receive returns to their investments in breeding, gene-rich countries would receive returns associated with their protection of germplasm from extinction and their discovery of useful previously unknown species. A system of property rights for wild or unimproved genetic resources would not be without significant implementation and enforcement problems. As with patents, a genetic resource must be defined in sufficient detail to distinguish it from similar but different resources. Conflicts are bound to occur. Nevertheless, the proposed system offers promise of providing an additional tool to induce social behavior to protect the earth's valuable genetic resources—resources that are currently under heavy pressure.

3. The Biodiversity Convention

INTERNATIONAL LAW AND THE PROTECTION OF BIOLOGICAL DIVERSITY

Daniel M. Bodansky
28 Vand. J. Transnatl. L. 623, 627 (1995)

Over the last twenty to twenty-five years, international environmental law has developed a number of general principles that are relevant to biodiversity protection. . . . Regardless of whether these principles have the status of customary international law . . . they represent an orientation or framework for discussions of environmental issues.

The three principles most relevant to biological diversity are: (1) the precautionary principle, (2) the principle of intergenerational equity, and (3) the principle of differentiated responsibilities. The precautionary principle says that the international community need not await scientific certainty before taking action to protect the environment, particularly when the potential environmental harms are irreversible. This principle is clearly relevant to the biodiversity question, given the substantial uncertainties about the magnitude of the problem. . . .

The second relevant principle is intergenerational equity, which says that people have a duty to conserve resources for the benefit not only of the present generation but of future generations as well. . . .

Finally, the principle of differentiated responsibilities addresses the concerns of developing countries, where most biodiversity is found. According to this principle, countries should contribute differently to international environmental efforts, depending on their capabilities and their historical responsibility. In practice, this principle has meant preferential treatment of poor, developing countries, and a greater contribution by wealthy, developed countries.

These three principles provide the general framework for efforts to conserve biological resources. However, they are not a panacea. They do not answer the hard questions about exactly how much evidence is needed before undertaking conservation measures or how much protection is warranted, nor do they dictate any particular regulatory policies.

The more specific rules and mechanisms to conserve biological diversity are found primarily in treaties. Over the last fifty to sixty years, a whole range of treaties has been negotiated. One general category includes wildlife protection treaties addressing particular species, such as migratory birds or whales. The primary purpose of these treaties is to protect against over-exploitation of species by humans. . . . The bigger threat to species, however, is not over-harvesting by humans but rather habitat loss. To protect biological diversity, emphasis needs to be placed not simply on protecting particular species, but on protecting the broader ecosystems in which they live. A number of international treaties have been developed to address the need for habitat conservation. . . . A final category of wildlife treaties are regional treaties that address nature conservation in a comprehensive fashion through both species protection and habitat protection. The first of these was developed in Africa. Subsequently, regional treaties have been developed for the Western Hemisphere, Europe, and Southeast Asia.

When the idea of developing a global biodiversity convention first began to gather momentum in the late 1980's, some suggested that it should serve as an umbrella agreement, consolidating and subsuming the many wildlife treaties developed since the turn of the century. Ultimately, this plan did not prove practicable. Instead, the 1992 Convention on Biological Diversity has served as a framework agreement that builds upon, rather than subsumes, existing treaties. In contrast to earlier treaties, it does not include any lists or annexes of protected species or areas. The Biodiversity Convention, however, goes beyond previous treaties by dealing with the problem of biodiversity in a more comprehensive fashion, addressing all aspects of biodiversity including access to biological resources, biotechnology, and financial resources.

The Convention on Biological Diversity was negotiated under the auspices of the United Nations Environment Programme and opened for signature at the United Nations Conference on Environment and Development in Rio de Janeiro, Brazil, in June 1992. The convention provides for national monitoring of biological diversity, the development of national strategies, plans and programs to protect biological diversity, national in situ and ex situ measures conservation measures, environmental impact assessments of projects for adverse effects on biological diversity, and national reports on implementing measures and the effectiveness of these measures.

The United States did not sign the convention when it opened for signature in Rio. (Brazil was the first country to sign.) Then-President Bush indicated that the United States was concerned about technology transfer and intellectual property rights under Articles 16 and 22, biotechnology and biosafety under Article 19, and the failure to designate the permanent financial mechanism under Articles 39 and 21. Subsequently, on Earth Day 1993, President Clinton announced that the United States would sign the agreement and provide an interpretive statement regarding the controversial provisions. The United States signing took place on June 4, 1993, just before the period for signing the agreement closed. As of July 1998, the United States was not among the 174 states that had ratified the convention.

The convention has entered into effect and parties have held several conferences.

Excerpts from the convention are reproduced below.

CONVENTION ON BIOLOGICAL DIVERSITY

UNEP/Bio. Div./CONF/L.2; reprinted in 31 ILM 818 (1992)
June 5, 1992

Article 15. Access to Genetic Resources

1. Recognizing the sovereign rights of States over their natural resources, the authority to determine access to genetic resources rests with the national governments and is subject to national legislation.

2. Each Contracting Party shall endeavor to create conditions to facilitate access to genetic resources for environmentally sound uses by other Contracting Parties and not to impose restrictions that run counter to the objectives of this Convention.

3. For the purpose of this Convention, the genetic resources being provided by a Contracting Party, as referred to in this Article and Articles 16 and 19, are only those that are provided by Contracting Parties that are countries of origin of such resources or by the Parties that have acquired the genetic resources in accordance with this Convention.

4. Access, where granted, shall be on mutually agreed terms and subject to the provisions of this Article.

5. Access to genetic resources shall be subject to prior informed consent of the Contracting Party providing such resources, unless otherwise determined by that Party.

6. Each Contracting Party shall endeavor to develop and carry out scientific research based on genetic resources provided by other Contracting Parties with the full participation of and where possible, in such Contracting Parties.

7. Each Contracting Party shall take legislative, administrative or policy measures, as appropriate, and in accordance with Articles 16 and 19 and, where necessary, through the financial mechanism established by Articles 20 and 21 with the aim of sharing in a fair and equitable way the results of research and development and the benefits arising from the commercial and other utilization of genetic resources with the Contracting Party providing such resources. Such sharing shall be upon mutually agreed terms.

Article 16. Access to and Transfer of Technology

1. Each Contracting Party, recognizing that technology includes biotechnology, and that both access to and transfer of technology among Contracting Parties are essential elements for the attainment of the objectives of this Convention, undertakes subject to the provisions of this Article to provide and/or facilitate access for and transfer to other Contracting Parties of technologies that are relevant to the conservation and sustainable use of biological diversity or make use of genetic resources and do not cause significant damage to the environment.

2. Access to and transfer of technology referred to in paragraph 1 above to developing countries shall be provided and/or facilitated under fair and most favorable terms, including on confessional and preferential terms where mutually agreed, and, where necessary, in accordance with the financial mechanism established by Articles 20 and 21. In the case of technology subject to patents and other intellectual property rights, such access and transfer shall be provided on terms which recognize and are consistent with the adequate and effective protection of intellectual property rights. The application of this paragraph shall be consistent with paragraphs 3, 4 and 5 below.

3. Each Contracting Party shall take legislative, administrative or policy measures, as appropriate, with the aim that Contracting Parties, in particular those that are developing countries, which provide genetic resources are provided access to and transfer of technology which makes use of those resources, on mutually agreed terms, including technology protected by patents and other intellectual property rights, where necessary through the provisions of Articles 20 and 21 and in accordance with international law and consistent with paragraphs 4 and 5 below.

4. Each Contracting Party shall take legislative, administrative or policy measures, as appropriate with the aim that the private sector facilitates

access to, joint development and transfer of technology referred to in paragraph 1 above for the benefit of both governmental institutions and the private sector of developing countries and in this regard shall abide by the obligations included in paragraphs 1, 2 and 3 above.

5. The Contracting Parties, recognizing that patents and other intellectual property rights may have an influence on the implementation of this Convention, shall cooperate in this regard subject to national legislation and international law in order to ensure that such rights are supportive of and do not run counter to its objectives.

Article 17. Exchange of Information

1. The Contracting Parties shall facilitate the exchange of information, from all publicly available sources, relevant to the conservation and sustainable use of biological diversity, taking into account the special needs of developing countries.

2. Such exchange of information shall include exchange of results of technical, scientific and socio-economic research, as well as information on training and surveying programmes, specialized knowledge, indigenous and traditional knowledge as such and in combination with the technologies referred to in Article 16, paragraph 1. It shall also, where feasible, include repatriation of information.

Article 18. Technical and Scientific Cooperation

1. The Contracting Parties shall promote international technical and scientific cooperation in the field of conservation and sustenance of biological diversity, where necessary, through the appropriate international and national institutions.

2. Each Contracting Party shall promote technical and scientific cooperation with other Contracting Parties, in particular developing countries, in implementing this Convention, inter alia, through the development and implementation of national policies. In promoting such cooperation, special attention should be given to the development and strengthening of national capabilities, by means of human resources development and institution building.

3. The Conference of the Parties, at its first meeting, shall determine how to establish a clearing-house mechanism to promote and facilitate technical and scientific cooperation.

4. The Contracting Party shall, in accordance with national legislation and policies, encourage and develop methods of cooperation for the development and use of technologies, including indigenous and traditional technologies, in pursuance of the objectives of this Convention. For this purpose, the Contracting Parties shall also promote cooperation in the training of personnel and exchange of experts.

5. The Contracting Parties shall, subject to mutual agreement, promote the establishment of joint research programmes and joint ventures for the development of technologies relevant to the objectives of this Convention.

Article 19. Handling of Biotechnology and Distribution of Its Benefits

1. Each Contracting Party shall take legislative, administrative or policy measures, as appropriate, to provide for the effective participation in biotechnological research activities by those Contracting Parties, especially developing countries, which provide the genetic resources for such research, and where feasible in such Contracting Parties.

2. Each Contracting Party shall take all practicable measures to promote and advance priority access on a fair and equitable basis by Contracting Parties, especially developing countries, to the results and benefits arising from biotechnologies based upon genetic resources provided by those Contracting Parties. Such access shall be on mutually agreed terms.

3. The Parties shall consider the need for and modalities of a protocol setting out appropriate procedures, including, in particular, advance informed agreement in the field of the safe transfer, handling and use of any living modified organism resulting from biotechnology that may have adverse effect on the conservation and sustainable use of biological diversity.

4. Each Contracting party shall, directly or by requiring any natural or legal person under its jurisdiction providing the organisms referred to in paragraph 3 above, provide any available information about the use and safety regulations required by that Contracting Party in handling such organisms, as well as any available information on the potential adverse impact of the specific organisms concerned to the Contracting Party into which those organisms are to be introduced.

Article 20. Financial Resources

1. Each Contracting Party undertakes to provide, in accordance with its capabilities, financial support and incentives in respect to those national activities which are intended to achieve the objectives of this Convention, in accordance with its national plans, priorities and programmes.

2. The developed country Parties shall provide new and additional financial resources to enable developing country Parties to meet the agreed full incremental costs to them of implementing measures which fulfil the obligations of this Convention and to benefit from its provisions and which costs are agreed between a developing country Party and the institutional structure referred to in Article 21 in accordance with policy, strategy, programme priorities and eligibility criteria and an indicative list of incremental costs established by the Conference of the Parties. Other Parties, including countries undergoing the process of transition to a market economy, may

voluntarily assume the obligations of the developed country Parties. For the purpose of this Article, the Conference of the Parties, shall at its first meeting establish a list of developed country Parties and other parties which voluntarily assume the obligations of the developed country Parties. The Conference of the Parties shall periodically review and if necessary amend the list. Contributions from other countries and sources on a voluntary basis would also be encouraged. The implementation of these commitments shall take into account the need for adequacy, predictability and timely flow of funds and the importance of burden-sharing among the contributing Parties included in the list.

3. The developed country Parties may also provide, and developing country Parties avail themselves of, financial resources related to the implementation of this Convention through bilateral, regional and other multilateral channels.

4. The extent to which developing country Parties will effectively implement their commitments under this Convention will depend on the effective implementation by developed country Parties of their commitments under this Convention related to financial resources and transfer of technology and will take fully into account the fact that economic and social development and eradication of poverty are the first and overriding priorities of the developing country Parties.

5. The Parties shall take full account of the specific needs and special situation of least developed countries in their actions with regard to funding and transfer of technology.

6. The Contracting Parties shall also take into consideration the special conditions resulting from the dependence on, distribution and location of, biological diversity within developing country Parties, in particular small island States.

7. Consideration shall also be given to the special situation of developing countries, including those that are most environmentally vulnerable, such as those with arid and semi-arid zones, coastal and mountainous areas.

Article 21. Financial Mechanism

1. There shall be a mechanism for the provision of financial resources to developing country Parties for purposes of this Convention on a grant or confessional basis the essential elements of which are described in this Article. The mechanism shall function under the authority and guidance of and be accountable to, the Conference of the Parties for purposes of this Convention. The operations of the mechanism shall be carried out by such institutional structure as may be decided upon by the Conference of the Parties at its first meeting. . . . The mechanism shall operate within a democratic and transparent system of governance.

2. Pursuant to the objectives of this Convention, the Conference of the Parties shall at its first meeting determine the policy, strategy and pro-

gramme priorities, as well as detailed criteria and guidelines for eligibility for access to and utilization of the financial resources including monitoring and evaluation on a regular basis of such utilization. . . .

Article 22. Relationship with Other International Conventions

1. The provisions of this Convention shall not affect the rights and obligations of any Contracting Party deriving from any existing international agreement, except where the exercise of those rights and obligations would cause a serious damage or threat to biological diversity.

2. Contracting parties shall implement this Convention with respect to the marine environment consistently with the rights and obligations of States under the law of the sea.

Notes and Questions

1. *Assuming responsibility for damages beyond one's borders.* Article 3 of the convention provides that

> **Principle**
>
> States have, in accordance with the Charter of the United Nations and the principles of international law, the sovereign right to exploit their own resources pursuant to their own environmental policies, and the responsibility to ensure that activities within their jurisdiction or control do not cause damage to the environment of other States or of areas beyond the limits of national jurisdiction.

This provision restates Principle 21 of the Stockholm Declaration on the Human Environment. It has been said that this is the first time that it has ever appeared as an explicit obligation in the text of a natural resources convention. Is it an explicit obligation? Note the title of the article. If it is, What is the significance of this? What legal differences does it make that the convention includes this provision in its text?

2. *Implementing the convention.* If you were asked to help draft implementing guidelines for the convention, what issues would you need to address and how would you address them?

3. *The Biodiversity Convention and intellectual property rights.* At the Rio Conference, the United States cited the proposed exchange of technology required by Articles 16(3) and 19(2) as a reason not to sign the Biodiversity Treaty. For a report on the United States's refusal to sign the Biodiversity Convention, *see* Industry Trade Groups Laud President Bush for Decision Not to Sign Biodiversity Treaty [Jan.-June], Chem. Reg. Rep. (BNA), at 571

(June 12, 1992) (quoting a State Department press memorandum stating that President Bush's refusal of " '[t]he convention focuses on [intellectual property rights] as a constraint to the transfer of technology,' " and warning that the provision would have encouraged " 'global pirating,' " that would " 'likely lead to a loss of intellectual property protection vital to all technologies' ").

On Earth Day 1993, President Clinton announced that the United States would sign the Biological Diversity Convention without requesting changes in Articles 16 and 19. When President Clinton submitted the convention to the Senate for ratification in November 1993, he included an interpretive statement to the convention: "with respect to technology subject to patents and other intellectual property rights," the United States understands that "the Convention requires all Parties to ensure that access or transfer of technology is consistent with the adequate and effective protection of intellectual property rights." *See* U.S. Treaty Doc. 103-20, November 16, 1993, VI-VII.

If you were advising a corporate client who relies on gathering natural plants in tropical forests for medicinal products, what protection does the Biological Diversity Convention give to the client?

4. *Who holds intellectual property rights?* Do you agree with the following characterization of the problem?

> Intellectual property rights are held by private corporations, not by the countries doing the negotiations for the creation of new global legislative regimes. The end result is that it is difficult to facilitate the transfer of these new technologies without expropriation, from the point of view of the holders of these property rights, or a new form of economic colonialism, from the point of view of the less developed countries. These, however, are some of the regulatory problems for which solutions must be found. Simply going about our business on a domestic level as if we were not tied to the global demands of an unequal world is no longer possible in the new global era.

Alfred C. Aman, Jr., The Earth As Eggshell Victim: A Global Perspective on Domestic Regulation, 102 Yale L.J. 2107, 2121-2122 (1993) (footnotes omitted).

For a thoughtful analysis of the problem of protecting intellectual property rights and transferring genetic resources, *see* John Barton, The International Breeder's Rights System and Crop Plant Invention, 216 Science 1071 (June 4, 1982).

5. *The intellectual property rights of indigenous people.* Indigenous people have invaluable information about how the environmental system functions in areas of biological diversity and about the usefulness of plant and animal life to people. The Western system of intellectual property is intended to encourage innovation and is not designed to protect the traditional knowledge of indigenous peoples. How do we protect their intellectual

property rights in the knowledge they have acquired? What measures should we adopt? *See* Andrew Jacoby and Charles Weiss, Recognizing Property Rights in Traditional Biocultural Contribution, 16 Stan. Envtl. L.J. 74 (1997). *See* Andrew Gray, The Impact of the Biodiversity Conservation on Indigenous Peoples, *in* Biodiversity: Social and Ecological Perspectives 59, 66-69 (Vandana Shiva et al., eds. 1991); Lee Breckenridge, Rights in Ecosystems Under International Environmental Law, 59 Tenn. L. Rev. 735, 757-758 (1992). In practice, research and conservation groups have developed model guidelines and research protocols to help indigenous peoples protect their interest. What benefit would an intergovernmental agreement provide? Are there any possible costs associated with such an agreement?

6. *Biodiversity conservation in review.* For a general review of international legal issues raised by biodiversity conservation, *see* Biodiversity and International Law 27 (Simone Bilderbeek, ed. 1992). For analysis of the Biodiversity Convention, *see* IUCN Environmental Law Centre, A Guide to the Convention on Biological Diversity (1994).

7. *Developments since the convention was opened for signature.* In May 1993, in Trondheim, Norway, countries met to begin preparations for implementing the Convention on Biodiversity. The meetings focused on drafting protocols to the Biodiversity Convention and debating questions that were not resolved in Brazil in 1992. The major issues in dispute were whether to have a biotechnology protocol, how to handle intellectual property rights in the context of conserving biological diversity, technology transfers, and how to develop a scheme to fund low-income states' efforts at protecting their biological resources.

a. The First Conference of the Parties (COP-1)

The First Conference of the Parties to the Biodiversity Convention took place in Nassau, the Bahamas, from November 28 to December 9, 1994. The UN Environment Programme (UNEP) was designated as the secretariat for the convention, the Global Environmental Facility (GEF) was designated as the interim financing arrangement, and a work program was developed for the years 1995-1997. The workplan included reports on biodiversity particularly under threat, coastal and marine biodiversity, and intellectual property; compilations of existing legislation regarding access to genetic resources and sharing of their benefits; investigation into the need for a biosafety protocol; and exploration of private funding sources to help developing countries. Agricultural biodiversity, linking decisions with the UN Commission on Sustainable Development (CSD), and promoting technology development and transfer were also key elements of the plan. Discussion of forest protection was postponed until the next Conference of the Parties.

b. The Second Conference of the Parties (COP-2)

The parties held their Second Conference in Jakarta, Indonesia, from November 6-17, 1995. They chose Montreal, Canada, as the home to the Biodiversity Convention's permanent secretariat. Failing to reach an agreement on a permanent financing mechanism, the parties agreed that GEF would continue as an "interim" financing mechanism and endorsed guidelines for preparing national biodiversity reports.

The most controversial issue at COP-2 was the decision to draw up a biosafety protocol to cover transfer, handling, and use of genetically modified organisms. An ad hoc working group was to complete work by 1998. Observers noted that any protocol was unlikely to be successful unless the United States ratified the treaty, as the United States houses a large majority of the biotechnology firms in the world.

The COP-2 also addressed forestry. The delegates agreed to ask the secretariat to carry out studies on forest biodiversity and to submit them to the Intergovernmental Panel on Forestry (IPF) but rejected establishing a working panel on forests for budget concerns and possible overlap with the IPF.

A controversial issue that has yet to be resolved is in the area of intellectual property rights: namely, reconciling fair and equitable access to biotechnology with legal patents over products. The conference called on the secretariat to work with the World Trade Organization (WTO) on a study of the relationship between the objectives of the Biodiversity Convention and those of the Uruguay Round Agreement on Trade-Related Aspects of Intellectual Property Rights (TRIPS). Environmental groups have claimed that any conflict between the two must be resolved in favor of the Biodiversity Convention, citing the rule that the general gives way to the specific to support the primacy of the Biodiversity Convention over TRIPS.

c. The Third Conference Of Parties (COP-3)

The contradictions regarding intellectual property rights intensified in the Third Conference of the Parties (COP-3) in Buenos Aires, Argentina, in November 1996. The COP-3 Declaration on Intellectual Property Rights called for increased cooperation with the TRIPS regime, despite strong criticism from environmental groups, developing countries, and indigenous peoples. Environmental NGOs were dismayed that the declaration did not assert the primacy of Biodiversity Convention over the TRIPS regime in matters relating to biodiversity in international law. Delegates from the developing countries and indigenous populations expressed frustration that the intellectual property rights direction of the conference failed to address their concerns regarding the equitable sharing of benefits arising from indigenous and local knowledge.

While debate over issues of transfer of technology and patent protections persisted, COP-3 found greater accord in its activities promoting agricultural biodiversity. The conference's decision on conservation and sustainable use of agricultural biological diversity championed the integrated land-use approach to agriculture and encouraged parties to develop national strategies for restoring biological diversity. In addition to encouraging the parties to implement the UN Food and Agriculture Organization's Global Plan of Action on Plant Genetic Resources for Food and Agriculture, the decision emphasized organic farming, integrated pest management, crop rotation, and support for indigenous systems of knowledge as key elements to be incorporated into national agriculture programs.

d. The Fourth Conference Of Parties (COP-4)

At the fourth conference of parties in Bratislava, Slovakia, in May 1998, the parties contunued to work on the biosafety protocol that they hope will be finalized by February 1999. The biosafety working group still must decide whether the protocol will apply to transboundary movement of modified organisms between convention parties, or whether it will also apply to transfer between parties and non-parties. The group also must work out the details of a system that will notify governments when transboundary transfers of modified organisms are taking place.

Among the more important results of the COP-4 was the establishment of an open-ended working group on "traditional knowledge." COP-4 also defined "benefit sharing" as the distribution of benefits arising from the use of genetic resources on mutually agreed terms, and recognized the private sector as a potential party to benefit sharing. Other conference topics included a biodiversity clearinghouse mechanism, in situ conservation, financing convention initiatives, inland water ecosystems, and the integration of conservation and sustainable use of biodiversity into national marine, coastal, agricultural, and forect management systems.

While the Biodiversity Convention and the subsequence conferences of the parties offer important means for protecting biological diversity, a number of studies suggest more urgent action is required. In December 1995, the Population Institute said that the world's population growth is likely to worsen environmental conditions related to biodiversity—namely loss of forests, erosion of topsoil, expansion of deserts, global warming, and thinning of the ozone layer. According to the Population Institute, the year 1994 showed the largest annual increase in population, with 100 million people added, ninety percent of those in developing countries. In addition, the winners of the 1996 UNEP Sasakawa Environment Prize claimed that an estimated 50,000 species are being lost each year, at a rate 1,000 to 10,000 times the rate occurring naturally over the last 65 million years. These estimates are far higher than those contained in the UNEP 1995 biodiversity report. The scientists said the Biodiversity Convention is a start in protecting these species, but they also urge immediate and drastic action to combat this massive extinction rate.

4. Ex Situ Conservation: Gene Banks

Ex situ conservation is the protection of genetic varieties by putting a small population of the species in a collection that people maintain. In this way, gene pools in the greatest danger of extinction can be saved in their present form, and potentially the population can be rebuilt. However, ex situ techniques, including greenhouses, botanical gardens, and zoos, stop any evolutionary development of a species that would be present in nature. *See* Walter V. Reid & Kenton R. Miller, Keeping the Options Alive: The Scientific Basis for Conserving Biodiversity 62 (1989) ("the evolution of the species is 'frozen' so no further adaptation to pests or environmental change can take place. For this reason, ex situ storage should be considered preservation" . . .).

Ex situ preservation is fundamental for conserving for future breeding the wild relatives of crop plants as well as traditional crop varieties that are being displaced by high-yielding varieties. But ex situ preservation has limitations. First, some crop species are difficult or costly to maintain ex situ. Second, important but rare genotypes are often absent from ex situ collections. Third, collections can be destroyed by mechanical breakdowns or accidents. Fourth, coevolution of a crop plant with other organisms, such as pollinators and potential pests and diseases, cannot continue ex situ. Fifth, the peculiar characteristics of each crop variety may be more difficult to study ex situ. Sixth, pollinators, propagule distributors (for example, birds that eat fruit and excrete the seeds), and other species specific necessities may be difficult or impossible to include in ex situ trials. For these reasons, wildlands that contain wild relatives of crops have a high priority as areas to be preserved. It is also advisable to encourage the planting of "museum strips" of traditional crop varieties alongside new high-yielding varieties.

For most other types of biological resources, ex situ preservation is simply not practical. The costs and difficulties of storage are too great, and, as noted above, a great proportion of the world's plants and animals have yet to be inventoried and collected. Furthermore, ex situ methods cannot preserve the numerous ecological interrelations among species that are so evident in natural systems and that encourage the evolution of new varieties. Plants and animals in a natural setting continuously coevolve, but when they are removed and isolated for any length of time, they are often maladapted or completely unable to survive when reintroduced into the wild. Maintaining dead specimens in museums and herbaria provides an historical record of their existence and structure but none of the benefits of living species.

For more detailed analysis of issues related to in situ conservation, *see* Walter V. Reid & Kenton R. Miller, Keeping the Options Alive: The Scientific Basis for Conserving Biodiversity, 61-66 (1989).

■ IN FAIRNESS TO FUTURE GENERATIONS: INTERNATIONAL LAW, COMMON PATRIMONY AND INTERGENERATIONAL EQUITY

Edith Brown Weiss
at 204-205 (1989)

Gene banks are a necessary complement to *in situ* conservation areas. The International Board for Plant Genetic Resources, established in 1974, has worked to develop an international network of gene banks for crop germplasm. As of 1986 about fifty such gene banks were operational. Most are field gene banks, which do not provide long-term storage of seeds. Less than 20 percent are banks that store collections for the long-term under low temperatures. The banks include both cultivated varieties and wild cultivars, although the emphasis to date has been upon the former. National centers for storing germplasm may consist of many local gene banks linked in a national network. Brazil, for example, has a national network under the Brazilian Enterprise for Agricultural Research (EMBRAPA) that includes about seventy gene banks, many of which have germplasm that is not stored at the central depository in Brasilia. There are now also efforts to conserve animal genetic resources, as by conserving embryos and semen of important races of bovines, poultry, etc. Some microorganisms are being conserved by the Microbiological Resources Centers, an international network of research centers supported by the United Nations Environment Programme.

Gene banks provide plant breeders with the genetic resources necessary to develop crops that will resist pests more effectively and produce higher yields. . . . Most of these banks store germplasm only of the major crops, such as cereals, grain legumes, and potatoes. There is as yet little attention to conserving the germplasm of medicinal herbs, fruit and timber trees, or plantation crops.

Notes and Questions

1. *Storing and sharing germplasm.* Who has access to germplasm stored in gene banks? Does it make a difference whether the banks are only under national auspices or whether they are part of an international network? Consider the following:

> Issues of access also arise in connection with the exchange of germplasm. Generally, countries exchange germplasm relatively freely, except for the germplasm of certain export-oriented cash crops. . . . The policy of the United States, which reportedly stores about 1/5 of the world's germplasm, has been "for many years to freely exchange germplasm with most countries of the world."[2] Developing countries exchange germplasm with each other, although a country may occasionally refuse to exchange germplasm of a particular commercially valuable crop, or if it exchanges germplasm, to provide that of a suboptimal strain. The cost to countries of such restrictions can be enormous.
>
> The experience with the international centers for storing germplasm reveals the evolution of an effective system of free gathering and exchange of germplasm, in the form of seeds. Again, the experience with the International Germplasm Center for Rice is instructive. While countries in the past expressed some reluctance to gather and send germplasm to the Center, they now do so routinely. Countries that may refuse to provide particular germplasm directly to their neighbor have been willing to provide it to an international center, even though they realize their neighbor will then have access to it. They are willing to provide the germplasm because they know that they, in turn, will have access to germplasm from other countries that they can use in improving their own crops. . . .

Edith Brown Weiss, In Fairness to Future Generations: International Law, Common Patrimony, and Intergenerational Equity 209-210 (1989).

2. *Will germplasm be available for future generations?* Gene banks are intended to preserve germplasm for future generations as well as the present. Does this raise any legal issues? Consider the following:

> Gene banks retain information on the physical characteristics of the stored germplasm and their native locations. They do not, however, collect photographs of the plants in their native habitats or otherwise keep a visual record. Such a record might be very useful to future generations, although perhaps difficult to obtain in dense tropical vegetation. . . .
>
> If we fail to allocate funds for maintaining gene banks, we will spend funds to construct a facility and to gather germplasm for the benefit of only the present generation. Equity demands that we make the benefits available to future generations. Moreover, the loss . . . may cause important economic losses to members of the present generation as well.

Edith Brown Weiss, In Fairness to Future Generations: International Law, Common Patrimony, and Intergenerational Equity 205-207 (1989).

As you read the next excerpt, consider the legal issues raised by efforts to establish an agreement governing ex situ gathering and storage

2. *See* A Battle Over Seeds, The Atlantic 36, 38 (Nov. 1985) (citing a 1977 letter from the head of the United States Agriculture Research Service to the Chairman of the International Board for Plant Genetic Resources).

of germplasm for plants. Note that the international legal instrument is an undertaking, not an international treaty. Ask yourself whether there is a need for a formal agreement governing international centers that store plant genetic material, or whether the international community is better served by the present, more informal arrangement, that operates under the Consultative Group on Agriculture Research under the auspices of the World Bank and UN member organizations.

■ THE LEGAL AND POLITICAL IMPLICATIONS OF THE INTERNATIONAL UNDERTAKING ON PLANT GENETIC RESOURCES

Harold J. Bordwin
12 Ecology L. Q. 1053, 1053-1054, 1059-1069 (1985)

INTRODUCTION

In November 1983, the biennial conference of the Food and Agriculture Organization of the United Nations (FAO) addressed the problem of international conservation and exchange of plant genetic resources. These resources include the vast assortment of seeds used by plant breeders to create the improved plant varieties that are the foundation of modern agriculture. Many nations are concerned about the increased destruction of and the increasing politicization of control over critical genetic resources. Out of the 1983 FAO conference emerged a controversial document: the International Undertaking on Plant Genetic Resources. While less developed countries (LDCs) supported the Undertaking, a number of developed countries opposed it. These developed countries opposed the Undertaking because they believed it called for decreasing their control over plant genetic resource activities and increasing the free international availability of special genetic stocks. . . .

I. THE INTERNATIONAL SEED INDUSTRY

Plant breeders crossbreed plants in the hope of uniting the best features of the parents in a new variety. To achieve this goal, breeders search for plants with desirable characteristics. "Primitive" varieties, varieties from other geographic areas, and wild relatives represent the only sources of additional desirable genes. Because glaciation during the ice-ages destroyed many plant varieties in higher latitudes, the tropics are the site of the greatest genetic diversity. Plant breeders send explorers to countries in the tropics, most of which are LDCs, to collect seed samples from plants with desirable traits. These plants may be weeds or primitively cultivated varieties called primitive cultivars. Through these practices, genetic resources flow from the LDCs to the developed nations. . . .

II. International Efforts to Conserve Plant Genetic Resources

A. The International Board for Plant Genetic Resources

1. The Structure of the Board

Until recently, the International Board for Plant Genetic Resources (IBPGR) provided the only international response to the problems of genetic erosion and genetic uniformity. The Consultative Group on International Agricultural Research (the Consultative Group) established the IBPGR in 1974. The Consultative Group is an international entity co-sponsored by the FAO, the World Bank, and the United Nations Development Programme, and it is comprised of forty-seven governments, international organizations, and foundations. The Consultative Group established the IBPGR to promote the "collection, conservation, evaluation, utilization and exchange of plant genetic resources." The IBPGR has seventeen members, thirteen of whom are elected by the Consultative Group upon the recommendation of the IBPGR. The FAO and the United Nations Environment Programme each designate one member, and the IBPGR elects an outsider to chair the Board. Finally, the Executive Secretary of the IBPGR is an ex officio member. The elected members serve in an individual capacity and not as government representatives. At least four of these elected members must be from LDCs; currently there are six such members.

2. Assessments of the IBPGR's Performance

Since 1974, the IBPGR has completed a number of important projects on an annual budget of only $3.8 million. The programs include sponsoring 250 germplasm collecting missions in more than seventy countries. A mission entails gathering samples of exotic germplasm, either in the form of seeds or seedlings, for the purpose of placing them in a storage facility. Missions usually focus on collecting varieties that are near extinction and have potential economic value. The IBPGR has also designated thirty-eight centers in twenty-nine countries for the long-term storage of thirty crops, sponsored advisory committees on major crop preservation subjects, and sponsored training courses and publications on conservation and use of plant genetic resources. The developed countries overwhelmingly support the IBPGR because of the effectiveness of these programs in combatting genetic erosion. The LDCs are less enthusiastic about the IBPGR, although their criticism is more political than scientific. Their discontent, arising from the perception that the IBPGR addresses the needs only of the developed countries, manifested itself at the November 1981 biennial conference of the FAO. . . .

B. THE INTERNATIONAL UNDERTAKING ON PLANT GENETIC RESOURCES

1. Policy Objectives and Rationale Guided by the Common Heritage Principle

Despite this conflict, in November 1983, the biennial FAO Conference adopted by resolution the International Undertaking on Plant Genetic Resources. The resolution was intended as a "strong formal commitment" by the FAO Conference to the principles of the Undertaking. The objective of the Undertaking, according to Article One, is "to ensure that plant genetic resources of economic and/or social interest, particularly for agriculture, will be explored, preserved, evaluated and made available for plant breeding and for scientific purposes."

The Undertaking is grounded on the "universally accepted principle that plant genetic resources are a heritage of mankind and consequently should be available without restriction." Neither the Undertaking nor the FAO Director General's Report to the Conference explains, however, precisely what is meant by "heritage of mankind." It is likely that this concept was adopted from the "common heritage principle" developed by the Law of the Sea Conference. Although developed for application to deep seabed resources this principle is also relevant in the context of plant genetic resources.

The common heritage principle is comprised of four elements:

1. No one should exploit the resource in question until rules have been agreed upon to ensure that exploitation will be in the common interest;
2. No state should acquire more than its equitable share of the resource;
3. The world community should determine what constitutes equitable sharing, taking into account the interests of those who did not have a chance to participate in exploiting the resource in the past;
4. An international body should have exclusive and comprehensive authority to administer the resource.

Only some of these elements can guide the application of the common heritage principle to plant genetic resources.

The first element makes little sense in the context of plant genetic resources, unlike the deep seabed which is as yet undeveloped, germplasm is already being exploited. Plants and their genetic material are already subject to the sovereignty of the state in which they are located. Plant genetic resources are being exploited, and their continued exploitation is economically and agriculturally necessary; therefore, exploitation should not be suspended pending the conclusion of rules to protect the common interest.

The second and third elements of the common heritage principle call for equitably shared resources in a manner determined by the world community, recognizing the interests of those countries that have not previously participated in exploiting the resources. Applying these elements to plant genetic resources first requires an examination of the Undertaking's definition of the plant genetic resources within its scope. Article Two of the Undertaking defines plant genetic resources as the "reproductive or vegetative propagating material of [five] categories of plants." The first four categories—cultivated varieties in current use and newly developed varieties, obsolete cultivars, primitive cultivars, and wild and weed species—are characterized either by their availability on the market or by their lack of significant economic value. The application of the common heritage principle of such germplasm already follows the customary practices of states and plant breeders. Equitably sharing germplasm does not mean its unlimited distribution. Access to germplasm is sometimes limited by governments through quarantine regulations, and through limits on the number of samples that are available only to "genuine users" from nations who practice reciprocity. Furthermore, certain countries do not release germplasm from some cash crops. Nonetheless, "[s]uch restrictions [do] not appear significantly to affect the availability of resources, particularly those of food crops."

The application of the common heritage principle to the fifth category of germplasm, "special genetic stocks," is controversial because it adversely affects developed countries and the seed industry. Special genetic stocks are those varieties or lines that the breeder uses to produce the variety sold on the market. In the case of hybrids, for example, the seed produced by the crop grown by farmers is not suitable for planting. Thus, farmers must return yearly to buy seed rather than plant seed saved from their own harvest. If farmers or seed companies had access to the parents of the hybrids, known as in-bred lines, then they would be able to produce the plantable hybrid seed on their own. Special genetic stocks typically represent large capital investments and are maintained by private breeders as trade secrets. Freely sharing such resources would radically undermine the property rights private breeders have traditionally possessed in special genetic stocks. Recognizing this threat, the American Seed Trade Association challenged the Undertaking for "strik[ing] at the very heart of free enterprise and intellectual property rights." The United States and New Zealand also opposed the Undertaking because they believed its inclusion of special genetic stocks threatened the property rights of plant breeders. Industry contends that the effect of the Undertaking's definition of plant genetics resources "would be to subject all private breeding materials to be made available to anyone."

Yet, the fear of a mandate for freely shared special genetic stocks may be unfounded because the Undertaking's scope is limited in Article Five to "adhering governments and [international or national] institutions." Many governments and institutions already share special genetic stocks. For example, stocks controlled by the United States government and public research institutions are freely exchanged through the National Plant Germplasm System (NPGS). Some international organizations, such as the thirteen International Agricultural Research Centers (IARCs) that operate under the auspices of the Consultative Group, make all breeding material freely available to public plant breeders, giving priority to those in LDCs. The special genetic stocks controlled by private companies, however, are arguably beyond the reach of the Undertaking.

The final element of the common heritage principle calls for an international body having "exclusive and comprehensive authority" to administer the resource in question. Articles Seven and Nine of the Undertaking address this principle by setting up the FAO as the central coordinator of plant genetics activities. Specifically, Article Nine proposed, and the Conference by a separate resolution required, that the FAO establish an intergovernmental commission on plant genetic resources. Article Seven calls for present national and international plant genetic resource activities to be "further developed and, where necessary, complemented in order to develop a global system" to protect plant genetic resources. Article Seven describes this system as including a network of international centers that will develop and maintain seed collections, a system for exchanging information on these collections, and the Board, pursuing and developing "its present activities, within its terms of reference, in liaison with FAO."

The mandate of the intergovernmental commission to "monitor" the activities listed in Article Seven, and to "take or recommend measures" to ensure the comprehensiveness of the global system, marks a potential shift in international authority over plant genetic resource activities from the Consultative Group and the IBPGR to the FAO. Both the United States and Canada objected to the Undertaking as a threat to the role of the board. The United States position is that responsibility for coordinating the international plant germplasm system lies with the IBPGR: "Our government is concerned . . . that the important work of the IBPGR . . . may be impeded by political factors or cumbersome procedures. . . . The autonomous technical nature of the IBPGR must be maintained and protected from political interference." . . .

2. The Legal Effect of the Undertaking

The Undertaking is not legally binding even on states that choose to adhere to it. The Conference only urges states to "give effect" voluntarily to the Undertaking. States adhere to the Undertaking by advising the Director-General of their intent to adhere and of their ability to effectuate the principles of the Undertaking. As of autumn 1984, the Director-General had received "replies" from approximately sixty countries. The contents of the replies, though, are unknown.

The Conference intentionally chose to adopt an undertaking rather than either a legally binding convention or a less formal code of conduct. The Conference and the Director-General rejected a legally binding international convention for two reasons. First, a convention would take too long to implement. Second, the binding nature of the convention could inhibit it from achieving the broadest possible support because "[s]tates may have difficulties in joining in a consensus on the text of a legally binding instrument and in committing themselves to implementing each one of its provisions." The FAO Conference and the Director-General also rejected incorporating their plant genetic resource agenda into an informal code of conduct with less force than an undertaking. A code of conduct "would reflect an international consensus on . . . principles;" in contrast, the Undertaking was intended to "establish specific commitments." Despite this intent, eight industrialized nations at the Conference reserved their position on the Undertaking. These countries were Canada, France, the Federal Republic of Germany, Japan, New Zealand, Switzerland, the United Kingdom, and the United States.

As a non-binding resolution, the Undertaking expresses the FAO Conference's support for a revised plant genetic resource system rather than any individual state's intent to commit itself to this system. Despite its lack of direct legal force, however, the Undertaking may have or may acquire international legal significance as "evidence of customary law." Customary law "reflects a [consistent] general practice accepted as law." The formulation of principles in a prescriptive resolution "may elucidate and develop the customary law" if those principles then become the general practice. In this way, nonbinding "[r]esolutions on new legal problems provide a means of corralling and defining the quickly growing practice of states. . . ." The gap between the content of the Undertaking and present international practice, together with the opposition of developed countries and the seed industry to the Undertaking, makes it doubtful, however, that international practice will change to conform to the Undertaking.

C. FORESTS

1. Introduction to the Value of Forests as a Natural Resource

Forests cover one-third of the land area of Earth. They cover 42 percent of the land in tropical countries and substantial portions in the temperate countries. About two-thirds of the forests are considered to be "closed forests," meaning that a substantially complete cover of trees exists over the whole land surface. The rest are "open forests." In the tropics and southern hemisphere, forests contain predominantly hardwoods; in the northern hemisphere, predominantly softwoods. The latter have been more readily viable commercially.

■ IN FAIRNESS TO FUTURE GENERATIONS: INTERNATIONAL LAW, COMMON PATRIMONY, AND INTERGENERATIONAL EQUITY

Edith Brown Weiss
219-223 (1989)

Forests have been exceedingly useful resources for people. As Spears and Ayensu note, "they protect watersheds and the natural environment as well as providing innumerable products vital to man. They provide sustenance, shelter, and employment as well as resources for the development of other sectors. They comprise the most biologically diverse, readily convertible, and potentially self-regenerating natural store of biological wealth on the planet. If all the shrubs, trees and forests in the developing countries were eliminated overnight, food production would decline by at least 20 percent in part because of the disruptive impact on irrigation water and fodder supplies." We may distinguish at least five classes of benefits that forests confer on present and future generations. First, they provide direct economic benefits through timber production and minor forest products, such as gums, resins, oils, medicines, fibers, fruits, wild nuts, etc., and through exploitation in tropical forests, in particular, for agricultural, medicinal, or industrial products. Secondly, they are important sources of fuelwood for people in rural areas of developing countries, of livestock, fodder, and even food. As population increases, the importance of tropical forests in particular will rise as people depend upon them increasingly to satisfy basic needs. Third, they provide amenity benefits, such as recreation and hunting, and have important cultural value for many societies, more or less independently of how frequently they are used. Fourth, they provide essential environmental services in conserving watersheds, as by preventing soil erosion, maintaining soil productivity, facilitating water recharge, harboring wildlife and buffering climate. They are important in the hydrological cycle and in regional, and perhaps global, climate systems. Finally, their environmental services provide direct economic benefits to areas downstream, such as increased electricity production or irrigation water due to reduced siltation of dams and streams, decreased need for dredging of navigable waterways and reduced risk of flood damage.

Today we are witnessing accelerated destruction of forests, particularly of tropical forests, at rates that will be difficult, perhaps impossible, to reverse. Forests in developing countries have declined by nearly half in this century. Over 11 million hectares of tropical forests, an area approximately the size of Austria and Switzerland combined, are being converted each year, primarily due to unplanned agricultural settlement. If this continues, the World Resources Institute estimates that at least 225 million hectares of tropical forests will be cleared by the year 2000. While the temperate climate forest area of most developed countries has stabilized in recent decades, recent studies indicate that pollution is affecting the quality of many forests in Europe and to a lesser extent in North America. Mismanagement of the forest ecosystem continues to be a problem.

Forests are threatened by several developments: population pressures, which lead to the denuding of nearby forests, destructive or unsustainable exploitation of forests for economic gain, and degradation by atmospheric pollution, which may lead to death of the forest. The first two reduce the volume of forest directly; the last indirectly.

I. Problems of Intergenerational Equity

Forests are renewable resources that can be used by present generations and also be available to future generations if they are exploited on a sustainable basis. The problem is that they are often exploited with little attention to sustainability or to their crucial role in protecting upland watersheds, and through this, lowland watersheds. The degradation of soils, which accompanies unsustainable forestry, and pollution, which changes the chemistry of forest soils, have long-term detrimental effects on future productivity. Mismanagement of forests and their soils, together with the elimination of the diverse genetic resources in tropical forests, raises serious problems of intergenerational equity, which must be addressed.

A. Depletion of Resources

The most serious form of depletion is the loss of the diverse genetic resources found in tropical forests. This occurs whenever primary forests are eliminated, even though they may be reforested with plantations of selected trees. Tropical forests have enormous as yet untapped genetic reserves, which are in danger of being eliminated before they are even known. These have great potential value for food and cash crops for medicines, for industrial applications, and for developing new strains resistant to disease and pests. They will become more valuable as biotechnology advances. Destruction of forests rich in genetic diversity impoverishes future generations by reducing the resource options available to them.

Depletion of resources also occurs in yet another form: the loss of the environmental services that forests provide. These include flood control, recharge of ground water, maintenance and restoration of fertility in the soils, control of erosion, prevention of sedimentation in rivers and irrigation systems, protection of navigation, stabilization of plant and animal populations, purification of air and water, promotion of hydrological cycling, and buffering of the climate system. When forests are destroyed, these services are lost, which results in extensive costs of present and future generations as they search for technological solutions to replace these services or adapt to changed rainfall patterns, waterways filled with sedimentation, etc. In particular, the denuding of forested slopes can lead to disastrous floods for future generations, as illustrated by those that have occurred in the Po River valley. Such floods can be expected in the hilly areas of Central America and other parts of the developing world.

Depletion occurs whenever forests are not used and maintained on a sustainable basis. Sometimes this may occur intentionally through the conversion of forests to other uses, such as pasture for cattle, which may reap a higher economic return. But in tropical areas with fragile soils this use may be unsustainable, with the result that the lands become barren and unproductive. Often forest depletion occurs inadvertently through mismanagement, as by harvesting of forest products with insufficient attention to maintenance of soils and sustainable reforestation, or as a consequence of population pressures. One of the most serious causes of deforestation is excessive removal of wood for fuel and for domestic use by rural populations living in poverty. U.N. Food and Agricultural Organization studies show that three-fourths of the two billion in developing countries depend on fuelwood and other traditional fuels for all their daily energy needs. One billion rural dwellers suffer increasing shortages and can meet minimum needs only at the expense of exhausting available resources. Such depletion may raise the real price of commercial forest products for future generations and imposes hardships upon those members of both present and future generations who depend upon nearby forests for basic needs.

B. DEGRADATION IN QUALITY OF RESOURCES

Loss in the quality of forests and their genetic resources occurs primarily from mismanagement in the exploitation of forests or from pollution. Mismanagement causes soil degradation, decline in productivity, and the triumph of undesired species of fauna and flora.

These effects of pollution on the quality of forests are only beginning to become known. Atmospheric pollution of forests can result in the disfigurement of existing trees, the stunting of tree growth, the acidification of soils, and the loss of productivity in the forests. It can also reduce the variety of uses to which the forest is put. The symptoms of decline in the forests due to pollution have been so stark that people have labeled the phenomenon "Waldsterben," or death of the forests.

Large portions of the forests in western and central Europe are now suffering severe damage from air pollution. The effects first became apparent in the mid-1970s in West Germany among the silver fir and Norway spruce trees. Now the decline is apparent in the forests of the other European countries and extends to deciduous trees such as oak and beech. In 1986, the estimated forest damage in Europe was more than thirty million hectares, or 22% of the total land area.

Extensive forest damage appears in Germany, Austria, Czechoslovakia, Poland, Yugoslavia, Belgium, France, the Netherlands, Sweden, Switzerland, Hungary and Romania and is believed to exist in the [former] Soviet Union. Forests in North America, in both Canada and the United States, are also affected.

While there is still some scientific controversy about the causes of the damage to forests in Europe and in North America, very substantial evidence indicates that sulphur dioxide, ozone and ammonia are major contributors. However, the pollutants causing forest damage in different areas may not always be the same, and different trees are affected in varying degrees by the stresses of air pollution. This makes the problem of controlling air pollution damage to forests more difficult. Moreover, some scientific uncertainty about the causes of "Waldsterben" persists. For example, a West German scientist has suggested that a virus may be responsible for some European forest damage. The scientific uncertainty which still surrounds some aspects of forest damage means that we must continue to conduct research to confirm cause and effect relationships and to identify all causes of damage. In the tropics, recent scientific work indicates that pollution from burning may contribute to the acidification of soils in forest areas. The air pollutants that cause the quality of forests to decline may come from distant areas outside national borders, which makes control more difficult, as illustrated by the experiences in western and central Europe.

2. *Rio Forest Principles*

At the Earth Summit, countries agreed upon a set of forest principles, which they called "[a] non-legally binding authoritative statement of principles for a global consensus on the management, conservation and sustainable development of all types of forests." These were negotiated under the auspices of the preparations for the United Nations Conference on Environment and Development or Earth Summit.

Excerpts from these principles are reproduced below:

Preamble

. . .

(b) The guiding objective of these principles is to contribute to the achievement of the management, conservation and sustainable development of forests, and to provide for their multiple and complementary function and uses.

. . .

(e) These principles should apply to all types of forests, both natural and planted, in all geographic regions and climatic zones, including austral, boreal, sub-temperate, temperate, sub-tropical and tropical.

Principles/Elements

1. (a) States have, in accordance with the Charter of the United Nations and the principles of international law, the sovereign right to exploit their own resources pursuant to their own environmental policies, and the responsibility to ensure that activities within their jurisdiction or control do not cause damage to the environment of other States or of areas beyond the limits of national jurisdiction.

(b) The agreed full incremental cost of achieving benefits associated with forest conservation and sustainable development requires increased international cooperation and should be equitably shared by the international community.

2. (a) States have the sovereign and inalienable right to utilize, manage and develop their forests in accordance with their development needs and level of socioeconomic development and on the basis of national policies consistent with sustainable development and legislation, including the conversion of such areas for other uses within the overall socioeconomic development plan based on rational land-use policies.

. . .

(c) The provision of timely, reliable and accurate information on forests and forest ecosystems is essential for public understanding and informed decision-making and should be ensured.

(d) Governments should promote and provide opportunities for the participation of interested parties, including local communities and indigenous people, industries, labor, non-governmental organizations and individuals, forest dwellers and women, in the development, implementation and planning of national forest policies.

3. (a) National policies and strategies should provide a framework for increased efforts, including the development and strengthening of institutions and programs for the management, conservation and sustainable development of forests and forest lands.

(b) The full participation of women in all aspects of management, conservation and sustainable development of forests should be actively promoted.

(c) Decisions taken on the management, conservation and sustainable development of forest resources should benefit to the extent practicable from a comprehensive assessment of economic and non-economic values of forest goods and services and of the environmental costs and benefits. The development and improvement of methodologies for such evaluations should be promoted.

(d) The role of planted forests and permanent agricultural crops as sustainable and environmentally sound sources of renewable energy and industrial raw material should be recognized, enhanced and promoted. Their contribution to the maintenance of ecological processes, to offsetting pressure on primary/old-growth forest and to providing regional employment and development with the adequate involvement of local inhabitants should be recognized and enhanced.

(e) Natural forests also constitute a source of goods and services and their conservation, sustainable management and use should be promoted.

. . .

7. (a) Efforts should be made to promote a supportive international economic climate conducive to sustained and environmentally sound development of forests in all countries, which include, *inter alia,* the promotion of sustainable patterns of production and consumption, and eradication of poverty and the promotion of food security.

(b) Specific financial resources should be provided to developing countries with significant forest areas which establish programs for the conservation of forests including protected natural forest areas. These resources should be directed notably to economic sectors which would stimulate economic and social substitution activities.

8. (a) Efforts should be undertaken towards greening of the world. All countries, notably developed countries, should take positive and transparent actions towards reforestation, afforestation and forest conservation, as appropriate.

. . .

(e) Forest management should be integrated with management of adjacent areas so as to maintain ecological balance and sustainable productivity.

(f) National policies and/or legislation aimed at management, conservation and sustainable development of forests should include the protection of ecologically viable representative or unique examples of forests, including primary/old-growth forests, cultural, spiritual, historical, religious and other unique valued forests of national importance.

(g) Access to biological resources, including genetic material, shall be with due regard to the sovereign rights of the countries where the forests are located and to the sharing on mutually agreed terms of technology and profits from biotechnology products that are derived from these resources.

(h) National policies should ensure that environmental impact assessment should be carried out where actions are likely to have significant adverse impacts or important forest resources, and where such actions are subject to a decision of a competent national authority.

. . .

11. New and additional financial resources should be provided to developing countries to enable them to sustainably manage, conserve and develop their forests resources, including afforestation, reforestation and combating deforestation, forest and land degradation.

12. In order to enable in particular developing countries to enhance their endogenous capacity and to better manage, conserve and develop their forest resources, and access to and transfer of environmentally sound technologies and corresponding know-how on favorable terms, including on confessional and preferential terms, as mutually agreed, in accordance with relevant provisions of Agenda 21, should be promoted, facilitated, and financed, as appropriate.

. . .

14. (a) Trade in forest products should be based on non-discriminatory and multilaterally agreed rules and procedures consistent with international trade law and practices. In this context, open and free international trade in forest products should be facilitated.

(b) Reduction or removal of tariff barriers and impediments to the provision of better market access and better prices for higher value-added forest products and their local processing should be encouraged to enable producer countries to better conserve and manage their renewable forest resources.

(c) Incorporation of environmental costs and benefits into market forces and mechanisms, in order to achieve forest conservation and sustainable development, should be encouraged both domestically and internationally.

15. (a) Unilateral measures, incompatible with international obligations or agreements, to restrict and/or ban international trade in timber or other forest products should be removed or avoided in order to attain long-term sustainable forest management.

16. Pollutants, particularly air borne pollutants, including those responsible for acidic deposition, that are harmful to the health of forest ecosystems at the local, national, regional and global levels should be controlled.

Notes and Questions

1. *Giving weight to the Rio forest principles.* What is the legal status of these principles? What weight must governments give these principles in making decisions about forests? Do these principles adequately address the forest problems outlined earlier? Are they consistent with the provisions of the new Convention on Biological Diversity?

2. *Codifying the Rio forest principles.* Some countries would like to see these principles codified into a convention. What difference would this make? Is it necessary in light of the Convention on Biological Diversity? Or could the forest principles become a protocol to the biological diversity convention?

3. *Who would facilitate negotiations for a new convention?* If a new convention were to be negotiated, under whose auspices should the negotiation take place? There are several potential hosts: the United Nations Food and Agricultural Organization, the United Nations Environment Programme, the International Tropical Timber Organization (headquartered in Japan), or the United Nations itself. Does the fact that the forest principles were negotiated as part of the Earth Summit suggest that it may not be easy to agree upon a forum? Why?

4. *Ecotourism.* Ecotourism has become one of the newest terms in the conservationist vocabulary. It refers to the tourism industry that brings people to enjoy the nature and wildlife of a particular region. If properly structured, it helps bring badly needed revenue to the local community and provides incentives to the local people to help conserve the area.

More importantly, the ecotourists bring money when they come. In the developing countries, where much of the world's most valuable natural resources lie, this money can encourage the governments to take an interest in protecting their heritage. *See* Hana Charny, Israel Hosts Global Environmental Parley, Jerusalem Post, June 2, 1993 (relaying the attitude expressed by the Bahamian Ministry of Tourism representative Cynthia Bowe, similar to that of other developing nations, when "[s]he stressed the need to develop ecotourism as the only true incentive and means of saving natural resources").

Some environmentalists are critical of ecotourism as a way to foster conservation of pristine forests and other areas. Not only do critics claim that the term "ecotourism" is used loosely, if not illegitimately, to lure customers, but they point to the real damage to the environment that occurs when so many visitors travel through it. *See* Keith C. Epstein, Climb Every Mountain, and You'll Find a Crowd, Plain Dealer, June 20, 1993 (reporting on Mount Everest's estimated 60 tons of garbage from climbers, Mount Rainier's problem with human waste, and the North Cascades National Park's efforts to stop the destruction of its natural grasses and wildflowers). Other environmentalists, however, see ecotourism as a benefit to the environment. The Sierra Club's trips are designed to preserve and foster the enjoyment of the environment, for example. *See Id.*

Governments and international financial institutions have been following the debate and addressing the issues. In August 1993, The World Tourism Organization and UNEP sponsored the Third International Symposium on Tourism, Ecology and Municipalities, held in Mexico. The intent was to help local authorities manage the tourist attractions that are endangered by the numbers of visitors they attract. The problems have been widely encountered for world natural and cultural sites on the World Heritage List (*see* Chapter 17).

What is the net effect of conserving biological diversity through wildlife parks that are open to tourists? Can the views that ecotourism destroys the biodiversity-saving value of the reserve and the recognition that tourism will help the general cause of saving biodiversity by generating funds for use in environmental projects be reconciled? What are the appropriate tools of international environmental law to use in dealing with this issue? How should the rights of future generations affect the decisions made?

Additional Readings

For an excellent discussion of the economics of ecotourism, *see* Brian Groombridge, ed., Global Diversity: Status of the Earth's Living Resources 407-438 (1992); D. Western & W. Henry, Economics and Conservation in Third World National Parks, 29 Bioscience 414 (1979); D. Tobias and R. Mendelsohn, Valuing Ecotourism in a Tropical Rain-Forest Reserve, 20 Ambio 91 (1991); J. Barnes, J. Burgess and D.W. Pearce, Wildlife Tourism, in Economics for the Wilds (1992); J.A. Dixon & P.B. Sherman, Economics of Protected Areas: A New Look at Benefits and Costs (1990); *see also*, K. Lindberg, Policies for Maximizing Nature Tourism's Ecological and Economic Benefits (1991).

3. The Intergovernmental Panel on Forests

As an outgrowth of the 1992 Rio Conference, the UN Commission on Sustainable Development created the UN Intergovernmental Panel on Forests (IPF) to produce recommendations on how to balance the need for forest protection with the commercial logging demands. The CSD scheduled the IPF recommendations for review in 1997 in order to forward them for consideration by the UN General Assembly during its Special Session to review environmental conditions five years after Rio. When the IPF concluded its work in February 1997, it had developed more than 100 proposals for action, which included national action programs, techniques for improved assessment and valuation of forests, improvements in identifying the causes of forest degradation, and means for integrating trade and sustainable development. Much of the IPF discussion focused on what in the end it did not propose—a binding international agreement on forests.

The IPF's deliberations on the merits of developing a forest convention involved significant debate and lobbying from several sides. Environmentalists, who lobbied for a convention on forests in 1992, argued against the idea of recommending a forest treaty in 1997 for fear it would enshrine weak, "lowest-common-denominator" standards in forest management. Additionally, they expressed no confidence in a new treaty when governments do not honor existing commitments to forest protection.

The European Union, on the other hand, insisted that a binding agreement would be the only way to establish uniformity in forestry conservation standards and mechanisms to enforce compliance. Due to the lack of consensus, the IPF left the issue unresolved. In its report to the CSD, it proposed three options: (1) continue the debate in existing UN bodies; (2) move the discussion into a new forum dedicated to forest action; and (3) begin immediate negotiations on a convention.

As the issue went before the CSD, developing countries also highlighted their concerns: financial assistance and technology transfer.

Developing countries conditioned their support for a pact upon the commitment of industrialized nations to assist them in providing the financing and technology necessary to implement sustainable forest management. The United States opposed the idea of a convention and pressed for the formation of an international forum on forests to continue dialogue on the IPF recommendations under CSD supervision. The CSD decided to send the IPF menu of options to the General Assembly for its consideration.

The General Assembly, in Special Session in June 1997 (Earth Summit +5), decided to continue the intergovernmental policy dialogue on forests through the establishment of an ad hoc, open-ended Intergovernmental Forum on Forests under the auspices of the CSD. The forum was charged with

a. promoting and facilitating the implementation of the panel's proposals for action;

b. reviewing, monitoring, and reporting on progress in the management, conservation, and sustainable development of all types of forests;
c. considering matters left pending regarding the program elements of the IPF (in particular, trade and environment related to forest products and services, transfer of technology, and the need for financial resources).

The forum was also commissioned to identify the possible elements of and work toward consensus on international arrangements and mechanisms, including a legally binding instrument on all types of forests. At the forum's first organizational session in New York, October 1-3, 1997, the forum agreed to structure its work program in three categories. Category I deals with promoting and facilitating IPF action proposals and reviewing, monitoring, and reporting on progress in management, conservation, and sustainable development of all types of forest. Category II includes pending matters, such as the need for financial resources, trade and environment, and technology transfer. Category III deals with building consensus for international arrangements and mechanisms to promote the management, conservation, and sustainable development of all forest types. The second session will take place in Geneva, August 24 to September 4, 1998. The forum will report on its work to the Commission on Sustainable Development in 1999. As of July 1998, electronic information about the International Forum on Forests could be found at the website address <http://www.un.org/esa/sustdev/iff.htm>.

Notes and Questions

1. *Binding or nonbinding agreements?* Should we have binding agreements on forests or continue with nonbinding mechanisms? Why would some countries favor the forum on forests as opposed to an international convention? In Rio, the United States pressed for a convention. As of September 1997, it preferred the forum. What might explain this change?

2. *Forests and the Biodiversity Convention.* How would a forest treaty intersect with the Biodiversity Convention?

3. *Forests as common patrimony.* Should forests be considered common patrimony? *See* A.-Ch. Kiss, La forêt et le patrimoine commun de l'humanité," in Forêt et environnement (M. Prieur, ed. 1984).

4. Trade in Tropical Timber

After World War II, Europe and Japan needed cheap timber to reconstruct their economies and turned to the tropical forests in Southeast Asia,

Africa, and South America. By 1978, world trade in tropical timber reached $7 billion annually.

In response to concerns about developing countries' abilities to process their own raw materials and about tropical deforestation, several UN bodies and NGOs began to advocate trade controls and higher timber prices. The United Nations Conference on Trade and Development (UNCTAD) requested its secretary-general to convene preparatory meetings for international negotiations on a new tropical timber agreement. In 1983 the International Tropical Timber Agreement (ITTA) was concluded under the auspices of UNCTAD and opened to both producer and consumer countries.

The International Tropical Timber Agreement

The 1983 treaty benefited both producer and consumer countries. For producer countries, it offered opportunities to expand trade and to receive technological transfers and financial assistance from consuming countries. Consumer countries enjoyed expanded and stable supplies of tropical timber as well as increased esteem in the eyes of domestic constituents and international organizations.

The treaty was opened for signature in November 1983 and went into effect in April 1985. As of June 1997, the treaty had 53 member countries: 26 producer countries and 27 consumer countries (including the European Union), accounting for 90 percent of the world's tropical forests and 90 percent of the world trade in tropical timber.

On January 26, 1994, countries concluded a successor treaty to the ITTA that entered into force on January 1, 1997. The 1994 ITTA pays more attention to sustainable forestry, particularly whether countries would be required to engage in sustainable forestry by the year 2000 and whether this would apply to all forests.

In the 1994 ITTA, those countries producing tropical timber agreed to try to export wood only from sustainably managed forests by the year 2000. In return, consumer countries agreed to establish a new fund, the "Bali Partnership Fund," to help producer countries meet the objective of sustainably managed forests. In addition, the consuming countries issued a separate formal statement (not a formal part of the treaty) pledging to respect comparable forest conservation guidelines for their own forests and committing themselves to the "national objective of achieving sustainable management of their forests by the year 2000."

The 1983 ITTA was designed to facilitate trade in tropical timber, defined as nonconiferous tropical wood for industrial uses, which grows or is produced in countries situated between the Tropic of Cancer and the Tropic of Capricorn. The treaty promoted research and development to improve forest management and wood utilization, to improve market intelligence, to encourage processing of tropical timber in producer countries, and to promote reforestation and forest policies to conserve tropical forests and their genetic resources. The treaty's preamble and Article 1, Objects, have served as the levers to advance conservation activities. Article 1 "encourages the development of national policies aimed at sustainable utilization and conservation of tropical forests and their genetic resources, and at maintaining the ecological balance in the regions concerned."

The ITTA tried to balance power between the producer and consumer countries. Almost all producers are developing countries located in the tropical belts of Latin America, Africa, and Asia. The consuming countries are for the most part developed countries from North America, Europe, and the Far East.

The ITTA obligates states to provide detailed information about their tropical timber trade to the secretariat, contribute to the administrative account (and for the developed countries, to the special projects account), and make their best efforts to promote the objectives of the treaty and comply with decisions made under the treaty.

To implement the treaty, parties established an International Tropical Timber Organization (ITTO), which functions through an International Tropical Timber Council (ITTC) and three permanent committees: the Committee on Economic Information and Market Intelligence; the Committee on Reforestation and Forest Management; and the Committee on Forest Industry. The council's voting system is designed to balance power between producer and consumer countries and among the various factions of each group. As a large consumer of tropical hardwoods, Japan has a significant share of the votes. However, matters are in fact settled by consensus. No decision has ever been put to a vote.

The ITTA's primary activities have been reporting on the international trade in tropical timber, formulating guidelines and criteria on various issues including the sustainable management of forests, and approving and implementating forestry projects in producer countries. The secretariat, housed in Yokohama, is independent and not attached to any international organization. It publishes comprehensive reports of its meetings and of other initiatives, which are available for the cost of postage.

Notes and Questions

1. *Assessing compliance with the guidelines.* How would you assess compliance with the ITTA and the Rio Forest Principles? Would it matter if the guidelines were made binding or remained nonbinding? What difference does it make that the goals of sustainable managed forests by the year 2000 is now enshrined in the 1994 ITTA? What legal effect does the statement by consumer countries have?

2. *Will the conventions work at cross-purposes?* With species of tropical timber, such as mahogany, listed as endangered species in CITES, how do countries ensure that the two conventions do not work at cross-purposes? Are additional implementing mechanisms required?

XIX

Conservation of Endangered Species

There has been much concern about the increasingly rapid disappearance of species. Traditionally this concern has taken the form of trying to protect certain species that are endangered, primarily through limiting international trade in them.

A. THE CONVENTION ON INTERNATIONAL TRADE IN ENDANGERED SPECIES (CITES)

International trade in endangered species has been very profitable. While this trade dates back centuries, the volume of trade greatly expanded several decades ago. In 1963 the International Union for the Conservation of Nature, a hybrid non-governmental/governmental organization, called for a convention to control the international trade in endangered species (CITES). The Convention was concluded ten years later. As of July 1998, 144 countries were party to the Convention, with more than 800 species on the Appendix I Endangered List and more than 4,000 species of animals and 24,000 plants on the Appendix II List of Threatened Species.

1. Basic Elements of the Convention

The Convention is designed to protect species of fauna and flora from extinction by commercial trade. States are required to give varying degrees of protection depending on the status of the particular species. Under the treaty, regulated species are listed on one of three appendices: those threatened with extinction (Appendix I), those that could face extinction if their trade is not controlled (Appendix II), and those facing over-exploitation in a particular country (Appendix III). Member countries decide multilaterally to list a species on the first two appendices; a country may unilaterally put one of its species on Appendix III.

The agreement operates through a permit system which requires export and import permits for species listed in Appendix I and export permits for species in the other two appendices. Every state is required to designate a Management Authority and a Scientific Authority to supervise the review of permit applications.

Traders in endangered species listed on Appendix I must present an export permit to the customs agency of the exporting country and both the export and import certificates to the importing country's custom officials. In theory this provides a double check against illegal trade. The Management Authority must certify that (1) the trade will not adversely affect species survival; (2) the specimen was not obtained illegally and will be transported in a manner minimizing the risk of death, damage, or cruel treatment; and (3) an import permit has been granted.

Species listed under Appendices II and III receive less protection. No import permit is required, and the specimens may be used for commercial purposes. But the same conditions for granting an export for Appendix I species apply to Appendix II species, and importation of them requires presentation of an export permit or re-export certificate prior to import. If a country has placed a species on Appendix III, an export permit is still required, but since the listing only means that the species is endangered in the listing country, no general assessment that the species is not endangered is needed for the export permit.

To implement the treaty, countries must designate ports of entry and exit, and create a detailed record of trade in specimens of listed species.

CITES provides six exceptions from the requirements of the three appendices: specimens owned as household or personal effects, bred or propagated in captivity for commercial purposes, acquired before regulation of them took effect, loaned noncommercially between registered scientific institutions, transshipped while in customs' control, or transported as part of a travelling exhibition. While these exemptions are intended to relieve the burden of CITES, the effect of the household use, captive bred, and prior acquisition exceptions have been particularly prone to abuse and have undermined the objectives of CITES.

To encourage countries to join CITES, countries can opt out of any listing of species on Appendix I or II—i.e., make a reservation to the listing—within 90 days before the listing becomes effective. In this case, the reserving country is not treated as a party to the agreement for purposes of trade in the particular species. From 1975 to 1990, countries filed 289 reservations to changes in the listing of species under CITES appendices. The most high profile reservations were those taken by five African countries (Botswana, Burundi, Malawi, Mozambique, and Zimbabwe) to the October 1989 decision of the CITES parties to move the African elephant from Appendix II to Appendix I, effectively banning trade in ivory and other elephant products. As a result these five countries were not bound by the Appendix I trade restrictions. You should consider this as you read the materials later in this chapter on the elephant controversy.

Non-governmental organizations have been integral to the operation of CITES. NGOs participate in the meetings of the parties and lack only the right to vote. Over time the number of NGOs participating in conference meetings has increased dramatically to the point where they significantly outnumber the state parties participating. In 1994, 96 percent of the parties (119 states) attended the Conference of the Parties, with 221 non-governmental observers and several nonparty governments attending as observers. The NGOs were highly influential in pushing for the listing of elephants on Appendix I.

NGOs have had a pivotal role in monitoring compliance with the agreement. The World Conservation Monitoring Unit, in Cambridge, England, has been responsible for the computerized tracking of exports and imports and provides the data to the CITES secretariat. TRAFFIC, a division of the World Wildlife Fund, has also been very active and effective in monitoring illegal trade in wildlife. NGOs have also assisted with scientific and technical studies and have provided valuable expertise.

Since the late 1980s there has been growing concern among countries and among secretariat staff with the enforcement of CITES. In September 1994 countries in southern Africa adopted the Lusaka Agreement on Cooperative Enforcement Operations Directed at Illegal Trade in Wild Fauna and Flora, which will provide a forum for a pilot experiment in a regional enforcement network.

As you read the following articles, consider the extent to which controlling trade in endangered species is an effective approach to species conservation.

■ THE CONVENTION ON INTERNATIONAL TRADE IN ENDANGERED SPECIES: NO CARROT, BUT WHERE'S THE STICK?

Laura H. Kosloff & Mark C. Trexler
17 Envtl. L. Rep. 10, 222 (1987)

The Convention on International Trade in Endangered Species of Wild Fauna and Flora (CITES), sets as its goal the prevention of the endangerment or extinction of species that could result from international trade in those species and their products.

For some species and products such as sea turtles, rhinoceros horn, and Asian elephant ivory, the trade is overwhelmingly illegal. For many other species and products, there are large components of both legal and illegal trade; examples here include African elephant ivory, parrots, and orchids. For items such as artificially propagated plants, ranched furs, and water buffalo horn jewelry, most shipments are legal, although there are exceptions. With thousands of plant and animal species in trade, a worldwide declared value of at least $5 billion is involved; the U.S. market accounts for up to one-third of that value.

Besides its diversity, the sheer volume of this trade is astounding. A minimum of 500,000 live parrots and 10 million cacti enter into international trade each year, along with over 500 tons of ivory, 50 million furs, and 350 million ornamental fish. Moreover, there is evidence that trade volume is growing in response to soaring demand. Given the volume of the trade, and its tendency to involve exotic and uncommon species, the biological threat to species posed by this trade cannot be discounted. When combined with the even more devastating impacts of worldwide habitat loss, it appears that millions of species will become extinct in coming decades. . . .

The Wisdom of Trade Controls as an International Response

To understand the potential impacts of the infrastructure established by CITES on species extinctions, it is important to remember the context of the extinction problem. At its best, CITES only regulates international trade. Domestic trade, even if its effects are felt internationally, is not addressed. Moreover, domestic activities that indirectly jeopardize endangered species, through habitat destruction, exotic species introduction, pesticide application, waste disposal, or otherwise, are also not covered by CITES.

Thus, the approach taken by trade controls as means of species conservation can be conceptually questioned on at least two levels. First, is focusing on the international wildlife trade an appropriate way to address species extinctions? Second, can the administrative infrastructure embodied in CITES achieve its goal of negating even just the impacts of international trade on a species' biological status?

Unfortunately, habitat loss is the primary threat facing species today, including many of the species for whom international trade is also seen as a significant threat. Much of this habitat loss is occurring, at devastating rates, in tropical forest regions. This habitat loss creates still other problems in a ripple effect, as cleared areas make the remaining forests and other sensitive areas much more accessible to resource exploiters. The net result is that many species are being lost or threatened, some before they are even discovered.

CITES, however, deals exclusively with wildlife and products that cross national borders. Not even a hortatory reference is made to the need to protect the species' habitats. This emphasis can be attributed to several factors. First, international agreements have historically focused on species that cross national boundaries, or species that are permanently outside of a particular nation's control. CITES' drafters no doubt saw the link between wildlife exploitation and the crossing of national boundaries in the form of wildlife trade as something susceptible to a tradition of international cooperation.

Second, regulation of the international wildlife trade impinges far less on the economic and political interests of sovereign nations than would international programs to regulate national land use practices, and hence generally receive more support (or less opposition) from national governments. Import and export permit requirements do not directly interfere with a nation's internal affairs, nominally affect all signatories equally, and tend to affect relatively small political interest groups, such as wildlife traders. Habitat conservation, on the other hand, requires the setting aside of land inside the boundaries of a state that could be used for other purposes, involves the displacement or exclusion of politically volatile interest groups, such as landless peasants, and requires disproportionately costly action on the part of biologically rich nations than biologically poor nations. Adherence to a habitat-conservation treaty would also implicitly involve the cession of a significant amount of national sovereignty to foreign nations.

These factors no doubt contributed to CITES' exclusive focus on international trade. Bolstering this approach was a string of wildlife and nature conservation failures in the form of earlier and generally broader treaties, and the perceived need to obtain as many nations as Parties to the Convention as possible. The net result, however, is an approach to the species extinction problem that in the vast majority of cases can only partially alleviate the threat facing a species, rather than solving the problem and restoring the species.

How much of even just a moderating influence CITES can achieve is the second of the conceptual questions one can ask of CITES.

To effectively control this trade, one would have to change the behavior of the hundreds of thousands of individuals involved in the harvesting, trading, processing, and marketing of relevant species. For many, the change would threaten their economic livelihood and is likely to be resisted. To actually monitor the trade controls would require tracking what leaves a particular country, what intermediate steps are made for processing, what products are manufactured from raw skins and other precursors to finished products, and where all these products ultimately go. Given the hundreds of thousands of shipments involved in the trade, and the many avenues by which they can move between a particular point of origin and their final point of consumption, this tracking presents an arguably insurmountable challenge.

Overall, the problems facing trade controls as a conservation measure are mammoth. As in the drug trade, the illegal wildlife trade can be so lucrative that people will always be willing to take the risk for some products literally worth their weight in gold, as is rhino horn. Also as with the drug trade, the primary countries of origin may be in no position to adequately track or control the trade and may be faced with many problems they perceive as more pressing than wildlife species.

Note

The Red List. The IUCN publishes a "Red List" of Threatened Animals, which the organization has tracked and recorded with the help of the World Conservation Monitoring Centre and the International Council for Bird Preservation. The list includes the family, genus, and species name, the common name, the area in which the species is found, and a rating indicating the severity of the threat of extinction. These categories, from least to most serious, are

> Commercially threatened—large populations exist, but will become reduced to a dangerous level if destruction is not regulated;
>
> Threatened—species categorized as "endangered," "vulnerable," "rare," "indeterminate," or "insufficiently known";
>
> Insufficiently Known—species that may be either "endangered," "vulnerable," or "rare," but whose exact status is not known;
>
> Indeterminate—those species that are either "endangered," "vulnerable," or "rare," but whose exact status is not known;
>
> Rare—species with small, at-risk populations;
>
> Vulnerable—species with probability of becoming endangered if no action is taken;
>
> Endangered—species with populations at critically low levels;
>
> Extinct—species of which no member has been found in 50 years.

From the 1990 IUCN Red List of Threatened Animals (1990) (an edition of the list published together with essays and documents upon which decisions were made).

For further information, *see generally* Simon Lyster, International Wildlife Law: An Analysis of International Treaties Concerned with the Conservation of Wildlife 239-277 (1985).

2. *The Elephant Controversy*

The elephant was moved to Appendix I of the Convention from Appendix II by a 1989 decision of the CITES parties which meant that international trade in the elephant or elephant products, namely ivory, was banned. Five African countries took reservations to the decision and were not, therefore, bound by the ban. Three of these countries, Botswana, Namibia, and Zimbabwe, proposed transfer of elephants to Appendix II in 1997 for the purpose of limited trade in elephant ivory to one trading partner, Japan, as well as limited trade in live animals as well as hides and hunting trophies, to other destinations. Satisfied with the precautions planned by these countries for controlling the elephant trade and with the strength of elephant populations, either stable or growing, in each country, the CITES secretariat recommended acceptance of the transfer, and the transfer was approved at the Tenth Meeting of the Conferences of the Parties (parties to CITES) in June 1997, in Zimbabwe. The following materials are intended to illuminate the controversy surrounding this ban. What legal problems can you identify in initiating and implementing a ban under the convention? Consider what conditions are needed in order for market incentives to be a viable approach to conserving elephants.

Consider carefully the provisions of CITES. If you were drafting the convention today, what changes would you make to the Convention and why?

For more on the controversial use of trade bans to save the elephant, *see* Curtis Bohlen, Face-Off: Elephants and Ivory; Save the Elephant-Stop the Ivory Trade, USA Today, Oct. 11, 1989, at 10A; Patrick Cox, Face-Off: Elephants and Ivory; Save the Elephant;—Keep the Ivory Trade, USA Today, Oct. 11, 1989, at 10A; John Waggoner, Ivory Market Loses Its Tusks After Bans, USA Today, June 11, 1990, at 1B; Annemarie Mannion, From Afar, Saving the African Elephant, Chicago Tribune, Nov. 4, 1990, at 2; Richard Littell, "Culling" Ivory, Saving Elephants: Relaxing the Trade Ban Can Only Help Africa's Dwindling Herds, The Washington Post, Feb. 23, 1992, at C5.

■ SAVE AN ELEPHANT—BUY IVORY

Randy Simmons & Urs Kreuter
The Washington Post, Oct. 1, 1989, at D3

On July 18, Kenyan President Daniel arap Moi set fire to $3 million worth of elephant tusks. This dramatic gesture, orchestrated by a Washington public-relations firm, was designed to demonstrate Kenya's dedication to saving the African elephant. In the belief that tourism should be the only commercial use of the animals, all other options were banned a decade ago. Since then, the Kenyan elephant population has fallen from 65,000 to 19,000. At that rate, all of them will be gone in five years. Kenyan wildlife experts blame poachers and the ivory trade.

In Zimbabwe, by contrast, the ivory trade is seen as an important tool for saving elephants. Shops openly sell ivory and hides from elephants culled to prevent overpopulation in the country's game parks. Part of the profit is returned to the parks. Elephants on tribal communal lands are managed similarly: Some two dozen Zimbabwean villages will earn a total of $5 million next year by selling ivory and elephant-hunting rights. Zimbabwe's policies are based on the belief that the best way to protect elephants is to ensure that people benefit from their use and thus have a vested interest in their preservation. In the decade during which Kenya's elephant population was dwindling, Zimbabwe's grew from 30,000 to 43,000.

The respective results of these antithetical strategies are visible across Africa. Elephant populations in those countries using a Zimbabwean approach—Botswana, Malawi, Namibia and South Africa—are increasing at a rate of 5 percent annually. The Zimbabwean approach, known as conservation through utilization, allows safari hunting and tourism on private, state and communal lands as well as the sale of ivory and hides. In Botswana, for example, safari-hunting permits are sold as part of that country's game-management program. South Africa's Kruger National Park earned $2.5 million last year—10 percent of its annual budget—by selling ivory and hides from 350 elephants culled to control herd size.

By contrast, East and Central African countries use the Kenyan approach. Their collective elephant populations have dropped from 866,000 in 1979 to 404,000 in 1989. Some projections indicate that elephants could be extinct in East and Central Africa as early as 2005.

Despite these failures, however, the Kenyan method now dominates international efforts to save the African elephant. Early this summer, Kenya, Tanzania and international conservation groups called for an immediate, worldwide ban on the ivory trade. The United States and the European Community responded by prohibiting imports. Japan and Hong Kong, the destination of most of the globe's raw ivory, instituted some controls as well.

Kenya and Tanzania also requested the secretariat of the Convention on International Trade in Endangered Species of Wild Flora and Fauna (CITES) to list the African elephant in its "Appendix I." [The parties subsequently agreed to do this.]

Best of Intentions

The African experience suggests that many wildlife preservationists are asking the wrong question. Instead of "How do we stop the ivory trade?" they should ask: "How do we make elephants valuable enough that people have an incentive to be careful stewards, rather than careless exterminators?"

But they don't, perhaps because a conservation ideology fueled by Western—and particularly American—opposition to commercial use has misled those who wish to save elephants. (American conservationists generally oppose relying on market forces to preserve wildlife.) A second possibility is less benign: An international ivory ban is expected to substitute for effective law enforcement at the national level and to cover up decades of mismanagement and corruption.

Regardless of motives, a government ban on a valued commodity never wholly eliminates demand. Three things do happen, however: Prices increase; people with a comparative advantage at avoiding detection—usually criminals and corrupt public officials—take over the formerly legal market; and in the case of a resource owned in common, the resource disappears. Legalizing trade and protecting property rights, however, reverses these outcomes: Prices drop as the legal supply grows; there is no incentive for criminality and corruption; and property rights encourage wise stewardship of the resource.

Trade bans have consistently failed to protect species for which there is a commercial demand. Many species of Latin American parrots, for instance, are "protected" by a CITES Appendix I listing. Prices skyrocketed after the trade ban and the legal market was taken over by poachers who make no effort to maintain birds on a sustainable basis. After all, the nest left today will, in all likelihood, be taken by someone else tomorrow. Native hunters go so far as to chop down nesting trees to get the parrots. The captured birds are drugged, hidden in automobile door panels (even hubcaps), and smuggled into the United States where the few that actually survive are sold on the black market for as much as $20,000. The return for trading in "protected" birds is often greater than what can be made from producing illegal drugs. Thus, rather than reduce the threat to native parrot populations, prohibition has increased it.

Prohibition has also failed to protect Africa's black rhino, which is valued for its horn. About 50,000 existed in Africa when the 1976 CITES ban went into effect. The rhinos dwindled to 14,800 by 1980 and 8,800 by 1984. Only about 3,500 exist today, most of them in Zimbabwe and South Africa. Rhino horn is prized by Arabs for dagger handles and by Asians for its supposed value as a medicine and aphrodisiac. Rhino horn currently sells for about $8,000 per pound and each horn weighs about 10 pounds, making a rhino worth about $80,000. Without economic incentives to save rhinos, even Zimbabwe has had poaching problems, and officials there are moving some rhino from the Zimbabwe Valley to privately owned ranches where they can be more actively protected. Black rhino populations have increased only in South Africa's well protected and funded game reserves.

All wild cats were listed on the CITES Appendix I in 1976. And the fact that some leopard populations grew and were subsequently "down-listed" to allow sport hunting and some export for non-commercial, personal use is sometimes claimed as an Appendix I success. But scientific data did not support listing these populations on Appendix I in the first place; and the listing predictably discouraged preservation. Zimbabwe's leopards, for example, were not endangered and they posed a serious threat to local livestock. Consequently, until the CITES downlisting was approved, leopards were killed in rural areas, not for their skins but for predator control.

Market Incentives

Contrary to the poor record of trade bans, commercial use has successfully protected a broad variety of species. Seabirds are farmed effectively in Iceland, crocodiles and butterflies in Papua New Guinea, ostriches in South Africa and Texas and a broad variety of species in Zimbabwe. Since Zimbabwe declared a reservation to the Appendix I listing for crocodiles, crocodile farming has become a multi-million dollar business there and is growing in Malawi.

The Northern white rhinoceros, also listed on Appendix I, declined from 1,500 animals spread among five countries in 1960 to just 20 animals in Zaire by 1989. Concurrently, the Southern white rhino increased tenfold in South Africa and now totals about 6,000 in parks, reserves and on privately-owned ranches. White rhinos are hunted in South Africa, and the horn derived from hunting and natural mortality totals several hundred kilograms each year. These horns are not presently traded, but could be the source of millions of dollars annually to be spent on additional rhino protection. South Africa's wildlife specialists are considering requesting a reservation under CITES and selling the horn.

All of Africa's elephants could be protected like those in the south if they were allowed to become part of the market economy. Elephant ivory has been prized for centuries and is now especially valued in the Far East. It is made into piano keys and carved into chess pieces, figures and the Oriental signature stamps known as "chops." Uncarved tusks like the ones burned by Kenya's government sell for $1,000 each; and the hide, which is made into a broad range of leather goods, is worth another $2,000.

When rural Africans can benefit from elephant hunts and from selling elephant products, they have an economic stake in elephant conservation. That stake can be sizable: $25,000 is the price of an average Zimbabwe hunt where elephant is the main trophy. Further income is generated for rural communities when animals that destroy property are killed by National Park personnel and the ivory and hide are given to the community. Income from hunting and ivory also helps finance enforcement of anti-poaching measures.

One Zimbabwean subsistence community recently curtailed poaching in Gona-re-Zhao National Park and villagers agreed to devote some of their land to wildlife in exchange for hunting permits for elephants and buffalo that overflowed from the park. The permits were sold to a safari operator. Part of the proceeds was used to develop community facilities and the rest distributed directly to community members who lost crops to animal damage.

Without such income, rural Africans kill elephants or destroy their habitat in order to survive. Elephants are dangerous competitors who drink water supplies dry, tear up trees and trample crops. In countries such as Kenya and Tanzania where over 80 percent of the people live off agriculture and human populations are rising at 3 or 4 percent each year, few families are willing to endure hunger so an elephant can live to provide a job for an urban-based tourist guide or a photo opportunity for a foreign tourist.

The simple reality is that elephants compete with people for scarce resources, and rural Africans must benefit if conservation is to be successful. Requests for trade bans ignore that reality and the incentive it creates for people to engage in poaching or to simply kill off local elephants.

The lessons from other species with commercial value that have been listed on CITES Appendix I suggest an Appendix I listing will make things worse for Africa's elephants. Some countries have already established ivory stockpiles in anticipation of a price rise. The Economist reports that Burundi has stashed 90-100 tons and Hong Kong has 500-700 tons. One effect of the price rise will be to encourage more people to be involved in poaching. Likely candidates include the Southern Somali Shifta, who roam and plunder at will in northeastern Kenya and who are suspected of killing conservationist George Adamson recently. A second effect will be to encourage greater political corruption as the returns from aiding illegal shipments will rise along with the price of ivory. Thus, virtually no one will have an incentive to preserve elephants and their habitat, but underpaid game guards, corrupt politicians, rural farmers and organized poachers will have an increased incentive to poach.

MONEY AND MORALITY

If those countries with effective conservation through utilization policies in place abide by a CITES trade ban, they will lose income, the incentive to protect elephants and eventually their elephants as well. To avoid this disaster, Zimbabwe, South Africa, Botswana, Malawi, Mozambique and Zambia have announced they would not honor a strict ban. Instead, they planned to develop their own ivory marketing and control system. This system included stringent controls and checks to reduce the chances of illegal ivory from other African countries being sold through the system. It introduced a form of ivory identification based on chemical analysis, X-ray spectrophotometry, electron microscopy and other forensic techniques. The identification technique will pinpoint the origin of the ivory. Only that ivory originating in the countries that join the regional marketing system will be allowed to be sold.

. . . Bans on hunting need to be replaced with policies that encourage game ranching, safari hunting and indigenous use of wildlife. Part of the income from these commercial activities can be used to fund expanded patrolling efforts to protect the newly established rights to wildlife.

Commercialization and intensive management of wildlife are difficult concepts for many members of the American wildlife lobby to accept. But there is still time to reconsider. Expanding elephant herds in Southern Africa shows there is no need for those in East and Central Africa to be rushing towards extinction.

■ DON'T LET THEM BUY IVORY

Michael Sutton
The Washington Post, Oct. 9, 1989, at A21

Having recently returned from Kenya and Botswana, I read with interest "Save an Elephant—Buy Ivory" by Randy Simmons and Urs Kreuter [Outlook, Oct. 1]. Their article espouses the prevailing philosophy of wildlife management in southern Africa: that exploiting the commercial value of wildlife through "conservation by utilization" is more likely to save endangered species than trade bans and strict protectionism. They contend this approach could be applied with equal success in East and Central Africa to save rapidly dwindling elephant populations. However, their idea is not new and is based on several mistaken premises that lead the authors to erroneous conclusions.

The southern African approach ignores the fundamental differences between the countries of East and Central Africa and those in the south. Zimbabwe, South Africa and to some extent, Botswana, are relatively rich countries that are able to put more money and effort into protecting and managing their wildlife resources. In contrast, Kenya, Tanzania, Uganda, Zaire and most other sub-Saharan countries are impoverished nations that simply cannot afford to adequately manage their national parks and wildlife. Partly as a result, the wildlife of East and Central Africa has historically been subjected to far greater poaching pressures than populations in the well-protected reserves of southern Africa. Kenya borders some of the poorest nations on earth—Somalia, Ethiopia, Sudan and Uganda, countries that provide an unlimited supply of poachers who make cross-border forays for ivory and rhino horn. The vigorous response of Zimbabwe and South Africa to move limited poaching there is only now being duplicated in East Africa, and it may be too little, too late.

It is not "conservation of utilization" that has succeeded in preserving the wildlife of Zimbabwe and South Africa, but effective antipoaching and park management. At best, wildlife utilization might succeed in conserving a few commercially valuable species under controlled conditions in southern Africa, but it is a mistake to assume that what works in Zimbabwe will also work in Kenya or Tanzania. There are no elephants left to cull for profit in East Africa. Most elephants are poached far from human settlements, where they compete with no one for habitat and where there are no local people to serve as "careful stewards" of wildlife. Even if there were, native villagers and subsistence farmers in East Africa are hardly a match for well-armed gangs of poachers. To most African countries, the value of elephant products such as ivory and skins is insignificant in comparison to their value on the hoof. According to recent estimates by Gardner Brown, professor and chairman of the economics department at the University of Washington, tourists spend $168 million to $200 million each year on wildlife-oriented safaris in Kenya alone, much of which is returned to local communities in the form of employment and purchases by visitors. Thus, African nations already have a significant incentive to preserve such wildlife as the elephant.

Simmons and Kreuter argue that trade bans simply drive the price of wildlife products up and encourage poaching and illicit commerce. This oft-quoted parallel to the narcotics trade probably holds true for some products such as rhino horn. But unlike narcotics and rhino horn, no one is addicted to ivory, and it has not been used in Oriental medicines for thousands of years. Ivory is a luxury item that is sold to the wealthy in jewelry and department stores. The publicity surrounding the plight of the African elephant and unilateral ivory import bans by the United States and other countries have already begun to lessen the demand for ivory and thus lower its price.

Further legal commerce such as that advocated by the authors would serve only to rekindle the demand for ivory, raise its price and encourage further poaching. Experts also fear that poached ivory from other African countries would be laundered through the loophole left open by continued legal trade in elephant products from southern Africa. Conservationists believe that, like spotted cat skins and egret plumes, ivory will eventually fall out of fashion and the demand will evaporate, provided continued trade in ivory from southern Africa is not allowed to perpetuate the market.

Taking Exception

Trade bans alone will not save the African elephant or any other species. The authors are correct in stating that an embargo on the international ivory trade is no substitute for effective law enforcement and better wildlife management at the national level in Africa. The two must go hand-in-hand. The recovery of the American alligator, cited by the authors as the result of successful commercialization, was in fact the result of effective enforcement of domestic and international trade sanctions that eventually allowed the resumption of limited, controlled hunting and export of skins. In

Zimbabwe and South Africa, only vigorous antipoaching measures have so far saved the elephant and the black rhino.

The nations of East Central Africa will require massive infusions of foreign assistance to similarly protect their elephants and other wildlife. To this end, Congress may soon appropriate $2.5 million for elephant conservation assistance. Some have even suggested that a United Nations antipoaching force be deployed to help Kenya and Tanzania deal with armed bands of poachers. In any event, the United States should continue to advocate a total ban on international trade in ivory and use government expertise to assist African countries with antipoaching programs and the wise management of their parks and wildlife.

Much has recently been written about the potential benefits of a free-market approach to conservation and parks management. But one has only to look at Ocean City, Md., to see the effects of market forces and for profit "stewardship" on natural resources. Left to the vagaries of the free market, Yellowstone would look like Coney Island with geysers.

Unbridled commercialism and human greed has often had disastrous impacts on natural resources, reducing such species as the American bison to near extinction and turning wildlife preserves into glorified zoos. We can all be thankful that Congress and the founders of our national parks had the foresight in 1872 to recognize and limit the invidious effects of commercialism on our protected areas and wildlife.

■ HAS INTERNATIONAL LAW FAILED THE ELEPHANT?

Michael J. Glennon
84 Am. J. Intl. L. 1, 3-4, 18-21, 22, 34-35, 37-43 (1990)

> Are we no longer capable of respecting nature, or of defending a living beauty that has no earning power, no utility, no object except to let itself be seen from time to time?
>
> *Roman Gary*

By far the greatest threat to the elephant's survival is poaching. . . . International conservation groups estimate that the illegal killing of elephants for their ivory has reduced Africa's elephant population from 1.5 million to fewer than 500,000 in the last decade. By some estimates, the poachers kill two to three hundred a day; at this rate, the African elephant could be extinct by the end of the century. The New York Times compared the elephant population in 1989 in countries where there were more than 50,000 in 1979:

Country	*1979*	*1989*
Central African Republic	63,000	19,000
Kenya	65,000	19,000
Mozambique	54,000	18,600
Sudan	134,000	40,000
Zaire	377,700	85,000
Zambia	150,000	41,000

Numbers, however, do not tell the whole story. They do not convey the brutality of the killing sometimes by paramilitaristic poachers who spray bullets from semiautomatic weapons over entire herds. They do not disclose the horror burned in the memories of survivors that have witnessed the hacking of parents and siblings they have lived with for decades and afterwards wander aimlessly in despair. Numbers—and dispassionate references to "ivory" and "offtake"—do not reveal what really is at issue. . . .

We know something about the persons engaged in poaching. In Kenya, some of the poaching has been done by Somali bandits, called shiftas, armed with modern automatic rifles. The gangs have gotten $6 a pound for tusks; a poacher can earn $100 in a single night. (The median income in Africa in 1988 was about $300 per year.)

Other poachers in Kenya have been outsiders; in February 1989, an armed band of Somalian soldiers entered the country and slaughtered six elephants. Kenyan security forces exchanged fire with the raiders, resulting in the death of one Somalian, the capture of another and the injury of three Kenyans. The Government of Kenya lodged a formal protest with the Somalian Embassy. The World Wildlife Fund determined that Somalia had sold or stockpiled about 29,000 tusks from 1986 to 1989—even though the country contained fewer than 4,500 elephants in 1987. The President of Somalia, Mohamed Siyaad Barre, explicitly authorized the import into Somalia of raw ivory from neighboring countries.

Poaching has been facilitated, through inadvertence or indifference, by developers. In 1981 the Shell Oil Company constructed roads in the previously isolated Selous game reserve in Tanzania. Its labor force "was not averse to poaching"; since the roads were built, elephants have declined rapidly in number.

Poaching has provided a source of revenue for guerrilla movements, which are well equipped to enter the business. Jonas Savimbi's UNITA, which is supported by the United States, has reportedly killed more than 100,000 elephants to finance its 14-year war against the Government of Angola.

We know from customs reports that an average of 800 metric tons of ivory has been leaving Africa annually. But in ivory exporting countries, the value of ivory to the export economy has rarely been greater than 1 percent. Relatively little raw ivory has gone directly to the United States or other end-user countries. For the most part, raw ivory has been transported to entrepots, way stations en route to final ports where ivory is worked and its origin easily concealed. Somalia, the United Arab Emirates and South Africa have been among the principal entrepots. Burundi has exported most of the ivory from East Africa, even though it has no elephant population itself. Macao and Singapore also have participated in the illegal ivory trade.

From these intermediary countries, the raw ivory has been shipped to countries where it is "worked," or carved. Hong Kong and Japan have been among the most prominent of such states. As controls in Hong Kong were tightened, the main carving industry appeared to be moving to Macao. Japan alone has consumed close to 75 percent of Africa's raw ivory production.

The worked ivory has then been either sold domestically or shipped to consumer states such as the United States. The United States has imported about 30 percent of worked ivory that enters the international trade. About a third of Hong Kong's worked ivory exports have been sent to the United States. It has been estimated that about 80 percent of the ivory sold in the United States was obtained illegally.

Why the Ivory Trade Flourished Under CITES

However incomplete our current picture of the international ivory trade, it nonetheless seems fair to conclude that throughout the 1980s, the trade boomed despite the CITES protective regime for a fairly obvious reason: CITES did not sufficiently diminish the incentives of producers, middlemen or consumers.

Producer states faced a variety of problems. The vast profits available from poaching, or merely looking the other way, made the corruption of enforcement personnel a recurrent difficulty. Game wardens, The Economist observed, "can make more from a couple of contraband tusks than they do in a year's honest work. Fat profits made government officials fairly easy to suborn." Grinding poverty, as noted above, also has played a major role.

Even producer states that purposefully undertook the task of protecting their elephant populations from poachers faced a shortage of resources. Their game wardens frequently were overwhelmed by the poachers' firepower, to the extent that Kenya—a nation that has come to take wildlife conservation seriously—asked Britain for helicopter gunships, spotter planes, transports and automatic weapons for its new, paramilitary Anti-Poaching Unit. By one estimate, the cost of surveillance, fencing and support equipment needed to halt poaching entirely in Kenya's Tsavo National Park was $200 per square mile per day—which worked out to $1.6 million a day.

Producer states seemed little affected by the quota system they established under CITES. The system has been entirely voluntary and had no binding effect on the parties. Consequently, if a producer state exceeded its quota or even declined to supply a quota to the CITES Secretariat, other CITES parties had no legal basis under CITES for refusing entry to that producer state's ivory. Moreover, the quotas have been based on ridiculously high estimates of sustainable yields provided by the producing countries. "The quota system," the World Wildlife Fund concluded, "has proved to be little more than a procedure for ivory-producing states to notify the CITES Secretariat of the number of tusks they plan to export in a given year.". . .

Prior to the Lausanne Conference in October 1989, therefore, CITES failed to protect the elephant. [Parties voted to put the elephant on the Appendix I list at the Lausanne Conference.]

These considerations suggest the outline of a general framework for the protection of endangered species under customary international law. Although such principles may still represent lex ferenda with regard to a particular species (or other resource), they appear to constitute emerging opinio juris on a broader structure of global environmental resources, rights and obligations that might be summarized as follows.

A global environmental resource is a natural resource located within the territory of one country but broadly enjoyed, and arguably needed, by the world community as a whole. Tropical rain forests, described as the "lungs of the world" by Indonesian President Suharto, are a good example. Unique cultural artifacts are another. That these exist within specific states is largely an accident of geography; but for their presence, the life of all would be diminished. For the reasons outlined in this article, and in light of the tremendous worldwide concern generated recently over its possible extinction, the elephant seems properly regarded as a global environmental resource.

A global environmental right arises in connection with a global environmental resource. It refers to the right of all states to expect that the resource will be protected by the state in which it is found. States are trustees, responsible for the preservation of species within their territories. That obligation runs to the international community as a whole: any state should be regarded as suffering legally cognizable injury when that obligation is breached by another state. That states have a global environmental right to expect that the elephant will be protected is confirmed by emerging norms of customary international law pertaining to endangered species, discussed above. "The protection of the elephant," UNEP has said, "is an obligation of humankind. . . ."

Global environmental obligation refers to the duty of states to share in preserving global environmental resources. There are two tiers of such obligations: custodial obligations, which refer to the preservation duties of states in which the resource is physically located; and support obligations, which refer to the duties of other states to contribute to the conduct of custodial obligations. First World states often complain about the failure of Third World states to meet their custodial obligations (concerning, for example, their elephant populations, rain forests and archaeological treasures), but few of the complainers have met their support obligations. The Economist put it well: "Logically, if the rest of the world wants the elephant to survive, then it should not only compensate Africa for $60 million of lost exports, but help to foot the bill—of perhaps $80m-$100m— for an effective war on poachers.". . .

Steps to Saving the Elephant

In sum, unless the elephant is to continue down the road of the black rhino, a number of steps must be taken.

1. The ivory trade must be stopped immediately. As discussed above, halting the ivory trade requires effective steps to dry up both supply and demand and to cut out middlemen. Kenya's President Moi put it well: "To stop the poacher, the trader must also be stopped and to stop the trader, the final buyer must be convinced not to buy ivory." States that do not comply with the international ban must be appropriately pressured into doing so, at least until the elephant is safe and an internationally controlled ivory-marking system is in place.

2. Antipoaching squads and other enforcement units must be strengthened. We ought not to be deluded into believing that domestic enforcement of the criminal law in producer countries can easily be tightened up. Corruption among law enforcement authorities is not unknown in those countries where the elephant is most threatened. This problem was exemplified by a 1989 incident involving the Indonesian Ambassador to Tanzania. The Ambassador, Joesoef Hussein, was caught trying to leave Dar es Salaam with 184 elephant tusks stowed in his luggage. He apparently expected no problem and claimed diplomatic immunity. Rather than asking the Indonesian Government for a waiver—so that Tanzania could prosecute, the local government officials reportedly tried to cover up the incident.

Even when there is a will to succeed, it is hard to take seriously a commitment to elephant conservation that sends game wardens armed with pre-World War I carbines against poachers using machine guns. A multilateral entity such as the CITES Secretariat or UNEP should undertake to arrange appropriate assistance. If that means some form of paramilitary or police training—or operational, down-in-the-trenches participation— that agency ought to be empowered to call upon appropriate countries to help, much as the Security Council may call upon members of the United Nations when military units are needed. The objective should be "united international police action to eliminate the illegal ivory trade."

3. Environmentally sustainable development must be supported as an essential prerequisite to elephant protection. The elephant simply will not be safe as long as unlawful conduct pays so much more than lawful conduct.

In the long term, enhanced law enforcement can only be a stopgap measure unless economic incentives to poach are greatly reduced. This is true even though, in the short run, development and conservation can conflict at times. A principal means of development in have-not countries, for example, is agriculturalization, but agriculturalization deprives the elephant of its habitat; funds spent to build a dam are not available to buy spotter planes for game wardens.

At a certain point, therefore, some weighing of the values of development relative to that of elephant protection remains unavoidable in determining how many elephant populations to protect, and at what price. The questions that arise here are difficult and timeless. Above all, development is directed at the preservation and enrichment of human life. It is easy for Americans, watching wildlife programs on color television in air-conditioned homes, to support elephant protection; it is not always so easy where the elephants actually live.

Yet, in the end, sustainable economic growth will be the elephant's best insurance, particularly growth that gives the local populace a concrete stake in the elephant's survival. It is no accident that relatively rich countries have been more able than relatively poor ones to protect the elephant.

4. An internationally operated ivory-marking system using the latest technology should be instituted. Recent advances in the science of wildlife forensics have been impressive. It is now possible not only to identify ivory by species of origin, but also to mark ivory tusks so that parts of lawfully taken tusks are subsequently identifiable—easily and inexpensively. In fact, secretly marked ivory is already in the stream of international commerce. The integrity of a tagging system depends upon that of the officials who operate it; if they are corrupt and accept bribes to mark poached ivory, or if they permit the tagging technology to fall into the hands of poachers, the system loses its reliability. For this reason, international control at this point seems essential. If it eventually proves desirable to move from the embargo model to a management model—that is, if the elephant someday gets "back on its feet" in countries where it is now threatened—such a system could operate in the following way: An international authority such as UNEP or the CITES Secretariat could be established at regular intervals in all countries where ivory is lawfully taken. The governments of those countries could then bring ivory, up to the amount permitted in their quota, to the marking authority's clearinghouse for tagging. Certain aspects would have to be public to avoid bribes and corruption, but the tagging itself would have to be conducted privately to keep the technology confidential. A comprehensive and enforceable marking system could not be put in place immediately; however, the upshot is that modern science seems finally to have eliminated the problem most responsible for the elephant's decline: the indistinguishability of lawfully and unlawfully taken ivory.

5. A long-term solution requires several modifications of CITES. First,

the CITES restrictions must be made applicable to worked, as well as raw, ivory. Middlemen, not producing states, have skimmed off the bulk of the profits of the ivory trade. They are able to do so in good part because CITES effectively carves out a role for them: inasmuch as CITES does not apply to the trade in worked ivory, it provides an incentive for "working" illegal tusks superficially so as to remove them from the CITES constraints. This incentive can and should be eliminated by the parties; indeed, the Convention itself already points the way. Article I(b)(3) provides for the express listing of "specified parts and derivatives" of already listed animals. A resolution was adopted at the first special session of the parties in Geneva that would have created a minimum list of readily recognizable parts and derivatives. However, no such list has been drawn up, in part because of concern that it would be a "maximum," rather than a "minimum," list. This concern, while perhaps valid at the time, seems to have been overtaken by events at Lausanne and should now give way to countervailing considerations—namely, that the failure to produce a "parts and derivatives" list has contributed mightily to the undoing of CITES. The parties should draw up a list, formalizing what was left implicit at Lausanne, and worked ivory should be on it.

This step is essential for another reason. The agility of middlemen at leapfrogging new restrictions has often been noted, though it takes little prescience to predict their next line of attack. If CITES continues to be construed as permitting international trade in worked ivory, middlemen will be encouraged to move their carving facilities to the producing states; as a result, the principal international trade will be in an uncontrolled item—worked ivory. There is evidence, in fact, that this movement has already begun. Some might applaud the establishment of carving facilities in producer countries; the economic boost would be welcome and some of the proceeds, at least theoretically, could be put to the best use in conserving remaining elephant populations. Yet, in the end, the move would only prolong the ivory trade and continue to threaten a species that CITES now officially views as "threatened with extinction." If the values sought to be vindicated by CITES are to be protected effectively, its application to the international trade in worked ivory is imperative.

Second, CITES must be further modified to permit the provisional listing of a species on Appendix I, and a new, broader treaty must be negotiated that is not tied to commerce. Because no such provisional listing is possible, the international system not only has failed the elephant, but also has inadvertently accelerated the killing of elephants. The flurry of unilateral bans on ivory importation announced by various governments in June 1989 derived from a justifiable concern that movement of the elephant to Appendix I by the CITES parties meeting in Lausanne the following October would result in an "orgy" of killing, as poachers anticipated tighter international controls. CITES provides no mechanism by which an international entity (such as the CITES Secretariat) can promulgate a provisional ban subject to subsequent approval by a conference of the parties. It may be that some parties would not delegate this much authority to the secretariat, at least as currently constituted. It may also be that the process of settling upon a provisional listing would itself generate anticipated killing; a measure of confidentiality would be required that could prove difficult to achieve. Yet without such a procedure, any public effort to move a highly visible species up to Appendix I to prevent poaching—and virtually every effort to do so will be public because international publicity generates the necessary support—is almost guaranteed, in the short term, to bring about more killing of the species, not less. If the elephant is safer today than it was a year ago, thanks are due to the individual governments that banned ivory imports and the international wildlife organizations that spurred them to act, not the international legal system.

Further lessons about CITES taught by the elephant's plight can be generalized only to a point. Some species are threatened by poachers. Others face threats apart from poaching, most often loss of habitat. The shortcomings of CITES that so hurt the elephant have little application to the difficulties those species confront. Yet the very inaptness of CITES to their problems is perhaps the most damning criticism of all: CITES does not even seek to protect those species, since its only concern is with endangerment posed by international trade. It is time for a new, worldwide treaty that broadly safeguards endangered species irrespective of commerce.

6. The broad-based educational campaign already successfully undertaken by nongovernmental organizations must be continued. It is not enough to educate buyers of ivory to the horrors of its origins. Ultimately, protection of the elephant and other endangered species will require a change in mind set by both individuals and governmental institutions that have viewed concern about animals with a certain derision. Robert Nozick began his review of Thomas Regan's book with the following observations: "Animal rights seems a topic for cranks. Who else would devote major energy to promote changes in our treatment of animals or write a book on the subject?" Past failures by the United States to pay its dues to organizations such as CITES, the Senate Foreign Relations Committee said, "have called into question its commitment to these agreements." When the committee added a provision to the Foreign Relations Authorization bill for fiscal year 1990 strengthening protection of the elephant, the Washington Post chided the senators for turning out a "global grab bag" of "hobbyhorses" reflecting a "somewhat disoriented world view."

The struggle to protect beings without reference to any "objective," mathematically quantifiable utility enriches our spirit. Even if this is not a struggle to ensure our own survival, it is a battle to clarify our character, to define what we hold dear, for ourselves and our descendants. It is the character of our species that is at issue. Who can say, on the day the last elephant dies, that the human race will ever again be the same?

Notes and Questions

1. *Updating the Endangered Species List.* The 112 members of CITES met March 2-13, 1992, in Kyoto, Japan. At this meeting, the parties extended protection to 45 additional species. Thirty-five that had been listed in Appendix II were switched to Appendix I, thereby prohibiting trade in these species. Approximately 17 species were dropped from either annex. Four were downgraded from Appendix I to Appendix II.

Among the additions to CITES, the Brazilian rosewood and the Central American mahogany became the first tropical tree species to come under the control of the Convention. The rosewood, which is used to make musical instruments and decorations, was placed in Annex I. Mahogany was listed in Annex II.

2. *Classifying the element.* Significantly, the controversial ban on ivory trade was retained at the Kyoto meeting. Five South African countries—Botswana, Malawi, Namibia, South Africa, and Zimbabwe—proposed an amendment that would downgrade the African elephant. They argued that the elephant population in their countries was stabilized and hunting should be strictly regulated, but not banned. A majority of CITES members however, opposed the amendment, arguing that allowing the elephant to be hunted would cause poaching to increase dramatically. In theory, the Bush administration supported removal of the ban, believing it to be a "means of providing African governments with an economic incentive to preserve the elephant herds." The United States, however, opposed the amendment at the conference, asserting that some countries would not be able to protect the herds sufficiently. Countries were concerned about enforcement of the Convention and unanimously adopted a resolution indicting the EEC for its illicit trading in endangered animals, mostly reptiles.

As noted in the introduction to this section, however, Botswana, Namibia, and Zimbabwe prevailed in the effort to downgrade protection of the elephant in 1997. The web-published text of the CITES secretariat's recommendations to the CITES parties regarding the elephant proposals stated, in part:

> If the proposals were adopted, the Secretariat believes that, as the intention is only to allow export of ivory from the registered stocks direct from the proponent States to Japan in secure containers, under strictly controlled conditions, in one supervised shipment a year, there would be no significant risk of ivory being illegally added to the shipments and thus traded in contravention of CITES.
>
> In this context, it is noteworthy that the Panel of Experts has concluded that the import and export controls in place in Japan are adequate, although there is a need to strengthen internal controls of the retail trade to prevent the laundering of illegally obtained ivory at this level.

> The proposed trade in live animals and hunting trophies seems unobjectionable. The same applies to the proposed trade in hides and the non-commercial trade (personal effects) in leather articles from Zimbabwe.
>
> There is speculation that renewed trade in elephant ivory may lead to an escalation of poaching and an increase in illegal trade in elephant ivory. There is no way to assess these risks but the Secretariat believes that the proposed conditions would minimize them. In this connection, the Secretariat is concerned that those who spread stories to indicate that the proposals are designed to re-open "free" trade in ivory are acting against the conservation of the African elephant. In fact they should make every endeavour to ensure that the public is well informed that this is not the case.
>
> Namibia and Zimbabwe have proposed that, in the event that their proposals are accepted and subsequently a Party becomes aware of abuses or aware that the proponent State is not honouring its commitments, the Standing Committee should be informed. If it is satisfied that there has been an abuse, it would request the Depositary Government to propose the retransfer of the population concerned to Appendix I by the postal procedure. A similar procedure could apply if the Standing Committee was satisfied that there was a significant increase in illegal trade in African elephant ivory as a result of the transfer to Appendix II.
>
> No trade in elephant products should be permitted from any of the proponent States until its reservation on the inclusion of the African elephant in Appendix I has been withdrawn.

The parties, by secret ballot, approved the proposals by an approximate ratio of 3:1. (*See* Doc.10.89 at http://www.unep.ch/cites/doc10-89.html)

3. *Trading in tiger bones.* The People's Republic of China is being condemned by environmental groups, such as Tiger Trust, for the large illegal trade in tiger bones that is carried on in contravention to its obligations under CITES. The number of wild tigers has dropped to only 6,000 as of May 1993, and they continue to be poached and traded from the Far East.

China is one of the largest markets for tiger bones, a major ingredient in traditional medicines. China is also the source of many illegal exports of tiger products to the West.

Declared by the Chinese government of the 1960s to be pests, the number of tigers dropped to 100 in the late 1980s, as the revived ancient medicinal values of the bones encouraged poaching. The number of tigers worldwide rose to 8,000 in 1991, but has fallen again recently, and according to one expert, tigers may be "virtually extinct in about 10 years" unless the poaching is stopped.

In 1986, China set up a tiger breeding farm, and is now petitioning the authorities of CITES for permission to export the products from it. The government argues that legalizing the trade will deprive the poachers of profits, and thus help save the species. *See* Sean Ryan, Health Shop Tablets Pose Threat to Tigers, London Sunday Times, May 2, 1993.

4. *Do trade bans work?* The article by Michael Sutton (Don't Let Them Buy Ivory, above) mentions the mistake of comparing the preservation

techniques of two countries, such as Kenya and Zimbabwe, which have great differences in geography and economic ability to protect their elephant populations. Additionally, however, there may be differences in conservation approaches between species. Consider the following:

> Do . . . trade bans [such as CITES] work? Not always. . . . A ban on commercial fishing may be an effective way of protecting threatened oceanic species from excessive farming, . . . but halting trade in elephant products is not.
>
> Whales are threatened with extinction for three reasons: they breed slowly; they are cheap to catch relative to the market price for whale products; and access is available to anyone with a boat and the necessary expertise. If access to whale farming were controlled by quotas, their numbers could theoretically be stabilised. In practice, a ban on commercial whaling is a more effective way of reducing the economic return for fishermen and thus discouraging their capture. But the success of this policy for preserving the whales depends on the assumption that, left to their own devices, whales would breed freely and flourish.
>
> The same argument does not apply to elephants, which do not have the luxury of living in huge oceans. The survival of land species, especially such large and potentially destructive animals as elephants, depends on the willingness of humans to preserve their habitat. This depends on their economic return, compared to other land uses.
>
> It is because investing in elephants has not been sufficiently profitable . . . that elephants are threatened. . . . Banning trade reduces the incentive for African countries to keep poachers out of the parks or to preserve elephant-friendly habitats. If African elephants are to be saved, the economic return on elephant farming must be increased, rather than lowered, perhaps by granting export quotas to countries willing to invest in keeping the poachers out. Free trade in ivory may not be environmentally friendly, but neither is a trade ban.

Timothy Swanson, Regulating Endangered Species, Economic Policy 16 (Apr. 1993).

Do you agree with the author's reasoning? Is there a greater danger in a failed policy of free trade than in a failed attempt at a trade ban?

5. *Privatizing animal ownership.* Also mentioned above, a new method of protecting endangered species is allowing animals to be placed on ranches guarded by the ranch owner. Giving an individual this job, it is assumed, provides greater protection than the protection the government can give. In Namibia, the government is starting a program of wildlife auctions to privatize ownership of animals. Specimens of elephant, buffalo, roan antelope, giraffe, eland, and rhino have been collected from national parks to be sold to the highest bidder. The species being auctioned have been successfully managed, and are now in surplus.

The buyers, having first proven that they are able to care for the animals, will thus have an economic stake in protecting their investments. Namibia to Auction Protected Species, Agence France Presse, Apr. 6, 1993.

Question: If privatizing ownership of wildlife proves to be an effective way to protect endangered species, should it be encouraged? What are the possible drawbacks to such a system?

6. *Don't forget the flora.* While the sentiment to "Save the Elephant" or "Save the Whale" is widespread among the general public in the industrialized world, one relatively ignored group of endangered species is the plant kingdom. Recently, however, there has been attention to at least one species of flora: orchids. At the Glasgow World Orchid Conference and Show in 1993, the plants' officer of CITES, Mr. Ger van Vliet, noted that since the late 1980s, the ban has begun to reduce the illegal trade of plants.

Mr. van Vliet reported that there have been "several cases of confiscations in the United States," that the European countries are "now moving in the right direction," and that Australia "does not hesitate to put anybody [who violates CITES] in jail for two years." Christopher Andreae, Orchids Have "Fatal Attraction" for Some Fans, The Christian Science Monitor, June 17, 1993, at 10.

3. Problems of Implementation of and Compliance with CITES

The Convention on International Trade in Endangered Species has frequently been criticized on the ground that countries do not enforce it effectively.

Consider the following article. Think about the issues of implementation and compliance in the framework of the tools that other international environmental conventions use and consider whether some would be more effective than the ones included in CITES.

■ THE CONVENTION ON INTERNATIONAL TRADE IN ENDANGERED SPECIES OF WILD FAUNA AND FLORA: IMPROVING THE PROSPECTS FOR PRESERVING OUR BIOLOGICAL HERITAGE

John B. Heppes & Eric J. McFadden
5 Boston U. Intl. L.J. 229, 232 234, 237-239, 241-242 (1987)

I. Party Implementation and Compliance with CITES: Problems and Prospects

A. National Record-Keeping

Article VII of CITES outlines the record-keeping and reporting requirements of the Treaty, providing:

6. Each Party shall maintain records of trade in specimens of species included in Appendices I, II and III which shall cover:

a) the names and addresses of exporters and importers; and

b) the number and type of permits and certificates granted; the States in which such trade occurred; the numbers or quantities and types of specimens, names of species as included in Appendices I, II and III and, where applicable, the size and sex of the specimens in question.

Accurate and detailed record-keeping and reporting of international wildlife transactions by national actors is a critical component of CITES. In the absence of such pertinent statistics, it is difficult for the Secretariat or parties to CITES to discern trends in the trade of endangered species or to become aware of suspicious transactions that may warrant further investigation. Trade statistics also are essential for updating the CITES Appendices and to gauge the effectiveness of the Treaty. Finally, records and reports provided by the parties to the Secretariat help to reveal discrepancies among the parties concerning the interpretation of treaty provisions or the regulation of trade in certain species. Despite the passage of several resolutions at the biennial conferences of the parties calling for improved record-keeping and reporting of wildlife trade statistics, national compliance has continued to be woefully inadequate.

A recent study by the World Wildlife Fund (WWF) of CITES record-keeping and of the reporting practices of the members of the European Economic Community (EEC) is emblematic of the problem.

In general, the WWF study found an appalling lack of compliance with CITES record-keeping and reporting requirements among EEC nations. In recent years most of the EEC's member states have failed to submit annual reports to the CITES Secretariat on time, severely hampering its effectiveness. In addition, virtually all of the EEC nations have neglected to provide any information about importation and exportation of plant species. The WWF found the quality of the data provided by most EEC nations to be poor, usually providing no indication of the contents or status of individual shipments and often based only on records or permits that have been issued, rather than actual trade data.

B. ENFORCEMENT OF THE CONVENTION BY MEMBER STATES

The efficacy of CITES has been hampered severely in most member nations by inadequate development of an infrastructure to enforce its provisions. Under the Convention, enforcement is vested solely in national authorities. One of the most severe problems in this context is an egregious shortage of personnel to conduct inspections of wildlife and wildlife products during the importation or exportation process. This problem is prevalent even in affluent member nations, such as the United States. For example, a recent study by the World Wildlife Fund of the psittacine importation process revealed that over 60,000 of such birds, many listed on Appendix I or II of CITES, may have entered the United States illegally in one year. One of the major factors contributing to this distressing situation is staff shortages at the Fish and Wildlife Service, the agency assigned to inspect psittacine shipments as they enter the United States. Because of manpower shortages, the Fish and Wildlife Service is unable to inspect the vast majority of psittacine shipments. As a consequence, the agency is compelled to rely upon importer's paperwork which purportedly certifies that the shipments are in compliance with CITES. Parrot smugglers have capitalized on this situation by exporting large numbers of endangered birds to the United States with inaccurate or wholly spurious documents obtained in other nations. As one analyst comments, "the bird market is extremely profitable and big importers have both the financial resources and the contacts in the countries of origin to ensure that the paperwork appears in order, regardless of which species may be involved. If FWS does not physically inspect the birds, they will not pick up on the illicit importation."

Manpower shortages are even more critical in member states with more limited economic resources. For example, in Argentina, national customs inspectors lack both the time and manpower to corroborate the legitimacy of transit documents for wildlife products that have been issued by provincial officials. This is distressing because provincial officials often establish quotas on the basis of market demand rather than the mandates of CITES. Similar problems plague efforts by Central American nations to staunch the flow of illegal exportation of endangered species.

Recent studies also indicate that national inspectors in most member nations lack adequate training to discharge effectively their responsibilities under CITES. In Bolivia the Forestry Development Center, a division of the Ministry of Agriculture, is responsible for issuing CITES permits. Unfortunately, most of the members of the Center have forestry backgrounds and often are unable to identify species by anything other than their common names. It is little wonder that Bolivia has had one of the worst records of compliance with CITES over the last decade.

Other nations are also plagued by similar problems. In Paraguay several government agencies that are authorized to issue import and export permits have no staff members with the expertise to ensure CITES compliance. Such shortcomings also are pervasive in developed countries such as the United States. For example, customs officials generally assign a low priority to wildlife law enforcement and only receive perfunctory training in species identification.

TRAFFIC, a program of the World Wildlife Fund which monitors international trade in animals and plants, conducted an experiment in an effort to assess the expertise of customs officials in CITES nations. TRAFFIC officials declared or displayed a cactus to customs officials in several countries, including the United Kingdom, the Soviet Union, Switzerland, Germany, Sweden, Denmark, and the United States. Despite the fact that virtually all cacti are protected under CITES, no questions were asked by officials in any of these countries about the species of the plant or its origins. While confiscation either occurred or was threatened, in the United States and the Soviet Union the officials' rationale was not related to possible CITES violations, but rather to health regulations. Officials in the United Kingdom also asked no questions when TRAFFIC sought to bring an orchid into the country from France, despite the fact that all species of orchids are listed in the CITES Appendices.

C. TRADE WITH NON-PARTIES

Under CITES, parties to the Treaty are permitted to trade listed species with non-party states. In recent years, it has been estimated that trade between CITES parties and non-parties comprises approximately thirty percent of all wildlife transactions. Article X of CITES conditions such trade merely upon the issuance of "comparable documentation" by the non-party state which "substantially conforms with the requirements of the present Convention for permits and certificates."

Unfortunately, the Convention does not define the terms "comparable documentation," or "substantially conforms." The absence of objective standards to govern trade between CITES parties and non-parties has proven to be extremely detrimental to the protection of endangered species. One of the primary reasons that many nations have refused to ratify CITES is because it enables them to maintain a virtual monopoly in trade of certain species. For example, Mexico exported more than 73,000 kilograms of turtle leather and skins over a five-year period utilizing "comparable documentation" most of which was derived from Appendix I species of sea turtles. Mexican trade currently threatens the green sea turtle (chelonia mydas) with extinction. Trade between CITES parties and non-parties has similarly pushed the saltwater crocodile perilously close to extinction in recent years.

Under CITES, wildlife or wildlife products cannot be imported or exported unless a scientific finding has been made that the transaction does not threaten the continued viability of the species in question. This crucial element of CITES is jeopardized when transactions with non-parties are contemplated.

Smugglers have capitalized on the vague standards of Article X to obtain "comparable documentation" from officials in nonparty states that often contains inaccurate or wholly falsified information. The decision of many CITES members to accept shipments supported by such fraudulent documents has contributed to the imperiled existence of many species.

Notes and Questions

1. *CITES enforcement officer.* The secretariat of CITES has included an Enforcement Officer. Is this consistent with the provisions of the Convention? What actions should such an officer be authorized to take?

2. *Enforcing CITES in the United States.* CITES is implemented through national legislation in the member countries. In the United States, The Endangered Species Act of 1973, 16 U.S.C. §1538, and regulations issued pursuant thereto, 50 C.F.R. §17.23 (1990) implement the Convention. How difficult is it to enforce the Convention in the United States? Consider Lujan v. Defenders of Wildlife, 60 U.S.L.W. 4495 (June 12, 1992), which made it significantly harder for environmental and other public-interest groups to gain standing to sue. The case involved the environmental group's challenge to a 1986 rule issued pursuant to the Endangered Species Act of 1973. The rule narrowed the scope of review of potentially threatening agency actions. The Defenders of Wildlife based its position on affidavits of two of its members, both of whose careers as professional naturalists who observed animals in their natural habitats were jeopardized by the rule. Writing for the Court, Justice Scalia dismissed the action for lack of standing, asserting that the plaintiffs did not exhibit the required injury in fact. In addition to narrowing the rule of standing, Lujan also put into doubt the constitutionality of citizen-suit provisions in many environmental laws and excluded some types of rules from judicial review.

3. *Reporting requirements.* Under CITES, parties are required to file annual reports to the secretariat on trade and permitting statistics. However, the compliance with the requirement has not been universal, as shown in Figure 19-1, below. Note that compliance with the reporting requirement increased after CITES declared that a failure to report would be considered as a formal violation of the agreement.

4. *Controlling trade in endangered species.* For articles on the effectiveness of controlling international trade in endangered species, *see* William C. Burns, CITES and the Regulation of International Trade in Endangered Species of Flora: A Critical Appraisal, 8 Dick. J. Intl. L. 203 (1990); S. Fitzgerald, The International Wildlife Trade: Whose Business Is It? (1989); David S. Favre, Tension Points Within the Language of the CITES Treaty, 5 B.U. Intl. L.J. 247 (1987); Note, Enforcement Problems in the Endangered Species Convention: Reservations Regarding the Reservation Clauses, 14 Cornell Intl. L.J. 429 (1981); Travalio & Clement, International Protection of Marine Mammals, 5 Colum. J. Envtl. L. 199 (1979); Note, International Trade in Endangered Species Under C.I.T.E.S.: Direct Listing vs. Reverse Listing, 15 Cornell Intl. L.J. 107 (1982) (advocating the rejection of Australia's proposal to implement reverse listing for CITES' scheme); Comment, The United States' Enforcement of the Convention on International

Figure 19-1
Annual Reports Required of CITES Parties: Received or Outstanding

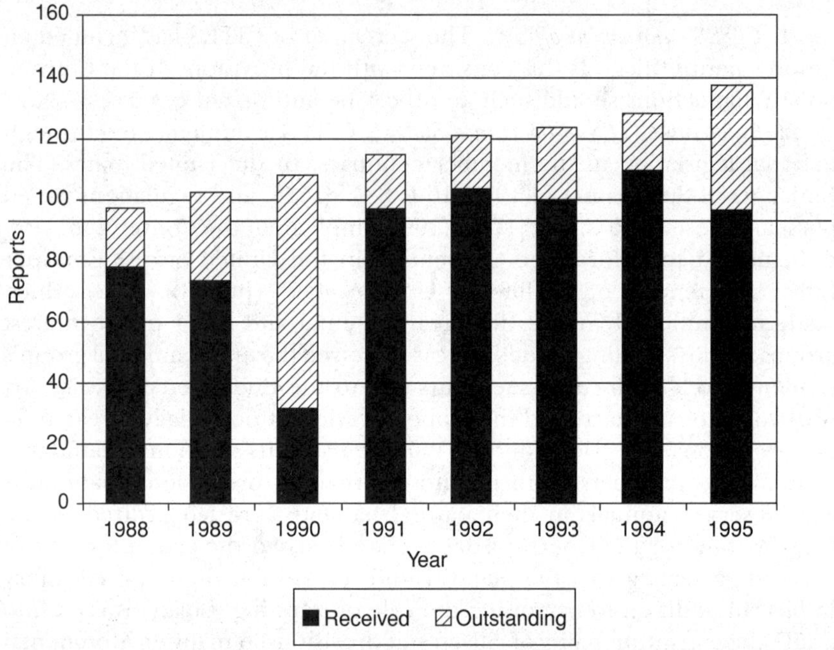

Note: Chart reflects status of 1991-1995 reports as of July 21, 1997. Reports for each year are due on October 31 of the following year; therefore, 1996 reports are due October 31, 1997. 1997 status of delinquent 1998-1990 reports is unknown; chart reflects status as of 1995 for those years' reports.

Source: Edith Brown Weiss and Harold K. Jacobson, (eds.) Engaging Countries: Strengthening Compliance with International Environmental Accords (MIT Press, 1998).

Trade in Endangered Species of Wild Fauna and Flora, 10 Nw. J. Intl. L. & Bus. 541 (1990).

B. REGIONAL AGREEMENTS

1. Western Hemisphere/OAS—The Convention on Nature Protection and Wildlife Preservation in the Western Hemisphere (Oct. 12, 1940, effective Apr. 30, 1942)

One of the earliest of the multilateral agreements concerning wildlife preservation is the 1940 Organization of American States' Convention on Nature Protection and Wildlife Preservation in the Western Hemisphere.[1]

1. T.S. 981, Bevans 630, U.N.T.S. 193.

This convention covers both flora and fauna and land areas of "extraordinary beauty."

Under the convention states have a duty to establish wildlife parks as nature reserves and to prohibit commercial profitmaking in them. They must notify the OAS when the reserves are established.

In the second half of the 1970s, in connection with the Panama Canal Treaty, parties adopted an Agreement Pursuant to Article VI of the Convention on Nature Protection and Wildlife Preservation in the Western Hemisphere to establish additional nature reserves, including one on Barro Colorado Island.[2]

Article IX of the 1940 Convention specifies that export permits must be required for trade of endangered species. However, there are no mechanisms for resolving disputes or ensuring compliance with the treaty's provisions. Since most of the parties are also members of CITES, the lack of enforcement of the 1940 Convention is less critical than it otherwise might be.

Note

CITES Implementation in the western hemisphere. For discussion of the implementation of CITES in the western hemisphere and the relation between national laws and CITES, *see* Kathryn S. Fuller & B. Swift, Latin American Wildlife Trade Laws (2d ed. 1985); Kathryn S. Fuller et al., Wildlife Trade Law Implementation in Developing Countries: The Experience in Latin America, 5 B.U. Intl. L.J. 289 (1987).

2. *Africa—African Convention on the Conservation of Nature and Natural Resources (Sept. 15, 1968, effective June 16, 1969)*

Africa is home to remarkable wildlife. To protect this resource, the members of the Organization of African Unity concluded the African Convention on the Conservation of Nature and Natural Resources. (1001 U.N.T.S. 3 (9/15/68).) Using language that sounds similar to a call for sustainable development and use, the convention calls for members to protect natural resources by "all necessary measures" (Article VI) in order "to ensure conservation, utilization and development. . . . in the best interests of the people." (Article II.)

2. United States International Trade Commission, International Agreements to Protect the Environment and Wildlife 5-33–5-36 (1991).

Trade in endangered species is addressed in Article IX, which calls for regulation of all trade of certain species.

Notes

1. *African wildlife laws.* An excellent source that lists and summarizes wildlife laws in Africa by country was produced by an IUCN project aimed at helping to implement CITES. *See* IUCN Environmental Law Centre, Cyril de Klemm, & Barbara Lausche, African Wildlife Laws (1987).

2. *Environmental conservation.* For an early work promoting environment conservation in Africa, *see generally* N.C. Pollock & B. Litt, Animals, Environment and Man in Africa (1975).

3. Association of South East Asian Nations (ASEAN) Agreement on the Conservation of Nature and Natural Resources, July 9, 1985 (not yet in force).

ASEAN members include Brunei, Indonesia, Malaysia, Philippines, Singapore, and Thailand.

The 1985 ASEAN agreement illustrates the evolution of regional natural resources protection agreements from ones that focus on controlling trade in endangered species to ones that rely primarily on protection of ecosystems. The agreement covers conservation of both species and ecosystems, however, including issues related to biological diversity, establishment of reserves, environmental impact assessment, scientific research, and public participation in the planning and implementation of conservation measures.

Article 5 of the convention regulates trade in both endangered and endemic species and obligates parties "wherever possible" to prohibit the taking of "endangered species recognized by the Contracting Parties as of prime importance to the Region and deserving special attention." However, the Agreement does not require export and import permits as does CITES.

Notes

1. *Asian compliance with CITES.* For compliance with CITES, *see* Eric McFadden, Asian Compliance with CITES: Problems and Prospects, 5 B.U. Intl. L.J. 311 (1987).

2. *Japan and CITES.* For a detailed discussion of Japanese compliance with CITES, *see* James V. Feinerman and Koichiro Fujikura, Japan: Consensus-Based Compliance in Engaging Countries: Strengthening Compliance with International Environmental Accords (Edith Brown Weiss and Harold K. Jacobson eds., forthcoming). For an overview of Japan's 1987 law regulating internal trade in endangered species and how it relates to

CITES, *see* Hiroji Isozaki, Japan's New Law on Endangered Species, 7 B.U. Intl. L.J. 211 (1989) (examining Law for Regulation, etc., of the Transfer of Endangered Species of Wild Fauna and Flora (No. 58), June 2, 1987 (Japan)). *See also* Gray-Schofield, Trends in Wildlife Trade from India to the United States, TRAFFIC (U.S.A.) (1983). (Neither India nor Japan are included in the ASEAN countries.)

3. *Citizen's group environmental advocacy.* For an account of how citizen groups in Asia are organizing to help preserve the environment, *see* James Rush, The Last Tree: Reclaiming the Environment in Tropical Asia (1991).

4. *Europe—Declaration on the Conservation of Flora, Fauna, and Their Habitats, 1988*

In 1988, the members of the Economic Commission for Europe (ECE) adopted a declaration to conserve endangered species and species native to Europe. (Declaration on the Conservation of Flora, Fauna and Their Habitats, ECE/ENVWA/6 (1988).) This declaration was intended to foster in situ conservation efforts in Europe and led to the creation of the European Red List of Globally Threatened Animals and Plants, which applies to any species put on the list, even if not threatened in that country. (ECE/ENVWA/20 (1991).) The EC has never joined CITES.

Most recently, the governments of the ECE have adopted a Code of Practice for the Conservation of Threatened Animals and Plants and Other Species of International Significance. (ECE/ENVWA/24 (1992).) This code, including a list of birds and mammals that live mainly in Europe, is to help member governments formulate and implement conservation policies for the protection of their biological resources.

Of particular importance are the basic principles set out in Part II of the Code, "[c]ountries should strive to maintain biological diversity within their jurisdiction and control"; "[m]easures to safeguard species should be based on the precautionary principle"; "[c]onservation of wild animals and plants should be integrated with economic activities as an integral component of sustainable development." (Code of Practice for the Conservation of Threatened Animals and Plants, ECE/ENVWA/24, II(10), (11), (12) (1988).)

Additionally, the Code includes a provision for updating the list of significant species. (Code, III (21).) While not explicit, the requirement of including the relevant data on each species' population seems to suggest that a species may be taken off, as well as put on, a list.

The Code includes separate provisions on public participation in implementing conservation measures. (Public awareness and participation. Code, IV (51)-(59).) The media, NGOs, and individual citizens are among those groups named specifically by the code, as are formal organizations and the scientific community.

Notes and Questions

1. *CITES and the European Community.* A report on implementation of CITES in the EC can be found in World Wildlife Fund, The EEC Annual CITES Report for 1984: A Preliminary Assessment of the Implementation of CITES in the European Economic Community (1986); *see also* Jorgen B. Thomsen & Amie Brautigam, CITES in the European Economic Community: Who Benefits? 5 B.U. Intl. L.J. 269 (1987). *See also* Fauna and Flora: Canadian Indians Uneasy about EC Trade Regulation, Europe Environment, Mar. 2, 1993 (reporting that native populations in Canada are dependent on trade in several species included in the EC restricted list, but not in CITES).

2. *CITES and habitat loss.* Many ecologists have noted that habitat loss is the primary threat facing species today. What implications does this have for the effectiveness of CITES as a way to preserve species?

3. *CITES, habitat loss and land use regulation.* Even if CITES were fully implemented, how much loss of biological diversity would occur due to habitat loss? Would an international legal regime controlling land use within a country be possible? Are there relevant precedents? What relevance does the Biological Diversity Convention have? (*See* Chapter 18, above).

C. PROTECTING WHALES AND OTHER SPECIES

1. Whales

Whales are mostly found in the marine area outside a state's territorial waters. Thus, protection of them raises intriguing legal issues regarding the conservation of marine mammals in shared areas and states' compliance with international resource regimes.

The following material provides a historical review of efforts to develop an effective regime to ensure the conservation of whales.[3]

a. Introduction

When Earth's whale population sharply decreased in the early 1900s, several countries attempted to regulate whaling off their coasts. They were not successful, however, because most whaling takes place on the high seas, where the traditional doctrine of freedom of the seas governed. This doctrine was interpreted to allow harvesting without restriction. The Inter-

3. The materials on whales and other species draws on a research note by Lainie Krop, 1992.

national Council for the Exploration of the Sea, established in 1902, tried to bypass the inability of individual countries to control the high seas by calling for an international effort to regulate whaling.[4] Resulting from this and other efforts, the 1931 International Convention for the Regulation of Whaling banned the harvest of two species and imposed other restrictions.[5] The absence of several major whaling states from the Convention, combined with the lack of enforcement devices, specific penalties, or basic amendment procedures to take account of new scientific data, rendered the Convention too weak to combat the severity of the whaling problem.

To remedy these defaults, countries concluded in 1946 the International Convention for the Regulation of Whaling (ICRW). In contrast to the earlier Convention, it introduced a schedule that annually identified protected species and set catch quotas, size limits, and whaling methods for various whale species in light of new scientific evidence. Further, it established the International Whaling Commission (IWC) to implement the guidelines set out in the schedule. However, the IWC, like the 1931 Convention, is not equipped with an enforcement mechanism adequate to ensure that its recommendations are followed. In addition, a provision was added that allows countries to opt out of whaling regulations by objecting to them in a timely manner. This provision has proved troublesome to the IWC, especially in enforcing a 1982 whaling moratorium.

Contrary to popular perception today, the convention was designed to preserve the whaling industry by initiating measures to conserve whale stocks, not to put a halt to whaling altogether. The preamble to the convention provides that it is the parties' desire "to establish a system of international regulation for the whale fisheries to ensure proper and effective conservation and development of whale stocks . . . and thus make possible the orderly development of the whaling industry."[6]

In 1982 the IWC adopted a moratorium on all commercial whaling, to which Japan, Norway, Peru, and the USSR objected. Peru since withdrew its objection, as has Japan with respect to commercial pelagic whaling and coastal whaling for minke, Bryde's, and sperm whales.[7] As long as the moratorium continues in force, the only whaling which is legal for the countries which have not objected must fall under the aboriginal whaling exception or the scientific research exception. Both exceptions have been troublesome. The first allows aborigines to take whales as long as they are used and consumed by the community alone. Because the term "aborigine" was never defined, some states, particularly Japan, argue that any commu-

4. For the history of ICES, *see* A. Went, 70 Years A-growing, ICES 1972; for a brief discussion of ICES functions, *see* P. Birnie, Problems Concerning Conservation of Wildlife including Marine Mammals in the North Sea, Intl. J. Estuarine & Coastal L. 252, 260 (1990).

5. 49 Stat. 3079, TS 880.

6. 3 International Convention for the Regulation of Whaling, Jan., 1964, 161 U.N.T.S. 2/24, at 14 [hereinafter ICRW].

7. Edith Brown Weiss, Daniel B. Magraw, & Paul C. Szasz, International Environmental Law: Basic Instruments and References 486 (1992).

nity that is culturally and economically dependent on whaling should qualify under the exception.[8] Such arguments have been continuously rejected by the IWC. States that claim to hunt under the scientific-research exception have been accused of hiding their commercial kills under the mask of "research" and thus undermining the moratorium. Although this problem is partially alleviated by having the scientific committee review all research applications, the committee's recommendations are not binding. In addition, the inefficiency of any type of observer scheme means that "pirating," taking whales clandestinely, goes largely unchecked.

In defiance of the IWC moratorium, Norway, which had objected to the IWC's whaling ban, announced in 1992 that it would allow commercial whaling of the minke whale beginning in 1993. Norway contended that sound scientific evidence exists that the minke whale was no longer endangered and hence should not be covered by the moratorium. The IWC questioned the reliability of this evidence. Moreover, a continuation of the moratorium would, in Norway's eyes, violate the basis of the Convention, which was intended to manage whales on a scientific basis not to prohibit their hunting indefinitely. The IWC, at its annual meetings in 1995 and 1996, urged Norway to stop whaling and to reconsider its objection to the moratorium. In 1996 this caused Norway to walk out of the IWC meeting, though the delegation maintained that they had no intention of withdrawing from the IWC permanently. Norway continued to hunt whales, with a 1996 quota almost double that of 1995,[9] and in April 1996, Norwegian ships were caught by Japanese officials trying to smuggle whale meat from Oslo marked "mackerel" into that country.[10]

At its meeting in 1996, the IWC passed a resolution that called on the commission to play a role in the development and monitoring of whale watching, a fast growing tourist industry.[11] The IWC feared that whale watching, a nonconsumptive and economically profitable use of whales, could pose a threat to whales if not correctly regulated. Increases in boat traffic can affect the behavior of whales and interrupt their breeding patterns. The noise and pollution, if excessive, could disturb the whales' sensitive hearing necessary for communication underwater. The World Wildlife

8. For further discussion on the exception, *see* Stephen M. Hankins, The United States' Abuse of the Aboriginal Whaling Exception: A Contradiction in United States Policy and a Dangerous Precedent for the Whale, 24 U.C. Davis L. Rev. 489 (1990).

9. Norway to Start Whale Hunt, AP (May 17, 1996) (Doug Mellgren, Associated Press Writer) (found on the Internet at http://whales.magna.com.au/FLASH/menuf.html); Norway Storms Out of IWC Meeting, Reuter News Service (June 28, 1996) (Helen Smith) (found on the Internet at http://whales.magna.com.au/FLASH/iwc3.html).

10. Smuggled 6 Tons of Whalemeat to Japan, Verdens Gang Newsagency (Apr. 25, 1996) (found on the Internet at http://whales.magna.com.au/FLASH/menuf.html).

11. Kate O'Connell, The 1996 International Whaling Commission Meeting (Cetacean Society International, July 1996) (found on the Internet at http://elfnetla.elfi.com/csi96301.html).

Federation estimated that more than four million people went on whale watching trips in 1992.[12]

b. Small Cetaceans

When most of us picture whales, we think of the large storybook creature or the calendar "pinup."[13] Yet other cetaceans include the dolphin and porpoise as well as smaller whales like the orca. Currently, the IWC regulates only a small percentage of the small cetaceans. In 1971, the IWC's Scientific Committee organized a Subcommittee on Small Cetaceans to monitor the status of small cetaceans and indicate which needed protection. The subcommittee recommended that a separate international body be set up to oversee those cetaceans not covered by the IWC, but no organization has yet been established. At its 1992 annual meeting the IWC adopted a resolution recognizing the need for international cooperation "to conserve and rebuild depleted stocks of small cetaceans."[14]

Specifically, the resolutions provided guidance on white whales, narwhals, pilot whales, and striped dolphins. Additionally, the IWC agreed to consider forming a body within the commission to address small cetaceans. Some officials, however, still doubt the IWC's legal competence on the issue of small cetaceans.[15] Patricia Birnie, an expert on the IWC, opposes that position, arguing that the commission does have authority to regulate small cetaceans. She asserts that because the ICRW listed no definitions for "whale" or "whaling," the terms could cover small cetaceans, allowing the IWC to regulate them. At its 1996 meeting, the IWC passed a resolution keeping the issue of small cetaceans on the agenda of the Scientific Committee and asking governments to provide information on kills of small cetaceans worldwide.[16]

12. Whaling Commission Faces New Moratorium Battle, Reuter News Service (June 19, 1996) (Helen Smith) (found on the Internet at http://whales.magna.com.au/FLASH/iwc.html).

13. Note that the name "whale" is

> not the scientific description of the species which are of the order Cetacean, but rather the term used by the whalers to describe those large numbers of this order that they actually hunted. They are: Greenland right whale or bowhead, North Atlantic right whale, North pacific right whale, Southern right whale, gray whale, blue whale, fin whale, sea whale, Bryde's whale, minke whale, humpback whale, and sperm whale.

Birnie, *supra* Footnote 4, at n.4.

14. Media release, *cited in* BNA Intl. Envtl. Daily (July 8, 1992).

15. After being ordered by the IWC to give a full briefing of its pilot whale harvesting methods in 1992, the Faroe Islands considered withdrawing, alleging that "The IWC is undermining its authority by meddling in Faroese pilot whaling, the body has no competence or brief to rule on small whale fishing." Statement of Prime Minister Atli Dam, *cited in* Faroese Consider Quitting International Whaling Commission, BC Cycle, July 21, 1992.

16. *See* O'Connell, *supra* footnote 11.

c. Scientific Research Exception

As discussed above, the scientific research exception to the moratorium allows states to issue special permits under Article VIII to take and process as many whales and in whatever manner as that state dictates, free from any restrictions of the convention. The potential for abuse of this exemption prompted the commission to amend the scientific committee's procedural rules and the schedule during the late 1970s. The amended version required states to submit all proposed permits to the committee for it to review them and recommend changes.[17] Because states could ignore the committee's comments, and sometimes did, concerns arose among the antiwhaling nations that the new provisions were not effective enough. To address these concerns, the IWC passed resolutions in 1986 and 1987 that set criteria for the scientific committee to analyze the merit of the proposed research. In addition, the commission could examine the scientific committee's analysis and when necessary, advise states to abstain from issuing the permit. A major legal debate ensued. Iceland, joined by Norway, Japan, and the former USSR, argued that by authorizing the commission to scrutinize the permits, Article VI of the ICRW was violated and the exclusive rights of the states were not being respected.[18] The United States, along with Australia and the United Kingdom, asserted that because no state was required to follow the commission's recommendations, the recommendations would likely activate certification under United States law.[19] Discussing the debate over national sovereignty, Dean Wilkinson suggests that "[i]t might be maintained that in the management of common resources, national sovereignty must be subsumed—otherwise the exhaustion of the resource becomes virtually inevitable."[20]

At its 1995 annual meeting, the IWC passed two resolutions with the intention of making scientific research whaling more difficult. The first requested that governments refrain from authorizing research programs unless they satisfy a review by the IWC's Scientific Committee using criteria contained in the resolution. The second requested that governments use nonlethal research methods in IWC whale sanctuaries. Japan and Norway voted against both resolutions.[21]

17. Birnie, *supra* footnote 4, at 931 & n.96.

18. Article VI reads "[t]he Commission may from time to time make recommendations to any or all Contracting Governments on any matters which relate to whales or whaling and to the objectives and purposes of this Convention." ICRW, footnote 6, above; *see* Birnie, *supra* footnote 4, at 931-933; IWC/39/39: Iceland: Legal Analysis.

19. *See* Dean M. Wilkinson, The Use of Domestic Measures to Enforce International Whaling Agreements: A Critical Perspective, 17 Denver J. Intl. L. & Poly. 271, 283 (Winter 1989). Wilkinson adds however, that "there are indications that the United States has backed off its determinations to use Article VI as a means of controlling 'research' whaling," at 285.

20. Id. at 291.

21. J. Frizell, Report on the 47th Annual Meeting of the International Whaling Commission (Greenpeace, June 1995) (found on the Internet at http://whales.magna.com.au/GOVERN/menug.html).

In practice, the IWC's ability to propose changes has had limited effect. Although proposals by Japan, Norway, and Iceland to increase their commercial quotas have continuously been rejected by the commission, catches continue.[22]

d. Aboriginal Whaling

The legal controversy surrounding the aboriginal whaling exception centers around the definition of "aboriginal," or more precisely, the lack of one. In 1977, the United States suffered political humiliation when the aboriginal exception for Alaskan Eskimos was hastily revoked after reports were issued of the severe depletion in the bowhead whale population, the Eskimos' primary hunt. The United States disputed the revocation on the grounds that the ban on whaling did not apply to the Eskimos, as they did not engage in "commercial" whaling.[23] The outcome of this dispute was a compromise, with the Eskimos allowed to hunt only a limited number of the bowheads. The confusion continued, however, as other countries question whether the exception covers small coastal communities with a cultural history of whaling. Japan, for instance, claimed that its fishing villages were culturally and economically dependent on whaling, thus qualifying as "aboriginal."[24] The IWC rejected the argument. The reason seemed to revolve around the Japanese sale of whale products commercially. Japan requested that a group be organized to define "commercial whaling," "aboriginal subsistence whaling," and other categories. This group was deemed the Definitions Working Group and was to work with the Aboriginal Subsistence Whaling Sub-Committee to clarify the problem. The confusion was apparent when trying to reconcile the IWC's dismissal of the United States's argument that the ban prohibits only commercial whaling with the explanation the commission gave for not recognizing an aboriginal exception for Japan's fishing villages.

Similar requests to permit aboriginal whaling were put forth by both Russia and the United States at the 1996 IWC meeting. Russia asked for a five whale quota for the Chukotka people of its polar region, who revere whales, and the United States asked for a five whale quota for the Makah tribe of its Olympic peninsula. Both requests were withdrawn after much discussion in the face of intense opposition, though the United States promised to renew its request in 1997. Despite the withdrawals, whaling

22. *See* Pete Aldhous, Commission to Keep Whaling Moratorium, 346 Nature 93 (July 12, 1990); Hankins, *supra* footnote 8, at 523.

23. *See* P. Birnie, *supra* footnote 4, at 930 & n.93. Birnie cites the legal opinion of D. Bowett, Q.C., who rejected the United States's argument by determining that the IWC's action was within the scope of the ICRW's Art. V; Opinion of Nov. 16, 1977 (on file IWC).

24. *See* Hankins, *supra* footnote 8, at n.201. Hankins explains that Japan uses a "cultural-dependence rationale" as grounds for an exception from the moratorium.

nations gained a toehold for their own requests for whaling permits, and the IWC lost ground in its efforts to keep the worldwide commercial whaling moratorium strongly in place. The dispute was a major issue at the 1996 meeting.[25]

e. Unilateral Sanctions

One of the most noticeably absent features of the IWC is any mechanism for enforcing its quotas or regulations. Although all members remain bound by regulation unless they object, there are no sanctioning or enforcement powers provided by the IWC. It must rely on national laws to enforce the IWC regulations. "The only effective sanctions to implement decisions of the IWC are provided by the United States. America pulled the IWC's teeth in the first place, and America now provides the IWC's dentition"[26] (referring to the ironic fact that the enforcement provision in the original draft of the ICRW was only taken out at the insistence of the United States). In 1971, the United States enacted the Pelly amendments to the U.S. Fisherman's Protective Act and the Packwood-Magnuson amendments to the Magnuson Fishery Conservation and Management Act 1979. These laws enable the United States Secretary of Commerce to certify, or identify, any foreign state that conducts fishing operations in a way that "diminishes the effectiveness" of the Whaling Convention. If a state is certified by the secretary, the president can respond as harshly as a full trade embargo against the state. Its quotas for access to fish within the 200 mile coastal waters of the United States, or Exclusive Economic Zone (EEZ), is automatically reduced by 50 percent. Access to the EEZ is completely restricted if by the next year the state has not altered its behavior.[27]

Beginning in 1984, the Pelly and Packwood-Magnuson amendments came under heated debate in the case of Japan Whaling Association v. American Cetacean Society.[28] In November of that year, Japan was harvesting sperm whale in direct violation of the zero quota. However, instead of certifying Japan and restricting their quota in America's EEZ under the Packwood-Magnuson amendment, the United States entered into a compromise with Japan. Under this deal, known as the Baldrige-Murazumi Agreement, the United States allowed Japan to hunt for two more seasons

25. IWC Receives Requests for Whaling Permits, AP (June 26, 1996) (Audrey Woods, Associated Press Writer) (found on the Internet at http://whales.magna.com.au/FLASH/iwal.html); IWC Conference Update, AP (June 29, 1996) (Audrey Woods, Associated Press Writer) (found on the Internet at http://whales.magna.com.au/FLASH/iwc2.html).

26. Jermey Cherfas, The Hunting of the Whale: A Tragedy That Must End 113 (1988), *cited in* Wilkinson, *supra* footnote 19, at 276-277.

27. *See* Wilkinson, *supra* footnote 19. For related issues, *see* Enforcement Ouestions of the International Whaling Commission: Are Exclusive Economic Zones the Solution?, 14 Cal. W. Intl. L.J. 114 (1984).

28. 78 U.S. 221 (1986).

despite the moratorium. Japan, in turn, agreed to withdraw its objection to the moratorium at the end of this period. A group of non-governmental organizations immediately challenged the agreement, arguing that when the secretary of commerce is notified by the Marine Mammal Commission of whaling violations, the secretary has no discretion to decide whether to certify the violator, but rather must do so. Although the NGOs were victorious in the lower courts, the United States Supreme Court held that certification was a discretionary matter. Not surprisingly there was criticism from some groups:

> The United States has provided enforcement leverage for IWC quotas through the Pelly and Packwood Magnuson Amendments. Most whaling nations, therefore, have based—or will base—their decisions on whether or not to observe an IWC quota on their assessment of the United States' intentions. They will watch to see whether the United States actually imposes the sanctions written in its laws. . . . Now that the United States has entered into a bilateral agreement with Japan that circumvents the IWC limits under which Japan may whale under objection without being certified, other whaling nations . . . may demand similar concessions.[29]

International politics, coupled with discretionary enforcement by the United States, has proven to be an obstacle to uniform enforcement of IWC rules. In December 1995, then Commerce Secretary Ron Brown certified that Japan was weakening the worldwide moratorium on whaling by killing them in the Southern Ocean Sanctuary, which had been created in 1994 by the IWC to provide whales with a safe mating habitat. The president was then authorized to impose trade sanctions on Japan. However, he decided not to do so, saying that there was not enough evidence to challenge Japan's claim that its research was scientific and required killing the whales. Groups claimed that the tenuous trade relationship between the United States and Japan was more likely the reason.[30]

Since then, the United States role in preventing whaling has come into question. Its lack of action against whaling nations and its 1996 request for an aboriginal whaling permit for a Native American culture have illustrated the unwillingness of the United States to take a strong stand on the issue of whaling and exposed the weakness of the IWC in enforcing its resolutions.[31]

Internationally, unilateral sanctions such as those imposed by the United States have met with a dual response. On the one hand, they have been welcomed for their deterrent effects. "The Pelly and Packwood-Magnuson Amendments unquestionably have had a salutary effect on the

29. Cristopher Gibson, Narrow Grounds for a Complex Decision: The Supreme Court's Review of an Agency's Statutory Construction in Japan Whaling Association v. American Cetacean Society, 14 Ecology L.Q. 509, 510 (1987).

30. Japan Lets Hunters Kill 30% More Whales, L.A. Times, Feb. 9, 1996 (found on the Internet at http://whales.magna.com.au/NEWS/menun.html).

31. *See* O'Connell, *supra* footnote 11.

ability of the IWC to achieve its conservation objectives."[32] On the opposite spectrum, "some members regard such action as an invasion of their sovereignty and contrary to UN Charter requirements on the use of force against the sovereignty of states."[33]

f. The Scientific Basis for Protecting Whales

In recent years, most of the debate in the IWC has centered around issues of science. Originally, whaling nations believed that scientific data would be applied so as to maximize the growth of the whaling industry while minimizing the threat to the species.[34] What occurred, however, was not a tempered and controlled harvesting, but an unrestrained worldwide slaughter of the whale, rationalized by its alleged "scientific" basis.[35] As the severity of this onslaught became known, antiwhaling nations pointed to the lack of accurate data and the need for a new system for measuring whale stocks, claiming that until such gaps were filled, commercial whaling would extinguish the whales. The success of their efforts culminated in 1982 with the adoption of the moratorium on commercial whaling. Purposefully kept out of the amendment was any language referring to a "permanent" ban, the mention of which would certainly have blocked its passage.[36] Rather, the "cessation" of commercial whaling was to begin in the 1985-86 season and be kept under review based upon "the best scientific advice" until 1990. By that year, the scientific committee was to assess the status of the whale stocks as well as develop a "Revised Management Procedure" (RMP) which would set optimum population and catch sizes. Based on this information, the convention would then determine whether to continue the moratorium, modify it, or end it altogether.[37]

32. Gene S. Martin, Jr. & James W. Brennan, Enforcinq the International Convention for the Regulation of Whaling: The Pelly and Packwood-Magnuson Amendments, 17:2 Den. J. Intl. L. & Poly. 293, 315 (1989).

33. Birnie, *supra* footnote 4, at 927.

34. *Id.* at 909.

35. *See* Whaling Leads the Way, New Scientist 11 (June 8, 1991) (arguing that science has been used to justify commercial interests).

36. *See* Birnie, *supra* footnote 4, at 925. Dr. Birnie explains that the amendment was passed "by subtle manipulation of the New Management Procedure combined with avoidance of any suggestion that the cessation would be permanent or indefinite." The amendment itself reads,

> Notwithstanding the other provisions of paragraph 10 catch limits for the killing for commercial purposes of whales from all stocks for the 1986 coastal and the 1985/86 pelagic seasons and thereafter shall be zero. This provision will be kept under review based upon the best scientific advice, and by 1990 at the latest, the Commission will undertake a comprehensive assessment of the effects of this decision on whale stocks and consider modifications of this provision and the establishment of other catch limits.

37. "It was up to science to provide the answers . . . whaling could only restart commercially once all the answers had been given." John Gummer, Norway's Minister of Agriculture, Times, July 4, 1992.

In 1991, the IWC adopted a management procedure that used computer models to set quotas. It determined that the moratorium should remain in force until the computer model was modified to incorporate more safety features. Whaling countries, particularly Iceland, Norway, and Japan, argued that this delay was simply a procrastination device, an attempt to "hide behind the science."[38] Their argument continued in 1992 since a resolution adopting the RMP was again made dependent upon obtaining more data and creating an inspection and observation system. The IWC was criticized by pro-whaling organizations for its "non-decision making process."[39] So angered was Iceland by the continuance of the moratorium that it withdrew from the commission. Norway, although still a member, announced that it would begin whaling by the 1993 season. Japan has also repeatedly expressed dissatisfaction. After the 1996 IWC meeting, the moratorium remained in effect, though more countries were rumored to favor weakening it. At the 1997 meeting, Ireland proposed the completion and adoption of the RMP. At the 1998 meeting the IWC adopted a resolution confirming how the RMP will take into account anthropogenic removals other than commercial catches, such as incidental catches, catches under scientific permit, and aboriginal whaling, but it decided not to fully adopt the RMP until an inspection and observer system is completed.

Even though the debate is usually framed in terms of science versus economics, some members of the scientific committee and analysts do not believe this to be the "true" argument. Rather, they believe that the controversy results from differences in ethics. In the viewpoint of the pro-whaling nations, the antiwhaling majority does not delay the use of scientific management procedures because the data is in any way incomplete, but because their true objections are grounded in morality, and thus outside the authority of the IWC.[40] They oppose whaling because they see whales as "special." Whether whales are in some way special is unknown, as theories of intelligence, compassion, and other "human" qualities are bandied about among scientists and biologists. As long as technology continues to expand and improve and until the antiwhaling regime identifies the genuine reason behind their stance, some argue that maintaining the ban will be difficult to sustain under the IWC's constitution.

Notes and Questions

1. *Are permanent bans possible?* Read the Convention carefully. Could the parties agree to a permanent ban on whaling? Of certain species?

38. Statement of Kevin Chu, from the United States State Department, *quoted in* Peter Aldhous & David Swinbanks, Whaling Ban versus Science, 351 Nature 259 (May 23, 1991).

39. Statement of the High North Alliance, a pro-whaling non-government organization, in BNA International Environment Daily, July 8, 1992.

40. *See* Nicholas Schoon, Delay and Dishonesty in Defense of the Whales, The Independent, July 6, 1992.

2. *Defeating the Convention's purpose?* Consider Article V carefully. Note how any state that does not wish to be bound by an amendment can file a timely objection and be exempted from it. Does this defeat the purpose of the Convention? (Consider the material on the Convention on International Trade in Endangered Species in this connection.)

3. *When is a species no longer endangered?* Changes in our scientific understanding of problems may indicate either that the risk is greater than we thought or that it is less. How can the international community effectively address the situation in which scientific evidence indicates a species is no longer endangered? Does the Whaling Convention adequately address this situation?

4. *NAAMCO v. IWC.* On September 15, 1992, Norway, Iceland, Greenland, and the Faroe Islands established the North Atlantic Marine Mammal Commission. The commission is in opposition to the International Whaling Commission. NAAMCO advocates sustainable commercial whale hunting. It will also control hunting of small cetaceans, including seals and small whales.

The problems outlined above are shared by many other marine mammals, including fur seals, polar bears, manatees, and dolphins. Hunting, marine pollution, habitat loss, oil drilling and pollution, incidental catches, and water recreation threaten all of these creatures.

2. *Fur Seals*

Seals have been overharvested since the nineteenth century. By the time the first international treaty was created to protect the animals, albeit for commercial purposes, their population had already plunged from several million to only thousands.[41] This first treaty, enacted in 1911, succeeded in guarding the North Atlantic fur seals sufficiently enough for their population to again reach into the millions. The 1911 Treaty was replaced by the 1957 Interim Convention on Conservation of North Pacific Fur Seals.[42] The Interim Convention was also begun out of commercial interests. This is clear from its preamble, which states that its desire "was to take effective measures towards achieving the maximum sustainable productivity of the fur seal resources of the North Pacific Ocean so that the fur seal populations can be brought to and maintained at the levels which will provide the greatest harvest year after year." Yet despite its commercial goals, the Interim Convention, like its 1911 predecessor, served to conserve fur seal

41. Treaty for the Preservation and Protection of Fur Seals, 7 July 1911, 37 Stat. 1542, TS 564.

42. Interim Convention on the Conservation of North Pacific Fur Seals, 9 February 1957, 8 U.S.T. 2283, T.I.A.S. No. 3948, 314 U.N.T.S. 105 [hereinafter Interim Convention].

stocks substantially. The Interim Convention was amended five times until 1984, when the United States declined from ratifying a protocol that would have extended it for another four years. The United States' decision not to ratify the agreement was due to the persuasive efforts of senators and environmentalists, who argued that "killing the animals is no longer justified on either economic or humane grounds."[43]

Although unprotected by international agreements, the North Pacific fur seal remains the subject of several national laws, including the Fur Seal Act of 1966[44] and the Marine Mammal Act of 1972.

Seals in the Antarctic region are protected through the Agreed Measures for the Conservation of Antarctic Fauna and Flora, which disallows the taking of indigenous animals from any "Specially Protected Area."[45] In addition, the 1972 Convention for Conservation of Antarctic Seals sets up a management system to monitor the status of the seal stock in order to maintain a healthy ecological balance.[46] The 1991 Protocol on Environmental Protection to the Antarctic Treaty, which entered into force on January 14, 1998, included fur seals in Appendix A of the list of "Specially Protected Species."[47] Once implemented, the Protocol is predicted to be the most stringent environmental protection measure in force.[48]

3. *Polar Bears*

While seals and whales are threatened by hunting, the survival of the polar bear is endangered by a different human activity—development. To address this hazard, the five circumpolar states—Denmark (including Greenland), the United States, the former USSR, Canada, and Norway—signed an Agreement on the Conservation of Polar Bears, which came into force on May 26, 1976.[49] The agreement requires countries in the Arctic region to cooperate in ensuring that polar bears are not hunted, captured, or killed.[50] Exceptions are made for scientific research and aboriginal hunting.

Equally if not more significant, Article II compels states parties to the agreement to preserve the natural ecosystems that make up the bears'

43. Statement by 44 senators urging Secretary of State Shultz to oppose the ratification, U.S. Senators Urge Defeat of Seal Treaty, Reuters North European Service, Apr. 23, 1985.

44. 16 U.S.C. §1151.

45. The 1964 Agreed Measures for the Conservation of Antarctic Flora and Fauna, June 13, 1964, 17 U.S.T. 991, T.I.A.S. 6058.

46. 1972 Convention for Conservation of Antarctic Seals, June 1, 1972, 29 U.S.T. 441, T.I.A.S. 8826; *reprinted in* 11 I.L.M. 251 (signed at London).

47. 30 I.L.M. 1455 (signed at Madrid, Oct. 4, 1991).

48. *See* Fact Sheet: Protecting the Antarctic Environment, U.S. Dept. of State Dispatch, Sept. 16, 1991.

49. Oslo Agreement on the Conservation of Polar Bears, May 26, 1976, 27 U.S.T. 3918, T.I.A.S. 8409, *reprinted in* 13 I.L.M. 13 (1973), UNEP3 #61, at 401, IPE 2276, IELMT 973:85.

50. *Id.* at art. I.

habitat. This would include not only regulating the number of people and human activities in the region, but also controlling the advancement of Arctic oil development. The United States Congress continually has considered the salvation of the polar bear and other wildlife in the ongoing debate over whether to open the coastal plain of the Arctic National Wildlife Refuge to oil drilling.[51] In addition to the 1973 Polar Bear Agreement, the bears are also included in Appendix II of CITES.

4. Dolphins and Driftnetting

With modern fishing technology, such as the purse seine net, or driftnet, fishermen efficiently catch tuna, but also incidentally catch other species such as dolphins. Used extensively in the Pacific, driftnet is attached to a boat or buoy where it floats along with the current. The nets can be up to 30 miles long and are made of plastic. This material is invisible and acoustically imperceptible, making the nets a cheap and effective means to catch fish and squid. Because no power is used during fishing, the driftnet is economically appealing. However, the very features that enable the net to produce a copious harvest (invisibility, strength, and silence) cause a high, unintended catch of marine mammals, birds, and fish. In addition, "ghost" nets, nets that have become lost or abandoned at sea, cause injuries to all types of species and become ensnared in vessels.[52] They also contribute to marine pollution.

In North America the driftnetting controversy has become a major political and diplomatic problem. Much of this controversy has been caused by the emotional nature of the issue. Groups usually at odds with each other, such as environmentalists, commercial fishermen, fish processors, Native American Indians, and sport fishermen, have been able to unite in an antidriftnet coalition to put pressure on their national and state governments.

a. International Action

The first effort to regulate driftnetting was made by Japan and the Soviet Union through the restriction of mesh size in 1953.[53] More recently, the United States and the former Soviet Union began discussing fishery

51. *See e.g.*, S. 531, 105th Cong. (1997), sponsored by Senator Roth (R-DE), supporting the designation of the coastal plain of the Arctic National Wildlife Refuge as wilderness, and thereby protecting it from industrial activities.

52. Douglas M. Johnston, The Driftnetting Problem in the Pacific Ocean: Legal Considerations and Diplomatic Options, 21 Ocean Dev. & Intl. L.J. 5, 10 (1990).

53. *Id.* at 11 & n.64.

questions in order to enter into a treaty in the near future.[54] In addition, several bilateral agreements have been negotiated among the North Pacific coastal states that provide for access to their zones for the harvesting of designated stocks or species.[55]

The main arena for international discussion of the high seas driftnetting problem in the North Pacific has been the International North Pacific Fisheries Commission (INPFC). The INPFC was established by Canada, Japan, and the United States in 1953 in an effort to regulate the Japanese high seas salmon fishery in the Northeast Pacific.[56] Although the INPFC was restructured in 1978, the rearrangement of the commission failed to resolve several disputes that have arisen between the INPFC members, especially between Japan and the United States.[57]

One of the most bitter of these disputes is over the high seas driftnet fishery.[58] Begun in 1979, the fishery was originally restricted to Japanese vessels, but since 1984 it has grown in scale and location. Vessels from Taiwan and South Korea, neither of which are INPFC members, largely caused this expansion. The Japanese insisted that Taiwan and South Korea are not permitted to engage in pelagic fishing of protected stocks in Convention waters.[59] Since 1987, all three of the INPFC member states have begun to discuss proposals for establishing an "international organization with broader membership" to deal with non-anadromous species, as foreseen in the amended version of the INPFC Convention.[60]

In July 1989, state and national government officials, NGOs, various observers and consultants, met in Victoria, British Columbia, to discuss the North American driftnetting problem. In November, the premier of British Columbia and the governors of the six affected U.S. states, issued the North Pacific Driftnet Proclamation, urging the federal governments to take diplomatic action against driftnetting in the North Pacific.[61] The proclamation listed six recommendations which would limit the impact of high

54. *Id.* at 12 & nn.66-67. "The principal treaty instrument is the Agreement between the United States and the Soviet Union on Mutual Fisheries Relations, May 31, 1988, reprinted in House Doc. 100-207, 100th Cong., 2d sess., 1988, which envisages cooperation on a wide variety of matters, including conditions of access to the fisheries in each other's EEZ, protection of marine mammals, management of anadromous species, boarding and inspection, scientific research, and joint ventures."

55. *Id.* at n.67.

56. *Id.* at 12.

57. The reconstitution of the INPFC was due to the new expansion of fishery jurisdiction and the fact that the principle of the coastal state's primacy of responsibility for salmon conservation secured consensus in UNCLOS III negotiations. *Id.*

58. Other disputes include: (1) the dispute over alleged Japanese illegal fishing in the U.S. zone; (2) the dispute over alleged Japanese intervention of salmon of North American origin on the high seas and; (3) the dispute over the scale of Japanese (and Polish) fishing for pollock in the high seas enclave ("doughnut hole") in the central Bering Sea. *Id.*

59. *Id.* at nn.71-73.

60. *Id.* at n.74. The former Soviet Union and the Republic of Korea have also expressed support for a broad-based organization.

61. *Id.* at 13 & n.85. The six states included Alaska, Washington, Oregon, California, Idaho, and Hawaii.

seas fisheries, form a multinational research organization, secure long-term commitments, and negotiate international agreements to prohibit illegally harvested salmon from entering commerce.

In the South Pacific, the political, economic, and diplomatic implications of the driftnet controversy were quite different from those in the North Pacific. Although the number of vessels using driftnets in the South Pacific was much smaller, the economic impact of driftnetting was actually greater because of the region's dependence on the tuna resources. The region was also politically distinct because of the existence of the South Pacific Forum, a political association made up of 13 developing island states, as well as Australia and New Zealand.[62] In order to represent its common interests, the forum established the Forum Fisheries Agency (FFA). The FFA has a limited ability to effectively handle the high seas driftnet problem largely because the FFA can primarily act only as a bargaining coalition. It lacks enforcement powers and has no means of collecting accurate scientific data.[63]

In July 1989, the heads of government of the South Pacific Forum issued the "Tarawa Declaration." In the declaration, the forum agreed to seek the establishment of a management regime for albacore tuna in the South Pacific "that would ban driftnet fishing from the region."[64] The declaration also called for a conference that would develop a convention to enforce the ban. This conference was hosted by New Zealand and resulted in the Convention for the Prohibition of Fishing with Long Driftnets in the South Pacific. The Convention area was defined broadly, including within it extensive high sea areas. However, because the Convention is confined to the coastal states of the region, only these states accept the obligation to "prohibit [their] nationals and vessels documented under [their] laws from engaging in driftnet fishing activities within the Convention Area."[65]

In Article 3(1) of the final act, the Convention listed measures which each party agreed to take against driftnet fishing activities. These measures included not to assist or encourage the use of driftnets within the Convention Area; and to take measures consistent with international law to restrict driftnet fishing activities within the Convention Area, including prohibiting the use of driftnets within areas under its fisheries jurisdiction; and prohib-

62. *See id.* The other members are the Cook Islands, the Federated States of Micronesia, Fiji, Kiribati, Nauru, Niue, Papua New Guinea, the Solomon Islands, Tonga, Tuvalu, Vanuatu, and Western Samoa.

63. *See id.* The FFA's most successful action was its conclusion of the Treaty on Fisheries between the Governments of Certain Pacific Island States and the Government of the United States of America concluded in 1987 and entered into force June 15, 1988. This was the first access agreement to include high seas as well as EEZ areas. The FFA has been working with Japan to negotiate a similar access agreement.

64. *See* The Proceedings of North Pacific Driftnet Conference, vol. 1 (Dept. of Fisheries and Oceans 1989), at 71-72.

65. Convention for the Prohibition of Fishing with Long Driftnets in the South Pacific, November 24, 1989, art. 2, *reprinted in* 29 I.L.M. 1449 (1990).

iting the transshipment of driftnet catches. Nothing in the Convention prevents a party from taking measures that are stricter than those required by the convention.[66]

On December 22, 1989, the UN General Assembly adopted a resolution on large-scale pelagic driftnet fishing.[67] The preamble to this resolution places a duty to cooperate globally and regionally in the conservation and management of living resources of the high seas and a "responsibility . . . to ensure the conservation and management of living marine resources and the protection and preservation of the living marine environment within their exclusive economic zones."

The operative part of the resolution, paragraph 3, calls upon all members of the international community to review the best available scientific data on the impacts of driftnet fishing and to "agree upon further cooperative regulation and monitoring measures, as needed," by no later than June 30, 1991.

Paragraph 4, perhaps the most important provision, contained three recommendations. The first was for all members of the international community to agree to a moratorium on all large-scale pelagic driftnet fishing by June 30, 1992.[68] The second recommendation was to take immediate action to reduce driftnetting activities by July 1, 1991. The last recommendation was addressed only to the North Pacific and is the most moderate. It calls for a cessation of further expansion of large-scale pelagic driftnet fishing on the high seas outside the Pacific Ocean. The United Nations General Assembly continued to recommend an international moratorium on large-scale pelagic driftnet fishing in resolutions in 1990, 1991, 1996, and 1997.

b. National Action

(i) United States Driftnet Act Amendments of 1990[69]

Congress's policy is that "the United States should implement the United Nations's moratorium, support the South Pacific Drift Net Conven-

66. *Id.* art. 3(3).

67. U.N. Doc. A/RES/44/225 (1989); For further discussion, *see* Ted McDorman, The GATT Consistency of U.S. Fish Import Embargoes to Stop Driftnet Fishing, and Save Whales, Dolphins and Turtles 24 Geo. Wash. J. Intl. L. & Econ. 477, 498 (1991); William T. Burke, Driftnets and Nodules; Where Goes the United States, 20 Ocean Dev. & Intl. L. 237, 238 (1989) (the general significance of the resolution is that the United States joined with other nations "to invoke the international machinery of the United Nations to recommend restrictions on the exercise of a fundamental right of all nations, that of fishing on the high seas.").

68. In addition to the UN action, several other international bodies have endorsed efforts to control driftnet fishing. Among these are the International Convention for the Conservation of Atlantic Tunas (25 member nations) and the International Whaling Commission. *See* Yearbook of International Law (1990).

69. 16 U.S.C. §1826 (1998).

tion, and secure a permanent ban on the use of high seas large-scale driftnets" (§107(c));[70] 16 U.S.C. §1826(c)(3). The secretary of commerce must report annually to Congress about all driftnet-related activities. In addition, the secretary must submit to Congress a list of nations diminish the effectiveness of any international driftnetting agreement to which the United States is a party. 16 U.S.C. §1826(e)(6). Any country listed will then be certified to the president and qualifies under the Pelly Amendment. *See* 16 U.S.C. §1826(f).

(ii) High Seas Driftnet Fisheries Enforcement Act[71]

This legislation was passed "to enhance the effectiveness of the UN international driftnet fishery conservation program." It would deny United States port privileges to any foreign driftnet fishing vessel and require the president to embargo all shellfish, fish, fish products, and sport fishing equipment from countries that do not comply with a UN-imposed moratorium on all large-scale driftnets.

Notes & Questions

1. *Marine Mammal Protection Act.* In addition to passing legislation to implement the UN moratorium, the United States also has taken unilateral measures to reduce dolphin kill rates through the enforcement of the Marine Mammal Protection Act (MMPA). Enforcement of the MMPA gave rise to a tuna-dolphin dispute between Mexico and the United States in 1990. GATT panels met on two occasions to assess the trade implications of the provisions of the MMPA, which bans the importation of yellowfin tuna cauught with high incidental dolphin kill rates, and found the primary and intermediary country embargoes against states that export yellowfin tuna and tuna products to the United States are inconsistent with GATT provisions. For a more detailed discussion of trade and the tuna-dolphin controversy, *see* Chapter 20.D.1.

2. *Addressing Driftnet Fishing.* If you were asked to draft a Convention on Driftnet Fishing, what would you include in the text and why? What problems do you foresee in turning the United Nations General Assembly resolution into a binding convention? Is there a need for a multilateral agreement, or should it be handled on a regional basis, as in the South Pacific?

70. *See* McDorman, *supra* footnote 67, at 500 and 16 U.S.C. §1826(c)(3).

71. Pub L. No. 102-582, 106 Stat. 4900 (1992) (codified in scattered sections of 16 U.S.C., 22 U.S.C., and 46 U.S.C.)

5. Migratory Species of Wild Animals

In 1972 at the Stockholm Conference on the Human Environment, countries recognized the need to conserve animals that migrate between countries or between areas of national jurisdiction and the sea. In 1979, states concluded the Bonn Convention on the Conservation of Migratory Species of Wild Animals (CMS), which became effective in 1983. As of July 1998, 55 countries from five continents were party to the Convention. As with CITES, the Convention operates by setting forth conservation obligations for species listed in two appendices: Appendix I for species that are in danger of extinction, and Appendix II for migratory species that have "an unfavorable conservation status or would benefit significantly from international cooperation." Under the Convention parties also agree to undertake joint research and monitoring activities.

Questions

How does this Convention intersect with CITES? What steps might be taken to ensure coordination between the two secretariats? Between the parties to the two conventions?

PART FOUR

TRADE AND FINANCE

Part IV addresses three issues that directly affect environmental protection and sustainable development: international trade law, transnational corporate environmental initiatives, and financial arrangements for environmental protection. The first two are addressed in chapter 20 and the last in chapter 21.

The international trade regime has important effects on both national and international efforts to protect human health and the environment. While countries party to GATT established a panel on the environment in 1979, the panel languished. Only since the late 1980s have countries and other actors begun to appreciate the importance of trade law on the envoronment. In 1991 for the first time the committees in the OECD addressing trade and environment issues met together to explore the linkages between the two fields. In November 1991, the GATT established a committee to address trade and environment issues met together to explore the linkages between the two fields. In November 1991, the GATT established a committee to address trade and environment issues. When the agreement establishing the World Trade Organization was concluded in 1994, it established a formal committee on trade and environmeent to pursue defined issues.

The environment and trade issues have proven to be very complex and not amenable to easy resolution. As of 1998, many fundamental questions (such as the relationship between international trade laws and multilateral enviromental agreements) remain unresolved. The two main trade agreements to which the United States is a party—the World Trade Organization (WTO) Agreement and the North American Free Trade Agree ment (NAFTA)—approach some of the related questions differently. The issues are expected to play out anew in the negotiations for a Free Trade Area of the Americas and in continued litigation in the WTO.

Increasingly, the private sector has become involved in negotiating interntional and transnational environmental codes of conduct and standards. Most of this activity has taken place since the United Nations Conference on Environment and Development in Rio de Janeiro, Brazil, in 1992. The Intenational Standards Organization's 14000 series, the European Union's Management Accounting Standards, and industry codes of conduct are important contributions to international environmental protection. Chapter 20 addresses these new developments.

The third set of issues in Part IV addresses the means of financing environmental protection and sustainable development. Some of these efforts, such as debt-for-nature swaps involve commercial banks. In other cases, multilateral development banks and binational initiatives, such as the Enterprise for America initiative, have significant roles. The World Bank (and regional development banks) critically affect the environment of developing countries through their lending programs. Chapter 21 addresses the legal issues raised by public and private financing of environmental protection and the efforts of the multilateral development banks to address environmental concerns in their lending programs. Financing sustainable development is the great challenge of the next century.

XX

Environment and Trade

Environmental protection and free trade are inherently linked. Measures to protect the environment often affect trade between countries; for example, protecting against pesticide-contaminated food may require regulating imports. Similarly, trade measures certainly affect environmental conditions; for example, trade disciplines place limits on what environmental protection measures are permissible, and trade may lead to the introduction of exotic species that alter local ecosystems, such as zebra mussels in the Great Lakes. Until recently, most discussions of trade and environmental issues have focused on facilitating freer trading relationships and on fitting environmental concerns into the framework of trade law. The traditional approach has been to identify trade issues raised by environmental measures, to assess their consistency with the General Agreement on Tariffs and Trade (GATT), and then to assess how the measures might be made consistent with GATT. Those concerned with environmental protection have criticized this approach as not giving sufficient weight to environmental concerns. The materials that follow are intended to introduce readers to some of the major environment-and-trade issues.

A. HISTORICAL INTRODUCTION

Modern international concern with trading relationships dates back to just after World War I. The first trade negotiations thereafter led to a 1927 agreement on abolishing import and export restrictions, which never came into effect. In 1929 countries faced a world depression, and in the 1930s national protectionism reigned, as exemplified by the U.S. Smoot-Hawley Tariff Act of 1930. After World War II, countries concerned with avoiding another world depression sought to create a regime that would promote free trade and squash protectionism. They tried to establish an International Trade Organization, but in the end settled in 1947 for the General Agreement on Tariffs and Trade (GATT), which eventually became the venerable framework for trading relationships. Only in 1994, after the end of the Cold War between the United States and the former Soviet Union, did countries successfully conclude a new World Trade Organization Agreement, which in fact includes several agreements and incorporates the GATT (now sometimes referred to as GATT 1994). Regional trade relationships had been created (e.g., the European Community in 1954 via the Treaty of Rome). Also, in the early 1990s Canada, Mexico, and the United States negotiated the North American Free Trade Agreement (NAFTA), an innovative regional trade agreement facilitating open and free trade among the three countries.

In contrast, countries were not as yet concerned in the immediate post-World War II period with environmental protection because they had not recognized their capacity to degrade the environment irreversibly on a large scale, except by using nuclear weapons. Rachel Carson's famous book, *The Silent Spring,* which promoted environmental consciousness in the United States and abroad, was published only in 1962. The first major piece of United States national environmental legislation, the National Environmental Policy Act, was enacted in 1969, and the United States Environmental Protection Agency was established only in 1971. Internationally, the picture is similar. In 1972 countries held the first United Nations conference concerned with environmental issues, which led directly to the formation of the United Nations Environment Programme. At the time there were only about three dozen multilateral environmental agreements concerned with the environment, and these included agreements primarily concerned with promoting use of living natural resources.

Unlike the trade area, where GATT has provided the basic law on tariffs and trade, there is no general international agreement on environmental and natural resource protection. Rather there are many separate legal instruments, some with overlapping provisions and each with a differing set of countries as parties. Thus, it is perhaps not surprising that the environment/trade debate has been focused on how environmental measures can fit into the one internationally accepted legal framework that exists—GATT, and now the WTO.

Beginning in 1991, the OECD recognized the need for the trade and the environment communities to talk to each other, and joint meetings of the OECD's committees on trade and on environment were initiated. The GATT also held in November 1991 the first meeting of its Working Group on Trade and Environment.

On April 14, 1994, parties to the GATT signed a Final Act embodying the results of the Uruguay Round of Multilateral Trade Negotiations at Marrakesh, Morocco. In this document, the Ministers decided "to direct the first meeting of the General Council of the WTO to establish a Committee on Trade and Environment open to all members of the WTO." The Committee was directed to address seven issues initially, as follows:

- the relationship between the provisions of the multilateral trading system and trade measures for environmental purposes, including those pursuant to multilateral environmental agreements;
- the relationship between environmental policies relevant to trade and environmental measures with significant trade effects and the provisions of the multilateral trading system;
- the relationship between the provisions of the multilateral trading system and
  - (a) charges and taxes for environmental purposes
  - (b) requirements for environmental purposes relating to products, including standards and technical regulations, packaging, labeling and recycling;
- the relationship between the provisions of the multilateral trading system with respect to the transparency of trade measures used for environmental purposes and environmental measures and requirements that have significant trade effects;
- the relationship between the dispute settlement mechanisms in the multilateral trading system and those found in multilateral environmental agreements;
- the effect of environmental measures on market access, especially in relation to developing countries, in particular to the least developed among them, and environmental benefits of removing trade restrictions and distortions;
- the issue of exports of domestically prohibited goods.

Little progress had been made as of June 1998.

Additional Readings

For general references generally on environment and trade issues, *see, e.g.*, Ernst-Ulrich Petersmann, International and European Trade and Environmental Law After the Uruguay Round (1995); Daniel C. Esty, Greening the GATT (1994); International Trade and the Environment (Patrick

Low, ed. 1992); Trade Environment and Competitiveness (John Kirton & Sarah Richardson, eds. 1992); 49 Wash. & Lee L. Rev. No. 4 (1992) (symposium on trade and the environment); Hillary F. French, Costly Tradeoffs: Reconciling Trade and the Environment (1993); Thomas Schoenbaum, International Trade and Protection of the Environment: The Continuing Search for Reconciliation, 91 Am. J. Intl. L. 268 (1997); Thomas Schoenbaum, Free International Trade and Protection of the Environment: Irreconcilable Conflict? 86 Am. J. Intl. L. 700 (1992); Edith Brown Weiss, Environment and Trade as Partners in Sustainable Development, 86 Am. J. Intl. L. 728 (1992); Jennifer Schultz, The GATT/WTO Committee on Trade and the Environment: Toward Environmental Reform, 89 Am. J. Intl. L. 423 (1995); Steve Charnovitz, Free Trade, Fair Trade, Green Trade: Defogging the Debate, 27 Cornell Intl. L.J. 459 (1994) (symposium); Robert C. Repetto, Trade and Sustainable Development (1994); C. Ford Runge, Freer Trade, Protected Environment: Balancing Trade Liberalization and Environmental Interests (1994); Trade and the Environment: Law, Economics, and Policy (Durwood Zaelke et al., eds. 1993); Asia Dragons and Green Trade (Simon S.C. Tay & Daniel C. Esty, eds. 1996); Robert Costanza, John Audley, Richard Borden, Paul Ekins, Carl Folke, Silvio O. Funtowicz, & Jonathan Harris, Sustainable Trade: A New Paradigm for World Welfare, 37 Environment 16 (June 1995).

B. DISPUTE SETTLEMENT IN THE WORLD TRADE ORGANIZATION[1]

The agreement establishing the World Trade Organization (WTO) brought important changes to the settlement of trade disputes. These changes are found in the Dispute Settlement Understanding (DSU), which is Annex 2 to the WTO agreement. The DSU is administered by the Dispute Settlement Body (DSB), which is basically the WTO Council. The importance of the DSU is reflected in Article III of the WTO Agreement, which states that a principal function of the WTO is administering the DSU. As a general matter, these changes were designed to increase the likelihood that disputes would be settled within the WTO and thereby to reduce the need for countries (such as the United States) to take unilateral measures to protect their rights.

There are up to ten steps in the full WTO dispute settlement process. The process starts with consultations between the parties to attempt to resolve their differences (Article 4.7). If these consultations are unsuccess-

1. The authors thank Richard Holbrook, Georgetown University Law Center, J.D. 1997, for his assistance with the dispute settlement section.

ful, parties may use the GATT conciliation or mediation services.[2] A party may also opt, however, to establish a panel to decide the dispute.[3] If parties opt to establish a panel, a panel is chosen[4] and terms of reference are decided.[5] The panel hears submissions by the disputing parties and other interested parties and issues a report.[6] Thereafter, the DSB must adopt the report unless there is a consensus against adoption.[7] If either of the disputing parties is dissatisfied with the results of panel decision, it may appeal the decision to the Appellate Body, which is composed of seven persons appointed for four-year terms, who serve in panels of three. Prior to the DSU, there was no Appellate Body. Appellate panels can only consider issues of law and legal interpretations developed by the original panel and must issue a report 60 to 90 days after hearing the submissions of the parties. Like the original panel, the report of the appellate panel is to be adopted automatically unless there is a consensus to the contrary, and the losing party must implement the recommendations and inform the DSB. The DSB monitors implementation and, in the event the recommendations are not implemented, may authorize the withdrawal of trade concessions.[8]

2. Article 5, DSU. Article 5 mentions the director-general of the WTO as one possible party who may provide good offices. These good offices may be used at the same time or in the alternative to the establishment of a panel.

3. Article 6.1. With the adoption of the WTO Agreement and the DSU, parties have the right to have a panel established unless there is a consensus of the DSB to the contrary.

4. Article 8.6 states that the secretariat of the WTO shall propose nominations for the membership of the panel. In the event that the parties are unable to agree who should sit on the panel, the WTO Director-General has the authority to appoint the panel by himself or herself, in consultation with the chairman of the DSB and the chairman of the relevant council or committee. Article 8.7. This change resolves a problem that sometimes arose under the GATT when a panel could not be established because the parties were unable to agree on its composition.

Panel members should be "well-qualified governmental and/or nongovernmental individuals, including persons who have served on or presented a case to a panel . . . or in the Secretariat, taught or published on international trade law or policy." Article 8.1.

5. Article 7. These terms of reference set forth what the panel is expected to decide. Under the DSU, terms of reference are standardized unless there is a consensus to the contrary. Article 7.1. Standardization of terms of reference removes the possibility for a party to delay the proceedings by disputing the terms of reference.

6. Third parties who have a "substantial interest" in a matter before a panel who have notified the DSB may intervene, but may only present issues raised by the parties. Article 10.1. Only third parties that are WTO members may so intervene, which, as discussed below, limits the opportunity for NGO's to present their opinions to panels. This limitation is further enhanced by the fact that panel proceedings are not public. In addition, under the DSU, a panel may also consult with a panel of experts either to assist in forming its opinion or to receive information on a technical matter raised by one of the parties. Article 13.

7. Under previous practice, a panel report could be adopted only by consensus, which meant that any party, even the losing party, could block implementation of the report. As described below, this was one of the most significant departures from previous parctice found in the DSU.

8. Article 22.1. The injured party may seek compensation or suspend trade concessions previously made to the offending party. Under previous practice, the GATT was entitled to authorize parties to suspend concessions, but as a matter of actual practice, the GATT only granted this authorization once. The DSU now automatically authorizes suspension of trading concessions unless there is a consensus to the contrary. Article 22.6. However, withdrawal of a nonconforming measure is preferred to compensation or suspension of trading concessions.

The new WTO dispute settlement process differs markedly from the GATT dispute settlement process. The GATT process offered multiple opportunities for parties to delay or prevent decisions. For example, prior to 1989, there was no right to have a panel established; the right was not completely clarified until the DSU came into effect. A party could also delay decisions by disputing composition of a panel and its terms of reference.

Most importantly, any party, even the losing party, could block adoption of a panel report. On the one hand, this led some countries, principally the United States, that were frustrated with inability to force compliance with a report to take action unilaterally. The United States usually acted under Section 301 of the Trade Act of 1974, as amended,[9] which was a source of intense friction with the United States's trading partners, who viewed the law as a heavy-handed means to allow the United States to enforce its will on them. On the other hand, the ability to block adoption of a panel report allowed countries to blunt the effect of panel reports they did not like, such as the tuna-dolphin reports (discussed in Section D, below). Under the DSU, panel reports will be adopted unless there is a consensus to the contrary; but in return, WTO members are required by Article 23.1 to use the DSU process exclusively if they "seek the redress of a violation of obligations or other nullification or impairment of benefits under the covered agreements."

Even though the DSU dramatically strengthened the WTO dispute resolution process, it has not resolved all problems with the process. Environmentalists have made three related complaints about the process.[10] First, although the DSU gives third parties who have a "substantial interest" in a dispute the right to make a presentation to the deciding panel, this right is extended only to WTO members. As a result, environmental groups are unable to present their views directly to a dispute resolution panel and can participate only indirectly by lobbying trade officials of their country to present their view.[11] Second, proceedings of panels are secret. Thus, the public is able to learn what is happening in the panel proceedings only if informed by an official of a party to the dispute or through leaks to the media. Third, and perhaps most importantly, panels are composed of trade experts, not environmental or scientific experts, with the result that needed expertise and perspective are missing, and so, the environmentalists argue, the decisions are flawed. The WTO Agreement provides for the use of subgroups of scientific experts, but the decisionmaking power still lies with the members of the panels.

Environmentalists are not the only group in the United States con-

9. Pub. L. No. 93-618 (Jan. 3, 1975), 19 U.S.C. §§2101-2487, 88 Stat. 1978.

10. *See, e.g.,* Daniel C. Esty, Greening the GATT (1994); Steve Charnovitz, The Environment vs. Trade Rules: Defogging the Debate, 23 Envtl. L. 475 (1993).

11. This procedure differs from that of the United States, where environmental groups may be able to submit *amici curae* briefs to courts hearing a case or intervene, either permissively or of right.

cerned about the DSU. Many conservatives have been afraid that the DSU will transfer United States sovereignty to the WTO. As a result, in order to secure United States participation in the WTO, President Clinton made a number of concessions to Congress, which are found in the statute implementing the WTO Agreement and the Statement of Administrative Action submitted by President Clinton to Congress. Key requirements include reporting and congressional consultation (to the House Ways and Means and Senate Finance Committees) concerning WTO decisionmaking and dispute settlement, five-year reviews of United States participation in the WTO, and support for consensus-based resolution of dispute.[12] More importantly, the implementing act establishes a three-judge panel to review all cases that the United States loses; in the event that the United States loses three or more cases, the panel is to decide whether to recommend continued United States participation in the WTO.

C. DOMESTIC ENVIRONMENTAL MEASURES

Most of the environmentally related disputes that have come before the GATT and now the WTO have involved domestic laws ostensibly directed to protecting the national environment. These have usually involved issues of consistency with the following GATT/WTO provisions: Article I (requirement of unconditional most favored nation treatment), Article III (requirement of national treatment of so-called like products), Article XI (prohibition of import restraints), and Article XX (b) and (g) (exceptions that apply should a violation of a GATT article occur). As Frieder Roessler has explained for Article I, "its fundamental function is to ensure that each contracting party accord access to its markets independently of *any* of the policies of the trading partner, including domestic policies." Frieder Roessler, Diverging Domestic Policies and Multilateral Trade Integration, 2 Fair Trade and Harmonization 21, 31 (J. Bhagwati & R. Hudec, eds. 1996). The relevant parts of Articles I, III, XI, and XX follow. Article XXI is also included.

The General Agreement on Tariff's and Trade 1994 Excerpts

ARTICLE I: GENERAL MOST-FAVOURED NATION TREATMENT

1. With respect to customs duties and charges of any kind imposed on or in connection with importation or exportation or imposed on the international transfer of payments for imports or exports, and with respect to the method of levying such duties and charges, and with respect to all rules and formalities in connection with importation and exportation, and with respect to all

12. Uruguay Round Agreements Act, §§124-127 (1994).

matters referred to in paragraphs 2 and 4 of Article III, any advantage, favour, privilege or immunity granted by any contracting party to any product originating in or destined for any other country shall be accorded immeditely and unconditionally to the like product originating in or destined for the territories of all other contracting parties. . . .

ARTICLE III: NATIONAL TREATMENT ON INTERNAL TAXATION AND REGULATION . . .

4. The products of the territory of any contracting party imported into the territory of any other contracting party shall be accorded treatment no less favourable than that accorded to like products of national origin in respect of all laws, regulations, and requirements affecting their internal sale, offering for sale, purchase, transportation, distribution or use. The provisions of this paragraph shall not prevent the application of differential internal transportation charges which are based exclusively on the economic operation of the means of transport and not on the nationality of the product.

ARTICLE XI: GENERAL ELIMINATION OF QUANTITATIVE RESTRICTIONS

1. No prohibitions or restrictions other than duties, taxes or other charges, whether made effective through quotas, import or export licenses or other measures, shall be instituted or maintained by any contracting party on the importation of any product of the territory of any other contracting party or on the exportation or sale for export of any product destined for the territory of any other contracting party. . . .

ARTICLE XX: GENERAL EXCEPTIONS

Subject to the requirement that such measures are not applied in a manner which would constitute a means of arbitrary or unjustifiable discrimination between countries where the same conditions prevail, or a disguised restriction on international trade, nothing in this Agreement shall be construed to prevent the adoption or enforcement by any contracting party of measures:

(a) necessary to protect public morals;
(b) necessary to protect human, animal or plant life or health;
(c) relating to the importations or exportations of gold or silver; . . .
(e) relating to the products of prison labour;
(f) imposed for the protection of national treasures of artistic, historic or archaeological value;
(g) relating to the conservation of exhaustible natural resources if such measures are made effective in conjunction with restriction on domestic production or consumption; . . .

ARTICLE XXI: SECURITY EXCEPTIONS

Nothing in this Agreement shall be construed

(a) to require any contracting party to furnish any information the disclosure of which it considers contrary to its essential security interests; or

(b) to prevent any contracting party from taking such action which it considers necessary for the protection of its essential security interests
  (i) relating to fissionable materials or the materials from which they are derived;
  (ii) relating to the traffic in arms, ammunitions and implements of war and to such traffic in other goods and materials as is carried on directly or indirectly for the purpose of supplying a military establishment;
  (iii) taken in time of war or other emergency in international relations; or
(c) to prevent any contracting party from taking any action in pursuance of its obligations under the United Nations Charter for the maintenance of international pease and security.

The materials presented here start with the Thai Cigarette Case, decided before the WTO was formed, and then look at the Beef Hormones Case (appellate report) decided after the WTO was concluded. Both address the issue of the compatibility of national regulations ostensibly directed to protecting domestic environmental health with the GATT/WTO. The issue of when the implementation of domestic environmental protection measures may conflict with the GATT/WTO is then considered in the context of the Reformulated Gasoline Case, the first dispute considered under the WTO dispute settlement procedures.

1. *The Thai Cigarette Case*

Thailand, Restrictions on Importation and Internal Taxes on Cigarettes, Report of the Panel adopted November 7, 1990.

In this dispute between the United States and Thailand, the Royal Thai Government enacted restrictions on imports of and internal taxes on cigarettes, under which all imports required a license. No license had been granted within the last decade. Thailand justified its import restrictions on grounds of public health, noting that the restrictions were to protect the public from harmful ingredients in imported cigarettes and to reduce the consumption of cigarettes in Thailand. Domestic cigarettes continued to be for sale. The United States contended that the import ban was in fact a protectionist measure directed to promoting local tobacco companies, in violation of GATT Article XI:1. The panel agreed but noted that a nondiscriminatory regulation requiring complete disclosure of ingredients, coupled with a ban on unhealthy substances, would be an alternative that would be consistent with the GATT.

In another important aspect of the case, the panel suggested that a ban on advertising of all cigarettes, both domestic and imported, would be consistent with the GATT. The United States tobacco companies contended that a ban on advertising would make it much more difficult for new, foreign suppliers to sell cigarettes within the country, even if imports were permitted. The panel noted that even if this argument were accepted, "such an inconsistency would have to be regarded as unavoidable and therefore necessary within the meaning of Article XX (b), because additional advertising rights would risk stimulating demand for cigarettes."(Panel report, para. 78).

Notes and Questions

1. Suppose that it could be shown that United States cigarettes contained much higher levels of nicotine than locally produced cigarettes and that these levels were intended to induce addiction, particularly in young people. Could a panel find the measure consistent with the GATT? Would the foreign cigarettes still be considered a "like product" for purposes of the national treatment required by Article III of the GATT? If so, would Article XX save the day? For an interesting and potentially important analysis of "like products," *see* the Euromotors case (also called the CAFE Standards case), brought under the GATT by the EC against the United States and decided in 1993.

2. In Canada, there has been a proposal to require plain packaging of all cigarettes sold in Canada. The proposed package would be white with only the brand name written in black letters on the package. Would such a measure be consistent with the GATT/WTO?

2. The Beef Hormones Case

In the WTO Beef Hormones Case, the United States and Canada lodged complaints in 1996 against the European Community (EC) on the ground that the EC prohibition on importing meat and meat products derived from cattle to which specific natural and synthetic hormones had been administered to promote growth violated one of the WTO agreements, viz. the Agreement on the Application of Sanitary and Phytosanitary Measures (the SPS Agreement). The 1997 panel report held against the EC on the grounds that a country could adopt a higher standard than the international standard but only in an exceptional case, that there was insufficient scientific basis for an exception here, and that the application of the SPS measure constituted a disguised restriction on trade because the EC accepted certain natural hormones but prohibited synthetic ones that had the same effect. The Appellate Body reversed some of the findings of the panel, although it ultimately found in favor of the United States.[13] Most importantly, the

13. World Trade Organization Appellate Body, EC Measures Concerning Meat and Meat Products (Hormones), WT/DS26/AB/R, WT/DS48/AB/R, 1998.

Appellate Body said that the right of a party (in this case the EC) to establish a higher standard was a basic rule, not an exception, and rejected the Panel's assessment of the scientific risk by noting that the issue was whether there was any scientific evidence to serve as a rational basis for the prohibition. This potentially provides broad latitude to states to adopt environmental measures that may be more environmentally protective than relevant international standards.

3. The Reformulated Gasoline Case

On January 17, 1996, the first panel decision was handed down by a WTO dispute resolution panel in a dispute between the United States and Venezuela/Brazil, which involved implementation of the U.S. Clean Air Act. The panel continued a trend of previous GATT panels in rejecting environmental justifications for laws that expressly discriminate between foreign and domestic producers to the disadvantage of the former, a position the Appellate Body upheld. However, in one sense the report of the Appellate Body was environmentally friendly in that it strengthened the hand of environmentalists against the protectionist interests of domestic producers who pressured Congress to require the discriminatory measures.

The dispute began in 1990 when Congress amended the Clean Air Act to instruct the United States Environmental Protection Agency (EPA) to issue regulations reducing vehicle emissions caused by gasoline.[14] The EPA subsequently promulgated regulations in December 1993 that tied gasoline emissions to the emission levels in effect in 1990. Conventional gasoline could have emission levels no higher than those in 1990. Reformulated gasoline had to reduce toxic air pollutants and volatile organic compounds by 15 percent compared with 1990 levels and have corresponding NOx emission levels no higher than those of 1990.

The problem in this case arose over how to determine the baselines for the reduction in air pollutants for reformulated gas. Domestic refineries that were in existence prior to 1990 could use one of several methods to determine their baseline, including an "individual baseline" derived from refinery specific data. In contrast, United States refineries built after 1990 and all foreign refineries were required to use a statutory baseline. This statutory baseline in some circumstances was more disadvantageous than the baselines used by domestic refineries. The EPA justified this discriminatory treatment of foreign refineries by arguing that there might be insufficient reliable information to determine the baseline for individual foreign refineries.

After the regulation was implemented in December 1993, Venezuela strongly protested the disparate treatment of domestic and foreign refiner-

14. Pub. L. No. 101-549 (1990).

ies and threatened to bring a complaint under the GATT (which was still in effect at that time). Instigation of a GATT action was avoided when the United States and Venezuela concluded an agreement in 1994 under which Venezuela dropped the action in return for the EPA's altering its regulations. The EPA then issued proposed regulations that would have permitted foreign refineries to use individual baselines. However, domestic oil producers joined with some United States environmental groups and successfully persuaded Congress to prevent the EPA from implementing the proposed regulations.[15] Following continued United States inaction, Venezuela (later joined by Brazil) brought an action in the WTO (which had by then gone into effect) in January 1995.

Venezuela's main allegation was that the EPA regulation violated Article III:4 of the GATT,[16] which states that imported products "shall be accorded treatment no less favorable than that accorded to like products of national origin in respect of all laws, regulations, and requirements affecting their internal sale." There are two key elements to finding a violation of Article III:4. The products in question must be "like" products and the imported product must be treated less favorably than the domestic product. The panel found that imported gas and domestic gas were "like" products and that by not giving foreign refineries the chance to use an individual baseline, the EPA regulation treated importers less favorably than domestic producers, and hence violated Article III:4.

The United States had argued that importers were not in fact treated less favorably because while some refineries were disadvantaged by use of the statutory baseline, other refineries were helped. However, the panel rejected this argument, stating that favorable treatment of some importers could not be used to counterbalance unfavorable treatment of other importers. Further, the United States contended that the EPA regulation only applied to annual shipments by refineries, so any particular shipment did not have to meet the baseline. However, the panel concluded that the EPA regulation nevertheless created a more favorable sales condition for domestic gasoline than for imported gasoline.

In addition to rejecting United States defenses to Venezuela's charges under Article III, the panel also rejected United States defenses based on Article XX(b) and (g) exceptions. Article XX(b) provides an exception for measures "necessary to protect human, animal or plant life or health." The panel agreed that the Clean Air Act fit within the general scope of Article XX(b) but said that the United States had not established that there was no "reasonably available" alternative measure that was consistent with GATT rules or less inconsistent with GATT rules. In particular, although the EPA claimed that it would be feasible neither to determine the refinery of origin for imported gasoline nor to compile enough information to

15. 108 Stat. 2322 (1994).

16. Although the WTO has replaced the GATT, the GATT rules have been absorbed into the WTO structure, and the GATT is referred to as GATT 1994.

create an individual baseline, the panel disagreed with these arguments. Instead, the panel suggested that the EPA could have given foreign refineries the chance to compile enough information to establish an individual baseline and apply the statutory baseline only in the event the refinery was unable to establish enough information.

The panel also rejected the United States' defense based on Article XX(g) and appeared to incorporate a "necessity" test into the article. Article XX(g) provides an exception for measures "relating to conservation of exhaustible natural resources if such measures are made effective in conjunction with restrictions on domestic production or consumption." According to previous GATT jurisprudence, for a measure to be "related" to the conservation of an exhaustible natural resource, it must be "primarily aimed" at such conservation. The panel recognized that clean air is an exhaustible natural resource. However, in determining whether the EPA regulation was "primarily aimed" at conservation, the panel did not examine the intent behind the whole statute but seemed to ask whether the "precise aspects" of the parts of the Act that violated Article III were necessary to achieve conservation. The panel determined that since the EPA could have implemented equivalent measures in a form that would have been consistent with Article III, the Article XX(g) exception did not apply. On appeal to the Appellate Body, the Appellate Body upheld the panel concerning Article XX(g) but rejected the implication that Article XX(g) contains a necessity test.

Note that the logical sequence of the legal argument is that first a violation of a provision of the WTO must be found and only then are the Article XX exceptions relevant.

The Reformulated Gasoline Case is especially noteworthy because the WTO dispute settlement bodies based their reports not on the characteristics of the product but on the treatment accorded to the producers of the product, namely the methods by which they were permitted to calculate their baselines for the reduction in air pollutants for reformulated gasoline.

Question

Can you argue that this case begins to lay a basis (if inadvertently) for finding that regulations based on the process by which products are produced could be consistent with the GATT/WTO? Why or why not?

D. UNILATERAL MEASURES TO PROTECT RESOURCES OUTSIDE NATIONAL BORDERS

As evidenced by the preceding materials, one of the major conflicts facing the environment and trade communities is the consistency with the

WTO Agreement (including GATT) of unilateral national measures to protect the environment. With the measures may have several characteristics, each of which raises different consistency issues: measures directed to products; measures targeting the process by which products are produced (so-called process and production methods or PPMs); and national measures targeting natural resources and environmental conditions located outside national boundaries. The following case study on the tuna-dolphin dispute raises these issues in the context of protecting resources outside national borders. As you read the material, consider what arguments you would marshall in support of the United States's measures to protect dolphins.

1. *The Tuna-Dolphin Controversy*

a. United States Actions and Court Decisions

■ EARTH ISLAND INSTITUTE v. MOSBACHER

329 F.2d 1449 (9th Cir. 1991)

Before SCHROEDER, CANBY, and NOONAN, Circuit Judges

SCHROEDER, Circuit Judge:

The government appeals from a preliminary injunction entered October 19, 1990, which enjoined the importation of yellowfin tuna from Mexico. The plaintiffs who sought the injunction are the Earth Island Institute, the Marine Mammal Protection Fund and David Brower, environmentalist (collectively termed "Earth Island"), all concerned with the enforcement of the Marine Mammal Protection Act ("MMPA" or "Act"). Congress amended the MMPA in 1988 to enhance protections for dolphins that were being killed in large numbers as a result of tuna fishing. *See* 16 U.S.C. §§ 1361-1401; *Caribbean Marine Servs. Co. v. Baldridge*, 844 F.2d 668, 670 (9th Cir. 1988). The district court granted the injunction because it concluded that the Secretary of Commerce had not made a positive finding, as required by the Act, that Mexico had met the applicable standards regarding the incidental killing of dolphins. We affirm.

Congress enacted the MMPA in 1972 to address, among other problems, the tremendous number of dolphins killed by the purse seine method of fishing for yellowfin tuna in the eastern tropical Pacific Ocean. For unknown reasons, yellowfin tuna swim below schools of dolphins in that area. Thus, fishing vessels often set their purse seine nets on dolphins to catch the tuna below. The dolphins are frequently killed or maimed in this process. In the early 1970s, the United States fishing fleet was responsible for the slaughter of over 300,000 dolphins annually. 134 Cong. Rec. S. 16336, 16344-45 (1988).

Although the Act brought about a material reduction in the number of dolphins killed by the United States fleet, dolphin slaughter by foreign nations remained a growing problem. By amendments to the Act in 1984 and 1988, Congress enacted specific standards intended to ensure that foreign tuna fishing fleets would reduce the number of dolphins killed and to protect certain endangered subspecies of dolphins. Such subspecies included the eastern spinner dolphin which is the subject of this lawsuit. The weapon Congress chose to bring about such reductions in killings was a mandatory embargo on the importation of yellowfin tuna to be imposed upon those countries whose fleets failed to meet the standards Congress established.

The statute mandates the Secretary of the Treasury to ban imports of yellowfin tuna products from a foreign nation until the Secretary of Commerce certifies that the nation's incidental kill rate of dolphins is comparable to that of the United States. The statute specifies that the total incidental kill rate of a foreign nation shall not be found comparable unless it is no more than 2.0 times the total incidental kill rate of the United States fleet. 16 U.S.C. § 1371(a)(2)(B)(ii)(III).

This dispute arises from a NMFS regulation promulgated March 26, 1990. This regulation provides that foreign countries must supply data to the NMFS by July 31 of each year regarding the number of dolphins killed during the previous calendar year. Thus, on July 31, 1990, data was due for 1989. 50 C.F.R. § 216.24(e)(5)(iv). The controversial portion of the regulation is the further provision that if a foreign nation has exceeded the limitations for a given year, and therefore remains under the embargo, the Secretary may nevertheless "reconsider" the embargo and certify compliance with the statute's provisions based upon data for only the first six months following the year the limits were exceeded.

1. The regulation states:

> The Assistant Administrator may reconsider a finding upon a request from and the submission of additional information by the harvesting nation, if the information indicates that the nation has met the requirements. . . . [T]he additional information must include data collected by an acceptable observer program which demonstrate that the nation's fleet marine mammal mortality rate improved to the acceptable level during the period including at a minimum January 1 through June 30 of the year following the year in which the nation's mortality rate was found to exceed acceptable levels.

50 C.F.R. § 216.24(e)(5)(viii), 53 Fed. Reg. 11.929 (Mar. 30, 1990).

On September 17, 1990, Earth Island applied for a temporary restraining order banning the import of yellowfin tuna from Mexico. Earth Island argued that NMFS had already found that Mexico had violated the eastern spinner kill comparability requirements for 1989, and that, under the plain language of the statute, the comparability finding for the eastern spinner dolphin limit must be based on an entire year of data.

On October 4, 1990, the district court granted the TRO. The district court held that the regulation allowing "reconsideration" of the 1989 embargo based on only six months of 1990 data violated the language and purpose of the statute and was thus beyond the agency's authority. The district court held that a year's data was required by the clear language of subsection III: "The Secretary of the Treasury *shall ban* the importation of . . . yellowfin tuna . . . *unless* . . . the total number of eastern spinner dolphin (Stenella longisrotris) incidentally taken by vessels of the harvesting nation during the *1989* and subsequent *fishing seasons* does not exceed 15 percent of the total number of all marine mammals incidentally taken by such vessels in *such year.*" Since the comparability finding for eastern spinner dolphins must be based on an entire year of data, and the limit was exceeded for 1989, the most recent year for which data were available, the court concluded that the embargo required by the 1989 data had to remain in effect until an evaluation of the data for all of 1990 demonstrated that the kills fell within the tolerated limits established by Congress.

On October 19, 1990, the court, at the government's request, converted the TRO into a preliminary injunction, and the government filed this appeal. The government challenges the district court's order on several grounds. The questions presented are essentially questions of law involving interpretation of the MMPA. Because we see no basis for overturning the district court's ruling, we affirm.

The government's primary argument is that the six-month "reconsideration" provision is within the discretion delegated by Congress to the agency for regulatory implementation of the Act. The government points to the deference the courts owe to agencies in matters of statutory interpretation. *See, e.g., Chevron,* 467 U.S. at 844, 104 S. Ct. at 2782.

The only textual support that the government advances for its position is the absence of any specific prohibition of "reconsideration" upon less than one year's data. The government argues that the lack of any explicit prohibition allows the agency to adopt an interpretation of the MMPA which permits such reconsideration. We reject this argument because the statute does require findings to be based on a full year's data. . . .

As the district court recognized, the language of the statute is clear: it requires an embargo unless "the total number of eastern spinner dolphins (Stenella longirostria) incidentally taken by vessels of the harvesting nation *during the 1989 and subsequent fishing seasons* does not exceed 15 percent of the total number of all marine mammals incidentally taken by such vessels *in such year.*" 16 U.S.C. § 1371(a)(2)(B)(ii)(III) (emphasis added); *see also* Marine Mammal Protection Act Amendments of 1988, S. Rep. No. 592, 100th Cong., 2d Sess. 6 (1988) [hereinafter S. Rep. No. 100-592] (referring to "annual quota" of dolphins killed). In the face of such a clear directive, the regulation in question is invalid.

The government also suggests that regardless of the language used in the statute, the reconsideration provision should be upheld as a matter of policy because it offers an incentive to foreign countries to speed up their efforts to meet the statutory standards. The record in this case belies the existence of any incentive effect. The record demonstrates that the six-month reconsideration allows foreign nations and NMFS to withhold the release of negative findings until they have available a subsequent set of positive findings, as occurred with the 1989-90 data for Mexico. The result in this case was that Mexico, which had exceeded MMPA standards for an entire year, was subject to embargo for less than one day. Under this regulation, foreign nations could thus continually exceed the MMPA limits for part of each year, yet never be subject to the ban. Because the reconsideration regulation creates such a potential for abuse, and has in fact already been used to circumvent the intent of Congress, we reject the government's argument that the reconsideration regulation offers a more effective incentive to foreign countries to reduce dolphin kill rates.

The agency's contention that it seeks only to provide additional incentives consistent with Congress' intent is further belied by the agency's own record of non-enforcement of congressional directives during the years which preceded the 1988 amendments. In enacting those amendments, Congress expressed its concern that the NMFS was not holding foreign vessels to U.S. dolphin protection standards. The agency's lax record of promulgating and enforcing standards for foreign fleets was alluded to repeatedly in the legislative history. The Senate Committee on Commerce, Science & Transportation pointed out that "[w]hile the U.S. industry has made dramatic improvements since enactment of the MMPA, unregulated tuna fleets of foreign nations now present a far more serious source of porpoise mortality." S. Rep. 100-592 at 7. The Senate Committee also stated:

> While the Committee is disappointed that the interim final regulations implementing the 1984 comparability amendments to the Act were issued only recently, it expects that these new amendments will be incorporated into the final regulations immediately. Recognizing that the foreign fleets harvest 60 percent of the yellowfin tuna in the [eastern Tropical Pacific] but kill 80 percent of the porpoise, the Committee intends these new requirements to reduce the foreign take of marine mammals, similar to those reductions made by the U.S. fleet.

100 S. Rep. 100-592 at 25. Individual members of Congress were more severe in their criticism of NMFS' performance. Senator Hollings, referring to the 1984 amendments, said "[T]he national marine fisheries service has failed to implement these requirements adequately." 134 Cong. Rec. S. 16336, 16344 (1988). According to Senator Adams, "[T]he administration has been inexcusably lax in implementing these laws." *Id.* at 16341. There is no basis in the history of the enforcement of the Act for us to conclude that the agency's policies are aimed at more stringent enforcement of Congressional policy.

Because the government's position is at odds with both the language and the purpose of the MMPA, and the agency's intended role under it, we affirm the district court's order of October 4.

AFFIRMED.

b. The First GATT Tuna/Dolphin Panel Report (Tuna-Dolphin I)

■ GENERAL AGREEMENT ON TARIFFS AND TRADE, *UNITED STATES—RESTRICTIONS ON IMPORTS OF TUNA, REPORT OF THE PANEL*

Sept. 3, 1991

1. Introduction

1.1. On 5 November 1990, Mexico requested consultations with the United States concerning restrictions on imports of tuna. These consultations were held on 19 December 1990. On 25 January 1991 Mexico requested the CONTRACTING PARTIES to establish a panel under Article XXIII:2 to examine the matter as the sixty-day period for consultations had expired without a mutually satisfactory adjustment having been reached. On 6 February 1991 the Council agreed to establish the Panel.

. . .

3. Prohibition of Imports of Certain Yellowfin Tuna and Certain Yellowfin Tuna Products from Mexico Categorization as Internal Regulations (Article III) or Quantitative Restrictions (Article XI) . . .

5.8. The Panel noted that Mexico had argued that the measures prohibiting imports of certain yellowfin tuna and yellowfin tuna products from Mexico imposed by the United States were quantitative restrictions on importation under Article III:A and the Note Ad Article III, namely that the prohibition of imports of tuna and tuna products from Mexico constituted an enforcement of the regulations of the MMPA relating to the harvesting of domestic tuna. . . .

5.14. The Panel concluded from the above considerations that the Note Ad Article III covers only those measures that are applied to the product as such. The Panel noted that the MMPA regulates the domestic harvesting of yellowfin tuna to reduce the incidental taking of dolphin, but that these regulations could not be regarded as being applied to tuna products as such because they would not directly regulate the sale of tuna and could not possibly affect tuna as a product. Therefore, the Panel found that the import prohibition on certain yellowfin tuna and certain yellowfin tuna products of Mexico and the provisions of the MMPA under which it is imposed did not constitute internal regulations covered by the Note Ad Article III.

5.15. The Panel further concluded that, even if the provisions of the MMPA enforcing the tuna harvesting regulations (in particular those providing for the seizure of cargo as a penalty for violation of the Act) were regarded as regulating the sale of tuna as a product, the United States import prohibition would not meet the requirements of Article III. As pointed out in paragraph 5.12 above, Article III:A calls for a comparison of the treatment of imported tuna *as a product* with that of domestic tuna *as a product.* Regulations governing the taking of dolphins incidental to the taking of tuna could not possibly affect tuna as a product. [The Panel then found that the ban on Mexican tuna was an import prohibition violating Art. XI.] . . .

ARTICLE XX

General

5.22. The Panel noted that the United States had argued that its direct embargo under the MMPA could be justified under Article XX(b) or Article XX(g), and that Mexico had argued that a contracting party could not simultaneously argue that a measure is compatible with the general rules of the General Agreement and invoke Article XX for that measure. The Panel recalled that previous panels had established that Article XX is a limited and conditional exception from obligations under other provisions of the General Agreement, and not a positive rule establishing obligations in itself. Therefore, the practice of panels has been to interpret Article XX narrowly, to place the burden on the party invoking Article XX to justify its invocation, and not to examine Article XX exceptions unless invoked. Nevertheless, the Panel considered that a party to a dispute could argue in the alternative that Article XX might apply, without this argument constituting *ipso facto* an admission that the measures in question would otherwise be inconsistent with the General Agreement. Indeed, the efficient operation of the dispute settlement process required that such arguments in the alternative be possible.

5.23. The Panel proceeded to examine whether Article XX(b) or Article XX(g) could justify the MMPA provisions on imports of certain yellowfin tuna and yellowfin tuna products, and the import ban imposed under these provisions. The Panel noted that Article XX provides that:

> Subject to the requirement that such measures are not applied in a manner which would constitute a means of arbitrary or unjustifiable discrimination between countries where the same conditions prevail, or a disguised restriction on international trade, nothing in this Agreement shall be construed to prevent the adoption or enforcement by any contracting party of measures . . .

(b) necessary to protect human, animal or plant life or health; . . .

(g) relating to the conservation of exhaustible natural resources if such measures are made effective in conjunction with restrictions on domestic production or consumption; . . .

ARTICLE XX(b)

5.24. The Panel noted that the United States considered the prohibition of imports of certain yellowfin tuna and certain yellowfin tuna products from Mexico, and the provisions of the MMPA on which this prohibition is based, to be justified by Article XX(b) because they served solely the purpose of protecting dolphin life and health and were 'necessary' within the meaning of that provision because, in respect of the protection of dolphin life and health outside its jurisdiction, there was no alternative measure reasonably available to the United States to achieve this objective. Mexico considered that Article XX(b) was not applicable to a measure imposed to protect the life or health of animals outside the jurisdiction of the contracting party taking it and that the import prohibition imposed by the United States was not necessary because alternative means consistent with the General Agreement were available to it to protect dolphin lives or health, namely international co-operation between the countries concerned.

5.25. The Panel noted that the basic question raised by these arguments, namely whether Article XX(b) covers measures necessary to protect human, animal or plant life or health outside the jurisdiction of the contracting party taking the measure, is not clearly answered by the text of that provision. It refers to life and health protection generally without expressly limiting that protection to the jurisdiction of the contracting party concerned. The Panel therefore decided to analyze this issue in the light of the drafting history of Article XX(b), the purpose of this provision, and the consequences that the interpretations proposed by the parties would have for the operation of the General Agreement as a whole. . . .

5.27. The Panel further noted that Article XX(b) allows each contracting party to set its human, animal or plant life or health standards. The conditions set out in Article XX(b) which limit resort to this exception, namely that the measure taken must be 'necessary' and not 'constitute a means of arbitrary or unjustifiable discrimination or a disguised restriction on international trade', refer to the trade measure requiring justification under Article XX(b), not however to the life or health standard chosen by the contracting party. The Panel recalled the finding of a previous panel that this paragraph of Article XX was intended to allow contracting parties to impose trade restrictive measures inconsistent with the General Agreement to pursue overriding public policy goals to the extent that such inconsistencies were unavoidable. The Panel considered that if the broad interpretation of Article XX(b) suggested by the United States were accepted, each contracting party could unilaterally determine the life or health protection policies from which other contracting parties could not deviate without jeopardizing their rights under the General Agreement. The General Agreement would then no longer constitute a multilateral framework for trade among all contracting parties but would provide legal security only in respect of trade between a limited number of contracting parties with identical internal regulations.

5.28. The Panel considered that the United States' measures, even if Article XX(b) were interpreted to permit extrajurisdictional protection of life and health, would not meet the requirement of necessity set out in that provision. The United States had not demonstrated to the Panel—as required of the party invoking an Article XX exception—that it had exhausted all options reasonably available to it to pursue its dolphin protection objectives through measures consistent with the General Agreement, in particular through the negotiation of international cooperative arrangements, which would seem to be desirable in view of the fact that dolphins roam the waters of many states and the high seas. Moreover, even assuming that an import prohibition were the only resort reasonably available to the United States, the particular measure chosen by the United States could in the Panel's view not be considered to be necessary within the meaning of Article XX(b). The United States linked the maximum incidental dolphin taking rate which Mexico had to meet during a particular period in order to be able to export tuna to the United States to the taking rate actually recorded for United States fishermen during the same period. Consequently, the Mexican authorities could not know whether, at a given point of time, their policies conformed to the United States' dolphin protection standards. The Panel considered that a limitation on trade based on such unpredictable conditions could not be regarded as necessary to protect the health or life of dolphins.

5.29. On the basis of the above considerations, the Panel found that the United States' direct import prohibition imposed on certain yellowfin tuna and certain yellowfin tuna products of Mexico and the provisions of the MMPA under which it is imposed could not be justified under the exception in Article XX(b).

ARTICLE XX(g)

5.30. The Panel proceeded to examine whether the prohibition on imports of certain yellowfin tuna and certain yellowfin tuna products from Mexico and the MMPA provisions under which it was imposed could be justified under the exception in Article XX(g). The Panel noted that the United States, in invoking Article XX(g) with respect to its direct import prohibition under the MMPA, had argued that the measures taken under the MMPA are measures primarily aimed at the conservation of dolphin, and that the import restrictions on certain tuna and tuna products under the MMPA are 'primarily aimed at rendering effective restrictions on domestic production or consumption' of dolphin. The Panel also noted that

Mexico had argued that the United States measures were not justified under the exception in Article XX(g) because, *inter alia,* this provision could not be applied extrajurisdictionally.

5.31. The Panel noted that Article XX(g) required that the measures relating to the conservation of exhaustible natural resources be taken 'in conjunction with restrictions on domestic production or consumption'. A previous panel had found that a measure could only be considered to have been taken 'in conjunction with' production restrictions 'if it was primarily aimed at rendering effective these restrictions. A country can . . . control the production or consumption of an exhaustible natural resource only to the extent that the production or consumption is under its jurisdiction. This suggests that Article XX(g) was intended to permit contracting parties to take trade measures primarily aimed at rendering effective restrictions on production or consumption within their jurisdiction.

5.32. The Panel further noted that Article XX(g) allows each contracting party to adopt its own conservation policies. The conditions set out in Article XX(g) which limit resort to this exception, namely that the measures taken must be related to the conservation of exhaustible natural resources, and that they not "constitute a means of arbitrary or unjustifiable discrimination . . . or a disguised restriction on international trade" refer to the trade measure requiring justification under Article XX(g), not however to the conservation policies adopted by the contracting party. The Panel considered that if the extrajurisdictional interpretation of Article XX(g) suggested by the United States were accepted, each contracting party could unilaterally determine the conservation policies from which other contracting parties could not deviate without jeopardizing their rights under the General Agreement. The considerations that led the Panel to reject an extrajurisdictional application of Article XX(b) therefore apply also to Article XX(g).

5.33. The Panel did not consider that the United States measures, even if Article XX(g) could be applied extrajurisdictionally, would meet the conditions set out in that provision. A previous panel found that a measure could be considered as "relating to the conservation of exhaustible natural resources" within the meaning of Article XX(g) only if it was primarily aimed at such conservation. The Panel recalled that the United States linked the maximum incidental dolphin-taking rate which Mexico had to meet during a particular period in order to be able to export tuna to the United States to the taking rate actually recorded for United States fishermen during the same period. Consequently, the Mexican authorities could not know whether, at a given point of time, their conservation policies conformed to the United States conservation standards. The Panel considered that a limitation on trade based on such unpredictable conditions could not be regarded as being primarily aimed at the conservation of dolphins.

5.34. On the basis of the above considerations, the Panel found that the United States direct import prohibition on certain yellowfin tuna and certain yellowfin tuna products of Mexico directly imported from Mexico, and the provisions of the MMPA under which it is imposed, could not be justified under Article XX(g).

Concluding Remarks

6.1. The Panel wished to underline that its task was limited to the examination of this matter "in the light of the relevant GATT provisions," and therefore did not call for a finding on the appropriateness of the United States' and Mexico's conservation policies as such.

6.3. The Panel further recalled its finding that the import restrictions examined in this dispute, imposed to respond to differences in environmental regulation of producers, could not be justified under the exceptions in Articles XX(b) or XX(g). These exceptions did not specify criteria limiting the range of life or health protection policies, or resource conservation policies, for the sake of which they could be invoked. It seemed evident to the Panel that, if the CONTRACTING PARTIES were to permit import restrictions in response to differences in environmental policies under the General Agreement, they would need to impose limits on the range of policy differences justifying such responses and to develop criteria so as to prevent abuse. If the CONTRACTING PARTIES were to decide to permit trade measures of this type in particular circumstances it would therefore be preferable for them to do so not by interpreting Article XX, but by amending or supplementing the provisions of the General Agreement or waiving obligations thereunder. Such an approach would enable the CONTRACTING PARTIES to impose such limits and develop such criteria.

6.4. These considerations led the Panel to the view that the adoption of its report would affect neither the rights of individual contracting parties to pursue their internal environmental policies and to co-operate with one another in harmonizing such policies, nor the right of the CONTRACTING PARTIES acting jointly to address international environmental problems which can only be resolved through measures in conflict with the present rules of the General Agreement.

7. Conclusions

7.1.

(a) The prohibition of imports of certain yellowfin tuna and certain yellowfin tuna products of Mexico and the provisions of the Marine Mammal Protection Act under which it is imposed are contrary to Article XI:1 and are not justified by Article XX(b) or Article XX(g).

(b) The import prohibitions imposed by the United States with regard to certain yellowfin tuna and certain yellowfin tuna products of "intermediary nations" and the provisions of the Marine Mammal Protection Act under which they are imposed are contrary to Article XI:1 and are not justified by Article XX(b), XX(d) or XX(g).

(c) The Panel *recommends* that the CONTRACTING PARTIES request the United States to bring the above measures into conformity with its obligations under the General Agreement.

7.2. The provisions of Section 8 of the Fisherman's Protective Act (the Pelly Amendment) as such are not inconsistent with the obligations of the United States under the General Agreement.

7.3. The tuna products labeling provisions of the Dolphin Protection Consumer Information Act relating to tuna caught in the Eastern Tropical Pacific Ocean are not inconsistent with the obligations of the United States under Article I:1 of the General Agreement.

Note that the panel focused on the fact that the United States was not regulating a product but the process by which the product was obtained, (i.e., a PPM), namely by the use of purse seine nets which captured dolphins in the process. Note also that the panel first determined whether Article III applied (no) and whether the import ban violated Article XI (yes) before considering whether Article XX exceptions applied. It is important to remember that Article XX becomes relevant only if there is a violation of some other provision of GATT/WTO.

The panel report in Tuna-Dolphin I was never adopted, presumably because the United States would block the consensus then needed to adopt a report. As it was, Tuna-Dolphin I inspired intense concern by environmentalists about the international trade regime.

c. The Secondary Boycott of Yellowfin Tuna (Tuna-Dolphin II)

On August 28, 1990, the United States District Court for the Northern District of California enjoined the United States from allowing the import of certain tuna products from countries that do not meet the statutory requirements of comparability in their incidental killing of dolphins during their tuna fishing operations. This was a primary embargo. Congress also provided for a secondary embargo against countries that import tuna from countries that do not satisfy the statutory requirements of the Marine Mammal Protection Act and then export the tuna to the United States. Congress wanted to protect against "tuna laundering."

The relevant section of the MMPA (§1371(a)(2)(C)) provided that the Secretary of the Treasury "shall require the government of any intermediary nation from which yellowfin tuna or tuna products will be exported to the United States to certify and provide reasonable proof that it has acted to prohibit the importation of such tuna and tuna products from any nation from which direct export to the United States of such tuna and tuna products is banned under this section within sixty days following the effective date of such ban on importation to the United States."

Earth Island brought suit to enforce the secondary embargo. The plaintiff argued, among other things, that the scope of the secondary embargo applies not *only* to yellowfin tuna and tuna products harvested with purse seine nets in the eastern tropical Pacific from countries not meeting MMPA comparability standards but applies to the import of *all* yellowfin tuna and tuna products containing yellowfin from intermediary countries, unless the secretary of the treasury obtains proof that the intermediary country has prohibited imports of tuna and tuna products from the embargoed country.

The court agreed with plaintiff's argument and ordered a preliminary injunction. Earth Island Institute v. Robert Mosbacher et al., January 31, 1992, 1992 U.S. Dis. LEXIS 1866.

The EC and the Netherlands, on behalf of the Netherlands Antilles, complained to the GATT that the embargoes were inconsistent with Article XI of the GATT, did not qualify as a border adjustment under Article III, and were not covered by Article XX exceptions. In July 1992 the GATT established a panel to hear the claims. The panel concluded that both the primary and the intermediary country embargoes against states that export yellowfin tuna or tuna products to the United States and import these items were inconsistent with Article XI, since they banned imports from countries not adopting certain policies and that Article III could not apply to restrictions based on practices and not the product. It rejected the Article XX exceptions but on the basis of reasoning that differed somewhat from that in the Tuna Dolphin I panel report. Most notably it concluded that Article XX(g) on conserving exhaustible natural resources does not limit the location of the resources that must be conserved, thus allowing for the possibility of extraterritorial jurisdiction under these exceptions. This differs from the reasoning of the Panel in the Tuna Dolphin I dispute. However, the panel rejected the argument that the measures were within Article XX. The panel concluded that, because the embargo went beyond prohibiting the import of tuna caught in a dophin-unsafe manner, to prohibiting the import of all tuna from countries that allowed any tuna to be caught in a manner endangering dolphins (or in this case, from countries that imported any tuna from such a country), the embargo was an impermissible attempt to force other countries to change their policy. This reasoning left open the possibility that a more narrowly drawn measure—(e.g., one aimed more precisely at preventing the United States's purchasing power from being an incentive to kill dolphins)—might be GATT/WTO-consistent. GATT, United States—Restrictions on Imports of Tuna (June 16, 1994),

33 I.L.M. 839 (1994). Like the panel report in Tuna-Dolphin I, this panel report was never adopted.

For further analysis, *see* Steve Charnovitz, Dolphins and Tuna: An Analysis of the Second GATT Panel Report, 24 ELR 10567 (Oct. 1994); Ernst-Ulrich Petersmann, International and European Trade and Environmental Law After the Uruguay Round (1995).

d. Subsequent Developments on the Tuna-Dolphin Controversy

In May 1992, the United States and nine other countries (Costa Rica, France, Japan, Mexico, Nicaragua, Panama, Spain, Venezuela, and Vanuatu) concluded a new Inter-American Tropical Tuna Commission Agreement. The agreement, which went into effect in January 1993, extends through 1999. Under the agreement parties aim to reduce dolphin mortality rates to near zero by the end of the century. Countries are to reduce the dolphin mortality rate by 30 percent in 1993, 24 percent in 1994, 19 percent in 1995, 14 percent in 1996, 11 percent in 1997, 10 percent in 1998, and 8 percent in 1999.

Questions

1. *Terminology: Extraterritoriality.* Is the term "extraterritorial" helpful in this context? Would it be more useful analytically to distinguish among efforts by one country: to protect its territory against a threat arising outside its territory; to protect the environment of another country; and to protect the global commons? Also, can (should) countries condition their acceptance of a multilateral environmental agreement on a change in other countries' domestic law?

2. *Environmental or ethical?* The eastern spinner dolphin was not an endangered or threatened species. Should this affect the characterization of the dispute as environmental? Was the United States legislation primarily ethically motivated?

3. *Protecting the commons.* Suppose a resource is found in the high seas, or suppose it is endangered: should this affect the WTO analysis? Does a country have no right to protect the global commons? Did countries give up any such right in joining the GATT in 1948 or the WTO in 1994?

2. The Shrimp-Turtle Dispute

There are seven species of sea turtles in the world, which are found in subtropical or tropical areas. All the species are included in Appendix

I of the Convention on International Trade in Endangered Species (CITES, examined in chapter 19, above) as endangered, and all except one species are listed in Appendices I and II of the 1979 Convention on Migratory Species of Wild Animals (CMS) and appear in the IUCN Red List as endangered or vulnerable.

In the United States, the Endangered Species Act lists all sea turtles as endangered or threatened and prohibits the taking of all endangered sea turtles within the United States, its territorial sea, or the high seas without authorizaiton by the Secretary of Commerce. One human activity that has proven highly dangerous to sea turtles is catching shrimp using mechanical shrimp trawlers.

In 1987, the United States issued regulations requiring all shrimp trawlers to use turtle excluder devices (TEDs), which are very effective in preventing turtles from being killed in the nets shrimp trawlers use; and in 1989 United States legislation (the Sea Turtle Protection Act) called upon the United States government to negotiate bilateral or multilateral agreements to protect sea turtles. The legislation banned imports of shrimp unless the president certified to Congress that the harvesting country had a regulatory program and incidental take rate for sea turtles comparable to that of the United States or that the fishing environment of the harvesting country did not pose a threat to sea turtles. The subsequent 1991 United States guidelines required countries to use TEDs or a program with comparable results but limited the application to the Caribbean/western Atlantic region. The 1993 Guidelines eliminated the alternative program option to TEDs.

The United States government conducted workshops around the world demonstrating the TEDs and how they could be made (cheaply) from local materials.

In December 1995, the United States Court of International Trade (CIT) found that the 1991 and 1993 Guidelines were contrary to law in limiting the geographical coverage and directed the Department of States to prohibit by May 1, 1996, the importation of shrimp or shrimp products harvested in the wild with commercial fishing technology that could affect sea turtles adversely. The subsequent regulations required all imports of shrimp to be accompanied by a declaration indicating that they were fished under conditions not adversely affecting sea turtles or in waters from a country that had been certified as sea turtle safe. The 1996 Guidelines required that certifications to other countries could be done only if they used TEDs at all times. The CIT ruled that the embargo applied to all shrimp and shrimp products from countries that had not been certified and nullified the alternative declaration method from noncertified countries. The United States government appealed that ruling to the U.S. Court of Appeals for the Federal Circuit.

India, Malaysia, Pakistan, and Thailand, which are large exporters of shrimp and shrimp products, brought a claim against the United States to the WTO in 1997. The dispute panel issued its final report to the parties on April 6, 1998, as this book went to press.

The panel held that the United States law restricting imports violates Article XI:1 of the GATT and did not rule on the claims that the law also violates Articles I:1 and XIII:1. Rather it proceeded directly to examine whether the measures could come within the Article XX exceptions and found they did not.

Contrary to all previous panels, which had first determined whether the measures came within any of the explicit exceptions (b) and (g) to Article XX, the Shrimp-Turtle Panel first determined whether the measures satisfied the chapeau (opening paragraph) of Article XX. This provides that

> [s]ubject to the requirement that such measures are not applied in a manner that would constitute a means of arbitrary or unjustifiable discrimination between countries where the same conditions prevail, or a disguised restriction on international trade, nothing in this Agreement shall be construed to prevent the adoption or enforcement by any contracting party of measures: . . .

Noting that the Sea Turtle Protection Act (as interpreted by the CIT) bans the import of all shrimp from a country that does not require that all its mechanized shrimp trawlers use TEDs—rather than banning the import only of shrimp caught by mechanized trawlers not using TEDs—the panel invoked reasoning somewhat similar to that used by the panel in Tuna-Dolphin II: the United States is impermissibly pressuring another country to change it policy. The panel's analysis was radically different in one sense, however, because it created a new test for applying the Article XX chapeau, *viz.* whether a challenged action would threaten the multilateral trading system. The panel stated:

> 7.43. Therefore, we are of the opinion that the chapeau Article XX, interpreted within its context and in the light of the object and purpose of GATT and of the WTO Agreement, only allows Members to derogate from GATT provisions so long as, in doing so, they do not undermine the WTO multilateral trading system, thus also abusing the exceptions contained in Article XX. Such undermining and abuse would occur when a Member jeopardizes the operation of the WTO Agreement in such a way that guaranteed market access and nondiscriminatory treatment within a multilateral framework—the primary objectives of the Agreement—would no longer be possible. . . .
>
> We are of the view that a type of measure adopted by a Member which, on its own, may appear to have a relatively minor impact on the multilateral trading system, may nonetheless raise a serious threat to that system if similar measures are adopted by the same or other Members. Thus, by allowing such type of measures even though their individual impact may not appear to be such as to threaten the multilateral trading system, one would affect the

> security and predictability of the multilateral trading system. We consequently find that when considering a measure under Article XX, we must determine not only whether the measure *on its own* undermines the WTO multilateral trading system, but also whether such type of measure, if it were to be adopted by other Members, would threaten the security and predictability of the multilateral trading system.

The panel expressed its strong opposition to unilateral measures:

> 7.44 In our view, if an interpretation of the chapeau of Article XX were to be followed which would allow a Member to adopt measures conditioning access to its market for a given product upon the adoption by the exporting Members of certain policies, including conservation policies, GATT 1994 and the WTO Agreement could no longer serve as a multilateral framework for trade among Members as security and predictability of trade relations under those agreements would be threatened.

The panel did not reach the question of whether the measures could come within the scope of either exception XX(b) or XX(g).

The panel noted that the preferred way to deal with international environmental problems is through multilateral agreements and cooperation, and it indicated that the United States had not adequately attempted to reach such agreement.

After the panel issued its report, the CIT decision was reversed by the United States Court of Appeals, on the ground that the plaintiff in the CIT case had withdrawn before the CIT issued its ruling. The Court of Appeals did not reach the question of how the ACT should be interpreted. More litigation appears likely, as of mid-1998.

The United States appealed the WTO panel's decision in July of 1998.

Notes and Questions

1. *A global standard?* The United States argued that the use of TEDs has become "a recognized multilateral environmental standard." Nineteen countries require TEDS on shrimp trawl vessels subject to their jurisdiction (either as a result of the Inter-American Convention on the Protection and Conservation of Sea Turtles or of countries' own initiatives). Why shouldn't this be sufficient to serve as the basis of legislation to ban shrimp imports caught by methods that desecrate the endangered sea turtles? What more could be required?

2. *Hypothetical.* Suppose a global agreement banning shrimp unless caught by TEDs or harvested through aquaculture were negotiated and the four claimant states did not join the agreement. Would a ban on their imports be consistent with the GATT, according to the Shrimp-Turtle Panel? Should it be?

3. *The panel's approach.* Do you agree with the panel's approach in analyzing Article XX's chapeau language before determining whether the measures could qualify under any of the exceptions to Article XX? Is it consistent with the language of the article? Is there any question about the applicability of paragarphs (b) and (g) in this case? Does the paragraph in Article XX providing an exception for goods made with prison labor have any implications for this case? Would it make any difference to address paragraphs (b) and (g) first and thereafter the chapeau language?

4. *Relationship to CITES.* In a situation in which species are already listed as endangered under Appendix I of CITES, why shouldn't countries be able to adopt legislation that discourages fishing methods that contribute to the extinction of the species? Or to put it another way, why should countries be forced to keep their markets open to fish that have been caught by methods that lead to the extinction of species that the international community has designated as endangered? Should the parties to the CITES take any action? Could they do so consistent with GATT 1994?

5. *"Same conditions".* Note/Questions 1 and 4 immediately above consider aspects of whether discrimination is "arbitrary or unjustifiable" (in the language of the Article XX chapeau). The chapeau also is limited by its terms to discrimination "between countries where the same conditions apply". Why isn't the use or non-use of TEDs a valid basis for determining whether the "same conditions prevail"? Hasn't the United States decided, in effect, that it is?

6. *The shoe on the other foot.* Suppose Canada or Brazil bans the import of forest products from the United States (or from the Pacific Northwest portion thereof) on the ground that U.S. forestry practices endanger the spotted owl and the marbled murelet (both endangered species). Would this be consistent with GATT 1994 and the WTO Agreement?

7. *The role of exceptions.* The Beef Hormones appellate decision, *see* above, referred to "abuses" of Article XX. The shrimp/turtle panel was concerned that recognizing exceptions within the plain meaning of Article XX would threaten the multilateral trading system as established by GATT 1994 and the WTO Agreement. How could that be? Isn't Article XX an essential component of that system? If so, would it be more accurate to say that failing to apply Article XX would threaten the multilateral trading system? The preamble to the WTO Agreement places trade liberalization in the context of sustainable development and also mentions the need to protect the environment. Does this affect your analysis?

8. *Unsustainable production and consumption patterns.* The Rio Declaration, Agenda 21, and various other international instruments call for countries, especially industrialized countries, to adopt production and consumption patterns that are sustainable. Is the Sea Turtle Protection Act an example of this? If so, how should that affect the legal analysis in the shrimp/turtle case?

3. *Unilateral Environmental Actions After the Rio Conference*

The 1992 Rio Declaration on Environment and Development addressed the acceptability of unilateral actions relating to extraterritorial environmental problems that have effects on trade. Principle 12 provides as follows:

> States should cooperate to promote a supportive and open international economic system that would lead to economic growth and sustainable development in all countries, to better address the problems of environmental degradation. Trade policy measures for environmental purposes should not constitute a means of arbitrary or unjustifiable discrimination or a disguised restriction on international trade. Unilateral actions to deal with environmental challenges outside the jurisdiction of the importing country should be avoided. Environmental measures addressing transboundary or global environmental problems should, as far as possible, be based on an international consensus.

Two other international legal instruments adopted at Rio also address the question of unilateral measures. The Framework Convention on Climate Change provides in Article 3(5) that measures to combat climate change should not constitute a means of arbitrary or unjustifiable discrimination or disguised restriction on international trade. Principles 13 and 14 of the Forest Principles provide as follows:

> International trade in forest products should be facilitated on the basis of non-discriminatory and multilaterally agreed rules and procedures consistent with international law and practices. Unilateral measures, incompatible with international obligations or agreements, to restrict and/or ban the international trade in timber or other forest products, should be removed or avoided.

The Forest Principles are explicitly nonbinding, but a similar provision is included in the newly adopted International Tropical Timber Agreement (which replaces the earlier agreement by that name).

The legitimacy of unilateral measures taken for environmental purposes remains an important issue. Can you think of situations where a state might want to take unilateral measures to protect an environmental resource before an international consensus on action could be reached? Under what conditions might these be allowed? One of the authors of this casebook has suggested the possibility of provisional unilateral measures (PUMs), which would be valid for only a few years pending an international arrangement, would be subject to scientific criteria as to the need for the measures, and would be accompanied by a dispute resolution procedure to evaluate the scientific need for the measures. What advantages would this approach have? What problems do you foresee? How would you apply

PUMs if a country wanted to impose a carbon tax to protect against global warming from greenhouse gases?

On the general issue of unilateral measures and the trade regime, *see* Office of Technology Assessment, Trade and Environment: Conflicts and Opportunities (1992); Daniel C. Esty, Greening the GATT: Trade, Environment and the Future (1994); Robert A. Reinstein, Trade and Environment: The Case for and against Unilateral Actions, Sustainable Development and International Law (Winfried Lang, ed. 1995). For a particularly thorough treatment of the use of trade measures as sanctions, *see* Howard F. Chang, An Economic Analysis of Trade Measures to Protect the Global Environment, 83 Geo. L.J. 2121 (1995).

Questions

Is the term "unilateral" a helpful one in this context? Isn't all domestic legislation (including that necessary to implement an international obligation) a unilateral act by a sovereign state? Suppose a country takes an action in support of a non-legally binding United Nations General Assembly resolution such as that condemning driftnet fishing? Suppose the action supports an international agreement but is not required by it? Suppose the action is in support of an international agreement to which the target country is not a party?

E. MULTILATERAL ENVIRONMENTAL AGREEMENTS

Some multilateral environmental agreements use trade restrictions as the primary instrument to accomplish the purposes of the agreements. These include the Convention on International Trade in Endangered Species (CITES), which restricts trade in species listed by countries in three appendices, and the International Whaling Convention. Regional agreements on conserving biological diversity also incorporate this approach. In the area of hazardous wastes, both the Basel Convention on the Transboundary Movement of Hazardous Wastes and regional/bilateral hazardous waste agreements restrict trade in covered wastes. Nonbinding legal instruments covering trade in toxic chemicals and in pesticides provide for prior informed consent from the importing country.

International agreements occasionally contain explicit provisions prohibiting import and export of products unless the exporting and importing countries are parties to the agreement or are complying with it. Such provisions provide incentives both to join the agreement and, in certain cases, to comply with the provisions of the agreement. *See e.g.,* Montreal Protocol on Substances That Deplete the Ozone Layer contains such provisions.

The question is whether such agreements, or the trade-related provisions in certain agreements, are consistent with the GATT/WTO. You should recall that the Tuna Dolphin I Panel report noted in the concluding remarks that

> [t]hese considerations led to the Panel to the view that the adoption of its report would affect neither the rights of individual contracting parties to pursue their internal environmental policies and to co-operate with one another in harmonizing such policies, nor the right of the CONTRACTING PARTIES acting jointly to address international environmental problems which can only be resolved through measures in conflict with the present rules of the General Agreement.

Was the panel implicitly suggesting that a multilateral agreement addressing the tuna-dolphin problem would survive scrutiny under the GATT?

1. The Multilateral Agreements

As a case study, consider whether the provisions in three international agreements restricting trade in controlled items to nonparties are consistent with the WTO: The Montreal Protocol on Substances That Deplete the Ozone Layer, the Basel Convention on Control of Transboundary Movements of Hazardous Wastes and Their Disposal, and the Convention on International Trade in Endangered Species of Fauna and Flora. As you read the provisions, note the differences among the conventions.

The Montreal Protocol, Article 4: Control of Trade with Non-Parties

> 1. Within one year of the entry into force of this Protocol, each Party shall ban the import of controlled substances from any State not party to this Protocol.
>
> 2. Beginning on 1 January 1993, no Party operating under paragraph 1 of Article 5 may export any controlled substance to any State not party to this Protocol.
>
> 3. Within three years . . . the Parties shall . . . elaborate in an annex a list of products containing controlled substances. Parties that have not objected to the annex in accordance with those procedures shall ban, within one year of the annex having become effective, the import of those products from any State not party to this Protocol.
>
> . . .
>
> 8. Notwithstanding the provisions of this Article, imports referred to in paragraphs 1, 3 and 4 may be permitted from any State not party to this Protocol if that State is determined, by a meeting of the Parties, to be in

full compliance with Article 2 [control measures] and this Article, and has submitted data to that effect as specified in Article 7 [reporting of data].

Convention on International Trade in Endangered Species, Article X: Trade with States not Party to the Convention

Where export or re-export is to, or import is from, a State not a party to the present Convention, comparable documentation issued by the competent authorities in that State which substantially conforms with the requirements of the present Convention for permits and certificates may be accepted in lieu thereof by any Party.

Basel Convention on the Control of Transboundary Movements of Hazardous Wastes and Their Disposal, Article 4(5)

A Party shall not permit hazardous wastes or other wastes to be exported to a non-Party or to be imported from a non-Party.

Note that the Montreal Protocol bans trade in the controlled substances with nonparties and allows parties to ban trade in products containing the substances and eventually products produced with the controlled substances (although parties have decided not to pursue the latter). However, Article 4(8) provides an escape: imports may be permitted from a nonparty if a meeting of the parties determines the state is in full compliance with the control measures and the reporting of data.

Article 4(5) of the Basel Convention simply restricts imports and exports of controlled hazardous wastes from/to nonparties, but Article 11 allows such trade if there is an agreement or arrangement in place between the countries that is consistent with the Convention. CITES permits export, re-export, or import from nonparty states only "if comparable documentation issued by the competent authorities in that State . . . substantially conforms with the requirements of the present Convention for permits and certificates." As an aside, who determines substantial conformance under CITES?

Notes and Questions

1. Do the differences in the provisions in the three agreements affect whether they are consistent with the WTO?

2. What if such provisions restricting trade with nonparties were incorporated in legal instruments that were not formal agreements but only guidelines or codes of conduct? What if there were a rule of customary international law that countries were using trade measures to enforce?

3. Does it matter whether trade provisions in international agreements are directed to products that would be in themselves harmful in the im-

porting country or rather to the processes by which the products are produced?

4. Does it matter whether the international agreement is directed to protecting the so-called global commons or to the environment (including species) within a country?

5. Must the measure adopted in the agreement be the least trade restrictive measure available to meet the environmental goal? *Cf.* Article 5 of the SPS Agreement, above. Should that be required?

6. Should it make any difference to the outcome of a dispute that the party complaining about the validity of a trade measure in an environmental agreement is or is not a party to the relevant environmental agreement?

7. In what forum should disputes over conflicts between provisions in environmental and in trade agreements be resolved? The protocol on deep seabed mining to the U.N. Convention on the Law of the Sea provides that trade-related disputes shall be brought in the WTO.

8. What means might be available to confirm that the multilateral environmental provisions limiting trade are consistent with GATT/WTO?

2. *The North American Free Trade Agreement and Multilateral Environmental Agreements*

The North American Free Trade Agreement addressed the question of the consistency of multilateral environmental agreements with it by including a provision by which the trade obligations set out in specific international agreements "trump" the NAFTA provisions to the extent of any inconsistency.

NAFTA, Article 104: Relations to Environmental and Conservation Agreements

1. In the Event of any inconsistency between this Agreement and the specific trade obligations set out in:

(a) the *Convention on International Trade in Endangered Species of Wild Fauna and Flora,* done at Washington, March 3, 1973, as amended June 22, 1979,

(b) the *Montreal Protocol on Substances that Deplete the Ozone Layer,* done at Montreal, September 18, 1987, as amended June 29, 1990.

(c) the *Basel Convention on the Control of Transboundary Movements of Hazardous Wastes and Their Disposal,* done at Basel, March 22, 1989, on its entry into force for Canada, Mexico and the United States, or

(d) the agreements set out in Annex 104.1,

such obligations shall prevail to the extent of the inconsistency, provided that where a Party has a choice among equally effective and reasonably available means of complying with such obligations, the Party chooses the alternative that is the least inconsistent with the other provisions of this Agreement.

2. The Parties may agree in writing to modify Annex 104.1 to include any amendment to an agreement referred to in paragraph 1, and any other environmental or conservation agreement.

Annex 104.1
Bilateral and Other Environmental Conservation Agreements

1. The *Agreement Between the Government of Canada and the Government of the United States of America Concerning the Transboundary Movement of Hazardous Waste*, signed at Ottawa, October 28, 1986.

2. The *Agreement Between the United States of America and the United Mexican States on Cooperation for the Protection and Improvement of the Environment in the Border Area*, signed at La Paz, Baja California Sur, August 14, 1983.

Questions

1. *Verbal agreements.* The United States received a verbal agreement from Canada and Mexico to add the Convention Between the U.S.-Mexican Convention for the Protection of Migratory Birds and Game Animals and the U.S.-Canada Convention on the Protection of Migratory Birds to Annex 104.1. What trade implications would arise if either Canada or Mexico did not agree to include their bilateral convention with the United States in Annex 104.1 while the other country did? Must all three countries agree to modify Annex 104.1?

2. *Does Article 104 really help?* What protection does Article 104 actually provide? Suppose Mexico or Canada complained about the Sea Turtle Protection Act, and the United States responded that the Act implements the objective of CITES. Would Article 104 protect against a challenge under NAFTA?

3. *WTO Article 104?* What problems do you foresee if the WTO were to include such a provision? Should only multilateral agreements be eligible? Must they be global or would regional ones qualify? Should there be a requirement that a certain number of WTO parties must also be party to the environmental agreement to qualify for listing? Who could decide and by what procedures whether to list the environmental agreement?

F. ENVIRONMENTAL LABELING

1. Introduction to Eco-Labeling

CRITERIA IN ENVIRONMENTAL LABELING: A COMPARATIVE ANALYSIS OF ENVIRONMENTAL CRITERIA IN SELECTED ECO-LABELING SCHEMES

United Nations Environmental Programme
2-6 (excerpts) (Feb. 1996) (reporting results of a study)

1. Introduction

Environmental labelling is defined as "the use of labels in order to inform consumers that a labelled product is environmentally more friendly relative to other products in the same category.[17] Labels may be granted by a government or privately sponsored agency to applicants from enterprises.

Environmental labelling represents a voluntary, market-based instrument of environment policy. Its major aims are to raise consumer awareness about environmental effects of products so as to inform consumers about the environmental characteristics of a product and to promote the adoption of more environmentally sound production methods and technologies. Environmental labelling is only one among a whole range of domestic environment policy tools. It is an example of informational tools, which have recently gained importance alongside with the more traditional legislative, administrative, and economic policy instruments.

In principle, eco-labels are awarded on the basis of an overall assessment of the environmental impact of a good during its entire life cycle, including the procurement of raw materials, production, distribution, consumption and disposal. Therefore, eco-labels differ from single-criteria labels, which address only one environmental quality of a product, or from "negative labels" containing warnings about the possible dangers of the product.

In recent years, the number of environmental labelling schemes in developed countries has multiplied rapidly, and several developing countries are in the process of establishing programmes. The majority of schemes are operated by the national authorities or bodies closely linked to them. The only international schemes at the moment are the European Union scheme, which is only in its developmental stage, and the Nordic scheme, operated jointly by the authorities from four Nordic countries (Finland, Iceland, Norway, and Sweden). Finally, some schemes are private, among the most well-known being the Good Environmental

17. International Cooperation on Eco-Labeling and Eco-Certification Programmes and Opportunities for Environmentally Friendly Products. 1994. UNCTAD Ad hoc Working Group on Trade, Environment and Development TD/B/WG.6/2.

Choice operated by the Swedish Society for Nature Conservation, the largest environmental organization in Sweden.

The criteria used for awarding eco-labels primarily reflect domestic environmental priorities. An issue of some concern is the extent to which environmental criteria of the importing country may and should be extended to imported products. Labelling might fail to have the desired effects of alleviating the environmental problems if the criteria address non-relevant environmental considerations (i.e., issues that are not of overriding concern to the producing/exporting country). Moreover, there is concern—which is now under study in the WTO Committee on Trade and Environment—that different eco-labelling schemes may constitute a technical barrier of trade, because domestic producers are better positioned to influence the choice of the product groups and the criteria used for awarding the labels, than exporters.

Thus, concerns have been raised that environmental criteria may discriminate against imports of like products. Finally labelling schemes are sometimes seen [as] problematic from the point of view of international trade agreements, because the criteria often include the process and production methods (PPMs) and not to the qualities of the product itself.

Developing countries may be particularly vulnerable to possible discriminatory trade impacts of labelling: on one hand, products earmarked for eco-labelling are often among the most important export items of developing countries (e.g., textiles); on the other, the developing country exporters frequently lack resources to undergo costly testing, verification, plant inspection, and certification procedures required.

1.1 TYPES OF ENVIRONMENTAL LABELLING

Three types of environmental labeling can be identified:

Type I based on criteria set by a third party;
Type II based on self-declaration by manufacturers;
Type III based on product information covering several environmental aspects, but without comparing or weighing such aspects.

Type I eco-labels are "third-party," typically voluntary schemes, which identify products that are relatively less harmful to the environment than similar products in the same category. The selection of product categories and determination of criteria for awarding the label are, in the case of official national schemes, generally undertaken by a national environmental authority. The criteria are defined by a Board, which uses a consultative process involving various interest groups and applying the existing scientific knowledge concerning the environmental effects. The right to use the eco-label is awarded for a fixed period, against a payment to cover the costs of running the labelling system.

Criteria are designed so as to allow only a certain proportion, usually 15-25 per cent, of the products in any one sector to be labelled. Criteria are normally revised every 3-5 years to accommodate developments in scientific knowledge and changes in production methods.

Type II labelling schemes are based on self-declaration by companies, claiming their products to have specific "environment-friendly" properties. For the moment there are no preestablished definitions or criteria with which products must comply to bear the label.

Type III labels do not establish pass/fail criteria on a product by product basis, but report the findings of a life-cycle assessment on a group of preset indices. It is suggested that the indices should include, at a minimum, information pertaining to extraction of natural resources, energy consumption, air and water pollution emissions, and generation of solid waste. These indices are directly reported in the label. Labelling is open to all products. A parallel can be drawn between the nutritional labels that provide information about the nutritional constituents of foods, and Type III labels containing information about the relative environmental burdens associated with products.

1.3 THE ECO-LABELLING SCHEMES STUDIED

The criteria for the following eco-labelling schemes were included in the study. The abbreviations following in the countries (or groups of countries) will be used in this report.

Austria (AU): The Austrian Eco-label. Initiated by the Federal Ministry of Environment, Youth and Family Affairs. Established in 1991.

Canada (CA): Environment Choice Programme. Founded in 1988 by the Ministry of Environment.

The European Union (EU): Coordinated by the European Commission. Instituted by a Council Resolution. The competent bodies at national level are responsible for, e.g., processing the applications. Established in 1992.

Germany (GE): The Blue Angel. Introduced by the Federal Minister and the Ministers for Environmental Protection of the Federal States. Administered by the Federal Environment Agency (FEA),the Environmental Label Jury (ELJ), and the Institute for Quality Assurance and Labeling (RAL). Established in 1977.

India (IN): ECOMARK. Introduced by the Ministry of Environment and Forests in 1991.

Japan (JA): ECO MARK. Established by the Japan Environment Association under the guidance of the Japanese Environment Agency (ministry).

Republic of Korea (KO): Eco-label. Conducted by the Ministry of Environment. Initiated by the Government in 1998.

The Netherlands (NL): Milieukeur. Initiated by the Ministries of Environment, and Economic Affairs, together with manufacturers' and retailers' organizations and consumer groups. Managed by the Stichting Milieukeur, subsidized by the above mentioned Ministries. Founded in 1992.

New Zealand (NZ): Environment Choice. Operated by Telarc, the national technical and quality system accreditation and certification authority. Programme launched as a result of Government initiative in 1992.

The Nordic Countries (NO): White Swan. Initiated by the Nordic Council of Ministers. Administered by the national agencies of Finland, Iceland, Norway, and Sweden, Denmark having an observer status. Established in 1989.

Singapore (SI): Green Label. Initiated and administered by the Secretariat of the Waste Minimization Department together with an Advisory Committee. Established in 1992.

Sweden (BM): Good Environmental Choice (Bra Miljoval). Initiated and operated by the Swedish Society for Nature Conservation together with the representatives of retail trade. Established in 1992.

The United States (US): Green Seal. Initiated and administered by an independent, non-profit organization, Green Seal. Established in 1989.

For general information on environmental labeling, *see* Nigel Dudley, Chris Elliott & Sue Stolton, A Framework for Environmental Labeling, 39 Environment 16 (July/August 1997).

2. *Environmental Labeling and Trade Regulation*

INTERNATIONAL ECONOMICS, TRADE AND THE ENVIRONMENT

Peter L. Lallas and Andreas R. Zeigler
International Occupational and Environmental Medicine
(Jessica Herzstein et al., eds., Mosby 1998)

1. Ecolabelling and the Trade Rules: An Overview

The relationship between ecolabelling and international trade has emerged rapidly, and in some respects surprisingly, as one of the most contentious issues of the day in the environment and trade debate. Indeed, in the not too distant past, ecolabelling was often cast as a more trade-friendly alternative to direct product restrictions. Chapter 4 of Agenda 21—an environment and development document— speaks positively about the potential value of ecolabelling in promoting more environmentally-sustainable patterns of production and consumption.

Part of the reason that ecolabelling has become a flashpoint in this debate lies in its expanding use as an environmental policy tool. The rising use of ecolabelling reflects a renewed emphasis in environmental policy on the right of the public to know about environmental issues, and of enlisting the market as a positive force for health and environmental protection. Ecolabelling programs can be a powerful tool to achieve these goals, by providing consumers environmental information and empowering them to choose products on the basis of their environmental characteristics, in some cases throughout the life cycle.

For this reason exactly (and certain others listed below), ecolabelling is now on the radar screen of both government ministries and industries concerned about protecting and enhancing sales and market share in international trade. U.S. industry, for example, has expressed strong and continuing concerns about the potential trade implications of a new European Union ecolabelling scheme. Many developing countries—who themselves are beginning to adopt ecolabelling programs—are concerned that they might not have an equitable opportunity to obtain ecolabels in developed country markets, and thus will face new obstacles to market access. Beyond this, some of these countries argue that to the extent ecolabels include information relating to PPMs, they constitute an unjustified and illegal intrusion into the sovereignty of exporting countries.

2. Types of Ecolabelling

Ecolabels generally refer to information printed on the label of products regarding the environmental characteristics associated with the product. In some cases, these characteristics are limited to the product itself (e.g., poisonous if swallowed). These types of labels have existed for many years, often in connection with domestic laws relating to hazardous wastes or products.

Other types of ecolabels describe or assess environmental impacts throughout some or all of the life-cycle of the product (e.g., impacts from producing and/or disposing of the product). These labels have garnered the most attention in trade and environment circles. They can be distinguished in several ways.

One point of distinction is the type of information offered in the label. In some cases, labels consist of a so-called "seal of approval" (e.g., blue angel, green seal logo), which conveys a judgment that the product is environmentally-preferred as compared with other similar products. The label may be conveyed on the basis of a full or partial life-cycle assessment. Other labels consist of a "report card" listing of the specific environmental characteristics of a product, focusing upon some or all of the product life-cycle. A final variation is labels identifying a single attribute (e.g., organically produced; dolphin safe). Some labels fall somewhere in between these categories (e.g., energy efficient).

A second point of distinction relates to whether or not the label is conferred by an independent entity. Recently, a number of independent certification entities have been established to confer labels, both within and outside the U.S. These entities establish a process and set of criteria by which to judge products and determine whether they merit a particular label. In other cases, producers or retailers themselves design and affix labels on their products; so-called "self-certification" schemes. These labels essentially represent product advertising or marketing claims.

A final point of distinction relates to whether the certification entity is governmental or private. In the U.S., certain ecolabels bear a governmental stamp-of-approval, such as the EPA-Energy Department Energy Star label and the EPA Pollution Prevention label. Other ecolabels are developed and certified by non-governmental entities, including the Green Seal labels.

Within the U.S., the Federal Trade Commission has jurisdiction to "police" the accuracy, truthfulness and reliability of labels, including self-certification claims. Beyond this, a number of states and in some cases the federal government have established by law certain definitions and/or minimum criteria that a product must meet before it is entitled to a particular label (e.g., organically produced; recyclable).

For its part, the European Union has recently commenced a major ecolabelling initiative, under which it will work with Member States to develop criteria to grant labels for a number of sectors and products, including paper products and textiles. The EU will use a "seal of approval" approach to label qualifying products, and has indicated that it will also make available additional explanatory information to consumers should they request it.

Other countries or regions with ecolabelling programs include the

Nordic countries, Japan, Chile (focused upon whether products are made using ozone-depleting substances) and Canada.

3. Application of WTO Rules

For reasons suggested above, the relationship between national ecolabelling programs and the WTO rules has been a priority topic in discussions of the WTO Committee on Trade and Environment, in joint meetings of UNEP/UNCTAD, and in other fora.

One issue in these discussions is whether ecolabels that include ppm-based criteria are and/or should be allowable under WTO rules, including in particular the TBT agreement.

Perhaps the most interesting aspect of this debate is not what arguments have been presented, but the underlying policy considerations. Many countries are concerned that interpreting TBT to cover ecolabels based on non-product related ppm-criteria might imply not only that such ecolabels could pass muster under WTO rules, but might also imply that other types of ppm-based trade measures (i.e., of the Tuna-Dolphin variety) would gain a foothold under WTO rules. This scenario awakens the core sense of opposition that many countries maintain against these latter types of measures. Accordingly, there is great reluctance to accept that such ecolabels are covered and—in particular—allowable under TBT.

By comparison, many environmental policy makers emphasize the importance of clarifying that such ecolabels either are not covered by TBT or—if they are—are allowable under TBT. There is concern that a WTO panel might not allow countries to differentiate (even for labeling purposes) between an imported product and a domestic product on the basis of a ppm criterion (e.g., whether one or the other is produced with ozone depleting substances), and instead would determine that these two products are "like" (based on physical characteristics of the product per se). This would, in effect, prevent ppm-based ecolabelling programs from being applied to imported products.

A basic policy issue underlying this analysis is whether ecolabelling schemes based on ppms should take into consideration the environmental conditions and priorities of other countries in determining whether to grant a label. The argument for this approach is that it would give the products of other countries an opportunity to gain an ecolabel on the basis of conditions most relevant to their environmental conditions and priorities, rather than those of the importing country. Such an approach might also, it is argued, discourage efforts to design ecolabelling criteria in a manner that "favors" domestic industry. The argument against it is, among other things, that it would be virtually impossible, and perhaps undesirable, for an ecolabelling entity to understand and judge individual approaches and priorities of all other countries with whom it trades.

Other issues involve whether to develop an "international" mechanism to police the truthfulness and accuracy of ecolabels, and how to ensure adequate and appropriate transparency in the ecolabelling process.

Of special importance in this regard will be creating opportunities for companies from developing countries to participate effectively in the development of ecolabelling programs. In today's world of sometimes complicated rules in a variety of ministries and fora, these companies might lack the capability even to learn about what is required to gain a label—not to mention the ability to meet the relevant criteria.

For analysis of the legal issues raised by environmental labels, *see* James Salzman, Informing the Green Consumer: The Debate Over the Use and Abuse of Environmental Labels, 1 J. Indus. Ecology 11 (1997).

Notes and Questions

As noted, the use of environmental labels on products is becoming increasingly common. Under what conditions are ecolabels consistent with the GATT/WTO provisions? In the 1991 GATT Panel Report on US Restrictions on Imports of Tuna, the panel found that the optional use of a "Dolphin Safe" label was consistent with the GATT because it did not restrict the sale of tuna products whether or not they carried a dolphin safe label nor did it grant any other governmental trade benefit. Does this mean that all labels that are not mandatory by governments are consistent with the GATT/WTO and the GATT Code on Technical Barriers to Trade? Are ecolabels developed by nongovernmental organizations and adopted by private industry always consistent with the GATT and the Code on Technical Barriers to Trade? What constraints should be permitted under the trading regime? Consider these issues as you read the materials below on forestry and the paper industry.

3. Environmental Labels and Paper Products

■ CRITERIA IN ENVIRONMENTAL LABELLING: A COMPARATIVE ANALYSIS OF ENVIRONMENTAL CRITERIA IN SELECTED ECO-LABELLING SCHEMES

United Nations Environment Programme
11-14 (excerpts) (Feb. 1996)

Part A. Discussion of the Environmental Impact of Paper Cycle

1. PRODUCTION, CONSUMPTION, AND TRADE OF PAPER PRODUCTS

Approximately 90 per cent of the wood fibre is estimated to originate in the developed countries, with North America accounting for over a half of world production. Almost 70 per cent of pulpwood comes from coniferous forests and only a small proportion is obtained from tropical areas. The share of fibre coming from forest plantations is increasing but is still believed to be at most one third of total pulp production. The growth in fibre and pulp production is considerably faster in developing countries than in the world in average. Chemical pulp accounts for about two thirds of the total production, whereas the share of mechanical pulp is a little over 20 per cent, and that of non-wood pulp approximately ten per cent.

With regard to paper products, more than 80 per cent of production takes place in the developed countries, but the share of developing countries is increasing, Brazil and Korea being main developing country producers. Finally, the rate of paper consumption in the developed world is several times higher than that of the South, but again, the percentage increase is fastest in the developing countries, particularly in Asia.

Less than one fourth of paper production enters international trade and most of the trade occurs between developed countries. The main importers are the U.S. and Germany, together accounting for over 30 per cent of world imports. The main exporters are Canada and Finland, although Germany and the U.S. are also significant exporters. The countries of the South import mainly unprocessed fibre, and their share of world paper trade is relatively small (19% of imports and 7% of exports). Most of the trade flows take place between neighboring countries or trading blocks (between the U.S. and Canada, among the EU countries, and from Scandinavia to EU and to Russia).

The importance of waste paper as a raw material for paper production has increased as a consequence of diminishing landfill capacity and the rising concern for the environment in most industrialized countries. Consequently, the trade in waste paper has gained importance. The main consumers of waste paper in absolute terms are the U.S. and Japan. The highest waste paper utilization rates (the share of recycled paper of the total paper production) are in Asian and Latin American countries such as Taiwan, Korea, and Mexico.

2. FORESTRY AND FIBRE SOURCING

The main environmental impacts of modern, large scale forestry practices include distortions in the global distribution of habitats and ecosystems; loss of habitat and species diversity; localized soil erosion, soil fertility, watershed instability and climatic change; increasing frequency of uncontrolled fires; and net transfer of carbon compounds to the atmosphere. Other environmental impacts that may be locally or occasionally important are watercourse pollution through herbicide, pesticide and fertilizer runoff, and through altering soil nutrient and water balances; acidification of water courses; silting of fish breeding areas; air pollution from machinery use; and species invasions and reduction of diversity outside forests.

Among the forestry practices most problematic from the environmental point of view are:

- clear felling over large areas;
- whole tree harvesting (removes 1.5 to 4 times more nutrients than harvesting the bole alone);
- excessive road networks, and poorly-aligned roads (fragmentation of forest areas);
- the use of heavy machinery (soil compaction, leading to increased run-off and erosion; pollution from machinery);
- excessive soil cultivation and drainage;
- poorly-controlled use of fire;
- poorly-managed monoculture plantations;
- monocultures using few clones (narrow genetic diversity tends to increase vulnerability of forest stand to extreme events, such as tree disease epidemics, or pest invasions);
- large-scale, homogeneous plantation layouts;
- afforestation on sensitive natural habitats (as opposed to degraded land or agricultural land);
- poorly-controlled chemical use, especially near water courses.

The scale and importance of the environmental impacts depend on many factors other than forestry practices. Such factors include site ecology, terrain and climate; current and previous land uses; surrounding ecology, water-sheds and land uses; types and numbers of uses and users; types and quantities of products harvested; timing of operations; and policy, market and institutional factors. Moreover, the relative importance of the environmental impacts differ along with the priorities accorded to different environmental values, and the importance of those values in relation to other goals. Finally, the importance of environmental impacts depends on from whose point of view they are viewed: e.g., forest owner, environmentalist, forest industry and civil servant may have fundamentally different perceptions of forests, environmental impacts, and the most appropriate ways of dealing with the impacts. These differences in perceptions seem to lie behind several of the conflicts related with forestry.

2.1 Efforts to Develop Criteria for Sustainable Forest Management

In the United Nations Conference on Environment and Development, held in 1992 Rio de Janeiro, a set of principles for forest management world-wide were adopted. These "Forest Principles" are non-binding and political, not technical or operational, in outlook. They express a consensus regarding general values related to the forest management. Since the adoption of the Forest Principles, work has been underway on several fora to establish more operational criteria and indicators for sustainable forest management. Such principles could in the future be incorporated in the criteria for eco-labeling of paper products.

The Helsinki Declaration of the Ministerial Conference on the Protection of Forests in Europe (1993) adopted resolutions concerning the general guidelines for the sustainable management and conservation of the biodiversity of European forests. It aims to implement the Forest Principles at European level, and improve upon them as a basis for international cooperation. The follow-up work of the Helsinki resolutions has resulted in the adoption of six criteria, and 27 qualitative indicators, and an acceptance by the parties of a number of descriptive indicators for possible use. The indicators are, to a large part, better suited for post-evaluation of policies and for establishing guidelines for the national forestry policies than for setting the criteria that the forestry practices need to meet in order to be established as sustainable. This is one of the main criticisms expressed by the environmental groups which would like to see the criteria to be established in the form of binding requirements.

The Forest Stewardship Council is an accreditation body, established in 1993 to sanction market-based claims by the growing number of forest product certification programmes. The FSC attempts to encourage voluntary efforts by the timber industry by establishing a strong framework for certification. The FSC is a non-governmental, non-profit assembly whose members include representatives from environmental institutions, foresters, timber traders, indigenous peoples' organizations, community forestry groups, and forest product certification organizations from 25 countries.

. . . The new forest management criteria could eventually be included in the criteria used for awarding eco-labels to paper products under the Nordic eco-labeling scheme. It is to be noted, however, that the general philosophy behind wood certification differs from that of eco-labeling in that the criteria are to be based on scientific knowledge and commonly agreed priorities concerning sustainable forest management. Reasons for changing the criteria are new scientific knowledge, and changes in the societal values and preferences. Therefore, all forest owners are in principle eligible for a wood certificate. The new eco-labeling schemes, in contrast, attempt to establish the criteria so that only a limited proportion (usually 15-25%) of the products are eligible for a label, and the criteria are periodically being revised in order to prevent a situation where all products would be labeled.

G. TRANSNATIONAL ENVIRONMENTAL CODES

Since 1992, the private sector has taken very significant initiatives in developing its own transnational environmental standards and practices. In some cases, these initiatives may effectively delay or preempt what governments might otherwise be tempted to do. Private codes of environmental practices have become a major force on the international scene. These include the International Standard Organization's environmental management standard, ISO 14000, the International Chamber of Commerce's (ICC) Business Charter for Sustainable Development, the Responsible Care Program of the Chemical Manufacturers Association, the Coalition for Environmentally Responsible Economies' (CERES) principles, and numerous private code initiatives within Europe. In addition, the European Union has developed the European Management Auditing System that applies to firms and is a counterpart to the ISO 14000 series.

As you read the following materials, consider how you would ensure that the private codes are viewed as legitimate by states and by the public, how compliance takes place, and whether the codes are consistent with GATT and the WTO.

■ ADAPTING TECHNOLOGY FOR A SUSTAINABLE WORLD

Robert A. Frosch
37 Environment 16, 16-17, 19-20, 21-22 (1995).

Throughout history, economic activity has taken place in what may be called an open system of materials flow. That is, people have taken natural materials (plants, animals, metals, and so forth), transformed them into products for their use, and then discarded worn-out products and any materials left over from the production process. In fact, archaeologists have found such remains from as long ago as Neolithic times. This practice, of course, often forced early peoples to change locations as the buildup of wastes rendered existing settlements uninhabitable. Even so, this was reasonable behavior when the human population was small and uncontaminated places were fairly easy to find. Now, however, the situation is very different. It is simply no longer possible to avoid the wastes that we create, and disposing of them is becoming more and more of a burden.

This suggests that an open industrial system such as ours cannot continue indefinitely, that it will have to be replaced by one that offers more control over the flow of materials. Such a system would involve, among other things, paying more attention to where materials end up, choosing materials and manufacturing processes to generate a more circular flow, and avoiding practices that could come back to haunt us. Until quite recently, industrial societies have attempted to deal with pollution and other forms of waste largely through regulation. Although this strategy has been partially successful, it has not really gotten to the root of the problem. To do so will require a new paradigm for our industrial system—an "industrial ecology" whose processes resemble those of a natural ecosystem.

Industrial Ecology

As suggested previously, the phrase "industrial ecology" connotes an industrial system that operates much like a natural ecosystem. In natural ecosystems, materials and energy circulate continuously in a complex web of interactions: microorganisms turn animal wastes into food for plants; the plants, in turn, are either eaten by animals or enter the cycle through death and decay. While ecosystems produce some actual wastes (by-products that are not recycled, such as fossil fuels), on the whole they are self-contained and self-sustaining.

In similar fashion, industrial ecology involves focusing less on the impacts of each industrial activity in isolation and more on the overall impact of all such activities. This means recognizing that the industrial system consists of much more than separate stages of extraction, manufacture, and disposal and that the stages are linked across time, distance, and economic sectors. It should also be stressed that industrial ecology incorporates elements of the regulatory approaches discussed in the previous section. Indeed, it places pollution control, pollution prevention, and recycling in a larger framework that includes additional types of environmentally responsible behavior.

The full relevance of the industrial ecology paradigm is best seen in simple box models of the modern industrial system, such as those in Figures 1a and 1b. . . .

Life Cycles and Closing the Loop

The production and consumption of products are increasingly being seen not as unrelated events but as stages in the flow of materials. As the more or less transient embodiment of materials and energy, a product can have a continuous "life cycle," always being transformed for a new purpose. Thus, the whole industrial process can become a closed loop in which manufacturers retain responsibility for their products until those products are reused. In other words, manufacturers become the stewards of industrial products. As it happens, this concept has already been embodied in law in Germany, which has imposed a stewardship requirement for some products. Similar measures are being discussed in the United States.

It is not clear whether the most useful level at which to regulate the flow of materials is the individual plant, the firm, the industrial sector, or industry as a whole. Optimization of a particular process or

Figure 1a.
An open system of materials flow.

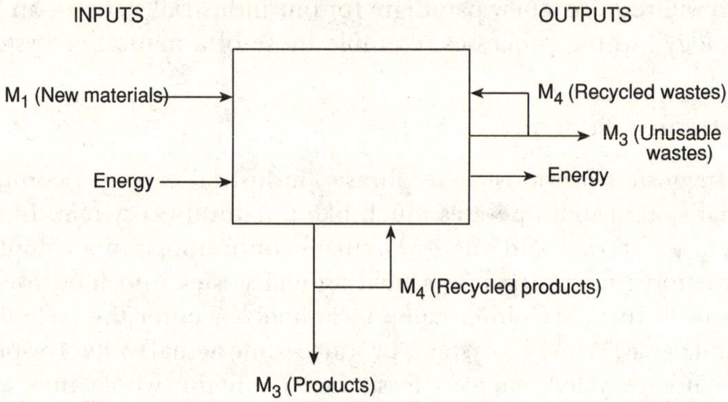

Figure 1b.
A closed system of materials flow.

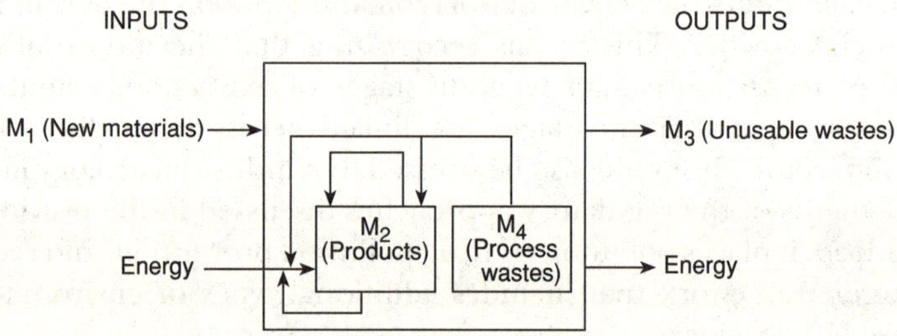

subsystem may be less efficient than optimization of the larger system because there are usually more opportunities to reuse materials (and thus attain more complete closure) at the industry level than at that of a single firm, process, or product. For example, while some of the alloys used in brass and bronze can be recycled within the foundry or between the foundry and the alloy supplier, others are more economical to recycle within the metal industry at large. This is generally the case with iron and steel as well as with aluminum. Often it is simply a matter of scale: The quantities used by a single manufacturer are not great enough to cover the capital costs of the recycling process. Similar complications arise in the recycling of plastics. While some plastics can be recycled into the same products (e.g., soda bottles), others are only economical to recycle if made into different products, which are frequently produced by different companies.

Product stewardship offers clear benefits for the environment. Preventing waste and pollution is a more natural impulse if firms retain a certain "ownership" of their products—that is, if the responsibility for those products remains inside the system.

CODE GREEN

Jennifer Nash & John Ehrenfeld
38 Environment 16, 19 (1996)

Over the past decade, private codes of environmental management practice have begun to emerge as a major force in corporate environmental programs. Examples of these codes include the Chemical Manufacturers Association's (CMA) Responsible Care program, the Coalition for Environmentally Responsible Economies' (CERES) principles, the International Chamber of Commerce's (ICC) Business Charter for Sustainable Development, and the international environmental management standard, ISO 14000. Although these codes differ in numerous ways, they have important features in common. First, each requires companies to adopt environmental management systems and to audit their progress toward the environmental goals they set for themselves. Second, to varying degrees, each calls upon firms to involve outside groups, such as suppliers, customers, and community groups, in their environmental programs. Importantly, however, none includes specific environmental performance standards that firms must meet, and only ISO 14000 requires third-party verification of firms' environmental systems. . . .

ISO 14000

The International Organization for Standardization (ISO) was formed in 1946 and is headquartered in Geneva, Switzerland. Its purpose is to

Figure 1.
Differences between Regulation and Private Codes.

Regulation	*Private Codes*
• Instituted by government	• Instituted by private sector
• Enforced by government	• Enforced by firms themselves with some third-party verification
• Compliance mandatory, with direct sanctions	• Compliance voluntary, with indirect sanctions such as peer pressure
• Largely medium specific (air, water, etc.)	• Integrative, focusing on life-cycle impacts "beyond the fence line"
• Places emphasis on product and process standards	• Places emphasis on management systems
• Defines standards for emissions or technology	• Lets each firm define own performance, with requirement for continuous improvement
• Provides public access to information on compliance	• Provides public access to information only in select cases

facilitate standardization as a means of promoting international trade. While its membership consists of the standards organizations of its 100 member nations, ISO has been an "industry-driven" organization.

ISO standards are documented agreements of technical specifications that companies use as guidelines to ensure that materials and products fit their purpose. For example, the format of credit cards, automatic teller machine (ATM) cards, and phone cards are derived from an ISO standard. Cards that adhere to the standard, which defines such properties as thickness, can be used worldwide. . . .

As ISO set up its environmental effort, many of the world's major manufacturing countries were in the process of developing environmental management standards of their own. Germany, Japan, and Canada were finalizing product eco-labeling programs. By 1992, approximately 15 countries had developed national environmental management standards. Perhaps most important, the European Union was moving rapidly to develop an international environmental management standard that would include strong provisions for public disclosure of corporate environmental activities. U.S. multinational corporations with European operations were unhappy about this requirement; they felt that because U.S. law already required disclosure of releases (through the Toxics Release Inventory), the European requirements would be unnecessary and burdensome. SAGE members saw these national efforts as potentially disruptive of international trade. In fact, the primary motivation for ISO 14000 was to rein in the standard-setting activities of individual countries through a program of international consensus building.

Some 400 representatives of U.S. industry, including ones from the chemical, petroleum, electronics, and consulting industries, have participated actively in the development of ISO 14000. Having seen the impact of ISO 9000, these firms are anxious to influence what they feel will be an important undertaking. In addition, about 20 representatives of government and public interest groups have been involved in developing the standard. . . .

ISO 14000, like ISO 9000 and other ISO standards, is intended to apply to a very wide range of organizations and to accommodate diverse geographical, cultural, and social conditions. The breadth of the standard thus limits how specific it can be. When completed, the ISO 14000 series will provide a very general schematic to firms of the management systems they should design and document. Like the other private codes discussed in this paper, ISO 14000 will not prescribe specific operational practices or set numerical or other kinds of performance standards that firms must meet. Its purpose will be to provide firms with the elements of an effective environmental management system, thereby helping them to achieve environmental and economic goals. . . .

TRANSNATIONAL NORMS OF ENVIRONMENTAL BEHAVIOR AND THE SPREAD OF THE INDUSTRIAL ECOLOGY ETHIC

Edith Brown Weiss & Charles Weiss, Jr., ©1997

Voluntary standards of environmental management, such as ISO 14000, the European Management Auditing System (EMAS), eco-labels, and sectoral programs like Responsible Care, bridge the gap between industrial ecology, technology management, and international law. In contrast to mandatory performance standards that are instituted and enforced by government and hence create an adversarial situation between government and business, these standards seek to use market, peer and public pressure to motivate firms to undertake major changes in their management procedures and indeed in their internal culture, including the introduction of life-cycle analysis and other techniques of industrial ecology. In this way, voluntary standards are hoped to effect a long-term improvement not only in the environmental performance of the firms that adopt them, but also in that of their suppliers and of other firms that are influenced by their example.

These voluntary environmental management standards offer a promising complement to existing national and international environmental law at a time when both the national and international legal systems are overburdened, and when proposals for new environmental laws are encountering political resistance all over the world. Nonetheless, these instruments raise important issues of public policy, precisely because they straddle the line between public and private international law.

Voluntary standards of environmental management are instruments of international law in the sense that they provide a normative framework and process for influencing international behavior over time in the direction of internationally accepted values. They are typical of a new generation of international legal instruments that originate, not with states, but with the "global civil society," in this case with industrial associations and non-governmental organizations, and rely on non-state actors (in this case other companies and individual consumers) for their development, interpretation and implementation.

Such instruments fill an important need in today's world, in which non-state actors often have expertise and freedom of action denied to governments that enable them to develop, interpret and implement international law. This newer, non-hierarchical view contrasts with the more traditional view of international law as consisting primarily of a set of binding legal instruments adopted by sovereign states and subject to immediate compliance. This traditional view makes a sharp distinction between public and private international law, and regards legally binding agreements, such as treaties, as inherently superior to and more effective to other measures.

Inducements to Adopt Voluntary Environmental Standards

Why do firms adopt voluntary environmental standards? In the complexity of the response to this question lies both the power of these standards to influence environmental behavior of firms and the public policy complications that result from relying on them to do so. Unlike traditional mandatory standards, voluntary environmental standards do not assume that a firm necessarily acts in its own best interests. Nor do they assume that a firm is a monolith, to be constrained by regulation and then left free to comply or evade as it decides.[18]

It is not necessary to convince industrial ecologists that improved environmental performance is likely to result in direct cash savings through improved resource management. Indeed, industrial environmental officers who were actually responsible for putting the voluntary standards into effect are generally convinced that their most important impact on the firm has been to increase its overall internal efficiency. Much of the work of these officers consists of convincing top management that this is indeed the case.

Management, however, is likely to view voluntary standards as a marketing tool, to be used to reassure customers and improve the public image of the firm, to gain competitive advantage through a "green" image or perhaps through proprietary products or technologies developed as a result of increased environmental emphasis, or at a minimum to ensure that they do not lose markets to competitors with a greener image or product line. Alternatively, they may be responding to peer pressure within an industrial association, or in certain countries, to political pressure from government, sometimes combined with the offer of technical assistance to enable smaller or weaker firms to implement the norm.

These motivations depend on the existence of an environment in which environmental regulations are expected to be enforced. Indeed, behind the immediate motivation for adoption may be a longer range strategy aimed at convincing government and the public to lessen the burden of environmental inspection or even exemption from compliance with regulatory procedures. Market pressures to adopt voluntary standards depend on the extent to which environmental awareness is well developed

18. It is worth recalling that a number of important environmental innovations in industry have resulted from the initiative of highly motivated individuals, independent of any commercial motivation. Here one may cite the establishment of a coding system to facilitate the disassembly and recycling of plastic devices by indicating the resin from which each part in a complicated assembly was made, an initiative of a Hewlett-Packard engineer, and the decision by Dupont to cease manufacture of chlorofluorocarbons, a decision that went against Dupont's immediate commercial interests and was taken at the urging of the then-head of the CFC manufacturing department.

on the part of the general public in the geographic areas in which the products of the firm are marketed.

Such environmental consciousness is well developed in Europe and North America, but not yet as well developed in Japan or in the rapidly expanding markets of Asia. On the other hand, experience in Brazil, a country where environmental consciousness was once almost entirely absent, raises hopes that customers in other countries may soon demand corporate environmental citizenship as a prerequisite for doing business. Indeed, there has been an extraordinary increase in environmental awareness in Brazil in the last few years, to the point where Brazilian companies now fear becoming the subjects of journalistic environmental exposes and are beginning to adjust their behavior accordingly.

Having decided to adopt a voluntary standard, management may appoint a vigorous environmental officer and give him or her the wholehearted support needed to effect thorough-going change in the company. This seems to be the case with the pioneering companies that have been the first to implement the new standards—the more so since these companies are already likely to be close to compliance. This is likely to give rise to a complicated "multi-level game," as the environmental officer, backed by top management, seeks to use the company's commitment to the voluntary standard to overcome remaining opposition from more traditional executives within the company, to whom environmental management may still be a bothersome irrelevance to the company's main mission of making a profit.

As more and more companies adopt voluntary standards, however, it is likely that the "second generation" of adopters will be motivated more by competitive pressures and market requirements than by purely environmental motives. Indeed, the idea underlying the voluntary standards is that companies will adopt them for any of a number of motives, and will absorb an environmental ethic in the course of implementing the standards.

This development is likely to put pressure on the integrity of the system by which environmental standards are devised and implemented. Absent rigorous oversight, we may expect a tendency for some of these firms to use ISO 14000 as "greenwash": i.e., to do as little as they can get away with to earn the certification they need to reassure the public and retain their markets. This is especially the case for environmental management standards which are less subject to objective verification than are performance-based standards like eco-labels. ISO 14000 is especially vulnerable to this kind of abuse, since its requirements for public reporting are less stringent than those of EMAS. This will create market opportunities for certifying firms—which depend for their income on fees from the firms to be certified—that are willing to cut corners and be less rigorous in their examination.

This last concern is of particular importance in many countries of the Far East, whose rapid economic growth is critically dependent on continued access to Western markets. These countries have embraced ISO 14000 as a universal standard that they hope will protect them against the danger that they will be accused of being environmental laggards and should therefore be banned from European or American markets. Several countries are considering making it mandatory for all companies that wish to export to qualify for ISO 14000, a requirement that could convert a voluntary standard into a mandatory one. Such a requirement would create major incentives for cheating or lip-service, possibly with the tacit approval of the government, and bring the issues of accountability discussed earlier into sharp relief.

These developments raise important issues of governance and accountability, which should be central concerns for the promoters of voluntary standards of all kinds. The public is being asked to believe that these non-binding norms will bring about socially desirable changes in behavior, and to modify its own buying behavior or even to allow public agencies to reallocate regulatory resources in recognition of the effectiveness and value of these norms. They need assurance that these norms are not an elaborate cover for lip-service or mutual back-scratching.

On the other hand, voluntary norms are a new development, and need to be allowed to evolve with experience. The hope is that they will build on themselves, as more and more firms observe the market and management advantages of an environmentally conscious company culture.

Notes and Questions

1. *The precautionary principle.* Does the precautionary principle apply to problems of industrial ecology? Consider the following three approaches:

> i. Prevention and/or reduction of environmentally damaging discharges at the source; ii. Transition from carbon-based energy sources to renewable sources or other sources, as well as the more efficient use of power; iii. Promotion of deposit-refunds and other incentives to spur innovation in product development.

In this context, can precaution be distinguished from pollution prevention? *See* discussion of scientific uncertainty and the precautionary principle in Chapter 4, supra at 156. For further discussion of the precautionary principle, *see generally* T. O'Riordan and J. Cameron, eds., Interpreting the Precautionary Principle, London: Cameron May (1994); T. O'Riordan and A. Jordan, The Precautionary Principle in Contemporary Environmental Politics, 3 Envtl. Values 191 (1995).

2. *Principles and code.* How are the principles of international environmental law relevant to the operations of the private codes?

3. *Legitimacy and accountability.* Do you agree that issues of legitimacy and accountability are central to public acceptance of the private codes?

How might these issues be addressed? What role, if any, should states have in their adoption and implementation?

4. *Enforcement.* How are private environmental codes of conduct enforced? Does compliance rely primarily on the market place? What are the benefits of market-based compliance? Do you foresee any problems? What steps could be taken to minimize these problems? Consider the following:

> Under the ISO scheme, compliance is to be enforced through audits and certification. While self-certification is a possibility, it will probably not be credible, and so many companies will turn to third-party certification by registered certifiers. These will be consultants with expertise in EMS, auditing and environment who will assure that the management systems are in place and are working as intended. Debates have focused on the nature and qualifications of verifiers and auditors: in terms of their geographic distribution (European vs. U.S.) and in terms of their competence (big auditing firms vs. environmental specialists.) Plans are underway to develop uniform guidelines for verifier selection and training, but as of now verifiers must meet national qualifications, and these differ significantly across countries.
>
> One of the weaknesses of ISO compared to other private codes of conduct, or to the European EMAS regulation, is that it does not require publication of information on environmental impacts. This reduces the possibilities of using information as a spur to compliance. In codes/standards that do rely on information provision, companies adhering to the code/standard must make public information regarding their impact on the environment, and their plans and policies for minimizing that impact. Through yearly reports on emissions, waste, resource use and other parameters, it is possible for interested parties to monitor whether adherence to the code/standard has resulted in improvements or has been an empty gesture. In this regard the scheme parallels monitoring and reporting requirements under public law: in the same way, monitoring and reporting are aimed at (1) making sure relevant decision-makers are aware of environmental information (here, the EMS requires organizations to ensure that top management has responsibility for decisions affecting environmental performance) and (2) using the publication of information as a way of shaming scofflaws and rewarding compliance. Only the first of these goals will be satisfied under ISO 14,000.
>
> Whether through information provision or third-party certification, adherence to the standard is to be encouraged through the market. In the first place, consumers (aided by watchdog NGOs, no doubt) will, hopefully, prefer environmentally aware and sensitive companies, other things being more or less equal. Second, intermediate goods purchasers, public procurement agencies and private companies seeking suppliers will require ISO certification or at least compliance with the standards before they will buy. Banks, insurers and institutional shareholders may require certification to reduce their own chances of excess liability. According to lawyers who represent transnational corporate clients, this is already beginning to happen, and they expect that within a short time adoption of the standards will be de facto mandatory for doing business in large global markets.

Naomi Roht-Arriaza, Compliance with Private Voluntary Agreements: The Example of the International Organization for Standardizations's ISO

14000 Environmental Management and Related Standards, in International Compliance with Non-Binding Accords 205-218 (Edith Brown Weiss, ed. 1998).

5. *WTO consistency.* Do these private transnational codes raise issues of consistency with GATT 1994 and the WTO? As of July 1998, this question was before the Technical Barriers to Trade Committee of the WTO.

H. REGIONAL TRADE AGREEMENTS: THE NORTH AMERICAN FREE TRADE AGREEMENT

The United States, Mexico, and Canada began negotiating the North American Free Trade Agreement (NAFTA) in 1991, with the goal of a free trade area. Free trade areas involve common internal tariffs but, unlike a customs union such as the European Union, no common external tariffs. Both free trade areas and customs unions are allowed by the WTO.

NAFTA was intended to lower tariffs (hopefully to zero) and to create more open markets for trade and investment among the three countries. It was designed to cover a wide variety of economic activity, including trade in goods, investment, agriculture (including sanitary and phytosanitary measures), standards-related measures, energy, and services. From the beginning of the negotiations, there was a debate about the environmental implications of NAFTA. This debate was fueled by the September 1991 Tuna-Dolphin GATT panel report, described above.

For references generally, *see e.g.*, NAFTA and the Environment (Daniel Magraw, ed. & contributor, 1995); Peter L. Lallas, NAFTA and Evolving Approaches to Identify and Address "Indirect" Environmental Impacts of International Trade, 5 Geo. Intl. L.J. 519 (1993); Gary Clyde Hufbauer & Jeffrey J. Schott, North American Free Trade Agreement (1992); Robert F. Housman, Reconciling Trade and the Environment: Lessons from the North American Free Trade Agreement (1994); Claudio Grossman et al., The Evolution of Free Trade in the Americas: NAFTA Case studies, 11 Am. U.J. Intl. & Poly. 687 (1996).

■ NAFTA AND THE ENVIRONMENT: SUBSTANCE AND PROCESS

Daniel Magraw, editor and contributor, 3-6 (1995) [footnotes omitted]

C. Environmental Concerns About a North American Free Trade Area

Threat to domestic environmental laws and to international environmental agreements. Perhaps the most significant environmental concern raised by the prospect of negotiating and implementing the NAFTA was the potential threat to U.S. domestic environmental laws and regulations posed by the "trade disciplines" contained in trade agreements. Trade disciplines are intended to prevent countries from unduly interfering with international trade by restricting imports or exports. These disciplines potentially affect environmental protection efforts because such efforts often require prohibiting trade in banned products. For example, to protect the U.S. health and environment from DDT (a toxic pesticide), it is necessary not only to prohibit DDT's use in the U.S., but also to prohibit the import of foodstuffs containing DDT residues.

A similar concern existed with respect to trade-related provisions in international environmental agreements. Several of these agreements, including the Montreal Protocol on Ozone Depletion, the Convention on International Trade in Endangered Species, and the Basel Convention on the International Transport of Hazardous Substances, provide for trade restrictions in order to achieve their fundamental objectives. The trade disciplines define the acceptability of measures taken to implement such provisions, and thus the effectiveness of the agreements. The trade disciplines in the General Agreement on Tariffs and Trade (GATT) formed the basis for the ruling by a GATT panel that the U.S. prohibition on importing tuna caught in a manner that killed dolphins at a higher rate than achieved by the U.S. fleet was inconsistent with the GATT. This challenge, which was brought by Mexico before the NAFTA negotiations began and was decided during the negotiations, did much to galvanize U.S. public opinion about the environmental implications of trade regimes. (A second tuna/dolphin challenge was subsequently filed by the European Union, resulting in another GATT panel report finding that the secondary aspects of the import ban also violated the GATT, though the reasoning differed from that of the first report.)

Harmonization. Harmonization (also referred to as compatibility) of rules and standards often occurs within trade regimes in order to facilitate trade. Although compatibility of environmental standards can also benefit health and the environment, there were fears that harmonization of environmental standards would be downward towards the least common denominator, and that federal, state, or local governments would be prohibited from exceeding international standards (where such standards existed or came to exist).

Pollution havens. The possibility that industry would be attracted to locales with low environmental protection standards or enforcement was another concern, especially given the risk that a government might lower its standards or reduce its enforcement in order to attract or retain investment. The antipathy towards pollution havens had both environmental and competitiveness underpinnings.

Environmentally damaging growth. The fact that liberalized trade would create economic growth and increased investment gave rise to other concerns. This was particularly the case along the U.S.-Mexican border. The growth of the *maquiladora* program—under which components may be imported duty-free into Mexico from the United States for processing or further manufacturing by factories (which are concentrated along the border) and then exported duty-free to the United States—had already caused serious health problems and environmental degradation. Some commentators were not convinced that the international trade paradigm of comparative advantage—the theory that free trade is good for all countries because it allows each country to exploit its particular advantage in inputs—makes environmental sense; some distrusted growth as a general matter; and others feared that the rapid pace of growth would outpace the creation of environmental infrastructure, some of which requires large capital outlays.

Other indirect effects. There were also other expected effects of increased trade and investment that have environmental implications, though several of these are positive. For example, increased trade in environment-friendly services and technologies will make pollution prevention and clean-up more efficient. Increased contact and information flow between companies will result in better environmental-management techniques. Perhaps most important, increased trade and investment was expected by some to result in increased resources being devoted to environmental protection, particularly in Mexico. This belief is based on historical evidence that the ratio of Gross National Product spent on environmental protection increased markedly once a country's per capita income exceeded $5000. Others are less optimistic, based on an assumption that the increased wealth from trade liberalization would not be spread equitably among the Mexican population.

Dispute settlement. Dispute settlement mechanisms in trade regimes, and the procedures under which they operate, were viewed by many as inherently biased against the environment. GATT panels are populated by trade experts, with no requirement of environmental expertise. GATT panels are not required to take into account international law, such as international environmental agreements, other than the GATT itself and customary international law in interpreting the GATT. The burden of proof, which can determine the outcome of a case, is sometimes on the country defending the environmental measure under attack. Moreover, trade dispute settlement mechanisms lack transparency and opportunity for public input.

Negotiating process and public input. A different type of concern involved the process of negotiating trade agreements. Historically, trade negotiations had been conducted with little input from either the environmental agencies of the U.S. (or any other) government or the environmental community; and previous trade negotiations had taken place in the context of very little public awareness of the impact of trade on the environment and on environmental protection efforts. The 1947 GATT, for example, did not contain the word "environment," and virtually no discussion of environmental issues accompanied the negotiation of the U.S.-Canada Free Trade Agreement in 1988, which treats environmental issues only briefly.

INTERNATIONAL ECONOMICS, TRADE, AND THE ENVIRONMENT

Adapted from Peter Lallas and Andreas Ziegler
International Occupational and Environmental Medicine
(Jessica Herzstein et al.,eds., Mosby 1998)

The U.S. Administrations, for their part, became very engaged in these debates [about NAFTA and the environment]. Both the Bush and the Clinton Administrations prepared an environmental review of the NAFTA, and carried out extensive public consultations on these issues.

In the end, a number of actions were taken. First, a political decision was made during the negotiation of NAFTA to diverge from the Uruguay Round "model" in order to address specific environmental concerns. This included, in particular, a new approach to provisions in the NAFTA Chapters on Standards, Sanitary and Phytosanitary measures, and Investment, as well as the introduction of a provision intended to safeguard the use of trade measures specified in MEAs from challenge under NAFTA, subject to a specified proviso.

Beyond this, the three countries transformed the NAFTA from a single trade agreement (the NAFTA) into a "package" of agreements focused more broadly on trade, environment and labor, with the broad objective of sustainable development. The core of this approach was the development of parallel environmental and labor-related agreements and initiatives. On the environmental side, these included:

- the North American Agreement for Environmental Cooperation (NACEC), designed *inter alia* to promote cooperation on environmental issues and maintain and enhance enforcement against violation of environmental laws;
- the Border Environmental Cooperation Commission and related NADBank, designed *inter alia* to identify and fund environmental infrastructure needs in the U.S.-Mexico Border Area.

In addition, the U.S. and Mexico reinforced existing efforts to address environmental problems in the U.S.-Mexico border area, including through the adoption of an integrated border environmental plan. This plan currently is being updated into a Border 21 Plan, with a view toward the 21st century.

■ NAFTA AND THE ENVIRONMENT: SUBSTANCE AND PROCESS

Daniel Magraw, editor and contributor
12-19 (1995) [footnotes omitted]

E. Provisions in the NAFTA Text

The NAFTA text contains several provisions intended to make it more environmentally sensitive. In almost every instance, these provisions (which are reprinted in Part II) are more protective of the environment than the equivalent provisions in the so- called Dunkel text, the then-operative text of the Uruguay Round of the GATT negotiations, which were occurring simultaneously with the NAFTA negotiations.

Although the Objectives article of the NAFTA does not refer to implementing the agreement in an environmentally protective manner, the NAFTA Preamble commits the countries to undertake the increased trade and investment envisioned by the NAFTA in "a manner consistent with environmental protection and conservation." It further commits the countries to "promote sustainable development" and "strengthen the development and enforcement of environmental laws and regulations."

Domestic environmental laws are protected in several ways. Provisions on Sanitary and Phytosanitary measures (SPS) (chapter 7B) and on Standards Related measures (chapter 9) ensure that the United States has the right to choose its own level of protection in those areas, and they establish committees to strive to enhance levels of protection. Domestic laws may exceed international standards and may exist in the absence of scientific certainty. The problem of downward harmonization is thus dealt with. The potential problem of "dueling science" in disciplines upon SPS measures is avoided by requiring that an SPS measure be supported simply by a scientific basis, rather than a standard that would allow a dispute over whose science is "better." The United States may determine whether another country's testing is equivalent to its own. States and localities retain their right to adopt standards that are stricter than federal and international standards.

Environmentalists expressed concern about several provisions in chapters 7B and 9, especially the use of the word "necessary" in article 712(5) as a trade discipline. The term "necessary" is problematic for many in the environmental community, because it has been interpreted narrowly by GATT dispute settlement panels when applying GATT article XX(b), which is the exception for trade measures taken to protect human, animal or plant life or health. In a letter dated September 13, 1993 to the Natural Resources Defense Council (reprinted in Part III), U.S. Trade Representative Michael Kantor explained this and several other points about the NAFTA text to the satisfaction of at least some in the environmental community.

Article XX of the GATT—which contains exceptions that permit otherwise-prohibited trade measures, inter alia, if they are necessary to protect human, animal, or plant life or health or if they relate to conserving exhaustible natural resources—formed the basis for the tuna/dolphin cases referred to above and is incorporated into NAFTA with respect to environment-based trade measures not already covered by chapters 7B and 9. Although new language clarifies that article somewhat in an environmentally sensitive manner, the outcome of the tuna/dolphin case, referred to above, most probably would remain unchanged. The inability to resolve this problem troubled many environmentalists deeply.

The trade-related obligations in specified international environmental agreements are protected by article 104, which gives them precedence over the NAFTA in certain circumstances. The list of such agreements can be added to by a relatively simple procedure. Some environmentalists believed, however, that the list in NAFTA was inadequate. During the political process leading to congressional approval of NAFTA, it was agreed to add the U.S.-Canada and U.S.-Mexico migratory birds treaties to the list and to consider adding other agreements.

Moreover, unlike those in the GATT, the dispute settlement provisions of NAFTA place the burden of proof in some circumstances on the country challenging an environmental regulation. In addition, a country defending an environmental standard under chapters 7B or 9 or article 104 may choose to have the case decided by a NAFTA dispute settlement panel, even if the challenging country desires to have the case decided by a GATT panel. This provision ensures the applicability of more environmentally sensitive rules and procedures. Finally, the provisions allow panels to obtain advice from scientific experts if such issues are present in a case. On the other hand, they embody the principle that panel hearings, deliberations, and written submissions shall be confidential. Environmentalists continue to be troubled by some aspects of dispute settlement. In particular, they argue for more environmental expertise on the panels and increased opportunities for public involvement in the process.

NAFTA also includes a provision regarding pollution havens, which states that countries should not encourage investment by relaxing or derogating from domestic health, safety or environmental measures. The article uses the hortatory word "should," rather than the normative "shall." Article 1114 further provides that if a country believes another country is engaging in this type of behavior, there shall be consultations if the first country requests them; but formal NAFTA dispute settlement is not provided.

F. North American Agreement on Environmental Cooperation

Pursuant to President Clinton's October 4, 1992 campaign statement (reprinted in Part III) about the need for additional environmental and labor protection before the NAFTA could be approved, negotiations commenced in April 1993 on what came to be referred to as the environmental and labor "side" or "supplemental" agreements. Because the U.S. government sought such strong agreements (particularly the establishment of an independent secretariat and the availability of trade sanctions for failure to enforce environmental and labor law), negotiations proved very difficult. They were also complicated by the fact that classified negotiating documents were repeatedly leaked to the press. Partly as a result of this, there was a rich dialogue between the governments and the environmental and business communities about precise negotiating positions (several documents illustrating the NGO Side of that dialogue are reprinted in Part IV).

After marathon bargaining at the highest levels of government the North American Agreement on Environmental Cooperation (NAAEC) and the North American Agreement on Labor Cooperation were agreed to on 13 August 1993; and the texts were finalized after a "lawyers' scrub" (in which lawyers from the three countries carefully scrutinized the text to ensure that it fully reflected the points that negotiators had agreed on and to remove inconsistencies and unintended ambiguities) in early September. The following discussion focuses on the environmental agreement—the NAAEC—although as noted above the labor agreement also has an environmental (worker health and safety) aspect to it.

The NAAEC contains unique normative and institutional elements that, once implemented, will provide new means of international environmental protection. The agreement establishes the Commission for Environmental Cooperation (CEC), which has three institutional components.

Council. The first institutional component is a Council to be composed of the environmental ministers of the three countries. The Council will convene annually—at which time it will meet in public—and at the request of any country that is a Party to the agreement. The Council will have strong government input since each environmental minister will be acting on behalf of his or her own country.

Secretariat. The second institutional component of the CEC is a Secretariat, which will have strong elements of independence. The Council will oversee the Secretariat and approve its budget; but the Secretariat, which will be located in Montreal, Canada, will be an international organization, with privileges and immunities. The Secretariat will be headed by an executive director, appointed by the Council for a renewable three-year term and removable only for cause. Victor Lichtenger, a Mexican, was chosen as the first executive director in summer 1994. The executive director will appoint the Secretariat staff which, like the executive director, will be international civil servants rather than employees of any of the three governments. The Council, by a two-thirds vote, can veto a staff appointment proposed by the executive director. The initial annual budget of Secretariat is approximately US$9,000,000 which will grow to US$15,000,000 per year, and the staff is expected to be about 30 professionals. It is expected that the Secretariat will continue to have the resources needed to fulfill its substantial responsibilities.

Conflicting concerns have been raised that the Secretariat represents an unacceptable loss of sovereignty by the United States or, in contrast, that the Secretariat is not independent enough. Concerns have also been raised about whether adequate funding will be available for the Secretariat as well as for other aspects of the NAFTA environmental package.

Joint Public Advisory Committee. The third institutional component of the CEC is a 15-member Joint Public Advisory Committee with five members appointed by each country. Its purpose is to ensure that the Council and Secretariat receive representative public input from persons from each of the countries. Optional national advisory committees are also provided for; the United States has set up both types—one composed of governmental representatives (the Governmental Advisory Committee (GAC)) and the other of members of the public (National Advisory Committee (NAC)).

Obligations. NAAEC also contains unprecedented new obligations that will foster environmental protection. Most notably, each country must "effectively enforce its environmental laws and regulations." In addition, each country is obligated to "ensure that its laws and regulations provide for high levels of environmental protection and to strive to continue to improve those laws and regulations." This provision, known colloquially as the anti-rollback provision, is intended to prevent a country from reducing its level of protection, although each country continues to be able to choose how to reach that level of protection. NAAEC also obligates each country to: publish laws, regulations, procedures and administrative rulings to ensure appropriate access by private persons to administrative and judicial proceedings; and ensure that its administrative and judicial proceedings are fair, open, and equitable.

CEC's Functions. Taken together, the institutions and norms just described lead to important and unusual or unique functions for the Commission for Environmental Cooperation. First, the Commission will facilitate cooperation between the countries. Because for these purposes the scope of the CEC is defined comprehensively to include virtually all environmental issues, this cooperation can occur with respect to any appropriate combination of environmental issues. Cooperation is likely to be especially important, however, with respect to transboundary issues such as air or water pollution, and investigations that encompass two or more countries. Cooperation is required in order to deal with such problems: downstream countries typically do not have the authority, and upstream countries do not have the incentive, to deal with transboundary problems unilaterally. Canada, Mexico, and the United States are both upstream and downstream countries with respect to each other—at least the United States is with respect to both of its neighbors. The importance of, and opportunity for, international cooperation are thus obvious. There are other institutions for environmental cooperation, but the many avenues for cooperation available to the Commission give it the potential to be unusually effective in this respect.

The Commission also provides a new and more effective forum for consultation on environmental issues. Any Party can call a special session of the Council to discuss issues. Certain environmental issues are given priority for discussion in the Council, and others are identified as appropriate for consultation. For example, one issue that is identified is life cycle management, which includes process and production methods (PPMs). Thus all the product and process methods, including the issues involved in the tuna/dolphin case, are appropriate for consultation, for discussion, and for recommendations at the Council level.

A third and somewhat more unusual function is reporting on different types of topics, primarily by the independent Secretariat. One type of report concerns particular environmental issues, such as pollution of the Rio Grande. That the kind of report may be prepared by the Secretariat, and the report will be made public unless two-thirds of the Council decides otherwise. The Secretariat will also prepare a periodic report on the state of the North American environment. These periodic reports will be included in the Commission's annual reports, which will be prepared by the Secretariat and reviewed by the Council. The annual reports are significant because, in addition to reporting on the activities of the Commission over the past year and the approved budget for the upcoming year, they will include the actions taken by the parties to fulfill their obligations under the Agreement (including environmental law enforcement) and relevant information submitted by the public. Through these various reports, an independent Secretariat, by identifying trends or analyzing a particular situation, may be able to focus governmental attention on a situation without pointing fingers, prevent disputes from arising, or create a common factual basis upon which to resolve a dispute.

The Council, with assistance from the Secretariat, is expressly tasked with monitoring the environmental effects of the NAFTA. Such a purpose is unique; and the Commission's reports on the topic should prove to be extremely important in elaborating the relationship between environment and trade generally, and in ensuring that the NAFTA is implemented in an environmentally sensitive fashion more particularly.

In addition, the Commission will encourage and make more effective the enforcement of environmental laws and regulations. Throughout the negotiations of the NAAEC, there was a consensus among the countries that the laws on the books in the three countries provided for high levels of protection and thus that the focus of these negotiations should be on strengthening enforcement (and preventing rollback) of those laws, rather than on improving them per se. Mechanisms for improving enforcement include cooperation, consultation, reporting, and monitoring. Also, a resident of any of the countries may complain to the Secretariat that a country is not enforcing its environmental laws. Under some circumstances, and if the Council by a two-thirds vote so directs, the Secretariat may prepare a factual record regarding the situation, based on information developed by the Secretariat and the use of outside experts. Critics have complained about the voting requirements and the fact that, for these purposes, the definition of "environmental law" excludes worker health and safety laws and laws relating to the commercial exploitation of natural resources. This limited definition also applies to dispute settlement, but not to other aspects of the commission's activities.

The obligation for countries to enforce their environmental laws reinforces the rule of law. It is enforceable through dispute settlement mechanisms in the agreement if two-thirds of the Council votes to institute the process. These mechanisms are elaborate; each stage of the process provides an opportunity to get countries to enforce their environmental law. This process can take many months to work through—almost three years if a country steadfastly refuses to enforce its law, the arbitral panel reconvenes to establish an action plan according to which the country must enforce its law, and the panel reconvenes again to determine whether the action plan is being fully implemented. Arbitral reports are public, and ultimately this obligation can be enforced against the United States and Mexico by trade sanctions and against Canada by enforcement in Canadian domestic courts. Moreover, these countries are physical neighbors and interact continuously in many ways, with the result that the countries have both strong incentives to live up to the Agreements obligations and a variety of means to attempt to persuade each other to comply with the provisions.

Providing trade sanctions in this context is unique. There are, of course, trade measures in many other international environmental agreements, but none addresses a persistent pattern of failure to effectively enforce a country's environmental laws.

A final important aspect of the NAAEC is that it furthers transparency and public participation in the development, adoption, application, and enforcement of environmental law and in international dispute settlement. Throughout this agreement, there are mechanisms for transparency and public participation—in other words, for democratization. These are very important. Although one can imagine more far-reaching provisions, the mechanisms in the agreement will lead to better environmental laws and more effective enforcement, and more generally to better government.

Notes and Questions

1. *Balance?* Does the NAFTA package provide proper balance to environmental and trade concerns?

2. *The FTAA.* In 1994, the 34 countries in the Western Hemisphere (all countries except Cuba) agreed to create a Free Trade Area of the Americas (FTAA). Would the NAFTA model fit the FTAA? Brazil, Argentina,

and Uruguay had formed their own regional trade area, MERCOSUR. These three countries, as well as others, were not enthusiastic about adopting the NAFTA model. Chile, however, was; and negotiations commenced in 1995 to accomplish that. Political disagreements in the United States interrupted these, however. By 1997, Chile had entered into bilateral trade agreements with Canada and Mexico.

3. *Enlarging the NAAEC.* What legal issues would be raised by bringing these countries into NAAEC? What policy questions? Would regional cooperation be enhanced?

4. *Public participation.* Suppose that you are a non-governmental organization in Canada, Mexico, or the United States. Could you make a submission to the NAAEC alleging that a contractor had failed to file a proper EIS if the case had already been litigated in the national court adversely to the plaintiff? What avenues for input are available to you under the NAAEC? By mid-1998, several submissions had been filed under NAAEC Article 14 by members of the public, asserting failure to enforce environmental law by Canada, Mexico, and the United States. These were processed according to the guidelines adopted by the CEC Council.

XXI

Financing Environmental Protection

A. INTRODUCTION

As earlier chapters indicate, the costs of international environmental protection can be great—in terms of the equipment, technology, and personnel required to abate pollution; the governmental infrastructure necessary to effectuate protection goals; and, often, the economic and social development opportunities resisted. Depending on the economic strength of a particular country, the impact of these costs in the short term can be devastating to a national economy or, at a minimum, beyond the capacity of some countries. Indeed a major concern facing the international community as it undertakes the tasks of global environmental protection is how to finance such efforts, especially when many of the necessary participants are developing countries.

As you have also seen in other chapters, the imposition of costs of environmental protection can involve issues of equity or fairness: why should developing countries sacrifice opportunities to industrialize to "save" the environment, when other countries already developed had no such care during their industrial development years ago and even had the largest role in causing environmental damage (such as depletion of the ozone layer)? Why should developing countries limit their development options when developed countries, which on a per capita basis pollute far more, will not proportionately curb their polluting activities? From the perspective of the industrialized world, the issue may be put differently: why should developed countries pay the costs of measures undertaken by developing countries, especially when developing countries argue that such aid should be in addition[1] to assistance already given by the developed countries? Part of the impetus to demanding *new* assistance is that during the past decade or so, the *real* amount of aid from developed countries, adjusted for inflation and so forth, has been decreasing.

While these issues remain subject to ongoing debate, the international community as a whole, and some developed countries unilaterally, endeavor to find ways to finance global environmental protection. Consider the following statement from Agenda 21,[2] the effort of the 1992 United Nations Conference on Environment and Development to prescribe an action plan to implement environmental and developmental cooperation, where financial arrangements were among the most contentious issues raised:

> 33.3. Economic growth, social development and poverty eradication are the first and overriding priorities in developing countries and are themselves essential to meeting national and global sustainability objectives. In the light of the global benefits to be realized by the implementation of Agenda 21 as a whole, the provision to developing countries of effective means, *inter alia,* financial resources and technology, without which it will be difficult for them to fully implement their commitments, will serve the common interests of developed and developing countries and of humankind in general, including future generations. . . .
>
> 33.9. For an evolving partnership among all countries of the world, including, in particular, between developed and developing countries, sustainable development strategies and enhanced and predictable levels of funding in support of longer term objectives are required.
>
> 33.10. The implementation of the huge sustainable development programmes of Agenda 21 will require the provision to developing countries of substantial new and additional financial resources. Grant or concessional financing should be provided according to sound and equitable criteria and indicators. . . .

1. This notion that the aid for global environmental protection be in addition to existing forms and amounts of assistance provided by developed countries is referred to as "additionally." It is not new. At the 1972 U.N. Conference on the Human Environment in Stockholm, this demand was also made by developing countries. *See* Peter Thatcher, The Role of the UN, in The International Politics of the Environment 194, 201 (A. Horrel & B. Kingsbury, eds. 1992) and Lytton K. Caldwell, Between Two Worlds 180 (1990).

2. Report of the United Nations Conference on the Environment and Development, A/CONF.151/26 (Vol. III), Section IV. ("Means of Implementation"), Chapter 33 ("Financial Resources and Mechanisms"), Aug. 14, 1992.

33.13. In general, the financing for the implementation of Agenda 21 will come from a country's own public and private sectors. For developing countries, particularly the least developed countries, ODA [Official Development Assistance] is a main source of external funding, and substantial new and additional funding for sustainable development and implementation of Agenda 21 will be required. Developed countries reaffirm their commitments to reach the accepted United Nations target of 0.7 per cent of GNP for ODA and, to the extent that they have no target, agree to augment their aid programmes in order to reach that target as soon as possible and to ensure prompt and effective implementation of Agenda 21. Some countries have agreed to reach the target by the year 2000. It was decided that the Commission on Sustainable Development would regularly review and monitor progress towards this target. This review process should systematically combine the monitoring of the implementation of Agenda 21 with a review of the financial resources available. Those countries that have already reached the target are to be commended and encouraged to continue to contribute to the common effort to make available the substantial additional resources that have to be mobilized. Other developed countries, in line with their support for reform efforts in developing countries, agree to make their best efforts to increase their level of ODA. In this context, the importance of equitable burden-sharing among developed countries is recognized. Other countries, including those undergoing the process of transition to a market economy, may voluntarily augment the contributions of the developed countries.

33.14. Funding for Agenda 21 and other outcomes of the Conference should be provided in a way that maximizes the availability of new and additional resources and uses all available funding sources and mechanisms. These include, among others:

(a) The multilateral development banks and funds:

(i) *The International Development Association (IDA).* Among the various issues and options that IDA deputies will examine in connection with the forthcoming tenth replenishment of IDA, the statement made by the President of the World Bank at the United Nations Conference on Environment and Development should be given special consideration in order to help the poorest countries meet their sustainable development objectives as contained in Agenda 21;

(ii) *Regional and subregional development banks.* The regional and subregional development banks and funds should play an increased and more effective role in providing resources on concessional or other favourable terms needed to implement Agenda 21;

(iii) *The Global Environment Facility,* managed jointly by the World Bank, UNDP and UNEP, whose additional grant and concessional funding is designed to achieve global environmental benefits, should cover the agreed incremental costs of relevant activities under Agenda 21, in particular for developing countries. Therefore, it should be restructured so as to, *inter alia:*

- Encourage universal participation;
- Have sufficient flexibility to expand its scope and coverage to relevant programme areas of Agenda 21, with global environmental benefits, as agreed;
- Ensure a governance that is transparent and democratic in nature, including in terms of decision-making and operations, by guaranteeing a balanced and equitable representation of the interests of developing countries and giving due weight to the funding efforts of donor countries;
- Ensure new and additional financial resources on grant and concessional terms, in particular to developing countries;
- Ensure predictability in the flow of funds by contributions from developed countries, taking into account the importance of equitable burden-sharing;
- Ensure access to and disbursement of the funds undermutually agreed criteria without introducing new forms of conditionality;

(b) *The relevant specialized agencies, other United Nations bodies and other international organizations,* which have designated roles to play in supporting national Governments in implementing Agenda 21;

(c) *Multilateral institutions for capacity-building and technical cooperation.* Necessary financial resources should be provided to UNDP [United Nations Development Program] to use its network of field offices and its broad mandate and experience in the field of technical cooperation for facilitating capacity-building at the country level, making full use of the expertise of the specialized agencies and other United Nations bodies within their respective areas of competence, in particular UNEP and including the multilateral and regional development banks;

(d) *Bilateral assistance programmes.* These programmes will need to be strengthened in order to promote sustainable development;

(e) *Debt relief.* It is important to achieve durable solutions to the debt problems of low- and middle-income developing countries in order to provide them with the needed means for sustainable development. Measures to address the continuing debt problems of low- and middle-income countries should be kept under review . . . .

(f) *Private funding.* Voluntary contributions through non-governmental channels, which have been running at about 10 per cent of ODA, might be increased.

33.15. *Investment.* Mobilization of higher levels of foreign direct investment and technology transfers should be encouraged through national policies that promote investment and through joint ventures and other modalities.

33.16. *Innovative financing.* New ways of generating new public and private financial resources should be explored, in particular:

(a) Various forms of debt relief, including greater use of debt swaps;

(b) The use of economic and fiscal incentives and mechanisms;

(c) The feasibility of tradeable permits;
(d) New schemes for fund-raising and voluntary contributions through private channels, including non-governmental organizations;
(e) The reallocation of resources at present committed to military purposes.

Notes and Questions

1. *The 0.7 percent commitment.* The conference estimated the annual cost (from 1993-2000) of implementing the Agenda 21 programs and projects in developing countries to be $600 billion. An accomplishment of this chapter is the pledge by developed countries to contribute 0.7 percent of their GNP for environmental and development assistance to developing countries. Of the industrialized countries, only the United States expressly stated that it refused to commit to the 0.7 percent level. As of 1997, only Denmark and Norway had met the 0.7 percent level.

2. *Is it enough?* Do you think $600 billion per year is enough? Should the entire amount be the responsibility of developed countries? Actually, this speculative figure was arrived at based on the expectation that developing countries would contribute the major portion, with developed countries giving about $125 billion (nearly double the current amount of additional grant and concessional financing). What criteria would you apply to disburse such an amount of money? How much would you give to which country, and what projects would you support?

3. *Where did it come from?* Is 0.7 percent of GNP (usually referred to in the United States as Gross Domestic Product, or GDP) too little or too much to require of developed countries? How do you suppose such a figure was calculated?

4. *Where is it going?* Developing countries frequently demand the removal of conditions on aid from developed countries (referred to as "conditionalities"). They argue that many bilateral aid agreements attach conditions so that the donor country's technology must be used and the price of such technology is inflated above market price. How did Agenda 21 deal with this matter? *See* paragraph 33.14 (a)(iii).

5. *How should it go?* What do you think the relationship should be between developed countries providing financial assistance to developing countries for environmental measures and their—as Agenda 21 put it—"transfer of environmentally sound technology, cooperation and capacity-building"? *See* Agenda 21, Ch. 34.

6. *Greenmail.* Some have written that the developing countries' demand for new aid to finance environmental protection, in addition to the current various assistance programs, is "greenmail." *See* Andrew Jordan, Financing the UNCED Agenda, 36 Envt. 16 (1994). What bargaining chips do Third World countries have? Is it important to the success of multilateral environ-

mental treaties to have the People's Republic of China and India as parties? What about San Moreno and Lesotho?

7. *How did it happen?* For an insider's view of the negotiations leading to adoption of Chapter 33, *see* Rubens Ricupero, Chronicle of a Negotiation: The Financial Chapter of Agenda 21 at the Earth Summit, 4 Colo. J. Intl. Envtl. L. & Poly. 81 (1993).

8. *MDBs, IFC and MIGA.* In addition to multilateral development banks (MDBs), discussed below, private sector sources may be developed through organizations such as the International Finance Corporation (IFC) and the Multilateral Investment Guarantee Agency (MIGA). The IFC was established to promote private sector development through financing of private enterprise in developing countries. IFC can make equity investments or loans within the private sector whether or not there is governmental participation and puts deals together that involve private banks and other lending institutions to leverage its capital. The World Bank established MIGA in 1988 to promote and protect private foreign aid direct investment for economic and social development in the World Bank member countries. MIGA provides investment guarantees against the risks of expropriation, war, civil disturbance, and breach of contract by the host government, thereby helping countries create an attractive investment climate for private foreign direct investment.

B. MULTILATERAL AND BILATERAL DEVELOPMENT BANKS

1. *General*

As mentioned in the Agenda 21 excerpt, MDBs play a significant role in financing major development projects in the Third World, and such development in turn can have significant environmental impacts. Consider the following description of MDBs and the brief critiques that follow to get an idea of the controversy that surrounds these institutions.

■ THE MULTILATERAL DEVELOPMENT BANKS, ENVIRONMENTAL POLICY, AND THE UNITED STATES

Bruce M. Rich

12 Ecology L.Q. 681, 682-688 (1985)

United States economic assistance to developing countries is administered bilaterally through federal agencies, primarily the United States Agency for International Development (AID), and through the multilateral development banks. In 1985, Congress appropriated nearly eight billion dollars for foreign economic assistance programs; of this amount, $5.45 billion were directed to AID for development assistance and $1.31 billion were contributed to the banks. The financial significance of this contribution to the banks is much more important than its dollar amount suggests, because it results in the mobilization of much larger amounts through matching funds from other countries and cofinancing arrangements. According to one estimate by the United States Treasury department, every dollar the United States appropriates to the banks is matched by a total investment by other countries, aid agencies, and commercial banks that ranges between 10 and 266 dollars, depending on the recipient bank.

The United States participates in four multilateral development banks: the World Bank, founded in 1945; the Inter-American Development Bank (Inter-American Bank), founded in 1959; the Asian Development Bank (Asian Bank), founded in 1966; and the African Development Bank (African Bank), founded in 1964. The Banks were established by Articles of Agreement that have the status of treaties, and United States participation in each bank was authorized by Congress. The authorizing acts have frequently been amended to provide for increased United States contributions and to promote certain policies within the banks.

The development banks are autonomous international institutions established to promote economic and social development in poorer nations by channeling financial resources, in the form of loans for specific projects, from the developed to the developing world. Structurally, the banks resemble closely held multinational corporations: each is managed by a president and a large internationally recruited staff, but authority is vested at the highest level in a board of governors. Each governor is a representative from an individual member country and is usually the finance minister or head of the central bank of that country. The voting power of each governor reflects the financial contribution made to the bank by the country represented.

The power of each board of governors is largely delegated to a board of executive directors. Each loan and all significant policy decisions must be approved by the executive directors or referred for the governors' approval. The board of executive directors of each bank consists of directors who individually represent the bank's largest shareholders and other directors who each represent several countries. The World Bank, for example, has 146 governors, each representing a member country, and a board of twenty-one executive directors. Each of the bank's five largest shareholders—the United States (19.3%), the United Kingdom (6.20%), the Federal Republic of Germany (6.02%), Japan (5.99%), and France (5.07%)—appoints its own director. The other sixteen directors are elected by the governors to represent groups of countries.

The banks lend money to governments of developing countries, usually for specific projects. A project is "a discrete investment program specified as to character, location and time." Each bank has a hard loan window, which provides loans for development projects at interest rates based on prevailing rates in international capital markets, and a soft loan window, which provides loans at reduced rates or no interest. Soft loans generally go to the poorest and least creditworthy member countries, which cannot afford the interest rates of hard loans.

No other international or bilateral institutions have more influence on development financing and policy in the developing world than do the banks, especially the World Bank. In 1983, the four banks together lent over twenty billion dollars to fund projects in developing countries, nearly four times the amount committed for economic development assistance by AID, the largest bilateral aid agency. In 1983, the World Bank alone committed over $15.3 billion in loans to three hundred projects in over eighty countries and disbursed $4.5 billion for ongoing loans. The net disbursements of the four banks accounted for more than twenty percent of all international development assistance in 1983.

In recent years, the majority of bank loans have supported projects in the environmentally sensitive areas of agriculture, rural development, power and irrigation schemes, and roadbuilding. In 1983, for example, 25.5% of World Bank lending was for agriculture and rural development, 15.5% for transportation projects, principally roads, and 12.2% for power projects. In the same year, 16.1% of Inter-American Bank lending was for agriculture, 24% for mining and industry, 5.6% for transportation, and 31.8% for energy, mainly hydroelectric projects.

The projects and policies of the banks have an impact on the ecological stability and environmental future of the developing world even greater than is indicated by the huge dollar amounts of their annual loan commitments. Funds lent by the banks are for the most part complemented by even greater sums provided by recipient countries, and the funding of many projects is further supplemented by cofinancing arrangements with other development agencies and with private banks. Thus, for every dollar the World Bank lends for a project, more than two additional dollars are raised from other sources; for the Inter-American Bank, this cofinancing ratio approaches three to one.

The influence of bank lending on development policy is also magnified by the banks' funding of research, training, technology transfer, planning, and other forms of institutional support in host countries. In addition, loan conditions and stipulations can be highly specific and often contain terms affecting more than just the implementation of a single project. The country and sector documents prepared by the banks to identify lending priorities often shape the planning discussions among the development banks, aid agencies, commercial banks, and the host countries, and thus profoundly affect the development efforts of those countries. Developing countries often modify their development policies and priorities for entire sectors of the economy in response to the suggestions and requirements of the banks.

This direct policy leverage is especially strong in structural adjustment and sector loans. Bank officials have commented on the superior policy leverage of structural adjustment lending, which is conditioned on structural reform of national economies. Sector lending seeks to promote policy changes in whole areas of economic activity, such as agriculture. In fiscal years 1983 and 1984, the World Bank committed ten percent of its loans for structural adjustment programs. This is the maximum amount of non-project lending that, according to the Bank's board of directors, is allowed under its Articles of Agreement. Both the World Bank and the United States wish to substantially increase structural adjustment lending in the future.

Notes

1. *Regional approach.* The World Bank has assisted with the development of some regional plans and programs such as the Mediterranean Environmental Technical Assistance Program, the Environmental Action Programme for Central and Eastern Europe, the Danube River Program, and the Black Sea Program. These are undertaken in conjunction with other bilateral and multilateral organizations.

2. *The World Bank and the environment.* The bank, while having the function of assisting development programs, has been criticized by conservation groups who charge that many of the activities funded by the bank have had a negative effect on the environment and the people living in development project regions. In the past years, there have been many cases in which development organizations have been responsible for carrying out programs that have had deleterious effects on rural populations, particularly those in the Third World. In many of these cases, local populations are excluded from discussions concerning their own homelands. In some areas, projects have ravaged farmlands and uprooted entire populations, placing hardships on the very people the projects were intended to help. World Bank countries have often come under fire for being shortsighted by exploiting the environments of lesser developed countries in an effort to strengthen their own economies. Conservation groups now charge that the World Bank itself is promoting and funding such unsound development projects. According to conservation group critics, the Singrauli construction and development project in India, backed by the World Bank in the amount of $850 million, is just one of several bank projects that have damaged the environment, ruined livelihoods, and even cost lives. *See* Bankrolling Debacles?, U.S. News & World Report, Sept. 25, 1989, at 43, 44.

3. *The World Bank and indigenous people.* Other criticized projects having

negative impacts on indigenous people include the National Land Management Project in Botswana, which resulted in dispossession of lands, impoverishment, and land use conflicts; the Chico Dams Project in the Philippines, which caused forced relocation and nonpayment of compensation; the Manantali Dam in Senegal, which resulted in dispossession of land and an increase in malaria; and the Ecuador Oil Developments Project, which resulted in the Waorani and other Indian tribes being forced off their land and massive environmental problems including oil spills and poisoned water sources. *See* Robert K. Hitchcock, International Human Rights, The Environment, And Indigenous Peoples, 5 Colo. J. Intl. Envtl. L & Poly. 1, 2-3 (1994).

4. *Indigenous people, NGOs, and foreign donors.* The question that a number of indigenous groups have is whether it is appropriate for environmental organizations and foreign donor agencies to be involved in promoting activities that have such a negative effect on the lives of the indigenous people and their environment. As one Tyua woman in Bulalima-Mangwe, Botswana, said, "Just because these people say they are helping preserve the environment does not mean that they should be able to violate our human rights." *Id.* at 18.

■ TROPICAL GANGSTERS

Robert Klitgard
8-12, 207 (1991)

Faced with these grave and worsening problems, most African countries are experimenting with radical economic reforms that can be compared to Eastern Europe's. (Few, however, are emulating Eastern Europe's move toward democracy.) Why the sudden upheaval in economic strategy? Bluntly put, most African countries have gone broke. Private banks will no longer lend to them, so they need financing of the International Monetary Fund and the World Bank. The IMF and the Bank are the preachers of free-market economic reforms. To get their blessing, the Africans are converting.

The influence of the Fund and the Bank has grown tremendously over the past decade. The two institutions work closely together—their headquarters are on adjacent streets in Washington. Both are multilateral organizations set up near the end of the Second World War to help the shattered global economy. Today both concentrate on the developing countries, to whom they offer low-interest loans with strings attached. But the two institutions tend to differ in their economic concerns. Although the lines have been blurring, the IMF tends to worry about economic stability in the short run—say, over a year or two—while the World Bank struggles with economic growth in the medium run—say, three to five years. The IMF tends to focus on money supplies and budget balances, whereas the Bank homes in on public investment and pricing policies. Both the Fund and the Bank emphasize exports as the key to growth, as opposed to the old strategy of import substitution, which promoted industries producing goods for domestic consumption. And both institutions stress the move toward free markets.

For a developing country, an agreement with the IMF has become something like a Good Housekeeping Seal of Approval. Unless the IMF says your economic strategy is sound, many aid donors and commercial lenders will not ante up. The World Bank's role is less dramatic, but having a structural adjustment program with the Bank is frequently a facilitator if not a prerequisite for aid from other sources.

An agreement with the IMF and a structural adjustment program with the Bank typically contain common elements. The country devalues its currency, cuts government spending, frees up domestic and international trade and turns public enterprises over to private management or joint ventures. In the parlance of the World Bank,

> The objective of structural adjustment programs is to restore rapid economic growth while simultaneously supporting internal and external financial stability. As such, these programs have macroeconomic and microeconomic aspects. The major macro objectives are to improve the external balance and domestic fiscal balance. An adjustment program thus commonly includes a combination of (1) fiscal and monetary policies to bring about overall demand reduction and (2) trade policies (mainly the exchange rate and import/export taxes and subsidies) to alter the relative incentives between tradable and non-tradable goods. On the micro side, the major objective is to improve efficiency in the use of resources by removing price distortions, opening up more competition, and dismantling administrative controls (deregulation). Such programs include those for government expenditures and the management of public enterprises, including reduction in the government's presence in areas where private enterprise can operate more efficiently.

Structural adjustment means less government, freer trade, and more private enterprise. But the change can be painful. It is often accompanied by a recession. Public spending on schooling and health collapses, while prices rise for food and housing and transport. Foreigners begin to play a greater role in the economy and the shift is ideologically traumatic: free-market reforms overthrow the gamut of socialist and nationalist policies of independent Africa's founding fathers, men like Ghana's Kwame Nkrumah, Guinea's Sékou Touré, Tanzania's Julius Nyerere.

Since so many poor countries are bankrupt and up to their eyes in debt, they virtually have to do what the IMF and the Bank say. Consequently, the Fund and the Bank often play the role of outside heavies. They insist on reform, design it, and monitor its implementation. No wonder such foreign aid is controversial: to many, it smacks of neo-imperialism. And there is controversy over the adequacy of the IMF-World Bank recipe. Not only politicians but also academicians and even Bank staff have qualms.

"I just don't have confidence in the formulas we prescribe, those standard remedies," an old friend, who had worked at the World Bank for years on various African nations, told me in 1985. "It's fine to praise export-led growth, but the evidence is that it doesn't work for a lot of countries. The Bank has terrible morale now, as you have noticed. One reason is that many of us doubt what we are doing. . . ."

Most societies share certain fundamental moral principles. Two such, I think, are the principles of beneficence and autonomy. Being beneficent means doing or producing good, specifically performing acts of kindness and charity. The word comes from the Latin word for favor. Autonomy comes from the Greek word for independence and means the quality or state of being self-governing. Sometimes the benefactor's role—his prescription—reduces the recipient's autonomy—as can occur, for example, in a medical setting. The physician wants to help, and the patient wants to be helped. But sometimes help becomes prescription, is required. The doctor may end up making and forcing the decisions—violating the patient's autonomy in the process . . .

First of all, the IMF and the World Bank do not exactly dictate. A country has to ask for loans from the Fund or the Bank. Some countries have not—Cuba, for example. It is in a strict sense voluntary that a nation submit to some impingements on its autonomy—as private companies sometimes do when they are in financial trouble and allow bankers to sit on their boards or venture capitalists to help manage the company. Or, as patients sometimes do with their physicians.

On the other hand, do bankrupt countries have a real choice?

Leverage can restrict sovereignty. Benevolence can undermine autonomy. Fundamental dilemmas like these often drive people to extremes. We seem to need to find bad guys, someone to blame, and to put ourselves on the other side. We seem to seek simple truths.

"Look," says one extreme position, "these countries want to borrow money and the only way they will be credit-worthy is if they follow this advice. We've seen our recipes work elsewhere. And by imposing these conditions, by using our leverage, we are doing good. Not least, we are saving the people of these countries a little bit from their corrupt and inefficient governments.["]"

"The governments of places like Equatorial Guinea are composed of predatory figures who cloak themselves in concepts of 'African socialism' and 'poorest of the poor' but spend their time with their hands in the till. Those beating the drum of sovereignty loudest are often, in the words of Kid Creole and the Coconuts, the truest tropical gangsters."

But consider another extreme interpretation.

"So-called 'foreign aid' and 'help in economic reform' are nothing more than neo-imperialism, the transgression of sovereignty, and the imposition of the dictates of international capitalism. The standard advice does violence to our country's realities. It also foments domestic monopolies as allies to the international monopolies, who wish again to tell the old colonies what to do.["]"

"The real tropical gangsters are the capitalists, both domestic and foreign, and the aid agencies who promote them. Perhaps even the expatriate so-called experts qualify—such as you."

Which side is right? Or are both? In most poor countries, as the first argument says, governments tend not to work well. But the second argument has a point, too. So-called free markets do not work well in most poor countries either. Nor does the machinery of international credit and foreign aid. Given Africa's poverty, ignorance, disease, and dictators, we should not be surprised to find rampant opportunism, deceit, and distrust; and these in turn foster flaccid and corrupt institutions—public, private, and international. The harsh conditions of underdevelopment encourage tropical gangsters of every variety—government, business, and international aid giver.

So there is no solace in extreme views. One cannot simply say, "Leave it to the market" or, "The World Bank knows best," just as one cannot say, "The government in its wisdom should run everything." In underdeveloped countries, the action is between the extremes of state domination and laissez-faire, between aid and dependency.

In these difficult circumstances, how can the outside world help without hurting, apply leverage without trampling sovereignty? Dilemmas of how to give and how to receive seem particularly stark in Africa, with so much need and so much leverage and so little understood about either. But this tension between benevolence and autonomy is also a fundamental human problem that in myriad ways and circumstances each of us encounters. How can we work for change while respecting what exists? How can we exercise analytical skills and make critical judgments while still affirming the imperfect people and situations we encounter? And how can we extend our limits in order to receive from the people to whom we are trying to give? . . .

In early 1988, we were descended upon by two World Bank missions. The term *mission* now seems to me curiously appropriate. One of its definitions evokes pilots over enemy terrain, flying in close formation, dropping their loads, and returning home. Another meaning has to do with missionaries, aliens who promise salvation to the natives if only certain, shall we say, structural adjustments are made. World Bank missions partake of both. Disciplined groups parachute in, carry out hectic sorties, advocate and even insist upon changed behavior and belief, and leave.

Notes and Questions

1. *Environmental Assessment.* What can be done to make the World Bank and other MDBs evaluate the environmental impacts of proposed projects

and to employ such data in funding decisions and project design? The World Bank does undertake projects after considering their environmental impacts, but their assessment process is not always adequate and the integration of the findings into the decisionmaking process and project design are apparently lacking. One explanation is that the Bank's personnel is largely composed of "economists, engineers, and agronomists—professionals who are not always sympathetic to environmental issues." John Horberry, The Accountability of Development Assistance Agencies: The Case of Environmental Policy, 12 Ecology L.Q. 817, 828 (1985). How can the professional predispositions of staff be overcome? *See generally* World Bank, Environmental Guidelines (1988) and the World Bank's Operational Directive 4.00, Annex A: Environmental Assessment (1989).

Professor David Wirth, formerly of the Natural Resources Defense Council, has argued: "Probably the most crucial feature in assuring the environmental sustainability of a development assistance project is the participation of environmental groups, human rights organizations, and the public generally at the planning stage. . . . Another procedural necessity . . . is effective monitoring and enforcement." David Wirth, Environment, Economic Development and Human Rights: A Triangular Relationship?, 1988 Proc. Am. Socy. Intl. L. Ann. Mtg. 40, 46-47. Consider the discussion on the World Bank's Inspection Panel, below. Does that institution adequately respond to the concerns expressed here?

2. *Private lending.* Twelve percent of the world's official development assistance is provided by the World Bank. But perhaps as significant is the fact that every $1 of World Bank support for a project usually means $2 are lent from commercial banks and countries. How can environmental concerns be part of the funding decisions taken by private lending sources?

3. *MDB decisionmaking.* Developing countries have criticized the undemocratic nature of the MDB decisionmaking process. "Weighted voting gives the major subscribers a majority of votes and makes their combined influence over matters of bank financial policies and practice particularly strong." Horberry, above, at 825. Is such criticism fair? Should not the donors of assistance have some control over which countries receive it? Moreover, why should not the donors be able to exercise some control over how the recipient uses the money?

2. The North American Development Bank (NADBank)

Pursuant to efforts to increase bilateral cooperation between the United States and Mexico in the border areas of the two countries, an "Agreement Between the Government of the United States of America and the Government of the United Mexico States Concerning the Establishment of a Border Environment Commission and a North American Development Bank" was entered into in October 1993 (Border Finance Agreement).

Newest among development banks, the NADBank will focus exclusively on financing in both countries environmental infrastructure projects that are certified by the Border Environment Cooperation Commission (BECC), also a new institution established by the Border Finance Agreement.

■ THE NAFTA: REPORT ON ENVIRONMENTAL ISSUES 23, 24 (1993)

reprinted in *Message from the President of the United States Transmitting North American Free Trade Agreement Supplemental Agreements and Additional Documents, H.R. Doc. 160, 103 Cong., 1st Sess. 179-80 (1993)*

The North American Development Bank will be capitalized and governed equally by the two countries. Its primary purpose is to finance projects certified by the Border Environment Cooperation Commission. Based on its paid-in capitalization, the parties envision that the NADBank will be able to make available some $2 billion or more in loans and guarantees for environmental infrastructure projects, with an upper limit of just under $3 billion.

The NADBank will use its own capital funds (contributed equally by the United States and Mexico), funds raised by it in the financial markets, and other available resources to finance public and private investment in environmental infrastructure projects, and to encourage and supplement private investment in environmental infrastructure projects. Initial paid-in capital will be $450 million, comprised of $225 million each from Mexico and the United States. The callable capital will amount to $2.55 billion, also contributed equally by the United States and Mexico.

Each country may apply up to ten percent of its capital to a community adjustment and investment "window," to supplement existing government assistance programs.

The NADBank is intended to supplement existing sources of financing. It will support, not impair, the ability of governments and investors to seek financing from other institutions. In conjunction with other sources of funds, such as existing governmental sources of funds in the United States for U.S. projects, as well as World Bank and Inter-American Development Bank loans to Mexico, a total of $7-8 billion of financing is expected to be available for environmental improvements in the border area over the next decade.

As of October 1996, the bank had $1.5 billion in capital paid in equal parts by both countries. By the end of December, capital increased to close to $2.25 billion. The bank's capital and reserves are invested through the Banco de Mexico and the U.S. Federal Reserve.

3. *The World Bank's Inspection Panel*

a. General

In 1993, in a NGO-led initiative touted as the first forum in which private parties can attempt to hold international organizations directly accountable for their actions, the executive directors of the International Bank for Reconstruction and Development (IBRD) and the International Development Association (IDA)—both institutions of the World Bank—established a three-member Inspection Panel. This independent panel provides private citizens access to the World Bank if they believe they are directly or adversely affected by a bank-financed project; in other words, it enables private parties to request that the bank act in accordance with its own policies and procedures. The panel investigates complaints and makes recommendations pursuant to its "Operating Procedures" (*See* <http://www.worldbank.org/html/ins-panel).

The Inspection Panel is composed of three members who are selected by the World Bank's Board of Executive Directors by weighted vote. The Inspection Panel members, since its operational inception in fall 1994, have been highly qualified; they are selected "on the basis of their ability to deal thoroughly and fairly with the requests brought to them, their integrity and independence from the bank's management, and their exposure to developmental issues and to living conditions in developing countries." Members must not work for the World Bank for two years before their service and may not work for the bank after expiration of their term. Each member must be a citizen of a different World Bank member country and is appointed to serve one nonrenewable five-year term.

b. Inspection Panel's Authority

The Operating Procedures specify that the panel is authorized to accept requests for inspection "which claim that an actual or threatened material adverse effect on the affected party's rights or interests arises directly out of an action or omission of the Bank as a result of a failure by the Bank to follow its own operational policies and procedures during the design, appraisal and/or implementation of a Bank-financed project." Also, before submitting a request, some exhaustion of administrative remedies is required: steps should have been taken to bring the matter to the attention of the management, and response received was unsatisfactory to the requester. Operating Procedures, Article 1. The panel is not authorized to deal with the following:

(a) complaints with respect to actions which are the responsibility of other parties . . . ;
(b) complaints against procurement decisions by Bank borrowers from suppliers of goods and services financed or expected to be financed by the Bank under a loan/credit agreement, or from losing tenderers for the supply of any such goods and services, which will continue to be addressed by Bank staff under existing procedures;
(c) requests filed after the Closing Date of the loan/credit financing the project . . . ; or
(d) requests related to a particular matter or matters over which the Panel has already made its recommendation after having received a prior Request, unless justified by new evidence. . . .

Operating Procedures, Article 2.

c. Who Can Request

The panel's processing of a request begins when a request is received complaining of a violation of the bank's policies and procedures. Any of the following persons or entities may file such a request:

- any group of two or more people in the country where the Bank financed project is located (e.g., an organization, association, society or other grouping of individuals would qualify);
- a duly appointed local representative;
- a foreign representative, where there is clear evidence that there is no adequate or appropriate representative in the country of the project; or
- an Executive Director of the Bank in special cases of serious alleged violations of the Bank's policies and procedures.

Operating Procedures, Arts. 4 and 11.

d. Timeline and Essential Aspects of the Investigation/ Recommendation Process

Within 21 days of notification of a request, the management of the project provides the panel with evidence that it has complied or intends to comply with the bank's policies and procedures. Operating Procedures, Article 27. After receiving management's response, the panel makes a recommendation to the executive directors as to whether the matter should be investigated. Operating Procedures, Article 30. The Board of the Executive Directors decides whether to accept or reject the panel's recommendation to investigate. Should an investigation occur, the panel may employ various approaches, including public hearings in the country of the project and visiting the project sites. Operating Procedures, Article 45. Consequently, a Panel Report is submitted summarizing the relevant facts and investigation and containing the panel's findings about whether the bank complied with relevant bank policies and procedures. Operation Procedures, Article 52. Within six weeks after receipt of this report, management submits a response; two weeks later, during which the executive directors have considered the Panel's Report and the management's response, the bank informs the requester of the results of the investigation and any proposed board action. Operating Procedures, Articles 54 and 55.

e. Experience of the Inspection Panel

In a report by a former Inspection panel member on the first three years of the panel's operation—from August 1994 to August 1997—the member reported that the panel had reviewed ten projects. During the first two years, five requests were received (from Nepal, Ethiopia, Tanzania, Brazil, and Chile), but only two went beyond the first stage of qualification. However, in the third year, the panel member reported that there was increasing complexity in the cases (two from Bangladesh; one each from Paraguay, Brazil, and India) and growth in the panel's influence over management's compliance with bank policies. (Richard E. Bissell, Recent Practice of the Inspection Panel of the World Bank, 91 Am. J. Intl. L. 741, 742 (1997); *see also* <http://www.worldbank.org/html/ins-panel/INS_PANEL.html>).

One of the more important requests, as reported by the World Bank press releases, follows. It illustrates the process and the complexity of the cases:

#7 Yacyreta Hydroelectric Project—Argentina/Paraguay

> On Octobert 1, 1996 the Panel Chairman registered a Request from SOBREVIVENCIA (Friends of the Earth, Paraguay) representing people living in Encarnacion, Paraguay. The Requester claims that their standards of living, health and economic well-being have been, and may be, directly and adversely harmed as a result of filling the Yacyreta Reservoir and the Bank's omissions and failures in preparation and implementation of the project.
>
> The Panel, on December 24, 1996, recommended an investigation which on February 28, 1997 was rejected by the Executive Directors. Instead, the Board chose to approve a review of the existing project problems and an assessment of agreed plans of action developed to remedy the effects of filling the reservoir. The Panel submitted this on September 16, 1997 and a date for Board consideration is to be determined.

<http://www.worldbank.org/html/ins-panel/INS_PANEL.html>

f. Issues of Enforcement

According to Bissell, above, and recognizing the outcome of the Yacyreta case as an example, the recommendations of Inspection Panels calling for a full investigation can be overridden by the Board of Executive Directors. On the other hand, there is evidence in this brief collection of cases that projects have been re-designed and even World Bank support has been withdrawn, due to panel investigations. For a description of the Requests for Inspection (as of July 1998 there were 13), *see* the website <http://www.worldbank.org/html/ins-panel/overview.html>

Notes and Questions

1. *Is it enough?* Do you think the World Bank Inspection Panel adequately responds to the criticisms levied at the World Bank regarding its attention to environmental concerns of its projects? For a book that analyzes the origins, functions, and objectives of the Inspection Panel, *see* Ibrahim F. I. Shihata, The World Bank Inspection Panel (1994).

2. *Who can participate?* The Operating Procedures indicates that access to the complaint process is available to a potentially large group of petitioners. What is not well known is the extent to which third parties may participate in the process. Under Article 50 of the Operating Procedures, "any member of the public may provide Inspector(s) with supplemental information that they believe is relevant. . . ." In fact, in the Indian NTPC Power Generation Project in Singrauli, India, NGOs in Switzerland and the United States submitted memoranda on the environmental issues of concern to the petitioners.

3. *What functions does it serve?* A recent article raises the issue of the enforcement efficacy of the Investigation Panel. It states:

> [T]he Panel has no enforcement power whatsoever. The Panel is only capable of recommending inspections and, if the inspection is approved, recommending changes in the projects. The Bank's Board decides whether to agree to a Panel investigation and whether to adopt the Panel's recommmendations. If the Board does not want an investigation, the Panel is unable to go forward with an investigation. In addition, if the Panel determines that no investigation is necessary, the Board does not have to abide by the Panel's findings and recommendations. Instead, the Board may continue to fund the project contrary to the Panel's findings and recommendation.

Kristine J. Dunkerton, Comment—The World Bank Inspection Panel and Its Effect on Lending Accountability to Citizens of Borrowing Nations, 5 U. Balt. J. Envtl. L. 226, 241-242 (1997).

Do you agree? If so, what function does the Inspection Panel serve? If not, how would you describe the function of the Inspection Panel in the World Bank bureaucracy?

4. *The NTC Power Generation Project.* In answer to the prior question, consider the following case:

> Local inhabitants of Singrauli, India challenged the Indian NTPC Power Generation Project, which they claim caused environmental damage and had provided inadequate resettlement compensation. Although the Inspection Panel recommended a full-fledged investigation, the bank's executive directors—upon submission of a corrective Action Plan presented by bank management—approved only a limited, restricted desk study in Washington.
>
> The report concluded that the World Bank committed "serious violations of its policies and procedures" in approving the loan for the project. Since the bank is charged with ensuring that borrowers have sufficient capacity to meet environmental standards and any people that must be involuntarily resettled must receive direct benefits from the project, the report found that neither of these conditions was met primarily due to the intense pressure that came from the World Bank's senior regional management to accelerate the loan approval process. The report specifically noted that regional advisers, acting on bank advice, had included promises of "land for land" and "jobs" in their final proposal, even though they knew both objectives were unrealistic. "Most of the displaced population does not appear to be receiving benefits from the project (for example, electricity) despite this being the express objective of the bank's resettlement policy." In addition, the bank did not properly consider alternatives to ash disposal plants, a byproduct of the power generation process, which have contaminated crops and farms. *See* Inspection Panel Report (Final) on NTPC Power Generation Project in Singrauli, India. (Panel investigation reports and Bank Management responses are available from the World Bank Public Information Centers.)

Does this case suggest that the Inspection Panel process makes the World Bank more accountable for its actions? Are its procedures and actions sufficiently transparent? What if the bank chooses to ignore the panel's report on the Singauli Power Plant Project?

5. *Independence.* Is the Inspection Panel really independent? Is independence from the bank necessary? Or does such a body tend to provide "cover" for bank actions?

6. *Other inspection panels.* The World Bank's efforts have apparently inspired other development banks to create institutions similar to the Inspection Panel. The private sector arm of the World Bank, the International Finance Corporation, has undertaken a major reform of its environmental, social, and disclosure of information policies of which the institution of

an "Inspection Panel" is a part. As of this writing (March 1998), a proposal for the formation of an IFC Inspection Panel is in draft and out for comment. However, in an early ad hoc application of the idea and in response to a complaint filed by a Chilean organization, the IFC commissioned an inspector to review the IFC's handling of the environmental and social aspects of the Pangue Hydroelectric project in Chile, for which the IFC approved debt and equity financing in 1992. Chilean environmentalists and Pehuenche Indians in 1995 alleged that the IFC had broken its own environmental and social rules in financing the dam, the first in a series of hydroelectric projects along the Bio Bio River that is planned by the country's privatized electric company, Endesa.

This was not a particularly good debut for the institution since only a heavily redacted version of the environmental report was released damning aspects of the project. IFC officials responded that it demonstrated the IFC was in compliance with most of the relevant policies and exercised a good influence on the project. The principal author of the inspection report, however, accused IFC officials of censoring the report in such a way as to reverse his findings. For more information about the IFC's efforts, see its website: <http://www.ifc.org/press/1998/policya.htm>.

The Asian Development Bank (ADB) has also taken the lead of the World Bank. In 1995, its Board of Directors adopted an inspection policy "to improve the quality and transparency of the Bank's operations, as well as its accountability." Overview of the Inspection Policy, at ADB website: <http://www.asiandevbank.org/policy/overview.html>. Although different in some of its structure, it is designed to establish a "formal channel through which local communities, organizations and other groups can request independent review or 'inspection' of the Bank's role in certain Bank-financed projects." Inspection Procedures, Art. 1. Under this policy, a committee comprised of six board members reviews requests for inspection and recommends to the board whether an inspection is warranted. If the board authorizes an inspection, the committee will select a panel of independent experts from an approved roster of experts to conduct the inspection to report to the committee. Based on the report and management's reponse to it, the committee makes recommendations to the board.

7. *Inspection panels and international law.* Some have characterized inspection panels as being a major development in international law in that they provide individuals and private groups access to the decisionmaking and adjudication processes of international organizations, where that access was traditionally reserved to states. *See, e.g.*, Shihata, above, at 119. Another commentator has argued that public international law "includes rules deriving from the operations of the MDBs [multilateral development banks] themselves, such as formal guidelines on the procurement of goods and services for MDB-financed projects; written interpretations of their own loan, guarantee, and project agreements; and principles drawn from cus-

tomary MDB practice in applying and enforcing key provisions of those agreements." John W. Head, Evolution of the Governing Law for Loan Agreements of the World Bank and Other Multilateral Development Banks, 90 Am. J. Intl. L. 214, 229-230 (1996) (citations omitted). Do you draw the same conclusions from your brief introduction to this new institution, or do you think these comments are overstated? Assuming Inspection Panels provide a new avenue of international environmental law development, as counsel to an NGO, how would you advise your organization to take advantage of the availability of such panels?

C. EXPORT CREDIT ANGENCIES

Most, perhaps all, industrialized countries have created institutions that assist in financing exports and investment opportunities abroad. In the United States, these include the Export-Import Bank (Ex-In Bank) and the Overseas Private Investment Corporation (OPIC).

Both Ex-In Bank and OPIC have internal policies directed at ensuring the environmental soundness of the activities. OPIC was a groundbreaker in this regard, once even attempting to terminate insurance of a project in Indonesia on environmental grounds.

The United States has tried to convince other countries to adopt similar policies, for example at the G-7 meeting in 1997. Unfortunately, it has had little success as of mid-1998: the other countries seem intent on emphasizing exports or foreign direct investment, without analyzing or otherwise taking into account the environmental implications of those activities.

D. DEBT RELIEF APPROACHES

1. *Debt-for-Nature Swaps*

■ DEBT-FOR-NATURE SWAPS, A NEW MEANS OF FUNDING CONSERVATION IN DEVELOPING NATIONS

Kathryn S. Fuller & Douglas F. Williamson
11 Intl. Envtl. Rep. (BNA) 301, 301-303 (May 11, 1988)

Developing nations owe more than one trillion dollars to lending institutions. The accelerating rate at which many banks are writing down portions of their loan portfolios—illustrated by the Bank of Boston's decision last December to write down 50 percent of its Latin American loans—shows fading confidence in the banking community that many of these loans will ever be repaid.

At the same time, deforestation in many tropical countries is occurring at an alarming rate. Developing countries, under pressure to meet domestic social needs as well as external financial obligations, may see no choice but to exploit their natural resource base at a pace that cannot be sustained. At the present rate of clearing, the forests of the tropics, which contain half of the animal and plant species on earth, could be destroyed in the next century. The result would be calamitous. In the tropics, rural people depend on these forests for food, fuel, building materials, medicines, fodder for livestock—indeed for many of their staples. In the developed world, too, people rely on the many agricultural, medicinal, and industrial products that originate in tropical forests.

In 1984, World Wildlife Fund's then vice-president for science, Dr. Thomas E. Lovejoy, proposed converting international debt into support for conservation. In an op-ed piece in the *New York Times*, Dr. Lovejoy drew a correlation between indebtedness and environmental degradation. In debtor nations, programs to manage natural resources were among the first slashed as governments struggled to reduce spending. As a consequence, these countries relied heavily on foreign donors to help support their biologically rich national parks. Development aid dollars, when made available, generally were channeled into export-oriented businesses that would yield foreign exchange to repay interest on the staggering debt. Because of pressing social needs, even under the best of circumstances debtor nations found it hard to address critical conservation needs. Why not, Lovejoy argued, use the debt crisis to help solve environmental problems? Why not convert tropical nations' debts directly into support for conservation—that is, swap debt for nature?

Exploring the Possibilities

At first, the idea was greeted with skepticism. Why would a debtor government or a lender bank be interested in such a proposal? How could a private conservation group involve itself in something as complex as the international debt crisis?

Indeed, a number of questions needed answers. The governments of debtor nations needed to be assured that debt swaps neither would jeopardize their economy—by contributing to inflation if large amounts of local currency were printed to redeem debt—nor would they threaten sovereignty by transferring control of land and other national assets to foreigners. Banks in both the creditor and debtor nations had to be convinced that debt-for-nature programs were in their self-interest and presented no undue financial risks. The governments of creditor nations needed to confirm that debt-for-nature swaps were compatible with regulations governing the activities of nonprofit organizations. And conservation organizations needed to be convinced that debt-for-nature swaps would be a better use of their own resources than conventional projects.

In 1987, several factors combined to provide impetus to debt-for-nature swaps. Opportunities emerged as a growing number of debtors and lenders, frustrated by the failure of standard approaches to alleviating debt, became open to unconventional solutions. Many debtor nations instituted "debt-for-equity swaps" through which they redeemed portions of their debt in local currency by allowing debt-holders to take equity positions in commercial and industrial projects. At the same time, a growing number of lender banks began to conclude that sizable portions of their debt portfolios, especially in Latin America, were uncollectible. These banks began to write down or sell high-risk debts at substantial discounts, fueling increased activity in what is called the secondary-debt market.

World Wildlife Fund and other conservation organizations began to discuss with debtor nations ways in which debt could be converted to benefit local conservation programs. Rather than swap debt for commercial or industrial expansion, these groups proposed that countries rich in biological resources agree to swap a portion of their debt for conservation.

The First Debt-for-Nature Swaps

In July 1987, Bolivia carried out the first debt-for-nature swap through an agreement between the Bolivian government and Conservation International. Conservation International purchased $650,000 of Bolivia's commercial debt through Citicorp Investment Bank for $100,000, that is, 15 cents on the dollar. In exchange for this debt, Bolivia's president agreed to set aside 3.7 million acres of tropical forest around the Beni Biosphere Reserve as a protected area and to establish a $250,000 fund in local currency for its management.

In October 1987, Ecuador announced its own $10 million debt-for-nature program. The concept behind the deal in Ecuador originated with Roque Sevilla, president of Fundacion Natura, Ecuador's leading private conservation organization. Under Ecuador's program, debt in a face amount of up to $10 million can be converted by the Central Bank into local currency bonds to be held by Fundacion Natura.

To date, World Wildlife Fund has purchased $1 million of Ecuadorean debt at 35 cents on the dollar with the help of both Citicorp and Bankers Trust Company. The interest on the nine-year bonds—33 percent in the first year—will be used to help manage Ecuador's new and existing parks, among them Cayambe-Coca Ecological Reserve, Podocarpus National Park, Pasochoa Nature Reserve, and the world famous Galapagos National Park. It will also be used to train national park personnel, strengthen local conservation institutions, and promote environmental education. Principal on the bonds, which is amortized over the life of the bonds, will provide an endowment for the Fundacion.

By issuing bonds rather than cash, Ecuador's Central Bank not only reduced the likelihood that the swap would have inflationary impacts locally but also provided a mechanism through which foreign donors could more than triple the value of their conservation investments. These donors could support the long-term development of a strong local conservation organization, while helping in a modest way to alleviate Ecuador's debt burden.

Because the bonds have a nine-year term, the planning and implementation of long-range programs can proceed without fear that project funding may be cut off next year.

Fundacion Natura actively sought contributions of the remaining $9 million of Ecuador's $10 million debt-for-nature program. This innovative program should substantially increase foreign investment in Ecuadorean conservation and provide much needed support not only to Fundacion Natura but also to other governmental and non-governmental groups throughout Ecuador. . . . [The second exchange under the Ecuadorean program involving the remaining $9 million took place in April 1989. The Nature Conservancy ("TNC") and the Missouri Botanical Gardens joined WWF-US as purchasers of the debt at twelve cents on the dollar—EDS.]

Also in 1987, Costa Rica announced a debt-for-nature program proposed by Alvaro Umana, Costa Rica's Minister of Natural Resources, Energy, and Mines. Under this initiative, the Central Bank of Costa Rica authorized up to $5.4 million in debt-for-nature swaps by autumn 1988. Contributions from a number of donors, including World Wildlife Fund, Conservation, International, and The Nature Conservancy have already resulted in the acquisition of the full face amount of debt at prices ranging between 15 to 17 cents on the dollar. As in the Ecuadorean program, the Central Bank has redeemed debt by issuing local currency bonds. Proceeds from the bonds are financing a wide range of conservation programs, including the acquisition by local Costa Rican groups of land to expand Guanacaste National Park and the Monteverde Cloud Forest Reserve, management of protected areas and their buffer zones, development of park facilities, and training of park personnel.

While the Fundacion de Parques Nacionales and the Fundacion Neotropica, two Costa Rican organizations, oversee payment of bond proceeds, a Costa Rican bank, the Banco Cooperativo, holds the bonds in trust. As a result of Costa Rica's quick success in securing the initial $5.4 million, the government plans to raise the ceiling on debt-for-nature swaps, perhaps up to $50 million. World Wildlife Fund has agreed to acquire up to $3 million of Costa Rican debt over a three-year period, and other prospective donors have also expressed interest in participating in further swaps. [These various swaps have brought the total face value of Costa Rican debt exchanged to

$79,253,631, according to figures provided by Anthony D'Amato, Kirsten Engel, International Environmental Law Anthology 465 (1996)—EDS.]

HOW BENEFICIAL ARE DEBT-FOR-NATURE SWAPS?

A question often asked is what makes these swaps more desirable as a means of funding conservation than merely providing cash payments directly.

At a glance, it might appear that the amount of work necessary to conclude a sound debt-for-nature swap outweighs the potential gain. The deals are extremely complex. Each step requires specialized talents. Approval must be obtained from the debtor country's government and central bank. An agreement must be fashioned, and the debt acquired and converted into a local financial instrument. The host government must decide what exchange rate to apply in converting debt into local currency, what conditions of payment to use in exchange for the debt, and whom to designate as a local agent to control the funds and dispense the proceeds. Only then can a conservation program be implemented.

For the conservation organization in the creditor country, the choices also are difficult. Acquiring debt is a technically complex transaction. It is not possible to purchase debt as one might buy commercial bonds. The expansion of the secondary-debt market has opened many options, making it necessary to shop for debt that is available in the right denomination, acceptable to the debtor country government, and with a satisfactory schedule of maturation.

If the aim of conservation organizations in debt-for-nature swaps is to achieve maximum conservation benefit with their scarce funds, why would they take on so much trouble involving lawyers, bankers, tax analysts, and extensive staff commitments?

The answer is straightforward: despite these administrative burdens, conservation still comes out ahead. Debt-for-nature swaps dramatically increase the impact of conservation dollars. At current exchange rates, one dollar face amount of acquired debt may yield many multiples over that in local currency. With the conversion of the debt into bonds, proceeds from the swap flow over a significant period of time. Good rates of return provide a strong incentive to foreign conservation donors to increase their contributions to countries that have approved debt-for-nature swaps.

In addition, debt-for-nature swaps promote and highlight the value of partnership between conservation organizations in the developed world and their counterparts in the developing world. It is of tremendous significance to conservation that the models in Ecuador and Costa Rica originated within those countries.

A third valuable aspect of these debt-for-nature swaps is the role they played in involving the business community in conservation. In the case of Ecuador and Costa Rica, for example, WWF was fortunate to receive pro bono legal services in negotiating the deal from the New York law firm of Shearman & Sterling and financial assistance in arranging the conversion and transfer of funds from Citibank, as well as several departments at Bankers Trust, the source bank for the debt.

THE FUTURE FOR DEBT-FOR-NATURE SWAPS

Debt-swap agreements in which WWF and other organizations have participated are the vanguard. Despite the complexity of these deals, debt swaps can be arranged successfully to meet the concerns of all parties. Bankers, government officials, and conservationists in debtor and creditor countries have managed to find the common ground necessary to conclude agreements. The possible inflationary impacts of swaps, for example, can be addressed not only through the use of bonds but also through the establishment of overall ceilings on debt-for-nature programs, although the amount of currency generated by debt swaps for conservation purposes is generally not large enough to have an appreciable impact on inflation.

Negotiators of debt-for-nature swaps may also face difficult questions when they work on setting up the delivery of conservation services. For example, should the money be channeled through one or two conservation groups in the debtor nation, or through a separately constituted trust? What criteria should be used to determine eligibility in the latter case?

These questions are important. Enormous sums of money suddenly made available may disrupt homegrown activities, among them a conservation movement deeply rooted in local needs and local culture. Experience has shown, however, that this can be avoided by listening to in-country partners, learning from them about their needs, and working with them to ensure that joint conservation efforts incorporate local views and experiences. The sovereignty concerns of debtor nations can thus be met through carefully constructed agreements.

Flexibility will be a key in any new debt-for-nature opportunities. Financial regulations vary from country to country. The particular value and structure of a country's debt may preclude debt-for-nature swaps from taking place, or necessitate innovative financial arrangements.

At the moment, prospects for additional swaps seem promising. Along with Bolivia, Ecuador, and Costa Rica, a growing number of debtor nations in Latin America and elsewhere in the developing world appear interested in exploring debt-for-nature programs. For many, the concept provides an opportunity to put more money into park and wildlife programs than they could through their normal budgeting processes.

The time frame for debt-for-nature swaps, however, is not open-ended. Debt-for-nature programs are responding to a specific situation that may not continue for very long. A solution to the debt burden may be negotiated by banks and debtor nations, or debt may be written down to a level that makes swaps impractical.

Conservation organizations are presently working with banks to assure their continued involvement in debt-for-nature programs. Debt that otherwise might simply be written down by banks as a loss can be put to productive use through debt swaps. In particular, World Wildlife Fund and other groups are encouraging commercial banks to donate a portion of their debt for use in swaps. Most of the debt used in swaps to date has been purchased with funds provided by foundations and individual donors.

In February 1988, Fleet/Norstar Financial Group became the first financial institution to donate debt for a debt-for-nature swap. It donated through The Nature Conservancy $254,000 (face amount) in Costa Rican debt paper towards conservation efforts in the Braulio Carillo National Park.

Recent actions by the Treasury Department may help encourage further debt donations. Previously, a bank that donated debt for conservation could deduct only the fair market value of the debt—generally, the discounted price for which debt notes have been selling. Thus, banks had a greater financial incentive to sell their debt, claim the loss as a deduction, and then donate the proceeds to conservation.

In November 1987, the Treasury Department issued Revenue Ruling 87-124, which provides lenders a full-cost-basis deduction (one based on the face value of the debt rather than on its fair market value) for donations of developing country debt to fund charitable activities in the debtor nations. In April, the Treasury Department clarified the ruling, enhancing debt-for-nature swap possibilities even further.

In Conclusion

Debt-for-nature swaps are among the most exciting recent developments in the field of international conservation. Yet the large number of players involved, as well as the complexity of some of the issues, suggest that it could take some time before these swaps become more common. They do provide, however, a very effective means of augmenting the operating budgets of natural resource agencies throughout the developing world. In so doing, they can become a major factor in helping these countries conserve their natural resource base—a base that will sustain the long-term economic productivity that is essential to their future well-being and to ours as well.

■ CONSERVATION INTERNATIONAL, THE DEBT-FOR-NATURE EXCHANGE: A TOOL FOR INTERNATIONAL CONSERVATION

11, 17-19, 23-30, 37-40 (1989)

The term "debt exchange," in general, refers to a form of financial transaction first used by multinational corporations, and now increasingly utilized by nonprofit organizations, to finance investments at a lower cost in less developed countries. The exportation of the debt exchange mechanism from the world of international corporate finance to the world of nonprofit conservation demonstrates the nonprofit organizations' growing recognition that they must become as savvy in generating and investing local currencies as their multinational corporate counterparts. Furthermore, by exploring the use of creative finance mechanisms such as debt-for-nature exchanges, conservation organizations acknowledge and act upon their responsibility, to both donors and projects, to generate the most value possible for their investments.

These new initiatives also illustrate the growing awareness—at home and abroad—that work in the "natural" environments of tropical rainforests and other ecosystems is affected profoundly by the surrounding "manmade" environments. For example, a heavy external debt burden clearly contributes to the economic and exploitative pressures placed upon a country's natural resource base. Although not an answer either to the debt or the conservation crises of the Third World, the debt-for-nature exchange does work to ameliorate these two interrelated issues, improving an otherwise gloomy scenario. As Dr. Thomas Lovejoy of the Smithsonian Institution noted as early as 1984, "Stimulating conservation while ameliorating debt would encourage progress on both fronts."

Debt-for-nature exchanges derive from the debt-equity exchange, a financial mechanism which allows corporations or commercial banks to exchange commercial debt of a less developed country for equity investments. In debt-for-nature exchanges something other than an equity stake is created as a result of the transaction. Defining that "something else" becomes a critical element of each debt-for-nature exchange. At a very minimum, every debt-for-nature exchange results in: 1) the reduction of a country's external debt and 2) a resulting commitment of additional local resources to conservation. . . .

Future Opportunities for Debt-for-Nature Exchanges

As the growing number of debt-for-nature transactions indicates, the window of opportunity for additional exchanges appears to be widening. Three factors make such transactions an increasingly viable means of supporting conservation in less developed countries (LDCs):

VOLUME OF LOAN TRADING

First, an increasing number of commercial debt holders are disposing of their Third World loan portfolios. From June 30, 1987 to June 30, 1988, for example, the ten largest U.S. banks cut their Third World loan exposure by 7.8 percent. Many regional U.S. banks have reduced their Third World loans by an even greater percentage. Much of this debt has been traded in a thin, but growing, secondary market for LDC commercial bank debt where banks trade and sell loans at sometimes substantial discounts to the loans' original face values. The 1988 trading volume of Third World loans reached about U.S. $55-60 billion, more than a tenfold increase in three years.

PRICE OF LOANS

Second, the price of Third World loans in the secondary market has dropped, increasing the possible leverage that can be achieved through debt-for-nature exchanges. According to Shearson Lehman Hutton analysts, the weighted average value of Third World loans in the secondary market dropped by 21.4 percent from June 30, 1987 to June 30, 1988. The secondary market price of this debt continued to fall steeply through the first quarter of 1989.

RECEPTIVITY OF HOST COUNTRIES

Third and perhaps most importantly, many LDC governments recognize that debt exchanges for nonprofit purposes such as advancing conservation and sustainable development are of equal or greater importance than many other profit-oriented investments. A growing receptivity to these exchanges is evident both informally and formally within many countries.

This growing recognition by host countries of the value of debt-for-nature exchanges has not been without some political backlash, however. For example, some initial press accounts in Bolivia of the first debt-for-nature exchange mischaracterized the exchange as a swap of debt for foreign ownership of land. Similar misconceptions regarding the debt-for-nature exchange mechanism have been voiced in Brazil where critics have charged that debt-for-nature exchanges may impinge on Brazil's national sovereignty in managing its natural resources. Such criticisms appear to be founded on serious misunderstandings of the purposes and uses to which the debt-for-nature exchange mechanism is put.

At least two positive consequences have followed from these politically charged reactions. First, the local beneficiaries of the proceeds of debt-for-nature exchanges (actual and potential) have been galvanized to present their case, in a public forum, for the commitment of government resources to a conservation agenda. Second, international conservation organizations have been reminded of the importance of developing these exchanges *in concert with* and *in response to* their local counterparts' needs. In short, debt-for-nature exchanges cannot be foisted upon unwilling participants. The process of negotiating and structuring a debt-for-nature exchange is a consensus building exercise.

Debt-for-nature exchanges may appeal to conservation organizations for a host of potentially competing reasons: they provide opportunities to generate publicity and raise money, as well as to finance creative conservation projects. The most compelling reason to use the debt-for-nature exchange, however, is to generate additional in-country support for conservation projects.

But project-responsive debt exchanges can be complicated to transact, particularly where there is also a non-monetary component to be gained. Even if the sole motivation for entering into a debt exchange is to generate a potentially cheap source of local currency for in-country conservation programs, many factors affect the appropriateness and viability of the debt exchange mechanism.

Nature of the Project

Before determining if a debt-for-nature exchange is an appropriate financing vehicle for a project, it is necessary to determine if the country in which the project is located has a debt exchange program. Even if the country lacks a formal program, it is still possible to pursue a debt exchange (given a receptive host country) if the applicable loan agreement does not preclude the contemplated exchange.

Availability and Cost of Debt

If the host country is both willing and able to exchange its debt for conservation purposes, the availability and cost of the country's debt must be determined. To date, while much commercial bank debt is eligible for debt-for-nature exchanges, multilateral and governmental organizations such as the World Bank or the U.S. government have not permitted debt owed to them to be used for such exchanges. Thus, in spite of a large amount of debt owed by African nations, limited amounts of it are available for debt-for-nature exchanges because most of the African sovereign debt is owed to multilateral or governmental institutions. In contrast, Latin American countries borrowed proportionally more from commercial banks in the 1970's, so a large amount of Latin American debt potentially could be exchanged for conservation purposes.

Assuming commercial bank debt is available, the next question becomes at what price to the conservation organization. Essentially, the nonprofit conservation organization either can purchase debt or receive a donation of debt. To purchase debt, a conservation organization can buy its debt from a financial institution that trades LDC commercial bank debt. Or, a nonprofit organization can seek donations of commercial bank debt from these same financial institutions.

Understandably, financial institutions are more receptive to making sales than donations. Under the current tax and regulatory schemes in the United States and elsewhere, there is little financial incentive to encourage financial institutions to make debt donations where they can sell the debt instead.

The U.S. tax code has been clarified to minimize some of the perceived disadvantages of debt donations, however. Revenue Ruling 87-124, issued in November, 1987, confirmed that U.S. financial institutions which donate debt to a U.S. non-profit 501(c)(3) organization may receive two tax benefits: 1) a bad loan loss deduction for any loss between the debt's original face value when the loan was made and its fair market value at the time of the donation, and 2) a charitable contribution deduction equal to the fair market value of the proceeds generated as a result of the exchange. These deductions effectively allow a donating bank to reduce its taxable income and, thus, its U.S. taxes.

While representing a step toward facilitating debt donations, Revenue Ruling 87-124 did not resolve a number of concerns of the potential bank donor. Still outstanding are questions of how to value both the bad loan loss and the charitable contribution deductions.[3] A related question of whether such deductions are to be taken against foreign source or domestic source income of the donor was addressed finally in late April, 1989.[4]

In part due to the lack of financial incentives, tax or otherwise, and in part due to banks' general reluctance to donate their assets, only two U.S. commercial banks to date have donated a portion of their debt to U.S. conservation organizations. The Fleet National Bank of Rhode Island made the first donation of debt to a conservation organization in late 1987 when it donated U.S. $254,000 face amount of Costa Rican debt to The Nature Conservancy. However, due to uncertainty over the tax consequences of Revenue Ruling 87-124, the bank took only a bad loan loss deduction instead of a charitable contribution deduction. More recently, in December, 1988, an affiliate of the Chase Manhattan Bank donated to CL approximately U.S. $400,000 face amount of Bolivian debt, the first donation of debt by a U.S. money center bank. Again tax motivations did not appear to be the primary catalyst for this donation.

Experience shows that without the creation of financial incentives for debt donations, donations alone will not fuel most debt-for-nature exchanges. Moreover, in light of the quantifiable financial and human resources expended in securing debt donations, they should not be treated as cost-free sources of debt.

3. Perhaps overly optimistic readings of Revenue Ruling 87-124 initially led some nonprofit organizations to believe that the combined value of the bad loan loss deduction and charitable contribution deduction available to a donor could exceed the donor's adjusted basis in the donated debt even where the debt had depreciated in value. Several tax experts, however, since have cautioned that such a windfall probably would be disallowed by the U.S. Internal Revenue Service and instead, the fair market value of the proceeds generated by an exchange may be calculated on the basis of the fair market value of the debt which was exchanged for these proceeds.

4. *See* Notice 89-58, 1989-20 I.R.B. I. Generally, charitable contribution deductions may be taken against domestic source income, while bad loan loss deduction shall be apportioned between domestic source and foreign source income. As many potential donors will prefer to take deductions against their domestic source income, there is some incentive for a donor of debt to value the charitable contribution deduction more highly than the bad loan loss deduction in order to allocate more of the deductions resulting from a donation against its domestic source income. It should be noted, however, that at least one major U.S. commercial bank has warned its U.S. Treasury Department that a possible consequence of requiring banks from conducting any disposal of their loans at a loss, be it through sales, swaps or donations.

Local Currency Needs of the Project

Where the primary purpose of a debt-for-nature exchange is to finance the conservation organization's local currency needs, it is necessary to determine exactly what those needs are. The timing, as well as the amount, of disbursements is paramount. Depending on the funding pattern of the particular conservation organization, such calculations can be made on a short or long-term basis or, preferably, both. The structure of the debt exchange then should reflect such funding patterns and needs.

Regardless of its other financial attractions, a debt exchange may not be desirable simply because the local currency funds are paid too slowly (or too quickly) to meet the needs of the project being financed. For example, if a project needs local currency to pay operating costs on a weekly or monthly basis, such as salaries or rent that require regular expenditures, a debt exchange may be too slow and inconsistent a finance mechanism. As an alternative, one large debt exchange could fund a trust or endowment from which the conservation organization would withdraw over time its needed local currency. Or, the debt could be exchanged for a long-term debt instrument, denominated in local currency, which has a schedule of interest and/or principal payments that coincides with the schedule of the costs being financed. Both types of exchanges require appropriate safeguards against the political and financial risks inherent in "stocking" local currency either in local currency endowments or in long-term debt instruments.

Economic Viability Exchanges

To determine if a debt exchange makes sense economically, at least three factors should be weighed against the costs of procuring local currency through other finance mechanisms. First, what is the cost of the debt? Second, what exchange rate will the host country government use to convert the debt into local currency? And third, what percentage of the face amount of the external debt will the host country government actually exchange into local currency? For example, suppose that a conservation organization purchased U.S. $100,000 face amount of Country X's debt for U.S. $50,000, then converted 90 percent of the debt at the official exchange rate of 100 pesos per dollar (rather than the free exchange rate of 300 pesos per dollar). The conservation organization would have spent U.S. $50,000 to acquire 9,000,000 pesos, for an effective exchange rate of 180 pesos per dollar.

That may be a good deal, but there is a better one for the conservation organization that simply converts U.S. $50,000 at the free exchange rate of 300 pesos per dollar into 15,000,000 pesos. Or, if such a purchase at the free exchange rate is not possible, another better option is to purchase blocked pesos from a multinational corporation at any exchange rate higher than the effective rate that can be obtained by using the debt exchange. This hypothetical example demonstrates that the financial advantages of debt exchanges, which largely result from the discounted value of the price of Third World debt in the secondary market, may be outweighed by disadvantageous factors such as a low effective exchange rate used by the debtor country in making its exchanges. When weighing the economics of debt-for-nature exchanges against other finance mechanisms, the conservation organization should (and can) be just as creative in looking for financing alternatives as its multinational corporate counterpart.

Transactional Costs of Exchanges

A final cost of debt-for-nature exchanges is the transactional costs, such as paying outside management fees to the bank or consultant that arranges the transaction, or hiring the in-house expertise necessary to close a transaction. Transactional costs also include less quantitative factors like the amount of human resources expended in the protracted negotiations often necessary for consummating debt exchanges. For example, the Bolivia debt-for-nature exchange has taken over two years to close.

Implementation of Exchanges

A key concern for both the conservation donor to a debt-for-nature exchange and the local recipient of the exchange is the long-term implementation of the transaction.

Implementation can be addressed most effectively in the way the transaction is structured. If the host country's long-term obligations with respect to the exchange are limited and the exchange serves the needs of a local constituency of conservationists, the transaction probably will be completed successfully without the need for enforcing legal remedies. If, however, the exchange involves an ongoing obligation, financial or otherwise, from the host government or if the local beneficiaries have a limited political voice, it may be necessary to build additional implementation measures into the debt-for-nature exchange agreement.

The legal documentation of a debt-for-nature exchange can help reassure the parties to the transaction. Governing law clauses, waivers of sovereign immunity and dispute settlement mechanisms, however, may be of limited use to the nonprofit conservation organization that has few financial resources available to enforce such clauses. Requiring bilateral or multilateral governmental institutions to consider a host country's observance of its debt-for-nature exchange agreements before providing foreign assistance might give the documentation more clout.

If such bilateral or multilateral governmental backing of debt-for-nature exchanges is not forthcoming, political risk insurance can be purchased from institutions like the U.S. Overseas Private Investment Corporation

(OPIC) or the World Bank's Multilateral Investment Guarantee Agency (MIGA). Such insurance, however, can be costly. And the usefulness of such coverage will depend on whether the structure of the debt-for-nature exchange gives rise to an insurable risk. For example, it is unlikely that any political risk insurer would insure a nonprofit organization against the risk that LDC government-owned "protect" lands are *not* being protected adequately. On the other hand, a government's nonpayment of amounts due from a conservation bond may be an insurable risk.

In short, investments made via debt-for-nature exchanges probably are neither less nor more inherently vulnerable to political risks than any other conservation investment in a foreign country, unless the debt-for-nature exchange requires a long-term financial commitment of the host government. Then such exchanges run the risk that a new government of a change in the country's national agenda may cause a host government to breach its contractual agreement. Legal documentation may discourage such breaches and political risk insurance may minimize the financial costs of such a breach, but the best protected debt-for-nature exchanges are those that are supported by a local and international constituency that would protest loudly at any breach of the debt-for-nature agreement.

Protection of Debt-for-Nature Proceeds

Less attention has been paid to the issue of the enforceability of such agreements. The financial advantages of a debt-for-nature exchange can be lost to high inflation just as easily as to the failure of a government to honor its contractual commitments. As noted earlier, there are inherent commercial risks in "stockpiling" local currency funds in countries prone to high inflation and/or currency devaluations.

Just as there is a need to structure debt exchanges to minimize political risks, it is equally important to structure exchanges that guard against commercial risks. These commercial risks will vary from country to country and thus the measures of protection depend, in part, on the sophistication of the country's financial markets. For example, if a debt exchange is expected to generate immediately a generous endowment of local currency that will be used slowly over the years, the beneficiary of the exchange should have access to local financial instruments that will adequately protect the endowment's spending power over the years. Such financial instruments may include bank accounts, certificates of deposit, or debt instruments that are indexed to the dollar or another relatively stable currency or commodity. Furthermore, this financial instrument may need to earn enough interest to counteract inflation so the principal amount of the endowment can remain relatively untouched. If these requirements cannot be addressed adequately, it may be necessary to structure a string of smaller debt-for-nature exchanges to take place as local currency is needed.

Debt-for-nature exchanges, like any contract, are flexible agreements.

The timing and amount of the exchange, and the form and timing of the proceeds' disbursement are some of the variables generally open to negotiation with the host country. It is the sum of these variables, together with the local financial proceeds, both on the day of the exchange and in subsequent years.

The debt-for-nature exchange has become an important mechanism for channeling in-country support toward the sustainable development of natural resources. The debt-for-nature exchange also has proved itself to be a viable form of the debt reduction initiative contemplated in the recently announced "Brady Plan."

The second generation of debt-for-nature exchanges offers opportunities to expand both the amount of in-country support generated for conservation and the amount of Third World debt reduced through these transactions. Structural developments in the exchanges and the involvement of bilateral and multilateral development institutions will share the degree to which these opportunities are explored and utilized.

Potential Role of Multilateral Development Banks

Just as AID may begin to play an increasingly catalytic role in financing debt-for-nature exchanges, the multilateral development banks ("MDBs") also may begin to play a pivotal role. Although their role has been negligible to date, MDBs potentially could facilitate exchanges both of their own outstanding loans to less developed countries and of commercial bank debt.

Facilitation of MDB Debt Exchanges

The most direct role that a MDB could play in the debt-for-nature exchange is to allow debt that is owed to the MDB to be used for an exchange. Principal or interest amounts of debt owed to MDBs could be extinguished in return for the advancement of conservation programs. Alternatively, MDBs could allow their debt obligations to be serviced with local currency payments. Then, instead of making such loan payments to the MDB, the host country could recycle this local currency to finance in-country conservation programs. Critics of MDBs playing such a direct role, however, note that these types of actions may jeopardize the MDBs' credit rating and hence, their capacity to raise money in the marketplace.

MDBs also can assist host countries in meeting their commitments, financial and otherwise, under debt-for-nature agreements. Like AID, MDBs from time to time may have access to local currency of the host country. A MDB could allow a host country to utilize this local currency to meet both its MDB and debt-for-nature agreement obligations. Just as importantly, MDBs also can assist a host country that has committed itself in a debt-for-nature exchange to meeting certain pollution control standards or to installing specific cleanup operations may need the financial, technical and scientific advice that a MDB could provide.

Assisting Commercial Bank Debt Exchanges

More indirectly, a MDB could provide transactional assistance to commercial bank debt-for-nature exchanges. This assistance could finance commercial bank debt buy-backs contingent on the host country's advancement of local conservation programs. A MDB also could purchase commercial bank debt for its own account and extinguish all or a portion of such debt in return for the host country or countries' adherence to national or regional conservation goals.

Furthermore, MDBs could provide banks with a financial incentive to make debt donations to nonprofit conservation organizations. MDBs could offer credit enhancements to commercial bank debt in return for the donation of certain portions of that debt. These credit enhancements could attach to a bank's existing stock of debt such as "exit bonds," or to newly incurred debt such as new money instruments.

By offering credit enhancements to exit bonds that have a debt-for-nature component, a "conservation exit bond" could be created. Essentially an exit bond allows banks to exchange all or a portion of their outstanding debt exchanged for an exit bond then can be subtracted from the formula on which the participating bank's share of future loans to the country will be calculated. Generic exit bonds have been included in the recent Argentine and Brazilian debt restructuring.

One way of increasing the perceived value of an exit bond, beyond interest rate adjustments, is to give the exit bond properties that the original debt may not have held: exemption from local taxes, availability in bearer form, eligibility for debt conversion programs or, as suggested here, incorporation of a credit enhancement by a MDB. The proposal of a "conservation exit bond" embellishes the type of exit bond for which outstanding debt could be exchanged.

Attaching a MDB credit enhancement to an exit bond—even a conservation exit bond—may run into difficulties, however, where banks also are being asked to make new loans to a country. Such banks may believe that any and all credit enhancements should accrue to the new loans that they are being asked to make, rather than to the existing but newly securitized, stock of debt held by banks "exiting" from the restructuring process. Like the conservation exit bond, a new money bond with a conservation component—a "Green Bond"—also could be created with an attached MDB credit enhancement.

Assuming that subscription to such a Green Bond is part of the menu of options available to a bank participating in new money lending to a country, the Green Bond would need to have sufficient financing incentives to be as attractive to new money lenders as the other form of lending offered in the new money package. Availability of a credit enhancement is one means of providing that financial incentive to the Green Bond.

Conservation exit bonds and/or Green Bonds could take many forms depending on the mutual interests of the host country and commercial creditors. Among the forms these instruments could take the conservation exit bond or Green Bond could have a repayment schedule divided among local currency payments donated to in-country conservation projects, and hard currency payments directed to commercial bank creditors. By attaching the guaranty or other credit enhancement of MDB to the hard currency portion of the bond, the economic viability and hence attractiveness, of the bond is assured, both to its commercial and conservation end-users. Alternatively, the conservation exit bond or Green Bond could have an expanding credit enhancement feature. As greater amounts of the conservation exit bond or Green Bond are donated by a holder for conservation purposes, a greater portion of the holder's remaining debt will be credit enhanced.

Irrespective of the form or instrument to which a credit enhancement is attached, it is clear that by granting a credit enhancement that is linked to either conservation exit bonds or Green Bonds, the participating MDB would stimulate the delivery of additional financial resources to the development and management of the natural resources of the participating host country. The host country that issues these new instruments would receive some debt relief and be enabled to redirect a portion of its debt servicing costs to support in-country conservation programs. And finally, participating commercial banks would receive the necessary incentive to make debt donations—the improved position of their remaining LDC loan portfolios.

Notes and Questions

1. Different types of debt-for-nature exchanges exist. The most common type is when a NGO purchases a lesser developed country's (LDC's) foreign debt on the secondary debt market and exchanges it for local currency or interest-bearing bonds to be managed by local environmental groups for designated conservation programs. A second type is similar to the first type, except that the lender bank donates the debt directly to the NGO rather than selling the debt in the secondary debt market. Another kind involves the sale of the debt to a corporate investor. Finally, the last kind provides continued funding for already established environmental programs in the debtor nations. To date, only the first two types have been used. Why is that?

2. What are the requirements for establishing debt-for-nature swaps? What are the key concerns of the conservation donor, the lending institution, and the LDC in formulating a debt-for-nature exchange? What are their long-term goals?

3. The debt-for-equity swap was an innovative response to the international debt crisis. Spurred by the skyrocketing oil prices in the mid-1970s, LDCs borrowed heavily in order to finance oil imports and development projects. Commercial banks, induced by the higher rates and fees that they could demand from the LDCs over those they could obtain from domestic borrowers, exceeded their legal lending limit and overextended loans to the LDCs. These debtor nations struggled to make the interest payments of their staggering foreign debt and often could not make the principal payments. Finally, in 1982, Mexico declared that it would be unable to pay its debt. Many other countries, such as Bolivia, Brazil, Costa Rica, Peru, Ecuador, and the Dominican Republic followed suit by unilaterally suspending part or all of their interest payments. In order to minimize the risk of defaults by LDCs on their payments, banks began writing down or selling debts that they had little hope of collecting, thereby providing impetus to increased transactions in the secondary debt market. The debt-for-equity exchange emerged as a creative solution for alleviating the debt problem. In a debt-for-equity swap, the creditor exchanges a nation's foreign debt for equity interests in local firms or assets. The transaction, therefore, allowed creditors to earn returns on nonperforming assets. Debt-for-equity exchanges served as precursors to debt-for-nature exchanges.

4. The Fuller and Williamson article points to the correlation made by Dr. Lovejoy between "indebtedness and environmental degradation." The requirement that international debt payments be made in hard currency further served to fuel the environmental degradation. In their efforts to raise the hard currency needed to service their foreign debt, some Latin American countries attempted to boost exports by clearing forests for timber and to create pasture lands for cattle grazing. A number of these countries switched from mixed farming to mainly cash crop agriculture. These practices resulted in soil erosion, diminishing water supplies, and the destruction of valuable wetlands, leading to extinction of plant and animal species.

5. Aside from avoiding defaults on the risky loans made to the LDCs, what motivates commercial banks to participate in debt-for-nature swaps? What about multilateral development banks? Does Revenue Ruling 87-124, which provides two tax benefits to organizations that donate debt (a bad loan loss deduction and a charitable deduction—*see* p. 1129), provide sufficient tax incentives for banks to donate debt? Why have banks not taken advantage of this tax measure? Would tax credits constitute a better alternative? If so, how could it be reconciled with the absence of tax credits to aid United States farmers?

6. If substantial administrative burdens accompany debt-for-nature transactions, why do NGOs promote them? How do NGOs choose the target areas for conservation, and how much input do the local environmental groups have in designing the type of conservation programs to be implemented? Does the national park model (which is more common in

western nations) work in the context of Latin America? Is setting aside reserve areas enough? How do NGOs monitor and ensure proper implementation of the conservation programs in the LDCs? What happens when the funds created by the debt-for-nature swap run out? Would it be better for NGOs to concentrate their efforts on a fewer number of well-chosen projects to ensure the projects' perpetuity rather than attempting more numerous projects?

7. If the debt relief provided by debt-for-nature swaps is so marginal in comparison to the total foreign debt of LDCs, what makes debt-for-nature exchanges an attractive option for LDCs? What concerns would make debt-for-nature swaps unattractive to LDCs? Would the benefits of the exchange outweigh the intrusions into the sovereignty and possible internal problems (i.e., inflation and increased domestic debt) of debtor nations?

8. Should national governments take part in debt-for-nature swaps by adopting loan forgiveness policies in order to facilitate "real" debt relief for LDCs and encourage their continued participation in future debt-for-nature exchanges? What political issues get implicated in subsidizing foreign debt, as compared to domestic debt?

9. The window of opportunity for continuing to make debt-for-nature swaps an attractive option for banks is narrowing. Banks are reducing their exposure to risky loans by restructuring debt, by increasing their loan loss reserves, and by selling discounted debt on the secondary debt market. Banks have now become less eager to sell remaining debt below market value. Would banks continue to finance debt-for-nature swaps mainly on the strength of gaining goodwill and publicity?

10. Can debt-for-nature agreements be enforced at all? Given the weaker bargaining position that NGOs occupy in international law as private individuals versus the superior position of nations as sovereign entities, how can the LDCs be influenced by the international community to adhere to debt-for-nature agreements? What factors must be considered in determining the best methodology for enforcement of the agreement? (Take into account the specific goal of the particular agreement along with the broad objectives of all the parties involved.) *See also* Laurie P. Greener (comment), Debt-for-Nature Swaps in Latin American Countries: The Enforcement Dilemma, 7 Conn. J. Intl. L. 123 (1991).

11. The language of debt-for-nature agreements is often vague and deliberately omits rigid enforcement terms. What is the rationale behind this? Should the agreements include provisions for foreseeable events/crises? What are they?

12. Why limit such exchanges to debt-for-nature? In a thought-provoking article, Professor Sunstein and Catherine O'Neill propose a technology-for-nature swapping. Catherine A. O'Neill & Cass R. Sunstein, Economics and the Environment: Trading Debt and Technology for Nature,

17 Colum. J. Envtl. L. 93 (1992). They state that such an exchange has considerable advantages over debt-for-nature kinds.

> Its major advantage is that it promises to bring about large-scale, long-term reform and thus to create structures for encouraging not only lower cost economic development, but also the production of energy by means of creating minimal damage to the environment. In its ideal form, it will also advance progress in energy efficiency, an area that is vital to sustainable development. . . .
>
> The proposed exchange raises some serious economic and ethical questions, and it is also fairly complex. For instance, developed countries may well be under an ethical obligation to transfer technology to developing countries for free or at significant reductions in price. This obligation might be justified by reference to general redistributive goals, environmental concerns, or the view that industrialized countries have profited from technological development producing environmental harms, that such countries benefit from environmental protection in developing countries, and that developing countries should not be placed under special economic disabilities because of environmental damage caused by others. These considerations suggest that at least a heavily discounted transfer of technology may be an ethical obligation of developed countries. . . .
>
> A transfer of technology for nature requires the cooperation of several parties, all of whom wish to advance different agendas. The arrangement we propose should serve the interests of each party, and the resulting advances in combatting global environmental and developmental problems should benefit all concerned. . . .

Id. at 150.

Do you agree?

In another article, the author argues that environmental infrastructure development can be enhanced through debt-for-development exchanges. Nicholas Kublicki, The Greening of Free Trade: NAFTA, Mexican Environmental Law, and Debt Exchanges for Mexican Environmental Infrastructure Development, 19 Colum. J. Envtl. L. 59 (1994).

> Such exchanges can be funded by official U.S. debt, donations of debt by institutional lenders, purchases of institutional debt on the secondary exchange through NGO fundraising, and USAID grants. Debt-for-EID [environmental infrastructure development] exchanges would allow creditors to recover a portion of their potentially uncollectible debt. At the same time, the mechanism would enable Mexico to develop its environmental infrastructure and reduce its massive foreign debt. Although Mexican debt-for-EID exchanges would need to generate a large amount of capital to contribute significantly to environmental infrastructure development, infrastructure construction represents a capital expenditure which must be amortized over the life of the physical infrastructure. Therefore, the effective annual cost

> of infrastructure projects may resemble annual environmental enforcement operating costs . . . [S]ome of the funds required for the exchanges currently are authorized, yet are being misallocated to natural resource preservation projects that will fail to alleviate human suffering caused by Mexican environmental degradation and poor sanitation, such as high infant mortality and cholera epidemics.

Id. at 138-139.

What do you think of this approach?

Finally, consider this optimistic note that environmental protection through debt reduction may in the future be more attractive to debtor-nations.

> The inescapable conclusion is that, to date, the world debt crisis has not been significantly alleviated by the myriad debt restructuring and conversion schemes, including debt-equity and debt-for-nature swaps. . . . There is, in fact, good reason to hope that debt-for-nature swaps, in particular, can be a more effective debt relief tool in the coming decade than they have been so far.
>
> This hope stems from two developments that took place in 1990. First environmental organizations began expanding debt-for-nature swaps beyond conservation to meet the specific environmental needs of debtor countries. . . . The second recent development in debt-for-nature swaps is the participation of sovereign creditors. Late in 1990, the Paris Club, a consortium of Western creditor countries, authorized its members for the first time to sell or donate debts for swaps. . . . The benefit from sovereign creditor-funded debt swaps would increase tremendously if other Paris Club members—such as Germany, Great Britain, France and Japan, each of whom hold billions of dollars in debt obligations of Latin American, Eastern European, African, and other countries—followed the lead of the United States. With debt donations from sovereign creditors, debt-for-nature swaps can be expected to proliferate greatly benefitting the environment and retiring truly significant amounts of debt.
>
> Largely as a result of these recent developments, debtor countries that formerly criticized debt-for-nature swaps have begun espousing them.

Daniel H. Cole, Debt-Equity Conversions, Debt-for-Nature Swaps, and the Continuing World Debt Crisis, 30 Colum. J. Transnatl. L. 57, 79-80 (1992).

13. Debt-for-education swaps have also been implemented as a way of reducing the amount of money owed by a debtor-nation. In 1990, Harvard University and Ecuador announced the signing of an agreement that instituted the first "debt-for-education" swap with a Third World nation. In this swap, Harvard uses heavily discounted debt to create scholarships for Ecuadorian students to study at Harvard and research areas concerning the environment.

As designed, the fund will yield approximately $150,000 annually for expenditures in the United States and Ecuador—scholarships in U.S. dollars for Ecuadorian students and grants in Ecuadorian sucres for Harvard faculty and students. The $2 million core of the fund will remain untouched. Fundacion Capacitar will divide the interest from the fund into two parts: 85 percent in U.S. currency for scholarships and the remaining 15 percent for local costs for research and study in Ecuador. In order to prevent "brain drain," a committee consisting of both Harvard faculty and Fundacion Capacitar will award scholarships in the form of loans that will automatically be forgiven when the student returns to Ecuador. Presently, Harvard has granted approximately four scholarships per year since 1991. Two Harvard graduate students participating in the program are presently in Ecuador to begin developing an organic farming system called the Harvard-Ecuador Farming Project.

Drawing from Harvard's experiences with its first debt-for-education swap, other universities, such as the University of California at Los Angeles and the University of Pittsburgh, are nearing completion of negotiations with Ecuador for a similar program. In addition, a consortium of southern and western universities has also established a fund in Mexico. *See* Jennifer F. Zaiser, Swapping Debt for Education: Harvard and Ecuador Provide a Model For Relief, 12 B.C. Third World L.J. 157 (1992).

14. The legal literature on debt-for-nature swaps is extensive. In addition to articles already cited, one could read: Congressional Research Service, Library of Congress, Debt-for-Nature Swaps in Developing Countries: An Overview of Recent Conservation (1988) (CRS Rep. No. 88-647 ENR); Derek Asiedu-Akrofi, A Comparative Analysis of Debt-Equity Swap Programs in Five Major Debtor Countries, 12 Hastings Intl. & Comp. L. Rev. 537 (1989); Marilyn Post, The Debt-for-Nature Swap: A Long-Term Investment for the Economic Stability of Less Developed Countries, 24 Intl. L. 1071 (1990).

2. *Enterprise for the Americas Initiative*

In July 1991 at the Group of Seven (G-7) Summit in Houston, Texas, the United States proposed what came to be known as the Enterprise for the Americas Initiative (EAI). Its intent was to reduce indebtedness to the United States for countries in Latin America and the Caribbean that satisfied certain economic criteria and to have the interest on the new loans paid in local currency to local governments for use in environmental projects.

The lead time between the initial proposal and the enactment of legislation by Congress for this initiative was unusually brief—less than six months.

Under the EAI, the United States reduces the amount of debt a Latin American or Caribbean country owes the United States under the Agricultural Trade Development and Assistance Act of 1954. In return, the debtor-nation must agree to pay the principal in dollars to the United States. The new interest payments, however, are disbursed in local currency to a jointly administered "Environmental Fund," which finances environmental projects in the debtor-country. The United States has entered into EAI agreements that provide for the funding of environmental projects in Argentina, Bolivia, Chile, Colombia, El Salvador, Jamaica, and Uruguay. (*See generally* Royal C. Gardner, Taking the Principle of Just Compensation Abroad: Private Property Rights, National Sovereignty, and the Cost of Environmental Protection, 65 U. Cin. L. Rev. 539 (1997)).

In order for a Latin American or Caribbean country to be eligible for debt relief the country must meet certain requirements and have in place an economic reform agreement with the IMF, a structural adjustment program through the World Bank, an Inter-American Development Bank (IDB) investment reform plan, and a restructuring agreement with its commercial creditors.

Management of funds shall be carried out by an Administering Body in each country. Members of the Administering Body will include one or more representatives appointed by the United States president, one or more appointees of the eligible country, and a majority of representatives from a broad range of local NGOs. The initiative also establishes the Environment for the Americas Board, which shall be composed of five representatives from the United States and four representatives from private NGOs with experience in Latin America and the Caribbean.

The board will be responsible for advising the president on negotiating the Environmental Framework Agreement, identifying a suitable Administrative Body in each eligible country, and reviewing the annual fiscal audits of each body. Each administering body will be responsible for receiving proposals and making grants in accord with the EAIs, managing the program and overseeing the grants, carrying out any annual independent fiscal audits, and submitting an annual report of activities to the board of the host country's government. Any grant over $100,000 will be subject to a veto by either government. Local NGOs have been guaranteed a role in all steps of the decisionmaking process.

The legislation initially included foreign assistance debt as well as loans with the Commodity Credit Corporation, but the former was deleted before the legislation was passed. The text of the legislation is given below.

■ ENTERPRISE FOR THE AMERICAS INITIATIVE

7 U.S.C.A. §1738

SUBCHAPTER VI—ENTERPRISE FOR THE AMERICAS INITIATIVE

§1738. Establishment of the Facility

There is established in the Department of the Treasury an entity to be known as the "Enterprise for the Americas Facility" (hereafter referred to in this subchapter as the "Facility").

§1738a. Purpose

The purpose of this subchapter is to encourage and support improvement in the lives of the people of Latin America and the Caribbean through market-oriented reforms and economic growth with interrelated actions to promote debt reduction, investment reforms, and community-based conservation and sustainable use of the environment. The Facility will support such objectives through the administration of debt reduction operations relating to those countries that meet investment reform and other policy conditions provided for in this subchapter.

§1738b. Eligibility for Benefits under the Facility

(a) Requirements

To be eligible for benefits from the Facility under this subchapter, a country shall—

(1) be a Latin American or Caribbean country;

(2) have in effect or have received approval for, or, as appropriate in exceptional circumstances, be making significant progress towards the establishment of—

(A) An International Monetary Fund (hereafter referred to in this subchapter as the "IMF") standby arrangement, extended IMF arrangement, or an arrangement under the structural adjustment facility or enhanced structural adjustment facility, or in exceptional circumstances, an IMF-monitorial program or its equivalent; and

(B) as appropriate, structural or sectoral adjustment loans from the International Bank for Reconstruction and Development (hereafter referred to in this subchapter as the "World Bank") or the International Development Association (hereafter referred to in this subchapter as the "IDA");

(3) have placed into effect major investment reforms in conjunction with an InterAmerican Development Bank (hereafter referred to as the "IDB") loan or otherwise be implementing, or making significant progress towards an open investment regime; and

(4) if appropriate, have agreed with its commercial bank lenders on a satisfactory financing program, including, as appropriate, debt or debt service reduction.

(b) Eligibility determination

The President shall determine whether a country is an eligible country for purposes of subsection (a) of this section.

§1738c. Reduction of Certain Debt

(a) Authority to reduce debt

(1) In general

Notwithstanding any other provision of law, the President may reduce the amount owed to the United States or any agency of the United States, and outstanding as of January 1, 1990 as a result of any credits extended under subchapter II of this chapter to a country eligible for benefits from the Facility.

(2) Availability[5] of appropriations

The authorities under this section may be exercised only to the extent provided for in advance in appropriation Acts.

(b) Limitation

A debt reduction authorized under subsection (a) of this section shall be accomplished, at the direction of the Facility, through the exchange of a new obligation under this subchapter for obligations of the type referred to in subsection (a) of this section outstanding as of January 1, 1990.

(c) Exchange of obligations

The Facility shall notify the Commodity Credit Corporation of an agreement entered into under subsection (b) of this section with an eligible country to exchange a new obligation for outstanding obligations. At the direction of the Facility, the old obligations that are the subject of the agreement may be canceled and a new debt obligation may be established for the country relating to the agreement. The Commodity Credit Corporation shall make an adjustment in its accounts to reflect a debt reduction under this section.

§1738d. Repayment of Principal

(a) Currency of payment

The principal amount owed under each new obligation issued under section 1738c of this title shall be repaid in United States dollars.

(b) Deposit of payments

Principal repayments on new obligations issued under section 1738c of this title shall be deposited in Commodity Credit Corporation accounts.

§1738f. Environmental Framework Agreements

(a) Authority

The President is authorized to enter into an environmental framework agreement with each country eligible for benefits from the Facility concerning the operation and use of an Enterprise for the Americas Environmental Fund (hereafter referred to in this subchapter as the "Environmental" Fund) established under section 1738g of this title for that country. The President shall consult with the Board established under section 1738i of this title when entering into such agreements.

(b) Requirements

An environmental framework agreement entered into under this section shall—

(1) require the eligible country to establish an Environmental Fund;

(2) require the eligible country to make interest payments under section 1738g(a) of this title into the Environmental Fund;

(3) require the eligible country to make prompt disbursements from the Environmental Fund to the body described in subsection (c) of this section;

(4) where appropriate, seek to maintain the value of the local currency resources deposited into the appropriate Environmental Fund in terms of United States dollars;

5. So in original.

(5) specify, in accordance with section 1738k of this title, the purposes for which the Environmental Fund may be used; and

(6) contain reasonable provisions for the enforcement of the terms of the agreement.

(c) Administering body

Funds disbursed from the Environmental Fund in an eligible country shall be administered by a body constituted under the laws of the country. Such body shall—

(1) be composed of—

(A) one or more representatives appointed by the President;

(B) one or more representatives appointed by the eligible country; and

(C) representatives from a broad range of environmental and local community development nongovernmental organizations of the host country; the majority of which shall be local representatives from nongovernmental organizations, and scientific or academic bodies;

(2) receive proposals for grant assistance from local organizations, and make grants to such organizations in accordance with the priorities agreed upon in the framework agreement and consistent with the overall purposes of section 1738k of this title;

(3) be responsible for the management of the program and oversight of grant activities funded from resources of the Environmental Fund;

(4) be subject to fiscal audits by an independent auditor on an annual basis;

(5) present an annual program for review by the Board established under section 1738i of this title each year;

(6) present an annual report on the activities undertaken during the previous year to the Chairman of the Board established under section 1738i of this title and the government of the eligible country each year, and

(7) have any grant over $100,000 be subject to veto by the United States and the government of the eligible country.

§1738h. Disbursement of Environmental Funds

Funds in an Environmental Fund shall be disbursed only pursuant to a framework agreement entered into pursuant to section 1738f of this title. . . .

§1738j. Oversight

The President may designate appropriate United States agencies to review the implementation of programs under this subchapter and the fiscal audits relating to such programs. Such oversight shall not constitute active management of an Environmental Fund.

§1738k. Eligible Activities and Grantees

(a) Eligible entities

Activities eligible to receive assistance through the framework agreements entered into under section 1738f of this title, shall include—

(1) activities of the type described in the Global Environmental Protection Assistance Act of 1989 (22 U.S.C. 462), and—

(2) agriculture-related activities, including those that provide for the biological prevention and control of animal and plant pests and diseases, to benefit the environment; and

(3) local community initiatives that promote conservation and sustainable use of the environment.

(b) Regulation

All activities of the type referred to in subsection (a) of this section shall, where appropriate, include initiatives that link conservation of natural resources with local community development.

(c) Setting of priorities

Appropriate activities and priorities relating to the use of an Environmental Fund shall be set by local nongovernmental organizations within the appropriate eligible country.

(d) Grants

Grants may be made by the body referred to in section 1738f(c) of this title from the Environmental Fund for environmental purposes to—

(1) host country nongovernmental environmental conservation, development, educational, and indigenous peoples organizations;

(2) other appropriate local or regional entities; or

(3) in exceptional circumstances, the government of the eligible country.

(e) Priority

In providing assistance from an Environmental Fund, the body established under section 1738f(c) of this title within the eligible country shall give priority to projects that are run by nongovernmental organizations and other private entities, and that involve local communities in their planning and execution.

§1738l. Encouraging Multilateral Debt Donations

(a) Encouraging donations from official creditors

The President should actively encourage other official creditors of an eligible country to provide debt reduction to such eligible country.

(b) Encouraging donations from other sources

The President shall make every effort to insure that programs established through Environmental Funds are able to receive donations from private and public entities, and private creditors of the eligible country.

§1738m. Annual Report to Congress

Not later than December 31 of each fiscal year, the President shall prepare and submit to the Speaker of the House of Representatives and the President Pro Tempore of the Senate an annual report concerning the operation of the Facility for the prior fiscal year.

Questions

1. Consider how you would implement this legislation. What are the issues that would arise in drafting a framework agreement between the debtor-country and the United States?

2. Why was the interest on the new debt to be paid in local currency to the local government?

3. What projects would qualify for financing?

E. FUNDS FOR THE ENVIRONMENT

1. General

Peter Sand, a commentator with extensive experience in international environmental organizations, recently wrote that efforts to institutionally respond to the space (transnational) and time-frame (intergenerational) concerns of environmental protection should suggest to lawyers that they consider the time-honored common lawyers' device called a "trust." *See* Peter H. Sand, Trusts for the Earth: New International Financial Mechanisms for Sustainable Development, Symposium on Sustainable Development and International Law, Baden Bei Wien, April 14-16, 1994. Indeed, according to Sand and other commentators such as Sir Joseph Gold, the trust fund approach, although historically alien to a number of legal cultures, has proliferated so that today there are approximately 1,600 trust funds currently administered by the World Bank worldwide. (*See generally* Joseph Gold, Trust Funds in International Law: The Contribution of the International Monetary Fund to a Code of Principles, 72 Am. J. Intl. L. 856 (1978).) Two major initiatives occurring at the end of 1990 involving the World Bank were the Global Environment Facility (GEF) and the Interim Multilateral Fund, which was the result of an amendment and adjustment to the Montreal Protocol on Substances that Deplete the Ozone Layer.

2. The Montreal Protocol Multilateral Fund (MPMF) and the Global Environment Facility (GEF)

■ THE MONTREAL PROTOCOL MULTILATERAL FUND: A MODEL FOR THE FRAMEWORK CONVENTION ON CLIMATE CHANGE

Donald M. Goldberg

16 Intl. Envtl. Rep. (BNA) 233, 233-235 (March 24, 1993)

a. The Montreal Protocol Multilateral Fund

The US $240 million MPMF was established on an interim basis in June 1990 to provide financial and technical assistance, including the transfer of relevant technologies, to eligible developing countries to enable them to comply with the control measures set out in the Montreal Protocol. Although the MPMF has links to the GEF, it operates as an independent entity with its own administrative structure, terms of reference, work programs, guidelines, and funding arrangements.

ORGANIZATIONAL STRUCTURE

The MPMF is administered by an Executive Committee made up of seven developed and seven developing country parties. The chair rotates annually between the developed and developing country members.

The committee's duties include: developing a three-year plan and budget and allocating resources among the implementing agencies; supervising and administering the fund; developing project eligibility criteria and guidelines; monitoring and evaluating operation of the fund; assessing bilateral arrangements to determine compliance with eligibility criteria; reporting annually and making recommendations to the parties; nominating the chief officer of the fund Secretariat; and performing all other functions assigned by the parties.

The Executive Committee reviews all country programs and projects and approves projects with agreed incremental costs in excess of $500,000. It also reviews any disagreements concerning funding requests under $500,000.

The MPMF is staffed by an independent Secretariat, which assists in discharging the day-to-day operations of the Executive Committee. Its responsibilities include: acting as a liaison with the parties, implementing agencies, and other institutions; helping the Executive Committee to develop the three-year plan and budget; monitoring and evaluating fund expenditures; and assessing country programs and work programs developed by the implementing agencies and making recommendations to the Executive Committee.

It also completes reports for the Executive Committee on projects over $500,000; prepares implementation performance reports for review by the Executive Committee; serves as liaison between governments, implementing agencies, and the Executive Committee; and monitors the activities of the implementing agencies.

The Executive Committee is assisted in its work by the fund's three implementing agencies: the United Nations Environment Programme (UNEP), the United Nations Development Programme (UNDP), and the World Bank.

UNEP is the fund's designated administrator, trustee, and treasurer. It receives and administers all contributions and disburses funds to the Secretariat and implementing agencies. UNEP also assists in the political promotion of the objectives of the protocol, as well as in research, data gathering, and clearinghouse functions.

UNDP provides technical assistance, including conducting feasibility and pre-investment studies, and cooperates on country studies and demonstration projects.

The World Bank assists the Executive Committee in administering and managing the program to finance agreed-upon incremental costs and approves projects under $500,000.

FINANCIAL STRUCTURE

Contributions to the MPMF are based on the U.N. scale of assessments, but countries can be credited up to 20 percent of their assessment for bilateral assistance. MPMF resources are to be independent of other World Bank funds allocated for ozone layer protection.

Assistance for investment projects is generally provided as a grant but may take the form of a highly concessional loan if the payback period is short and if the Executive Committee agrees. All technical assistance and pre-investment activities must be provided in the form of grants.

In some cases, countries are permitted to make their contributions in kind. At the request of the recipient country, in-kind support can be provided in the form of expert personnel, technology, technology documentation, and training.

PROJECT DEVELOPMENT

Before they can obtain assistance from the fund, countries must prepare a country study to determine their production and consumption of ozone-depleting substances (ODS), and a country program describing their ODS regulatory framework, activities undertaken in response to protocol requirements, a strategy statement, action plan, timetable, and budget for eliminating ODS. They may receive help from the implementing agencies in preparing their country study and program.

The Executive Committee reviews country programs and individually reviews all projects costing more than U.S. $500,000. Upon approval, the agencies proceed with full preparation, appraisal, and implementation. The agencies also prepare annual work programs which include technical assistance and training. These programs also require Executive Committee approval.

Although countries have yet to do so, they may prepare their own projects and apply directly to the fund without the participation of the implementing agencies.

In November 1992 during the Agreement on Accelerater Phase-Out, the Montreal Multilateral Fund was created to replace the interim fund. The structure of the Fund remains the same as described. As of July 1998, 165 countries have ratified the Montreal Protocol on Substances that Deplete the Ozone Layer.

b. The Global Environment Facility

The GEF was established in November 1990 as a three-year pilot program to provide grants and concessional financing to developing countries to help them implement environmental programs in four problem areas:

ozone depletion; global warming; loss of biodiversity; and pollution of international waters. The GEF is operated jointly by the World Bank, UNDP, and UNEP.

ORGANIZATIONAL STRUCTURE

The World Bank is the GEF administrator and is responsible for all investment projects. UNDP is responsible for pre-investment studies, technical assistance projects, and a small grants program. UNEP provides environmental expertise and ensures project consistency with existing environmental treaties.

The GEF chairman, who comes from the World Bank staff, is responsible for the operation of the facility and promotes cooperation between the implementing agencies. The chairman is assisted by the GEF administrator, also from the bank, who manages the day-to-day operation of the facility and coordinates the work programs.

Delegates from contributor countries—the "Participants"—meet twice a year to oversee the GEF's activities and review and approve work programs. The Participants set terms and conditions for use of GEF funds and assess work programs developed by the implementing agencies.

An implementation committee composed of GEF operational and managerial staff from all three implementing agencies meet regularly to review policy, program, and project issues. It screens project proposals to determine eligibility for GEF assistance and identifies and reviews policy issues for the work programs.

A Scientific and Technical Advisory Panel (STAP) advises the three implementing agencies on technical issues including available technology options, technical criteria for project approval, and evaluation of performance reports.

[The assembly, to which each participating country appoints a representative, is to meet every three years. Its functions include review of the general policies of the GEF and evaluation of the operation of the GEF on the basis of reports submitted by the council. *See* discussion of restructured GEF on p. 1152.

Each member of the council may separately cast the votes of each participant in the constituency represented. Voting is intended to be made by consensus. A formal vote is to be taken on any matter of substance only as a last resort, if all practicable efforts by the council and its chairperson have been made and no consensus was met. Decisions requiring a formal vote by the council are taken by a double weighted majority, an affirmative vote representing both a 60 percent majority of the total number of participants and a 60 percent majority of the total contribution.—EDS.]

FINANCIAL STRUCTURE

The GEF began with an initial funding commitment of 1 billion Standard Drawing Rights (about U.S. $1.3 billion). Funding is on a grant or concessional basis and is additional to existing aid flows.

The GEF is actually made up of three separate funding arrangements: the Core Fund; bilateral funding arrangements known as 'co-financing' and 'parallel financing'; and the Ozone Projects Trust Fund (OTF).

Roughly speaking, 40-50 percent of Core Fund and bilateral funds are for global warming, 30-40 percent to conserve biodiversity, and 20 percent to protect international waters. All the money from the OTF goes to protect the ozone layer.

[The United States contributed $90 million to the fund in 1995 and $35 million in 1996, despite the earlier United States pledge of $100 million to the fund for 1995 through 1998. Japan is also under a pledge of $400 million for four years.—EDS.]

PROJECT DEVELOPMENT

Projects may be proposed by governments, the implementing agencies, non-governmental organizations, the private sector, and others. Project proposals must be endorsed by the recipient government, which submits the proposal directly to the appropriate implementing agency. Normally proposals are initiated outside the GEF, but the implementing agencies may also solicit proposals for projects they are interested in funding.

Projects can be 'freestanding' or linked to regular World Bank loans. Eighty percent of investment projects (projects administered by the bank) are linked.

All technical assistance projects (projects administered by UNDP) are freestanding. Freestanding projects are limited to $10 million, while linked projects may receive up to $30 million. These amounts may be increased through co-financing or parallel financing.

Each of the three implementing agencies develops its own work programs containing new projects it is administering. After individual project review by the STAP for technical and scientific merit and by the Implementation Committee to ensure they meet established criteria, work programs are submitted to the Participants for their approval.

Upon approval by the Participants, projects undergo further development. Final approval of investment projects is by World Bank management and the appropriate regional vice president. Linked investment projects must also be approved by the bank's executive directors.

UNDP project development takes place in the recipient country and may involve outside participation from NGOs and local people.

[Under a joint IFC/GEF program, mechanisms are being developed to provide financing to enable Small and Medium-sized Enterprises (SMEs) to address GEF initiatives. IFC has selected five of six intermediaries that will each identify and fund several SMEs undertaking biodiversity conservation and global warming projects. Each intermediary will receive subsidized loans that it will then use to provide debt or equity financing to SME projects that address GEF objectives. If successful, the mechanisms for selecting, funding, supervising, and evaluating SME projects will become the basis of a larger program.—EDS.]

GEF RESTRUCTURING AND REPLENISHMENT

The GEF pilot phase was over at the end of 1993, and the GEF's funds were replenished and its mandate extended.

At the U.N. Conference on Environment and Development (the Rio Earth Summit), several countries indicated they would be willing to support account concerns regarding, among other things, governance, management, participation, and access to information.

Reflecting similar concerns, the Climate Convention calls for restructuring the GEF to provide for 'universal' membership (Article 21.3).

[The GEF now provides for universal membership, continued and enhanced involvement between non-governmental organizations (NGOs) and the private sector and a new decisionmaking structure. As restructured, the GEF has an Assembly, a Council, and a Secretariat. The Assembly consists of Representatives of all Participants (approximately 142 countries) and will meet for the first time in India in 1998. The Council consists of 32 Members, representing constituency groupings formulated and distributed taking into account the need for balanced and equitable representation of all Participants and giving due weight to the funding efforts of all donors. There are 16 Members from developing countries, 14 Members from developed countries, and 2 Members from countries of central and eastern Europe and the former Soviet Union. The Secretariat is under the direction of a Chief Executive Officer and reports to the Council and the Assembly.—EDS.]

It also requires that the financial mechanism have an "equitable and balanced representation of all parties within a transparent system of governance" (Article 11.2). NGOs generally oppose replenishment until a thorough, open, and independent review has demonstrated that the GEF is performing as intended and all significant problems have been identified and corrected.

Notes and Questions

1. Note that both Funds have similar institutional frameworks, but there are significant differences. Consider the following comparison, especially as it relates to concerns of voting and governance—some of the most contentious issues surrounding these institutions.

While there are certain similarities between the MPMF and the GEF, there are also important differences. For example:

- Representation. All Parties to the Montreal Protocol on Substances that Deplete the Ozone Layer are eligible to participate in the MPMF, whereas to participate in the GEF, countries must contribute a minimum of SDR 4 million (about U.S. $5.7 million). The GEF has proposed dropping this requirement but would still require Participants to contribute to administrative costs of the facility.

- Voting. The MPMF Executive Committee votes by consensus, when possible; otherwise, it votes by two-thirds majority plus simple majorities of both developed and developing country blocs. In the GEF Governing Council, however, the Participants vote by member state (one-nation, one-vote) and by weighted votes (allocated according to contribution). Decisions require 60% weighted vote and 60% of member states. The 32-seat Governing Council of GEF is composed of 14 seats for industrialized states, 16 for developing countries and 2 for transition economics (Eastern and Central Europe).
- Segregation of Funds. The MPMF is designated only for ozone depletion projects. The Core Fund—which the GEF proposes to utilize for the climate and biodiversity conventions—is designated for projects in three areas: global warming, biodiversity protection, and protection of international waters.
- Contributions. MPMF contributions are based on the U.N. scale of assessments, while contributions to the GEF are discretionary—GEF Participants are only required to meet the SDR 4 million minimum. Furthermore, GEF Participants have the option of providing all funds bilaterally, while Montreal Protocol parties are only permitted to provide 20 percent of their assessment bilaterally.
- NGO Participation. NGOs are permitted to attend MPMF Executive Committee meetings as observers but are barred from GEF Participants' meetings. The GEF has instituted an NGO consultation immediately before each Participant meeting, to which Participants have been invited. Few have accepted, however, and those who do attend have been reluctant to participate in discussions.
- Project Approval. The MPMF Executive Committee approves projects on a project-by-project basis and has final say on all projects over $500,000. In contrast, GEF Participants approve work programs, not individual projects, and review programs early in the project cycle, after which they have no role in project development or approval.
- Role of the World Bank. The World Bank plays a considerably more prominent role in the GEF than in the MPMF. The bank staff administers the GEF and gives final approval to all GEF investment projects. Currently, 80 percent of GEF investment projects are linked to regular World Bank loans. The role of the bank in the MPMF is limited primarily to assisting countries in the preparation of their programs, preparing and supervising investment projects, and approving projects costing less than U.S. $500,000.

Goldberg, above, at 15-16.

2. The restructuring of the GEF, a necessary condition to its becoming the permanent financing mechanism of the Climate Change Convention and the Biodiversity Convention (*see* the Climate Change Convention, Article 21 (3), and the Biodiversity Convention, Article 39), required reconsideration of its institutional structure, its system of governance, the

transparency of that system, and the accessibility of NGOs. Many of these have occurred and are described above. Do you have any other suggestions?

3. For additional information on this subject, *see* John C. Dernback, The Global Environment Facility: Financing the Treaty Obligations of Developing Nations, 23 Environ. L. Reptr. 10124 (1993); C. Miner, The World Bank Global Environmental Facility: First Project Approved in Poland, 33 Harv. Intl. L. J. 642 (1992); Lin Gan, The Making of the Global Environmental Facility: An Actor's Perspective, 3 Global Envtl. Change 256 (1993); and E. Helland-Hansen, The Global Environment Facility, 3 Intl. Envtl. Affrs. 137 (1991).

F. OTHER FINANCING APPROACHES

1. *"Innovative financing."* Returning to the excerpt of Agenda 21 at the beginning of this chapter, which identifies possible funding sources and mechanisms, note the reference to "innovative financing" at Ch. 33.16. Can you add any to the list there? What is the relationship of technology transfer to financing arrangements?

2. *Tradeable permits.* At a follow-up Working Group of the Commission on Sustainable Development (CSD) in early 1994 charged with developing policy options/recommendations to the CSD, the Group encouraged further examination of tradeable permits; removing subsidies; reducing military spending; and the feasibility, legal modalities, and administrative aspects of such measures as international emission charges, internationally tradeable permits, taxes on air travel, and fees and arrangements to cover international environmental disasters, including those related to transportation of hazardous wastes and materials. Do you think these approaches have promise?

3. *Carbon taxes.* The European Union is considering the adoption of a carbon/energy tax that would be based on the harmonization of excise taxes on energy consumption. Described as an effort to rely on market-based approaches (rather than "command-control" approaches), such a measure is designed to ensure that by 2000 carbon dioxide emissions would be brought down to their 1990 level. The tax would apply to all fuels and would be equivalent to $10 per barrel of oil by 2000. The new proposal (put forth in March 1997) would be phased in over three two-year stages and would ultimately be based on the energy value of fuels such as oil, coal, natural gas, kerosene, and electricity. Such "green" taxes, inspired by efforts to find longer-term sustainable development solutions rather than to generate revenues, would replace labor-based taxation approaches. What are the implications of the tax? Is it an appropriate application of the pollutor-pays-principle?

4. *Insurance.* Consider the possible role that insurance plays in financ-

ing environmentally sensitive activities. It can affect the calculation of risk of liability for environmental harm and therefore might be determinative in whether to undertake certain environmentally risky projects. In other words, the availability of insurance for environmental risk arguably could make it easier for environmentally dangerous projects to be undertaken. On the other hand, it can also improve the protection of the environment should damage occur (i.e., guaranty that various kinds of injury to the environment are covered). Can you think of any ways by which companies insuring environmentally sensitive activities (e.g., the building of a nuclear power plant or hydroelectric dam) might play an effective role in making projects less environmentally damaging? What effect could insurance have on the financing of environmental protection?

5. *Tax subsidies.* What impact would tax subsidies given to individuals and corporations for pollution control facilities and equipment have on international trade? Would they be consistent with the WTO?

APPENDIX I

Researching International Environmental Law[1]

Researchers in public international law, including international environmental law, encounter challenges not present in most domestic law research. Citations are more likely to be impenetrable. Pertinent authorities (e.g., books, articles, international agreements, and foreign laws) sometimes exist only in languages other than that of the researcher or may be published only outside the researcher's country. Documents prepared by international organizations may not be readily available or their existence easily ascertainable, and international indexes and digests may not be as complete as their domestic law counterparts.

While Internet and commercial online databases of international and foreign law have proliferated over the last five years and have indeed made some of these materials more accessible, these online sources have not necessarily overcome the barriers of language and reliability. Researchers should use these sources judiciously and (as with print sources) consider both the authority of the source of the documents provided and the editorial integrity of the publisher. To evaluate the reliability of the texts of documents mounted on the Internet, for example, researchers should determine

1. The Editors are grateful to Susan Van Syckel of the Gordon D. Schaber Law Library, University of the Pacific, McGeorge School of Law, for her work in updating and filling out an earlier version of this appendix.

the following: Has the text been provided by the official source, in the official language? If the text is a translation, what is the identity and expertise of the translator? Has the text been accurately digitalized? How current are the documents provided, and how frequently is the site updated? Who (private or public entity) is responsible for maintaining the site? Is this information made available at the site itself? And while editorial integrity may be assumed for the commercial online legal databases, researchers should check the online scope notes of these databases to determine coverage (comprehensive or selective publication of documents) and source (particularly where documents are provided as English-language translations).

With these caveats in mind, researchers are directed to the sources below as starting points only. The works cited represent a much larger body of literature: the research guides and bibliographies included here identify additional excellent sources. Because an integrated approach—use of print *and* online sources—is essential to thorough legal research, citations to sources in both media have been provided.

REFERENCE WORKS

The Guide to International Legal Research, published by the George Washington University Journal of International Law and Economics (Washington, D.C., 1993), provides an overview of public international law research sources and techniques. A supplement to this work, Guide to International Legal Research, 2d Edition: 1996 Supplement: A Guide to Internet and Commercial Online Research (1996), identifies relevant online sources: an annotated list of Internet sites for foreign and international law organized by source of law, by jurisdiction, and by area of law (including environmental); and an annotated list of primary and secondary sources available on LEXIS and Westlaw organized by geographical region and by topic. Legal Research on International Law Issues Using the Internet, by Foreign and International Law Librarian Lyonette Louis-Jacques, is available at the University of Chicago Law School Internet site: <http://www.lib.uchicago.edu/~llou/forintlaw.html>. The site provides hyperlinks (with annotations) to relevant primary and secondary sources on the World Wide Web and includes links to additional research guides.

Guides to conducting research on foreign law exist for at least some countries, although researchers typically require assistance by a person trained in the law of the particular jurisdiction whose law or practices are at issue. The five-volume compendium Foreign Law: Current Sources of Codes and Basic Legislation in Jurisdictions of the World by Thomas H.

Reynolds and Arturo A. Flores (Littleton, CO: Rothman, 1991-) provides citations to *current* primary and some secondary sources (and to English translations when available), to multijurisdictional works where appropriate and reliable, and to country-specific guides and handbooks. Titles of works addressing "environmental protection" and "natural resources" are included for many jurisdictions. Germain's Transnational Law Research Guide: A Guide for Attorneys, by Claire M. Germain (Yonkers, NY: Juris Publishing, 1991-), provides citations to primary and secondary sources (English language) for 17 European countries and the United States along with individual research guides for several areas of international law including "Antarctica," "Law of the Sea," and "Environmental Law."

Two articles concentrate solely on research methodology in the field of international environmental law: Ellen O. Creagar, Research Strategy and Sources for International Environmental Law, Colorado Journal of International Environmental Law and Policy 141-181 (1991); Ellen G. Schaffer, Researching International Environmental Law, 1 Georgetown International Environmental Law Review 199-216 (1988). An ambitious pathfinder to primary and secondary sources that addresses the linkage between environment and development is provided by Margaret Aycock, International Trade and the Environment: A Research Guide, in Introduction to Transnational Legal Transactions (Marilyn J. Raisch & Roberta I. Shaffer, eds. New York: Oceana, 1995).

Three subject-specific bibliographies are available to researchers: International Environmental Law, Robert J. Munro (Dobbs Ferry: Oceana 1990), which contains a bibliographic survey of twentieth century works on international environmental legal issues; Alberto Szekely, The International Law of Natural Resources and the Environment: A Selected Bibliography, Part I: 30 Natural Resources Journal 765-917 (1990), Part II: 31 Natural Resources Journal 265-427 (1991); World Environment Law Bibliography: Non-Periodical Literature in Law and the Social Sciences Published Since 1970 in Various Languages with Selected Reviews and Annotations from Periodicals, Virginia Evans Templeton & Howard J. Taubenfeld (Littleton, CO: Rothman, 1987). Public International Law: A Current Bibliography of Books and Articles, published biannually by the Max Planck Institute in Heidelberg (1975-), includes works on "Environmental Protection" and the "Sea."

Citations to relevant articles are also provided by the legal periodical indexes: Index to Foreign Legal Periodicals (Berkeley, CA: University of California Press for the American Association of Law Libraries, 1960-); Index to Legal Periodicals (New York: H.W. Wilson Co., 1928-); and the Current Law Index (Foster City, CA: Information Access Company for the American Association of Law Libraries, 1980-). Descriptive word search capability is available for the electronic versions of the Current Law Index: LegalTrac (CD-ROM); Legal Resource Index, on LEXIS and Westlaw. Likely subject headings include "environmental law, international," "international environmental law and practice," "international law," "natural resources," and "transnational pollution."

SOURCES OF INTERNATIONAL ENVIRONMENTAL LAW

A comprehensive index of references to international environmental instruments (900 of them), reproductions of 85 important environmental instruments, and an index to popular names of such instruments are provided in International Environmental Law: Basic Instruments and References (Edith Brown Weiss, Daniel Barstow Magraw, & Paul C. Szasz, eds. Dobbs Ferry: Transnational Publishers, 1992). The references and reproduced instruments are organized by subject in a manner that allows for orthogonal research. Texts of these instruments are also available on Westlaw in its *INTLENVL* database.

The Register of International Treaties and Other Agreements in the Field of the Environment, issued biennially in all the official languages and published in softbound report style by the United Nations Environment Program (UNEP), contains important data (e.g., date entered into force, depository, language(s)) about many international environmental agreements; it should be noted that the lists of "Parties" in the *Register* sometimes include states that have signed but not yet expressed final consent to be bound (e.g., by ratification).

The largest compendium of international environmental law instruments is the 31-volume International Protection of the Environment: Treaties and Related Documents (Bernd Ruster, Bruno Simma, & Michael Bock, eds. Dobbs Ferry: Oceana, 1975-1983), updated with the six-volume second series (1989-).

Over 100 documents (including judicial and arbitral decisions) are provided in Documents in International Environmental Law (Philippe Sands, Richard Tarasofsky & Mary Weiss, eds. New York: Manchester University Press, 1995-), a two-volume companion set to the textbook Principles of International Environmental Law (1994). The fourth volume begins regional coverage, Documents in European Community Environmental Law. Conventions, soft law texts, and some judicial and arbitral decisions are available in the Supplement of Basic Documents to International Environmental Law and World Order (Lakshman D. Guruswamy, Geoffrey W.R. Palmer & Burns H. Weston, eds. St. Paul, MN: West Pub. Co., 1994).

Basic Documents of International Environmental Law (Harald Hohmann, ed. London: Graham & Trotman, 1992) provides the texts of environmental conventions and draft conventions, and documents generated by international organizations and associations undertaking codification of international environmental law. Access to soft law texts is also provided by International Environmental Soft Law: Collection of Relevant Documents (Wolfgang Burhenne & Marlene Jahnke, eds. Boston: M. Nijhoff, 1993-).

Versions of multilateral environmental conventions in French and German (as well as English) are available in International Environmental Law—Multilateral Treaties (Wolfgang E. Burhenne, ed. Berlin: Erich Schmidt Verlag, 1974-).

Useful summaries and the official texts of pertinent multilateral conventions concluded in the period to 1990 are provided by the United Nations Environment Program (UNEP) in a two-volume compilation, Selected Multilateral Treaties in the Field of the Environment (Cambridge: Grotius, 1983-), vol. 1 1933-1979 (Alexander C. Kiss, ed.), vol. 2, 1979-1989 (Ivana Rummel-Bulska & Seth Osafo eds.). UNEP has mounted the texts of some of these conventions at its Internet site: <http://www.unep.ch/>.

The texts and status of all the multilateral treaties deposited with the Secretary-General of the United Nations may now be accessed on the Internet at the United Nations Treaty Collection (United Nations): <http://www.un.org/Depts/Treaty>. The United Nations Home Page provides links to some soft law texts—General Assembly resolutions; reports on the work of the International Law Commission with some documentation: <http://www.un.org>.

ENTRI: Environmental Treaties and Resource Indicators (Consortium for International Earth Science Information Network's (CIESIN's) Policy Instruments Database on the Internet) provides the texts, summaries, and status of international environmental conventions accessed with either a free text index (treaty texts) or a searchable index (summaries): <http://sedac.ciesin.org/entri>. ENTRI is a collaborative undertaking by CIESIN, the World Conservation Union (IUCN), UNEP, Freedom House, the Multilaterals Project at Tufts University's Fletcher School of Law and Diplomacy, the World Resources Institute, and the Antarctic Cooperative Research Centre.

Globelaw International and Transnational Law provides the texts of these treaties, links to other international environmental treaty sites and to commentary on international environmental law and policy: <http://www.globelaw.com>.

The Multilaterals Project (Fletcher School of Law and Diplomacy at Tufts University) makes available on the Internet the texts of multilateral treaties and other instruments: <http://www.tufts.edu/fletcher/multilaterals.html>. Subject organization of the database provides access to conventions addressing biodiversity, marine and coastal areas, and "other environmental." Texts can be downloaded in a number of formats.

Pace Virtual Environmental Library (Pace University School of Law

Internet site) contains links to texts of international environmental treaties, other instruments, and background information: <http://www.law.pace.edu/env/vell6.html>. Topical organization provides access to conventions concerning climate change, hazardous substances, impact assessment, Antarctica, biodiversity, pollution control, seas, and fish and fisheries.

Print versions of more specialized collections of international environmental instruments also exist: Philippe Sands, Chernobyl: Law and Communications (Cambridge: Grotius, 1988); Simon Lyster, International Wildlife Law (Cambridge: Grotius, 1985); Gregorios Timagenis, International Control of Marine Pollution, vols. I & II (Dobbs Ferry: Oceana, 1980); Barbara Kwiatkowski and Alfred H.A. Soons, Transboundary Movements and Disposal of Hazardous Wastes in International Law: Basic Documents (Boston: M. Nijhoff, 1993).

Texts of selected international environmental law instruments are available on Westlaw in the INTLENVL database; texts of treaties to which the United States is a party (including some multilateral environmental conventions) are available in the USTREATIES database. Texts of some multilateral conventions are available on LEXIS in the INTLAW and WORLD Libraries.

International Legal Materials (Washington, D.C.: American Society of International Law, 1962- , issued bimonthly) provides the official text of recently concluded conventions along with reports on the status of existing treaties, International Court of Justice (ICJ) decisions, and other developments in international law; available on Lexis in the INTLAW Library; available on Westlaw as the ILM database.

Reports on recently concluded treaties, the work of international organizations, and national pollution control policies and programs (for the industrialized nations) are provided by the bi-weekly International Environment Reporter: Current Report, published by the Bureau of National Affairs (Washington, D.C.: BNA, 1978-); available on Lexis in the ENVIRN Library. BNA also provides a daily electronic current awareness service, BNA International Environment Daily, available on Lexis in the ENVIRN and NEWS Libraries, and on Westlaw as the BNA-IED database.

The Environmental Law Reporter, published by the Environmental Law Institute (Washington, D.C. 1971-) also provides the texts of international environmental agreements with weekly and monthly updates; it is available on Lexis in the ENVIRN Library and on Westlaw in the ELR family of databases.

Yearbook of International Environmental Law (London: Graham & Trotman, 1990-) reviews developments in the field, the work of international organizations and tribunals, and the literature for the year. The texts of significant documents are appended, and an accompanying diskette provides texts of documents not included in the print volume.

Reports of selected environmental law cases from international and national tribunals are provided by these works: International Environmental Law Digest: Instruments for International Responses to Problems of the Environment and Development, 1972-1992 (A.O. Adede, ed. Amsterdam: Elsevier, 1993); and Environmental Law Reports (Richard Wade-Smith, ed. London: Sweet & Maxwell, 1992-). International Law Reports (E. Lauterpacht, ed. London: Butterworth, 1919-) does not report environmental law cases exclusively, but periodic indexes and a consolidated index (1996) provide access to cases concerning the "environment," "marine pollution," "natural resources," "nuclear energy."

The International Court of Jusice (ICJ) publishes its decisions in Reports of Judgments, Advisory Opinions and Orders (the Hague, 1947-). The court now has its own web site: <http://www.icj-cij.org>. With the documentary assistance of the ICJ, the Law Library at Cornell University Law School has mounted the official texts of the ICJ's judgments, advisory opinions, and orders (in English and French) at its International Court of Justice Internet site: <http://www.law.cornell.edu/icj/home.htm>. ICJ cases are available as well on Westlaw in the INT-ICJ database.

SOURCES OF FOREIGN LAW

Two comparative law works provide useful summaries and analysis of the environmental laws and regulations of selected foreign jurisdictions: International Encyclopedia of Laws: Environmental Law (Mark Boes, ed. Boston: Kluwer, 1991-); and Comparative Environmental Law and Regulation (Nicholas A. Robinson, ed. Dobbs Ferry: Oceana, 1996-). The Robinson text also provides, as a separate chapter, an annotated list of Internet sites for the texts of some of these laws (organized by jurisdiction), along with criteria for determining the reliability of texts of laws available on the Internet generally. This collection of sites will be regularly updated at the publisher's Web Page.

The Internet hosts a number of multijurisdictional sites that provide direct access to the texts (official and English translations) of municipal environmental law. Pace Virtual Environmental Law Library (Pace University School of Law) provides access to links abroad where countries have placed environmental legal materials on the Internet: <http://www.law.pace.edu/env/vell6.html>. Additional links provide access to the texts of international environmental law documents and to United States federal and state environmental law sources.

U.S. House of Representatives Internet Law Library: Laws of Other Nations provides links to the texts of laws (including environmental) of foreign jurisdictions along with links to other international environmental law sites: <http://law.house.gov/52.htm>.

Environmental Law Around the World (Environmental Law Alliance) provides links to the texts of environmental laws of foreign jurisdictions

(English translations when available) along with links to other international environmental law sites: <http://www.igc.apc.org/envlaw/otherlaw.html>. Environmental Law Alliance (E-LAW) is an international, professional association of public interest environmental specialists (attorneys, scientists, and advocates).

GLIN: Global Legal Information Network (a United States Library of Congress project) provides links to the full texts of national laws of participating countries, searchable English language abstracts, links to other sites providing international legal sources: <http://lcweb2.loc.gov:8081/glin/glinhome.html>.

The *ENFLEX* family of databases on Westlaw provides access to the texts of selected environmental regulations for certain foreign jurisdictions. These texts are available as well on Lexis in the *ENVIRN* Library. The texts of some municipal laws (that may include environmental laws) for selected foreign jurisdictions are available on Lexis (Canada, Mexico, Australia, New Zealand, People's Republic of China, United Kingdom and Commonwealth countries, France, Italy, Russia, Eastern Europe, and the European Union), and on Westlaw (the European Union, Russia, and Mexico). Users should consult the Database Directories for Lexis and Westlaw for specific database identifiers.

APPENDIX II

International Organizations

This appendix supplements the material in Chapter 5, section D, on international organizations. It follows the same general organizational structure found in that chapter. The following sections deal with the basic characteristics of intergovernmental organizations (IGOs) and non-governmental organizations (NGOs); UN organs, other than the principal environmental institutions discussed in Chapter 5.D, with environmental functions; procedural aspects of environmental conferences; other agencies in the UN system with functions related to the environment; other nonregional IGOs; regional and subregional IGOs; and international NGOs.

A. INTERGOVERNMENTAL ORGANIZATIONS: BASIC CHARACTERISTICS

IGOs are (with very few exceptions) created by written international treaties between the states that are the members of the organization. These treaties serve as the constitutional instruments of their respective IGOs.

The members of IGOs are for the most part states, or sometimes particular governmental organs (e.g., environmental ministries), though recently the constitutional treaties of some IGOs have permitted certain other IGOs to become parties; the latter are usually defined as "regional integration organizations," such as the European Union (EU), which in effect are supranational organizations to which its members have delegated certain governmental (legislative, executive, and judicial) functions that these organizations then carry out on behalf of their member states—including as participants in other IGOs (e.g., environmental ones).

Each IGO has its own international legal personality, which is independent of that of its members—somewhat like corporations have a national legal personality independent of their shareholders.

An important aspect of IGOs is how they are financed, which may be by assessing (i.e., taxing) member states according to some formula; by voluntary contributions, mostly by members; by capital contributions or periodic "replenishments" (characteristic of financial institutions, such as the World Bank and regional development banks); or sometimes by income from operations. Many IGOs use several of these sources of financing for different types of operations. The independence and effectiveness of an IGO depends to a considerable extent on how it is financed—with those having to rely substantially on voluntary contributions usually being in the weakest position.

In most IGOs decisions are taken by votes (usually requiring a simple majority for procedural matters and two-thirds for important and/or substantive ones), each member having just one vote. However, in financial institutions (i.e., those that are financed by capital contributions or replenishments, such as the World Bank and the regional development banks) voting strength is normally distributed in accordance with each member's contribution to or investment in the institution.

Finally, it should be noted that most significant IGOs are parts of groups. Thus the UN System consists of the United Nations and of its specialized and related agencies, such as WHO, FAO, IAEA, and the World Bank—which itself consists of a cluster of some five IGOs. There are also important regional clusters, particularly in the Americas, in Africa, in Europe, in the Middle East, and in South-Eastern Asia.

B. NON-GOVERNMENTAL ORGANIZATIONS: BASIC CHARACTERISTICS

Unlike IGOs, which have legal structures and a status well-grounded in international law, INGOs not only lack such assured positions but do not even have any generally accepted definition. The most that can be said is that on the one hand they are not IGOs (i.e., they are not established by treaty and generally their members are not states) and that on the other they have certain attributes that make it possible to characterize them as being both international (as opposed to merely national) and as organizations (which requires a certain stability and regularity of structure).[1] INGOs can thus take many different forms, such as organizations that have individual members in several countries, or that constitute a federation of parallel membership organizations that are established in several countries.

INGOs therefore come in many sizes and shapes. Some represent, in effect, tens of thousands of individuals in many countries, while others only a handful from a few closely related ones. Most are nonprofit, but some represent powerful business interests. Some engage in activities, such as relief work or environmental cleanup, while many are partially or primarily engaged in lobbying—which may be addressed both to IGOs or to national governmental organs on behalf of certain transboundary concerns.

There is no international law, whether customary or treaty-based, for the establishment of INGOs. Thus, to the extent that an INGO has a legal basis, it must be grounded in the domestic law of one or more states. Many states require that any domestic organization be established according to specified rules and procedures (e.g., registration with some governmental authority) and even may require that foreign organizations that wish to operate domestically, register in some way.[2] Other countries (e.g., the United States) have no such requirements, though if an INGO wishes to engage in ordinary business transactions (e.g., open a bank account, buy real estate) it may have to establish its legal personality. Nevertheless, some INGOs probably have no formal legal status at all.

The one aspect of INGOs that is to some extent regulated by international law are their relationships with IGOs. In the United Nations these are in part grounded in Article 71 of the Charter and in a number of ECOSOC resolutions adopted pursuant thereto. These resolutions classify NGOs[3] into three categories:

(1) Category I: NGOs with a basic interest in most of the activities of ECOSOC;
(2) Category II: NGOs with a special competence but concerned with only a few of ECOSOC's activities;
(3) Roster: NGOs with which *ad hoc* consultations may take place

A number of other UN organs and other IGOs also have standing rules (often in their rules of procedure) concerning their relations with NGOs

1. *See* the annual Yearbook of International Organizations (Edited by the Union of International Associations), Appendices 3 and 5.

2. The European Convention on the recognition of the legal personality of international non-governmental organizations, adopted by the Council of Europe on April 24, 1986, provides that the legal personality and capacity of NGOs that meet certain specified requirements, including establishment by an instrument governed by the internal law of a party to the convention, are to be recognized by other parties.

3. UN Charter Article 71, which principally concerns INGOs, nevertheless also allows for the recognition by ECOSOC of NNGOs under specified conditions. Indeed, in 1996 ECOSOC considerably relaxed its distinction between NGOs that are worldwide, regional, subregional (all INGOs) or national (NNGOs).

and may also adopt ad hoc arrangements concerning a particular conference or set of meetings. In recent years these rules and criteria have been considerably relaxed to widen the circle of NGOs participating in IGO activities and broaden the scope of such participation.

C. UN ORGANS, OTHER THAN THE PRINCIPAL ENVIRONMENTAL BODIES, WITH ENVIRONMENTAL FUNCTIONS

The principal environmental organs of the United Nations were discussed in Chapter 5.D. Other UN organs with environmental functions are identified in this section.

1. Principal UN Organs

Several of the six UN principal organs perform or stand ready to perform miscellaneous functions in respect of the environment, though for each of them these are generally rather minor and peripheral.

a. General Assembly

The General Assembly considers environmental issues for the most part in its overburdened Second (Economic and Financial) Committee, largely in odd-numbered years; at recent sessions this consideration has taken place under a main agenda item titled "Environment and sustainable development" with several subitems. These are debated at a few plenary meetings before private consultations start on the texts of the ever more numerous environmental resolutions that emerge from each regular session of the Assembly—including some resolutions giving specific programmatic guidance and administrative directives to UNEP.[4] Some environmental mat-

4. *See, e.g.,* the followinhg resolutions adopted in 1997 at the 52nd regular session of the General Assembly: A/RES/52/28 (Agreement for the implementation of the Provisions of the United Nations Convention on the Law of the Sea of 10 December 1982 relating to the Conservation and Management of Straddling Fish Stocks and Highly Migratory Fish Stocks), /29 (Large-scale pelagic drift-net fishing: unauthorized fishing in zones of national jurisdiction and on the high seas, fisheries by-catch and discards; and other development), /172 (Strengthening of international cooperation and coordination of efforts to study, mitigate and minimize the consequences of the Chernobyl disaster), /173 (Assistance in Mine Clearance), all adopted without reference to a main committee; A/RES/52/198 (Implementation of the United Nations Convention to Combat Desertification in Those Countries Experiencing Serious Drought and/or Desertification, Particularly in Africa), /199 (Protection of the global climate for present future generations of mankind), /200 (International cooperation to reduce the impact of the El Niño phenomenon), /201 (Convention on Biological Diversity), /202 (Implementation of the outcome of the Global Conference on the Sustainable Develop-

ters are considered directly in plenary, notably the marine environment, which is treated as an aspect of the Law of the Sea.

In spite of the relatively scant attention that the General Assembly has until recently devoted to the environment, it has from time to time issued or endorsed important directives designed to set the environmental agenda of the international community: first the convening of the 1972 Stockholm Conference (Ch.5.D.2.c(i)(1))(1)(a)(i) and then the endorsement of its Declaration and the implementation of its structural recommendations, as well as the de facto establishment of UNEP (Ch.5.D.2.a(i)); ten years later, the promulgation of the World Charter for Nature;[5] in 1987, the approval of Environmental Perspective for the Year 2000 and Beyond (evaluating the outlook and setting detailed goals and recommended actions on ten key environmental issues)[6] and the endorsement of the report of the UNEP-established World Commission on Environment and Development (the Brundtland Commission);[7] and, most recently, the convening of UNCED (Ch.5.D.2.c(i)(2)) and then the implementation of its structural recommendations, including the establishment of CSD (Ch.5.D.2.a(ii)) and the Advisory Board (Ch.5.D.2.a.(iii)). It has also convened more narrowly focused environment-related conferences, including most of those listed in Chapter 5.D.2.c(ii), below, as well as intergovernmental negotiating fora, such as the climate change, biodiversity, desertification, and fisheries conferences.

b. Economic and Social Council (ECOSOC)

ECOSOC receives the reports of the UNEP Governing Council, the CSD, and the Advisory Board on each of their sessions, as well as those of most other quasi-autonomous UN subsidiaries active in areas relevant to the environment and also those of the specialized and related agencies of the UN System. However, the Council itself has rarely performed any significant work or conducted any decisive debates in this field. Instead, it merely passes the CSD and UNEP reports, and those of several other of the above-mentioned organs, to the General Assembly.

---

ment of Small Island Developing States), all adopted on the report of the Second Committee; as well as A/RES/52/38 (General and Complete Disarmament) /[38] A (Convention on the Prohibition of the Use, Stockpiling, Production and Transfer of Anti-personnel Mines and on Their Destruction), /38 H (Contribution towards banning anti-personnel landmines), /38 I (Prohibition of the dumping of radioactive wastes), all adopted on the report of the First Committee.

5. A/RES/37/7 of Oct. 28, 1982.

6. A/RES/42/186 of Dec. 11, 1987, Annex.

7. A/RES/42/187 of Dec. 11, 1987. The Commission's Report is set out in A/42/427 (also published as *Our Common Future*).

c. Secretary-General

The Secretary-General is the nominal supervisor of the UNEP Executive Director, though in effect the former can exercise little influence over an official who is responsible to and has the support of his own political body (the UNEP Governing Council) the representatives to which are located far from UN Headquarters.[8] The Secretary-General does have more influence over those offices of the central (or headquarters) secretariat that are charged with environment-related tasks, but these are generally peripheral to the main activities in this field.

d. International Court of Justice (ICJ or World Court)

The World Court has from time to time been faced with disputes that had an environmental tinge or that caused it to make pronouncements significant in respect of the environment.[9] In September 1997 it decided its first case in which environmental issues have been directly raised, between Hungary and Slovakia concerning the Gabcíkovo-Nagymaros Project, in which a principal issue was whether a state can be required to proceed with a major project on an important international watercourse (the Danube) to which it had committed itself by treaty, in spite of subsequent environmental objections. In addition, in its advisory opinion on the legality of the use of nuclear weapons (*see* Chapter 15, section C.1 and 8), the Court made several important statements concerning the importance of environmental protection.

In July 1993, in anticipation of more environmental cases, the Court established, pursuant to Article 26(1) of its Statute, a seven-judge Chamber for Environmental Matters. So far, no cases have been submitted to it.

e. Security Council

The Security Council does not really have any directly relevant functions. But it should be noted that in its resolution relating to the cease-fire

8. Most members of the UNEP Governing Council maintain special representatives in Nairobi to deal with UNEP business, and these naturally establish close relations with its staff and Executive Director. Aside from the few formal meetings of the Governing Council, the Executive Director from time to time convenes the Permanent Representatives to UNEP to advise them of new developments and to consult on certain matters requiring decisions, a procedure finally formalized by a 1997 decision of the Council.

9. *See* Chapter 5.B.7.a, as well as the cases in Chapter 6, and in particular the *Corfu Channel, Merits, Judgment,* 1949 *I.C.J.* 4. As will be seen, this case was not really about the environment at all (unless one considers that placing mines in international straits an environmental offense), but is frequently cited by international environmental lawyers, for its strong affirmation of the *sic utere* principle, later put into environmental terms as the oft-cited Stockholm Principle 21, which was later reformulated as Principle 2 of the Rio Declaration.

in the Gulf War, the Council held Iraq specifically responsible for any environmental damage it had caused as a result of its invasion of Kuwait[10] and established a Compensation Commission charged, inter alia, with determining the amount of that liability towards particular claimants.

2. *Other UN organs*

A number of UN subsidiary organs, such as the five Regional Commissions,[11] the UN Development Programme (UNDP), the UN University (UNU), the UN Institute for Training and Research (UNITAR), and many parts of the central Secretariat perform environment-related activities. From time to time other permanent or temporary environmental bodies have been established, such as the UN Scientific Committee on the Effects of Atomic Radiation (UNSCEAR).[12]

D. ENVIRONMENTAL CONFERENCES: PROCEDURAL ASPECTS

A number of environmental conferences are dealt with in Chapter 5.D.2.c. The present section provides additional information on how they function.

The full set of arrangements for environmental conferences is likely to consist of:

(1) A preparatory body, which may be an ad hoc representative organ established for just that purpose or a standing representative organ especially tasked (and whose composition may sometimes even be increased for that function); in any event it is assisted by a secretariat, often headed by the official designated to become the Secretary-General of the conference. The preparatory body holds a

10. S/RES/687 of Mar. 2, 1991, para. 16—quoted in Chapter 15 (Military Activities), section D.3.

11. For example, the Economic Commission for Europe (ECE)—for many decades the only body in which East and West European States, as well as Canada and the United States, regularly collaborated—in 1974 established as a subsidiary organ the Senior Advisers to ECE Governments on Environmental Problems (ECE/DEC/8(XXIX) of Apr. 29, 1974). Under the sponsorship of the latter, the Co-operative Programme for Monitoring and Evaluation of the Long-Range Transmission of Air Pollutants (EMEP) was established, followed by the 1979 Geneva Convention on Long-Range Transboundary Air Pollution (LRTAP) and its successive protocols; the secretariat for implementing LRTAP is part of that of ECE.

12. A/RES/913(X) of Dec. 3, 1955. Originally UNSCEAR was established to monitor the fallout from nuclear test explosions, but with the waning number of these tests (particularly of atmospheric ones) it has long since become a primarily environmental body. Its secretary therefore now functions within the UNEP Secretariat.

number of sessions, often over a period of several years, and reports from time to time to the parent representative organ that is convening the conference.

(2) Other preparatory meetings, of representative or expert organs, may be convened during the preparatory period, usually by the preparatory body itself but sometimes by other organizations (e.g., UN regional commissions or specialized agencies) that are interested in the subject and wish to advance its consideration in the light of their own special concerns. Such meetings may be regional or thematic, addressing particular aspects of the general subject.

(3) A set of informal organizational meetings immediately preceding the conference proper, at which procedural details are worked out (rules of procedure; distribution of offices) so that these need not intrude on the conference.

(4) The conference itself. Thematic ones usually have a duration between one and two weeks; treaty-making ones may last much longer and may require several sessions—the number of which may not be predictable at the time the process starts.

(5) Ever since the 1972 Stockholm Conference, each thematic conference has been accompanied by a parallel, INGO-organized, public gathering, whose venue is as close as practicable to that of the formal conference. These gatherings consist of a great number of workshops, exhibitions, study sessions, and usually also some formal meetings of INGO representatives that endeavor to reach conclusions that are then communicated to the formal conference. A great deal of networking and consciousness-raising is typically accomplished.

(6) Depending on the type of conference, there are different types of follow-ups. Treaty-making ones require domestic steps and international pressures to get the agreements ratified and in force; sometimes the treaties will provide for the establishment of a new IGO or treaty organ, and until entry into force some preparatory body established by the conference may function to advance the process. Thematic conferences are often followed by the establishment by the convening IGO of one or more organs, which are tasked with encouraging and monitoring the implementation of substantive and administrative recommendations of the conference. For this purpose these organs may rely on the national governmental structures that had been established or especially charged during the preparations for the conference, and that are likely to remain in place indefinitely as long-time domestic bureaucratic champions of the objectives of the conference.

Thus international conferences are much more than merely short-term meetings whose proceedings and decisions are soon forgotten. The often years-long preparatory process and the follow-up arrangements usually ensure that the recommendations of the conference are carefully formulated and that, once adopted, they continue to be taken into account, both internationally and domestically. They thus definitely constitute part of the international institutional environmental regime.

E. ELSEWHERE IN THE UN SYSTEM

Even before the establishment of UNEP, a number of the specialized and related agencies of the United Nations were assigned or gradually assumed some environment-related functions incidental to carrying out their principal tasks. As international environmental concerns became more prominent on the world's agenda, because of or at least accelerated by the Stockholm Conference, most of these agencies have increased these activities.

1. Food and Agriculture Organization of the United Nations (FAO)[13]

Some important pre-1972 FAO initiatives in the field of the environment include the 1949 Rome Agreement for the Establishment of a General Fisheries Council for the Mediterranean (GFCM),[14] the 1951 Rome International Plant Protection Convention,[15] the 1956 Rome Plant Protection Agreement for the Asia and Pacific Region,[16] the 1969 Rome Convention on the Conservation of the Living Resources of the South-East Atlantic,[17] and several agreements for the establishment of various regional Commissions for Controlling the Desert Locust.[18]

Later important FAO instruments include the 1981 World Soil Charter,[19] the 1983 International Undertaking on Plant Genetic Resources,[20] the 1985 Tropical Forest Action Plan (TFAP),[21] and the 1985 International Code of Conduct on the Distribution and Use of Pesticides[22] (along with numerous guidelines relating to pesticides).

13. *See generally* FAO and the Environment, booklet published by FAO in 1986 (M/R 9910E).
14. 126 U.N.T.S. 237.
15. 150 U.N.T.S. 67.
16. 247 U.N.T.S. 400.
17. 801 U.N.T.S. 101.
18. Southwest Asia, 1963, 529 U.N.T.S. 217; Near East, 1965, 592 U.N.T.S. 215; Northwest Africa, 1970, 797 U.N.T.S. 97.
19. 21 FAO Conference Resolution 8/81.
20. 22 FAO Conference Resolution 8/83.
21. FAO Publication M-30.
22. 23 FAO Conference Resolution 10/85.

FAO has also convened a number of environment-related conferences, such as the 1984 World Conference on Fisheries Management and Development, Rome, which adopted the Strategy for Fisheries Management and Development, as well as related action programs.

The organization has also become a major implementing agency for the Biodiversity Convention because of its mandates on forests, fisheries, and plant genetic resources.

2. *United Nations Educational, Scientific and Cultural Organization (UNESCO)*

UNESCO may be credited with early intellectual leadership in respect of environmental questions. In 1968 it convened the Rational Use of the Biosphere Conference, and in 1971 it initiated what may be considered as the precursor of broad-based environmental programs: Man in the Biosphere (MAB).[23]

In 1972 UNESCO promulgated the convention concerning the Protection of the World Cultural and Natural Heritage,[24] which established the Intergovernmental Committee for the Protection of the Cultural and Natural Heritage of Outstanding Universal Value (the World Heritage Committee) and provides that its secretariat be appointed by the UNESCO Director-General, which thus in effect functions as part of the UNESCO secretariat.

3. *World Bank*

In the World Bank (formally the International Bank for Reconstruction and Development (IBRD)), which is at the center of a group of four other IGOs, whose establishment it itself had sponsored, environmental sensitivity grew with that of the rest of the world community. For development institutions, such as the Bank, there are two principal issues:[25]

(1) To what extent environmental considerations enter into the planning and implementation of projects supported by the Bank. To charges that the Bank has all too often disregarded concerns of this type, its response has been:

(a) It is not for the Bank to set priorities for its borrowers, who can be presumed to have the best interests of their peoples in mind. Whether this is always a valid presumption, the Bank

23. *See* Man Belongs to the Earth (UNESCO 1988).
24. 11 I.L.M. 1358 (1972).
25. *See also* Chapter 20.

now recognizes that the internationalization of environmental concerns has meant that, even assuming that a particular government may be willing to prefer economic development to protecting some aspects of its country's environment, that tradeoff may not appear to be advantageous to the world community, and therefore should not be supported by international financial institutions.

(b) The critics are often wise after the fact, reproaching the Bank and the borrowing governments for environmental consequences that were not readily foreseeable when a project was initiated or that only became recognized as problems as a result of later scientific insights or of outside developments (e.g., rising worldwide levels of pollution) that now make dangerous actions that when initiated seemed and actually were safe. As a positive response, that Bank has steadily been investing more in scientific and other research designed to signal in advance possibly deleterious consequences of proposed projects or of the means to implement them.

(2) To encourage borrowers to engage in projects primarily designed to protect or improve the environment.

In 1980 the World Bank joined with numerous other multilateral development institutions in a Declaration of Environmental Policies and Procedures relating to Economic Development[26] and in founding the Committee of International Development Institutions on the Environment (CIDIE) (*see* 8(2) below). In 1991 it joined with UNEP and UNDP in establishing the Global Environment Facility (GEF) (discussed in Chapter 21).

As to its internal affairs, the Bank in 1989 adopted an Operational Directive on Environmental Assessment.[27] In 1993 it established an Inspection Panel, which is primarily charged with considering charges made from any source (e.g., persons to be displaced by a Bank-financed project) that the Bank's own environmental guidelines have been disregarded in a particular operation.[28] Since 1990 the Bank has issued annual Progress Reports on *The World Bank and the Environment.*[29]

4. *World Health Organization (WHO)*

Although many of WHO's public health measures evidently have an environmental aspect, its specifically environmental activities are mostly undertaken in collaboration with UNEP, such as the 1981 WHO/FAO/

26. 19 I.L.M. 524 (1980).
27. World Bank Operational Manual, OD 4.00, Annexes A, A1, A2.
28. *See* I. Shihata, The Inspection Panel of the World Bank (1995).
29. The World Bank's Fiscal 1994 report was titled, Making Development Sustainable.

UNEP Memorandum of Understanding Governing Collaboration in the Control of Water-Borne and Associated Diseases in Agricultural Water Development Activities. Other concerns include those on pesticides and chemicals.

5. *World Meteorological Organization (WMO)*

WMO's monitoring activities were originally simply weather-related, but their importance for environmental affairs was soon recognized. It was instrumental in organizing the 1979 and 1990 World Climate Conferences and in November 1988 co-established, with UNEP, the Intergovernmental Panel on Climate Change (IPCC) in which the negotiations of what became the 1992 Framework Convention on Climate Change were initiated (though not concluded) and which still continues its activities to assist in implementing the Convention. Earlier it had been instrumental in gathering data on ozone depletion, which were important in connection with the 1985 Vienna Convention and the 1987 Montreal Protocol and its amendments.

6. *International Maritime Organization (IMO*[30])

IMO is responsible for the negotiation and/or the administration of a number of important conventions relating to ocean pollution, including the 1954 International Convention for the Prevention of Pollution of the Sea by Oil[31] plus its 1971 London Amendment concerning the Protection of the Great Barrier Reef;[32] the 1972 Convention on the Prevention of Marine Pollution by Dumping of Wastes and Other Matter (London Ocean Dumping Convention);[33] and the 1990 London International Convention on Oil Pollution Preparedness, Response and Co-operation.[34] In 1973 the IMCO Assembly established the Marine Environment Protection Committee as a standing organ.

7. *International Atomic Energy Agency (IAEA)*

The IAEA's statutory concern for nuclear safety evidently always had an environmental aspect, which became more evident as a result of the Chernobyl disaster. Of special importance are: the 1980 Convention on

30. IMO was originally established as the Inter-Governmental Maritime Consultative Organization (IMCO).
31. 327 U.N.T.S. 3.
32. IMCO/RESA.232(VII), 1 IPE 378.
33. 1046 U.N.T.S. 120, 11 I.L.M. 1294 (1972).
34. 30 I.L.M. 735 (1990).

the Physical Protection of Nuclear Material;[35] the 1983 IAEA Guidelines for Mutual Emergency Assistance Arrangements in Connection with a Nuclear Accident or Radiological Emergency;[36] the 1986 (post-Chernobyl) Conventions on Early Notification of a Nuclear Accident and on Assistance in the Case of a Nuclear Accident or Radiological Emergency;[37] the 1990 IAEA Code of Practice on the International Transboundary Movement of Radioactive Waste;[38] and the 1994 Convention on Nuclear Safety.[39] The Agency has no specifically environmental organ.

8. *Other UN System Organs with Environmental Functions: Joint Bodies*

As environmental concerns have proliferated, such functions have in many organizations increased in response to the demands of member states or of other intergovernmental and non-governmental international organizations. For the purpose of carrying out such functions, these organizations have from time to time established joint organs or other arrangements, such as:

(1) Joint Group of Experts on the Scientific Aspects of Marine Pollution (GESAMP), a joint organ of UN, UNEP, FAO, UNESCO, WHO, WMO, IMO, and IAEA;
(2) Committee of International Development Institutions on the Environment (CIDIE), a joint organ of by now 16 multilateral development/finance institutions, including several outside the UN System;
(3) Intergovernmental Panel on Climate Change (IPCC), jointly sponsored by UNEP and WMO;
(4) Second World Climate Conference, Geneva, cosponsored by WMO, UNESCO and UNEP.

F. OTHER NONREGIONAL IGOs

A number of IGOs have been established to protect certain aspects of the environment, such as a particular group of animals or plants, which organizations are tied neither to the UN System nor to any regional group

35. IAEA INFCIRC/274.
36. IAEA INFCIRC/310.
37. Respectively, IAEA INFCIRC/335, 25 I.L.M. 1370 (1986), and IAEA INFCIRC/336, 25 I.L.M. 1377 (1986).
38. IAEA INFCIRC/386.
39. IAEA INFCIRC/449; 33 I.L.M. 1518; IAEA Legal Series No. 16 (IAEA, Vienna, 1994).

of organizations; often these relate to a global commons, such as the oceans or Antarctica. Some of the more prominent of these organizations are:

(1) International Whaling Commission (IWC);
(2) The European and Mediterranean Plant Protection Organization;
(3) International Council for Local Environmental Initiatives;
(4) Committee for Environmental Protection of the Antarctic Treaty System (which is an organ of the Antarctic Treaty System, itself an environment-oriented IGO, nonregional in the sense that its membership comes from all regions of the world).

G. REGIONAL AND SUBREGIONAL IGOs

There are a number of regional IGOs or groups of IGOs, covering in particular Africa, the Americas, and Europe.[40] There are also subregional ones, such as those for Africa South of the Sahara, for the Caribbean and for the Nordic States, which cover areas also encompassed by regional ones, as well as several ones for various parts of Asia (which does not have an overall regional IGO), such as for the Middle East or for South-East Asia.

For the most part, these regional and subregional IGOs, with the exception of those for Europe, do not include any prominent environmental ones or have any strong specifically environmental organs. This reflects the lesser emphasis that most of the developing states place on environmental concerns, which they probably consider sufficiently met by the regional and subregional activities sponsored by a number of the above-mentioned UN System IGOs and organs.

Europe, on the other hand, has a number of environmental IGOs or IGO organs. Many of these are associated with one or another of the somewhat concentric systems of European IGOs: the 15-member European Union (EU—formerly the European Communities), the 29-member Organization for Economic Cooperation and Development (OECD—which also has six non-European members), the 40-member Council of Europe (CoE), and the 55-member Organization for Security and Co-operation in Europe (OSCE—formerly the CSCE—with seven North American and Asian members); others relate to particular common resources, such as a river or lake. Some of the more prominent of these organizations and organs are:

40. These regional IGOs are to be distinguished from the UN Regional Commissions established by ECOSOC (for Africa, for Asia and the Far East, for Europe, for Latin America and the Caribbean, and for Western Asia), which are all part of the UN System. Their interaction with corresponding regional IGOs is a complex one.

(1) International Commission for the Protection of the Mosel [River] against Pollution;
(2) International Commission for the Protection of the Rhine against Pollution;[41]
(3) European Environment Agency of the EU;
(4) European Environment Information and Observation Network of the EU;
(5) Environment Committee of OECD.

H. INTERNATIONAL NGOS

In Chapter 5.D.3 we listed some international NGOs in Category II status with ECOSOC. Below we list some other important international NGOs active in the environmental field.

A. *Organizations on the ECOSOC Roster* (organizations to be consulted by the Council on an ad hoc basis):
   1. Caribbean Conservation Association;
   2. Environmental Coalition for North America;
   3. Fauna and Flora Preservation Society;
   4. Friends of the Earth International;
   5. Habitat International Council;
   6. International Association Against Noise;
   7. International Association on Water Pollution Research and Control; and
   8. International Institute for Environment and Development.

B. *Not in consultative status:*
   1. European Council on Environmental Law; and
   2. World Wildlife Fund (WWF).

41. It should be noted that there also are agreements for protecting the Danube against pollution, but their implementation has been entrusted to the multifunctional Danube Commission.

APPENDIX III

General Steps in Formulating Multilateral Agreements

The general steps in formulating multilateral agreements are normally as follows:

(1) The **initiation** of the process begins on the proposal of some state, IGO organ, NGO, or even individual. That proposal is then examined by an appropriate organ of the IGO to which that proposal was made to determine the need for and the potential utility of the proposed instrument, its relationship to existing international law, the chances of successfully negotiating a useful instrument likely to be acceptable to a significant number of states, and the expected length and cost of the project. If there is a conclusion to proceed, decisions are taken as to how to do so, and in particular as to which organ(s) of the IGO the principal or at least the initial work should be assigned.

(2) The **formulation** of the proposed treaty is often a multistage process. It normally starts with any necessary preliminary studies and then proceeds to the preparation of an initial draft (at least of the central provisions) by: the proposing state(s); an organ consisting of governmental representatives or of experts; the secretariat of the sponsoring IGO; a special rapporteur; or possibly even interested NGO(s). This draft is then considered by bodies with expertise in the substance of the proposed treaty (e.g., environ-

ment or disarmament) or in purely legal matters. Thereupon it is normally submitted one or more times to governments or to organs consisting of governmental representatives and, since many stages of the treaty-making process take place in public (particularly in respect of environmental agreements), may be subject to NGO, media, and other forms of public scrutiny. Finally, a drafting committee may perfect the text, as far as it has been agreed, ensuring both internal consistency as well as concordance between the various language versions in which the treaty is to be concluded.[1]

(3) Once the formulating process has been completed, resulting either in a perfected text or in one that has merely a restricted number of open questions—often signalled by the inclusion of disputed or alternative passages within square brackets—the project is transmitted to a senior IGO organ. That organ must then decide whether to proceed to the **conclusion** of the instrument, which requires a decision as to whether the then existing text is likely to result in a treaty that a sufficient number of interested states will ratify. If the decision is negative, the project may be turned back for further formulation, perhaps to another expert or political organ; or it may be abandoned. If, as is usual after substantial work has been invested in a project, it is decided to go forward, then a forum has to be chosen in which the concluding steps are to be taken. If little further work is required, this may be done in the most representative IGO organ itself. If the required work is still extensive (especially if major differences must be resolved) then a conference of states may be convened to meet (perhaps after some more preliminary work by a preparatory organ) to finish the work, adopt the treaty, and open it for signature. This concludes the substantive international phase of the international legislative process.

The following tables show the chronology of the steps taken by various international organs in connection with the adoption of the instruments relevant to protection: (1) against transboundary air pollution; (2) of the ozone layer; and (3) of the climate—including postadoption steps (such as those discussed in Chapter 5.A.3.b(iv), above) for keeping these instruments up to date.

1. For restricted multilateral agreements, normally an equally authentic or authoritative version is prepared in each of the official languages of the participating states. For those formulated within an IGO, normally the official or working languages of that IGO are used; in case of the UN these have for some time been: Arabic, Chinese, English, French, Russian, and Spanish.

TABLE APP. III-1
Chronology of Principal Development in International Legislation Concerning the Atmosphere*

A. PROTECTION AGAINST TRANSBOUNDARY AIR POLLUTION

1969	*Eric Oden, studies on acidification of Scandinavian lakes by long-range pollution*
Jun. 1972	*Swedish case-study on "Air Pollution Across National Boundaries: Impact on the Environment of Sulfur in Air and Precipitation" (submitted to the Stockholm Conference)*
18 Jun. 1974	**OECD Council Recommendation on Guidelines for Action to Reduce Emissions of Sulphur Oxides and Particulate Matters from Fuel Combustion in Stationary Sources**
14 Nov. 1974	**OECD Council Recommendation on Measures Required for Further Air Pollution Control**
1 Aug. 1975	**Helsinki Final Act of the Conference on Security and Co-operation in Europe (calling, *inter alia*, for promoting international law in respect of long-range air pollution)**
	OECD study on long-range transboundary air pollution in Europe
1978	Establishment of the Co-operative Programme for Monitoring and Evaluation of the Long-Range Transmission of Air Pollutants in Europe (EMEP), by ECE in co-operation with WMO and UNEP
1978	Negotiation of a long-range transboundary air pollution convention within the framework of the Senior Advisors to ECE Governments on Environmental Problems
13 Nov. 1979	CONVENTION ON LONG-RANGE TRANSBOUNDARY AIR POLLUTION, GENEVA
Jul. 1982	Ministerial Conference on Acidification, Stockholm
28 Sep. 1984	PROTOCOL ON LONG-TERM FINANCING ON THE CO-OPERATIVE PROGRAMME FOR MONITORING AND EVALUATION OF THE LONG-RANGE TRANSMISSION OF AIR POLLUTANTS IN EUROPE, GENEVA

A. PROTECTION AGAINST TRANSBOUNDARY AIR POLLUTION

21 Mar. 1984	Ministerial Conference on Acid Rain, Ottawa
27 Jun. 1984	Multilateral Conference on Environment, Munich
8 Jul. 1985	PROTOCOL ON THE REDUCTION OF SULPHUR EMISSIONS OR THEIR TRANSBOUNDARY FLUXES BY AT LEAST 30 PER CENT, HELSINKI
Oct. 1985-Aug. 1988	Negotiation of a Protocol on Nitrogen Oxides
31 Oct. 1988	PROTOCOL CONCERNING THE CONTROL OF EMISSIONS OF NITROGEN OXIDES OR THEIR TRANSBOUNDARY FLUXES, SOFIA
31 Oct. 1988	Declaration on 30 Per Cent Reduction of Nitrogen Oxide Emissions, Sofia
24 Nov. 1988	**EEC Directive on the Limitation of Emissions of Certain Pollutants in the Air from Large Combustion Plants**
Feb. 1989-Aug. 1991	Negotiation of a Protocol on Volatile Organic Compounds
18 Nov. 1991	PROTOCOL CONCERNING THE CONTROL OF EMISSIONS OF VOLATILE ORGANIC COMPOUNDS OR THEIR TRANSBOUNDARY FLUXES, GENEVA
14 Jun. 1994	PROTOCOL ON FURTHER REDUCTION OF SULPHUR EMISSIONS
14 Jun. 1998	PROTOCOL ON HEAVY METALS
14 Jun. 1998	PROTOCOL ON PERSISTENT ORGANIC CHEMICALS

B. PROTECTION OF THE OZONE LAYER

1973-1974	*Richard Stolarski and Ralph Cicerone, studies of release of chlorine in the atmosphere*
1974	*Mario Molina and Sherwood Rowland, studies of CFCs in the atmosphere and stratosphere*
8 Mar. 1977	**UNEP's World Plan of Action on the Ozone Layer, Washington**
Apr. 1980	**UNEP Governing Council resolution on restriction of CFC usage**
May 1981	UNEP Governing Council resolution initiating negotiations towards an ozone agreement

B. PROTECTION OF THE OZONE LAYER

1981	Meeting of legal experts convened by UNEP, Montevideo
Jan. 1982	First session of Ad Hoc Working Group of Legal and Technical Experts for the Preparation of a Global Framework Convention for the Protection of the Ozone Layer, convened by UNEP, Stockholm (NB: There were seven sessions, until 1985)
1983	**Establishment of the "Toronto Group"**
22 Mar. 1985	VIENNA CONVENTION OF THE PROTECTION OF THE OZONE LAYER
1986	*WMO/UNEP Report on Atmospheric Ozone*
May 1986	*Workshop on CFC production and consumption trends, convened by EEC and UNEP, Rome*
Sep. 1986	*Workshop on alternative regulatory strategies on protection of ozone, convened by USA and UNEP, Leesburg (USA)*
Dec. 1986	First negotiating session on a protocol to the Vienna Convention, convened by UNEP, Geneva
Feb. 1987	Second negotiating session on a protocol to the Vienna Convention, convened by UNEP, Vienna
Apr. 1987	Third negotiating session on a protocol to the Vienna Convention, convened by UNEP, Geneva
Jun. 1987	Meeting of heads of key delegations, convened by UNEP, Brussels
8-13 Sep. 1987	Preliminary meetings preceding the Montreal Conference, convened by UNEP, Montreal
16 Sep. 1987	MONTREAL PROTOCOL ON SUBSTANCES THAT DEPLETE THE OZONE LAYER
Apr.-May 1989	First Meeting of Parties to the Vienna Convention and the Montreal Protocol, Helsinki
27-29 Jun. 1990	Second Meeting of Parties to the Montreal Protocol, London (adoption of ADJUSTMENTS AND AMENDMENTS TO MONTREAL PROTOCOL)
Jun. 1991	Second Meeting of Parties to the Vienna Convention and the Third Meeting of those to the Montreal Protocol, Nairobi (also Executive Committee of Interim Multilateral Fund)
23-25 Nov. 1992	Fourth Meeting of Parties to the Montreal Protocol, Copenhagen (adoption of Amendments to Montreal Protocol)

B. PROTECTION OF THE OZONE LAYER

17-19 Nov. 1993	Third Meeting of Parties to the Vienna Convention and Fifth Meeting of those to the Montreal Protocol, Bangkok
16 Sep. 1994	**First International Ozone Day**
Oct. 1994	Sixth Meeting of Parties to the Montreal Protocol, Nairobi
Dec. 1995	Seventh Meeting of Parties to the Montreal Protocol, Vienna
Nov. 1996	Fourth Meeting of Parties to the Vienna Convention and Eighth Meeting of those to the Montreal Protocol, San Jose
Sep. 1997	Ninth Meeting of Parties to the Montreal Protocol, Montreal (adoption of Amendments to the Montreal Protocol)
16 Sep. 1997	**Celebration of the Tenth Anniversary of the Montreal Protocol, Montreal**

C. PROTECTION OF THE CLIMATE

12-23 Feb. 1979	**First World Climate Conference, convened by WMO**
9-15 Oct. 1985	**International Conference on the Assessment of the Role of Carbon Dioxide and Other Greenhouse Gases in Climate Variations and Associated Impacts, Villach (Austria), sponsored by UNEP, WMO, and ICSU**
28 Sep.-2 Oct. 1986	**Conference on Developing Policies for Responding to Future Climatic Change, Villach (Austria)**
1986	**Establishment of the UN system inter-agency Advisory Group on Greenhouse Gases (AGGG)**
Nov. 1987	**Policies Issues Workshop on Developing Policies for Responding to Climatic Change, Bellagio (Italy)**
27-30 Jun. 1988	**Conference on the Changing Atmosphere: Implications for Global Security, convened by the Canadian Department of External Affairs, Toronto**
Nov. 1988	First Session of the Intergovernmental Panel on Climate Change (IPCC), Geneva, established by UNEP and WMO

C. PROTECTION OF THE CLIMATE

6 Dec. 1988	**UNGA Resolution: Protection of Global Climate for Present and Future Generations of Mankind (A/RES/43/53)**
20-22 Feb. 1989	**Meeting of Legal and Policy Experts on the Changing Atmosphere, convened by the Canadian Department of External Affairs, Ottawa**
11 Mar. 1989	**Declaration of the Hague**
28-30 Jun. 1989	Second Session of IPCC, Nairobi
7 Nov. 1989	**Noordwijk Declaration of the Ministerial Conference on Atmospheric Pollution and Climate Change**
1990	Third Session of IPCC
27-31 Aug. 1990	Fourth Session of IPCC, Sundsvall (Sweden)
29 Oct.-7 Nov. 1990	**Second World Climate Conference, convened by WMO, Geneva, and Ministerial Declaration**
21 Dec. 1990	Establishment of Intergovernmental Negotiating Committee for a Framework Convention on Climate Change (INFCCC) (A/RES/45/212)
4-14 Feb. 1991	First Session of the INFCCC, Washington
13-15 Mar. 1991	Fifth Session of IPCC, Geneva
19-28 Jun. 1991	Second Session of the INFCCC
9-20 Sep. 1991	Third Session of the INFCCC
29-31 Oct. 1991	Sixth Session of IPCC
9-20 Dec. 1991	Fourth Session of the INFCCC
10-12 Feb. 1992	Seventh Session of IPCC, Geneva
18-28 Feb. 1992	Fifth Session of the INFCCC, New York
Apr. 1992	Informal consultations among principal delegations to INFCCC, Paris
30 Apr.-8 May 1992	Fifth Session (resumed) of the INFCCC
4 Jun. 1992	UNITED NATIONS FRAMEWORK CONVENTION ON CLIMATE CHANGE (UNFCCC) opened for signature in Rio de Janiero (UNCED)
Nov. 1992	Eighth Session, IPCC, Harare
7-10 Dec. 1992	Sixth Session of INFCCC,** Geneva

C. PROTECTION OF THE CLIMATE

15-20 Mar. 1993	Seventh Session of INFCCC, New York
16-27 Aug. 1993	Eighth Session INFCCC, Geneva
21 Mar. 1994	Entry into force of UNFCCC
7-18 Feb. 1994	Ninth Session INFCCC, Geneva
22 Aug.-2 Sep. 1994	Tenth Session INFCCC, Geneva
Nov. 1994	IPCC completes special report to the First Conference of States Parties to UNFCCC
10-12 Nov. 1994	Tenth Session IPCC, Nairobi
6-17 Feb. 1995	Eleventh Session INFCCC, New York
28 Mar.-7 Apr. 1995	First Conference of States Parties to UNFCCC, Berlin. Adoption of Berlin Mandate
28 Aug.-1 Sep. 1995	First Session of the Subsidiary Body for Scientific and Technological Advice, Geneva
31 Aug.-1 Sep. 1995	First Session of the Subsidiary Body for Implementation, Geneva
21-25 Aug. 1995	First Session of the Ad Hoc Group on the Berlin Mandate, Geneva
30 Oct.-3 Nov. 1995	Second Session of the Ad Hoc Group on the Berlin Mandate, Geneva
27 Feb-4 Mar. 1996	Second Session of the Subsidiary Body for Scientific and Technological Advice and Second Session of the Subsidiary Body for Implementation, Geneva
5-8 Mar. 1996	Third Session of the Ad Hoc Group on the Berlin Mandate, Geneva
8-19 Jul. 1996	Second Conference of the States Parties to UNFCCC, Geneva
9-16 Jul. 1996	Third Session of the Subsidiary Body for Scientific and Technological Advice and Third Session of the Subsidiary Body for Implementation, Geneva
11-16 Jul. 1996	Fourth Session of the Ad Hoc Group on the Berlin Mandate, Geneva
9-13 Dec. 1996	Fifth Session of the Ad Hoc Group on the Berlin Mandate, Geneva

C. PROTECTION OF THE CLIMATE

10-11 Dec. 1996	Fourth Session of the Subsidiary Body for Implementation, Geneva
16-18 Dec. 1996	Fourth Session of the Subsidiary Body for Scientific and Technological Advice, Geneva
25 Feb.-7 Mar. 1997	Fifth Session of the Subsidiary Body for Implementation, Bonn
25-28 Feb. 1996	Fifth Session of the Subsidiary Body for Scientific and Technological Advice, Bonn
3-7 Mar. 1997	Sixth Session of the Ad Hoc Group on the BERLIN MANDATE, Bonn
28 Jul.-5 Aug. 1997	Sixth Session of the Subsidiary Body for Scientific and Technological Advice, Geneva and Sixth Session of the Subsidiary Body for Implementation, Bonn
20-29 Oct. 1997	Seventh Session of the Subsidiary Body for Implementation, Bonn
31 Jul.-7 Aug. 1997	Seventh Session of the Ad Hoc Group on the BERLIN MANDATE, Bonn
22 Sep. 1997	Thirteenth Session IPCC, Maldives
20-29 Oct. 1997	Seventh Session of the Subsidiary Body for Scientific and Technological Advice, Bonn
22-31 Oct. 1997	Eighth Session of the Ad Hoc Group on the BERLIN MANDATE, Bonn
1-10 Dec. 1997	Third Conference of the States Parties to UNFCCC, Kyoto; (adoption of KYOTO PROTOCOL)

* **Code for Table:**

Scientific Developments and Meetings Not Part of International Legislative Process.

Legal and Political Meetings and Statements Not Part of Non-Regional International Legislative Process.

Meetings Relating to the International Legislative Process

LEGAL INSTRUMENTS ADOPTED.

**NB: The Intergovernmental Negotiating Committee (INFCCC) retained its name and certain functions, even though its task of negotiating the Framework Agreement had been completed and even after the UNFCCC had entered into force.

Index